NAVAIR 01-40ATA-1

DOUGLAS A-3 SKYWARRIOR
PILOT'S FLIGHT OPERATING INSTRUCTIONS

NATOPS

Flight Manual

NAVY MODEL

A-3A AND A-3B

AIRCRAFT

THIS PUBLICATION IS INCOMPLETE WITHOUT
CONFIDENTIAL SUPPLEMENT NAVAIR 01-40ATD-1A

©2012 Periscope Film LLC
All Rights Reserved
ISBN #978-1-937684-85-3

ISSUED BY AUTHORITY OF THE CHIEF OF NAVAL OPERATIONS
AND UNDER THE DIRECTION OF THE COMMANDER,
NAVAL AIR SYSTEMS COMMAND

THE AIRCRAFT	1
INDOCTRINATION	2
NORMAL PROCEDURE	3
FLIGHT CHARAC	4
EMER PROCEDURE	5
ALL-WEA OPERATION	6
COMM PROCEDURE	7
WEAPONS SYSTEMS	8
FLT CREW COORD	9
NATOPS EVAL	10
PERFORM DATA	11

CHANGE NOTICE

THESE ARE SUPERSEDING OR SUPPLEMENTARY PAGES TO SAME PUBLICATION OF PREVIOUS DATE

Insert these pages into basic publication
Destroy superseded pages

NAVAIR 01-40ATA-1

NATOPS
Flight Manual
NAVY MODEL
A-3A AND A-3B
AIRCRAFT

THIS PUBLICATION IS INCOMPLETE WITHOUT
CONFIDENTIAL SUPPLEMENT NAVAIR 01-40ATD-1A

ISSUED BY AUTHORITY OF THE CHIEF OF NAVAL OPERATIONS
AND UNDER THE DIRECTION OF THE COMMANDER,
NAVAL AIR SYSTEMS COMMAND

1 August 1968
Changed 15 July 1970

NAVAIR 01-40ATA-1

Reproduction for non-military use of the information or illustrations contained in this publication is not permitted without specific approval of the issuing service (NAVAIR or USAF). The policy for use of Classified Publications is established for the Air Force in AFR 205-1 and for the Navy and Marine Corps in OPNAVINST 5510.1 Series.

LIST OF EFFECTIVE PAGES

INSERT LATEST CHANGED PAGES. DESTROY SUPERSEDED PAGES.

NOTE: The portion of the text affected by the current change is indicated by a vertical line in the outer margins of the page.

TOTAL NUMBER OF PAGES IN THIS PUBLICATION IS 554, CONSISTING OF THE FOLLOWING:

Page No.	Issue	Page No.	Issue	Page No.	Issue
*Title	15 Jul 1970	1-34 - 1-35	1 Aug 1968	*1-115	15 Jul 1970
*A	15 Jul 1970	*1-36 - 1-37	15 Jul 1970	1-116 - 1-117	1 Aug 1968
*B	15 Jul 1970	1-38	1 Jun 1969	1-118	1 Jun 1969
C Blank	1 Jun 1969	*1-39 - 1-43	15 Jul 1970	1-119 - 1-128	1 Aug 1968
LOP	1 Aug 1968	1-44	1 Aug 1968	*1-128A - 1-128B	15 Jul 1970
LOP Blank	1 Aug 1968	1-45	1 Jun 1969	1-129	1 Jun 1969
*Flyleaf 1	15 Jul 1970	1-46	1 Aug 1968	1-130 - 1-131	1 Aug 1968
Flyleaf 2 Blank	1 Aug 1968	*1-47 - 1-48	15 Jul 1970	*1-132	15 Jul 1970
*i - ii	15 Jul 1970	*1-49 - 1-60 Deleted	15 Jul 1970	1-133 - 1-135	1 Jun 1969
iii - iv	1 Aug 1968	1-61 - 1-62	1 Aug 1968	1-136	1 Aug 1968
1-1	1 Jun 1969	*1-63 - 1-64	15 Jul 1970	*1-137 - 1-138	15 Jul 1970
1-2 Blank	1 Jun 1969	1-65 - 1-66	1 Jun 1969	1-139	1 Aug 1968
*1-2A	15 Jul 1970	1-67 - 1-70	1 Aug 1968	*1-140	15 Jul 1970
1-2B Blank	1 Jun 1969	*1-71	15 Jul 1970	*1-141 - 1-148 Deleted	15 Jul 1970
*1-3	15 Jul 1970	1-72	1 Aug 1968	1-149	1 Jun 1969
1-4 - 1-6	1 Aug 1968	1-73	1 Jun 1969		

This manual is sold for historic research purposes only, as an entertainment. It is not intended to be used as part of an actual flight training program. No book can substitute for flight training by an authorized instructor. The licensing of pilots is overseen by organizations and authorities such as the FAA and CAA. Operating an aircraft without the proper license is a federal crime.

Page No.	Issue	Page No.	Issue	Page No.	Issue
1-18	1 Aug 1968	*1-94 - 1-96	15 Jul 1970	1-164 Blank	1 Jun 1969
*1-19 - 1-20	15 Jul 1970	1-97	1 Aug 1968	1-165	1 Jun 1969
1-21	1 Aug 1968	*1-98	15 Jul 1970	1-166 - 1-169	1 Aug 1968
*1-22	15 Jul 1970	1-99	1 Jun 1969	1-170 Blank	1 Aug 1968
1-23	1 Aug 1968	1-100	1 Aug 1968	1-170A	1 Jun 1969
*1-24 - 1-25	15 Jul 1970	*1-101	15 Jul 1970	1-170B Blank	1 Jun 1969
1-26	1			- 1-176	15 Jul 1970
*1-27	15	*This book has been digitally*		- 1-178	
1-28	1	*watermarked to prevent illegal duplication.*		ted	15 Jul 1970
*1-29	15			2-1 - 2-3	1 Jun 1969
1-30 Blank	1 Aug 1968	1-110	1 Aug 1968	*2-4	15 Jul 1970
*1-30A - 1-30B	15 Jul 1970	*1-111	15 Jul 1970	2-5 - 2-6 Deleted	15 Jul 1970
*1-30C - 1-30D Deleted	15 Jul 1970	1-112	1 Aug 1968	3-1	1 Jun 1969
1-31 - 1-33	1 Jun 1969	*1-113	15 Jul 1970	3-2 Blank	1 Jun 1969
		1-114	1 Aug 1968		

Current Pilot's Pocket Checklist - NAVAIR 01-40ATA-1B, 15 June 1968, Changed 15 July 1970

*The asterisk indicates pages changed, added, or deleted by the current change.

ADDITIONAL COPIES OF THIS PUBLICATION MAY BE OBTAINED AS FOLLOWS: NAVAIR

USAF ACTIVITIES.—In accordance with Technical Order No. 00-5-2.
NAVY ACTIVITIES.—Use DD FORM 1348 and submit in accordance with the instructions contained in NAVSUP PUBLICATION 437—Military Standard Requisitioning and Issue Procedure.
For information on other available material and details of distribution refer to NAVSUP PUBLICATION 2002, SECTION VIII, PART C and NAVAIR 00-500A.

A   Changed 15 July 1970

NAVAIR 01-40ATA-1

LIST OF EFFECTIVE PAGES ISSUED (Continued)
INSERT LATEST CHANGED PAGES. DESTROY SUPERSEDED PAGES.

NOTE: The portion of the text affected by the current change is indicated by a vertical line in the outer margins of the page.

Page No.	Issue	Page No.	Issue
3-3 - 3-5	1 Jun 1969	8-5 - 8-7	1 Aug 1968
3-6 - 3-7	1 Aug 1968	8-8 - 8-9	1 Jun 1969
3-8 Blank	1 Aug 1968	8-10	1 Aug 1968
*3-8A	15 Jul 1970	9-1	1 Jun 1969
3-8B Blank	1 Jun 1969	9-2 Blank	1 Aug 1968
*3-9	15 Jul 1970	10-1 - 10-2	1 Jun 1969
3-10 - 3-11	1 Aug 1968	10-3 - 10-21	1 Aug 1968
*3-12 - 3-15	15 Jul 1970	10-22 Blank	1 Aug 1968
3-16	1 Aug 1968	11-1	1 Aug 1968
*3-17	15 Jul 1970	11-2 Blank	1 Aug 1968
3-18	1 Jun 1969	11-3 - 11-5	1 Jun 1969
*3-19	15 Jul 1970	11-6 - 11-14	1 Aug 1968
3-20 - 3-21	1 Aug 1968	11-15 - 11-16A	1 Jun 1969
3-22	1 Jun 1969	11-16B Blank	1 Jun 1969
3-23	1 Aug 1968	11-17 - 11-40	1 Aug 1968
3-24	1 Jun 1969	11-41 - 11-43	1 Jun 1969
3-25	1 Aug 1968	11-44 - 11-56	1 Aug 1968
*3-26 - 3-27	15 Jul 1970	11-57 - 11-58	1 Jun 1969
3-28	1 Aug 1968	11-59 - 11-90	1 Aug 1968
3-29 - 3-32	1 Jun 1969	11-91	1 Jun 1969
3-33 - 3-34	1 Aug 1968	11-92 - 11-97	1 Aug 1968
*3-35	15 Jul 1970	11-98 Blank	1 Aug 1968
3-36 - 3-38	1 Aug 1968	11-99	1 Jun 1969
3-39	1 Jun 1969	11-100 - 11-101	1 Aug 1968
3-40 Blank	1 Aug 1968	11-102 Blank	1 Aug 1968
*4-1	15 Jul 1970	11-103	1 Jun 1969
4-2 Blank	1 Jun 1969	11-104 - 11-110	1 Aug 1968
4-2A - 4-2B	1 Jun 1969	11-111	1 Jun 1969
4-3	1 Jun 1969	11-112 - 11-114	1 Aug 1968
4-4 - 4-17	1 Aug 1968	11-115	1 Jun 1969
4-18	1 Jun 1969	11-116 - 11-121	1 Aug 1968
4-19 - 4-21	1 Aug 1968	11-122 Blank	1 Aug 1968
*4-22	15 Jul 1970	11-123	1 Jun 1969
*4-23 - 4-30 Deleted	15 Jul 1970	11-124 - 11-133	1 Aug 1968
4-31	1 Aug 1968	11-134 Blank	1 Aug 1968
4-32	1 Jun 1969	11-135 - 11-136	1 Jun 1969
4-33 - 4-34	1 Aug 1968	11-137 - 11-143	1 Aug 1968
*5-1 - 5-5	15 Jul 1970	11-144 Blank	1 Aug 1968
5-6 - 5-8	1 Aug 1968	11-145 - 11-147	1 Jun 1969
5-9	1 Jun 1969	11-148 - 11-176	1 Aug 1968
*5-10 - 5-14	15 Jul 1970	11-177	1 Jun 1969
5-15	1 Jun 1969	11-178 - 11-181	1 Aug 1968
*5-16	15 Jul 1970	11-182 Blank	1 Aug 1968
5-17	1 Jun 1969	11-183	1 Jun 1969
5-18 - 5-21	1 Aug 1968	11-184 - 11-186	1 Aug 1968
*5-22	15 Jul 1970	11-187	1 Jun 1969
5-23	1 Jun 1969	11-188	1 Aug 1968
5-24 - 5-25	1 Aug 1968	11-189	1 Jun 1969
*5-26	15 Jul 1970	11-190 - 11-192	1 Aug 1968
5-27 - 5-29	1 Aug 1968	*Index 1 - Index 25	15 Jul 1970
*5-30	15 Jul 1970	*Index 26 Blank	15 Jul 1970
6-1 - 6-4	1 Jun 1969		
6-5 - 6-7	1 Aug 1968		
6-8 Blank	1 Aug 1968		
7-1	1 Jun 1969		
7-2 - 7-10	1 Aug 1968		
*8-1	15 Jul 1970		
8-2 - 8-3	1 Aug 1968		
8-4	1 Jun 1969		

*The asterisk indicates pages changed, added, or deleted by the current change.

Changed 15 July 1970

NAVAIR 01-40ATA-1

INTERIM CHANGE SUMMARY

The following Interim Changes have been canceled or previously incorporated in this manual:

INTERIM CHANGE NUMBER(S)	REMARKS/PURPOSE
1 thru - 45	Canceled or previously incorporated

The following Interim Changes have been incorporated in this Change/Revision:

INTERIM CHANGE NUMBER	REMARKS/PURPOSE
46	Engine temperature operating limitations
47	Launching restriction from waist catapult

Interim Changes Outstanding - To be maintained by the custodian of this manual:

INTERIM CHANGE NUMBER	ORIGINATOR/DATE (or DATE/TIME GROUP)	PAGES AFFECTED	REMARKS/PURPOSE
none	Msg R 192328Z	3-35	Slot Failure Warning

Changed 15 July 1970   Flyleaf 1/(Flyleaf 2 Blank)

THIS ERRATA INCOMPLETE WITHOUT MANUAL INDICATED BELOW

NOTICE

NAVAIR 01-40ATA-1

1 AUGUST 1968

Changed 1 June 1969

Please remove and destroy the following pages, which are in error, from your manual:

1-139, 1-140, 1-141, 1-142

Insert the corrected pages, which are attached.

24 JULY 1969

DEPARTMENT OF THE NAVY
OFFICE OF THE CHIEF OF NAVAL OPERATIONS
WASHINGTON, D.C. -20350

1 August 1968

LETTER OF PROMULGATION

1. The Naval Air Training and Operating Procedures Standardization Program (NATOPS) is a positive approach towards improving combat readiness and achieving a substantial reduction in the aircraft accident rate. Standardization, based on professional knowledge and experience, provides the basis for development of an efficient and sound operational procedure. The standardization program is not planned to stifle individual initiative but rather, to aid the Commanding Officer in increasing his unit's combat potential without reducing his command prestige or responsibility.

2. This manual standardizes ground and flight procedures but does not include tactical doctrine. Compliance with the stipulated manual procedure is mandatory except as authorized herein. In order to remain effective, NATOPS must be dynamic and stimulate rather than suppress individual thinking. Since aviation is a continuing progressive profession, it is both desirable and necessary that new ideas and new techniques be expeditiously evaluated and incorporated if proven to be sound. To this end Type/Fleet/Air Group/Air Wing/Squadron Commanders and subordinates are obligated and authorized to modify procedures contained herein, in accordance with the waiver provisions established by OPNAVINST 3510.9 series, for the purpose of assessing new ideas prior to initiating recommendations for permanent changes. This manual is prepared and kept current by the users in order to achieve maximum readiness and safety in the most efficient and economical manner. Should conflict exist between the training and operating procedures found in this manual and those found in other publications, this manual will govern.

3. Checklists and other pertinent extracts from this publication necessary to normal operations and training should be made and may be carried in Naval Aircraft for use therein. It is forbidden to make copies of this entire publication or major portions thereof without specific authority of the Chief of Naval Operations.

THOMAS F. CONNOLLY
Vice Admiral, USN
Deputy Chief of Naval Operations (Air)

NAVAIR 01-40ATA-1   Table of Contents

TABLE OF CONTENTS

SECTION I	THE AIRCRAFT	1-1
SECTION II	INDOCTRINATION	2-1
SECTION III	NORMAL PROCEDURES	3-1
SECTION IV	FLIGHT CHARACTERISTICS	4-1
SECTION V	EMERGENCY PROCEDURES	5-1
SECTION VI	ALL-WEATHER OPERATION	6-1
SECTION VII	COMMUNICATIONS PROCEDURES	7-1
SECTION VIII	WEAPONS SYSTEMS*	8-1
SECTION IX	FLIGHT CREW COORDINATION	9-1
SECTION X	NATOPS EVALUATION	10-1
SECTION XI	PERFORMANCE DATA	11-1
	A-3B AIRCRAFT PERFORMANCE DATA CHARTS (J57-P-10 ENGINES)	11-1
	A-3A AIRCRAFT PERFORMANCE DATA CHARTS (J57-P-6B ENGINES)	11-115
	ALPHABETICAL INDEX	Index 1

*Also refer to the Supplemental NATOPS Flight Manual (NAVAIR 01-40ATD-1A)

Changed 15 July 1970   i

Introduction NAVAIR 01-40ATA-1

FOREWORD

SCOPE

The NATOPS Flight Manual is issued by the authority of the Chief of Naval Operations and under the direction of the Commander, Naval Air Systems Command in conjunction with the Naval Air Training and Operating Procedures Standardization (NATOPS) Program. The manual provides the best available operating instructions for most circumstances, but no manual is a substitute for sound judgment. Multiple emergencies, adverse weather, or terrain may require modification of the procedures contained herein. Read this manual from cover to cover. It's your responsibility to have a complete knowledge of its contents.

HOW TO GET COPIES

Automatic Distribution

To automatically receive future changes and revisions to this manual, a unit must be established on the automatic distribution list maintained by the Naval Air Technical Services Facility (NATSF). To become established on the list, a unit must submit its requirement to NATSF on NAVWEPS Form 5605/2 listing this manual and all other NAVAIR publications required. For additional instructions, refer to BUWEPSINST 5605.4 series and NAVSUP Publication 2002, Section VIII, Part C.

Additional Copies

Additional copies of this manual and changes thereto may be procured by submitting a DD Form 1348 to NPFC Philadelphia in accordance with the instructions contained in NAVSUP PUBLICATION 437-Military Standard Requisitioning and Issue Procedures. For information on other available material and details of distribution, refer to NAVSUP PUBLICATION 2002, Section VIII, Part C, and NAVAIR 00-500A.

UPDATING THE MANUAL

To ensure that the manual contains the latest procedures and information, a review conference will be held periodically as necessary.

YOUR RESPONSIBILITY

NATOPS Flight Manuals are kept current through an active manual change program. If you find anything you do not like about the manual, if you have information you would like to pass along to others, or if you find an error in this manual, submit a change recommendation to the Model Manager.

CHANGE RECOMMENDATIONS

Recommended changes to this manual or other NATOPS publications may be submitted by anyone in accordance with OPNAV INSTRUCTION 3510.9 (series). Change recommendations of an URGENT

Changed 15 July 1970

nature (safety of flight, etc) should be submitted directly to the NATOPS Advisory Group Member in the Chain of Command by priority message.

Submit routine change recommendations to the Model Manager on OPNAV Form 3500-22.

Address routine changes to:

      Commanding Officer
      VAH-123
      NAS Whidbey Island
      Oak Harbor,
      Washington 98277

NATOPS FLIGHT MANUAL INTERIM CHANGES (FMIC'S)

FMIC'S are changes or corrections to the NATOPS Flight Manual promulgated by CNO or NAVAIRSYSCOM. FMIC'S may be received by the individual custodian as a printed page or pages, or by the commands as a naval message. After the completion of the action directed by an interim change, the interim change shall be retained in front of the Interim Change Summary Page of the Manual unless the interim change contains authorization to discard the change.

INTERIM CHANGE SUMMARY

The interim change summary in each manual is provided for the purpose of maintaining a complete record of all interim changes issued to the manual. Each time the manual is changed or revised, the interim change summary will be updated to indicate disposition and/or incorporation of previously issued interim changes. When a regular change is received, the interim change summary should be checked to ascertain that all outstanding interim changes have been either incorporated or cancelled; those not incorporated should be re-entered and noted as applicable.

CHANGE SYMBOLS

Revised text is indicated by a black vertical line in either margin of the page, like the one printed next to this paragraph. The change symbol shows where there has been a change. The change might be material added or information restated.

WARNINGS, CAUTIONS, AND NOTES

The following definitions apply to WARNINGS, CAUTIONS, and NOTES found throughout the manual.

Operating procedures, practices, etc, which may result in injury or death, if not carefully followed.

Operating procedures, practices, etc, which, if not strictly observed, may damage equipment.

              NOTE

An operating procedure, condition, etc, which is essential to emphasize.

WORDING

The concept of word usage and intended meaning which has been adhered to in preparing this manual is as follows:

    1. "Shall" has been used only when application of a procedure is mandatory.

    2. "Should" has been used only when application of a procedure is recommended.

    3. "May" and "need not" have been used only when application of a procedure is optional.

    4. "Will" has been used only to indicate futurity, never to indicate any degree of requirement for application of a procedure.

Introduction   NAVAIR 01-40ATA-1

NATOPS CHANGE RECOMMENDATION
OPNAV FORM 3500/22 (8-65) 0107-722-2001

TO BE FILLED IN BY ORIGINATOR

ORIGINATORS CHANGE RECOMMENDATION IDENT. NO.	DATE	☐ NATOPS MANUAL	☐ NATOPS FLIGHT MANUAL	☐ FLIGHT MANUAL
MODEL AIRCRAFT	SECTION/CHAPTER	PAGE NUMBER	PARAGRAPH NUMBER	

RECOMMENDATION (be specific)

SAMPLE

☐ CHECK IF CONTINUED ON BACK

JUSTIFICATION

NAME	UNIT
ADDRESS	

TO BE FILLED IN BY MODEL MANAGER (Return to Originator)

FROM	DATE
TO	

REFERENCE
(a) Your Change Recommendation Number _____

☐ Your change recommendation number _____ is acknowledged. It will be held for action of the review conference planned for _____ to be held at _____

☐ Your change recommendation is reclassified URGENT and forwarded for approval to _____ by my DTG _____

/S/ _____ FOR MODEL MANAGER. _____ AIRCRAFT

GPO 931-057   A – 8345

NAVAIR 01-40ATA-1 Section I

SECTION I
THE AIRCRAFT

TABLE OF CONTENTS

Part	Page	Part	Page
1 GENERAL DESCRIPTION	1-2A	3 AIRCRAFT SERVICING	1-128A
2 SYSTEMS	1-30A	4 AIRCRAFT OPERATING LIMITATIONS.	1-170A

NAVAIR 01-40ATA-1

Section I
Part 1

PART 1
GENERAL DESCRIPTION

TABLE OF CONTENTS

TEXT

	Page		Page
Description	1-3	Emergency Escape Chute and	
Main Differences	1-3	Entrance — A-3A	1-5
General Arrangement	1-3	Escape Chute Test Switch — A-3A	1-8
Aircraft Dimensions	1-5	Emergency Escape Chute and	
Seats	1-5	Entrance — A-3B	1-8
Pilot's Seat	1-5	Escape Chute Test Switch —	
Plane Captain's Seat (PC)	1-5	A-3B	1-8
Navigator's Seat (Nav)	1-5	Escape Hatch	1-8
Shoulder Harness and Inertia Reel	1-5	Pilot's Assist Handle	1-8
Entrance Door	1-5	Crew Movement	1-8

ILLUSTRATIONS

Figure		Page	Figure		Page
1-1	Aircraft Dimensions	1-4	1-14	Pilot's and Plane Captain's Seats — A-3B (Typical)	1-20
1-2	General Arrangement	1-6	1-15	Plane Captain's Station — A-3A	1-21
1-3	Crew Movement and Compartment Diagram	1-9	1-16	Plane Captain's Station — A-3A	1-22
1-4	Pilot's Instrument Panel — A-3A/B Typical	1-10	1-17	Plane Captain's Console — A-3A	1-23
1-5	Deleted.		1-18	Plane Captain's Console — A-3B	1-24
1-6	Pilot's Left-Hand Console — A-3A	1-11	1-19	Navigator's Station — A-3A/B (Typical)	1-25
1-7	Pilot's Left-Hand Console — A-3B	1-13			
1-8	Deleted.		1-20	Circuit Breaker and Fuse Panels — A-3A	1-26
1-9	Pilot's Center Console — A-3B	1-15			
1-10	Navigator's Typical Right-Hand Console — A-3A	1-16	1-21	Circuit Breaker and Fuse Panels — A-3B	1-27
1-11	Navigator's Typical Right-Hand Console — A-3B	1-17	1-22	Pilot's Circuit Breaker Panel — A-3A	1-28
1-12	Aft Cockpit — A-3A	1-18	1-23	Pilot's Circuit Breaker Panel — A-3B	1-29
1-13	Aft Cockpit — A-3B	1-19			

Changed 15 July 1970

1-2A/(1-2B Blank)

DESCRIPTION

The Navy Model A-3A/B aircraft (figure 1-1), manufactured by the Aircraft Division of McDonnell Douglas Corp., are three-place, jet propelled, sweptwing monoplanes designed for attack and air refueling operations. The aircraft is powered by two Pratt and Whitney J57-P-6B[1] or J57-P-10[2] series turbojet engines installed in underwing nacelles. The aircraft is equipped with retractable tricycle landing gear with a steerable nosewheel. The aircraft is designed for carrier operations, utilizing catapult assistance for takeoff and conventional arresting gear for deck landings. JATO assistance is available for airfield takeoff. KA-3B aircraft technical data will be updated and incorporated into the EKA-3B NATOPS Flight Manual.

MAIN DIFFERENCES

The A-3A/A-3B series aircraft are basically the same; therefore, this handbook applies generally to all aircraft of these designations. Certain differences do exist, however, and the information in this flight manual concerns two relatively separate groups. These groups are characterized by one or more variations in equipment, system operation, or structural detail. For this reason, the problem of effectivity — always important — becomes vital. The main differences that characterize the two groups are as follows:

Group I

A-3A
- Aircraft BuNo. 135407 through 135444
- a. Modified instrument panel
- b. Liquid oxygen system
- c. Aileron-spoilers
- d. Bomb bay spoiler
- e. Drag chute
- f. Level launch configuration designed for carrier operation
- g. J57-P-6B engines
- h. Hydraulic fluid heat exchanger
- i. Angle-of-attack indicator system

Group II

Aircraft BuNo. 138922, 138938, 138968, 142246, 142630, 142653, 142655, 142658, 142663, 142665, 144626-144627, 144629, 147650-147651, 147653-147654, 147661-147662, 147664, and 147668.

A-3B
- a. All items in Group I apply to this group.
- b. J57-P-10 engines replace J57-P-6B series engines
- c. Increased design load factor and elevator boost ratio
- d. Improved radio/ICS capabilities
- e. Aileron caging mechanism (some aircraft)
- f. Provisions for a fourth crewmember
- g. DECM equipment
- h. Additional liquid oxygen supply

Certain changes exist that affect only a portion of the aircraft in one or more groups, and these differences will be indicated by footnotes. When no footnote is indicated, the information given is applicable to all aircraft.

GENERAL ARRANGEMENT

For general arrangement of the aircraft, including location of external power receptacles, battery water

---
[1] Aircraft prior to BuNo. 138902
[2] Aircraft BuNo. 138902 and subsequent.

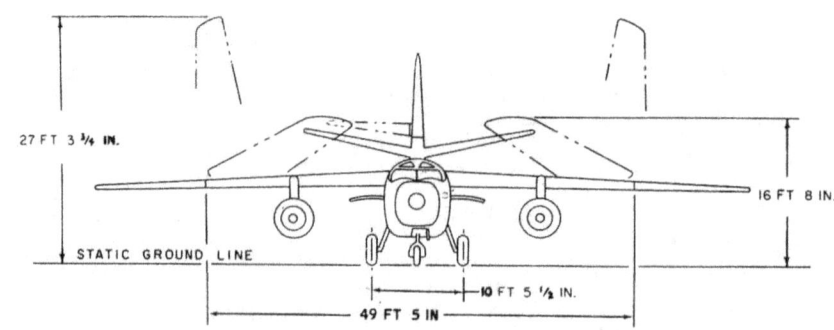
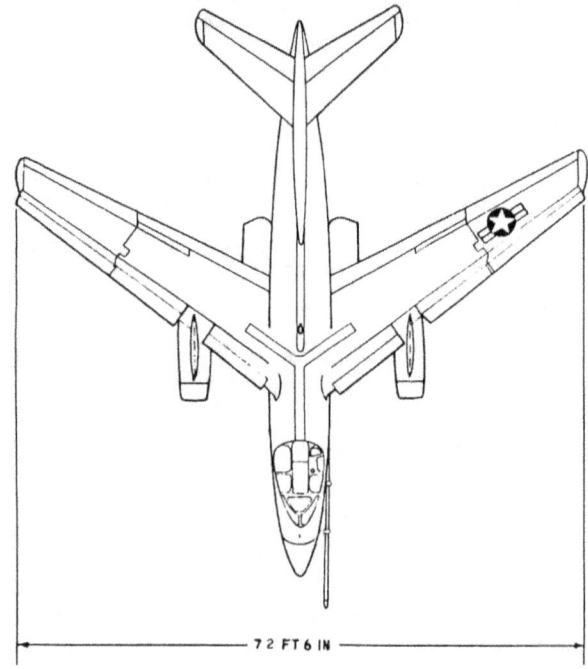
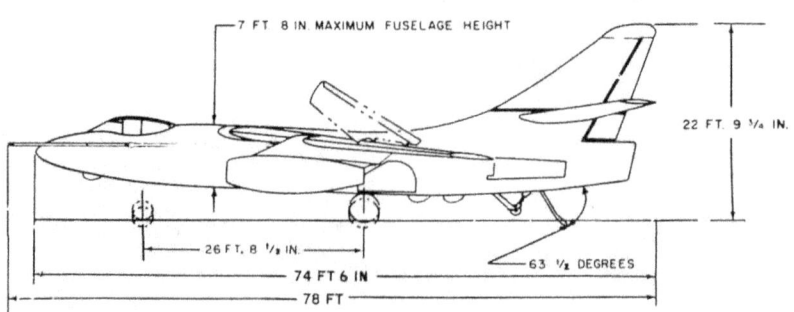

Figure 1-1. Aircraft Dimensions

containers, hatches, fuel tanks, etc, refer to figure 1-2. For a description and location of each compartment, refer to figure 1-3. Only the cockpit companionway, and bomb bay are accessible during flight; all other compartments are neither accessible nor inhabitable except when the aircraft is on the ground.

AIRCRAFT DIMENSIONS

The principal dimensions of early aircraft are:

Length (fin erect)..............75 ft 10 3/4 in.

Length (fin folded) ....75 ft 11 7/8 in.

Wing span (wings spread).........72 ft 6 in.

Wing span (wings folded) ....49 ft 1 1/8 in.

Height (fin erect) ....23 ft 10 3/8 in.

Height (fin folded) ....16 ft 6 5/8 in.

Maximum height during folding.....27 ft 6 in.

Height over wings (wings folded)....16 ft 9 1/4 in.

The principal dimensions of later aircraft are:

Length (fin erect and
probe installed)...............78 ft

Length (fin folded) ....74 ft 6 in.

Wing span (wings spread).........72 ft 6 in.

Wing span (wings folded) ....49 ft 5 in.

Height (fin erect) ....22 ft 9 3/4 in.

Height (fin folded) ....15 ft 9 3/8 in.

Maximum height during folding.....27 ft 3 3/4 in.

Height over wings (wings folded)....16 ft 8 in.

SEATS

The aircraft is equipped with a pilot's seat, a navigator's seat, a plane captain's (PC) seat, and a seat for a fourth man in the aft cockpit (figure 1-13).

Pilot's Seat

The pilot's seat is equipped with a lap safety belt, inertia reel, and shoulder harness, and is adjustable in height. An electrical actuator moves the seat up or down, as desired, when a control handle (figure 1-14), located on the right-hand side of the seat, is actuated. The pilot's seat is also equipped with an adjustable headrest.

Plane Captain's Seat (PC)

The PC's seat is equipped with a lap safety belt, shoulder harness, and inertia reel. The shoulder harness and inertia reel are controlled by a handle (figure 1-14) on the left-hand side of the seat. The upper entrance door opening handle is on the lower left-hand side of the seat, and the bomb indicator lights panel is on the upper left-hand side.

Navigator's Seat (Nav)

The navigator's seat is manually adjustable fore and aft on slides with four lock positions. The adjustment lever is on the forward end of the seat. The seat is provided with a lap safety belt and a shoulder harness with an inertia reel. The shoulder harness and inertia reel are controlled by a handle on the left-hand side of the seat.

Shoulder Harness and Inertia Reel

Each seat is equipped with a shoulder harness. The two free ends of the harness fit into the safety belt catch and are held securely as long as the catch is closed. The harness and safety belt are released by opening the safety belt catch. Buckles on the front of the harness permit it to be adjusted. An inertia reel shoulder harness takeup mechanism is provided with each harness. The harness may be locked in position by movement of a control handle at the left-hand side of each seat. When unlocking the harness, it may be necessary to move the lever from one position to the other several times to obtain disengagement within the reel. In the UNLOCKED position, the reels are automatically locked when subjected to a deceleration along the thrust line of the aircraft in excess of 2.5 g's.

NOTE

If the inertia reel fails to unlock while any load is applied to cable, relax the load and recycle the handle.

ENTRANCE DOOR

Emergency Escape Chute and Entrance—A-3A

The emergency escape chute (figure 5-2) serves as the normal entrance and exit on the ground and provides for emergency exit from the aircraft in flight.

Section I
Part 1

NAVAIR 01-40ATA-1

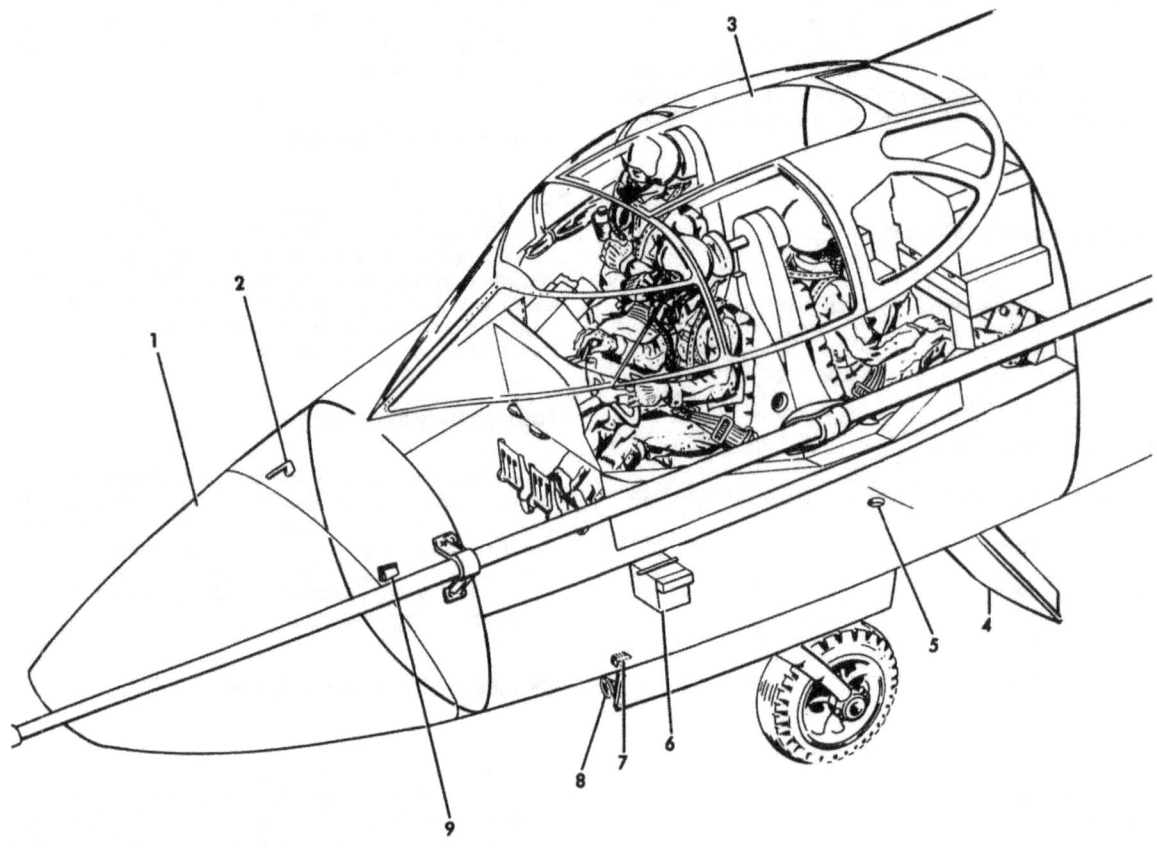

1. Radome
2. Pitot tube
3. Ditching hatch
4. Outer escape chute door
5. External ac and dc electrical power receptacle
6. Battery
7. Angle-of-attack light
8. Taxi (or landing) light
9. Air refueling probe light

FF1-4460-2F

Figure 1-2. General Arrangement (Sheet 1)

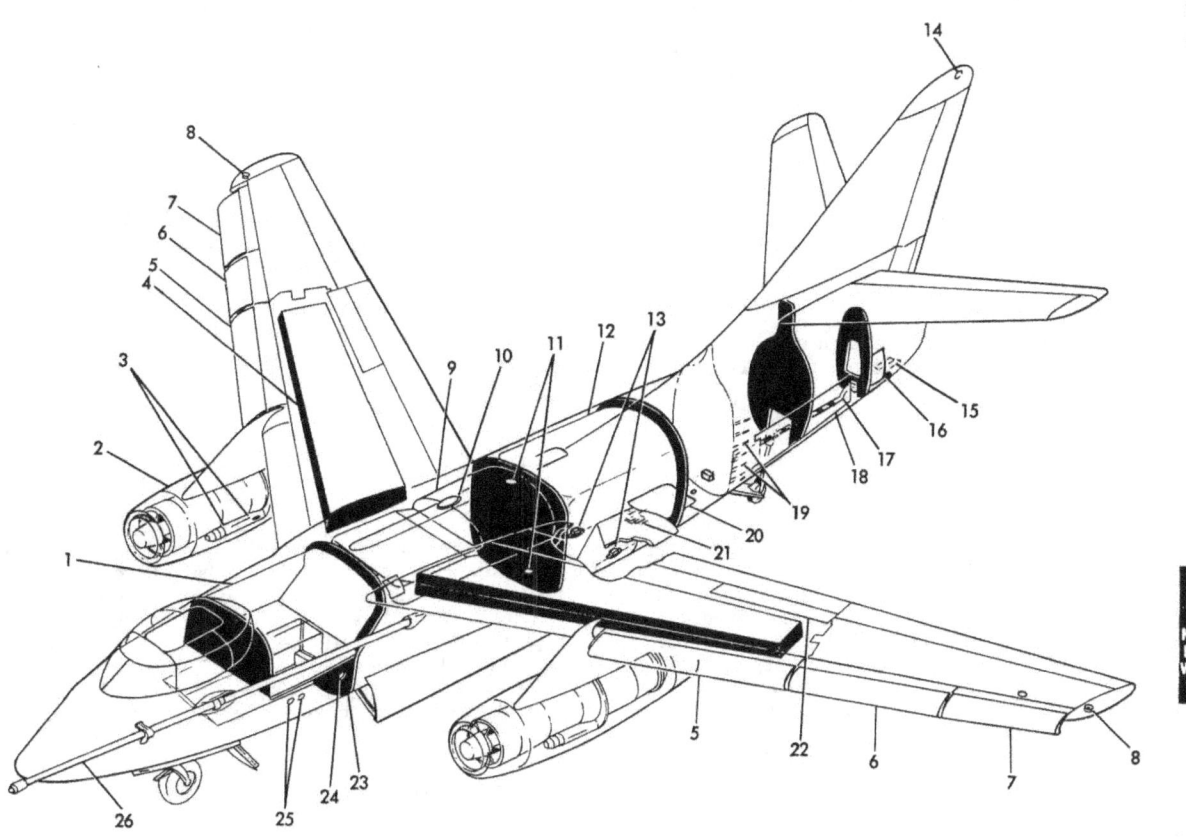

1. Forward fuselage fuel tank
2. J57-P-6 or J57-P-10 series engine
3. Engine starter and connection port
4. Wing fuel tank
5. Center wing outboard slats
6. Outer wing inboard slats
7. Outer wing outboard slats
8. Wing navigation lights
9. Upper bomb bay auxiliary tank
10. Upper anticollision rotating beacon
11. Exterior fuselage lights
12. Aft fuselage fuel tank
13. Lower anticollision rotating beacons
14. Fin navigation lights
15. Drag chute receptacle
16. Tail compartment access door
17. Arresting hook
18. Speedbrake
19. JATO mounting hooks
20. Aft compartment access door
21. Catapult holdback fitting
22. Wing spoilers (1)
23. Catapult hook (later aircraft)
24. ATM external power receptacle
25. ATM exhaust ports
26. Air refueling probe

(1) Aircraft BuNo. 135407 and subsequent.

Figure 1-2. General Arrangement (Sheet 2)

The inner and outer emergency escape chute doors, when extended together, serve as a chute for emergency abandonment of the aircraft. The EMER LOWER ESCAPE handle (figure 1-14), on the right-hand side of the pilot's seat, controls the emergency chute actuating system. Pulling up on the handle mechanically releases the door uplatches and electrically fires four cartridges which create and direct expanding gas into the escape chute actuating cylinders to extend the doors.

NOTE

When the ELEC PWR switch is in the OFF position, maximum battery power is available to fire the cartridges that open the emergency escape chute doors.

Escape Chute Test Switch —A-3A

A circuit test switch, labeled LH-RH, and two indicator lights, labeled SEAT and PASSAGEWAY, are located in the lower door locking handle recess (figure 3-2) on the right-hand side of the companionway. To test the escape chute circuit, position the LH-RH toggle switch to each position. If the indicator lights come on for each position when the switch is operated, the lights indicate circuit continuity from the test switch to the firing cartridges.

Emergency Escape Chute and Entrance

The emergency escape chute (figure 5-2) serves as the normal entrance and exit on the ground and provides for emergency exit from the aircraft in flight.

The inner and outer emergency escape chute doors, when extended together, serve as a chute for emergency abandonment of the aircraft. The emergency escape chute doors can be actuated by the EMER LOWER ESCAPE handle (figure 1-14) on the right-hand side of the pilot's seat, or by the companionway EMER EXIT T-handle (figure 5-3) located on the right-hand side of the companionway aft of station 204.000. Pulling up on either handle mechanically releases the door uplatches, actuates two arming switches, and electrically fires four cartridges which create and direct expanding gas into the escape chute actuating cylinders to extend the doors.

Escape Chute Test Switch

A circuit test switch, labeled LH-RH, and two indicator lights, labeled SEAT and PASSAGEWAY, are located in the lower door locking handle recess (figure 3-2) on the right-hand side of the companionway. To test the escape chute circuit, place the LH-RH toggle switch in each position. If the indicator lights come on for each position when the switch is operated, the lights indicate proper operation of the escape chute circuit. The escape chute system receives power from the battery bus.

Escape Hatch

The escape hatch (figure 5-2) serves as the primary ditching route and an alternate bailout route for both controlled and uncontrolled bailout. The escape hatch is opened in an emergency by an independent pneumatic system (figure 1-45). Two controls are provided for emergency opening of the hatch: T-handle above the pilot's head (figure 5-2), and a recessed handle above the plane captain's position.

Pilot's Assist Handle

A handle located above the pilot on the overhead windshield support beam (figure 5-2) facilitates emergency escape by the pilot.

Crew Movement

Certain operating conditions and emergency procedures (figure 1-3) require movement of one or more crewmembers from the cockpit to the companionway or bomb bay areas. The cockpit must be depressurized before opening the inner escape chute door. To open the companionway safety door (figure 1-3), depress the companionway safety door latch (figure 1-3), lowering the companionway safety door to overlap the inner surface of the outer escape chute door, and crawl into the companionway (figure 1-3) or into the bomb bay.

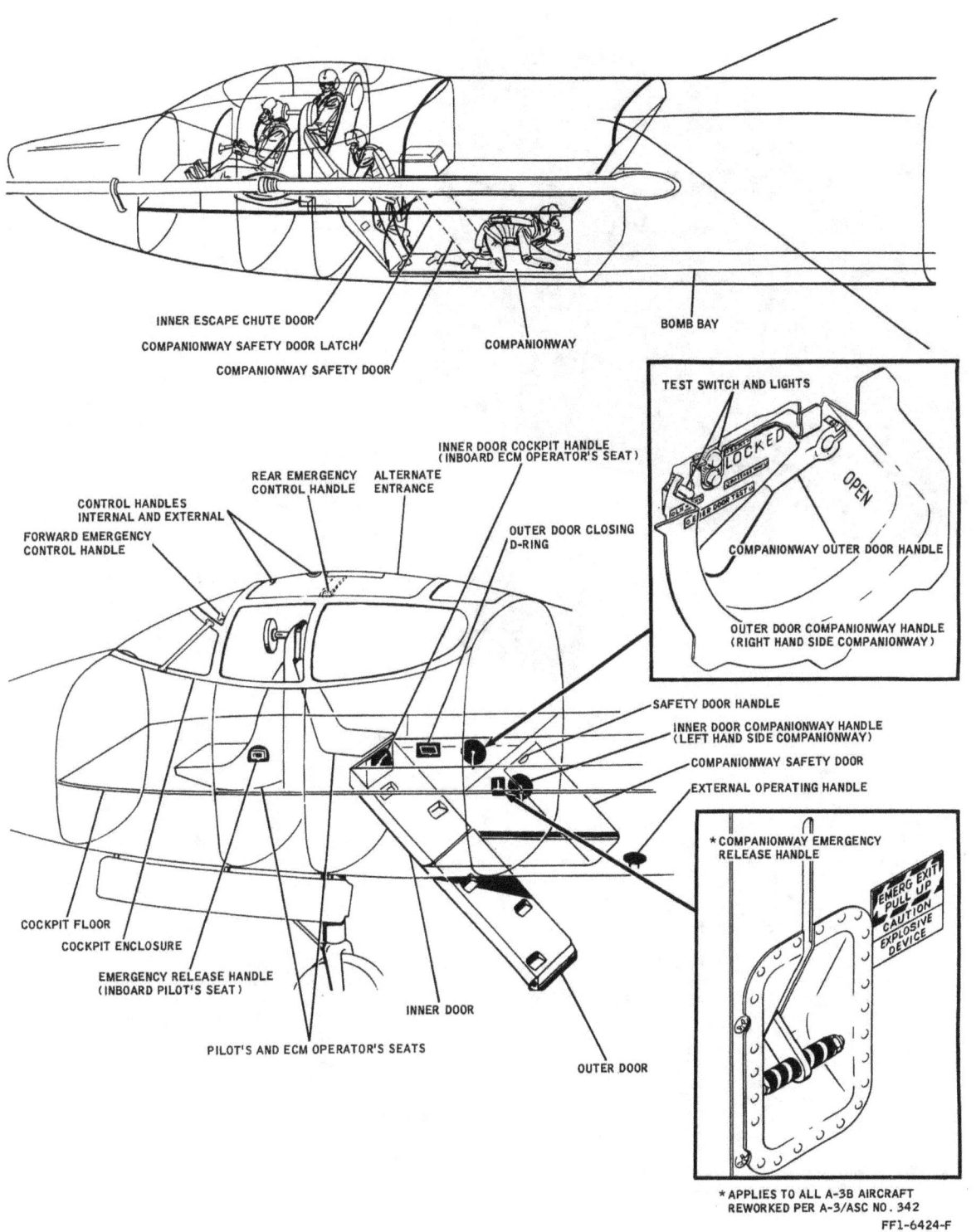

Figure 1-3. Crew Movement and Compartment Diagram

Section I
Part 1

NAVAIR 01-40ATA-1

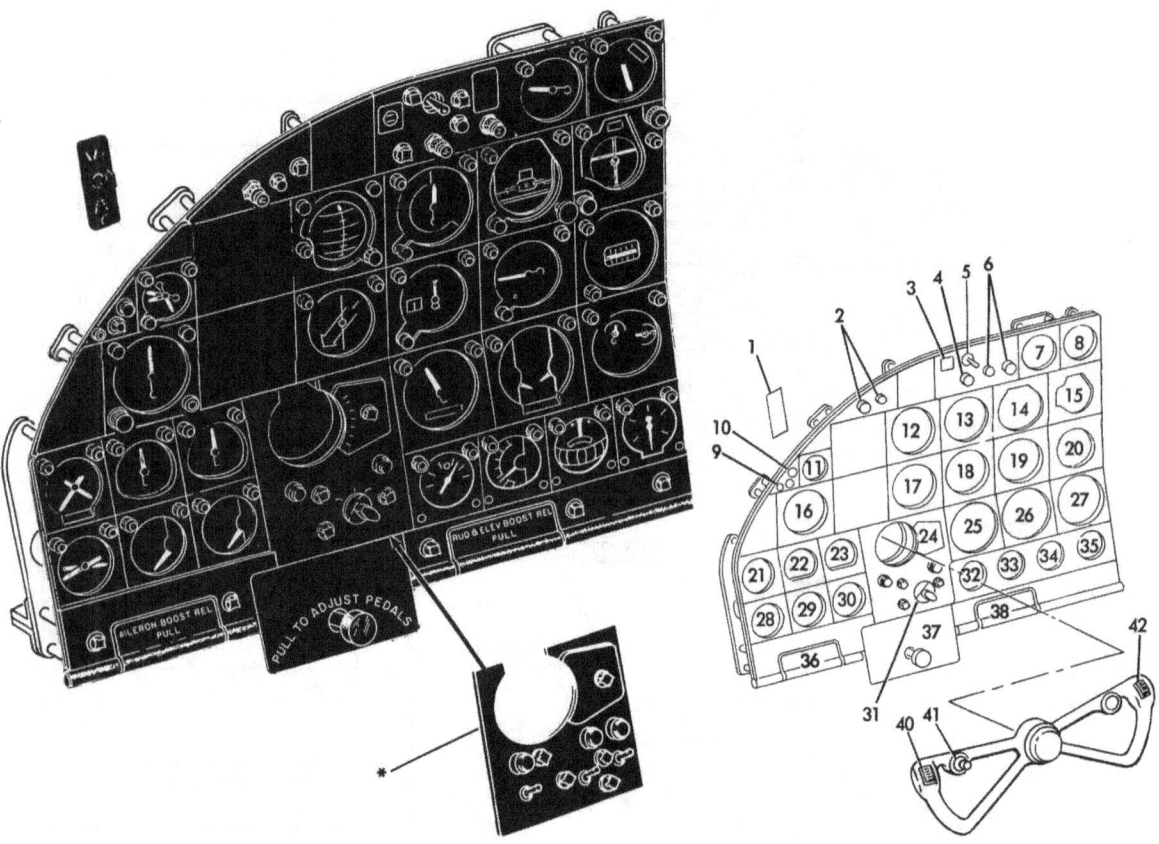

1. Angle-of-attack indexer
2. Left-hand fire warning light and circuit test switch
3. Utility hydraulic system pressure indicator
4. Lateral control warning light
5. Windshield wiper switch
6. Right-hand fire warning light and circuit test switch
7. Dual fuel flowmeter
8. Angle-of-attack indicator
9. ATM compartment temperature warning light
10. Fuel low level warning lights
11. Accelerometer
12. Vertical gyro attitude indicator (VGI)
13. Airspeed indicator
14. Standby gyro attitude indicator
15. ID-249A/ARN course indicator
16. ID-257/APN-22 radar altimeter
17. ID-250A/ARN radio magnetic indicator
18. Counter pointer pressure altimeter
19. Vertical velocity indicator
20. ID-310/ARN-21 range indicator
21. Dual oil pressure gage
22. Left engine turbine tachometer
23. Right engine turbine tachometer
24. Aileron trim position indicator
25. Fuel quantity indicator
26. Dual engine oil temperature indicator
27. Rudder and elevator trim position indicator
28. Dual fuel boost pressure indicator
29. Left engine turbine outlet temperature gage
30. Right engine turbine outlet
*31. Bleed air shutoff rotary switch
32. Liquid oxygen quantity gage
33. Free air temperature gage
34. Turn and slip indicator
35. Cabin pressure altimeter
36. Aileron power boost release handle
37. Rudder pedal adjust knob
38. Rudder and elevator boost release handle
39. Deleted
40. Horizontal stabilizer ac control switch
41. Autopilot release switch
42. Radio-ICS switch

* Bleed air shutoff rotary switch to be replaced with toggle switches when available.

FF1-4463-5F

Figure 1-4. Pilot's Instrument Panel — A-3A/B Typical

1-10

Changed 1 June 1969

NAVAIR 01-40ATA-1

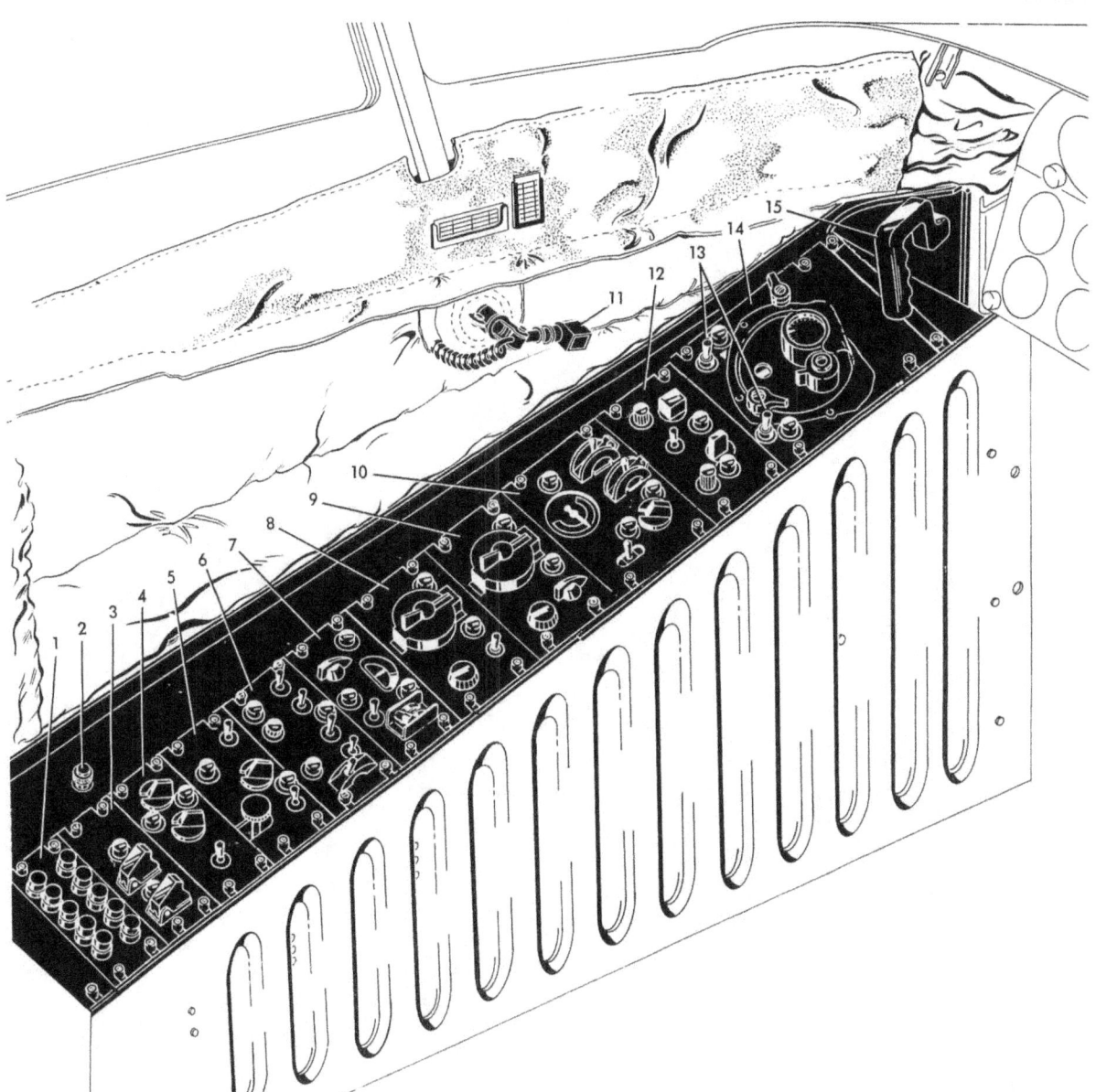

1. Cockpit lights fuse panel
2. Fin unlocked indicator light
3. ATM switches
4. Interior lights control panel
5. Cabin pressure and temperature control panel
6. Exterior lights control panel
7. S-5 pilot compass control panel
8. AN-760/ARN-14E control panel
9. AN-C-1763/ARN-21A control panel
10. Fuel system switch panel
11. Console floodlight
12. Interphone control panel
13. ADF-navigation selector switches
14. Oxygen regulator panel
15. Nosewheel steering control

Figure 1-6. Pilot's Left-Hand Console — A-3A

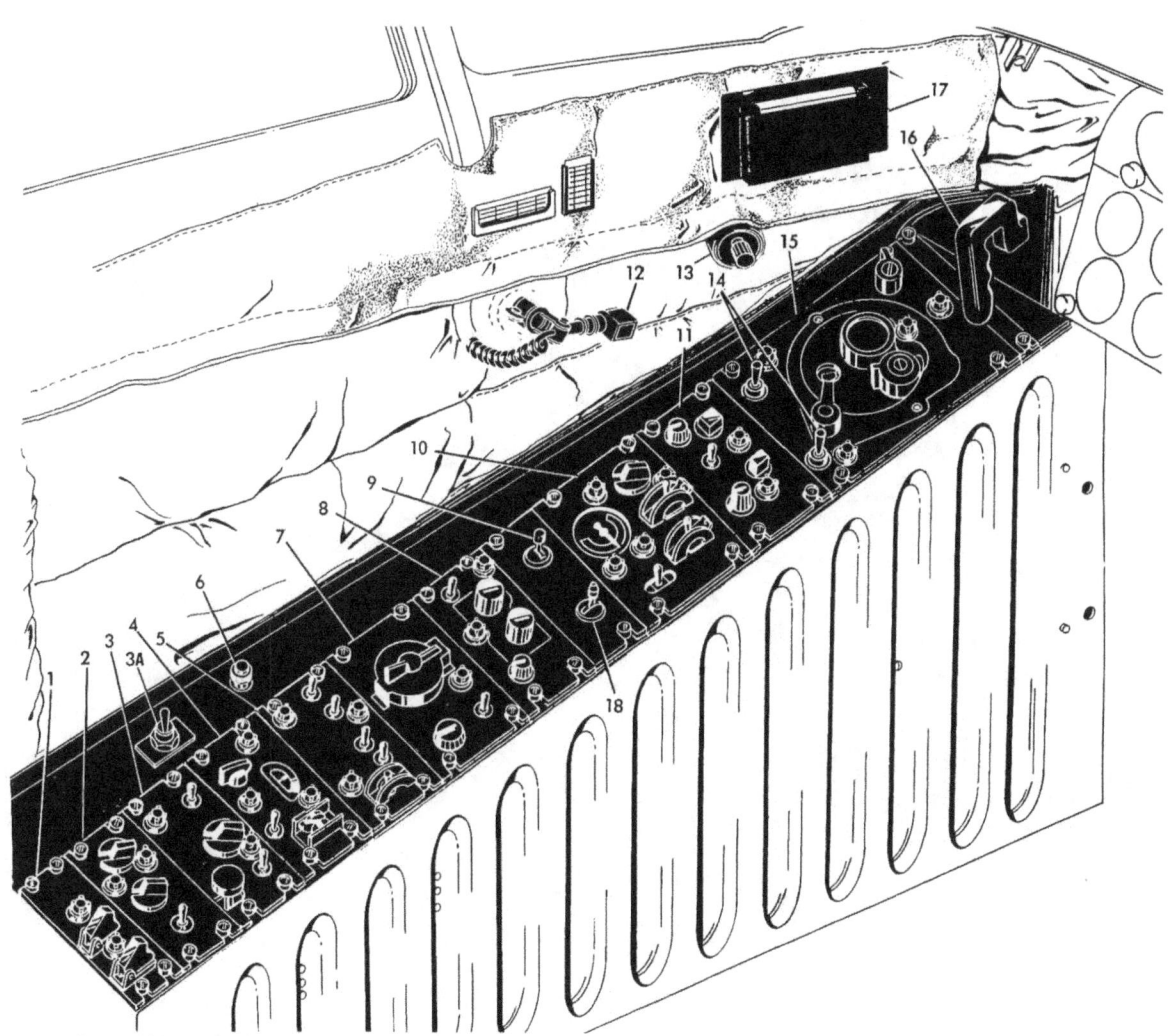

1. ATM switch panel
2. Interior lights control panel
3. Cabin pressure and temperature control panel
3A. AUX UHF receiver control switch
4. S-5 pilot compass control panel
5. Exterior lights control panel
6. Fin unlocked indicator light
7. AN-760/ARN-14E (VOR) control panel
8. AN-866/ARN-21 control panel
9. Fuel dump switch
10. Fuel system switch panel
11. Interphone control panel
12. Console floodlight
13. Pilot's white floodlight control switch
14. ADF-Navigation selector switches
15. Oxygen regulator panel
16. Nosewheel steering control
17. Engine trim card holder
18. Fuel crossfeed control

Figure 1-7. Pilot's Left-Hand Console — A-3B

NAVAIR 01-40ATA-1

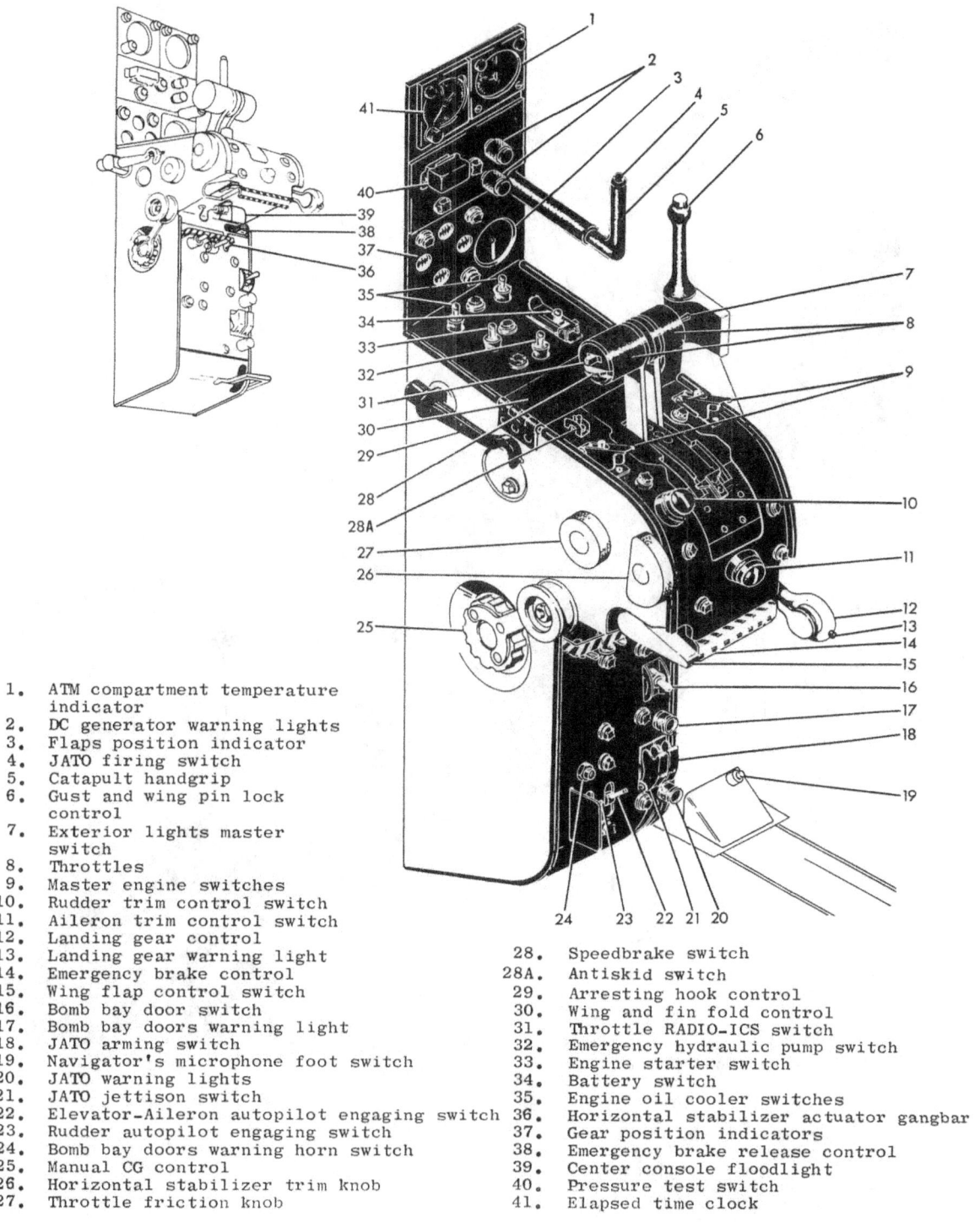

1. ATM compartment temperature indicator
2. DC generator warning lights
3. Flaps position indicator
4. JATO firing switch
5. Catapult handgrip
6. Gust and wing pin lock control
7. Exterior lights master switch
8. Throttles
9. Master engine switches
10. Rudder trim control switch
11. Aileron trim control switch
12. Landing gear control
13. Landing gear warning light
14. Emergency brake control
15. Wing flap control switch
16. Bomb bay door switch
17. Bomb bay doors warning light
18. JATO arming switch
19. Navigator's microphone foot switch
20. JATO warning lights
21. JATO jettison switch
22. Elevator-Aileron autopilot engaging switch
23. Rudder autopilot engaging switch
24. Bomb bay doors warning horn switch
25. Manual CG control
26. Horizontal stabilizer trim knob
27. Throttle friction knob
28. Speedbrake switch
28A. Antiskid switch
29. Arresting hook control
30. Wing and fin fold control
31. Throttle RADIO-ICS switch
32. Emergency hydraulic pump switch
33. Engine starter switch
34. Battery switch
35. Engine oil cooler switches
36. Horizontal stabilizer actuator gangbar
37. Gear position indicators
38. Emergency brake release control
39. Center console floodlight
40. Pressure test switch
41. Elapsed time clock

Figure 1-9. Pilot's Center Console – A-3B

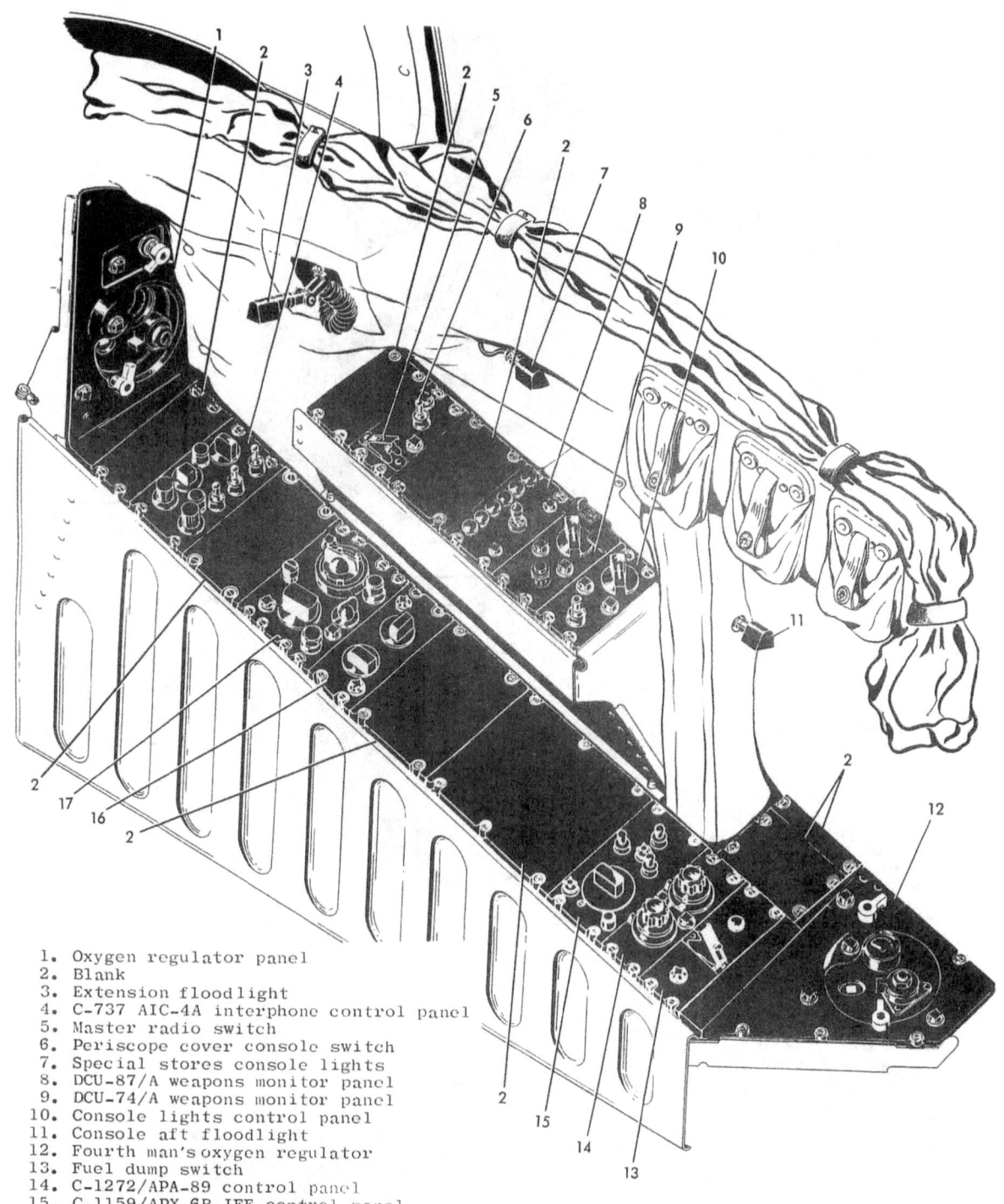

1. Oxygen regulator panel
2. Blank
3. Extension floodlight
4. C-737 AIC-4A interphone control panel
5. Master radio switch
6. Periscope cover console switch
7. Special stores console lights
8. DCU-87/A weapons monitor panel
9. DCU-74/A weapons monitor panel
10. Console lights control panel
11. Console aft floodlight
12. Fourth man's oxygen regulator
13. Fuel dump switch
14. C-1272/APA-89 control panel
15. C-1159/APX-6B IFF control panel
16. C-ARC-1 VHF radio control panel
17. C-1015/ARC-27A UHF radio control panel

Figure 1-10. Navigator's Typical Right-Hand Console — A-3A

NAVAIR 01-40ATA-1

Section I
Part 1

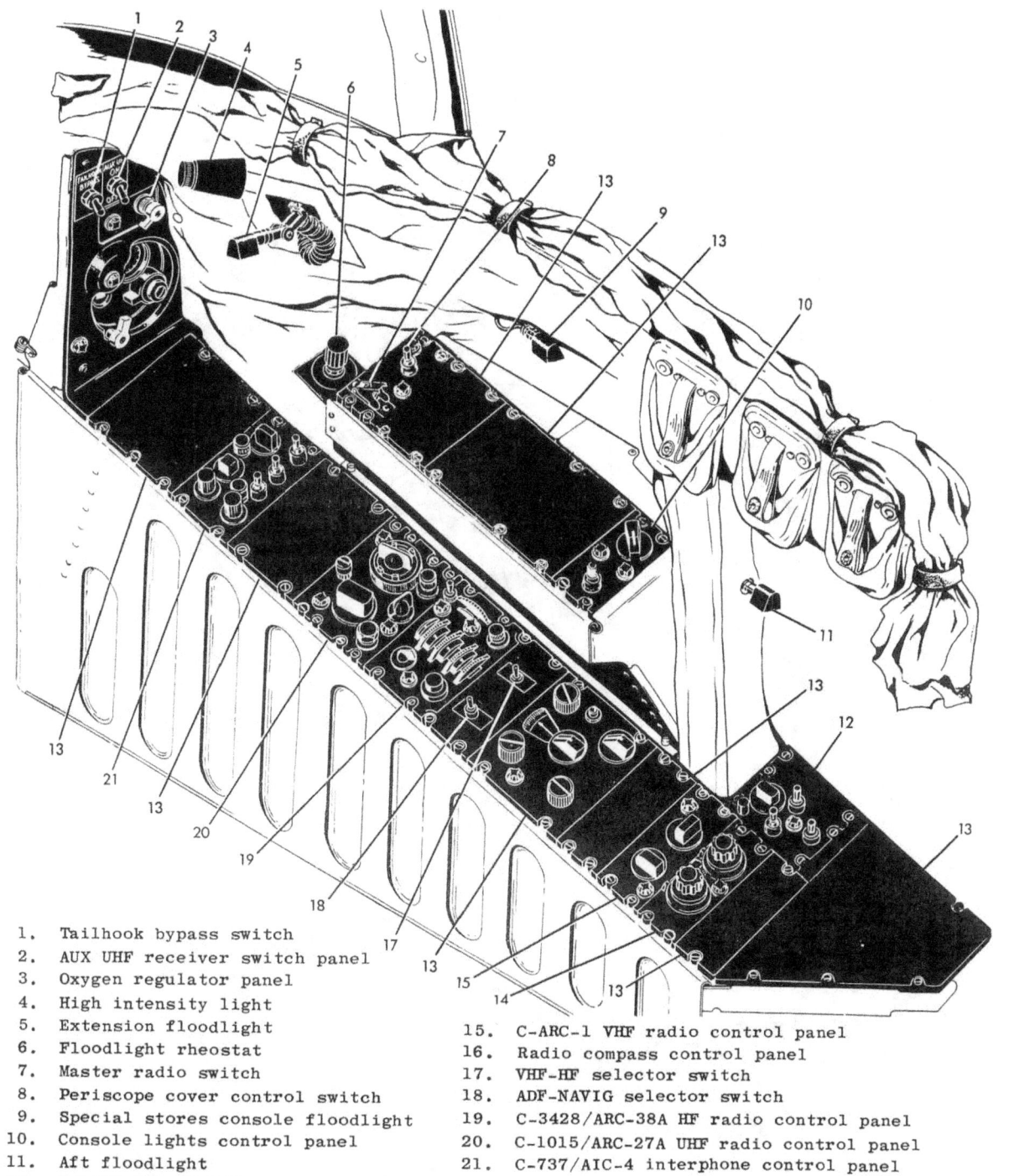

1. Tailhook bypass switch
2. AUX UHF receiver switch panel
3. Oxygen regulator panel
4. High intensity light
5. Extension floodlight
6. Floodlight rheostat
7. Master radio switch
8. Periscope cover control switch
9. Special stores console floodlight
10. Console lights control panel
11. Aft floodlight
12. C-1159 APX-6B IFF control panel
13. Blank
14. C-1272/APA-89 control panel
15. C-ARC-1 VHF radio control panel
16. Radio compass control panel
17. VHF-HF selector switch
18. ADF-NAVIG selector switch
19. C-3428/ARC-38A HF radio control panel
20. C-1015/ARC-27A UHF radio control panel
21. C-737/AIC-4 interphone control panel

FF1-4472-3K

Figure 1-11. Navigator's Typical Right-Hand Console — A-3B

Changed 15 July 1970

1-17

Section I
Part 1

NAVAIR 01-40ATA-1

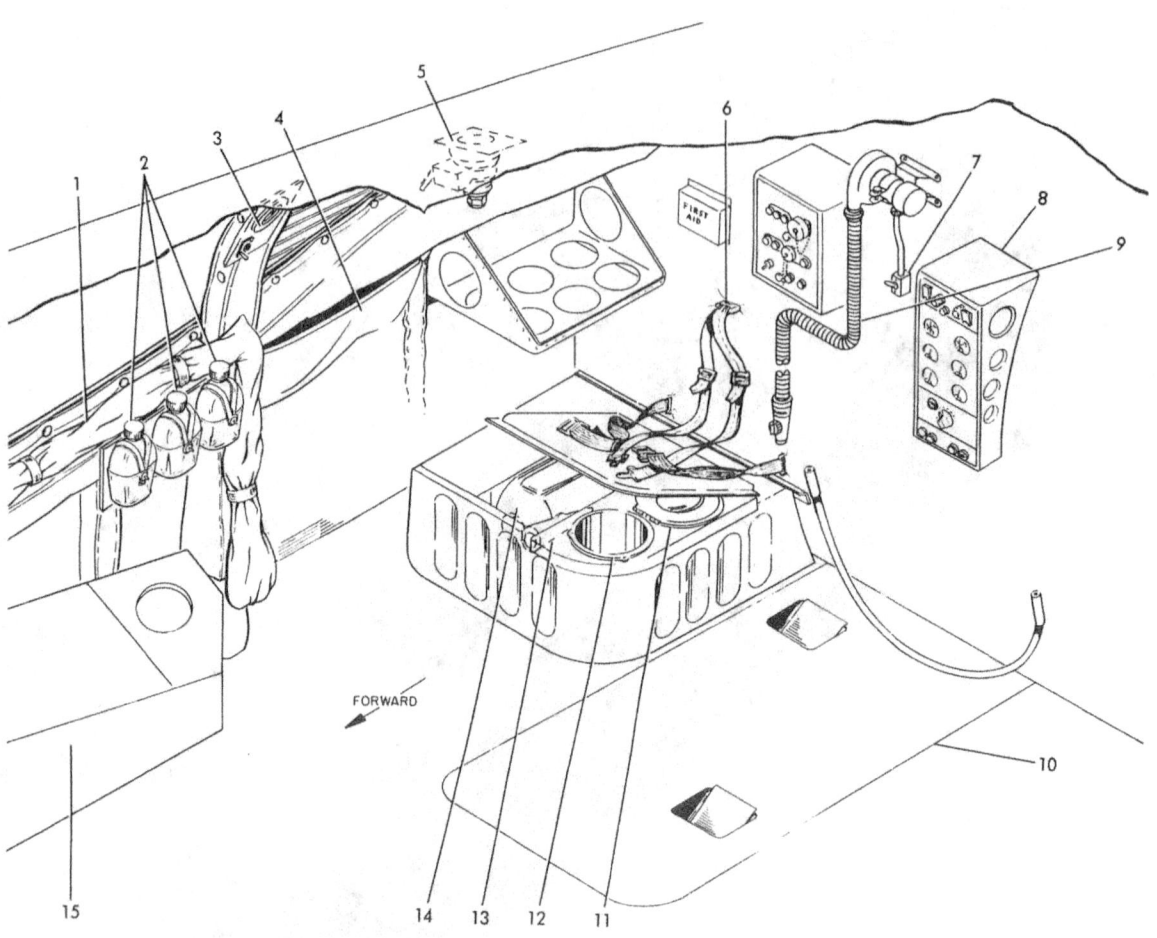

1. Navigation curtain
2. Canteens
3. Dome light
4. Tissue storage receptacle
5. Sextant mount
6. Lap belt and shoulder harness
7. Fourth man's antiexposure suit blower switch
8. Aft power panel
9. Fourth man's antiexposure suit blower hose
10. Inner emergency escape chute door
11. Waste receptacle
12. Toilet
13. Relief tube
14. CN-100/ASB-1 gyroscope
15. Right-hand console (Ref.)

Figure 1-12. Aft Cockpit — A-3A

NAVAIR 01-40ATA-1

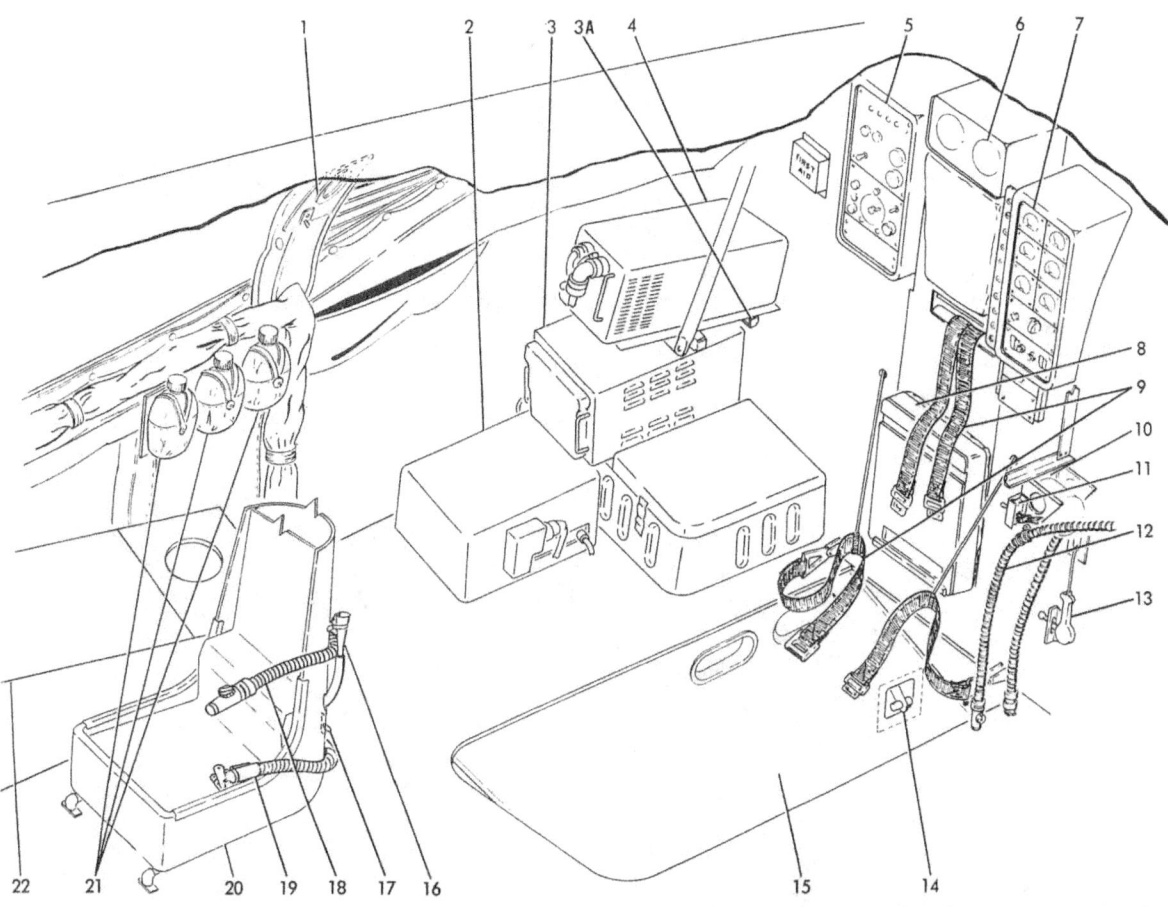

1. Dome light
2. R-101/ARN-6 radio compass unit
3. RT/ARC-1 VHF receiver-transmitter
3A. Recorder bracket and receptacle
4. Automatic pilot amplifier
5. Power distribution panel
6. Time meter
7. Aft power panel
8. Fourth man's seat
9. Fourth man's seat shoulder harness and lap belt
10. Fourth man's oxygen control panel
11. Fourth man's antiexposure suit blower switch
12. Fourth man's antiexposure suit blower air hose
13. Fourth man's seat shoulder harness lock
14. Companionway emergency exit T-handle (RH side of companionway aft of station 204)
15. Inner emergency escape chute door
16. Relief tube
17. Navigator's antiexposure suit blower switch
18. Navigator's antiexposure suit blower air hose
19. Navigator's oxygen hose
20. Navigator's seat
21. Canteens
22. Navigator's right-hand console

Figure 1-13. Aft Cockpit — A-3B

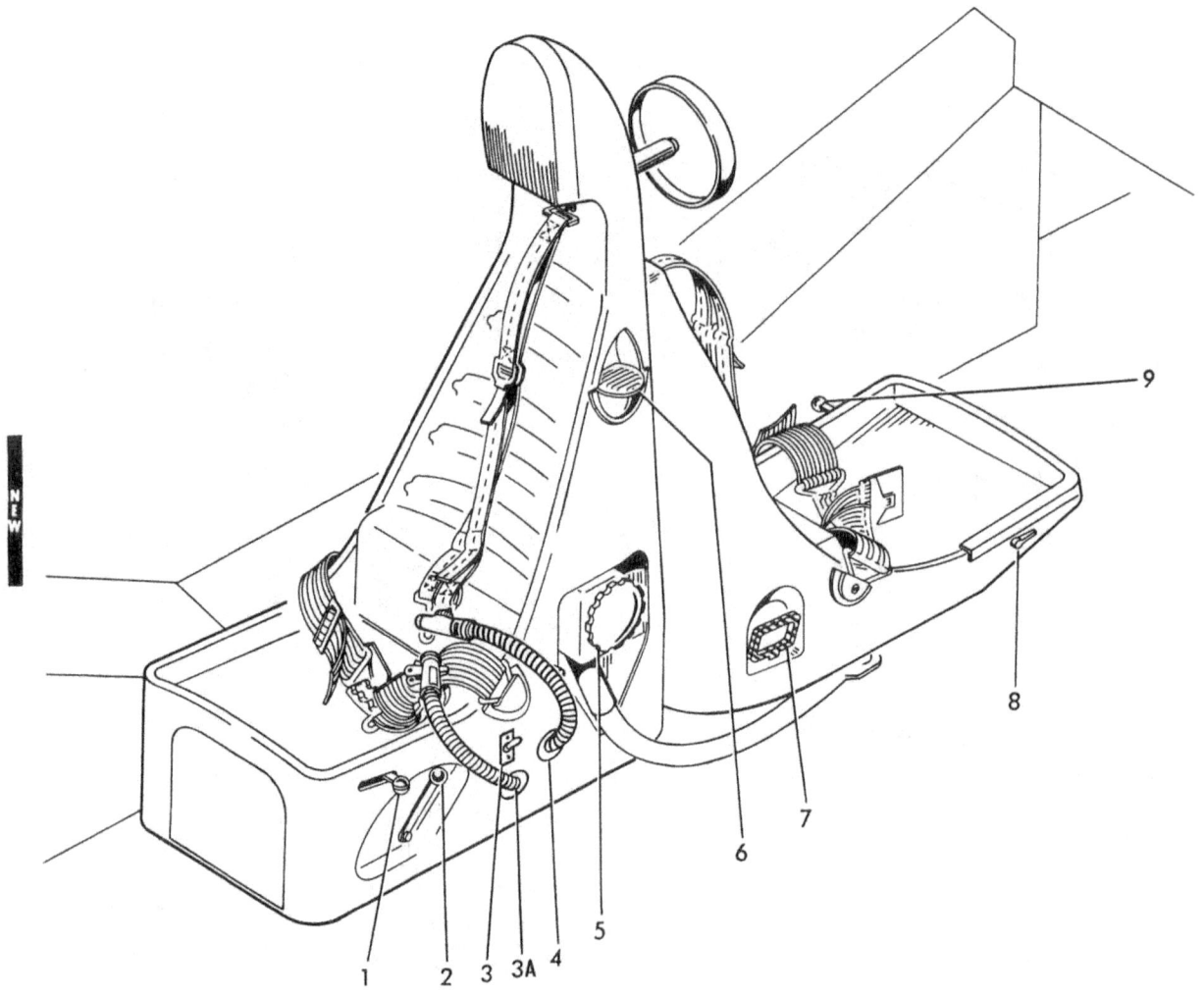

1. Shoulder harness lock
2. Upper entrance door lock
3. Antiexposure suit blower switch
3A. Plane captain's oxygen hose
4. Antiexposure suit blower air hose
5. Gyropilot pedestal controller (stowed)
6. Upper hatch step
7. Emergency escape chute control handle
8. Pilot's seat adjustment control
9. Pilot's shoulder harness lock

Figure 1-14. Pilot's and Plane Captain's Seats — A-3B (Typical)

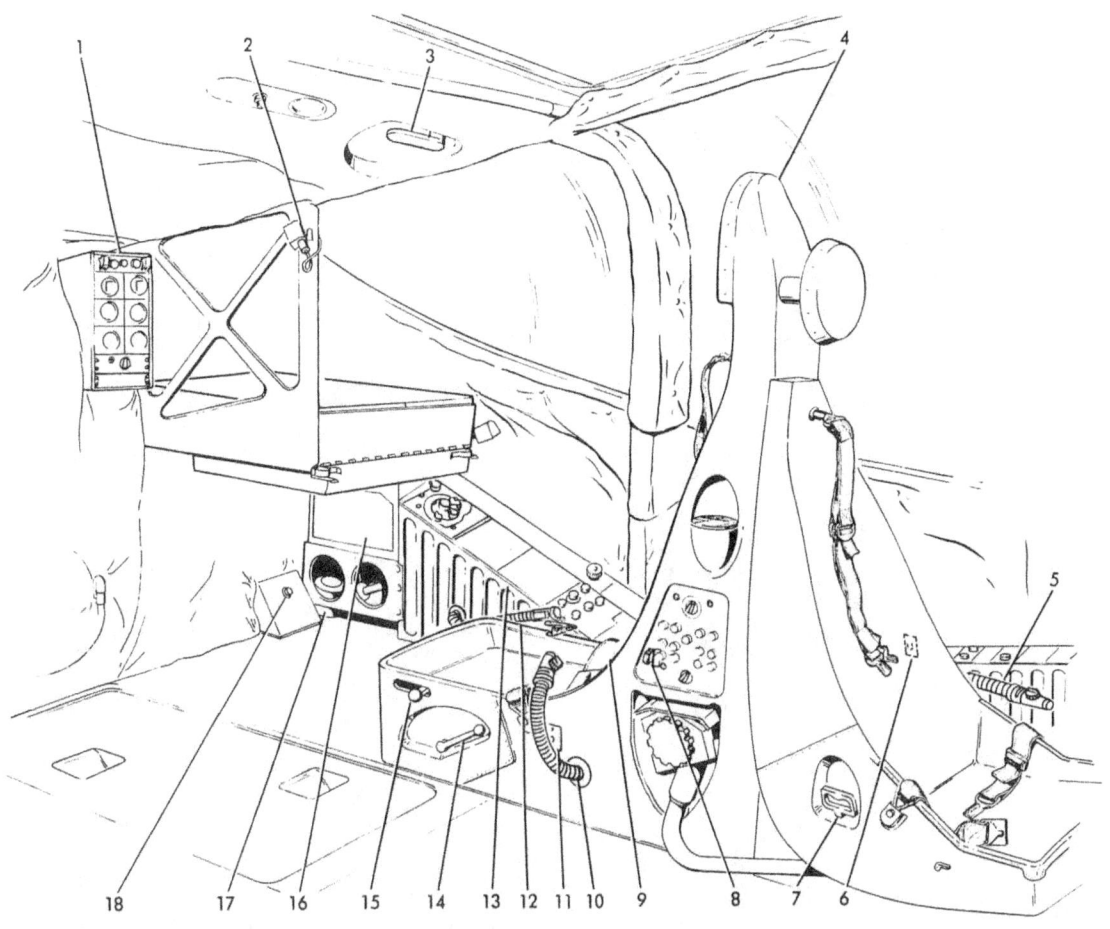

1. Aft power panel
2. Aft power panel floodlight
3. Escape hatch control handle
4. Plane captain's seat
5. Pilot's antiexposure suit blower air hose
6. Pilot's antiexposure suit blower switch
7. Emergency escape chute control handle
8. Emergency bomb release safety switch
9. Lap belt and shoulder harness
10. Antiexposure suit blower air hose
11. Antiexposure suit blower switch
12. Oxygen hose
13. Console
14. Inner emergency escape chute door lock
15. Shoulder harness lock
16. Storage compartment
17. Cabin pressurizing valve
18. ICS/Radio foot microphone switch

Figure 1-15. Plane Captain's Station — A3-A

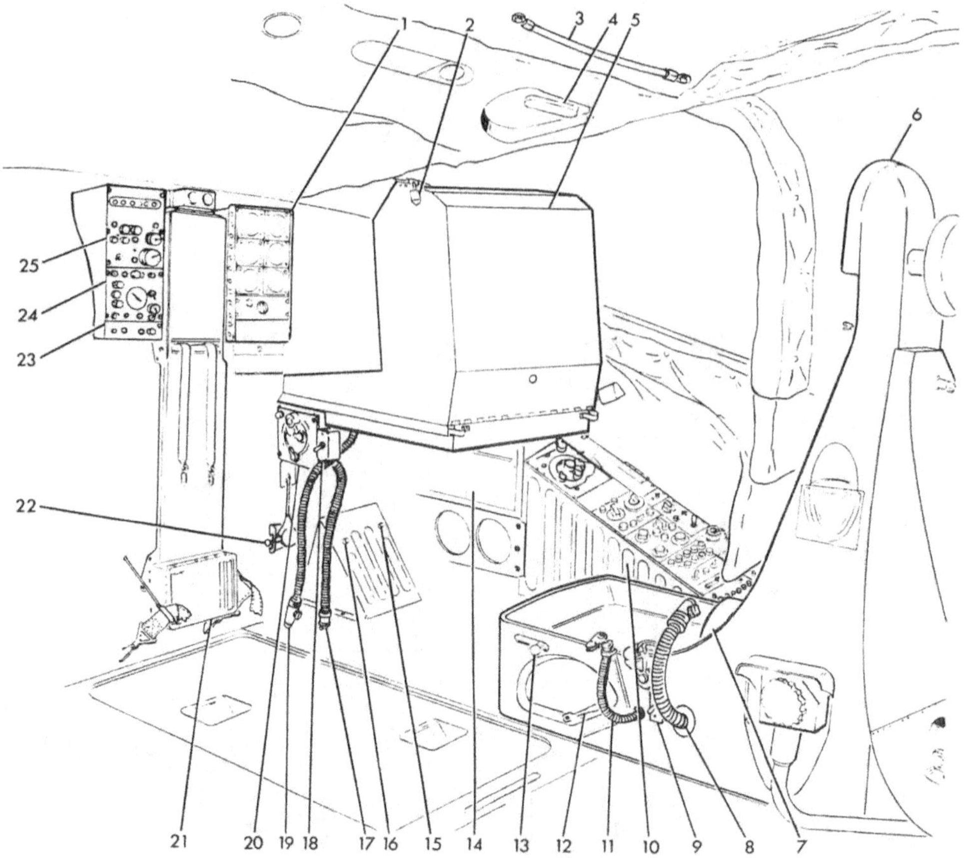

Section I
Part 1

NAVAIR 01-40ATA-1

1. Aft power panel
2. Aft power panel floodlight
3. Bailout assist bungee
4. Escape hatch control handle
5. DECM equipment panel
6. Seat
7. Lap belt and shoulder harness
8. Antiexposure suit blower air hose
9. Antiexposure suit blower switch
10. Console
11. Oxygen hose
12. Inner emergency escape chute door lock
13. Shoulder harness lock
14. Storage compartment
15. Radio foot microphone switch (late A-3B)
16. ICS Switch (early A-3B)
17. Fourth seat oxygen hose
18. Fourth man's antiexposure suit blower switch
19. Fourth man's antiexposure suit blower air hose
20. Fourth man's oxygen regulator
21. Fourth man's seat
22. Fourth man's seat shoulder harness lock
23. Control boost latch test panel
24. ASB pressure monitor panel
25. Power distribution panel

Figure 1-16. Plane Captain's Station — A-3B

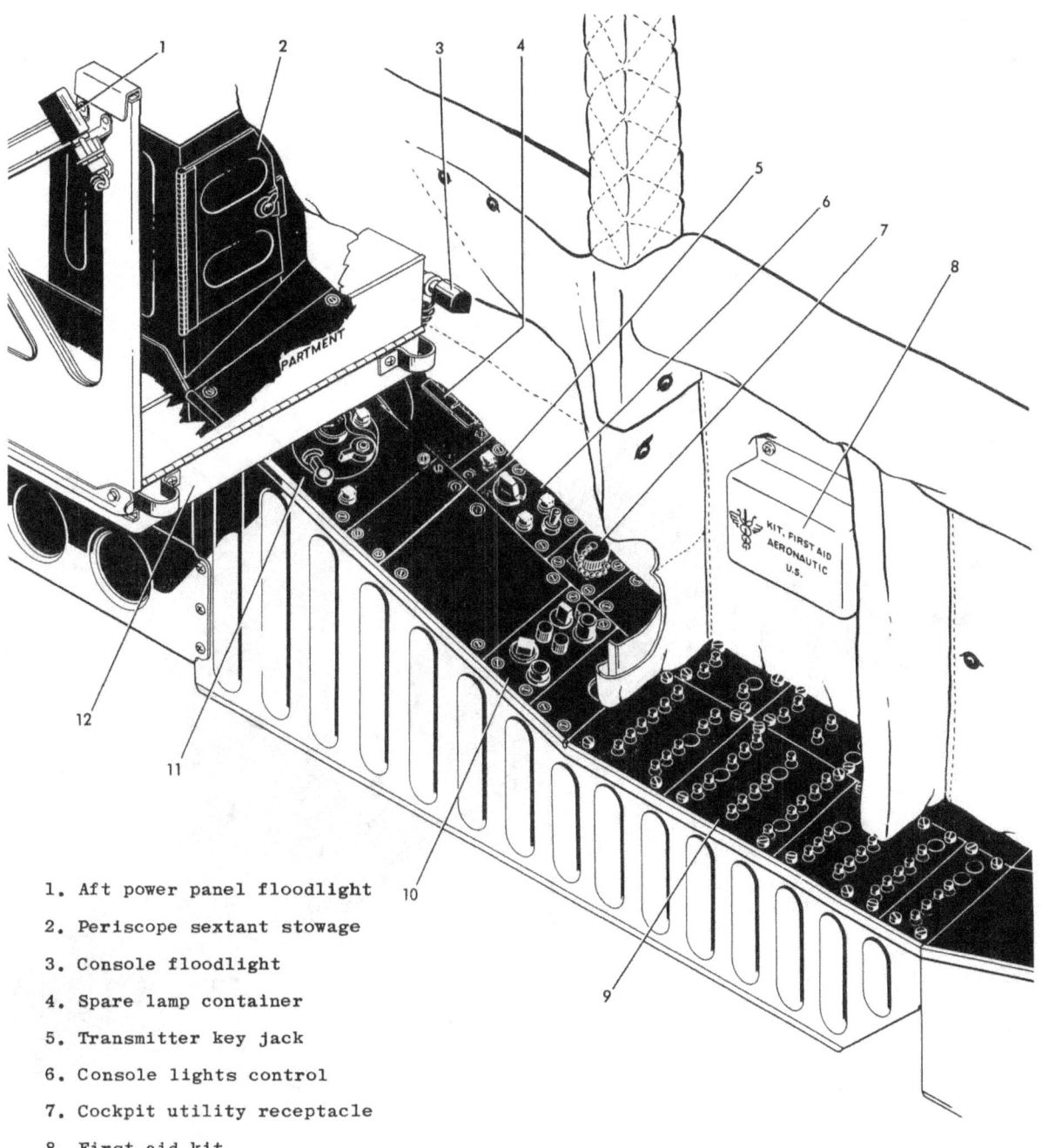

1. Aft power panel floodlight
2. Periscope sextant stowage
3. Console floodlight
4. Spare lamp container
5. Transmitter key jack
6. Console lights control
7. Cockpit utility receptacle
8. First aid kit
9. Cockpit circuit breaker panel
10. C-736/AIC-4A interphone control panel
11. Oxygen regulator panel
12. Navigation equipment container

Figure 1-17. Plane Captain's Console — A3-A

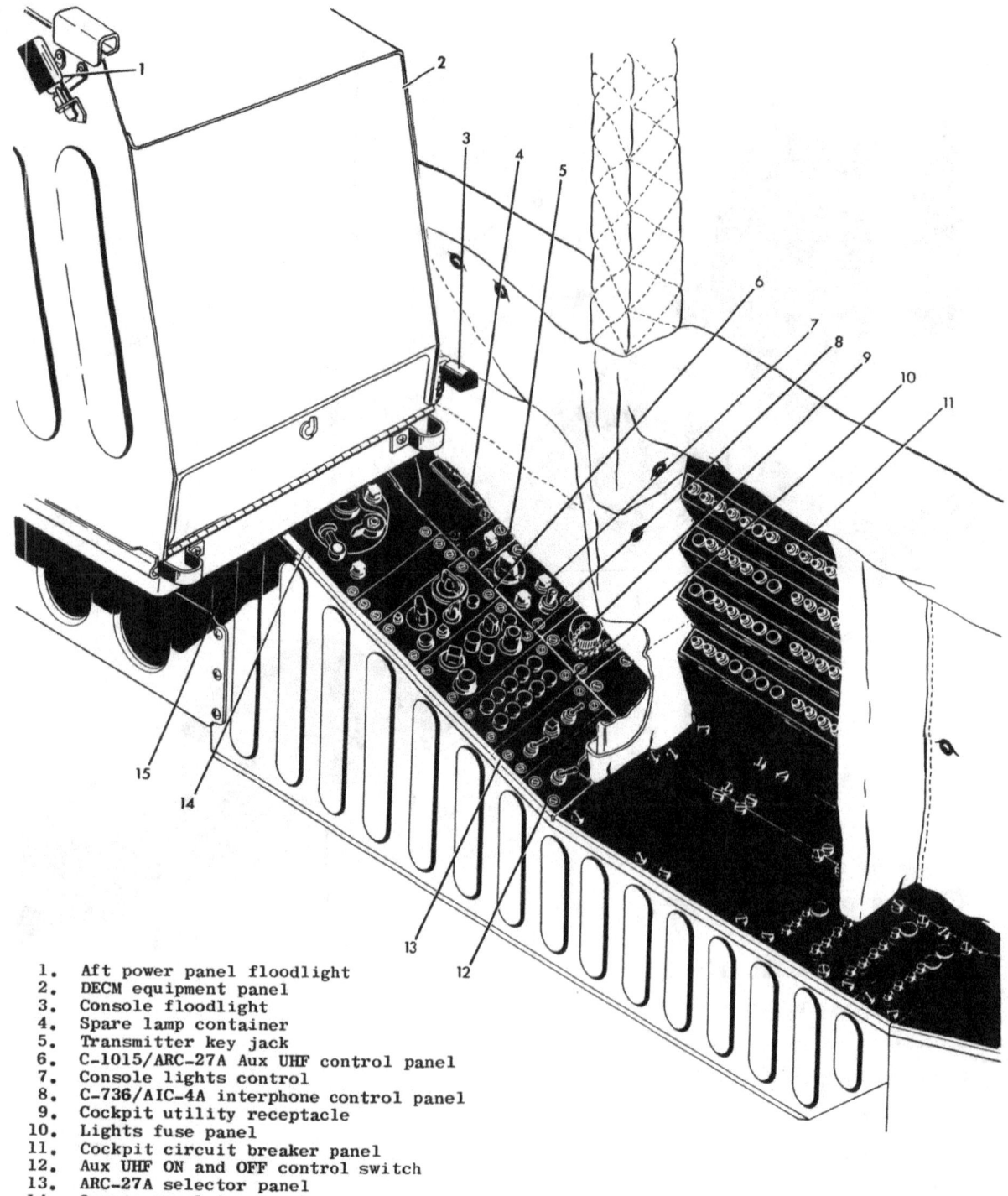

1. Aft power panel floodlight
2. DECM equipment panel
3. Console floodlight
4. Spare lamp container
5. Transmitter key jack
6. C-1015/ARC-27A Aux UHF control panel
7. Console lights control
8. C-736/AIC-4A interphone control panel
9. Cockpit utility receptacle
10. Lights fuse panel
11. Cockpit circuit breaker panel
12. Aux UHF ON and OFF control switch
13. ARC-27A selector panel
14. Oxygen regulator panel
15. Navigation equipment container

Figure 1-18. Plane Captain's Console – A-3B

NAVAIR 01-40ATA-1 Section I
Part 1

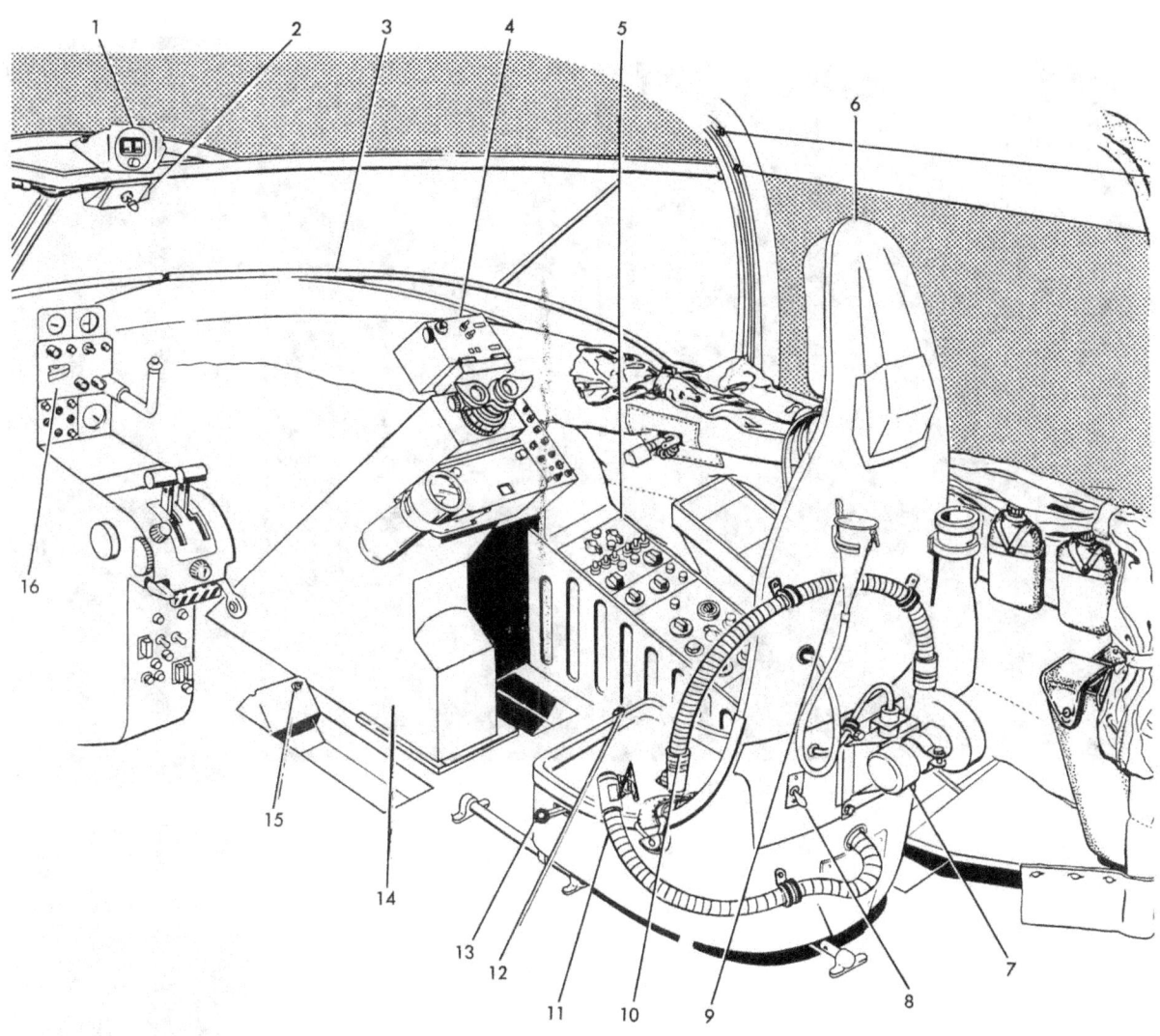

1. Standby magnetic compass
2. Drag chute switch
3. Glareshield
4. MK 97 modified computer control
5. Console
6. Seat
7. Antiexposure suit blower motor
8. Antiexposure suit blower switch
9. Relief tube
10. Antiexposure suit blower air hose
11. Oxygen connection
12. Seat control
13. Shoulder harness control
14. ASB-1A equipment
15. ICS microphone switch
16. ATM monitor panel

FF1-6742-P

Figure 1-19. Navigator's Station — A-3A/B (Typical)

Changed 15 July 1970

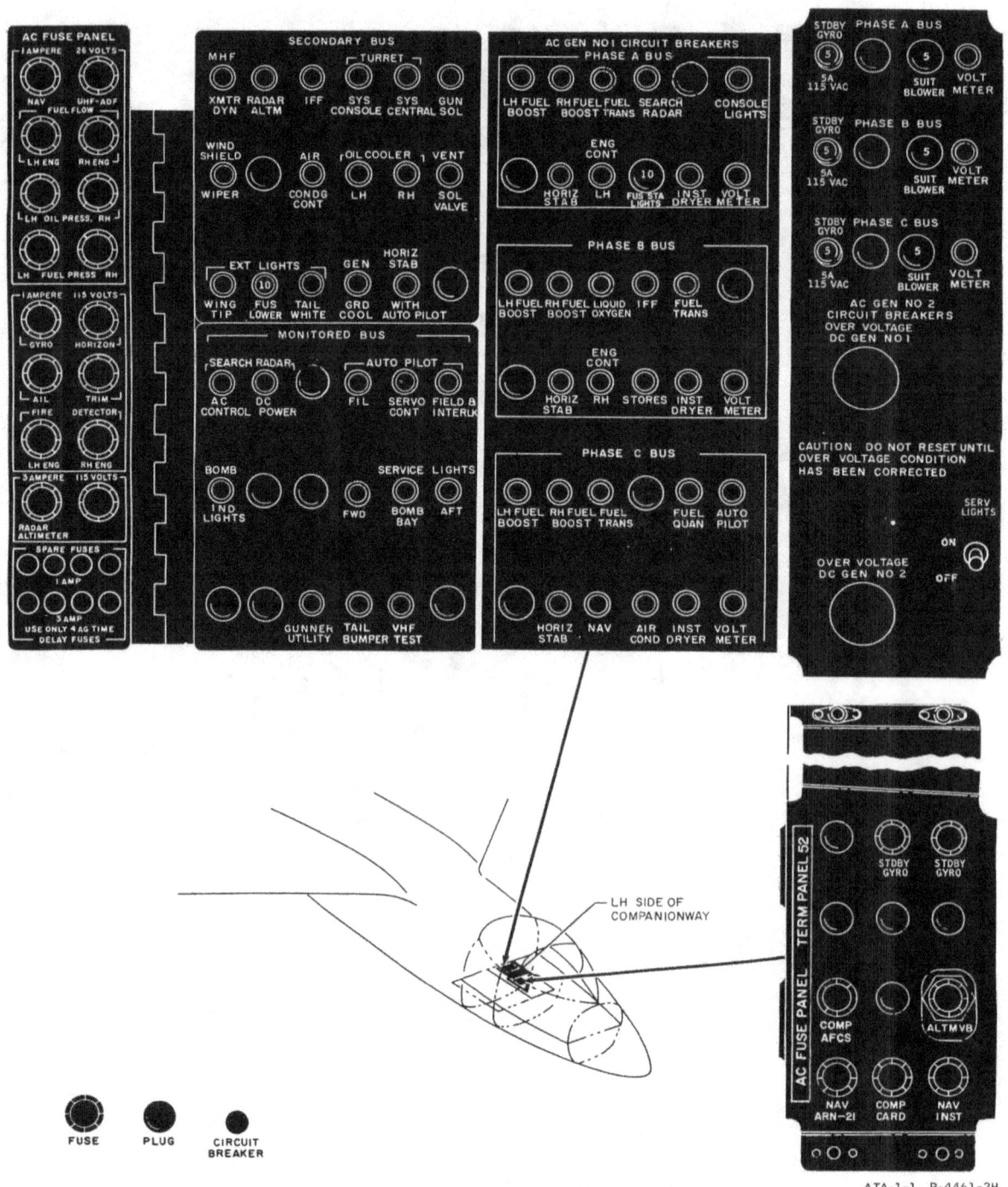

Figure 1-20. Circuit Breaker and Fuse Panels — A-3A

NAVAIR 01-40ATA-1

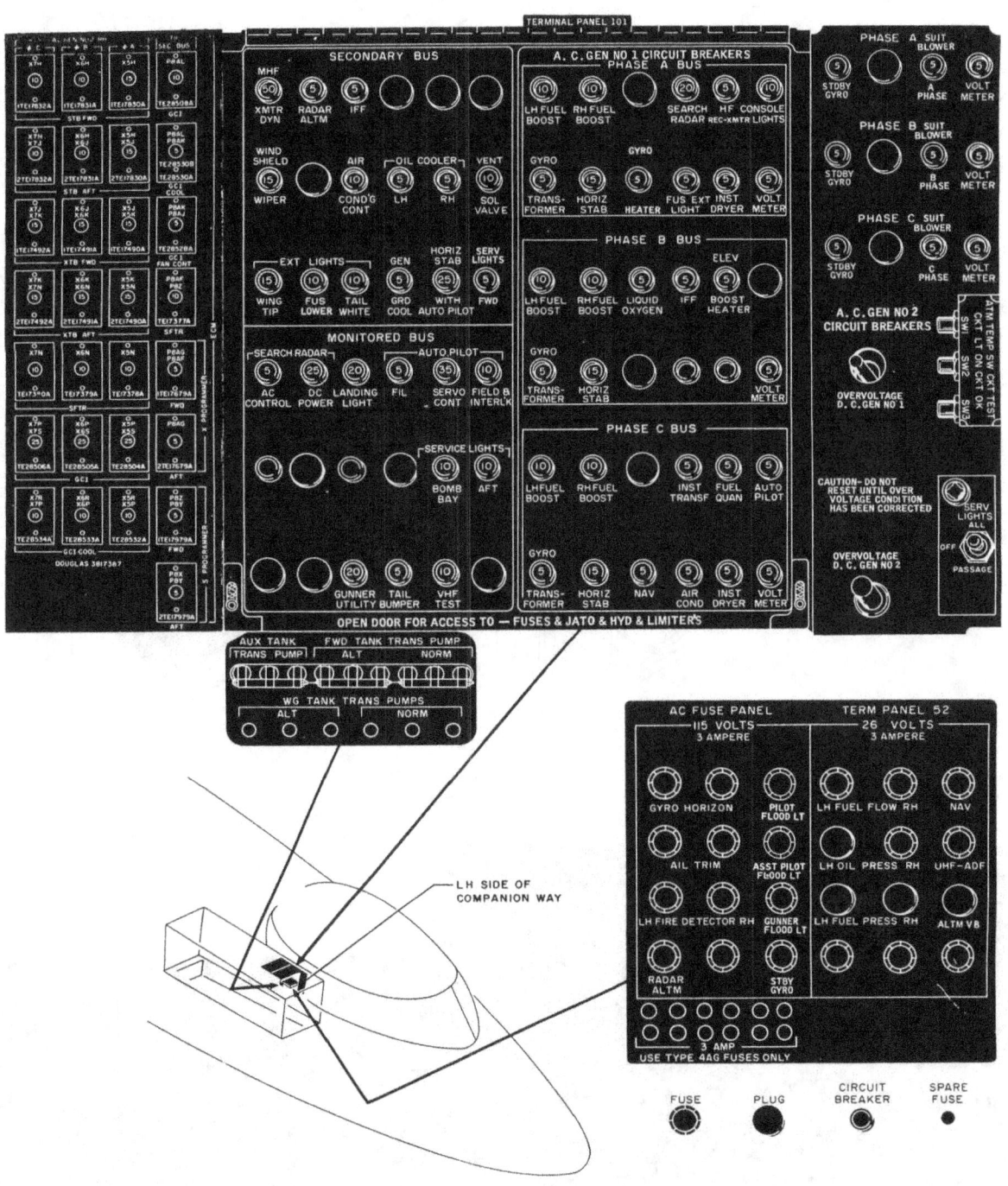

Figure 1-21. Circuit Breaker and Fuse Panels — A-3B

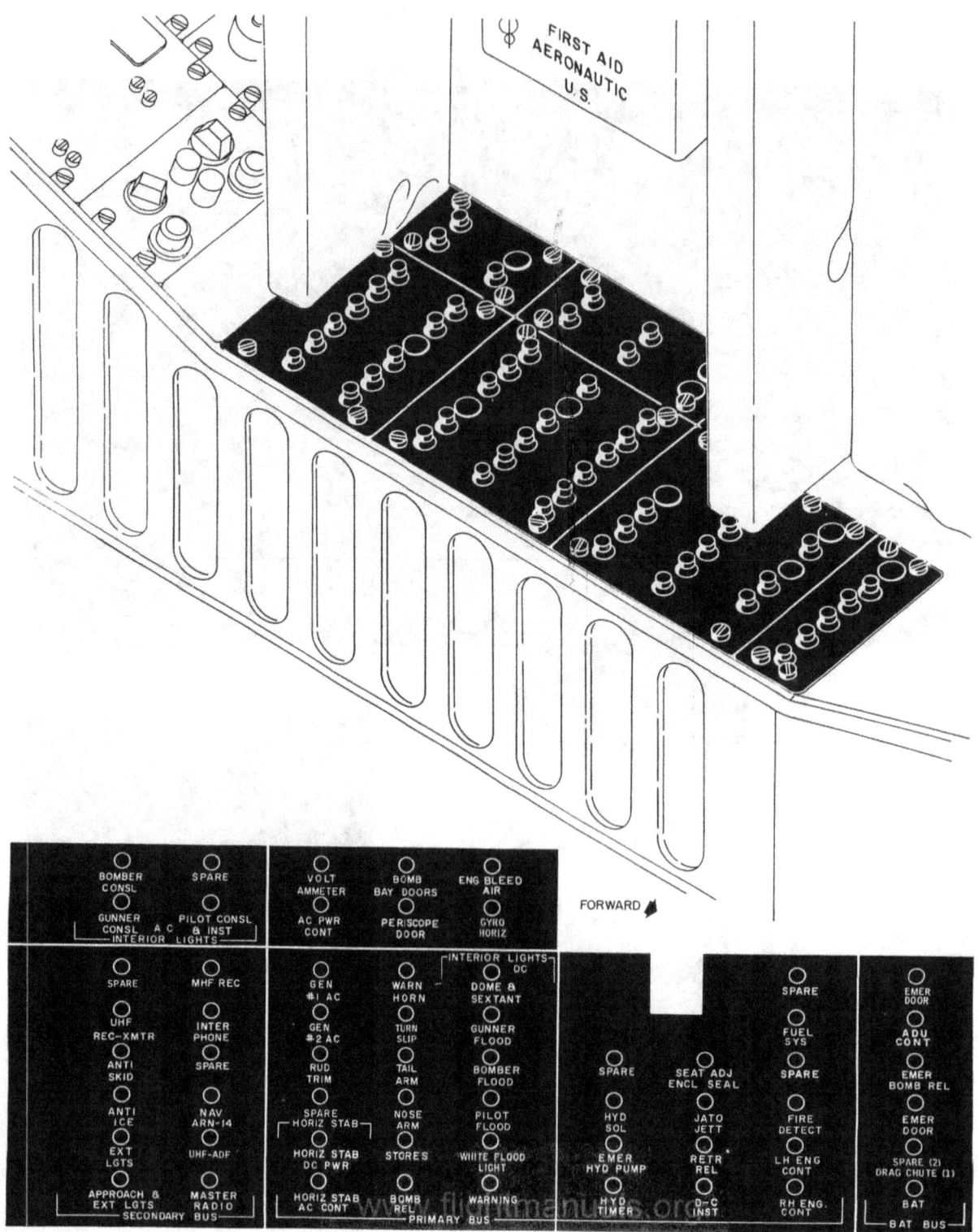

Figure 1-22. Pilot's Circuit Breaker Panel – A-3A

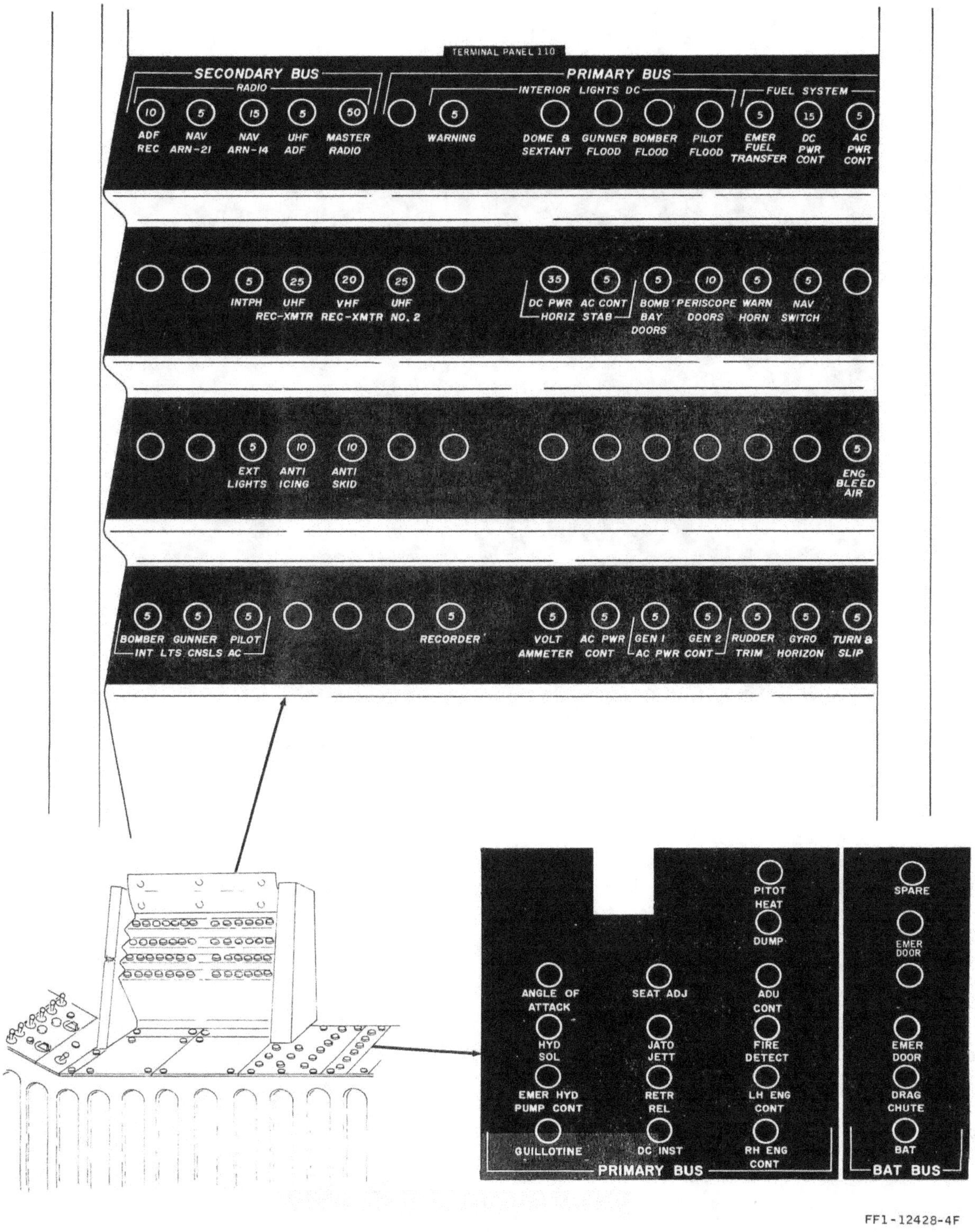

NAVAIR 01-40ATA-1

Section I
Part 1

Figure 1-23. Pilot's Circuit Breaker Panel — A-3B (Typical)

Changed 15 July 1970

1-29/(1-30 Blank)

PART 2
SYSTEMS

TABLE OF CONTENTS

TEXT

	Page		Page
Engine	1-31	Antiexposure Suit Ventilation	1-72
Engine Operation	1-31	Electrical System	1-72
Engine Malfunction/Failure	1-31	DC Power System	1-72
Engine Fire-Detection System	1-32	DC Power Distribution	1-72
Ignition System	1-33	DC Generator Switches	1-73
Engine Starter	1-33	Generator Warning Lights	1-73
Engine Fuel Control System	1-33	Electrical System Emergency Operation	1-73
Engine Controls	1-33	AC Power System	1-76
Engine Instruments	1-34	AC Power Distribution	1-76
Engine Starting	1-34	AC Power Control	1-77
Engine Oil System	1-36	AC Power Failure	1-81
Oil Pressure Gage	1-37	Hydraulic System	1-81
Oil Cooler Door Control	1-37	Utility Hydraulic System	1-81
Dual Engine Oil Temperature Indicator	1-37	Emergency Hydraulic System	1-85
Oil System Malfunction	1-37	Flight Control System	1-85
Fuel Systems	1-37	Aileron Control System	1-85
General (All Aircraft)	1-37	Aileron/Spoiler and Surface Control	
Basic A-3A/B Fuel System	1-39	Pressure Warning Light	1-91
Fuel Tanks	1-39	Aileron and Rudder-Elevator	1-91
Pressure Fueling System	1-39	Horizontal Stabilizer Trim System	1-92
Wing Tank Fuel Transfer Control	1-42	Horizontal Stabilizer Trim Control	1-92
Auxiliary Tank Fuel Transfer Control	1-42	AC High-Speed Stabilizer Trim	1-92
Fuel Trim Control System	1-43	Autopilot Stabilizer Trim	1-93
Fuel System Switch Panel	1-43	Wing and Fin-Folding System	1-94
Fuselage Fuel Trim Switch	1-43	Wing Flaps	1-95
CG Indicator	1-44	Speedbrakes	1-96
Manual CG Fuel Control Valve	1-44	Landing Gear System	1-96
Wing Tank Fuel Dumping System	1-44	Landing Gear Emergency Operation	1-97
Fuel Quantity Indicating System	1-44	Bomb Bay to Main Gear Access	1-97
Fuel Tank Pressurizing and Venting System	1-45	Nosewheel Steering System	1-97
Fuel System Management – Basic A-3A/B		Arresting Hook	1-98
Fuel System	1-45	Wheel Brakes System	1-98
Fuel Trim Control – Automatic	1-45	Pneumatic Emergency Systems	1-99
Fuel Trim Control – Selective	1-45	Escape Hatch Air System	1-99
Fuel Trim Control – Manual	1-47	Wing Slats	1-99
Fuel Transfer	1-47	Drag Chute	1-99
Fuel Quantity Indicator	1-48	Instruments	1-101
Fuel Low-Level Warning Light	1-48	Airspeed Indicator	1-101
Engine Compressor Bleed Air System	1-48	Counterpointer Pressure Altimeter	1-101
Bleed Air Shutoff System (Toggle Switches)	1-48	Vertical Velocity Indicator	1-102
Bleed Air Shutoff System (Rotary Switch)	1-63	Turn-and-Slip Indicator	1-102
Air Turbine Motors (ATM's)	1-63	Accelerometer	1-102
Air-Conditioning and Pressurizing System	1-66	Vertical Gyro Attitude Indicator (VGI)	1-102
Electronic Temperature Controller	1-66	Standby Gyro Horizon Indicator	1-103
Cabin Air Contamination	1-69	Standby Compass	1-103
Windshield Defogging	1-71	Angle-of-Attack Approach Light System	1-103
Emergency Operation	1-71	Engine Trim Card	1-104
Equipment Ground Cooling	1-71	Clocks	1-104
Windshield Wiper	1-71	Radio and Electronics Equipment	1-104
Anti-Icing System	1-71	Radio Master Switch	1-104
Engine Air Inlet	1-71	ARN Radio Selector Switch	1-105
Anti-Icing Control	1-71	UHF Communication and Direction Finding System	1-105

Changed 15 July 1970

Section I
Part 2

NAVAIR 01-40ATA-1

TEXT (Continued)

	Page
AN/ARC-27A UHF Radio Receiver-Transmitters	1-105
RT-178/ARC-27A Receiver-Transmitters	1-105
UHF Radio Control Panel	1-107
AN/ARA-25 *Automatic Direction Finding* System	1-109
Dual AN/ARC-27A UHF Radio Receiver-Transmitter Installation	1-109
Security Equipment	1-111
AN/ARC-38A HF Radio Receiver-Transmitter	1-111
AN/APX-6B Transponder (IFF)	1-112
C-1159/APX-6B Control Panel (IFF)	1-112
AN/APA-89 (SIF)	1-113
AN/AIC-4A Interphone	1-113
Pilot's and Plane Captain's Interphone Control Units (ICS)	1-113
Navigator's Interphone Control Unit (ICS)	1-113
Fourth Man ICS Switch	1-114
AN/APN-22 Radar Altimeter	1-114
Height Indicator	1-114
Radio Compass Indicator	1-114
Omnibearing Equipment (VOR)	1-114
AN/ARN-14E Receiver (VOR)	1-114
Control Panel C-760A/A	1-115
Course Indicator ID-249A/ARN	1-115

	Page
Radio Magnetic Indicator ID-250A/ARN	1-115
AN/ARN-21B TACAN	1-115
TACAN Air-to-Air Ranging	1-116
AN/ARC-1 Receiver-Transmitter	1-116
Lighting Equipment	1-116
Interior Lights	1-116
Exterior Lights	1-117
Oxygen System	1-118
Liquid Oxygen System	1-118
Oxygen System Controls (Panel-Mounted Regulator)	1-119
Autopilot	1-120
Automatic Trimming	1-121
Autopilot Pedestal Controller	1-121
To Engage Autopilot	1-124
To Disengage Autopilot	1-124
Altitude Hold Operation	1-124
Emergency Procedures	1-125
Autopilot Use Following Boost Disconnect	1-125
Navigation Equipment	1-125
Slaved Gyro Magnetic Compass System	1-125
Bomb Bay	1-127
Bomb Bay Doors	1-127
Jet-Assisted Takeoff System	1-127
JATO Arming Switch	1-128
Catapult Equipment	1-128

TABLES

Table		Page
1-1	Communications and Associated Electronics Equipment	1-110

ILLUSTRATIONS

Figure		Page
1-24	J57-P-10 Engine	1-35
1-25	Fuel System Schematic – Basic A-3A/B Aircraft	1-40
1-26	Fuel System Switch Panel	1-43
1-27	Fuel Distribution Schedule	1-46
1-28	Deleted.	
1-29	Deleted.	
1-30	Deleted.	
1-31	Engine Compressor Bleed Air Schematic A-3A/B and KA-3B	1-61
1-32	ATM Monitor Panel	1-65
1-33	ATM Restart	1-67
1-34	Air-Conditioning and Pressurizing System	1-68
1-35	Cockpit vs Aircraft Altitude Comparison	1-70
1-36	DC Electrical System	1-74

Figure		Page
1-37	Aft Power Panel	1-76
1-38	AC Power Panel	1-77
1-39	AC Electrical System	1-78
1-40	Utility Hydraulic System Schematic	1-82
1-41	Companionway Hydraulics Panel	1-86
1-42	Aileron Power Boost Assembly	1-88
1-43	Wing Spoiler System Schematic	1-89
1-44	Flight Controls Boost Schematic	1-90
1-45	Emergency Pneumatic System Schematic	1-100
1-46	Deleted.	
1-47	Radio and Radar Equipment and Antennas	1-106
1-48	Liquid Oxygen Duration	1-120
1-49	Gaseous Oxygen Duration – Portable Cylinder	1-122
1-50	Autopilot Pedestal Controller	1-123

1-30B

Changed 15 July 1970

NAVAIR 01-40ATA-1

Section I
Part 2

ENGINE

The Pratt and Whitney J57 Turbo-Wasp engine is a continuous flow, gas turbine engine consisting of two multistage, axial flow compressors; eight combustion chambers; and a split, three-stage turbine assembly. The engine consists of three main sections: the compressor section; the accessory section; and the combustion chamber, turbine, and exhaust section. The compressor section consists of a low-pressure, nine-stage unit driven by the second and third stages of the turbine assembly, and a high-pressure, seven-stage unit driven by the first stage of the turbine assembly. The eight combustion chambers are interconnected by crossover tubes to allow flame passage and continuous burning in all chambers. The main accessory section is located beneath the engine at the point of smallest diameter and contains those components necessary for proper operation of the engine. These components are the fuel control unit, fuel pump, oil system pressure and scavenging pumps, and the air turbine starter. These components are all geared to the high-pressure compressor rotor.

The J-57-P-6B engine installed in earlier aircraft is rated at 9500 pounds military thrust and at 10,000 pounds maximum (takeoff) thrust. The J57-P-10 engine is rated at 10,500 pounds for both military and maximum thrust.

Engine Operation

The pilot's management of the engine consists of setting engine power by positioning the throttle and of observing the engine instrumentation to ensure that the operating limitations (tables 1-8 and 1-9) are not exceeded. The engine rotor speed, rpm, and exhaust gas temperature (EGT) show how hard the engine is working to produce the desired thrust. A worn engine will require higher than average rotor speeds and EGT to produce a given thrust. If any of the engine limits are exceeded, the throttle must be retarded until all engine parameters are within limits.

The engine instrumentation is a valuable aid to the pilot in recognizing possible engine malfunction. The engine performance parameters shown have a definite relationship to each other which the pilot will learn to recognize. He will therefore be able to recognize abnormal engine behavior. Engine life is dependent on the length of time the engine is operated at high turbine inlet temperatures. A given power setting corresponds to a specific level of turbine temperature which is indirectly measured by EGT. Strict attention should be paid to the 30-minute time limit that applies to military power to ensure that the engine will not be subject to premature removal due to overtemperature problems.

In the interest of future safety, all instances of abnormal engine behavior should be reported. It is of particular importance to note abnormally high levels of EGT and the length of time the engine operated at these levels.

Engine Malfunction/Failure

Indication of impending engine failure will usually be in the form of unstable engine operation and may be manifested by one or a combination of the following symptoms:

1. Erratic increase in turbine outlet temperature

2. Fluctuation of engine rpm at a constant throttle setting

3. No increase in engine rpm when throttle is advanced

4. Compressor pulsation

5. Loss of thrust.

WARNING

- Continued operation of an unstable engine is dangerous. Maximum temperature limits should be observed under all conditions. If overtemperaturing cannot be controlled, shut down affected engine.

- Engine failure or malfunction can, in instances, result in toxic fumes being introduced into the cockpit. At first sign of engine trouble, all crewmembers shall switch to 100% OXYGEN.

If unstable engine operation occurs during acceleration or deceleration, retard the throttle to IDLE until engine operation becomes stable. When engine operation becomes stable, slowly advance the throttle to

Changed 1 June 1969

1-31

the desired power setting. If unstable operation occurs during steady-state operation, immediately reduce power, reduce altitude, and increase airspeed by changing the attitude of the aircraft. If necessary, due to continued excessive instability, shut down the malfunctioning engine.

Engine Fire-Detection System

The engine fire-detection system indicates fire and hazardous temperature conditions in the engine nacelles and pylons by making appropriate fire warning lights come on. Components of the system include:

Name	Type	Location
Heat-sensing elements (2)	Six-section thermistors	Engine nacelles and pylons, LH and RH (inside)
Heat-sensing-element guards (4)	3/8-inch aluminum tubing	Forward doors, LH and RH engine nacelles (inside)
Fire-detection control units (2)	Two-stage amplifier first stage, thyratron second stage	Engine pylons, LH and RH (inside)
Fire-warning lights (2)	Press-to-test	Cockpit, pilot's instrument panel
Fire-detection test switch	Press-to-test	Cockpit, pilot's instrument panel
Fire-detection test relays (2)	Double-pole, double-throw	Engine pylons, LH and RH (inside)

The engine fire-detection system consists of two identical fire-detection circuits, one for each engine nacelle, with a press-to-test switch for each circuit. Each circuit operates independently of the other to make its associated left- or right-hand fire warning light come on when the circuit is affected by excessive heat in the nacelle and pylon which it serves.

Each fire detection circuit utilizes a six-section heat-sensing element located in the engine nacelle and in the engine pylon. The electrical resistance of the sensing element varies inversely with the temperature of the nacelle, so that an increase in heat results in a decrease of sensing element resistance. The resistance of the sensing element is continuously monitored by the fire-detection control unit which indicates, by means of a red warning-light for each engine (figures 1-4 and 1-5), labeled FIRE WARN, any great decrease in resistance caused by an excessive temperature along some section of the sensing element.

Each fire detection circuit receives 115-vac power (phase C for left- and phase A for right-hand circuit) from the left-hand ac generator essential bus on terminal panel 101. A supply voltage for the test switch is provided by the 28-vdc essential bus on terminal panel 100. Circuit protection for the fire detection circuits is provided by the 3-ampere LH FIRE DETECTOR and RH FIRE DETECTOR fuses on terminal panel 101; circuit protection for the test switch is provided by the 5-ampere FIRE DETECTOR circuit breaker on terminal panel 100.

HEAT-SENSING ELEMENTS

The heat-sensing element provided in each fire detection circuit is installed within its related (left- or right-hand) engine nacelle and pylon. The sensing element is constructed in six sections, with mated connectors and four flexible interconnectors, and is protected by two aluminum guards. The sensing element is essentially a thermistor, consisting of two wires embedded in a ceramic core with an inconel (nickel alloy) casing. The ceramic core has a high negative temperature coefficient of resistance; at extremely high temperatures, the electrical resistance of the ceramic material decreases sufficiently to permit current flow. The wires within the ceramic core facilitate heat conductivity throughout the sensing element. At normal temperatures, the resistance within the sensing element is such that the fire-detection control unit is inoperative. Only at excessively high temperatures does the resistance within the sensing element decrease sufficiently to permit the control unit to supply an output voltage that energizes the fire warning lights.

FIRE-DETECTION CONTROL UNIT

The fire-detection control unit in each fire detection circuit is installed within the related engine pylon aft of the front spar, and is accessible through an access door on the inboard side of the pylon. The control unit monitors the heat-sensing element and electrically energizes the fire warning light when the electrical resistance of the heat-sensing element is lowered by a fire or hazardous temperature condition in the nacelle or pylon.

The fire-detection control unit is a two-stage unit with a transformer power supply that contains four secondary windings and receives single-phase, 115-vac, 400-cycle power. The first stage of the unit consists of an amplifier in the form of a triode tube (V101) whose bias is controlled by the current flow in the heat-sensing element. The amplifier-grid voltage is always the same value when the tube is conducting, and is dependent on the resistance of the potentiometer (R102). Under normal operating conditions, the amplifier is effectively biased by the voltage appearing across the R104 resistor so that there is no current flow through the amplifier. As temperature increases within the areas monitored by the heat-sensing element, the resistance of the heat-sensing element is lowered and allows an increased current flow. When current flow from the heat-sensing element is sufficient, the bias is lifted and the amplifier conducts.

The second stage of the control unit includes an electronic relay, in the form of a thyratron tube controlled by the output of the triode amplifier, and an output transformer. The thyratron is biased below cutoff by the voltage across windings 9 and 10 of the power transformer. At the firing point (the point at which the output voltage of the amplifier is sufficient to fire the thyratron) the bias is lifted by the output of the amplifier. The thyratron then conducts, and its plate current in the form of half-wave pulses passes through the output transformer to energize the fire warning light.

Ignition System

Each engine ignition system consists of two spark-igniters and an ignition timer. The spark-igniters are located in the lower two combustion chambers of each engine. The ignition timers, which automatically energize the igniters for a 30-second firing cycle, are located in the engine nacelles. The MASTER ENGINE switch and the ignition switch control the ignition system.

Engine Starter

An air turbine starter (figure 1-2) is located in each engine accessories section. The starter is powered by an external compressed air supply unit. Shutoff is by pilot hand signal when engine acceleration reaches 35 percent.

Engine Fuel Control System

Each engine has an independent fuel control system. The function of the system is to maintain automatically a fixed percentage of trimmed engine speed for a given throttle setting. The system consists of the throttle, the two-stage engine fuel pump, the fuel flowmeter, the fuel pressurizing and dump valve, the fuel manifold, and the hydromechanical fuel control unit.

HYDROMECHANICAL FUEL CONTROL UNIT

The function of the hydromechanical fuel control unit is to schedule the quantity of fuel flow required by the engine to deliver the desired amount of thrust, as dictated by the position of the throttle in the cockpit and by particular operating conditions of the engine. Fuel flow must be maintained within certain limits which vary, depending upon operating conditions. These limits imposed upon the hydromechanical fuel control unit are those of air inlet temperature, compressor discharge pressure, and engine turbine rpm. Subject to these limits, the control is capable of accurately maintaining engine rpm during steady state operation by the use of a permanent droop system in conjunction with the speed setting governor.

Engine speed selection is accomplished mechanically by means of throttle movement which positions a throttle fuel valve within a fuel metering orifice. A positive minimum flow adjustment is provided in this valve. The percent of trimmed engine speed selected by throttle position is closely regulated for all operating conditions through the action of a flyball governor which governs fuel flow through a servo. During acceleration, the hydromechanical control senses burner static pressure, engine inlet temperature, and engine speed and combines these variables to limit fuel flow to the maximum allowable for a given engine to prevent compressor surge and overtemperaturing. When operating at a steady state for a given throttle setting, the hydromechanical unit compensates automatically for variations in altitude, airspeed, compressor inlet temperature, engine speed, and burner pressure to prevent overspeeding, overtemperaturing, and compressor surge. During deceleration the control schedules a minimum fuel flow as a function of burner pressure to prevent flameout. This minimum flow schedule also provides a low limit of fuel flow for altitude idle and the starting operation.

ENGINE FUEL CONTROL MALFUNCTION

Malfunction of certain components of the engine fuel control can result in either a rapid uncontrollable increase in rpm or a rapid decrease to minimum fuel flow. In both instances, the only recourse is to shut down the engine (throttle OFF, master engine switch OFF) immediately, particularly in case of an overspeed condition, since complete destruction of the engine may occur.

Engine Controls

THROTTLES

The throttles (figure 1-9) are located on the pilot's center console. Each throttle is mechanically linked to the engine-mounted fuel control units. The left-hand throttle contains the SPEED BRAKE switch (figure 1-9) and the radio-ICS switch (figure 1-9). Mounted outboard on the right-hand throttle is the three-position, exterior lights master switch. A friction control knob (figure 1-9) controls the freedom of movement of the throttles. The engine ignition system control is incorporated in the throttle assembly. Outboard movement of either throttle from the OFF position energizes the ignition system for the corresponding engine. Gates in the throttle channel prevent the throttles from being inadvertently retarded below the IDLE position. Each throttle is mechanically linked to a fuel flow shutoff valve in the fuel control unit. The linkage provides a positive shutoff of fuel flow to the engine when the throttle is moved to the OFF position. This action permits a fuel manifold drain valve in the engine to open and allows complete drainage of all residual fuel in the manifold within 10 seconds.

IGNITION SWITCH

The ignition switch, which energizes the ignition timer, is incorporated in the throttle system. The switch is a momentary-contact switch and is actuated by movement of the throttle toward the engine to be started, when the throttle lever is in the OFF position. The ignition switch is energized (30 seconds) by dc power from the primary bus through the ON position of the MASTER ENGINE switch.

ENGINE STARTER SWITCH

The ENG STARTER switch (figure 1-9) is located on the center console. This switch has three positions: momentary LH, momentary RH, and center OFF. The switch utilizes dc power from the primary bus through the ON position of the MASTER ENGINE switch to energize a relay that then supplies dc primary bus power through the starter cutoff speed switch to the air shutoff valve solenoid.

CARTRIDGE STARTER

The ATSC 100-83 cartridge starter (figure 1-24) may be installed on A-3 aircraft that are deployed to areas not having pneumatic starters available. The addition of the cartridge starter significantly increases the versatility of any squadron A-3 aircraft. See Section III, Part 3, for operating procedures for the cartridge starter.

MASTER ENGINE SWITCHES

The MASTER ENGINE switches on the center console (figure 1-9) control the ac powered fuel boost pumps, the fuel shutoff valves, the ignition timers and spark-igniters, and the engine starter cutoff speed switches. In the ON position, the fuel boost pump control relays are energized and the fuel shutoff valves in the engine nacelles are open. Through relays energized by the momentary-contact ENG STARTER and ignition switches, the MASTER ENGINE switches control power to the spark-igniter and timer system and to the starter cutoff speed switch. The MASTER ENGINE switches receive power from the primary bus through the engine control circuit breakers on the pilot's console circuit breaker panel.

Engine Instruments

TACHOMETERS

The engine tachometers (figure 1-4) are located on the pilot's instrument panel. These instruments reflect the rpm of the high-pressure rotor as a percentage of 9700 rpm.

FUEL BOOST PRESSURE INDICATOR[1][2]

A dual fuel boost pressure indicator (figure 1-4) is located on the instrument panel. This instrument indicates the pressure of fuel being delivered to the engine fuel pumps.

ENGINE FUEL PUMPS

A two-stage, engine-driven fuel pump supplies the fuel pressure necessary for proper engine performance. Fuel is delivered to the pump at boost pump pressure (12 to 30 psi) when the pressure is increased for delivery to the combustion chambers. Fuel is filtered prior to entering each of the two stages of the pump. No control or pressure indicator for the pump is provided.

FUEL FLOWMETER

A dual needle fuel flowmeter (figure 1-4) installed on the pilot's instrument panel indicates the rate of fuel flow to the engines in pounds per hour. The dual flowmeter dials are marked from 0 to 3 in 100-pound increments and from 3 to 12 in 1000-pound increments.

TURBINE OUTLET TEMPERATURE INDICATORS

The turbine outlet temperature indicators (figure 1-4) are located on the instrument panel. These instruments indicate the temperature of the exhaust gases at the turbine outlet.

Engine Starting

During an engine start, the maximum EGT specified in tables 1-8 and 1-9 is permitted only momentarily. After lightoff, EGT rises steadily until a peak is reached, then drops gradually to stabilize at the normal value for idle. If the start is normal, this peak is well below the starting maximum; if the start is

---
[1] Aircraft BuNo. 135407-135444
[2] Aircraft BuNo. 138902-138962, 138964-138976, 142236-142255, 142400-142407, 142630-142649.

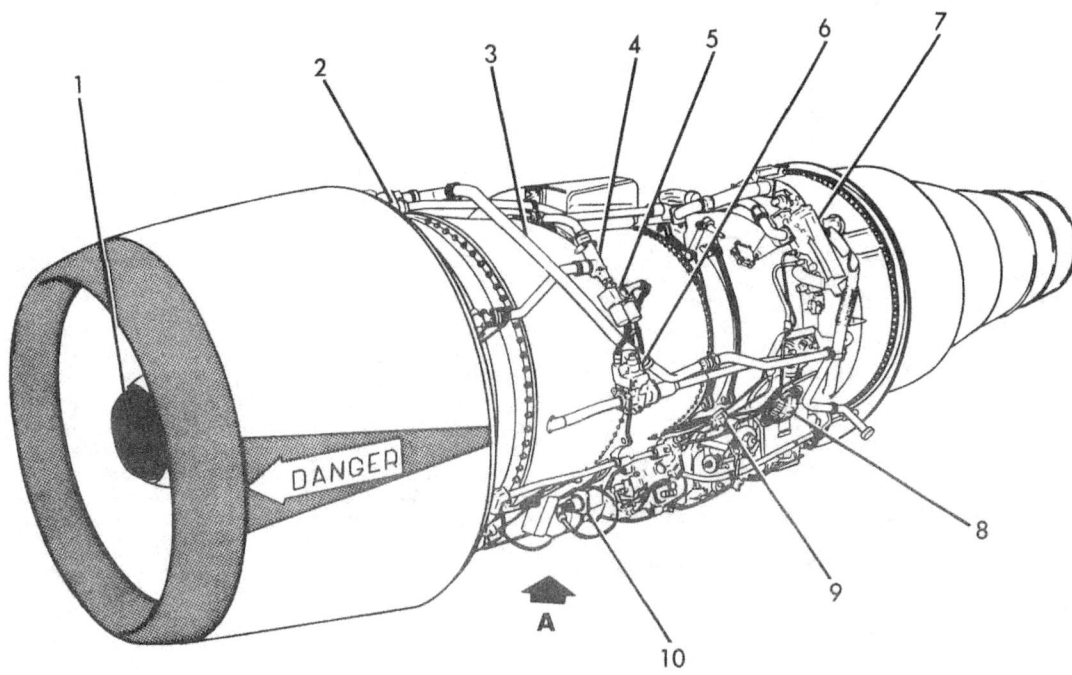

1. Oil cooler fairing
2. Breather pressure valve
3. Oil vent line
4. Oil temperature control adapter
5. Oil temperature regulator
6. Anti-icing air valve
7. Fuel heater
8. Compressor bleed valve
9. Automatic oil-drum valve
10. Oil pressure switch
11. Cartridge starter location (when installed)

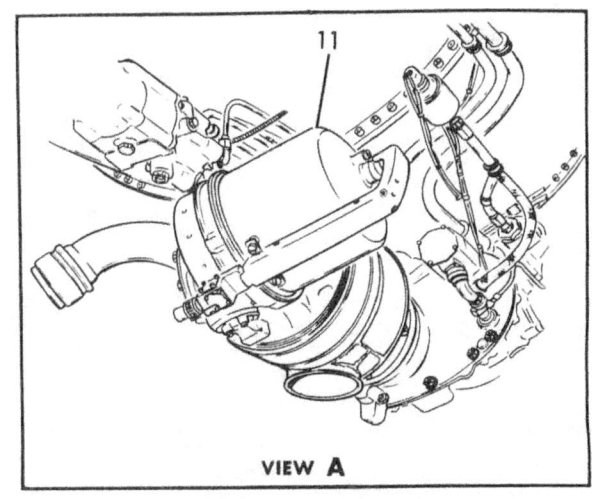

VIEW A

Figure 1-24. J57-P-10 Engine

abnormal, this peak may exceed that maximum. The momentary starting time limit will probably never be exceeded unless some abnormal condition like a hung start results. In such a start, rpm hangs at some value below idle, and the engine cooks at some high internal temperature at or above the starting temperature limit. The engine starting attempt must be discontinued immediately, and the reason for the hot or hung start should be determined.

The EGT tendency may be more significant than the EGT itself. Thus, a ground starting EGT of 400°C and rising rapidly should concern the pilot more than one of 440°C and falling. The 400°C value, fortunately, is sufficiently below the allowable starting EGT to permit the pilot to abort the start before the starting temperature limit is reached.

ACCELERATION

The acceleration temperature limit and corresponding 2-minute time limit apply, of course, to engine rpm, but not to aircraft speed acceleration. Although the EGT limit specified in tables 1-8 and 1-9 applies to both cold and hot engines, a relatively high value was set to take care of cold engines. A cold engine is defined as one that has just been started or has been permitted to cool at idle for at least 5 minutes before an acceleration. The time limit applies to the period between the time that the throttle is advanced and the time that the EGT first starts falling after reaching its peak. Another criterion of a properly functioning engine is that the EGT should stabilize at or near the normal operating temperature for the higher thrust setting within 5 minutes after the throttle is advanced for an acceleration.

The performance of an engine is not acceptable if it violates either the EGT or time limit. The acceleration temperature limit applies only when an acceleration is made over the full thrust range of the engine, as from idle to military rated. For an acceleration from idle to normal rated, the EGT limit for normal rated instead of for acceleration applies. Throttle movement during acceleration should be smooth and continuous.

STEADY-STATE OPERATION

Exhaust gas temperatures for normal rated (tables 1-8 and 1-9) should not be considered limits, but the temperatures, if attained or exceeded during routine operations, should warn the pilot of a possible engine malfunction. An engine which exceeds the maximum EGT for cruise conditions when it is operated below normal rated can be expected also to exceed the temperature limits when it is operated at higher thrust settings. The same assumption can be made about EGT at idle, which is intended only as a guide and is not a firm operating limit. Nevertheless, the temperatures shown for military rated and normal rated

are positive limits that can not be exceeded without compromising the engine's service life. A normally functioning engine should operate somewhat below the EGT limits published for the several operating conditions.

Specified temperature limits serve two purposes. They assure than an engine will always be operated at internal temperatures that will not shorten the service life expectancy of engine components; and they enable the pilot to detect an engine fuel control system or instrumentation malfunction in time to take proper corrective action.

The length of time that an engine may be operated at each thrust setting (operating condition) was established to conserve the life of the engine and to make the time between overhauls predictable. Without these time limits to guide him, the careless or insensitive pilot might literally wear out an engine in a few hours of operation and would certainly disrupt the logistic structure of any large-scale operation predicted on fixed overhaul periods.

An engine that is always operated conservatively will last many times longer than one that is habitually operated at maximum limits. In the high thrust range, an increase of only 5°C may double the rate of turbine blade creep. Just so much creep can be tolerated by each blade. How fast the blade life is depleted depends on the pilot. Unfortunately, no operational technique can reverse the effect of blade creep.

The time limit for operation at military rated is specified not so much to permit a cooling period between intervals of operation at high thrust as to distribute the rate of blade creep throughout the engine's normal life. Nothing is gained, therefore, by reducing a high thrust setting only momentarily before repeating it — just to be able to report that time limits were not violated.

An engine's service life budget has only so many hours of operation at high thrust. Whether these hours are used up quickly or are distributed throughout a normal calculated period depends on how conscientiously the EGT and time limits are observed by the pilot.

ENGINE OIL SYSTEM

Each engine is lubricated and partially cooled by an independent oil system. The oil tanks are located in the engine nacelles. Each tank, when fully serviced, contains 5 1/2 gallons of oil in addition to approximately 3 gallons in each engine oil system. See figure 1-52 for engine oil grade and specification. An engine-driven oil pressure pump and five gear-type scavenger pumps supply a constant flow of oil to the seven main bearings of each engine. Scavenged oil is filtered and routed through the oil cooler (figure 1-52) before re-entering the system. Maximum oil consumption of each engine is estimated to be approximately 2 quarts per hour at normal rated power.

Oil Pressure Gage[1]

The dual oil pressure gage (figure 1-4) reflects the pressure differential between system oil pump discharge pressure and engine accessory drive case internal pressure. A pressure relief valve in the system maintains a relatively constant 45-psi differential oil pressure at the bearing orifices. When the aircraft engine is at idle rpm, the oil pressure gage should not indicate less than 35 psi.

Oil Cooler Door Control[1]

While airborne, the volume of air passing through the oil cooling system is regulated by the ENG OIL COOLER switches (figure 1-9) on the center console. Each switch has four positions: OFF, OPEN, AUTO and CLOSE. In the AUTO position, the oil cooler doors are automatically controlled by a sensing and transmitting element in each system. The element senses the temperature of cooled oil as it is returned to the system and regulates the position of the oil cooler door to maintain the temperature below $112 \pm 3^{\circ}$C. The OPEN and CLOSE positions of the switch provide manual control of oil temperature. The maximum allowable oil temperature is 121°C at which point the oil cooler doors remain open.

The ENG OIL COOLER switches are inoperative when the weight of the aircraft is on the landing gear. Dc power normally supplied to the switches is transferred by the landing gear retraction release relays to the CLOSE side of the oil cooler doors circuits, causing the doors to close and remain fully closed during all operations with the main gear struts compressed. During ground operation when no ram air is available for oil cooling, closing the oil cooler doors allows air to be drawn through the oil cooler by engine suction by way of the open trailing edges of the nose ring pylon air exits.

NOTE

When the MASTER ENGINE switch is secured in flight and the oil cooler door switch is in the AUTO position, oil cooler door will open and remain open.

Dual Engine Oil Temperature Indicator[2]

The dual engine oil temperature indicator (figure 1-4) indicates the temperature of scavenged and cooled oil as it enters the engine oil pump. The normal temperature, with the oil cooler doors in AUTO, may range from 40° to 121°C. The maximum allowable oil temperature is 121°C at which point the oil cooler doors remain open. The average oil temperature range is 70° to 90°C. Operation of the anti-icing system will cause a slight increase in the engine oil temperature.

Oil System Malfunction

Malfunction of the engine oil system will be indicated by erratic or reduced oil pressure and/or an increase or decrease in oil temperature. In case of erratic or reduced oil pressure, operate the affected engine at lowest possible rpm and land as soon as practicable. If engine oil pressure fails completely, shut down the engine. In case of increasing or decreasing oil temperature from normal indications, manually operate the engine oil cooler door by placing the ENG OIL COOLER switch of the affected engine in OPEN or CLOSE as required. If this action fails to remedy excessive oil temperatures, operate the engine at some reduced power setting or perform the shutdown procedure outlined in Section V.

FUEL SYSTEMS

The basic A-3A/B aircraft fuel system that is currently in service is discussed in detail in the following pages under title defined below:

Basic A-3A/B Fuel System. Applies to all basic aircraft not designated as tankers. All have Avien fuel balance and quantity indicating systems with gravity transfer from forward to aft tank.

General (All Aircraft)

FUEL CROSSFEED CONTROL VALVE

The fuel crossfeed control valve is controlled by the FUEL X FEED switch located on the pilot's left-hand console. The switch has two positions: OPEN and CLOSED. In the CLOSED position, fuel is supplied

---

[1]Aircraft BuNo. 135407-142649.

[2]Aircraft BuNo. 138963.

Section I
Part 2

NAVAIR 01-40ATA-1

to each engine from each respective fuel boost pump system. In the OPEN position, the fuel crossfeed valve is opened, and the operative boost pump system supplies fuel to both engines. This provides the best fuel flow as long as one boost pump is operating. If both boost pumps become inoperative, refer to Fuel Boost Failure with Continued Engine Operation. The fuel crossfeed control valve may be functionally checked by pulling the circuit breaker for either fuel boost pump and then opening the fuel crossfeed valve to regain pressure.

FUEL BOOST PUMP CONTROL

Transfer of fuel from the aft fuel tank to each engine fuel pump is through an independent fuel boost and supply system. Two ac electrically driven boost pumps, mounted internally in the aft tank, supply fuel to the engine fuel pumps mounted in the engine nacelles. Each boost pump has one shutoff valve located in the engine pylon. The boost pumps and shutoff valves are actuated by the MASTER ENGINE switches. The systems (figure 1-30) are interconnected by a fuel crossfeed control valve, making possible the operation of both engines from either boost pump.

FUEL BOOST FAILURE WITH CONTINUED ENGINE OPERATION

If the engine continues to operate normally, loss of fuel boost pressure can generally be regarded as boost pump failure, but may also be caused by a faulty indicator. Place the FUEL CROSSFEED switch in OPEN position. If fuel pressure returns to normal (12 to 30 psi is acceptable), the pressure loss is the result of pump failure.

NOTE

The FUEL CROSSFEED switch should remain in the OPEN position for the remainder of the flight as long as fuel boost pressure is indicated. If complete loss of fuel boost pressure occurs, indicating failure of both boost pumps, place the FUEL CROSSFEED switch to CLOSED position to obtain the best fuel flow. The engine fuel pumps will supply fuel to the engines through the failed boost pumps if flight altitude is not extremely high. Contractor tests indicate that engine performance with boost pumps inoperative is satisfactory to altitudes above 30,000 feet. As critical altitudes are reached, engine symptoms are erratic fuel flow, RPM fluctuations, and compressor stalls. Rapid power changes and maneuvering flight increase the symptom severity. If symptoms are encountered, descend to an altitude at which steady-state operation can be maintained.

FUEL BOOST FAILURE WITH ACCOMPANIED ENGINE FLAMEOUT

Engine flameout with simultaneous loss of fuel boost pressure indication can be due to a failed boost pump or ruptured fuel boost line. However, boost pump failure should not cause engine flameout at cruise power since the engine fuel pump will continue to draw fuel from the tank by suction except at extremely high altitude. If a ruptured fuel line is suspected, a check may be made for this condition before attempting an air start of the flamed out engine. Proceed as follows:

1. Throttle, inoperative engine . . . . . . OFF

2. Master engine switch, inoperative engine . . . . OFF

3. Fuel crossfeed switch . . . . OPEN

Although both fuel boosts should read 12 to 30 psi, closely observe fuel boost indicator of operative engine, since possibility of fuel starvation on engine exists.

NOTE

When the fuel crossfeed switch is placed in the OPEN position, a momentary drop in fuel boost pressure may occur. If the boost pressure of the operative engine does not return almost immediately, such a pressure loss indicates a leaking or severed fuel line between the crossfeed valve and the pylon shutoff valve of the inoperative engine. A second attempt may be made to make sure the pressure drop was not caused by the filling of an empty fuel line.

4. Fuel boost, inoperative engine, check . . . . 12 to 30 psi

5. If boost pressure not indicated, immediately return fuel crossfeed switch to . . . . CLOSED

6. If fuel boost indicators of both engines stabilize between 12 to 30 psi after step 4, place MASTER ENGINE switch of inoperative engine tentatively in ON.

7. Fuel boost, inoperative engine . . . . . CHECK

8. If boost pressure is not indicated, immediately return MASTER ENGINE switch to . . . . OFF

NOTE

When the MASTER ENGINE switch is placed in ON position, a momentary drop in pressure may again occur if the fuel line between the pylon shutoff valve and the engine is empty. If the fuel boost indicators fluctuate or pressure is not indicated, a leaking or severed fuel line is indicated.

1-38

Changed 1 June 1969

9. If the fuel boost indicators of both engines stabilize after step 7, an air start of the inoperative engine may be attempted.

WARNING

- If fuel boost pressure is less than 12 psi and engine operation is regained by means of crossfeed, circuit breakers for affected fuel boost pump shall be pulled. If engine operation is not regained, and fuel boost pressure on the affected engine remains below 12 psi, place MASTER ENGINE switch in OFF

- Failure to perform this operation can lead to a loss of approximately 15,000 pounds of fuel per hour from a ruptured fuel line.

FUEL LINE HEAT EXCHANGER

Under certain atmospheric conditions, ice may form in the fuel filter of A-3 aircraft, resulting in aircraft fuel starvation. For this reason all A-3 aircraft have a fuel heater incorporated in the fuel line upstream of the low-pressure fuel filter.

BASIC A-3A/B FUEL SYSTEM

The aircraft fuel system consists of four fuel tanks, with a combined total of 4421 usable gallons, installed in the wings and fuselage. See figure 1-25 for the fuel system schematic. These tanks may be serviced through a three-point, high-pressure fueling system, or through four gravity fuel tank filler caps, one located in each tank. Each engine is provided with an independent fuel boost pump system. These systems are interconnected through a crossfeed valve, making possible the operation of both engines from either fuel boost pump system.

Two self-sealing main fuel tanks are located in the fuselage. An automatic fuel control feature between the main tanks maintains fuel distribution within a given cg envelope for the fuel system and provides flight stability within its limitations. See figure 1-52 for fuel grades and specifications of approved and emergency fuels.

NOTE

An ac fuel control circuit breaker is installed on the pilot's circuit breaker panel. This circuit breaker is powered by phase A ac power from the No. 1 bus and controls ac power to all fuel pumps. Loss of electrical power to the circuit will automatically shut down all boost and transfer pumps.

Fuel Tanks

One of the two fuselage tanks is located forward of the bomb bay above the companionway and the other, immediately aft of the bomb bay. The forward tank has a usable capacity of 1214 gallons; the aft tank, 1909 gallons. A tank with a usable capacity of 649 gallons is located in the inboard section of each wing as an integral part of the wing structure. The forward fuselage tank and both wing tanks feed into the aft fuselage tank through a transfer system, which also functions as the fuel trim system when this automatic feature is turned on.

AUXILIARY UPPER BOMB BAY TANK

ASC 28 INC II provides for installation of an upper bomb bay auxiliary tank (figure 1-25) to increase the operational capabilities of the aircraft. With the incorporation of this service change, the aircraft can carry an additional 748 gallons of usable fuel.

Pressure Fueling System

The pressure fueling system is designed to permit fueling at approximately 250 gallons per minute through each of three pressure fueling receptacles (figure 1-52) with 60 psi measured at the reel for carrier installations, at the truck for mobile ground units, and at the filter for fixed ground installations. At the pressure fueling nozzle under full flow conditions, the maximum pressure should never exceed 50 psi. A separate pressure fueling receptacle and stop valve is provided for each fuselage tank and the two wing tanks being fueled through a single receptacle and individual stop shutoff valves. Each fuel tank contains two float valves; a primary float valve which is the pilot valve for the fueling receptacle stop valve, and a secondary float valve which is a standby for the stop valve. A three-position switch at each receptacle provides a means for checking the operation of both valves. Moving the switch from OFF to either the PRIMARY or SECONDARY position causes the float valve solenoids to raise the floats to simulate the normal stop valve action at the maximum fuel capacity level. This check can be made only after fueling has begun.

Pressure defueling of the fuselage fuel tanks may be accomplished through either the aft tank pressure

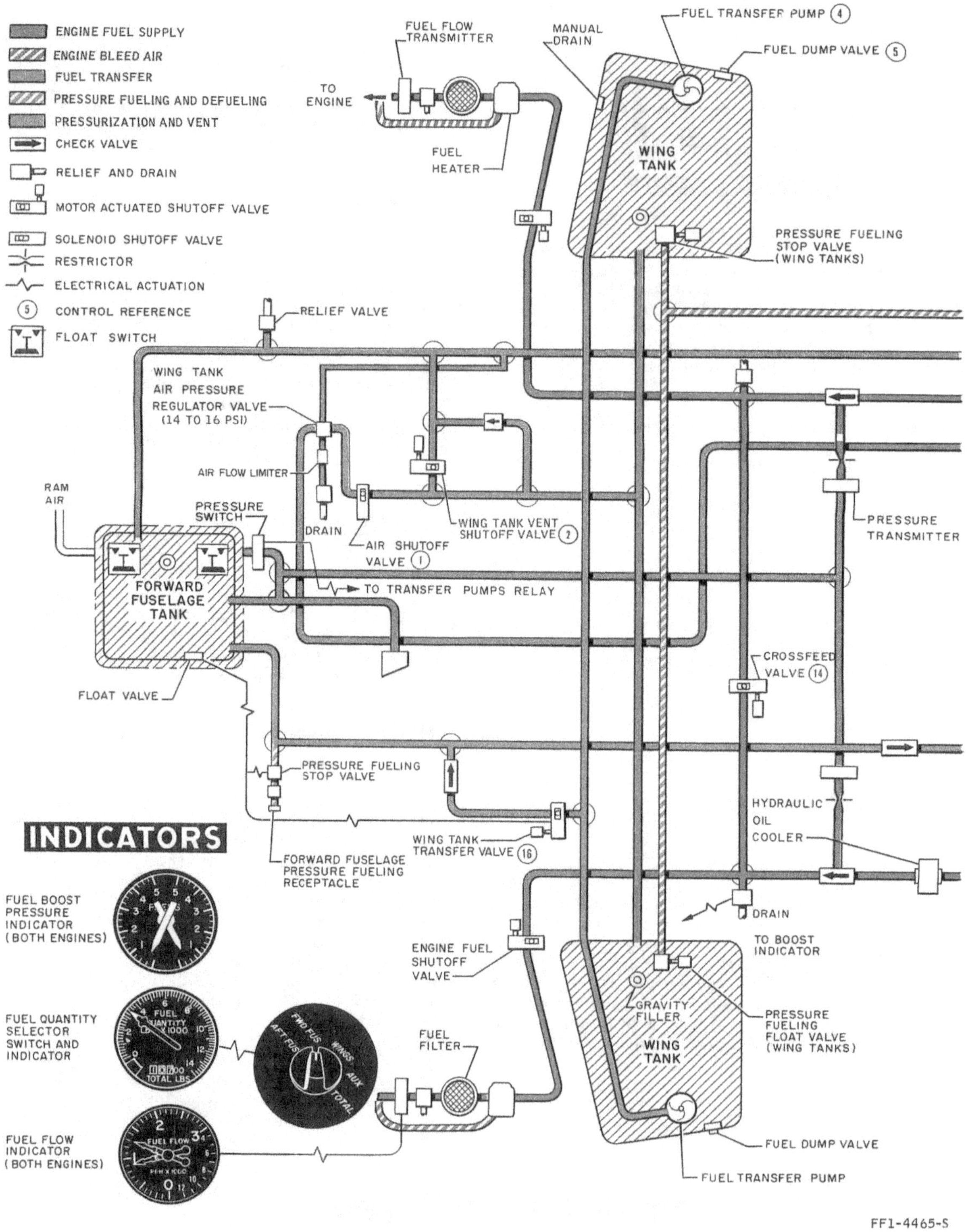

Section I
Part 2

NAVAIR 01-40ATA-1

Figure 1-25. Fuel System Schematic — Basic A-3A/B Aircraft (Sheet 1)

NAVAIR 01-40ATA-1

Section I
Part 2

CONTROLS

WING TRANSFER SWITCH

ON TRANSFER —
OPENS WING TANK FUEL TRANSFER VALVE (16)
TURNS ON WING FUEL TRANSFER PUMPS (4)

WING FUEL DUMP SWITCH

OPENS AIR SHUTOFF VALVE (1)
OPENS FUEL DUMP VALVE (5)
CLOSES WING TANK VENT SHUTOFF VALVE (2)

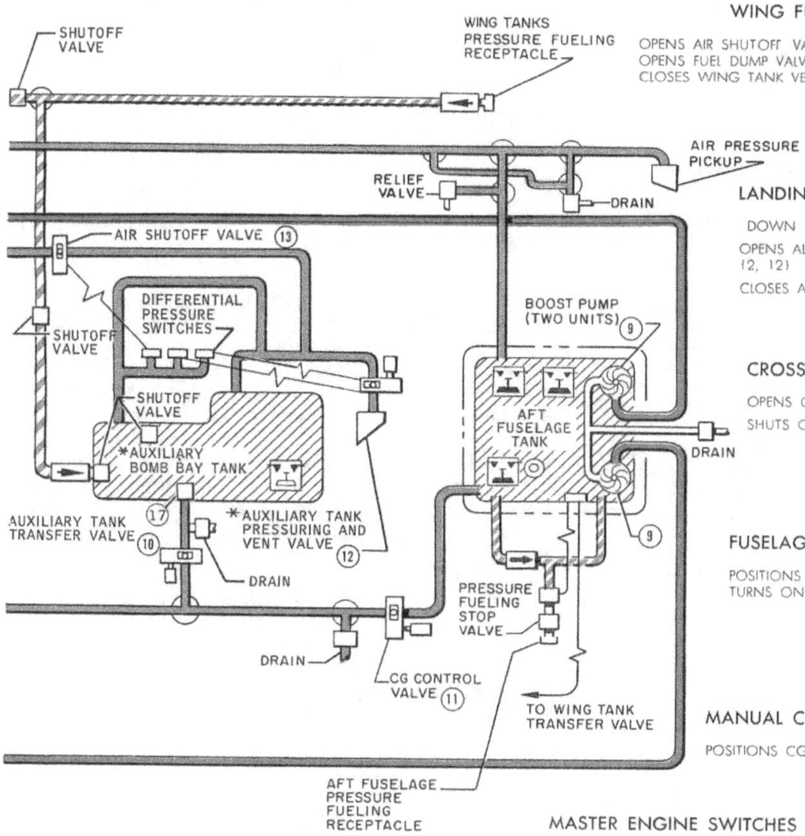

LANDING GEAR HANDLE

DOWN —
OPENS ALL TANK VENT VALVES (2, 12)
CLOSES AIR SHUTOFF VALVE (1)

CROSSFEED VALVE SWITCH

OPENS CROSSFEED VALVE (14)
SHUTS OFF EITHER BOOST PUMP (9)

FUSELAGE FUEL TRIM SWITCH

POSITIONS CG CONTROL VALVE (11)
TURNS ON AUTOMATIC CG CONTROL

MANUAL CG CONTROL HANDLE

POSITIONS CG CONTROL VALVE (11)

MASTER ENGINE SWITCHES

LEFT-HAND SWITCH —
OPENS LEFT-HAND ENGINE FUEL SHUTOFF VALVE (15)
TURNS ON LEFT-HAND ENGINE BOOST PUMP (9)

RIGHT-HAND SWITCH —
(CORRESPONDING OPERATION OF R.H SYSTEM COMPONENTS)

*** BOMB BAY AUXILIARY TANK TRANSFER SWITCH**

ON TRANSFER –
OPENS AUXILIARY TANK TRANSFER VALVE (10)
OPENS AIR SHUTOFF VALVE (13)
OPENS AUXILIARY TANK VENT VALVE (12)
TURNS ON ELECTRIC PUMP (17)

* AIRCRAFT BUNO.
138902 THROUGH 142649

FF-1-4665-2Q

Figure 1-25. Fuel System Schematic — Basic A-3A/B Aircraft (Sheet 2)

Changed 15 July 1970

1-41

fueling receptacle or both aft and forward fuselage tank pressure fueling receptacles. The aircraft can be defueled at the rate of 100 gallons per minute through these two pressure fueling receptacles (figure 1-52). To defuel the forward tank through the aft tank pressure fueling receptacle, a source of external electrical dc power must be connected to the aircraft and the FUSELAGE (FUS) FUEL TRIM switch (figure 1-26) must be in the NOSE UP position. This may also be accomplished by manually placing the cg control valve in NOSE UP position.

PRESSURE FUELING POWER SWITCH

The two-position PRESSURE FUELING POWER SWITCH is located in the right-hand wheel well adjacent to the pressure fueling receptacle. The switch is energized when the primary bus is energized and the FUSELAGE (FUS) FUEL TRIM switch (figure 1-26) on the fuel control panel is placed in the NOSE DN position. The PRESSURE FUELING POWER switch is then placed in the ON position to provide power to the float valves and fueling receptacle stop valves. This procedure prevents fuel flow from one fusealge tank to the other and places the float valves and stop valves in control of the fueling of each individual tank.

Wing Tank Fuel Transfer Control

Fuel transfer is controlled by the three-position WING TANK switch (figures 1-6, 1-7, and 1-26) on the fuel system switch panel. In the center OFF position, the wing tanks motor-operated fuel transfer valve is closed to prevent fuel flow from the wing tanks to the fuselage tanks. The wing tanks fuel transfer valve is controlled during transfer by a float switch in each fuselage tank, which opens or closes the valve to prevent loss of fuel through the fuel vent system.

Transfer of fuel is accomplished by an electrical transfer pump in each wing fuel tank. The transfer pumps are powered from the ac generator No. 1 bus through a wing fuel transfer relay and are controlled by the WING TANK switch. With the switch in the OFF position, the wing fuel transfer relay is opened, disrupting the flow of electrical power to the transfer pumps. When the WING TANK switch is moved to TRANSF, the wing fuel transfer valve is opened, the pumps are energized, and fuel is transferred from the wing tanks to the fuselage tanks by pump pressure.

CAUTION

To ensure complete transfer of wing fuel, leave WING TANK switch in TRANSF position for 5 minutes after fuel gage pointer indicates zero. At certain attitudes, 50 to 100 gallons can remain in the wing tanks after the pointer reaches zero. After 5 minutes, turn WING TANK switch OFF to return to normal cg control.

Auxiliary Tank Fuel Transfer Control

Fuel transfer is controlled by the two-position, OFF and TRANSF, AUX tank transfer switch on the fuel system switch panel.

In the OFF position the auxiliary tank motor-operated shutoff (transfer) valve is closed and the auxiliary tank transfer pump is off to prevent fuel flow from the auxiliary tank to the aft fuselage tank. In the TRANSF position, the auxiliary tank shutoff valve and the auxiliary tank transfer pump are opened and fuel is pumped into the aft fuselage tank if cg valve is in proper position. Low-level switches turn off the transfer pumps when the auxiliary tank is empty. The auxiliary tank transfer pump receives power from the No. 2 ac bus.

CAUTION

Wing tank fuel transfer is inoperative until the AUX tank transfer switch is placed in OFF.

NOTE

There are no gravity transfer provisions from the auxiliary tank to the aft tank.

NAVAIR 01-40ATA-1

Section I
Part 2

Fuel Trim Control System

The fuel trim control system provides automatic (electronic), selective (electrical) and manual (mechanical) control of fuel transfer to maintain the proper fuel distribution. A cg control valve (figure 1-25), which can be opened and closed by any of these three methods, is located in the fuel line between the forward and aft fuel tanks. Since fuel flows from the forward to the aft tank because of gravity, the cg control valve is used to control the flow. When the cg control valve is open, the fuel in the forward tank is decreased by gravity flow to the aft tank; when the valve is closed, the quantity of fuel in the aft tank decreases through normal engine consumption.

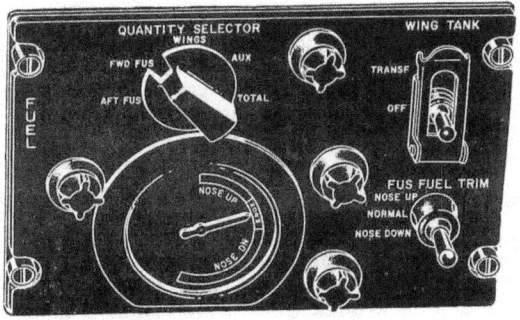

AIRCRAFT BUNO. 135407 THROUGH 135444

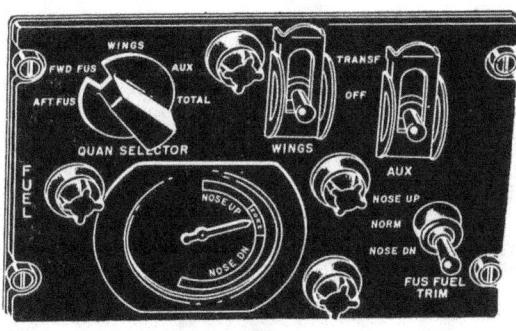

AIRCRAFT BUNO. 138902 THROUGH 138927, 138929 THROUGH 138931, 138933 THROUGH 138976

Fuel System Switch Panel

A fuel system switch panel (figure 1-7), labeled FUEL, is installed on the left console and contains the switches for pilot operation of the fuel system. The fuel QUANTITY SELECTOR switch, the FUS FUEL TRIM switch, the WING TANK switch, a cg indicator, and an auxiliary tank switch labeled AUX, are located on the panel (figure 1-26). In addition to the cg indicator and the auxiliary tank switch, the fuel system switch panels vary from earlier panels in that different nomenclature is used to designate several switch positions. The functions of these controls will be discussed in the following paragraphs where most appropriate.

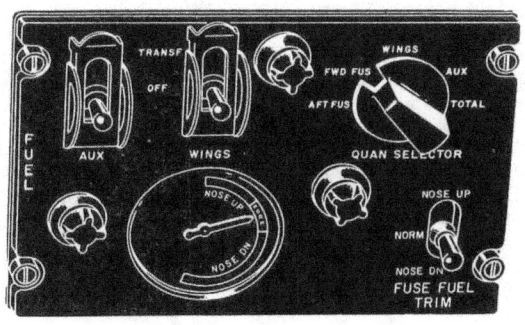

AIRCRAFT BUNO. 138963, 142236 THROUGH 142255, 142400 THROUGH 142407, AND 142630 THROUGH 142649

FF1-8544-D

Fuselage Fuel Trim Switch

A three-position toggle switch (figure 1-7), labeled FUS FUEL TRIM and located on the fuel system switch panel, is used for both automatic and selective operation of the cg control valve. The positions of the FUS FUEL TRIM switch are marked NORM, NOSE UP, and NOSE DN. When the switch is in NORM, the cg control valve is automatically operated by the electronic cg control system to maintain the proper fuel distribution as shown in figure 1-25. The NOSE UP position electrically opens the cg control

Figure 1-26. Fuel System Switch Panel

Changed 15 July 1970

1-43

valve, allowing fuel to flow from the forward to the aft fuel tank, causing a noseup condition. Placing the FUS FUEL TRIM switch in NOSE DN closes the cg control valve, permitting fuel to be used from the aft fuel tank only. This results in a nosedown trim condition.

CG Indicator

The cg indicator contains a single pointer that moves radially through marked ranges on the indicator face to present the existing condition of fuel distribution. These ranges are NORM, NOSE UP and NOSE DN. The NORM range signifies that fuel distribution is within the schedule established for automatic operation of the cg control system (figure 1-25). The NOSE UP range signifies that too much fuel is contained in the aft fuel tank for the amount in the forward tank, thus, a noseup condition exists. Conversely, the NOSE DN range shows that too much fuel is contained in the forward fuel tank for the quantity in the aft tank; therefore, a nosedown condition is present. Normally, during automatic operation of the cg control system, the cg indicator pointer will remain within the NORM range and no action is required by the pilot.

Manual CG Fuel Control Valve

An emergency control (figure 1-9) for manual operation of the cg fuel control valve is located on the pilot's side of the center console. Labeled MANUAL CG FUEL CONTROL VALVE, the control handle has three positions: NORMAL, NOSE UP, and NOSE DN (figure 1-25). Operating the cg control valve through a system of cables, pulleys, and cranks, the manual control must be pulled out from NORMAL, which is a neutral position, before it can be moved to either of the other two positions. When moved to the NOSE UP position, the manual control handle opens the cg control valve, allowing fuel to flow from the forward to the aft fuselage fuel tank. The NOSE DN position closes the cg control valve, and fuel is then used only from the aft fuel tank. It should be remembered when using the manual control that placing the MANUAL CG FUEL CONTROL VALVE handle in the NORMAL position will not change the position of the cg control valve. The valve will remain in the previously selected position until the opposite position is selected.

> **CAUTION**
>
> Do not use the MANUAL CG FUEL CONTROL VALVE if automatic and/or selective trim control is available. The manual control will prevent fuel transfer by automatic or selective means but will not shut off the cg control valve motor. However, if manual selection is required, reposition the fuel trim switch to coincide with console handle to preclude damage to cg valve motor.

Wing Tank Fuel Dumping System

> **CAUTION**
>
> The maximum recommended speed for wing fuel dumping is 250 knots, due to fuel impingement on the ailerons and flaps.

The wing tank fuel dumping system (figure 1-7) permits fuel to be jettisoned from the wing tanks to rapidly reduce the weight of the aircraft. Fuel dumping is controlled by a guarded or lever lock fuel dump switch on the FUEL panel located on the pilot's left-hand console. When the switch is moved to DUMP, a dump valve in each wing fuel tank is opened, allowing fuel to flow overboard through a dump outlet extending below the surface of each wing. Placing the fuel dump switch in OFF closes the wing tank dump valves. Wing tank fuel dump effectiveness is a function of engine rpm and wing tank pressurization. Six to 12 minutes will be required to dump wing tank fuel with sufficient rpm (80 percent on both engines) and 12-psi wing tank pressurization. At idle rpm (65 percent on both engines), fuel flow will be negligible.

Fuel Quantity Indicating System

The rotary fuel QUANTITY SELECTOR switch on the FUEL panel (figure 1-7) has five fuel tank positions: AFT FUS, FWD FUS, WINGS, AUX, and TOTAL (figure 1-26). The switch is used with the FUEL QUANTITY indicator on the pilot's instrument panel (figure 1-4) to indicate the amount of fuel aboard. To determine the weight of the fuel in a particular tank, the pilot must place the fuel QUANTITY SELECTOR switch in the desired position. The FUEL QUANTITY indicator pointer will then show, in pounds, the weight of the fuel in the selected tank. When the fuel QUANTITY SELECTOR switch is placed in TOTAL, the fuel tank pointer of the indicator will move to a point below the 0 mark on the dial and be concealed by a blacked out area on the glass cover of the indicator. The total weight of the fuel aboard will be shown on a fuel remaining counter seen through a window cut out in the face of the dial.

> **CAUTION**
>
> When the QUANTITY SELECTOR switch is moved from TOTAL, the fuel counter will be inoperative and will not indicate total fuel until QUANTITY SELECTOR switch is again placed in TOTAL.

The fuel QUANTITY SELECTOR switch must be left in the AFT FUS position during normal flight operations except for frequent checking of the fuel quantity in other tanks. Fuel for both engines is obtained from the AFT FUS tank; therefore, it is important to monitor this tank at all times.

CAUTION

The quantity of fuel in all tanks may vary considerably from the actual fuel quantity, depending upon the ground or flight attitude of the aircraft. In the clean configuration, a level flight airspeed or approximately 250 KIAS will place the aircraft in the normal ground attitude for which the fuel quantity indicating system is calibrated. With the wheels and wing flaps extended, 135 KIAS should be used for determining the quantity of fuel aboard.

Fuel Tank Pressurizing and Venting System

The aft fuselage tank and the forward tank are pressurized to a greater pressure than the atmosphere to prevent collapse of the tanks. This pressure is created by ram air from the fuel vent mast located on the left-hand side of the fuselage under the left-hand stabilizer.

The wing fuel tanks are pressurized to 12 to 16 psi during fuel dumping by engine compressor bleed air and vented through a pressurizing and venting system. The wing tanks vent shutoff valve is closed only during dump. The wing tanks pressurization relief valve relieves the wing tanks pressurization in excess of 14 to 16 psi. The entire fuel system is also vented when the landing gear control is moved to the DOWN position and the fuel dump switch is OFF. All fuel tanks are pressurized by ram air pressure from the fuel vent mast.

FUEL VENT MAST ICING

Fuel vent mast or line icing, which is a remote possibility, can cause the following sequence of events:

1. As fuel is consumed, the normal slight pressure maintained on the forward and aft fuel tank by the vent system is reduced below ambient.

2. Ambient pressure tends to collapse both fuselage tanks; the aft cell is more susceptible to volume reduction by collapsing.

3. Aft tank volume is reduced faster than fuel level, giving erroneous fuel quantity reading and precluding functioning of low fuel level light and automatic transfer of fuel to aft tank. Aft fuel cell quantity could be reduced to a dangerously low level without warning to the pilot.

Fortunately, the pilot can easily recognize the sequence of events because of the following indications: fuel consumption, as indicated by fuselage quantity gages, will be unrealistic; in advanced stages, abnormal amounts of noseup trim will be required at approach airspeeds. For recommended action, refer to Section V.

FUEL SYSTEM MANAGEMENT—BASIC A-3A/B FUEL SYSTEM

Fuel Trim Control — Automatic

Normally, fuel distribution between the forward and aft fuselage fuel tanks is automatically regulated, and no selective or manual control is required of the pilot. With the FUS FUEL TRIM switch in NORMAL (figure 1-26), the electronic cg control system maintains the distribution of fuel between the forward and aft tanks at the respective schedules shown in figure 1-27. This modified schedule is obtained by keeping the amount of fuel in the aft tank at 1 1/2 times that in the forward tank plus 3000±500 pounds to avoid any possibility of entering a dangerous cg condition through misunderstanding of proper fuel distribution when various store loadings are carried. This schedule is with the Avien balance amplifier adjusted to provide modified fuel distribution and should be strictly followed.

NOTE

The normal fuel distribution schedule before adjustment of the Avien balance amplifier is with the aft tank at 1 1/2 times the amount in the forward tank plus 1500±500 pounds.

Responsibility for operating A-3 aircraft within published weight and balance limitations lies with the operator. Pilots should be aware of the revised fuel scheduling and effect on weight and balance. Attention is invited to aircraft launching bulletins with emphasis on using the correct trim settings for catapult shots with partial fuel loads and/or bomb bay loads with the modified fuel distribution.

Fuel Trim Control — Selective

Should automatic control of fuel distribution no longer be available, or if the pilot should desire to depart from automatic control, fuel trim can be regulated selectively through the FUS FUEL TRIM switch to maintain the fuel distribution at the recommended schedule. The cg indicator is used with the FUS FUEL TRIM switch to selectively control fuel distribution. Keep in mind that the labeled ranges of the indicator convey to the pilot the existing trimmed condition (in relation to fuel distribution) of the aircraft. The marked positions of the FUS FUEL TRIM

Section I
Part 2

NAVAIR 01-40ATA-1

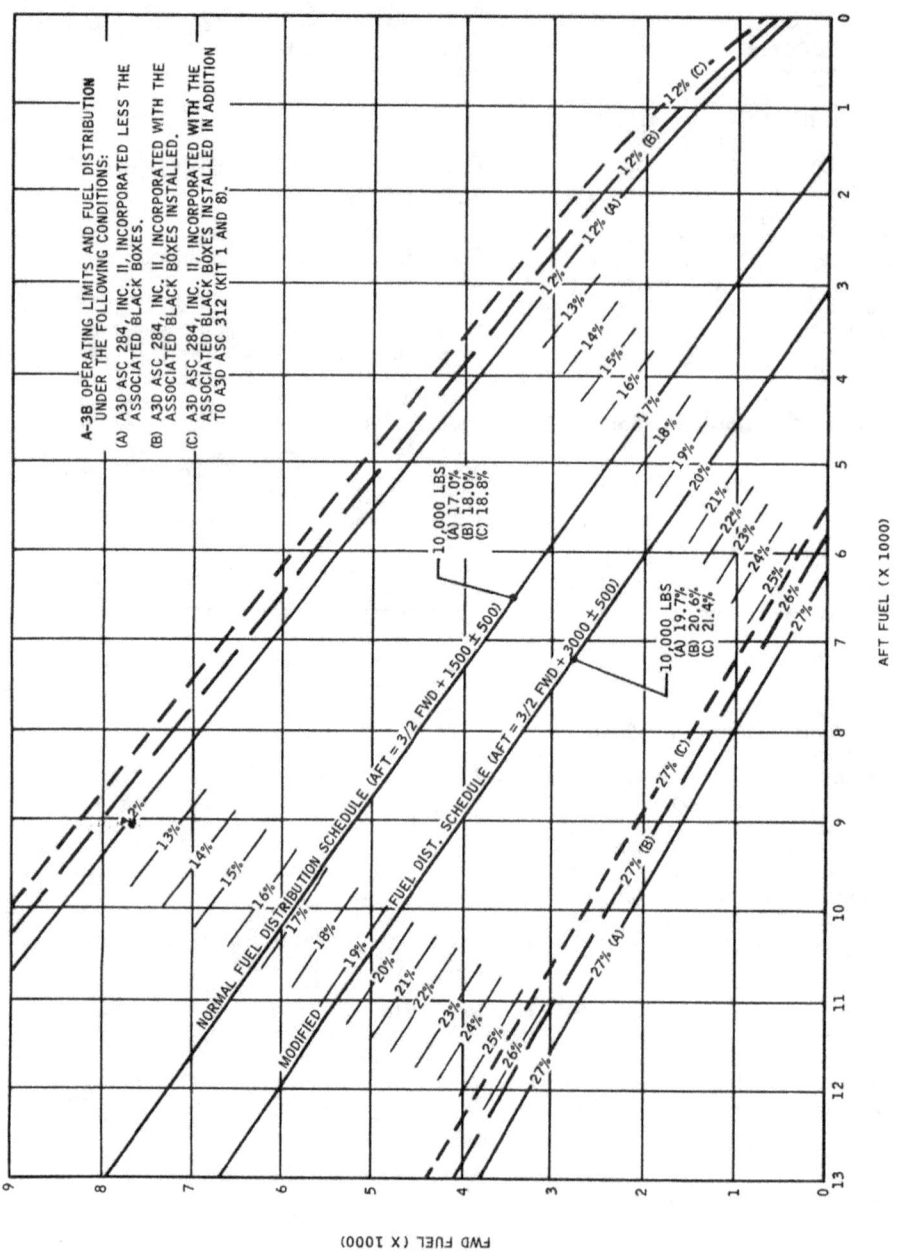

Aircraft BuNo. 135407-135444, 138902-138927, 138929-138931, 138933-138976, 142236-142255, 142400-142407, 142630-142649
Figure 1-27. Fuel Distribution Schedule

switch denote the trimmed condition (again in relation to fuel distribution) which will result from moving the switch to that position. On selective fuel trim control when the cg indicator moves from the NORM to the NOSE DN range, for instance, it will indicate that the present fuel distribution has caused the aircraft cg to move into a nosedown condition. Therefore, the FUS FUEL TRIM switch should be placed in NOSE UP to rectify the situation. The cg pointer will then gradually move back into the NORM range. The pointer should be allowed to move to the end of the NORM range toward the NOSE UP range before placing the FUS FUEL TRIM switch in NOSE DN. This procedure will allow more time for operation before having to repeat the sequence. For noseup conditions, reverse the procedure.

Since the flow of fuel from the forward to the aft fuel tank is affected by gravity, the pitch attitude of the aircraft can have a marked affect on the rapidity with which the fuel distribution can be changed. With the cg valve opened (FUS FUEL TRIM switch at NOSE UP, or MANUAL CG FUEL CONTROL VALVE handle at NOSE UP), a nosedown attitude can reduce or even stop the fuel flow to the aft tank. Therefore, during selective or manual operation, it is recommended that deviations from level flight be held to a minimum and assumed only for short periods.

Frequent cg checks should be made, preferably during level flight at an airspeed of 250 KIAS when the aircraft is clean, or at 135 KIAS during a power approach when the gear and flaps are down. An aft cg can be overcome more quickly by placing the FUS FUEL TRIM switch in NOSE DN and operating at a high power setting. This switch position will stop all fuel flow to the aft fuel tank, and the high power setting will burn the fuel more quickly. Conversely, a forward cg can be overcome more quickly by placing the FUS FUEL TRIM switch in NOSE UP and operating at a low power setting.

Fuel Trim Control—Manual

Manual control of fuel distribution should become necessary only if a dc electrical failure occurs. The procedure for manual operation of the fuel trim control system is essentially the same as that for selective operation, except that it is accomplished mechanically instead of electrically. Monitor the fuel levels in both the forward and aft fuselage fuel tanks and move the MANUAL CG FUEL CONTROL VALVE handle to NOSE UP or NOSE DOWN as necessary to maintain the required fuel distribution. NOSE UP is used to relieve a nose-heavy condition, and the NOSE DOWN position will relieve a tail-heavy condition. Do not, after selecting one of these positions, return the manual control to NORMAL, as this position will leave the cg control valve in the previously selected position. Instead, move the MANUAL CG FUEL CONTROL VALVE handle to the opposite position until it is necessary to again control fuel distribution.

WARNING

The quantity of fuel in the aft tank must at all times be equal to 1 1/2 times the quantity of fuel in the forward tank and must not exceed this ratio by more than 3000±500 pounds with modified fuel system.

CAUTION

If manual operation of the cg valve is required, reposition the fuel trim switch to coincide with console control handle to preclude possible damage to the cg valve motor.

The following warning is applicable to all DECM equipped basic wing.

WARNING

Manual operation of the gravity-transfer gate valve to the open position will be required when the fuel loading reaches 19,000 pounds for model A-3B aircraft with store-loadings in excess of 8000 pounds. The gravity-transfer gate valve should remain open until a fuel loading of 3100 pounds is reached. Manual operation of the gravity-transfer gate valve in this manner will prevent the forward cg limit from being exceeded. Manual operation of the gravity-transfer gate valve will not be required after release of stores.

Fuel Transfer

Fuel transfer from the wing tanks to the fuselage tanks can be accomplished as desired by the pilot within the capability of the fuselage tanks and the cg of the aircraft. If hot fuel is being used (27°C (80°F) or higher), delay fuel transfer as long as practicable, or until half of the fuselage fuel is consumed, so that the wing can act as a heat exchanger to cool the fuel. To transfer fuel, place the WINGS tank switch in TRANSF. The WING TANK switch should be placed in OFF after transfer is accomplished. The AUX switch (A-3B aircraft) will be operative if the auxiliary tank is installed. The FUS FUEL TRIM switch should be in the NORMAL position during the fuel transfer operation (figure 1-26).

Fuel Quantity Indicator

The FUEL QUANTITY indicator (figure 1-4) is controlled by the FUEL QUANTITY SELECTOR switch panel (figure 1-26). The indicator normally indicates the quantity of fuel remaining in the fuel cell selected by the fuel QUANTITY SELECTOR switch. However, when in flight the pitch attitude of the aircraft will have considerable effect on WINGS and TOTAL fuel quantity indications when the wing tanks are only partially full. Accurate readings can be obtained only during level flight with airspeed at 250 KIAS if the wing tanks are more than half full. Therefore, it is recommended that the pilot make certain before takeoff that the aircraft has been fueled properly and that all tanks are fully serviced.

Fuel Low-Level Warning Light

A red push-to-test fuel low-level warning light (figure 1-4) is located on the pilot's instrument panel. The purpose of the fuel low-level light is to warn the pilot of a low fuel state in the aft fuselage tank. When the fuel in the aft tank decreases to 3000±400 pounds or 460 gallons, a fuel low-level float switch is actuated, which lights a warning light on the instrument panel. The warning light and the fuel quantity indicating system are on separate electrical systems to ensure dual fuel indication when the fuel state reaches the low-level point.

When the low-level warning light comes on, the pilot must assume that no more than 3000±400 pounds of fuel remain in the aft tank, regardless of higher fuel quantity indicator readings.

ENGINE COMPRESSOR BLEED AIR SYSTEM

The engine compressor bleed air system draws compressed air from the high-pressure compressor rotor case of both engines and distributes this compressed air through an interconnected ducting system containing check valves, pressure regulators, shutoff valves, and relief valves, to power or pressurize certain aircraft components. Engine compressor bleed air powers the air turbine motors (ATM's), air conditioning system, and generator ground cooling ejector pump. This bleed air also pressurizes the wing fuel tanks for dump, hydraulic reservoirs, upper hatch seal, inner escape chute door seal, ASB receiver transmitter, and ASB modulator. Two check valves, one located between each engine and the common ducting to the various operating components, serve to prevent loss of airflow in case of failure of one engine. One operative engine will provide sufficient airflow to power the engine compressor bleed air system when operated at 85 percent rpm or above. For operating pressures of pressure regulated components of the engine compressor bleed air system, see figure 1-31.

An air-conditioning air filter is installed in the ducting which makes it possible to use main compressor bleed air from both engines for the air-conditioning and pressurization system.

NOTE

It is possible that cabin air contamination may occur under certain circumstances. For information on operation of the compressor bleed air system if contamination occurs, refer to Cabin Air Contamination.

Bleed Air Shutoff System (Toggle Switches)

VALVES

Motor-operated valves (figure 1-31) are installed in the pylon section of each engine bleed air duct and upstream of the air-conditioning filter. The purpose of the valves is to control the escape of high-temperature/pressure air in the event of air duct rupture. These valves are powered by the 28-vdc PRIMARY BUS.

SWITCHES

Three switches are installed (one for each valve) and are located on the pilot's instrument panel

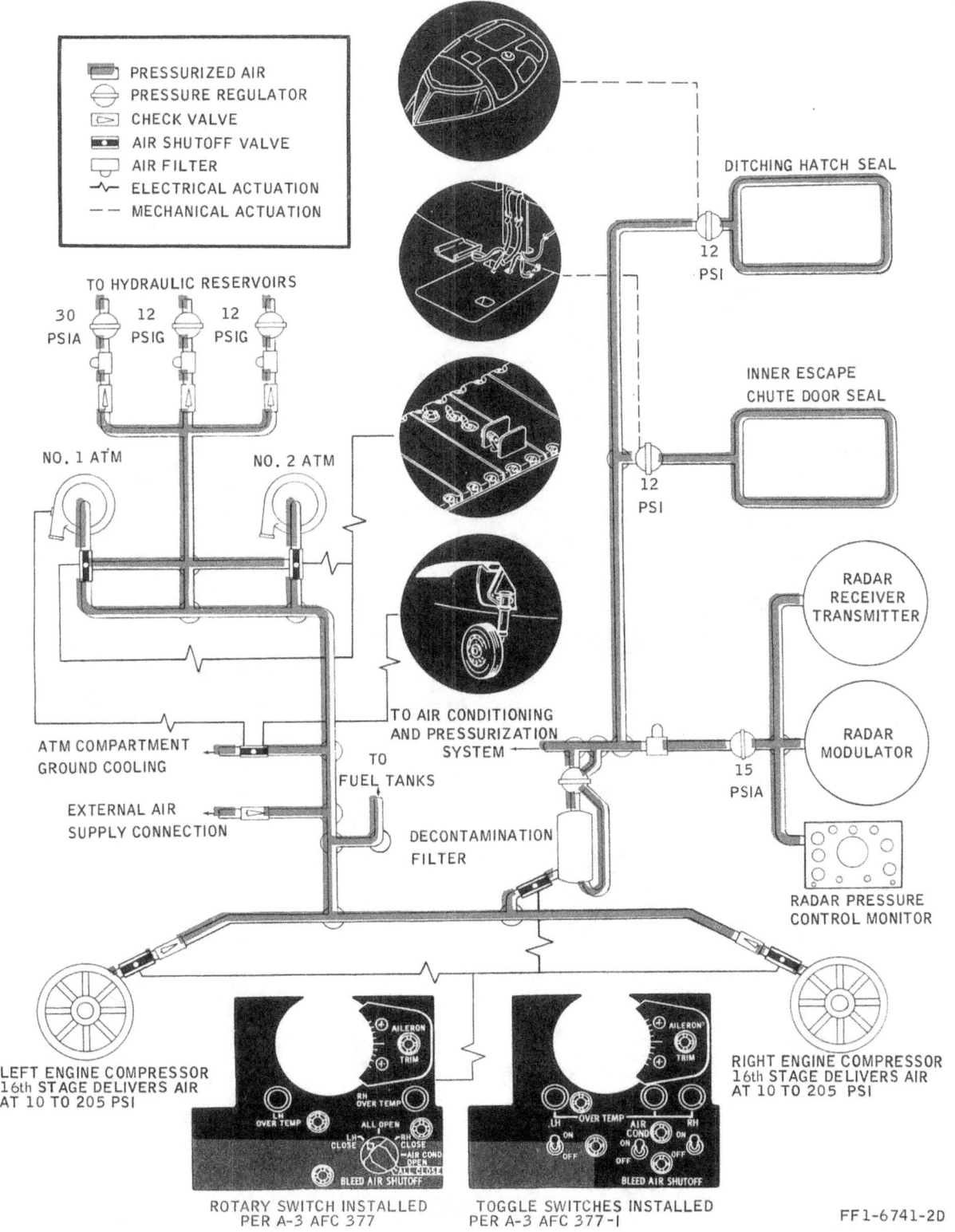

Figure 1-31. Engine Compressor Bleed Air Schematic A-3A/B and KA-3B (Sheet 1)

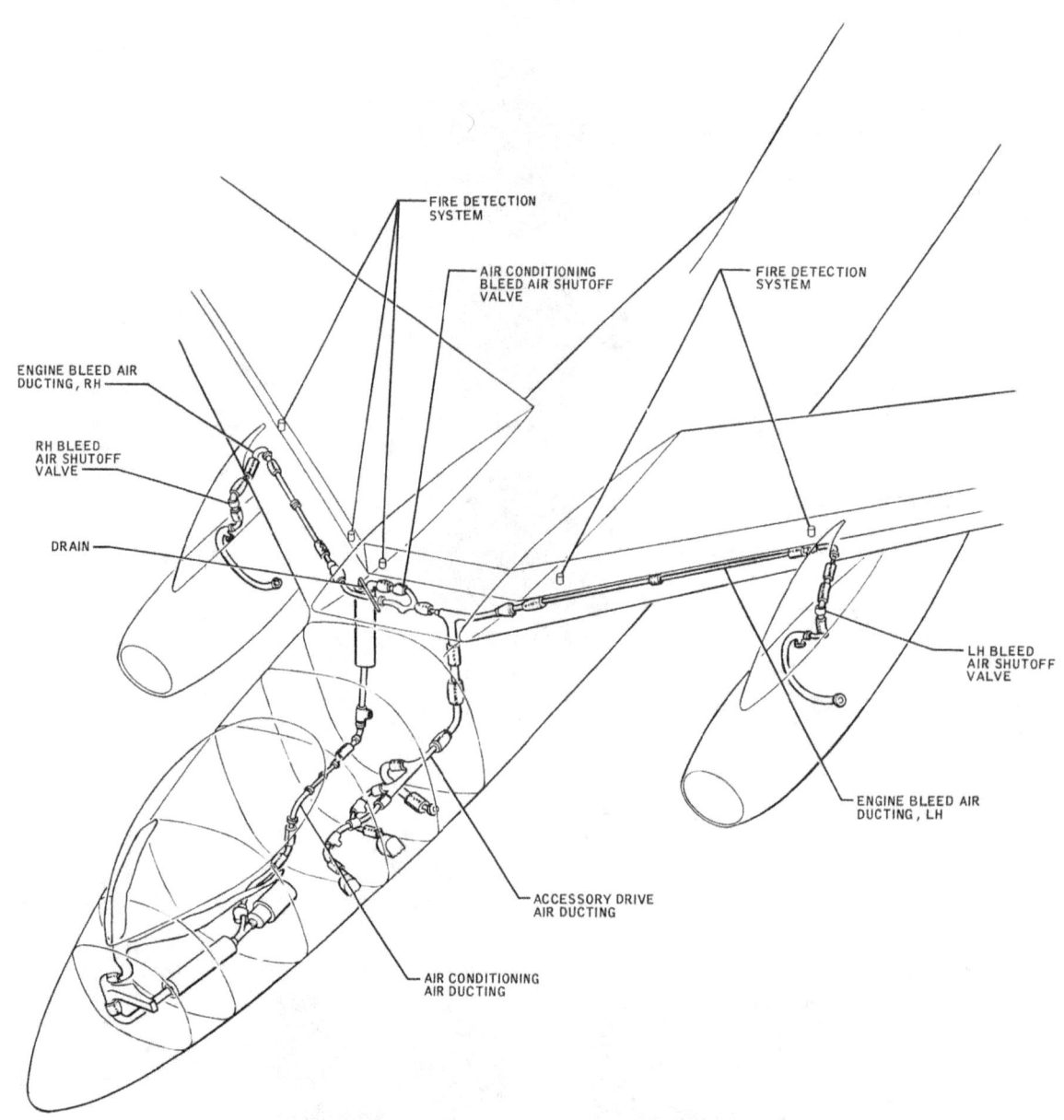

Figure 1-31. Engine Compressor Bleed Air Schematic A-3A/B and KA-3B (Sheet 2)

below the control wheel and are labeled OVER TEMP. These switches function as follows:

1. LH on............ LH VALVE OPENS
   LH off............ LH VALVE CLOSES

2. Air Cond on......... AC VALVE OPENS
   Air Cond off........ AC VALVE CLOSES

3. RH on............. RH VALVE OPENS
   RH off............ RH VALVE CLOSES

WARNING LIGHTS AND THERMOSWITCHES

Three warning lights, one for each switch, are placarded OVER TEMP and are located on the pilot's instrument panel. The LH and RH lights are lighted by two thermoswitches located inboard and two thermoswitches located outboard of each wing. The third light, AIR COND, is lighted by a thermoswitch located in the bomb bay adjacent to the air-conditioning filter can cap.

OPERATION

Refer to Section V for Emergency Operation and to Section III, Part 3, for Normal Operation.

Bleed Air Shutoff System (Rotary Switch)

VALVES

Motor-operated valves are installed in the pylon section of each engine bleed air duct and upstream of the air-conditioning filter. Their purpose is to control the escape of high-temperature/pressure air in the event of catastrophic air duct rupture. The valves are powered by the 28-vdc bus.

SWITCHES

A BLEED AIR SHUTOFF rotary switch to control the valves is located on the pilot's instrument panel below the control wheel. See figure 1-4. The switch is labeled and functions as follows:

1. LH close.......... CLOSES LH PYLON VALVE

2. All open.......... ALL OPEN (NORMAL OPERATION)

3. RH close......... CLOSES RH PYLON AND AIR-CONDITIONING VALVE.

4. Air cond OPEN...... CLOSES RH PYLON VALVE ONLY, OR REOPENS AIR-CONDITIONING VALVE AFTER CLOSING BY RH CLOSE.

5. All close.......... CLOSES ALL THREE VALVES.

WARNING LIGHTS AND THERMOSWITCHES

Two warning lights are located on the pilot's instrument panel (figure 1-4) adjacent to the rotary control switch. These are lighted by two thermoswitches (figure 1-31) located outboard in each wing leading edge. A fifth thermoswitch, connected to the RH light, is located in the bomb bay adjacent to the air-conditioning filter can cap.

OPERATION

Refer to Section V for Emergency Operation and to Section III, Part 3 for Normal Operation.

Air Turbine Motors (ATM's)

Two air turbine motors (ATM's) with gear trains, and mounting pads, are driven by the engine compressor bleed air and provide necessary power for driving the ac and dc generators, the utility hydraulic pumps, and the flight controls power boost pumps. The No. 1 (forward) ATM drives the No. 1 dc generator, the No. 1 ac generator, the aileron/spoiler power boost pump, and a utility hydraulic pump. The No. 2 (aft) ATM drives the No. 2 dc generator, the No. 2 ac generator, the surface control power boost pump, and a utility hydraulic pump. The ATM's are located in the hydraulics compartment on the left-hand side of the companionway. In normal operation, compressed air bled from the compressor outlet pressure sections of the engines is directed through a common duct to the ATM's. At each ATM, the air passes through a solenoid-operated (fail safe) shutoff and pressure regulating valve and is directed through a variable-vane nozzle to a turbine wheel, which in turn drives the accessory units. Speed of the turbine wheel is controlled by a flyball governor and a servomotor, which uses oil pressure supplied by an integral oil pump to vary the area of the air inlet nozzle vanes and thus maintain a constant turbine speed. A hydraulically actuated microswitch in the governor oil pressure system provides protection against overspeeding due to failure of the governor. The microswitch, when closed by excessive oil pressure due to overspeed, actuates the shutoff valve in the air intake duct of the overspeeding unit which cuts off all airflow to the ATM. As a protection against excessive bleed air pressure within the units, an overpressure sensing circuit is provided in each ATM. The overpressure circuit consists of a pressure-actuated switch, wired in series with each air-driven unit control switch and located within the bleed air duct of each ATM. The switch, when closed by pressure within the duct in excess of 70 psi, actuates the air shutoff valve in the bleed air duct to shut down the affected unit. A test switch, for checking operation of the overpressure sensing circuit, is provided on the ATM monitor panel (figure 1-32). Refer to PRESSURE SWITCH TEST in this section. In the event of a shutdown of an ATM, either by overpressure or by the test switch, the air shutoff valve is held in a shutdown position by means of an interlock relay. The air shutoff valve may be recycled by placing the applicable ATM switch (figure 1-6) in the OFF position and then back to the ON position. Two one-way flapper valves, one located between each engine and the common ducting, serve to prevent a loss of airflow during single-engine operation, thus permitting both ATM's to operate from one engine.

At 85 percent rpm on one engine, the ATM's will provide sufficient drive to the accessory units for normal operation of the electrical and hydraulic systems. Normal operation of the ATM's is indicated by the ac generator frequency meter located on the pilot's AC POWER panel (figure 1-38). A frequency of 400±20 cps indicates normal operating ATM rpm.

During ground operation, cooling air is drawn through the accessory chamber by pneumatic actuation of the generator ground cooling ejector pump. This pump is turned on by a microswitch, which is governor-actuated when the No. 1 ATM reaches sufficient rpm, and is shut off when the weight is off the landing gear.

Limit ground operation of the air turbine motors to 15 minutes if:

  1. Dc loads are above 50 amps

  2. Engine power settings are above 70 percent rpm.

Continuous ground operation under the above conditions results in ATM oil temperatures in excess of 250°F or overheating of the generators.

CAUTION

- During ground operation, never start No. 2 ATM until No. 1 ATM has been placed in operation. Overheating of generators can create serious fire hazard.

- With external power connected, ac frequency meter cannot be used as indication that ATM's are operating. Engine rpm must be at least 85 percent when ATM's are operated on one engine.

- During single-engine flight, do not operate engine at IDLE as engine bleed air may not be sufficient to operate ATM's.

An air inlet is provided in the fuselage (figure 1-2) to permit the use of an external air supply, consisting of one GTC 85 air compressor, to operate the ATM's during ground check of the electrical and hydraulic systems. Ground operation of the ATM's requires the use of the battery or an external source of dc power to provide overspeed protection.

ATM SWITCHES

Two switches (figure 1-7) located on the ATM panel of the pilot's left-hand console, control the air supply to the ATM's. These two-position switches, marked NO. 1 and NO. 2, supply power from the primary bus to the air shutoff valve solenoids and the overspeed microswitch. Switch positions are ON and OFF.

ATM MONITOR PANEL

The ATM monitor panel (figure 1-9) provides the pilot with a means for checking and monitoring the operation of the ATM's and components. The panel contains the dc generator warning lights, a test switch for checking operation of the ATM overpressure sensing circuit, and an ATM compartment temperature indicator. The dc generator warning lights are located on the center console (figure 1-9).

The dc generator warning light indicates a loss of output from the associated generator which, in turn, may indicate failure of the associated ATM. Refer to Section V, ATM Failure.

PRESSURE SWITCH TEST SWITCH. The three-position PRESS SWITCH TEST switch provides a means for checking proper operation of the ATM overpressure sensing circuit when the ATM's are operating. The switch, when moved from OFF to either momentary-contact ATM NO. 1 or ATM NO. 2 position, introduces a simulated overpressure signal

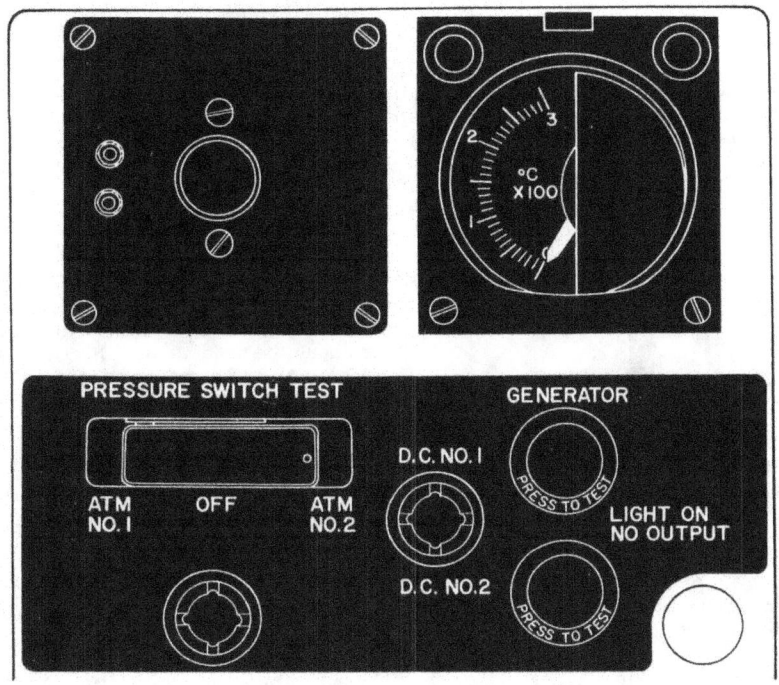

Figure 1-32. ATM Monitor Panel

into the applicable ATM overpressure sensing circuit. Proper operation of the overpressure circuit is immediately indicated by shutdown of the ATM being tested, as evidenced by loss of ac frequency and lighting of the dc generator warning light. On later aircraft, the PRESS SWITCH TEST switch is located on the center console (figure 1-9) below the ATM COMPT TEMP indicator.

ATM COMPARTMENT TEMPERATURE INDICATOR. The temperature indicator on the ATM monitor panel, identified as ATM COMPT TEMP, indicates the temperature of the air in the ATM compartment. The indicator is used with the ATM compartment temperature warning light (figure 1-9) on the pilot's instrument panel.

WARNING

- If an abrupt rise in compartment temperature occurs, closely monitor ATM's. Compartment temperature in the 230° to 315°C range is dangerously close to autoignition of hydraulic fluid. ATM compartment temperature, in this temperature range and rising, is an emergency situation which may, at discretion of the pilot, necessitate abandonment of aircraft.

- Experience has shown that ATM compartment temperature in excess of 100°C is a valid indication of bleed air leaks.

On later aircraft, the ATM compartment temperature indicator is located on the center console (figure 1-9).

ATM COMPARTMENT TEMPERATURE WARNING LIGHT

A warning light, located on the pilot's instrument panel (figure 1-4) and identified as ATM COMPT TEMP WARN, serves to warn of excessive temperature in the ATM compartment. Three thermoswitches, located at sensitive points in the ATM compartment, are parallel-wired in the warning light circuit between the dc primary bus and the light. If the temperature in the immediate area of any one of the switches exceeds 177°±11°C, the thermoswitch closes to complete the circuit between the primary bus and the warning light. Subsequent monitoring of ATM compartment temperatures is accomplished by observing the ATM COMPT TEMP indicator on the ATM monitor panel. Refer to ATM Compartment Temperature Indicator.

Three press-to-test switches (SW1, SW2, and SW3 figure 1-21) are provided to test the three ATM compartment temperature warning light circuits. With dc power applied to the primary bus, actuation of each switch should cause the ATM compartment temperature warning light to come on. The press-to-test circuits shall be checked during the PRETAXI check.

Changed 1 June 1969

ATM FAILURE

Failure of an ATM will be evidenced by the loss of a hydraulic boost pump, a dc generator, and an ac generator. An ATM failure is not necessarily indicated unless all three of these power losses occur. Malfunction or stoppage may be due to any of several causes: overpressure, overspeed, failure of ducting, negative g conditions, or internal failure.

WARNING

The ATM's may become inoperative if flight maneuvers beyond 1 negative g are maintained for 15 seconds.

In the case of overpressure, shutdown will be accomplished automatically through actuation of the overpressure cutout circuit. An attempt may be made to restart the unit by first throttling back to a lower power setting, and then recycling the applicable ATM control switch; however, if the unit again shuts down, no further attempt should be made to restart the unit and the ATM compartment temperature should be carefully monitored for the remainder of the flight.

NOTE

The ATM overpressure cutout circuit can be overridden, in an emergency, by pulling out the ATM CONT circuit breaker on the pilot's circuit breaker panel.

If stoppage is due to duct or internal failure, the pilot has no choice but to shut the unit down. Depending upon the location, failure of the ducting may be indicated by the ATM COMPT TEMP warning light coming on. In this event, the temperature of the ATM compartment must be closely monitored on the ATM COMPT TEMP indicator on the ATM monitor panel.

If the ATM governor fails, the ac frequency will oscillate from approximately 370 to 450 cps, being limited to this range by the overspeed control cutting in and out. The oscillating ATM should be shut down if the remaining ATM is operating satisfactorily. If the speed governors of both ATM's fail, it is possible to operate on overspeed control although the accuracy of some ac electrical components may be compromised.

A dual flameout or severance of the common portion of the ATM air duct will result in a complete hydraulic and electrical failure except for the battery and the emergency electrical hydraulic pump. The most immediate indications of failure of the No. 1 ATM are appearance of the gyro horizon warning flag, illumination of the DC NO. 1 warning light, loss of wing spoilers, and partial loss of the aileron power boost. Failure of No. 2 ATM will be indicated by a loss of voltage on No. 2 ac generator, the DC NO. 2 warning light coming on, loss of rudder-elevator power boost, and partial loss of aileron boost.

With one ATM inoperative, the remaining ATM will operate satisfactorily on bleed air from one engine at 85 percent rpm. In such a situation, the ac frequency meter should be used as an indication of proper ATM operation. An ac frequency reading of 400±20 cycles must be obtained to indicate normal operating speed of the remaining ATM.

ATM RESTART AFTER A NEGATIVE G CONDITION

If a negative g condition is inadvertently entered, the ATM nozzle vanes will close and cause the loss of an ATM. The nozzle vanes must be repositioned before a restart attempt will succeed. A crewman must go back in the companionway, remove the panel to the ATM compartment, and reposition the servo piston rod (figure 1-33). Pulling out on the rod will reposition the nozzle vanes, and a restart can then be accomplished by recycling the applicable ATM.

AIR CONDITIONING AND PRESSURIZING SYSTEM

An interconnected air conditioning and pressurizing system (figure 1-34) heats, cools, ventilates, and pressurizes the cockpit as required to maintain the most efficient operating conditions for the pilot and crew. Hot compressed air, bled from the engine compressor section, is passed through a decontaminating filter, a pressure regulator, (1) and an air conditioning unit, and then is mixed with a regulated amount of hot compressed air, which has bypassed the air conditioning unit, to provide the desired cockpit temperature. The cockpit is pressurized by automatic regulation of the release of cockpit air. Part of this air is passed through the electronic equipment compartment for cooling of radio and radar equipment; the remainder of the air is vented overboard forward of the periscope cover and serves to defrost the periscope.

Electronic Temperature Controller

The electronic air conditioning temperature controller regulates the position of the cabin air temperature control valve. The position of the C'PIT TEMP switch on the pilot's AIR COND & C'PIT PRESS

---
(1) Aircraft BuNo. 138902 and subsequent.

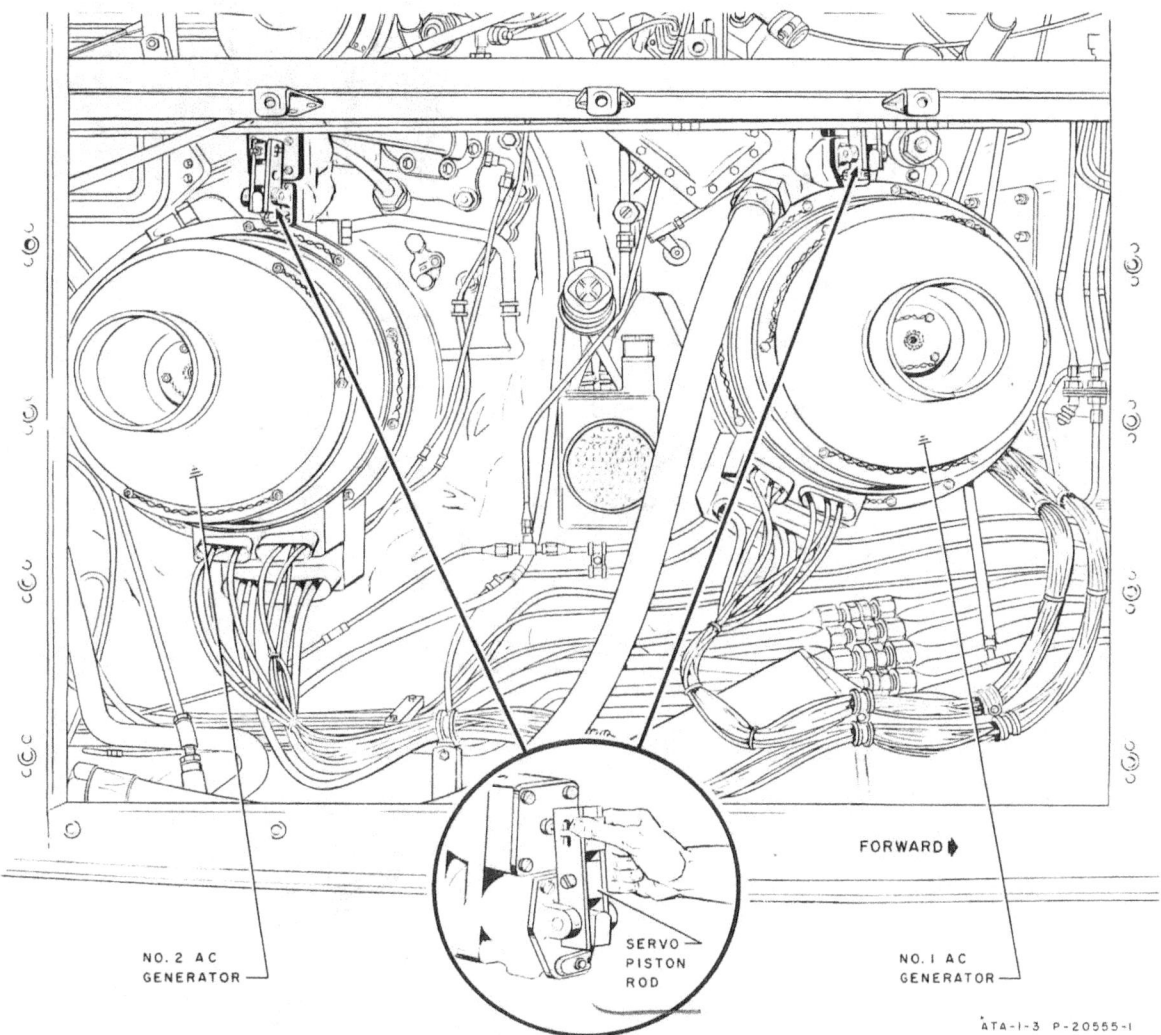

Figure 1-33. ATM Restart

panel on the left-hand console (figure 1-6) establishes the desired cabin temperature as a reference voltage in the electronic temperature controller, which then maintains the desired temperature by opening or closing the air temperature control valve in response to signals received from three temperature-sensing elements: the cabin air temperature pickup, the cabin air temperature high limit pickup, and the cabin air temperature anticipator. The cabin air temperature pickup is the basic sensing unit of the control system and provides regulating signals to the electronic temperature controller which in turn opens or closes the air control valve to maintain the desired cabin temperature. The cabin air temperature high limit pickup acts to limit the temperature of the air entering the cabin to 190±5°F in order to protect the windshield and other heat-sensitive materials. Whenever the electronic temperature controller calls for excessively hot conditioned air, the high limit circuit overrides the electronic temperature controller signals to limit the air supply temperature to 190±5°F. The cabin air temperature anticipator controls the rate of change of the cabin temperature. If a relatively small change of temperature is called for, the anticipator prevents an excessive amount of hot air from entering the cabin by modifying the degree to which the cabin air temperature control valve opens or closes, thus preventing the cabin temperature from

NAVAIR 01-40ATA-1

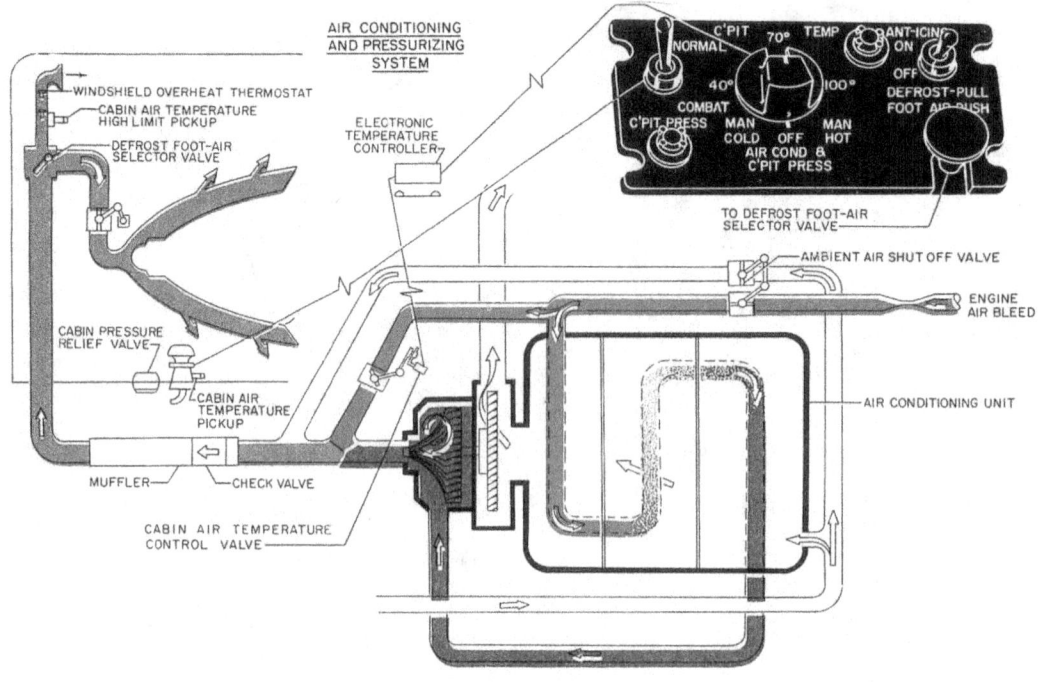

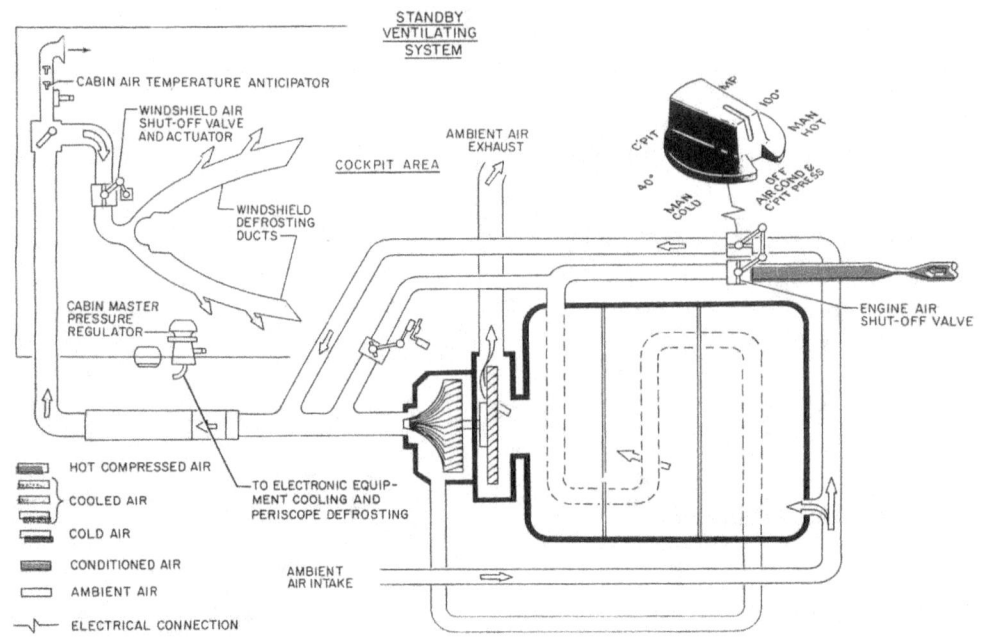

Figure 1-34. Air-Conditioning and Pressurizing System

fluctuating above and below the desired temperature before establishing and maintaining the desired temperature.

NOTE

During ground operation of the air conditioning system, both ac and dc power must be provided for operation of the cabin air temperature pickups and the electronic control units.

AIR-CONDITIONING CONTROL

The C'PIT TEMP switch on the pilot's left-hand console provides manual or automatic selection of cockpit temperature, or manual selection of ambient air. The rheostat portion of the control provides for selection of an electronically regulated cockpit temperature through a range of 40° to 100°F. The MAN COLD and MAN HOT positions are momentary-contact positions. Full hot or full cold air is supplied when the control is held in the desired position. On later aircraft[1] the MAN COLD position of the C'PIT TEMP switch is a momentary-contact switch that is spring loaded to a neutral position slightly above MAN COLD. The switch must be held in the MAN COLD position as long as necessary (approximately 30 seconds) to allow the cockpit temperature control valve to move to the cold position. If the switch is released during the travel of the cockpit temperature control valve, the switch will spring to the neutral position above MAN COLD and stop the valve at whatever position has been reached in the valve's travel to MAN COLD. The MAN HOT position of the switch, on later aircraft,[1] is not spring loaded and will remain in the MAN HOT position when released. If less than MAN HOT air is desired, the C'PIT TEMP switch should be placed in MAN HOT momentarily and then rotated to a position slightly above MAN HOT. Repeat this procedure until the desired temperature level is reached. In either MAN HOT or the automatic control range, a windshield overheat thermostat and a shutoff valve in the windshield defrosting duct automatically prevent overheating of the windshield by diverting defrosting air to the air-conditioning outlet at the pilot's floor until the temperature is reduced to below 210°F. A manual control is provided on the AIR COND & C'PIT PRESS panel for selecting the greater portion of air directed to the windshield or to the pilot's floor. The positions of this knob control, identified as DEFROST – PULL and FOOT AIR – PUSH, provide mechanical setting of a flapper valve in the windshield defrosting duct. The windshield overheat thermostat operates only in the event of failure of the cabin air temperature high limit pickup. The OFF position of the C'PIT TEMP switch turns on ambient ventilating air, depressurizes the cockpit, and closes the engine air shutoff valve. On some aircraft, the C'PIT TEMP switch must be pushed down to enter the OFF position (figure 1-34).

{ CAUTION }

The C'PIT TEMP switch must be left in the OFF position during ground operation of the ATM's with external power to prevent contaminated (hot bleed) air from the external power source from entering the cabin.

COCKPIT PRESSURE CONTROL

The C'PIT PRESS switch on the air-conditioning and pressurizing control panel (figure 1-6) of the pilot's left-hand console controls cockpit pressurization. In the NORMAL position, the switch selects and maintains a cockpit pressure altitude of 5000 feet up to a flight altitude of 13,500 feet, and above that point maintains a cockpit pressure differential of 3.3 psi above flight altitude pressure (figure 1-35). The COMBAT position of the switch causes a gradual reduction of the 3.3-psi pressure differential from an altitude of approximately 36,500 to 48,000 feet and thereafter remains constant at 1.3 psi pressure differential with further gain in altitude. The C'PIT TEMP switch should be placed in OFF within 60 seconds if for any reason the cabin becomes depressurized in flight. This causes air pressure to be retained in the cabin master pressure regulator, thus making rapid pressurization possible whenever the cause of depressurization no longer exists. If the switch is not turned OFF, pressurization may require as much as 5 minutes.

Cabin Air Contamination

Cabin air contamination may occur periodically. This contamination can consist of smoke, visible oil vapor, or irritating fumes caused by the combustion of residual oil collected in the engine compressor section due to small leaks and seepage around the rotor bearings. After the engine is started, the residual oil is carried through the compressor and subsequently contaminates the air bled off to operate the air-conditioning unit.

The occurrence of cabin air contamination is most likely when the aircraft has been shut down for several days or when the engines have been operated at idle rpm for extended periods. Under these circumstances, contamination will probably occur for approximately 30 seconds to 2 minutes when the throttles are advanced to military power for takeoff. When this condition arises, the cockpit may be ventilated by placing C'PIT TEMP switch in OFF for several minutes.

If cabin air contamination from the air-conditioning system persists or becomes severe, a leak or failure in the engine oil system is indicated. It is possible to

---

[1] Aircraft BuNo. 142236-142255, 142400-142407, 142630-142665, 144626-144629.

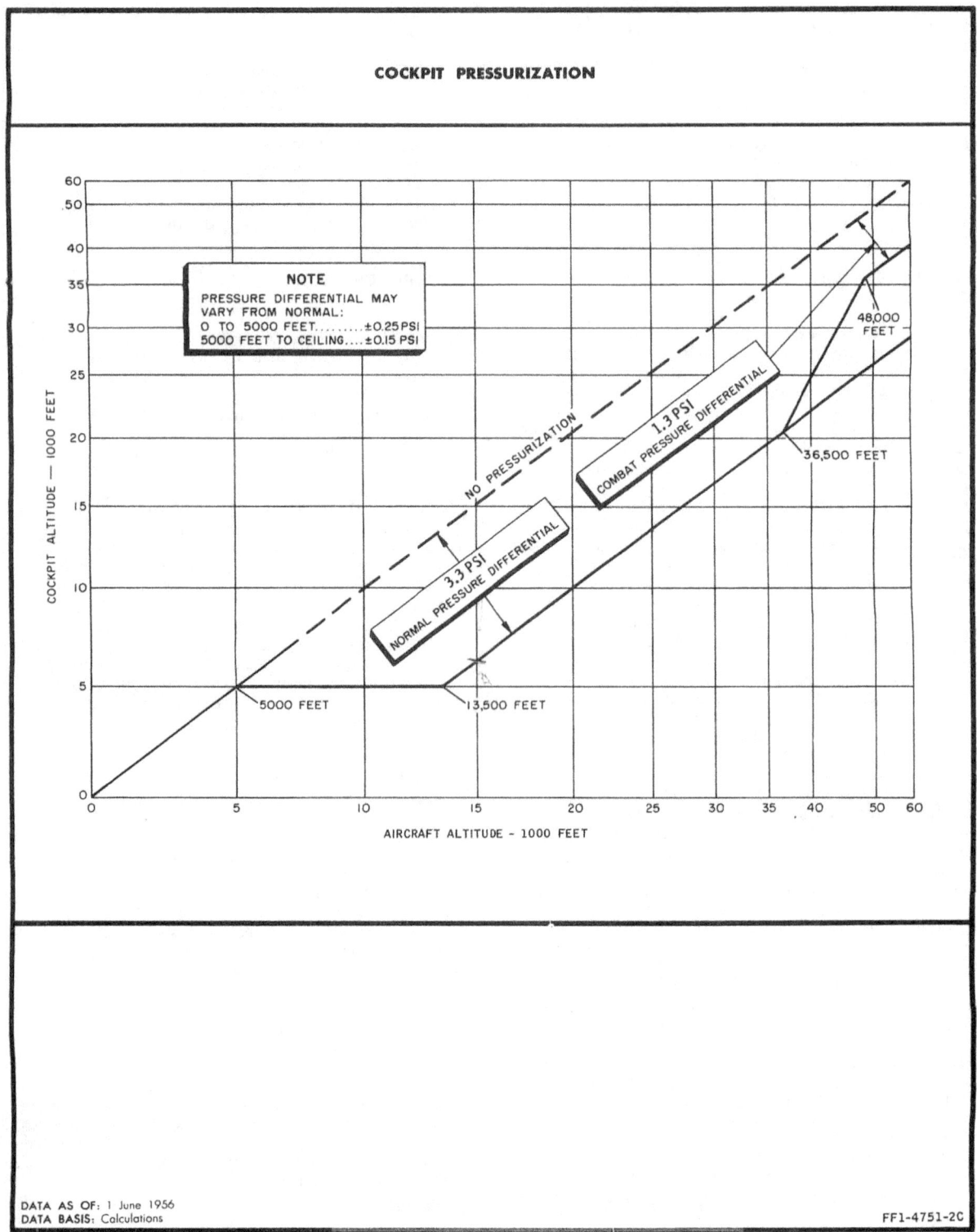

Figure 1-35. Cockpit vs Aircraft Altitude Comparison

correct this condition without depressurizing the cabin by retarding the throttle of the engine having the suspected oil leak. If this action has no noticeable effect, return the power setting to its original position and reduce rpm on the other engine. If neither procedure is successful in eliminating the contamination, place the C'PIT TEMP switch in OFF.

CAUTION

If cabin air contamination has been prolonged in nature, even though corrected by the foregoing procedure, maintain close observation of engine oil pressure and temperature, as the indicated oil leak will eventually deplete the engine oil supply.

WINDSHIELD DEFOGGING

The windshield defogging system normally requires no control. Small amounts of fog, however, or even finely divided snow will, on numerous occasions, appear at the windshield defroster and air-conditioning outlets. While this is a normal condition resulting from the rapid cooling of air by the refrigeration unit, an excessively large volume of fog, which obstructs vision, can occur under extreme conditions of high humidity and warm outside air temperature at very low altitudes. This fog may be eliminated by turning the cabin air temperature control up to increase the temperature of cabin air. In some cases the ducting may have cooled to a point where fog will persist for a short time after the cockpit temperature has been increased. After the fog has dispersed, a temperature setting should be selected that will provide the most comfortable temperature above the fogging point. In takeoffs or landings during which fogging conditions exist, it is suggested that the C'PIT TEMP switch be turned to the OFF position until the climb is established or the landing is completed.

Emergency Operation

AIR-CONDITIONING CONTROL

If the air conditioning unit fails, the cabin air temperature will become excessively high and operation of the MANUAL COLD position of the C'PIT TEMP control will be ineffective. In this event, place the C'PIT TEMP control in the OFF position.

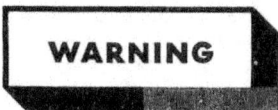

Placing the C'PIT TEMP control in the OFF position depressurizes the cabin. Aircraft flight altitude should not be higher than 43,000 feet as this altitude would exceed oxygen regulator limitations.

EQUIPMENT GROUND COOLING

The aircraft is equipped with five installation locations for equipment cooling blowers. Blowers can be temporarily installed for the cooling of aircraft equipment during prolonged ground operation. Two installation points are located in the nosewheel well for radome and left-hand equipment compartment cooling; one, externally on the right-hand side of the aircraft at the entrance door for right-hand equipment compartment cooling; and one each, externally on the left- and right-hand sides of the tail bumper for aft compartment cooling. Sliding plates cover the blower inlets when blowers are not installed.

WINDSHIELD WIPER

The windshield wiper is controlled by a four-way toggle switch located on the top of the instrument panel (figure 1-4). The switch positions are: OFF, SLOW, FAST, and PARK. The PARK position is a momentary-contact position used to position the blade after the wiper motor has been shut off. Do not operate the windshield wiper at airspeeds in excess of 200 KIAS.

ANTI-ICING SYSTEM

Engine Air Inlet

To prevent dangerous icing of the engine air inlet surfaces, an anti-icing system is incorporated in the engine. High temperature compressor discharge air is piped forward to the compressor case and inlet guide vanes through external tubes on each side of the engine. An anti-icing air regulator and air valve are incorporated in each tube system. The regulator automatically controls the volume of air flowing through the tubes, permitting maximum flow at 70°F bleed air temperature and minimum flow at 560°F.

Anti-Icing Control

The ANTI-ICING switch on the air-conditioning and pressurizing control panel (figure 1-4) controls selection of the anti-icing system. This ON-OFF switch actuates the anti-icing valves to permit temperature-regulated air to flow through the engine inlet guide vanes and controls heat to the pitot tube and the angle-of-attack probe.

Section I
Part 2

NAVAIR 01-40ATA-1

PITOT HEAT CONTROL

Heat for the pitot tube is supplied by an electrical resistor coil in the pitot tube head. The system is controlled by the ANTI-ICING switch on the pilot's left-hand console.

ANGLE-OF-ATTACK PROBE

Heat for the angle-of-attack probe is supplied by an electrical resistor coil in the probe. The system is controlled by the ANTI-ICING switch on the PILOT'S left-hand console.

ANTIEXPOSURE SUIT VENTILATION

An antiexposure suit ventilation control panel is installed on each flight crewmember's position (figure 1-15) for use with the Mark 5 antiexposure suit.

The control panel contains the EXPOSURE SUIT VENT and OFF toggle switch, a ventilation blower, and a quick-disconnect flexible hose for connection to the antiexposure suit. The suit hose disconnect coupling contains a butterfly valve to control the flow of ventilating air to the antiexposure suit or to close off the opening when the suit is not used.

ELECTRICAL SYSTEM

The aircraft has two electrical systems: a 28-vdc and a 115/200-vac, 400-cycle, three-phase system (figure 1-36). Two ATM-driven generators are incorporated into each system. An external power receptacle (figure 1-2) is provided for employment of an external ac and dc power source during engine starting or ground operation of the electrical equipment.

DC Power System

The dc power supply consists of a 24-v, 36-ampere-hour battery (figure 1-2) and two 28-v, 300-ampere generators. The generators are mounted on and driven by the ATM's. Five buses are used for power distribution. These are the battery, primary, secondary, radio, and monitor buses. Control of the system is provided by the ELEC PWR (battery) switch (figure 1-9) on the pilot's center console and the dc GENERATORS switches on the aft power panel (figure 1-37). Each generator circuit is protected by a voltage regulator, an overvoltage relay, and a reverse current cutout relay. Power from the generators passes through these devices to the primary bus and to two interconnected bus control relays,

which govern distribution of power to the secondary and monitor buses. Circuit breakers for the dc powered units are located on the pilot's console circuit breaker panel and the companionway circuit breaker panel (figures 1-20 and 1-21).

DC Power Distribution

PRIMARY BUS

The primary bus is located in the cockpit circuit breaker panel (figures 1-22 and 1-23). The bus is energized by the battery when the electrical power switch is in the BAT or EMER position, by the generators when either dc generator is ON and operating, or by external power.

SECONDARY BUS

The secondary bus is located at the companionway circuit breaker panel (figures 1-20 and 1-21) and in the cockpit circuit breaker panel (figures 1-22 and 1-23). This bus is energized when either dc generator is ON and operating. The bus is also energized with both dc generators OFF or inoperative, whenever:

1. The ELEC PWR switch is in the EMER position

2. The landing gear is extended and the ELEC PWR switch is in the BAT position

3. An external power supply is connected. See figure 1-36 for details.

RADIO BUS

The radio bus is located at the cockpit circuit breaker panel on the pilot's left-hand console (figures 1-14 and 1-23). This bus is energized by the secondary bus, through the MASTER RADIO switch (figures 1-10 and 1-11) on the navigator's right-hand console.

MONITOR BUS

The monitor bus is located at the companionway circuit breaker panel (figures 1-20 and 1-21). The bus is energized when either generator is ON and operating, or by external power.

BATTERY BUS

The battery bus, located at the pilot's console circuit breaker panel (figures 1-22 and 1-23) on the center console, controls the distribution of battery power. The switch has three positions: OFF, BAT, and

EMER. With the switch in BAT, the battery energizes the primary bus and, with the landing gear extended, the secondary bus. When switched to EMER, the battery energizes the primary and secondary buses. The battery bus is energized at all times, when a charged battery is installed and connected, regardless of the position of the ELEC PWR switch.

NOTE

Full battery power is available for actuating the emergency escape chute and drag chute circuits when the battery is installed and connected regardless of the position of the ELEC PWR switch.

DC Generator Switches

The dc GENERATORS switches (figure 1-37) are located on the aft power panel at the gunner's station. These ON, OFF switches are labeled DC NO. 1 and DC NO. 2. The switches control the flow of current from the generators to the primary bus and the bus control relays, which in turn distribute generator power to the secondary and monitor buses and to the battery.

Generator Warning Lights

A warning light (figure 1-37) for each dc generator is located adjacent to the generator switches on the aft power panel. These lights are on when the primary bus is not receiving power from the generator.

DC GENERATOR WARNING LIGHTS

A warning light for each dc generator, identified as DC NO. 1 and DC NO. 2, is located on the ATM monitor panel (figure 1-32). These lights are on when the primary bus is not receiving power from the applicable generator. The lighting of either warning light may indicate failure of an ATM (ATM Monitor Panel).

NOTE

An inoperative dc generator may be brought "on the line" to assume the dc electrical load, by either actuating the dc stabilizer trim or by turning off the operating dc generator. If neither method is successful, do not attempt to take off.

VOLTAMMETERS

A voltammeter (figure 1-37) for each generator is located directly below the generator switches on the

aft power panel. The voltmeter side of the instrument is calibrated from 15 to 33 volts. The voltmeters of both instruments indicate primary bus voltage, and both voltmeters will, if operating normally, indicate the same voltage regardless of the source of power to the primary bus. The ammeter side indicates ampere load on each generator from 0 to 450 amperes.

GENERATOR MANUAL RESET

The dc generator overvoltage relays are equipped with a manual reset control. The OVERVOLTAGE reset pushbuttons are located on the circuit breaker and fuse panel in the companionway (figures 1-20 and 1-21). Should the overvoltage relay of either generator trip, one attempt to reset the relay may be made by pushing in momentarily on the pushbutton. If the relay does not reset immediately, as indicated by the generator instruments and warning light on the aft power panel, no further attempt should be made until the cause of the malfunction has been found and corrected.

Electrical System Emergency Operation

DC POWER FAILURE

Failure of a dc generator will be indicated by a warning light on the aft power panel and the ATM monitor panel coming on. The operative generator will supply sufficient power for operation of essential equipment, but the load must be maintained at a level below 300 amperes. If both generators fail, switching the ELEC PWR switch on the pilot's center console to EMER will energize the primary and secondary buses directly from the battery.

NOTE

If the ELEC PWR switch is left in the BAT position, only the primary bus will be energized by the battery until the landing gear control is moved to the DOWN position.

The battery will supply sufficient power for operation of the essential equipment for a period dependent upon the ampere load placed on it. Extreme conservatism will prolong the life of the battery; indiscriminate use of such high-drain equipment as the emergency hydraulic pump or UHF transmitter can drain the battery completely in a very few minutes. All electrical equipment not essential to operation of the aircraft should be turned off before placing the ELEC PWR switch in EMER.

Changed 1 June 1969

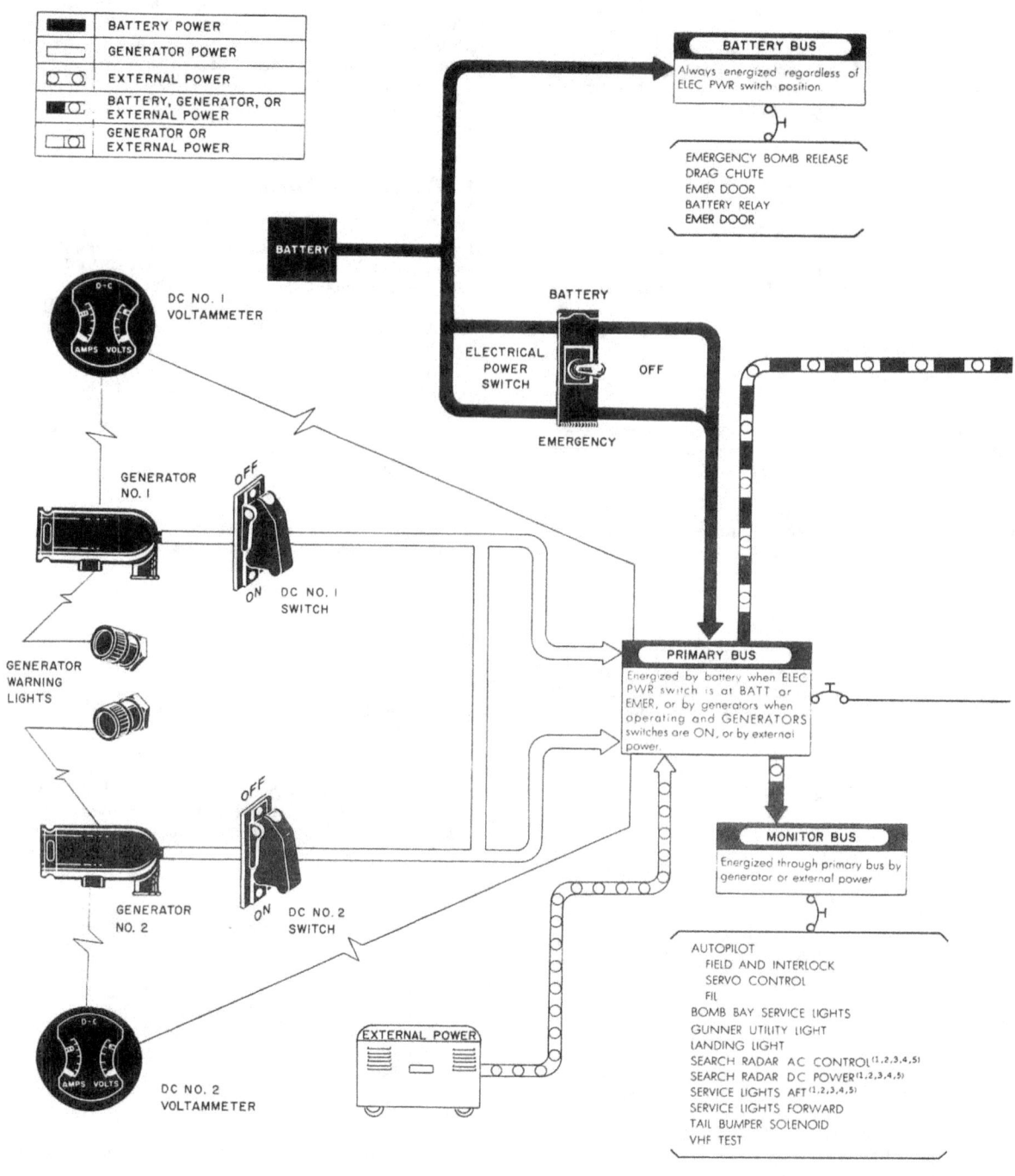

Figure 1-36. DC Electrical System (Sheet 1)

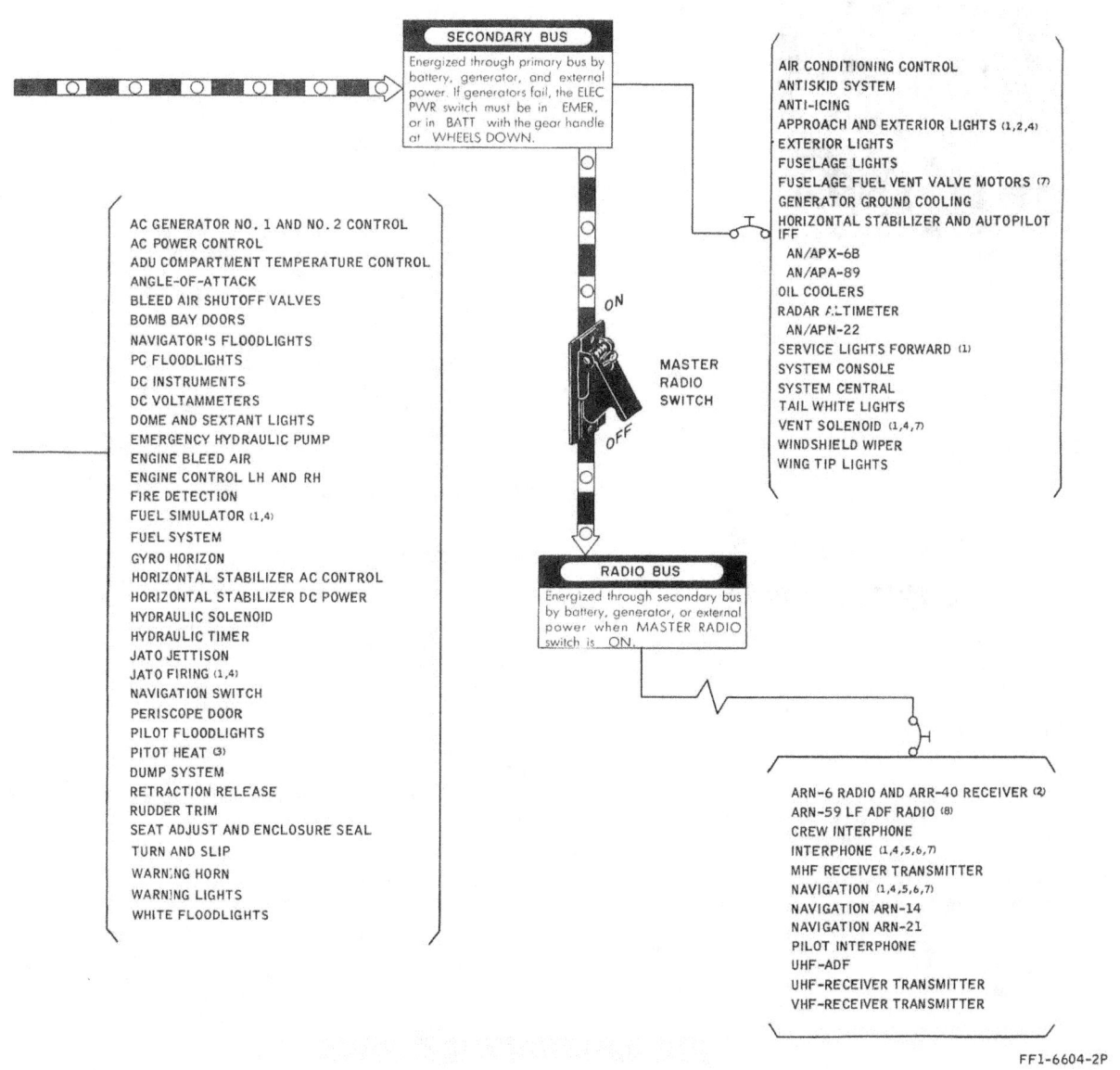

Figure 1-36. DC Electrical System (Sheet 2)

three-phase distribution bus if an overvoltage condition exists. Each ac generator is rated for continuous duty at 15 kva. Generators must not be loaded in excess of 150 percent of rated capacity for more than 2 minutes, or in excess of 200 percent for more than 5 seconds.

- The overvoltage relay automatically protects the ac generator circuit from an overvoltage condition. For any other malfunction of a generator or its circuit, disconnect the generator with the generator switch.

- During two-engine operation, maintain rpm about 70 percent to ensure adequate ac frequency and voltage.

No protection is provided against an undervoltage or an overfrequency or underfrequency condition. The ac frequency meter and switches for controlling the operation of the ac power system are located on the AC POWER panel (figure 1-38) below the pilot's instrument panel. A voltammeter for each generator is installed on the aft power panel (figure 1-37). Circuit breakers for the ac powered equipment are located on the companionway circuit breaker and fuse panel.

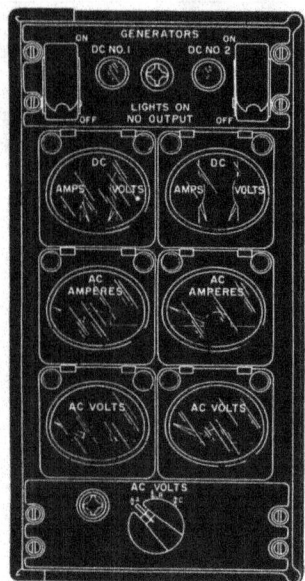

AIRCRAFT BUNO. 135407-135444, 138902-138976, 142236-142255, 142400-142407, 142630-142649, 144626-144629

FF1-4745-F

Figure 1-37. Aft Power Panel

AC Power System

WARNING

The ac electrical power system contains voltages dangerous to life. Do not rely on interlocks for protection. The ac system and equipment may be serviced only by qualified personnel on the ground.

The electrical power supply (figure 1-39) consists of two 115/200-vac, three-phase, 400-cycle, 15-kva generators. Each generator is essentially three 115-volt generators combined into one unit. They are Y-connected with the common grounded. The voltage between any line (or phase) and ground is 115 volts, and between any two lines is 200 volts. Each generator is driven directly by an ATM whose constant governed speed drives the generator at the rpm required to furnish ac power at 400±20 cps. Dc power is supplied to the generator controls from the dc primary bus through the AC PWR-CONT circuit breaker on the pilot's left-hand console. Each generator output is regulated by a voltage regulator, and protected from overvoltage by an overvoltage relay which automatically disconnects the generator from its

AC Power Distribution

AC GENERATOR NO. 1 BUS

The ac generator No. 1 power distribution bus, consisting of three separate 115-volt buses designated the A, B and C phases, is energized by the ac No. 1 generator through the No. 1 generator circuit breaker relay. The No. 1 bus may also be energized by an external ac power source if dc power is available, the EXT PWR switch is ON, the BUS TIE switch is in AUTO, both GEN switches are OFF, and an external ac power source is plugged into the external power receptacle.

AC GENERATOR NO. 2 BUS

The ac generator No. 2 power distribution bus, consisting of three separate 115-vac phases (A, B and C), is energized by the ac No. 2 generator through the No. 2 generator circuit breaker relay, or by an external ac power source if dc power is available, the EXT PWR switch is ON, the BUS TIE switch is in AUTO, the ac power source is plugged into the external power receptacle, and both GEN switches on the AC POWER panel are OFF.

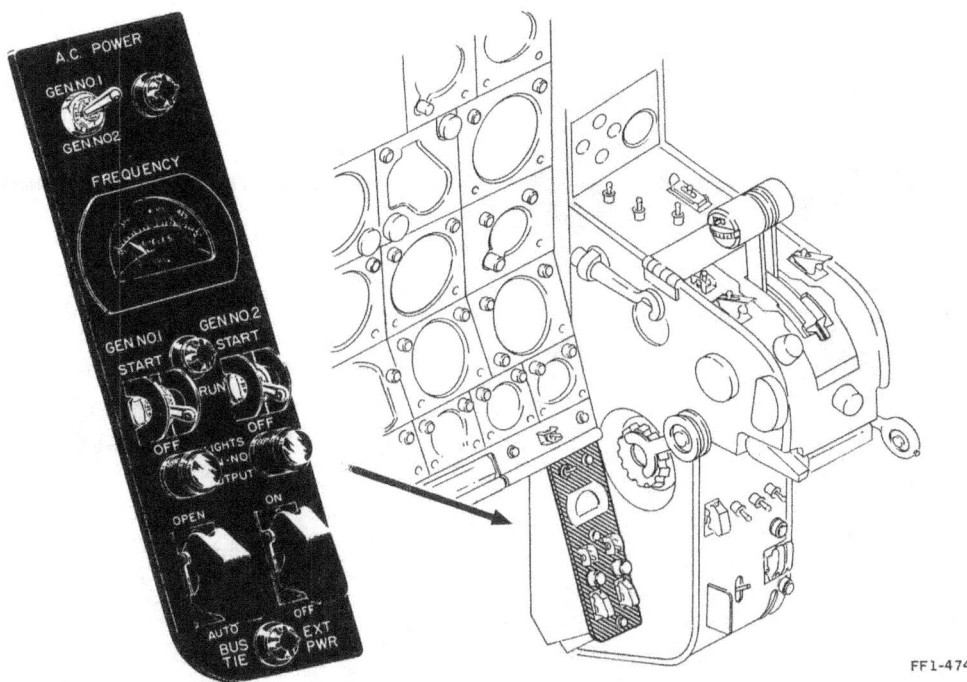

Figure 1-38. AC Power Panel

AC Power Control

The ac power supply and distribution system is controlled by dc power from the primary bus, which must be energized before the ac power control switches become effective. Distribution of ac generator power to the ac buses is controlled by three major power control relays: a circuit breaker relay for each generator and a bus tie breaker relay. These relays are controlled by switches on the pilot's AC POWER panel (figure 1-38).

GENERATOR CIRCUIT BREAKER RELAYS

The generator circuit breaker relays serve as a control between the generators and the generator buses. These relays are of the push-pull type with a coil at either end. When either coil is energized momentarily, the relay moves toward that coil and is latched in that position until the opposite coil is energized. The "close" coil of each relay, which completes the circuit between the generator and its bus, is energized by dc power supplied to the coil when the applicable GEN switch is cycled to START and RUN, but only if the BUS TIE switch is in the OPEN position and the EXT PWR switch is OFF. The "open" coil of each circuit breaker relay is energized by dc power either through the OFF position of the ac GEN switch or through action of the overvoltage relay, which automatically opens the generator circuit breaker relay to disconnect the generator from its bus if a generator overvoltage occurs. If either generator circuit breaker relay is "opened" by the overvoltage relay of its respective generator circuit while the BUS TIE switch is in the AUTO position, a circuit is completed between the dc primary bus and the bus tie relay. The bus tie relay will then be energized to "tie" the ac generator No. 1 and No.2 buses together, thus supplying power to the deenergized bus from the powered bus.

CAUTION

A malfunction within either generator will not cause the circuit breaker relay of the failed generator to "open." The most immediate warning of such a failure of the No. 1 generator will be the loss of fuel flow indications, appearance of the gyro horizon warning flag, and indication of the frequency meter due to its switch being spring loaded in the No. 1 position. Such a failure of the No. 2 generator will be indicated most immediately by the appearance of STANDBY gyro horizon warning flag. (Refer to Ac Power Failure, Section V.

Dc power for energizing the ac generator warning lights (refer to Generator Warning Lights) and the external ac power relay is also supplied through the

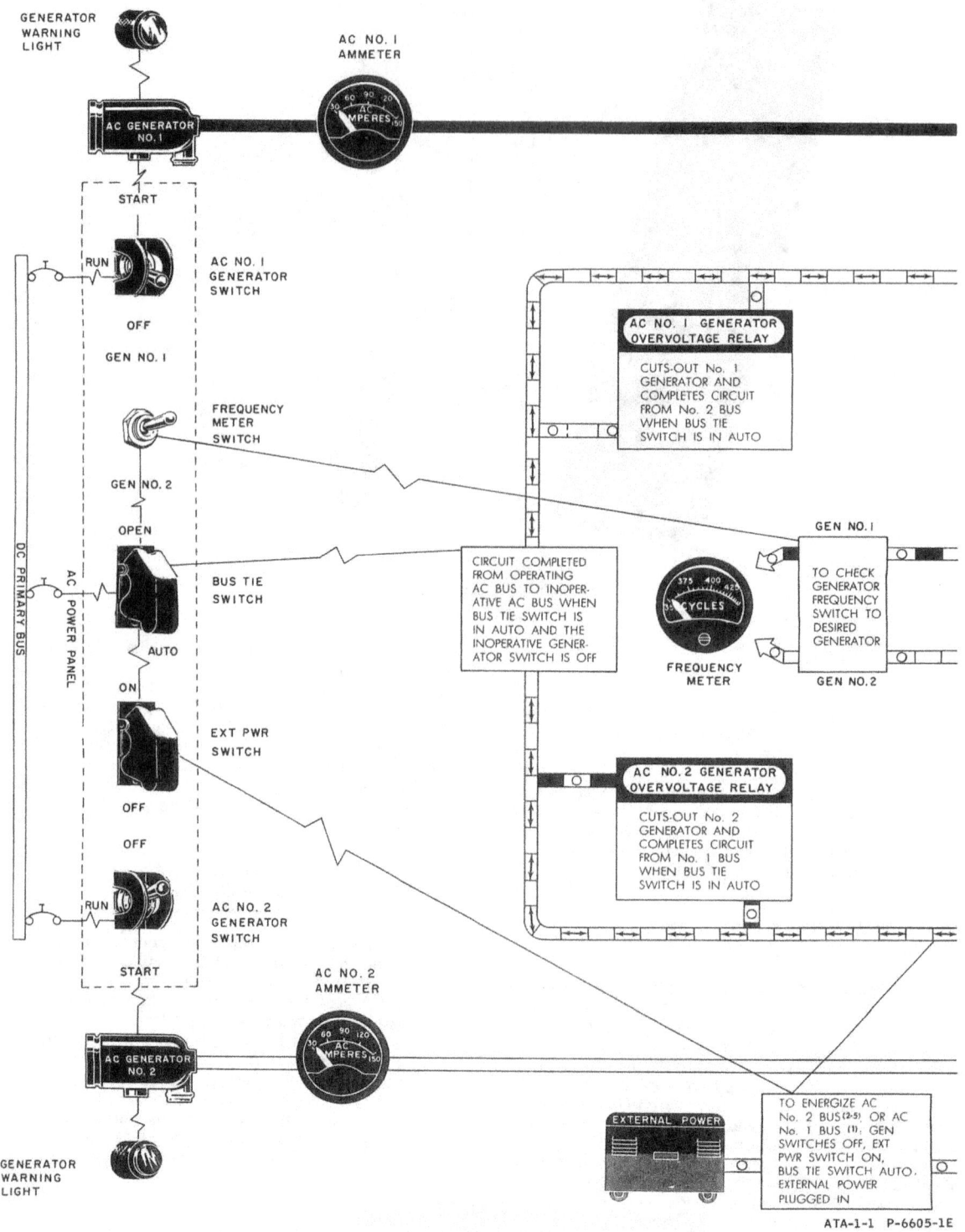

Figure 1-39. AC Electrical System (Sheet 1)

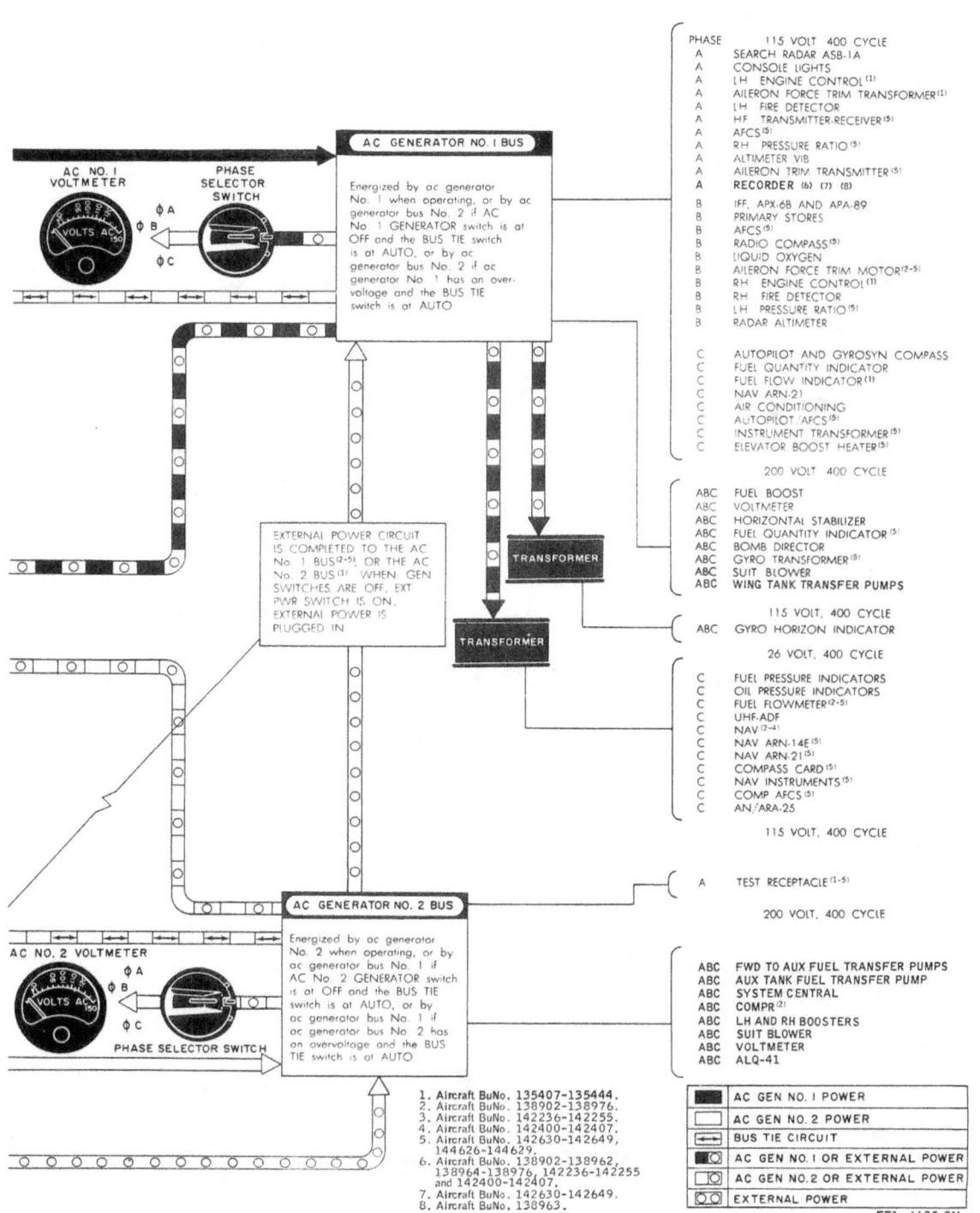

Figure 1-39. AC Electrical System (Sheet 2)

"open" position of the generator circuit breaker relays. Both generator switches must be OFF before dc power is supplied to energize the external power relay, which then completes a circuit between the external ac power receptacle and the ac No. 1 bus in early aircraft[1] or the ac No. 2 bus in later aircraft[2].

GENERATOR WARNING LIGHTS

The ac generator warning lights on the AC POWER panel (figure 1-38) are energized by dc power through the generator circuit breaker relays only when the relays are in the open position, and therefore indicate only that the circuit breaker relay of the indicated generator circuit is "open." If the warning light is on during normal flight, the generator switch may be turned OFF, then recycled through the normal starting procedure. If the warning light comes on again, the generator must be turned OFF and power must be supplied to the bus of the inoperative generator through the BUS TIE switch.

BUS TIE BREAKER RELAY

The two-position BUS TIE switch on the AC POWER panel, controls the bus tie breaker relay which provides a means of energizing both the ac generator No. 1 and 2 buses from one generator. With the switch in the OPEN position, both ac generator circuits function normally as independent circuits. When the switch is placed in the AUTO position, part of a circuit is completed between the dc primary bus and the bus tie breaker relay. This circuit is completed if either generator circuit breaker relay is opened during normal operation of the ac power system, thus energizing the bus tie relay which in turn closes to complete a direct circuit between the No. 1 and 2 buses.

NOTE

A generator circuit breaker relay will open only when its open coil is energized by the overvoltage relay or by the OFF position of the generator switch. If a generator is lost for any reason other than overvoltage, the generator switch must be turned OFF before the bus tie relay will be energized to close and tie the ac No. 1 and 2 generator buses together.

External power is supplied directly through the external power receptacle to the ac generator No. 1 bus on early aircraft(1). Subsequent aircraft(2) provide external power directly to the ac generator No. 2 bus. To energize the ac generator No. 1 bus(1) or the ac generator No. 2 bus(2) for ground operation of ac equipment; the GEN switches must be OFF, the EXT PWR switch ON, the BUS TIE switch in AUTO, and the external power plugged in.

NOTE

The BUS TIE switch must always be placed in the OPEN position to accomplish a start of the ac generators.

The BUS TIE switch is powered from the dc primary bus through the AC PWR CONT circuit breaker on the left-hand console circuit breaker panel.

GENERATOR SWITCHES

Two three-position GEN switches on the AC POWER panel, labeled GEN NO. 1 and GEN NO. 2, control the output and distribution of ac generator power. The three positions of each switch are OFF, START, and RUN. The OFF position of each switch energizes the open coil of the generator circuit breaker relay and the exciter relay, which in turn cuts off the dc power supply to the generator controls and opens the generator field to deenergize the generator and circuit. The momentary-contact START position of each switch supplies dc power to the exciter relay, which closes a part of the circuit between the dc primary bus and the generator controls. This circuit, including the generator field, is not completed and the generator circuit breaker relay close coil is not energized until the generator switch is released to fall into the RUN position. The generator switches are dc powered through the GEN NO. 1 and GEN NO. 2 circuit breakers on the pilot's left-hand console.

NOTE

If an AC generator drops off the line, flick the applicable ac GEN switch momentarily to START. Generators with high residual will go overvoltage and cannot be placed on the line if the start switch is held too long in the START position. An overvoltage during start does not constitute a reason for rejection and/or replacement of the generator.

EXTERNAL POWER SWITCH

The EXT PWR switch on the AC POWER panel (figure 1-38) supplies dc power from the primary bus to close a relay that connects the AC NO. 2 bus(1) or the AC NO. 1 bus(2) to the ac external power receptacle.

---

(1) Aircraft BuNo. 135407-135444.
(2) Aircraft BuNo. 138902 and subsequent.

The relay can be energized only if both GEN switches are OFF and the external power supply is plugged into the receptacle.

The BUS TIE switch must be placed in the AUTO position after the EXT PWR switch is turned ON, to energize the AC NO. 1 bus[1] or the AC NO. 2 bus[2] from the external power supply.

FREQUENCY METER

An ac frequency meter is located on the pilot's AC POWER panel (figure 1-38). The meter indicates the A-phase frequency of the generator selected by the switch on the meter panel. The two-position ac generator switch is spring loaded to the GEN NO. 1 position. Normal operating frequency of both generators is 400±20 cps.

No protection against an underfrequency condition is provided. Much of the electronic equipment operated by ac power is frequency-sensitive; therefore, a generator producing less than 380 cps must be turned OFF and necessary equipment operated from the remaining generator through the bus tie.

An underfrequency condition on either generator indicates that the corresponding ATM is operating at an rpm lower than the normal governed speed. Refer to Air Turbine Motors.

VOLTMETERS

The ac generator bus voltage is indicated by voltmeters (figure 1-37) on the aft power panel. A phase selector switch on the lower power panel provides a means of checking the voltage of each phase of the bus. The voltmeters are calibrated from 0 to 150 volts. Normal indication is 115 volts on each phase.

AMMETERS

An ammeter for each generator circuit is located adjacent to the voltmeters. The ammeter reflects the ampere load on the A phase only. Normal ammeter indication may range from approximately 10 to 30 amperes on the AC No. 1 GENERATOR ammeter, and from 12 to 35 amperes on the AC No. 2 GENERATOR ammeter. Maximum continuous rated amperage is 43 amperes.

---

[1] Aircraft BuNo. 135407-135444.
[2] Aircraft BuNo. 138902 and subsequent.

AC Power Failure

Under normal conditions (BUS TIE in AUTO), illumination of an ac generator light indicates loss of the generator due to overvoltage only and the bus tie transfer to the operating generator will be automatic. Loss of a generator through overvoltage with the BUS TIE in the OPEN position will cause the applicable warning light to come on but there will be no bus transfer. An additional indication, if the overvoltage is on the AC NO. 1 generator, will be the appearance of the gyro horizon warning flag. Overvoltage on an ac generator will be indicated most immediately by the applicable warning light. The BUS TIE switch may be turned to the AUTO position to energize the appropriate generator bus until the inoperative generator is recycled. In either case, the generator may be brought back on the line by the normal starting procedure. Loss of either ac generator through a malfunction, other than overvoltage, will not cause the generator light to come on. There will be no bus tie transfer regardless of whether the bus tie switch is in the OPEN or AUTO position. The most obvious indication of a malfunction in the AC NO. 1 generator will be the appearance of the gyro horizon warning flag. A malfunction of the AC NO. 2 generator will be indicated by the standby gyro horizon warning flag. Malfunction of either AC generator will also be indicated on the appropriate voltmeter. On early aircraft[1] to complete a bus tie transfer, the following steps must be accomplished in the order presented.

1. BUS TIE switch . . . . OPEN
2. Inoperative generator switch . . . . OFF
3. BUS TIE switch . . . . AUTO

To complete a bus tie transfer in later aircraft[2], perform the following steps:

1. BUS TIE switch . . . . AUTO
2. Inoperative generator switch . . . . OFF

HYDRAULIC SYSTEM

The aircraft is equipped with three independent hydraulic systems for normal operation (figure 1-40), and one hydraulic system for emergency operation.

The systems are: the main, or utility hydraulic system, the emergency hydraulic system, the surface control system, and the aileron spoiler control system. The reservoirs, pressure gages, and filler valves are located in the hydraulics compartment on the left-hand side of the companionway (figure 1-41) except the surface controls system reservoir which is located on the left forward side of the bomb bay.

Utility Hydraulic System

The utility hydraulic system fluid and pressure supply consists of two interconnected ATM-driven variable

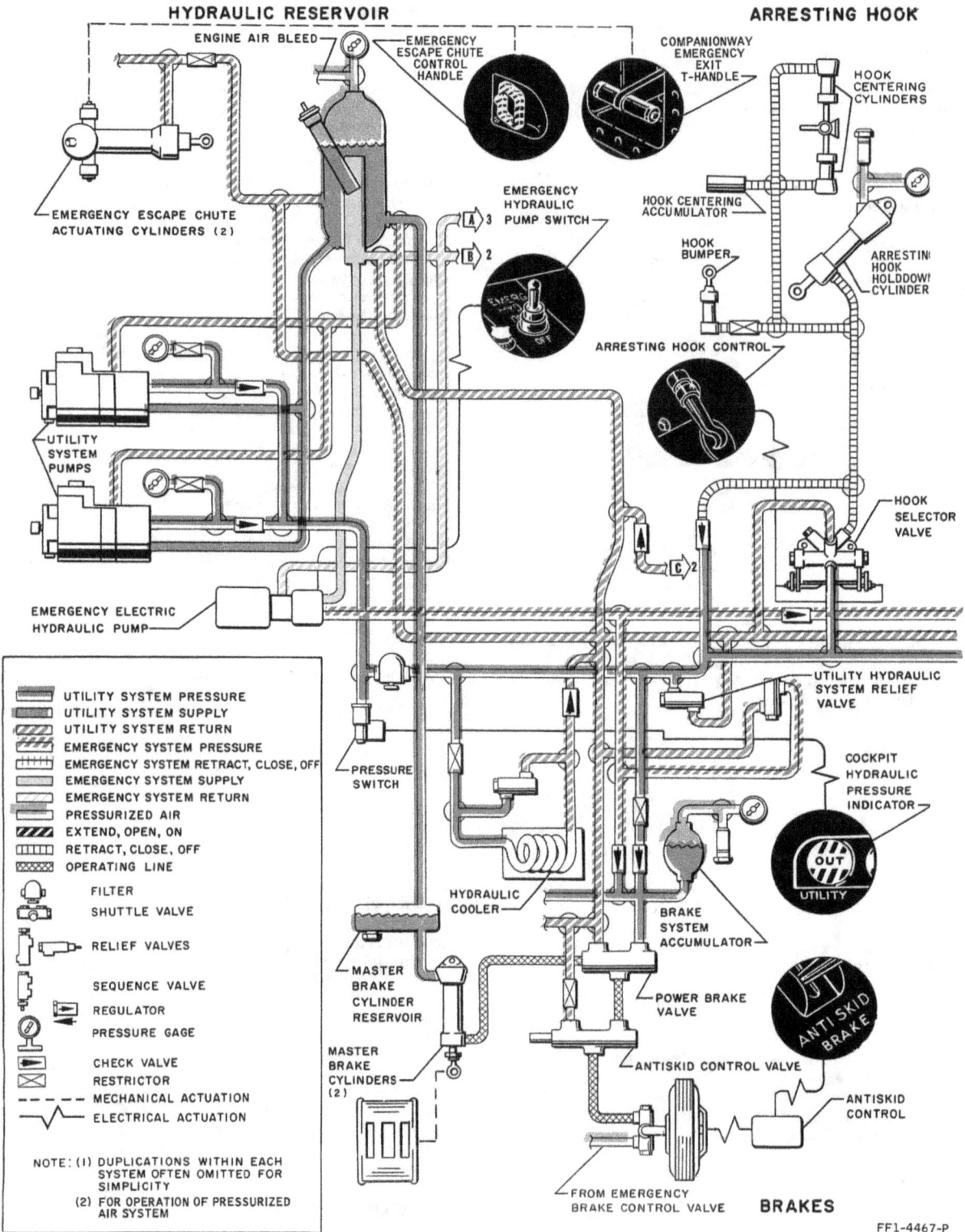

Figure 1-40. Utility Hydraulic System Schematic (Sheet 1)

NAVAIR 01-40ATA-1

Section I
Part 2

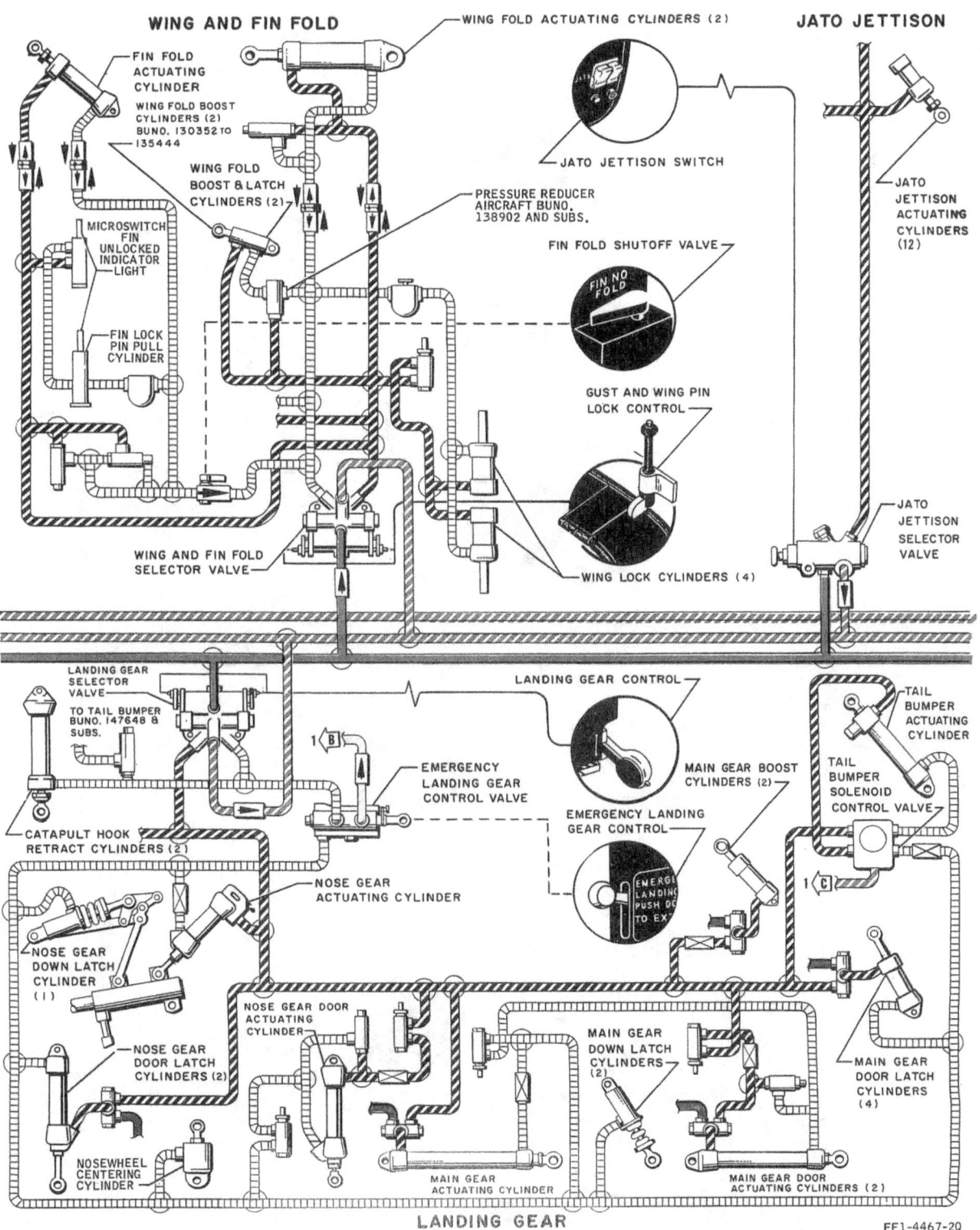

Figure 1-40. Utility Hydraulic System Schematic (Sheet 2)

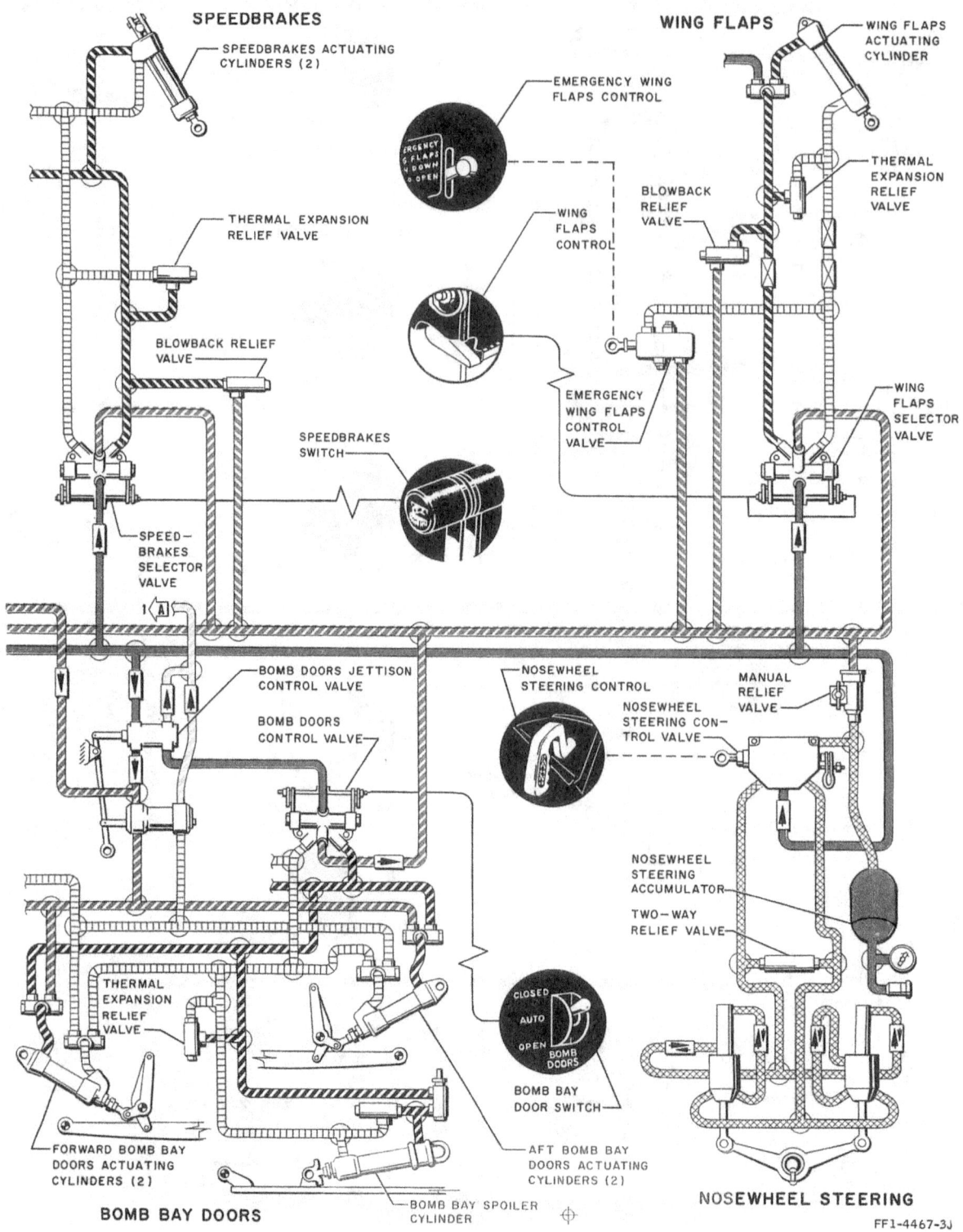

Figure 1-40. Utility Hydraulic System Schematic (Sheet 3)

displacement pumps and a single hydraulic reservoir. The utility system is of the demand type and operates at a normal pressure of 3000 psi. Each hydraulic pump is full feathering.

Either pump can supply sufficient pressure to the system for normal operations. A partial or complete failure of either pump has no effect on the system other than to require more time to operate the hydraulically actuated units. The utility system supplies pressure for normal operation of the landing gear, arresting gear, wing flaps, speedbrakes, wheel brakes, bomb bay doors, and bomb bay spoiler, JATO jettison, wing and fin folding, nosewheel steering, and catapult hook retraction.

WARNING

- Prior to entering the companionway to activate any hydraulic override handle during ground operation, ensure that landing gear safety pins are installed.

- Operation of Solenoid Override Handles to correct malfunctions of the Electrical Solenoid Controlled Systems is hazardous. Minute movements of the override handle are sufficient to reposition the control slide when hydraulic pressure is on the system and can result in accidental actuation of an undesired system. The override handle bypasses all electrical safety devices. Extreme caution should be exercised when working with or near the companionway Hydraulic Control Panel. Accidental actuations of various valves have resulted from misreading handle labels, bumping handles, or catching on loose clothing.

The selector valves for utility system operation of these functions, except JATO jettison and the wheel brake, are located in the hydraulic compartment in the companionway and are electrically actuated by solenoids powered from the dc primary bus. Solenoid override knobs are provided at the companionway hydraulics panel for manual actuation of the selector valves in case of electrical failure. In addition to the pressure gages in the companionway, a utility system pressure indicator (figure 1-4) is located on the pilot's instrument panel. This indicator reads PRESS when system pressure is above approximately 1000 psi, and OUT when system pressure drops below 900±25 psi.

Emergency Hydraulic System

An electrically driven hydraulic pump supplies hydraulic pressure for operation of the wheel brakes during deck handling without engine power and, at other times, for emergency operation of the brakes and bomb bay doors operation. For emergency operation of the brakes, or for limited operation of the brakes in deck handling, the pump must be turned on with EMER HYD PUMP switch (figure 1-9) on the center console. The ELEC PWR switch must be in the BAT position during ground operation. For emergency operation of the bomb bay doors, the pump is energized when the EMER BOMB REL handle (figure 1-9) on the lower center console is positioned out of the normal detent. This system utilizes hydraulic fluid from an emergency supply standpipe in the utility system reservoir and electrical power from the dc primary bus. No pressure indicator is provided for the emergency hydraulic system. For use of the emergency hydraulic system during a landing, refer to Wheel Brake Emergency Operation, Section V.

CAUTION

- Use of the emergency hydraulic pump during ground handling can discharge the battery completely within a very few minutes. Use of this system must be held to an absolute minimum when the dc generators are not operating.

- When operating the emergency hydraulic pump on dc generator or external power, a 30-minute time limit must be observed to prevent overheating the electrical motor. When such operation is required, a 30-minute cooling period should be observed before resuming operation.

FLIGHT CONTROL SYSTEMS

The aircraft is equipped with conventional flight controls operated from a single station in the cockpit. Two 2000-psi hydraulic systems are provided to reduce or provide the control force required in high-speed flight. The flight control surfaces are of conventional design and operation. Trim is provided through a trim tab on the rudder, a controllable horizontal stabilizer, and an aileron force trim mechanism. Wing slats are provided to delay loss of lift and aileron control at low airspeeds and high angles of attack. To eliminate aerodynamic buzz of the ailerons during high-speed flight, an independent self-contained snubber system is provided for each aileron. Primarily, each snubber system consists of an accumulator, two snubber cylinder assemblies, and two one-way restrictors. The accumulator contains a piston which is spring loaded against hydraulic pressure in the snubber system. The snubber cylinders are anchored to the wing structure, and each cylinder contains a piston whose end rod is attached to the aileron. An orifice in the piston provides the snubbing action by restricting the flow of fluid from one side of the piston to the other as the aileron is displaced. The speed at which the ailerons are moved determines the degree of damping action provided. When the ailerons are rapidly displaced, high snubbing action is provided; when moved slowly, less damping is supplied. A Sperry S-5 autopilot and yaw damping system is incorporated in the flight control system.

Aileron Control System

AILERON CONTROL

The ailerons are controlled by a conventional control wheel in the cockpit. Control forces are applied by

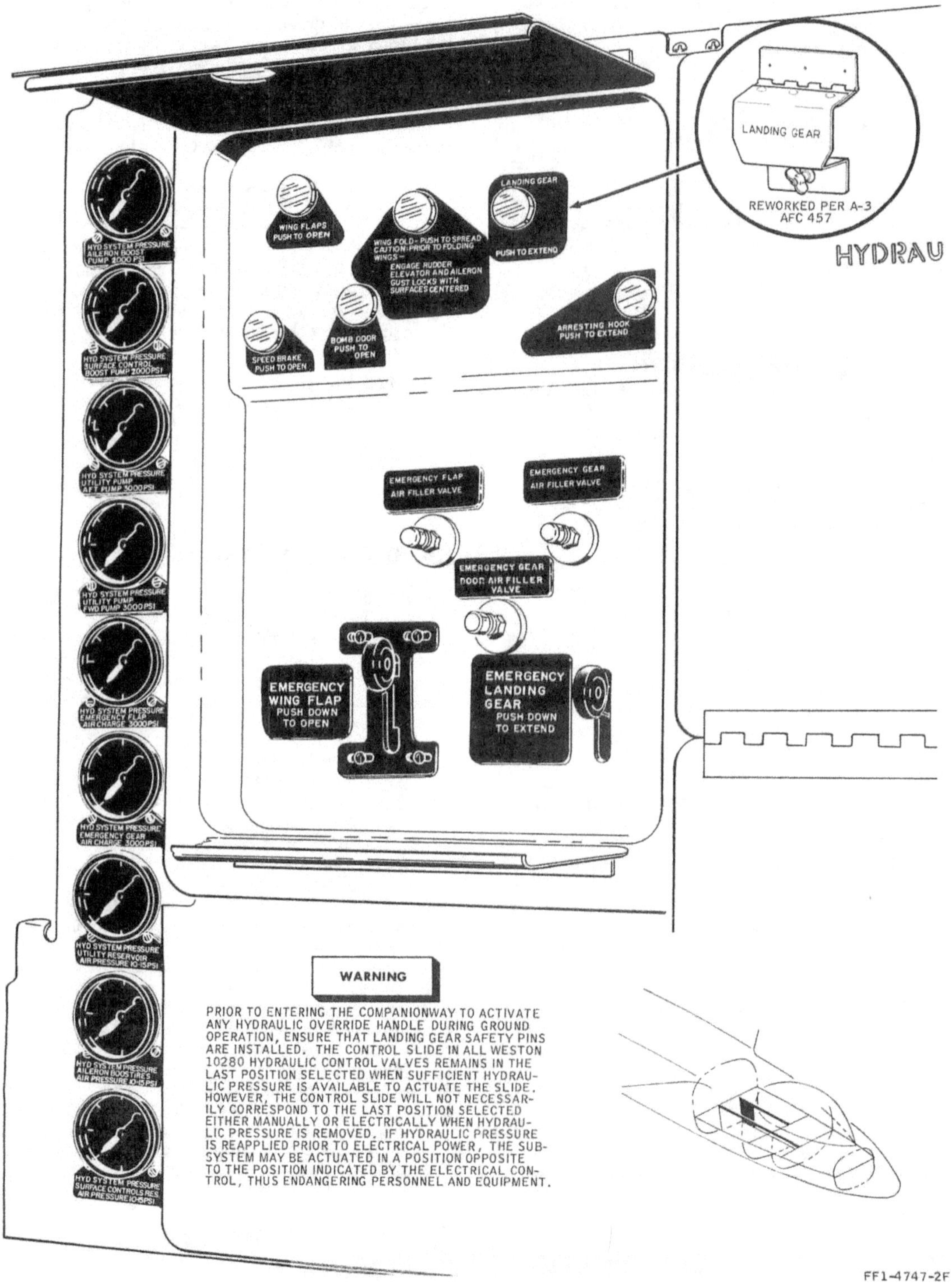

Section I
Part 2

NAVAIR 01-40ATA-1

Aircraft BuNo. 135407 and Subsequent
Figure 1-41. Companionway Hydraulics Panel

WARNING

PRIOR TO ENTERING THE COMPANIONWAY TO ACTIVATE ANY HYDRAULIC OVERRIDE HANDLE DURING GROUND OPERATION, ENSURE THAT LANDING GEAR SAFETY PINS ARE INSTALLED. THE CONTROL SLIDE IN ALL WESTON 10280 HYDRAULIC CONTROL VALVES REMAINS IN THE LAST POSITION SELECTED WHEN SUFFICIENT HYDRAULIC PRESSURE IS AVAILABLE TO ACTUATE THE SLIDE. HOWEVER, THE CONTROL SLIDE WILL NOT NECESSARILY CORRESPOND TO THE LAST POSITION SELECTED EITHER MANUALLY OR ELECTRICALLY WHEN HYDRAULIC PRESSURE IS REMOVED. IF HYDRAULIC PRESSURE IS REAPPLIED PRIOR TO ELECTRICAL POWER, THE SUBSYSTEM MAY BE ACTUATED IN A POSITION OPPOSITE TO THE POSITION INDICATED BY THE ELECTRICAL CONTROL, THUS ENDANGERING PERSONNEL AND EQUIPMENT.

1-86

Changed 15 July 1970

2000-psi hydraulic pressure supplied by two independent hydraulic systems to the aileron tandem actuating cylinder. This cylinder, which is basically two independent actuating pistons on a single piston rod, is provided with pressure to one piston by the aileron control system and to the other piston by the surface controls system. The aileron control system, unlike the rudder and elevator control system, does not permit a feedback of airloads to the pilot's control linkage to simulate the approximate airload normally encountered throughout the airspeed range of the aircraft.

Since the aileron control system is a tandem system, failure of either side of this tandem system at high speeds will result in some reduction of the maximum roll rate available. This is due to the 50 percent reduction of the effective actuating cylinder force available. However, aileron deflection will still be available under all conditions within the flight envelope of the aircraft. The pilot's control wheel force is simulated and will not be affected. Should both systems fail, the aileron tandem actuating cylinder can be disconnected from the aileron control linkage by use of the AILERON BOOST REL handle on the lower left side of the pilot's instrument panel. Pulling out on the release handle will mechanically disconnect the aileron tandem actuating cylinder and shift to mechanical advantage. This provides double the no-boost ratio while reducing aileron deflection to one-half normal travel.

NOTE

Since it is possible for the aileron power boost to become disengaged, the assembly must be carefully inspected prior to takeoff (figure 1-42). If the latch is not properly engaged, any unusually heavy control force can disengage the power cylinder, leaving the pilot to manually overcome the aileron load feel bungee as well as the airload without the benefit of a mechanical advantage. In such a condition, pull the AILERON BOOST REL handle, thereby cutting off all power control and obtaining the 2:1 mechanical advantage.

AILERON TRIM CONTROL. Because of the irreversible control system, conventional aileron trim tabs are not required. Actuation of the aileron force trim switch (figure 1-9) on the pilot's center console causes the center or neutral position of the pilot's control wheel to be relocated, thus repositioning the simulated airload at the control wheel and positioning the ailerons to trim the aircraft about the roll axis. The aileron trim indicator (figure 1-4) is calibrated to indicate the displacement of the ailerons in relation to the displacement of the control column.

AILERON MANUAL CONTROL CAGING HOOK

An aileron manual control caging hook has been added in certain aircraft to the power boost cylinder latch crank assembly (figure 1-42). When the AILERON BOOST REL handle is pulled to disengage the power boost system, the caging hook is actuated to engage a pin on the input crank. This caging hook reduces the amount of "slop" in the controls during manual operation of the ailerons and assures the pilot of adequate control of the aircraft.

CAUTION

Aileron trim is not available with aileron boost disconnected.

WING SPOILER CONTROL

The wing spoilers (figure 1-2) are powered by the No. 1 ATM aileron hydraulic system spllemented by accumulator pressure, and controlled by the pilot's control wheel. Movement of the aileron push-pull tube by the aileron tandem actuating cylinder in the center wing is transmitted through two bungees and a cable system to the spoiler control valves. The spoilers operate from the faired position in an upward direction only.

Movement of the pilot's control wheel (approximately 20 degrees) to the left of neutral causes the left spoiler to open in proportion to the displacement of the control wheel while the right spoiler remains in the faired position. Displacement of the pilot's control wheel (approximately 20 degrees) to the right of neutral reverses this movement. Since the wing spoiler system is a hydraulic power system, no airloads on the spoilers are transmitted back to the pilot's control wheel. If the aileron tandem actuating cylinder is disconnected by pulling the AILERON BOOST REL handle, the spoilers are mechanically disconnected (figure 1-43), at the aileron tube motion pickup. In the event of hydraulic failure, the spoilers automatically move to, and remain in, the faired position.

RUDDER CONTROL

The rudder is controlled by conventional rudder pedals in the cockpit. Rudder pedal forces are transmitted through a hydraulic boost system which provides a boost ratio of 7:1 to the rudder. Hydraulic pressure for rudder boost (figure 1-44) is provided by the surface controls system through a pressure reducer supplying 750 psi to the rudder. Directional stability is aided by a yaw damper system, which is engaged through the autopilot (refer to YAW DAMPING SYSTEM). The rudder hydraulic boost can be disengaged by pulling out on the RUD AND ELEV

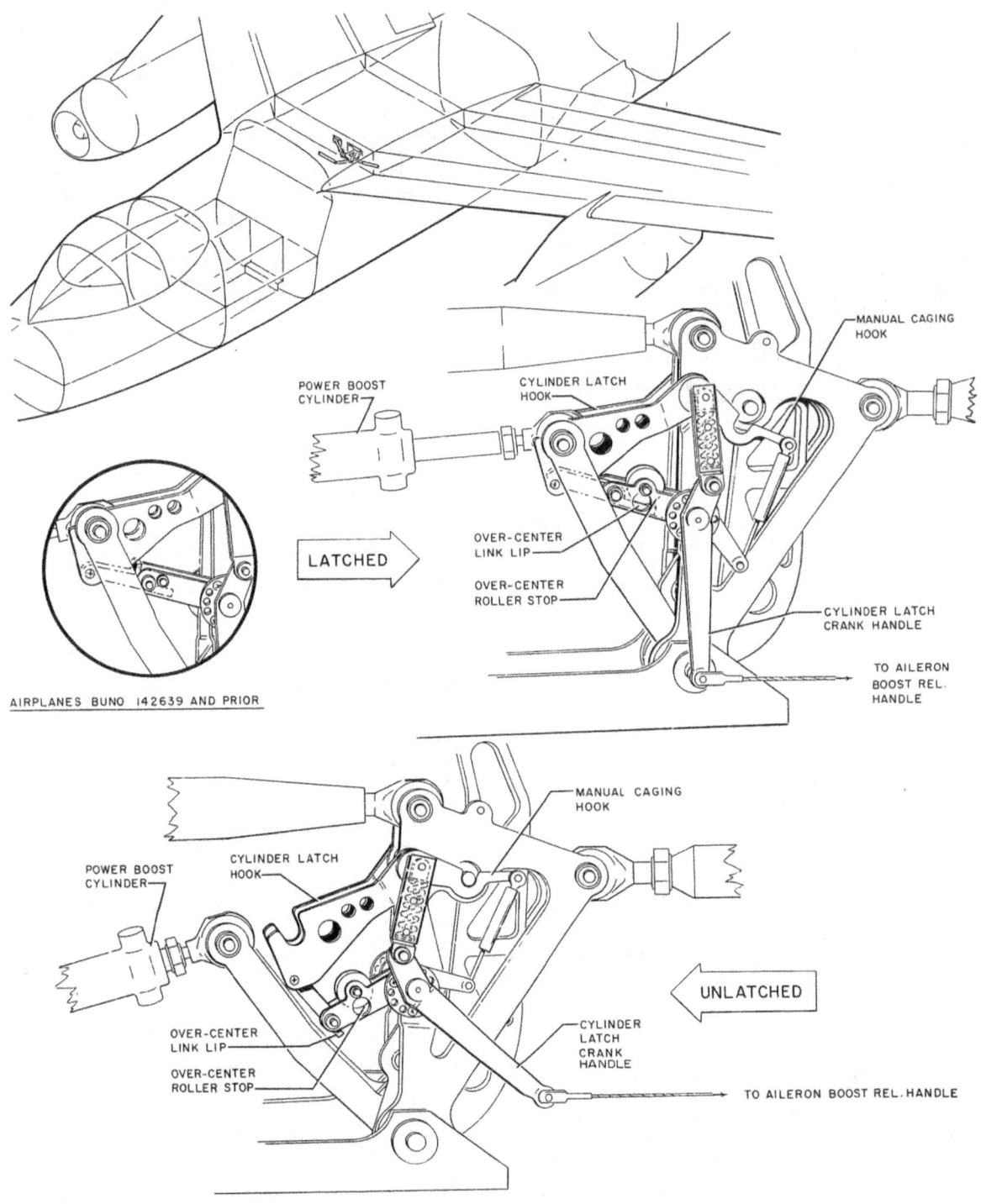

Figure 1-42. Aileron Power Boost Assembly

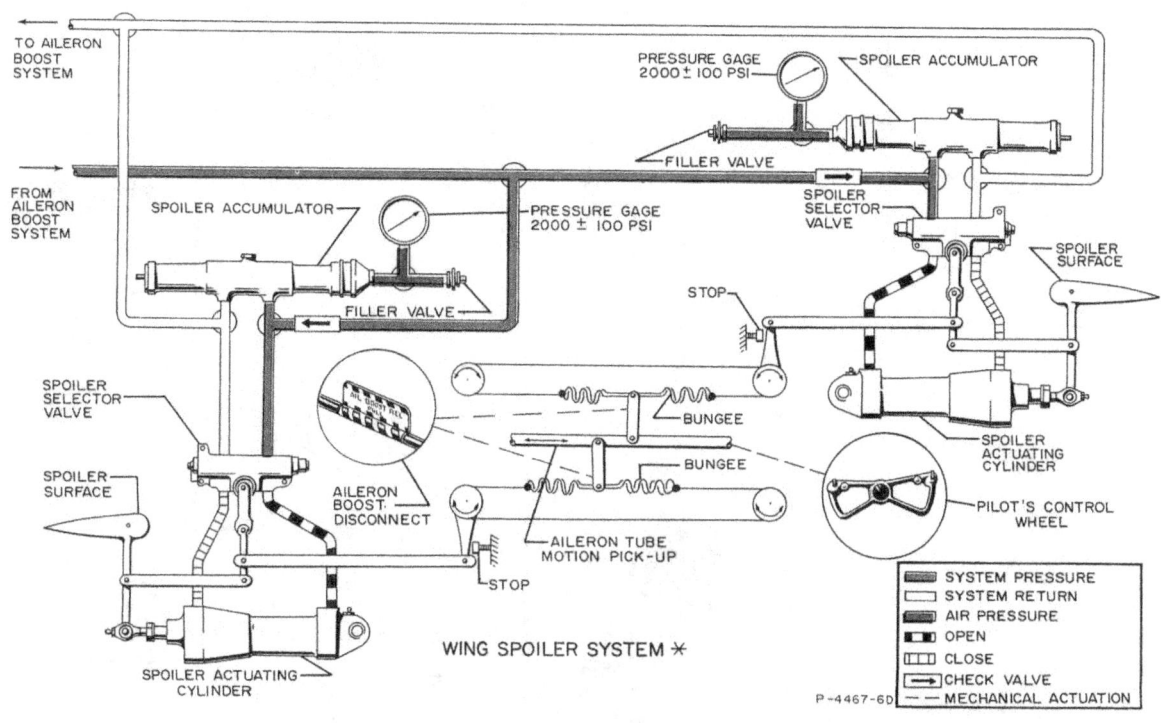

Figure 1-43. Wing Spoiler System Schematic

BOOST REL handle (figure 1-4) on the lower center of the pilot's instrument panel. This action also disengages the elevator hydraulic boost.

RUDDER TRIM CONTROL. The rudder is provided with a conventional trim tab that is electrically controlled by a switch (figure 1-9) on the pilot's center console. The switch is turned in direction of the desired turn.

ELEVATOR CONTROL

The elevators are of conventional design and are controlled through the pilot's control column in the cockpit. The surface controls hydraulic system, through a pressure reducer set at 1150 psi, provides a boost ratio of 7:1 to the elevators.

NOTE

- On recent aircraft a 10:1 boost ratio supplied to the elevators affords the pilot improved control at high speeds by reducing the required force on the wheel (fwd and aft movement of the control column). However, with the increased boost ratio in the system, a bobweight has been added to the mechanical linkage to increase resistance to aft wheel movement during pullups at the rate of 5 pounds per g. This synthetic load is effective in preventing excessively fast pullups which would impose dangerous loads on the wing structure.

- The RUD AND ELEV BOOST REL cannot be reset in flight after having been disengaged.

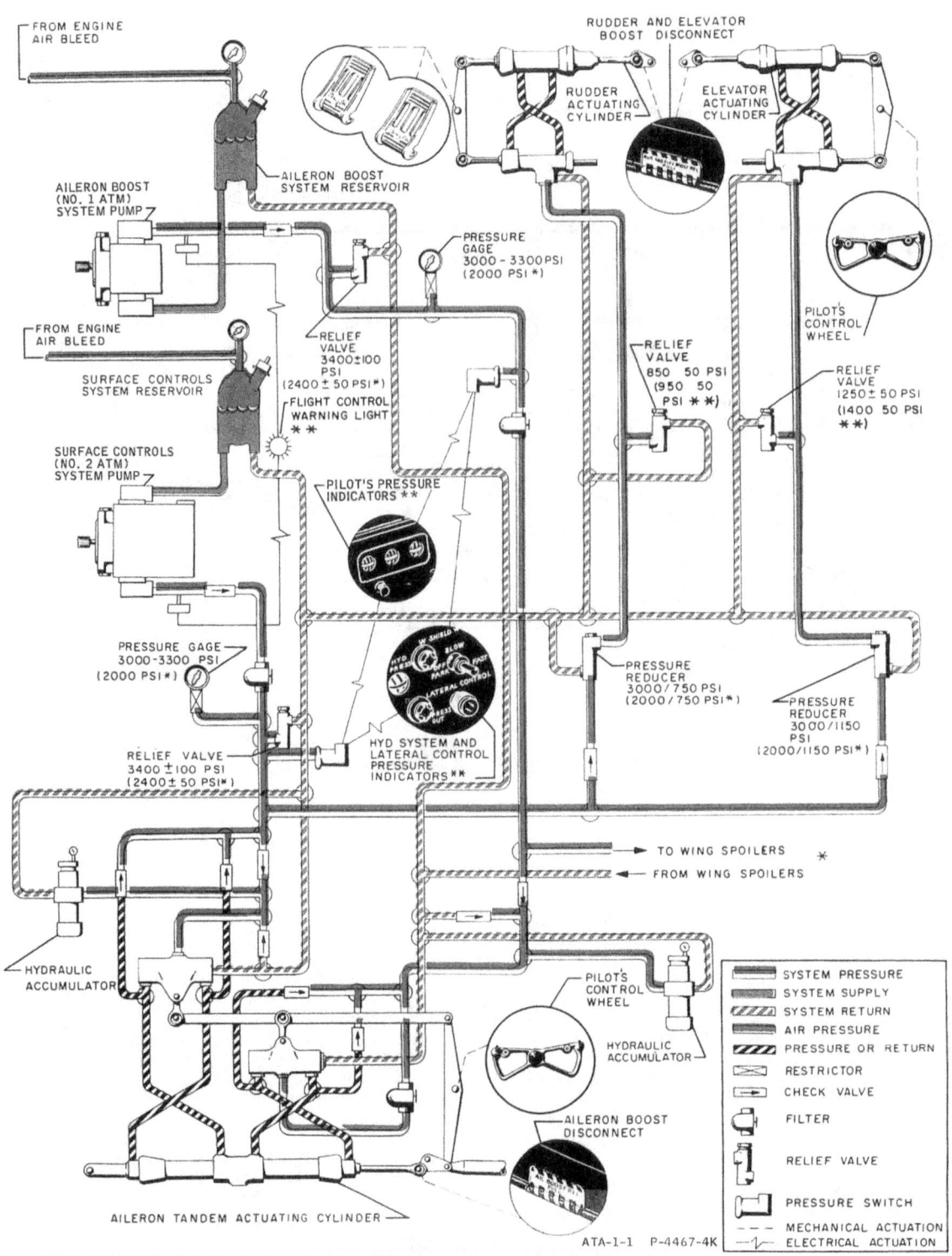

*Aircraft BuNo. 135407 and subsequent
**Aircraft BuNo. 138902 and subsequent

Figure 1-44. Flight Controls Boost Schematic

FROZEN ELEVATOR BOOST MECHANISM

An accumulation of moisture inside the fold area may cause freezing of the elevator boost mechanism as the aircraft ascends. A frozen elevator boost mechanism can be recognized by heavy elevator control forces and/or stiffness of the elevator control column. In the event the elevator boost mechanism does become frozen, a cross trim condition could be reached by trimming the horizontal stabilizer to maintain level flight. This cross trim condition should be avoided because of the possibility of erratic trim change should the elevator boost mechanism suddenly break free. When flying in or above the freezing level, the pilot should ensure that the degree of horizontal stabilizer trim indicated by the trim indicator is compatible with the condition of flight.

The following procedure is recommended to free the elevator control in the event freezing is suspected:

1. Reduce altitude, if practical, keeping in mind that cross trim exists.

2. Reduce airspeed and cautiously move control column fore and aft through small amplitude to break ice loose from elevator boost mechanism.

CAUTION

Anticipate erratic trim change when elevator boost mechanism becomes free.

ELEVATOR BOOST HEATERS. Electrical heater blankets are installed on the elevator boost mechanism to prevent frozen elevator controls. These blankets will prevent icing of the mechanism at high altitudes and low temperatures. They also keep the viscosity of the hydraulic fluid more nearly constant. The blankets are heated by phase C current from the ac generator No. 1 bus, through the elevator boost circuit breaker on the companionway circuit breaker and fuse panel.

Aileron/Spoiler and Surface Control Pressure Warning Light

On some aircraft an aileron/spoiler and surface control hydraulic pressure light, labeled LATERAL CONTROL PRESS OUT (figure 1-4), is located on the pilot's instrument panel next to the RH FIRE WARN light. The purpose of this light is to indicate pressure failure in either the aileron/spoiler or the surface control hydraulic systems. When the hydraulic pressure in either system drops to 1000 psi, a pressure-sensing switch closes completing an electrical circuit and causing the LATERAL CONTROL PRESS OUT light to come on. If the LATERAL CONTROL PRESS OUT light is on, it is possible to determine which flight control hydraulic system has failed by movement of the control surfaces. If the surface control system has failed, movement of the elevator and rudder would be extremely difficult. If the aileron control system has failed, aileron deflection will still be available under all conditions within the flight envelope of the aircraft. Hydraulic volume for the aileron control system will be reduced one-half because the aileron tandem actuating cylinder is provided with pressure from both the aileron and surface control systems.

Aileron and Rudder-Elevator

If both flight control systems fail, elevator control forces can be easily trimmed out if the horizontal stabilizer is operative (dc or ac power is available), and some elevator control is possible even though the rudder-elevator boost is inoperative and still connected. Aileron control will be lost, and the primary problem will be one of maintaining or returning to wings level flight. Small roll rates may be obtained by rudder deflection, rudder trim (if dc generator power is available), or with asymmetric thrust. Unless loss of control occurs or is imminent, immediate pulling of the AILERON BOOST REL handle is not recommended. If conditions permit, time should be taken to analyze the failure and attempts made to regain power.

Under complete boost-out conditions, the ailerons are quite limited in effectiveness, but lateral control can be substantially increased by combined use of the ailerons and rudder. Using ailerons alone, the maximum rate of roll is approximately 6 to 8 degrees per second over the speed range of the aircraft. This rate of roll requires a control wheel force of approximately 80 pounds. As airspeed is increased, control wheel forces become rather large for a small increase in rate of roll. If rudder only is used for lateral control, the maximum rate of roll under the same conditions can be raised to 20 or 30 degrees per second; however, the pressure on the rudder pedals required to achieve this rate of roll reaches from about 260 to 300 pounds. As these forces are exhaustively high, combined use of the rudder and ailerons will effectively reduce the control forces and will also produce a higher rate of roll than can be achieved when rudder or ailerons are used independently.

With wheels and flaps extended, damping of the characteristic lateral-directional oscillation is virtually nil; but, with flaps retracted, damping, although still difficult, can be accomplished to a better extent than with lowered wing flaps.

NOTE

The yaw damper will be inoperative under rudder-elevator boost-out conditions.

Horizontal Stabilizer Trim System

The A-3 aircraft is trimmed longitudinally by varying the incidence of the horizontal stabilizer surface. The actuator which drives the stabilizer surface can be operated by either a high-speed ac trim system or a fail-safe, slow-speed dc trim system. There are two pilot-operated controls: a thumb switch on the pilot's control wheel that supplies high-speed ac trim, and a manual override knob on the center console that controls both the ac and dc systems. The autopilot also provides control of the dc system, although only at one-half the normal dc rate. In addition, an emergency cutoff is located on the center console (figure 1-9) which interrupts all electrical power to the actuator.

The thumb switch on the control wheel directs 28-vdc power from the primary bus to the noseup or nosedown coil of the relay-type contactor in the center console, which in turn directs three-phase, 200-vac power to the ac motor and rectified ac to the clutch coil. The manual override knob directs dc current to the dc motor providing trim in either direction from neutral. If the rotation of the knob is continued beyond the point where dc trim occurs, the dc clutch disengage and the ac system will be energized (the dc motor will continue to operate although declutched from the actuator). There is no marked position to indicate where this change from dc to ac operation occurs; however, a greatly increased trim rate can be noted by aircraft response and by observing the stabilizer position indicator on the instrument panel. The manual control knob operates the same relay switch ac contacts that the yoke switch operates, except that it does so by mechanical linkage rather than energizing the switch solenoids. It can thus be used to override the electrical (thumbswitch) operation or as an alternate control if the thumb switch circuit fails. The ac and dc clutches are mounted on the same shaft, which travels axially in one direction to engage the ac motor and in the opposite direction to engage the dc motor. The shaft is spring loaded to the dc engaged position at all times except when ac power is directed to the actuator, at which time the clutch coil is energized by rectified ac and overcomes the spring to move the shaft into the ac engaged position. Automatic dc engagement is thus provided in the event of ac failure, and since the dc motor may be operated from the battery or the dc generator, slow-speed trim will be available. The dc system provides an additional safeguard in that the dc motor brake makes the actuator irreversible (i.e., it cannot be back-driven by stabilizer airloads) provided the clutch is engaged.

Horizontal Stabilizer Trim Control

A controllable horizontal stabilizer provides longitudinal trim through a range of 2 degrees nosedown to 6 degrees noseup. On later aircraft[1] the

---
[1] Aircraft BuNo. 142643 and subsequent.

horizontal stabilizer provides a longitudinal trim range of 2 degrees nosedown to 10 1/2 degrees noseup.

AC High-Speed Stabilizer Trim

The ac electrical trim may be actuated by the thumb switch on the control wheel or the second position of the manual override trim knob on the center console (figure 1-9). Normal actuation of the horizontal stabilizer trim system is initiated through the use of the three-position switch on the pilot's control wheel. Placing the normally open switch to NOSE UP or NOSE DOWN triggers the following events:

1. Dc power from the primary bus is routed through the thumb switch to the appropriate limit switch on the horizontal stabilizer actuator.

2. If there is additional surface travel left in the desired direction, the limit switch is closed and the dc power is directed to the proper horizontal stabilizer relay coil.

3. The energized coil closes switches allowing three-phase, ac power to be directed to the ac trim motor and rectified ac to be directed to the clutch which engages the ac trim motor to the actuator jackscrew.

If the pilot wishes to override the trim signal initiated by the thumb switch, the manual override trim knob should be used. Placing the trim knob in the second position in the NOSE UP or NOSE DOWN direction mechanically forces the closed relay contacts open and closes the contacts for driving in the opposite direction, which reverses the stabilizer trim through a sequence of events as previously described. It should be noted that when the second position of the manual override trim knob is selected, dc power is also routed to the actuator (refer to paragraph on dc electrical trim system). A lost motion device incorporated in the switching linkage results in simultaneous application of power to both the ac and dc motors of the actuator. The dc trim motor is turning over but is not engaged to the jackscrew because of the clutching arrangement. Thus the ac trim motor drives the stabilizer unless ac power is interrupted, causing dc power to be supplied automatically. Application of the ac electrical power either by the thumb switch or the second position of the manual override trim knob will also override any autopilot signal if so desired.

The symptom of a high-speed runaway is a sudden and rapidly increasing requirement for the pilot to assume a load on the control column in either the NOSE UP or NOSE DOWN direction coupled with an indication of changing stabilizer setting without the pilot moving any trim controls.

DC SLOW-SPEED STABILIZER TRIM

The purpose of the dc electrical trim system is twofold. It is an alternate trim system in the event of ac power failure and provides slow-speed stabilizer travel for autopilot operation. To manually initiate the dc trim system, the horizontal stabilizer manual override trim knob (figure 1-9) is moved to the first position in the NOSE UP or NOSE DOWN direction. The following events occur:

1. Through linkage from the trim knob, the shaft on the dc trim switch is mechanically rotated to close the switch contacts.

2. Dc power from the primary bus is routed to the switch through the closed contacts and to the dc trim motor on the actuator.

The first position of the center console trim knob does not affect the ac electrical circuit in any manner.

A runaway dc slow-speed trim is more difficult to perceive than a high-speed runaway. The symptom of a dc runaway is a requirement for frequent and constant trimming utilizing normal ac trim consistently in the same direction over some period of time.

CAUTION

- Either in flight or on the deck, prolonged operation of the horizontal stabilizer trim actuator in either high speed (ac) or low speed (dc) can cause overheating of the motor. Observe the following operating limitations to avoid motor failure.

    1. High speed .... Maximum period of steady operation is 15 seconds. Allow 3-minute cooling period before continuation.

- If maximum period is repeated for another 15 seconds, allow 15-minute cooling period.

    2. Low speed .... Maximum period of steady operation is 40 seconds. Allow 4-minute cooling period before resuming operation.

Autopilot Stabilizer Trim

The autopilot horizontal stabilizer trim system is a dc powered circuit that receives its source of power from the secondary bus. With the autopilot engaged, the trim system functions as follows:

1. When a hinge moment is present across the elevator surface, a voltage is generated across the elevator servomotor.

2. A sensor picks up the voltage across the elevator servomotor and closes the appropriate gyro-pilot signal relay.

3. Dc power is routed from the secondary bus through the gyro-pilot signal relay to the proper limit switch in the actuator.

4. If there is available travel left in the actuator in the required direction, the limit switch is closed and the dc power is routed to the gyro-pilot signal relay.

5. The gyro-pilot engage relay is normally closed when the autopilot is engaged (through appropriate interlocks), thus dc power is directed to the dc trim motor.

The autopilot trim may be overridden by the use of the ac trim system. Refer to the paragraph on ac high-speed trim for the manner in which this may be accomplished. Use of the first position of the manual override trim knob will not affect the autopilot trim in any manner since the autopilot engage relay, which is actuated when the autopilot is turned on, breaks the emergency dc circuit.

The symptoms of a runaway trim when the autopilot is on consists of three items which the pilot will note in the course of monitoring flight on autopilot. The first item is a change in attitude and prescribed altitude. The second item is an unusual trim setting indication for flight at the gross weight, speed, and altitude prescribed.

The third and most important symptom is an unusual deviation of the control column from its normal trimmed flight position for the flight condition. On early aircraft corrective action, in case of emergency, consists of disengaging the autopilot by pressing the GYRO-PILOT REL switch (figure 1-4) on the control wheel. Another method is to place the ELEVATOR-AILERON servo switch (figure 1-9), located on the lower center console in DISENGAGE.

Upon complete disengagement of the autopilot, the HORIZ STAB WITH AUTO-PILOT circuit breaker, located on the companionway panel (figures 1-20 and 1-21), should be pulled. Under these circumstances the pilot must expect to pick up the load on the elevator when the autopilot is disengaged and hold it until retrimmed using normal ac power. The maximum output of the autopilot is within the pilot's force capability, and no problem should result if the pilot is aware the condition exists. After completing these operations, the aircraft will be without autopilot.

Section I
Part 2

NAVAIR 01-40ATA-1

HORIZONTAL STABILIZER ACTUATOR GANGBAR

A horizontal stabilizer trim emergency shutoff gangbar (figure 1-9) controls the HOR STAB ACT ac power cutoff switch and the HOR STAB ACT dc power cutoff switch. Downward actuation of this gangbar provides emergency disconnection of electrical power to the horizontal stabilizer trim motors should a runaway trim occur.

TRIM POSITION INDICATORS

The trim position indicator on the pilot's instrument panel (figure 1-4) indicates the direction and degree of displacement of the rudder trim tab and the horizontal stabilizer. An aileron force trim position indicator (figure 1-4) is located at the base of the control wheel column on the pilot's instrument panel.

HORIZONTAL STABILIZER TRIM SYSTEM – GENERAL

It should be borne in mind that the rates at which the stabilizer moves, particularly on ac trim, leave a small but sufficient amount of time for quick action by the crew that is thoroughly trained. The normal maximum no load ac rate is 0.5 degree per second which means 20 seconds minimum are required for the stabilizer to run from full NOSE UP to full NOSE DOWN setting. The normal maximum no load dc rate is 0.1 degree per second or 100 seconds minimum stop to stop. The dc rate on autopilot is 0.05 degree per second or 200 seconds minimum stop to stop. A good practice in the case of a runaway which the pilot cannot immediately classify is to follow the procedure as outlined in Emergency Horizontal Stabilizer Trim, Section V.

Wing and Fin-Folding System

The wings and fin are folded and spread by hydraulic pressure from the utility hydraulic system. Hydraulically actuated wing locking pins are safetied by a mechanically operated safety latch mechanism which also controls extension and retraction of the wing and fin fold warning flags.

GUST AND WING PIN LOCK CONTROL

The GUST AND WING PIN LOCK control (figure 1-9) on the center console controls the gust locks and the wing and fin locking pin safety latches. The control has detents in the vertical and horizontal positions and is released from either detent position by a push-button release on the end of the control. The GUST AND WING PIN LOCK control is mechanically interconnected with the WING FOLD control, and operation of either control is dependent upon the position of the other control. The horizontal position of the GUST AND WING PIN LOCK control mechanically engages the gust locks and releases the wing and fin locking pin safety latches. The wings and fin may then be folded. Release of the wing and fin locking pin safety latches is accompanied by mechanical extension of the wing fold warning flags, located at the lower forward inboard section of each wing at the hinge point, and the fin-fold warning flag, located on the forward right-hand side of the fin below the hinge point. The vertical position of the GUST AND WING PIN LOCK control releases the gust locks and engages the wing and fin locking pin safety latches. Movement of the wing and fin locking pin safety latches to the full lock position causes mechanical retraction of the wing and fin fold warning flags. The GUST AND WING PIN LOCK control can be placed in the vertical position only if the wings and fin have been spread. While in the horizontal position, the control forms a barrier to prevent the throttles from being moved into the takeoff power range. For engine runup with the wings folded, the spring-loaded barrier tab may be lifted to make throttle travel possible.

WING AND FIN-FOLDING CONTROL

The WING FOLD control (figure 1-9), located on the center console, controls the hydraulic folding and spreading of the wings and vertical fin. Placing the WING FOLD control in the vertical position causes the unlatched locking pins to be pulled and the wing and fin to be folded. When the control is positioned horizontally, the wings and fin are extended and the locking pins are thrust home. Through a mechanical interlock with the GUST AND WING PIN LOCK control, the WING FOLD control is prevented from being moved to either the vertical or horizontal position out of the proper sequence (refer to GUST AND WING PIN LOCK CONTROL). In addition, limit switches at the ailerons, rudder and elevators gust locks prevent the wing and fin-fold hydraulic solenoid from being energized until the control surfaces are centered and locked. The system uses utility hydraulic system pressure electrically controlled by a solenoid-operated selector valve located on the hydraulic control panel in the companionway. In the event of control switch or solenoid failure, the wings and fin may be positioned by manual operation of the solenoid override knob (figure 1-41) on the companionway hydraulics panel and moving the WING FOLD control as in normal operation. A fin-fold shutoff valve, accessible to ground personnel through the aft compartment access door (figure 1-2), permits folding and spreading the wings while the fin is secured erect.

CAUTION

- The maximum relative wind for operation of wing and fin-fold is 50 knots.
- To reduce wing fold fitting loads, do not spread or fold wings during taxi.

1-94

Changed 15 July 1970

FIN-UNLOCKED INDICATOR LIGHT

The fin-unlocked indicator light (figure 1-6) is located on the pilot's left-hand console. Two microswitches, one each located on the fin lockpin pull and fin-fold latch cylinders, activate the light when the fin is not erect and latched, and the fin lockpin secured.

AUTOMATIC JURY STRUT

Certain aircraft are equipped with a locking device in the wings that eliminates the need for a jury strut. The operation of this locking device is controlled by the wing and fin fold control on the center console. This locking device consists of a latch roller in the outboard wing and a latch hook and overcenter linkage located in the inboard wing.

NOTE
Wings folded and in latched position are secure in winds up to 100 knots.

WING SPREAD TO WING FOLD

To fold the wings the pilot must actuate the gust lock control and move the wing and fin-fold control to the wing fold position. This will enable the main wing fold cylinder, located in the outboard wing section, to fold the wings to approximately the 156-degree position. The latch roller, located in the outboard wing section, trips the overcenter linkage and then engages the latch hook. The latch hook is then moved by hydraulic power to pull the outboard latch roller into a locked position. The latch hook will be held in a locked position by the overcenter linkage and will remain locked until hydraulic power is applied to the wing spread position.

WING FOLD TO WING SPREAD

To spread the wings the pilot must actuate the wing and fin-fold control to the wing spread position. Hydraulic power then moves the mechanical latch hook from the overcenter position. The latch hook, located in the inboard wing section, then cams the latch roller up about 4 degrees. When this point in the wing spread cycle is reached, the main wing spread cylinder, located in the outboard wing section, takes over the wing spread operation and moves the outboard wing section to the fully spread position. A spring then forces the overcenter linkage to the overcenter position thus locking the latch hook open. The latch hook remains in the open position until it is tripped by the latch roller during the next wing fold cycle.

Wing Flaps

The aircraft is equipped with single-slotted type wing flaps which extend from the fuselage to the inboard edge of the ailerons. The flaps are normally extended by utility hydraulic system pressure which is controlled by a switch on the center console and by a solenoid-operated selector valve located in the hydraulics compartment. The solenoid is mounted on the hydraulic control panel in the companionway and, in the event of failure of the flaps control switch, can be manually operated by pushing in on the solenoid override knob on the panel and moving the wing flaps switch to DOWN. A blowback relief valve in the flaps control system allows the flaps to blow back when the airload against the flaps exceeds the hydraulic pressure extending them. With the flaps fully extended (36 degrees), blowback begins between 215 and 250 KIAS. In normal operation, the flaps require approximately 10 seconds to fully extend and 25 seconds to retract from the full down position.

WING FLAPS CONTROL SWITCH

The wing flaps are controlled by a switch (figure 1-9) on the pilot's center console. The switch has three positions: UP, STOP, and DOWN. The STOP position is used for regulating flaps travel for partial flaps settings.

WING FLAPS POSITION INDICATOR

The FLAPS position indicator is located above the pilot's center console and is marked in increments of one-quarter of full flap travel.

WING FLAPS EMERGENCY OPERATION

An emergency 3000-psi pneumatic system is provided for extension of the wing flaps if failure of the utility hydraulic system occurs. The wing flap emergency extension control is located on the companionway hydraulic panel. The control is marked EMERGENCY WING FLAPS PUSH DOWN TO LOWER. Downward movement of the control causes residual hydraulic pressure to bypass the wing flaps hydraulic selector valve and directs pneumatic pressure through independent pressure lines to the wing flap actuating cylinders. Partial extension of the flaps is not possible, since returning the emergency control handle to the up position will relieve all pneumatic pressure in the actuating cylinders. In case of a go-around or wave-off, it is possible to relieve the pneumatic pressure extending the flaps by moving the control upward, which will allow the flaps to blow back into free trail and thus relieve a part of the drag effect of the flaps. However, subsequent attempts to operate the flaps

Changed 15 July 1970

by pneumatic pressure may result in only a partial extension since the pneumatic pressure remaining in the system may not be great enough to completely overpower the air load against the flaps.

CAUTION

- Following extension of the flaps by emergency system air pressure, do not actuate the normal hydraulic flap control handle until the emergency control is first returned to the up position, thus bleeding the air out of the lines. Failure to observe this procedure can cause an explosion of the hydraulic reservoir.

- Use the wing flaps air system as late in the landing pattern as possible and at the lowest practicable airspeed. The wing flaps will begin to blow back after a time due to dissipation of the air in the system.

EMERGENCY FLAP RETRACTION

In the event of a utility hydraulic failure after flap extension and if flaps must be raised to increase range, the following procedures are recommended:

1. Place emergency flap handle in DOWN position for 3 seconds.

2. Return emergency flap handle to UP position.

CAUTION

When emergency flap handle is returned to UP position, flaps may immediately fair as all restriction has been bypassed.

NOTE

If the initial operation was accomplished with a full 3000-psi charge, the remaining air in the flap bottle will be sufficient for one additional emergency actuation.

Speedbrakes

The speedbrakes, located on the aft fuselage, are actuated by utility hydraulic system pressure. The selector valve for the speedbrakes is electrically controlled through a solenoid which is powered by the dc primary bus.

SPEEDBRAKE SWITCH

The SPEEDBRAKE switch (figure 1-9) is located on the pilot's left-hand throttle. The switch has two marked positions: OPEN and CLOSE. No neutral center position is provided; therefore, the switch will remain in the selected position. This feature allows the position of the speedbrakes to be checked merely by reference to the SPEEDBRAKE switch position.

The speedbrakes can be extended only if utility hyraulic system pressure is available. In the event of a speedbrake switch or selector valve failure, however, a hydraulic selector valve solenoid override on the hydraulic control panel may be used for manual control of the speedbrakes hydraulic selector valve. The override control is marked SPEEDBRAKE PUSH TO OPEN. If it is desired to close the speedbrakes after they have been opened by using the manual override control, pull the SPEEDBRAKE PUSH TO OPEN control out to its original position. The speedbrakes switch must be operated in the normal manner during this operation. There are no airspeed restrictions on opening or closing the speedbrakes.

Landing Gear System

The aircraft is equipped with hydraulically actuated tricycle landing gear, doors, and tail bumper. The system is normally operated by utility hydraulic system pressure, which is electrically controlled by a solenoid-actuated hydraulic selector valve. If electrical failure occurs, the solenoid can be actuated manually by pressing a knob located on the hydraulic control panel in the companionway. On aircraft reworked per A-3 AFC 457, a hinged guard marked LANDING GEAR (figure 1-41) covers the knob to prevent inadvertent actuation. To uncover the knob, a fastener on the lower portion of the guard must be loosened before the guard can be lifted. The knob is marked LANDING GEAR PUSH TO EXTEND.

CAUTION

- To ensure that no system component reverses itself if electrical system is restored, ensure that normal landing gear control handle is first placed in position corresponding to desired operation before positioning solenoid.

- Recycling of landing gear system shall not be attempted when in-flight difficulties involving slow extension of gear occurs. When gear is down and indicating locked, gear shall remain down and a landing shall be accomplished.

Operation of the doors, latches, and tail bumper is through separate actuating cylinders whose operation is timed through the landing gear sequence valves. The landing gear doors remain in the open position when the landing gear is extended.

LANDING GEAR CONTROL

Operation of the landing gear is controlled by a handle (figure 1-9) on the pilot's center console. The handle has a wheel-shaped knob for identification. The control must be left in the position selected for the gear as indicated by the two marked positions UP or DOWN. A safety latch on the handle prevents inadvertent lowering of the gear and must first be compressed before moving the handle from the UP position to DOWN. A solenoid-operated safety lock prevents inadvertent retraction of the gear when the weight of the aircraft is on the gear. The safety lock can be manually released by pressing the solenoid release button in the landing gear control handle recess.

LANDING GEAR POSITION INDICATORS. Landing gear position indicators (figure 1-9) are located directly above and forward of the center console. These indicators reflect the position of the three landing wheels and the tail bumbper. The indicators are actuated by limit switches, which are operated by the landing gear and bumper when in the up or latched down position. The indicator circuit receives electrical power from the primary bus through the dc instruments 10-ampere circuit breakers.

LANDING GEAR WARNING LIGHT. A landing gear warning light (figure 1-9) is located in the end of the landing gear control handle. The light will come on when the handle is moved to UP or DOWN position and remain on until the landing gear is latched up or down.

NOTE

A solenoid control valve and timing device has been introduced into the landing gear system which causes the tail bumper to retract 15 seconds after touchdown.

Landing Gear Emergency Operation

The emergency landing gear air bottle, filler valve, and pressure gage are located in the hydraulics compartment. A separate air bottle, filler, and pressure gage located in the forward left-hand side of the bomb bay are provided for operation of the main gear doors. Both bottles normally contain a pressure of 3000 psi. The use of separate air systems for main gear and gear doors is a precaution against loss of main gear pressure if, in the event of door failure, the hydraulic lines are damaged.

The landing gear emergency extension control is located on the companionway hydraulic control panel. The control is marked EMERGENCY LANDING GEAR PUSH DOWN TO EXTEND. Downward movement of the control causes residual hydraulic pressure to bypass the landing gear system and directs pneumatic pressure through independent pressure lines to release the main and nose gear uplatches and to extend and lock the main gear. The nose gear door extends by free fall to the down and locked position, aided by the airload against the gear. The main gear doors are extended by pneumatic pressure; the nosewheel door is opened by the nosegear as it extends; the tail bumper is not extended by the emergency pneumatic system.

CAUTION

Do not attempt to retract the gear following extension by emergency air pressure. Raising the landing gear handle before air is bled from the lines can cause an explosion of the hydraulic reservoir.

Bomb Bay to Main Gear Access

An access hole is located in the aft bomb bay bulkhead forward of each wheel well. These access holes enable the flight crew to check the position of the main gear. If the landing gear is extended, a black line painted on the down latch linkage should be visible to the crew on inspection. A continuous black line across the down latch linkage indicates that the main gear is latched down. The main gear is not latched down when the black line appears to be broken. The pilot should reduce airspeed to lessen the airload on the landing gear. On earlier aircraft[1] there are no access holes to the wheel well; however, two decals have been placed on the aft bulkhead to indicate where holes can be cut. A sharp instrument such as a crowbar will be required to cut through the bulkhead.

Nosewheel Steering System

The steerable nosewheel provides directional control through 80±3 degrees to either side of center during ground operation of the aircraft. Control of the nosewheel steering system is through a handle (figure 1-6) on the pilot's left-hand console, which, through a mechanical linkage, positions the nosewheel control valve to direct utility hydraulic system pressure to the hydraulic control cylinders. Due to the caster angle of the nosewheel strut, the steering control must be held at the desired rate of turn. The wheel is automatically centered and the steering control locked when the gear handle is placed in the UP position. However, care must be taken to ensure that the nosewheel is centered before initiating the retraction cycle. When the arresting hook is extended, a

---

[1] Aircraft BuNo. 135408, 135411-135444, 138904-138949, 138954-138967.

centering detent in the nosewheel steering linkage is engaged to prevent nosewheel swivel during arrested landings. The centering detent prevents movement of the linkage within the limits of the heart-shaped centering cam. Tests indicate that limited steerage may be available with the hook down. Consideration should be given to the possibility of utilizing this limited steerage in the event of aborted takeoff or missed field arrestment; however it should not be relied upon as a primary directional control measure. The nosewheel steering system is provided with an accumulator which supplies hydraulic fluid pressure to the control cylinders for nosewheel shimmy damping. The nosewheel is free to caster when the steering system is not operated.

CAUTION

Do not touch nosewheel steering control at touchdown. Steering control must be free to swivel to prevent possible damage from extreme loads.

NOSEWHEEL STEERING EMERGENCY OPERATION

During operation of the aircraft on the emergency hydraulic system, there is no hydraulic pressure available for the nosewheel steering system. Rudder control and alternate use of the brakes should be used for steering.

Arresting Hook

An arresting hook of conventional design and operation is provided for carrier operations. The hook is retracted by 3000-psi utility hydraulic system pressure. An arresting hook holddown unit consists of an air chamber containing 675- to 700-psi air pressure. The air gage is located aft on the external left-hand side of the fuselage. This unit also supplies air pressure for extending the hook. The hook is mechanically latched in the up position.

ARRESTING HOOK CONTROL

The arresting hook control handle (figure 1-9) is located on the left-hand side of the center console. The handle is hook-shaped for easy identification. Movement of the handle to the HOOK DOWN position mechanically releases the hook uplatch and actuates the solenoid-operated hydraulic selector valve to relieve hydraulic pressure in the actuating piston, thereby allowing the hook to extend by air pressure in the holddown unit. A solenoid override, located on the companionway hydraulics panel, may be manually positioned to relieve hydraulic pressure in case of electrical failure or selector valve sticking. In such a case the hook control must be placed in the HOOK DOWN position in order to mechanically release the hook uplatch. A fail-safe mechanism allows the hook to extend if the uplatch control cable is severed. If the control cable should bind on the aircraft structure, it is possible that the fail-safe mechanism would not

be actuated. A warning light at the end of the arresting hook control comes on when the hook control is moved to the HOOK DOWN position and goes out when the hook is fully extended. There is no indication of hook position during the retracting cycle.

ARRESTING HOOK EMERGENCY OPERATION

Emergency operation of the arresting hook is accomplished by pulling the arresting hook cable in the bomb bay. A cable identification decal is located at station 295 pointing to the proper cable to be pulled. Emergency operation is as follows:

1. Cycle arresting hook control handle to DOWN.

2. Actuate arresting hook override PUSH. If solenoid returns to retract position, disconnect Cannon plug at valve. (Essential only if arresting hook returns to UP when override button is released.)

3. Have crewman pull arresting hook cable in bomb bay.

Wheel Brakes System

Hydraulically operated wheel brakes are provided for the main gear only and are controlled conventionally by toe pressure on the upper portion of the rudder pedals. The wheel brake system is powered by utility hydraulic system pressure when the engines are operating. For emergency brake operation following depletion of utility system pressure during deck handling, hydraulic pressure for the brakes is provided by the electrical emergency hydraulic pump.

ANTISKID BRAKE SYSTEM

The wheel brake system, alone, is very sensitive to skid. It is difficult for the pilot to determine when this condition exists, and for this reason it is supplemented with a hytrol antiskid system. This equipment is effective in preventing blowouts as it applies control in braking operation by relieving pressure when either wheel of the main gear approaches a skid condition.

Braking should not be used until both main wheels are firmly on the runway, after which full braking may be applied down to 50 knots. Below 50 knots, the wheel detector units are less sensitive, and less than full braking should be used or blowouts can occur.

If the malfunction prevents braking of the aircraft, the guarded ANTISKID BRAKE switch (figure 1-9) must be turned OFF to restore normal braking, and the pilot should apply braking pressure judiciously to prevent skidding and blowouts.

WHEEL BRAKE EMERGENCY OPERATION

Two emergency systems supply pressure for the wheel brakes. If the utility hydraulic system fails, the EMER HYD switch on the upper center console must be turned ON to energize the emergency electrical hydraulic pump, which then supplies hydraulic pressure for operation of the wheel brakes.

> **CAUTION**
>
> Operation of the emergency hydraulic pump without dc generator or external power available can completely discharge the battery within a few minutes.

NOTE

- Do not use the emergency electrical hydraulic pump during normal landings and takeoffs. It results in unnecessary use of the emergency hydraulic system.

- The emergency hydraulic pump can also be energized by the EMER HYD switch to supply pressure for the brakes during ground handling without engine power.

- Utilization of antiskid with the emergency hydraulic pump on during a utility hydraulic system failure will rapidly deplete the standpipe hydraulic fluid in the utility hydraulic reservoir.

In the event of a complete dc power failure, or if an immediate stop is necessary, a 2000-psi pneumatic emergency brakes system is available. This compressed air system is controlled by the EMERGENCY BRAKE handle (figure 1-9) on the center console. Pulling out on the handle applies compressed air from the emergency upper escape hatch air bottle directly to the brakes, locking the brakes. The EMERGENCY BRAKE control latches in the extended position. The control can be released and pressure on the brakes can be relieved by outboard movement of the EMER BRAKES RELEASE handle which is located on the center console (figure 1-9) underneath and forward of the EMERGENCY BRAKE control. Sufficient air pressure is available in the system for three full applications of the brakes, with diminished pressure being available after each application.

NOTE

It is imperative that the emergency upper escape hatch air bottle be filled after using the emergency brakes.

Pneumatic Emergency Systems

Compressed air bottles are provided for the emergency operation of the following systems: landing gear extension, wing flap extension, and brake operation. For emergency operation of the individual systems, refer to applicable discussion in this section. For a schematic presentation of the pneumatic emergency systems, see figure 1-45.

> **CAUTION**
>
> Following pneumatic emergency operation of a system, air must be exhausted from lines before normal hydraulic controls are actuated. Failure to follow this sequence can cause rupture of the system hydraulic reservoir.

Escape Hatch Air System

The upper escape hatch emergency system is powered by compressed air. The air supply bottle, filler valve, and pressure gage (figure 1-45) are installed directly aft of the hatch. Normal pressure in the air bottle is 2000 psi. The control valve for the upper hatch is adjacent to the pressure gage, and is opened by a handle on the valve (figure 5-2) or by a T-handle above the pilot's head (figure 5-2).

Wing Slats

NOTE

The nomenclature for slat location is: outer wing outboard, outer wing inboard, and center wing outboard. Division point between outer wing and center wing is the wing fold.

The wing slats form a part of the leading edge of each wing. The slats on each wing are in three sections and extend from each engine pylon outboard to the wing tips. No manual control over the slats is provided, and their position is entirely dependent upon the flight attitude and airspeed of the aircraft. At high angles of attack the slats extend automatically, directing airflow over the wing and ailerons, thus reducing loss of lift and aiding control. The slats retract to their normal faired position when the angle of attack is reduced and airspeed increased. The center slats on each wing are mechanically extended when the wings are folded.

Drag Chute

A drag chute is installed to provide rapid deceleration during the initial part of the landing roll or for emergency use on aborted takeoffs. To deploy the drag chute, the pilot operates the two-position DRAG CHUTE switch located directly beneath the standby compass at the top center of the windshield. The switch is normally set on the JETTISON-STOWED position and must be pulled out of a detent and moved

Changed 1 June 1969

Section I
Part 2

NAVAIR 01-40ATA-1

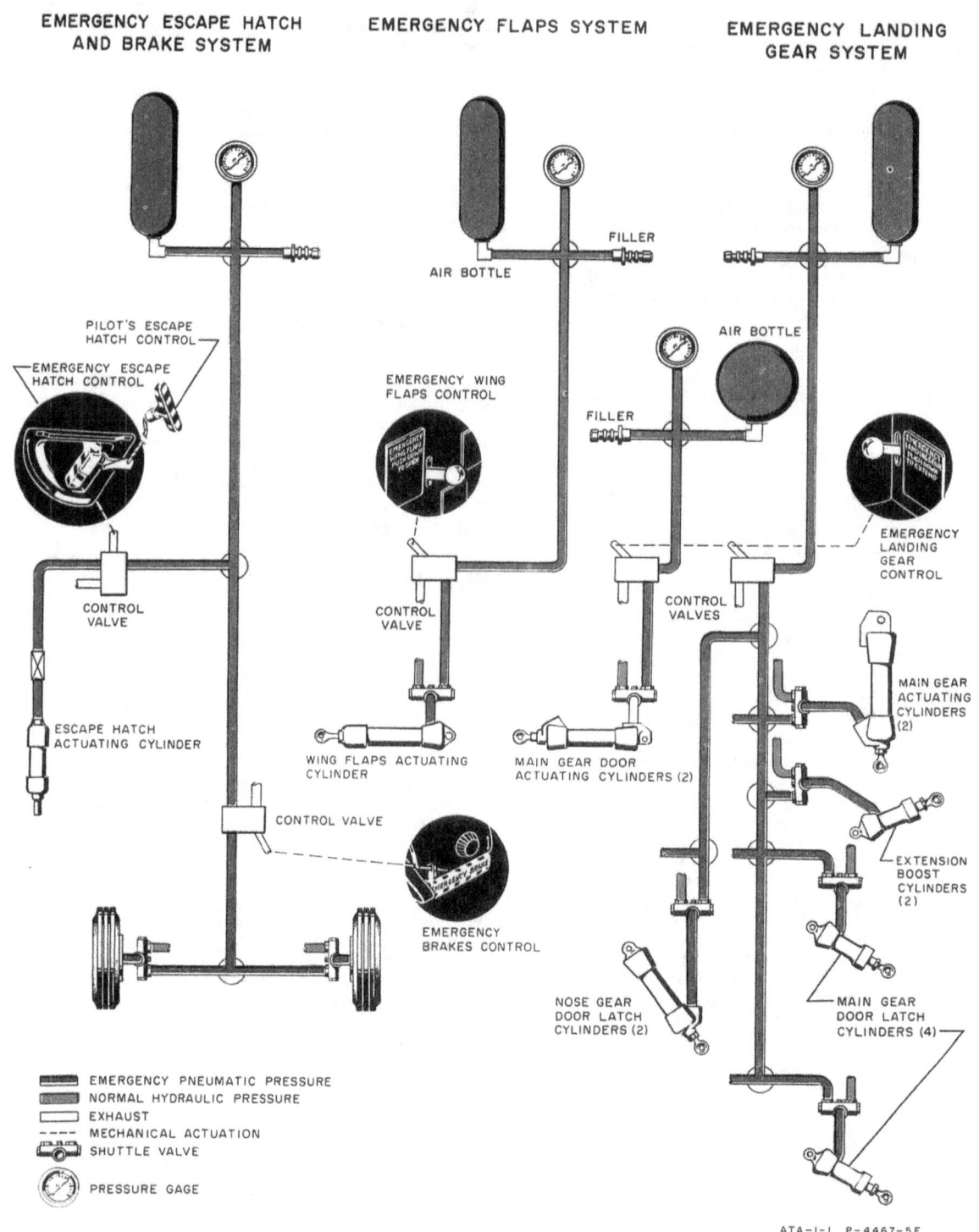

Figure 1-45. Emergency Pneumatic Systems Schematic

upward to DEPLOY for drag chute operation. This electrically positions a locking arm to lock the drag chute riser link to the aircraft and triggers open the two spring-loaded doors on the lower aft fuselage receptacle, releasing the pilot chute, which carries aft the deployment bag containing the canopy. As the deploying bag clears the aircraft, the pilot chute pulls the canopy into the slipstream. The drag chute may be jettisoned by returning the DRAG CHUTE switch to the JETTISON-STOWED position, unlocking the drag chute riser link and disengaging the drag chute from the aircraft. Emergency provisions for jettisoning the parachute are also incorporated in the chute system. If the control circuit is prematurely energized to deploy the chute, a shear pin connecting the riser link to the parachute fails at approximately 170 KIAS and jettisons the parachute. If the parachute doors should open without electrical actuation of the locking mechanism, a shear rivet in the latch mechanism will fail at a latch load of 250 pounds and jettison the drag chute.

For operating techniques, refer to Section III, LANDINGS, MINIMUM ROLL WITH DRAG CHUTE.

Drag chute failures should be thoroughly investigated. Particular attention shall be given all drag chute equipment, fittings, and installation features to ensure that all available safety features have been utilized.

INSTRUMENTS

The instruments are of conventional design and operation. All are located on the instrument panel or above the center console. The instruments and sources of power are listed below.

DC POWERED INSTRUMENTS

Hydraulic pressure flip-flop indicators

Wheel position indicators

Wing flap position indicator

Trim position indicators

Oil temperature gage

Free air temperature gage

CG indicator [1]

ATM compartment temperature gage

Angle-of-attack indicator [1]

Turn-and-slip indicator

Fuel boost pressure indicator

Vertical gyro attitude indicator (VGI)

AC POWERED INSTRUMENTS

Position deviation indicator

[1] Aircraft BuNo. 135407 and subsequent.

Changed 15 July 1970

Stby gyro horizon

Gyrosyn compass repeater indicator

Fuel flowmeter

Fuel quantity indicator

Liquid oxygen quantity gage [1]

Vertical gyro attitude indicator (VGI)

Oil pressure gage

SELF-GENERATING INSTRUMENTS

Tachometers

Turbine outlet temperature indicators

PITOT STATIC INSTRUMENTS

Altimeter

Vertical velocity indicator

Airspeed indicator

DIRECT PRESSURE INSTRUMENTS

Cabin pressure altitude indicator

Pneumatic pressure gages

Hydraulic pressure gages

Airspeed Indicator

A combination airspeed indicator and machmeter (figure 1-4) is mounted on the instrument panel. The airspeed portion of the dial is fixed in position and is calibrated from 80 to 650 knots. The machmeter scale is a rotating disc, marked from 0.50 to 2.20, turning beneath the airspeed dial. Only a portion of the disc can be seen through a cutout in the airspeed dial. Both airspeed and corresponding Mach number are indicated simultaneously by a single-needle pointer. On the Mach number disc is a movable index which is used to set the limiting Mach number of the aircraft by depressing and turning a PUSH MACH LIMIT knob on the lower left corner of the instrument case. An airspeed index pointer on the edge of the airspeed dial, is adjustable through a range of from 80 to 145 knots merely by turning the PUSH MACH LIMIT knob. The airspeed index pointer is used as a reference point to indicate the minimum safe airspeed for a particular gross weight during approach and landing or slow-speed flight. See figure 4-2 for stalling speeds at various gross weights, aircraft configurations, and angles of bank.

Counterpointer Pressure Altimeter

A counterpointer pressure altimeter is located on the pilot's instrument panel (figure 1-4). When properly set, the altimeter will indicate the height of the aircraft above mean sea level. Altitude in units of a hundred feet and altitude in units of thousands of feet are indicated by the instrument. The barometric scale and the altitude pointer are adjustable to barometric pressure variation and field elevation. Adjustment is controlled by a knob on the lower left-hand corner of the instrument case. The counter is shown through a cutout in the face of the instrument and will add or subtract as altitude is gained or lost.

Vertical Velocity Indicator

A conventional vertical velocity indicator (figure 1-4) is installed on the pilot's instrument panel.

Turn-and-Slip Indicator

A conventional needle-and-ball type turn-and-slip indicator (figure 1-4) is provided for basic instrument flight. The instrument is dc powered.

NOTE

Because of the 15-degree tilt of the instrument panel, the turn-and-slip indicator is operating partially as a rate of roll indicator and partially as a turn indicator. Because of this, the turn-and-slip indicator lags and reverses until the turn is established, at which time the indicator will indicate properly. The amount of error in the indications is dependent upon the rate of roll.

Accelerometer

The accelerometer (figure 1-4) provides a record of the g forces applied to the aircraft structures both during and after maneuvers. The instrument uses three pointers for recording g: a free pointer, which indicates the g force being applied at any given moment; a pointer indicating the greatest positive g applied to the aircraft during a given period; and a pointer indicating the greatest negative g during a given period. The last two pointers hold their greatest indication until reset to their base position by use of the knob on the lower left of the instrument.

Vertical Gyro Attitude Indicator (VGI)

The vertical gyro indicator (figure 1-4) provides the pilot with constant visual indication of aircraft pitch and roll. Aircraft attitude indication signals are transmitted to the indicator from a remotely located vertical gyro. The indicator will show the aircraft attitude accurately and continuously through 360 degrees of roll and 85 degrees of climb or dive. Pitch and roll attitudes are shown on the indicator by the motion of a universally mounted sphere in relation to a miniature reference aircraft mounted on the instrument case. The horizon is represented on the sphere as a white line dividing the top and bottom halves. The upper half of the sphere, labeled CLIMB, is painted light gray to symbolize the sky. The lower half, labeled DIVE, is painted black to symbolize the earth. The climb and dive sections of the sphere are graduated every 5 degrees. A pitch trim knob, located on the lower right face of the indicator, is used to center the sphere horizon line with respect to the miniature aircraft. A power failure warning flag displaying the word OFF will be visible at the lower left of the indicator if No. 1 ac power or dc power is lost.

CAUTION

The power failure flag is actually what its name implies: a warning device indicating loss of ac and/or dc power to the VGI system. The flag does not indicate other failures that might occur within the VGI system. Do not use indicator for attitude reference if OFF flag is visible.

The VGI system is powered by both the No. 1 ac bus and the dc primary bus. The system is always in operation when the ac and dc gyro horizon circuit breakers are depressed and both the ac and dc buses are energized. When power is applied to the system, pitch axis erection starts immediately, roll axis erection starts approximately 15 seconds later. After 2±1/2 minutes, the indicator should show the ground attitude of the aircraft and the OFF warning flag should be raised out of view. If not, pull and reset the dc gyro horizon circuit breaker.

CAUTION

To ensure proper gyro erection, both the ac and dc gyro horizon circuit breakers may be pulled before applying electrical power to the aircraft. After applying power, reset ac circuit breakers first; then reset the dc circuit breaker. Fast erection can be accomplished during ground checks or when the aircraft is in a level flight attitude by pulling momentarily and then resetting the dc circuit breaker, with both ac and dc power on.

VERTICAL GYRO ATTITUDE INDICATOR (VGI)
OPERATION AFTER ELECTRICAL POWER LOSS

If either No. 1 ac or dc power is lost; the power OFF warning flag will appear on the face of the indicator. If dc power is lost momentarily, the warning flag will appear. When dc power is regained, the system will automatically recycle. Recycle time is 2±1/2 minutes.

If ac power is lost longer than 5 minutes, pull and reset the dc gyro horizon circuit breaker on the pilot's circuit breaker and fuse panel to obtain the fast, slaving rate feature of the VGI system. When No. 1 ac power is regained, the VGI system will automatically recycle. Recycle time is 2±1/2 minutes.

CAUTION

- The indicator must not be used for attitude reference during the recycle period or when the OFF flag shows on the instrument face.

- During the recycle period, the aircraft should be flown straight and level.

For operating procedure and checks, refer to Preflight Checklists, Section III.

Standby Gyro Horizon Indicator

The standby gyro horizon indicator (figure 1-4) is an electrically driven flight instrument with a manual control mechanism for fast erection. The instrument is nontumbling and provides indications of roll attitude through 360 degrees and is powered from the No. 2 ac bus. The horizon bar pitch attitude indicators are mechanically limited to ±27 degrees; an auxiliary indicator of pitch is provided up to ±80 degrees by a subdial mounted in the center of the mask. Quick erection of the gyro is accomplished by means of a momentary mechanical erection device which is controlled by a knob on the front bezel. The knob should be pulled out steadily and firmly and held extended until the horizon bar and bank index cease to oscillate, at which time they should indicate zero roll and pitch within 3 degrees. The time required for mechanical erection should not exceed 10 seconds. For initial erection, the gyro should be manually erected 10 to 15 seconds after power is applied to obtain rapid settling of the gyro to the vertical.

WARNING

- The erection device erects the gyro to the true aircraft attitude and not to the true vertical.

- The aircraft must be in straight and level flight during the entire erecting procedure.

A power warning flag is incorporated within the instrument and is visible when the power supply is not sufficient for proper operation of the gyro. The flag is not visible when the unit is operating properly.

WARNING

Do not rely on instrument indications when the warning flag is visible. Appearance of warning flag during flight may indicate ac power failure. Check the voltage and frequency of No. 2 ac generator immediately.

Standby Compass

A standard magnetic compass (figure 1-19) is mounted on the canopy between the pilot and navigator. The compass light may be controlled by the pilot's INT LTS, CONSOLES switch.

Angle-of-Attack Approach Light System

The angle-of-attack approach light system consists of a sensing probe, a transmitter unit, an ANGLE-OF-ATTACK indicator, a tricolored external approach light, and a cockpit approach indexer light. The probe extends outboard, forward of the cockpit on the right side, and senses the attitude of the aircraft to the relative airstream. Angle-of-attack information gained by the probe is transmitted to the ANGLE-OF-ATTACK indicator (figure 1-4) located in the upper right-hand corner of the instrument panel. This indicator will be in operation during the entire flight, presenting optimum cruise information. The external APPROACH LIGHT (figure 1-2) and cockpit approach indexer light (figure 1-4) are in operation only when dc power is available and the landing gear and hook are extended in flight. The system may be used for FCLP landings with the hook retracted if the hook bypass switch in the cockpit is used. The hook bypass switch is a momentary contact-type switch and must be reactuated after each touch and go landing.

NOTE

Readings on the ANGLE-OF-ATTACK indicator represent attitude of the aircraft to the relative airstream only and do not relate to the flight path or attitude with respect to the terrain.

ANGLE-OF-ATTACK INDICATOR

The angle-of-attack indicator includes a graduated dial, a pointer, and an OFF warning flag. The instrument provides visual indication of the angle-of-attack in units marked from 0 to 30 on the face of the dial.

1-103

The position of the pointer in relation to the various index units determines which of the three lights on the external APPROACH LIGHT will come on, and also controls the cockpit light. The OFF warning flag will be visible when dc power is lost.

APPROACH LIGHT

The external approach light (figure 1-2) is mounted on the nose gear door and consists of red, green, and amber lights. Only one of these lights will come on at any one time. The position of the pointer on the angle-of-attack indicator determines which light comes on. When the pointer is lined up with the correct angle-of-attack index on the dial, the amber or optimum approach angle-of-attack light comes on. The approach light gives the following visual information to the LSO.

1. Amber light comes on when the aircraft is within the optimum angle-of-attack limits.

2. Red light comes on when the angle-of-attack is too low.

3. Green light comes on when the angle of attack is too high.

The lights are bright for daytime use, but automatically dim when the EXTERIOR LIGHTS master switch is turned on for night flying.

ARRESTING HOOK BYPASS SWITCH

The arresting hook bypass switch is installed on the navigator's right-hand console. To use the approach light during landing, the bypass switch must be actuated after each touchdown. The approach light will then operate with the wheels down and locked and the arresting hook up. Turning the electrical power switch to OFF or placing the arresting hook control in the hook down position releases the bypass switch relay and restores normal operation of the approach light.

COCKPIT INDEXER

The cockpit approach indexer (figure 1-4) is mounted on the pilot's glareshield. The unit consists of three vertically mounted, shielded lights, and a dimming adjustment wheel. The top light shield has a V-slit pointing downward, the center light shield has a circular hole, and the lower light has a V-slit pointing upward. At low angles of attack only the lower light will be on and the external approach light will be red. As the angle of attack increases and approaches the optimum, both the lower light and the center light will be on, and the external approach light will change to amber. When the optimum angle-of-attack is reached,

only the center light will be on and the external approach light will remain amber. As the angle of attack is increased above the optimum, both the center and the upper light will be on; and, as the limits of the optimum angle of approach are passed, the center light will go out, the upper V-light will be on, and the external approach light will change to green. At any time the center light is on, the external approach light will be amber and the aircraft is within the optimum angle of attack limits. (See angle-of-attack charts in Section IV.)

Engine Trim Card

An engine trim card (figure 1-7) shall be posted in the cockpit of each aircraft.

The card must contain the following information:

	LH Engine	RH Engine
TRIM RPM	(% RPM on last trim)	(% RPM on last trim)
EGT	(From last eng trim)	(From last eng trim)
Fuel Flow	(From last eng trim)	(From last eng trim)

Date_____

Allowable tolerances from the last trim are listed in Section III, Part 3. Maximum operating limitations are listed in Section I, Part 4.

When used in an engine trimmed for JP-5, JP-4 will have the following effects:

Max Rated (trim) RPM . . . . . 1% decrease

EGT . . . . 4% decrease

Fuel Flow . . . . 4% decrease

Clocks

A combination 8-day and elapsed time clock (figure 1-9) is located on the center console.

RADIO AND ELECTRONICS EQUIPMENT

Radio Master Switch

The MASTER RADIO switch (figure 1-10) located on the navigator's right-hand console, is a two-position guarded switch with positions ON and OFF. The switch controls the power input to the AN/ARC-27A UHF receiver-transmitter, the AN/ARN-6 radio compass, the AN/AIC-4 interphone, the AN/ARC-38A HF radio receiver-transmitter,[2] and the AN/ARN-14E omnirange receiver,[2] and the AN/ARN-21 receiver-transmitter.[2]

---
[1] Aircraft BuNo. 142236-142255, 142400-142407, 142630-142649
[2] Aircraft BuNo. 135407 and subsequent

NAVAIR 01-40ATA-1

Section I
Part 2

ARN Radio Selector Switch.[1]

Selection of the ARN-21B or the ARN-14E radio receivers may be accomplished by operating the ARN radio selector switch (figure 1-7) located on the pilot's left-hand console.

NOTE

When the ARN-21B (TACAN) is on T/R, the ID-310 indicator will show the distance to the selected TACAN station regardless of the position of the selector switch. If the ARN-14E (OMNI) has been selected, it must be remembered that the ID-249 and the ID-310 DO NOT refer to the same station.

UHF COMMUNICATION AND DIRECTION FINDING SYSTEM

The UHF system provides direction finding and communication in the range of 225 to 399.9 megacycles (figure 1-47). The system consists of dual AN/ARC-27A receiver-transmitters, and the AN/ARA-25

---

[1] Aircraft BuNo. 138963, 142630 and subsequent

direction finder. UHF direction finding information will be shown by the No. one needle of the ID-250/ARN indicator (figures 1-4 and 1-5).

AN/ARC-27A UHF RADIO RECEIVER-TRANSMITTERS

The AN/ARC-27A radio sets provide radio telephone communication in the ultra-high-frequency range of 225 to 400 megacycles. A manual selection of 1750 frequency channels is possible in this operating range. The pilot is provided with selection of any one of 20 preset frequencies, or operation on a guard channel frequency. Transmission and reception is on the same frequency and antenna.

RT-178/ARC-27A Receiver-Transmitters

Two RT-178/ARC-27A receiver-transmitters are located in the empennage of the aircraft. A control panel is installed on the front of each unit. Sensitivity of both the main and guard receivers is controlled at this panel. The front panel of the receiver-transmitter contains the sensitivity controls for both the main and guard receivers, a meter jack and metering switch, squelch controls, and headset and microphone jacks. These controls are not accessible in flight but are used for preflight operating checks.

Changed 1 June 1969

Figure 1-46 Deleted.   1-105

Section I
Part 2

NAVAIR 01-40ATA-1

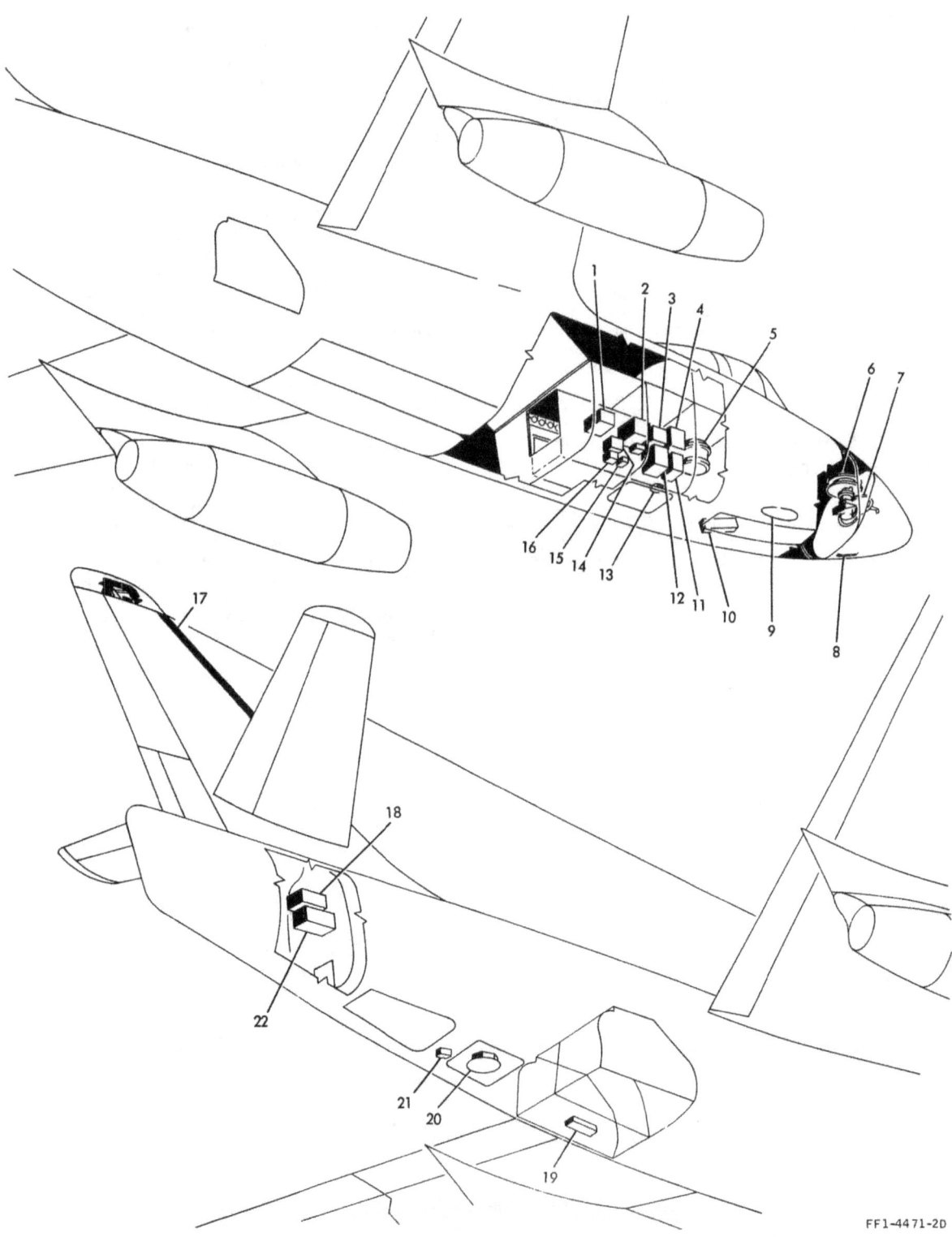

Aircraft BuNo. 135407 through 135444
Figure 1-47. Radio and Radar Equipment and Antennas (Sheet 1)

1-106

Key to Figure 1-47 (Sheet 1)

1. PP-451/ASB-1 power unit
2. AM-632/ASB-1 amplifier
3. SN-116/ASB-1 electrical synchronizer
4. J-335/ASB-1 junction box
5. MD-106/ASB-1 radar modulator
6. RT-170/ASB-1 receiver-transmitter
7. AS-473/ASB-1 antenna
8. ARN-14E antenna
9. Periscope door
10. AN-R-540/ARN-14E radio receiver
11. KY81/APA-89 equipment
12. RT-82A/APX-6B receiver-transmitter
13. AT-234/APX-6B antenna
14. AM-40/AIC-4 amplifier
15. AM-291/APN-22 radio altimeter
16. ID-269/ASB-1 time meter
17. AN/ARC-38A antenna
18. AN/ARC-38A transmitter-receiver
19. RT-160/APN-22 radar receiver-transmitter and antenna
20. AS-578/ARA-25 antenna
21. AN/ARC-27A UHF receiver-transmitter antenna
22. RT-178/ARC-27A UHF receiver-transmitter

UHF Radio Control Panel

C-1015/ARC-27A radio control panels (figures 1-11 and 1-18), identified as UHF and located on the NAV's and PC's consoles, provide the pilot and crew with 20 preset channels, 1750 manual channels, or the guard channel, all of which are selected from the 1750 frequency channels in the 225- to 400-megacycle range. The channel selector (CHAN) provides selection of No. 1 through No. 20 preset channels, the guard channel (G), or the manual position (M). In the manual position (M), the three concentric dials (frequency selections) on the right side of the panel control the equipment frequency directly. The outer dial sets the first two digits of the frequency, the center dial sets the third digit, and the inner dial sets the digit to the right of the decimal point.

The frequency of a preset channel is normally set by maintenance personnel. However, the procedure is as follows:

1. Set channel selector (CHAN) to desired preset channel number.

2. Set three concentric dials (frequency selectors) to desired frequency.

3. Turn preset button (PUSH TO SET CHAN) in direction shown by arrow next to word UNLOCK, until stop is felt; then, push button into panel until another stop is felt, and release to lock.

A standard function switch provides for mode of operation as follows:

Setting	Function
OFF	Set inoperative
T/R	Transmitter and main receiver in operation
T/R + G	Guard receiver in standby ADF in standby
	Transmitter and main receiver in operation
	Guard receiver in operation ADF in standby
ADF	Transmitter in standby
	Guard receiver in standby ADF in operation through main receiver

TO TRANSMIT OR RECEIVE

1. MASTER RADIO switch . . . . ON

NOTE

Allow a 60-second warmup prior to transmission on the AN/ARC-27A.

2. Turn channel selector switch to channel number giving desired frequency.

3. OFF-T/R-T/R + G-ADF switch . . . . T/R

NOTE

If monitoring the guard channel is desired, the OFF-T/R-T/R + G-ADF switch must be on T/R + G. If transmission on the guard channel is desired, the channel selector switch must be on G.

1-107

Section I
Part 2

NAVAIR 01-40ATA-1

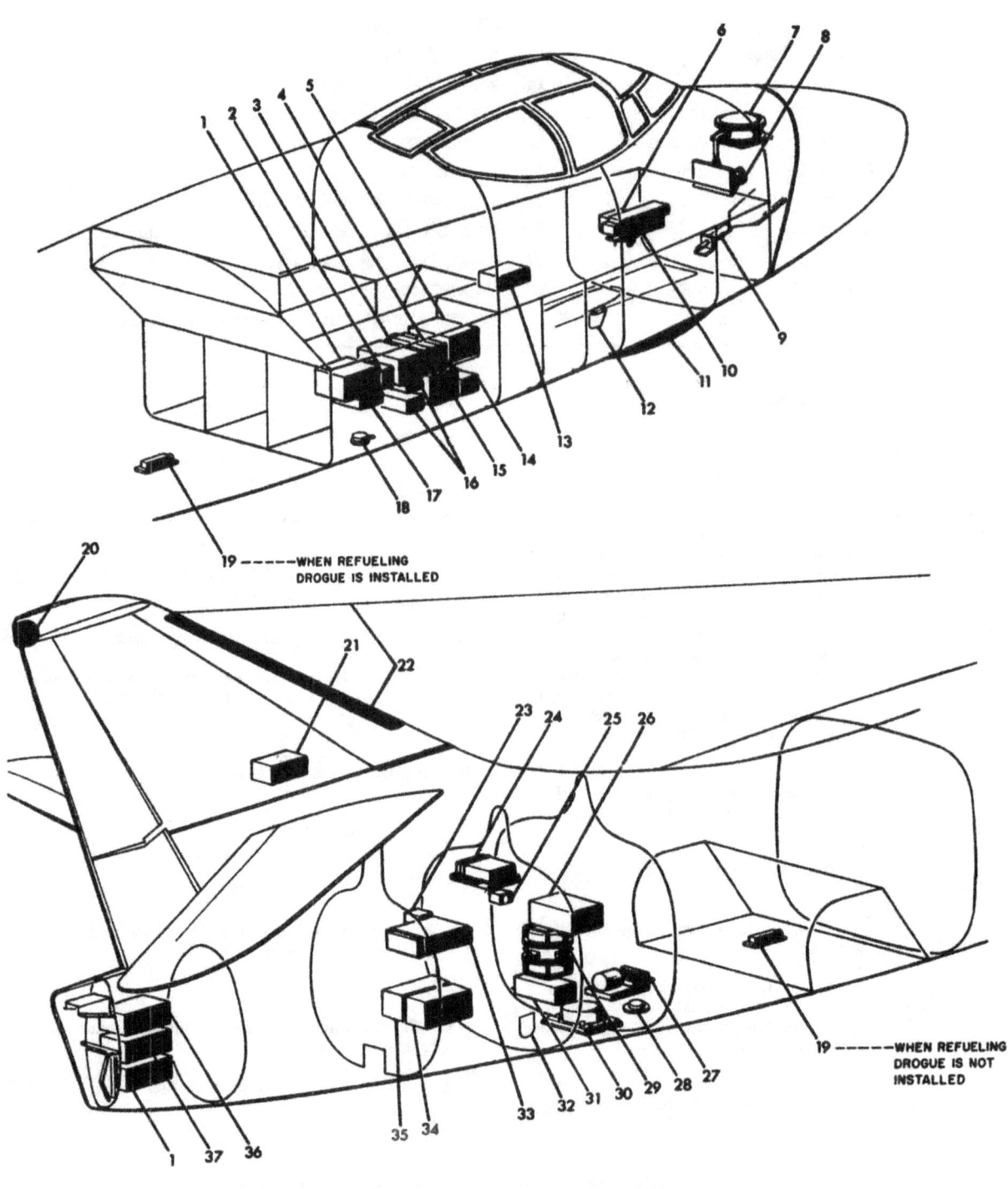

Figure 1-47. Radio and Radar Equipment and Antennas (Sheet 2)

Key to Figure 1-47 (Sheet 2)

1. RT-600/ALQ-51 receiver-transmitter
2. AN-40A/AIC interphone amplifier
3. AM-632/ASB-1 amplifier
4. SN-116A/ASB-1 synchronizer
5. J-335/ASB-1 junction box
6. ARN-14E dynamotor
7. RT-170A/ASB-1 receiver-transmitter
8. AS-473B/ASB-1 antenna
9. ARN-14E antenna
10. R-540/ARN-14C radio receiver
11. Periscope fairing
12. ARC-27A No. 2 antenna
13. ARC-1 VHF receiver-transmitter
14. KY-81/APA-89 equipment
15. RT-82/APX-6B receiver-transmitter
16. AM-291/APN-22 radar control equipment
17. ID-269/ASB-1 time meter
18. AT-234/APX-6B antenna
19. RT-160/APN-22 receiver-transmitter antenna
20. ALQ-51 receiver antenna
21. CU-509 AN/ARC-38A coupler
22. AN/ARC-38A antenna
23. AM-608/ARA-25 electronic amplifier
24. RT-220/ARN-21 radio receiver transmitter
25. ID-307/ARN-21 course indicator
26. PP-3067/ALQ-41 power supply
27. DY-118/ARC-38 dynamotor
28. ARN-21 antenna
29. MD-106/ASB-1 radar modulator
30. AS-578/ARA-25 antenna
31. PP-451/ASB-1 power unit
32. ARC-27A UHF No. 1 receiver-transmitter antenna
33. AN/ARC-38A transmitter-receiver
34. RT-178/ARC-27A No. 1 UHF receiver-transmitter
35. RT-178/ARC-27A No. 2 UHF receiver-transmitter
36. RT-631/ALQ-41 receiver-transmitter
37. T-846/ALQ-41 transmitter

AN/ARA-25 Automatic Direction Finding System

The AN/ARA-25 homing adapter is installed in later aircraft and operates with the AN/ARC-27A UHF communication equipment. Continuous indication of the relative direction of the signal source is provided by the No. 1 pointer of the ID-250/ARN indicator (figure 1-4). Signals are received in the 225.0- to 400.0-megacycle band. The system is placed in operation when the OFF-T/R-T/R+G-ADF selector switch on the UHF control panel is placed in ADF position.

NOTE

If monitoring the guard channel is desired, the OFF-T/R-T/R + G-ADF switch must be in T/R + G. If transmission on the guard channel is desired, the channel selector switch must be in G.

Dual AN/ARC-27A UHF Radio Receiver – Transmitter Installation

The A-3B aircraft is equipped with dual ARC-27A's to provide normal and automatic airborne relay UHF communications. The UHF audio is mixed with the TACAN audio in the ICS. The control box for the No. 1 ARC-27A is located on the Nav's console; the control box for the No. 2 ARC-27A, and the NORMAL/RELAY, UHF select switches are located on the Nav's and PC's consoles (figures 1-11 and 1-18). Physical location of components are:

No. 1 ARC-27A blade antenna – aft and right of aft equipment compartment access door

No. 2 ARC-27A blade antenna – immediately forward of cockpit entrance door

Both ARC-27A receiver-transmitter units are located in the aft equipment compartment.

NOTE

Allow a 1-minute warmup period before keying transmitter when AN/ARC-27A is first energized.

OPERATION

Either ARC-27A may be used for normal communication by selection No. 1 or 2 UHF on the control panel on the PC's console and by placing the NORMAL RELAY switch in the NORMAL position. When the

TABLE 1-1. COMMUNICATIONS AND ASSOCIATED ELECTRONICS EQUIPMENT

Type	Designation	BuNo. 135407-135444	138902-138962 138964-138976	142236-142255 142400-142407 142630-142649	Function	Primary Operator	Range	Location
Communication								
HF Radio	ARC-38A	*	*	*	Tr/Rec Voice, CW or CWS	Nav	Horizon up to 2000 nautical miles	Nav's console
UHF Dual ARC-27A	ARC-27A	*	*	*	Short range Tr/Rec		Horizon	
VHF Radio	ARC-1		*	*	Short range Tr/Rec		Line of sight	
Interphone								
Interphone	AIC-4A	*	*	*	Communication between crewmembers	All crew-members	Interphone	Each crewmember's position
	Transistor ICS							
Navigation								
UHF Homing Adapter	ARA-25	*	*	*	Provides homing on UHF transmissions	Nav	Line of sight	Nav's console
OMNIRANGE Receiver	ARN-14E	*	*	*	Directional homing on VOR, and localizer signals	Pilot		Pilot's console
TACAN	ARN-21B	*	*	*	Tr/Rec distance signals, receives radial bearing signals, and air-to-air ranging	Pilot	Horizon: 198 nautical miles maximum for distance measuring	
RADAR Altimeter	APN-22	*	*	*			Overland: 0 to 10,000 Ft Overwater: 0 to 20,000 Ft	Indicator on instrument panel. Altitude limit switch on indicator.
Identification								
IFF Transponder	APX-6B	*	*	*	Identification	Nav	Horizon	Nav's console
SIF Coder	APA-89	*	*	*				
Radar								
Modified RADAR Sys	ASB-1A	*	*	*	Navigation aids, Automatic search	Nav	Horizon	Nav's console
	ASB-7			*(1)				

(1) Aircraft BuNo. 142400, 142402-142407, 142633, 142635, 142642, 142644, 142647, 142649

No. 1 UHF is being used, frequency selection and audio levels are controlled by the UHF control box on the Nav's console.

The frequency selection and audio volume for No. 2 UHF is controlled by the control box on the PC's console.

An ON-OFF toggle switch labeled AUX UHF is located on the pilot's left-hand console. This switch enables the pilot to select either normal or AUX UHF operation.

AUTOMATIC RELAY FUNCTION

By placing the NORM/RELAY switch on the PC's console to the RELAY position any communication received on No. 1 or 2 UHF will be automatically retransmitted on the opposite UHF. For relay operation, the two ARC-27A's must be set up on different frequencies.

NOTE

Considering the difference in the ARC-27A receivers sensitivity transmitter power output and the location of the blade antenna on the aircraft, switching the functions of either ARC-27A may produce better communication.

Security Equipment

The security equipment, which is supplementary to the UHF, consists of either Romero 8 or Juliet 28. The security equipment control panel (figure 1-11) is located on the Nav's right-hand console. Power for the security equipment is 28 vdc. Any further description of the security equipment or its function is above the security classification of this manual.

AN/ARC-38A HF Radio Receiver-Transmitter

Radio set AN/ARC-38A provides radio communication between aircraft and a ground station or another aircraft. Voice and CW operation from 2.0 to 25.0 megacycles are provided by the equipment. Frequencies from 2.0 to 14.2495 megacycles may be selected in 500-cps steps. From 14.250 to 25.0 megacycles, channels may be selected in steps of 1000-cps. A selection of 20 frequencies may be preset on a drum within the control panel. Transmission and reception are on the same frequency and antenna.

AN/ARC-38A CONTROL PANEL. The HF radio control panel (figure 1-11), located on the navigator's console, contains the operating controls for the ARC-38A radio. A four-position rotary function switch, labeled OFF, AME, CW, SSB/FSK (C-3428/ARC-38A), is used to select type of emission and receiver selectivity, and to control application of power to the equipment. A three-position frequency mode knob marked MAN, LOCAL, REMOTE, permits use of the manual frequency selection feature when positioned at MAN, or use of the preset channels when positioned at LOCAL. The REMOTE position is not used in this aircraft. Four thumb wheel manual frequency selectors are used in conjunction with the MAN position. A 20-position thumb wheel channel selector is used to select one of the preset channels in conjunction with the LOCAL position of the frequency mode knob. A two-position CW RECPT-CW XMSN switch permits monitoring the received signal without operating the dynamotor when positioned at CW RECPT. A beat frequency oscillator (BFO) control knob is used for remote control of the beat frequency oscillator. A volume control knob controls the audio gain in the AME position and controls the rf gain in CW positions. The sensitivity control knob, regulates rf gain in the AME position. Accessible by lifting a hinged door on the panel are the following: a drum for presetting 20 channels, a tool for presetting the drum, and a code book with the instructions and code needed to set up the desired frequencies on the drum or the manual frequency selectors.

OPERATION OF AN/ARC-38A RADIO

For operation with the preset channels, proceed as follows:

1. Aircraft electrical system . . . ENERGIZED

2. ICS panel, HF switch . . . . . . REC ON

3. To transmit, ICS panel transmitter switch . . . . HF

4. Frequency mode knob . . . . . . LOCAL

5. Turn channel selector thumb wheel to channel of desired frequency. (The frequency of the 20 preset channels may be logged on the chart on the hinged door of the control panel.)

6. Energize equipment and select type of emission on function knob.

7. Regulate rf gain to comfortable level with volume or sensitivity knob.

8. For CW or CWS operation, regulate signal pitch with beat frequency oscillator control knob.

9. To transmit, press microphone button and speak into mike. Sidetone should be heard in headset. Release the mike button to hear incoming signals. If operating in CW, press the key. A 400-cps sidetone

Section I
Part 2

is monitored in this case. Release the key to receive incoming signals. For CW transmission, the cw xmsn-cw recpt function knob should be at CW XMSN. When a CW signal is being received, the cw xmsn - cw recpt toggle switch should be placed in CW RECPT which disables the dynamotor to permit monitoring the received signal without operating the dynamotor.

For operation with manual selection of frequency:

1. Turn frequency mode knob to MAN.

2. Use code book to set up the desired frequency on the four manual frequency selection thumb wheels. Proceed with steps 5 through 8 of the procedure for operation with preset channels.

NOTE

Automatic tuning circuits in the AN/ARC-38A radio receiver-transmitter require time to perform their tuning and loading functions. Fifteen seconds are required to tune the receiver-transmitter and a slightly longer time to load the antenna. Certain relays in the receiver-transmitter open the keying circuits during tuning so that no transmission may be made. A 400-cycle note will be audible in the headset during the antenna coupler loading cycle. Do not attempt transmission until the tuning cycle is complete, and the 400-cycle tone is no longer heard in the headset.

To secure the equipment, position the function knob in OFF.

AN/APX-6B TRANSPONDER (IFF)

The radar identification set AN/APX-6B (figure 1-10 and 1-11) is an airborne transponder and is one of several units that may be operated together to provide a system of electronic identification and recognition. The purpose of the AN/APX-6B transponder is to identify the aircraft in which it is installed as friendly, when correctly challenged by friendly radar, and to permit surface tracking control of aircraft. Functionally, the receiver portion of the AN/APX-6B equipment receives the challenges initiated by an interrogator responder, and applies a single pulse corresponding to each interrogation to the AN/APA-89 coder. In response to interrogations in modes 1, 2, or 3, the AN/APA-89 provides coded pulse train replies (the coding of which can be selected for each of the three modes) back to the AN/APX-6B. This pulse train is transmitted by the transmitter portion of the AN/APX-6B to the interrogator responder where proper replies, decoded or as raw video, are

displayed along with the associated radar targets on the radar indicator. When a radar echo is accompanied by a proper IFF reply, that target is considered friendly.

C-1159/APX-6B Control Panel (IFF)

The IFF control panel (figure 1-11) is located on the navigator's console. The panel contains a rotary master selector knob with positions marked: OFF, STBY, LOW, NORM, and EMERGENCY.

APX-6B OPERATION

The system is energized when the master knob on the IFF control panel is set in any position other than OFF. A pushbutton below and to the left of the function selector switch must be pressed before the EMERGENCY position can be entered. This prevents inadvertent entering of the EMERGENCY position. Two lights on the panel provide lighting of the master selector control and the three toggle functional switches. The master knob functions as follows.

Position	Function
OFF	Set is inoperative
STBY	Set is ready for operation but transponder-receiver is not sensitized and no replies can be transmitted.
NORM	Transponder-receiver is given full sensitivity and transponder operates with maximum performance. Transmitted power from transponder is same for both LOW and NORM positions of switch.
EMERGENCY	Emergency replies are transmitted upon receipt of any IFF interrogation regardless of mode of interrogation or settings of MODE toggle switches on control panel.

NOTE

To enter the EMERGENCY position, first depress the dial stop button.

I/P-OUT-MIC SWITCH

The I/P-OUT-MIC switch is a three-position switch that allows identification of individual aircraft. This switch is functional only with the MODE 3 selector switch forward. The I/P position is momentary and, when actuated, initiates a two-train coded MODE 3 response to any MODE 3 interrogations received for approximately 30 seconds. When the switch is placed in MIC position, the 30-second period is commenced each time the UHF microphone is depressed, and the same two-train coded MODE 3 response occurs as in the I/P position.

AN/APA-89 (SIF)

The AN/APA-89 coder is used with the AN/APX-6B transponder to supply multiple coded replies to the transmitter portion of the AN/APX-6B. Selective and individual identification of aircraft is possible, thus facilitating ground control and providing flexibility to the identification process. The AN/APA-89 coder accepts the decoded output of the AN/APX-6B transponder and generates coded information pulse trains, enabling the transponder to reply on SIF. The AN/APA-89 has two supplementary purposes: to provide two-train coded replies automatically for I/P purposes; to provide four-train coded emergency replies. Emergency and I/P replies occur only for MODE 1 and MODE 3 interrogations.

SIF CONTROL PANEL

The C-1272/APA-89 SIF control panel (figure 1-10) is located on the navigator's console. The panel contains two coaxial type switches identified as MODE 1 and MODE 3. Each switch has an inner and an outer rotary dial. The MODE 1 inner dial is numbered from 0 to 3 and the outer dial is numbered from 0 to 7. The MODE 3 selector switch has both inner and outer dials numbered from 0 to 7. Positioning of these switches provides the pilot with a selection of various codes in MODE 1 or MODE 3. Four rotary switches for the selection of codes in MODE 2 are located behind a door on the face of the AN/APA-89 coder and are normally preset on the ground. When the APX-6B is switched to EMERGENCY with MODE 3 selected, the APA-89 coder will provide automatic transmission of code 77.

AN/AIC-4A INTERPHONE

The AN/AIC-4A intercommunication radio system provides ratio communication between crewmembers. Microphone and headset jacks are located strategically in the tail section, the bomb bay, the engine nacelles, and the fuselage nose section for use during ground test or bomb bay operations in flight.

Pilot's and Plane Captain's Interphone Control Units (ICS)

A C-736/AIC-4A control unit is installed on the pilot's left-hand console (figure 1-7) and the PC's right-hand console (figure 1-11). Both are designated SEL and have RADIO VOL and ICS VOL controls. A transmission selector switch, labeled TRANS, has ICS, UHF, and HF positions. On the pilot's panel, however, the ICS position is covered and the pilot may transmit on ICS at any time by moving the throttle or control wheel switch to ICS. A receiver switch on the interphone panels, labeled RCVR, has UHF, HF, NAVIG, and OUT positions. The UHF position is for AN/ARC-27A UHF reception; HF, for AN/ARC-38A, MHF and VHF reception; and NAV for the AN/ARN-6 radio compass, and OMNI/TACAN.

Navigator's Interphone Control Unit (ICS)

The C-736/AIC-4A control unit, designated MIX, is installed on the navigator's right-hand console (figure 1-10). The control unit has ICS VOL and RADIO VOL controls and three receiver selector switches marked RCVR-OUT. One is for UHF reception, one for HF and VHF, and the third is used for ARN-6/ARN-21/ARN-14/ARA-25. UHF or HF reception may be discontinued by placing the respective switches in the OUT position. An HF SENS switch governs the volume of the HF radio. The TRANS switch has ICS, UHF, and HF positions.

MICROPHONE HEADSET EXTENSIONS

The pilot's and crewmember's microphone and headset extensions are incorporated into the personal gear adapters at each crew station.

PILOT'S MICROPHONE CONTROLS

The pilot's microphone controls are located on the left-hand throttle (figure 1-9) and the control wheel (figure 1-4). Both controls are spring-loaded switches and have three positions, OFF, RAD, and ICS.

FOOT MICROPHONE SWITCHES

The foot microphone switches, located on the cockpit floor forward of the navigator (figure 1-9) and aft of the PC (figure 1-15), are used for ICS, UHF, or VHF/HF depending on the position of the TRANS switch on the respective control panel.

OPERATION

TO RECEIVE. When transmission is made on the interphone system, all stations receive interphone communication regardless of switch position if the ICS VOL controls are turned up.

TO TRANSMIT. The pilot can transmit over the interphone system regardless of the position of the TRANS switch on his SEL panel by switching to ICS

Changed 15 July 1970

Section I
Part 2

NAVAIR 01-40ATA-1

on either the throttle or control wheel microphone switch and talking into the microphone. Before either crewmember can transmit over the interphone system, the TRANS switch on his control panel must be in the ICS position.

Fourth Man ICS Switch

With the installation of a low-pressure oxygen system regulator (figure 1-16), the FOURTH MAN's ICS switch is located on the oxygen hose. This will enable the fourth man to communicate with other crewmembers without the necessity of the PC depressing the MIC switch on his footrest.

AN/APN-22 RADAR ALTIMETER

The AN/APN-22 radar altimeter is designed to provide reliable indications of altitude from 0 to 10,000 feet over land and from 0 to 20,000 feet over water. The accuracy of indication is plus or minus 2 feet from 0 to 40 feet, and plus or minus 5 percent of the corrected pressure altitude from 40 to 20,000 feet. Corrected pressure altitude is to be computed using OAT corrected for compressibility.

The AN/APN-22 receiver-transmitter on KA-3B aircraft gives erratic altitude indications because of close proximity to the air refueling drogue fairing. On KA-3B aircraft, the APN-22 will be moved forward to the bomb bay spoiler area when the drogue fairing is installed and returned to the wheel well area when the fairing is removed. A decal will be placed in the wheel well indicating that the APN-22 is operating forward.

Height Indicator

The ID-257/APN-22 height indicator (figure 1-4) is located on the pilot's instrument panel and shows the true altitude of the aircraft above the surface. An ON-LIMIT switch, located on the indicator, is used to turn the equipment on and off and to select the limit altitude by adjusting of a bug pointer on the outside of the calibrated scale.

1-114

LIMIT INDICATOR SYSTEM

An altitude limit indicator system is included to provide a visual indication of flight at, or below, a preset altitude. When at or below a preset altitude as selected by the ON-LIMIT switch, a red warning light on the indicator comes on.

DROPOUT

The dropout altitude (altitude at which the signal becomes too weak to operate the radar altimeter) is above 10,000 feet over land, and 20,000 feet over water. The dropout altitude decreases in banks, climbs, and dives of 50 degrees or more. When dropout occurs, an electrical circuit disables the indicator and moves the indicator needle behind a mask to prevent the pilot from depending on an unreliable reading.

OPERATION OF THE RADAR ALTIMETER AN/APN-22

1. Turn ON-LIMIT CONTROL in clockwise direction.

2. Allow approximately 3 minutes for equipment to begin operating.

3. Set bug pointer to desired altitude limitation, using ON-LIMIT switch.

4. To stop the equipment, turn ON-LIMIT switch in counterclockwise direction to fullest extent.

Radio Compass Indicator

A navigation selector switch (figure 1-7), located on the pilot's left-hand console, is used to select output from the ARA-25 for display on the No. 1 needle of the ID-250.

OMNIBEARING EQUIPMENT (VOR)

AN/ARN-14E Receiver (VOR)

The AN/ARN-14E (VOR) receiver provides reception of all VHF omnirange, tone localizer, and voice transmissions in the 108.0- to 136.0-megacycle spectrum. Navigational information is registered on two course indicators located on the pilot's instrument panel. (Refer to Course Indicator ID-249A/ARN and Course Indicator ID-250/ARN No. 2 needle.) Voice transmissions are received on communications channels or superimposed on navigation signals in the omnirange bands.

Control Panel C-760A/A

The control panel (figure 1-6) for the AN/ARN-14E receiver contains a POWER switch with marked positions of ON and OFF, a FREQUENCY selector control, and a VOLUME control. The ON position of the POWER switch is used for VHF omnirange and tone localizer reception. Frequency selection is accomplished by setting the desired frequency into the vertical window with the concentric knobs provided. Vertically downward the numbers represent hundreds, tens, units, and the tenths of megacycles.

NOTE

On aircraft that utilize the simultaneous installation of the AN/ARN-21 and the AN/ARN-14E radio receivers, the ARN radio selector switch (figure 1-6) must be positioned to AN/ARN-14 in order to operate the AN/ARN-14E radio receiver.

Course Indicator ID-249A/ARN

The ID-249A/ARN course indicator (figure 1-4) located on the pilot's instrument panel contains a COURSE window and a SET control for setting the desired course to or from the VHF omnirange station; a window with a TO-FROM indicator to signal whether the aircraft is heading toward or away from the station; a vertical bar which indicates left or right to guide the pilot onto the desired course which is set in the COURSE window with a TO-FROM indicator to signal whether the aircraft is heading toward or away from the station; a vertical bar which indicates left or right to guide the pilot onto the desired course which is set in the COURSE window; a relative heading indicator consisting of a pointer with a white circle on the end which moves to either side of top or bottom center as much as 45 degrees to indicate the angle between the heading of the aircraft and the course set in the COURSE window. The horizontal bar which is used for glide path control is inoperative. On the upper right corner of the instrument case is a marker beacon indicating light which is inoperative also, as no marker beacon receiving equipment is installed in the aircraft.

Radio Magnetic Indicator ID-250A/ARN

The ID-250A/ARN course indicator (figure 1-4), located on the pilot's instrument panel, provides navigational information in conjunction with the AN/ARN-14E and AN/ARN-21 radio receivers. This instrument contains a rotating compass card slaved to the S-2 gyrosyn compass to provide magnetic heading of the aircraft. Two needle pointers are contained in the indicator. The No. 1 pointer gives visual indication of the direction of signals received by the AN/ARA-25 homing adapter set, while the No. 2 pointer indicates similar information for the AN/ARN-14E receiver and the AN/ARN-21 NAV receiver. An ARN radio selector switch is provided for operational selection of the AN/ARN-14E receiver or the AN/ARN-21 NAV receiver on later aircraft. Readings thus observed are magnetic bearings to the selected stations, provided the S-2 compass is correctly set, when the AN/ARA-25 radio is not in use.

AN/ARN-21B TACAN

Provisions and equipment are incorporated in later aircraft for simultaneous installation of the AN/ARN-21B TACAN radio equipment and the AN/ARN-14E radio receiver. The AN/ARN-21B TACAN radio equipment is an airborne navigation interrogator-responsor that operates in conjunction with a surface navigation beacon transponder (TACAN station). The TACAN navigation system provides bearing, distance, and station identification information to the pilot. The No. 2 needle of the ID-250/ARN compass indicates the magnetic bearing to the station. The ID-249A/ARN indicates the relative position and TO-FROM indication of a selected radial as with OMNI equipment. The ID-310/ARN (figure 1-4) indicated the slant range in nautical miles from the ground station to the aircraft. The ground (or ship-based) station transmits identification signals at regular intervals.

The AN/ARN-21B TACAN navigation system has 126 two-way operating channels of 1-megacycle spacing. Each of these 126 channels can provide service to 120 aircraft simultaneously. Ground stations transmit on a frequency between 962 and 1024 and also on the frequency between 1151 and 1213 megacycles. These transmissions are converted by the airborne receiver into the azimuth indications displayed on the ID-249 and ID-250. When T/R is selected, the transmitter portion of the airborne equipment sends out paired interrogation pulses on one of 126 frequencies between 1025 and 1150 megacycles. The ground station receives the interrogation pulses and replies with similar pulses on the transmitting frequency. The airborne receiver converts the time between transmission of the interrogation pulses and reception of the ground station reply into distance for display on the ID-310. The design of the airborne transmitter is such that the time between paired pulses varies widely between individual sets of equipment. Thus, each set has an individual characteristic which enables it to distinguish between replies to its distance interrogations and replies to ARN-21 equipment in other aircraft. Distance reception is limited to line of sight and extends from 0 to 198 nautical miles. Bearing information extends to over 200 nautical miles. Atmospheric conditions limit the use of the AN/ARN-21B to altitudes up to 50,000 feet.

C-866/ARN-21B NAV CONTROL PANEL

The C-866/ARN-21B control panel (figure 1-6) is identified as NAV and located on the pilot's left-hand console. Operating controls include the power switch with OFF-REC-T/R positions, two CHAN (channel selector) knobs, and a VOL (volume) control.

OPERATION OF AN/ARN-21B NAV RADIO. After a 90-second warmup in the REC position, the power switch may be placed in the T/R position. Observe the following procedure for operating the equipment:

1. MASTER RADIO switch . . . ON

2. AN/ARN-21 power switch . REC

3. CHAN selector . . . . Set channel number in indicator dial.

4. ARN radio selector switch ARN-21B

Identify beacon by tone signals in headset and read bearing to station on the No. 2 pointer of the ID-250 indicator. Directional information will also be supplied by the ID-249 indicator. For distance information, the power switch must be turned to T/R. Distance will be indicated on the ID-310 instrument in nautical miles.

TACAN Air-to-Air Ranging

Air-to-air (A/A) ranging requires cooperating aircraft to be within line-of-sight distance. The A/A mode enables the TACAN installation to provide range indications between two aircraft, or between one lead aircraft and up to five others. TACAN displays normal range and azimuth information in the T/R mode and range information only is obtained in the A/A mode with azimuth indicator (No. 2 needle) rotating continuously. If A/A operation is desired between aircraft, the channel selected by one aircraft must be separated by exactly 63 channels from the other aircraft; e.g., No. 1 aircraft is set to channel 64, No. 2 aircraft is set at channel 1. Both aircraft must then select A/A on the TACAN function switch. Range between aircraft will then be displayed on the DME indicator in each aircraft. The maximum lock-on range is 198 miles. However, due to the relative motion of the aircraft, the initial lock-on range will usually be less.

If A/A operation is desired between one lead aircraft and five others, the channel selected by the lead aircraft must be 63. The other five aircraft must be separated by exactly 63 channels. The A/A mode must then be selected on the TACAN selection switch.

AN/ARC-1 Receiver-Transmitter

The AN/ARC-1 receiver-transmitter provides two-way communication between the ground and an aircraft or between aircraft. There are nine prearranged main channel communication frequencies and a guard channel frequency. Incoming signals can be received on the AN/ARC-1 radio at any time except when transmission is desired. The change from receiving to transmitting is accomplished by operating the microphone switch.

C-865/ARC-1 RADIO CONTROL PANEL

The C-865/ARC-1 control panel (figure 1-11) located on the navigator's console provides a CHANNEL selector switch for selecting one of the nine channels and a GUARD-MAIN switch. The GUARD-MAIN switch provides choice of operation on the selected main channel or the guard channel, or operation on the selected main channel and monitoring on the guard channel. The GUARD-MAIN switch is labeled MAIN T/R, MAIN T/R & G REC, and GUARD. The GUARD-MAIN switch knob has a radial line on it to indicate selection in use, and the CHANNEL switch has an index, on the panel, opposite the channel selected on the CHANNEL dial.

OPERATION OF AN/ARC-1 RECEIVER TRANSMITTER

The C-865/ARC-1 radio is operated in the following manner:

1. MASTER RADIO switch . . . . ON

2. GUARD-MAIN switch . . . . MAIN T/R & G REC

3. CHAN selector switch . . . . Desired channel

The radio will be ready for reception of incoming signals on the guard channel and the selected main channel, after at least 20 seconds when the vacuum tubes will reach operating temperature. It is possible that while operating on the main channel and monitoring on the guard channel, reception on either channel will be prevented by interfering noise passed by the other channel. This interference may be suppressed by turning the GUARD-MAIN switch to the MAIN T/R position as required.

LIGHTING EQUIPMENT

Interior Lights

The interior lighting system includes all instrument and console lights, dome light, floodlights, service lights, and necessary controls. The instrument and console lights operate on ac while the floodlights operate on dc, thus providing standby lighting in case of failure of either system.

PILOT'S INSTRUMENT AND CONSOLE LIGHTS

The pilot's instrument and console lights are controlled from the INT LTS control panel (figure 1-6) on his left-hand console. Two selector switches marked INST and CONSOLES may be rotated clockwise from OFF toward BRIGHT to provide illumination of variable intensity for the instruments and consoles. Turning the INST light switch from OFF toward BRIGHT operates a warning light dimming relay which automatically dims all cockpit warning lights for night flying.

NOTE

When flying during the hours of daylight, ascertain that the INST light switch is turned OFF so that the warning lights dimming relay will be deenergized.

NAVIGATOR'S CONSOLE LIGHTS

The navigator's console lights are controlled from the PANEL LIGHTS control panel (figure 1-10) on the navigator's right-hand console. To operate the console lights, the CONSOLES switch is turned from the OFF position toward BRIGHT until the desired intensity is obtained.

PLANE CAPTAIN'S CONSOLE LIGHTS

The plane captain's console lights are controlled from the PANEL LTS control panel (figure 1-17) on the PC's console. Turning the switch on the panel from OFF toward BRIGHT turns on the console lights and regulates their intensity.

FLOODLIGHTS

Floodlights are provided for the pilot's instrument panel and console, the center console, AN/ASB-1 bombing equipment, navigator's consoles, PC's console, and the aft electrical power panel. A FLOOD lights switch on the pilot's INT LTS control panel operates the pilot's instruments and consoles lights. The switch has three positions: BRIGHT, MEDIUM, and DIM. The FLOOD lights switch on the navigator's PANEL LIGHTS control panel operates the AN/ASB-1 navigator's console, and special weapons console floodlights. The switch has three positions: BRT, MED, and DIM. The FLOOD lights switch on the PC's PANEL LTS control panel operates the PC's console and aft power panel floodlights. The switch has three positions: BRT, MED, and DIM. The FLOOD lights switches will not operate the floodlights unless their respective CONSOLES switch is moved out of the OFF position.

CABIN DOME LIGHT

The cabin dome light (figures 1-12 and 1-13) is located above the navigator's seat and contains both a white and a red lamp. The control switch has three positions: RED, OFF, and WHITE.

SERVICE LIGHTS

Service lights are located in the accessory compartment, the bomb bay, the turret compartment, and the armament accessory compartment. Switches are located adjacent to the light at all stations.

Exterior Lights

The exterior lighting system includes navigation lights on wingtips and tail; formation lights on lower surface of the outer wing panels; fuselage lights on the lower fuselage surfaces; three anticollision lights, two located on the bottom of the fuselage and one on top of the fuselage; and a taxi light on the nosewheel door. The exterior lights system receives power from the secondary bus through five circuit breakers.

EXTERIOR LIGHTS CONTROL

The exterior lights master control switch is located on the right-hand throttle. This three-position toggle switch provides on-off control of the exterior lights and acts as a catapult signal when switched to the aft, momentary position. Selective operation of the lights is controlled at the EXTR LTS panel (figure 1-6) on the pilot's left-hand console. On early aircraft[1] two switches labeled FUSELAGE are located on the panel. The outboard switch has two positions: FLSH and STDY. The inboard switch has three positions: BRT, MAN, and DIM. The navigation and formation lights are controlled by the WING & TAIL and FORM switches, each with three positions: BRT, OFF, and DIM. These switches are located inboard of the FUSELAGE switch.

The EXTR LTS panel on later aircraft contains four switches. The outboard switch has three positions: labeled ALL, OFF, and TOP. Inboard of this switch is a two-position ON, OFF FUEL PROBE switch. Inboard of the FUEL PROBE switch, some aircraft have two switches labeled WING & TAIL and FORM. The three-position switch labeled BRT, OFF, and DIM, control the formation and navigation lights.

---

[1] Aircraft BuNo. 135407-135444

The tanker aircraft do not have the FORM or TAXI light switches. The WING and TAIL lights are controlled by separate switches.

AIR REFUELING PROBE LIGHT

An air refueling probe light is recessed within the nose and is capable of lighting both the probe and the drogue from a distance of approximately 50 feet. The light can be turned ON or OFF without affecting the aircraft's refueling capability.

ANTICOLLISION LIGHTS

The high intensity tandem oscillating type anticollision beacons are controlled by a three-position switch (figure 1-7) located on the exterior lights panel. The switch positions are labeled ANTICOLL, OFF, and FUS. Two anticollision lights are located on the bottom of the fuselage, one under each wheel well. An additional anticollision light is located on top of the fuselage near the trailing edge of the wing. The two white steady fuselage lights are located on the bottom of the fuselage in line with the tanker fairing.

TAXI (OR LANDING) LIGHT

The taxi light (figure 1-2) is mounted on the forward edge of the nosewheel door immediately below the approach light. To operate the taxi light, the TAXI switch on the EXTR LTS control panel is placed in the ON position. The taxi light is powered by the dc monitor bus, through the LANDING LIGHT circuit breaker on the companionway circuit breaker panel.

APPROACH LIGHT

The approach light (figure 1-2) is mounted on the nosewheel door. The approach light will operate when the landing gear is locked down and the hook is fully extended or if the tailhook bypass switch is actuated. The lights are bright for daytime use, but automatically dim when the EXTERIOR LIGHTS master switch is turned ON.

OXYGEN SYSTEM

An automatic, positive-pressure, diluter-demand oxygen system is provided with oxygen from a liquid oxygen converter. The quantity gage provides the pilot with an indication of the level of the liquid oxygen in the container. A flexible oxygen breathing tube with incorporated radio connections is mounted on the left side of the back of each crewmember's seat. In addition, an oxygen-radio tube is mounted in the sextant position directly behind the navigator's seat and on the right companionway bulkhead just forward of the bomb bay. An oxygen regulator is supplied with each oxygen-radio tube. The pilot's regulator is located on the forward left-hand console, the navigator's regulator is located on the forward right-hand console, and the PC's regulator is mounted aft of the seat on the PC's console. A portable oxygen cylinder and regulator assembly (figure 1-14) can be stowed beneath the PC's seat and should be carried if operations require a crewmember to be away from an oxygen outlet. The portable cylinder has a capacity (figure 1-49) of 96 cubic inches and must be removed from the aircraft for filling.

Each oxygen regulator automatically mixes varying quantities of air and oxygen in ratios proportionate to the altitude up to 30,000±2000 feet, and delivers the quantity demanded upon inhalation. Above 35,000 feet, the regulators automatically supply 100-percent oxygen under positive pressure. A flow indicator and oxygen cylinder pressure gage are incorporated in each regulator.

Due to limiting features of oxygen regulator, do not exceed 43,000 feet cabin pressure altitude except during operational emergencies.

Liquid Oxygen System

The liquid oxygen converter unit (figure 1-52), located in the forward equipment compartment beneath the pilot's floor, contains an insulated storage tank with a nominal capacity of 8 liters. However, the total supply that can be placed in the system is 9.5 liters, utilizing additional space in the converter. Duration time of the oxygen supply is calculated on 8 liters only (figure 1-48), allowing for evaporation over a 24-hour period.

In later aircraft[1] the liquid oxygen system consists of two 10-liter interconnected, liquid oxygen tanks, check valves, relief valves, filler valves, shutoff valves, regulators, associated piping, and a quantity gage. The two insulated tanks (figure 1-52) are mounted in the aft compartment. Access to the aft compartment is through a door in the lower fuselage. Individual filler valves for each tank are located in the aft compartment. Evaporation of the liquid oxygen is constant when the system is not in use and this evaporation loss is used to pressurize the system. By venting any excess pressure overboard through relief valves, pressure is kept below 112 psig. When

---
[1] Aircraft BuNo. 138902 and subsequent.

the system is being used, liquid oxygen flows through noninsulated lines in the aft compartment and between the converter and the cockpit. As it flows, the liquid oxygen warms and changes to gaseous oxygen.

CAUTION

The following instructions must be followed to prevent malfunction or contamination of the liquid oxygen system:

1. Liquid oxygen converter should be left in buildup condition with supply valve in OFF position, except when filling system.

2. Liquid oxygen system must not be permitted to go dry and be exposed to surrounding atmosphere. If converter system is exposed, water vapor or other gases may condense in the liquid oxygen bottle causing malfunction of system valves or odors in oxygen supply.

3. If liquid oxygen quantity has become nearly depleted and aircraft remains for over 2 hours without refilling, maintenance crew should purge system with dry oxygen prior to further use.

WARNING

Liquid oxygen can injure the skin on contact. When oxygen storage tank is being filled, stay clear of overflow vent on bottom side of fuselage aft of aft compartment access door.

The liquid oxygen quantity gage (figure 1-4) is located on the pilot's instrument panel. A capacitance transmitter mounted on the storage tank is used to measure the liquid level in the tank. The gage registers the amount of liquid oxygen in the following calibrations: F (full), 3/4, 1/2, 1/4, and E (empty). When the supply system is serviced in excess of 8 liters, the gage will read F until the quantity decreases to less than 8, which is the capacity of the storage tank. In later aircraft[1] the liquid oxygen quantity gage is calibrated to 20 liters.

Oxygen System Controls (Panel-Mounted Regulator)

OXYGEN AIR VALVE

In the NORMAL OXYGEN position of the oxygen air valve knob, diluted oxygen is supplied upon demand.

----
[1] Aircraft BuNo. 138902 and subsequent

The amount of dilution depends upon cabin altitude up to 30,000 feet, above which altitude 100 percent oxygen is supplied. Turning the control to 100 % OXYGEN supplies undiluted oxygen upon demand, regardless of altitude.

OXYGEN SUPPLY VALVE

An OXYGEN SUPPLY shutoff valve is incorporated in each oxygen regulator. The valve is installed to provide a positive shutoff between the oxygen supply cylinders and the normal regulator controls. Be careful to ensure the valve being OPEN prior to each flight. Upon completion of each flight, turn the shutoff valve to OFF.

During flight, make sure the companionway oxygen regulator's OXYGEN SUPPLY valve is OFF when the regulator is not in use.

CAUTION

On early aircraft there is a possibility of the oxygen supply valve being inadvertently positioned to OFF when the nosewheel steering handle is actuated.

SAFETY PRESSURE CONTROL

A manual safety pressure control is also located on the face of the regulator. When the safety pressure control is placed in the ON position, breathing volume will be delivered at a slight positive pressure, thus permitting a pressure buildup in the mask to prevent air leakage into the mask. Since positive pressure is supplied automatically at altitudes above 35,000 feet, the utility of the safety pressure control is for emergency at lower altitudes only. Routine use of safety pressure reduces the effectiveness of the air dilution and causes increased oxygen consumption. However, if anoxia is suspected, the safety pressure control should be used. The Type A-13A mask must be used with this regulator in order to gain full benefit of the safety pressure feature.

NOTE

At cabin pressure altitudes above 35,000 feet when the regulator is delivering automatic positive pressure, the oxygen flow indicator will remain in the open position. In this case, proper operation of the regulator can be readily determined by "feeling" the positive pressure against the face.

LIQUID OXYGEN DURATION
8-Liter System

MAN HOURS PER GAGE READING

Cabin Pressure Altitude Feet	Air Valve	Liquid Oxygen Quantity Gage			
		Full	3/4 Full	1/2 Full	1/4 Full
40,000	Normal	48.2	36.4	24.2	12.1
	100% Oxygen	48.5	36.4	24.2	12.0
35,000	Normal	29.6	22.2	14.8	7.4
	100% Oxygen	29.6	22.2	14.8	7.4
30,000	Normal	21.7	16.3	10.9	5.4
	100% Oxygen	21.8	16.4	10.8	5.4
25,000	Normal	28.8	21.6	14.4	7.2
	100% Oxygen	16.4	12.4	8.2	4.0
20,000	Normal	48.2	36.4	24.2	12.1
	100% Oxygen	12.8	9.6	6.4	3.2
15,000	Normal	56.0	42.0	28.1	14.1
	100% Oxygen	10.2	7.2	5.2	2.6
10,000	Normal	63.0	47.2	31.4	15.7
	100% Oxygen	8.0	6.0	4.0	2.0
5000	Normal	53.4	40.0	27.4	13.3
	100% Oxygen	6.6	5.0	3.2	1.6
Sea Level	Normal				
	100% Oxygen	5.6	4.2	2.8	1.4

REMARKS:

(1) Based on 800 liters of gaseous oxygen per liter of liquid oxygen.
(2) Data assume the use of a properly fitted mask.

DATA AS OF: 15 October 1957

DATA BASIS: Specification MIL-I-19326(WEPS) taken from NAVWEPS 03-50-517

Aircraft BuNo. 135407-135444
Figure 1-48. Liquid Oxygen Duration (Sheet 1)

AUTOPILOT

The Sperry S-5 autopilot is electrically controlled and receives signals from the directional gyro for control about the yaw axis. Lateral and longitudinal control is supplied by the vertical gyro.

The Sperry S-5 gyropilot system is a standard autopilot which has been modified to provide damping about the aircraft yaw axis when the aircraft is under manual control and for automatic longitudinal trim control through the aircraft horizontal stabilizer trim actuator. The autopilot is completely electrical and in automatic flight is controlled directionally by the directional gyro, which furnishes simultaneous signals to the autopilot and gyrosyn compass repeater indicator, and laterally and longitudinally by a vertical gyro. In addition, the aircraft can be controlled manually through the autopilot by use of the pedestal controller (figure 1-50) which is mounted on a swinging arm.

LIQUID OXYGEN DURATION

Cabin Pressure Altitude Feet	MAN HOURS REMAINING GAGE READING (LITERS)									
	20	18	16	14	12	10	8	6	4	2
40,000	121.2	109.1	97.0	84.8	72.6	60.6	48.5	36.4	24.2	12.0
35,000	74.0	66.6	59.2	51.8	44.4	37.0	29.6	22.2	14.8	7.4
30,000	54.4	49.0	43.6	28.0	32.6	27.2	21.8	16.4	10.8	5.4
25,000	40.8	36.8	32.8	28.6	24.4	20.4	16.4	12.4	8.2	4.0
20,000	32.0	28.8	25.6	22.4	19.2	16.0	12.8	9.6	6.4	3.2
15,000	25.6	23.0	20.4	18.0	15.4	12.8	10.2	7.6	5.2	2.6
10,000	20.0	18.0	16.0	14.0	12.0	10.0	8.0	6.0	4.0	2.0
8000	18.8	16.8	15.0	13.0	11.2	9.4	7.4	5.6	3.7	1.8
Sea Level	14.0	12.6	11.2	9.8	8.4	7.0	5.6	4.2	2.8	1.4

REMARKS:

(1) Based on 800 liters of gaseous oxygen per liter of liquid oxygen.
(2) Data assume the use of a properly fitted mask.

DATA AS OF: 15 October 1957

DATA BASIS: Specification MIL-I-19326(WEPS) taken from NAVWEPS 03-50-517

Aircraft BuNo. 138902 and Subsequent
Figure 1-48. Liquid Oxygen Duration (Sheet 2)

For use, the pedestal is swung forward from a recessed position in the side of the PC's seat to a position at the lower left of the center console. The pedestal controller receives electrical power through the YAW DAMPER switch on the S-5 PILOT COMPASS panel (figures 1-6 through 1-8) on the pilot's left-hand console.

Coordinated turns, climbs, dives, climbing turns, and diving turns are accomplished through the use of the pedestal controller. A signal system alines itself continuously with the attitude of the aircraft so that the autopilot may be engaged with the aircraft in any normal flight attitude except a turn. Electrical and mechanical interlocks are provided so that the autopilot cannot be turned on and engaged unless the proper engaging procedure is followed. When engaged, the autopilot will maintain without change the attitude and heading which existed at the time of engagement. The aircraft can be returned to manual control by methods described under Autopilot Engaging and Disengaging Controls.

Automatic Trimming

Automatic trimming of the horizontal stabilizer provides continuous trim about the pitch axis. Trimming the aircraft, therefore, after maneuvers or autopilot-controlled flight of long duration is not necessary. The aircraft should be trimmed manually, however, for "hands off" flight before engaging the autopilot. After engagement, changes in trim about the yaw and roll axes must not be corrected by any means except the autopilot. An out-of-trim condition about any axis is indicated visually to the pilot by the trim signal indicators on the pedestal controller. A sustained small deflection of the elevator trim signal indicator does not signify a malfunction of the automatic trim. As an out-of-trim condition develops, the autopilot corrects with elevator deflection until the signal required reaches a preset value. Automatic trim occurs at this point.

Autopilot Pedestal Controller

The autopilot pedestal controller (figure 1-50) incorporates controls for turning the autopilot on or off and

GASEOUS OXYGEN DURATION

MINUTES ON ONE 96-CUBIC INCH PORTABLE CYLINDER

Cabin Altitude Feet	Air Valve	Gage Pressure PSI								
		1800	1600	1400	1200	1000	800	600	400	Below 300
30,000	NORMAL	44	38	31	26	20	15	9	2	Operationally Empty
	100% Oxygen	44	38	31	26	20	15	9	2	
25,000	NORMAL	50	42	37	30	23	17	9	3	
	100% Oxygen	30	26	21	18	13	10	6	2	
20,000	NORMAL	56	52	45	37	29	20	12	3	
	100% Oxygen	21	19	16	12	10	7	4	1	
15,000	NORMAL	69	60	50	41	32	23	13	4	
	100% Oxygen	16	13	11	9	7	6	3	1	
10,000	NORMAL	68	58	49	40	31	22	13	4	
	100% Oxygen	12	10	9	7	6	3	2	1	
5000	NORMAL	50	44	37	30	24	18	10	3	
	100% Oxygen	8	7	6	4	3	2	1	1	

REMARKS:

The altitude indicated by the cabin altimeter must be used for all oxygen duration calculations.

Figure 1-49. Gaseous Oxygen Duration – Portable Cylinder

for maneuvering the aircraft. The PILOT-YAW DAMPER switch on the front face of the controller has two positions, PILOT and YAW DAMPER. (Refer to YAW DAMPING SYSTEM.) Turning the switch to the PILOT position provides electrical power to the autopilot if the YAW DAMPER switch on the pilot's left-hand console is ON. Rotating the AIL control knob clockwise or counterclockwise from the centering or neutral mark adjusts the lateral reference point for the autopilot and will result in a right or left wing down action. The ALT CONT switch on the pedestal controller permits the pilot to maintain a specific pressure altitude as long as desired. Placing the switch in the ALT CONT position during a climb or descent will tend to make the aircraft level off and hold pressure altitude.

CAUTION

Level aircraft prior to turning on ALT CONT, if aircraft is in a climb. If altitude control is turned on during climb, aircraft tends to overshoot desired altitude momentarily, which may damage bellows in altitude-sensing mechanism.

Returning the switch to the OFF position will not affect the level flight attitude thus assumed, since the automatic trim feature of the autopilot will have trimmed out the original climb or descent trim within 20 seconds. Attain the desired cruising altitude and attitude before turning on the altitude control. Of further note is that altitude will be maintained during turns.

Pitch control knobs are mounted on each side of the controller and provide control of pitch attitude. Interlocks prevent the pitch control knobs from having effect while the ALT CONT switch is in the ALT CONT position. The TURN knob on the top of the controller provides directional control. Rotating the knob out of the centering detent in the desired direction of turn applies both aileron and rudder into the turn, resulting in coordinated turns at any airspeed. Rate of turn depends upon the degree of rotation of the TURN knob from the center position.

AUTOPILOT ENGAGING AND DISENGAGING CONTROLS

The autopilot is engaged by using the AUTOPILOT switches on the lower center console (figure 1-9).

The left-hand switch, labeled RUDDER, is used to engage the rudder only, and the right-hand switch, labeled ELEVATOR AILERON, engages both the elevators and ailerons. The ELEVATOR AILERON switch cannot be moved to the ENGAGE position unless the PILOT-YAW DAMPER switch on the pedestal controller is in the PILOT position. The RUDDER and ELEVATOR-AILERON switches will not lock in the ENGAGE position unless they are engaged simultaneously. The PILOT-YAW DAMPER switch cannot be moved to the PILOT position unless the YAW DAMPER switch on the left-hand console is in the ON position.

NOTE

The YAW DAMPER switch, which is a master switch for the AUTOPILOT, is always spring loaded to the OFF position when the aircraft is on the ground. In order to preflight the autopilot, it is necessary for the pilot to hold the YAW DAMPER switch in the ON position.

The autopilot is disengaged by turning the PILOT-YAW DAMPER switch on the controller to YAW DAMPER or, in an emergency, by pressing the electrical GYROPILOT REL switch on the pilot's control wheel. The GYROPILOT REL switch also releases the yaw damper.

YAW DAMPING SYSTEM

Automatic yaw damping, through control of the rudder alone, is provided to increase the aircraft directional stability during manual flight. This is effected by making rudder servo movement a function of the rate of change of the aircraft heading, which is sensed by two accelerometers, one located in the aft fuselage and one located in the flight compartment.

If an uncoordinated maneuver is to be performed, the yaw damping system can be overpowered by rudder pedal pressure exceeding 25±10 pounds. The yaw damping system can be engaged when the aircraft is on the ground only by holding the YAW DAMPER switch in ON and placing the RUDDER switch in ENGAGE. The system is disengaged by placing the YAW DAMPER switch on the pilot's left-hand console off, which automatically causes the RUDDER switch to fall to DISENGAGE. Yaw damping may be released in an emergency by pressing the GYROPILOT REL switch on the control wheel.

TO ENGAGE YAW DAMPER:

1. Left-hand console YAW DAMPER switch . . . . ON

2. Center console RUDDER servo switch . . . . ON

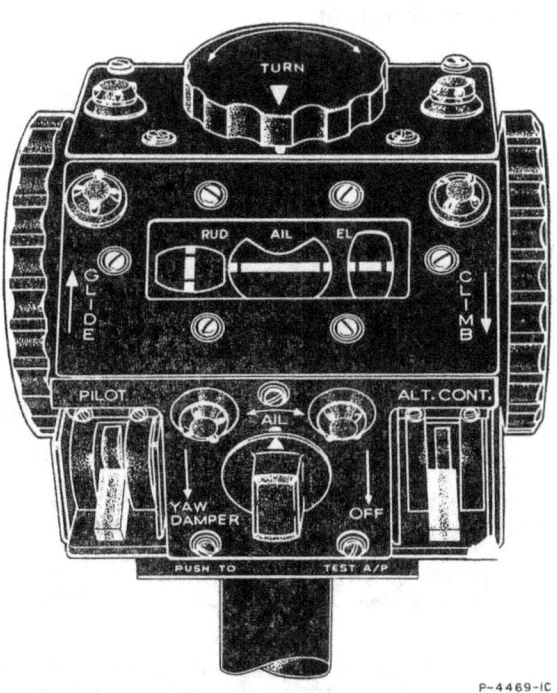

Figure 1-50. Autopilot Pedestal Controller

TO DISENGAGE YAW DAMPER

1. Move YAW DAMPER switch, S-5 PILOT COMPASS panel, to OFF, or

2. Move RUDDER servo switch to OFF, or

3. Move TURN knob, autopilot pedestal controller, out of detent position, or

4. Press GYROPILOT REL switch on pilot's control wheel.

NOTE

If the yaw damper is engaged when the aircraft is brought in for a landing, the yaw damper will be turned off automatically by the landing gear retraction release relay upon right main gear shock strut compression.

1-123

To Engage Autopilot

CAUTION

Do not engage the rudder servoswitch while aircraft is in a turn.

In the following procedure, engaging of the yaw damper switch is included because it is an integral part of the autopilot system. If the yaw damper has previously been engaged, steps 1 and 3 may be disregarded:

1. TURN knob, pedestal controller .... Centered

2. AIL knob, pedestal controller...... Centered

3. YAW DAMPER switch, S-5 PILOT COMPASS panel................. ON

4. PILOT-YAW DAMPER switch, pedestal controller................ PILOT

If the YAW DAMPER was previously engaged, placing the PILOT-YAW DAMPER switch in the PILOT position will cause the RUDDER servoswitch to drop to the OFF position.

5. Trim aircraft manually with normal trim controls and check to see that trim meters on pedestal controller are approximately in their neutral position. (Allow up to 20 seconds for loss of transmit signal.)

6. RUDDER and ELEVATOR AILERON servoswitches, simultaneously move to....... ENGAGE

OPERATION

1. Use pitch knobs on sides of pedestal controller to make climbs or descents.

2. Use TURN knob to perform coordinated turns.

3. Use AIL knob during straight and level flight to keep wings level.

4. Use ALT CONT switch to maintain constant pressure altitude.

NOTE

With the ALT CONT switch in the ALT CONT position, the pitch knobs are inoperative.

To Disengage Autopilot

1. Move PILOT-YAW DAMPER switch, autopilot pedestal controller, to YAW DAMPER, or

2. Move YAW DAMPER switch, S-5 PILOT COMPASS panel, to off position, or

3. Move either RUDDER, or ELEVATOR AILERON servoswitch to DISENGAGE, or

4. Press GYROPILOT REL switch on pilot's control wheel.

EMERGENCY PROCEDURE

In the event of any autopilot system emergency, such as erratic operation or horizontal stabilizer trim runaway, the pilot should overpower and disengage the autopilot as follows:

1. GYROPILOT REL BUTTON..... PRESS

The pilot must retrim the aircraft by using the

2. HORIZONTAL STABILIZER THUMB SWITCH .... NOSEUP or NOSEDOWN

If this does not immediately reverse the direction of trim:

1. Rotate center console horizontal stabilizer trim knob to full travel (ac) position in desired direction.

If this method is not effective, break the horizontal stabilizer actuator ac and dc trim circuits as follows:

2. HORIZONTAL STABILIZER ACTUATOR GANGBAR .... EMER OFF

If necessary to regain stabilizer trim prior to landing, place dc EMER OFF switch in ON and trim with the center console horizontal stabilizer trim knob.

Altitude Hold Operation

Certain conditions may permit a constant-rate loss or gain of altitude during autopilot operation in the altitude during autopilot operation in the altitude hold mode. The altitude transducer will saturate if the aircraft pitch attitude at engagement is 4.8 degrees greater or less than the level flight pitch attitude. To counter this, the recommended practice is to attain a level-flight attitude at the desired cruising altitude before engaging the altitude mode, and to avoid large airspeed variation after engagement. A loss of altitude may occur during turns even when in the altitude hold mode; however, this is prevalent only near the top of the flight envelope.

Emergency Procedures

HARDOVER FAILURES

Hardover failures are indicated by abrupt movement of flight controls and by g forces. Because hardovers are limited in magnitude by saturation of the autopilot amplifier, they can be overpowered by the pilot. Maximum manual overpowering forces are 90 pounds in the rudder channel, 60 pounds in the aileron channel, and 45 pounds in the elevator channel. Moreover, an aileron limit switch automatically disengages the autopilot whenever the single aileron deflection exceeds 10 degrees.

PITCH TRIM FAILURES

An automatic pitch trim failure can cause the horizontal stabilizer to become inoperative or to run away. An inoperative horizontal stabilizer reduces the capability of the longitudinal channel to maintain attitude through varying flight conditions, such as airspeed or cg changes. A loss of altitude may result. The horizontal stabilizer runs away at 0.05 degree per second. The autopilot will compensate for this runaway to the limit of its output torque (45 pounds at the control column); then, the aircraft will respond slowly to the horizontal stabilizer movement. The pilot should immediately correct the aircraft attitude and disengage the autopilot. Disengagement will stop this type of stabilizer runaway. The pilot should attempt to retrim the aircraft with the pitch trim button.

If this method is not effective, break the horizontal stabilizer actuator ac or dc trim circuits as follows:

1. Horizontal stabilizer actuator gangbar . . . . EMER OFF

Reenergize each trim circuit, in turn, to determine which circuit is functioning properly.

2. DC TRIM SWITCH . . . . ON

If this action alleviates the malfunction, the remaining sequence will not be necessary. If the malfunction continues, proceed as follows:

1. DC TRIM switch . . . . EMER OFF

2. AC TRIM switch . . . . ON

If the ac trim system is functioning properly, trim the aircraft and leave the malfunctioning circuit open for the remainder of the flight.

Autopilot Use Following Boost Disconnect

The autopilot may be used with the control boost disconnected to prevent pilot fatigue; however, the rate of response will be slow. In calm air cruising, no problem will be encountered, as control inputs will be of small magnitude. Turbulence should be avoided, as the autopilot will not be capable of the greater control deflections required. Response of the aircraft to control inputs will be rather sloppy. Since the autopilot is designed for saturation loads, it will not be damaged when used with boost disconnected.

NAVIGATION EQUIPMENT

Slaved Gyro Magnetic Compass System

The slaved gyro magnetic compass system is similar to the S-2 gyrosyn compass system in principle and operation. In addition to providing a visual indication of the heading of the aircraft, the compass system is integrated into the S-5 automatic pilot. The compass system consists of a magnetic flux valve, amplifier, directional gyro, compass controller, and a repeater indicator. In addition to its normal function as a gyro-stabilized magnetic compass, the system may be used as a free directional gyro indicator and/or the directional control component of the S-5 automatic pilot system.

COMPASS CONTROLLER

The S-5 PILOT COMPASS controller (figure 1-7) is located on the pilot's left-hand console and consists of a SLAVED GYRO-FREE GYRO selector switch, a SET HDG FREE GYRO switch, a SYNC SIGNAL indicator, and a YAW DAMPER switch. The SLAVED GYRO-FREE GYRO switch has two positions, SLAVED GYRO and FREE GYRO. In the SLAVED GYRO position of the switch, the gyroscope is automatically slaved to the position of the magnetic flux valve and, once correctly set, will indicate the actual magnetic heading of the aircraft on the pilot's repeater compass indicator (figure 1-4). If incorrectly set, the gyroscope automatically precesses toward the correct magnetic heading at a slaving rate of approximately 90 degrees per minute during the first 2 or 3 minutes after ac and dc electrical power is supplied to the system. After this time, interlocks and relays operate to reduce the automatic slaving rate to approximately 3 degrees per minute for any subsequent deviations between the gyroscope and the flux valve. With the switch in the FREE GYRO position, the gyroscope is not slaved to the flux valve and operates as a free directional gryo. During this operating condition the compass repeater indicator shows the position of the directional gyroscope and no indication of the magnetic heading of the aircraft is available, except by reference to the standby compass mounted on the canopy above the glare shield. In addition, with the SLAVED GYRO-FREE GYRO switch in the FREE GYRO position, the gyroscope may be manually slaved to the magnetic heading of the aircraft at a slaving rate of 90 degrees per minute by use of the SET HDG FREE GYRO switch. Positions of the switch are INC and DEC. With the SET HDG FREE GYRO switch in the INC position, the dial card on the compass repeater indicator will move upscale (increase heading) and the SYNC SIGNAL indicator needle will move toward the right. With the SET HDG FREE GYRO switch in the DEC position, the dial care on the compass repeater indicator will move downscale (decrease heading) and the SYNC SIGNAL indicator needle will move toward the left. When the SLAVED GYRO-FREE GYRO switch is in the SLAVED GYRO position, the SET HDG FREE GYRO switch is inoperative. For information regarding the function and use of the YAW damper switch, refer to Automatic Pilot.

GYROSYN COMPASS OPERATIONAL CHECK

Immediately after energizing aircraft ac and dc electrical power, perform the following:

1. WINGS . . . . SPREAD

2. SLAVED GYRO-FREE GYRO switch . . . . SLAVED GYRO

3. Observe that compass repeater indicator moves toward actual magnetic heading of aircraft at slaving rate of 60 to 90 degrees per minute.

4. When compass card on repeater stops rotating, observe that SYNC SIGNAL indicator needle is centered.

5. SLAVED GYRO-FREE GYRO switch . . . . FREE GYRO

6. SET HDG FREE GYRO switch. . INC

7. Observe that compass repeater card moves upscale (counterclockwise) at 60 to 90 degrees per minute and that SYNC SIGNAL indicator needle moves to right.

8. SET HDG FREE GYRO switch. . DEC

9. Observe that compass repeater card moves downscale (clockwise) at 60 to 90 degrees per minute and that SYNC SIGNAL indicator needle moves to left.

10. Release SET HDG FREE GYRO switch when SYNC SIGNAL indicator needle is centered.

11. SLAVED GYRO-FREE GYRO switch . . . . SLAVED GYRO

NOTE

A 60- to 90-degree slaving rate in SLAVE position will occur for the first 2 minutes after power is applied. After 2 minutes a 2- to 30-degree minimum slaving rate is used.

NORMAL OPERATION

For field takeoff, flight, and landing, place the SLAVED GYRO-FREE GYRO switch in SLAVED GYRO. For carrier-based operations, due to shipboard magnetic disturbances, perform the following:

1. SLAVED GYRO-FREE GYRO switch . . . . FREE GYRO

2. Manually slave the gyro to the estimated heading of the aircraft by placing the SET HDG FREE GYRO switch in INC or DEC as required. Make no effort to center the SYNC SIGNAL indicator needle.

3. After wings are spread, manually slave gyroscope to flux valve by placing SET HDG FREE GYRO switch in INC or DEC as required until SYNC SIGNAL indicator needle is centered on index mark.

4. SLAVED GYRO-FREE GYRO switch . . . . SLAVED

NOTE

Operation of the SET HDG FREE GYRO switch with the SLAVED GYRO-FREE GYRO switch in the FREE GYRO position with either the yaw damper or the automatic pilot engaged will release the AUTOPILOT servo engage switches.

NAVAIR 01-40ATA-1

Section I
Part 2

BOMB BAY

- Opening and closing of bomb bay doors poses an extremely hazardous problem. Therefore, it is mandatory that all signals between outside observers and the cockpit be given and acted upon only by qualified A-3 personnel.

- Only qualified A-3 plane captains or crewmembers will initiate signals from outside observer's position. Before any signals are given, the outside observer will first ensure that all personnel are well clear of the limits of travel of the bomb bay doors. In addition, a second observer should be stationed on the opposite side of the aircraft within line of sight of the controlling observer. The pilot, after receiving an actuation signal from the outside observer, shall personally sight all crewmembers prior to actuating the bomb bay door switch.

Bomb Bay Doors

The bomb bay doors are normally actuated by utility hydraulic system pressure through a solenoid-operated selector valve. The solenoid, located on the companionway hydraulics panel, may be manually operated in case of bomb doors switch or solenoid failure. The bomb doors switch must be operated normally after the valve is positioned. The doors normally require 1 1/2 seconds, using both hydraulic systems or approximately 20 seconds using the emergency system only, to open or close. Emergency operation of the doors is through hydraulic pressure supplied by the utility hydraulic system and/or electrically driven emergency hydraulic pump. The doors may be operated automatically through the bombing equipment. The bomb doors are provided with adjustable ground safety locks located at each of the forward bomb bay door actuating cylinders. The safety locks, normally stowed and held in a vertical position by clips, may be swiveled down from the stowed position and placed against the door arm elbows to secure the doors during loading.

The bomb door safety locks must be installed and adjusted in the safety position during all ground operations.

NOTE

Operation of the bomb bay doors with the electrically driven emergency hydraulic pump requires that dc power be supplied to the PRIMARY DC BUS. If the ATM's are not operating, either the battery switch must be actuated (BATT or EMER) or external power must be supplied.

BOMB BAY DOORS CONTROL

The bomb bay doors are controlled by positioning the guarded three-position BOMB DOORS switch (figure 1-9) on the lower center console. The OPEN and CLOSED positions of the BOMB DOORS switch provide the pilot with control of the doors. The AUTO position was deactivated by removal of the AN/ASB-1A bomb director set. A warning light (figure 1-9) located immediately below the BOMB DOORS switch, comes on when the doors are in a position other than fully open or fully closed. The bomb bay doors will reverse direction at any point of travel by moving the BOMB DOORS switch momentarily to the opposite marked position.

BOMB DOORS WARNING HORN

A warning horn is provided to warn personnel of the imminent opening or closing of the bomb bay doors. The horn is controlled by the BOMB BAY WARNING HORN pushbutton (figure 1-9) on the lower center console.

The horn must be sounded prior to every operation of the bomb bay doors.

JET-ASSISTED TAKEOFF SYSTEM

A 12-bottle JATO system is installed to provide the aircraft with additional thrust during takeoff. Six MK 7 Mod 2 5KS-4500 JATO units (15° nozzle) or six MK 7 Mod 1 5KS-4500 JATO units (30° nozzle) may be mounted on each side of the fuselage aft of the bomb bay (figure 1-2). Combinations of 2, 4, 6, or 12 units may be utilized depending on the operational demand as shown in JATO Firing Delay and Minimum Takeoff Distance, Section XI, and figures 11-11 through 11-26. Each bottle is capable of producing 4500 pounds of thrust for 5 seconds. The bottles are fired electrically and are jettisoned hydraulically

1-127

by utility hydraulic system pressure applied through a solenoid-operated selector valve.

The MK 7 Mod 2 JATO units may be used in lieu of MK 7 Mod 1 JATO units with established operating parameters and safety precautions applicable. Partial JATO loading stations for both Mod 1 and 2 are the same: two JATO units — station 3, four JATO units — stations 2 and 3, and six JATO units — stations 2, 3, and 4. JATO takeoff with MK 7 Mod 2 bottles may require very slight reduction in trim setting from MK 7 Mod 1 standards to alleviate pitchup. This trim reduction setting is 1 unit for a 12-bottle takeoff. During takeoff, pilots should use nosewheel steering for initial seconds of JATO firing.

To prevent possible JATO accidents, the JATO arming switch in the cockpit must be in SAFE and a no-voltage test should be made at all aircraft igniter terminals prior to attaching the JATO igniter leads.

JATO Arming Switch

The JATO arming switch (figure 1-9) is located on the lower center console. The switch has two positions: ARM and SAFE. In the ARM position the switch energizes a limit switch in the catapult handgrip which, when turned to the horizontal position, energizes the JATO firing switch in the end of the handgrip.

JATO WARNING LIGHT

A warning light (figure 1-9), located directly below the JATO ARM-SAFE switch, comes on when the arming limit switch is energized. The light also serves as a preflight check of the JATO arming and firing circuit, since the light is wired in series with the JATO circuit breaker and current limiter. On later aircraft, the JATO warning light is located on the pilot's annunciator panel.

JATO FIRING SWITCH

The JATO firing switch (figure 1-9) is located in the end of the catapult handgrip. To fire the JATO bottles, move the catapult handle to a horizontal position and press the switch. This switch energizes a relay which completes a circuit between the firing mechanism and the dc primary bus.

JATO JETTISON SWITCH

The JATO jettison switch (figure 1-9) is located adjacent to the JATO arming switch on the lower center console. The switch has two positions: SAFE and JETTISON. In the JETTISON position the switch energizes a solenoid-controlled hydraulic selector valve which in turn supplies pressure to the JATO mounting hooks actuating cylinders. The mounting hooks are actuated to release all the JATO bottles simultaneously.

Catapult Equipment

The catapult hooks (figure 1-2) are located immediately forward of the bomb bay doors. Hook extension is accomplished by manually releasing the mechanical uplatch. Retraction is accomplished hydraulically as landing gear is raised. In later aircraft, retraction is simultaneous with tail bumper retraction.

The catapult holdback fitting is located at bottom center of the fuselage and at the aft end of the main gear well.

CATAPULT HANDGRIP

A catapult handgrip, located on the center console, enables the pilot to maintain a secure grasp on the throttles during a catapult takeoff. When the handgrip is moved to the horizontal position and the throttles are moved to the MILITARY position, they may be grasped together. The JATO firing control is incorporated in the handgrip.

FIRST AID KIT

A first aid kit (figure 1-13) is provided for emergency use. The kit is located in the aft part of the cockpit.

NAVAIR 01-40ATA-1

Section I
Part 3

PART 3
AIRCRAFT SERVICING

TABLE OF CONTENTS

TEXT

	Page
Introduction	1-129
Towing, Pushing, and Parking	1-129
Pressure Fueling and Defueling – Basic System	1-129
Safety Precautions	1-134
Pressure Fueling – Basic System	1-134
Pressure Defueling – Basic System	1-135
Fueling – Multiple Point	1-137
Pressure Fueling with Engines Operating (Hot Refueling)	1-140
Gravity Fueling – Procedures	1-140
Fuel Quantity Measurement	1-140
Fuel Measurement Stick	1-140
Oil System – Servicing	1-149
Servicing Engine Oil Tank	1-149
Hydraulic Reservoir Servicing	1-149
Brake System – Servicing	1-149
Master Brake System Reservoir – Filling and Bleeding	1-149
Power Brake Valves – Bleeding	1-149
Main Landing Gear Brake – Bleeding	1-152
Accumulator – Charging	1-153
Nose Gear Steering Accumulator	1-153
Brake Accumulator	1-153
Spoiler System Accumulators (Two)	1-153

	Page
Aileron System Accumulator	1-153
Emergency Air System – Servicing	1-153
Servicing Completely Empty Systems	1-153
Servicing Low Systems	1-153
ATM Oil Sump – Servicing	1-157
Oxygen System – Servicing	1-157
Filling Liquid Oxygen Converter – 8-Liter System	1-157
Filling Liquid Oxygen Converter – 20-Liter System	1-158
Emergency Oxygen Bottle	1-160
Oxygen System Check	1-160
Rain Repellent	1-160A
Rain Repellent Application	1-160A
Antifogging Compound	1-161
Antifogging Compound Application	1-161
Deicing-Defrosting Fluid	1-161
Deicing-Defrosting Fluid Application	1-161
Ground Support Starting Equipment	1-165
Engine-Mounted Starters	1-165
Danger Areas	1-165
Turning Radii	1-165
Securing Aircraft	1-165

TABLES

Table		Page
1-2	Fuel Capacity Data Pressure Fueling	1-135
1-3	Pressure Fueling and Defueling – Basic System	1-136
1-4	Fuel Float Valve and Shutoff Valve Test – Basic System	1-137
1-5	Deleted.	
1-6	Deleted.	

Table		Page
1-7	Deleted.	
1-7A	Guide to the Elimination of Ice, Snow or Frost from Parked Aircraft	1-162
1-7B	Deicing-Defrosting Fluid Application Precautionary Data	1-163
1-7C	Engine Mounted Starter – Operating Parameters	1-165

Changed 15 July 1970

1-128A

Section I
Part 3

NAVAIR 01-40ATA-1

ILLUSTRATIONS

Figure		Page	Figure		Page
1-51	Towing, Pushing, and Parking	1-130	1-59	Brake System – Servicing	1-152
1-52	Servicing Diagram	1-132	1-60	Accumulator – Charging	1-154
1-53	Pressure Fueling and Defueling – Basic System	1-138	1-61	Emergency Air Systems – Servicing	1-156
1-54	Deleted.		1-62	ATM Oil Sump – Servicing	1-158
1-55	Gravity Fueling	1-149	1-63	Oxygen System – Servicing	1-159
1-56	Fuel Quantity Measurement	1-150	1-64	Emergency Oxygen Bottle – Servicing	1-160A
1-57	Oil System – Servicing	1-150	1-65	Danger Areas	1-166
1-58	Hydraulic Systems – Servicing	1-151	1-66	Mooring	1-169

Changed 15 July 1970

INTRODUCTION

NOTE

The NATOPS Flight Manual is not intended as a maintenance manual. For detailed information, refer to the appropriate section of the applicable Handbook of Maintenance Instructions for the system desired.

The aircraft will be serviced by qualified maintenance personnel, and servicing will not require crew supervision. However, navigation flights, diversions, weather alternates, and NATO operations may require the use of various bases. Therefore, the crew must have a knowledge of aircraft servicing procedures sufficient to accomplish normal aircraft turnaround type servicing. Reference to the following procedures, and figure 1-52, should be sufficient to ensure proper aircraft servicing by transient maintenance personnel under the supervision of the pilot or one of the crewmembers. Detailed procedures for fueling (pressure and gravity) and defueling the aircraft are also included.

TOWING, PUSHING, AND PARKING

Towing and Pushing (figure 1-51)

CAUTION

Do not use nose gear towing if aircraft cannot be moved with normal effort. Instead, use cable bridle attached to main gear tiedown rings or arresting hook. Do not tow or push aircraft with one engine removed; overbalance can transmit excessive side loads to nose gear.

1. Install landing gear locking pins.

2. Disconnect nose gear torque link.

3. Verify that arresting hook is retracted and latched.

4. Attach tow bar with extension to nosewheel axle.

5. Verify that nose gear shock strut is extended sufficiently to provide clearance between nose gear door and tractor on turns.

6. Verify that brake accumulator pneumatic pressure is 400 psi and emergency hatch and brake pneumatic pressure is 2000 psi.

7. Connect source of electrical dc power to aircraft from towing tractor.

8. With emergency hydraulic pump circuit breaker engaged and EMER HYD switch on cockpit center console in ON position, apply brakes as required.

9. Station man in cockpit to operate brakes and a man at either wingtip to watch for clearance.

CAUTION

Operation of emergency hydraulic pump without external electric power will completely discharge battery within 4 minutes.

Parking (figure 1-51)

1. Head aircraft into the wind if possible.

2. Engage gust locks.

3. Install main and nose gear ground locking pins.

4. Chock wheels fore and aft.

5. Fold wings and fin, if desired.

NOTE

For applicable tiedown procedures, see figure 1-66.

CAUTION

Close cockpit enclosure and chute door at night and when washing aircraft. Install jury struts on aircraft when exposed to high wind velocities and jet blast.

PRESSURE FUELING AND DEFUELING — BASIC SYSTEM

General

JP-5 or JP-4 is recommended for all normal operations afloat and ashore. AVGAS is approved as an emergency fuel. For additional information, reference should be made to current Bureau of Naval Weapons directive on the utilization of aircraft fuels.

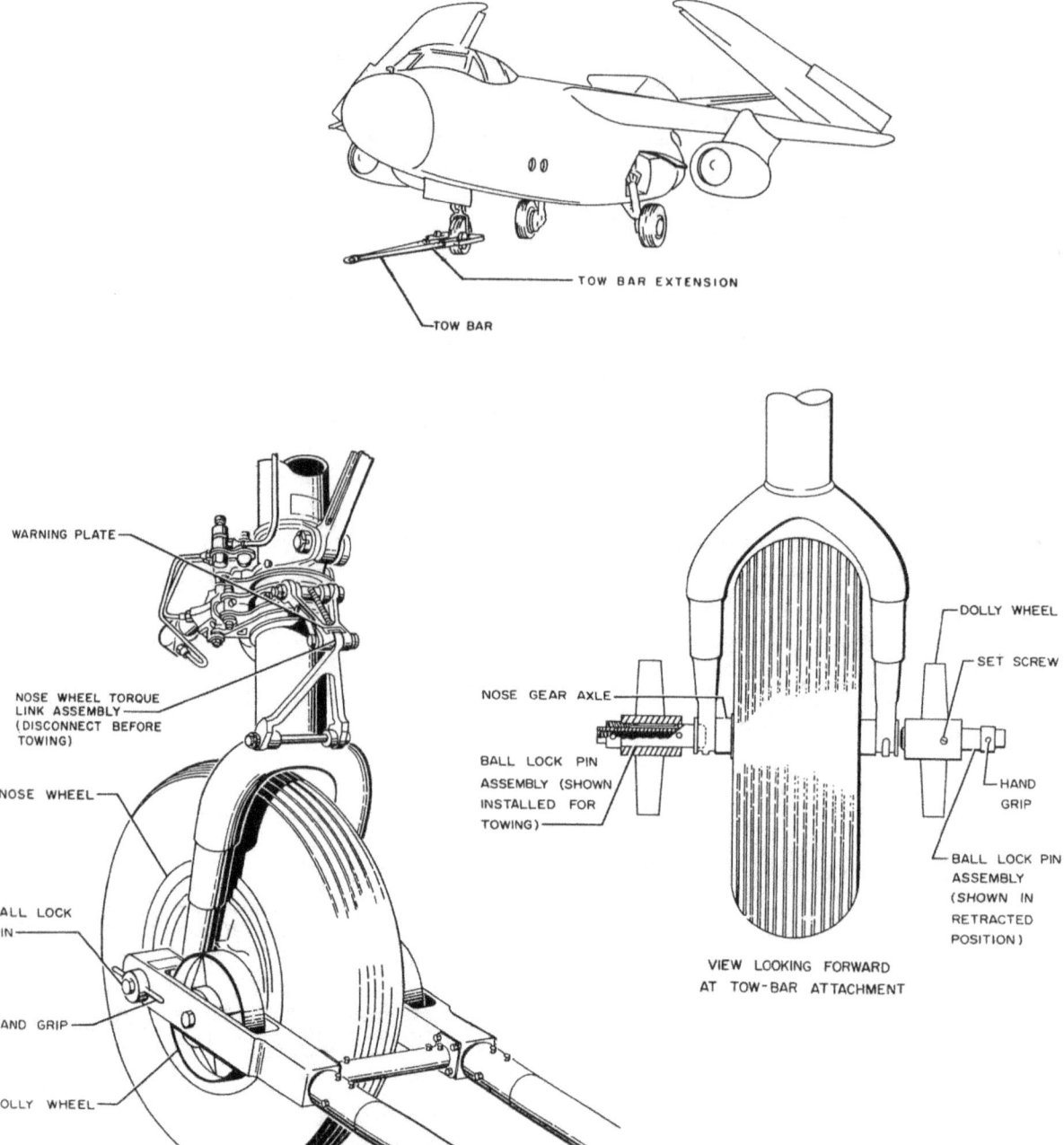

Figure 1-51. Towing, Pushing, and Parking (Sheet 1)

NAVAIR 01-40ATA-1

Section I
Part 3

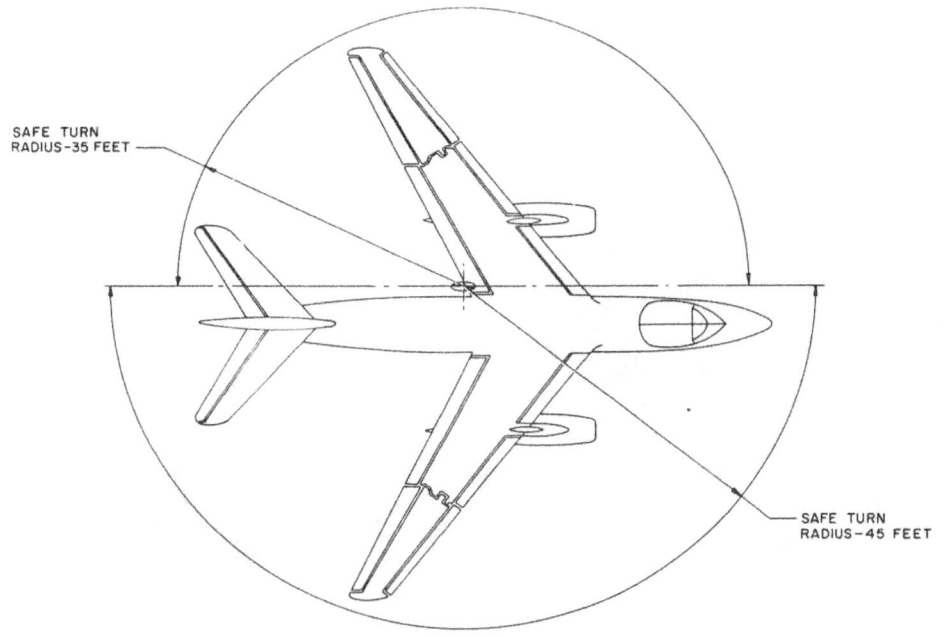

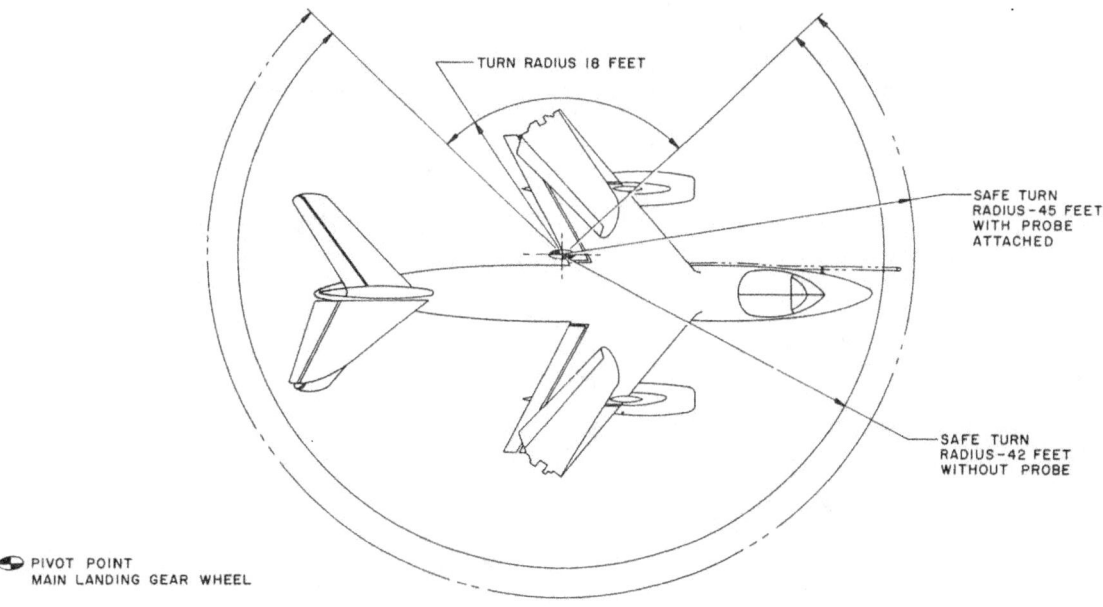

Figure 1-51. Towing, Pushing, and Parking (Sheet 2)

1-131

Section I
Part 3

NAVAIR 01-40ATA-1

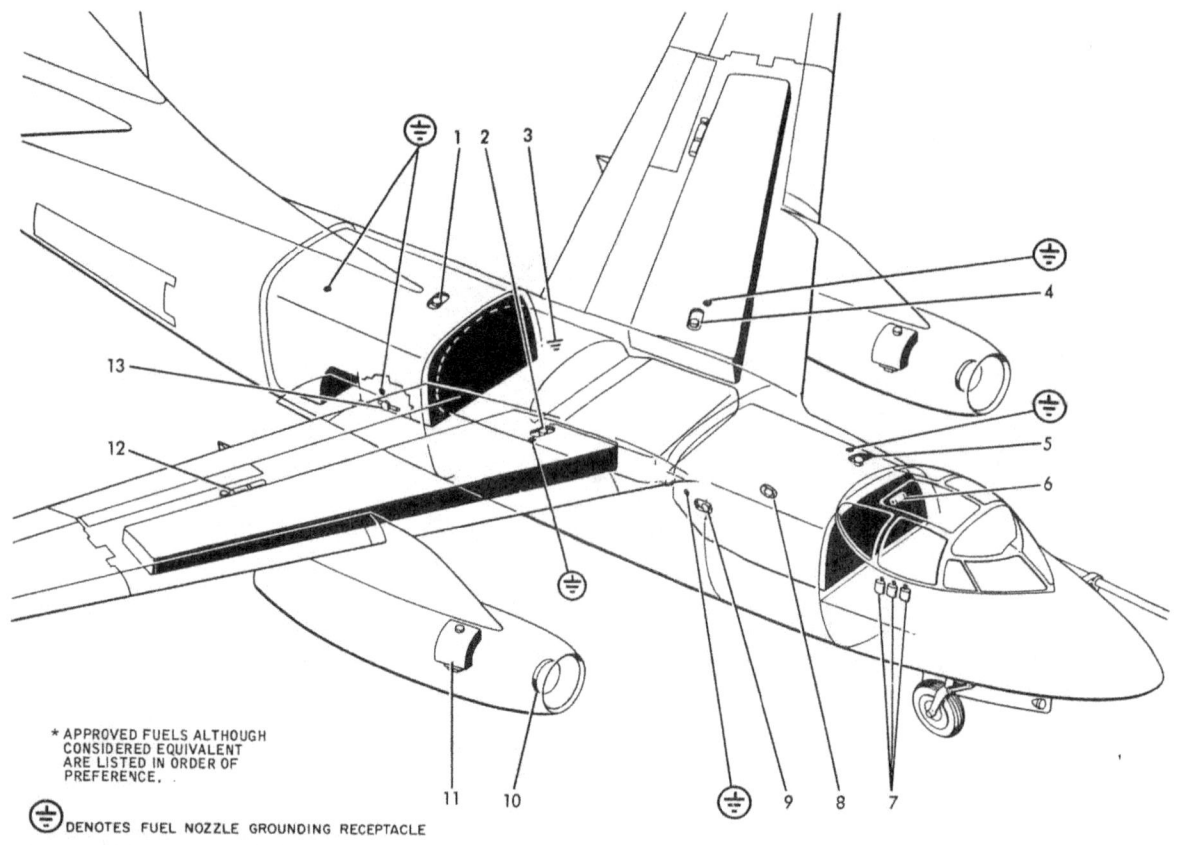

* APPROVED FUELS ALTHOUGH CONSIDERED EQUIVALENT ARE LISTED IN ORDER OF PREFERENCE.

⏚ DENOTES FUEL NOZZLE GROUNDING RECEPTACLE

KEY	UNIT DESCRIPTION	NORMAL CAPACITY PER UNIT	REPLENISHING SPECIFICATION		
1.	Aft fuel tank gravity filler	1928 U.S. gallons	Recommended	ASHORE	AFLOAT
2.	Right wing tank gravity filler	668 U.S. gallons	MIL-T-5624	JP-5	JP-5
3.	Auxiliary bomb bay tank	793 U.S. gallons	MIL-T-5624	JP-4	
4.	Left wing tank gravity filler	668 U.S. gallons	Emergency fuel	AVGAS	
5.	Forward fuel tank gravity filler	1225 U.S. gallons			
6.	Upper escape hatch/emergency brake and air bottle	2000 psi	Dry nitrogen		
7.	Canteens	1 quart	Drinking water		
8.	Fwd fuel tank press. fueling receptacle				
9.	Wing tanks pressure fueling receptacle				
10.	Engine oil cooler				
11.	Engine oil tank	5 1/2 U.S. gallons	MIL-L-23699 lubricating oil		
12.	Spoiler system accumulator and pressure gage	1000 psi			
13.	Aft fuel tank pressure fueling receptacle				

FF1-4466-M

Figure 1-52. Servicing Diagram (Sheet 1)

NAVAIR 01-40ATA-1

Section I
Part 3

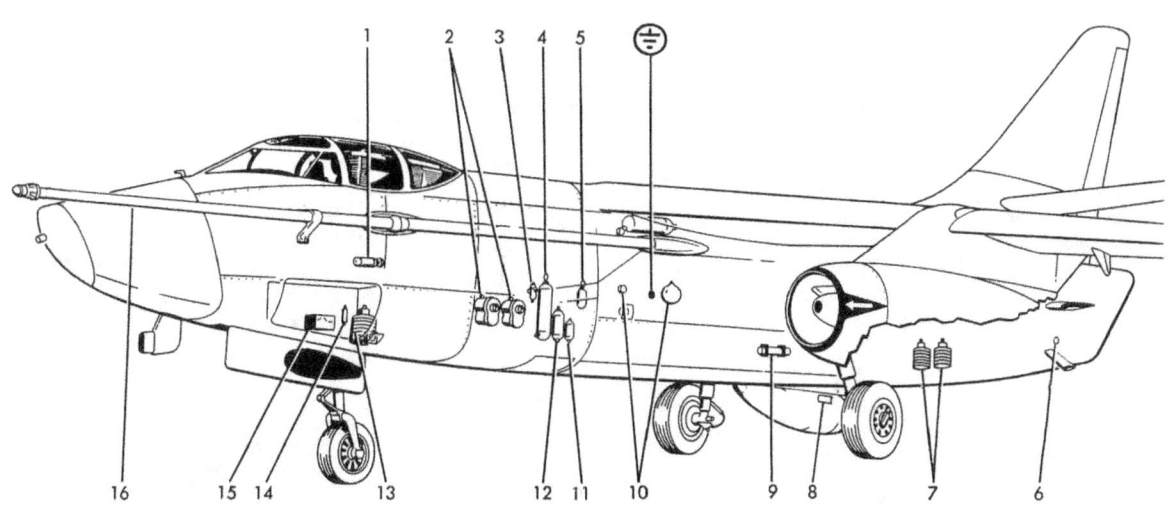

⊕ DENOTES FUEL NOZZLE GROUNDING RECEPTACLE

KEY	UNIT DESCRIPTION	NORMAL CAPACITY PER UNIT	REPLENISHING SPECIFICATION
1.	Portable oxygen bottle	96 cu in.	Dry breathing oxygen
2.	ATM's	2 to 2.6 quarts	MIL-L-6081 lube oil grade 1005 (-54°C. to -18°C.) MIL-L-6081 lube oil grade 1010 (-18°C. to +54°C.)
3.	Rudder-elevator boost reservoir	0.15(2) or 0.324(1) U S gallon	MIL-H-5606 hydraulic fluid
4.	Utility hydraulic system reservoir	5.8 U S gallons	MIL-H-5606 hydraulic fluid
5.	Aileron power boost reservoir	0.15(2) or 0.324 U S gallon	MIL-H-5606 hydraulic fluid
6.	Arresting hook holddown pressure gage	675 to 700 psi	
7.	Liquid oxygen converters and filler valve	20 liters (2)	Liquid oxygen
8.	Air refueling dump boom accumulator(2)	3000 psi	
9.	Antiskid brake system accumulator and pressure gage	400 psi	Dry nitrogen
10.	Landing gear doors air bottle and pressure gage	3000 psi	Dry nitrogen
11.	Emergency wing flaps air bottle	3000 psi	Dry nitrogen
12.	Emergency landing gear air bottle	3000 psi	Dry nitrogen
13.	Liquid oxygen converter and filler valve (1)	8 liters	Liquid oxygen
14.	Nosewheel steering accumulator	350 psi	Dry nitrogen
15.	Battery		Distilled water
16.	Air refueling probe (2)		

(1) Aircraft BuNo. 135407-135444.
(2) Aircraft BuNo. 138902 and subsequent.

FF1-4466-2L

Figure 1-52. Servicing Diagram (Sheet 2)

Changed 1 June 1969

Emergency fuel is to be used only under emergency conditions and for a minimum of flight time.

CAUTION

When different approved fuels are mixed in fuel cells, maximum engine operating limits, particularly rpm and tailpipe temperature, must not be exceeded. In some cases, fuel controls should be reset to obtain maximum engine efficiency.

Fuel	NATO Symbol	Remarks
Recommended JP-5	F-44	MIL-T-5624
JP-4	F-40	MIL-T-5624
Emergency AVGAS		Lowest possible grade

Safety Precautions

1. Make certain supply hose nozzle is grounded (figure 1-55) before making contact with aircraft.

2. When filling tanks or cells, clean up any spillage, especially fuel spilled on tires or other rubber material. If any amount of fuel is spilled during refueling operation, tow aircraft a safe distance before starting engines, or allow sufficient time for evaporation of spillage.

3. Accomplish all fueling operations out of doors and prohibit smoking within 75 feet of fueling area.

4. Use only fuel trucks equipped with static ground chain. If chain has become fouled and has not recently touched ground, ground truck to suitable ground connection.

5. Observe all safety precautions when handling jet fuel. Vapor spaces in jet fuel tanks contain easily ignited, highly explosive mixture.

6. Do not fuel aircraft while radio or radar transmitting equipment is in operation except for hot refueling.

7. Do not make dipstick readings until fuel flow has subsided for at least 30 seconds. Failure to do so could result in static discharge and explosion.

Pressure Fueling—Basic System

NOTE

When fueling the wing, forward, or aft fuselage tanks, on aircraft with upper bomb bay auxiliary tank installed, use wing tank pressure fueling receptacle to fuel auxiliary tank. Auxiliary tank can be filled simultaneously with wing tanks or individually. When filling auxiliary tank individually, omit step 2. If wing tanks or auxiliary are empty and are to remain empty, place applicable check switch in PRIMARY OFF.

CAUTION

To maintain aircraft center of gravity, do not fuel aft fuel tank first.

1. In cockpit, place FUSELAGE FUEL TRIM switch (1) in NOSE DOWN (tables 1-2 and 1-3). In right-hand main gear wheel well, place FUELING POWER ALL TANKS switch (9) in ON (figure 1-53).

2. Remove applicable gravity filler cap (4).

3. Remove applicable pressure fueling receptacle cap (8, 11, or 12) and connect pressure fueling nozzle.

4. Begin pressure fueling. During first minute of fueling, check fuel shutoff valves for proper operation. Position test switch (5, 6, 7, 10, or 13) as applicable. (Refer to table 1-4.)

CAUTION

Failure to check fuel shutoff valves can result in extensive fuel spillage or rupture of fuel tank.

5. Continue fueling until tank is full and fueling stops.

6. Disconnect pressure fueling nozzle and install pressure fueling receptacle cap.

7. Install gravity filler cap (4).

8. Position FUELING POWER ALL TANKS switch (9) to OFF.

TABLE 1-2. FUEL CAPACITY DATA PRESSURE FUELING

Applies to Aircraft BuNo. 135407-135444, 138902-138927, 138929-138931, 138933-138976, 142236-142255, 142400-142407, 142630-142649

Fuel Container	Total Volume (US Gallons)	Expansion Space (US Gallons)	Residual Fuel (US Gallons)	Service Capacity			
				US Gallons	Imperial Gallons	Liters	Pounds†
Fuselage – Forward Fuel Cell	1225	8	3	1214	1011	4595	8255
Fuselage – Rear Fuel Cell	1928	16	3	1909	1590	7226	12,981
Wing Fuel Tanks (2)	668	18	1	649	540	2456	4413
	668	18	1	649	540	2456	4413
Upper Bomb Bay Auxiliary Fuel Cell*	793	37	8	748	623	2831	5086
Total (Upper bomb bay auxiliary fuel cell not installed)	4489	60	8	4421	3681	16,733	30,063
Total (Upper bomb bay auxiliary)	5282	97	16	5169	4304	19,565	35,149

NOTE: Service capacity is the amount of usable fuel that may be stored in fuel containers by pressure fueling. An additional 60 US gallons may be added to forward and aft fuselage tank and wing tank.

*Upper bomb bay auxiliary fuel cell provisions installed in aircraft BuNo. 138902 and subsequent.

†Calculated at 6.8 pounds of fuel per US gallon.

Pressure Defueling—Basic System

NOTE

On aircraft BuNo. 138902-138927, 138929-138931, 138933-138976, 142236-142255, 142400-142407 and 142630-142649 incorporating upper bomb bay auxiliary tank, place auxiliary fuel switch (3) in TRANSFER and defuel simultaneously with aft tank.

CAUTION

To maintain aircraft center of gravity, do not defuel forward tank first.

AFT OR FORWARD FUSELAGE FUEL TANK

1. Remove applicable pressure fueling receptacle cap (11 or 12) and connect pressure fueling nozzle.

2. Apply defueling pressure.

3. Shut off defueling pressure when tank is empty.

4. Disconnect pressure fueling nozzle and install pressure fueling receptacle cap.

WING TANKS

1. Remove left-hand pressure fueling receptacle cap (12) at station 302 and connect defueling nozzle.

2. Position WING TANK switch (2) to TRANSFER.

3. Begin pressure defueling.

Changed 1 June 1969

TABLE 1-3. PRESSURE FUELING AND DEFUELING – BASIC SYSTEM

CONDITIONS FOR FUELING AND DEFUELING

Operation and Tank	Receptacle Used			Wing Tank Switch	Auxiliary Tank Switch	Fueling Power All Tanks	Wing Tanks Check Switch	Forward Tank Check Switch	Auxiliary Tank Check Switch	Aft Tank Check Switch	Fuel Dump Switch	External Power	
	Forward LH	RH	Aft									DC	AC
Pressure Fueling Forward Tank	X			OFF	OFF	ON	FUELING ON	FUELING ON	FUELING ON	FUELING ON	OFF	X	
Pressure Fueling Aft Tank			X	OFF	OFF	ON	FUELING ON	FUELING ON	FUELING ON	FUELING ON	OFF	X	
Pressure Fueling Wing Tanks		X		OFF	OFF	ON	FUELING ON	FUELING ON	PRIMARY OFF	FUELING ON	OFF	X	
Pressure Fueling Auxiliary Tank		X		OFF	OFF	ON	PRIMARY OFF	FUELING ON	FUELING ON	FUELING ON	OFF	X	
Pressure Fueling Wing and Auxiliary Tank		X		OFF	OFF	ON	FUELING ON	FUELING ON	FUELING ON	FUELING ON	OFF	X	
Defueling Forward Tank	X			OFF	OFF	OFF	FUELING ON	FUELING ON	FUELING ON	FUELING ON	OFF	X	
Defueling Aft Tank			X	OFF	OFF	OFF	FUELING ON	FUELING ON	FUELING ON	FUELING ON	OFF		
Defueling Auxiliary Tank			X	OFF	ON	OFF	FUELING ON	FUELING ON	FUELING ON	FUELING ON	OFF	X	
Defueling Aft and Auxiliary Tank			X	OFF	ON	OFF	FUELING ON	FUELING ON	FUELING ON	FUELING ON	OFF	X	
Defueling Wing Tanks	X			ON	OFF	OFF	FUELING ON	FUELING ON	FUELING ON	FUELING ON	OFF	X	X

NAVAIR 01-40ATA-1

Section I
Part 3

TABLE 1-4. FUEL FLOAT VALVE AND SHUTOFF VALVE TEST – BASIC SYSTEM

CAUTION

Test each tank individually to ensure proper operation of fuel shutoff valves.

Position	Desired Result
1. Place applicable check switch in PRIMARY OFF.	Fuel flow to tank will stop within 30 seconds.
2. Verify fuel flow stoppage by observing pulsation in fueling hose. Check flowmeter or fuel counter for 30 seconds to determine leakage rate.	Leakage rate to be less than 3 gpm for wing tanks, 6.5 gpm for auxiliary tank, 1.5 gpm for forward or aft fuselage tank.
3. Place check switch in FUELING ON.	Fuel flow to tank will resume.
4. Place check switch in SECONDARY OFF.	Fuel flow to tank will stop within 30 seconds.

NOTE

Verify stoppage of fuel flow as in step 2.

5. Position check switch to FUELING ON.	Fuel flow to tank will resume.

WARNING

If fuel flow (leakage greater than indicated in step 2) does not stop when check switch is in either primary or secondary OFF position, stop fueling immediately and replace defective component. If fuel flow stops in one OFF position but not in other position, fueling may be continued with caution. Station man at gravity filler to watch for overflow should remaining component malfunction. Correct malfunction prior to next pressure fueling.

---

4. Watch wing tank fuel quantity indicator. When tanks are empty, position WING TANK switch (2) to OFF.

5. Disconnect defueling nozzle and install pressure fueling receptacle cap.

Fueling — Multiple Point

CAUTION

To maintain aircraft center of gravity, do not fuel aft tank first.

FORWARD FUSELAGE AND UPPER BOMB BAY AUXILIARY TANK:

1. Remove left-hand pressure fueling receptacle cap (14) (station 302), and connect pressure fueling nozzle.

2. Begin pressure fueling. During first minute of fueling, check fuel shutoff valves and vent system for proper operation. (Refer to Fuel Float Valve, Shutoff Valve and Vent System Test – Multiple Point Fueling.)

3. Continue fueling until tanks are full and fueling stops.

4. Disconnect pressure fueling supply hose and install pressure fueling receptacle cap.

NOTE

If it is desired to fuel either the forward fuselage fuel tank or the upper bomb bay auxiliary tank only, hold shutoff check switch of tank to remain empty to PRIMARY OFF during fueling.

AFT FUSELAGE FUEL TANK

1. Position FUEL POWER AFT TANK switch (6) in ON.

2. Remove pressure fueling receptacle cap (8) and connect pressure fueling nozzle.

3. Begin pressure fueling. During first minute of operation, check fuel shutoff valves and vent system for proper operation. (Refer to Fuel Float Valve, Shutoff Valve and Vent System Test – Multiple Point Fueling.)

4. Continue fueling until tank is full and fueling stops.

5. Disconnect pressure fueling nozzle and install pressure fueling receptacle cap (8).

6. Place FUEL POWER AFT TANK switch (6) in OFF.

WING TANKS

1. Remove pressure fueling receptacle cap (5), located at station 300 right-hand side, and connect pressure fueling nozzle.

2. Begin pressure fueling. During first minute of fueling, check fuel shutoff valves and vent system for proper operation. (Refer to Fuel Float-Valve, Shutoff Valve, and Vent System Test.)

3. Continue fueling until tanks are full and fueling stops.

4. Disconnect pressure fueling nozzle and install pressure fueling receptacle cap (5).

Changed 15 July 1970

1-137

Section I
Part 3

NAVAIR 01-40ATA-1

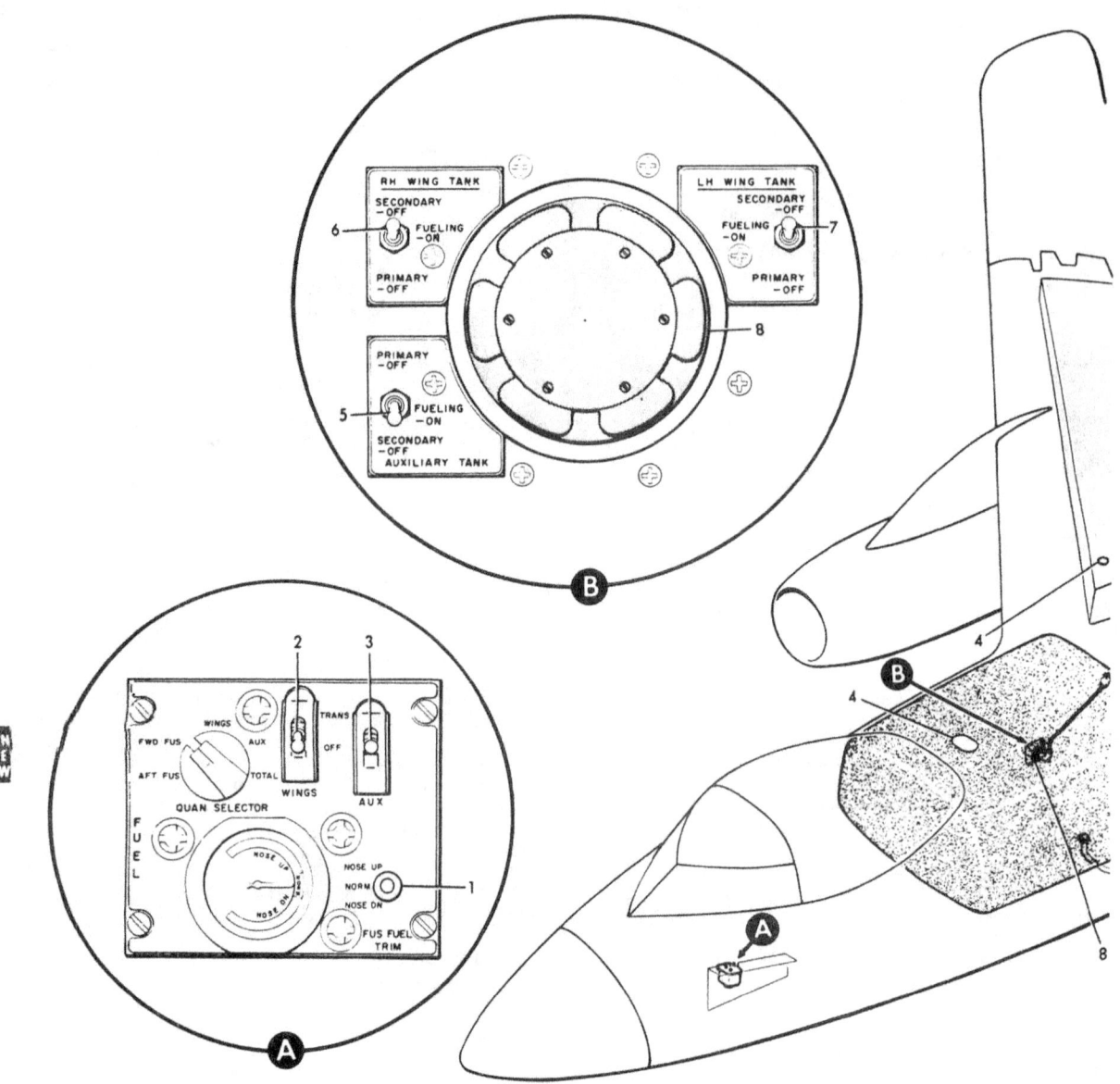

Figure 1-53. Pressure Fueling and Defueling — Basic System (Sheet 1)

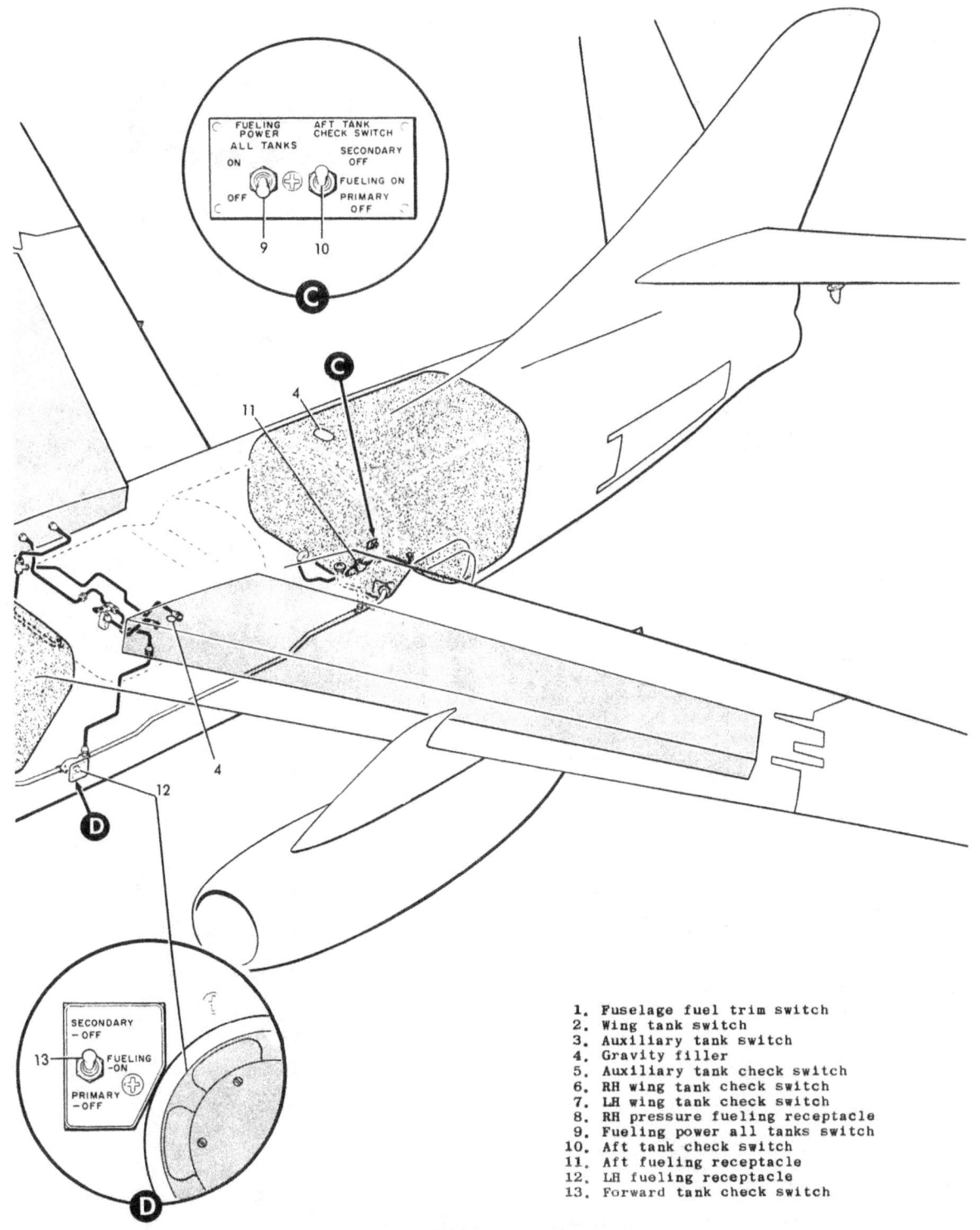

Figure 1-53. Pressure Fueling and Defueling — Basic System (Sheet 2)

Pressure Fueling with Engines Operating (Hot Refueling)

1. Check aircraft for hot brakes prior to entering fuel pit.

2. Turn off all electrical and electronic equipment that is not necessary for refueling.

3. Pilot must maintain UHF radio contact with control tower during fueling operation to report any emergency that might arise.

CAUTION

To maintain aircraft center of gravity, do not fuel aft fuel tank first.

Aircraft refueling while engines are running (hot refueling) is used during carquals, shipboard refresher, and in some instances during FCLP training operations. The use of this procedure is dangerous, and extreme precautionary measures are mandatory regarding fuel spillage, adequate ventilation to dissipate fuel vapors emanating from fuel vent masts, and movement of personnel in the vicinity of the aircraft. Fuel shall be pumped into the forward tank. The pilot will ensure that aircraft center-of-gravity limitations are observed by monitoring transfer of fuel into the aft tank. A normal "hot refueling" load should not exceed 10,000 pounds.

When the aircraft is in control of the plane captain, chocked (afloat, tied down), the pilot will indicate that he is ready to take on fuel by using thumb to open mouth signal (night use red flashlight). The pilot shall monitor fuel on board by tank and/or totalizer fuel quantity readings and signal fueling completed by horizontal movement of left hand at eye level (night use red flashlight).

Gravity Fueling—Procedures

The fuselage fuel cells and the wing fuel tanks can be gravity fueled individually or simultaneously in accordance with the same fueling procedures except that the applicable gravity-type filler unit or units must be used. If the tanks and cells are fueled individually, it is recommended that they be filled in the following order to maintain aircraft center of gravity

safely forward of the main gear: forward fuel cell, wing tanks, and rear fuel cell.

Make certain supply hose nozzle is grounded before making contact with aircraft.

1. Remove applicable filler-unit cap and insert supply hose nozzle into filler unit.

CAUTION

Be cautious when servicing fuel tanks or cell to avoid damage to filler necks. Nozzle must be held by servicing crew and must not be allowed to remain in filler neck without support.

2. Fill fuel cell or tank to capacity.

3. Remove supply hose nozzle, and ground, from aircraft and install filler cap.

FUEL QUANTITY MEASUREMENT

Fuel Measurement Stick

NOTE

Measurement stick is to be used to measure forward and aft tanks only.

1. Open filler access doors.

Before removing cap, ground measuring stick guard to fuel tank filler cap to discharge static electricity.

2. Remove applicable filler cap.

3. Sink entire measuring stick into fuel tank until guard rests on filler neck (figure 1-56). Depress button and hold approximately 5 seconds to allow fuel level to stabilize.

NOTE

During fueling operation, depress valve for a longer period to allow air bubbles to rise. Verify prior reading with second dipping if evidence of air pocket exists.

Figure 1-54, Tables 1-5 through 1-7, Pages 1-141 through 1-148 Deleted.

FUELING – MULTIPLE POINT

CAUTION

To maintain aircraft center of gravity, do not fuel aft tank first.

FORWARD FUSELAGE AND UPPER BOMB BAY AUXILIARY TANK:

1. Remove left-hand pressure fueling receptacle cap (14) (station 302), and connect pressure fueling nozzle.

2. Begin pressure fueling. During first minute of fueling, check fuel shutoff valves and vent system for proper operation. (Refer to Fuel Float Valve, Shutoff Valve and Vent System Test – Multiple Point Fueling.)

3. Continue fueling until tanks are full and fueling stops.

4. Disconnect pressure fueling supply hose and install pressure fueling receptacle cap.

NOTE

If it is desired to fuel either the forward fuselage fuel tank or the upper bomb bay auxiliary tank only, hold shutoff check switch of tank to remain empty to PRIMARY OFF during fueling.

AFT FUSELAGE FUEL TANK

1. Position FUEL POWER AFT TANK switch (6) in ON.

2. Remove pressure fueling receptacle cap (8) and connect pressure fueling nozzle.

3. Begin pressure fueling. During first minute of operation, check fuel shutoff valves and vent system for proper operation. (Refer to Fuel Float Valve, Shutoff Valve and Vent System Test – Multiple Point Fueling.)

4. Continue fueling until tank is full and fueling stops.

5. Disconnect pressure fueling nozzle and install pressure fueling receptacle cap (8).

6. Place FUEL POWER AFT TANK switch (6) in OFF.

WING TANKS

1. Remove pressure fueling receptacle cap (5), located at station 300 right-hand side, and connect pressure fueling nozzle.

2. Begin pressure fueling. During first minute of fueling, check fuel shutoff valves and vent system for proper operation. (Refer to Fuel Float-Valve, Shutoff Valve, and Vent System Test.)

3. Continue fueling until tanks are full and fueling stops.

4. Disconnect pressure fueling nozzle and install pressure fueling receptacle cap (5).

Changed 1 June 1969

Pressure Defueling—Tanker-Receiver System

NOTE

All fuel tanks can be defueled simultaneously from right-hand main gear wheel well pressure fueling receptacle.

DEFUELING – SINGLE POINT

1. Remove right-hand main gear wheel well pressure fueling receptacle cap (8) and connect defueling nozzle.

2. Place SINGLE POINT FUEL and DEFUEL switch in ON. WING TANKS switch in TRANS NORM, AUX TANK switch in TRANS, and PRESS FUEL CHECK TANKS switch in PRI OFF.

3. Begin pressure defueling.

4. Shut off defueling pressure when all tanks are empty.

5. Place SINGLE POINT FUEL and DEFUEL switch (10) in OFF, WING TANK switch (2) in OFF, and AUXILIARY TANK switch (1) in OFF.

6. Disconnect defueling nozzle and install pressure fueling receptacle cap (8).

NOTE

Approximately 250 gallons of fuel will remain in the aft section of the aft fuel cell when defueling operations are complete.

DEFUELING – MULTIPLE POINT

Aft Fuselage, Fwd Fuselage, and Upper Bomb Bay Auxiliary Tank

1. Remove pressure fueling receptacle cap (8) and connect defueling nozzle.

2. Begin pressure defueling.

NOTE

When defueling upper bomb bay auxiliary tank, place auxiliary tank switch (1) in TRANSFER. Ac and dc power is required.

3. Stop defueling pressures when tank or tanks are empty.

4. Disconnect defueling nozzle and install pressure fueling receptacle cap (8).

NOTE

Approximately 250 gallons of fuel will remain in the aft section of the aft fuel cell when defueling operations are complete.

FORWARD FUSELAGE AND WING TANKS

1. Remove left-hand pressure fueling receptacle cap (14) (station 302), and connect defueling nozzle.

TABLE 1-6. PRESSURE FUELING AND DEFUELING – TANKER-RECEIVER SYSTEM

CONDITIONS FOR FUELING AND DEFUELING

Operation and Tank	Receptacle Forward LH	RH	Aft	External Power AC	DC	Wing Tank Switch	Aux Tank Switch	IFR Switch	Fuel Dump Switch
Fueling Forward Tank	X				ON	OFF	OFF	NORMAL	OFF
Fueling Upper Aux Tank	X				ON	OFF	OFF	NORMAL	OFF
Fueling Upper Aux and Forward Tank	X				ON	OFF	OFF	NORMAL	OFF
Fueling Wing Tanks		X			ON	OFF	OFF	NORMAL	OFF
Fueling Aft Tank			X		ON	OFF	OFF	NORMAL	OFF
Fueling All Tanks	X				ON	OFF	OFF	NORMAL	OFF
Defueling Aft Tank			X		OFF	OFF	OFF	NORMAL	OFF
Defueling Upper Aux Tank			X	ON	ON	OFF	TRANSFER	NORMAL	OFF
Defueling Aft and Upper Aux Tank			X	ON	ON	OFF	TRANSFER	NORMAL	OFF
Defueling Forward Tank	X			ON	ON	OFF	OFF	NORMAL	OFF
Defueling Wing Tank	X			ON	ON	TRANSFER	OFF	NORMAL	OFF
Defueling Wing Tank		X		OFF	OFF	OFF	OFF	NORMAL	OFF
Defueling All Tanks			X	ON	ON	TRANSFER NORMAL	TRANSFER	NORMAL	OFF

TABLE 1-6. PRESSURE FUELING AND DEFUELING – TANKER-RECEIVER SYSTEM (Continued)

CONDITIONS FOR FUELING AND DEFUELING

Fwd Tank Switch	Wing Purge Switch	Fueling Power Aft Tank	Single Point Fuel and Defuel	Fuel Shutoff Check Switch				
				Upper Aux Tank	Fwd Tank	Aft Tank	Wing Tank	Press. Fuel Check Tanks
NORMAL	OFF	OFF	OFF	PRI OFF OR SEC	FUEL ON	FUEL ON	FUEL ON	FUEL ON
NORMAL	OFF	OFF	OFF	FUEL ON	PRI OFF	FUEL ON	FUEL ON	FUEL ON
NORMAL	OFF	OFF	OFF	FUEL ON	FUEL ON	FUEL ON	FUEL ON	FUEL ON
NORMAL	OFF	OFF	OFF	FUEL ON	FUEL ON	FUEL ON	FUEL ON	FUEL ON
NORMAL	OFF	ON	OFF	FUEL ON	FUEL ON	FUEL ON	FUEL ON	FUEL ON
NORMAL	OFF	OFF	ON	FUEL ON	FUEL ON	FUEL ON	FUEL ON	FUEL ON
NORMAL	OFF	OFF	OFF	FUEL ON	FUEL ON	FUEL ON	FUEL ON	FUEL ON
NORMAL	OFF	OFF	OFF	FUEL ON	FUEL ON	FUEL ON	FUEL ON	FUEL ON
NORMAL	OFF	OFF	OFF	FUEL ON	FUEL ON	FUEL ON	FUEL ON	FUEL ON
NORMAL	OFF	OFF	ON	FUEL ON	FUEL ON	FUEL ON	FUEL ON	PRI OFF OR SEC OFF
OFF	OFF	OFF	OFF	FUEL ON	FUEL ON	FUEL ON	FUEL ON	FUEL ON
OFF	OFF	OFF	OFF	OFF	OFF	OFF	OFF	OFF
NORMAL	OFF	OFF	ON	FUEL ON	FUEL ON	FUEL ON	FUEL ON	FUEL ON

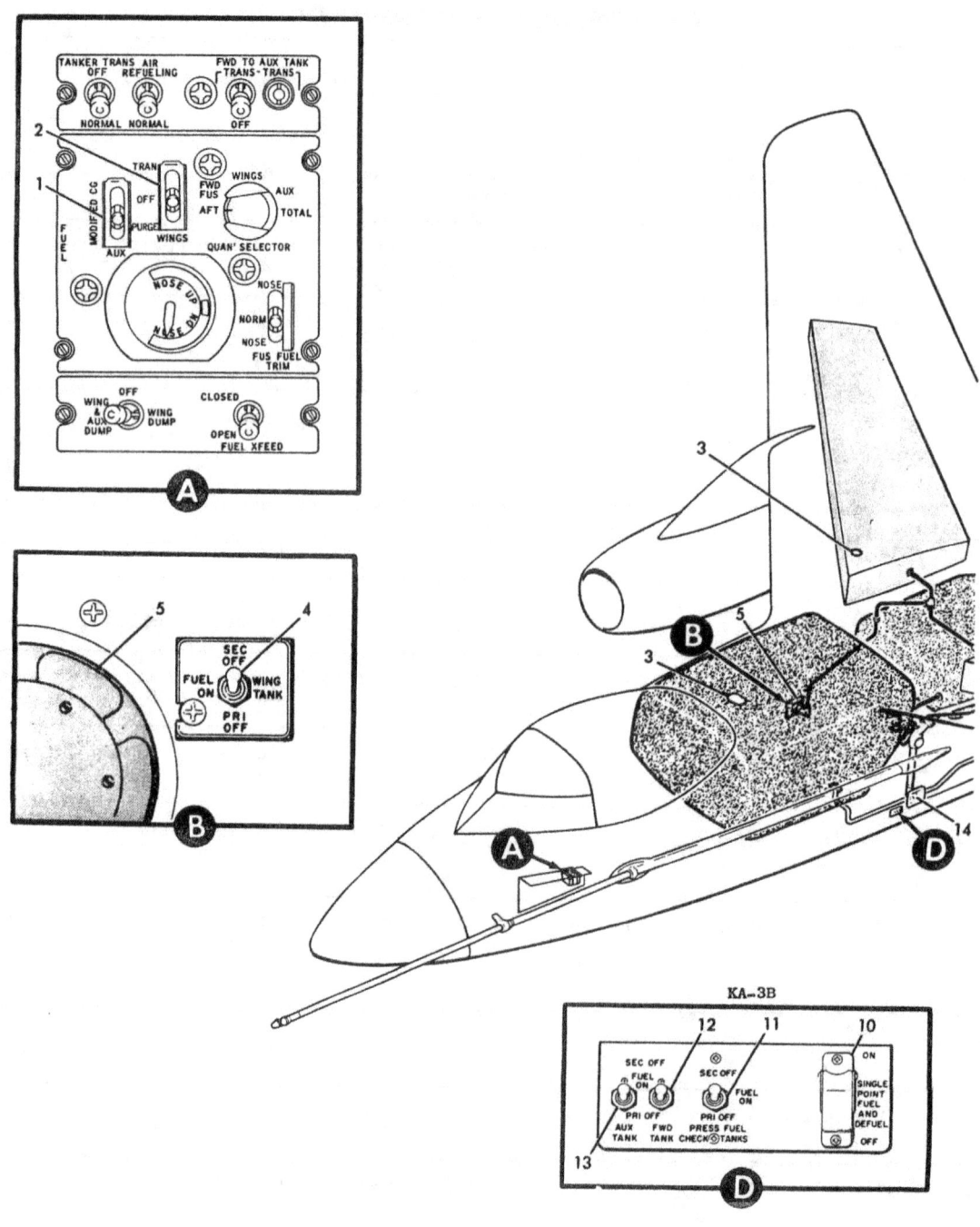

Figure 1-54. Pressure Fueling and Defueling – Tanker-Receiver System (Sheet 1)

NAVAIR 01-40ATA-1

Section I
Part 3

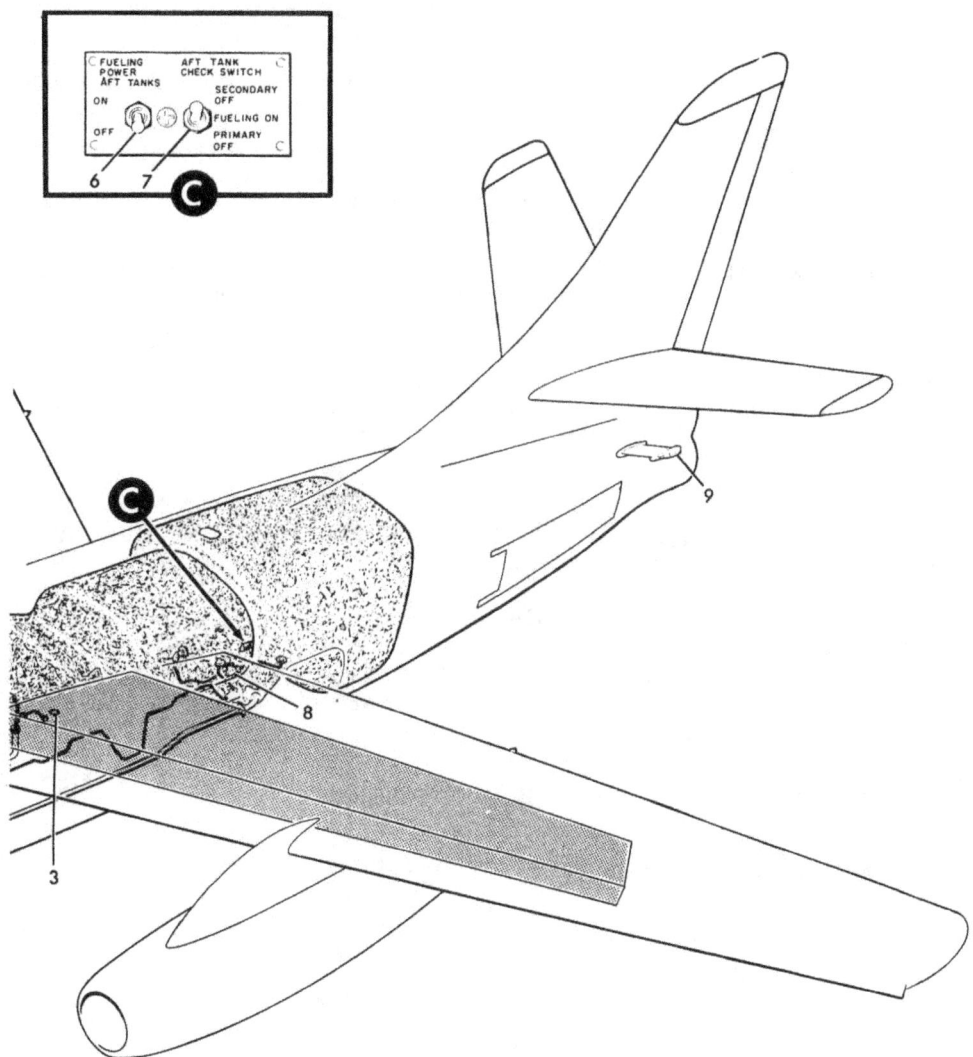

1. Auxiliary tank switch
2. Wing tank switch
3. Gravity filler
4. Wing tank check switch
5. RH fueling receptacle cap
6. Fueling power aft tank switch
7. Aft tank check switch
8. Aft fueling receptacle cap
9. Vent outlet
10. Single point fuel and defuel switch
11. Pressure fuel check all tanks switch
12. Forward tank check switch
13. Auxiliary tank check switch
14. LH fueling receptacle cap

FF1-28278-2A

Figure 1-54. Pressure Fueling and Defueling – Tanker-Receiver System (Sheet 2)

1-145

2. Place PRESSURE FUEL CHECK ALL TANKS switch (11) in PRIMARY OFF.

3. Place SINGLE POINT FUEL and DEFUEL switch (10) in ON.

4. Begin pressure defueling.

5. When tank is empty, stop defueling pressure.

6. Place SINGLE POINT FUEL and DEFUEL switch (10) in OFF.

7. Place PRESSURE FUEL CHECK ALL TANKS switch (11) in FUELING ON.

8. Disconnect defueling nozzle and install pressure fueling receptacle cap (8).

WING TANKS

1. Remove right-hand pressure fueling receptacle cap (5) (station 302), and connect defueling nozzle.

2. Place WINGS tank switch (2) in OFF position.

3. Begin pressure defueling.

4. Turn off defueling pressure when wing tanks are empty.

5. Disconnect defueling nozzle and install pressure fueling receptacle cap (5).

Pressure Fueling with Engines Operating (Hot Refueling)

1. Check aircraft for hot brakes prior to entering fuel pit.

2. Turn off all electrical and electronic equipment that is not necessary for refueling.

3. Pilot must maintain UHF radio contact with control tower during fueling operation to report any emergency that might arise.

CAUTION

To maintain aircraft center of gravity, do not fuel aft fuel tank first.

Aircraft refueling while engines are running (hot refueling) is used during carquals, shipboard refresher, and in some instances during FMLP training operations. The use of this procedure is dangerous, and extreme precautionary measures are mandatory regarding fuel spillage, adequate ventilation to dissipate fuel vapors emanating from fuel vent masts, and movement of personnel in the vicinity of the aircraft. Fuel shall be pumped into the forward tank. The pilot will ensure that aircraft center-of-gravity limitations are observed by monitoring transfer of fuel into the aft tank. A normal "hot refueling" load should not exceed 10,000 pounds.

When the aircraft is in control of the plane captain, chocked (afloat, tied down), the pilot will indicate that he is ready to take on fuel by using thumb to open mouth signal (night use red flashlight). The pilot shall monitor fuel on board by tank and/or totalizer fuel quantity readings and signal fueling completed by horizontal movement of left hand at eye level (night use red flashlight).

FUEL FLOAT VALVE, SHUTOFF VALVE AND VENT SYSTEM TEST—TANKER-RECEIVER SYSTEM

General

For information on fuel float valve, shutoff valve, and vent system test for the tanker-receiver system, refer to table 1-7.

GRAVITY FUELING

Safety Precautions

1. Make certain supply hose nozzle is grounded before making contact with aircraft (figure 1-55).

2. When filling tanks or cells, clean up any spillage, especially fuel spilled on tires or other rubber material. If any amount of fuel is spilled during the refueling operation, tow aircraft safe distance before starting engines, or allow sufficient time for evaporation of spillage.

3. Accomplish all fueling operations out-of-doors and prohibit smoking within 75 feet of fueling area.

4. Use only fuel trucks equipped with static ground chain. If chain has become fouled and has not recently touched ground, ground truck to suitable ground connection.

5. Observe all safety precautions when handling jet fuel. Vapor spaces in jet fuel tanks contain easily ignited, highly explosive mixture.

6. Do not fuel aircraft while radio or radar transmitting equipment is in operation.

NAVAIR 01-40ATA-1

Section I
Part 3

TABLE 1-7. FUEL FLOAT VALVE, SHUTOFF VALVE, AND VENT SYSTEM TEST –
TANKER-RECEIVER SYSTEM

FUEL FLOAT VALVE, SHUTOFF VALVE, AND VENT SYSTEM TEST – MULTIPLE POINT FUELING

CAUTION

Test each tank individually to ensure proper operation of fuel shutoff valves and vent system.

Position	Desired Results
1. Place applicable check switch in PRIMARY OFF.	Fuel flow to tank and exhaust airflow from vent outlet will stop within 30 seconds.
2. Verify fuel flow stoppage by observing pulsation in fueling hose. Check flowmeter or fuel counter to determine leakage rate for 30 seconds.	Leakage rate to be less than 1.5 gpm for forward or aft fuel tank, 6.5 gpm for upper bomb bay auxiliary tank or 3 gpm for wing tanks.
3. Place check switch in FUELING ON.	Fuel flow to tank and exhaust airflow from vent outlet will resume.

NOTE

Verify exhaust airflow from vent outlet by visual observation of fuel vapor.

Position	Desired Results
4. Place check switch in SECONDARY OFF.	Fuel flow to tanks and exhaust airflow from vent outlet will stop within 30 seconds.

NOTE

Verify fuel flow stoppage as in step 2.

Position	Desired Results
5. Place check switch in FUELING ON.	Fuel flow to tanks and exhaust airflow from vent outlet will resume.

WARNING

If fuel flow (leakage greater than indicated in test) does not stop when check switch is in either PRIMARY or SECONDARY OFF position, stop fueling immediately and replace defective component. If fuel flow stops in one OFF position but not in the other, fueling may be continued with caution. Remove applicable gravity filler cap, station man at filler to watch for overflow, should remaining component malfunction. Place placard in cockpit to warn pilot against performing inflight fueling operation. Correct malfunction prior to next pressure fueling.

FUEL FLOAT VALVE, SHUTOFF VALVE, AND VENT SYSTEM TEST – SINGLE-POINT FUELING

CAUTION

Test each tank individually to ensure proper operation of fuel shutoff valves and the vent system.

Position	Desired Results
1. Place and hold AUXILIARY, FORWARD, and AFT TANK check switches (left-hand fueling receptacle, station 302) and WING TANK check switches right-hand fueling receptacle, station 302) in PRIMARY OFF.	Fuel flow to all tanks will stop within 30 seconds.
2. Verify fuel flow stoppage by observing pulsation in fueling hose. Check flowmeter or fuel counter to determine leakage rate for 30 seconds.	Leakage rate to be 12 gpm or less.

CAUTION

A leakage rate greater than 12 gpm indicates a system malfunction. Test each tank individually to determine defective component.

Position	Desired Results
3. Place AUXILIARY TANK check switch in FUELING ON.	Fuel flow to auxiliary tank and exhaust airflow from vent outlet will resume.

NOTE

Verify exhaust airflow from vent outlet by visual observation of fuel vapor. If there is no indication of vapor exhaust at vent outlet, stop fueling and correct malfuntion.

Position	Desired Results
4. Place AUXILIARY TANK switch in PRIMARY OFF.	Fuel flow to auxiliary tank and exhaust airflow from vent outlet will stop within 30 seconds.
5. Verify fuel flow stoppage.	Leakage rate to be 12 gpm or less.
6. Place AUXILIARY TANK switch in SECONDARY OFF.	Fuel flow to auxiliary tank and exhaust air from vent outlet will stop within 30 seconds.

Changed 1 June 1969

1-147

TABLE 1-7. FUEL FLOAT VALVE, SHUTOFF VALVE, AND VENT SYSTEM TEST – TANKER-RECEIVER SYSTEM (Continued)

Position	Desired Results
7. Verify fuel flow stoppage.	Leakage rate to be 6.5 gpm or less.
8. Repeat steps 3 through 7 for WING TANKS.	Leakage rate to be 3 gpm or less.
9. Repeat steps 3 through 7 for FORWARD TANK.	Leakage rate to be 1.5 gpm or less.
10. Repeat steps 3 through 7 for AFT TANK.	Leakage rate to be 1.5 gpm or less.

WARNING

If fuel flow (leakage greater than indicated in test) does not stop when check switches are in either PRIMARY or SECONDARY OFF position, stop fueling immediately and replace defective component. If fuel flow stops in one OFF position but not in the other, fueling may be continued with caution. Remove applicable gravity filler cap, station man at filler to watch for overflow, should remaining component malfunction. Place placard in cockpit to warn pilot against performing inflight fueling operations. Correct malfunctions prior to next pressure fueling.

Gravity Fueling—Procedures

The fuselage fuel cells and the wing fuel tanks can be gravity fueled individually or simultaneously in accordance with the same fueling procedures except that the applicable gravity-type filler unit or units must be used. If the tanks and cells are fueled individually, it is recommended that they be filled in the following order to maintain aircraft center of gravity safely forward of the main gear: forward fuel cell, wing tanks, and rear fuel cell.

WARNING

Make certain supply hose nozzle is grounded before making contact with aircraft.

1. Remove applicable filler-unit cap and insert supply hose nozzle into filler unit.

CAUTION

Be cautious when servicing fuel tanks or cell to avoid damage to filler necks. Nozzle must be held by servicing crew and must not be allowed to remain in filler neck without support.

2. Fill fuel cell or tank to capacity.

3. Remove supply hose nozzle, and ground, from aircraft and install filler cap.

FUEL QUANTITY MEASUREMENT

Fuel Measurement Stick

NOTE

Measurement stick is to be used to measure forward and aft tanks only.

1. Open filler access doors.

WARNING

Before removing cap, ground measuring stick guard to fuel tank filler cap to discharge static electricity.

2. Remove applicable filler cap.

3. Sink entire measuring stick into fuel tank until guard rests on filler neck (figure 1-56). Depress button and hold approximately 5 seconds to allow fuel level to stabilize.

NOTE

During fueling operation, depress valve for a longer period to allow air bubbles to rise. Verify prior reading with second dipping if evidence of air pocket exists.

4. Remove stick and read. Insert stick end into tank. Depress button to drain fuel back into tank. Tap stick gently against filler neck to release trapped fuel in tube.

5. Replace tank filler cap.

6. Secure filler access doors.

OIL SYSTEM — SERVICING

(See figure 1-57.)

Servicing Engine Oil Tank

CAUTION

Service engine oil system within 15 minutes after engine shutdown. Do not add oil after false start or dry cranking run.

1. Remove oil tank filler access plate from right-hand side of upper engine nacelle.

2. Remove cap and dipstick from oil tank.

3. Fill oil tank to capacity with oil (MIL-L-23699).

4. Wipe oil cap off and install on oil tank.

5. Install access plate.

Hydraulic Reservoir Servicing

Relieve reservoir air pressure and add hydraulic fluid (MIL-H-5606) through filler neck on reservoir. Fill slowly until proper level, as shown on instruction plate, is obtained on the sight gage (figure 1-58).

BRAKE SYSTEM—SERVICING

(See figure 1-59.)

Master Brake System Resevoir — Filling and Bleeding

1. Service utility reservoir with hydraulic fluid.

2. Pressurize utility reservoir to 5 psi.

3. In nosewheel well, remove brake reservoir bleed cap. Bleed until fluid appears and is free of air.

4. Tighten brake reservoir bleed cap.

Power Brake Valves — Bleeding

1. Service utility reservoir with hydraulic fluid.

2. Pressurize utility reservoir to 30 psi.

3. Place absorbent rags around power brake valves in bomb bay to absorb excess fluid during bleeding operation.

4. Station one crewmember in cockpit, and one crewmember in bomb bay; then, depress right brake

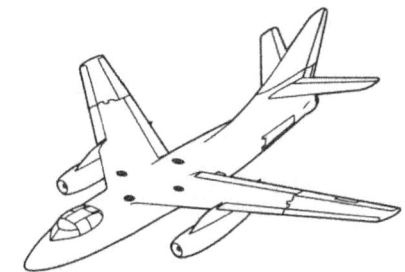

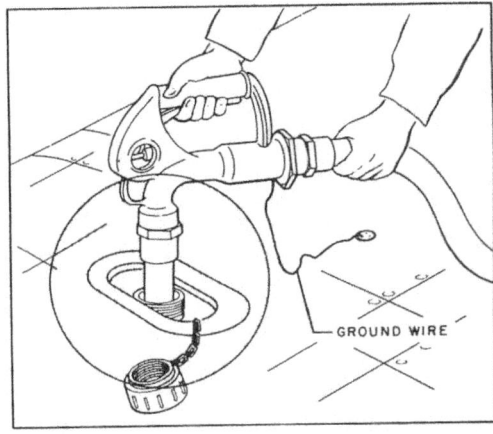

FORWARD FUSELAGE FUEL CELL GRAVITY FILLER UNIT

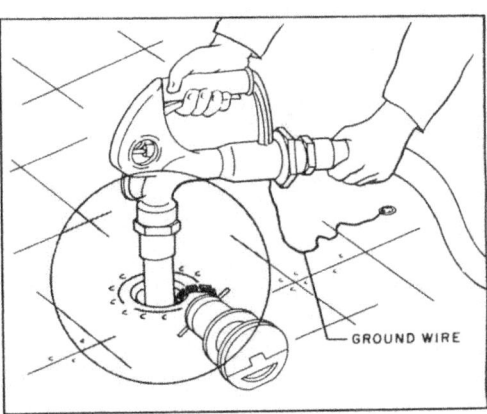

WING TANK GRAVITY FILLER UNIT

ATA-1-1 P-28279-1

Figure 1-55. Gravity Fueling

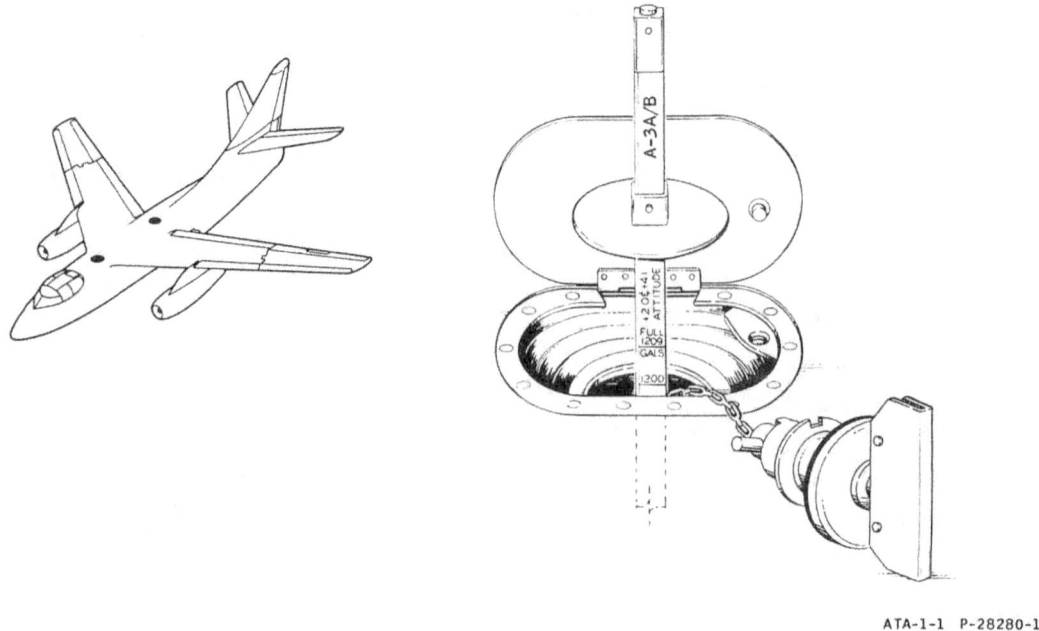

Figure 1-56. Fuel Quantity Measurement

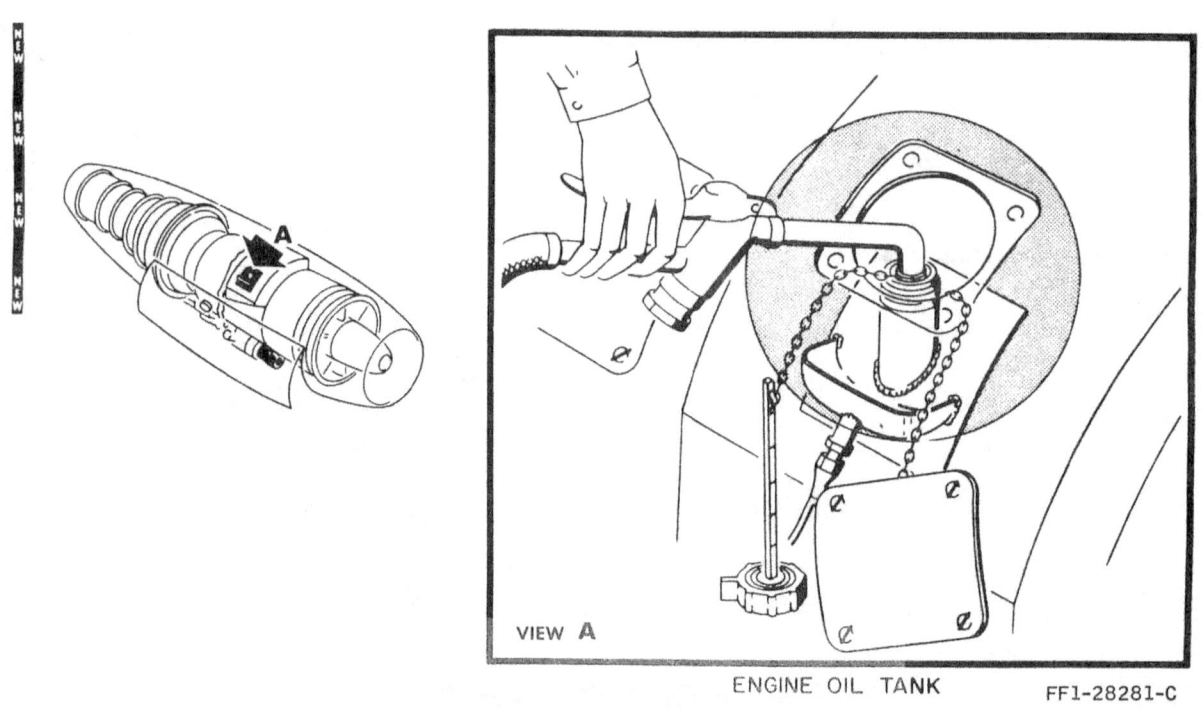

Figure 1-57. Oil System — Servicing

NAVAIR 01-40ATA-1

Section I
Part 3

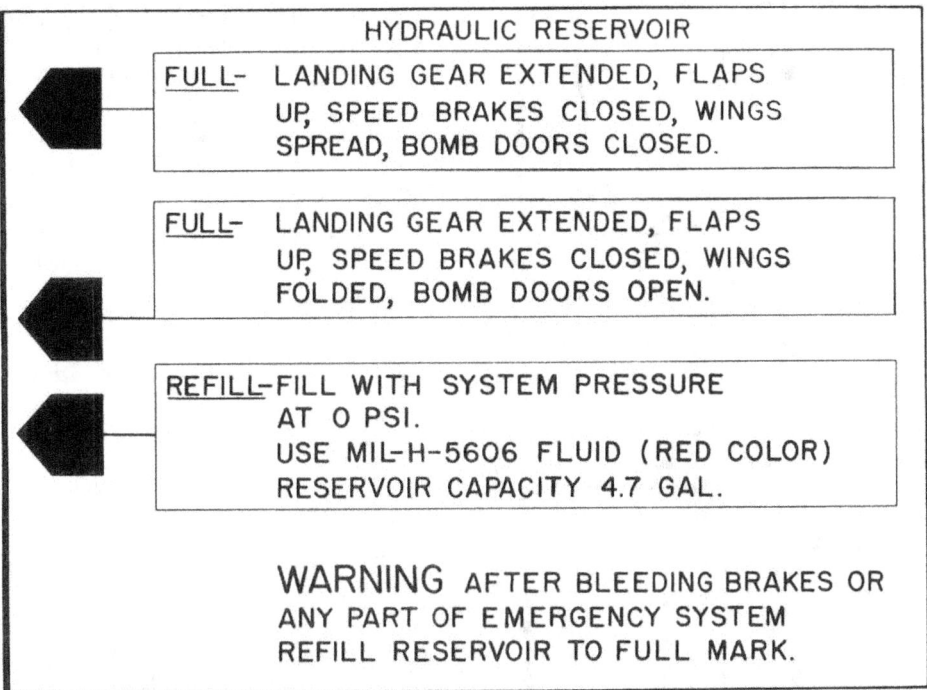

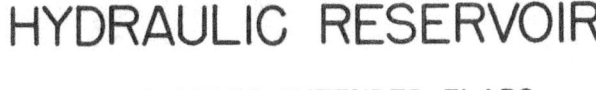

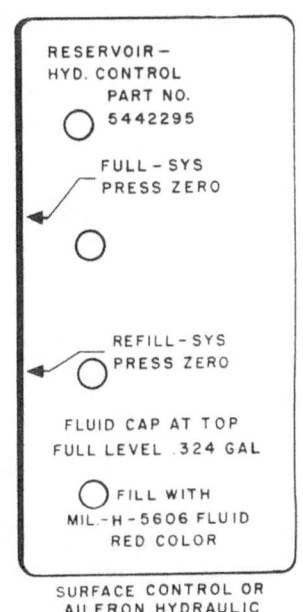

Figure 1-58. Hydraulic Systems – Servicing

1-151

Section I
Part 3

NAVAIR 01-40ATA-1

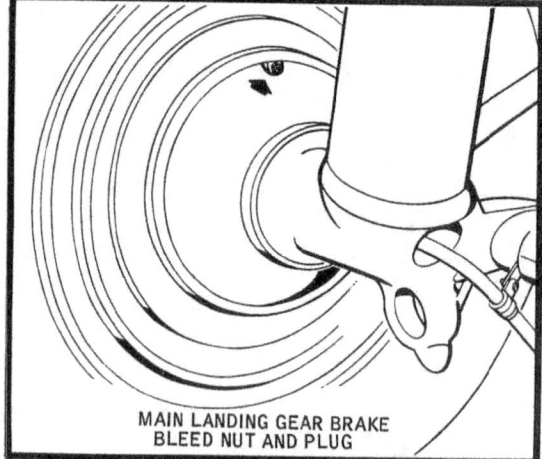

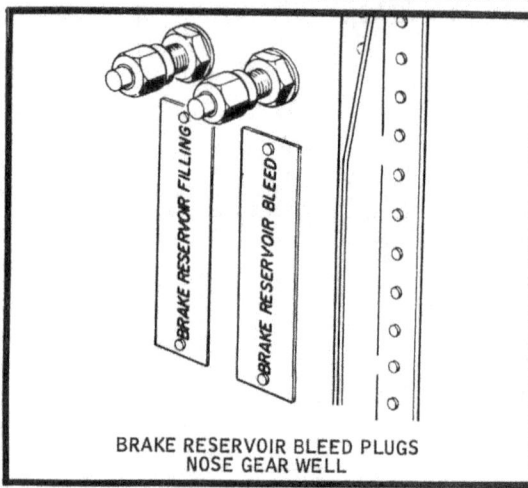

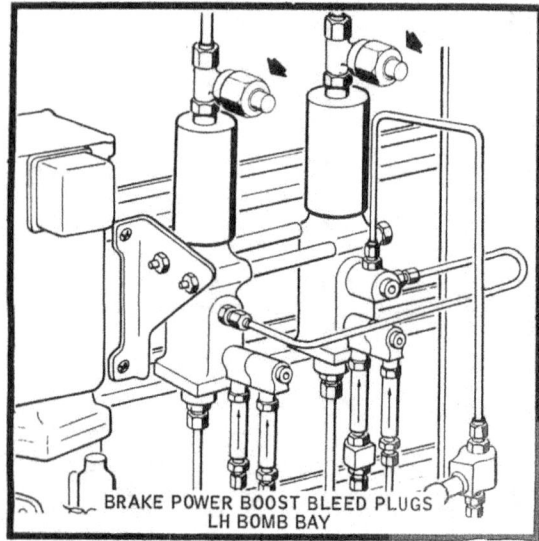

Figure 1-59. Brake System – Servicing

pedal and crack appropriate brake valve bleeder cap to allow hydraulic fluid and/or air to escape. Tighten bleeder cap when hydraulic fluid is free of air. Check brake pedal pressure. If pressure is spongy, repeat bleeding operation until brake pedal pressure is firm. Repeat bleeding operation with left brake pedal and appropriate power brake valve bleeder cap until both pedals have firm, nonspongy, feel.

5. Remove excess or spilled hydraulic fluid from bomb bay area.

Main Landing Gear Brake—Bleeding

1. Service utility reservoir with hydraulic fluid (MIL-H-5606).

2. Remove top bleeder screw (plug) from brake housing and install bleeder hose.

3. Submerge free end of bleeder hose in container partially filled with clean hydraulic fluid.

4. Release nut (figure 1-59) around base of bleeder port.

5. Energize utility hydraulic system or pressure brake system, using EMERGENCY HYDRAULIC PUMP.

NOTE

Use external electrical power (dc) to operate the emergency hydraulic pump. The battery will be discharged in approximately 4 minutes if used to operate the emergency hydraulic pump.

6. Depress brake pedal and bleed wheel brake assembly until hydraulic fluid is free of air.

7. Tighten nut around base of bleeder plug.

8. Remove hose from brake assembly and replace screw in bleeder plug.

9. Repeat steps 2 through 8 for opposite brake assembly.

10. Service utility reservoir with hydraulic fluid.

Changed 1 June 1969

ACCUMULATOR—CHARGING

(See figure 1-60.)

Use plastic face shield in front of gage for protection while servicing air systems. Ensure that space exists between gage and shield.

Nose Gear Steering Accumulator

1. Thirty minutes after shutdown, check pressure reading on accumulator gage. The gage should read 625 psi minimum to 825 psi maximum, with no leakage.

2. Relieve nose gear steering system pressure by turning relief valve handle clockwise.

3. Hold valve in open position and charge accumulator to 350±25 psi (figure 1-60).

4. Release relief valve handle to closed position.

Brake Accumulator

Have one man depress brake pedals while second man charges accumulator to 400±25 psi. See figure 1-60 for air bottle vs temperature chart information.

Spoiler System Accumulators (Two)

1. Open spoiler controls access door in right and left wing lower surface.

2. Charge each accumulator in accordance with instruction plate adjacent to valve (figure 1-60).

Aileron System Accumulator

NOTE

Air filler valve is located in bomb bay at lower right-hand side, station 283.

Charge accumulator in accordance with instruction plate adjacent to valve.

EMERGENCY AIR SYSTEMS—SERVICING

(See figure 1-61.)

Use plastic face shield in front of gage for protection while servicing air systems. Ensure that space exists between gage and shield.

Servicing Completely Empty Systems

1. Charge bottle to 200±50 psi.

2. Open bottle drain valve to release any trapped hydraulic fluid.

3. Close drain valve and charge air bottle to pressure shown on temperature correction chart for appropriate system (figure 1-61).

Servicing Low Systems

1. Charge bottle to pressure shown on temperature correction chart for appropriate system (figure 1-61).

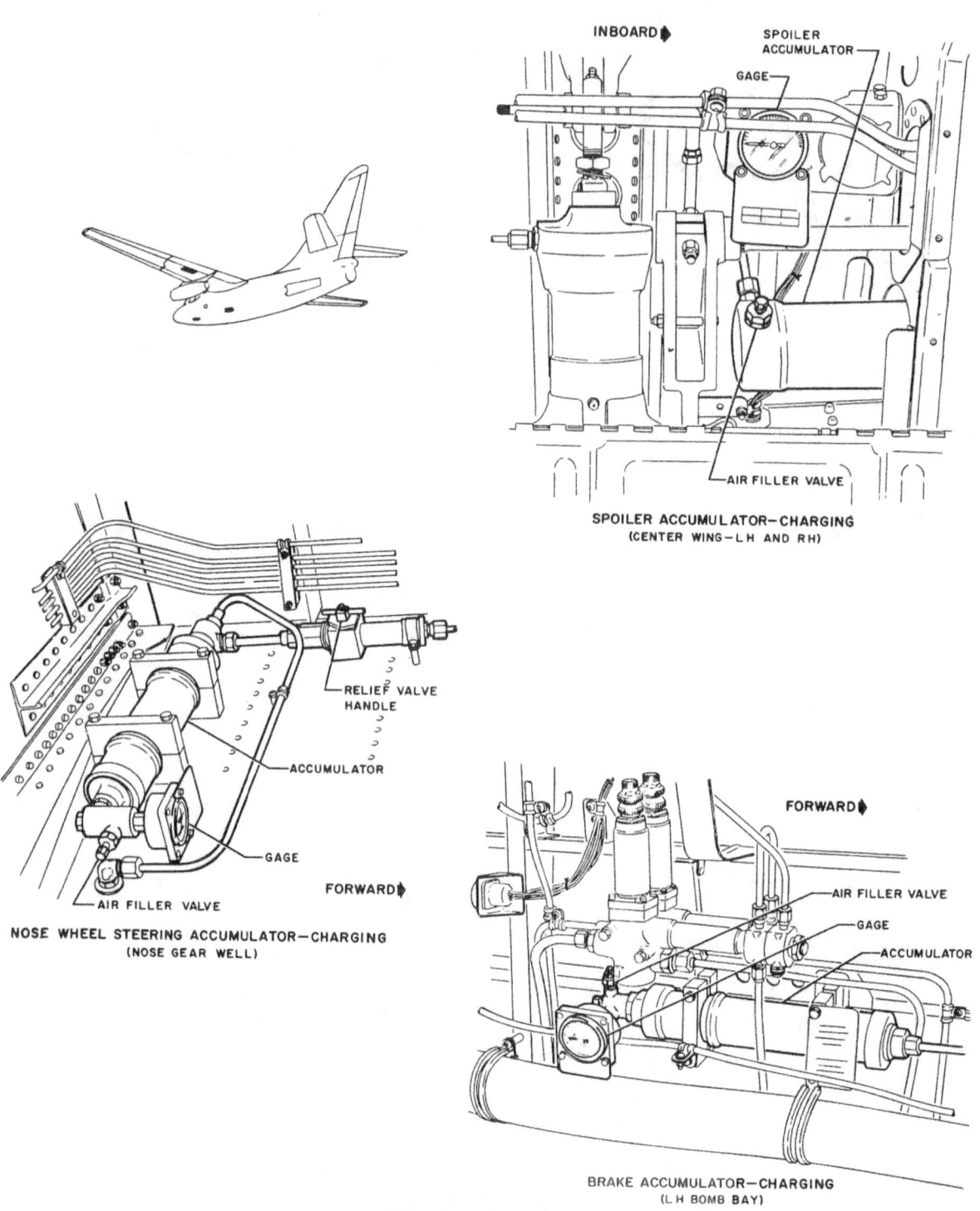

Figure 1-60. Accumulator – Charging (Sheet 1)

NAVAIR 01-40ATA-1

Section I
Part 3

AILERON ACCUMULATOR CHARGING
INSTRUCTION PLATE
(R.H., LOWER BOMB BAY, STA. 283)

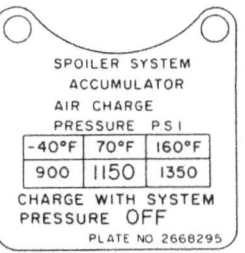

SPOILER ACCUMULATOR CHARGING
INSTRUCTION PLATE

CAUTION

WITH HYDRAULIC SYSTEM PRESSURE OFF, CHARGE 60 CUBIC INCH ACCUMULATORS TO 1150 PSI AIR PRESSURE. CHARGE 18 CUBIC INCH ACCUMULATORS TO 1000 PSI AIR PRESSURE.

NOTE

THE 60 CUBIC INCH ACCUMULATORS ARE INSTALLED IN AIRCRAFT BUNO. 135407, 135409, 135410, 138902, THROUGH 138905, 138918, 138928, 138932, 138938, 138947, 138967, 139871, 138972, 142236-142255, 142400-142407, 142630.

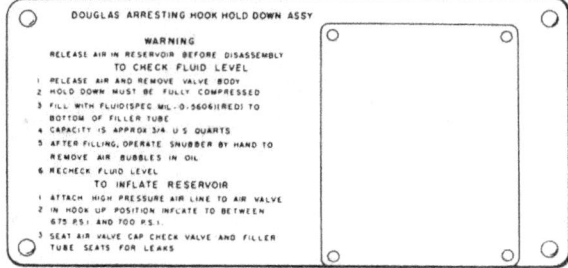

ARRESTING HOOK HOLD DOWN ASSY
INSTRUCTION PLATE

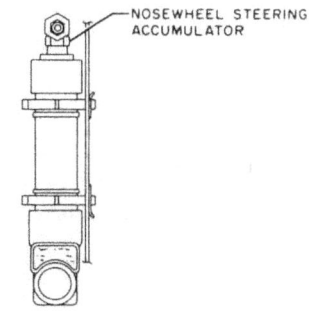

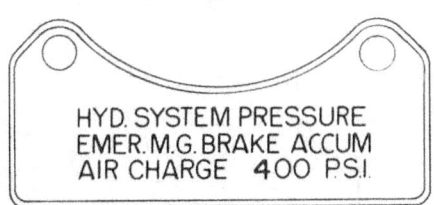

BRAKE ACCUMULATOR CHARGING
INSTRUCTION PLATE

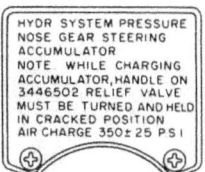

NOSEWHEEL STEERING ACCUMULATOR
CHARGING INSTRUCTION PLATE

Figure 1-60. Accumulator — Charging (Sheet 2)

Section I
Part 3

NAVAIR 01-40ATA-1

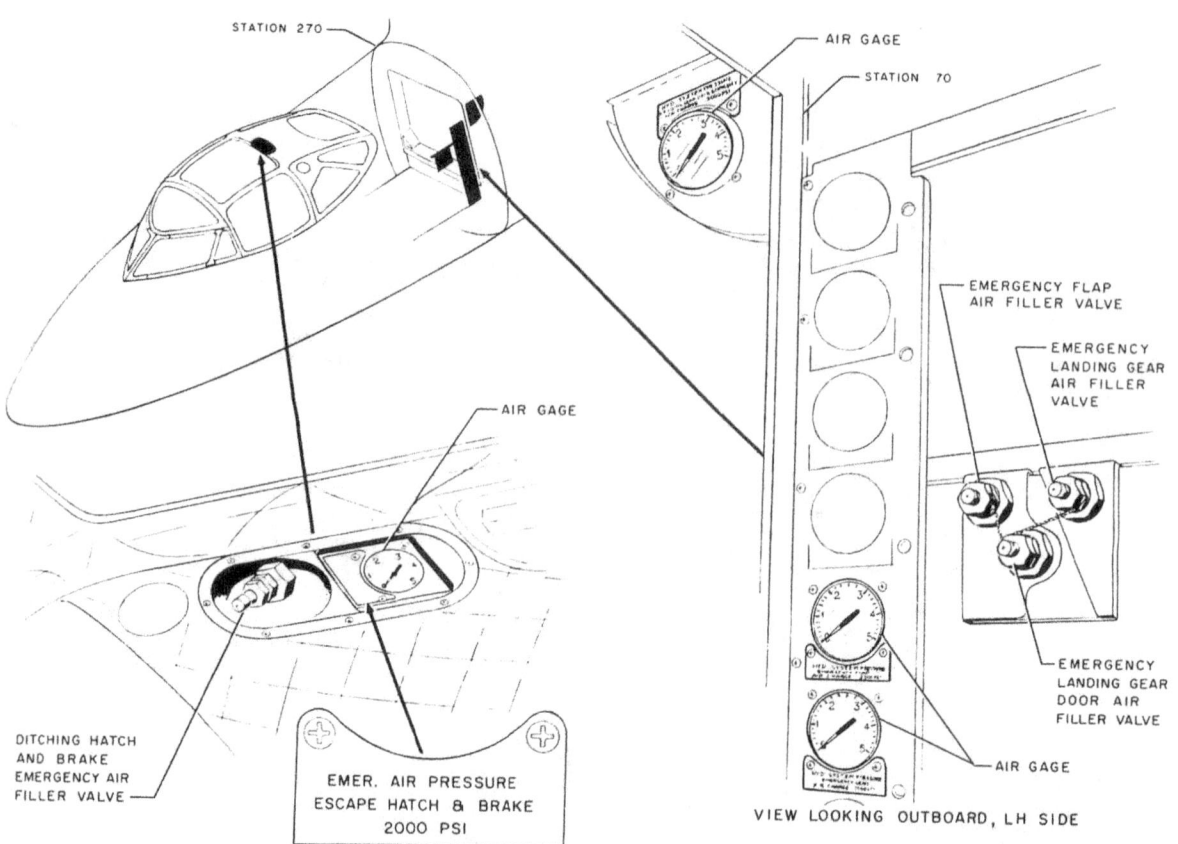
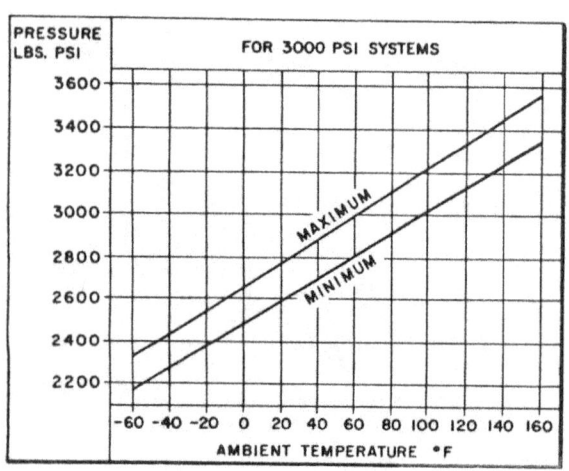
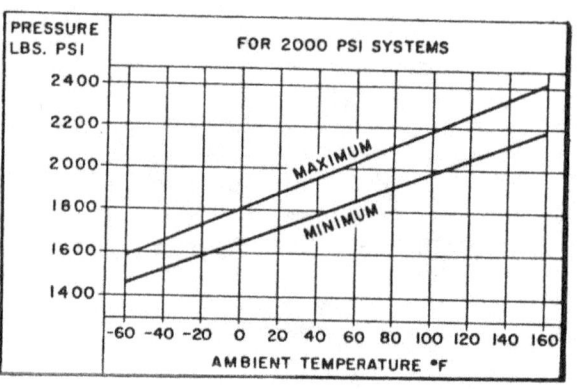

TEMPERATURE CORRECTION CHARTS

ATA-1-1 P-28285-1A

Figure 1-61. Emergency Air Systems – Servicing

ATM OIL SUMP—SERVICING

(See figure 1-62.)

WARNING

Do not overfill oil sump because lubricant cavitation at reduction gearing will cause overloading and/or failure of ATM.

1. Remove filler cap and fill to full mark on dip stick with the following oil:

Temperature	Grade	Reference
-18°C to 54°C (0°F to 127°F)	1010	MIL-L-6081
-18°C to -54°C (0°F to -45°F)	1005	MIL-L-6081

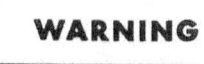

Do not mix 1010-grade oil with 1005-grade oil.

2. Replace filler cap and inspect dipstick for proper oil level.

OXYGEN SYSTEM—SERVICING

(See figure 1-63.)

Filling Liquid Oxygen Converter—8-Liter System

WARNING

Before filling system make certain filler valve, transfer hose, and adjacent area are free from all contamination. Clear area of unauthorized personnel and rigidly comply with all LOX safety precautions.

1. Close shutoff valve at each regulator station.

2. Remove filler valve access plate at left-hand forward fuselage station 152.

3. Slowly open vent and buildup valve until any excessive pressures have been released, then turn handle fully to VENT.

4. Remove filler valve cap and connect electrical ground to aircraft.

Some spillage or leakage is to be anticipated at filler valve. When disconnecting service hose from filler valve, stand as far to one side as possible. The spring-loaded check in filler valve may freeze in open position when filling and allow liquid oxygen to spew out of filler valve after removal of servicing hose.

5. Connect filler hose from liquid oxygen supply unit to filler valve.

6. Transfer liquid at rate of approximately 35-psi pressure until liquid (blue in color) begins to come out of overboard vent at bottom of fuselage beneath converter. Filling time should be about 10 minutes. If filling time exceeds 10 minutes, faulty flask may exist. If frost has collected on outside of flask, it must be replaced.

7. Carefully remove filler hose.

8. Replace filler valve cap, turn vent and buildup valve to BUILD-UP, and secure cap in position with lockwire.

NOTE

If filler valve leaks, heat from cap and ambient air will free mechanism and stop leakage. When leakage stops, verify proper operating pressure. System purging can be delayed until time for routine ground maintenance.

9. Replace filler valve access plate and fasten with camloc fasteners.

10. Perform regulator flow test.

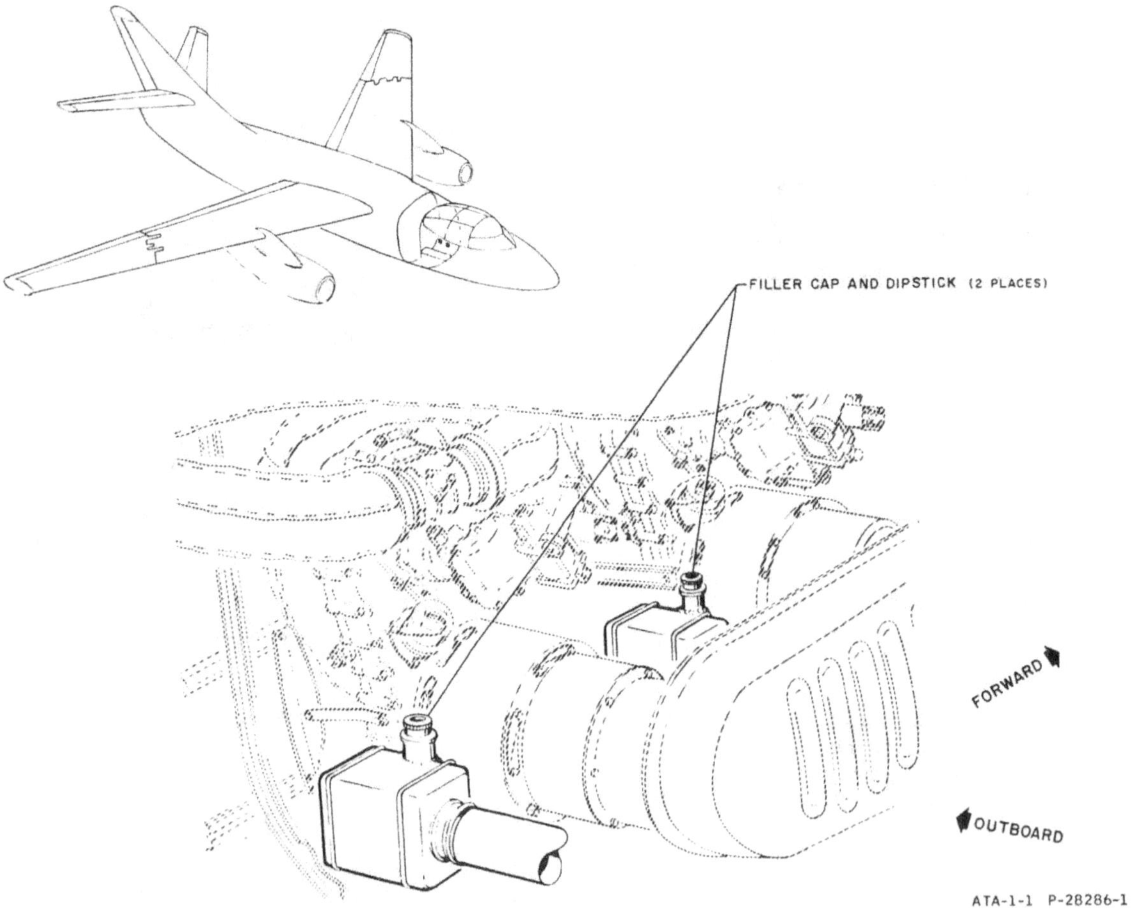

Figure 1-62. ATM Oil Sump — Servicing

Filling Liquid Oxygen Converters — 20-Liter System

(See figure 1-63.)

WARNING

- If the oxygen system is empty and exposed to the surrounding atmosphere, water vapor or other gases may condense in the converter bottle, causing contamination of the oxygen system. The system must be purged prior to further use.

- Before filling system, make certain filler valve, transfer hose, and adjacent area are free from all contamination. Clear area of unauthorized personnel and rigidly comply with all LOX safety precautions.

NOTE

Converters may be filled in or out of aircraft. If converters are filled out of aircraft, provide suitable vent line at combination filler, buildup, vent and relief valve.

1. Close oxygen shutoff valves at each crew station.

2. Open lower aft access door to aft equipment compartment (station 657).

3. Open door on converter compartment and latch with strap provided on overhead structure.

NAVAIR 01-40ATA-1

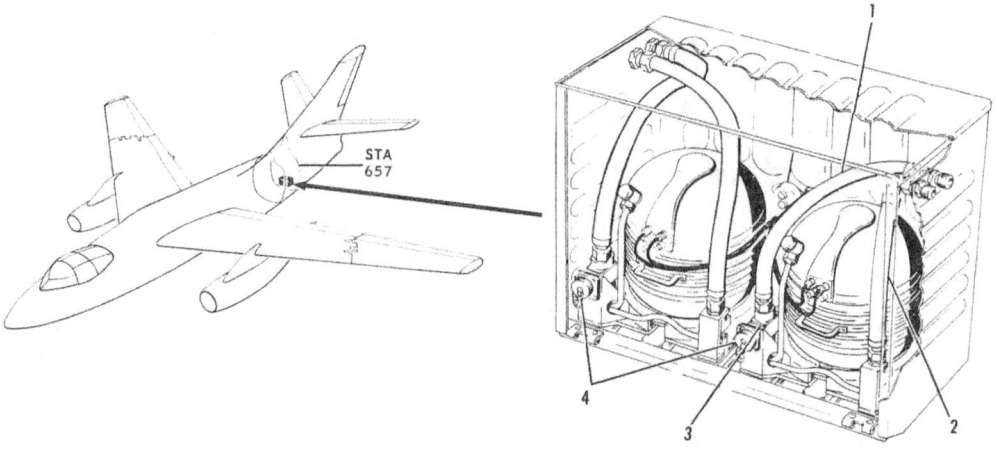

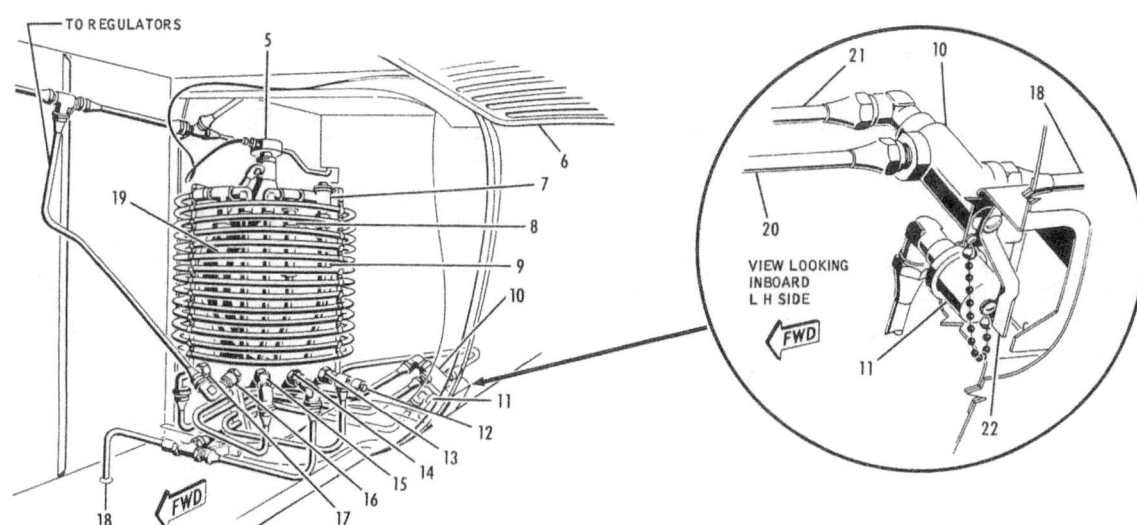

1. Oxygen vent line
2. Oxygen supply line
3. Filler, buildup, vent, and relief valve
4. Liquid oxygen filler ports
5. Quantity transmitter
6. LH forward compartment door
7. Pressure close valve (70 ± 5 PSI)
8. Low pressure relief valve (85 ± 5 PSI)
9. Flask
10. Vent and buildup valve
11. Filler valve and cap
12. Pressure test T-connection
13. Filler port
14. Relief vent port
15. Buildup port
16. Supply port
17. Filler vent port
18. Overboard vent line
19. High pressure relief valve (95 ± 5 PSI)
20. Filler vent line
21. Buildup line
22. Handle (buildup position)

FF1-28287-B

Figure 1-63. Oxygen System — Servicing

4. Remove filler valve cap on one converter.

Some spillage or leakage is to be anticipated at filler valve.

5. Purge filler hose before connecting to filler valve to ensure steady stream of liquid at filling nozzle.

6. Connect filler hose from liquid oxygen supply unit to filler valve on converter.

NOTE

Connecting filler nozzle automatically opens vent line and closes buildup circuit. Disconnecting filler nozzle automatically opens buildup circuit and closes vent line.

7. Transfer liquid at rate of approximately 40 to 50-psi pressure until liquid (blue in color) begins to come out of overboard vent at bottom of fuselage (station 657) beneath converters. Filling time should be about six minutes.

Stand clear of overboard vent.

8. Remove filler hose nozzle and replace cap on filler valve.

NOTE

If filler valve leaks, heat from cap and ambient air will free mechanism and stop leakage. When leakage stops, verify proper operating pressure. System purging can be delayed until routine ground maintenance.

9. Repeat steps 4 through 8 for second converter.

Emergency Oxygen Bottle

(See figure 1-64.)

1. Secure release pin in regulator actuating mechanism.

NOTE

Apply slight pressure on pin to overcome resistance of ball-bearing lock.

2. Remove filler valve cap. Connect high-pressure (minimum 1800-psi) gaseous oxygen source to filler valve.

3. Charge bottle to 1800 psi.

4. Remove high-pressure line and install filler valve cap.

Oxygen System Check

Check the following to ensure proper functioning of the system:

The quantity gage should read 20 liters for 24 hours after servicing, as the total supply will be in excess of the "full" measurement of the tank. Indication of system pressure on the small gage located on the high pressure-type regulators will be almost negligible, as the low-pressure supply system is maintained at only 65 to 90 psi.

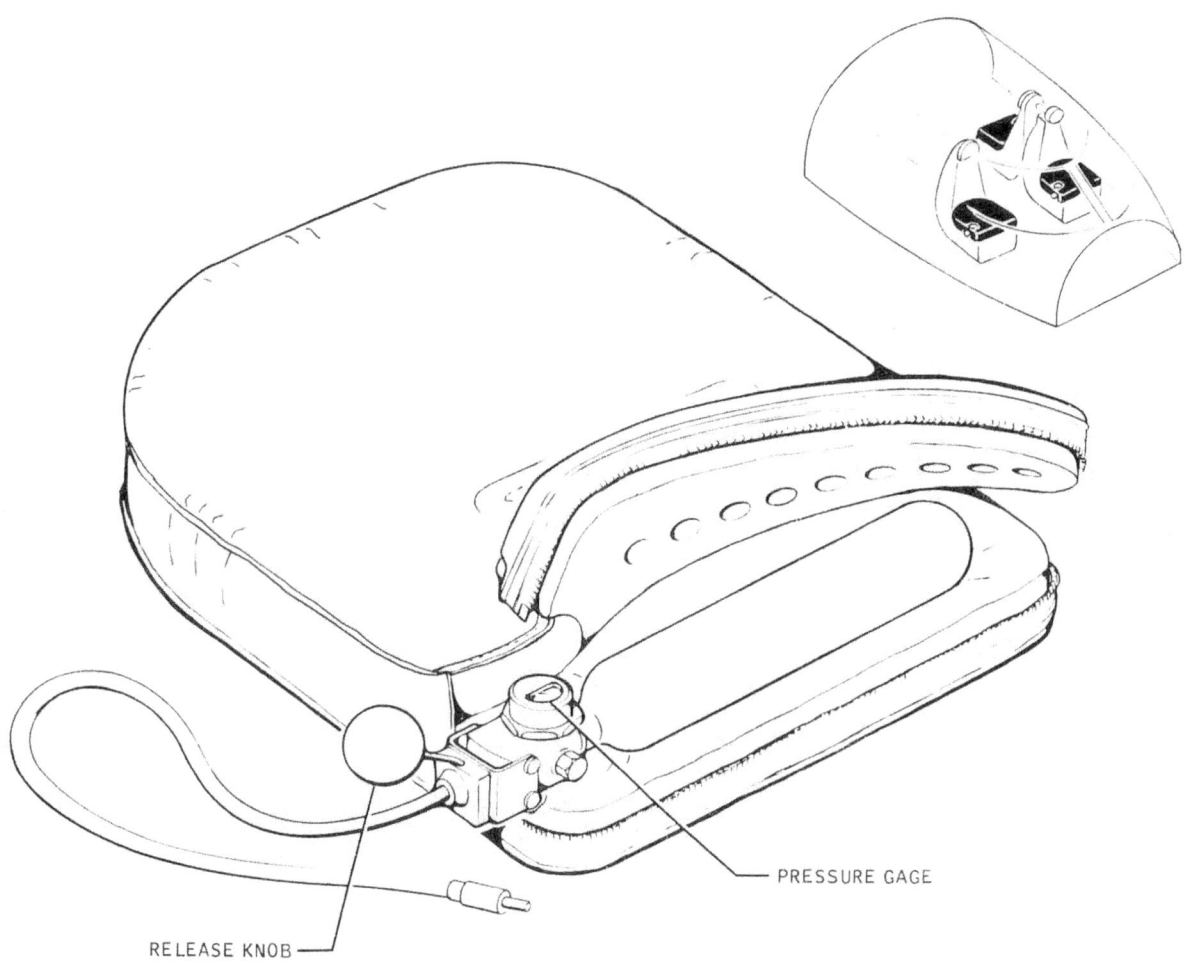

Figure 1-64. Emergency Oxygen Bottle Servicing

RAIN REPELLENT

A rain repellent kit, stock number RM6850-661-1821-LA20, is available through normal supply channels for coating the external surfaces of the windshield and canopy. The function of the repellent is to increase visibility through windshields and canopies during rainstorms. The kit consists of a can of solvent cleaner, a tube of bonding paste, and a stick of repellent.

Rain Repellent Application

1. Wash surface, if excessively soiled, in accordance with existing instructions.

2. Clean surface with kit-supplied cleaner. Use clean, soft cloth; then, dry surface.

3. Polish cleaned surface with clean soft cloth.

4. Apply kit-supplied bonding paste very sparingly with clean, soft cloth, working paste completely over the surface.

NOTE

Do not apply the bonding paste to a wet surface. A satisfactory bond will not be obtained.

5. Polish surface with clean, soft cloth until all black color disappears.

6. Apply kit-supplied rain repellent by rubbing side of stick lightly over surface.

NOTE

Do not apply rain repellent stick endwise. An excessive amount of film will be deposited.

7. Polish surface with clean, soft cloth until film is clear.

CAUTION

Do not apply rain repellent to interior of windshield or canopy.

ANTIFOGGING COMPOUND

An antifogging compound, stock number RN6850-200-2397-G500, is available through normal supply channels for coating the interior surfaces of the windshield and canopy. The function of the compound is to absorb the moisture and prevent fogging of the surfaces.

Antifogging Compound Application

1. Wash surface, if excessively soiled, in accordance with existing instructions.

2. Apply antifogging compound to interior of windshield by means of application unit.

3. Wipe interior surface with clean, lintless cloth until surface is clear.

CAUTION

- Do not permit compound to contact instrument panel finish.

- Do not permit compound to remain on windshield and canopy sealant.

NOTE

One application of compound is effective for a minimum of 10 fogging and drying cycles, or approximately 7 hours of continuous fogging conditions.

DEICING-DEFROSTING FLUID

Material

Deposits of frost on the exterior surfaces of the aircraft on the ground may be removed by the application of deicing-defrosting fluid (MIL-A-8243). When the deposits have been removed, the fluid remaining on the treated surfaces should provide protection for approximately 12 hours.

Deicing-Defrosting Fluid Application

The deicing-defrosting fluid may be applied by swabbing, brushing, or spraying. (Refer to table 1-7B.) If wind conditions permit, a back-pack pump, 5-gallon, water-type, or similar spray pump, is convenient application equipment. However, other types of spray equipment may be used. At low temperatures and under unfavorable wind conditions, swabs or brushes should be used, but care must be taken to prevent their freezing to aircraft surfaces. (Refer to table 1-7A.) The defrosting fluid is supplied mixed ready for use; but it may be diluted, if required for spraying, up to the proportion of one part water to two parts fluid. It should be noted, however, that dilution decreases the ice or frost-melting efficiency of the fluid.

If the recommended deicing-defrosting fluids are not available, anti-icing fluid (isopropyl alcohol), stock number FSN R-51F-516/-519, or specially denatured alcohol, stock number FSN R-51-A-1946/-1947, may be used. These alcohols are volatile, and protection to aircraft surfaces will not be afforded for an extended period after application.

Changed 1 June 1969

Section I
Part 3

NAVAIR 01-40ATA-1

TABLE 1-7A. GUIDE TO THE ELIMINATION OF ICE, SNOW,
OR FROST FROM PARKED AIRCRAFT

Type Deposit	Typical Weather Conditions	Prevention Method (Other than Hangaring)	Removal Procedure	Precautions
Dry Snow	1. Overcast skies 2. Temperature below 30°F	1. Protective covers 2. Frequent removal of snow prevents packing.	1. Sweeping 2. Cloth strip 3. Ground run	1. Chemicals are wasteful in removing dry snow. 2. Check all air intakes and openings for blown snow.
Wet Snow	1. Overcast skies 2. Temperature 30° to 35°F	1. Waterproof protective covers 2. Frequent removal more important	1. Sweeping 2. Mopping 3. Cloth strip	1. Check all openings and moving parts where snow may collect and freeze. 2. Dry surface *after removal* of snow. 3. Check for frozen slush on underside of surfaces.
Frozen Snow	1. Temperature drop after wet snowfall	1. Do not allow wet or dry snow to remain on surface, thaw, and refreeze. 2. Do not remove aircraft from hangar during snowfall.	1. Sweep to remove loose deposits. 2. Apply chemicals by mop or spray. 3. Use heat under cover as alternative method.	1. Check surfaces for frozen snow after wet or dry snow has been removed.
Ice	1. Uniformly overcast skies 2. Temperature 25° to 32°F	1. Frequent application of deicing fluid may prevent freezing. 2. Remove water or slush that may freeze.	1. Allow ice to melt off in hangar. 2. Beat off with short rubber hose. 3. Apply chemicals generously. 4. Use heat under cover.	1. Check all openings and removable parts. 2. Check for runoff that has frozen between or on underside of surface. 3. Avoid damage to surface when heating.
Frost	1. Temperature near freezing 2. Clear skies – night 3. High relative humidity 4. Little or no wind	1. Protective covers 2. Application of deicing fluid (temporary protection only)	1. Chemicals, mop or spray 2. Cloth strip 3. Place aircraft in bright sun.	1. Do not underestimate effect of frost. Remove from top and bottom of all flight surfaces and antennas.
Frozen Mud	1. Thawing conditions	1. Avoid taxiing through water or mud.	1. Hot water, mop or spray 2. Use chemicals if temperature is below freezing.	1. Check movable parts. 2. Leave no water to freeze after cleaning.

NOTES:

1. Where chemicals are specified in the removal procedure column, the use of MIL-A-8243A deicing defrosting fluid is authorized.

2. Mixture to ensure at least -10°F should be mixed half and half with water. For temperatures below -10°F, refer to NAVWEPS 01-1A-520, Anti-Icing, De-Icing and Defrosting of Parked Aircraft.

NAVAIR 01-40ATA-1

Section I
Part 3

TABLE 1-7A. GUIDE TO THE ELIMINATION OF ICE, SNOW,
OR FROST FROM PARKED AIRCRAFT (Continued)

NOTES (Continued):

3. Closely check the following items during and after removal operations:

    a. Top and bottom of all flight surfaces
    b. Air intakes and vents
    c. Static vents
    d. Controls surface gaps and seals
    e. Hinge points
    f. All movable external parts.

WARNING

Prior to LOX servicing, the fluid will be removed from areas adjacent to the LOX filler and overflow tubes and vents, by flushing and wiping methods. Contact of fluid with LOX, a powerful oxidizing agent, may result in fire or explosion. Although the flash point of the fluid is above 93° Centigrade (200°F), the fluid should be used with care when sprayed around heater or engine exhaust. Special care shall be taken to prevent the excessive use of fluid around all engine and intake ducts. This precaution is essential to minimize the possibility of toxic fumes from entering the cockpit during taxi prior to takeoff.

TABLE 1-7B. DEICING-DEFROSTING FLUID APPLICATION PRECAUTIONARY DATA

DO	DON'T
1. Remove fluid from around LOX filler and overflow tubes prior to servicing aircraft with LOX.	1. Apply fluid when LOX carts are in vicinity of aircraft.
2. Position stabilizers and elevators so that liquid will be drained from surface.	2. Apply fluid by spray method unless all personnel are clear of spray areas.
3. Remove ice from leading edge first, and then move progressively aft.	3. Use fluid for removal of heavy snow or ice deposits.
4. Remain on windward side during spray or brush applications.	4. Use alcohols on acrylic turret domes or canopies.
5. Wear adequate eye protection when applying fluid.	
6. Operate spray boom slowly and cautiously. (Boom operator should be thoroughly trained in his job.)	
7. Reapply fluid as needed during severe weather or when takeoff is delayed.	
8. Use covers whenever possible.	
9. Inspect control surfaces for complete removal of ice, snow, and slush.	
10. Manually check control surfaces through their full range of travel to ensure freedom of movement.	

WARNING

- Be careful to keep alcohols away from fire, sparks, etc, since they are flammable and are known to have caused fires when trapped in engine nacelles. Be careful to ensure that alcohols do not contact acrylic plastic (Plexiglas or Lucite) canopies, etc, since they will crack or craze transparent plastic material. The alcohols are toxic and shall not be taken internally, and excessive breathing of the vapors shall be avoided.

- All these fluids have an irritating effect on eyes, throat, nasal passages, etc, and care shall be taken to prevent contact with mucous membranes, especially if sprayed. Personnel applying these fluids shall wear approved type respirator and eye protector.

Changed 1 June 1969

1-163/(1-164 Blank)

GROUND SUPPORT STARTING EQUIPMENT

During the past few years pneumatic starting equipment has become so varied that the listings of suitable equipment for use in the safe starting of the J57-P-10 engine is no longer valid. The MA-1A series of starting units, can include many types, built by different manufacturers, some of which are suitable and some marginal. Ground support starting equipment that adheres to the operating parameters are listed in table 1-7C and can be used when starting A-3 aircraft engines.

All pneumatic air supply starting equipment used today incorporates a flow control valve that governs the air supply in a manner compatible with various aircraft engine-mounted starters, even though the maximum rated output values of the supply units are greater than the maximum limits of the particular starter.

CAUTION

Some of the latest types of ground support starting equipment, both portable and stationary, have controls that permit the operator to select HIGH or LOW pressure air. To prevent damage to engine-mounted starters, it is imperative that the LOW pressure setting be selected when starting engines on A-3 aircraft.

Engine-Mounted Starters

The J52-P-10 engine, installed in A-3 aircraft, utilizes a BUWEPS Model A-21 starter. The Model A-21 starters manufactured by AiResearch and Bendix vary only slightly in operating limitations. Table 1-7C considers both AiResearch and Bendix models of A-21 engine-mounted starters and does not exceed the limitations of either.

DANGER AREAS

During ground operation certain hazardous areas exist. These areas are shown in figure 1-65.

TURNING RADII

For turning radii of the A-3A/B and KA-3B aircraft, see figure 1-51.

SECURING AIRCRAFT

1. Chock wheels.

2. Install ATM exhaust plugs.

3. If gusty wind conditions exist or are anticipated, moor aircraft securely (figure 1-66). Install engine exhaust covers, inlet duct covers, and compressor bleed port plugs. Install bomb bay door safety locks landing gear locking pins, fin jury struts, ATM air outlet duct plugs, and covers for cockpit enclosure, folded fin, and folded wing butts.

CAUTION

When the aircraft is secured for the night at an airfield or on the upper deck of a carrier, it is recommended that the fin not be folded. It is possible for moisture to form in the horizontal stabilizer power boost mechanism and cause deterioration of the unit or freezing of the controls when the aircraft climbs to altitude.

TABLE 1-7C. ENGINE-MOUNTED STARTER – Operating Parameters

Ambient Outside Air Temp °F	Duty Cycle	Air-Flow PPM	Inlet Press. PSIA			Inlet Temp °F		
			Rated	Max	Min	Rated	Max	Min
-65 to +160	3 min on, 15 min off 3 1-min cycles with 2-min rest 3 starts in 5 min	60	50	70	45	345	650	250

Starter Units

The following is a partial listing of suitable starting units that can be used when starting the A-3A/B and KA-3B aircraft:

GTC-85	MA-3MP
MA-1	M-32A-60
MA-1A	MA-1E
MA-2	Wells Airstart
MA-2MP	NC-PP105

Changed 1 June 1969

Section I
Part 3

NAVAIR 01-40ATA-1

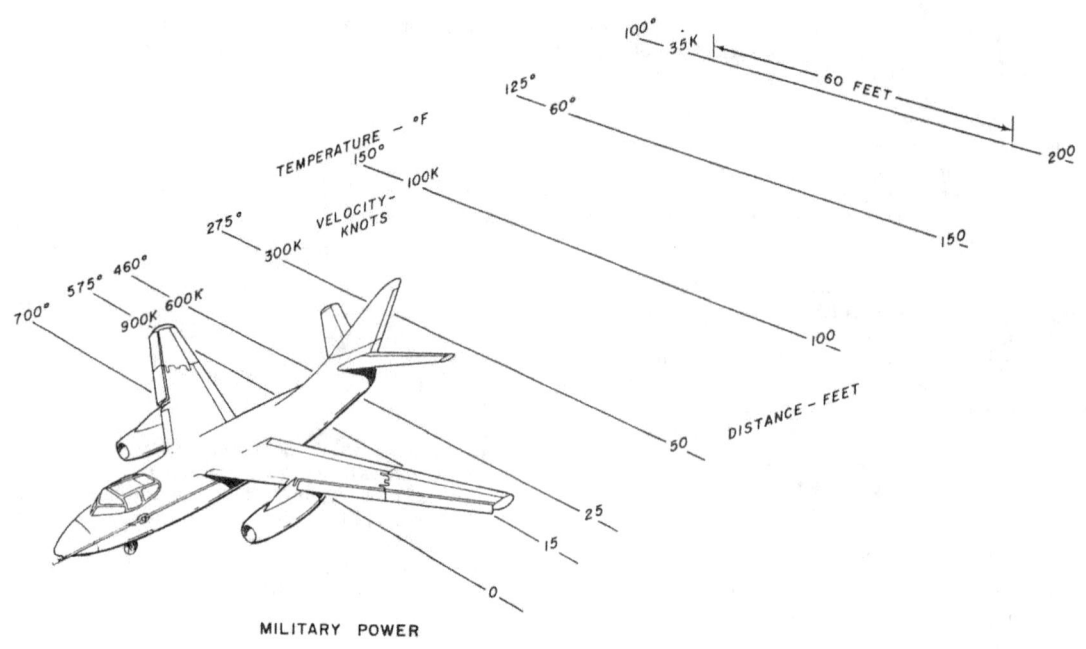

MILITARY POWER

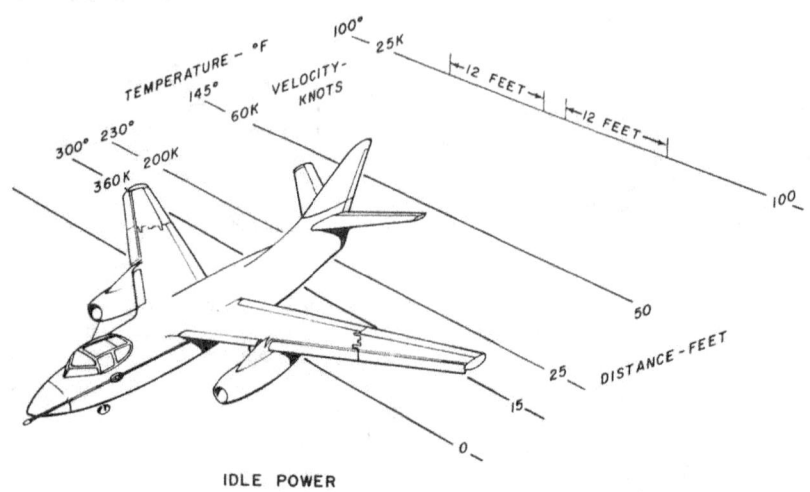

IDLE POWER

ATA-1 P-4470-1E

Jet Blast
Figure 1-65. Danger Areas (Sheet 1)

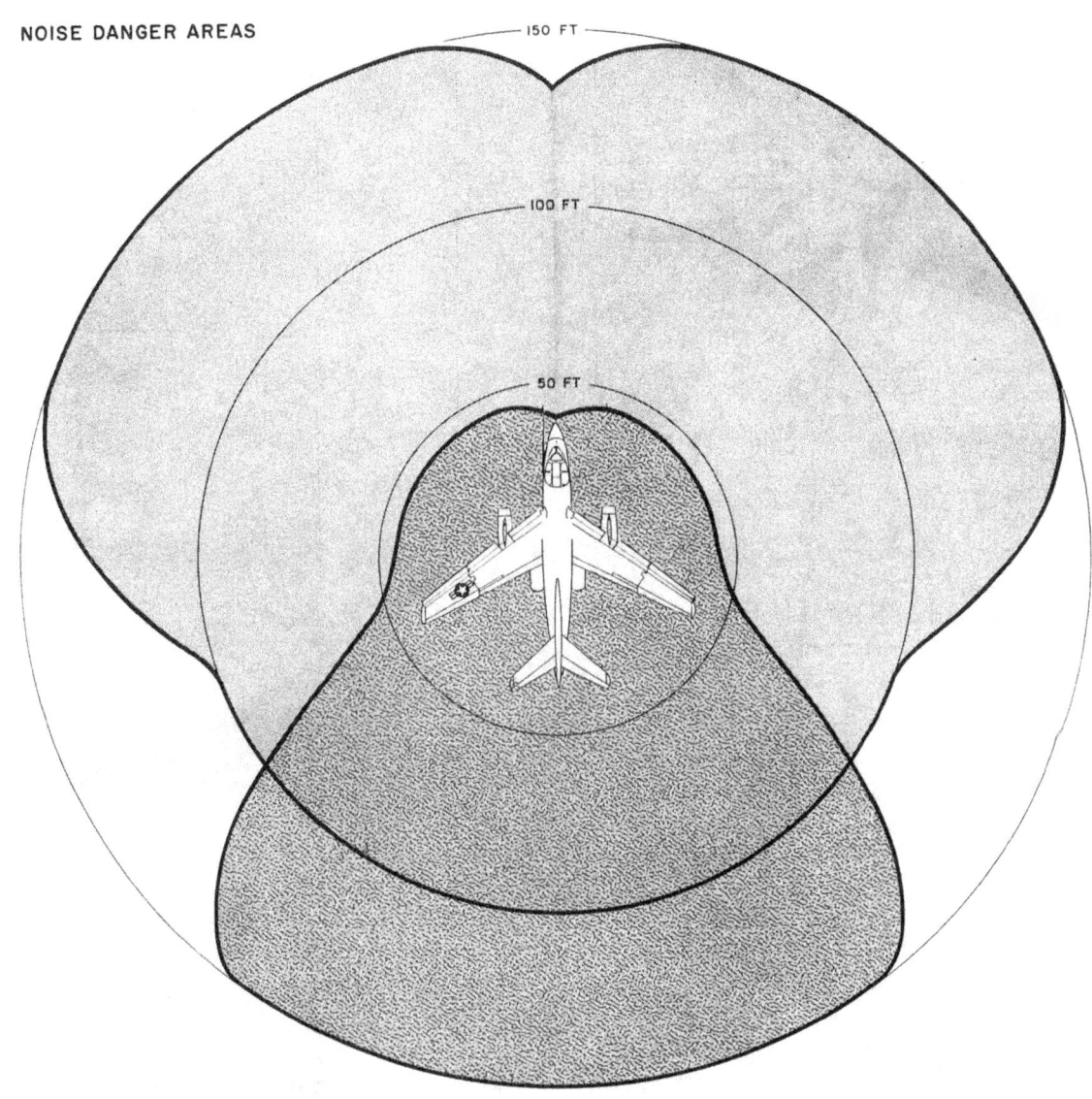

Noise
Figure 1-65. Danger Areas (Sheet 2)

Section I
Part 3

NAVAIR 01-40ATA-1

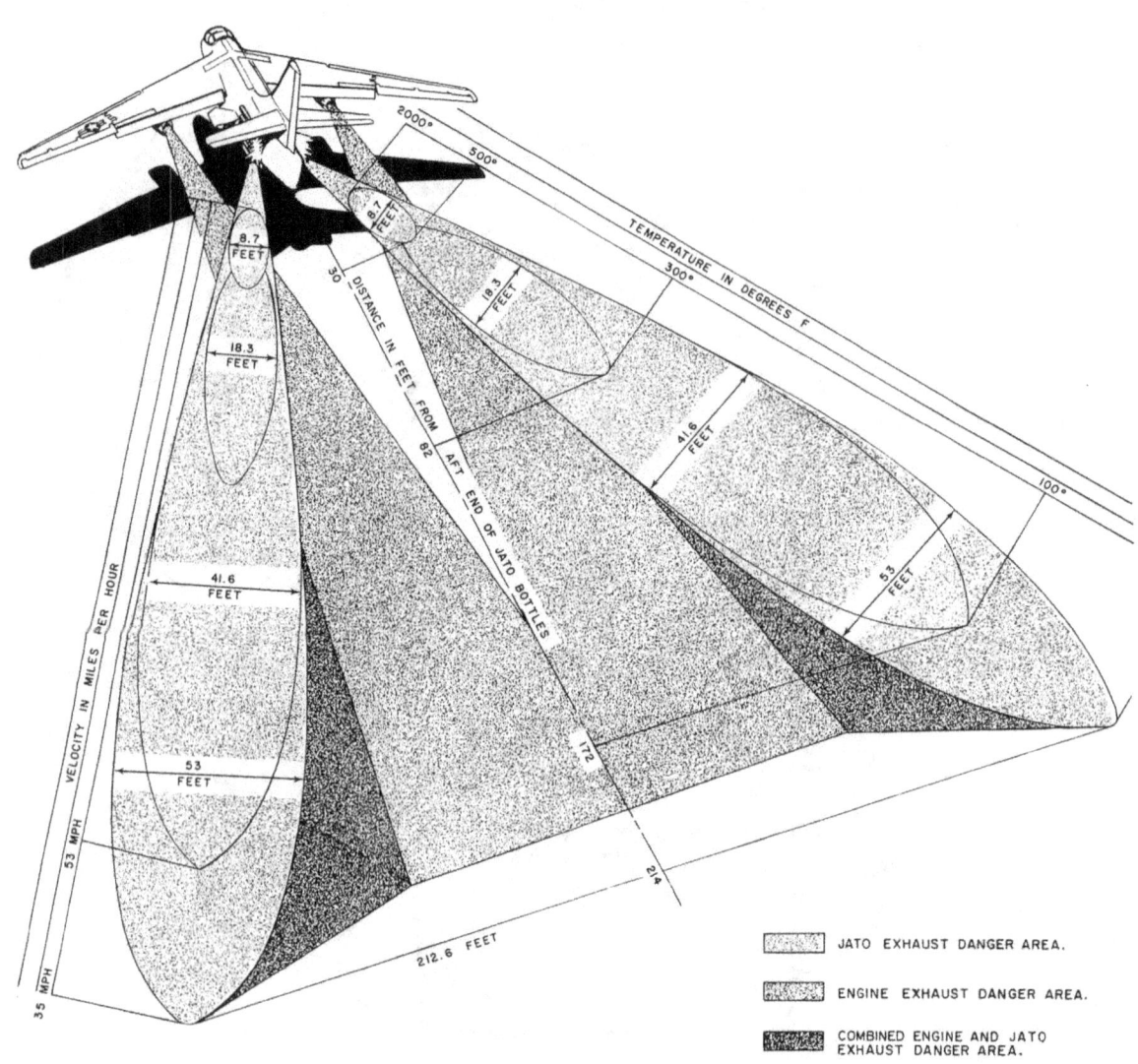

JATO Blast
Figure 1-65. Danger Areas (Sheet 3)

NAVAIR 01-40ATA-1

Section I
Part 3

Figure 1-66. Mooring

NAVAIR 01-40ATA-1

Section I
Part 4

PART 4
AIRCRAFT OPERATING LIMITATIONS

TABLE OF CONTENTS

TEXT

	Page		Page
Introduction	1-171	Acceleration Limitations	1-175
Engine Limitations	1-171	Weight Limitations	1-175
Engine Operating Limitations	1-171	Carrier Operations	
Normal Flight	1-171	Limitations	1-175
Airspeed Limitations	1-171	Center-of-Gravity Limitations	1-175
Maneuvers	1-171	JATO Limitations	1-175

TABLES

Table		Page	Table		Page
1-8	J57-P-6B Engines	1-174	1-9	J57-P-10 Engines	1-174

ILLUSTRATIONS

Figure		Page	Table		Page
1-67	Instrument Markings	1-172	1-68	Operating Flight Strength (VN) Diagrams	1-176

Changed 1 June 1969

1-170A/(1-170B Blank)

NAVAIR 01-40ATA-1

Section I
Part 4

INTRODUCTION

This section describes operating limitations that shall be observed during normal aircraft operation. It is mandatory that the prescribed limitations be observed at all times, not only for the safety of the pilot and crew but also to obtain the most satisfactory operation of the aircraft. Cognizance shall be taken of the instrument markings illustrated in figure 1-67, since limitations represented in the figure are not necessarily repeated in the text.

ENGINE LIMITATIONS

The engines and their supporting structure will mechanically withstand any flight maneuver or landing forces within the design load factor limitations of the aircraft structure.

Engine Operating Limitations

The engine limitations are based on a combination of engine speeds and exhaust gas temperatures. The maximum allowable engine rpm under any condition is red-lined at 105.2 percent of maximum rated (9700) rpm. Should this limiting rpm be exceeded, reduce power and land as soon as possible. Adhere strictly to maximum allowable exhaust gas temperatures to prolong the life of the engine. Tables 1-8 and 1-9 show maximum engine speeds and exhaust gas temperatures under various operating conditions.

Normal Flight

Except for combat and carrier operations, normal flight consists of normal takeoffs and landings, horizontal flight in normal attitudes, "g" factors not in excess of 2g, angles of bank not in excess of 60 degrees and inclined flight upward to an angle not in excess of that angle which the aircraft can maintain for a prolonged period at maximum power.

AIRSPEED LIMITATIONS

The maximum permissible indicated airspeeds are as follows:

1. In smooth or moderately turbulent air:

   a. With arresting hook, landing gear, and wing flaps retracted, and speedbrakes retracted or extended, and except that airspeeds shall be kept below that at which airframe vibration is encountered:

13,000 feet and below	480 knots
13,000 to 33,000 feet	0.85 IMN
33,000 feet and above	0.88 IMN

   b. With landing gear extended:

   With ASC 39 or 39A incorporated .... 225 knots

   c. With wing flaps fully or partially extended .... 255 knots

   d. Drag chute should be deployed only when aircraft is on the ground and below 150 knots.

   e. It is recommended that fuel dumping be conducted in unyawed, straight, and level flight or unabrupt coordinated level turns. Optimum airspeeds for dumping fuel with landing gear and wingflaps are:

   Retracted .... 250 knots
   Extended .... 150 knots

   f. JATO bottles shall be jettisoned at airspeeds below 200 knots, in a level flight attitude, with flaps down.

   g. Maximum speed for windshield wiper operation .... 200 KIAS

   #### NOTE

   JATO bottles can be carried safely at airspeeds up to 300 KIAS but not jettisoned above 200 KIAS.

2. In severe turbulence the maximum permissible airspeeds are: aircraft should not be operated in conditions of severe turbulence because gusts can be encountered that impose excessive loads. However, if flight in severe turbulence cannot be avoided, indicated airspeeds in range of 190 to 300 KIAS are recommended. Airspeeds of 220 to 250 KIAS are recommended for thunderstorm penetration.

MANEUVERS

The following maneuvers are not permitted:

1. Normal and accelerated stalls

2. Loft maneuvers

3. Loops

Changed 1 June 1969

1-171

Section I
Part 4

NAVAIR 01-40ATA-1

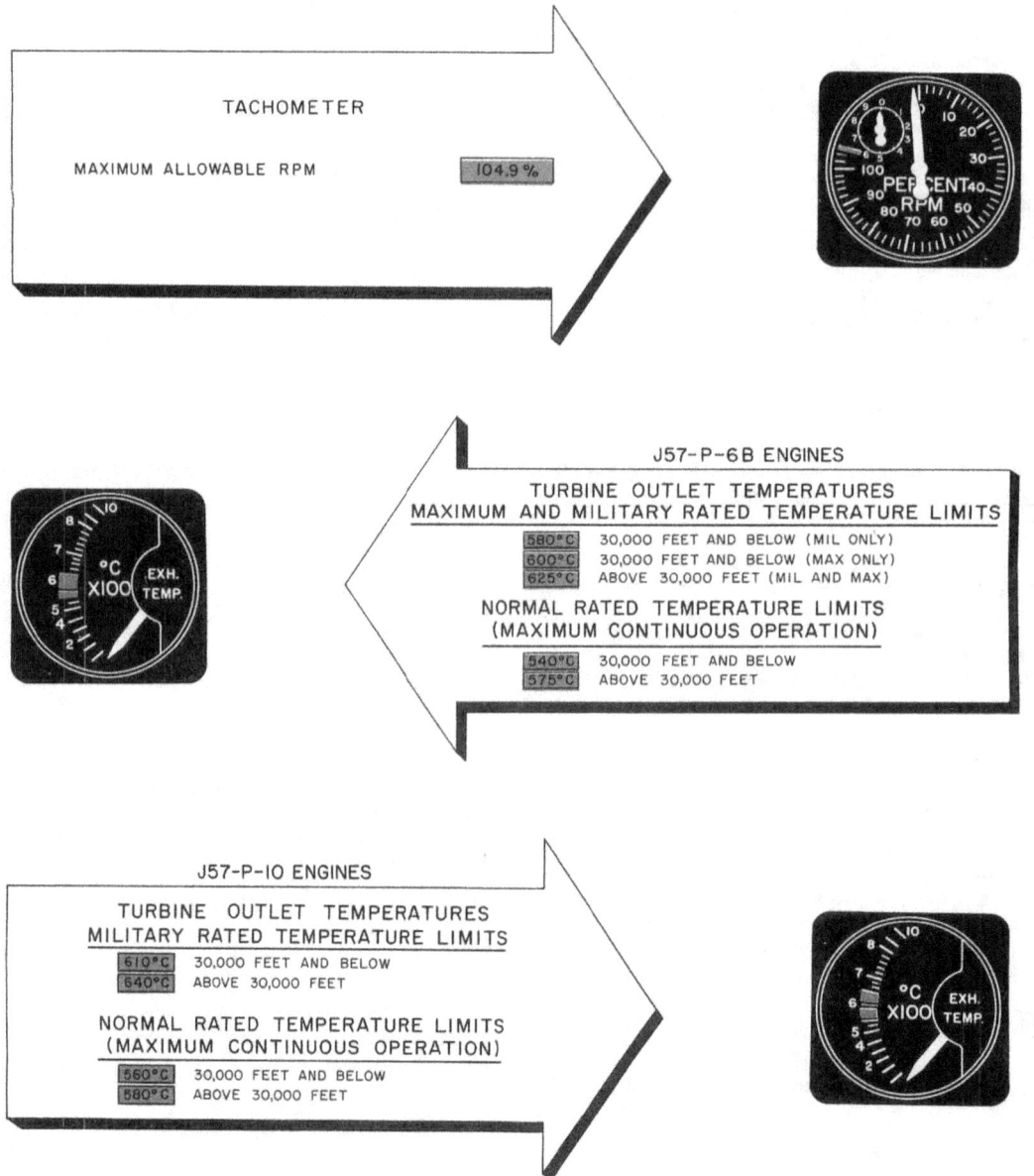

Aircraft BuNo. 135407-135444,
138902-138962, 138964-138976, 142400-142407, 142630-142649
Figure 1-67. Instrument Markings (Sheet 1)

1-172

Changed 15 July 1970

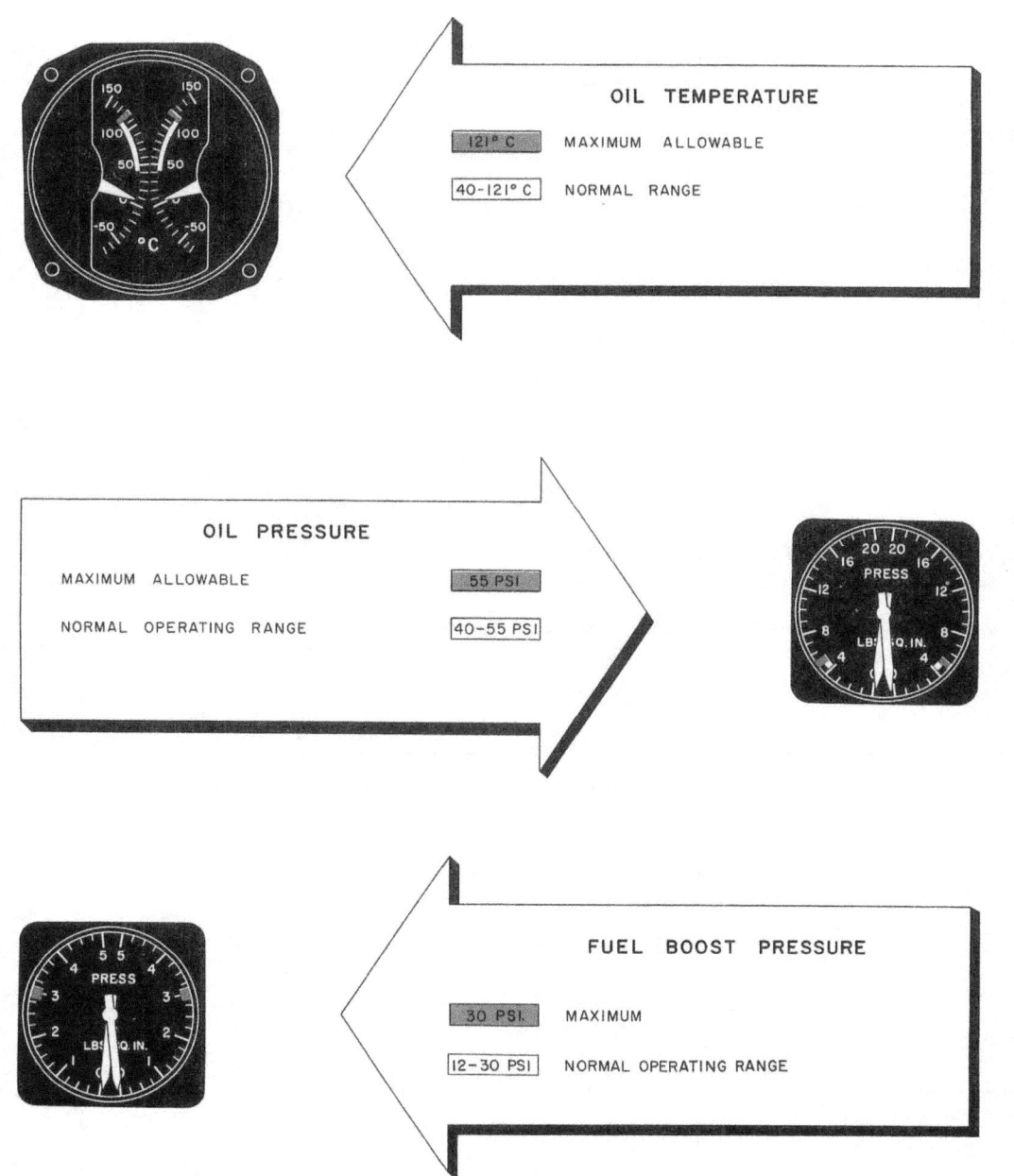

Aircraft BuNo. 135407-135444,
138902-138962, 138964-138976, 142400-142407, 142630-142649
Figure 1-67. Instrument Markings (Sheet 2)

Section I
Part 4

NAVAIR 01-40ATA-1

TABLE 1-8. J57-P-6B ENGINES

Operating Conditions	% of Max Rated RPM	Maximum Exhaust Gas Temperature °C		Time Limit (Minutes)	Fuel Boost Pressure		Oil Pressure
		30,000 Ft & Below	Above 30,000 Ft		Min	Max	Normal
Maximum	104.9	600	625	5 to 15[1]	12	24	40 55
Military rated	104.9	580	625	30	12	24	40 55
Normal rated (Max continuous)	104.9	540	575	--	12	24	40 55
Idle	60 to 62	340 (Ground)	---	--	12	24	35 minimum
Starting	--	430-450 (Ground)	---	Momentary	12	24	-- --
Acceleration	104.9	625	625	2	12	24	40 50

[1] 5 minutes for takeoff or ground operation; 15 minutes in flight.

TABLE 1-9. J57-P-10 ENGINES

Operating Conditions	% of Max Rated RPM	Maximum Exhaust Gas Temperature °C		Time Limit (Minutes)	Fuel Boost Pressure		Oil Pressure
		30,000 Ft & Below	Above 30,000 Ft		Min	Max	Normal Range
Military rates	104.9	610	640	30	12	30	40 55
Normal rated (Max continuous)	104.9	560	580	--	12	30	40 55
Idle	60 to 62	340 (Ground)	---	--	12	30	35 minimum
Starting	--	450 (Ground)	610	Momentary	12	30	-- --
Acceleration	105.2	650	650	2	12	30	40 55

4. Bank angles in excess of 60 degrees.

5. Under asymmetric power conditions, intentional slips or skids into dead engine at airspeeds in excess of 350 KIAS.

NOTE

A maximum of 300 KIAS shall not be exceeded when intentionally securing an engine during routine operations.

6. Abrupt uncoordinated maneuvers, especially abrupt rudder kicks.

ACCELERATION LIMITATIONS

Positive acceleration limits of A-3B aircraft vary with aircraft gross weight and velocity (figure 1-68). The maximum acceleration load factor is 3.4g for smooth air at an aircraft gross weight of 56,000 pounds. At 1.0g negative, a time limit of 15 seconds must be observed to prevent loss of ATM power. The maximum positive design load factor is 4.77g without wing fuel at a landing gross weight of 44,000 pounds. The maximum gust acceleration limit shall be 2.0g when operating in moderate turbulence at a gross weight of 56,000 pounds or less. Limit load factors versus gross weights are shown in figure 1-68. At any gross weight above 55,942 pounds, the limit load factor is significantly reduced. Acceleration at which buffeting is encountered shall not be exceeded. Figure 4-1, illustrates the load factor for buffet onset versus altitude and Mach number. Operation to the limits of buffet onset, prior to incorporation of A-3 AFC 200, is not permitted. Skin and rib cracks in the cove area along the center wing trailing edge can result from flight involving buffet.

NOTE

Figure 1-68 is not to be used for A-3A aircraft. The acceleration curve is calculated for A-3B aircraft with a maximum acceleration load factor of 3.4g, while the A-3A aircraft, limited to 2.67g, will not coincide with the curve depicted in figure 1-68.

WEIGHT LIMITATIONS

The maximum recommended gross weights are as follows:

1. Field takeoff — A-3A . . . . . 70,000 pounds
   A-3B . . . . . 78,000 pounds

2. Field landing. . . . . 56,000 pounds

3. Catapulting — A-3A . . . . . . 70,000 pounds
   A-3B . . . . . . 73,000 pounds

4. Arrested landings, both shipboard and shore-based, including touch and go and FCLP . . . . 50,000 pounds

CARRIER OPERATIONS LIMITATIONS

Arrested landings with fuel in the wing tanks are not permitted. Catapulting and arrested landings in the tanker configuration with fuel in the lower bomb bay tank are not permitted.

Catapult shots with partial wing fuel are not permitted.

Barricade engagements are permitted to a maximum gross weight of 50,000 pounds. The applicable recovery bulletin contains the permissible arresting gear engaging speeds.

CENTER-OF-GRAVITY LIMITATIONS

The aircraft cg must never exceed the established center of gravity limitations.

The center of gravity for all currently permissible gross weight and configurations must be kept between 12 percent and 27 percent of mean aerodynamic chord. Refer to the Weight and Balance Handbook, AN 01-1B-40, for details regarding the center-of-gravity loadings.

JATO LIMITATIONS

JATO bottles shall be jettisoned at airspeeds below 200 KIAS in a level flight attitude with flaps full down.

NOTE

JATO bottles can be carried safely at airspeeds up to 300 KIAS but should not be jettisoned at airspeeds above 200 KIAS.

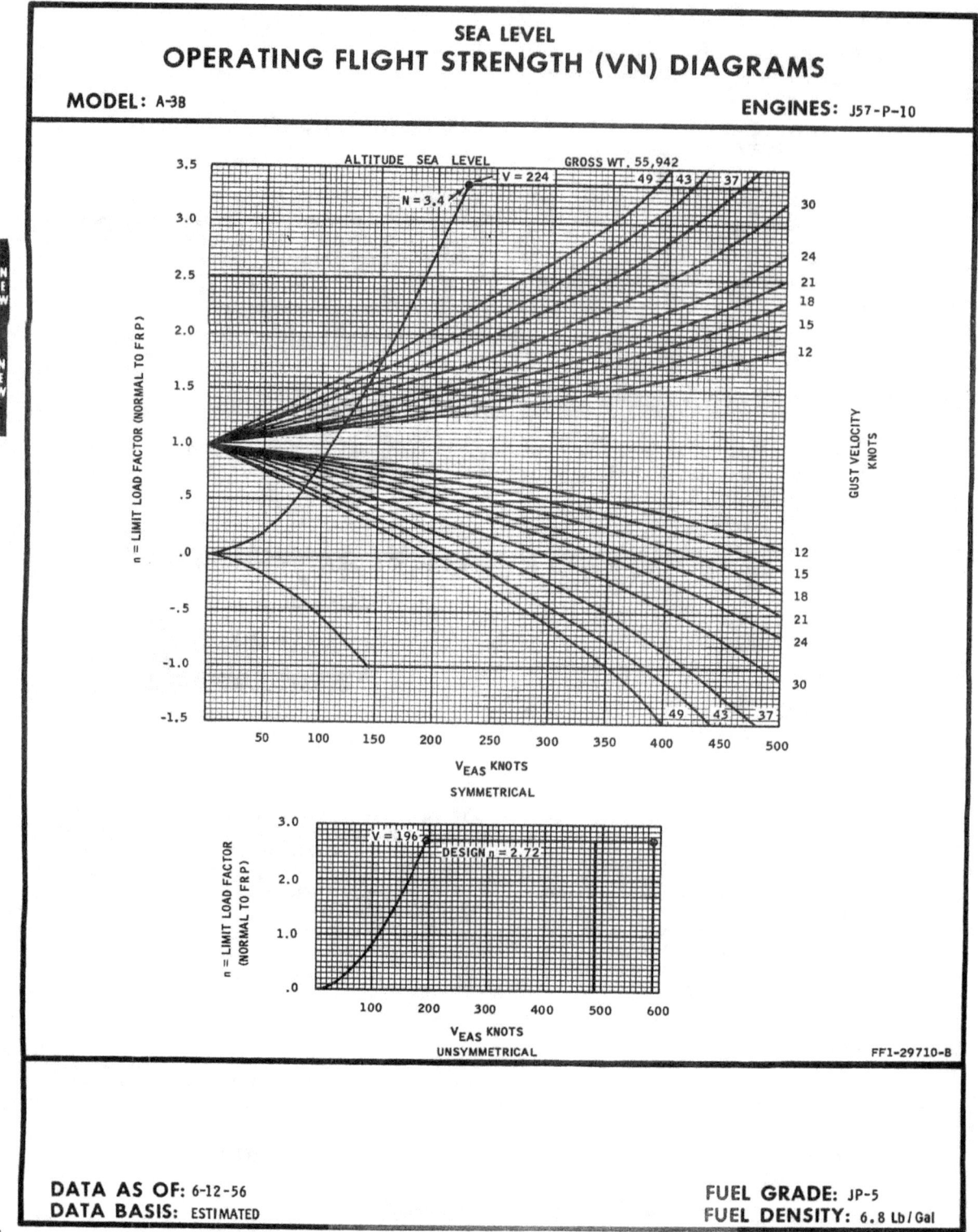

Figure 1-68. Operating Flight Strength (VN) Diagrams

SECTION II
INDOCTRINATION

TABLE OF CONTENTS

TEXT

	Page		Page
Introduction	2-1	Oxygen Equipment Check	2-3
Ground Training	2-1	Parachute	2-3
Survival Training	2-1	Pararaft Kit	2-3
Flight Crew Requirements	2-1	Pararaft Deployment	2-3
Personal Equipment Requirements	2-2	Emergency Transceiver	2-3

ILLUSTRATIONS

Figure		Page
2-1	Personal Gear	2-5

INTRODUCTION

This section establishes minimum requirements for training, initial qualification, and currency. Subsequent sections when used with the Naval Warfare Publication series provide the operational information considered necessary to ensure safe and efficient operation of A-3 aircraft. Unit commanders are authorized to waive, in writing, flight hour minimums and/or OFT/WST training requirements where recent experience in similar models warrants. However, adequate preparation and guidance of the pilot for initial and subsequent flights, so that he safely attains and maintains a reasonable degree of proficiency in a safe manner, is of prime importance. Too often, under pressure of operational commitments, the groundwork is abbreviated or deleted. This can result only in a deterioration of individual and unit effectiveness. For this reason, commanding officers must continuously ensure adherence to these basic criteria whenever possible. Procedures for submitting changes to and requesting waivers from the provisions of this section are contain in OPNAV Instructions 3510.9 (current revision). Training requirements, checkout procedures, evaluation procedures, and weather minima for ferry squadrons are governed by the provisions contain in OPNAVINST 3710, 6 Series. Separate qualifications are required for each model of A-3 aircraft.

GROUND TRAINING

Ground training should be continuous throughout the tour of the A-3 pilot and crew. The overall syllabus will vary according to local conditions, facilities, directives from higher authority, and the unit commander's estimation of squadron readiness. However, there are certain specific requirements that must be met to ensure that the crew is properly indoctrinated and briefed prior to flight.

SURVIVAL TRAINING

The requirements for and frequency of survival training shall be as directed by the type commander. Survival training will normally require the following minimum training of all A-3 flight personnel:

1. Low pressure chamber .... EVERY 2 YEARS

2. Night vision .... AS REQUIRED

3. Swimming tests .... AS REQUIRED

4. Underwater breathing ..... AS REQUIRED

5. Helicopter rescue .... AS REQUIRED

6. Parachute harness release and drag .... AS REQUIRED

7. Ditching and bailout ...... AS REQUIRED

FLIGHT CREW REQUIREMENTS

The crew of the A-3A/B and KA-3B aircraft will normally consist of the pilot, navigator, and plane captain. A fourth crewmember (observer, plane captain

Changed 1 June 1969

trainee, etc) may be included as deemed necessary. For hazardous operations, the minimum crew required to perform the mission safely will be used. The minimum crew, consisting of the pilot and qualified additional crewman (navigator, or plane captain), may be used during initial FMLP and carrier qualification, etc. A pilot must complete the following ground syllabus conducted by the RCVW training squadron prior to commencing A-3 flight transition:

Naval air maintenance training	(8 days)
Prefamiliarization ground training	(3 1/2 days)
A-3 operational flight trainer (OFT)	(10 hours)

The minimum flight training requirements will normally be completed in the RCVW training squadron. However at the discretion of the commanding officer, nonoperational pilots (those who are not ordered to operational A-3 squadrons) may complete the A-3 flight training requirements at their parent activity under the supervision of a currently qualified A-3 pilot. The RCVW squadron will maintain a detailed flight syllabus to be available on request for the conduct of such training. The minimum pilot time requirements while undergoing TCVW training are as follows:

10 hours OFT prior to SOLO

10 hours pilot time prior to SOLO

20 hours pilot time prior to NIGHT SOLO

20 hours pilot time prior to ACTUAL INSTRUMENT FLIGHT

30 hours pilot time prior to CROSS COUNTRY

30 hours pilot time prior to FCLP

50 hours pilot time prior to CARRIER QUAL.

Commanding officers may waive these minimums where previous or recent experience is indicated.

Fourth Seat

The use of the fourth seat for other than official purposes is not authorized. The following criteria should be followed when authorizing a flight requiring occupancy of the fourth seat:

1. Presence of fourth seat crewman in aircraft must be essential to successful completion of flight or be in support of squadron's mission or assigned tasks.

2. Fourth crewman must be equipped in accordance with minimum personnel equipment requirements given in this manual.

3. Fourth crewman must complete survival training requirements of this manual.

NOTE

While it is not intended to discourage flight by legitimate, qualified observers, flight by sightseeing, nonproductive passengers is prohibited.

PERSONAL EQUIPMENT REQUIREMENTS

The equipment (figure 2-1) indicated below shall be worn on all flights in naval aircraft unless other safety considerations or the design characteristics of the model aircraft dictate otherwise:

1. Flame retardant coveralls

2. Identification tags

3. Flight gloves

4. Flight safety boots/field shoes (ankle-high lace type)

5. Antibuffet helmet

6. Life preserver. The preserver will be equipped in accordance with applicable NAVAIR technical bulletins.

7. An approved survival knife and sheath

8. Personal survival kit

9. Parachute

10. Oxygen mask

11. Antiexposure suit or full pressure suit shall be provided on all overwater flights beyond gliding distance from land when water temperature is 59°F or below, OAT is 32°F or below, or the combined air/water temperature is 120°F or below.

NOTE

Antiexposure suit is not required when the water temperature is 50°F and aircraft is within gliding distance of land. When high ambient cockpit temperature would create a hazardous debilitating effect on the crew, type commanders are authorized to grant a waiver in accordance with current OPNAVINST 3710.7 series.

12. A pistol with tracer ammunition for all flights, night or day, over water or over sparsely populated areas. An approved signaling device is authorized as a substitute for the pistol when operational and/or security conditions warrant.

13. Flashlight for all night flights.

All survival equipment must be secured so that it is easily accessible and will not be lost in an emergency.

Oxygen Equipment Check

Procedures for checking proper operation of the oxygen mask are as follows:

1. When initially positioning oxygen mask for use, direct mask away from face as a precaution in the event of flash fire.

2. Turn oxygen supply valve ON and place diluter knob to 100% position.

3. Turn safety pressure knob to ON and listen for flow of oxygen.

4. Place safety pressure switch in OFF.

5. Fit and adjust mask. (Inhalation should not be difficult if regulator is functioning properly.)

6. Check flow indicator for proper operation. (Indicator will blink black with each inhalation.)

PARACHUTE

The NB7D parachute is used in the aircraft. An automatic opening device is actuated by a lanyard attached to the actuator and snapped to an O-ring fitting on the inboard side of each crewmember's seat. The baro-release lanyards for the navigator and plane captain can drop straight down from their left side and snap on the end fitting. The pilot's lanyard must pass behind his back and fasten to the fitting. Upon bailout, the lanyard will extend fully to a length of 51 inches before arming the automatic parachute actuator. Each crewmember should be sliding down the chute before the lanyard tightens and arms the actuator. The automatic parachute actuator is set to deploy the parachute at 14,000 feet MSL. If the bailout is accomplished below 14,000 feet MSL, the actuator will open the parachute 3 seconds after the lanyard is pulled.

Pararaft Kit

All crewmember seats are designed to accommodate a pararaft kit. This kit is installed beneath the seat pan and is secured in the kit (high-speed container) by a ripcord located at the right rear of the high speed container. In addition to normal survival equipment, the kit also contains an emergency locator transceiver. Additional locator transceivers may be carried depending on local area commander requirements. Operating instructions and frequencies will be contained in applicable survival bulletins (OPNAVINST 3710.7 series).

Pararaft Deployment

The pararaft and survival equipment can be removed from the high-speed container in the following manner.

During parachute descent, release the lower left rocket jet fitting. This will allow the high-speed container to swing to the right somewhat. Located on the right rear of the container is a 4-inch yellow snap tab attached to the pararaft lanyard. Pull the tab and connect the pararaft lanyard to the lower right rocket jet fitting or the MK-3C lifevest. After the pararaft lanyard has been secured, pull the ripcord handle on the right rear of the high-speed container to separate the pararaft and survival equipment from the container.

NOTE

Securing and deployment of the pararaft and survival equipment should be completed prior to inflation of the MK-3C lifevest and water entry. If the MK-3C lifevest is inflated, some difficulty may be encountered when trying to secure the pararaft lanyard. If the pararaft lanyard is not attached prior to water entry, the raft and attached survival equipment may be lost during parachute/seat pan separation.

Emergency Transceiver

The emergency radio transceiver (AN/PRC-32 or AN/PRC-17A) is located in the equipment container of the pararaft. Both transceivers are battery operated. The AN/PRC-32 has an approximate range of 40 miles, with a battery operating life of 8 hours.

The AN/PRC-17A has an approximate range of 20 miles, with a battery operating life of 15 hours.

Section II NAVAIR 01-40ATA-1

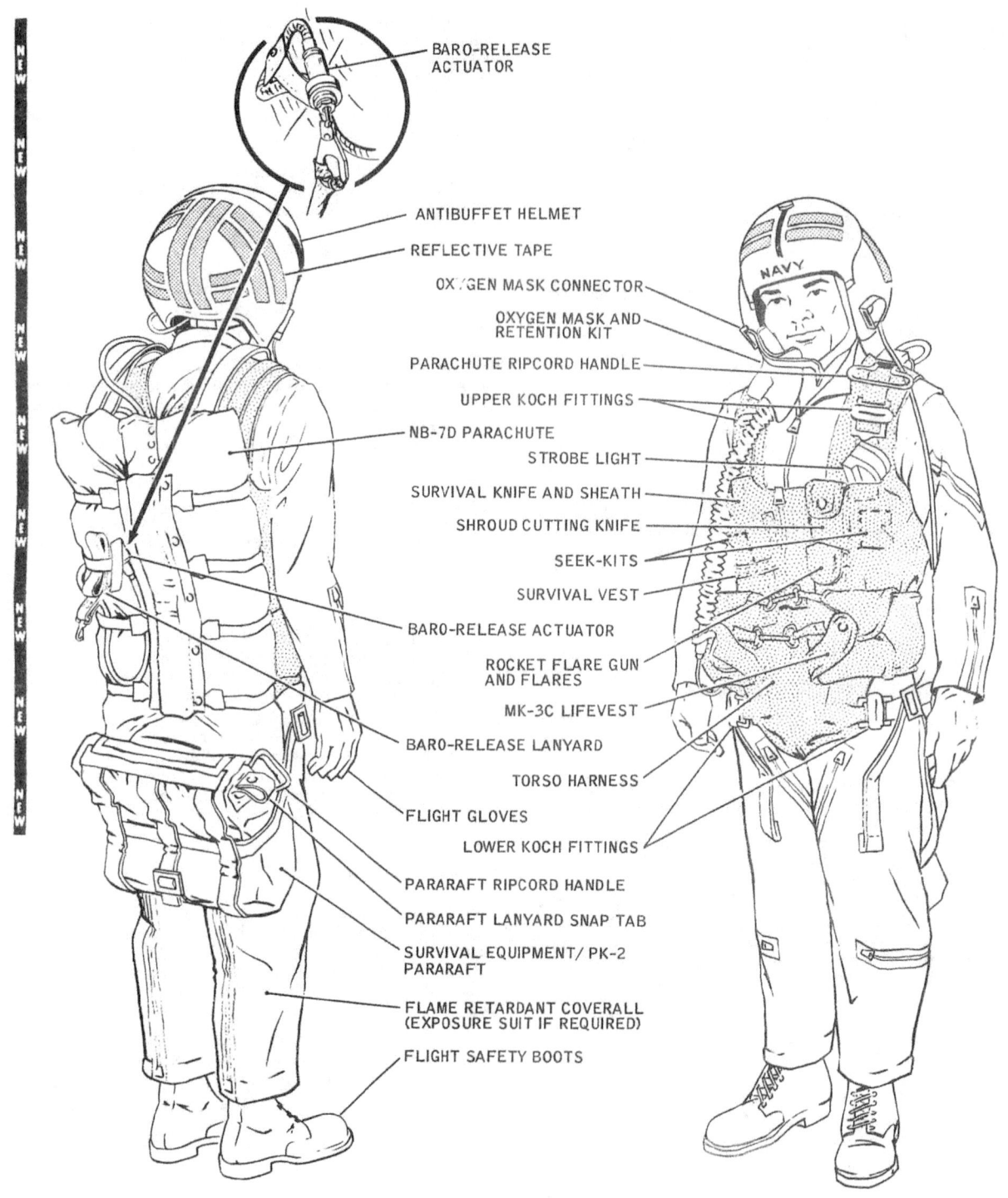

Figure 2-1. Personal Gear

NAVAIR 01-40ATA-1   Section III

SECTION III
NORMAL PROCEDURES

TABLE OF CONTENTS

Part		Page	Part		Page
1	BRIEFING/DEBRIEFING	3-3	3	SHORE-BASED PROCEDURES	3-8A
2	MISSION PLANNING	3-5	4	CARRIER-BASED PROCEDURES	3-35

Changed 1 June 1969   3-1/(3-2 Blank)

NAVAIR 01-40ATA-1

Section III
Part 1

PART 1
BRIEFING/DEBRIEFING

TABLE OF CONTENTS

TEXT

	Page		Page
Introduction	3-3	Navigation and Flight Planning	3-3
General Briefing	3-3	Takeoff Abort Computations	3-3
Mission Planning Briefings	3-3	Emergencies	3-4
Operational Mission Plan	3-3	Air Intelligence and Special Instructions	3-4
Communications	3-3	Debriefing	3-4

INTRODUCTION

Successful execution of an assigned mission depends upon complete familiarity with its specific requirements. The nature of the assigned mission will determine briefing format and persons responsible for delivering the briefing. If possible, all crewmembers will attend mission briefings. It is the responsibility of the Operations Officer to see that correct and complete briefings are conducted. The Operations Officer will assign briefing duties to specific individuals of the various squadron departments. For air refueling missions, the tanker pilot shall brief all receiver pilots concerning rendezvous, receiver aircraft movements, amount of fuel to be transferred, interplane signals, and emergency procedures.

GENERAL BRIEFING

The briefing shall be conducted using a briefing guide. Each pilot shall maintain a knee pad and record data necessary to complete the assigned mission. The briefing guide shall include the following items:

1. Aircraft assigned, call signs, and deck spot
2. Engine start, taxi, and takeoff time
3. Rendezvous instructions.

MISSION PLANNING BRIEFINGS

Operational Mission Plan

1. Primary
2. Secondary
3. Operation area
4. Control agency
5. Time on station
6. Air refueling requirements.

Communications

1. Frequencies
2. Radio procedure and discipline
3. Navigational aids
4. Identification and ADIZ procedures
5. Tactical IP codes/call signs
6. Visual signals
7. Encryption and authentication.

WEATHER

1. Present weather
2. Forecast weather
3. High altitude weather for jet stream, temperature, inversion layers, and contrail band width.

Navigation and Flight Planning

1. Climbout
2. Navigation track
3. Mission plan, including fuel/oxygen management
4. Marshal
5. Penetration
6. GCA or CCA
7. Recovery.

Takeoff Abort Computations

1. Takeoff airspeed
2. Takeoff roll

Changed 1 June 1969

3-3

3. Distance from lift-off point to arresting gear (if applicable)

4. Line speed check

5. Refusal speed (if applicable)

6. Safe single-engine speed for takeoff gross weight

7. Single-engine performance (Section XI)

8. Surrounding terrain and obstruction altitudes

9. Fuel dumping considerations.

NOTE

For takeoff on runways not rigged with arresting gear or distance markers, a refusal speed must be computed. For takeoff on runways where arresting gear is rigged, sufficient distance remains to drop the hook.

Emergencies

1. Aborts

2. Divert fields

3. Bingo and low-state fuel

4. Waveoff pattern

5. Ready deck

6. Radio failure

7. Loss of visual contact with flight

8. Down-pilot and aircraft emergencies

9. System failures.

Air Intelligence and Special Instructions

1. Friendly or enemy force disposition

2. Current situation

3. Safety precautions.

DEBRIEFING

Immediately after securing the aircraft, the crew shall proceed to the line shack or ready room to sign off the yellow sheet and debrief. Postflight debriefing is necessary to obtain maximum value from training flights. Postflight debriefings of actual missions are a primary source of operational intelligence. Debriefs shall be conducted in a concise and orderly manner immediately following recovery of the flight and shall include mission accomplishment, crew performance, and pertinent recommendations for improving crew coordination.

NAVAIR 01-40ATA-1

Section III
Part 2

PART 2
MISSION PLANNING

TABLE OF CONTENTS

TEXT

	Page		Page
Introduction	3-5	Navigation Planning	3-6
Briefings	3-5	Cross-Country Flights	3-6
Weight and Balance	3-5	Navigation Bag Contents	3-6
Operational Mission Planning	3-5	Fuel Planning	3-6
Mission Checklist	3-5		

INTRODUCTION

The success and ease with which a mission can be accomplished depends on the planning that precedes it. Thorough and detailed mission planning is mandatory. The planning of the mission is a crew function and will serve as a guide for the flight. Training must emphasize the necessity for crew coordination and shared responsibility in preparation and conduct of all flights.

Briefings

All briefings shall be attended by the entire crew. Planning should begin with a briefing that outlines the objectives of the mission to the crew. The preflight crew brief is the responsibility of the pilot. He shall ensure that mission requirements are known and methods to be used are understood. Mission planning briefs shall include air intelligence, operational, air refueling requirements, and individual crew briefings.

Weight and Balance

Check gross weight and center of gravity for takeoff and anticipated loading for landing. Refer to Section I, part 4, for weight limitations to be observed. Loading data are furnished in AN 01-1B-40 Handbook of Weight and Balance Data.

Operational Mission Planning

When proper planning precedes the mission, the crew primarily conducts the mission by means of checklists and logs. The following mission checklist will be used to ensure complete planning and accurate, timely accomplishment of each specific item. The mission checklist which is normally completed after extensive study, establishes in detail the conduct of the flight in chronological order. Applicable portions of the mission checklist shall be used on all flights.

Mission Checklist

The following items are to be used as a guide by the navigator in the preparation of the mission checklist. Only those applicable items required for the type mission flown need be considered.

NAVIGATION

1. PIM
2. TAS checks
3. Deviation checks
4. Drift readings
5. Fix times
6. Checkpoint coordinates
7. Bearings/distance en route
8. Variation
9. Control lines
10. Rendezvous.

FUEL MANAGEMENT

1. Wing tank transfer
2. Climb and cruise data
3. Tanker fuel management

DETECTION

1. EW detection
2. GCI detection
3. Aircraft interception point.

TACTICAL

1. EMCON:
   Radar
   Navaids OFF/ON
2. Radio signals/visual signals
3. Periscope cover
4. DECM operation
5. Abort procedure.

Changed 1 June 1969

REPORTS

1. ADIZ
2. Broadcast control.

Navigation Planning

The crew must use every means at their disposal in navigating the aircraft. Navigation must be planned to place the aircraft in the desired position for the air refueling mission and return to base.

Responsibilities of the crew in planning navigation are:

1. Pilot must have a general knowledge of air navigation and be thoroughly familiar with particular procedures and problems inherent in navigating the A-3 aircraft.

2. Navigator is responsible to the pilot for navigation planning of all flights. The following is a minimum listing of navigation planning duties:

Receive operational briefing.

Receive weather briefing. Obtain cross section from aerology for the flight.

Prepare chart of suitable scale, depicting intended flight path, suitable diversionary fields, and such other data as may be pertinent to mission.

Prepare route cards and parts of DD 175 or ship's flight plan that pertain to navigation.

When operating from a carrier, navigator shall know PIM and state of its navigation aids prior to launch.

Ensure that all needed navigation publications, devices, charts, as well as pertinent code books, crosscountry packets, etc, are aboard aircraft.

Cross-Country Flights

Pilots must have a minimum of 30 hours in type, must have completed night and instrument familiarization in type, and must possess a valid instrument card. Flights should be conducted in accordance with instrument flight rules.

The pilot in command of the aircraft shall ensure that proper measures are taken to safeguard the aircraft and any classified equipment whenever the aircraft is landed at other than its home base.

Information in sufficient detail to permit proper servicing of the aircraft must be carried on all flights.

Navigation Bag Contents

1. Current NATOPS Flight Manual NAVAIR 01-40ATA-1 and NATOPS Pocket Checklist NAVAIR 01-40ATA-1B
2. Flashlight with red lens
3. Flight packet
4. En route supplement
5. En route high altitude charts
6. En route low-altitude charts
7. Instrument approach procedures charts
8. ONC charts (or equivalent)
9. Navigation computer
10. REST computer
11. Dividers and plotters.

Fuel Planning

All methods of fuel transfer should be checked for proper operation after level-off.

HOWGOZIT

A HOWGOZIT is a plan of predicted and actual fuel consumption versus distance from which the pilot can determine whether the flight can be safely continued or must be aborted or diverted for landing. A HOWGOZIT shall be prepared for all flights other than local flights.

For flights conducted with periodic fixes determined from electronic navigation aids, the HOWGOZIT may consist of a fuel check and comparison of predicted and actual fuel remaining at each navigational fix.

The HOWGOZIT shall be prepared using the latest winds for the flight route. Specific cruise altitudes can be selected.

FUEL RESERVES

Flights shall be planned and whenever possible, conducted in such a manner that the aircraft will be on deck with a minimum of 3000 pounds of usable fuel remaining. At any time usable fuel remaining reaches 3000 pounds indicated, or is projected to be 3000 pounds or less at the destination, an emergency shall be declared. The HOWGOZIT for long-range overwater flights shall show the equal time point, based on internal fuel only. All modes of wing fuel must be checked prior to proceeding beyond this point. When the destination is forecase to be IFR on arrival, reserve fuel must be sufficient to proceed to the destination airport and then to the alternate field at penetration altitude with sufficient fuel to hold for 20 minutes and land with 3000 pounds remaining. It is to be noted that this fuel reserve is greater than that required by OPNAV Instruction 3710.7 series.

FUEL COMPUTATIONS

Fuel graphs are contained in Section XI.

NAVAIR 01-40ATA-1

Section III
Part 3

PART 3
SHORE-BASED PROCEDURES

TABLE OF CONTENTS

TEXT

	Page		Page
Familiarization and Transition	3-9	Post Takeoff Checklist	3-25
Line Operations	3-9	General In-Flight Considerations	3-25
Manning the Aircraft	3-9	Climb Schedule	3-25
Preflight Checklists	3-9	CG/Icing	3-25
Entrance	3-12	Cruise Procedures	3-25
Companionway Access	3-13	Cruise Climb	3-25
Prestart Checklist	3-13	Level-Off/In-Flight Checklist	3-26
Starting Aircraft	3-14	Descent Checklist	3-26
Equipment Required for Starting	3-14	Descent	3-26
Starting Procedure	3-14	Landing Checklist	3-26
Cartridge Start	3-15	Landings	3-27
Start Checklist	3-16	Crosswind Landing	3-27
Bleed Air Check (Toggle Switches)	3-17	High Crosswind Landings	3-28
Bleed Air Check (Rotary Switch)	3-17	Touch-and-Go Landing	3-29
Ground Emergencies	3-17	Single-Engine Approach/Landing	3-29
Companionway and Hot Bleed Air Check	3-18	Minimum Roll without Drag Chute	3-29
Pretaxi/Taxi Checklist	3-19	Minimum Roll with Drag Chute	3-29
Controls Check	3-19	Hydroplaning	3-29
Horizontal Stabilizer Trim Check	3-20	Antiskid Braking Techniques	3-30
Autopilot Preflight Check	3-20	Postlanding Checklist (Field)	3-32
Taxi	3-21	Shutdown Checklist	3-32
Taxi Procedure	3-21	Field Arrestments	3-32
Pretakeoff	3-22	Field Barrier	3-33
Trim, Flaps, and Fuel Trim	3-22	FMLP and CQ	3-33
Takeoff Checklist	3-22	General Requirements	3-33
Full Power Check	3-23	Landing Weight	3-33
Takeoff Procedures	3-24	Day FMLP	3-33
JATO Takeoff	3-24	Speed, Pattern, and Technique	3-33
JATO Jettisoning	3-24	Night Taxi and Takeoff	3-34

ILLUSTRATIONS

Figure		Page	Figure		Page
3-1	Exterior Inspection Diagram	3-10	3-3	Elevator Trim Setting vs CG Position	3-23
3-2	Entrance to the Aircraft	3-13	3-4	Landing and Waveoff Pattern	3-31

Changed 15 July 1970

3-8A/(3-8B Blank)

FAMILIARIZATION AND TRANSITION

The professional approach to flying requires that the entire operation, ground and air, be conducted as safely as the mission permits. Aircraft accidents caused by personnel error cannot be tolerated. Flight safety means:

1. Thorough training and standardization

2. Complete planning and flight preparations

3. Knowledge of the aircraft

4. Constant alertness

5. Common sense.

Flying the A-3 aircraft presents problems typical of any swept-wing, high-performance aircraft. Approach speed and sink rates must be carefully controlled. (Stall warning in the CLE aircraft is much less intense than in the basic wing.) At altitude, the aircraft has a slight "dutch roll," which becomes unimportant as the pilot gains experience in the aircraft. Transition will normally be accomplished in the Fleet Replacement Training Squadrons. For a description of flight characteristics, refer to Section IV.

LINE OPERATIONS

Manning The Aircraft

The aircraft should be manned at least 30 minutes prior to launch to ensure sufficient time for a thorough preflight inspection. Before the aircraft is manned, the yellow sheet shall be examined for previous discrepancies and completed insofar as practicable for information relative to the current flight.

Preflight Checklists

A preflight inspection shall be made in accordance with the following checklists. For a suggested inspection sequence, see figure 3-1.

FORWARD FUSELAGE AND RADOME (AREA A)

1. Deleted

2. Access plates and covers . . . . SECURED

3. ATM exhaust vanes . . . . FREE

4. Generator intake and exhaust vents . . . . CLEAR

5. Fuselage for hydraulic leaks . . . . . CHECK

6. Oxygen-battery compartment access door . . . . SECURE

7. Battery compartment intake scoop . . . . CLEAR

8. Static vents (port) . . . . CLEAR

9. Refueling probe . . . . CHECK

10. Radome and temperature-sensing element . . . . NO BREAKS, CLEAR

11. Pitot tube cover . . . . REMOVED

12. Static vents starboard and angle-of-attack probe . . . . CLEAR

13. Air-conditioning compartment intake scoop . . . . CLEAR

14. Air-conditioning compartment door . . . . SECURE

15. Periscope cover . . . . SECURE

16. Catapult hooks . . . . UP

NOSEWHEEL AREA (AREA B)

1. Nosewheel and tire condition, inflation, slippage . . . . CHECK

2. Strut inflation, and condition . . . . . CHECK

3. Nosewheel steering components . . . CHECK

4. Scissors connected . . . . CHECK

5. Nosewheel steering accumulator . . . . 350 PSI

Changed 15 July 1970

3-9

Section III
Part 3
NAVAIR 01-40ATA-1

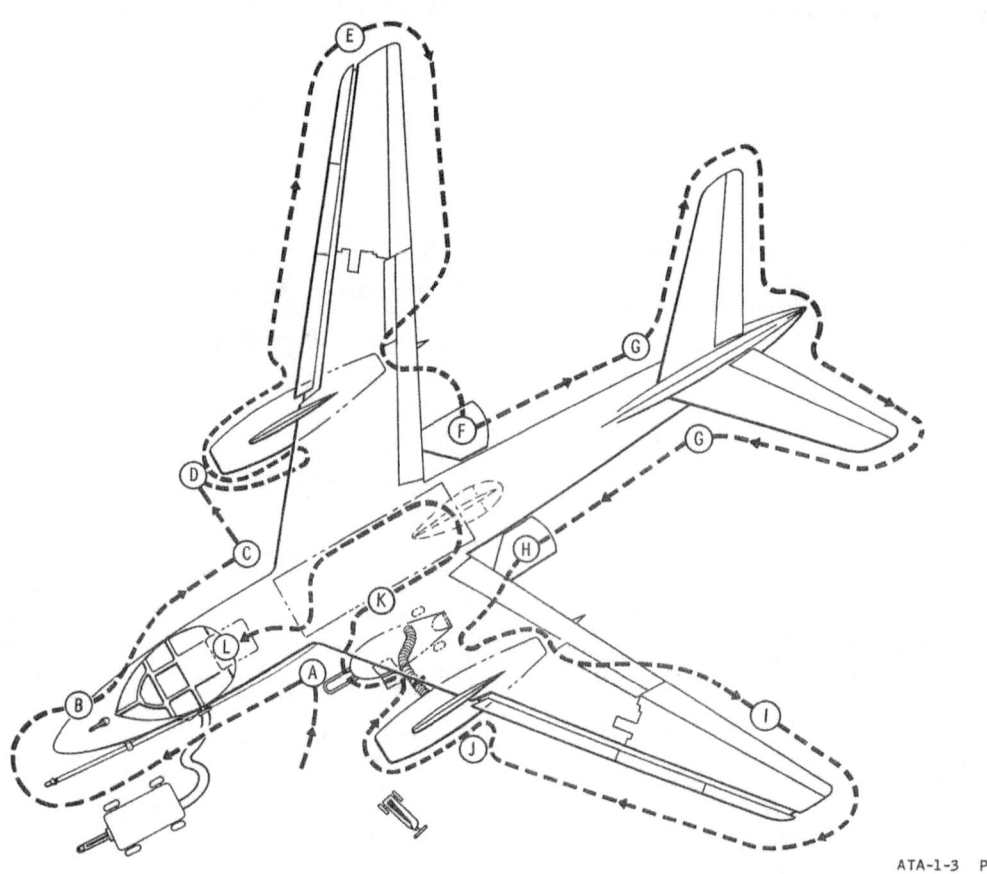

Figure 3-1. Exterior Inspection Diagram

6. Ground lockpin . . . . INSTALLED

7. Taxi and approach light . . . . CHECK

8. Radome lock handles . . . . SECURE

9. Nosewheel door condition . . . . . . SECURE

STARBOARD SIDE (AREA C)

1. Exhaust ducts . . . . CLEAR

2. Access plates and covers . . . . . . CHECK

3. Bomb bay door and fuselage . . . . CHECK

4. Inboard wing, access plates,
and fuel leaks . . . . CHECK

STARBOARD ENGINE (AREA D)

1. Left bleed air valve and screen . . . . . CHECK

2. Pylon, access plates, and doors . . . . CHECK

3. Nacelle fasteners . . . . CHECK

4. Inlet duct and oil cooler . . . . CHECK

5. Oil cooler door . . . . CHECK

6. Right bleed air valve and screen . . . . CHECK

STARBOARD WING (AREA E)

1. Jury strut . . . . CHECK

2. Access plates and covers . . . . CHECK

3. Slats, condition . . . . CHECK

4. Wing fold, hydraulic leaks, and condition . . . . CHECK

5. Wingtip condition . . . . CHECK

6. Ailerons, static wicks, and bonding . . . . CHECK

7. Fuel dump and drain outlets . . . . CHECK

8. Flaps and hinges . . . . CHECK

9. Tailpipe condition . . . . CHECK

STARBOARD WHEEL (AREA F)

1. Wheel and tire condition . . . . CHECK

2. ANTISKID detector . . . . CHECK

3. Hydraulic brake lines . . . . CHECK

4. Strut condition . . . . CHECK

5. Ground lockpin . . . . INSTALLED

6. Hydraulic actuating components . . . . CHECK

7. Bumper pad . . . . CHECK

8. Wheel well (free of fuel, oil, and foreign objects) . . . . CHECK

9. Pressure fueling receptacle and switches . . . . CHECK

10. Boost pump ground wire . . . . CHECK

11. Wheel well door and components . . . . CHECK

AFT FUSELAGE AND EMPENNAGE (AREA G)

1. Access plates and covers . . . . . . CHECK

2. Fuel vent and drain points . . . . . CHECK

3. JATO hooks (stbd) . . . . CHECK

4. Speedbrakes condition (stbd) . . . . CHECK

5. Tail bumper condition . . . . CHECK

6. Tailhook . . . . CHECK

7. Horizontal stabilizer and trim mark (stbd) . . . . CHECK

8. Elevator, curtain, static wicks, and bonding (stbd) . . . . CHECK

9. Vertical stabilizer . . . . CHECK

10. DECM radome/tail turret and drag chute installed . . . . CHECK

11. Rudder, curtain, static wicks, and bonding . . . . CHECK

12. Elevator curtain, static wicks, and bonding (port) . . . . CHECK

13. Horizontal stabilizer and trim mark (port) . . . . CHECK

14. Fuel vent tube . . . . CHECK

15. Tail access door . . . . CHECK

16. Tailhook holddown pressure (if hook up) . . . . CHECK

17. Speedbrakes condition (port) . . . . CHECK

18. JATO hooks (port) . . . . CHECK

19. Radio compartment access door . . CHECK

PORT WHEEL (AREA H)

1. Wheel well door and components . . CHECK

2. Boost pump ground wire . . . . CHECK

3. ANTISKID and radar altimeter boxes . . . . CHECK

4. Wheel well (free of fuel, oil, and foreign objects) . . . . CHECK

5. Bumper pad . . . . CHECK

6. Hydraulic actuator components . . . CHECK

7. Ground lockpin . . . . INSTALLED

8. Strut condition . . . . CHECK

9. Hydraulic brake lines . . . . CHECK

10. ANTISKID detector . . . . CHECK

11. Wheel and tire condition . . . . CHECK

12. Tailpipe condition . . . . CHECK

PORT WING (AREA I)

1. Jury strut . . . . CHECK

2. Flap and hinges . . . . CHECK

3. Fuel dump and drain outlets . . . . CHECK

4. Aileron, static wicks, and bonding . . . . CHECK

3-11

5. Wingtip condition . . . . CHECK

6. Wing fold, hydraulic leaks,
and condition . . . . CHECK

7. Slats condition . . . . CHECK

8. Access plates and covers . . . . CHECK

PORT ENGINE (AREA J)

1. Left bleed air valve and screen . . . . CHECK

2. Pylon, access plates and doors . . . . CHECK

3. Nacelle fasteners . . . . CHECK

4. Inlet duct and oil cooler . . . . CHECK

5. Oil cooler door . . . . CHECK

6. Right bleed air valve and screen . . . CHECK

BOMB BAY (AREA K)

1. Bomb bay door safety pins . . . . CHECK

2. 16th stage bleed ducting . . . . CHECK

3. Control cables, hydraulic,
fuel, and vent lines . . . . CHECK

4. Center-of-gravity simulator
and amplifier . . . . CHECK

5. Starboard bomb bay door hinge . . . . CHECK

6. Deleted

7. Center-of-gravity valve . . . . CHECK

8. Flapper valve (squeeze check) . . . . . CHECK

9. Hydraulic cooler area . . . . CHECK

10. ANTISKID brake accumulator . . . . . 400 PSI

11. Port bomb bay door hinge . . . . CHECK

12. Main wheel door emergency
air pressure . . . . 3000 PSI

13. Spoiler disconnect . . . . CHECK

14. Aileron boost disconnect . . . . CHECK

15. Deleted

16. Aileron accumulator pressure . . . . . CHECK

17. Surface control hydraulic
reservoirs . . . . CHECK

18. Aileron control hydraulic
reservoirs . . . . CHECK

19. Emergency flap and gear
air pressure . . . . 3000 PSI

20. Bomb bay oxygen station . . . . . . WIRED OFF

ENTERING COCKPIT (AREA L)

1. Companionway emergency
exit handle . . . . CHECKED

2. Escape chute circuit . . . . TESTED

3. Companionway circuit breakers
and fuses . . . . CHECK

4. Upper escape hatch pressure . . 2000 PSI

5. Cockpit circuit breakers . . . . . . CHECK

6. Oxygen equipment . . . . CHECKED

7. Baro release lanyard . . . . ATTACHED
TO ACTUA-
TOR

Entrance

Entrance into the aircraft is through the emergency escape chute. To gain access to the cockpit, perform the following steps (figure 3-2):

1. Unlatch outer escape chute door by turning latch handle aft of hatch. Manually lower outer escape chute door to extended position.

2. Unlatch inner escape chute door by turning latch release handle on left-hand side of escape chute liner. Manually lower inner escape chute door until it latches in extended position. Enter cockpit.

3. Close outer escape chute door by pulling up on D-ring on right-hand side of escape chute liner.

4. Before releasing door closing control, latch outer escape chute door by turning latch handle aft of D-ring on right-hand side of escape chute liner. Stow D-ring in clip provided in recess.

5. Close inner escape chute door by manually raising door to close position.

6. Before releasing inner door, latch door by operating latch handle on inboard side of PC seat.

This procedure is reversed for leaving the cockpit by using the latching controls to unlock the doors.

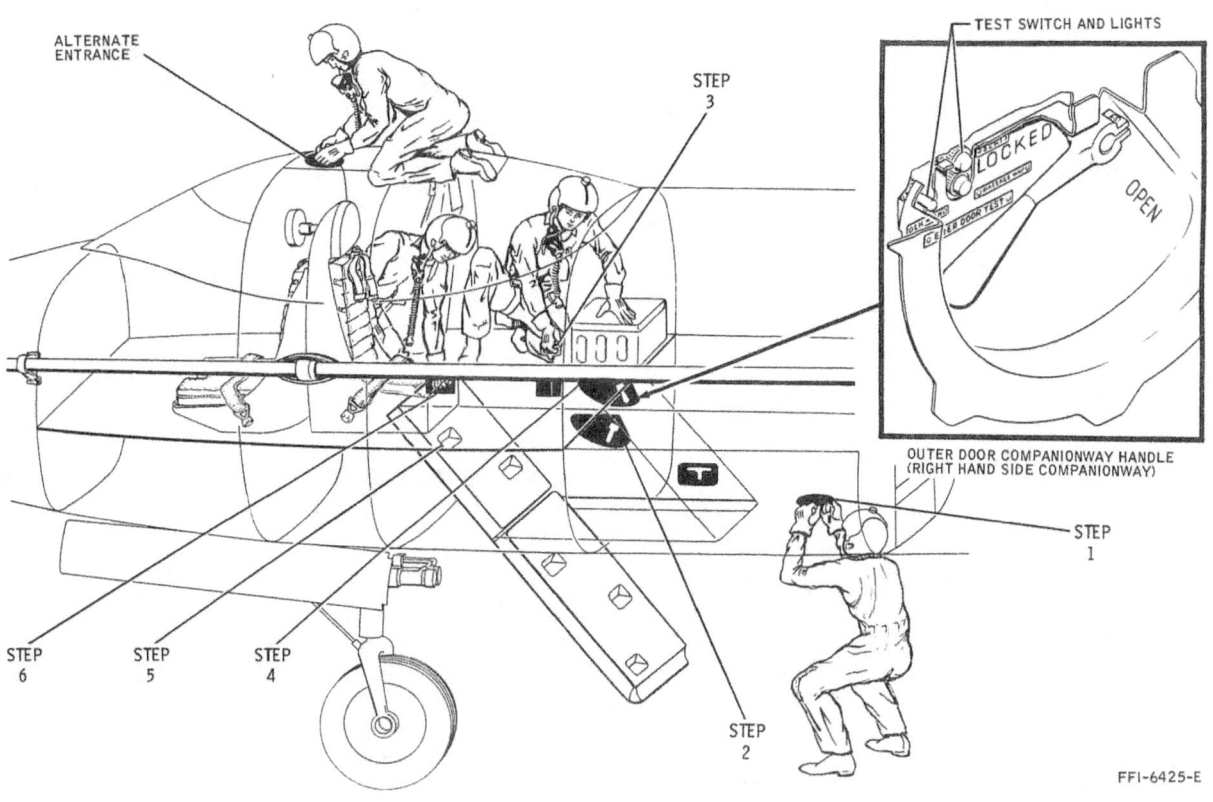

Figure 3-2. Entrance to the Aircraft

ALTERNATE ENTRANCE

Entrance to the cockpit may also be gained through the ditching hatch. The hatch is unlocked by a latch handle recessed in the forward center section of the hatch. The hatch may then be opened manually by sliding it aft.

Companionway Access

The aft face of the emergency escape chute is formed by the companionway safety door. The door is unlocked by means of a squeeze-type latch handle (figure 1-3) in the aft upper center section of the door. The door may be lowered to the horizontal position, thus overlapping the outer escape chute door and forming a part of the center equipment compartment floor.

Prestart Checklist

1. Preflight	....	COMPLETE
2. Escape chute circuit	....	TESTED
3. Hydraulic solenoid overrides	....	NORMAL
4. Hydraulic reservoirs	....	FULL/CLOSED
5. Companionway/cabin circuit breakers/fuses	....	CHECKED/IN
6. Dc generators	....	ON
7. DECM	....	OFF
8. VGI/STBY gyro horizon/LH or RH fuel boost circuit breakers	....	OUT
9. ASB/IFF	....	OFF/SET/OFF
10. Radio master	....	ON
11. ATM switches	....	OFF

Section III
Part 3

NAVAIR 01-40ATA-1

12. Air conditioning/anti-icing/pressurization	OFF/OFF/NORMAL	
13. Interior lights	AS DESIRED	
14. Compass/yaw damper	FREE/OFF	
15. Exterior lights/anticollision ..	AS DESIRED	
16. Radios/Navaids	OFF	
17. Fuel panels:		
a. Fuel dump	OFF	
b. Crossfeed	CLOSED	
c. Fuel trim switch........	NOSEDOWN	
d. Aux tank transfer	OFF	
e. Wing tank transfer........	OFF	
18. Bleed air switches	ALL OPEN/ON	
19. ANTISKID	OFF	
20. Ac control panel	SET	
21. Manual fuel trim	SET	
22. Hook	POSITIONED	
23. Drag chute switch	STOWED	
24. Oil coolers	AUTO	
25. Battery (check battery voltage)	ON	
26. Emer hydraulic pump (check battery voltage)	ON	
27. Emer hydraulic pump/battery	OFF/OFF	
28. Wing/fin fold	POSITIONED	
29. Master engine switches/throttles	OFF/OFF	
30. Light master/speedbrakes................	POSITIONED	
31. Gear handle/solenoid	DOWN/LATCHED/OUT/FREE	**NEW**
32. Flaps	POSITIONED	
33. Bomb bay door switch	POSITIONED	
34. JATO switches............	SAFE	
35. Oxygen equipment..........	CHECKED	
36. Baro-release lanyards	AS REQUIRED	

STARTING AIRCRAFT

Aircraft should be started in sufficient time to allow for completion of the pretaxi checklist and to taxi and take off at the scheduled time. To minimize fuel consumed on the deck, instrument clearances may be copied prior to engine start for long-range flights.

Equipment Required for Starting

The aircraft requires a gas turbine compressor (GTC) for starting. Engine ignition is normally provided by the battery. Dc external power may be used whenever available.

CAUTION

Use of ac external power may damage frequency sensitive instruments if frequency cannot be maintained within 400±20 cps.

Starting Procedure

Starting procedures contained in the prestart and start checklists will be used. The starting procedure, in general, is as follows:

1. Wheel chocks will be in place and fire extinguisher readily available before starting engines. The battery will be turned ON to ensure an uninterrupted ignition and backup dc power in the event of external malfunctions. The emergency airbrakes may be used in case either engine accelerates past normal-idle during start.

2. Normally, the start will be a manual (ground crew controlled) start. The plane captain indicates ready to start by a giving thumbs-up signal with one hand and, at the same time, indicating which engine to start by holding up one or two fingers of the other hand. On signal from the pilot, the plane captain signals the ground crew to initiate starting of the engine. At 12 to 16 percent, the pilot actuates the igniters by moving the throttle outboard (ignition will continue automatically for 30 seconds). Immediately after actuating the igniters, the pilot brings the throttle to the idle position. Fuel is then admitted to the engine in the proper amount for ignition. Following ignition, the tailpipe temperature will start increasing. The pilot must ensure that the starting compressor is shut off before 38 percent, to prevent shearing off the starter pawls. The starter shutoff signal is a horizontal motion of the fist away from the open palm of the other hand. The engine should continue to accelerate to an idle rpm of about 58 to 65 percent. Tailpipe temperature will normally rise to a peak of about 450°C, and then settle back to about 340°C. TPT must be monitored closely, since a temperature in excess of 450°C for J57 engines constitutes a hot start, requiring engine shutdown and, in accordance with applicable handbook of service instructions, approval or disapproval of the engine for flight.

CAUTION

Only the No. 1 ATM has provisions for ground cooling of the ATM compartment.

3. The second engine is started exactly as the first.

CAUTION

Seventy percent rpm should be sufficient to sustain frequencies between 400±20 cps except in extremely hot weather. If more than 75 percent rpm is required, the aircraft should be downed and the system should be inspected.

REMOTE (PILOT CONTROLLED) START

Although seldom used, the pilot, rather than the ground crew, may control the start. The electrical plug is connected from the starting unit to the receptable on the engine. The procedure is the same, except the pilot actuates the starter switch momentarily to the desired engine. Although, with this type start, the compressor should disconnect automatically at 36 to 40 percent rpm, it is good practice to signal for shutoff at 30 to 35 percent rpm. The engine is then at an rpm that will sustain acceleration to idle.

Cartridge Start

SAFETY PRECAUTIONS

The following safety precautions shall be observed when operating or servicing the ATSC 100-83 cartridge starter:

1. MXU-4/A starter cartridges shall not be removed from their containers in the immediate area of high-powered radio or radar transmitters.

2. Asbestos gloves or welders gloves shall be worn whenever handling live or spent cartridges.

3. Cartridges shall not be loaded while power is on the aircraft.

4. It is possible for a cartridge to hangfire (take an abnormally long time to ignite or burn). This condition will usually be evidenced by smoke in less than normal amounts and may last for a number of minutes. In this case, wait at least 10 minutes after the last signs of combustion before removing the cartridge chamber.

5. If a cartridge misfires (shows no evidence of combustion), wait at least 10 minutes before opening the cartridge chamber.

6. After a normal cartridge start, allow the chamber to cool for at least 5 minutes before removing the cartridge.

7. Personnel shall remain clear of the starter exhaust during starts and when removing cartridges that have misfired or hangfired.

8. Do not attempt to use a cartridge that has been dropped or damaged as the burning rate may be altered.

9. Do not use solvent for cleaning the cartridge chamber or breech. If deposits cannot be removed with a dry cloth or steel wool, a dry brush shall be used.

10. For pneumatic starts, do not use a compressed air source that is not regulated to less than 68 psig. The GTC-85 and MA-1A compressors are acceptable.

11. Do not attempt a pneumatic start with a cartridge in the chamber.

OPERATING PROCEDURES

The following procedures will be used for a normal cartridge start:

> **CAUTION**
>
> If the engine nacelle doors are not configured for cartridge starts (holes cut to allow escape of exhaust gasses), the nacelle doors shall be latched in the open position until engine start is completed.

1. Open engine nacelle doors and remove cartridge chamber from starter. Inspect starter exhaust port and secondary air inlet screen to ensure that they are clean and free from debris.

2. Place cartridge can on ground near the cartridge chamber.

3. Ensure that no high-power radar sets or radio transmitters are operating in the immediate area.

4. Open cartridge can with key provided.

5. Invert can and, with cartridge resting on ground, remove can and wrapping.

6. Wear asbestos or heavy leather (welder's) gloves when handling live or spent cartridge.

7. Remove safety clip from top of cartridge and bend ground tabs slightly upward.

8. With cartridge setting on ground, slide cartridge chamber onto cartridge. Pick up cartridge and chamber, grasp perforated end of cartridge and rotate it at least 180 degrees while maintaining firm pressure against cartridge. This action will ensure good electrical contact to igniter.

9. Ensure that mating surfaces of starter breech and chamber are free of carbon deposits. Install and lock chamber on starter.

10. Secure engine nacelle doors.

11. Attach 24-vdc power to external receptacle. Ac power, 115/200-volt, 3-phase, 400-cycle, may be applied at this time but is not required for cartridge start.

12. Position cockpit switches and levers as for a normal start.

13. Engage all power plant and fuel system circuit breakers. Place engine master switch for desired engine ON.

14. To ignite starter cartridge, press LH/RH engine starter control switch to appropriate position.

15. When engine rotation is indicated by movement of tachometer needle, release starter control switch. Move throttle to start ignition cycle, then forward to IDLE position.

16. Light-off will occur within 15 seconds after throttle is placed in IDLE position.

17. After flight, remove spent cartridge by opening engine nacelle doors and detaching chamber from starter. Interior of chamber and breech should be wiped with dry cloth to remove cartridge deposits.

PNEUMATIC STARTS WITH ATSC 100-83 STARTER INSTALLED

1. Pneumatic starts must not be attempted with a cartridge in the chamber.

2. The operating air pressure of the pneumatic starter unit must be 68 psig or less.

3. Only ground controlled starts can be made.

4. Attach compressed air source to the pneumatic air inlet on the starter.

5. Proceed as for a ground controlled start with the ATS 70 starter.

DUTY CYCLES AND START INTERVALS

The interval between any two successive cartridge starts are as follows:

1. The interval between any two successive cartridge starts must be at least 5 minutes.

2. No more than two cartridge starts may be attempted in any 1-hour period.

3. If cartridge starts and pneumatic starts are interspersed, no more than three starts may be attempted in a 15-minute period. The 5-minute limitation of successive cartridge starts applies.

4. Do not attempt more than three pneumatic starts in a 15-minute period.

5. Do not motor the starter from a compressed air source for more than 5 minutes during a 15-minute period. The starter may be continuously motored for 5 minutes.

Start Checklist

1. External power . . . . AS REQUIRED

2. Aft area/fire guard . . . . CLEAR/POSTED

NAVAIR 01-40ATA-1
Section III
Part 3

3. Wing caps/sextant cover/spoilers .... CHECKED

4. Battery switch .... ON

5. Master engine switches ...... ON

6. Start engine .... ON SIGNAL

7. Ignite 12-16%

8. Disconnect 35%

9. ATM switches (75%) .... ON

10. Bleed air check .... COMMENCE

11. External power .... OFF/DISCONNECT

12. Ac generators .... ON

13. Frequencies/bus tie .... STABLE/AUTO

14. Utility hydraulic pressure .... CHECKED

15. Start second engine. (Repeat items 6 through 8.)

Bleed Air Check (Toggle Switches)

Start RH engine, 75 percent RPM, both ATM switches – ON, Air Conditioning – ON

Bleed Air Shutoff Switch Test Positions	Required Result
ALL – ON	ATM's – RUN/AIR COND – RUN
AIR COND – OFF	AIR COND – OFF/ATM's – RUN
AIR COND – ON	AIR COND – RUN/ATM's – RUN
RH – OFF	ATM's – STOP/AIR COND – STOP
START LH ENGINE RUN AT 75%	ATM's – RUN/AIR COND – RUN
LH – OFF	ATM's – STOP/AIR COND – STOP
LH – ON	ATM's – RUN/AIR COND – RUN

Bleed Air Shutoff Switch Test Positions	Required Result
RH – ON	ATM's – RUN/AIR COND – RUN

Both ac generators – ON

Retard throttles – TO IDLE.

If both ATM's do not continue to run, or AC frequencies drop, suspect RH bleed air pylon valve did not reopen, turn off air conditioning.

Bleed Air Check (Rotary Switch)

Start RH engine, 75 percent RPM, ATM switches – ON, Air Conditioning – ON

Bleed Air Shutoff Switch Test Positions	Required Result
ALL OPEN	ATM's RUN, AIR COND – ON
RH CLOSE	ATM's STOP, AIR COND – OFF

Start LH engine (Both at 70%), ATM's RUN

AIR COND OPEN	AIR COND – ON
ALL CLOSE	ATM's STOP, AIR COND – OFF
ALL OPEN	ATM's RUN, AIR COND – ON
AIR CONDITIONING – OFF START BOTH AC GENERATORS	

Ground Emergencies

WET STARTS

A wet start occurs when the fuel in the burner baskets fails to ignite. This is usually caused by the pilot failing to strike the igniter microswitch with the throttle when coming around the horn to idle position. One way to tell if the igniters are operating is to have the hard hat on and earphones plugged in during the start. As the throttle is moved out against the igniter microswitch, operate the ICS switch. The igniters, if operating, will give a cycling, buzzing sound on ICS. If the throttle has been moved to idle and ignition is not accomplished, secure the engine master switch, return the power lever to off, and continue to crank the engine for 20 to 30 seconds. If the engine master switch is not secured prior to moving the throttle to off, the igniters could be set in operation by striking the microswitch which would cause an explosion of raw fuel collected in the engine. The engine should be dried out thoroughly by cranking, draining, and swabbing out the tailpipe prior to attempting another start.

NOTE

To prevent overheating, the starter should not be run continuously longer than 3 minutes.

HOT START AND INTERNAL ENGINE FIRES

In case of hot start or internal engine fire during start, place throttles in the OFF position and, if it is a ground-controlled start, turn engine master switch OFF, and continue turning the engine with the starter. This procedure should normally extinguish an internal engine fire. If the fire persists, abandon the aircraft and use all available means to extinguish the fire.

FALSE START

False starts result from failure of the engine to accelerate to idle rpm during the start. This malfunction is usually the result of insufficient boost from the starting unit and occurs between 12 and 30 percent rpm. The engine fails to reach the autoacceleration rpm and burns idle fuel at an rpm much lower than idle. The pilot must closely monitor the tachometer and tailpipe temperature during the early stages of the start. The first indication of a false start will normally be a stall or near-stall, with the tachometer in the 12 to 22 percent range. The next indication will be a rapidly rising TPT. The throttles should be brought around the horn to OFF position; and, if it is a ground-controlled start, engine master switch should be turned OFF. The engine should be turned over until the TPT drops to within the normal range. Do not attempt a restart until the cause of the malfunction is remedied.

WARNING

If the throttle should at any time be inadvertently retarded to the OFF position, an immediate flameout will occur. In this case, the throttle must remain in OFF until a new start is made, since introducing unburned fuel into the engine will create a serious fire hazard.

ENGINE CLEARING PROCEDURES

1. Continue engine cranking until fuel stops coming out of tailpipe or until fire is out.

2. Inspect tailpipe.

NOTE

If engine starting is unsuccessful after 2 minutes of rotation, the front engine oil sump becomes full and leaks into the compressor section. This sump should be drained before continuing rotation. Failure to observe this procedure allows oil to accumulate which will contaminate the air conditioning system or overload the filter in that system.

Companionway and Hot Bleed Air Check

When the companionway check is commenced, and after the bomb bay door circuit breaker is pulled, the ATM temperature warning circuits shall be checked by depressing, in turn, each of the three test switches (figure 1-21). Proper operation of the temperature warning system will be reflected by the ATM temperature warning light (figure 1-4) on the pilot's instrument panel, coming on each time that a test switch is depressed. The fuel crossfeed control valve may be functionally checked by pulling the circuit breaker for either fuel boost pump, and then opening the crossfeed valve to regain pressure. Prior to taxi, the ATM compartment shall be checked for hydraulic and hot air leaks. When this check is completed and the ATM compartment access doors are secured, the bleed air ducting in the forward part of the bomb bay will be checked. This is best accomplished by standing or kneeling on the tunnel ledge and passing the hands along the ducting. Particular attention should be given to that area around the air-conditioning filter, located in the upper right-hand side of the bomb bay, and the 4-inch ducting on the left-hand side. The crewmember shall report completion of the check to the pilot.

1. Bomb bay door circuit breaker .... PULL

2. Surface controls boost system reservoir air pressure gage .... 10 to 15 PSI

3. AILERON BOOST RESERVOIR AIR PRESSURE gage .... 10 to 15 PSI

4. UTILITY RESERVOIR AIR PRESSURE gage .... 10 to 15 PSI

5. AILERON PUMP BOOST PRESSURE gage .... 2000 PSI

6. SURFACE CONTROL PUMP gage .... 2000 PSI

7. UTILITY PUMP AFT PUMP gage .... 3000 PSI

8. UTILITY PUMP FWD PUMP gage .... 3000 PSI

9. Hot air leaks .... CHECKED

10. Bomb doors ground safety locks .... REMOVE

11. Emergency landing gear bottle .... 3000 PSI

12. Emergency flap bottle .... 3000 PSI

13. ATM temperature warning circuits .... TEST

14. Crossfeed control valve ..... CHECKED

15. Landing gear lockpins .... ABOARD

16. Outer escape chute door ..... LATCHED

17. Inner escape chute door...... CLOSED AND LATCHED

18. Bomb bay door pins/circuit breaker .... STOWED/IN

6. Oxygen quantity .... RECORD

7. Warning lights/test circuits .... CHECKED

8. Trim tabs .... CHECKED/SET

9. Ac-dc gang bar/switches ...... UP/ON

10. ASB/IFF .... SET/STBY

11. Radar/pressure altimeters ..... SET

12. PC's report:

   a. Voltages .... CHECKED

   b. Hydraulic gages .... CHECKED

   c. Three pins .... ABOARD

   d. Escape doors .... CLOSED

   e. Overhead hatch .... LOCKED OPEN/MANNED

Controls Check

Pretaxi/Taxi Checklist

1. VGI/STBY gyro horizon circuit breakers............... IN/SET

2. Radios/Navaids/ASB gyros ... ON

3. Bomb bay door circuit breaker .... OUT

4. On signal (70%)

   a. Crossfeed .... CHECKED

   b. Companionway/hot bleed air leaks .... CHECKED

   c. Speedbrakes........... CYCLED/CLOSED

   d. Flaps .... CYCLED/DOWN

   e. Hook .... CYCLED/UP

   f. Bomb bay door pins/circuit breaker .... STOWED/IN

   g. Bomb bay doors (actuate warning horn)........... CYCLED/CLOSED

5. Fuel quantity............. RECORD

WARNING

Bomb bay doors, speedbrakes, flaps, wing fold, and tailhook shall not be operated while the aircraft is stationary on the deck unless the appropriate signal is given by a qualified lineman stationed outside the aircraft in a position to see that all affected areas are clear of personnel and obstructions. When home based, the lineman shall normally be the assigned plane captain; when away from home base, the signals will be given from the lineman's position by a crewmember if an A-3 qualified lineman is not available.

1. Spread and lock wings and fin. See that GUST & WING PIN LOCK control is in vertical position and that WING FOLD control is flush with center console. Red warning indicators (cans) on the lower surface and inboard of each wing fold joint, and below the fin fold joint, must be faired to indicate that unfolded wings and fin are locked. (A crewmember may view the fin-lock warning indicator by standing in cockpit and looking aft from open upper hatch.)

2. Check controls for freedom of movement.

3. Check spoiler operation. (A crewmember may check spoiler operation by viewing spoilers through upper hatch.)

Section III
Part 3
NAVAIR 01-40ATA-1

4. After wings and fin are spread, proper operation of aileron power boost and elevator and rudder boost systems may be checked manually by feel when controls are moved to full extent of their travel.

Horizontal Stabilizer Trim Check

CAUTION

To avoid exceeding 15-second continuous operating limit of stabilizer trim motor in fast trim mode, steps outlined in this check must be performed in rapid succession.

NOTE

If the repeat-back trim mode of the autopilot has just been operated, allow adequate cooling time before energizing the manual dc trim. Ground operation duty cycle for autopilot trim is 15-seconds, followed by a 3-minute cooling period.

1. Emergency ac/dc gangbar . . . . . OFF (DOWN)

   a. Actuate ac/dc trim switches; observe trim indicator positions for . . . . NO MOVEMENT

   b. Emergency gangbar & switches . . . . UP (ON)

2. Position dc console trim knob UP then DOWN while monitoring trim position indicator for proper movement.

3. Position ac console trim knob UP then DOWN while monitoring trim position indicator for proper movement.

4. Ac yoke trim switch UP then DOWN while monitoring trim position indicator for proper movement.

5. Position aileron trim knob LEFT then RIGHT, monitor trim indicator.

6. Position rudder trim knob LEFT then RIGHT, monitor trim indicator.

Autopilot Preflight Check

The pilot's preflight check of the autopilot system can be performed quickly when the pilot is familiarized with the controls. This check is not a complete procedure such as the regular preflight check performed by ground personnel, since it is impractical to simulate an in-flight condition required to check the circuit breaker action of the YAW DAMPER (master) switch. To operate the autopilot system for a ground check, proceed as follows:

1. Check freedom of all controls through full travel.

CAUTION

Do not perform autopilot check with wings and fin folded, as control stops restrict operation of rudder and ailerons.

2. Make certain that electrical system is operating normally and that all circuit breakers are pressed in.

NOTE

After starting engines, it is necessary to wait approximately 3 minutes for the vertical gyro to erect and the directional gyro to level. The YAW DAMPER switch cannot be moved until this occurs.

3. YAW DAMPER switch . . . . HOLD ON

4. Rudder position indicator on pedestal controller should be centered and stationary. Do not engage RUDDER switch if indicator shows any significant degree of deflection.

5. RUDDER servoswitch (on center console AUTOPILOT panel) . . . . ENGAGE

This action engages yaw damping system.

6. Rotate SET HDG FREE GYRO switch momentarily to release autopilot. RUDDER servoswitch should drop to DISENGAGE.

7. Check directional gyro for alignment with magnetic (repeater) compass. It may be necessary to reslave directional gyro by operating SET HDG FREE GYRO switch.

8. PILOT-YAW DAMPER switch . . . . . PILOT

9. RUDDER and ELEVATOR-AILERON servoswitches on AUTOPILOT panel center console, simultaneously . . . . ENGAGE

3-20

This action engages autopilot.

10. Rotate top of pitch knob forward and then aft. The wheel (control column) should move fore and aft to indicate normal nosedown and noseup control, respectively.

11. Rotate AIL knob left and right, and check related movement of control wheel.

12. Rotate TURN knob to left and to right to check coordination of controls. For left turn, control wheel rotates left and left rudder pedal moves slightly forward. It is necessary to move TURN control knob in opposite direction to return rudder pedals to neutral.

13. Turn ALT CONT switch to ALT CONT. There should be little or no ELEV control movement. To check automatic trimmer operation, both hands are required to hold control wheel. Since this cannot be done without releasing YAW DAMPER switch, another crewmember should assist pilot. Otherwise, omit step 14.

14. Manually pull elevator control column aft, applying about 50 pounds of pressure. Horizontal trim indicator (on instrument panel) should move toward nosedown trim. Manually push control column forward and observe noseup trim indication.

15. Check overpowering of automatic trim control unit in both directions by applying pilot's wheel and console trim switches.

16. Push electrical release button momentarily. PILOT-YAW DAMPER switch should snap automatically to YAW DAMPER position; ALT CONT switch, to OFF position and lock; and autopilot servoswitches on the center console, to DISENGAGE position and lock.

17. Release YAW DAMPER switch.

18. Manually check aircraft controls for freedom of movement.

TAXI

The following brake check procedure shall be utilized. When leaving the chocks, check hydraulic brake action by depressing the brake pedals, and then releasing. (Afloat, do not turn ON ANTISKID.) Ashore, turn ANTISKID ON and check brakes again. Leave the ANTISKID switch in the ON position. If brakes fail during taxi, place ANTISKID switch in OFF for normal hydraulic brake action. If malfunction continues, the emergency hydraulic pump must be turned ON. If hydraulic brake system fails completely, utilize the pneumatic brake system to stop aircraft.

Taxi Procedure

The aircraft can be taxied using minimum power and nosewheel steering. To start taxiing, it will usually be necessary to increase rpm to about 70 to 80 percent. Once the aircraft is moving, reduce power to idle. Idle rpm produces sufficient power for normal taxi speeds, even with heavy loads. Excessive power required to taxi may indicate dragging brakes. If brakes are dragging, return to the line.

LOOKOUTS

When taxiing in congested areas, a director in front of the aircraft and a wingtip walker at each wingtip will be provided to ensure safe clearance from obstructions. The crew must be alert for obstructions. The PC shall man the upper hatch until clear of congested areas. The pilot should be ready to turn ON the emergency hydraulic pump at any indication of brake failure.

BRAKING PROCEDURES

With the aircraft at light weight, intermittent braking will be necessary to stay at an acceptable taxi speed.

CAUTION

Continual riding of the brakes will cause overheating which could result in loss of brake effectiveness and possible fire or explosion in the wheel well when the wheels are retracted after takeoff. If brake overheating is suspected, proceed to designated hot brake area.

NOSEWHEEL STEERING PROCEDURES

To steer the aircraft, a smooth, steady application is used on the nosewheel steering control handle. Asymmetrical braking, although helpful in tight spots or on a carrier deck, is usually unnecessary and tends to overheat the brakes. Do not brake against the nosewheel steering. The nosewheel steering control handle rotates through an arc of 160 degrees to obtain the limits of steering. If possible, the nosewheel should be returned to the center position before stopping. Avoid abrupt, high-speed operation of the nosewheel steering system.

TAXIING AT NIGHT

Night taxiing demands extreme care. The plane captain is in a better position to see from the upper hatch

Section III
Part 3

NAVAIR 01-40ATA-1

than the pilot. He should constantly check ahead and from side to side on each wingtip. The taxi light must be used judiciously for all night taxiing.

Pretakeoff

PRESSURIZATION, AIR-CONDITIONING, AND DEFROSTING PROCEDURES

Pressurization is not normally used during takeoff but may be necessary in areas of high humidity. The defrost/foot control shall be in the FOOT position for takeoff and for the initial operation of the air conditioning system. These precautions are necessary since the air conditioning system often will produce fog and snow initially, regardless of the control position. Turn the air conditioning ON when comfortably established in the climb and when clear of other traffic. The control should be rotated to the full HOT position, and the defrost/foot control should remain in the FOOT position until satisfactory operation has been ensured. The air conditioner may be operated on the ground as a defogger when heavy condensation persists in forming on the inside of the windshield. However, the precautions enumerated above must be followed for takeoff. It is recommended that the pilot keep his hand on temperature control knob until integrity of the system filter is assured.

CONSERVATION OF FUEL PRIOR TO TAKEOFF

When taxiing to the takeoff position, the takeoff checklist may be completed, flight instruments and radios tested, compasses set, and the instrument clearance obtained. Normally, on long-range flights or where delay in obtaining IFR clearance is expected, the clearance should be obtained prior to starting engines. Ground operation is costly in fuel and should be held to a minimum. Idle rpm fuel consumption is approximately 1000 pounds per hour per engine.

Trim, Flaps, and Fuel Trim

For normal takeoffs, between 0 to 3 degrees of noseup elevator trim will be used (figure 3-3), depending on aircraft cg. For abnormal cg of 15 percent MAC or less, use 5 degrees of noseup trim. The aileron and rudder trim must be neutral. Flaps must be full down for all takeoffs. All takeoffs will be made with fuel trim switch in the NOSEDOWN position. With forward and aft fuel tanks full, normal cg indications will be observed at the 6 o'clock position. Normal elevator trim settings will be used.

Takeoff Checklist

1. ANTISKID .... ON FIELD/ OFF SHIP

2. Wings/fin/gust locks .... SPREAD/ UNLOCKED

3. Controls .... CHECKED/ FREE

4. Compass .... SET/ SLAVED

5. Clock/altimeter .... SET

6. Takeoff performance data ..... COMPUTED

    a. Lift-off speed

    b. Ground roll

    c. Line speeds

    d. Refusal speed or distance to abort gear

    e. Minimum single-engine control speed

    f. Single engine, half-flap transition speed

7. Radios/Navaids/IFF .... ON/ CHECKED/ SET

8. Speedbrakes .... CLOSED

9. Flaps .... FULL DOWN

10. Trim tabs .... SET

11. Anti-icing .... AS DESIRED

12. CG position/fuel trim .... CHECKED/ NOSEDOWN

13. Shoulder harness/seat belts/ headrest .... LOCKED/ CREW READY

14. Full power check:

    a. Compass alignment .... CHECKED

    b. Engine instruments .... CHECKED

    c. ATM temperature .... CHECKED

    d. Ac frequencies .... CHECKED

    e. Hydraulic pressure .... CHECKED

Changed 1 June 1969

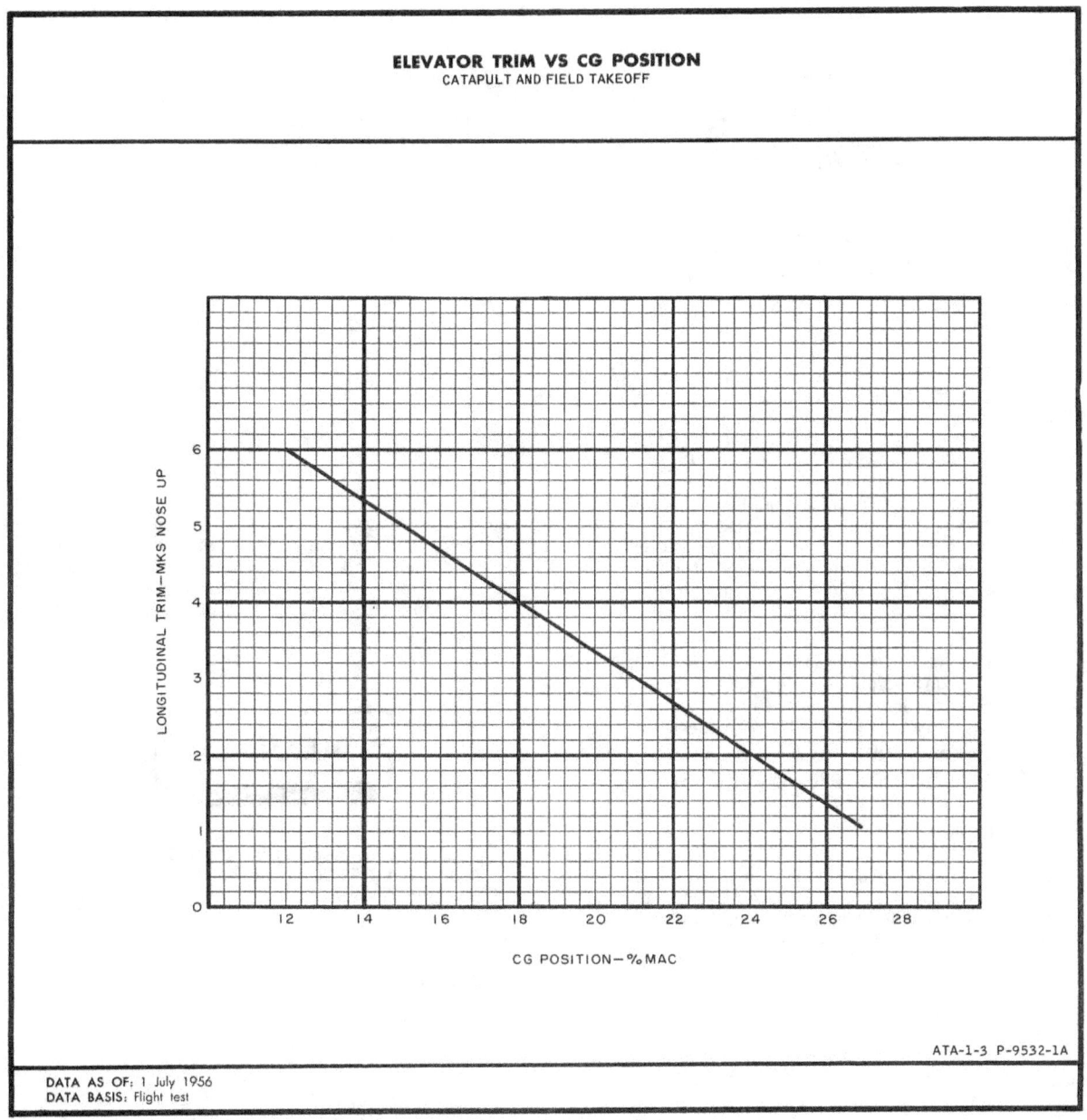

Figure 3-3. Elevator Trim Setting vs CG Position

Full Power Check

After assuming the takeoff position and ensuring that the nosewheel is straight, apply the brakes and advance the throttles to full power. Check compass alignment, ATM compartment temperature, hydraulic pressure, and ac frequencies. When engines have stabilized at full power, check engine instruments as follows: percent rpm on both engines within 2 percent of trim rpm; TPT within 25 degrees of the temperature recorded when engine was last trimmed (maximum TPT for J57-P-6B engines is 600°C and for J57-P-10 engines is 610°C); fuel pressure 12 to 24 psi (P-6), 12 to 30 psi (P-10), or "normal;" oil pressure 40 to 50 psi or normal; fuel flow 7,000 to 10,000 pounds.

Takeoff Procedures

Recent flap hinge failures indicate a need for the following interim procedures as a means of reducing exposure time of flaps to high load conditions. These procedures should be followed only until incorporation of A-3 AFC 390.

(1) Takeoffs and instrument departures: Unless an immediate turn after takeoff is required for terrain clearance or traffic separation, climb straight ahead at 180 KIAS maximum. Initiate flap retraction at 500 feet above ground level. During flap retraction, maintain runway heading, positive rate of climb and maximum of 15 units angle of attack. When flaps are fully retracted, turn and accelerate as required to conform to SID procedures and/or climb schedule.

(2) Landings: Reduce airspeed below 180 KIAS before lowering flaps and maintain wings-level attitude while flaps are extending. Do not exceed 15 units angle-of-attack.

(3) Avoid prolonged gear up, flaps down operation.

Normal Takeoff

Section takeoffs are prohibited. When individual takeoffs are made with two or more aircraft at close interval, the second aircraft shall not commence takeoff roll until the first is airborne.

When instrument readings are satisfactory at full power turnup, release the brakes and start the takeoff roll; position the left hand on the nosewheel steering control and the right hand on the control wheel. At approximately 80 knots, rudder control becomes effective. At this point, shift the left hand to the control wheel and the right hand to the throttles. (Extreme turbulence or gusty conditions may require both hands on the control wheel.) During heavy-load takeoffs on rough runways, the nosewheel may have a tendency to bounce. If this happens, forward pressure on the control wheel may be necessary. Line speed checks will be called by the navigator at the 2000- or 3000-foot marker. When takeoff speed is reached, rotate the nose smoothly. Be cautious to prevent the aircraft from being overrotated just prior to becoming airborne. After lift-off, tap brakes lightly prior to actuating the landing gear. Assume a climbing attitude to maintain 200 KIAS.

The landing gear must not be raised until a positive rate of climb has been established. The navigator will assist the pilot by calling the gear up and locked as it occurs after takeoff. As the aircraft accelerates through 200 KIAS and with at least 500 feet altitude above the terrain, raise the flaps. Avoid raising flaps in a turn. When comfortably airborne, complete the post takeoff checklist. During touch-and-go landings when the gear and full flaps are to remain down, make the initial climb with full power.

NOTE

Landing gear retraction time is a maximum of 12.5 seconds. For landing gear airspeed limitations, refer to Section I, part 4.

JATO Takeoff

The use of JATO is restricted to airfield takeoffs. The most effective use of JATO will be during the last 5 seconds of the takeoff run. Refer to performance charts in Section XI for detailed information concerning JATO takeoff procedures, JATO firing time data, and FIELD takeoff with JATO.

Simultaneous installation of MK 7 Mod 1 and MK 7 Mod 2 JATO bottles can cause dangerous asymmetrical thrust condition on firing.

JATO Jettisoning

Jettison the JATO bottles as soon as possible in a level flight attitude, with landing flaps full down and at airspeeds below 200 KIAS. A slight nosedown pitch will occur upon jettisoning a battery of 8, 10, or 12 bottles.

JATO bottles can be carried safely at speeds up to 300 KIAS but cannot be jettisoned at speeds above 200 KIAS.

Post Takeoff Checklist

1. Gear .... 4 UP
2. Overhead hatch .... CLOSED/LOCKED
3. Flaps .... UP
4. Fuel trim .... NORMAL
5. External inspection .... CLEAN
6. Pressurization .... ON
7. Bailout bottles, baro-release lanyards .... HOOKED UP

General In-Flight Considerations

The following items apply to all flights:

1. Checklists shall be used.

2. At least one crewmember shall maintain an alert watch for other aircraft.

3. Oxygen shall be used during takeoff and landing by all crewmembers.

All crewmembers shall remain on oxygen and strapped in seat after leveling off at cruising altitude until sufficient time has elapsed to ensure maintenance of a cabin altitude less than 10,000 feet and windshield panel integrity. Oxygen masks may be removed for short periods for crew comfort but must be connected and immediately available.

4. In-flight checks shall be performed at level-off and every 30 minutes thereafter.

5. On other than local flights, heading check shall be performed at least once each leg.

NOTE

The pilot must be prepared to divert the flight if necessary, and initiate appropriate action while fuel still remains to reach an adequate alternate airfield. Altitude must be maintained until a suitable field is available.

6. Baro-release lanyards and bailout bottle shall be connected at all times when above 10,000 feet MSL. It is recommended that the liferaft lanyard remain disconnected during flight and connected after bailout.

NOTE

For shore-based operation, lanyards should be hooked up at all times; for carrier-based operation, they should be connected after takeoff and disconnected prior to landing.

Climb Schedule

After becoming airborne (and aircraft is clean), trim for acceleration to 300 KIAS unless tactical or operational considerations require otherwise. Hold 300 KIAS (or assigned/required airspeed) until reaching cruising Mach. Maintain cruising Mach until reaching assigned altitude. When established in the climb, the posttakeoff checklist will be completed. To achieve maximum rate of climb, unnecessary turns, particularly at high altitude, should be avoided. Full power should be used within engine operating limitations.

CG/Icing

If constant longitudinal retrimming is necessary during climb, investigate the possibility of faulty fuel transfer. At level-off, be especially conscious of excessive nosedown elevator trim requirement. If more than 1 degree of nosedown trim is required, either a poor cg condition or icing of the elevators is indicated. If the fuel distribution is normal, icing is likely.

Cruise Procedures

Performance is affected primarily by gross weight and secondarily by engine performance, aircraft cleanliness, and cg trim. When a constant airspeed and altitude are to be maintained, it will be necessary to decrease fuel flow as gross weight decreases. The angle-of-attack indicator is a valuable aid in all conditions of flight. While a primary landing approach instrument, the angle-of-attack indicator should be used only as a secondary cruise control instrument. (See figures 4-4 and 4-5.)

Cruise Climb

Cruise climb trades reduction in gross weight for a gain in altitude and a resultant decrease in fuel flow for the same Mach number. No hard and fast rules can be established, as cruise climb is dependent on

3-25

Section III
Part 3

aircraft cleanliness, engine performance, temperature, and winds aloft. The general procedures for cruise climb are as follows:

1. At optimum altitude, set power levers to establish appropriate IAS, TAS, or Mach.

2. Maintain established Mach.

Level-Off/In-Flight Checklist

1. Fuel quantity/transfer/
cg indicator . . . . RECORD/
CHECKED

2. Oxygen quatity . . . . RECORD

3. Cabin altitude/altimeter . . . . . CHECKED

4. Engine instruments . . . . CHECKED

5. ATM temperature . . . . CHECKED

6. Compasses . . . . CHECKED

7. Trim tabs . . . . CHECKED

8. Hydraulic pressure . . . . CHECKED

9. Ac frequencies/ac-dc
voltages . . . . CHECKED

10. Anti-icing (level off only) . . . . AS DESIRED

Descent Checklist

1. Fuel quantity . . . . CHECKED

2. Radar/pressure altimeters . . . SET

3. Air conditioning/defrost . . . . . HOT/
WINDSHIELD

4. Anti-icing . . . . AS REQUIRED

5. Loose gear . . . . STOWED

6. Exterior lights . . . . AS DESIRED

7. Pilot's circuit breakers . . . . . CHECKED

8. Autopilot . . . . AS DESIRED

9. Bailout bottles/baro-release
lanyards . . . . AS REQUIRED

10. 5000-/1000-foot intervals . . . . RIGHT SEAT
MONITOR

Descent

TACAN/VOR penetrations are made at 250 KIAS, speedbrakes extended, and 1500 pounds per hour per engine fuel flow. This configuration produces a rate of descent of approximately 4000 fpm. Throttle adjustments must be made as altitude decreases to maintain 1500 pounds per hour per engine fuel flow. En route descents may be made at en route airspeeds, 1500 pounds per hour per engine fuel flow with or without speedbrakes depending on the rate of descent desired. Consideration must be given to encountering possible icing conditions, in which event a rapid descent is required.

Idle descents are made when fuel conservation is the primary consideration. Refer to performance data for maximum range descent performance data.

WARNING

During idle descent, engine bleed air to ATMs may not be sufficient to permit operation of utility system hydraulic equipment without considerable drop in ac generator frequency and power output. Low-frequency operation can result in loss of electrical system, including all ac electrical flight instruments.

Landing Checklist

1. Autopilot. . . . . OFF

2. Pressurization . . . . AS REQUIRED

3. ANTISKID . . . . ON FIELD/
OFF SHIP

4. Fuel dump . . . . OFF

5. Deleted

*6. ASB/periscope cover/DECM . . SET/
CLOSED/OFF

*7. Hook . . . . UP FIELD/
DOWN SHIP

*8. Slats . . . . WORKING

*9. Flaps. . . . . DOWN

*10. Gear . . . . 4 DOWN

*11. Tailhook bypass switch . . . . . ON FIELD/
OFF SHIP

*12. Fuel quantity/approach speed . . CHECKED/
SET

*13. Hydraulic pressure . . . . CHECKED

---
*For touch-and-go/FCLP landings, repeat items 6 through 17.

*14. Nosewheel steering .... CENTERED

*15. Shoulder harness (all) .... LOCKED

*16. Overhead hatch .... LOCKED
OPEN

*17. Speedbrakes .... OPEN

LANDINGS

(See figure 3-4.)

Complete the landing checklist up to "slats" prior to pattern entry. Enter the landing pattern for the "break" at 250 KIAS at the prescribed altitude. At the "break," open the speedbrakes and reduce fuel flow to 1500 pounds per engine. The angle of bank should be between 30 and 45 degrees. At 200 KIAS, lower the flaps. The aircraft will tend to pitch up and climb during the last part of the flap extension. This tendency can be controlled with forward pressure on the control wheel to hold the required altitude. When the flaps are down, lower the landing gear. At the proper altitude and at an airspeed of 135 knots, retract the speedbrakes and increase fuel flow to approximately 3000 pounds per engine. It is necessary that fuel flow be used as a measure of power adjustment during the approach. Smaller and more precise power changes can be made using fuel flow as opposed to rpm. When the aircraft is level at 135 knots in the typical landing configuration and gross weight, make a fuel-remaining check. The aircraft should arrive at the 180-degree position with 13 units angle of attack at the prescribed altitude. Plan the turn from the 180-degree position to have approximately a 1 1/4-mile "final." Extend the speedbrakes and adjust power to arrive at the 90-degree position at 700 to 800 feet of altitude. When turning into final and sighting the meatball, adjust fuel flow to give approximately a 500- to 700-foot per minute rate of descent. Ensure that the landing checklist is complete at this time. Fuel flow should be about 2700 to 3100 pounds per hour per engine, depending on landing weight. Fly the aircraft onto the runway in the approach attitude (15 units angle of attack) and at the approach speed for the landing weight. Touchdown target should be approximately 500 feet from the touchdown end.

A waveoff SHALL NOT be attempted after drag chute deployment, because the aircraft may be unable to maintain a positive rate of climb.

NOTE

If touchdown is not effected within the first 1000 feet from the touchdown end of the runway, a waveoff shall be taken.

---
*For touch-and-go/FCLP landings, repeat items 6 through 17.

Immediately after touchdown, pull the throttles to IDLE. If the rate of descent is slightly high at touchdown, the aircraft will normally take a short skip as the main gear oleos are compressed and extended. This is a very critical point in successfully landing the aircraft. If the control wheel is allowed to move forward at the start of the skip, a porpoise will be induced and further pumping of the control wheel will aggravate the porpoise. The only reasonable correction for a porpoise is a full-power waveoff. The porpoise can be prevented by holding the control wheel as is at touchdown and throughout the skip. If the aircraft bounces moderately, a slight back pressure on the control wheel must be maintained and the aircraft relanded MAIN GEAR FIRST. After the throttles are brought to IDLE, continue flying the aircraft, keeping the wings level with the ailerons. If the landing speed, rate of descent, and attitude were satisfactory, the aircraft will rock forward on the nosewheel and run smoothly down the runway. If the airspeed is too high, the attitude too shallow, or the rate of descent too high, the aircraft will bounce into the air. Do not use forward pressure on the control wheel to force the aircraft to remain on the runway. When it is ensured that the landing has been safely accomplished, deploy the drag chute. After the chute has been deployed, fly the aircraft down the runway, using ailerons as necessary to keep the wings level and using the rudder to maintain directional control. Use the brakes during the runout as necessary. At about 50 knots, nosewheel steering may be used to help maintain a straight rollout. For landing on a wet and/or slippery runway, use the normal landing technique. No-chute landings for training purposes may be made at the commanding officer's discretion.

CAUTION

- Do not touch the nosewheel steering control at touchdown. The steering control must be free to swivel as the nosewheel casters to prevent damage to the nose gear scissor linkage.

- The nosewheel steering is extremely sensitive at high speeds. Make directional changes with caution until speed is lost.

Crosswind Landing

Crosswind landings are critical due to the narrow landing gear and the closeness of the wingtips to the ground. The best crosswind technique is as follows: Make the same approach as for a normal landing. When on final, a wing-down or crab can be used to compensate for drift. Level wings or remove crab just prior to touchdown. After landing, continue to fly the aircraft, keeping the wings level with aileron and maintaining directional control with rudder and nose gear steering. Until slowed to approximately 60 knots, the aircraft tends to tip, bank, and drift downwind. After the aircraft is firmly on the landing gear, lead the aileron to keep the up-wind wing level or slightly low. Some lateral control is available through use of the ailerons above 60 knots. Below this speed, the aircraft tends to weathercock. Align the aircraft longitudinal axis with the runway on touchdown. Slowing through the critical airspeeds is effected in less time than flap retraction; so raising the flaps in crosswinds up to 15 knots 90 degrees to the runway with drag chute deployed is of little practical value and should not be attempted. However, if the drag chute fails to deploy in a crosswind landing, raise the flaps.

CAUTION

- The flap handle and gear handle are in close proximity.

- Do not exceed 10-degree angle of bank or the low wingtip may drag on the runway upon landing.

Crosswind landings are controllable in wind up to 15 knots, 90 degrees to the runway, with full flaps. In the event of the loss of No. 1 ATM and/or wing spoilers are not operating, the acceptable crosswind component is lowered to 7 knots, 90 degrees to the runway, with full flaps. If existing crosswind exceeds these limits, request another runway or proceed to an alternate airfield where acceptable wind conditions are available.

High Crosswind Landings

This presentation of alternative action shall not be construed as preventing the pilot from ordering a bailout.

When 90-degree crosswind exceeds 15 knots, and a divert field with a suitable runway is not available, the pilot must make a decision as to the best course of action. In all cases, a short field arrestment would be the most advantageous solution, with other types of field arrestments only slightly less desirable. If no such arrestment facilities are available, consideration must be given to the problems associated with high crosswind landings.

To aid the pilot in making a decision, the following aircraft characteristics in high crosswinds are presented:

1. The aircraft has a marked tendency to arc downwind during rollout, in an amount directly proportional to the crosswind until slowed to below 60 KIAS at which time it begins to weathercock.

2. Pitchup of the upwind wing will occur immediately after touchdown and will require prompt corrective aileron control to prevent severe wing rock.

3. The speed range where control will be most difficult extends from touchdown to approximately 60 KIAS. While in this speed range, the pilot must continue to "fly" the aircraft even though on the runway.

Use of the nosewheel steering above 50 KIAS should be avoided, as loads can be imposed on the nose gear scissors linkage that are of sufficient magnitude to cause structural damage.

The following techniques can be employed to optimize these characteristics:

1. Take full advantage of tendency to arc downwind by landing wing-down on downwind side of runway with aircraft pointed into wind as much as possible. This will:

   a. Cause aircraft to roll out toward upwind side of runway prior to beginning its arc downwind. This technique serves to lengthen the effective distance of the runway.

   b. Lessen crosswind component to degree that aircraft can be pointed successfully into the wind.

2. Raise flaps after touchdown. This will decrease lift, thereby increasing effective weight of aircraft on landing gear, tire footprint area, friction, and braking effectiveness.

3. Deploy drag chute as soon as decision is made to remain on runway rather than attempt another approach. The chute will have a stabilizing effect by pointing the aircraft more nearly down the runway.

4. Use brakes as judiciously as the situation will permit, taking note of probability of blown tires if full braking is initiated before aircraft has firmly settled on landing gear.

Touch-and-Go Landing

Accomplish touch-and-go practice using the same technique as described above. Complete the landing checklist prior to each landing. The landing gear and flaps normally will not be retracted after a touch-and-go. It will be necessary to reduce power shortly after the takeoff if a comfortable climb attitude is desired. After each landing, pull the throttles to the idle position, allowing the aircraft to settle down on a short runout prior to the takeoff. Be cautious when advancing throttles for takeoff to prevent asymmetrical acceleration. Approximately 500 pounds of fuel are required for each circuit. Touch-and-go landings shall not be practiced with less than 3000 pounds of fuel remaining.

Single-Engine Approach/Landing

Single-engine landings can be accomplished with ease. If time permits, the fuel load should be burned down to a gross weight of 50,000 pounds. A GCA approach is recommended if available. LSO assistance in short final is also desirable. If short field arresting gear is available, consider making an arrestment as this would eliminate braking and control problems if ATM's drop off line when power is reduced.

NOTE

Under poor field conditions (wet runway, short runway, crosswind, etc), consider making a short field arrestment. Tests indicate that limited nosewheel steering may be available with the hook down. Consideration should be given to the possibility of utilizing this limited steering in the event of aborted takeoff or missed field arrestment. However, it should not be relied upon for primary directional control. If an arrested landing is not attempted, braking and control problems may occur if ATM's drop off the line when power is reduced.

Upon entry downwind, the flaps should be lowered to 1/2 flaps at 200 KIAS. The landing gear should be lowered at the 180-degree position and the aircraft slowed to 15 units angle of attack, or the approach speed for gross weight as indicated in Pocket Checklist (NAVAIR 01-40ATA-1B). Speedbrakes normally should be closed during the approach; however, they may be used, as necessary, to slow the aircraft. Approximately 2800 to 3400 pounds per hour fuel flow will be required by the operating engine during approach. Full rudder trim against the good engine should be used in order to control the aircraft during a waveoff. Waveoffs can be accomplished at any time up to and including touchdown.

Caution must be taken to prevent the aircraft from going below the normal glide slope, as considerable power and trim changes are required to recover from a low, slow final. After touchdown and when power is reduced to IDLE, the loss of both ATM's may result. Engine rpm requirements will vary according to temperature. Maintain sufficient power on the good engine to support both ATM's. The aircraft will be landed normally main gear first. At touchdown, direction control will be maintained with rudder as the power is slowly reduced to IDLE. Deploy the drag chute as soon as the aircraft is firmly on the deck. During the approach if doubt of the success of the landing arises, an early waveoff will be initiated by applying full power and full rudder into the good engine. Yaw must be controlled during the waveoff. The landing gear will be raised as soon as altitude and directional control can be maintained. Directional control can be aided by a shallow turn into the good engine as full power is applied. After the airspeed has increased to 150 KIAS a shallow climb back to landing pattern altitude will be established. Simulated single-engine approaches will be practiced periodically with one engine in the IDLE position. (Refer to Carrier-based Procedures, Section III, part 4.) If a single-engine approach to a short runway is necessary, lower full flaps prior to intercepting glideslope. Do not slow to below minimum single-engine control speed until landing is assured.

Minimum Roll Without Drag Chute

For minimum roll landings without drag chute, use approach speed shown in the landing charts (figure 11-57). As soon as the aircraft is firmly on the runway, retard the throttles to IDLE, place nosewheel on the runway, and smoothly apply maximum braking effort. Maximum antiskid braking effectiveness occurs between 90 and 50 knots.

Minimum Roll With Drag Chute

Deployment of the drag chute can be safely accomplished immediately after main gear touchdown.

NOTE

Minimum ground roll charts are based on deployment of drag chute at touchdown.

Observe the recommended approach and landing technique for minimum roll and place the DRAG CHUTE switch in DEPLOY as soon as both main gear are firmly on the runway. Deployment of the chute will require 3 seconds at the maximum before deceleration takes effect.

Hydroplaning

When tires of an aircraft roll over water-covered or flooded runways, hydrodynamic pressures develop between the tire footprint and the runway. The pressures grow larger as the ground speed increases. At a critical speed, hydrodynamic lift resulting from the buildup of pressure under a tire will equal the weight riding on the tire. When this occurs, hydroplaning speed has been reached. Any increase in groundspeed above this critical value lifts the tire completely off the pavement, leaving it supported by the fluid alone. The result is called total tire hydroplaning. Total tire hydroplaning speed may be determined by means of the simple relation $V_H = 9\sqrt{p}$, where V_H = tire hydroplaning speed in knots and p = tire inflation pressure in pounds per square inch. (The equation is valid for smooth tires or for grooved tires where fluid depth exceeds tread groove depth.) For example, an operating tire pressure of 230 to 240 psi would give a total hydroplaning speed of 136 to 139 KIAS.

NOTE

Bald or smooth tread tires will hydroplane on a very smooth pavement if only 1/10 inch of water is present. Ribbed treads on rough textured pavement may hydroplane in 2/10 or 3/10 inch of water.

CONSEQUENCES OF TIRE HYDROPLANING

During total tire hydroplaning, tire-ground friction forces drop to insignificant values because the fluid cannot develop large shear forces. In addition, hydrodynamic lift tends to shift the vertical ground reaction on the tire in a way that produces a spin-down tendency on the tire. These two major effects combine to produce the following consequences:

1. Nearly complete loss of braking and cornering capability

2. Greatly increased stopping distances

3. Crosswind can cause severe skidding

4. Partial hydroplaning can occur at speeds well below total tire hydroplaning speed in deep fluids.

Avoid hydroplaning conditions if possible. If hydroplaning conditions cannot be avoided, the pilot should determine field conditions prior to approach; i.e., braking action, runway conditions, crosswind component, type, status, and location of arresting gear.

If landing must be made where field conditions may produce hydroplaning, proceed as follows:

1. Land on longest runway available that is acceptable to aircraft crosswind and arresting gear limitations.

2. Land on end of runway, DO NOT flair, deploy drag chute at touchdown.

3. Be prepared for field arrestment if drag chute fails to deploy.

Antiskid Braking Techniques

There should be no braking attempted before the main mounts are firmly on the runway. Maximum antiskid braking effectiveness occurs between 90 and 50 knots.

Excessive pedal force should not be applied, but rather, normal braking procedures should be used to preclude tire failure in the event of antiskid malfunction. The normal procedure is to apply light brake pressure and to increase pressure steadily as the aircraft decelerates. On normal landings, heavy braking may be used down to a speed of 50 knots. Below this speed, heavy pedal force may result in tire failure due to the decreased sensitivity of the antiskid system.

If antiskid failure occurs at speeds in excess of 70 knots, the pedal force should be released, antiskid turned off, and no antiskid braking methods used. Since the pedal feel in the A-3 is completely artificial and the skidding of the main mounts cannot be felt by the pilot, possibility of tire failure is great.

Even with the antiskid in perfect operating order, tire failure is still possible, due to one or a combination of the following:

1. ANTISKID switch not ON

2. Application of brakes before touchdown

3. Locked brakes due to material failure

4. Application of brakes before both main mounts are firmly on runway

5. Application of brakes during a long bounce

6. Application of brakes with one wing held high (due to crosswind, etc)

7. Application of brakes with wings rocking

8. Application of brakes at high speeds on rough runway.

The first four types of tire failure with an operating antiskid are self-explanatory; the last four types are caused by a wheel lifting clear of the runway while the brakes are applied. For example, if a gust of wind lifts a wing and one wheel leaves the ground for an appreciable time, that wheel may be turning slow enough, due to brake pressure, to stop rotating. If a skid signal is not received from the wheel still on the ground, the airborne wheel will lock, if full brake pressure is applied at touchdown, and will blow a tire before a skid signal is transmitted from the rotating wheel, which has been in contact with the runway.

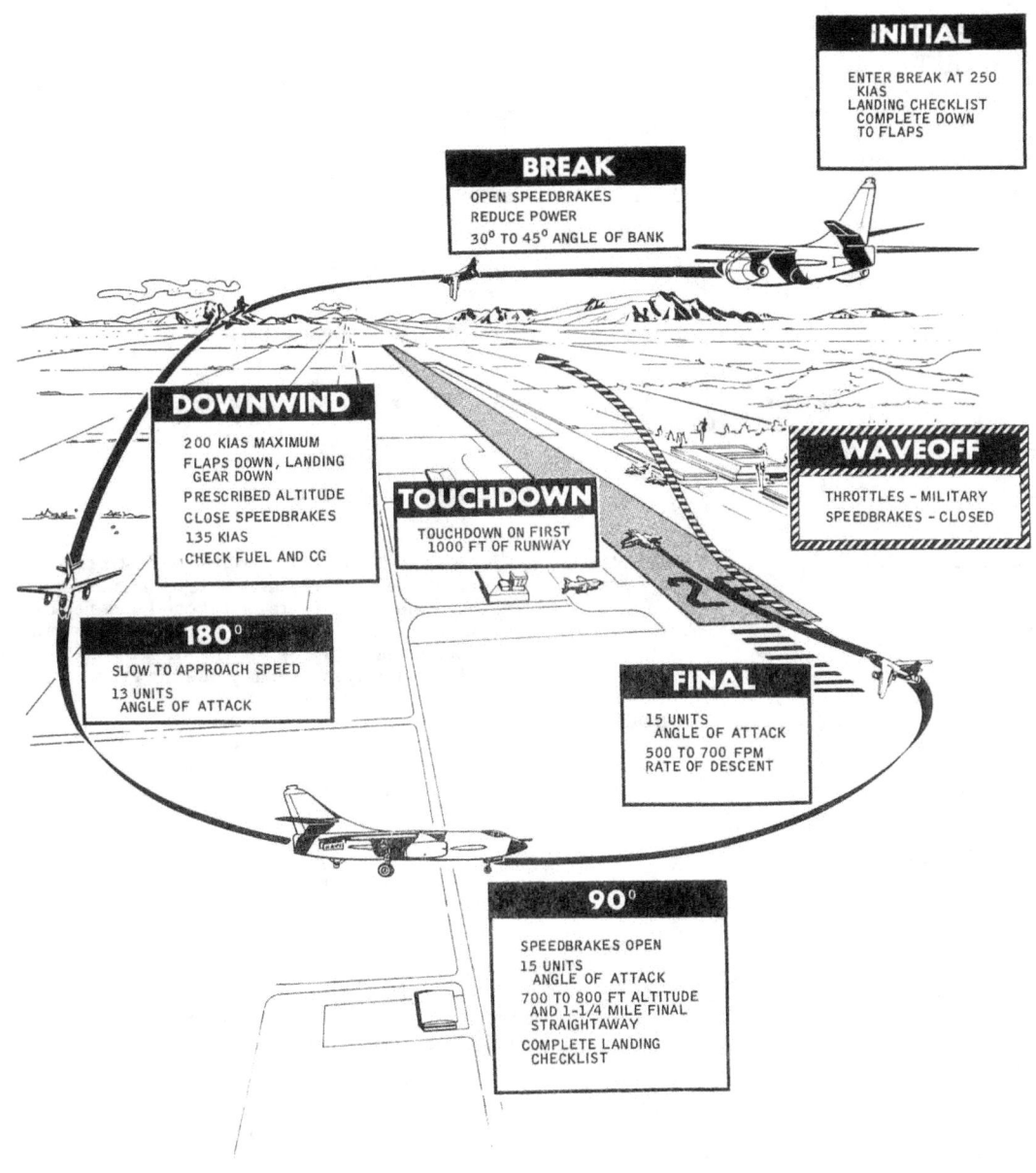

Figure 3-4. Landing and Waveoff Pattern

Section III
Part 3

In the event of a long bounce when both wheels are airborne, the wheels may lock; and, if the brake pressure is not released, a skid signal will not be transmitted to the antiskid system. The reason for the skid signal not being transmitted is that the skid contacts will not close unless there is sufficient wheel rotation to generate flywheel action in the units.

Postlanding Checklist (Field)

(When clear of runway,

1. Speedbrakes (70% rpm) . . . . . . CLOSED

2. Gust locks . . . . LOCKED

3. ANTISKID . . . . OFF

4. Anti-icing . . . . OFF

5. Unnecessary radios/Navaids/ radar alt/IFF . . . . OFF

6. Trim tabs . . . . SET

7. Fuel trim . . . . NOSEDOWN

8. Upper hatch . . . . MANNED

9. Wings (70% rpm, aircraft stopped) . . . . AS REQUIRED

10. Flaps (70% rpm) . . . . AS DESIRED

Shutdown Checklist

1. Lights . . . . OFF

2. Warning lights/test circuits . . . CHECK

3. VGI/STBY gyro horizon circuit breakers . . . . OUT

4. Bomb bay doors (on signal) . . . OPEN

5. ASB/radio master . . . . OFF

6. Ac generators/bus tie . . . . OFF/OPEN

7. ATM switches . . . . OFF

CAUTION

Allow the engine to idle for 5 minutes, if the engine has been operating at 85 percent rpm or higher for 1 minute during the previous 5 minutes.

8. Advance throttles to 75% rpm for approximately 30 seconds.

9. Throttles/master engine switches . . . . OFF/OFF

10. Bleed air switches . . . . ALL OPEN/ON

11. Oxygen control valves . . . . OFF

12. Battery . . . . OFF

FIELD ARRESTMENTS

There are several types of field arresting gear including the anchor chain cable, water squeeze, and Morest-type equipment. All these types require engagement of the arresting hook in a cable pendant rigged across the runway. Location of the pendant in relation to the runway classifies the gear as follows:

1. Short-field gear. Located at the approach end of the runway. In some instances, prior notification may be required to rig for arrestment in direction desired.

2. Midfield gear. Located near the halfway point of the runway. Usually requires prior notification in order to rig for arrestment in direction desired.

3. Abort gear. Located 1500 to 2500 feet short of the upwind end of the duty runway and usually will be rigged for immediate use.

4. Overrun gear. Located shortly past the upwind end of the duty runway. Usually will be rigged for immediate use.

Some fields will have all these types of gear; others, none. For this reason, it is imperative that all pilots be aware of the type, location, and compatibility of the gear in use with the aircraft, and the policy of the local air station with regard to which gear is rigged for use and when.

The approximate maximum permissible engaging speed, gross weight, and off-center engagement distance for field arrestment of aircraft are listed in the Pocket Checklist.

WARNING

- Under no circumstances should pilot decision to abort a takeoff be delayed because of knowledge that an emergency arresting gear is available at the end of the runway. Decision to abort should be based on the usual parameters of remaining runway and distance required for stopping, using wheel brakes. The arresting gear will then serve as an assist to stop the aircraft from rolling off the runway onto unprepared surfaces.

- If off center just prior to engaging arresting gear, do not attempt to go for center of runway. Continue straight ahead parallel to centerline.

- As various modifications to the basic types of arresting gear are made, exact speeds will vary accordingly. Certain aircraft service changes may also affect engaging speed and weight limitations.

- Severe damage to the aircraft is usually sustained if an engagement is made in the wrong direction into the chain gear.

Field Barrier

Land in a 3-point attitude and secure engines prior to entering the barrier.

FMLP AND CQ

General Requirements

FMLP is required for all pilots prior to engaging in basic carrier qualifications or refresher carrier landings. The exact number of FMLP periods required depends on the experience and ability of the individual pilot and is determined by the squadron commanding officer and landing signal officer. A pilot shall not engage in day FMLP until he has become proficient in emergency procedures, slow flight characteristics, and instrument flying. A minimum of 50 hours pilot time in A-3 aircraft shall be accumulated prior to commencing carrier qualifications.

The final decision in regard to a pilot's readiness rests with the squadron commanding officer.

Landing Weight

Current landing weight restrictions for each model are published in this Flight Manual and shall not be exceeded. Approach may be made in an overweight condition but shall be terminated in a waveoff.

Day FMLP

Prior to taxiing onto the runway for takeoff, make a radio check with the LSO and the tower. Aircraft shall not engage in FMLP unless two-way communications with both the tower and the LSO have been established. After takeoff, make an initial landing gear check to the tower on paddles frequency. The LSO will assume control of aircraft in the FMLP pattern until the aircraft are ready for a final landing, at which time the LSO will pass control back to the tower. Leave the landing gear and flaps in the down position throughout the pattern. Upon touchdown, apply full power, close the speedbrakes, and climb-out straight ahead, accelerating to 150 KIAS. The upwind turn may be started at 300 feet altitude, continuing the climb to 600 feet actual altitude if terrain permits. Roll the aircraft smoothly into a 25-degree bank and hold this bank for the upwind turn to establish proper distance abeam. When the upwind turn has been completed, slow to 135 KIAS and make a fuel quantity check. Make the final landing with at least 3000 pounds of fuel remaining.

Speed, Pattern, and Technique

An angle-of-attack setting of 15 units should be used. Approach speed will vary with gross weight at 15 units angle of attack.

The 180-degree position will vary on the field with the wind velocity but can generally be considered to have been reached when the mirror is 45 degrees aft of the abeam position. With practice, this position can be determined and checked by TACAN bearing and distance. Upon reaching the 180-degree position, initiate a turn, increasing the angle of bank to about 20 degrees parallel to the runway, at 600 feet actual altitude and at the proper approach speed. At this point, terrain permitting, make a cross-check between the radar and pressure altimeters.

The angle of bank may be varied as necessary to fly a rounded pattern. Altitude should be constant and power adjusted as required to roll out on the landing line at 600 feet at the proper approach speed. As soon as the "meatball" is sighted (this should be a few seconds prior to rolling wings level), rate of descent is set up by extending speedbrakes and

3-33

reducing power slightly. Set up the approach speed no later than the 180-degree position. Extend the speedbrakes upon sighting the meatball. Report to the LSO: "Side number, aircraft model, fuel state meatball."

Three things are necessary to fly a "Roger" approach: The meatball must be kept in the center, the proper approach speed must be maintained, and the aircraft must be lined up with the center of the landing area. Power changes, when necessary, should always be minor and monitored by fuel flow. Altitude and power must be varied in order to correct for a meatball not in the center. The correction for a low meatball is an addition of power to slow the rate of descent to bring the meatball back to the center. A readjustment of power to hold the proper rate of descent will then be required. A slightly high meatball can be centered by taking a "high dip." With a very high meatball, reduce power to decrease altitude. To keep from accelerating, maintain proper approach attitude. When quite close to the ramp, there should be no attempt to correct for a high meatball; "hold what you have" and land long. This is extremely important inasmuch as aboard ship a late correction for a high meatball can easily result in a hard landing or even striking the ramp if the deck is pitching. Establish proper lineup early in the approach. Lineup must be monitored constantly on every approach. Trim aircraft during the approach as necessary to lighten control pressure (4- to 5-degree noseup trim usually being sufficient). Good landings usually feel quite hard as the aircraft is actually flown into the deck in its approach attitude. Avoid tendency to flare the aircraft. Flaring just before touchdown will usually extend the touchdown point by as much as 100 feet which, aboard ship, will normally result in a bolter. As soon as the aircraft touches the deck, advance the throttles to full power and close the speedbrakes in the same motion. The waveoff is a mandatory signal, is answered by immediately adding full power and closing the speedbrakes. Keep the aircraft lined up with the angled deck during late waveoffs, as a possibility of an inflight engagement exists. Normally, no change in attitude should be made. A slight rotation causes the tail to drop considerably before any gain in altitude is experienced and may possibly result in an inflight engagement. The application of power should stop the rate of descent immediately. Shortly after the aircraft has begun to accelerate, raise the nose slightly to establish a climb.

NIGHT FMLP

The pattern and approach speeds are identical to those for day FMLP. Turn all lights on bright and steady. Once again, the essential ingredients of a "Roger" pass are: be properly set up at 180, fly the meatball, and monitor airspeed and lineup. <u>Fly the angle-of-attack indicator</u>, cross-checking with the airspeed indicator.

BUFFET-ONSET CHECK

Make buffet-onset (nibble) check on the downwind leg when doubt exists as to the accuracy of the angle-of-attack or airspeed systems. See Flight Procedures, Section IV, for buffet-onset check procedures.

Night Taxi and Takeoff

Prior to leaving the line, ensure that exterior lights are functioning normally. Turn all exterior lights on bright. Ensure that cockpit lights, both ac instrument lights and dc floodlights are operating satisfactorily, and that a flashlight with red lens is readily available. Taxi the aircraft slowly, using idle power once rolling. It is very easy to taxi at excessive speeds at night without realizing it. Have the navigator man the upper hatch. Use the taxi light as required.

The aircraft will be lined up in center of the runway. Takeoff is accomplished exactly as during daylight, using preplanned acceleration checks, and lift-off speed.

NIGHT FORMATION AND RENDEZVOUS

Night rendezvous technique is similar to day operations. Extra caution is necessary, however, since closing rates are difficult to judge. Approach the lead aircraft slowly but deliberately. During join-up, keep the exterior lights on bright. Once joined, switch lights to dim. The last aircraft in the formation will keep lights on bright.

General considerations of day formation operations are applicable. If possible, use radios to keep all pilots prepared for heading, altitude, or power changes. Use small angles of bank and smooth power changes. Refer to Section IV for rendezvous instructions.

NIGHT BREAKUP AND LANDING

Breakup will be signaled by the leader flashing his running lights and by radio, if practical. Following break, each aircraft must turn running lights on bright. A long interval for break will be necessary to enable aircraft ahead to clear the runway.

The landing is accomplished exactly as in daylight. Maintain a normal rate of descent with power until the aircraft touches down. The use of the taxi light is optional during its approach when shore based but is prohibited aboard ship. Avoid the tendency to use the light to pick out the runway for a flared landing. Power should remain on until touchdown.

CZ CVHA 686
RTIEZYUW RULSSAA5544 3232328-EEEE--RUWMHVA.
ZNY EEEEE
R 192328Z NOV 69   ----FILLER
FM NAVAIRSYSCOMHQ
INFO RUWMHVA/TACELECWARWG THIRTEEN
RUWJMUA/NAVAIRSYSCOMREPAC
RUWMHVA/NAVAIREWORKFAC ALAMEDA
P R 142301Z NOV 69
FM NAVSAFECEN   ----FILE
TO COMNAVAIRPAC
COMNAVAIRLANT
NAVAIRSYSCOMHQ
INFO CNO
HATRON ONE TWO THREE
NAVTACDOCACT
NAVAIRTESTCEN
BT
UNCLAS E F T O
3510 URGENT CHANGE RECOMMENDATIONS TO A-3A/B, KA/EKA/EA/TA/RA-3B
NATOPS FLIGHT MANUALS
A. NAVAIRSYSCOMHQ 222258Z AUG 69 NOTAL
B. NAVAIR 01-40-ATA-1 CHANGED 1 JUN 69

PAGE TWO RULSSAA5544 UNCLAS E F T O
C. NAVAIR 01-40ATD-1 CHANGED 15 JUN 68
D. NAVAIR 01-40-ATE-1 CHANGED 1 JUN 69
E. NAVAIR 01-40-ATB-1 CHANGED 15 SEP 68
1. REF A RECOMMENDED A-3 ACFT BE LAUNCHED FROM BOW CATS WHENEVER
POSSIBLE; HOWEVER, THE USE OF WAIST CATAPULTS WITH RESULTANT SLAT
FAILURES CONTINUES TO OCCUR. ADDITIONALLY, INCIDENTS HAVE NOT BEEN
LIMITED TO BASIC (NON-CLE) WING
2. IN VIEW OF THE ABOVE, THE FOL CHANGES TO REF B THROUGH E ARE
RECOMMENDED:
  A. SECTION III PART 4 LAUNCHING PARA
    (1) DELETE: NA
    (2) ADD: WARNING. PROBABILITY OF SLAT FAILURE A RESULT OF
TURBULENCE ASSOCIATED WITH NR 3 CATAPULT PRECLUDES THE
UTILIZATION OF THIS CATAPULT FOR LAUNCHING A-3 ACFT.
3. FOR NAVAIRSYSCOMHQ. REQUEST ADVISE ALCON RESULTS OF EFFORTS
OUTLINED PARA 4 REF A
BT
5544

CVAQW13   NARF   //SK//

PART 4
CARRIER-BASED PROCEDURES

TABLE OF CONTENTS

TEXT

	Page		Page
Introduction	3-35	Minimum Fuel (Bingo Fuel)	3-38
Aircraft Inspection	3-35	Emergency (Low State)	3-38
Engine Starting	3-35	Arrestment and Taxiing	3-38
Flight Deck Operations	3-35	Carqual Checklist	3-38
Taxiing	3-35	Barricade Engagement	3-39
Rendezvous	3-35	Postlanding Checklist (Ship)	3-39
Breakup and Landing	3-35	Shutdown Checklist (Ship)	3-39
Carrier Landing	3-36		
Night Carrier Operations	3-36		
CCA Night Recovery	3-38		
Single-Engine Carrier Landing	3-38		

ILLUSTRATIONS

Figure		Page
3-5	Typical Carrier Landing Pattern	3-37

INTRODUCTION

The CVA-CVS NATOPS Manual governs general aircraft operations with aircraft carriers. This section contains carrier operating procedures peculiar to A-3B aircraft.

AIRCRAFT INSPECTION

It is the responsibility of the pilot, in conjunction with the crewmembers, to conduct a thorough preflight inspection of the aircraft. These procedures are outlined in part 3 of this section.

ENGINE STARTING

The procedure for starting the engines is covered in part 3.

FLIGHT DECK OPERATIONS

Taxiing

CAUTION

- Should improper wheelbrake operation be indicated or suspected, turn on EMER HYD PUMP. The emergency airbrake handle should be pulled whenever the brakes do not respond properly.

- A wet, rolling, and/or pitching deck requires extreme caution while taxiing or towing. The aircraft shall not be taxied or towed while the ship is in a hard turn. The antiskid switch shall remain OFF.

A flight deck director will signal "hold brakes" when the tiedowns and chocks are removed. The pilot must be particularly alert for this signal so that brakes can be held firmly. The director will bring the aircraft out of the spot and pass control from director to director up to the catapult. The pilot will complete the takeoff checklist, secure all loose gear, and position headrest. Taxiing onto the catapult is a precision maneuver, and every signal must be answered smoothly and promptly. Use small corrections with nosewheel steering. A power setting of 80 percent will normally provide adequate thrust to roll the nosewheel over the shuttle. Once over the shuttle, the director will signal for an immediate stop to allow the holdback bar to be installed. A very slow come ahead will then be directed to apply tension to the holdback cable. Caution should be taken to tension the holdback cable as gently as possible. When the taxi director gives the signal to the catapult crew for tension to be applied to the launching bridle, the throttles will be advanced to a minimum of 80 percent.

WARNING

Launching of NON-CLE aircraft should be restricted from the waist catapult except for urgent operational requirements until aircraft is reworked per wing slat A-3 AFC 465.

NOTE

Refer to A-3 aircraft launching bulletins for additional information.

Rendezvous

Rendezvous and departure shall be in accordance with Section IV and CVA/CVS NATOPS Manual.

Breakup and Landing

The sector for climbout, rendezvous, letdown, and orbiting (figure 3-5) in the vicinity of each carrier varies according to number of carriers in the formation as well as the position of a specific carrier in formation. This information is contained in ATP-1 (A), Volume L, and the CVA/CVS NATOPS Manual.

Upon sighting the carrier on an independent flight or after rendezvous in a group flight, the flight leader shall call the ship on the assigned frequency to give a "see you" report which must include the leader's call and the number of aircraft in the flight. In VFR weather and at the proper time, CATTC will clear the flight leader to contact "_____" on land/launch frequency. Landing order will be given at this time. Under IFR conditions, CATTC will maintain control and give marshal instructions, expected approach clearance times, and expected initial and final bearings for the CCA. Each carrier has an established recovery order by aircraft type. As the aircraft return to the ship and are shifted to tower (land/launch) frequency, a Charlie time should be specified by the ship. Charlie time is the time at which the addressed flight leader is to cross the ramp in landing configuration. It is expressed as the number of minutes from the time of the transmission that the ship expects to be ready to recover the addressed flight leader. This message is usually addressed only to the leader of the first flight to be recovered, and leaders of subsequent flights must then compute their own Charlie time. A good thumb rule is to allow 1 minute for recovery of each aircraft scheduled to be taken aboard. As experience increases, this will be reduced to approximately 35 seconds. Landing interval for night operation should be about 1 minute. The landing pattern is entered by flying along the starboard beam at 800 feet and 250 KIAS. The leader should break, extend speedbrakes, and reduce fuel flow to about 1500 pounds per hour per engine. When straight and level downwind, lower flaps, gear, and hook, while slowing to 135 KIAS. The break interval shall be one-half the desired ramp interval. Upon slowing to 135 KIAS on the downwind leg, close speedbrakes, adjust power to hold altitude and airspeed (about 3000 pounds fuel flow per engine), and complete the landing checklist. After obtaining the fuel state at 135 KIAS, continue slowing to approach speed. Arrive at the 180-degree position at 600 feet, 13 units angle of attack. Start the approach turn abeam of the ship. Make all approaches at an angle-of-attack setting of 15 units.

Carrier Landing

Carrier landings on angled deck ships (figure 3-5) should be made with particular attention to achieving a good lineup and avoiding landings with right to left drift which, when associated with the increased runout of angled deck arresting gears, can result in the aircraft coming to rest in the port catwalk even though a pendant is engaged.

A burble effect, present under all wind conditions, produces a definite tendency for the right wing to drop as the aircraft approaches and passes the round-down at the forward end of the landing area on angled deck ships.

The maximum carrier landing weight is 50,000 pounds; however, limitations of shipboard arresting gear may further reduce this figure. The average fuel required for a circuit of the landing pattern after a touch-and-go is 600 pounds. The average fuel used from an arrested landing, catapult shot, and flying the pattern back to an arrested landing is 800 pounds. Approach the 90-degree position at 600 feet altitude and on approach speed. As the final is approached at approximately 600 feet altitude, pick up the meatball, extend speedbrakes, and adjust power to commence the proper rate of descent. LSO voice signals during the mirror approach are advisory except for the waveoff which is mandatory. Until crossing the ramp, the pilot may take his own waveoff but must be careful of a late waveoff. On a late waveoff, do not rotate but maintain the landing attitude to ensure clearing the ramp and to prevent an inflight engagement. Flying a good approach will require precise control and attention to procedures learned in FMLP. The following rules should become second nature to the pilot.

1. Fly the meatball – not the deck; the meatball is stabilized and the deck is not.

2. Establish the following scan pattern – meatball, lineup, airspeed (angle of attack); meatball, lineup, airspeed (angle of attack); etc. Check fuel-flow settings every third or fourth scan. Fuel-flow settings for an average pass will be 2800 to 3000 pounds.

3. If the meatball is low, add power and adjust rate of descent to let the ball come into position.

4. If the meatball is lost in close, take a waveoff.

5. Do not dive for the deck.

6. Make small corrections in close.

7. Do not flare or push over just prior to touchdown. Hold the approach attitude. Fly the meatball all the way to the deck.

8. If it is known or suspected that the hook has struck the ramp or should a cross deck pendant break and a divert field is within range, the aircraft shall be immediately diverted. If a divert field is not available, the aircraft shall be recovered into the barricade.

Night Carrier Operations

Operations on the flight deck at night are slower than during the day. It is imperative that pilots be thoroughly familiar with every signal used on the deck at night. If in doubt as to the meaning of a signal, hold brakes and wait for clarification.

Set up the exterior light control panel prior to taxiing onto the catapult. Place the wing and taillight switch in BRIGHT, the fuselage switch in MANUAL, the flashing-steady switch in STEADY, and all others in

NAVAIR 01-40ATA-1

Section III
Part 4

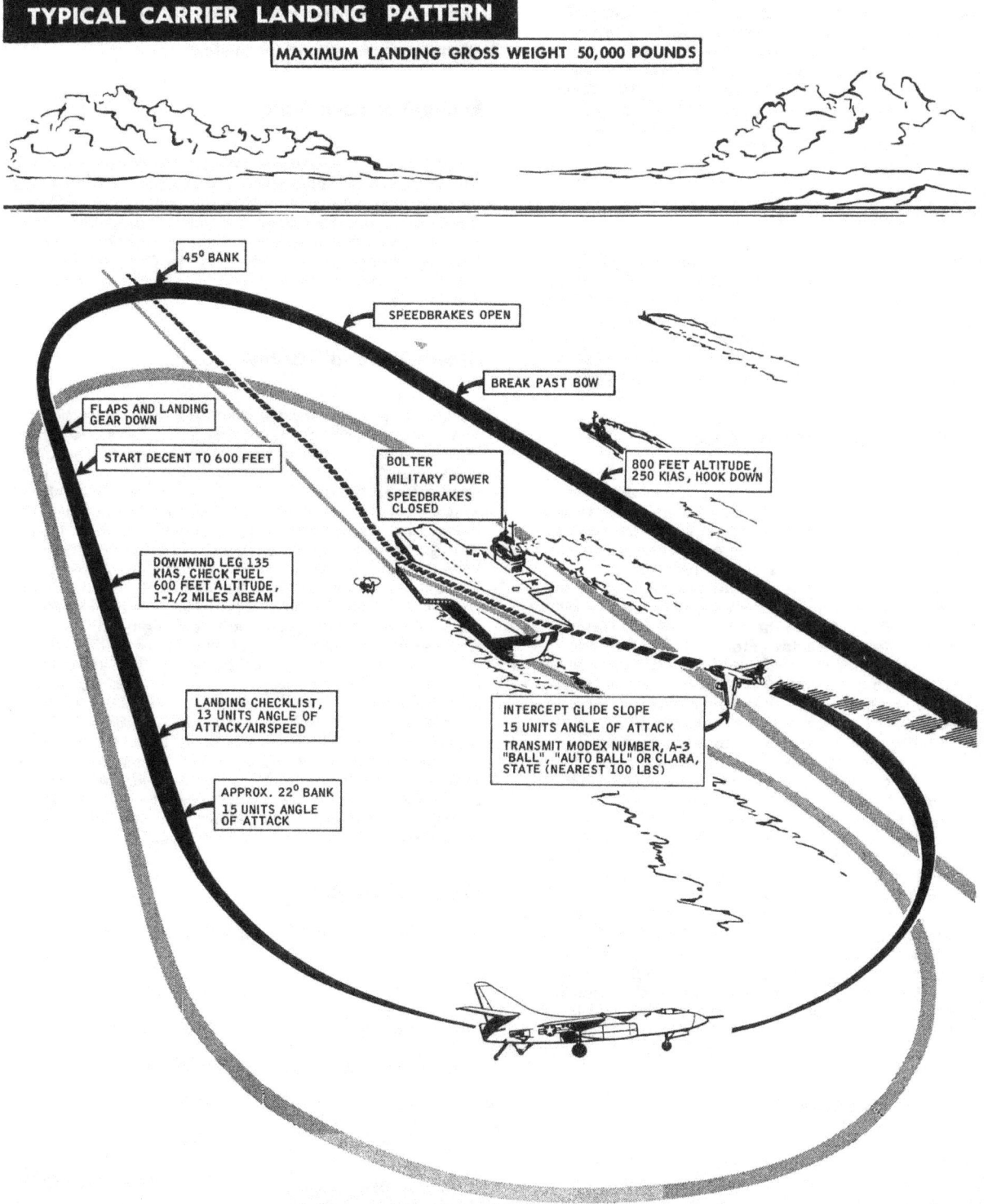

Figure 3-5. Typical Carrier Landing Pattern

3-37

OFF. Until ready for the catapult shot, all exterior lights must remain off. Signal ready for catapult launch by turning on the exterior lights, with the throttle master light switch. Once airborne, lights may be adjusted as desired. If the aircraft goes down on the catapult, notify primary fly immediately by radio. Do not reduce power until the catapult officer steps in front of the aircraft and gives the retarded power-lever signal.

CCA Night Recovery

CCA standard night recovery procedure employs a TACAN penetration with a CCA pickup. The pattern procedures and terms for CCA will be in accordance with CVA/CVS NATOPS MANUALS. Upon entering the landing pattern, all exterior lights must be turned on bright and steady. Turn the lower anticollision light OFF. After arrestment turn off exterior lights.

Single-Engine Carrier Landings

Single-engine carrier landings can be made by an experienced A-3 pilot. The pattern should be flown a little wider at the 180-degree position and with a longer final to compensate for the higher approach speeds. Gross weight should not be over 50,000 pounds. Fly the aircraft downwind at 13 units angle of attack with 1/2 flaps extended. At the 180-degree position, extend the gear. Use full rudder trim into the good engine prior to final approach. This may require the use of some rudder against the overtrimmed condition. Fly the final approach at 15 units angle of attack or the approach speed for gross weight as indicated in Pocket Checklist (NAVAIR 01-40ATA-1B) with speedbrakes in. About 2800 to 3400 pounds per hour fuel flow will be required on the operating engine. A waveoff or touch-and-go can be made successfully if full rudder is used into the good engine (full rudder trim is already in effect) simultaneously with power application. This technique will affect heading control during the waveoff or touch-and-go maneuver. Retract the gear upon commencing climb and accelerate to 150 KIAS. Aircraft gross weights and engaging speeds must fall within current launch/recovery bulletin limits. It is recommended that this procedure be practiced by experienced A-3 pilots prior to deployment aboard ship. It should be practiced only after a thorough briefing and then under the supervision of a qualified LSO.

Minimum Fuel (Bingo Fuel)

During carrier operations, bingo fuel is the remaining usable fuel adequate to reach the destination approach fix or the point of commencing a VFR idle descent with 3000 pounds usable fuel remaining. This fuel state precludes any delay in landing at the destination such as holding, a circling approach, or a waveoff. When communications with controlling agencies ashore are established, the pilot shall declare an EMERGENCY, requesting priority handling for approach and/or landing.

Emergency (Low State)

During carrier operations when a diversionary field is not available, 3000 pounds usable fuel is considered an emergency situation and is defined as that situation when the usable fuel is so low that an immediate landing is required and no delay can be accepted. When fuel remaining reaches 2000 pounds, the decision must have been made to rig the barricade or to bail out the crew.

Arrestment and Taxiing

Smart and precise aircraft handling on deck is the mark of an experienced carrier pilot. Every carrier landing must be treated as if it were a touch-and-go, even though a wire has been engaged. As soon as the wheels touch the deck, apply FULL power with deliberate but positive action, closing speedbrakes at the same time. If a wire is engaged and it should break during arrestment, the aircraft must be in the best possible position to become airborne. If a bolter occurs, adequate speed is maintained to regain flight before reaching the end of the deck. Once forward motion has been stopped, deck handling begins. Reduce throttles to idle, brakes off, and allow the aircraft to roll back so that the hook will disengage the wire. When the hook is clear, the director will give the brake signal, followed by the hookup signal. As the hook is raised, lock the controls and fold the wings as directed. At night, the exterior lights must be turned off as soon as arrestment is complete. The power added on receipt of the brake signal will be sufficient to provide hydraulic pressure for folding the wings. Through a succession of plane directors, the aircraft will be directed to a parking spot.

Carqual Checklist

(To be used between Trap and Catapult Shot)

1. Controls . . . . CHECKED/FREE
2. Compass . . . . SET/SLAVED
3. Speedbrakes . . . . CLOSED
4. Flaps . . . . DOWN
5. Trim tabs . . . . SET
6. CG/fuel trim . . . . CHECKED/NOSEDOWN
7. Fuel/gross weight . . . CHECK/SET
8. Full power check.

Barricade Engagement

Successful barricade engagements (both day and night) have been made. The barricade engagement shall be attempted only if a divert field is not available. Experience level of the pilot, sea conditions, and location of barricade are all factors to be considered. The normal pass is made with the lense set at the barricade lense setting. During the last portion of the approach, the barricade stanchions will obscure the meatball. An LSO talk-down will be given throughout the approach.

Lower the hook if possible. Engagement of the hook with a wire will help ensure a successful barricade arrestment by:

1. Keeping the aircraft firmly on deck as the barricade is entered.

2. Lowering airspeed at barricade entry.

3. Minimizing damage incurred by the airframe.

NOTE

LSO guidance is mandatory to ensure an on-glide slope approach and to direct an early waveoff if necessary.

Postlanding Checklist (Ship)

On trap:

1. Speedbrakes .... CLOSED

2. Lights .... OFF

After rollback

1. Hook (on signal)............ UP

2. Gust locks .... LOCKED

3. Wings (70%) on signal .... FOLDED

4. Flaps (70%)............... AS DESIRED

5. Anti-icing............... OFF

6. Unnecessary radios/Navaids/radar alt/IFF .... OFF

7. Trim tabs................ SET

8. Fuel trim .... NOSEDOWN

Shutdown Checklist (Ship)
(When chocked 75%)

1. Lights .... OFF

2. Warning lights/test circuits.... CHECK

3. VGI/STBY gyro horizon circuit breakers .... OUT

4. Bomb bay doors (on signal) .... OPEN

5. ASB/radio master .... OFF

6. Ac generators/bus tie......... OFF/OPEN

7. ATM switches .... OFF

CAUTION

Allow engine to idle for 5 minutes if engine has been operating at 85% rpm or higher for 1 minute during previous 5 minutes.

8. Advance throttles to 75% rpm for approximately 30 seconds

9. Throttles/master engine switches..................... OFF/OFF

10. Bleed air switches .... ALL OPEN/ON

11. Oxygen control valves........ OFF

12. Battery .... OFF

NAVAIR 01-40ATA-1

Section IV

SECTION IV
FLIGHT CHARACTERISTICS

TABLE OF CONTENTS

TEXT

	Page
Introduction	4-2A
Control Surface Characteristics	4-2A
Flight Controls	4-2A
Trim Devices	4-2B
Wing Flaps	4-2B
Speedbrakes	4-2B
Wing Slats	4-2B
Flight Characteristics	4-3
Cruising Flight	4-3
High-Speed Flight	4-3
Low-Speed Flight	4-5
Stalls	4-5
Spins	4-6
Engine Shutdown In Flight	4-6
Single-Engine Flight Characteristics	4-7
Cruise After Climb	4-7
Air Starting	4-7
Immediate Air Start	4-8
Engine Failure Under Specific Conditions	4-8

	Page
Conditions	4-8
Maneuvering Flight	4-9
Angle-of-Attack Relationship	4-9
Pitchup Characteristics	4-9
Boost-Off Flight	4-9
Boost-Off Carrier Landing	4-13
Boost-Off Airfield Landing	4-14
Boost-Off Single-Engine Landing	4-22
Formation	4-15
General	4-15
Rendezvous	4-15
Wing Position	4-16
Basic Formation	4-16
Air Refueling	4-18
Rendezvous Procedures	4-18
Altitudes, Airspeed, and Engagement	4-18
Air Refueling Checklist	4-22

ILLUSTRATIONS

Figure		Page
4-1	Load Factor for Buffet Onset	4-4
4-2	Stalling Speeds	4-6
4-3	Approximate Indicated Angle-of-Attack	4-10
4-4	Angle-of-Attack Relationship — A-3A	4-11
4-5	Angle-of-Attack Relationship — A-3B	4-12

Figure		Page
4-6	Air Refueling Speed	4-19
4-7	Deleted.	
4-7A	Deleted.	
4-8	Deleted.	
4-9	Deleted.	
4-10	A-3 Receiver Capabilities	4-31
4-11	Fuel Transfer Rate	4-34

Changed 15 July 1970

4-1/(4-2 Blank)

INTRODUCTION

The data presented herein are limited in scope and the latest service directives and orders concerning this aircraft should be consulted regularly. Control about all three axes is very good throughout the normal airspeed range, and stall warning is early and positive. The control forces required during flight with hydraulic power are not excessive, and trim effectivity is positive at all normal airspeeds.

CONTROL SURFACE CHARACTERISTICS

Flight Controls

AILERONS-SPOILERS

The ailerons are operated by an irreversible dual power system; the spoilers are operated by one-half of this dual system. Control feel is artificially furnished by a load-feel bungee. In the event of a failure of one of the completely independent power systems, one-half of the full power output of the aileron tandem actuating cylinder will be lost. The spoilers may remain operative or become inoperative depending upon which portion of the dual aileron system fails. When inoperative, the spoilers remain faired. With the spoilers operative, the loss of one-half of the power output of the ailerons will have little effect on lateral control; with the spoilers inoperative lateral control effectiveness decreases but is considered adequate up to speeds approaching 500 knots. Manual operation of the ailerons, at a mechanical advantage of 2:1 over the no-boost ratio, is available in the event of a double power failure. If it becomes necessary to revert to manual operation, it is recommended that whenever possible pilots acquaint themselves with the aircraft's lateral control characteristics at low speed at altitude prior to landing. When operating with the manual control system, the approach and landing should be made at speeds higher than those used for normal operation. Manual control is obtained by pulling out on the AILERON BOOST REL handle on pilot's instrument panel. This handle also releases the spoilers load-feel bungee and the aileron force trim mechanism, making it necessary for the pilot to hold in the aileron trim desired.

NOTE

During rapid lateral control deflections it is possible to exceed the rate capacity of the aileron actuating cylinder. This will appear as a temporary, abrupt increase in lateral control force. However, the rolling performance of the aircraft will not be impaired.

ELEVATOR

The elevator boost system increases the force transmitted by the control wheel approximately 10 times. However, the addition of a bob-weight to the mechanical linkage of the elevator is provided to prevent excessively fast pullups which would impose dangerous loads on the wing structure.

If boost failure occurs provision is made for direct manual control of the elevators. Because of the increased control forces that will be encountered during manual control, it is important that the out-of-trim forces be kept small. Adequate control can be maintained with the elevator in conjunction with the adjustable stabilizer. The elevator and rudder disconnect are actuated by the same handle. If a disconnect is required on either system, both systems will be disconnected.

The aircraft cg must never exceed the limits established in Center of Gravity Limitations, Section I, Part 4.

RUDDER

The rudder boost system increases the force transmitted by the rudder pedals approximately seven times. Provision is made for direct control of the rudder in case of a failure of the rudder boost system. The elevator and rudder disconnect are actuated by the same handle. If a disconnect is required on either system, both systems will be disconnected.

The RUD AND ELEV BOOST REL cannot be reset in flight after having been disengaged.

Trim Devices

AILERON TRIM

Because of the irreversible control system, conventional trim tabs are not required. Since the hydraulic surface actuators prevent the transmission of air loads to the pilot's control wheel, actuating the aileron trim switch merely relocates the wheel center position so that wheel forces supplied by the load feel bungee are zeroed. Since the aileron trim range is within the spoiler actuation deadband, operation of the trim switch will not actuate the spoilers. However, spoiler operation will no longer be symmetrical about the new neutral aileron position. Spoiler action will begin with less aileron displacement in the direction in which the ailerons have been trimmed. No provision is made for lateral trim when the ailerons are operated manually.

ELEVATOR TRIM

Elevator forces are trimmed out by the adjustable horizontal stabilizer. Two actuation speeds are available: a high speed, powered by an ac source and actuated by the control wheel switch or by a switch on the pilot's center console; and a slow speed, powered by a dc source and actuated by the console switch. The high-speed trim control is used for normal trimming while the slow speed acts as standby.

NOTE

With ac trim failure dc trim will be available through the console trim switch in either detent.

CAUTION

When the cg is between 12 and 16 percent at speeds below 1.2 times the stalling speed, a pull force of approximately 12 pounds will have to be exerted on the control column in order to maintain level flight, as full noseup trim is not sufficient under these cg conditions. For later aircraft with increased stabilizer throw, this does not apply.

RUDDER TRIM

An electrically dc operated trim tab is provided to trim rudder pedal forces to zero for all normal flight conditions.

Wing Flaps

Two speeds are used for wing flap operation: a slow speed for retraction and a fast speed for extension. The slow retraction speed minimizes the trim changes necessary after takeoff or waveoff. The fast extension speed ensures a rapid full flap extension upon demand. The fast flap extension speed causes a more abrupt noseup trim change. The flap control is a three-position lever UP, STOP, and DOWN, thus providing infinite flap positioning.

Speedbrakes

Opening the speedbrakes will result in a slight but controllable pitchup at all airspeeds.

Wing Slats

Aerodynamically operated wing slats are installed on the leading edge of the wings to improve the stalling characteristics during both accelerated and unaccelerated flight. The slats are fully automatic in operation. A reduction in airspeed causes the slats to extend; an increase in airspeed causes them to retract. Up to a Mach number of approximately 0.45, an increase in g will cause the slats to extend and a decrease in g will retract them. Above Mach 0.45 the slats will not open.

NAVAIR 01-40ATA-1   Section IV

WARNING

Slats can stick in either the open or closed position as a result of mechanical malfunction or icing. The result of outer wing outboard and/or outer wing inboard slats failing to open will be a severe pitchup, with little or no buffet warning, at approximately approach speed. The outer wing slats should begin to open at 20 to 25 KIAS above normal approach speed and should be approximately half open at approach speed. If a visual check indicates a probable malfunction of any outer wing slats, approach speed should be increased 35 KIAS above normal. (For recommended procedures, refer to No-Slat Landing, Section V.) Center wing slats should begin to open at or slightly above normal approach speed but will not fully open until just above stall speed. The pitchup due to retracted center wing slats is mild and easily controlled. A slight increase in approach speed may be required if buffet or mild pitchup is encountered.

NOTE

The nomenclature for slat location is outer wing outboard, outer wing inboard, center wing outboard, and center wing inboard.

SLAT PULSE CHECK PROCEDURES

Slat pulse check procedures shall be accomplished on all flights before transitioning to the landing configuration. Assuming a gross weight of 50,000 pounds, slat checks shall be performed at the following landing pattern positions.

IFR PENETRATIONS. Prior to the fix before the "gate", or prior to controller instructions to "dirty up", decelerate the clean aircraft to 15 units angle-of-attack (approximately 200 KIAS), using power as required with speedbrakes closed. Momentarily pulse the elevator in a 5 to 7 degree pitchup. The outboard slats should be seen popping out. Visual inspection of pop out will not be possible at night. If slats fail to extend, a noticeable buffet will occur and is easily controlled. In CLE aircraft, buffet will not occur, but a noticeable wallow will be encountered. Full power should be applied and slat emergency procedures promptly executed.

VFR IN THE BREAK. As the aircraft decelerates through 200 KIAS in a 30-degree to 45-degree bank angle, outer wing slat operation should be noted. Pulsing is not necessary due to the bank angle and application of g force.

FLIGHT CHARACTERISTICS

The stability characteristics of the aircraft in level flight are positive. Any increase in airspeed from a trimmed attitude will require nosedown trim, while a decrease in airspeed will require noseup trim in order to maintain the original trimmed attitude.

Flying the A-3 presents problems typical of any swept-wing, high performance aircraft. Approach speed and sink rates must be carefully controlled. At altitude, the aircraft has a slight "dutch roll", which becomes unimportant as the pilot gains experience in the aircraft.

Cruising Flight

The handling characteristics of the A-3 are good about all three axes during normal cruise. The ailerons are very effective at high altitude and at moderate airspeeds.

High-Speed Flight

To ensure maximum safety during high-speed flight, full knowledge of certain characteristics of the aircraft is essential, particularly when operating at low altitudes. With spoilers, lateral control is adequate up to maximum permissible speeds.

NOTE

In the following description, the inclusion of flight characteristics at airspeeds above maximum permissible does not imply authorization to exceed the airspeed limitations of the aircraft.

At approximately 425 KIAS and continuing at higher speeds, a slight buffet is transmitted through the rudder pedal and a slight directional trim change occurs. This trim change is small and is easily corrected by the rudder trim tab. The estimated load factor for buffet onset for various altitudes, Mach numbers, and a gross weight of 55,942 pounds is presented in Load Factor for Buffet Onset charts, figure 4-1. When the aircraft is rolled into a turn above 400 KIAS without the use of elevators, a pitchup will occur as a result of spoiler deflection. The magnitude of the pitchup will increase with airspeed up to approximately 450 KIAS. At this airspeed, the incremental load factor resulting from full lateral throw of the control wheel is approximately 1 g. From 450 KIAS to the maximum permissible airspeed, the maximum pitchup resulting from full throw of the control wheel remains at approximately 1 g. Because the pitchup is a result of spoiler deflection, partial throw of the wheel will cause less pitchup.

At high Mach numbers, a reduction in elevator effectiveness and an increase in control wheel force per g are encountered. At medium and high altitude, the control wheel force per g increases from a nominal value of 29 pounds to 61 pounds at Mach number of 0.90. At low altitudes, it increases from 29 pounds to 82 pounds at a Mach number of 0.90. At Mach numbers appreciably above 0.90, elevator effectiveness virtually disappears, and aft wheel deflection does not impose any significant load factor. Under these conditions, the speedbrakes should be extended and as the aircraft slows below 0.90 effect recovery with the

Changed 1 June 1969   4-3

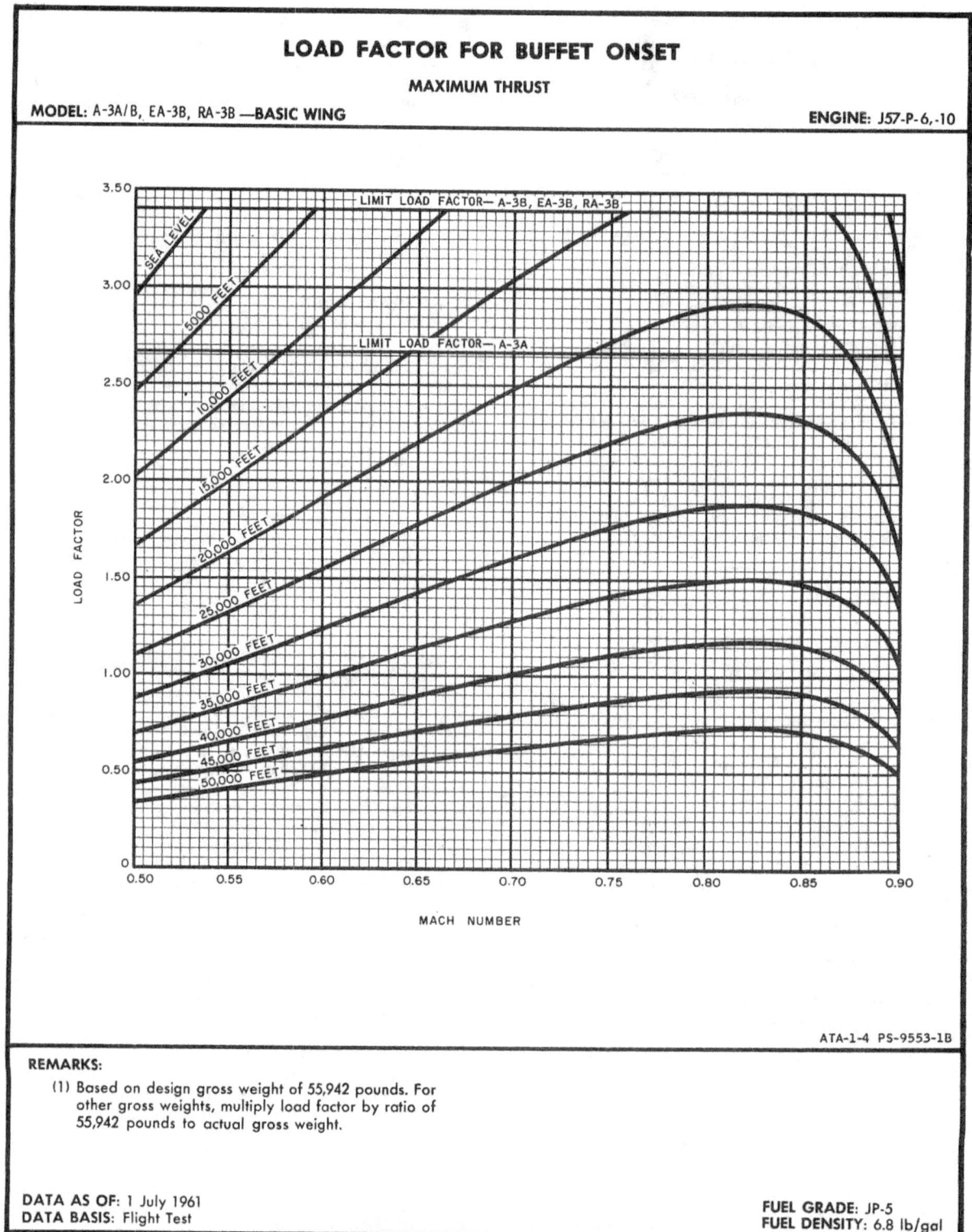

Figure 4-1. Load Factor for Buffet Onset

elevator. In an emergency, the horizontal stabilizer can be used, but it should be used with caution, since a pitchup will occur near 0.90 Mach number if there is too much noseup trim. Regardless of the means by which Mach number is reduced, it is important to remember that elevator effectiveness will be regained near 0.90 Mach number, and a noseup pitch will occur if aft wheel deflection is being held. Dives up to the maximum permissible Mach number and airspeed can be accomplished with safety, provided reasonable precautions are taken. The longitudinal trim should be adjusted during the dive to a position that requires a moderate push force on the control wheel to hold the aircraft in the dive: this will decrease the control wheel force required to execute the pullout. Except as noted above, the elevator trim control should not be used as a pullout device unless an emergency exists, such as loss of elevator boost, because of the lack of control feel and the possibility of overstressing the aircraft. At high indicated airspeeds, the aircraft is extremely sensitive to trim changes, and trim adjustments must be made very carefully to avoid excessive load factors.

WARNING

Failure of either the surface control hydraulic system or the aileron control hydraulic system makes it imperative that airspeed be reduced below 510 KIAS, which is the speed at which aileron reversal normally occurs.

Low-Speed Flight

In general, the handling characteristics of the aircraft during low-speed flight are good, although aileron effectiveness decreases quite rapidly with a decrease in airspeed when in the power approach configuration. In the landing configuration a lateral-directional oscillation or "dutch roll" appears. When the flight control boost systems are operative, this "dutch roll" can be adequately controlled through combined use of the ailerons and rudder. Control of the oscillations is extremely difficult with the boost systems inoperative since damping of the "dutch roll" is virtually zero. If the wing flaps are retracted damping is considerably better than when the flaps are extended; therefore, it is recommended that landings with the boost systems inoperative be conducted with the wing flaps retracted if runway length permits (refer to section V).

BUFFET-ONSET

BUFFET-ONSET (NIBBLE) CHECK. The buffet phenomenon (figure 4-1) in basic wing aircraft can be used to establish best approach speed whenever angle of attack and/or airspeed are erratic or out. When required, this check shall be made following the fuel check on the downwind leg as follows:

1. Reduce power to 2500 pounds per hr per engine.

2. Speedbrakes extended.

3. Ease nose up smoothly to maintain altitude as aircraft decelerates.

4. When nibble is felt (note IAS), add power, retract speedbrakes, and accelerate to buffet plus 5 knots for approach.

Stalls

POWER-OFF STALLS

The power-off stalling characteristics (see figure 4-2) of the aircraft are good. Early warning occurs in the form of light tail and general airframe buffeting. With the gear and flaps extended, buffeting starts at 15 to 20 knots above the stall. With gear and flaps up, buffeting occurs at 25 to 30 knots above the stall. An increase in buffet intensity to heavy should be accepted as the stall. If airspeed reduction is continued, a pitching oscillation will begin at 4 to 12 knots (depending on flap deflection) below the onset of heavy buffet. Slightly below the speed at which pitching oscillations begin, a slow rolloff, mild pitchup, or very mild pitchdown will occur. A normal recovery is easily accomplished by moving the wheel forward. During recovery, both elevator and rudder control are good, and although aileron control effectiveness is low, wing position can be controlled with rudder. If speed reduction is carried into the pitch oscillation region, wheel deflections causing spoiler operations should be avoided as they increase the possibility of spin entry on rollout. Application of power will serve only to reduce the stalling speed as shown in figure 4-2.

CAUTION

Flight at speeds below that for prestall buffet onset shall be avoided because of possible fatigue failure of the vertical fin fold fitting.

ACCELERATED STALLS

No unusual characteristics will be experienced at low Mach numbers. At airspeeds above Mach 0.45

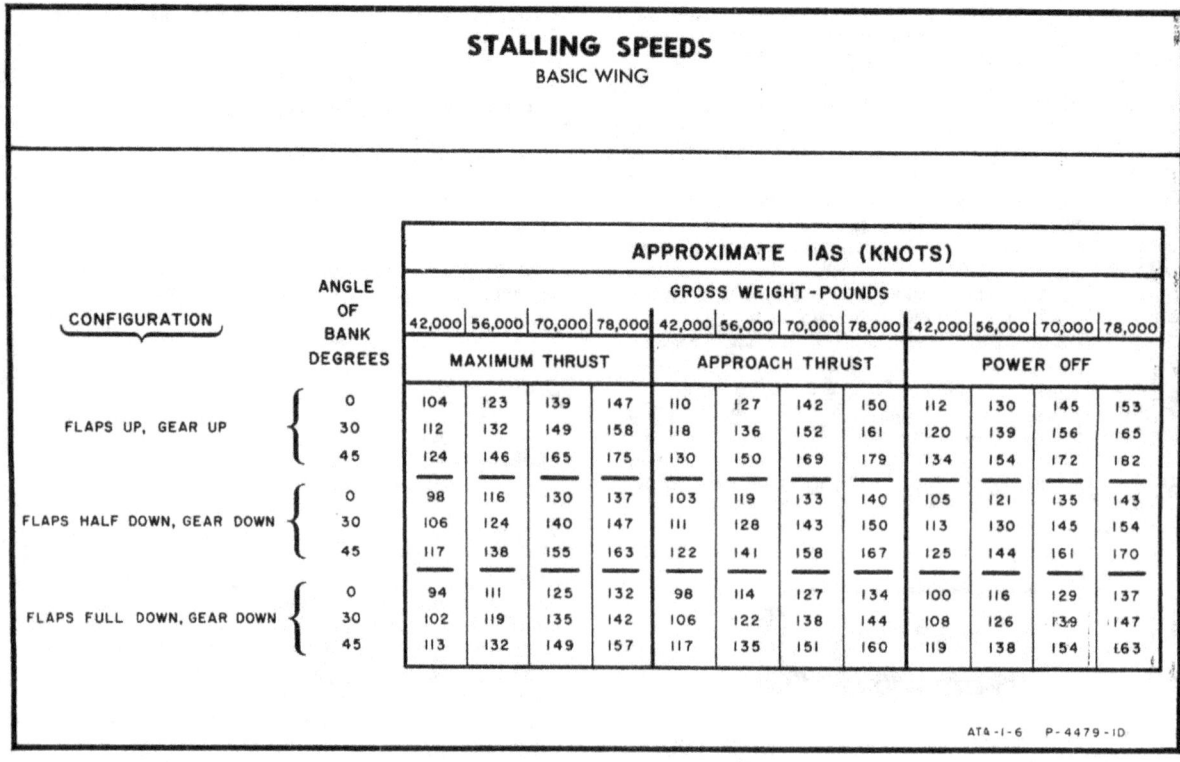

Figure 4-2. Stalling Speeds

the slats do not open, and a mild pitchup will occur in accelerated turns.

CAUTION

In accelerated turns, a tendency for the aircraft to dig into the turn is to be regarded as a warning of the approach to a stall and an immediate recovery must be made. Additional warning is present in the form of airframe buffeting.

Spins

Intentional spins are prohibited. There should be no difficulty in avoiding inadvertent spins because of the strong buffet preceding the stall. If a spin is inadvertently entered the normal recovery technique, consisting of down elevator followed by full rudder reversal, shall be executed immediately. Ailerons should be maintained at neutral during spin recovery since incorrect usage of ailerons may slow recovery. Retract flaps and landing gear immediately if extended at spin entry. Retard both throttles to IDLE immediately after spin entry.

ENGINE SHUTDOWN IN FLIGHT

NOTE

A maximum of 300 KIAS shall not be exceeded when intentionally securing an engine during routine operations.

An engine may be shut down in flight at the discretion of the pilot, to increase the cruising range for endurance operation or, possibly, to practice in-flight engine relights and pilot proficiency training with either engine inoperative. The engine is shut down much the same way as on the ground except that the throttle should be retarded to IDLE for 1 minute to cool the engine before moving it to the OFF position. If the engine is shut down from a setting above cruising thrust, it is advisable to increase the cooling period by permitting the engine to remain at IDLE for as long as 2 or 3 minutes before moving the throttle to OFF. Whenever the engine is to remain shut down for an appreciable length of time, the throttle should be moved to the IDLE position for 3 minutes every hour to open the main fuel valve and permit fuel to circulate in the fuel system. This reduces excessive temperatures in the engine driven fuel pump, prevents vapor lock and helps lubricate the pump. During such periods the MASTER ENGINE switch must be left ON to prevent damage to the engine driven fuel pump.

The engine may be started again by following the procedure outlined under AIR STARTING. For emergency procedures to be followed if engine failure of flameout occurs, refer to Section V.

SINGLE-ENGINE FLIGHT CHARACTERISTICS

NOTE

Single-engine operations shall be practiced at an altitude not to exceed 30,000 feet. Single-engine operations may be simulated in the landing pattern with waveoffs at no lower than 300 feet altitude.

The MASTER ENGINE switch should be left in the ON position at all times during single-engine practice.

The single-engine flight characteristics of the aircraft are good. Altitude can be maintained up to approximately 20,000 feet, under standard day conditions, at the normal gross weight for takeoff if the aircraft is in the "clean" configuration. However, the problem of holding altitude or climbing will be markedly increased with a high outside air temperature or with the landing gear and flaps down. The flight controls boost and power systems provide adequate control during single-engine flight at all airspeeds above 1.2 times the power-off stall speed. While attempting to maintain straight-and level flight, use a minimum angle of bank to avoid sideslip. In this event, rudder pedal forces may be high, but bending loads at the vertical stabilizer will be small.

If an engine has been shut down in flight for a period of 1 hour and the windmilling rpm exceeds 25 percent, perform the following to cool the engine fuel pump:

1. MASTER ENGINE switch, inoperative engine . . . . ON

2. Throttle, inoperative engine, 3 minutes at . . . . IDLE

NOTE

Do not move the throttle outboard when moving from OFF to IDLE as such action will start the ignition cycle.

3. Throttle, inoperative engine . . . . OFF

4. MASTER ENGINE switch, inoperative engine, leave at . . . . ON

WARNING

Failing to cool the engine fuel pump at one hour intervals can cause excessive temperatures in the pump, leading to subsequent failure.

Cruise After Climb

SINGLE-ENGINE CRUISE. When the left engine is shut down during practice or endurance flight, fuel is not normally supplied through the hydraulic oil cooler. In this case the pilot must keep the left MASTER ENGINE switch ON and the fuel CROSSFEED at RH ENG to enable the fuel to flow through the hydraulic cooler. If the left engine is shut down because of engine failure, the left MASTER ENGINE switch must be turned OFF and the hydraulic pumps must be inspected for damage when the aircraft lands.

NOTE

When MASTER ENGINE switch is secured in flight and the oil cooler door switch is in the AUTO position, oil cooler door will open and remain open.

AIR STARTING

CAUTION

No attempt should be made to restart an engine unless it can be determined that it would be reasonably safe to do so and only if it is suspected that the loss of combustion was due to flameout. If the loss of combustion was accompanied by symptoms that indicated engine malfunction or failure, an attempted relight may result in an engine fire.

Consistently successful air starts are dependent upon windmilling rpm. Listed below are the indicated air speeds at various altitudes that will produce windmilling rpm within the best air starting rpm range.

PRESSURE ALTITUDE	KIAS RANGE
40,000	150-170
35,000	150-180
30,000	150-205
25,000	150-230

PRESSURE ALTITUDE	KIAS RANGE
20,000	150-255
15,000	160-285
10,000	170-310
5,000	180-335
Sea Level	200-360

NOTE

- Successful relights may sometimes be obtained at any altitude or airspeed by taking advantage of the high airflow through the engine immediately following a flameout. The minimum rpm for successful air starts will vary with altitude and airspeed.

- If the engine ignition timer holding relay has failed, the engine ignitors will cease firing when the throttle quadrant ignition microswitch is released as the throttle is moved to IDLE. If such is the case, the ignition microswitch must be manually held closed and the throttle placed at IDLE. The microswitch is to be released whenever the start is completed or that start attempt abandoned.

Immediate Air Start

If a flameout occurs, the following procedure should be accomplished as quickly as possible:

1. Throttle, inoperative engine. . . OFF

2. Throttle, inoperative engine, move outboard to start the ignition cycle.

3. Throttle, inoperative engine. . . IDLE

The procedure for a normal air start is as follows:

1. Throttle, inoperative engine. . . OFF

2. Master engine switch, inoperative engine . . . . ON

3. Fuel pressure . . . . NORMAL

4. Tachometer . . . . 12 to 30 PERCENT

5. Throttle . . . . IGNITE, THEN IDLE

6. Oil Pressure . . . . NORMAL

NOTE

- An air start may be attempted without oil pressure indication. If oil pressure indication does not return to normal after air start, secure the engine at pilot's discretion.

- If fuel boost pressure reads LOW, place CROSSFEED switch to affected engine. If boost pressure does not return, place CROSSFEED switch to normal and continue air start attempt.

7. If excessive fuel flow is noted, control the fuel flow by positioning the throttle between OFF and IDLE.

8. When lightoff occurs, follow the normal procedures outlined in Starting Procedures, Section III. During an air start, the idling rpm will be 60 to 70 percent.

CAUTION

If lightoff does not occur within 30 seconds after the throttle has been moved to IDLE, or if an unsatisfactory start is indicated, retard the throttle to OFF and allow the engine to windmill for 30 seconds minimum before attempting another start.

Engine Failure Under Specific Conditions

DURING TAKEOFF. Failure of an engine during takeoff before flying speed is attained normally will necessitate aborting the flight.

NOTE

At light gross weights a single-engine takeoff can be completed under normal atmospheric conditions. (Refer to the takeoff and climb charts in Section XI for critical field lengths and single-engine climb performance.)

The one engine will normally provide sufficient power for climbing out; however, at heavy gross weights and high outside air temperatures, climb performance right after takeoff is marginal. Aircraft directional control is adequate for single-engine operation at all airspeeds above 1.2 times the power-off stall speed if the required rudder and directional trim are combined with banking of the aircraft. Use a minimum angle of bank to avoid sideslip. Rudder pedal forces may be high, but bending loads at the vertical stabilizer will be small.

In flight planning the pilot should keep in mind the following conditions: Aircraft gross weight, air temperature, pressure altitude, wind conditions, runway length, and necessary airspeed. In the following situation aircraft climb performance would be marginal. Assume an aircraft of 70,000 pounds gross weight, standard day temperature, at sea level, on a 4000-foot runway with a 10-knot headwind. Under these conditions the recommended takeoff speed is 140 KIAS. If an engine fails, immediate landing gear retraction and acceleration to at least 150-KIAS is necessary to enable the aircraft to continue flying. If the landing gear isn't retracted soon enough, the aircraft will not be able to maintain altitude. If the conditions were similar at a lower gross weight the chances of climbing to a safe altitude would be better. It is unlikely that the airspeed would be sufficient immediately after takeoff to enable the aircraft to zoom to a high enough altitude to permit safe bailout. If safe flight cannot be continued, keep the wings level and land straight ahead.

Maneuvering Flight

The stick force per g increases at higher Mach numbers as outlined in HIGH SPEED FLIGHT discussion. During any flight maneuver, a tendency of the aircraft to dig into a turn must be regarded as a warning of approach to a stall and an immediate recovery must be made. In the event airspeed indications are lost, see figure 4-3 for approximate indicated angle of attack to be flown.

ANGLE-OF-ATTACK RELATIONSHIP

The angle-of-attack relationship for the operational envelope of the aircraft is illustrated in figures 4-4 and 4-5.

Pitchup Characteristics

High angle-of-attack pitchup can occur when maneuvering the aircraft in heavy buffet. This pitchup is defined as an increase in load factor without an increase in elevator column pull force. It is most likely to occur at high altitudes; however, in this case aircraft stall would be reached prior to limit load factors. At intermediate altitudes (20,000 to 35,000 feet) limit load factor can be attained if corrective action is not taken immediately. At low altitudes the aircraft load factor limit prevents the aircraft from attaining the angle of attack for pitchup, and the maneuvering characteristics are normal.

Should pitchup be encountered, immediate corrective action should consist of forward elevator and if necessary, aircraft nosedown stabilizer. If engine stalls are encountered in the pitchup region, they will be relieved as the angle of attack is reduced.

CAUTION

Due to the possibility of pitchup, maneuvering flight which carries the aircraft beyond moderate to heavy buffet in the Mach range of 0.50 to 0.90 should be avoided.

As described in High-Speed Flight, transonic noseup trim change will occur when making recoveries from speeds above Mach 0.9. This trim change, which is due primarily to the return of elevator effectiveness when slowing down, is aggravated by use of full aft yoke. Care should be used in returning from the transonic region with full aft yoke, as the return of elevator effectiveness can be very abrupt.

Boost-Off Flight

AILERON

The aileron tandem actuating cylinder is provided with pressure from both the aileron control hydraulic system and the surface control hydraulic system. Failure of either of these systems causes a partial loss of power, but adequate lateral control is available. Failure of both systems, however, necessitates a complete mechanical release of the tandem actuating cylinder from the aileron control linkage. Aileron control forces are extremely high with both of the dual hydraulic systems inoperative; but are reduced considerably when the tandem actuating cylinder is disconnected. Pulling the aileron power boost release handle on the pilot's instrument panel mechanically disconnects the tandem actuating cylinder thus providing direct manual control of the ailerons through a mechanical advantage shifter. This shifter doubles the boost-off mechanical advantage ratio of the controls. The actuating cable system of the two spoilers is disconnected when the aileron power boost release handle is pulled, and the spoilers cannot operate until the actuating cable system lock is re-connected. Aileron trim is not available during manual control of the ailerons, and aileron load is transmitted directly through the aileron control linkage.

Lateral control by use of the ailerons alone is negligible above 350 KIAS. Above this speed, lateral trim can be maintained by asymmetric power or rudder trim. Below this speed, lateral control can be substantially increased by combined use of the ailerons and rudder, and control will be sufficient to make satisfactory turns at low speeds; however, forces required will be high. Speeds in excess of 0.80 IMN should be avoided because of an occasional random wing-drop characteristic. If this characteristic develops, an immediate airspeed reduction will be required to maintain control. Large rudder inputs should be avoided in this speed range. During an approach in the landing configuration, moderate to heavy lateral-directional oscillations are inherent.

4-9

Section IV

NAVAIR 01-40ATA-1

APPROXIMATE INDICATED ANGLE-OF-ATTACK AIRSPEED RELATIONSHIP

	Pressure Altitude ~1000 ft	Climb KCAS	Angle of Attack for Gross Weight ~1000 lb			
			80	70	60	50
Max Rate of Climb			AOA	AOA	AOA	AOA
	SL	375	6.1	5.6	4.9	4.2
	10	345	6.6	6.0	6.4	4.7
	20	315	6.8	6.2	5.6	5.0
	30	285	7.4	6.9	6.1	5.1
	40	245	–	–	8.1	7.2

	Pressure Altitude ~1000 ft	Angle of Attack: KCAS for Gross Weight ~1000 lb							
		80		70		60		50	
Max Range		AOA	KCAS	AOA	KCAS	AOA	KCAS	AOA	KCAS
	SL	7.0	330	6.7	315	6.3	305	5.9	290
	10	7.7	310	7.8	290	7.1	285	6.8	270
	20	6.9	320	7.2	300	7.7	270	7.7	250
	30	7.3	295	6.9	290	6.5	280	7.0	255
	40	–	–	9.1	245	7.9	245	7.2	225

	Pressure Altitude ~1000 ft	Angle of Attack: KCAS for Gross Weight ~1000 lb							
		80		70		60		50	
Max Endurance		AOA	KCAS	AOA	KCAS	AOA	KCAS	AOA	KCAS
	SL	10.2	275	10.3	255	10.3	235	10.4	215
	10	9.9	275	10.1	255	10.2	240	10.3	215
	20	9.6	275	9.7	260	9.8	240	10.0	220
	30	8.5	280	8.7	265	9.1	245	9.6	220
	40	–	–	9.3	245	9.0	235	8.5	225

Penetration 250 KCAS 50,000 lb Gross Wt	Angle of Attack
	7.5

Landing Transition 200 KCAS	SL Angle of Attack
	10

Figure 4-3. Approximate Indicated Angle-of-Attack

NAVAIR 01-40ATA-1　　Section IV

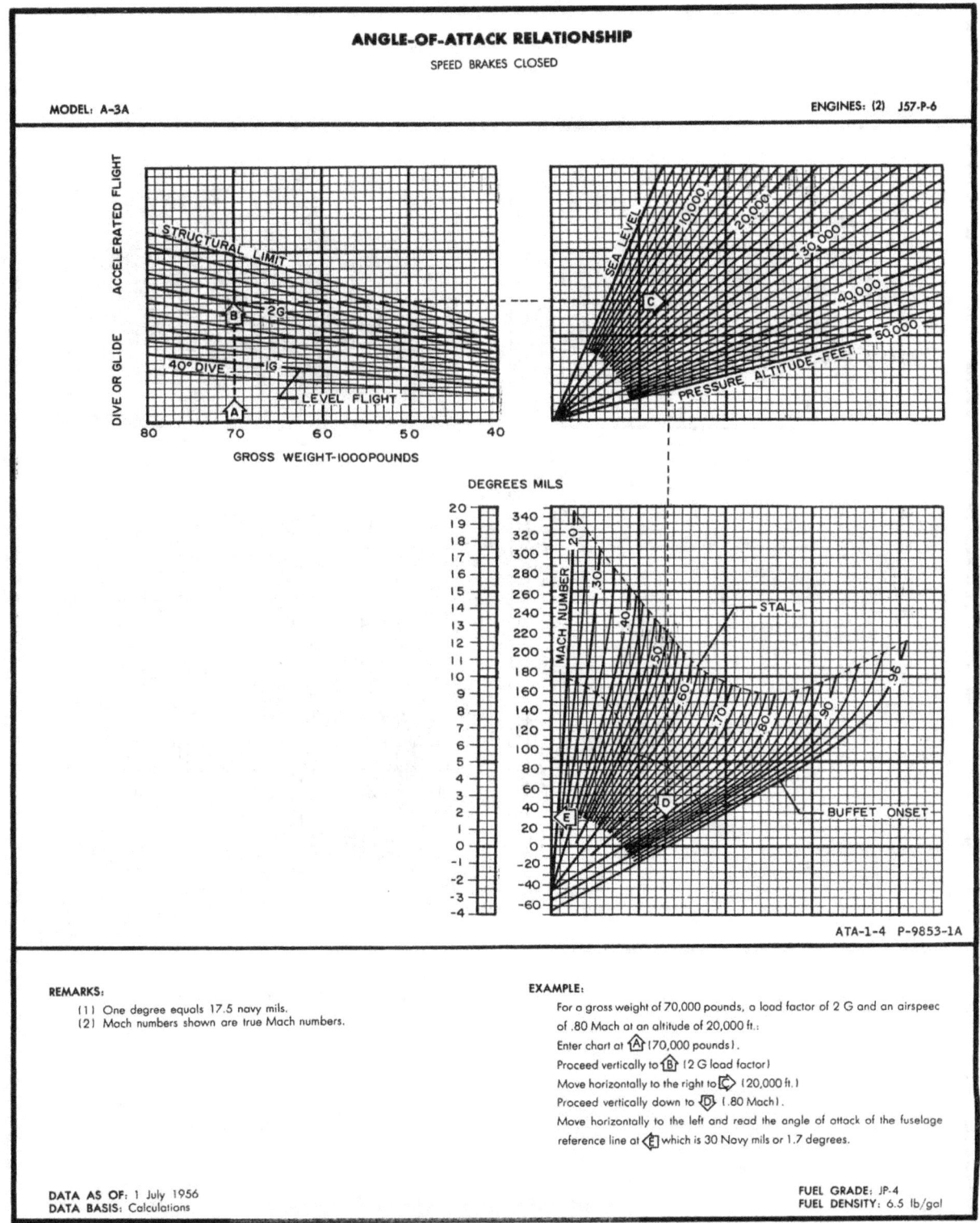

Figure 4-4. Angle-of-Attack Relationship — A-3A

Section IV NAVAIR 01-40ATA-1

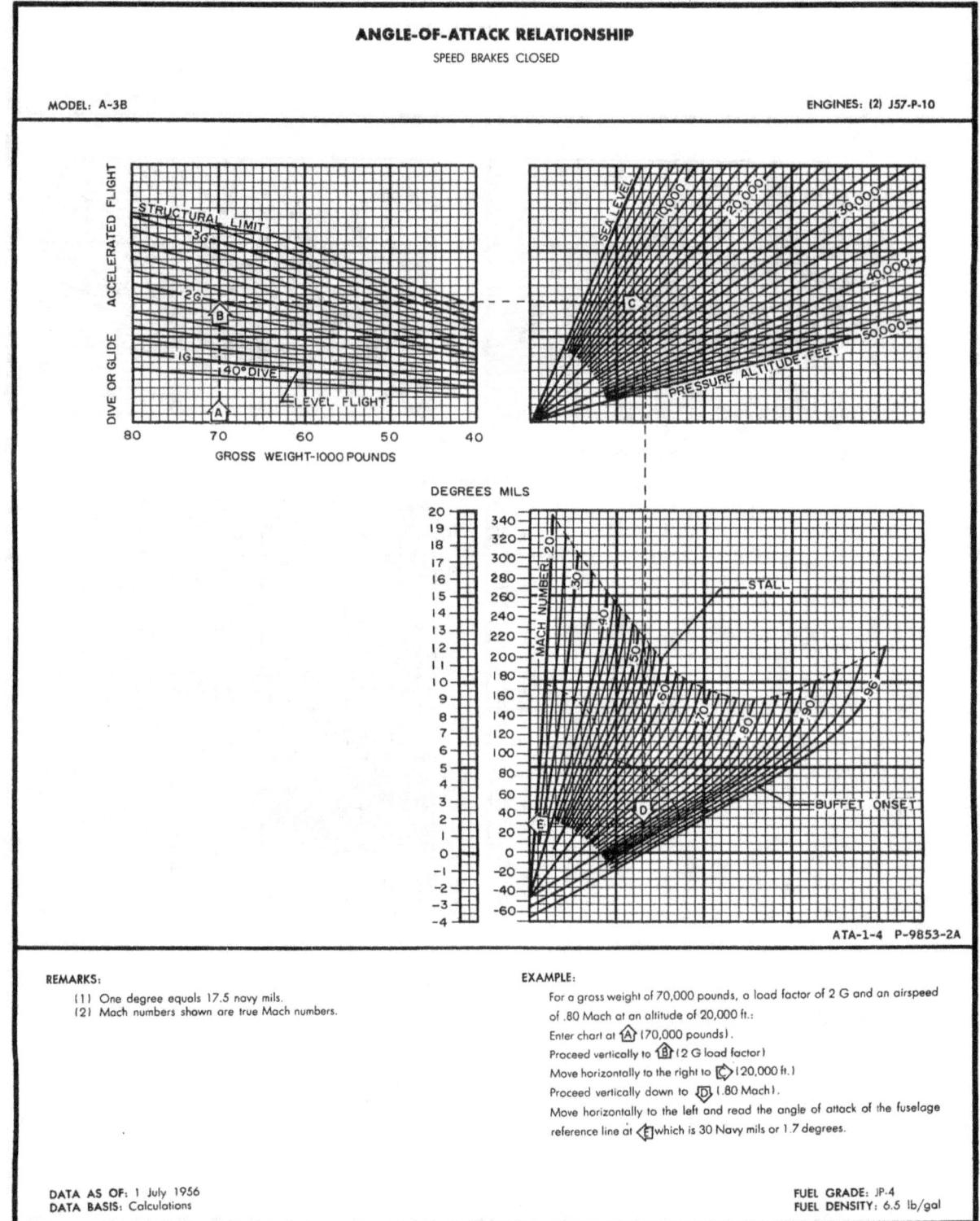

Figure 4-5. Angle-of-Attack Relationship — A-3B

RUDDER-ELEVATOR

The rudder and elevators are supplied with hydraulic boost pressure from the surface control hydraulic system. The surface control hydraulic system can be disconnected from the flight controls linkage by pulling the RUD AND ELEV BOOST REL handle on the pilot's instrument panel. This will provide direct mechanical control of the rudder and the elevators.

Under normal conditions an increase in elevator and rudder forces will be experienced during boost-off flight, but extremely high rudder forces are required for directional control if a yaw condition exists. In the event the rudder/elevator boost system becomes inoperative, the actuating cylinders should be disengaged by pulling out the RUD AND ELEV BOOST REL handle on the pilot's instrument panel, thus providing direct manual control of the rudder and elevator controls. Direction control can be maintained adequately by the use of the rudder or rudder trim during normal flight. During an approach in the landing configuration, lateral-directional oscillation will be apparent which cannot be dampened out by use of the rudder pedals due to high forces and sluggishness within the controls. Directional oscillation is of lesser magnitude at higher speeds, and at slower approach speeds wheel forces are noticeably lighter. During normal boost-off flight, longitudinal control can be adequately maintained by the use of the elevators. During a boost-off approach, longitudinal trim can be maintained easily by the horizontal stabilizer trim system if electrical power is available. Longitudinal trim should be maintained at all times. For information on the use of the rudder and elevator during boost-off approach and landing, refer to Flight Controls Emergency Operation, Section V.

AILERON AND RUDDER-ELEVATOR

If both flight control systems fail, elevator control forces can be easily trimmed out if the horizontal stabilizer is operative (dc or ac power is available); and some elevator control is possible even though the rudder-elevator boost is inoperative and still connected. Aileron control will be lost and, hence, the primary problem is one of maintaining or returning to wings-level flight. Small roll rates may be obtained by rudder deflection, rudder trim (if dc generator power is available) or with asymmetric thrust. Unless loss of control occurs or is imminent, immediate pulling of the AILERON BOOST REL handle is not recommended. If conditions permit, time should be taken to analyze the failure and attempts made to regain power.

Under complete boost-off conditions, the ailerons are quite limited in effectiveness, but lateral control can be substantially increased by combined use of the ailerons and rudder. Using ailerons alone, the maximum rate of roll throughout the speed range of the aircraft is 6 to 8 degrees per second. This rate of roll requires a control wheel force of approximately 80 pounds. As airspeed is increased, control wheel forces become rather large for a small increase in rate of roll. If rudder only is used for lateral control, the maximum rate of roll under the same conditions can be raised to 20 to 30 degrees per second, however the pressure on the rudder pedals required to achieve this rate of roll reaches from about 260 to 300 pounds, depending on which direction the rudder is deflected. As these forces are exhaustively high, combined use of the rudder and ailerons will effectively reduce control forces and will also produce a higher rate of roll than can be achieved when rudder or ailerons are used independently. With wheels and flaps extended, damping of the characteristic lateral-directional oscillation is virtually nil, but with flaps retracted, damping, although still difficult, can be accomplished to a better extent than with lowered wing flaps.

NOTE

The yaw-damper will be inoperative under rudder-elevator boost-off conditions. Complete boost-off manual control is provided to make possible emergency landings.

Boost-Off Carrier Landing

Complete boost-off carrier landings shall not be attempted.

AILERON

Carrier landings may be safely accomplished with the failure of one of the aileron tandem power control cylinders (one ATM). With failure of both ATM's, however, carrier landings are unsafe because of excessively high lateral control forces and loss of the rudder-elevator boost systems. The maximum rolling velocity attainable in the approach configuration at normal approach airspeed with further increase in wheel force up to approximately 80 pounds will not significantly increase available rolling velocity. Small rudder inputs will greatly assist in maintaining the wings level. Conditions existing at the carrier and the diversionary field should be considered as to their effect on landing with aileron boost inoperative.

RUDDER-ELEVATOR

Loss of the rudder-elevator boost system will result in high control forces for out-of-trim conditions. During an approach in the landing configuration, lateral-directional oscillations will be apparent which

Section IV

NAVAIR 01-40ATA-1

cannot be damped out by use of the rudder pedals. This is a result of high rudder pedal forces and sluggishness within the controls. Carrier landings will not, however, be appreciably complicated provided that longitudinal and directional trim controls are available. Abrupt power adjustments should be avoided during the final stages of approach because of pronounced trim changes resulting from thrust effects.

NOTE

The yaw damper will be inoperative under rudder-elevator boost-off conditions.

Boost-Off Airfield Landing

AILERON

Lateral control forces are high during the approach to landing with both aileron-boost systems out. Sufficient controllability, however, is available to land the aircraft safely under normal operating conditions. Aileron boost-off landings in light crosswinds (below 7 knots) and in light turbulence can be accomplished without difficulty. Landings are more difficult in higher crosswind components or increased turbulence. Depending upon the degree of turbulence, moderate to extreme lateral-directional oscillations will occur during the approach. The "dutch roll" characteristic is, however, less pronounced with flaps retracted. If neither short field arrestment nor suitable divert field are available, a no-flap landing is recommended.

NOTE

If a no-flap approach is made, the approach should be 17 to 20.5 units angle of attack or 20 KIAS above normal. Deploy drag chute after landing, and make a long field arrestment.

With flaps extended, there is no advantage to be gained with an increase in normal approach airspeed. Due to an overall decrease in lateral control effectiveness with the boost inoperative, directional control is extremely marginal during landing rollout with crosswind components in excess of 7 knots. Landings in high crosswind components should be accomplished with drag chute or field arresting gear when available.

RUDDER-ELEVATOR

With rudder-elevator boost-off, field landings will not be appreciably complicated provided that longitudinal and directional trim controls are available. Abrupt

power adjustments should be avoided during the final stages of approach due to pronounced trim changes resulting from thrust effects.

NOTE

The yaw damper will be inoperative under rudder-elevator boost-off conditions.

AILERON AND RUDDER-ELEVATOR

In the power approach configuration, with complete boost failure, the aircraft is marginally controllable in moderate turbulence and essentially uncontrollable in severe turbulence. Where existing turbulence levels are moderate to severe, landings should be accomplished with landing flaps retracted and using drag chute if possible.

WARNING

Field landings in crosswinds of 7 knots or greater, or in moderate to severe turbulent air are hazardous and should not be attempted unless an alternate airport with more favorable weather is not available. If it is necessary to land under adverse conditions, then consideration should be given to utilizing field emergency arresting gear to shorten the landing run and assist in directional control.

To land on a short runway or to alleviate high elevator forces, lower the wing flaps and attempt to control the lateral-directional oscillations with the rudder. With flaps extended, use an approach speed of approximately 140 KIAS at 56,000 pounds gross weight. Sideslips not to exceed 5 degrees can be accomplished in this configuration with control wheel and rudder pedal forces of approximately 60 to 200 pounds, respectively. Should the horizontal stabilizer actuator fail in conjunction with complete failure of the flight control boost systems, the pilot can counteract control surface forces only by application of his flight controls. Because control forces are extremely high with the boost systems inoperative, a landing under this condition is difficult. The degree of difficulty will be increased if the stabilizer actuator should fail while the aircraft is trimmed for a nosedown attitude. In this situation, when reducing airspeed for a landing, the back pressure on the control wheel necessary to counteract the heavy nosedown trim setting may be so excessive as to require an extremely fast approach speed. Extension of the wing flaps and speed brakes will help to relieve the nose-heavy condition, since a noseup trim change results from use of these devices. It should be remembered though, that with the flaps extended, damping of the lateral-directional oscillation is less effective than with the flaps retracted.

Boost-Off Single-Engine Landing

AILERON

Single-engine approach and landing may be safely accomplished with both aileron boost systems inoperative. For a landing gross weight of approximately 55,000 pounds, it is possible to maintain steady, straight flight at normal approach speeds with approximately 5 degrees of bank and 130 pounds of rudder pedal force (full rudder with maximum available directional trim). A wheel force of approximately 50 pounds is required to maintain the required bank angle. At lighter landing weights the wheel force required to maintain straight flight is reduced. Any decision to waveoff should be made well out on final. The dynamic yawing maneuver resulting from application of thrust on the operating engine is extremely difficult to control because of the excessive lateral control force required to maintain straight flight. The landing gear and flaps should be retracted as soon as practical and the airplane accelerated to at least minimum directional trim speed. Near sea level the minimum directional trim speed for stabilized level flight with landing gear and flaps retracted varies from 160 KIAS to 50,000 pounds gross weight to 175 KIAS at 55,000 pounds gross weight.

RUDDER-ELEVATOR

Single-engine approach and landing may be safely accomplished with the rudder-elevator boost system inoperative. The normal technique of maintaining directional control, primarily with rudder, is impossible. Directional control can be maintained by side slipping and banking (wing down towards operating engine) with zero rudder pedal force. With high side slip angle, i.e., high asymmetric power, stabilizing the aircraft is complicated because of excitation of lateral-directional oscillations. For this reason, it is recommended that single-engine approaches with rudder-elevator boost inoperative be accomplished at light gross weights and 10 knots above normal approach airspeed.

NOTE

The yaw damper will be inoperative under rudder-elevator boost-off conditions.

Any decision to waveoff should be made well out on final approach. Upon application of power on the operating engine, directional control can be maintained with aileron alone; however, an extreme lateral-directional oscillation may result. This oscillation is mildly divergent and characterized by intermittent airframe buffet. The landing gear and flaps should be retracted as soon as practical and the aircraft accelerated to at least minimum directional trim speed.

AILERON AND RUDDER-ELEVATOR

Normal approach and landing procedures, i.e., with gear and flaps down throughout the approach, will result in prohibitive control forces with the aileron and rudder-elevator boost systems inoperative. As a result of the prohibitive control forces and associated pilot fatigue factors the following approach and landing procedure is recommended. The approach pattern should be flown with landing gear and flaps retracted 3 miles abeam with a 2 mile final. Maintain airspeed at or near the directional trim speed. Extend landing flaps at a point, dictated by surface wind velocity and airspeed (or approximately 1.5 miles out on the final), where there is no risk of landing short of the runway with the approach power setting. Care must be taken to avoid ballooning during flap extension. Therefore, a low approach is recommended. On approaching the runway threshold or landing area, gradually retard power and retrim the aircraft directionally. Touchdown should be accomplished at idle thrust.

Waveoff should not be attempted after the landing gear is extended unless utility system pressure is available and the landing gear can be retracted. Waveoff should also not be attempted after decelerating 15 knots below the minimum directional trim airspeed as determined with landing gear and flaps retracted. Under no circumstances should a waveoff be attempted after the landing gear is down and the flaps have been completely extended. The dynamic yawing and rolling maneuver resulting from application of asymmetric thrust is virtually impossible to overcome.

FORMATION

General

Flyaways or other mass flights also require proficiency in formation flight. Formation practice shall be scheduled while the squadron is shore-based. Formation flying is not difficult or hazardous, but lack of knowledge of proper procedures, inadequate briefing, and sloppy flying can make it extremely dangerous.

Rendezvous

The rendezvous is potentially the most hazardous of all maneuvers since it involves relative motion on a constant bearing. Observance of established safety procedures is mandatory. Keep the aircraft ahead constantly in view. Keep the nose of the aircraft slightly ahead of the leader's with speed equal to or slightly in excess of the leader. As the wingman approaches the leader, he should ensure that he is aft of the leader's beam. To avoid overshooting, excess speed must be reduced before reaching the wing position. As necessary, the wingman should abort rendezvous by leveling his wings, sighting all aircraft ahead, and moving to the outside of the formation. During rendezvous, only enough stepdown should be used to ensure separation of the aircraft ahead. If one plane is "sucked" during rendezvous, the pilot shall move to the outside of the leader. All relative motion should be stopped prior to joining up to the inside wing position. A cross-under to the outside can then be made. During a running rendezvous, caution must be observed in the final steps of joining up since relative motion is difficult to discern when approaching from the rear. The rendezvous shall be conducted in one of four ways, depending on the circumstances involved.

CIRCLING RENDEZVOUS

The leader establishes an easy orbit around the rendezvous point and other aircraft cross the circle to effect the rendezvous. The wingman places himself well aft of the leader's beam, then puts the nose of his aircraft ahead of the leader, gains a slight speed advantage (10 to 25 knots), and slides into position. As the leader is closed, the speed advantage must be reduced by use of throttles and speedbrakes. Succeeding wingmen should rendezvous on the leader rather than the plane ahead. All planes ahead must be kept in sight or the rendezvous discontinued.

RENDEZVOUS AFTER TAKEOFF

When a number of aircraft take off together and rendezvous for a flight, the first aircraft airborne flies straight ahead for a period of 1 minute plus 20 seconds for each aircraft in the flight, climbing to the designated rendezvous altitude and maintaining 275 KIAS. At the end of this leg, a 180-degree turn to the left or right is made at a 20-degree bank, and the leader flies the reciprocal of the outbound heading. Succeeding planes follow the leader until his turn is started. When the leader bears 30 to 45 degrees off the bow, a turn is started to place the nose slightly ahead of the leader. If the nose is kept in this position with a speed equal to the leader's, the plane will be drawn into the leader for the join-up. As the wingman nears the leader's position, he should ensure that he is aft of the leader's beam. A slight turn in the direction of the leader will move the line of bearing aft, at which time the nose of the aircraft should again be placed ahead of the leader.

RUNNING RENDEZVOUS

The first aircraft launched assumes temporary lead. When safely airborne, he should reduce fuel flow 1000 pounds below takeoff fuel flow, climbing on the course or vector assigned for the mission, and maintaining climb-schedule airspeed. The other aircraft in the flight join, using military power. The rates of closure thus developed are high, and pilots must be alert to avoid overrunning the lead aircraft.

ON-TOP RENDEZVOUS

This rendezvous consists of individual climbs through the overcast and an ontop join-up at a briefed altitude and TACAN position.

Wing Position

A good wing position permits the leader to see all aircraft in the formation. It is close enough to make relative motion and signals easy to see. It should permit the wingman to follow the maneuver and permit relaxed flying. Stepdown should be sufficient to place the top of the wingman's fuselage below the bottom of the leader's fuselage. When the proper bearing is maintained, the leader's cockpit will be visible just ahead of the engine nacelle. If the formation is widened, it should be done by moving out on bearing but not by moving aft and out of the leader's sight.

Basic Formation

The basic unit of formation flying is the two-plane section. Two sections operating together form a division. Two or more divisions comprise a flight. Squadrons use one of three types of formations described below:

PARADE FORMATION

The parade formation is used for all flight demonstrations and in the landing pattern around the ship. The position is fixed and cross-unders are to be executed on signal from the leader. The distance between aircraft is close, and aircraft dress on each other rather than flying a rigid bearing on the leader. The section leader flies a close-wing position on the leader. The four-plane division or combination of divisions shall be used unless special formations are prescribed. If only two divisions are involved, the second division flies to the unbalanced side of the first.

TACTICAL FORMATION

When flying the tactical or cruise formation, the section leader operates from a loose position and all aircraft are free to slide or cross under as necessary to hold position with a minimum of effort. The section leader will always choose the side on which he wishes to cruise and the wingman is required to take the other side. Although this formation is free and flexible, the proper bearing must be maintained to permit the leader to maintain visual contact.

ECHELON FORMATION

The echelon formation is one of special purpose and normally shall only be used prior to breakup, rendezvous, or demonstrations. An echelon to the right or left must be signaled by the leader. If the leader's wingman is on the side on which the echelon is to be formed, the section must cross under and join on him. If the section is on the side on which the echelon is to be formed, the section must move out to make room for the wingman. Turns shall never be made into the echelon.

NIGHT FORMATION FLYING

The same general rules for day rendezvous can be applied to night formation flying. It is difficult to determine relative motion at night; for this reason, no abrupt maneuvers should be attempted and crossunders should be held to a minimum. Turns for rendezvous should be wide and closing speeds low. Keep lights on BRIGHT during rendezvous. After rendezvous, the last plane in the formation shall use bright lights and all others shall place wing and taillights on DIM. At night it is easier to fly close enough to see the outline of the plane ahead rather than attempting to fly position on the lights.

CLOUD FLYING

Normally, approaches and penetrations shall be made by single aircraft, but should a formation enter a cloud it can be kept intact if proper wing positions are maintained. If necessary to make a section instrument approach for any reason (lost radios, navigation aids, etc.), the aircraft requiring assistance shall assume the starboard wing position. The lead aircraft shall advise the controlling agency of the situation. When the lead aircraft has the landing area in sight, he shall pass the lead (day—hand signal; night—flash navigation lights) to the wingman, increase power, and wave-off to the left. The wingman shall continue straight in and land. Should any aircraft lose sight of the plane ahead, a 30-degree turnaway shall be made and held for 1 minute prior to returning to base heading. Power settings must remain unaltered, and after leaving the cloud the formation shall be rejoined. The leader of the formation must concentrate on smooth instrument flying while maintaining base course. Penetrations involving more than one section shall not be made.

PENETRATION AND APPROACHES BY DISSIMILAR AIRCRAFT

In an emergency when it is necessary for dissimilar aircraft to make a section penetration, transition to landing configuration should be attempted only when VFR. If the ceiling precludes transition during the approach phase and fuel state permits, transition to the landing configuration should be made before penetration is commenced.

ODD NUMBERS IN FORMATION

When all aircraft are not launched, it may be necessary to rearrange the formation to replace missing aircraft. This is done according to the following rules:

1. Fill in the first division from the wingman of the last division.

2. Fill in the first section, using the wingman of the second section.

3. Maintain the integrity of the four-plane division.

4. Not more than four aircraft shall operate as a division.

5. When a division consists of less than four aircraft, it shall continue to operate as if it were a full division, with one plane acting as the second section.

Maneuvering

The formation leader should avoid abrupt and violent maneuvers unless the planes in the formation are forewarned. No difficulty should be encountered in following any smooth, coordinated maneuver which the leader might make if each aircraft is free to slide and tail-in during steep, prolonged turns. The formation leader can make the wingmen's job easier by observing the following rules:

1. Make all attitude changes smooth and coordinated, and use a constant power setting when possible.

2. Never use full power for climb or idle power with speedbrakes out for descent.

3. When possible, advise the flight by radio before operating the speedbrakes (signal "Speedbrakes — Now").

AIR REFUELING

Rendezvous Procedures

Normally the tanker aircraft should be at the prescribed rendezvous point 5 minutes prior to the time that refueling is scheduled to commence. Upon arrival at a designated static rendezvous point, the tanker aircraft should set up a left-hand 30-degree bank orbit at 250 KIAS. A running rendezvous may be performed if operationally necessary. The rendezvous point may be selected geographically or given with respect to radio navigation aids. A ship's CIC, early warning aircraft, GCI stations, and air to air TACAN may be used to expedite or control a static on course rendezvous. The ARA-25 should not be overlooked as a possible rendezvous aid when the rendezvous is being conducted without the aid of control stations.

Receiver aircraft should rendezvous with the tanker and escort or tanker and other receiver aircraft in a loose echelon (standby position). Following join-up, a refueling base course and altitude should be taken up. For rendezvous procedures refer to CVA/CVS NATOPS Manual and the NATOPS Air Refueling Manual.

Altitudes, Airspeed, and Engagement Procedures

ALTITUDES

The altitude for refueling may vary from sea level to more than 35,000 feet; however, the desirable minimum altitude is 1500 feet. Refueling may be performed at airspeeds of from 220 to 300 KIAS. The altitudes and airspeeds selected should be those best suited to the receiver aircraft and within the operating limitations of the tanker.

AIRSPEED

Air refueling KA-3B to A-3 is most comfortably accomplished at an altitude of 20,000 feet and at an indicated airspeed of 250 knots. After the receiver aircraft is engaged and refueling, turns using 30 degrees of bank or less can be made and climbs and descents of 500 feet per minute can be performed comfortably. Following initial checkout and practice, engagements may be performed while the tanker aircraft is turning.

EXAMPLE

The air refueling speed chart (figure 4-6) illustrates the speeds, altitudes, and weights at which the KA-3B tanker can satisfactorily operate. The shaded area on the chart indicates the speed ranges at which satisfactory operation of the fueling gear can be expected. To illustrate: follow the 70,000-pound gross weight tanker speed envelope line. The KIAS range of the aircraft at sea level is from 220 to 480 KIAS. However, the fueling gear will only operate in the speed range of 220 to 300 KIAS. The fueling gear speed range for satisfactory operation remains constant from sea level to 28,500 feet. Above 28,500 feet the maximum speed for satisfactory operation of the fueling gear is limited to Mach 0.8.

NOTE

Emergency aerial refueling is possible below 220 KIAS down to a low of approximately 180 KIAS. At approximately 180 KIAS the air load on the drogue is lowered to the point where the auto retraction feature of the tanker system will pull the drogue away from the receiver aircraft.

RECEIVER ENGAGEMENT PROCEDURES

Do not engage drogue unless an amber light is on. The reel response will be inoperative, no fuel will be transferred and an engagement will damage both aircraft.

Receiver aircraft will rendezvous in echelon abeam the tanker ensuring that aft area of tanker is clear. Receiver aircraft should be briefed to remain well clear of the tanker during all drogue actuations. Should a reel malfunction occur, the drogue and hose assembly may be carried away. Normal drogue deployment is rapid and smooth. When signaled by flight leader, the tanker will deploy drogue. After drogue extension the flight leader should move the flight to a position abeam the drogue. When the drogue is fully extended, an amber light is visible on the drogue fairing. In the event that the amber light is not on, the tanker shall be notified and receiver aircraft shall not engage the drogue until proper cockpit indications are obtained by the tanker (amber light – ON, reel lock indicator – OUT). At this time the receiver aircraft may be cleared to engage drogue. The following transmissions shall be made by all receiver aircraft as applicable: lining up, contact, clear and breakaway.

The tanker pilot, as leader of the refueling formation, has the primary responsibility for maintaining a good lookout for aircraft. Other members of the flight shall assist as lookouts to the maximum extent possible.

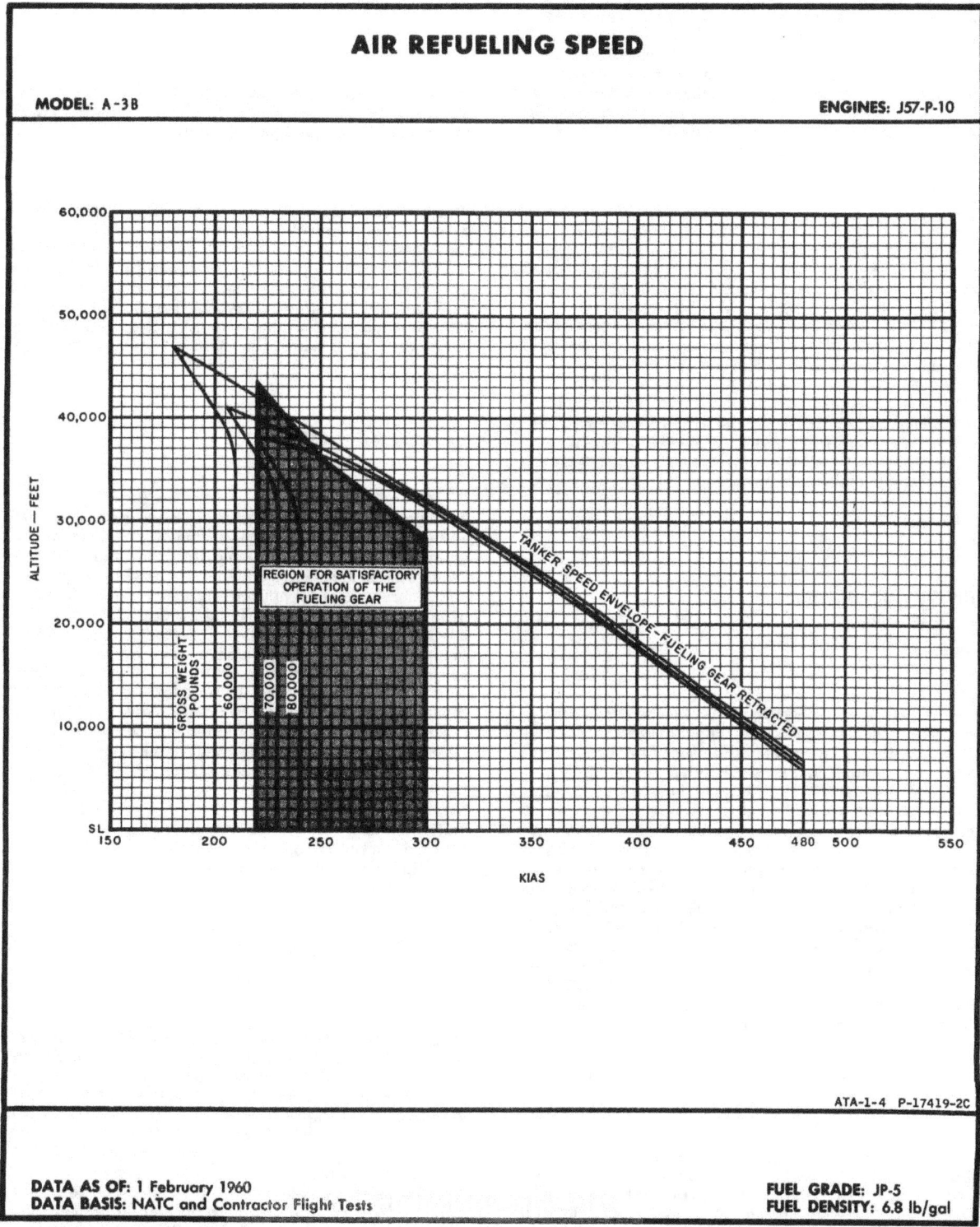

Figure 4-6. Air Refueling Speed

The receiver aircraft will assume the ready position, approximately 50 feet behind and slightly below the drogue. The receiver aircraft should be stopped relative to the tanker and trimmed at this position prior to closing the drogue. The position of the drogue relative to the tanker aircraft should be noted in order that the receiver aircraft may assume the proper disengagement position following refueling.

A small amount of power should be added by the receiver pilot to commence a rate of closure with the drogue. The desired rate of closure is approximately equal to a walking pace. The vertical displacement of the probe to the drogue should be decreased smoothly in order that the last few feet of travel may be level. A positive rate of closure must be maintained until the drogue and probe are engaged and locked or until the decision is made to abort the attempt. Completely stopping the rate of closure a few feet from the drogue in the area of maximum turbulence is undesirable and will invariably result in overcontrolled oscillation of the receiver aircraft preventing a successful engagement.

DROGUE OSCILLATION

As the drogue is closed by the probe the oscillation appears to become greater. The increase in motion of the drogue is due to the influence of the probe assembly. Small and slowly applied corrections to lineup will generally lead to a good engagement. Turbulence behind the tanker aircraft may require the receiver aircraft to be flown in unbalanced flight during engagement. If the drogue is overshot, or lineup corrections are out of phase, or if the receiver pilot is overcontrolling corrections, it is best to abort the attempt and reopen to about 30 feet aft of the drogue, using throttles and speedbrakes. The receiver pilot should stop all relative motion at this position and analyze the mistakes made prior to attempting another engagement. Generally, failure to engage properly results from errors made in closure rate or in overcontrolling lineup corrections.

Occasionally the locking mechanism on the probe will hang up on the lip of the drogue basket and continued closure will cause the drogue to tilt on the probe. Some slack may be formed in the hose and, unless the probe can be freed inside of the drogue immediately, it is best to withdraw completely and reclose the drogue.

DROGUE CLOSURE

Some pilots have found it helpful to commence closure using the tanker aircraft as reference and including the drogue in the peripheral scan.

When the probe is firmly seated in the drogue, the rate of closure should be slowed by the use of throttles. The drogue must be pushed forward along its neutral catenary until approximately 5 feet of hose are rewound on the hose reel. White stripes on the hose painted at 1-foot intervals from the fairing may be used to determine the amount of hose rewound. A probe light is provided for night refueling operations.

REFUELING OPERATIONS

When approximately 5 feet of hose are rewound, the amber fairing light will go off and if fuel is to be transferred the green fairing light will come on, indicating fuel transfer. Fuel flowing into the tanker hose in excess of 20 gpm turns a flow sensing device which lights the drogue fairing green light. Small movements in the hose may make the light blink even though transfer is taking place. The receiver aircraft should be flown in a trail position on the tanker with the hose maintained in its natural trail position (exclusive of the 5 feet of retracted hose). Minor throttle and control adjustments will be required to maintain position. During the transfer operation the receiver aircraft will require trim changes and throttle adjustment as gross weight and fuel distribution are changed. If refueling is commenced at high altitudes, descents during refueling may be required in order for the receiver to maintain adequate and comfortable control.

TANKER TRANSFER RATE

If fuel is being received from the KA-3B tanker aircraft and sufficient fuel is transferred to deplete the fuel in the auxiliary tank of the tanker, the green fairing transfer light will go off and the amber light will come on. The receiver aircraft must back out to approximately 5 feet from the full trail position or disengage completely. The refueling operation may recommence after a delay of approximately 2 1/2 minutes during which time the tanker auxiliary tank will refill. For transfer of a small amount of fuel the completion of transfer will be indicated to the receiver pilot by the green fairing light going off, and the amber light coming on.

The rate at which the receiver will accept fuel and the tanks into which fuel will be received is dependent upon the receiver fuel remaining and the fuel distribution. KA-3B tanker transfer rate is dependent on tanker fuel state and distribution. The fueling rates for various situations are given in figure 4-11.

DISENGAGEMENT PROCEDURES

To disengage from the drogue, the receiver pilot should first endeavor to return the drogue to the position at which it was first engaged and then establish a slow opening rate by use of throttles. The use of speedbrakes is not recommended. Backing out should be done slowly and directly aft of the above described position with no vertical or lateral motion. A slight tug will be felt as the probe and drogue disengage and some fuel may be sprayed back into the windshield of the receiver aircraft if fuel has been received. In the event that the receiver is not in the proper position to disengage, the drogue may whip violently and damage either the receiver or tanker aircraft. The receiver probe may be bent or broken or the tanker drogue may be damaged by improper disengagement techniques. Following final drogue disengagement, the receiver aircraft should take up loose left echelon position. In the event that he is the last aircraft presently rendezvoused to receive fuel, the receiver pilot will observe the drogue while it is retracted and stowed prior to departing the tanker. All departures from the tanker will be made to port. Elements may depart from the tanker when refueling is completed and after joining in left echelon.

EMERGENCY DISENGAGEMENT PROCEDURES

Emergency breakaway action by the receiver aircraft may become necessary due to difficulties in either the tanker or the receiver aircraft. Emergency breakaway signals are by radio transmission and/or turning on the lower anticollision lights. The action taken will be prompted by the nature of the emergency; however, if at all possible the receiver aircraft should make an expeditious return to the normal disconnect position and disengage without delay using the normal disconnect procedures. If normal disconnect procedures are followed, disconnecting slowly, the possibilities of damage to the tanker and or receiver aircraft are reduced. Possible damage which may occur to either the tanker and or receiver due to improper disconnect procedures includes damaged fueling package, broken hose or probe, and external airframe damage to either aircraft from whipping hose and drogue.

RECEIVER PROCEDURES FROM TANKERS OTHER THAN KA-3B

- When tanking from a KC-130, the receiver must be positioned, after engagement, so that the tanker's jet exhaust does not impinge on the receiver's engine intakes causing EGT to exceed the maximum.

- Simultaneous tanking of two KA-3B aircraft from the KC-130 should be avoided. If required, staggered tanking positions must be maintained, as there is no horizontal wing clearance between receivers. Aircraft flying the aft position must engage last and disengage first.

- When tanking from a KC-135, the maximum total fuel on board shall not exceed 27,000 pounds of JP-4 or 28,500 pounds of JP-5. Failure to observe these limitations may result in catastrophic rupture of fuel tanks by over pressure.

In receiving fuel from tanker aircraft other than KA-3B, the KA-3B receiver procedures outlined herein will generally apply. In refueling from the wing pod of a KC-130, or from the A-4 buddy store, cross trim conditions may have to be set up by the receiver aircraft due to the aircraft control surfaces being in the wingtip vortex or jet exhaust of the tanker aircraft. In the event that the tanker airspeed is less than desired, partial flaps may be used by the receiver aircraft to improve aircraft stability and to operate in a more responsive engine operating range.

Place forward looking radar to OFF or RAD STBY and position receiver pilot's visor down prior to assuming the ready position. Techniques for receiver engagement may vary in minor areas depending on the aircraft performance and configuration. See NATOPS Air Refueling Manual for additional information.

Following engagement of the drogue, the receiver aircraft may find it desirable to slightly displace the position of the drogue laterally or vertically away from the position at which it was engaged in order to maintain a more comfortable position during refueling. Care must be exercised by the receiver pilot in repositioning the drogue, since the effects of tanker jet exhaust and turbulence are unpredictable and any rapid movements of the receiver may become violent and uncontrollable due to these effects.

Section IV   NAVAIR 01-40ATA-1

Air Refueling Checklist

TANKER LIGHT IDENTIFICATION SIGNALS

Tanker aircraft are equipped with green rotating beacons to facilitate tanker location and operation. When all (upper and lower) rotating beacons are ON, the tanker system is up and the tanker is ready for air refueling. When the upper rotating beacon only is ON, refueling operations are in progress.

RECEIVER

The receiver pilot should observe proper drogue deployment. The pilot shall place all forward looking radar on standby, lower the helmet visor, and place cockpit switches as follows:

1. Air refueling switch ..... AIR REFUELING

2. Fuel dump switch .... OFF

RECEIVER CAPABILITY

3. Wings tank transfer
switch................... OFF

The time interval capabilities of the receiver aircraft to receive fuel from the tanker depend upon the amount of fuel in the various tanks of the receiver. The elapsed time in minutes for receiving fuel is illustrated in the A-3B Receiver Capabilities charts. (See figure 4-10.)

4. Aux tank transfer .... OFF

5. FWD to AUX transfer
switch................... OFF

WARNING

Do not engage drogue unless an amber light is on.

Figure 4-10, sheet 1. A-3 Receiver Capability. With the A-3 receiver wing tanks empty, FWD tank empty, AUX tank empty, and AFT tank containing 315 gallons, the receiving rate will be approximately 420 gpm for the first 6.1/2 minutes. At this time approximately 2900 gallons will have been received and AUX tank and wing tanks of the receiver will be full. The receiving rate then drops to 228 gpm until the receiver FWD tank fills. After a total elapsed time of 10 minutes, approximately 3650 gallons has been received by the receiver aircraft. All action above the 2650-gallon line of the chart is hypothetical because of the tanker capacity limitation and will not be discussed.

EMERGENCY BREAKAWAY PROCEDURES

If an emergency breakaway is required, the tanker should continue straight ahead and maintain altitude if possible, while the receiver aircraft disengages. Emergency breakaway signals are made by radio transmission and/or by activation of the lower anti-collision lights. In an extreme emergency, the tanker should add power and accomplish breakaway by pulling ahead.

Figure 4-10, sheet 2. A-3 Receiver Capability. With the A-3 receiver wing tanks empty, AUX tank empty, FWD tank containing 965 gallons, and AFT tank containing 1150 gallons, the receiving rate will be approximately 420 gpm for the first 6 1/2 minutes. At this time, 2840 gallons will have been received and all tanks of the receiver except the AFT tank will be

COMMUNICATIONS AND SIGNALS

For correct radio and visual signals, refer to NATOPS Air Refueling Manual.

4-22   Figures 4-7 through 4-9, Pages 4-23 through 4-30 Deleted.   Changed 15 July 1970

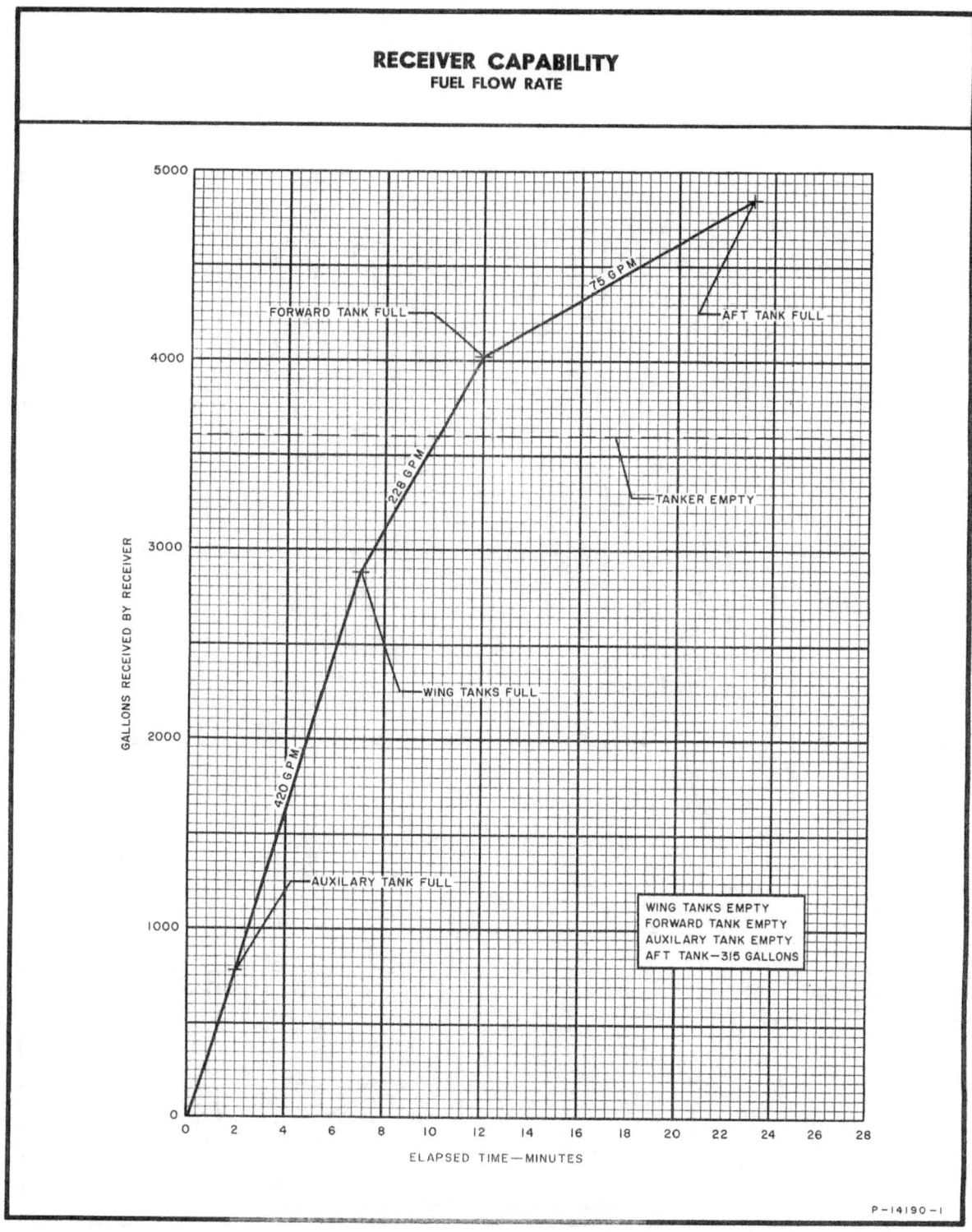

Figure 4-10. A-3 Receiver Capabilities (Sheet 1)

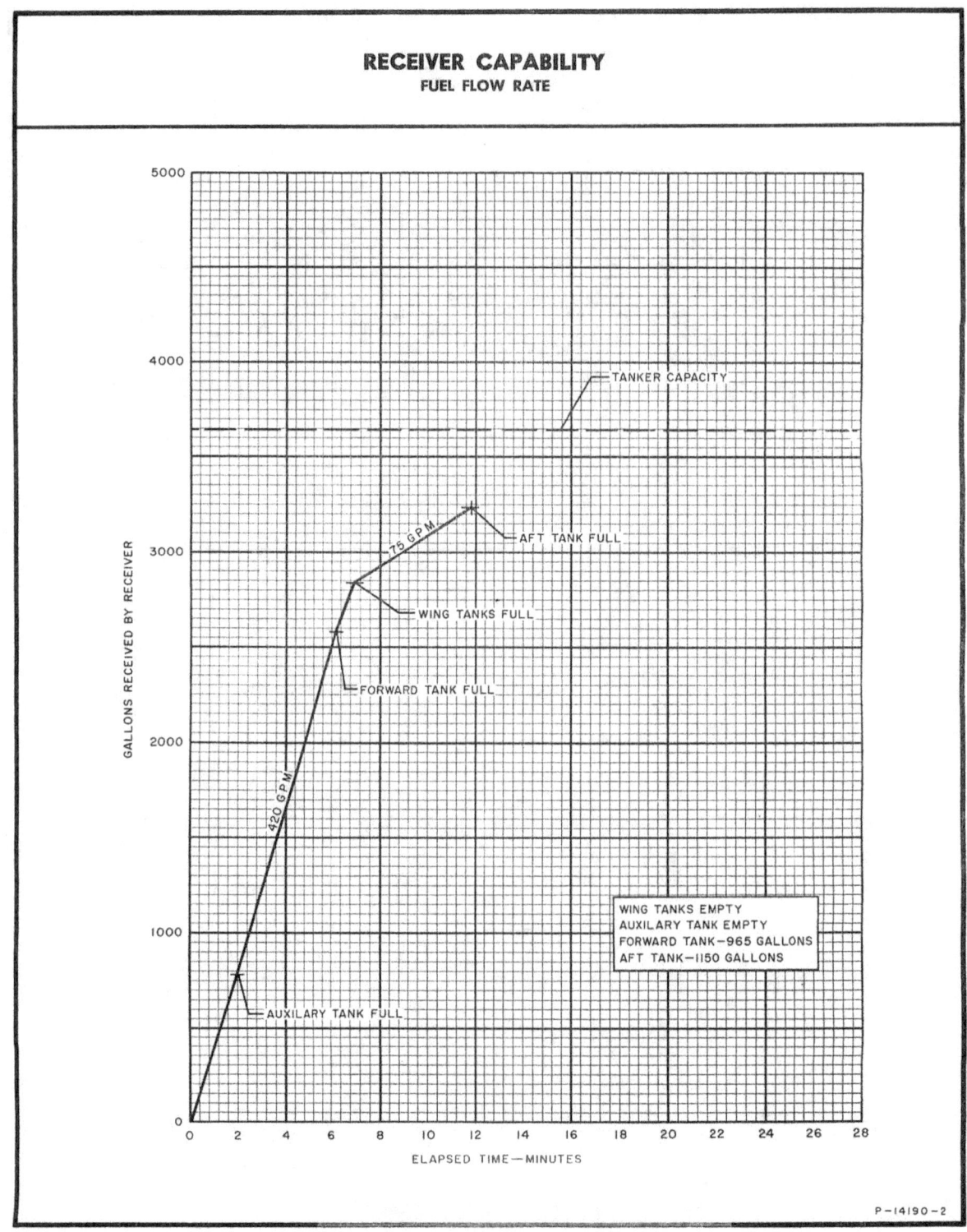

Figure 4-10. A-3 Receiver Capabilities (Sheet 2)

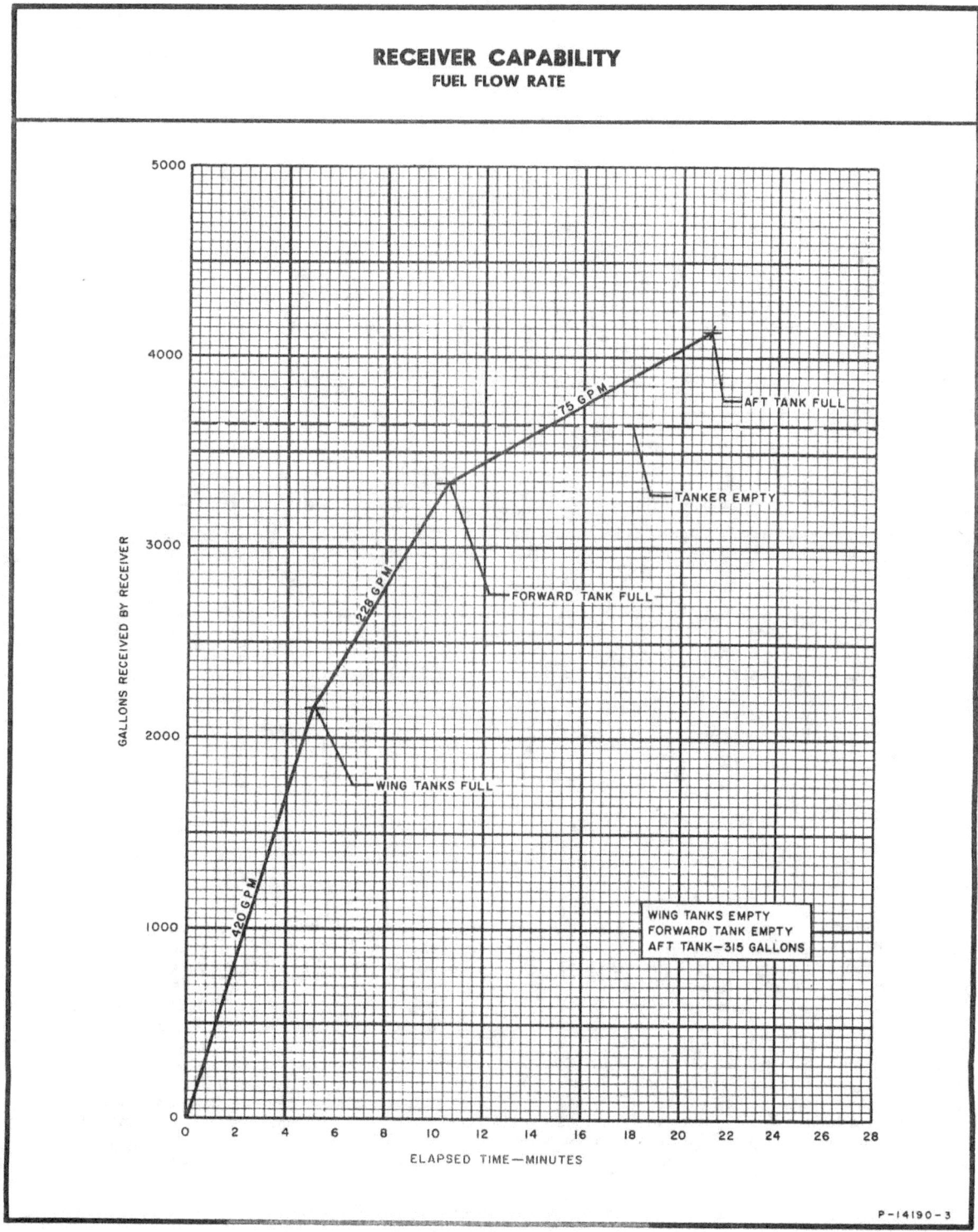

Figure 4-10. A-3 Receiver Capabilities (Sheet 3)

FUEL TRANSFER RATE

			INTERNAL TRANSFER RATE			RECEIVER TRANSFER RATE				
				Transfer Rate to Aux Tank			Receiver Rate			
	Tank	Capacity	Alone	With Wing	With Forward	Alone	All Tanks	With Wing	With Forward	With Aux
T A N K E R	Forward	1178	137	120		228 (153 If Aft Tank Not Full)	420	420		420
	Wing	649 Each	169		160	373	420		420	420
	Aux	773				420	420	420	420	
	Aft	1907	None	None	None	88 GPM From Forward Tank				
KA-3B	Wing	649 Each				373	420		420	
	Forward	1178				228	420	420		
No Aux Tank	Aft	1907				75 GPM From Forward Tank	420			

Figure 4-11. Fuel Transfer Rate

full. The receiving rate then drops to 75 gpm and the AFT tank will fill. After a total elapsed time of 12 minutes, approximately 3200 gallons will have been received and all tanks will be full.

Figure 4-11. The Fuel Transfer Rate chart is divided into two sections; TANKER and RECEIVER. The TANKER portion of the Fuel Transfer Rate chart illustrates the capacity of the fuel tanks and the transfer rate to the AUX tank of the various tanks alone, then the rate of wing tank transfer and FWD tank transfer combined. As is shown, all of the AFT tank fuel is for tanker engine consumption and cannot be transferred to the AUX tank for air refueling operations. The RECEIVER portion of the Fuel Transfer Rate chart illustrates the receiver rate in gallons per minute of the KA-3B. When all tanks but the aft tank of the receiver are empty, the receiving rate at the start of the refueling is 420 gpm. If only the FWD tank is empty, the rate is 228 gpm (153 gpm if AFT tank is not full). If only the wing tanks are empty, the rate is 373 gpm. In order to receive fuel at 400 gpm, the AUX tank must be low, or if the AUX tank is not installed, then the wing tanks plus any other tank must be low.

NAVAIR 01-40ATA-1 Section V

SECTION V
EMERGENCY PROCEDURES

TABLE OF CONTENTS

TEXT

	Page
Introduction	5-2
Ground Emergencies	5-2
Unsatisfactory Start	5-2
Takeoff Emergencies	5-2
In-Flight Emergencies	5-3
Engine Malfunction/Failures	5-3
Air Starting	5-3
Single-Engine Flameout/Failure	5-4
Dual Engine Flameout/Failure	5-4
Maximum Glide (Two Engines Inoperative)	5-5
Fire Warning Indications (Lights On)	5-5
Engine Fire	5-5
Fuselage Fire	5-5
Electrical Fire	5-5
Hot Bleed Air Leaks	5-6
Wing Fire or Hot Bleed Air Leak	5-6
Bleed Air Rotary Shutoff Switch	5-6
Bleed Air Toggle Shutoff Switches	5-7
ATM Compartment Fire or Hot Bleed Air Leaks	5-7
Air-Conditioning/Upper Bomb Bay Hot Bleed Air Leaks (Light On)	5-7
Bomb Bay/Companionway Fires or Hot Bleed Air Leaks	5-7
Air-Conditioning Turbine Failure	5-7
Smoke and Fume Elimination	5-8
Utility Hydraulic System Failure	5-8
Shore-Based Considerations	5-8
Shipboard Considerations	5-8
Wing Flap Emergency Operation	5-9
Landing Gear Emergency Operation	5-9
Hook Emergency Operation	5-10
Speedbrake Emergency Operation	5-10

	Page
Wheel Brake Operation After Utility Failure	5-10
ATM Malfunction/Failure	5-10
Electrical System Malfunction/Failure	5-11
DC Generator Malfunction/Failure	5-11
AC Generator Malfunction/Failure	5-12
Complete AC and DC Generator Failure	5-12
Complete AC and DC Failure Including Battery	5-12
Runaway Trim Procedure	5-12
Oil System Malfunction/Failure	5-13
Fuel System Malfunctions/Failure	5-13
Aircraft Fuel Trim Control Malfunction/Failure	5-13
Fuel Vent Icing	5-14
Landing Emergencies	5-14
Single-Engine Landings	5-14
No-Boost Field Landings	5-16
No-Boost Carrier Landings	5-17
No-Flap Field Landings	5-17
No-Flap Carrier Landings	5-17
No-Slat Field Landings	5-17
No-Slat Carrier Landings	5-18
Wheel Brakes Emergency	5-18
Bailout/Ditching Doctrine	5-18
Bailout/Ditching Procedures	5-18
Emergency Field Arrestment	5-24
Recommended Runway Foaming Procedure	5-27
Emergency Crew Removal	5-27
Aircraft Upright or Inverted	5-27

TABLES

Table		Page	Table		Page
5-1	Emergency Landing/Diversion Recommendations	5-25	5-2	A-3 Field Maximum Engagement (KIAS) vs Gross Weight X 1000	5-26

ILLUSTRATIONS

Figure		Page	Figure		Page
5-1	Single-Engine Landing and Waveoff Pattern (Typical)	5-15	5-3	Secondary Emergency Exit – With Rake Fully Extended	5-23
5-2	Emergency Exit	5-22	5-4	Fire Fighting	5-28
			5-5	Emergency Access and Crew Evacuation	5-29

Changed 15 July 1970

5-1

Section V   NAVAIR 01-40ATA-1

INTRODUCTION

The course of action pilots and crewmembers will take when faced with an emergency situation is based upon their knowledge of the aircraft and emergency procedures. For this reason, initial training must be thorough in this area, but should not be considered complete. Aircraft systems and procedures must be frequently reviewed on a regular basis. Periodic emergency drills in the Operational Flight Trainer are ideally suited for realistic simulation of almost all emergencies that may be experienced. Above all, the pilot must be able to recognize emergency situations. In analyzing possible course of action, the crew will not only be aware of aircraft systems operations but remain aware of external factors affecting emergencies such as terrain features, weather conditions, divert fields, etc. The pilot shall keep the crew informed of airspeed and altitude during bailout situations.

1. NWP 41( ) contains general considerations which are applicable in various emergency situations.

2. NWP 37(A) discusses SAR organization and procedures.

3. The FLIP En Route Supplement covers current procedures for any emergency phase (uncertainty, alert, distress, lost), and procedures for use with a rescue interceptor, both day and night.

4. Operation plans and orders of carrier-force commanders and commanders of other forces employing aircraft contains provisions for handling aircraft in distress and for rescue of personnel.

5. When an emergency is experienced while operating in the continental limits of the United States, the IFF-function select knob will be placed in the EMERGENCY position, with MODE 3 selected, unless otherwise directed by competent authority.

This chapter contains the specific step-by-step procedures to be used for all emergencies likely to be encountered in the A-3. Use it as the primary guide for studying remedial procedures for various emergencies. The information contained in Section I, part 2 of this manual must be used to provide additional knowledge of system operation and malfunctions. In general, the emergencies a pilot will encounter fall into one of four categories. These are: GROUND EMERGENCIES, TAKEOFF EMERGENCIES, IN-FLIGHT EMERGENCIES, and LANDING EMERGENCIES. It is likely that most emergencies will require some deviation from the procedure set forth for a simple failure because of varied conditions; i.e., compounded emergencies, facilities available, weather factors, etc; consequently, thoughtful analysis of each situation is necessary. The selection of the course of action to be taken rests with the pilot.

For the common understanding of all, it is necessary to define the meaning of failure, malfunction, and flameout as used in this section. Failure is considered to be the complete, non-regainable loss of function or performance of any component, unit, or system installed in the aircraft. Malfunction is defined as improper performance of the intended purpose of a device in one or more of three aspects; quality, quantity, or consistency. The definition of flameout is limited to loss of combustion due to external influences upon the engine, such as interruption of fuel or air supply.

NOTE

In instances where it is indicated that the proper procedure is: Land, using short field arresting gear, if available. It is intended that the pilot should exercise his judgment and land as soon as conditions permit on the end of the runway or as directed by the LSO, using the first available arrestment gear that is compatible with aircraft and arresting gear limitations.

GROUND EMERGENCIES

Unsatisfactory Starts

WET STARTS

1. Master engine switch .... OFF
2. Throttle .... OFF
3. Continue cranking engine .. 20 TO 30 SECONDS

NOTE

The engine should be dried thoroughly by cranking, and/or swabbing out the tailpipe prior to attempting another start.

FALSE START

1. Throttle .... OFF
2. Master engine switch .... OFF
3. Continue cranking until TPT drops to normal
4. Do not attempt restart until the cause of malfunction has been corrected.

HOT START

1. Throttle .... OFF
2. Master engine switch .... OFF
3. Continue cranking to extinguish fire.
4. If fire persists, abandon aircraft and use all available means to extinguish fire.

TAKEOFF EMERGENCIES

TAKEOFF ABORT PROCEDURES

1. Throttles .... IDLE
2. Hook .... DOWN
3. Drag chute .... DEPLOY
4. Braking .... MAXIMUM ANTISKID

5-2   Changed 15 July 1970

NAVAIR 01-40ATA-1   Section V

> **CAUTION**

- If off center just prior to engaging arresting gear, do not attempt to go for center of runway. Continue straight ahead parallel to centerline.

- When engagement is outside the permissive limitations of the arresting gear, the gear may fail before the aircraft is stopped.

- With hook down, nose gear steering will be centered, however, limited steering may be available within the limits of steering linkage and centering detent.

- Raise hook if field arresting gear will not be needed to stop aircraft on runway.

- Do not raise landing gear if aircraft is going to overrun runway.

ENGINE FAILURE DURING TAKEOFF RUN

1. Use abort procedures should an engine fail during takeoff run before becoming airborne.

2. Continue single-engine takeoff if unsafe to abort and sufficient runway remains to become safely airborne using procedures listed below:

ENGINE FAILURE AFTER LIFTOFF

1. Landing gear . . . . UP
2. Accelerate
3. Fuel Dump. . . . . WINGS/ AUX
4. Flaps . . . . BLEED UP

NOTE

Half flap transition speed is approximately 25 KIAS above computed takeoff speed.

5. Throttle, affected engine . . . . OFF

NOTE

- Maximum acceleration will be obtained by keeping the wings level and allowing the aircraft heading to drift, if field and terrain conditions permit.

- If heading must be maintained, an increase in bank angle is preferred over a reduction in power on the operative engine.

6. If no engine fire or other abnormal indications exists, attempt air start of second engine. Jettison and/or consume fuel to reach a gross weight of 50,000 pounds or less.

7. Land using both engines if available, but using single-engine pattern, speeds, and techniques.

IN-FLIGHT EMERGENCIES

Engine Malfunction/Failures

Indication if impending engine failure will usually be in the form of unstable engine operation and may be manifested by one or a combination of symptoms. (Refer to Section I, Part 2.)

Air Starting

Successful air starts may sometimes be obtained at any altitude or airspeed by taking advantage of the high airflow through the engine immediately following a flameout. The minimum rpm for successful air starts will wary with altitude and airspeed.

IMMEDIATE AIR START

The following procedures should be accomplished as quickly as possible:

1. Throttle inoperative engine:

   a. OFF

   b. Outboard for ignition

   c. IDLE position

> **CAUTION**

If air start does not occur within 30 seconds after the THROTTLE has been moved to IDLE, or if an unsatisfactory start is indicated in any way, retard the THROTTLE to OFF and allow the engine to windmill for 30 seconds minimum before attempting another start.

NORMAL AIR START

1. Throttle, inoperative engine . . . . OFF

2. Master engine switch . . ON

Changed 15 July 1970   5-3

Section V
NAVAIR 01-40ATA-1

3. Fuel pressure . . . . NORMAL

4. Tachometer . . . . 12 to 30 percent

5. Throttle . . . . IGNITE, THEN IDLE

6. Oil pressure . . . . NORMAL

NOTE

• An air start may be attempted with no oil pressure indications. If indications do not return to normal after air start, secure the engine.

• If fuel boost pressure reads low/out, position CROSSFEED switch to affected engine. If boost pressure does not return, place CROSSFEED switch to normal and continue air start attempt.

Single-Engine Flameout/Failure

WARNING

If fuel boost indicates OUT/ZERO and engine operation is regained by means of crossfeed, circuit breakers for affected fuel boost pump shall be secured. If engine operation is not regained and fuel boost on affected engines indicates OUT/ZERO, return crossfeed switch to closed and master engine switch to OFF. Failure to perform this operation can lead to loss of as much as 15,000 pounds of fuel within an hour from ruptured fuel line.

Attempt immediate air start if conditions warrant. If unable:

1. Throttle, operative engine . . . . . AS DESIRED

2. Throttle, inoperative engine . . . . OFF

3. Master engine switch, inoperative engine . . . . OFF

4. Retrim

5. Attempt NORMAL air start, if conditions warrant.

Dual Engine Flameout/Failure

HIGH ALTITUDE (ABOVE 10,000 FEET AGL)

1. Immediate air start . . . . IF POSSIBLE

2. Battery switch . . . . EMERGENCY

3. Transmit . . . . MAYDAY

NOTE

• If conditions permit, reduce altitude and attempt additional air starts.

• When necessary to maintain control of the aircraft, pull AILERON and RUDDER/ELEVATOR BOOST REL.

4. If air start unsuccessful, bailout prior to 10,000 feet AGL.

MEDIUM ALTITUDE (BETWEEN 3000 AND 10,000 FEET AGL)

1. Trade airspeed for altitude, attempt one air start, each engine, at pilot's discretion.

2. Battery switch . . . . EMERGENCY

3. Transmit . . . . MAYDAY

4. If airstart is unsuccessful . . . . . BAILOUT

LOW ALTITUDE (3000 FEET AGL AND BELOW)

1. Trade airspeed for altitude . . . . BAILOUT

NOTE

Ditch aircraft if safe bailout altitude (1000 feet) cannot be reached.

5-4

Changed 15 July 1970

Maximum Glide (Two Engines Inoperative)

Maximum glide performance is obtained by use of a constant speed in the clean configuration. Should a dual engine failure occur, establish optimum glide speed.

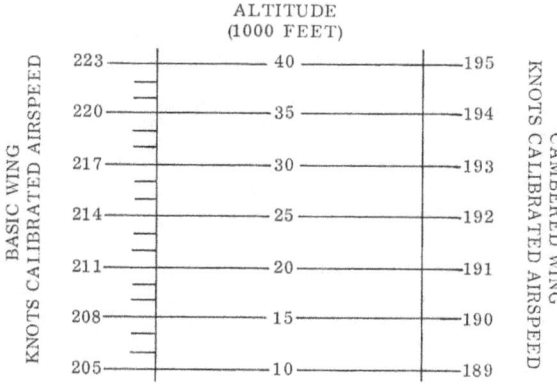

RECOMMENDED SPEED FOR MAXIMUM RANGE GLIDE
TWO ENGINES INOPERATIVE
GROSS WEIGHT = 50,000 POUNDS

NOTES: BASIC WING AIRCRAFT
1. For weights greater than 50,000 pounds, add 10 knots for each 5000 pound increase.
2. Glide ratio = 12.3/1.

CAMBERED WING AIRCRAFT
1. For weights freater than 50,000 pounds, add 8 knots for each 5000 pound increase.
2. Glide ratio = 13.6/1.

Fire Warning Indications (Lights On)

NORMAL FLIGHT CONDITIONS

1. Engine and instruments . . . . CHECK

2. Power, affected engine . . . . REDUCE

3. Continue engine operation at pilot's discretion.

CRITICAL FLIGHT CONDITIONS

During takeoff, climbout under instrument conditions, or approach/GCA, no power reduction shall be made until the aircraft is under full control, and single engine performance speed can be maintained.

Engine Fire

If above safe single-engine speed, shut down the engine:

1. Throttle . . . . OFF

2. Master engine switch . . . . OFF

3. Do not attempt air start.

4. If fire persists, bailout or land immediately using short field arresting gear, if available.

Fuselage Fire

No system for extinguishing a fuselage fire is provided. If the fire is accessible, use any means available to extinguish.

Electrical Fire

KNOWN ORIGIN

1. Secure applicable equipment or isolate by circuit breaker.

2. If fire persists, treat as fire of unknown origin.

UNKNOWN ORIGIN

1. In critical flight conditions or IFR, secure all electrical equipment switches except:

   a. Master engine switches

   b. ATM switches

   c. Battery switch

   d. Ac and dc generator switches

   e. Bleed air switches

2. Oxygen regulators 100%

3. Upper hatch, lower access and bomb bay doors . . . . KEEP CLOSED

4. If fire persists, bail out or land immediately using short field arresting gear, if available.

NOTE

If VFR, secure the battery and generators to rapidly eliminate all electrical power. If fire persists, bail out or land immediately using short field arresting gear, if available. If fire is eliminated, secure all electrical equipment and pull associated circuit breakers. Restart dc and ac generators. Systematically restore electrical power to equipment essential for safe flight.

LANDING GEAR SOLENOID FAILURE

If the landing gear control handle solenoid fails, an excessive amount of smoke is invariably emitted from the center console. When this failure is suspected, proceed as follows:

1. RETRACT RELEASE circuit breaker. . . PULL

NOTE

Once this circuit breaker has been pulled, the following will be affected in the manner indicated:

   a. Power will be removed from the landing gear solenoid.

   b. Landing gear solenoid may extend.

   c. Oil cooler doors will close, and no longer function.

   d. The angle-of-attack indexer and approach lights will be inoperative.

   e. Tail skag may not be in proper sequence with landing gear.

   f. Autopilot will be inoperative.

 *g. Antiskid will be inoperative.

2. If any of the above items are required for landing, reset RETRACT RELEASE circuit breaker just prior to landing.

---

*Aircraft BuNo. 138904, 138906-138937, 138954-138962, 135408-135444

HOT BLEED AIR LEAKS

NOTE

● Hot air leaks are usually indicated by progressive deterioration of electrical and communications system, i.e., loss of ICS and/or radios, popped circuit breakers, erratic engine instruments indications, rising ATM temperature, fire warning light and/or overtemp indicator lights coming on, etc.

● Simultaneous loss of both ATM's indicates probable catastrophic failure of the bleed air ducting. Place bleed air switches ALL OFF, investigate, and prepare for:

   a. VFR . . . . No boost landing

   b. IFR . . . . To abandon aircraft

● The reduction in pressure and temperature within the hot air system is significant with a reduction in power.

Wing Fire or Hot Bleed Air Leak
(Overtemp indicator light on)

1. Appropriate bleed air switch . . . . OFF

2. Wing lights . . . . OFF

3. Wing tanks . . . . PURGE
(DUMP VALVE OFF)

4. If fire or light persists and above single-engine performance speed:

   a. Throttle . . . . OFF

   b. Master engine switch . . . . OFF

   c. If fire persists, bail out or land immediately using short field arresting gear, if available.

Bleed Air Rotary Shutoff Switch

FIRE WARNING LIGHT (WING) LH

1. Bleed air shutoff . . . . LH CLOSE

FIRE WARNING LIGHT (WING) RH

1. Bleed air shutoff . . . . RH CLOSE

2. If light goes off:

   a. Bleed air shutoff . . . . . . AIR COND OPEN

   b. If light stays out . . . . . . LAND AS SOON AS PRACTICABLE

3. If light comes on again:

   a. Bleed air shutoff . . . . . . RH CLOSE, LAND AS SOON AS PRACTICABLE

Bleed Air Toggle Shutoff Switches

FIRE WARNING LIGHT(S) (wing(s) and/or air cond)

1. Appropriate switch(es) . . . . OFF

ATM Compartment Fire or Hot Bleed Air Leaks

1. Throttles . . . . RETARD TO MINIMUM REQUIRED FOR SAFE FLIGHT

2. All hatches . . . . KEEP CLOSED

3. Prepare for bailout or immediate landing.

4. If temperature rise is slow and below 200°C:

   a. No. 2 ac generator . . . . . . OFF (BUS TIE AUTO)

   b. No. 2 ATM. . . . . OFF

5. If no noticeable drop in ATM compartment/ temperature:

   a. No. 2 ATM. . . . . ON

   b. No. 2 ac generator . . . . . . ON (BUS TIE OPEN)

6. Bus tie . . . . AUTO

   a. No. 1 ac generator . . . . . . OFF

   b. No. 1 ATM. . . . . OFF

7. If temperature rise is stopped or controlled after the securing of an ATM, land as soon as possible, leaving the upper hatch closed until on short final.

8. If temperature rise is rapid:

   a. Bleed air shutoff switch(es) . . . . ALL OFF

   b. If temperature rise still cannot be controlled . . . . BAIL OUT

ATM temperature of 230°C is dangerously close to the auto ignition point of hydraulic fluid. ATM compartment temperature above 100°C and rising rapidly, is an emergency situation, which may, at the discretion of the pilot, necessitate abandonment of the aircraft. If bailout is necessary, the engines shall be secured before evacuation.

Air-Conditioning/Upper Bomb Bay Hot Bleed Air Leaks (Light On)

1. AIR-COND bleed air switch . . . . OFF

2. If light goes off, investigate. If light persists, handle as a bomb bay/companionway hot bleed air leak.

Bomb Bay/Companionway Fires or Hot Bleed Air Leaks

1. Throttles . . . . RETARD TO MINIMUM REQUIRED FOR SAFE FLIGHT

2. Use bleed air shutoff switches . . . . AS NECESSARY

3. All hatches . . . . KEEP CLOSED

4. If controllable, land immediately using short field arresting gear, if available.

   a. On short final, upper hatch . . . . . . OPEN PNEUMATICALLY

5. If uncontrollable. . . . . BAIL OUT, USING UPPER HATCH

Air-Conditioning Turbine Failure

If the air-conditioning unit cooling turbine fails, the cabin air temperature may become excessively high, and operation of the MAN COLD position of the

C'PIT TEMP knob will be ineffective. In this event, place the C'PIT TEMP knob in the OFF position.

WARNING

Placing the C'PIT TEMP knob in the OFF position depressurizes the cockpit. Aircraft flight altitude should be reduced to one which will assure crew safety and comfort and to avoid possible harmful effects of decompression. The pilot shall ensure that all crewmembers are wearing oxygen masks prior to depressurizing.

Refer to Air Conditioning and Pressurization System, Section I, part 2 for other malfunctions.

Smoke and Fume Elimination

Smoke and fumes may be eliminated from the cockpit area by turning the C'PIT TEMP knob on the pilot's left-hand console to OFF. This will depressurize the cockpit and ventilate the cockpit area with ambient air. Except as a last resort, the upper hatch, escape chute or bomb bay doors shall not be opened for the purpose of smoke elimination. Refer to Air Conditioning and Pressurization, Section I, part 2, for additional system description and operating procedures.

WARNING

When smoke or gases are present or suspected, turn all oxygen regulators immediately to 100% OXYGEN regardless of altitude. Do not switch back to NORMAL OXYGEN until the danger is past or the flight completed. The AIR COND and C'PIT TEMP system shall not be turned OFF at altitudes in excess of 43,000 feet because of the oxygen regulator limitations.

UTILITY HYDRAULIC SYSTEM FAILURE

Shore-Based Considerations

Failure of the utility hydraulic system results in the loss of speedbrakes, nosewheel steering, JATO jettison, wing fold, tail bumper and ability to raise the landing gear and arresting hook. Utility system failure requires the use of the emergency hydraulic pump to actuate bomb bay doors and wheel brakes. Wing flaps and landing gear can be extended pneumatically using procedures listed below, but extra time is required for actuation. When utility hydraulic system failure requires the use of the pneumatic systems, extend and check the flaps down before extending the landing gear.

No particular difficulty will be encountered, except that the approach will be made without speedbrakes. The aircraft will have to be towed from the landing area with the arresting hook tied up and the wings spread. Insert landing gear ground safety pins prior to moving the aircraft. A landing on a runway shall always be made into the short field arresting gear, if available. An LSO should assist the pilot in picking up the short field gear. The pilot shall be prepared for a waveoff if the arresting gear is missed. Crosswinds and/or braking problems may make directional control difficult on rollout if a short field arrestment is not made.

The ANTISKID shall be off and EMERGENCY HYDRAULIC PUMP shall be ON prior to touchdown. In the event of ineffective braking, continue with wheelbrake emergency operation.

Shipboard Considerations

If divert field is beyond dirty bingo range, the decision to divert shall precede lowering landing gear.

No particular difficulty will be encountered except that the approach will be made without speedbrakes. The hook will have to be tied up and landing gear ground safety pins inserted before aircraft is moved from the landing area with the wings spread.

1. Emergency hydraulic pump
(After Arrestment)......................ON

- Prior to entering the bomb bay/companionway in flight, descend to 10,000 feet or below, except when operational requirements dictate otherwise, and pull the bomb bay door circuit breaker.

- A parachute shall be worn by any crewmember entering the bomb bay while the aircraft is in flight. When a crewmember is in the bomb bay or companionway, he must be kept in sight and/or be required to make a voice check every minute. Oxygen must be used above 10,000 feet MSL during the day or 5000 feet MSL at night.

Wing Flap Emergency Operation

WARNING

Prior to entering the companionway to activate any hydraulic override handle during ground operation, ensure that landing gear safety pins are installed. The control slide in all Weston 10280 hydraulic control valves remains in the last position selected when sufficient hydraulic pressure is available to actuate the slide. However, the control slide will not necessarily correspond to the last position selected either manually or electrically when hydraulic pressure is removed. If hydraulic pressure is reapplied prior to electrical power, the subsystem may be actuated in a position opposite to the position indicated by the electrical control, thus endangering personnel and equipment.

EMERGENCY WING FLAP EXTENSION

1. Slow aircraft . . . . 200 KIAS OR LESS

2. Flap handle . . . . RECYCLE DOWN

3. Hydraulic solenoid circuit breaker . . . . CHECK IN

4. With hydraulic pressure indicated:

   Wing flap override . . . . PUSH TO LOWER

5. Without hydraulic pressure indicated:

   Wing flaps emergency air bottle control handle . . . . DOWN

CAUTION

- Following extension of the flaps by emergency air pressure, do not actuate the normal flaps control level until the emergency flaps level is first returned to the UP position, thus exhausting air out of the lines.

- Failure to observe this sequence can cause a rupture of the utility hydraulic system reservoir.

NOTE

Flaps may begin to blowback to trail position 10 to 15 minutes after being blown down pneumatically.

EMERGENCY WING FLAP RETRACTION

NOTE

Whenever the emergency flap handle is returned to the UP position, the flaps may immediately become faired.

1. Hydraulic failure after normal (hydraulic) extension:

   a. Wing flaps emergency air bottle control handle . . . . . . DOWN

   b. Wait . . . . 3 SECONDS

   c. Wing flaps emergency air bottle control handle . . . . . . UP

   d. Flap handle . . . . UP

NOTE

Providing the initial operation was accomplished with a full (3000 psi) air bottle, one more emergency extension is possible.

2. With hydraulic failure prior to pneumatic extension:

   a. Wing flap emergency air bottle control . . . . HANDLE UP

   b. Flap handle . . . . UP

NOTE

Subsequent emergency air pressure extension of the flaps is possible, but may result in only partial extension, since the pressure remaining in the flaps emergency pneumatic bottle may not be great enough to overpower the air load against the flaps. It is recommended that the flaps not be extended by the emergency system until a successful landing is assured.

Landing Gear Emergency Operation

1. Slow to minimum safe airspeed.

2. Landing gear handle . . . . RECYCLE DOWN

3. Hydraulic solenoid circuit breaker . . . . CHECK IN

4. With utility hydraulic pressure indicated:

   a. Landing gear hydraulic override . . . . PUSH TO EXTEND

NOTE

If the solenoid returns to the retracted position, disconnect the cannon plug at the valve. (Essential only if the landing gear returns to up when the landing gear override is released.)

5. Without utility hydraulic pressure indicated:

   a. Landing gear handle . . . . DOWN

Changed 1 June 1969

Section V NAVAIR 01-40ATA-1

b. Landing gear emergency
air bottle control handle . . . . DOWN

> **CAUTION**
>
> - Recycling of the landing gear system shall not be attempted when in-flight difficulties involving slow extension of the gear occurs. When gear is down and indicating locked, the gear shall remain down and a landing accomplished.
>
> - Following emergency gear extension, do not place the landing gear handle in the UP position prior to bleeding air from the system. Failure to observe this sequence can cause rupture of the utility system hydraulic reservoir.

NOTE

In the event a main gear is down but unlocked, yawing, banking, positive g's or slowing the aircraft to buffet airspeed may help lock the gear down.

Hook Emergency Operation

1. Hook handle . . . . RECYCLE
 DOWN

2. Hook hydraulic override. . . . . . . PUSH

NOTE

If the solenoid returns to the retracted position, disconnect the cannon plug at the valve. (Essential only if the hook returns to UP when the override button is released.)

3. Bomb bay hook latch
control cable . . . . PULL

Speedbrake Emergency Operation

1. Utility hydraulic pressure must be available.

2. Speedbrake control switch . . . . . . OPEN/
 CLOSED

3. Hydraulic speedbrake
override . . . . PUSH TO
 EXTEND/
 PULL TO
 CLOSE

Wheel Brake Operation After Utility Failure

(No field arresting gear available.)

1. ANTISKID . . . . OFF

2. Emergency hydraulic pump
on short final . . . . ON

3. Make normal landing

4. Drag chute . . . . DEPLOY

5. Emergency airbrake as last
resort . . . . PULL

6. If emergency airbrake handle has been pulled, the aircraft must be stopped with the pneumatic system.

7. Insert landing gear pins and have aircraft towed to the line.

ATM Malfunction/Failure

1. Affected ac generator control switch . . . OFF

2. Recycle affected ATM control switch . . ON

3. If the ATM restarts, bus tie open,
affected ac generator . . . . ON

4. If the ATM does not restart,
ATM switch . . . . OFF

5. Continue flight or land, as determined by existing conditions.

6. If the No. 2 ATM cannot be restarted, pull the RUD AND ELEV BOOST disconnect prior to commencing an approach. (Refer to **NO BOOST FIELD LANDINGS.**)

NOTE

- The spoilers and one half of the aileron boost will be inoperative, if the No. 1 ATM cannot be restarted and the MAXIMUM CROSSWIND COMPONENT is reduced to 7 knots.

- Rudder and elevator boost will be inoperative if the No. 2 ATM cannot be restarted.

DOUBLE ATM MALFUNCTION/FAILURE

Double ATM failure will result in complete electrical, utility hydraulic, and flight control boost system failure. Airspeed should be limited to less than 250 KIAS.

Changed 15 July 1970

If double ATM failure occurs without loss of engine power, it is likely that the hot air ducting has failed between the bleed air check valves and the ATM's, with a resultant major hot air leak. If this condition is substantiated by high ATM compartment temperature gage indications, warning light, or by inspection, refer to emergency procedures listed under hot bleed air leaks. In addition:

1. Bleed air shutoff switch(es) . . . . ALL OFF

2. Battery power . . . . CONSERVE

3. Ac generator switches. . . . . . OFF

4. Cg/gravity transfer valve . . . . AS REQUIRED

   a. Manually control fuel distribution, using battery power, to maintain aircraft trim.

NOTE

Aft tank fuel quantity can be maintained between 3000 and 4000 pounds by monitoring fuel low level warning lights.

   b. Investigate and if ducting permits, bleed air shutoff switches . . . . ALL OPEN OR AS SELECTED

5. ATM(s) . . . . RESTART

6. When necessary to maintain control of the aircraft and/or the ATM(s) cannot be restarted . . . PULL AILERON/RUDDER AND/OR ELEVATOR BOOST DISCONNECT PRIOR TO COMMENCING AN APPROACH (REFER TO BOOST-OFF FLIGHT)

7. If VFR, continue flight and land as soon as possible.

8. If IFR, bail out before an unusual attitude occurs.

NOTE

If ATM's were lost due to negative g condition, a restart can be attempted after a crewmember repositions the servo piston rod. Refer to figure 1-33 for recocking procedures.

ELECTRICAL SYSTEM MALFUNCTION/FAILURE

NOTE

If overvoltage is the suspected cause of generator failure, one attempt to restore the generator may be made with the applicable dc overvoltage relay switch located on the companionway circuit breaker panel.

DC Generator Malfunction/Failure

SINGLE DC GENERATOR MALFUNCTION/FAILURE

1. Apply dc load or cycle operable generator to check for nonparallel.

2. If load not sustained applicable generator switch control . . . . OFF

NOTE

Safe flight is possible since one generator is more than adequate.

DUAL DC GENERATOR MALFUNCTION/FAILURE

1. Dc generator switches . . . . . RECYCLE

2. If generators do not sustain load dc generator switches . . . . . OFF

3. Nonessential electrical equipment . . . . SECURE

4. Battery switch . . . . EMERGENCY AS REQUIRED

NOTE

With landing gear handle down, leave switch in battery.

5. Radio transmissions . . . . . KEEP TO MINIMUM

AC Generator Malfunction/Failure

SINGLE AC GENERATOR MALFUNCTION/FAILURE

1. Affected generator control switch . . . . OFF

2. If VFR, attempt restart

   a. Bus tie . . . . OPEN

Changed 15 July 1970

Section V NAVAIR 01-40ATA-1

3. If the generator does not start

   a. Generator switch . . . . . OFF

   b. Bus tie . . . . AUTO

4. If DECM equipment is required, reduce other ac load. (For example, ac trim).

5. Continue flight or land as determined by existing conditions.

DUAL AC GENERATOR MALFUNCTION/FAILURE

1. Bus tie . . . . OPEN

2. Secure all unnecessary electrical equipment.

3. Both ac generator switches . . . . RECYCLE

4. If one or both regained, bus tie . . . . AUTO

5. If neither regained, continue VFR flight . . . . LAND AS SOON AS POSSIBLE

6. Gravity transfer/cg valve . . . . AS REQUIRED (ELECTRICALLY CONTROLLED WITH DC POWER)

CAUTION

Ensure that electrical fuel trim switch remains in same position as that selected with manual fuel time control handle to prevent continuous cycling of cg valve motor.

7. If IFR and control of the aircraft is in question . . . . . . BAIL OUT

Complete AC and DC Generator Failure

1. VFR . . . . LAND AS SOON AS POSSIBLE

2. Battery switch . . . . EMER

3. Manual fuel trim control handle. . . . . AS REQUIRED TO MANUALLY CONTROL FUEL DISTRIBUTION

4. If IFR and control of the aircraft is in question . . . . . . BAIL OUT

Complete AC And DC Failure Including Battery

1. If VFR . . . . LAND AS SOON AS POSSIBLE

NOTE

Manual control of fuselage fuel is possible, but no means exist to monitor fuel distribution.

2. Manual fuel trim control handle . . . . MANUAL OPEN

3. If IFR and control of aircraft is in question . . . . BAIL OUT

Runaway Trim Procedure

If horizontal stabilizer trim becomes uncontrollable:

1. Trim gangbar . . . . OFF

2. Attempt to reestablish trim control using dc system first. If trim is regained with dc control, do not reengage ac trim. If dc trim system is causing the difficulty, attempt to retrim with ac trim.

3. If normal trim conditions can be regained, proceed in normal flight and land as soon as practicable.

4. If malfunction continues and aircraft can be controlled, perform simulated approaches at altitude to determine if aircraft can be safely landed.

5. Carrier landings in out-of-trim conditions shall not be attempted if a divert field is available.

6. If trim failure occurs during takeoff or in approach configuration, pilot can control aircraft with manual controls if runaway is nosedown; however, control pressures are very great if runaway trim is full noseup. A clean configuration will allow greater bank angles while controlling nose attitude and should be considered.

7. If trim cannot be regained, an intentional out-of-cg fuel condition may help to balance stabilizer trim condition. Approximate fuel distribution can be determined, for noseup out-of-trim condition, by using catapult trim chart in reverse.

5-12 Changed 15 July 1970

Oil System Malfunction/Failure

1. Consider the possibility that a malfunction of the gage, transmitter or circuitry may be causing the malfunction.

2. If low oil pressure is indicated and confirmed by rising oil temperature or by visual inspection, shut down the affected engine and treat as a single engine failure.

3. Land as soon as practicable.

NOTE

With progressive engine oil loss, oil temperature will rise until all oil is lost, at which time oil temperature readings will decrease.

Fuel System Malfunctions/Failure

FUEL BOOST FAILURE WITH CONTINUED ENGINE OPERATION

If the engine continues to operate normally, loss of fuel boost pressure can generally be regarded as boost pump failure, but may also be caused by a faulty indicator. Turn the FUEL CROSSFEED switch to OPEN. If fuel pressure is returned to NORM (12 to 30 psi is acceptable), the pressure loss is due to pump failure.

NOTE

- Continue necessary flight, since engine performance is not affected by the loss of one boost pump.

- The FUEL CROSSFEED switch should remain in the OPEN position for the remainder of the flight as long as the fuel boost pressure is indicated. If complete loss of fuel boost pressure occurs, indicating failure of both boost pumps, return the FUEL CROSSFEED switch to CLOSED to obtain the best fuel flow. The engine fuel pumps can supply fuel to the engines through the failed boost pumps if flight altitude is not extremely high. Contractor tests indicate that engine performance with boost pumps inoperative is satisfactory to altitudes above 30,000 feet. As critical altitudes are reached, engine symptoms are erratic fuel flow, RPM fluctuations, and compressor stalls. Rapid power changes and maneuvering flight increase the symptom severity. If these symptoms are encountered, descend to an altitude at which steady-state operation can be maintained.

FUEL BOOST FAILURE WITH ACCOMPANIED ENGINE FLAMEOUT

Engine flameout with simultaneous loss of fuel boost pressure indication can be due to fuel boost pump failure or a fuel line rupture. However, fuel boost pump failure should not cause engine flameout at cruise power since the engine fuel pump will continue to draw fuel from the tank by suction, except at extremely high altitudes. If a ruptured fuel line is suspected, a check may be made for this condition before attempting an air start of the flamed out engine. Proceed as follows:

1. Throttle (inoperative engine) . . . . OFF

2. MASTER ENGINE switch (inoperative engine). . . . . OFF

3. Fuel CROSSFEED switch. . . . . OPEN

WARNING

Although both fuel boost windows should read NORM after this procedure, it is imperative in this operation that the fuel boost indicator of the operative engine be observed closely since there is the possibility of fuel starvation on this engine.

NOTE

Upon placing the fuel CROSSFEED switch at OPEN, a momentary drop in fuel boost pressure may be expected. If the boost pressure of the operative engine does not return to NORM almost immediately, such a loss of pressure indicates a leaking or severed fuel line between the crossfeed valve and the pylon shutoff valve of the inoperative engine. A second attempt may be made to make sure the pressure drop was not due to the filling of an empty fuel line.

4. Fuel boost (inoperative engine) check . . . . NORM or OUT

5. If OUT, immediately return fuel CROSSFEED switch to . . . . CLOSED

6. If the fuel boost indicators of both engines stabilize at NORM after step 4, place MASTER ENGINE switch of inoperative engine ON.

7. Fuel boost (inoperative engine) check . . . . NORM or OUT

8. If OUT, immediately return MASTER ENGINE switch to. OFF

Section V NAVAIR 01-40ATA-1

NOTE

Upon placing the MASTER ENGINE switch ON, a momentary drop in pressure may again occur if the fuel line between the pylon shutoff valve and the engine is empty. If the fuel boost indicators fluctuate or remain at OUT, a leaking or severed fuel line is indicated.

9. If the fuel boost indicators of both engines stabilize at NORM after step 7, an air start of the inoperative engine may be attempted.

WARNING

If fuel boost pressure indicates OUT/ZERO and engine operation is regained by means of crossfeed, circuit breakers for affected fuel boost pump shall be secured. If engine operation is not regained and fuel boost on affected engine indicates OUT/ZERO, return crossfeed switch to closed and master engine switch to OFF. Failure to perform this operation can lead to loss of as much as 15,000 pounds of fuel per hour from ruptured fuel line.

1. If normal pressure (12 to 30 psi) is not indicated for both engines, return switch to original position.

2. Check fuel system (dc) and boost pump (ac) circuit breakers . . . . IN

Fuel Vent Icing

While operating in moderate to heavy icing conditions, the pilot should be alert for fuel vent icing. When the fuel vent is obstructed the aft fuel cell will collapse as fuel is pumped to the engine. Symptoms of fuel vent icing may be:

1. Abnormal NOSEUP trim although cg indications are normal.

2. Total fuel quantity/total readouts greater than predicted fuel consumed over a specific period.

3. Loss or erroneous aft fuel quantity indications. Recommended action:

    a. Cg valve . . . . OPEN

    b. Obtain a warmer flight level

    c. Maintain nose high attitude

    d. Land as soon as possible

LANDING EMERGENCIES

NOTE

In instances where it is indicated that the proper procedure is: Land, using short field arresting gear, if available, it is intended that the pilot should exercise his judgment, and land as soon as conditions permit, on the end of the runway or as directed by the LSO. Utilize the first available arrestment gear that is compatible with aircraft and arresting gear limitations.

Single-Engine Landings

- A successful single-engine waveoff at slow airspeeds with landing gear and full flaps down is marginal and should not be attempted unless absolutely necessary.

- A successful single-engine waveoff with landing gear and half flaps down is possible up to maximum gross landing weights provided the airspeed is not below minimum single engine control speed.

- Immediate retraction of the landing gear will reduce drag and increase the margin of safety during a waveoff.

SINGLE-ENGINE FIELD LANDINGS

Time, weather, and engine operating conditions permitting, jettison or consume fuel until reaching a gross weight of 50,000 pounds or less. If possible, plan a straight-in mirror or GCA approach (figure 5-1). Consider a short field arrestment, if available.

NOTE

When poor field conditions exist, such as wet runway, high crosswinds, or short runway (6000 feet or less) a short field arrestment is recommended.

NOTE

When gross weights exceed 50,000 pounds and/or landing on a short runway, consider extension of full flaps prior to glide slope to reduce landing speed or arresting gear engagement speed.

5-14 Changed 15 July 1970

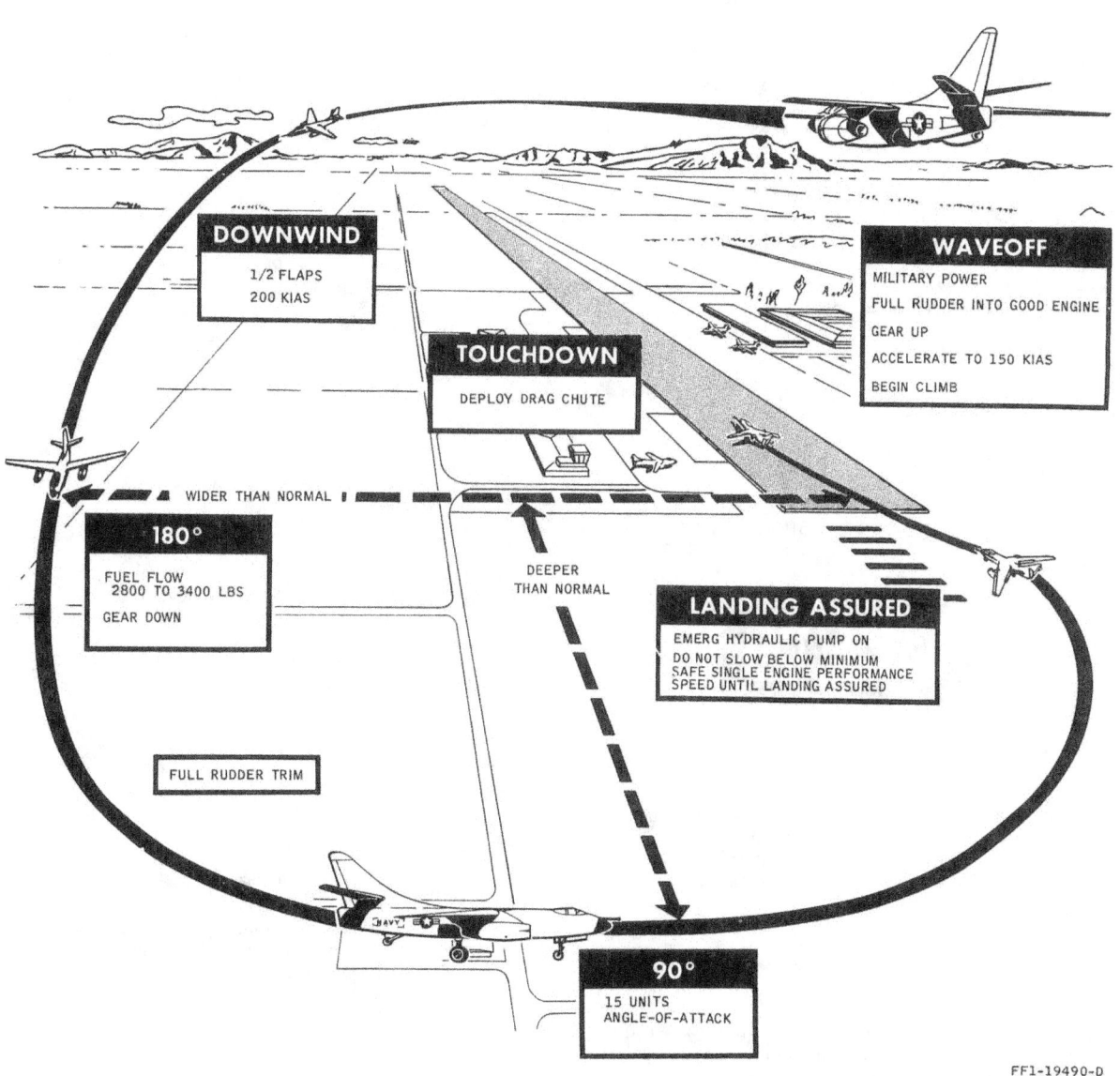

Figure 5-1. Single-Engine Landing and Waveoff Pattern (Typical)

Proceed as follows:

1. Slow aircraft . . . . . . 200 KIAS OR LESS

2. Half flaps . . . . DOWN

3. Landing gear . . . . . . DOWN (PRIOR TO GLIDE SLOPE OR AT 180-DEGREES POSITION)

4. Hook . . . . DOWN (FOR SHORT FIELD ARRESTMENT)

5. Speedbrakes . . . . . . IN (MAY BE ACTUATED OUT FOR SHORT PERIODS TO CONTROL AIRSPEED)

6. Fly angle of attack . . 15 UNITS

7. Do not slow below minimum single-engine performance speed until landing is assured.

8. Emergency hydraulic pump . . . . ON

9. After touchdown

   a. Throttle . . . . RETARD SLOWLY TO IDLE

   b. Drag chute . . . . . . DEPLOY, IF NOT SHORT FIELD ARRESTED

WARNING

- Be alert for a swerve on reduction of power.

- Braking and/or control problems may occur if ATM rpm decreases due to low power settings. A very slight power increase is usually sufficient to restore normal ATM operation.

SINGLE-ENGINE CARRIER LANDINGS

Use the procedures listed under single-engine field landings, with the exception of Item 9. Maximum gross weights, engagement speeds and wind over deck (WOD) must be observed.

No-Boost Field Landings

Time and weather permitting, jettison or consume fuel until reaching a gross weight of 50,000 pounds or less. Plan a straight-in approach to a short field arrestment, if available. Landing should be made in minimum crosswind conditions to reduce lateral control oscillations.

CAUTION

Directional control with loss of spoilers is marginal when crosswind component exceeds 7 knots. If short field arrestment is not available, divert to a suitable field. If neither short field arrestment nor suitable divert field are available, a no-flap landing is recommended.

Proceed as follows:

1. Attempt to regain boost, pull aileron and/or rudder/elevator boost release handles only if control prior to commencing an approach.

2. Slow aircraft . . . . 200 KIAS OR LESS

3. Wing flaps . . . . DOWN

4. Landing gear . . . . DOWN

5. Hook (for short field arrestment) . . . . DOWN

6. Speedbrakes . . . . OUT, IF POSSIBLE

7. Fly angle of attack/airspeed . . . . 15 UNITS OR NORMAL APPROACH

8. Expect high control pressures when damping lateral directional oscillations during final approach.

9. Drag chute . . . . DEPLOY IF NOT SHORT FIELD ARRESTED

NOTE

- If no flap approach is made, use above listed procedure except approach should be 17 to 20.5 units angle of attack or 20 KIAS above normal. Deploy drag chute after landing and make a long field arrestment.

- If stabilizer actuator should fail with the aircraft trimmed for nosedown attitude, consider extension of wing flaps, and speedbrakes if possible, to reduce approach speed and amount of back pressure required. A high landing speed may be required to lower the pull force to a manageable amount. Utilize manual control of fuel distribution to create a more aft cg.

No-Boost Carrier Landing

Carrier landings shall not be attempted when both aileron and rudder/elevator boosts are not available. If landing with only rudder/elevator boost inoperative, be extremely cautious. Loss of damping and delayed elevator response to yoke movement increase possibility of overcontrolling nose position in close and/or during bolter/waveoff.

No-Flap Field Landings

Weather and fuel permitting, practice no-flaps flight in landing configuration at altitude. Jettison and/or consume fuel until reaching a gross weight of 50,000 pounds or less. Plan a straight-in approach, on the longest suitable runway, to a long field arrestment. Proceed as follows:

1. Slow aircraft . . . . 180 KIAS OR LESS

2. Landing gear . . . . DOWN

3. Speedbrakes . . . . OUT

4. Fly angle of
attack/airspeed . . . . 17 TO 20.5 UNITS OR 20 KIAS ABOVE NORMAL

5. After touchdown

   a. Drag chute . . . . DEPLOY

   b. Antiskid braking . . . . . . MAXIMUM

   c. Hook . . . . DOWN, PRIOR TO LONG FIELD ARRESTING GEAR

No-Flap Carrier Landings

No-flap carrier landings shall not be attempted.

No-Slat Field Landings

Partial or no extension of the wing slats may be experienced during the approach due to icing, binding, etc.

NOTE

The nomenclature for slat location is outer wing outboard, outer wing inboard, and center wing outboard. Division point between outer wing and center wing is the wing fold.

If center wing slats fail to extend, a mild pitchup and slight buffet will be experienced, but controllability will be only slightly affected. Normal approach speed should be increased about 10 KIAS to remain above the buffet or pitchup zone.

If the outer wing outboard and/ outer wing inboard slats fail to extend, a severe pitchup prior to buffet warning will be encountered. Increased drag and loss of airspeed develop quite rapidly, and controllability will be extremely marginal. If any outer wing slats fail to extend, normal approach speed should be increased about 35 KIAS. This should correspond to an angle of attack of approximately 4 units.

If both center wing and outer wing slats fail to extend, aircraft characteristics will be essentially the same as with the outer wing slats only in the retracted position. If it is suspected that the slats are sticking or will not fully extend, proceed as follows:

1. Continue to destination if approach can be executed VFR. If not, divert to suitable VFR alternate. If neither, then selection of the field should be made consistent with weather, runway length, arresting gear, etc.

2. Avoid abrupt transition to approach configuration.

3. Monitor wing slats as much as possible during the approach, particularly when transitioning to landing configuration.

4. Do not slow below normal approach speed plus 35 KIAS or 4 units angle of attack unless it can be determined that all outer wing slats are beginning to extend. If outer wing slats fail to extend, slats function may be checked by pulsing elevators before reducing airspeed. A moderate momentary back pressure should cause slats to extend far enough for a visual check. If slats still do not extend, continue approach (at 160 KIAS i.e. 50,000 pounds gross

Changed 1 June 1969

5-17

weight). Continued flight in temperatures above 32°F should free frozen slats.

> **CAUTION**
>
> Approach speeds and angles of attack are for clean airfoils; thus, if wing ice is present, buffet and pitchup will be experienced at appreciably higher airspeeds and lower angles of attack.

5. Be alert for porpoise on touchdown. If practicable, make touch-and-go landings. Icing may break on touchdown, allowing normal landing on next attempt.

6. If unable to free slats during touch-and-go landings, a short field arrestment should be made if available.

No-Slat Carrier Landings

Arrested carrier landings will not be attempted when a divert field is available, if outer wing slats fail to extend. If possible, touch-and-go landings should be made in an attempt to free slats. If this fails, divert to suitable field. If divert field is not available, decision to attempt barricade engagement will depend on the wind over deck and limitations on specific ship's barricade equipment. A successful barricade engagement in this condition is considered extremely marginal and decision to attempt it or bailout will rest with the pilot. Limited experience (shore-based) has been used to develop above procedures and has been projected for carrier procedures.

Wheel Brakes Emergency

If wheelbrake failure occurs on landing, with throttles at IDLE and the drag chute deployed, proceed as follows:

1. Hook . . . . DOWN

2. Emergency hydraulic pump . . . . ON IF BRAKING INEFFECTIVE

3. Remove pedal pressure and turn antiskid . . . . OFF IF BRAKING STILL INEFFECTIVE

4. Actuate airbrakes as last resort.

Bailout/Ditching Doctrine

UNCONTROLLED FLIGHT

If the aircraft becomes uncontrollable, it shall be abandoned prior to reaching 10,000 feet AGL if possible.

DUAL-ENGINE FAILURE LOW ALTITUDE/LOW AIRSPEED

If dual-engine failure occurs at or below 3000 feet above the terrain and below 250 KIAS the crew will immediately abandon the aircraft. After dual flameout, the rapid rate of descent coupled with engine acceleration lag, makes a successful recovery improbable.

LOW LEVEL TAKEOFF AND LANDING

Airspeed should be traded for altitude whenever possible. If a safe bailout altitude cannot be reached, the standard ditching procedures should be followed.

NOTE

Safe bailout altitude is 1000 feet above the terrain with the aircraft in a level or climbing attitude. If below, 1000 feet and unable to climb, the aircraft should be ditched.

Bailout/Ditching Procedures

CONTROLLED BAILOUT

PRIMARY AND SECONDARY ESCAPE ROUTES

Reduce airspeed to lowest possible speed not to exceed 250 KIAS (220 KIAS with hook extended). Head aircraft to crash clear of the force or any populated area. If situation and time permit, obtain an altitude between 8000 and 10,000 feet AGL. Crewmembers shall bail out in the following order:

Fourth crewmember (when aboard), plane captain, navigator and pilot. In a controlled bailout, the command "PREPARE TO BAILOUT" shall be issued by the pilot.

1. The pilot shall: (Prior to issuing the command "BAIL OUT").

    a. Battery switch . . . . . EMERGENCY

    b. Transmit . . . . ON APPROPRIATE FREQUENCIES

        (1) Mayday, Mayday, Mayday

        (2) Identification

        (3) Position

        (4) Situation

        (5) Intentions

    c. Secure . . . . COCKPIT PRESSURIZATION

    d. Actuate . . . . EMERGENCY ESCAPE CHUTE HANDLE

2. The navigator shall:

    a. Select IFF . . . . EMERGENCY

    b. Visually check . . . . . BOMB BAY DOORS/ RAKE CLOSED, IF POSSIBLE

    c. Guillotine drogue . . . IF EXTENDED

    d. Position seat . . . . . . FULL AFT

    e. If directed by the pilot:

        (1) Transmit . . . . MAYDAY, MAYDAY, MAYDAY

        (2) Actuate . . . . EMERGENCY ESCAPE CHUTE HANDLE

3. The plane captain shall:

    a. Turn on . . . . COCKPIT WHITE DOME LIGHT (NIGHT)

    b. If directed by pilot. . . ACTUATE EMERGENCY EXIT T-HANDLE

4. Each crewmember shall check the following:

    a. Helmet . . . . TIGHT

    b. Bailout bottle . . . . . . CONNECTED

    c. Parachute . . . . HARNESS TIGHT

    d. Baro-release . . . . . . HOOKED UP

5. At the command "BAIL OUT" issued by the pilot, each crewmember shall:

    a. Actuate . . . . BAILOUT BOTTLE

    b. Disconnect . . . . . OXYGEN HOSE AND COMMUNICATION JACKS

    c. Release . . . . LAP BELT

    d. Lower . . . . HELMET VISOR

    e. Bail out . . . . IN ORDER

6. Escape through escape chute should be made:

    a. Feet first facing aft

    b. Legs together

    c. Arms tight to the body

    d. Hands grasping parachute harness at the D RING

    e. Head turned to side

7. Prior to landing:

    a. Release lower left rocket jet fitting

    b. Attach pararaft to torso harness

    c. Inflate MK-3C

    d. Loosen oxygen mask

    e. Turn on strobe light

    f. Place hands on risers, ready to release parachute from torso harness.

ALTERNATE ESCAPE ROUTE

When necessary to use the upper escape hatch for bailout, reduce to lowest practicable airspeed not to exceed 250 KIAS. If situation and time permit,

Section V NAVAIR 01-40ATA-1

obtain an altitude between 8000 and 10,000 feet AGL. Crewmembers shall bail out in the following order:

Navigator, fourth crewmember, plane captain, and pilot.

WARNING

Procedures for the use of the upper hatch are predicated on a limited amount of empirical data and informed opinion. It is assumed that crewmember will exit as far to the right of centerline as possible.

1. The pilot shall: (Prior to issuing the command BAIL OUT)

    a. Battery switch ..... EMERGENCY

    b. Transmit .... ON APPROPRIATE FREQUENCIES

    (1) Mayday, Mayday, Mayday

    (2) Identification

    (3) Position

    (4) Situation

    (5) Intentions

    c. Secure .... COCKPIT PRESSURIZATION

    d. Flaps .... DOWN

    e. Upper escape hatch .. BLOW OPEN

    f. Place aircraft in gentle starboard turn if consistent with considerations for surrounding populated areas.

2. The navigator shall:

    a. Select IFF .... EMERGENCY

    b. Drogue (if extended) .. GUILLOTINE

    c. Seat .... FULL AFT

    d. If directed by pilot:

    (1) Transmit .... MAYDAY, MAYDAY, MAYDAY

3. The plane captain shall:

    a. Turn on .... COCKPIT WHITE DOME LIGHT (NIGHT)

    b. If directed by pilot, emergency escape hatch .... BLOW OPEN

4. Each crewmember shall check the following:

    a. Helmet .... TIGHT

    b. Bailout bottle ..... CONNECTED

    c. Parachute .... HARNESS TIGHT

    d. Baro-release lanyard .... HOOKED UP

5. At the command "BAIL OUT" issued by the pilot each crewmember shall:

    a. Actuate .... BAILOUT BOTTLE

    b. Disconnect .... OXYGEN HOSE AND COMMUNICATION JACKS

    c. Release .... LAP BELT

    d. Lower .... HELMET VISOR

    e. Bail out .... IN ORDER

6. Prior to landing:

    a. Release lower left rocket jet fitting

    b. Attach pararaft to torso harness

    c. Inflate MK-3C

    d. Loosen oxygen mask

    e. Turn on strobe light

    f. Place hands on risers, ready to release parachute from torso harness.

EMERGENCY BAILOUT

In an emergency situation requiring immediate bailout

1. The pilot shall:

    a. Actuate .... EMERGENCY ESCAPE CHUTE HANDLE (IF ABLE)

    b. Command .... "BAIL OUT – NOW"

2. The navigator shall:

   a. Select IFF . . . . EMERGENCY

   b. If directed by the pilot:

      (1) Actuate . . . . EMERGENCY ESCAPE CHUTE HANDLE

3. Each crewmember shall:

   a. Actuate . . . . BAILOUT BOTTLE

   b. Disconnect. . . . . . . OXYGEN HOSE AND COMMUNICATION JACKS

   c. Release. . . . . LAP BELT

   d. Check parachute . . . HARNESS TIGHT

   e. Bail out . . . . IN ORDER, WITHOUT FURTHER COMMAND FROM PILOT

4. If ICS is lost:

   a. Command "BAIL OUT — NOW" shall be given by pointing down escape chute or by using UHF/VHF if available.

CONTROLLED BAILOUT-ESCAPE ROUTES

1. Primary exit . . . . EMERGENCY LOWER ESCAPE CHUTE

   a. If emergency lower escape chute fails to open when actuated proceed as follows: (see figure 5-2.)

      (1) Upper escape hatch . . . . CLOSED

Do not open the upper escape hatch prior to manually opening the inner escape chute door since the resulting negative pressure will make manual opening extremely difficult.

      (2) Actuate . . . . INNER ESCAPE CHUTE DOOR LATCH RELEASE, EMERGENCY EXIT T-HANDLE

2. Secondary exit . . . . . . BOMB BAY (SEE FIGURE 5-3.)

   a. Inner escape chute . . RELEASE LATCH OPEN DOOR

   b. Bomb bay doors . . . OPEN

   c. Companionway safety door . . . . . . RELEASE LATCH OPEN DOOR

   d. Crawl through companionway

   e. Rollout of bomb bay head first

3. Alternate exit . . . . . . UPPER ESCAPE HATCH (SEE FIGURE 5-2.)

   a. Upper escape hatch . BLOW OPEN

   b. Bail out . . . . ALONG RIGHT SIDE OF FUSELAGE

WARNING

- If bomb bay doors and/or rake are open and cannot be closed, use secondary or alternate exit escape routes.

- Although the alternate exit has been used successfully, it should only be used in an extreme emergency.

EMERGENCY BAILOUT ESCAPE ROUTES

1. Primary exit . . . . EMERGENCY LOWER ESCAPE CHUTE

2. Alternate exit . . . . . . UPPER ESCAPE HATCH

   a. Use alternate exit if:

      (1) Emergency lower escape chute fails to open when actuated.

      (2) Companionway, ATM, or bomb bay fire exists.

      (3) Bomb bay doors and/or rake are open.

5-21

Section V NAVAIR 01-40ATA-1

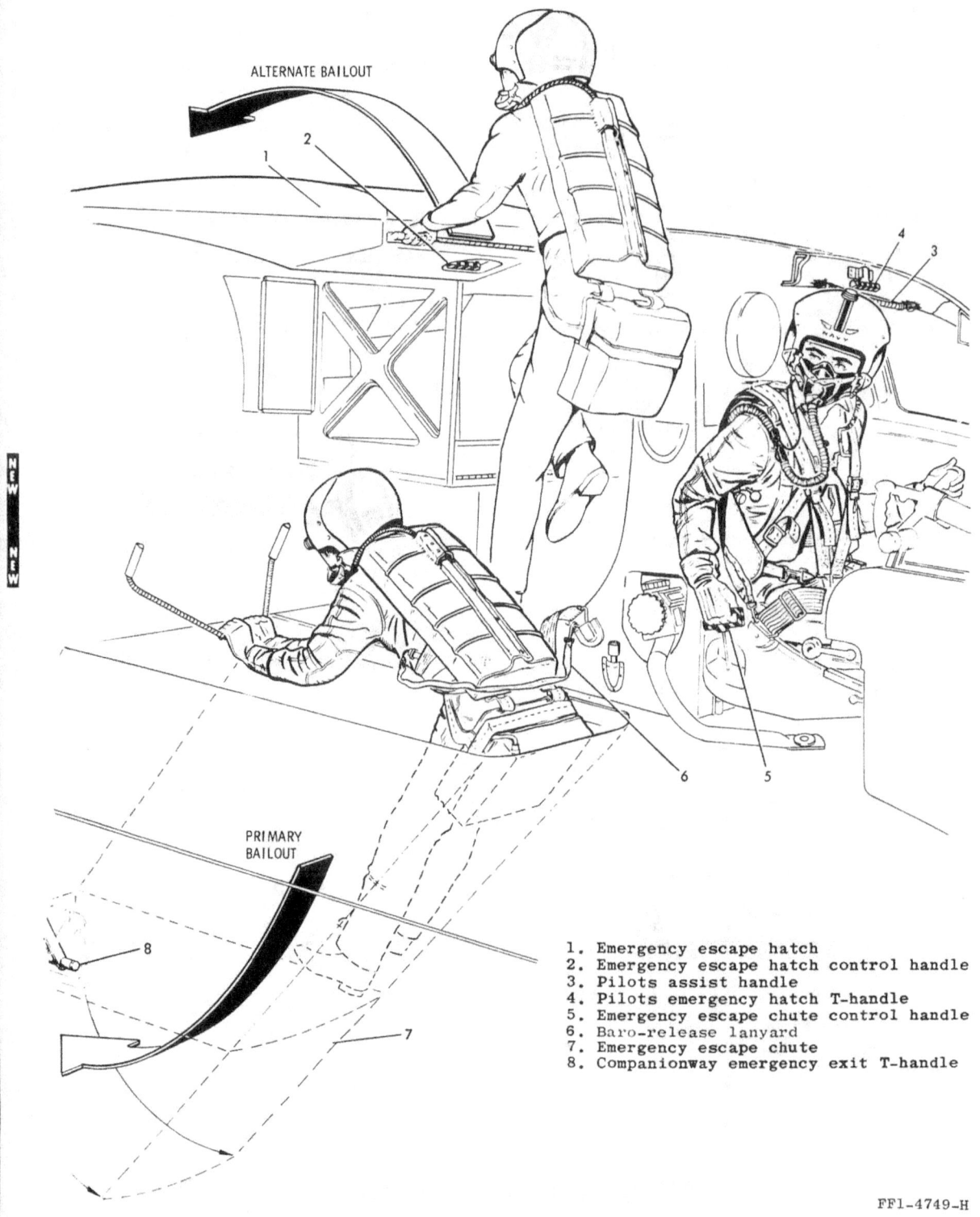

1. Emergency escape hatch
2. Emergency escape hatch control handle
3. Pilots assist handle
4. Pilots emergency hatch T-handle
5. Emergency escape chute control handle
6. Baro-release lanyard
7. Emergency escape chute
8. Companionway emergency exit T-handle

Figure 5-2. Emergency Exits

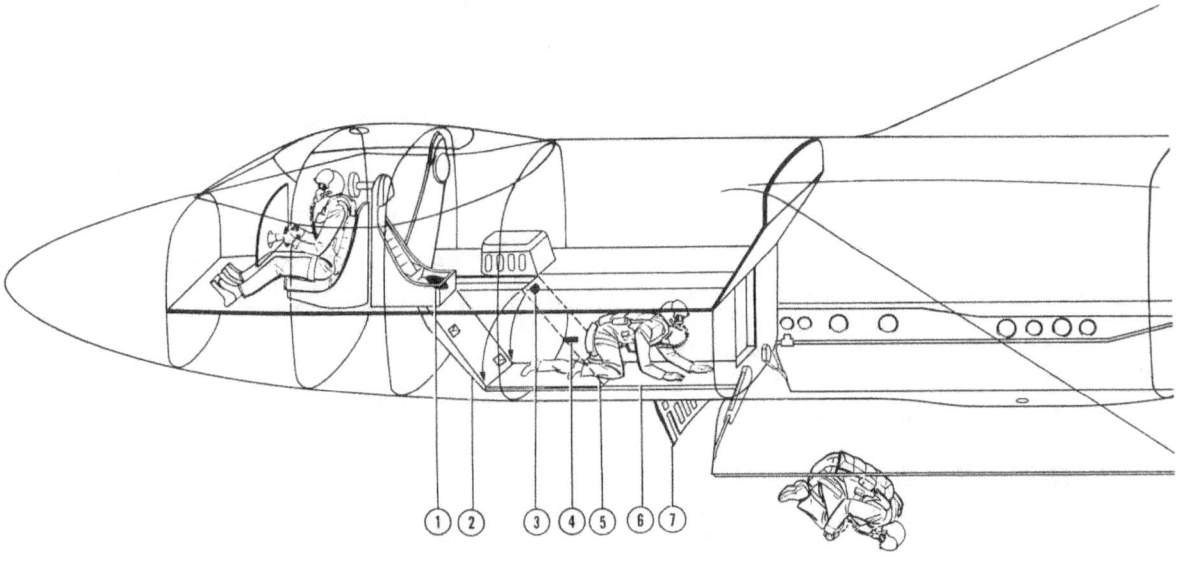

1. Inner escape chute door latch release
2. Inner escape chute door
3. Companionway safety door latch release
4. Companionway emergency exit T-handle
5. Companionway safety door
6. Companionway
7. Bomb bay spoiler

Figure 5-3. Secondary Emergency Exit — With Rake Fully Extended

EMERGENCY DITCHING-LAND

WARNING

Ditching shall not be attempted if altitude is available for safe bailout.

Proceed as follows:

1. Maintain . . . . FLYING SPEED AND HEADING
2. Shoulder harness/lap seat belts . . . . CHECK TIGHT/LOCKED
3. Lower seat . . . . AS FAR AS POSSIBLE
4. Disconnect . . . . PARACHUTES, BAILOUT BOTTLE HOSES, BARO-RELEASE LANYARDS
5. Wing flaps . . . . DOWN
6. Landing gear . . . . DOWN
7. Arresting hook . . . . DOWN
8. Upper hatch . . . . OPEN (EMERGENCY AIR)

9. Land wings level on approach speed/angle-of-attack sink rate 200 to 300 fpm optimum.

10. After touchdown (if possible)
   a. Drag chute . . . . DEPLOY
   b. Throttles . . . . OFF
   c. Master engine switch . . OFF

11. Do not release lap belts until forward movement of aircraft has stopped.

Section V NAVAIR 01-40ATA-1

EMERGENCY DITCHING-SEA

Follow the procedures listed for EMERGENCY DITCHING-LAND, except:

1. Do not . . . . LOWER LANDING GEAR

2. Do not . . . . DEPLOY DRAG CHUTE

EMERGENCY LANDING-DIVERSION RECOMMENDATIONS

1. Emergency landing-diversion recommendations are listed in table 5-1.

2. These recommended actions are based on statistical data and are of an advisory nature. Deviations may be authorized by the on-the-scene commander if sufficient time is available for an on-the-spot analysis of the emergency and the attendant conditions of landing, the facilities, weather, seastate, and pilot ability.

3. These recommendations should be used as a guide.

4. Fouled deck data for endurance or diversion are contained in Section XI, Performance Data.

5. A field will be considered VFR with 1000 feet broken or better cloud coverage and visibility 3 miles or greater. Approach to the field should be possible under visual flight rules.

6. The operational commander has authority to divert an aircraft to a suitable field for an emergency landing or to arrest it on board. It is recommended that a suitable divert field meet the following criteria:

   a. Sufficient length to effect a landing with antiskid only.

   b. Hard-surface of macadam, concrete, or compacted coral (gravel-surface runways not acceptable).

   c. Crash crews available, preferably English speaking.

   d. Either foam or arresting gear available.

   e. Weather above minimum compatible with NAVAIDS available in the aircraft and at the field.

Emergency Field Arrestments

There are several types of field arresting gear, including anchor chain cable, water squeeze, and Morest-type equipment. All these types require engagement of the arresting hook in a cable pendant rigged across the runway. The gear is classified as follows by the location of the pendant in relation to the runway.

1. Short-field gear. Located at approach end of runway. In some instances prior notification may be required to rig for arrestment in the direction desired.

2. Midfield gear. Located near halfway point of runway. Usually requires prior notification in order to rig for arrestment in the direction desired.

3. Abort gear. Located 1500 to 2500 feet short of upwind end of duty runway and usually will be rigged for immediate use.

4. Overrun gear. Located shortly past upwind end of duty runway. Usually will be rigged for immediate use.

Some fields have all four types of gear; others, none. For this reason, it is imperative that all pilots be aware of the type, location, and compatibility of the gear in use with the aircraft, and the policy of the local air station with regard to which gear is rigged for use and when.

The approximate maximum permissible engaging speed, gross weight, and off-center engagement distance for field arrestment of aircraft are listed in the Pocket Checklist.

WARNING

- Under no circumstances should pilot decision to abort a takeoff be delayed because of knowledge that an emergency arresting gear is available at the end of the runway. Decision to abort should be based on the usual parameters of remaining runway and distance required for stopping, using wheel brakes. The arresting gear will then serve as an assist to stop the aircraft from rolling off the runway onto unprepared surfaces.

- If off center just prior to engaging arresting gear, do not attempt to go for center of runway. Continue straight ahead parallel to centerline.

As various modifications to the basic types of arresting gear are made, exact speeds will vary accordingly. Certain aircraft service changes may also affect engaging speed and weight limitations.

TABLE 5-1. EMERGENCY LANDING/DIVERSION RECOMMENDATIONS

Configuration	Shore Based and/or Divert Field Available	Action if Carrier Based and no Divert Field Available	Remarks
1. No Hook			
*a. All gear down	Normal landing	Barricade	
*b. One main wheel gone	Land (foam, if available)	Barricade	
*c. Nosewheel missing, nose mount up or down and unlocked.	Land (foam, if available)	Barricade	
d. All gear up	Land (foam, if available)	Bail out	
*e. Nose and one main mount down, other mount up or unlocked	Land (foam, if available)	Barricade	
f. Nosewheel only down	Land (foam, if available)	Bail out	At field, deploy drag chute just before touchdown.
g. One main mount only down	Bail out	Bail out	
h. Both ATM's failed	Land, if VFR	Bail out	Land ashore under ideal conditions.
†i. Single engine	Land	Bail out	
j. No flaps	Land	Bail out	
k. No. 2 ATM failed	Land	Barricade	
2. Hook Down			
*a. One main wheel gone	Land in arrest gear and foam, if available	Barricade	
b. All gear up	Land in arrest gear and foam, if available	Bail out	
c. Nosewheel missing, nose mount up or down and unlocked	Land in arrest gear and foam, if available	Barricade	Attempt normal carrier landing if entire strut is down and locked with only wheel missing.
*d. Nose and one main mount down, other mount up or down and unlocked	Land in arrest gear and foam, if available	Barricade	
e. Nosewheel only down	Land in arrest gear and foam, if available	Bail out	At field, deploy drag chute just before touchdown.
f. One main mount only down	Bail out	Bail out	
g. Both ATM's failed	Land in arrest gear VFR only	Bail out	
*h. Single engine	Land	Land	Refer to Section V single engine landing.
i. No flaps	Land	Bail out	
j. No. 2 ATM failed	Land	Land	

*If pilot performance or deck conditions are marginal, consider bailing out.
†If survival appears marginal because of sea state and water conditions, consider barricade arrestment.

TABLE 5-2. FIELD ARRESTING GEAR DATA

Arresting Gear Type	40	44	48	52	56	60	64	68	72	76	80	Maximum Offcenter Engagement (Feet)
M-2	97	93	89	86	83	81	79	76	74	71	68	20
M-21	125					→	Varies with Arresting Gear Setting					10
E5/E5-1	148	144	140	136	132	129	126	122	119	116	114	(b)
E5/(a)	150						→	147	143	139	132	(b)
E5-1(a)	165			→	161	157	152	147	143	139	132	(b)
E14-1	160		→	151	140	133	128	123	119	116	114	50
E15 (200 ft. Span)	160						→	158	153	146	140	35
E15 (300 ft. Span)	160										→	50
E-27	147	143	139	134	130	126	122	118	114	100	82	35
E-28	160						→		159	158	157	40
BAK-6	153	150	147	145	140	135	131	127	123	120	117	15
BAK-9	160	160	160	155	148	138	130	123	118	112	108	30
BAK-12	160			→		159	152	147	143	138	135	50

(a) Heavy chain
(b) May not exceed 25 percent of runway span — Shaded areas are extrapolated.
(c) Values given are for dry tapes. If tapes are wet, speed must be kept under 100 KCAS.

CAUTION

If offcenter prior to engagement, parallel runway centerline.

Severe damage to the aircraft is usually sustained if an engagement is made in the wrong direction into the chain gear.

SHORT FIELD ARRESTMENTS

If a directional control problem exists or a minimum rollout is desired, a short field arrestment should be made (refer to table 5-2) and the assistance of an LSO requested. The hook should be lowered while airborne and a positive hook-down check should be made. A constant glide slope approach to touchdown is recommended with touchdown on centerline just prior to the arresting wire. Landing approach power will be maintained until arrestment is assured or a waveoff is taken. Be prepared for a waveoff if the gear is missed. If LSO assistance is not available, land on the approach end of the runway.

LONG FIELD ARRESTMENTS

Lower hook, allowing sufficient time for the hook to extend fully prior to engagement (normally 1000 to 2000 feet prior to reaching the arresting gear.) Line up the aircraft on the runway centerline. Inform the control tower of intentions.

CAUTION

If aircraft is off center just prior to engaging arresting gear, do not attempt to go for center of runway. Continue straight ahead parallel to centerline.

Recommended Runway Foaming Procedures

FACILITIES

The following information is provided as a guide for runway foam patterns, based upon the availability of 3000 gallons of water and 250 gallons of foam, producing 160,000 sq. feet of wet foamed runway.

CONDITIONS AND BACKGROUND

Experience with arrestment and landings of the A-3 aircraft indicates that the maximum rollout following arrestment has not exceeded 2200 feet. One A-3 unarrested landing, nose gear missing, resulted in a 4000-foot rollout. It is concluded that this is the best planning figure for an A-3 aircraft unarrested landing with less than three landing gear extended.

ARRESTED LANDINGS

The foaming patterns for arrested landings depend primarily upon aircraft landing configuration. Namely, the aircraft landing configuration will allow a straight rollout when both main gears are retracted and/or the nose gear is missing while a swerve will result when only one main gear is extended. One of three patterns should be used:

1. Centerline
2. Right of centerline
3. Left of centerline

Based upon maximum rollout, all patterns should extend 2200 feet from the arresting gear cross-deck pendant. The left and right patterns should be parallel with the centerline for approximately 1200 feet, and then angled to the runway edge an additional 1000 feet. The width of the standard pattern should be 50 feet.

UNARRESTED LANDINGS

The following three patterns are recommended, depending upon the aircraft landing configuration:

1. Centerline
2. Right of centerline
3. Left of centerline

Based upon a maximum 160,000 square feet of available foam, the three patterns should be 4000 feet long and 40 feet wide. Foaming should commence 1000 feet from the approach end of the runway. The left and right patterns should be parallel to the centerline for the first 2000 feet and then angled to the runway edge.

EMERGENCY CREW REMOVAL

Aircraft Upright or Inverted

1. Open outer and inner escape chute doors by turning handles clockwise (figure 5-5). If aircraft inverted, escape chute doors must be held in OPEN position.

2. If escape chute doors cannot be opened, mount top of fuselage, open ditching hatch by turning external handle counterclockwise and sliding hatch aft.

NOTE

If ditching hatch or escape chute doors cannot be opened by external means, use power saw to cut out rear or middle, right-hand side sections of cockpit canopy.

3. Enter cockpit and secure engine controls; throttles OFF, engine master switches OFF, and battery switch OFF.

4. If aircraft was entered through ditching hatch or is inverted, ensure cockpit area clear of leaking fuel. Clear all personnel from areas of escape chute doors and on positive signal from outside observer PULL yellow emergency release handle located on lower right-hand side of pilots seat.

If escape chute doors do not open when the emergency handle is pulled, keep all personnel clear of escape chute doors, open forward left-hand equipment bay and disconnect battery.

5. Remove crewmembers oxygen masks, release or cut lap belt and shoulder harness. (Aircraft inverted, support crewmembers to cushion fall before releasing lap belt and shoulder harness.)

6. Disconnect shoulder torso harness koch fittings and seat pan rocket-jet fittings.

7. Remove crewmembers from seats and evacuate aircraft.

LANDING GEAR COLLAPSED

Repeat steps 2 through 7 of above, except DO NOT pull emergency release handle.

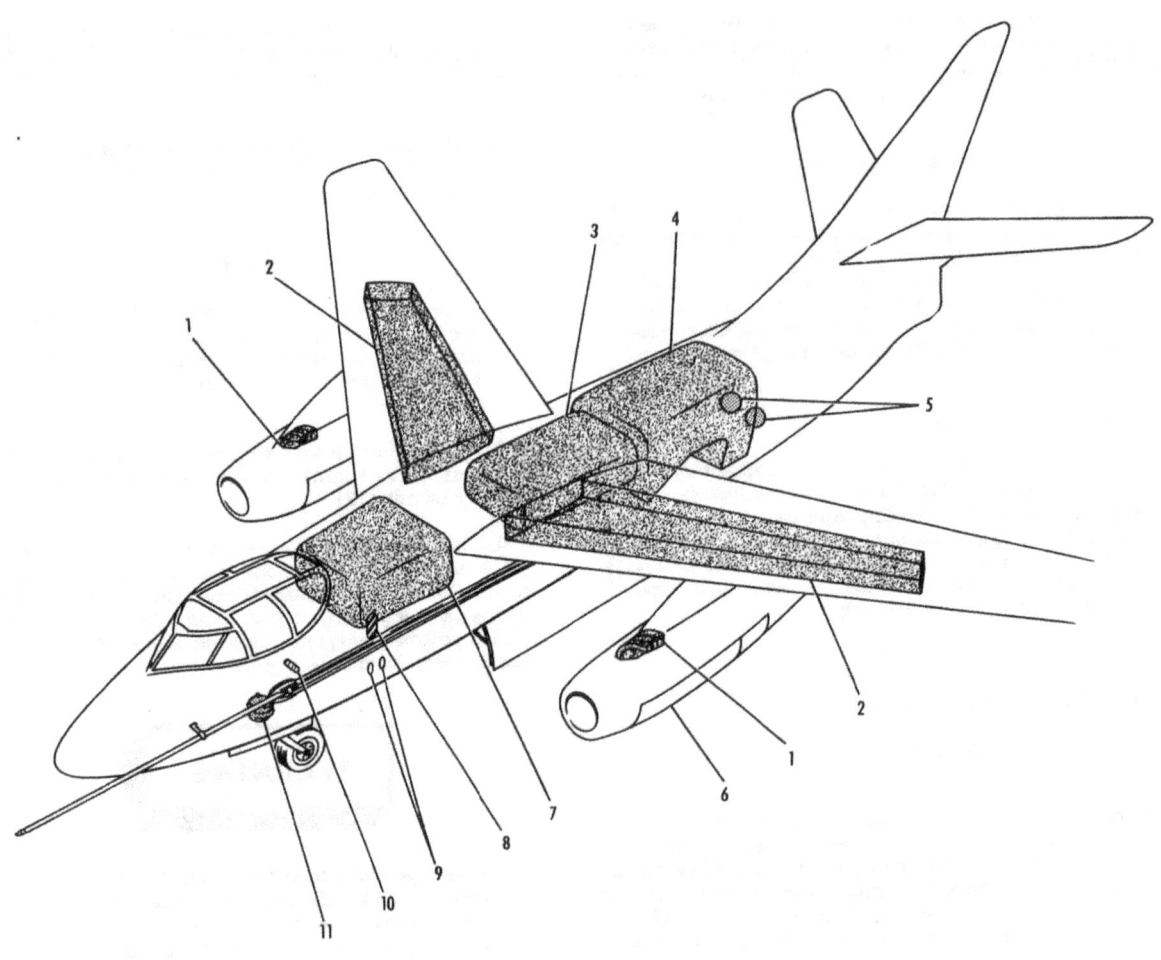

1. Engine oil reservoirs
2. Wing fuel tanks
3. Upper bomb bay auxiliary fuel cell
4. Aft fuel cell
5. Liquid oxygen converters (A-3B, KA-3B)
6. Forward engine nacelle access door
7. Forward fuel cell
8. Utility hydraulic reservoir
9. Auxiliary turbine motors exhaust
10. Portable gaseous oxygen unit (located under plane captain's seat)
11. Liquid oxygen converter (A-3A)

Figure 5-4. Fire Fighting

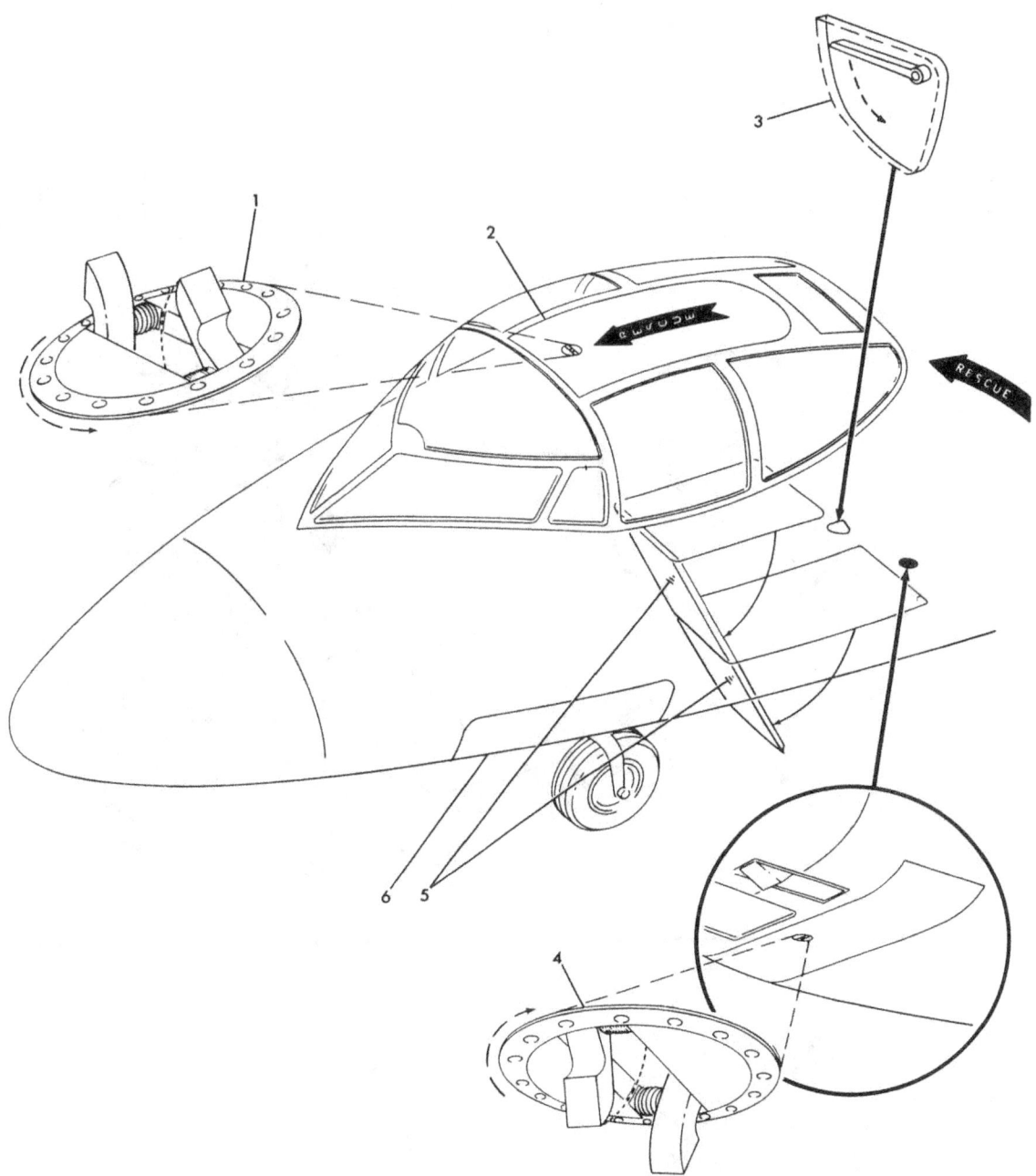

1. External ditching hatch handle
2. Ditching hatch
3. Handle, inner door, cockpit escape chute (located on left side of fuselage)
4. Handle, outer door, cockpit escape chute (located on underside of fuselage)
5. Doors, inner and outer, cockpit escape chute
6. Forward left hand equipment bay (battery)

Figure 5-5. Emergency Access and Crew Evacuation (Sheet 1)

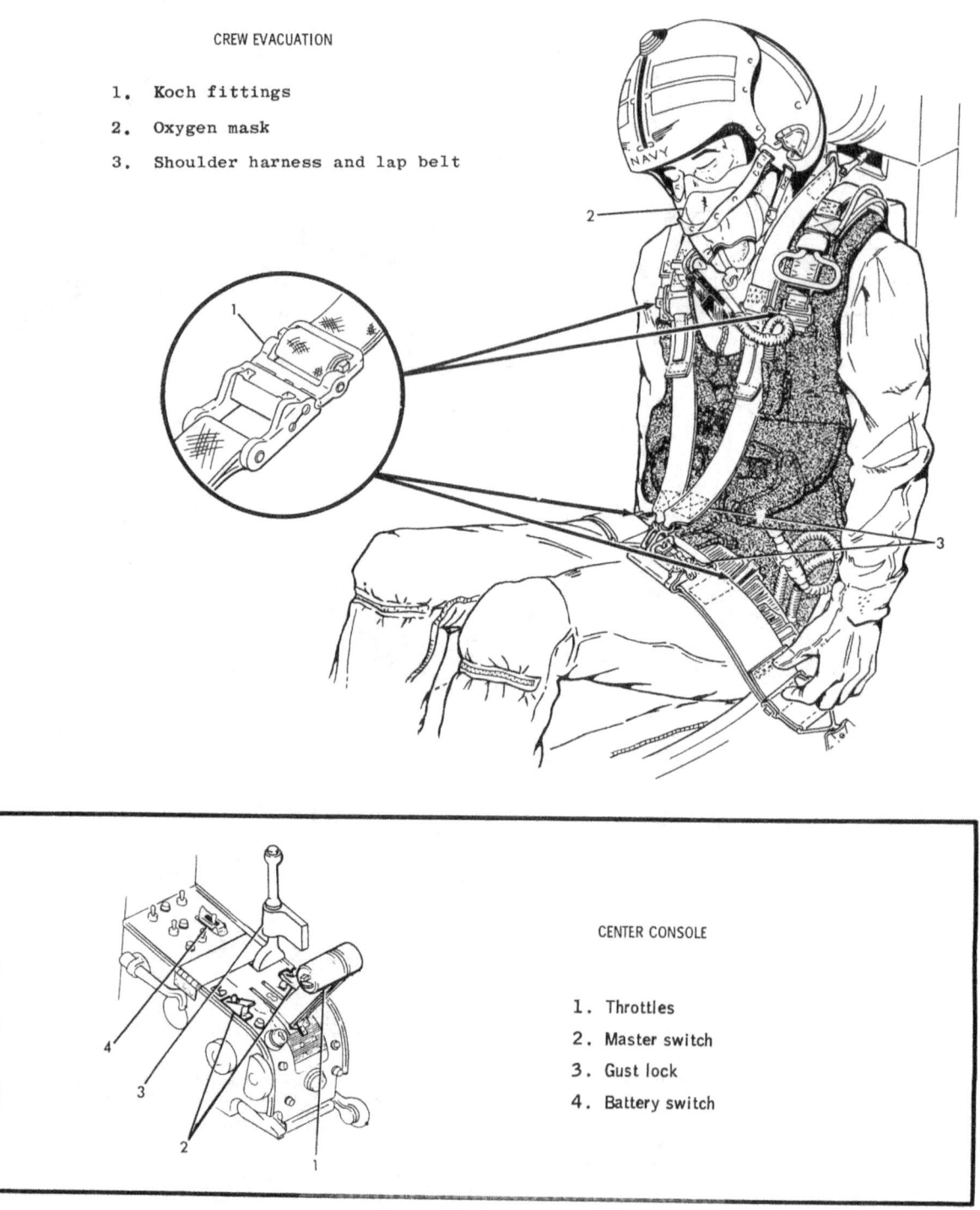

Figure 5-5. Emergency Access and Crew Evacuation (Sheet 2)

NAVAIR 01-40ATA-1   Section VI

SECTION VI
ALL-WEATHER OPERATION

TABLE OF CONTENTS

TEXT

	Page		Page
Introduction	6-1	Before Takeoff	6-5
Simulated Instrument Flying	6-1	Takeoff	6-5
Instrument Flight Procedures	6-1	During Flight	6-6
Jet Penetrations	6-2	Descent	6-6
Weather Considerations	6-3	Landing	6-6
Ice	6-3	Shutdown and Postflight	6-6
Thunderstorms	6-4	Hot Weather and Desert Operation	6-6
Icing of Pitot-Static Instruments	6-4	Before Entering Aircraft	6-6
Cold Weather Operation	6-4	On Entering Aircraft	6-6
Ice, Snow, and Rain	6-4	Starting Engines	6-6
Before Entering Aircraft	6-4	Taxi and Takeoff	6-7
On Entering Aircraft	6-5	Climb	6-7
Before Starting Engines	6-5	Descent and Landing	6-7
Starting and Warmup	6-5	Postflight	6-7
Taxiing	6-5		

INTRODUCTION

This section contains procedures that differ from or are additional to the normal operating instructions in Section III. In a few instances, repetition is necessary, either to establish the proper sequence of operation or to stress the importance of an operation.

Simulated Instrument Flying

Simulated instrument flights shall be scheduled for pilots preparing for their annual instrument flight check. A qualified (instrument qualified) aviator or crewmember will be assigned to fly in the navigator's seat as pilot observer and lookout. Other flight personnel will be assigned to fly in the plane captain's seat to act as lookout.

PILOT INSTRUMENT PROFICIENCY

Pilots must maintain instrument proficiency by requesting practice instrument departures, penetrations, and controlled approaches on all normal training flights. Flight crews must be aware of the critical importance of maintaining proper lookout at all times during climbouts and descents. During this portion of flight, high-density traffic is normally encountered. The pilot must refer to his instruments frequently, even though flying contact, and therefore must rely upon the crewmembers for lookouts.

Instrument Flight Procedures

For instrument clearance purposes, the A-3 is a multipiloted aircraft, providing the right seat occupant is instrument qualified in accordance with OPNAVINST 3710.7 series.

Changed 1 June 1969

Since standard jet instrument procedures must be used, only procedures that require special precautions or are peculiar to this aircraft will be described.

If any possibility of rain is anticipated during the time of takeoff and/or approach and landing, ensure that the aircraft has an operating windshield wiper before takeoff. If adverse weather conditions are anticipated, ensure that the anti-icing system is operative before takeoff.

ANTI-ICING SYSTEM OPERATION

Actuate the anti-icing system prior to entering clouds or other visible moisture. Icing conditions should be anticipated, as this system is primarily an anti-icing system rather than a deicing system. If anti-icing system is operating properly, a noticeable drop in pressure ratio readings can be observed when the anti-icing switch is turned ON and oil temperature readings will be higher than normal. For climbs and descents in warm, humid climates and in other situations when necessary, place the air conditioning switch to HOT (not manual hot) and the manual defrost knob to the windshield.

CHANGING RADIO CHANNELS

While on instruments or at night, the pilot must not change radio channels below 2500 feet AGL unless required by the mission and then only in level flight. The navigator may change radio channels at any altitude as directed by the pilot.

6-1

INSTRUMENT TAKEOFF

Recent flap hinge failures indicate a need for the following interim procedures as a means of reducing exposure time of flaps to high load conditions. These procedures shall be followed only until incorporation of A-3 AFC 390.

(1) Takeoffs and instrument departures: Unless an immediate turn after takeoff is required for terrain clearance or traffic separation, climb straight ahead at 180 KIAS maximum. Initiate flap retraction at 500 feet above ground level. During flap retraction, maintain runway heading, positive rate of climb and maximum of 15 units angle of attack. When flaps are fully retracted, turn and accelerate as required to conform to SID procedures and/or climb schedule.

(2) Landings: Reduce airspeed below 180 KIAS before lowering flaps and maintain wings level attitude while flaps are extending. Do not exceed 15 units angle-of-attack.

Because the A-3 is a single-control aircraft, hooded ITO's shall not be practiced. Practice nonhooded ITO's during normal takeoff. The takeoff speed and technique for ITO is the same as for VFR takeoff.

INSTRUMENT DEPARTURE

When safely airborne, retract the landing gear and maintain 200 KIAS with full flaps extended. When the initial turn of the instrument departure is completed (not below 1000 feet above the terrain), retract flaps, and proceed in compliance with the departure clearance.

CLIMB

Normal climb schedule shall be adhered to during climb under instrument conditions. The aircraft radar may be used to monitor the climbout course to avoid thunderstorms. GCA or control-center radar monitor track-out should be used where available.

CRUISING

Cruising procedures and techniques are the same under instrument conditions as under VFR. When on instruments in thunderstorm areas, the ASB radar and/or flight-following service shall be used continuously to avoid flying through thunderstorms.

HOLDING

Use 230 KIAS for standard jet holding patterns unless gross weight and/or altitude requires higher holding speed.

Jet Penetrations

ALTITUDE MONITORING

During a penetration or any letdown, the navigator shall monitor the approach on ASB radar to ensure terrain clearance. During IFR or simulated IFR conditions, the navigator shall call out passing each 5000 feet of altitude, and below 5000 feet AGL the navigator shall call out passing each 1000 feet as the aircraft descends. Each altitude check shall be confirmed by the pilot.

PENETRATION DESCENT

COMMUNICATIONS

Communications must be established before commencing penetration.

AIR-TO-GROUND COMMUNICATIONS. The pilot may delegate communication functions to his crewmembers except when being directed by radio from external sources i.e. approach control, GCA etc. In such instances it is essential that the pilot personally acknowledge instructions received from the controlling agency.

Complete the predescent checklist prior to commencing penetration. TACAN/VOR penetrations are made at 250 KIAS, speedbrakes extended and 1500 pounds per hour per engine fuel flow. This configuration produces a rate of descent of approximately 4000 feet per minute. Throttle adjustments must be made as altitude decreases to maintain 1500 pounds per hour per engine fuel flow.

En route descents may be made at en route airspeeds at 1500 pounds per hour per engine fuel flow, with or without speedbrakes depending on the rate of descent desired. Consideration must be given to encountering possible icing conditions in which a rapid descent is required.

Idle descents are made when fuel conservation is the primary consideration. Refer to appendix charts for maximum range descents performance data.

During idle descent, engine bleed air to the ATM's is not sufficient to permit operation of the utility system hydraulic equipment without a considerable drop in ac generator frequency and power output. Such low-frequency operation can result in loss of the electrical system, including all ac electrical and flight instruments.

TRANSITION FROM PENETRATION

When transitioning to level flight and desiring to maintain descent airspeed:

1. Retract speedbrakes 1000 feet above level-off altitude.

2. Leave throttles at 1500 pounds per hour and maintain 250 KIAS by smoothly raising the nose.

3. As aircraft reaches level-off altitude, add power to maintain desired airspeed.

NOTE

Rate of descent should never exceed actual altitude above terrain.

TRANSITION TO LANDING CONFIGURATION

When transitioning to the landing configuration:

1. Commence raising nose smoothly at 10 percent of the rate of descent above level-off altitude with speedbrakes out.

2. Conduct slat check clean at 15 units angle-of-attack. (Refer to Slat Check procedure, Section IV.)

3. At 200 KIAS, lower flaps. Lower gear after flaps are down.

4. Continue descent and add power as required to level off. Maintain at least 135 KIAS until on glide slope or on final.

APPROACH

The final approach fix, aircraft speed/configuration shall be determined as follows:

1. For TACAN approaches, airspeed shall be 250 KIAS clean, until reaching the fix corresponding to the 10-mile gate of a CCA approach.

2. For VOR or UHF/ADF approaches when the final approach fix and the runway are at least 10 nautical miles apart, airspeed shall be 250 KIAS and aircraft clean until reaching the fix.

3. For VOR or UHF/ADF approaches where the final approach fix and the runway are less than 10 nautical miles apart, the aircraft will be in the landing configuration and slowed to 135 KIAS when inbound out of the penetration turn.

4. For CCA approach, refer to Section III, Part 4.

GCA APPROACHES

GCA approaches shall be used whenever possible, even in visual weather. Fly the GCA pattern at 135 KIAS with the aircraft in the landing configuration until approaching final, then slow to landing approach speed.

Waveoffs shall be as directed by the GCA controller; however, the aircraft must climb straight ahead to a minimum of 1000 feet AGL before commencing a turn. The aircraft shall normally remain in the landing configuration while in the GCA pattern.

WEATHER CONSIDERATIONS

Ice

The A-3 aircraft is not equipped to fly continuously in icing conditions. All flights must be planned to avoid areas of continuous icing. The rate of climb and descent are great enough that icing should be encountered for only a short time. The pitot heat and bleed air heat to the engine-inlet guide vanes are anti-icing equipment, NOT deicing equipment, and shall be turned on before entering area where icing is expected. If considerable ice builds up on the wings and other areas, it is important to maintain the proper airspeed. The standard climb schedule should be adequate for climbout, and 250 KIAS should be adequate for penetration. If ice is encountered during penetration, do not slow below the recommended no slat approach speed until it is ascertained that slats are functioning properly.

Thunderstorms

Fuel state and mission permitting, thunderstorms or suspected areas of severe turbulence shall be avoided. Aircraft and ground radar should be used. In areas of severe turbulence such as tropical thunderstorms and typhoons, rain is frequently encountered well above the middle third of the storm. Above 35,000 feet, reduced power available and limited bleed air for engine anti-icing make engine icing and compressor stalls a distinct hazard.

THUNDERSTORM PENETRATION

Use radar to circumnavigate or pick the weakest area of the storm. The storm should be penetrated at recommended speeds (220 to 250 KIAS) and at an altitude at which the least turbulence is expected. When the severity of turbulence is unknown, penetrate at an altitude above or below the middle third of the storm. High altitude penetrations between 30,000 and 35,000 feet have proved to be the most desirable, offering the best combination of engine power available and controllability. Once in a storm, it is advisable to level off at the recommended altitude with cruise power rather than to continue a full power climb in an attempt to top the storm. Engine icing, compressor stalls, flameout, and loss of control have resulted from flying through thunderstorms above 35,000 feet.

Prior to entering the storm, turn instrument lights on bright, including white floodlights. Reset accelerometer, turn on anti-icing, set power, and trim to maintain level flight at recommended penetration speed. Once in the storm, fly attitude. Do not attempt to chase airspeed, altitude, or heading transients in turbulence. Make power changes only when necessary to maintain positive control. Speedbrakes have been effectively used to prevent exceeding design Mach limits. However, speedbrakes should be used cautiously as the VN area of control becomes very narrow at high altitudes. The angle-of-attack indicator provides a backup for the airspeed in the event of pitot icing. On aircraft reworked per AFC 267 and 268, the S-5 autopilot is designed to maintain control inputs within the stress envelope of the airframe. When operating normally, the autopilot may be used in turbulence. The altitude-hold feature SHALL NOT be used. If penetrating on autopilot, monitor the autopilot servo trim indicators in conjunction with normal flight instruments.

Icing Of Pitot—Static Instruments

Icing may sometimes result in loss of static pressure to the instruments. This may be recognized by simultaneous failure of airspeed, altimeter, and rate of climb. If necessary, fly the aircraft on angle of attack.

COLD WEATHER OPERATION

The majority of cold weather operating difficulties are encountered on the ground. Extreme diligence must be exercised by both ground and flight personnel if operations are to be successful. The procedures presented herein are intended to supplement those outlined for normal operations in Section III.

Ice, Snow, and Rain

Ice, snow, and rain may be encountered both in flight and on the ground. Ground protection consists mainly of a thorough postflight inspection and the provision of adequate cover for the aircraft. The aircraft is not equipped to prevent ice formation on the wings or fuselage and should not be flown in areas where heavy icing is likely to be encountered. Rain and dry snow present no particular problem except that of restricted vision. The aircraft is equipped with engine anti-icing equipment, and pitot and angle-of-attack probe heat for the prevention of ice formation during normal operation; however, this equipment is not sufficient protection should prolonged exposure to icing conditions become necessary. The engine anti-icing system uses hot air bled from the engine compressor section, and the amount of heat available is dependent upon engine rpm.

GROUND CREW

Ground crew personnel must ensure that the following preflight is performed:

1. Drain fuel tanks of all water prior to fueling.

2. After fueling allow sufficient time for entrapped water to settle (optimum time 8 hours); drain again prior to flight.

3. If the aircraft is fueled with fuel 40° Fahrenheit or below, ice formation is slight due to the small amount of dissolved water, assuming steps 1 and 2 have been followed.

Before Entering Aircraft

In addition to a thorough preflight inspection by the ground crew, the following checks should be made:

1. See that all protective covers and plugs are removed.

2. Check engine intakes for evidence of ice. Make sure the compressors are free to rotate; engine heat on shutdown melts ice accumulated during the previous flight, and the moisture may refreeze in the lower sections of the low-pressure compressor blades. Apply external heat if necessary, and start the engines as soon as possible after they are free.

3. Check fuel tank vents, pitot tube, angle-of-attack probe, temperature sensing element, fuselage and wing drainage and vent outlets, and remove all evidence of ice.

4. Make sure fuel sumps have been drained. Check lines and shutoffs.

5. Clean dirt and ice from struts and exposed actuating cylinder pistons.

6. Thoroughly check control surfaces and hinges.

7. Check the entire aircraft for freedom from frost, snow, and ice. Remove frost or snow by light brushing, ice by application of heat.

CAUTION

Ensure that ice melted by external heat does not reform. Recheck control hinges thoroughly. Do not scrape or chip ice from any surface.

8. Check landing gear and struts for freedom from ice, snow, or dirt. Inspect limit switches and fairing door hinges, actuating cylinder pistons, and wheels.

9. Check landing flap hinges, rollers, and limit switches.

10. Check battery for full charge.

11. Use external power for operating and ground checking all electrical and radio equipment.

On Entering Aircraft

1. Check operation of upper and lower escape hatches.

2. Make a thorough check of the controls, both by feel and visually.

Before Starting Engines

Make certain wheels are securely chocked to prevent slippage during the start.

Starting and Warmup

1. Start the engines using normal starting procedure. Heating of jet engines is seldom required unless external power source is weak. If necessary, apply external heat to accessory section to reduce starter loads.

2. Check oil pressure for indication within 30 seconds. Pressure may exceed maximum limits temporarily during extreme cold weather starts.

3. Turn on necessary electrical equipment only after positive indication of generator operation.

4. Check all instruments for normal operation and indications within allowable limits.

5. Recheck hydraulic system. Each control should be operated through its complete cycle several times for assurance of proper pressure and operation.

6. Check windshield wiper and anti-icing system for proper operation.

Taxiing

1. Exercise extreme caution when passing other aircraft, buildings, and other obstructions when ice is present. Fast turns or heavy crosswinds can cause skidding. Brakes are ineffective on ice.

2. Be particularly careful in maneuvering near other aircraft, since exhaust heat and blast will blow melted snow and slush which will refreeze on contact.

3. Avoid taxiing in deep snow or slush. Steering will be more difficult and brakes, gear, and flaps may freeze after takeoff.

Before Takeoff

1. Windshield defogging shutoff valve – OPEN.

Do not attempt takeoff with frosted windshield, or with snow, ice, or frost formation on wings or control surfaces.

2. Recheck nosewheel steering if takeoff is not begun immediately after taxiing.

3. Pitot heat, if required – ON.

Takeoff

1. Apply brakes and advance throttles to MILITARY. If aircraft starts to skid, release brakes and begin takeoff run. Continue engine check during early part of takeoff run. If takeoff must be aborted, use brakes lightly.

2. After takeoff from a snow or slush-covered runway, operate landing gear and flaps through several cycles to prevent their freezing in the up position.

3. Watch closely for signs of icing. Engine icing will be indicated by excessive tailpipe temperatures and loss of thrust.

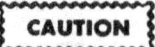

At low outside air temperatures, turbine outlet temperatures may exceed operating limits at a lower engine rpm than at normal OAT, and flight instruments may be inaccurate. Maintain a reasonable margin of safety on all indicators.

During Flight

Under certain atmospheric conditions it is possible for fog to accumulate in the cabin while pressurized, causing a serious restriction to visibility. Turn the cabin temperature rheostat to the full increase position or the momentary MAN HOT position. After the cabin has cleared, readjust the temperature control rheostat to a temperature higher than the original. If a comfortable temperature cannot be maintained without fogging, depressurize the cabin until more favorable atmospheric conditions exist. Refer to Air Conditioning and Pressurizing System, Section I, Part 2.

Descent

Follow the normal procedure for letdown. Operation of engine anti-icing equipment will require an increase in engine rpm to offset the resulting loss of thrust.

Landing

When slowing to approach speed following a penetration through icing conditions, failure of the outboard slats to extend may cause a severe pitchup.

During adverse weather, at landing fields where braking difficulty may be expected, it is recommended that the pilot request the current runway conditions and anticipated braking effectiveness from the controlling agency and recheck the landing roll data prior to landing.

Follow normal landing procedures, exercising extreme caution at touchdown.

Shutdown and Postflight

1. Follow normal procedure for shutdown.

2. See that wheels are securely chocked.

3. Have aircraft serviced and fuel sumps drained.

4. See that all covers and plugs are securely installed and that aircraft is tied down.

5. If aircraft is not to be flown for several days, remove battery.

HOT WEATHER AND DESERT OPERATION

Proper protection of the aircraft while on the ground is of primary importance during hot weather operation. The following procedures supplement the normal operating procedure outlined in Section III.

Before Entering Aircraft

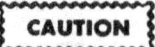

Metal surfaces exposed to the sun are often hot enough to cause serious burns. It is advisable to use gloves when contact with these surfaces is necessary.

1. Check tires and struts for proper inflation, as high temperatures may cause overinflation.

2. Check thoroughly for accumulation of sand or dust.

3. Check for fuel, oil and hydraulic leaks which may have been caused by expansion of valves or packing.

4. In locations where high humidity is encountered, nonmetallic equipment is subject to corrosion, fungus, and moisture absorption. See that such equipment is completely dry and in operating condition.

5. Cool cabin with a portable cooler, if available.

On Entering Aircraft

If necessary, apply heat to dry instruments and controls which may be damp with condensation moisture.

Starting Engines

Use normal starting procedures. Engines will accelerate to idle much more slowly than on a normal or cold day.

Taxi and Takeoff

1. Use brakes as little as possible during taxi and takeoff.

2. Hold taxi time to a minimum and watch turbine outlet temperatures closely.

3. Stalling speeds are increased in extremely hot weather. Strict adherence to recommended takeoff and climbing speeds is necessary, as takeoff distances are considerably increased in hot weather. The total impulse provided by JATO, however, is not affected significantly.

Climb

Extremely high OAT has a considerable effect on climb performance. On a very hot day, military rated thrust may be required to give the same rate of climb as normal rated thrust on a standard day. However, since fuel vaporization losses are high during rapid climbs to altitude, the rate of climb should be held as low as practicable.

CAUTION

Thunderstorms occurring during hot weather are extremely hazardous and should be avoided if at all possible. If penetration cannot be avoided, follow Thunderstorm instructions in this section.

Descent and Landing

Use normal letdown and landing procedure. True airspeed will be higher than normal for a given indicated airspeed, and touchdown speed will be higher than usual. Turbulence during the final approach and flare-out may be expected, and the landing roll will be considerably longer.

Postflight

1. Have wheels securely chocked.

2. See that protective covers and plugs are installed.

3. Leave ditching hatch and emergency escape chute doors open on calm days to provide ventilation. If sandstorms or other foul weather is anticipated, close hatches and doors, and moor aircraft (see figure 1-66).

4. Have aircraft serviced. Fuel tanks must not be topped since excessive heat will cause the tanks to overflow, thereby creating a fire hazard.

5. In dusty or sandy areas, interior equipment should be covered.

NAVAIR 01-40ATA-1   Section VII

SECTION VII
COMMUNICATIONS PROCEDURES

TABLE OF CONTENTS

TEXT

	Page		Page
Introduction	7-1	Emergency Communications	7-1
Pilot Responsibility	7-1	Radio Communications Equipment	7-2
Radio Communications	7-1	Electronic Navigation Equipment	7-2
Air-to-Ground Communications	7-1	IFF/SIF Procedures	7-2
Radio Discipline	7-1	Visual Communications Procedures	7-2

TABLES

Table		Page	Table		Page
7-1	General Conversation	7-2	7-5	Aircraft and Engine Operation	7-8
7-2	Takeoff, Changing Lead, Leaving Formation, Breakup, Landing	7-3	7-6	Air Refueling	7-8
7-3	Formation Signals	7-4	7-7	Emergency Signals Between Aircraft	7-8
7-4	Electronic Communications and Navigation	7-6	7-8	JATO Procedures	7-9

INTRODUCTION

Because of the nature of jet operations, voice radio is normally used for communications between aircraft. Occasionally conditions of radio silence are prescribed for certain operations. Proficiency in the use of visual signals must therefore be maintained by all pilots. Information and additional references concerning radio and electronic communications are outlined in Chapter VI of NWP 41 (A) and Chapter III of the CVA/CVS NATOPS Manual.

Pilot Responsibility

It is the responsibility of the pilot to ensure that all radio and electronic transmissions from his aircraft are in compliance with applicable directives and squadron doctrines. It is imperative that all crewmembers be thoroughly and properly indoctrinated in the use of all communications equipment installed.

RADIO COMMUNICATIONS

Air-to-Ground Communications

The pilot may delegate communication functions to his crewmembers except when being directed by radio from external sources i.e. approach control, GCA etc. In such instances it is essential that the pilot personnally acknowledge instructions received from the controlling agency.

Radio Discipline

Adherence to the following instructions will ensure the desired degree of radio discipline.
1. Do not interrupt another transmission.
2. Keep all transmissions brief and concise.

3. Use the phonetic alphabet and approved phraseology. Be familiar with the use of the fighter director vocabulary, ACP-135.

4. Be familiar with the communications sections of the flight planning document.

5. Maintain a listening watch on GUARD frequencies at all times (121.5 and 243.0 mc.); do not transmit on GUARD except in actual emergency.

Emergency Communications

Comply with OPNAV instructions and the steps listed on the inside back cover of the FLIP En Route Supplement. The steps are repeated for convenience:

1. MAYDAY (or PAN, as applicable) three times. This is followed by the aircraft call sign (three times) and the frequency on which the transmission is being made (243.0 UHF or 121.5 mc VHF).

2. Type of aircraft

3. Position and time

4. Heading

5. True airspeed

6. Altitude

7. Fuel remaining (in hours and minutes)

8. Nature of emergency

9. Pilot's intentions (bail out, etc.)

10. Assistance desired.

Changed 1 June 1969

RADIO COMMUNICATIONS EQUIPMENT

UHF is the primary means of voice communications. The AN/ARC-27A UHF set has 20 preset channels with a control head located in the cockpit to the right of the navigator. All aircraft will have a current frequency plan for UHF, VHF, and HF.

VHF is normally a secondary means of voice communication and has nine preset channels plus GUARD. In the event of a UHF failure, however, the VHF may become the sole means of communication.

All A-3 aircraft are equipped with the AN/ARC-38A HF radio which gives additional communication capabilities. The operation of this equipment, as well as the UHF-VHF, is fully covered in Section I.

Electronic Navigation Equipment

The aircraft contains four electronic aids to navigation in addition to the ASB radar. They are:

1. UHF direction finder
2. LF direction finder (Bird-dog)
3. OMNI
4. TACAN.

IFF/SIF Procedures

Aircraft operating within the continental U.S. shall operate the IFF/SIF equipment to conform with OPNAV/FAA regulations, unless otherwise directed by competent authority. During carrier operation, all aircraft must operate IFF as prescribed by appropriate directives.

When an aircraft is lost or has an in-flight emergency and is unable to obtain assistance by other means, select emergency IFF.

VISUAL COMMUNICATIONS PROCEDURES

Communications between aircraft will be conducted visually whenever practicable, provided no sacrifice in operational efficiency is involved. Flight leaders shall ensure that all pilots in the formation receive and acknowledge signals when given. The visual communications section of NWP 41 must be reviewed and practiced by all pilots and crew.

TABLE 7-1. GENERAL CONVERSATION

Signal		Meaning	Response
Day	Night		
Thumbs up, or nod of head	Flashlight moved vertically up-and-down repeatedly	Affirmative. ("Yes," or, "I understand.")	
Thumbs down, or turn of head from side to side	Flashlight moved horizontally back-and-forth repeatedly	Negative. ("No," or, "I do not understand.")	
Hand cupped behind ear as if listening		Question. Used in conjunction with another signal, this gesture indicates that the signal is interrogatory	As appropriate
Hand held up, with palm outward		Wait	
Hand waved back and forth in an erasing motion in front of face, with palm turned forward	Letter N in code, given with external lights	Ignore my last signal.	

NAVAIR 01-40ATA-1 Section VII

TABLE 7-1. GENERAL CONVERSATION (Continued)

Signal		Meaning	Response
Day	Night		
Hand held up, with thumb and forefinger forming an 0 and remaining fingers extended		Perfect, well done.	
Employ fingers held vertically to indicate desired numerals 1 through 5. With fingers horizontal, indicate number which added to 5 gives desired number from 6 to 9. A clenched fist indicates 0. (Hold hand near canopy when signalling.)		Numerals as indicated	A nod of the head ("I understand"). To verify numberals, addressee repeats. If originator nods, interpretation is correct. If originator repeats numerals, addressee should continue to verify them until they are understood.

TABLE 7-2. TAKEOFF, CHANGING LEAD, LEAVING FORMATION, BREAKUP, LANDING

Signal		Meaning	Response
Day	Night		
1. Two aircraft on runway. Takeoff-leader raises either forearm to vertical position.		1. I have completed my take-off check list and am ready for takeoff.	1. Stands by for reply from wingman, holding arm up until answered.
2. Wingman raises forearm.		2. I have completed my take-off check list and am ready for takeoff.	2. Wingman lowers arm and stands by for takeoff.
3. Leader lowers arm.		3. Takeoff path is clear, I am commencing takeoff.	3. Execute takeoff. Ten-second interval.
1. Leader pats self on the head, points to wingman.	2. If external lights are inoperative, leader shines flashlight on hard-hat, then shines light on wingman.	Leader shifting lead to wingman.	1. Wingman pats head and assumes lead. 2. Wingman shines flashlight at leader, then on his hard-hat. Turns external lights to DIM/STDY and assumes lead.
Leader pats self on head and holds up two or more fingers.		Leader shifting lead to division designated by numerals.	Wingman relay signal; division leader designated assumes lead.
Pilot blows kiss to leader.		I am leaving formation.	Leader nods ("I understand") or waves goodby.

7-3

Section VII NAVAIR 01-40ATA-1

TABLE 7-2. TAKEOFF, CHANGING LEAD, LEAVING FORMATION, BREAKUP, LANDING (Continued)

Signal		Meaning	Response
Day	Night		
Leader blows kiss and points to aircraft.		Aircraft pointed out leave formation.	Wingman indicated blows kiss and executes.
Leader points to wingman, then points to eye, then to vessel or object.		Directs plane to investigate object or vessel.	Wingman indicated blows kiss and executes.
Division leader holds up and rotates two fingers in horizontal circle, preparatory to breaking off.		Section break off	Wingman relays signal to section leader. Section leader nods ("I understand") or waves goodby and executes.
Leader describes horizontal circle with forefinger.	Series of I's in code, given by external lights.	Breakup (and rendezvous)	Wingman take lead, pass signal after leader breaks, and follow.
Landing motion with open hand: 1. Followed by patting head. 2. Followed by pointing to another aircraft.		Refers to landing of aircraft, generally used in conjunction with another signal. 1. I am landing. 2. Directs indicated aircraft to land.	 1. Nods. ("I understand") or waves goodby. 2. Aircraft indicated repeats signal, blows a kiss and executes.

TABLE 7-3. FORMATION SIGNALS

Signal		Meaning	Response
Day	Night		
Open hand held vertically and moved forward or backward, palm in direction of movement.		Adjust wing-position, forward or aft.	Wingman moves in direction indicated.
Open hand held horizontally and moved slowly up or down, palm in direction of movement.		Adjust wing-position up or down.	Wingman moves up or down as indicated.
Open hand used as if beckoning inboard or pushing outboard.		Adjust wing-position laterally toward or away from leader.	Wingman moves in direction indicated.

7-4

TABLE 7-3. FORMATION SIGNALS (Continued)

Signal		Meaning	Response
Day	Night		
Hand opened flat and palm down, simulating dive or climb		I am going to dive or climb.	Prepare to execute.
Hand moved horizontally above glareshield, palm down		Leveling off.	Prepare to execute.
Head moved backward		Slow down.	Execute.
Head moved forward		Speed up.	Execute.
Head nodded right or left		I am turning right or left.	Prepare to execute.
Thumb waved backward over shoulder	Series of 00's in code, given by external lights	Take cruising formation or open up.	Execute.
1. Holds up right (or left) forearm vertically, with clenched fist of single wing-dip.	1. Single letter R (or K) in code, given by external lights.	1. Wingman cross under to right (or left) echelon or in direction of wing-dips.	1. Execute.
2. Same as above, except with pumping motion or double wing-dip.	2. Series of RR's (or KK's) in code, given by external lights.	2. Section cross under to right (or left) echelon or in direction of wing-dips.	2. Execute.
Triple Wing-dip		Division cross under.	Execute.
	Series of VV's in code, given by external lights	Form a Vee or balanced formation.	Execute.
Series of zooms	Series of XX's in code, given by external lights	Close up or join up; join up on me.	Execute.
Rocking of wings by leader		Prepare to attack.	Execute preparation to attack.
Rocking of wings by any other member of flight		We are being, or are about to be, attacked.	Standby for and execute defensive maneuvers.
Lead plane swishes tail		All aircraft in this formation form step-down column in tactical order behind column leader.	Execute. Leader speeds up slightly to facilitate formation of column.
Shaking of ailerons	Long dash, given with external lights	Execute signal; used as required in conjunction with another signal.	Execute last signal given.

Section VII NAVAIR 01-40ATA-1

TABLE 7-4. ELECTRONIC COMMUNICATIONS AND NAVIGATION

Signal		Meaning	Response
Day	Night		
Tap earphones, followed by patting of head, and point to other plane.		Take over communications.	Repeat signals, pointing to self, and assume communications lead.
Tap earphones, followed by patting of head.		I have taken over communications.	Nod ("I understand").
Tap earphones and indicate by finger-numerals, number of channel to which shifting.		Shift to radio frequency indicated by numerals.	Repeat signal and execute.
Tap earphones, extend forearm vertically, and rotate fingers, formed as if holding a grapefruit, followed by 4 numbers.		Manually set up ARC-27A on frequency indicated.	Repeat signal and execute.
Tap earphones, followed by question signal.		What channel (or frequency) are you on?	Indicate channel (or frequency) by finger-numerals.
Tap earphones and point to plane being called, followed by finger-numbers indicating frequency.		You are being called by radio on channel indicated by finger numbers.	Repeat numbers. Check receiving frequency and switch to channel indicated by originator. Dial in manually, if necessary.
Vertical hand, with fingers pointed ahead and moved in a horizontal sweeping motion, with four fingers extended and separated.		What is bearing and distance to the TACAN station?	Wait signal, or give magnetic bearing and distance with finger-numerals. The first three numerals indicate magnetic bearing and the last two or three, distance.
Vertical hand, with 4 fingers extended and separated, pointed ahead in a fore-and-aft chopping motion, followed by a question signal.		What is bearing to TACAN station?	Repeat signal and give bearing in three digits.
Arm and vertical hand, with 4 fingers extended and separated, moved ahead in a fore-and-aft circular motion, followed by question signal.		What is distance to TACAN station?	Repeat signal and give distance in two or three digits.
TACAN bearing or distance signal, followed by thumbs up or down.		TACAN bearing or distance, up or down.	Thumbs up or nod ("I understand").

7-6

TABLE 7-4. ELECTRONIC COMMUNICATIONS AND NAVIGATION (Continued)

Signal		Meaning	Response
Day	Night		
TACAN-bearing signal, followed by finger-numerals.		Switch to TACAN station indicated.	Repeat and execute.
Hand held up. First and fourth fingers extended; moved in fore-and-aft chopping motion, followed by:			
1. 4 numbers.		1. Set up UHF/ADF on frequency indicated.	1. Repeat signal and execute.
2. Question signal.		2. What is UHF/ADF bearing?	2. Repeat chopping motion, followed by wait, or three numerals indicating magnetic bearing.
3. Up or down signal.		3. My UHF/ADF is up or down.	3. Thumbs up or nod ("I understand").
Two fingers pointed toward eyes (meaning IFF/SIF signals), followed by:			Repeat, then execute.
1. "CUT."		1. Turn IFF/SIF to "STANDBY."	
2. 3-digit numerals.		2. Set mode and code indicated: first numeral-mode, second and third numerals - code.	
1. Open hand held up, fingers together, moved in fore-and-aft chopping motion (by leader).		1. Course to be steered is present compass heading.	1. Nod of head ("I understand").
2. Followed by question signal.		2. What is your compass heading?	2. Repeat signal and give compass heading in finger-numerals.
3. Followed by three-finger numerals.		3. My compass heading is as indicated by finger-numerals.	3. Nod or clarify, as appropriate.

Section VII NAVAIR 01-40ATA-1

TABLE 7-5. AIRCRAFT AND ENGINE OPERATION

Signal		Meaning	Response
Day	Night		
Raise fist with thumb extended in drinking position.		How much fuel have you?	Repeat signal, then indicate fuel in hundreds of pounds by finger-numbers.
Rotary movement of clenched fist in cockpit as if cranking wheels, followed by head nod.	Letter W in code, given by external lights.	Lower or raise landing gear and flaps, as appropriate.	Repeat signal. Execute when leader changes configuration.
Leader lowers hook.	Letter H in code, given by external lights.	Lower arresting hook.	Wingman lower arresting hook. Leader indicate wingman's hook is down with thumbs-up signal.
Open and close from fingers and thumb.		Extend or retract speed brakes, as appropriate.	Repeat signal. Execute upon head-nod from leader or when leader's speed brakes extend/retract.

TABLE 7-6. AIR REFUELING

(Refer to NATOPS Air Refueling Manual for Air Refueling Signals)

TABLE 7-7. EMERGENCY SIGNALS BETWEEN AIRCRAFT*

Signal		Meaning	Response
Day	Night		
Arm bent across forehead, weeping.		I am in trouble.	Escort disabled plane, assuming lead, if indicated and return to base or nearest suitable field.
1. Followed by HEFOE signal and code.	1. HEFOE signal and code.	1. I am having trouble with indicated system.	
2. Followed by landing signal.	2. HEFOE signal and code, followed by wheels-signal.	2. I must land immediately.	

*Refer to NWP 41 (A) for all Emergency Aircraft-to-Carrier and Carrier-to-Aircraft Signals.

TABLE 7-7. EMERGENCY SIGNALS BETWEEN AIRCRAFT* (Continued)

Signal		Meaning	Response
Day	Night		

Malfunctioning Of Equipment (HEFOE Code)

Day	Night	Meaning	Response
Clenched fist held to helmet-visor and then indicating by finger-numbers 1 to 5 the affected system.	Flashlight held close to top of canopy, pointed toward wingman, followed by 1 to 5 dashes to indicate system affected.	Number of fingers or dashes means: 1. Hydraulic system 2. Electric system (including TACAN and flight instruments) 3. Fuel system 4. Oxygen system 5. Engine.	Day: Nod, or thumbs up ("I understand"). Night: Vertical movement of flashlight. Pass lead to disabled plane or assume lead, if indicated.

*Refer to NWP 41 (A) for all Emergency Aircraft-to-Carrier and Carrier-to-Aircraft Signals.

TABLE 7-8. JATO PROCEDURES

NOTE

If an emergency situation arises, not covered by the following procedures, a crossed arms signal will be given by person(s) involved. Upon receipt of this signal the pilot will shutoff all JATO switches. The safety officer will proceed to the aircraft and verbally communicate with the pilot.

Crew Chief	Pilot	Action/Response

Positive Electrical Voltage Test

Crew Chief	Pilot	Action/Response
Hand horizontal	Both hands in view	JATO arming ON JATO arming light ON
	Thumb down	JATO arming light not ON
Clenched fist		Rotate catapult lever down, depress and hold firing button
Point to JATO crew		JATO crew conduct voltage test
Fingers clenched thumb horizontal		Release firing button
	Both hands in view	Firing button released

7-9

TABLE 7-8. JATO PROCEDURES (Continued)

NOTE

If an emergency situation arises, not covered by the following procedures, a crossed arms signal will be given by person(s) involved. Upon receipt of this signal the pilot will shutoff all JATO switches. The safety officer will proceed to the aircraft and verbally communicate with the pilot.

Crew Chief	Pilot	Action/Response
No Voltage Electrical Test		
Point to JATO crew		JATO crew conduct NO voltage test
Grasp thumb and pull rearward		Rotate catapult lever UP JATO arming switch OFF JATO arming light OFF Hold brakes HARD
	Both hands in view	Catapult lever UP JATO arming switch OFF JATO arming light OFF Brakes being held HARD
Connection of JATO Igniters		
Thumb extended up into palm of other hand	Both hands in view	JATO crew connect igniters
Thumbs Up		JATO plug-in completed JATO crew clear of aircraft

NAVAIR 01-40ATA-1 Section VIII

SECTION VIII
WEAPONS SYSTEMS

TABLE OF CONTENTS

TEXT

	Page		Page
Introduction	8-1	Radar System Preflight	8-1
AN/ASB-1A Modified Radar	8-1	ASB Modified Radar System	8-1
Radar Ground Operation	8-1		

ILLUSTRATIONS

Figure		Page	Figure		Page
8-1	AN/ASB-1A Modified Radar System - Cockpit Arrangement	8-2	8-3	AN/ASB-7 Modified Radar System - Cockpit Arrangement	8-4
8-2	C-852B/ASB-1A Radar Control Panel	8-3	8-4	AN/ASB-7 Radar Control Panel	8-6

INTRODUCTION

The A-3A/B and KA-3B AN/ASB-1A and AN/ASB-7 radar systems have been modified to be used as an aid to navigation, weather avoidance, and to provide a visual means for monitoring tanker operations.

AN/ASB-1A Modified Radar

The AN/ASB-1A modified radar system (figures 8-1 and 8-2) is a combined airborne search and navigation radar system. The major operating controls for the AN/ASB-1A radar system are located on the bombing data computer and the modified MK-97 computer. The modified radar system has four radar presentations. Two of the presentations are PPI over a 150-degree or 25-degree sector, and are non-stabilized. The two remaining presentations are expanded presentations over a 25-degree scan in azimuth. An optical presentation (periscope) with a fixed field of view aft, is combined with the AN/ASB-1A modified system to provide visual observations during air refueling operations. The fixed field view aft is controlled by a switch placarded CLOSED-STOP-OPEN located on the forward end of the navigator's upper right-hand console (figure 1-11). The AN/ASB-1A modified radar system is operated on 28-volt dc from the monitor bus, and ac from Phase A of the No. 1 ac generator through three SEARCH RADAR circuit breakers.

WARNING

Operation of this equipment involves the use of high voltages that are dangerous to life. Do not make internal adjustments, remove covers, or rely on interlocks for protection while high voltage is on. Under certain conditions, dangerous potentials may exist in circuits due to charge retained by capacitors when power controls are in the OFF position. Discharge and ground circuits before working on them.

Radar Ground Operation

When necessary to radiate during ground operations, the aircraft should be placed in a position that will permit the radar antenna to be directed into a suitable absorbing screen or open area. An open area is interpreted as follows:

1. An area clear of large obstructions such as buildings, parking lots, or residential areas for a distance of one-half mile.

2. An area clear of ordnance material for a distance of 300 feet.

3. An area clear of personnel.

Radar System Preflight

The preflight of the aircraft's radar system should, in addition to the normal checks, include a review of recent system history.

ASB-7 Modified Radar System [1]

The AN/ASB-7 radar system is planned to give increased capability through the use of proven components. The set has both high- and low-altitude capabilities. The ECM/navigator is provided with the equipment to accurately navigate to any desired target area. In the target area it gives ECM/navigator a high-resolution radar presentation of the target area. The navigational features aid in finding the target and returning home. The system's tunable radar and video features afford high immunity to radar countermeasures (figure 8-3).

---

[1] Aircraft BuNo. 142400, 142402-142407, 142633, 142635, 142642, 142644, 142646, 142647, 142649, 147648-147668.

Changed 15 July 1970 8-1

Section VIII   NAVAIR 01-40ATA-1

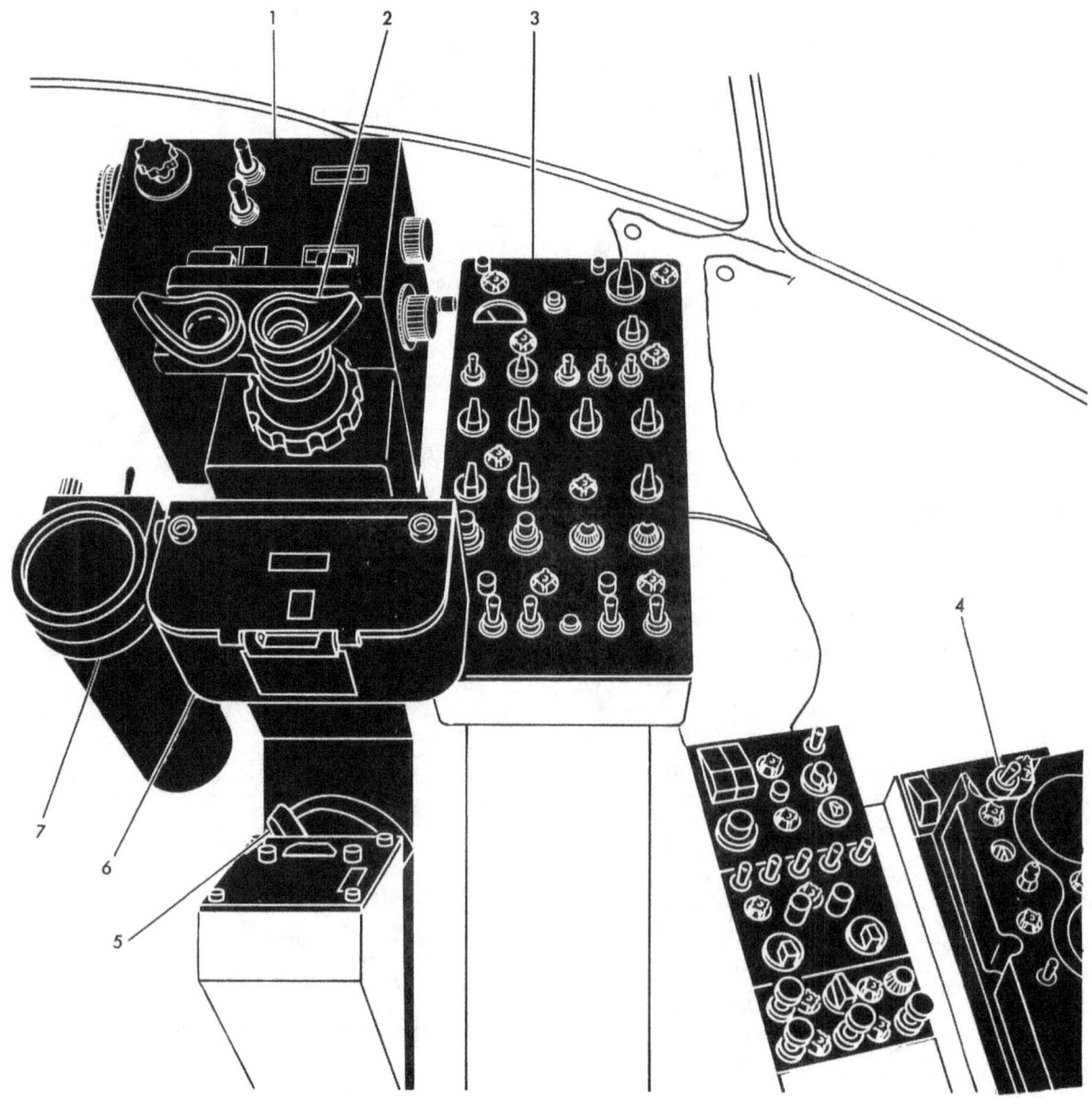

1. Modified MK-97 computer
2. MX-1295/ASB-1A periscope
3. C-582B/ASB-1 bomb director control
4. Periscope cover control switch
5. Magnification control lever
6. MX-1295/ASB-1A tracking recorder
7. IP-187A/ASB-1 auxiliary indicator

FF1-28293-C

Figure 8-1. AN/ASB-1A Modified Radar System - Cockpit Arrangement

NAVAIR 01-40ATA-1 Section VIII

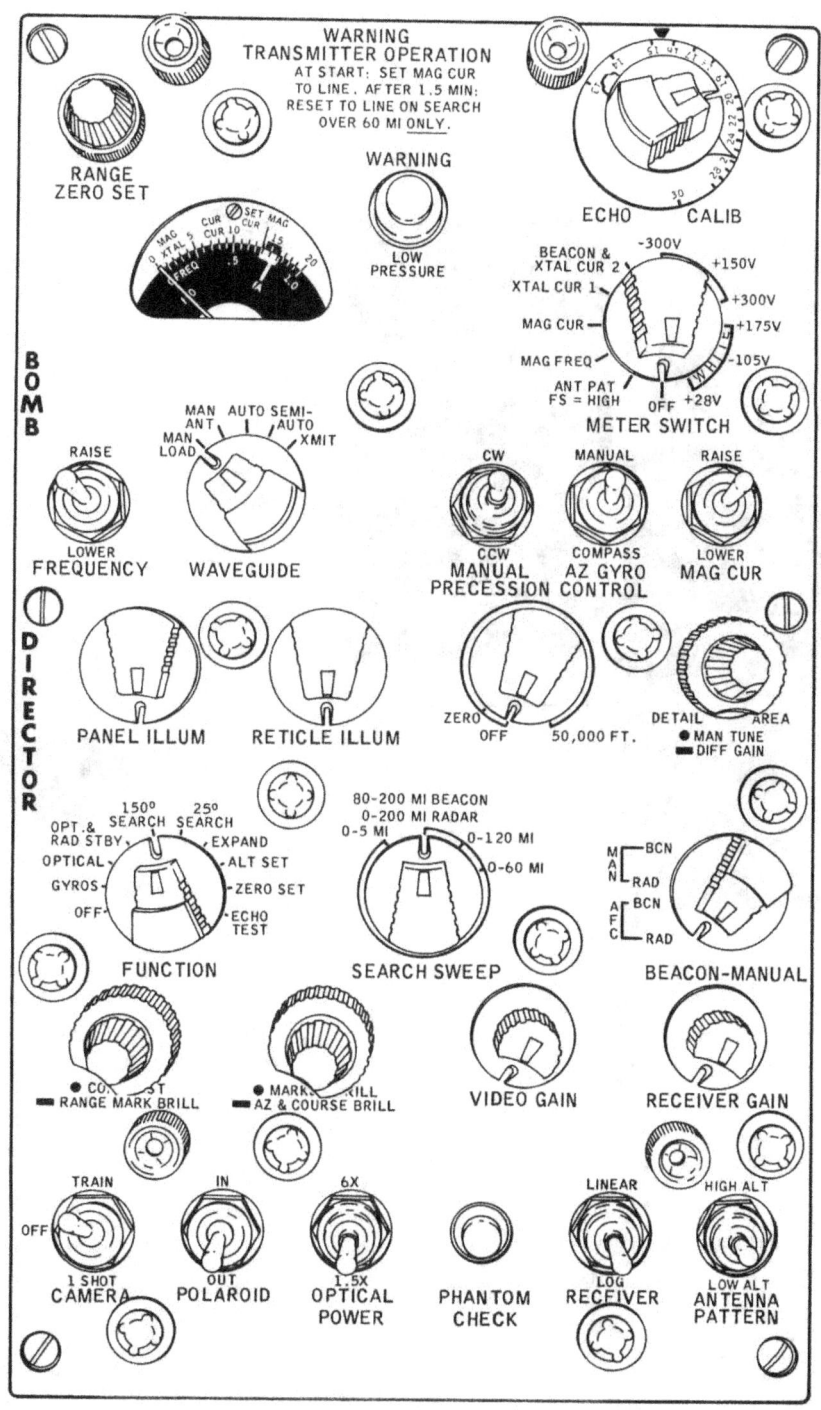

Figure 8-2 C-852B/ASB-1A Radar Control Panel

Section VIII NAVAIR 01-40ATA-1

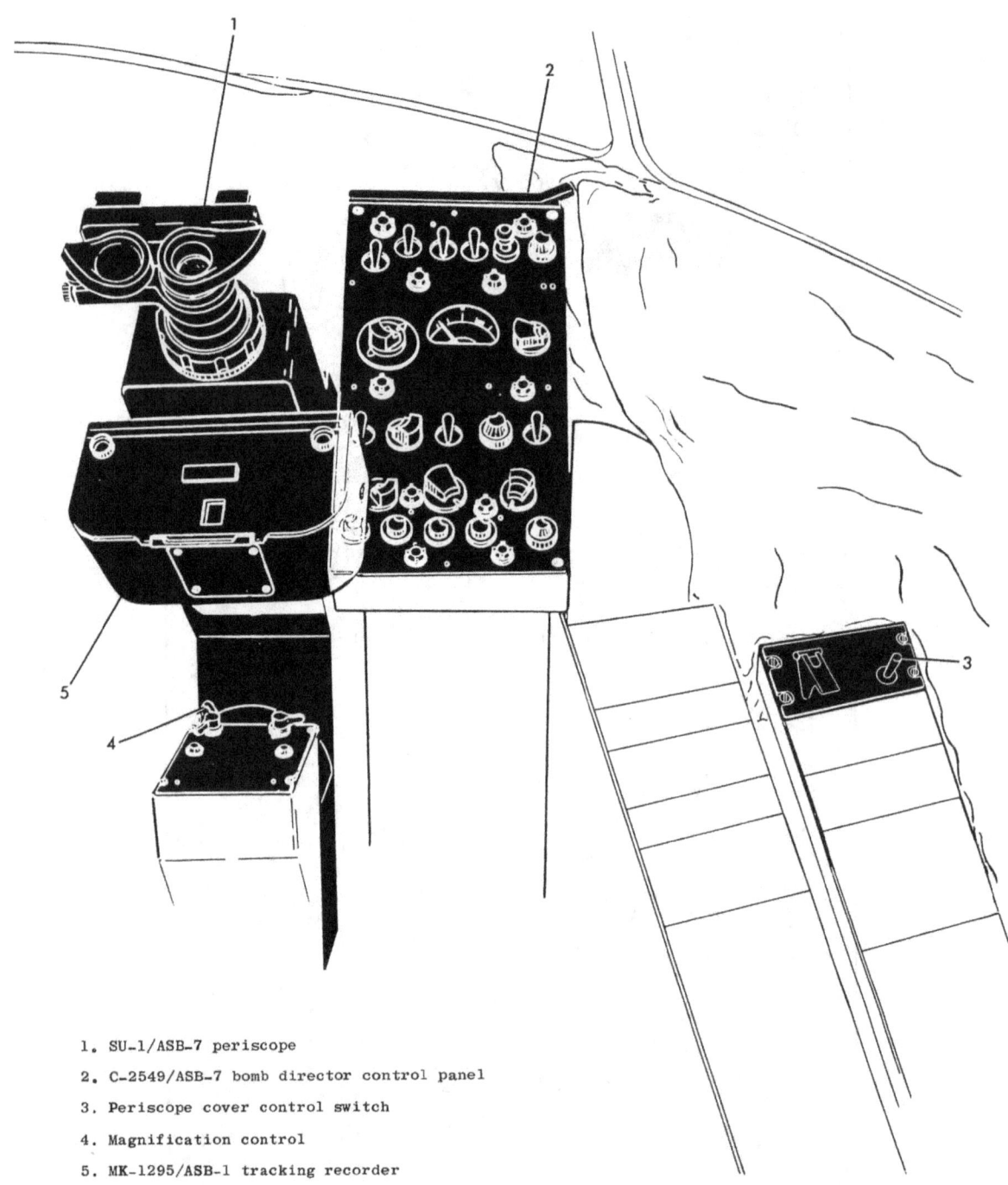

1. SU-1/ASB-7 periscope
2. C-2549/ASB-7 bomb director control panel
3. Periscope cover control switch
4. Magnification control
5. MK-1295/ASB-1 tracking recorder

FF1-28622-C

Figure 8-3. AN/ASB-7 Modified Radar System — Cockpit Arrangement

C-2549/ASB-7 RADAR CONTROL PANEL

The modified radar control panel C-2549/ASB-7 (figure 8-4) is the basic control unit for the system as well as the control for the tunable radar subsystem.

STARTING PROCEDURE

    FUNCTION switch . . . . GYROS

After aircraft is airborne, place FUNCTION switch in OPT and RAD STBY to place radar units in standby operation.

STOPPING PROCEDURE

    FUNCTION switch . . . . GYROS

The FUNCTION switch must be turned from OFF to GYROS before set becomes operational. Do not move FUNCTION switch from GYROS position for at least 3 minutes as this amount of time is necessary to allow the gyros to erect. When the switch is turned to the OPTICAL position, dc power is supplied to the periscope, data computer, power unit gyro stabilization system, and the electronic control amplifier. When the function switch is turned to the OPT and RAD STBY position, the radar system becomes ready for operation and optical viewing of tanking operation is possible. In the 150° SEARCH position, the antenna scans a 150-degree sector at one-half look per second centered about the aircraft centerline. The antenna scans a 25-degree sector at two looks per second centered about the azimuth line when in the 25° SEARCH position. If the BEACON-RADAR-PHANTOM CHECK switch is in the BEACON position at the time the FUNCTION switch is in EXPAND position, the antenna will scan the 25-degree sector at two looks per second if under 33 miles. In the ZERO SET position the antenna scans a 25-degree sector at five looks per second, and delays the transmitter pulse so that it can be brought into coincidence with the precision range line on the CRT screen. When switched to the ECHO TEST position, the antenna scans a 25-degree sector at five looks per second and varies the delay of the precision range line until the end of the ringing signal on the indicator presentation may be brought into coincidence with the precision range line. The SEARCH SWEEP switch has three positions: 5MI-60MI, 120MI, and 200MI. The sweep range is varied as the control knob is rotated to each position. The SEARCH SWEEP switch switch is in operation only when the FUNCTION switch is set at either 150° SEARCH or 25° SEARCH positions.

The BEACON-RADAR-PHANTOM CHECK switch is operated in conjunction with the RECEIVER-TUNING switch. The RECEIVER-TUNING switch has two positions: AFC and MAN. If the BEACON-RADAR-PHANTOM CHECK switch is in the BEACON position and the RECEIVER-TUNING switch is in the MAN position, beacon operation is selected, but AFC beacon circuits are disabled. When the BEACON-RADAR-PHANTOM CHECK switch is in the BEACON position and the RECEIVER-TUNING is in the AFC position, beacon AFC operation is selected and beacon search is disabled. When the BEACON-RADAR-PHANTOM CHECK switch is in the RADAR position and the RECEIVER-TUNING switch is in the MAN position, radar search operation is selected and the AFC circuits are disabled. When the BEACON-RADAR-PHANTOM CHECK switch is in the RADAR position and the RECEIVER-TUNING switch is in the AFC position, radar search is disabled and the receiver AFC circuits are placed into operation. When the BEACON-RADAR-PHANTOM CHECK switch is placed in the PHANTOM CHECK position, it permits a reduction of the pulse repetition frequency for checking to determine if the echo is a phantom.

The WAVE-GUIDE switch has six positions: XMIT OFF, MAN LOAD, MAN ANT, AUTO, SEMI AUTO, and XMIT. In the XMIT OFF position, rf energy is not supplied to the antenna. When the switch is turned to the MAN LOAD position, rf energy is directed to a dummy load. This position is used for test purposes only. If the switch is changed to the MAN ANT position, rf energy is directed to the antenna. This position is used for test purposes of the antenna. In the AUTO position, rf energy is directed to the antenna except when the MAG FREQ switch is set at either RAISE or LOWER. The rf energy is removed from the antenna and directed to the dummy load until the MAG FREQ switch is returned to the center (off) position. In the SEMI-AUTO position, rf energy is directed to the antenna until tuning is started. If the MAG FREQ switch is positioned at either RAISE or LOWER, the rf energy is diverted from the antenna and directed to the dummy load. The rf energy will remain diverted even though the MAG FREQ switch is centered (off). To return the rf energy to the antenna, advance the WAVE-GUIDE switch to the momentary XMIT position. The MAG-CUR switch has two positions: RAISE and LOWER. The two positions are necessary to increase or decrease the amplitude of the modulating pulse of the magnetron. The METER SWITCH must be in the MAG-CUR position to raise the magnetron current. Lowering of the current is not affected by the position of the METER SWITCH. The MAG FREQ switch provides a means of changing the operating frequency during search operations by tuning the magnetron and local oscillator. The ALT DELAY switch is adjusted to introduce the proper delay for illumination of the "hole" in the center of the indicator presentation. Delay can be introduced only when the SEARCH SWEEP is in the 5MI-60MI position. The RECEIVER GAIN switch, when in the log position, selects logarithmic operation so that the receiver if amplifier output is approximately proportional to the log of the inputs. Logarithmic operation is available only in the RADAR position of the

8-5

Section VIII NAVAIR 01-40ATA-1

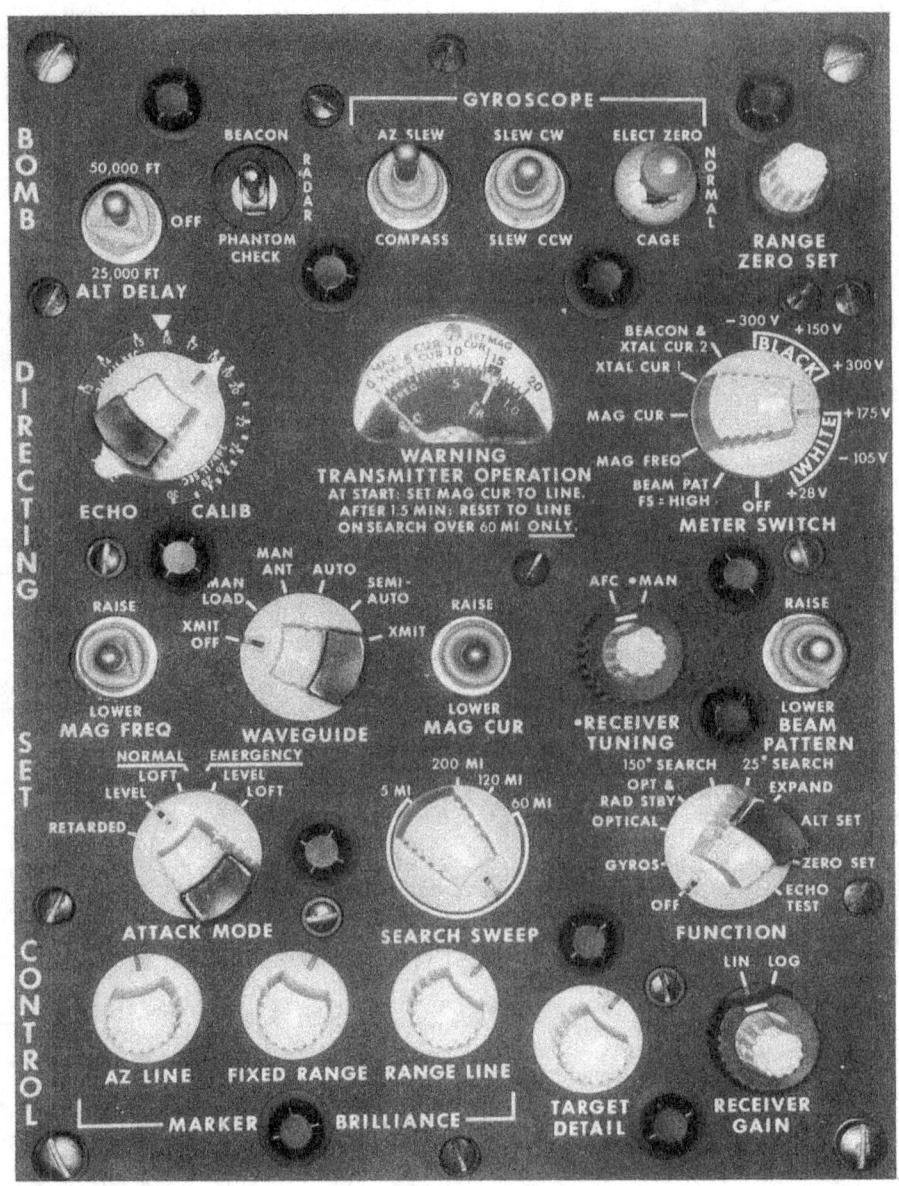

Figure 8-4. AN/ASB-7 Radar — Control Panel

BEACON-RADAR-PHANTOM CHECK switch. When switched to the BEACON position, linear if operation is automatically selected regardless of the position of the RECEIVER GAIN switch. In all other cases the LIN position of the RECEIVER GAIN switch selects the linear characteristics of the if amplifier.

TUNABLE RADAR SUBSYSTEM

The tunable radar subsystem provides four major functions: (1) It provides facilities for radar search at ranges up to 200 nautical miles through a 150-degree or 25-degree scanning sector. (2) It provides an expanded presentation for precision location and identification of an aimpoint. (3) As an aid to navigation, it supplies facilities to locate radar beacons or known check points, providing range and bearing information relative to the aircraft. (4) It provides for inflight calibration of the barometric altitude of the aircraft above the ocean or terrain. In addition to providing high resolution search and expanded presentations of the target area or surrounding terrain, the tunable radar holds a distinct advantage over fixed frequency radars in its relative immunity to radar countermeasures. In the presence of jamming signals, the navigator can tune the magnetron between the operating limits of 8600 and 9600 megacycles. During the tuning operation, the receiving system remains fully operative and is capable of receiving the jamming signals, while the transmitted output is completely absorbed by a dummy load. By observation of the indicator presentations and the magnetron frequency meter on the bomb director control panel, the navigator can determine the frequency of the jamming signals and select a jam-free frequency at which to operate.

ASB-1A Radar Equipment Checklist

COCKPIT

1. Accessible electrical cables, cannon connectors, static and pitot lines . . . . SECURE

CAUTION

Prior to application of external power, ensure that items 2 through 14 have been accomplished.

2. Gyro horizon ac circuit breakers . . . . PULLED

3. Dc generators . . . . OFF

4. Fuel trim switch . . . . NOSEDOWN

5. Throttles . . . . FULL AFT

6. Master engine switches . . . . . OFF

7. Battery switch . . . . OFF

8. Bus tie . . . . OPEN

9. External power switch . . . . . . OFF

10. Ac generators . . . . OFF

11. Radar function switch . . . . . . OFF

12. Radio master . . . . OFF

13. IFF . . . . OFF

14. Fuel dump switch . . . . OFF

RADAR CONTROL SETTINGS (POWER APPLIED)

1. Waveguide switch . . . . MANUAL LOAD

2. Azimuth gyro control . . . . . . MANUAL

3. Meter switch 28V

4. Altitude delay . . . . OFF

5. Differential gain . . . . AREA

6. Search sweep . . . . 0 TO 120 NM

7. Beacon/manual . . . . AFC/RAD

8. Contrast, markers, video, receiver gain . . . . CCW

9. ASB circuit breakers . . . . . . IN

10. Function switch . . . . GYROS (28V)

VOLTAGE CHECK (3 MINUTES AFTER INITIAL POWER APPLICATION)

1. Function switch . . . . OPT & RAD/STBY

2. Meter switch (voltages and currents) . . . . NORMAL

RADAR CONTROL PANEL CHECK

1. Mag switch . . . . LOWER/10 SEC

2. Function switch . . . . 150-DEGREE SEARCH

3. Mag current . . . . SET TO LINE

4. Crystals No. 1 and No. 2 . . . . CHECKED

Section VIII
NAVAIR 01-40ATA-1

5. AFC, crystal No. 2 . . . . LOCKED

6. Set scope controls.

7. Check sweeps.

8. Check scope presentations.

9. Antenna pattern . . . . HIGH/LOW ALTITUDE

ASB-1A Radar Taxi and Pretakeoff Checklist

TAXI

1. Check for targets. (If forward area clear and EMCON conditions permit)

PRETAKEOFF (SHIPBOARD)

1. Antenna scan . . . . 25-DEGREE SEARCH

2. Range . . . . AS DESIRED

3. Waveguide . . . . MANUAL LOAD

ASB-1A Radar Prelanding and Shutdown Checklist

PRELANDING

1. Antenna scan . . . . 25-DEGREE SEARCH

2. Range . . . . AS DESIRED

3. Waveguide . . . . MANUAL LOAD

CAUTION

Maintain prelanding switch positions until aircraft is in chocks.

SHUTDOWN (IN CHOCKS)

1. All scope controls . . . . CCW

2. Function switch . . . . OFF

ASB-1A Radar Malfunction Checklist

1. Antenna sticks. Change antenna scan rate; or, if freezing is suspected, descend to lower altitude, if possible.

2. Loss of targets on expanded-under-25 NM. Depress and hold phantom button to maintain 800 PRF.

3. Loss of AFC. Adjust MAN TUNE for maximum crystal current, and return to AFC. Change frequency. If AFC still inoperative, operate in MAN.

4. Arcing magnetron current. Check pressurization; if normal, decrease magnetron current until stable, or increase magnetron current and then reduce to level where current remains stable. If pressurization is low, reduce altitude as required to stabilize magnetron current.

5. Loss of presentation. Switch to 25-degree search, using search sweep to keep crosshairs in outer one-third of scope.

6. Loss of range or azimuth line. Use grease pencil or string under eyepiece as reference.

7. Loss of magnetron current. Attempt frequency change, PRF change, recycle radar system.

8. Loss of sweeps. Change PRF.

ASB-7 Radar Equipment Checklist

COCKPIT

1. Accessible electrical cables, cannon connectors, static and pitot lines . . . . SECURE

CAUTION

Prior to application of external power, ensure that items 2 through 14 have been accomplished.

2. Gyro horizon ac circuit breakers . . . . PULLED

3. Dc generators . . . . OFF

4. Fuel trim switch . . . . NOSEDOWN

5. Throttles . . . . FULL AFT

6. Master engine switches . . . . . OFF

7. Battery switch . . . . OFF

8. Bus tie . . . . OPEN

9. External power switch . . . . . OFF

10. Ac generators . . . . OFF

11. Radar function switch . . . . . . OFF

12. Radio master . . . . OFF

13. IFF . . . . OFF

14. Fuel dump switch . . . . OFF

RADAR CONTROL SETTINGS (POWER APPLIED)

1. Alt delay . . . . OFF

2. Beacon/radar . . . . RADAR

3. Gyroscope . . . . AZ SLEW/NORMAL

4. Meter switch 28V

5. Waveguide . . . . MANUAL LOAD

6. Receiver tuning . . . . AFC

7. Attack mode . . . . EMERGENCY LEVEL

8. Search sweep . . . . 0 TO 20 NM

9. Function switch . . . . GYROS

10. Marker brilliance . . . . ALL CCW

11. Differential gain . . . . CCW

12. Receiver gain . . . . CCW

13. Video gain/brightness . . . . . . OFF

VOLTAGE CHECK

1. Function switch . . . . OPT. AND RAD. STBY

2. CP209 blowers . . . . OPERATING

3. Meter switch (voltages and currents) . . . . NORMAL

RADAR CHECK (ZERO PDI WITH EMERG. LOS CONTROL)

1. Meter switch . . . . MAG CURRENT

2. Function switch . . . . 150-DEGREE SEARCH

3. Mag current . . . . SET TO LINE

4. Crystal current No. 1 and No. 2 . . . . CHECKED

5. Set scope controls.

6. Check sweeps.

7. Check presentation.

8. Beam pat . . . . RAISE/LOWER

ASB-7 Radar Taxi and Pretakeoff Checklist

TAXI

1. Check for targets.

PRETAKEOFF (SHIPBOARD)

1. Function switch . . . . 25-DEGREE SEARCH

2. Waveguide . . . . MANUAL LOAD

ASB-7 Radar Prelanding and Shutdown Checklist

PRELANDING

1. Function switch . . . . 25-DEGREE SEARCH

2. Waveguide . . . . MANUAL LOAD

SHUTDOWN

1. Scope controls . . . . OFF

2. Marker brill receiver gain . . . . CCW

3. In the chocks, function switch . . . . OFF

Changed 1 June 1969

8-9

ASB-7 Radar Malfunction Checklist

1. Antenna sticks. Change scan rate.

2. Loss of expanded presentation. Switch 25-degree search and use search-sweep control to maintain cross hairs in outer one-third of scope.

3. Loss of AFC. Change frequency or adjust manual tuning for maximum target returns.

4. Arcing magnetron current. Decrease magnetron current until arcing stops, then increase to the level of infrequent arcing.

5. Loss of sweeps. Change PRF.

6. Loss of receiver gain. Adjust camera gain controls.

SECTION IX
FLIGHT CREW COORDINATION

TABLE OF CONTENTS

Text	Page	Text	Page
Introduction	9-1	Duties of Flight Crewmembers	9-1

INTRODUCTION

To achieve the maximum possible crew coordination, each crewmember must have a thorough knowledge of NATOPS procedures and his crew duties and responsibilities. In addition, he should be familiar with the duties and responsibilities of the other crewmembers, and be prepared to anticipate demands on his crew position. This applies in particular to each crewmember's knowledge of emergency systems and procedures. Comprehension of instrument flight procedures will minimize distraction in the cockpit and interference with external communications during critical phases of flight. The most critical phases of flight involve in-flight emergencies when survival may depend on crew coordination and crew knowledge of emergency systems and procedures.

Duties of Flight Crewmembers

PILOT

1. Complete responsibility for the aircraft and its assigned mission and for the performance of the crew in their specified flight duties

2. Safe and proper operation of the aircraft in accordance with standard procedures

3. Supervise adequate and continued training of his crew

4. Delegate duties within his crew and ensure that all duties are properly designated and understood.

5. Inspection of crew flight gear prior to each flight.

NAVIGATOR

1. Complete preparation for and execution of the air refueling problem

2. Complete preparation for and proper conduct of required navigation

3. Ensure that the navigation bag with appropriate contents (Section III, part 2) is available in the aircraft

4. Train and supervise additional crewmember trainees

5. Assist in preflight of the aircraft

6. Assist in any other matters, as directed by the pilot (lookout, radio communications, etc).

PLANE CAPTAIN

1. Ensure completion of aircraft preflight inspection 1 hour prior to flight

2. Keep aircraft clean and serviced for mission assigned

3. Have personal knowledge of all aircraft discrepanices

4. Check stowage, availability, and condition of all survival equipment required in aircraft

5. Ensure that frequency cards and cockpit checklists are up to date, neat, and legible

6. Assist pilot and navigator in preflight inspection

7. Assume navigator's in-flight duties, excluding navigation, when flying in lieu of the navigator or when directed by pilot to do so

8. Have a thorough working knowledge of A-3 systems, emergency systems, radios, all flight equipment, and the procedures required for servicing the aircraft

9. Ensure adequate indoctrination and supervision of plane captain trainees assigned.

NAVAIR 01-40ATA-1 Section X

SECTION X
NATOPS EVALUATION

TABLE OF CONTENTS

TEXT

	Page		Page
Introduction	10-1	Radar Equipment Preflight Checklist	
Concept	10-1	(Area II)	10-11
Applicability	10-1	Taxi and Pretakeoff (Area III)	10-11
Definitions	10-1	Navigation (Area IV)	10-12
Implementation	10-2	Equipment Malfunction (Area V)	10-12
Ground Evaluation	10-2	Airmanship (Area VI)	10-12
Grading Instructions	10-3	Prelanding and Shutdown Procedures	
Flight Evaluation	10-3	(Area VII)	10-12
Pilot Flight Evaluation Grading Criteria	10-4	Debrief (Area VIII)	10-13
Mission Planning (Area I)	10-4	Plane Captain Flight Grading Criteria	10-13
Preflight Inspection of Aircraft (Area II)	10-5	Mission Planning (Area I)	10-13
Turnup and Taxi (Area III)	10-5	Preflight (Area II)	10-13
Takeoff (Area IV)	10-5	Pretaxi and Taxi (Area III)	10-14
Climbout and Level-Off (Area V)	10-6	Airmanship (Area IV)	10-14
Cruise (Area VI)	10-6	Checklist (Area V)	10-14
Instruments (Area VII)	10-6	Postlanding (Area VI)	10-14
Emergencies (Area VIII)	10-8	Flight Evaluation Grade Determination	10-15
Crew Coordination (Area IX)	10-8	Final Grade Determination	10-15
VFR Landing Pattern (Area X)	10-9	Critique	10-15
Postlanding and Shutdown (Area XI)	10-10	NATOPS Evaluation Forms	10-15
Postflight Debrief (Area XII)	10-10	Records and Reports	10-15
Navigator Flight Grading Criteria	10-10	NATOPS Evaluation Question Bank	10-16
Mission Planning (Area I)	10-10	A-3 NATOPS Flight Manual Question Bank	10-16

INTRODUCTION

Concept

The standard operating procedures prescribed in this manual represent the optimum method of operating A-3 aircraft. The NATOPS evaluation is intended to evaluate compliance with NATOPS procedures by observing and grading individuals and units. This evaluation is tailored for compatibility with various operational commitments and missions of both NAVY and Marine Corps units.

The prime objective of the NATOPS evaluation program is to assist the unit commanding officer in improving unit readiness and safety through constructive comment. Maximum benefit from the NATOPS program is achieved only through vigorous support of the program by commanding officers as well as flight crewmembers.

Applicability

The NATOPS evaluation shall be administered annually to pilots, navigators, and plane captains.

Definitions

The following terms, used throughout this section, are defined as to specific meaning within the NATOPS program.

NATOPS EVALUATION

A periodic evaluation of individual flight crewmember standardization consisting of an open book examination, a closed book examination, an oral examination, and a flight evaluation.

NATOPS REEVALUATION

A partial NATOPS evaluation administered to a flight crewmember who has been placed in an Unqualified status by receiving an Unqualified grade for any of his ground examinations or the flight evaluation. Only those areas in which an unsatisfactory level was noted need be observed during a reevaluation.

MINOR DISCREPANCIES AND/OR OMISSIONS

Minor discrepancies and/or omissions, as may be referred to in the grading criteria, are defined as those that would not adversely affect the successful completion of the mission or jeopardize the safety of the crew and/or equipment.

Changed 1 June 1969

Section X   NAVAIR 01-40ATA-1

MOMENTARY DEVIATIONS

A momentary deviation may be defined as very brief deviation from the tolerances set forth in the grading criteria, which will not be considered in marking, are permissible provided the evaluee is alert in applying corrective action, and the deviation does not jeopardize the safety of the aircraft or crew, and does not exceed the limitations prescribed for conditionally qualified grade. Cumulative momentary deviations, however, will result in downgrading.

QUALIFIED (Q)

That degree of standardization demonstrated by a very reliable flight crewmember who has a good knowledge of standard operating procedures and a thorough understanding of aircraft capabilities and limitations.

CONDITIONALLY QUALIFIED (CQ)

That degree of standardization demonstrated by a flight crewmember who meets the minimum acceptable standards. He is considered safe enough to fly as a pilot in command or to perform normal duties without supervision but more practice is needed to become Qualified.

UNQUALIFIED (U)

That degree of standardization demonstrated by a flight crewmember who fails to meet minimum acceptable criteria. He should receive supervised instruction until he has achieved a grade of Qualified or Conditionally Qualified.

AREA

A routine or preflight, flight or postflight.

SUBAREA

A performance subdivision within an area, which is observed and evaluated during an evaluation flight.

CRITICAL AREA

Any area or subarea that covers items of significant importance to the overall mission requirements, the marginal performance of which would jeopardize safe conduct of the flight. These items are identified with an * asterisk in the Flight Evaluation Criteria, contained in this section.

EMERGENCY

An aircraft component, system failure, or condition that requires instantaneous recognition, analysis, and proper action.

MALFUNCTION

An aircraft component or system failure or condition which requires recognition and analysis, but which permits more deliberate action than that required for an emergency.

Implementation

The NATOPS evaluation program shall be carried out in every unit operating naval aircraft. The various categories of flight crewmembers desiring to attain/retain qualification in the A-3 aircraft shall be evaluated initially in accordance with OPNAVINST 3510.9 series and at least once during the 12 months following initial and subsequent evaluations. Individual and unit NATOPS evaluation will be conducted annually; however, instruction in and observation of adherence to NATOPS procedures must be on a daily basis within each unit to obtain maximum benefits from the program. The NATOPS coordinators, evaluators, and instructors shall administer the program as outlined in OPNAVINST 3510.9 series. Evaluees who receive a grade of Unqualified on a ground or flight evaluation shall be allowed 30 days in which to complete a reevaluation. A maximum of 60 days may elapse between the date the initial ground evaluation was commenced and the date the flight evaluation is satisfactorily completed.

Ground Evaluation

The ground evaluation consists of two parts: Phase I, the open and closed book examination, and Phase II, the OFT/15Z5 evaluation. The OFT evaluation will consist of a graded simulated flight with emphasis on emergencies for the pilot; the 15Z5, an optional radar navigation evaluation for the navigator. For squadrons based at locations without access to the OFT/15Z5, Phase II evaluations are waived; however, the pilot will be given an oral examination. The ground evaluation shall be completed with a grade of qualified prior to commencement of the flight evaluation, Phase III.

OPEN BOOK EXAMINATION

Up to 50 percent of the questions used may be taken from the question bank. The number of questions on the examination will not exceed 75 or be less than 25. The purpose of the open book examination portion of the written examination is to evaluate the pilot's, navigator's, and plane captain's knowledge of appropriate publications and the aircraft. The maximum time for this examination should not exceed 3 hours.

CLOSED BOOK EXAMINATION

The closed book examination may be taken from the question bank and shall include questions concerning normal and emergency procedures and aircraft limitations. The number of questions on the examination will not exceed 75 or be less than 25. Questions designated critical will be so marked. An incorrect answer to any question in the critical category will result in a grade of Unqualified being assigned to the examination.

10-2   Changed 1 June 1969

ORAL EXAMINATION

The oral questions may be taken from this manual and drawn from the experience of the instructor/evaluator. Such questions should be direct and positive and in no way opinionated.

OFT/WST PROCEDURES EVALUATION

An OFT shall be used to assist in measuring the pilot's efficiency in the execution of normal operating procedures and his reaction to emergencies and malfunctions. In areas not served by the OFT facilities, evaluation may be made with the pilot in the cockpit, while the instructur/evaluator asks appropriate questions.

Grading Instructions

WRITTEN EXAMINATION

Examination grades shall be computed on a 4.0 scale and converted to an adjective grade of Qualified or Unqualified.

OPEN BOOK EXAMINATION

To obtain a grade of Qualified, an evaluee must obtain a minimum score of 3.5.

CLOSED BOOK EXAMINATION

To obtain a grade of Qualified, an evaluee must obtain a minimum score of 3.3.

ORAL EXAMINATION

A grade of Qualified or Unqualified shall be assigned by the instructor/evaluator using the following criteria:

Q - Demonstrated thorough knowledge of proper cockpit procedures, both normal and emergency; was thoroughly familiar with aircraft systems.

U - Indicated an obvious lack of understanding of proper cockpit procedures, both normal and emergency; was unfamiliar with aircraft systems.

OFT EVALUATION

Emergency procedures must be memorized.

Q - Recognized emergency situation with minimum delay; took timely and appropriate action as specified by governing directives; completed applicable checklists without errors or omissions.

U - Failed to recognize situation; used improper procedures or deviated from specified procedures to the extent of endangering safety of flight.

Flight Evaluation

The flight evaluation is designed to measure with maximum objectivity the degree of standardization demonstrated by pilot and crewmembers. It is not intended to measure the proficiency and/or ability of those evaluated beyond a point necessary to assure safety of flight. Within reasonable limits, any individual evaluated should be able to attain a qualified grade based upon demonstrated knowledge without regard to special proficiency or ability.

The process uses three integrated parts: the flight evaluation worksheet, the flight evaluation grading criteria, and the evaluation report form.

The flight evaluation worksheet is designed to enable the evaluator/instructor to record pertinent information for the purpose of a comprehensive postflight reconstruction and critique. Following completion of the evaluation, data from the worksheet are compared with the grading criteria to determine the numerical/adjectival equivalent for entry on the evaluation report form.

Missions flown shall be adequate for evaluation purposes. Only observed areas will be graded. The first flight will be an air refueling mission with the navigator evaluator/instructor grading the navigator, the target planning and delivery portion of the pilot's grading criteria, and a portion of the plane captain's in-flight duties. The second flight will be a local flight with the pilot evaluator/instructor grading the pilot and the remaining portion of the plane captain's in-flight duties not observed by the navigator evaluator/instructor. All ground phase duties of the plane captain, including aircraft preflight and postflight inspection, will be graded by the plane captain evaluator/instructor.

FLIGHT EVALUATION GRADING CRITERIA

The grades assigned for a subarea shall be determined by comparing the degree of adherence to standard operating procedures with adjectival ratings listed below. Momentary deviations from standard operating procedures should not be considered as unqualifying provided such deviations do not jeopardize flight and the evaluee applies prompt corrective action.

NOTE

The term "mission," as it appears in the following text, applies to ECM and/or air refueling procedures.

PILOT FLIGHT EVALUATION GRADING CRITERIA

Mission Planning (Area I)

TARGET PLANNING (SUBAREA a)

- Q - Supervised and coordinated the planning of the flight route and mission profile; ensured that the crew received adequate mission briefing in accordance with governing directives.

- CQ - Prepared with minor errors or omissions.

- U - Prepared with major errors or omissions which adversely affected mission accomplishment.

FLIGHT PLAN (SUBAREA b)

- Q - Completed flight plan and other applicable clearance forms without error or omission, in accordance with governing directives. Considered weather factors including departure, destination, and alternate weather in requesting flight clearance; Included other weather factors, such as cruise winds and severe weather warnings, en route planning. Chose route with regard to warning, restricted, prohibited, or controlled areas; reviewed Flight Planning Document and NOTAM file for information which would affect the mission, obtained copies of applicable IFR departures/routes.

- CQ - Prepared with minor errors or omissions.

- U - Prepared with major errors or omissions which adversely affected mission accomplishment.

FUEL PLAN (SUBAREA c)

- Q - Prepared in accordance with current doctrine; included bingo fuel, adequate checks, and sufficient fuel remaining at destination and alternates.

- CQ - Prepared with minor errors or omissions which did not jeopardize mission or aircraft safety.

- U - Did not prepare fuel plan or prepared an inadequate fuel plan.

TAKEOFF COMPUTATIONS (SUBAREA d)

- Q - Computed all performances within tolerances listed below.

- U - Made computation errors exceeding tolerances listed:

Data	Tolerance
Takeoff roll	±500 feet
Takeoff speed	±5 knots
Refusal speed	±5 knots
Line speed	±5 knots
Minimum single-engine speed	+5 knots

CREW PROMPTNESS (SUBAREA e)

- Q - Crew met scheduled briefing time.

- U - Crew failed to meet scheduled briefing time.

PERSONAL EQUIPMENT (SUBAREA f)

- Q - Pilot was equipped as required.

- U - Not up to the standards of qualified.

Preflight Inspection of Aircraft (Area II)

ACCEPTANCE OF AIRCRAFT (SUBAREA a)

Q - Listed all entries on yellow sheet without errors. Properly inspected section B of yellow sheet.

CQ - Filled out yellow sheet with errors or omissions that would not affect safety; accepted aircraft with minor discrepancy not cleared up for flight.

U - Accepted aircraft with downing discrepancy; failed to check section B discrepancies on yellow sheet.

PREFLIGHT INSPECTION (SUBAREA b)

Q - Received plane captain's report of preflight, ordnance, fuel distribution, and equipment for mission. Completed preflight inspection with no errors or omissions.

CQ - Accomplished preflight with minor errors or omission.

U - Accomplished preflight with major errors or omissions.

PRESTART (SUBAREA c)

Q - Used checklist properly.

U - Used checklist improperly.

Turnup and Taxi (Area III)

ENGINE START AND PRETAXI (SUBAREA a)

Q - Used checklist properly.

U - Omitted item affecting safety. Did not observe engine starting limitations.

TAXI AND PRETAKEOFF (SUBAREA b)

Q - Commenced taxi in time to meet scheduled takeoff. Taxied prudently at all times; used checklist properly.

CQ - Commenced taxi after minor pilot/crew-caused delays; omitted checklist items not affecting safety of flight.

U - Pilot/crew caused taxi delay in excess of 10 minutes of scheduled takeoff time, taxied too fast and/or failed to observe proper precautions, omitted checklist item affecting safety of flight.

CLEARANCE/COMMUNICATIONS (SUBAREA c)

Q - Used proper voice procedures and initiated timely clearance request.

CQ - Made minor errors in communications and/or untimely requests.

U - Failed to initiate clearance requests. Made gross errors in communications procedures.

Takeoff (Area IV)

*PROCEDURE AND TECHNIQUE (SUBAREA a)

Q - Performed full power check. Maintained smooth control during takeoff roll. Performed line speed check. Rotated to takeoff attitude at computed takeoff speed.

CQ - Was rough on control without compromising safety. Had tendency to drift off takeoff heading. Failed to rotate at takeoff speed but rotated within 10 knots after reaching computed takeoff speed.

U - Failed to perform full power check. Was erratic enough on control during takeoff roll tending to compromise safety. Failed to perform line speed check. Overrotated takeoff.

*AFTER LIFTOFF (SUBAREA b)

Q - Maintained smooth control. Established optimum climb attitude. Retracted wheels and flaps in accordance with established procedures.

CQ - Was rough on control without compromising safety. Unnecessarily delayed retraction of gear or flaps, but did not exceed established limits.

Section X   NAVAIR 01-40ATA-1

U - Exceeded the gear and flap tolerances. Was erratic enough on control to compromise safety.

Climbout and Level-Off (Area V)

CLIMB SCHEDULE (SUBAREA a)

Q - Maintained climb schedule within 10 knots.

CQ - Maintained climb schedule within 15 knots.

U - Exceeded climb schedule more than 15 knots.

CHECKLISTS (AFTER TAKEOFF, 23,500 FEET, LEVEL-OFF) (SUBAREA b)

Q - Completed checklists in proper sequence without errors or omissions.

CQ - Completed checklists with errors or omissions not affecting safety of flight.

U - Completed checklists with errors or omissions not affecting safety of flight.

LEVEL-OFF AND TRANSITION TO CRUISE (SUBAREA c)

Q - Made smooth transition to cruise altitude and airspeed.

CQ - Leveled off more than 100 feet but less than 300 feet from assigned altitude and more than 10 but less than 20 knots of cruise airspeed.

U - Exceeded limits established for CQ. Made rough transition to cruise condition.

Cruise (Area VI)

AIRCRAFT CONTROL (SUBAREA a)

Maintained airspeed, heading, and altitude within following limits:

	AIRSPEED	HEADING	ALTITUDE
Q -	±10	±5°	±200
CQ -	±15	±10°	±300
U -	Exceeded CQ limits	Exceeded CQ limits	Exceeded CQ limits

INFLIGHT CHECKS (SUBAREA b)

Q - Performed complete inflight checks at least every 30 minutes.

CQ - Performed inflight checks with minor errors or omissions.

U - Failed to perform checks as required for conditionally qualified.

POSITION REPORTS (SUBAREA c)

Q - Made timely reports using proper procedures and exact phraseology.

CQ - Submitted reports as required but with procedures and phraseology containing minor errors.

U - Made improper or wrong report, or failed to make report.

Instruments (Area VII)

NOTE

The instrument area is quite detailed in nature, with its subareas broken down into items. This breakdown was designed to be used as an instrument check if desired.

COMPLETE MISSION PLANNING (SUBAREA a)

NOTE

Omit items graded in Mission Planning (Area 1).

DEPARTURE (SUBAREA b)

*COMPLIANCE WITH CLEARANCE

Q - Complied with departure clearance with no navigation deviations in excess of ±5 degrees from assigned track or heading and with no altitude deviations in excess of ±200 feet of assigned altitude. Made all voice reports as required.

10-6

CQ - Complied with departure clearance with no navigational deviations in excess of ±10 degrees from assigned track and with no altitude deviations in excess of ±300 feet of assigned altitude(s). Voice reports made with minor errors or omissions not affecting safety of flight.

U - Did not meet criteria for CQ.

CLIMBOUT

Q - Completed after-takeoff checklist with no errors or omissions. Established climb schedule without delay and maintained schedule within 10 knots.

CQ - Completed after-takeoff checklist with minor errors or omissions not affecting safety of flight. Established climb schedule with little delay and maintained schedule within 15 knots.

U - Did not meet criteria for CQ.

LEVEL-OFF PROCEDURES (See Area V, b and c)

NOTE

Do not grade here if previously graded in Area V.

HOLDING AND PATTERN ENTRY (SUBAREA c)

Q - Smoothly entered and maintained position in the pattern in accordance with governing directives.

CQ - Was late stabilizing holding IAS. Maintained position in the pattern within prescribed limits, but occasionally overcontrolled.

U - Did not comply with current directives entering pattern. Deviated in excess of 300 feet from assigned altitude. Did not obtain holding IAS until after crossing fix. Constantly overcontrolled.

PENETRATIONS (SUBAREA d)

*PROCEDURES

Q - Completed descent checklist without error or omission prior to commencing descent.

Complied with penetration clearance without error or omission. Remained within 5 degrees of penetration radial after initial interception. Maintained penetration IAS within 5 knots and rate of descent within 500 fpm (where assigned).

CQ - Made minor deviations or omissions in descent checklist not affecting safety of flight. Completed checklist before penetration turn. Remained within 7.5 degrees of penetration radial after initial interception. Deviated from clearance, but not enough to affect traffic control or safety of flight. Maintained penetration IAS within 10 knots and rate of descent within 750 fpm (where assigned).

U - Exceeded limits specified for CQ. Exceeded published limits of penetration.

*TRANSITION TO LEVEL-OFF

Q - Made smooth transition to level flight in accordance with governing directives.

CQ - Transition to level flight in accordance with governing directives, but occasionally overcontrolled. Maintained level-off altitude within limits of -100 to +300 feet.

U - Failed to follow current directives and/or constantly overcontrolled aircraft. Exceeded limits specified for CQ.

APPROACH (SUBAREA e)

*TRANSITION TO LANDING CONFIGURATION

Q - Completed smooth transition to landing configuration. Completed landing checklist to speed brakes without error or omission. Observed aircraft limitations regarding the lowering of gear and flaps. Did not go below minimum or assigned approach altitude throughout the approach.

CQ - Occasionally overcontrolled aircraft during transition. Checklist completed to speed brakes with minor variations or deviations not affecting safety of flight or ability to complete the approach. Deviated below minimum or assigned approach altitude by no more than 100 feet.

U - Continually overcontrolled aircraft during transition. Failed to complete landing checklist to speedbrakes or made major error or omission affecting safety of flight or ability to complete the approach. Exceeded 100 feet below minimum or assigned altitude. Exceeded aircraft limitations on flaps and gear.

*FINAL

Q - Smoothly established and maintained approach airspeed/angle of attack. Made smooth transition to final descent path without descending below minimum altitude until establishing visual contact. Completed landing checklist.

CQ - Occasionally overcontrolled and/or had difficulty maintaining final approach airspeed. Did not exceed 50 feet below minimum altitude.

U - Continually overcontrolled power and/or altitude during approach. Overlooked extending speedbrakes causing difficulty in controlling aircraft and resulting in a missed approach.

*GCA/CCA PROCEDURES

Q - Made all required voice reports using proper procedures and phraseology. Followed all instructions without delay or deviation. Maintained position on GCA/CCA final with minor deviations of assigned heading or altitude.

CQ - Made all necessary voice reports but with minor deviations or delays not affecting safety of flight or ability to complete the approach. Maintained position on GCA/CCA final with minor deviations which did not result in a missed approach.

U - Used improper voice procedures resulting in a missed approach or endangering safety of flight, or failed to make a required report or acknowledge when so required. Failed to follow instructions received and acknowledged. Overcontrolled aircraft and/or power to the extent that a waveoff was given. Continued approach beyond minimums without visual contact.

*MISSED APPROACH

Q - Recognized missed approach situation within 30 seconds of published position/time for initiating missed approach. Made required voice report using proper procedure and exact phraseology when executing missed approach. Made smooth transition to missed approach pattern with minor deviations in heading and altitude. Requested clearance to alternate if required.

CQ - Recognized missed approach situation more then 30 seconds but not more than 1 minute from published position/time. Made necessary report with minor errors or omissions not affecting safety of flight. Occasionally overcontrolled during transition to missed approach pattern but with no deviations affecting the safety of flight or traffic control.

U - Failed to recognize missed approach situation within one minute of published position/time. Failed to make required voice report executing approach and/or failed to request necessary further clearance. Overcontrolled aircraft to the extent that safety of flight or traffic control was endangered.

*Emergencies (Area VIII)

Q - Recognized emergency situation with minimum delay. Took timely and appropriate action as specified by governing directives. Completed applicable checklists without error or omissions.

CQ - Recognized emergency situation with delay not endangering safety of flight. Successfully coped with emergency situation but with deviations from specified directives.

U - Failed to recognize situation. Used improper procedures or deviated from specified procedures to the extent of endangering safety of flight.

*Crew Coordination (Area IX)

NONCRITICAL IF CREW NONTACTICAL

Q - The crew was well coordinated, and the pilot was well aware of the responsibility of each crewmember. Crew's performance as a team reflected pilot's emphasis of conformance to standard procedures by all crewmembers.

CQ - The crew was coordinated. Pilot was generally aware of crewmembers' responsibilities. Crew performance as a team reflected some lack of emphasis on conformance to standard procedures but did not jeopardize safety of flight or ability to complete the mission.

U - The crew was not coordinated. Pilot was generally unaware of crewmembers' responsibilities. Crew performance as a team reflected lack of emphasis on conformance to standard procedures to the extent that safety of flight and/or ability to complete the mission was jeopardized.

VFR Landing Pattern (Area X)

*ENTRY AND BREAK (SUBAREA a)

Q - Properly planned entry to the pattern on speed and altitude. Made proper voice report prior to entry and followed instructions received. Was aware of other traffic in the vicinity of the field. Smoothly executed break maneuver in accordance with specified procedure.

CQ - Entered pattern with slight deviations in speed and/or altitude. Occasionally overcontrolled. Voice report prior to entry was late or incomplete but did not affect flight safety or traffic control. Executed break maneuver with minor deviations from specified procedure. Occasionally overcontrolled.

U - Made poorly planned or improperly executed entry to the pattern. Failed to make voice report prior to entry. Was not aware of other traffic in the vicinity. Executed break maneuver with major deviations from specified procedure and/or exceeded aircraft limitations.

*SIMULATED SINGLE-ENGINE (SUBAREA b)

Q - Followed applicable procedures as specified in governing directives without error or omission. Smoothly controlled aircraft at all times, and maintained minimum single-engine speed, and pattern spacing and altitude with minor deviations. Completed landing checklist as modified by single-engine situation. Initiated waveoff at specified altitude and smoothly controlled aircraft through waveoff transition. Did not exceed aircraft limitations.

CQ - Followed applicable procedures as specified in governing directives with minor deviations or omissions not affecting safety of flight or ability to complete the landing. Occasionally overcontrolled with minor deviations not exceeding 300 feet below standard pattern altitude or 10 knots below safe single-engine approach speed. Completed landing checklist as modified by single-engine situation but with additonal deviations and/or omissions not affecting safety of flight or ability to complete the landing. Initiated waveoff no more than 100 feet below specified altitude. Occasionally overcontrolled during waveoff transition but did not exceed aircraft limitations.

U - Failed to follow applicable procedures as specified or made major deviations from the specified procedures which endangered safety of flight or the ability to complete the landing. Continually overcontrolled or made major deviations in pattern spacing and/or altitude and/or airspeed exceeding the limits specified for conditionally qualified. Failed to complete the landing checklist as modified by the single-engine situation or made major deviations or omissions that affected safety of flight or the ability to complete the landing. Delayed initiation of waveoff below the limits specified for conditionally qualified. Continually overcontrolled during waveoff transition and/or exceeded aircraft limitations.

*FMLP (SUBAREA c)

Q - Smoothly controlled aircraft throughout pattern in accordance with specified FMLP pattern procedures. Completed landing checklist without error or omission. Maintained pattern altitudes and airspeeds with minor deviations not exceeding ±100 feet altitude and ±10 KIAS until turning off the 180. (Speed deviation on final did not exceed ±2 units angle of attack.) Did not lose meatball throughout final after initial sighting. Made touchdown in safe attitude and with centerline not outside of either main mount.

CQ - Occasionally overcontrolled aircraft in the pattern. Made minor deviations from specified procedures and/or landing checklist. Maintained pattern altitudes and airspeeds with deviations not exceeding ±150 feet and ±20 KIAS until entering the final. Speed deviation on final did not exceed ±4 units angle of attack but touchdown was made within ±2 units of approach setting. Lost meatball no more than one time on final after initial sighting, and recovered before reaching 300 feet.

U - Continually overcontrolled aircraft in the pattern. Made major deviations from specified procedures and/or landing checklist, jeopardizing safety of flight or ability to complete the landing. Exceeded altitude and/or airspeed limits specified for conditionally qualified. Made touchdown in unsafe attitude or with centerline outside of either main mount. Received technique waveoff.

*NORMAL FINAL LANDING (SUBAREA d)

Q - Smoothly controlled aircraft throughout pattern in accordance with specified landing pattern procedures. Completed landing checkoff list without error or omission. Maintained pattern altitudes and speeds with minor deviations not exceeding ±150 feet and ±10 KIAS until entering the final. Speed deviation on final did not exceed 2 units angle of attack. Made touchdown between 200 and 800 feet down the runway. Made touchdown in safe attitude, with the aircraft smoothly controlled during the rollout.

Section X   NAVAIR 01-40ATA-1

CQ - Occasionally overcontrolled aircraft in the pattern. Made minor deviations from specified procedures and/or landing checklist. Maintained pattern altitudes and airspeeds with deviations not exceeding ±200 feet and ±20 knots until entering the final. Speed deviation on final did not exceed ±4 units angle of attack and touchdown made within ±2 units of approach setting. Touchdown made on runway short of 200-foot mark or beyond 800-foot mark but within first 1000 feet or a waveoff taken. (If waveoff is taken to prevent landing short or long on the first pass, a maximum grade of conditionally qualified will be assigned regardless of outcome of the second pass. If touchdown is made short of the runway or beyond 1000-foot mark or an excessive sink rate is intiated to land within the 1000-foot mark, a grade of unqualified will be assigned.)

U - Continually overcontrolled aircraft in the pattern. Made major deviations from specified procedures and/or landing checklist, jeopardizing safety of flight or ability to complete the landing. Exceeded airspeed or altitude limits specified for conditionally qualified. Made touchdown short or runway or beyond 1000-foot mark. Touchdown attitude unsafe. Aircraft control during rollout unsafe. Failed to take waveoff following third divergent porpoise.

Postlanding and Shutdown (Area XI)

TAXI PROCEDURES (SUBAREA a)

Q - Taxied aircraft smoothly to the parking area. Observed specified taxi techniques and procedures. Did not commence postlanding checklist until clear of the duty runway.

CQ - Was rough on control while taxiing to the parking area. Deviated slightly from specified taxi techniques and procedures.

U - Was rough on control while taxiing to the parking area, resulting in overstress of the nose gear or injury to personnel or taxiing of aircraft off of taxi area. Failed to follow taxi instructions. Commenced postlanding checklist prior to clearing duty runway.

SHUTDOWN PROCEDURES (SUBAREA b)

Q - Completed all items on the postlanding checklist without error or omission, and did not proceed with shutdown checklist until in the chocks.

CQ - Completed shutdown checklist with minor deviations not affecting aircraft safety.

U - Failed to complete shutdown checklist or made major deviations that affected aircraft safety. Proceeded with shutdown checklist before being chocked.

Postflight Debrief (Area XII)

YELLOW SHEET (SUBAREA a)

Q - Filled out yellow sheet properly without error or omission. Included clear, concise description of discrepancies.

CQ - Yellow sheet filled out with minor deviations or omissions not affecting pilot or aircraft record keeping. Wrote up discrepancies in understandable manner.

U - Made major errors in filling out yellow sheet, which would affect pilot or aircraft record keeping. Wrote up aircraft discrepancies in ambiguous manner.

CREW DEBRIEF (SUBAREA b)

Q - Debriefed crew by covering:

　　1. Mission accomplishment

　　2. Crew performance

　　3. Pertinent recommendations

　Made debriefing short, clear, and concise.

CQ - Debriefing unnecessarily long and detailed. Made irrelevant comments.

U - Failed to debrief crew or did not cover, even briefly, the three areas listed under Q above.

NAVIGATOR FLIGHT GRADING CRITERIA

Mission Planning (Area I)

CHARTS (SUBAREA a)

Q - Properly scaled charts for the type of mission flown. Plotted an accurate intended course with DR positions or tick marks as appropriate. Plotted suitable enroute diversionary fields.

CQ - Prepared charts with minor errors or omissions.

U - Prepared charts with major errors or omissions, with positions grossly misplotted or courses and distances in error.

NAVIGATION LOG (SUBAREA b)

Q - Prepared navigation log and route cards with no errors or omissions. Included all items on the standard navigation log.

CQ - Prepared navigation log and route cards with minor errors or omissions.

U - Prepared navigation log and route cards with major errors or omissions that adversely affected mission accomplishment.

CHECKLISTS (SUBAREA c)

Q - Suitable checklists were available. These included:

1. Radar equipment checklist

2. Mission checklist

The mission checklist listed was complete, with accurate timely accomplishment of each specified item listed. It established in detail the conduct of the flight in chronological order.

CQ - The checklists were available. The mission checklist was prepared with minor errors or omissions.

U - The checklists were not available. The mission checklist was prepared with major errors or omissions which adversely affected mission accomplishment.

AIR REFUELING (SUBAREA d)

Q - Completed Air Refueling checklists in a timely manner, demonstrated thorough knowledge of tanker fuel system capabilities, and corrective procedures for system malfunction.

CQ - Completed Air Refueling checklists with minor errors or omissions, could have been better versed on fuel system capabilities, hesitant in corrective procedures for system malfunction.

U - Air Refueling checklists were not available or not utilized, unsure of system capabilities and corrective procedures for system malfunction.

*MISSION CHECKLIST (SUBAREA e)

Q - Mission checklist included those items from Section III, part 2 and Section VIII that were pertinent to the flight.

U - Omissions noted which would jeopardize the successful completion of the flight.

PERSONAL FLYING EQUIPMENT (SUBAREA f)

Q - Crewmember was equipped as required (refer to Section II).

U - Crewmember lacked required equipment.

NAVIGATION BAG CONTENTS (SUBAREA g)

Q - Navigation bag contained all required items (refer to Section III, part 2).

U - Navigation bag lacked required items.

Radar Equipment Preflight Checklist (Area II)

Q - Checked ASB system in accordance with the radar equipment preflight checklist. Reviewed recent system history.

CQ - Conducted preflight with minor errors or omissions.

U - Conducted preflight with major errors or omissions which adversely affected mission accomplishment.

Taxi and Pretakeoff (Area III)

Q - Conducted taxi and pretakeoff in accordance with radar equipment taxi and pretakeoff checklist.

CQ - Used taxi and pretakeoff checklist but made minor errors or omissions.

U - Completed checklist with major errors or omissions which adversely affected mission accomplishment.

Navigation (Area IV)

Minimum navigational standards for evaluation purposes are defined as follows:

1. For overwater flights, comply with ICAO rules as set forth in current flight planning documents.

2. For flight on US airways or off-airways flights over the U.S., comply with FAA rules as set forth in current flight planning documents.

3. For training and operational flights, minimum standards will be those set forth by the controlling authority for the flight under evaluation.

4. The minimum standards for plotting when required are: A DR position be plotted every 10 minutes and a fix be obtained and plotted at least every 30 minutes.

   Q - The navigational requirements of the mission were met. Navigational information was properly obtained, evaluated and plotted.

   CQ - The navigational requirements of the mission were met; however, navigational information was not properly obtained, not properly evaluated, or not properly plotted.

   U - The navigational requirements of the mission were not met.

Equipment Malfunction (Area V)

   Q - Equipment malfunctions were recognized and handled in an orderly manner in accordance with the equipment malfunction checklist.

   CQ - Equipment malfunctions were recognized; however, the best corrective action was not taken.

   U - Failed to recognize and take proper corrective action where equipment malfunctions existed.

Airmanship (Area VI)

*CREW COORDINATION (SUBAREA a)

(Noncritical if crew nontactical)

   Q - Coordinated smoothly and effectively in all crew endeavors. Anticipated demands upon his crew position. Enhanced overall performance of the crew by continual alertness.

   U - Coordinated at a level sufficiently low to hinder crew performance. Was unfamiliar with crewmembers' duties and/or was continually interrupting them to a degree that team work was definitely retarded and mission requirements were lost.

RADIOTELEPHONE PROCEDURES (SUBAREA b)

   Q - Demonstrated the ability to copy, understand, and read back FAA airways clearances in minimum time. Was familiar with communications equipment and procedures.

   CQ - Met the criteria for Q, except for discrepancies or delays that indicated lack of familiarity with procedures, equipment, or facilities.

   U - Failed to transmit or receive mandatory reports through omission or lack of familiarity with equipment or procedures.

AIRWAYS CHARTS AND PUBLICATIONS (SUBAREA c)

   Q - Demonstrated complete familiarity with en route charts and publications. When in flight, was able to assist pilot with changes to the flight plan through proper use of en route charts and publications.

   CQ - Generally understood the procedures for proper use of airways publications and charts. Was slow in rendering assistance required by the pilot.

   U - Was completely unfamiliar with en route publications and charts. Gave the pilot no assistance in handling documents.

Prelanding and Shutdown Procedures (Area VII)

   Q - Completed prelanding and shutdown checklist in an orderly manner.

   CQ - Completed checklist with minor errors or omissions which would not normally affect future operation of the equipment.

   U - Did not complete checklist, or made an error that would affect safety of flight or be damaging to the equipment.

Debrief (Area VIII)

YELLOW SHEET (SUBAREA a)

Q - Assisted pilot by providing a clear concise description of discrepancies. Debriefed ASB maintenance ground crew clearly and comprehensively.

CQ - The ASB debrief sheet was filled out with minor deviations or omissions not affecting future operation and maintenance of the system. Discrepancies were written in an understandable manner.

U - Omitted equipment malfunctions from the writeup or wrote them up improperly.

MISSION (SUBAREA b)

Q - Completed all required debriefing forms, charts, cards, and logs. Recorded in-flight data accurately. Made it possible to reconstruct the mission from available information. Conducted the debrief in a concise, clear, and intelligent manner.

CQ - Made minor errors or omission in log keeping that did not, however, make it impossible to reconstruct the mission from available information.

U - Failed to complete required forms, charts, cards, and logs, so that it was impossible to reconstruct the mission from available information.

PLANE CAPTAIN FLIGHT GRADING CRITERIA

Mission Planning (Area I)

ASSISTANCE TO PILOT AND NAVIGATOR (SUBAREA a)

Q - Assisted pilot and navigator in preparation of mission. Was familiar with all forms and checklists used in mission planning.

CQ - Assisted pilot and navigator in preparation of mission. Required some supervision. Was familiar with most forms and checklists used in mission planning.

U - Failed to assist pilot and navigator or needed constant supervision. Was not familiar with forms and checklists used in mission planning.

PERSONAL FLYING EQUIPMENT (SUBAREA b)

Q - Reported for flight briefing in proper flight gear.

U - Reported for flight briefing lacking required flight gear.

Preflight (Area II)

YELLOW SHEETS (SUBAREA a)

Q - Checked yellow sheets before proceeding to the aircraft for preflight and daily inspections. Checked aircraft limitations and other pertinent information concerning the aircraft.

U - Failed to comply with requirements for Q.

*EXTERIOR (SUBAREA b)

Q - Completed exterior preflight inspection without error or omission 45 minutes prior to scheduled takeoff time. Took timely and appropriate action regarding discrepancies found.

QC - Completed exterior preflight inspection with some minor errors or omissions not affecting flight safety and/or no later than 35 minutes prior to takeoff time. Took appropriate action regarding discrepancies found.

U - Failed to complete exterior inspection properly. Make major error or omissions affecting flight safety. Did not complete inspection within 35 minutes of scheduled takeoff time.

NOTE

In grading for time, the evaluator will consider the time by which the inspection would have (in his opinion) been completed if circumstances beyond the plane captain's control had not intervened.

*ENTERING COCKPIT (SUBAREA c)

Q - Completed items 1 through 6 on the prestart checklist prior to commencing the reading of the checklist to the pilot.

U - Failed to comply with requirements for Q.

10-13

Pretaxi and Taxi (Area III)

*COMPANIONWAY CHECK (SUBAREA a)

Q - Completed companionway check in accordance with Section III of this manual and operating checklist.

U - Failed to complete companionway check and/or failed to report discrepancies to the pilot.

MANNING UPPER HATCH (SUBAREA b)

Q - Manned upper hatch and established ICS contact with the pilot. Read control position properly during control check. Was in position in the hatch before aircraft left the chocks. Kept vigilant lookout during taxi until clear of congested areas.

U - Failed to meet requirements for Q.

Airmanship (Area IV)

*CREW COORDINATION (SUBAREA a)

Q - Coordinated smoothly and effectively in all crew endeavors. Anticipated demands upon his crew position. The overall performance of the crew was enhanced by his continual alertness in performing his duties.

U - Coordination was at a level sufficiently low so as to hinder crew performance. Was unfamiliar with crew members duties and/or was continually interrupting them to a degree that team work was definitely retarded. Mission requirements were lost due to his failure to coordinate properly.

ICS AND LOOKOUT PROCEDURES (SUBAREA b)

Q - Well qualified as an airborne lookout. Thoroughly understood established lookout doctrine. Well versed in and utilized generally accepted ICS procedures.

CQ - Generally understood established lookout procedures but was occasionally lax in following doctrine. Could have been better versed in proper ICS procedures.

U - Not up to the standards of CQ.

AIRWAYS CHARTS AND PUBLICATIONS (SUBAREA c)

Q - Demonstrated complete familiarity with en route charts and publications. When required was able to assist the pilot through proper use of en route charts and publications.

CQ - Generally understood the procedures for proper use of airways publications and charts. Was slow in rendering assistance required by the pilot when questions concerning the airways flight came up or when changes to the flight plan occurred.

U - Completely unfamiliar with en route publications and charts. Gave the pilot no assistance in handling subject documents in flight.

Checklist (Area V)

Q - Use of operating checklist was timely with no errors or omissions. Did not interrupt radio communications. Initiated inflight checks at 30-minute intervals.

CQ - Use of checklists was timely with minor errors or omissions not affecting flight safety.

U - Did not meet standards for CQ.

Postlanding (Area VI)

TAXI PROCEDURES (SUBAREA a)

Q - Manned upper hatch and established ICS with the pilot expeditiously after turning off the duty runway. Kept pilot informed of obstructions, drag chute position, etc. Did not leave upper hatch until in the chocks unless called down previously by the pilot.

CQ - After slight, but not unsafe, delay in manning upper hatch, kept pilot informed of obstacles and drag chute position.

U - Delayed excessively in manning upper hatch and/or was unsatisfactory as lookout for pilot.

POSTFLIGHT (SUBAREA b)

Q - Conducted a visual postflight after shutdown and reported the results to the pilot.

U - Failed to conduct a visual postflight inspection after shutdown or failed to report the results of a postflight inspection to the pilot.

FLIGHT EVALUATION GRADE DETERMINATION

The following procedure shall be used in determining the flight evaluation grade: A grade of unqualified in any critical area will result in an overall grade of Unqualified for the flight. Otherwise, flight evaluation (or area) grades shall be determined by assigning the following numerical equivalents to the adjective grade for each subarea. Only the numerals 0, 2, or 4 will be assigned in subareas. No interpolation is allowed.

Unqualified 0.0

Conditionally Qualified 2.0

Qualified 4.0

To determine the numerical grade for each area and the overall grade for the flight, add all the points assigned to the subareas then divide this sum by the number of subareas graded. The adjective grade shall then be determined on the basis of the following scale.

0.0 to 2.19 — Unqualified

2.2 to 2.99 — Conditionally Qualified

3.0 to 4.0 — Qualified

EXAMPLE: (Add Subarea numerical equivalents)

$$\frac{4+2+4+2+4}{5} = \frac{16}{5} = 3.20 \text{ Qualified}$$

Final Grade Determination

The final NATOPS evaluation grade shall be the same as the grade assigned to the flight evaluation. An evaluee who receives an Unqualified on any ground examination or the flight evaluation shall be placed in an Unqualified status until he achieves a grade of Conditionally Qualified or Qualified on a reevaluation.

CRITIQUE

The critique is the terminal point in the evaluation. The results of the evaluation are presented to the individual at this time. Critique preparation involves processing, reconstructing data collected, and presentation of the evaluation report form. The critique will be given by the evaluator/instructor administering the evaluation. Deviations from standard operating procedures will be covered in detail using all collected data and the worksheet as a guide.

NATOPS Evaluation Forms

In addition to the NATOPS Evaluation Report, a NATOPS Flight Evaluation Worksheet, OPNAV FORM 3510/_____ is provided for use by the Evaluation/Instructor during the evaluation flight. All flight areas and subareas are listed on the worksheet with space for related notes.

RECORDS AND REPORTS

A NATOPS Evaluation Report (OPNAV Form 3510-8) shall be completed for each evaluation and forwarded to the evaluee's commanding officer.

This report shall be filed in the individual flight training record and retained therein for 18 months. In addition an entry shall be made in the pilot/NFO flight logbook under "Qualifications and Achievements" as follows:

QUALIFICATION			DATE	SIGNATURE	
NATOPS EVAL.	(Aircraft Model)	(Crew Position)	(Date)	(Authenticating Signature)	(Unit which Administered Eval.)

In the case of enlisted crewmembers, an entry shall be made in the Administrative Remarks of his Personnel Record upon satisfactory completion of the NATOPS Evaluation as follows:

(Date) Completed a NATOPS Evaluation in (Aircraft Designation) as (Flight Crew Position) with an overall grade of (Qualified or Conditionally Qualified).

Section X   NAVAIR 01-40ATA-1

NATOPS EVALUATION QUESTION BANK

The following bank of questions is intended to assist the unit NATOPS Instructor/Evaluator in the preparation of ground examinations and to provide an abbreviated study guide. The questions from the bank should be combined with locally-originated questions as well as questions obtained from the Model Manager in the preparation of ground examinations.

A-3 NATOPS Flight Manual Question Bank

1. The A-3B is powered by two Pratt and Whitney _____ engines.

2. The A-3B has a wing span (spread) of _____ ft, length of _____ and a height of (fin erect) _____ .

3. The inner and outer _____, when extended together, serve as a chute for emergency abandonment of the aircraft.

4. The J57-P-10 engine is rated at _____ for both military and maximum thrust.

5. In the event of an electrical failure of the AUX tank motor-operated transfer valve, how can AUX tank fuel be transferred? _____

6. Each engine ignition system consists of _____ and an _____ which automatically energizes the _____ for a _____ firing cycle.

7. The master engine switches control what five items?

    1. _____ .

    2. _____ .

    3. _____ .

    4. _____ .

    5. _____ .

8. The MASTER ENGINE switches receive power from the _____ bus through the _____ circuit breaker, located _____ .

9. The engine tachometers indicate the RPM of the _____ as a percentage of _____ rpm.

10. The capacity of the engine oil system is _____ gallons in each engine.

11. When the main landing struts are compressed, the engine oil cooler doors are in the _____ position.

12. Illumination of the emergency fuel transfer light located on the pilot's console indicates that _____

13. If a refueling hose must be guillotined, what position shall the reel control switch and fuel control switch be in prior to the guillotine operation? _____

14. If it is desired to dump some portion of the WING tanks fuel and then secure the dump and transfer the remaining fuel to the FWD tank, what must be accomplished before WING fuel will transfer? _____

15. In the KA-3B, transfer of wing tanks fuel is accomplished by _____ of _____ located in each wing tank.

10-16

NAVAIR 01-40ATA-1   Section X

16. List the fuel cells and their usable capacities in gallons for the A-3B (pressure fueling):

   1. _____ GAL _____

   2. _____ GAL _____

   3. _____ GAL _____

   4. _____ GAL _____

17. From which tank is fuel supplied directly to the engines? _____

18. An indicated airspeed of _____ knots is used to compute the fuel load in the clean condition. _____ knots is used with the wheels and flaps down.

19. If the drogue is lost while the hose is deployed, what mandatory procedure shall be observed? _____

20. The pressure fueling system is designed to permit fueling at approximately _____ gallons per minute through each of _____ receptacles.

21. Wing fuel is transferred to the fuselage tanks by _____.

22. The wing tank transfer switch should be left on for _____ after the fuel quantity reads zero.

23. A complete wing tank purge can be assured if accomplished at an altitude _____ with _____.

24. The "Auto-Retraction" feature of the A-3 tanker package is operative whenever the reel control switch is in _____.

25. Are the wing ranks pressurized by bleed air for dumping? _____

26. The fuel trim system can be controlled by three methods. Name them.

   1. _____.

   2. _____.

   3. _____.

27. When the fuel dump switch is selected to ALL LESS AFT, fuel in the fwd fuel cell may be dumped by _____.

28. When the emergency fuel transfer system is utilized, cg is controlled _____.

29. The NORM range on the CG indicator signifies that fuel distribution is _____.

30. The manual CG fuel control valve handle is located _____.

31. Wing fuel tanks are pressurized to _____ to _____ psi during fuel dumping by _____.

32. The aux tank is pressurized by _____ from the _____.

33. Two _____, mounted internally in the aft tank, supply fuel to the fuel pumps located on _____.

34. Each boost pump has one shutoff valve located _____.

35. The ATM's are driven by _____.

10-17

Section X NAVAIR 01-40ATA-1

36. Name the four units driven by the No. 1 ATM:

   1. _____ .

   2. _____ .

   3. _____ .

   4. _____ .

37. Name the four units driven by the No. 2 ATM:

   1. _____ .

   2. _____ .

   3. _____ .

   4. _____ .

38. The ATM is protected from excessive bleed air pressure by _____ .

39. One engine will drive both ATM's for normal operation at _____ percent rpm.

40. Normal operation of the ATM is indicated by _____ .

41. The ground cooling ejector pump operates off the _____ requiring the _____ to be placed in operation prior to _____ during ground operations.

42. The ATM switches are located _____ .

43. A temperature in the _____ range is dangerously close to the auto ignition point of hydraulic fluid.

44. The fuel flow level warning lights come on when the fuel in the aft tank decreases to _____ and _____ .

45. The A-3A/B is equipped with _____ electrical systems.

46. Name the five dc buses utilized for power distribution.

   1. _____   4. _____

   2. _____   5. _____

   3. _____

47. Circuit breakers for the dc power units are located:

   1. _____

   2. _____

48. The primary bus can be energized in three ways. Name them.

   1. _____

   2. _____   3. _____

49. When both dc generators are inoperative, how can the secondary bus be energized?

   1. _____

   2. _____

   3. _____

10-18

NAVAIR 01-40ATA-1 Section X

50. The emergency position of the battery switch energizes which two buses?

    1. _____ 2. _____

51. The _____ bus energizes the radio bus when the _____
    _____ .

52. Dc power is supplied to the ac generator controls from the _____ through the
    AC PWR-CONT circuit breaker located _____ .

53. What must be done to regain the use of units powered by an ac generator when that generator is lost due to overvoltage? _____

54. Will the bus tie operate automatically in the event of a malfunction other than overvoltage? _____ .
    What must be done to regain the use of the inoperative units under these conditions? _____
    _____

55. The bus tie switch must be in the _____ position in order to start the ac generators.

56. Name the three positions of the ac generator switches.

    1. _____ 2. _____ 3. _____

57. What is the normal operating frequency of the generators? _____ .

58. What protection is provided for an underfrequency? _____ .

59. What must be done in the event a generator is producing less than 380 cps? _____
    _____

60. Name the three independent hydraulic systems used in normal operations of the A-3B.

    1. _____

    2. _____

    3. _____

61. Name nine units operated by the utility hydraulic system:

    1. _____ 6. _____

    2. _____ 7. _____

    3. _____ 8. _____

    4. _____ 9. _____

    5. _____

62. The emergency hydraulic system is _____ powered from the _____ bus.
    It supplies pressure to the _____ and _____

63. When operating the emergency hydraulic pump on the dc generator or external power a _____
    time limit must be observed.

64. The surface control hydraulic system operates three units. Name them.

    1. _____

    2. _____

    3. _____

65. The upper hatch air bottle has a normal pressure of _____ psi. What other emergency system
    utilizes the upper escape hatch air bottle?

Section X　　　　　　　　　　　　NAVAIR 01-40ATA-1

66. What is the normal pressure of the emergency wing flaps air bottle? _____ psi.

67. The emergency landing gear control handle is located _____ , and when actuated releases air pressure to the _____ and the _____ normally charged to a pressure of _____ psi.

68. The horizontal stabilizer trim control on the console has two speeds.

    1. _____　　2. _____

69. With the flaps fully extended (36°) blowback begins between _____ and _____ knots.

70. Normally, the flaps require approximately _____ seconds to extend and _____ seconds to retract from the full down position.

71. The speedbrake switch is located on the _____ .

72. Retraction of the main landing gear control following emergency extension of the landing gear may result in _____ .

73. The nosewheel steering provides directional control through _____ degrees either side of center during ground operations.

74. Is nosewheel steering available without utility hydraulic pressure? _____ .

75. The arresting gear hook is extended by _____ and retracted by _____ .

76. Name six dc powered instruments located on the instrument panel or above the center console.

    1. _____　　4. _____

    2. _____　　5. _____

    3. _____　　6. _____

77. Name six ac powered instruments located on the instrument panel or above the center console.

    1. _____　　4. _____

    2. _____　　5. _____

    3. _____　　6. _____

78. During extreme cold weather starts, oil pressure may _____ temporarily. Press indicators should be acquired within _____ .

79. The engine should be idled for 5 minutes before shutting down if it has operated at _____ percent rpm or higher for more than _____ minute(s) during the previous 5 minutes.

80. When the cockpit pressure control switch is set at normal, the cabin pressure altitude is maintained at _____ up to a flight altitude of 13,500 feet, and above that point maintains a cockpit pressure differential of 3.3 psi.

81. What three items are affected by the anti-icing control?

    1. _____　　3. _____

    2. _____

82. The accuracy of the APN-22 is _____ from 0 to 40 feet, and _____ from 40 to 20,000 feet.

83. The instrument and console lights operate on _____ electrical power and the floodlights operate on _____ electrical power.

84. The capacity of the liquid oxygen system is _____ liters.

85. What is the duration of a full tank of oxygen with a crew of four at a cabin altitude of 20,000 feet breathing 100 percent oxygen? _____

86. The maximum allowable engine RPM under any conditions is _____ percent rpm.

87. Give the following J57-P-10 engine limitations:

OPERATION CONDITION	MAX RPM	TOT BELOW 30,000	TOT ABOVE 30,000	TIME LIMIT
MILITARY				
MAX. Continuous				
Idle				

88. What are the limitations on the J57-P-10 engine to be observed during acceleration?

    RPM _____ TOT _____ TIME LIMIT _____

89. What is the maximum permissible airspeed with the wing flaps fully or partially extended? _____.

90. What is the maximum recommended gross weight for a field landing? _____.

91. What is the maximum g loading on the A-3B in smooth air at a gross weight of 56,000 pounds? _____.

92. What is the takeoff roll for an A-3B under the following conditions: Gross weight, 76,000 pounds pressure altitude 2000 feet, air temperatures +20°C, headwind 10 knots? _____

93. Under the above conditions, figure the takeoff distance to clear a 50-foot obstacle. _____.

94. The takeoff airspeed is _____ KIAS.

95. What is the 2000 foot normal line speed? _____ kts.

96. What is the single-engine control speed? _____ kts.

97. With a gross weight of 60,000 pounds, and a true airspeed of 480 knots at sea level, the fuel flow per engine is _____.

98. What is the cruise ceiling with a gross weight of 65,000 pounds for twin engine operations? _____ ft.

99. What is the two engine maximum endurance altitude for a gross weight of 45,000 pounds? _____.

100. Emergency extension of the hook may be accomplished by _____ on the port side of the bomb bay.

NAVAIR 01-40ATA-1   Section XI

SECTION XI
PERFORMANCE DATA

TABLE OF CONTENTS

Part		Page
1	GENERAL	11-3
2	TAKEOFF	11-15
3	CLIMB	11-41
4	RANGE	11-57
5	ENDURANCE	11-91
6	DESCENT	11-99
7	LANDING	11-103
8	COMBAT PERFORMANCE	11-111

Part		Page
1A	GENERAL	11-115
2A	TAKEOFF	11-123
3A	CLIMB	11-135
4A	RANGE	11-145
5A	ENDURANCE	11-177
6A	DESCENT	11-183
7A	LANDING	11-187
8A	COMBAT PERFORMANCE	11-189

A-3B/KA-3B AIRCRAFT
PERFORMANCE DATA CHARTS (J57-P-10 ENGINES)

INTRODUCTION

The operating data charts contained in this section provide the pilot with information enabling him to realize the maximum performance capabilities of the aircraft. Use of the chart material for preflight planning and application of the prescribed operating procedures will result in optimum effectiveness of the aircraft.

Section XI is divided into several parts to present performance data in proper sequence for preflight planning. Parts 1 and 1A (General) contain data pertinent to the complete section. Parts 2 through 8 contain performance data for A-3B aircraft equipped with J57-P-10 engines. Parts 1A through 8A contains performance data for A-3A aircraft equipped with J57-P-6B engines. Sample problems and charts are provided (in Parts 1 through 8 only) to present the sequence of steps required to find the proper values and solution of a given problem. Performance data is presented in graphical and profile type charts for ICAO standard day conditions. In some instances, temperature corrections for non-standard atmosphere have been included.

NOTE

Operating data charts contained in this section that apply to the A-3B aircraft, also apply to the KA-3B aircraft even though the KA-3B designation does not appear as one of the aircraft listed under the model heading of the chart concerned.

11-1/11-2

NAVAIR 01-40ATA-1

Section XI
Part 1

PART 1
GENERAL

TABLE OF CONTENTS

TEXT

	Page		Page
Performance Data Basis	11-3	Cruise Control Computer	11-4
Abbreviations, Symbols, and Definitions	11-3	Airspeed and Altitude Correction Charts	11-4

ILLUSTRATIONS

Figure		Page	Figure		Page
11-1	Airspeed vs Mach Number	11-6	11-5	Airspeed and Altitude Correction for Position Error	11-11
11-2	Temperature Correction for Compressibility	11-7	11-6	Mach Number for Correction for Position Error	11-13
11-3	Density Altitude Chart	11-9			
11-4	ICAO Standard Altitude Table	11-10			

PERFORMANCE DATA BASIS

Performance data is based on aircraft characteristics obtained from Navy and Contractor flight tests, calculations, and engine data from Pratt and Whitney specifications. All charts are presented for ICAO standard atmosphere conditions, although ambient temperature correction scales are provided in a number of charts where temperature effects are significant. If the fuel control has been properly adjusted to the fuel type, all charts are applicable to JP-4 or JP-5 fuel, having a nominal density of 6.5 and 6.8 pounds per gallon, respectively.

ABBREVIATIONS, SYMBOLS, AND DEFINITIONS

Abbreviation	Definition
a/a_o	Ratio of speed of sound at altitude to speed of sound at sea level, ICAO standard day
ac	Alternating current
ADF	Automatic direction finding
Alt	Altitude
°C	Degrees Centigrade
CAS or V_c	Calibrated airspeed = IAS corrected for position error
CG	Center of Gravity
dc	Direct current
Deg	Degrees

Abbreviation	Definition
EAS or V_e	Equivalent airspeed = CAS corrected for compressibility effect
EGT	Exhaust gas temperature
EPR	Engine Pressure Ratio
°F	Degrees Fahrenheit
Flt	Flight
FPM or fpm	Feet per minute
Freq	Frequency
Ft or ft	Feet
g	Gravity force
H or h	Altitude
hg	Mercury
hr	hour
IAS or V_i	Indicated airspeed = instrument reading corrected for instrument error
ICAO	International Civil Aviation Organization
In.	Inches
KCAS	Knots calibrated airspeed
KEAS	Knots equivalent airspeed
KIAS	Knots indicated airspeed

Changed 1 June 1969

11-3

Abbreviation	Definition
KTAS	Knots true airspeed
Kts	Knots
lb	Pounds
M	Mach number
MAX	Maximum
min	Minutes
mm	Millimeter
NM or N. Mi.	Nautical Miles
OAT	Outside air temperature
P	Static atmospheric pressure at any altitude
P_o	Static atmospheric pressure at sea level ICAO standard day = 29.92 inches of mercury
psi	Pounds per square inch
RPM	Revolutions per minute (Engine speed)
SL	Sea level
Std	Standard
T	Static absolute temperature at any altitude
T_o	Static absolute temperature at sea level ICAO standard day = 288.2 degrees Kelvin
TAS	True airspeed
Vol	Volume
Wt	Weight
Δ	Delta – change in (e.g., gross weight)
δ or P/P_o	Delta – Ratio of static air pressure to ICAO standard sea level static air pressure
ρ	Rho – Density of atmosphere in slugs/foot at any altitude
ρ_o	Rho – Density of atmosphere at sea level ICAO standard day = 0.002378 slugs per foot
σ or ρ/ρ_o	Sigma – Ratio of density of any altitude to density at sea level, ICAO standard day
θ or T/T_o	Theta – Ratio of absolute temperature of any altitude to absolute temperature at sea level. ICAO standard day.

Cruise Control Computer

A cruise control computer is available for use with this aircraft. Its use provides a means for the rapid solution of mission planning problems and in-flight problems involving the determination of Range, Endurance, Speed, and Time quantities. Operating instructions are packaged with each computer. A supply of REST Computers is provided each Navy operating activity upon first procurement of each new design computer. Additional supplies may be ordered from the Naval Supply Center. For the manufacturer's part number, see REST Computers listing.

Airspeed and Altitude Correction Charts

AIRSPEED CORRECTIONS

To obtain true airspeed, several corrections must be applied to the airspeed indicator reading. Instrument error, which varies for each airspeed indicator as a result of manufacturing tolerances, is noted on the instrument calibration card. This error is usually small and normally may be disregarded, in which case the instrument reading is the actual indicated airspeed (IAS).

The position error correction determined for each location of the static pressure source is added to indicated airspeed to obtain calibrated airspeed, or CAS as indicated in figure 11-5, sheets 1 and 2. A Mach meter correction for position error is included in figure 11-6, sheets 1 and 2.

True airspeed (TAS) and Mach number are read directly from figure 11-1, using known calibrated airspeed, outside air temperature and true pressure altitude. To obtain equivalent airspeed (EAS), true airspeed is multiplied by $\sqrt{\sigma}$ corresponding to pressure altitude and ambient temperature.

True ambient temperature is obtained by applying a temperature correction increment, which includes installation and compressibility error, to the cockpit temperature indicator reading (which is always high). This temperature correction increment may be obtained from figure 11-2, Temperature Correction for Compressibility. Using the corrected temperature, the value for $\sqrt{\sigma}$ may then be obtained from figure 11-3. Similar data may be obtained from the Standard Altitude Table, figure 11-4, when standard atmospheric conditions are desired.

EXAMPLE: Assume the aircraft is at a pressure altitude of 20,000 feet, with an airspeed indicator reading of 460 knots and with a temperature indicator reading of +37°C. Assuming zero instrument error, correct ambient temperature and true airspeed are then found as follows:

Airspeed indicator reading . . . . 460 knots

Correction for instrument error . . . . . 0 knots

NAVAIR 01-40ATA-1

Section XI
Part 1

REST COMPUTER

Aircraft	Federal Stock No.	Manufacturer's Part No.	Configurations
A-3B	RM6605-703-2499-V170	APN-71	(Basic Wing)

Indicated airspeed .... 460 knots

Correction for position error
(figure 11-5, sheet 1) .... -5 knots

Calibrated airspeed .... 455 knots

Temperature indicator reading ...... +37°C

Correction for instrument error 0

Indicated temperature .... +37°C

Correction for compressibility
(see figure 11-2, sheet 2) .... -37°C

Ambient temperature .... 0°C

Then Mach No. = 0.96 and true airspeed = 492 knots under standard day conditions (figure 11-1).

At 20,000 feet pressure altitude with an ambient temperature of +0°C, true airspeed - 617 knots (figure 11-1).

ALTITUDE CORRECTIONS

Instrument error and position error corrections similar to those applied for airspeed indicator readings, must be applied to the indicated altimeter readings to obtain true pressure altitude. Figure 11-5, sheet 1 provides the correction necessary to compensate for the installation.

EXAMPLE: Assume the A-3B/KA-3B basic wing aircraft is at an indicated pressure altitude of 20,000 feet with an airspeed indicator reading of 460 knots. The true pressure altitude, assuming zero instrument error, is obtained by the following method:

Altimeter reading.............. 20,000 feet

Correction for instrument error
(assumed).................... 0 feet

Indicated airspeed .... 460 knots

Altimeter correction for position
error (figure 11-5, sheet 1)........ -600 feet

True pressure altitude........... 19,400 feet

Conversely, the indicated pressure altitude required to establish a selected true pressure altitude can be determined by subtracting algebraically the position error correction provided by figure 11-5, sheet 1.

EXAMPLE:

Selected true pressure altitude ..... 20,000 feet

Instrument error (assumed) .... 0 feet

Indicated airspeed .... 450 knots

Altitude correction .... -200 feet

Required indicated pressure
altitude 20,000 - (-200) .... 20,200 feet

MACH NUMBER CORRECTIONS

Instrument error and position error corrections must be applied to the indicated Mach number readings (IMN) to obtain a true Mach number reading (TMN). Figure 11-6, sheet 1 incorporates the position error correction to make possible direct reading of true Mach number. For all flight in the permissible airspeed range, this correction is virtually zero.

Changed 1 June 1969

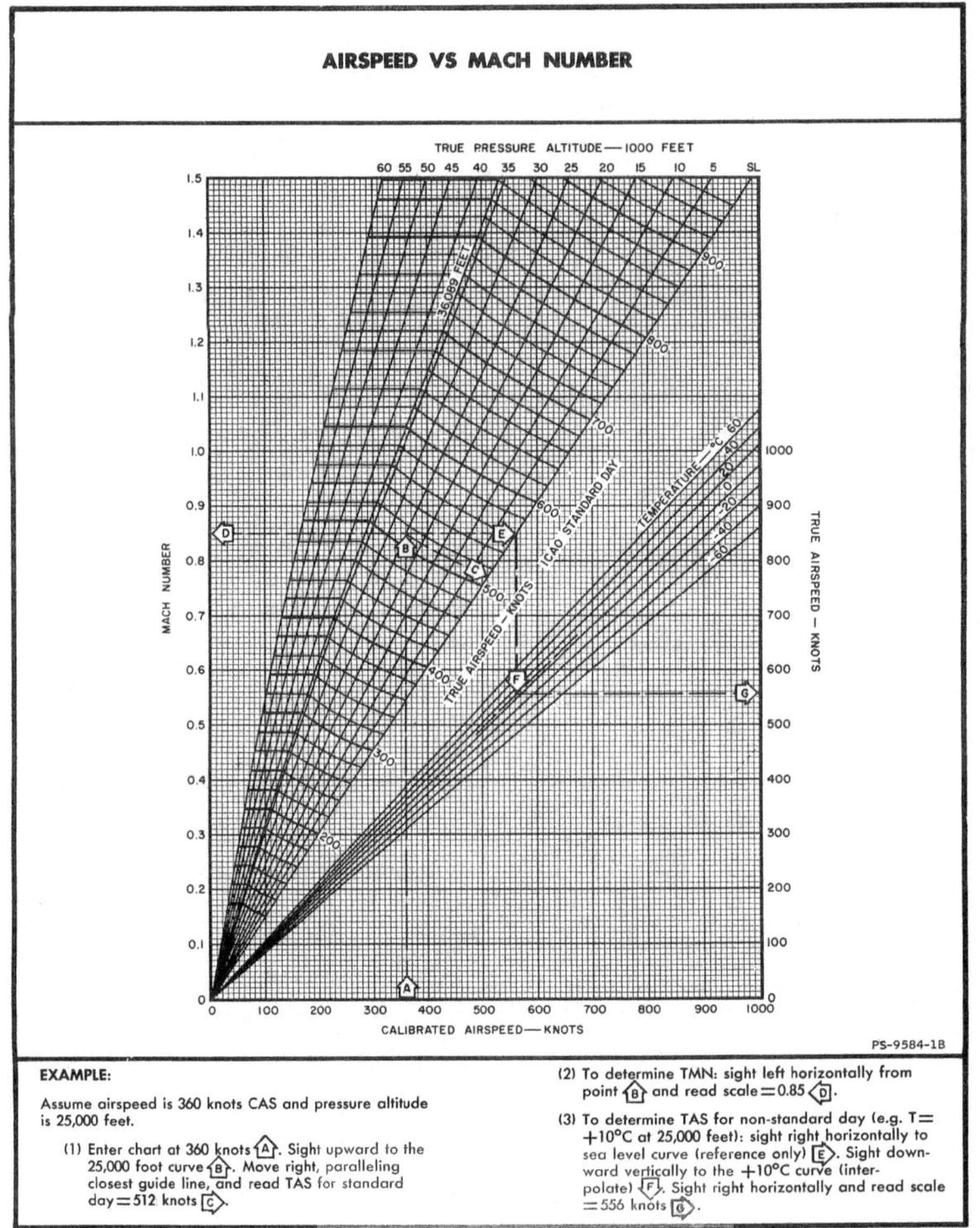

Figure 11-1. Airspeed vs Mach Number

NAVAIR 01-40ATA-1
Section XI
Part 1

TEMPERATURE CORRECTION FOR COMPRESSIBILITY

Pressure Altitude Feet	Calibrated Airspeed – Knots										
	100	150	200	250	300	350	400	450	500	550	600
Sea Level	1	2	4	7	10	13	17	21	26	32	38
5,000	1	3	5	8	11	15	19	24	30	36	42
10,000	1	3	6	9	13	17	22	28	34	41	48
15,000	2	4	7	10	15	20	25	32	39	46	54
20,000	2	4	8	12	17	23	29	36	44	52	
25,000	2	5	9	14	20	26	33	41	50		
30,000	3	6	11	16	23	30	38	47			
35,000	3	7	13	19	27	35	44				
40,000	4	9	16	24	32	42					
45,000	5	11	20	29	39						
50,000	7	14	24	35							

Remarks:

(1) Based on 80 percent of full adiabatic temperature rise.
(2) Indicated temperatures read high.
(3) Subtract correction from indicated air temperature (°C) to obtain free air temperature (°C).

Data as of: 1 April 1954
Data Basis: Estimates

Fuel Grade: JP-4
Fuel Density: 6.5 lb/gal

Figure 11-2. Temperature Correction for Compressibility (Sheet 1)

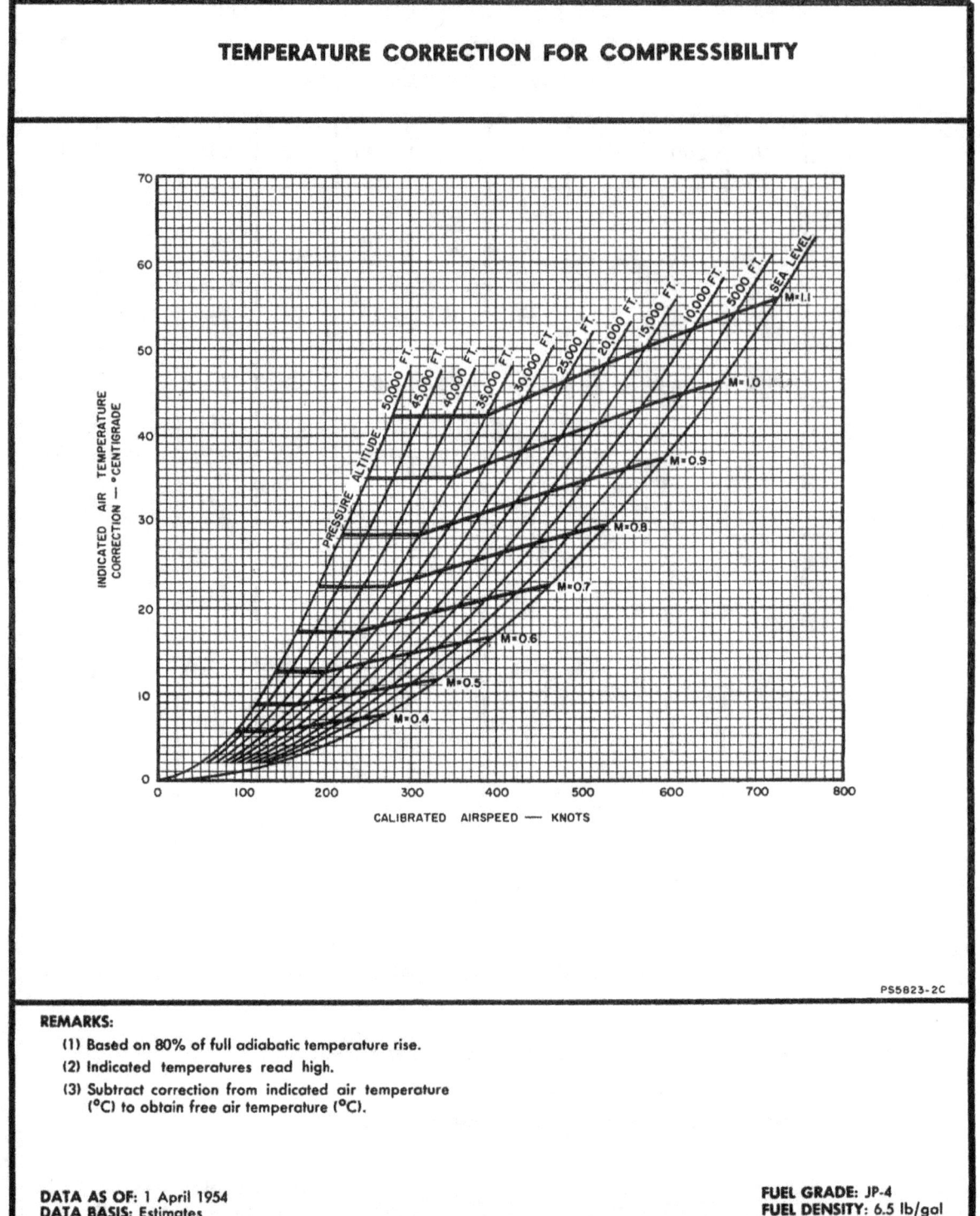

Figure 11-2. Temperature Correction for Compressibility (Sheet 2)

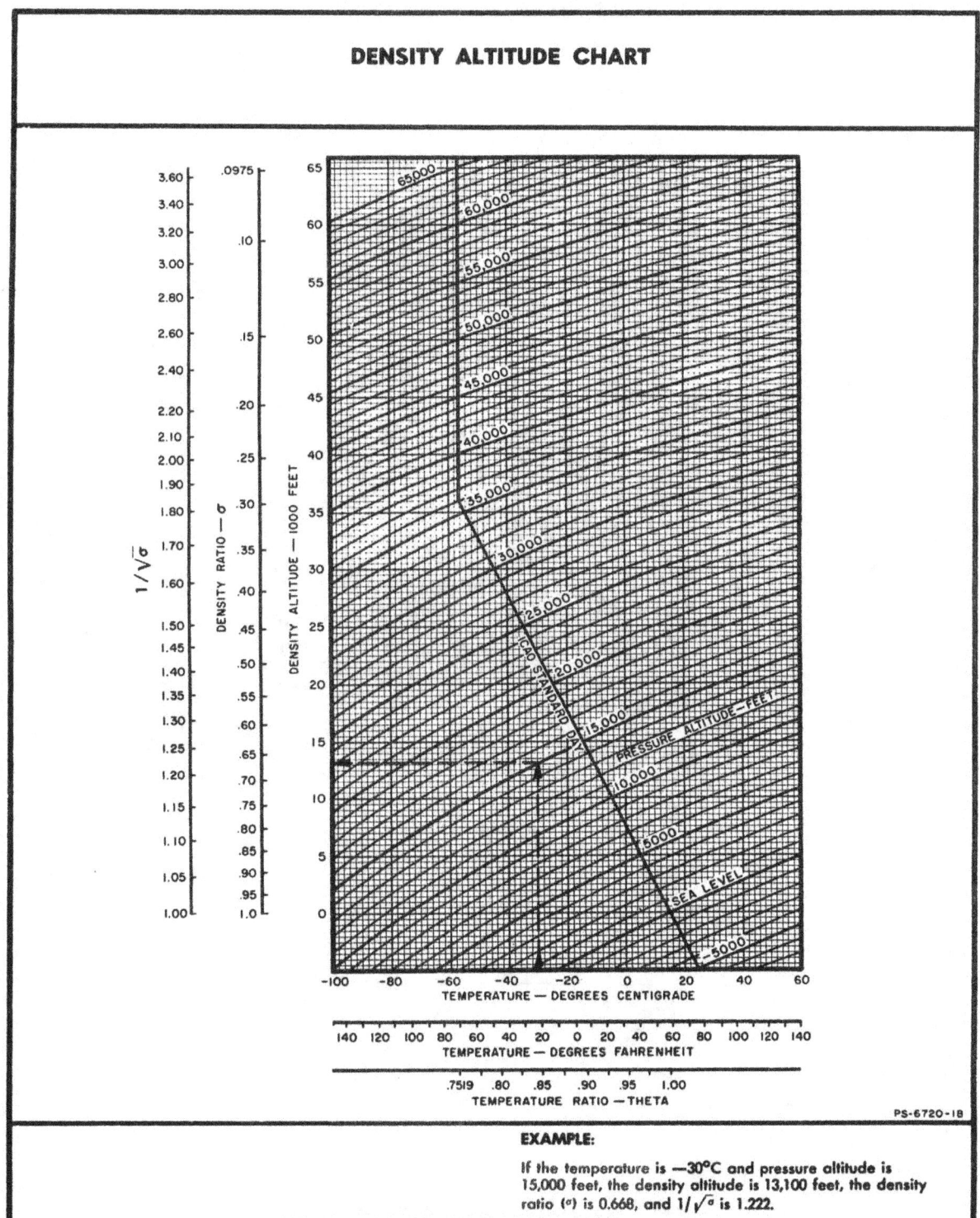

Figure 11-3. Density Altitude Chart

ICAO STANDARD ALTITUDE CHART

ALTITUDE FEET	DENSITY RATIO $\sigma = \rho/\rho_o$	$\frac{1}{\sqrt{\sigma}}$	TEMPERATURE DEG. C	TEMPERATURE DEG. F	TEMPERATURE RATIO $\theta = T/T_o$	SPEED OF SOUND RATIO a/a_p	PRESSURE IN. OF Hg	PRESSURE RATIO $\delta = p/p_o$
Sea Level	1.0000	1.0000	15.000	59.000	1.0000	1.000	29.921	1.0000
1000	.9711	1.0148	13.019	55.434	.9931	.997	28.856	.9644
2000	.9428	1.0299	11.038	51.868	.9862	.993	27.821	.9298
3000	.9151	1.0454	9.056	48.302	.9794	.990	26.817	.8962
4000	.8881	1.0611	7.075	44.735	.9725	.986	25.842	.8637
5000	.8617	1.0773	5.094	41.169	.9656	.983	24.896	.8320
6000	.8359	1.0938	3.113	37.603	.9587	.979	23.978	.8014
7000	.8106	1.1107	1.132	34.037	.9519	.976	23.088	.7716
8000	.7860	1.1279	-0.850	30.471	.9450	.972	22.225	.7428
9000	.7620	1.1456	-2.831	26.905	.9381	.969	21.388	.7148
10,000	.7385	1.1637	-4.812	23.338	.9312	.965	20.577	.6877
11,000	.7156	1.1822	-6.793	19.772	.9244	.961	19.791	.6614
12,000	.6932	1.2011	-8.774	16.206	.9175	.958	19.029	.6360
13,000	.6713	1.2205	-10.756	12.640	.9106	.954	18.292	.6113
14,000	.6500	1.2403	-12.737	9.074	.9037	.951	17.577	.5875
15,000	.6292	1.2606	-14.718	5.508	.8969	.947	16.886	.5643
16,000	.6090	1.2815	-16.699	1.941	.8900	.943	16.216	.5420
17,000	.5892	1.3028	-18.680	-1.625	.8831	.940	15.569	.5203
18,000	.5699	1.3246	-20.662	-5.191	.8762	.936	14.942	.4994
19,000	.5511	1.3470	-22.643	-8.757	.8694	.932	14.336	.4791
20,000	.5328	1.3700	-24.624	-12.323	.8625	.929	13.750	.4595
21,000	.5150	1.3935	-26.605	-15.889	.8556	.925	13.184	.4406
22,000	.4976	1.4176	-28.586	-19.456	.8487	.921	12.636	.4223
23,000	.4807	1.4424	-30.586	-23.022	.8419	.918	12.107	.4046
24,000	.4642	1.4678	-32.549	-26.588	.8350	.914	11.597	.3876
25,000	.4481	1.4938	-34.530	-30.154	.8281	.910	11.104	.3711
26,000	.4325	1.5206	-36.511	-33.720	.8212	.906	10.627	.3552
27,000	.4173	1.5480	-38.493	-37.286	.8144	.902	10.168	.3398
28,000	.4025	1.5762	-40.474	-40.852	.8075	.899	9.725	.3250
29,000	.3881	1.6052	-42.455	-44.419	.8006	.895	9.297	.3107
30,000	.3741	1.6349	-44.436	-47.985	.7937	.891	8.885	.2970
31,000	.3605	1.6654	-46.417	-51.551	.7869	.887	8.488	.2837
32,000	.3473	1.6968	-48.399	-55.117	.7800	.883	8.106	.2709
33,000	.3345	1.7291	-50.379	-58.683	.7731	.879	7.737	.2586
34,000	.3220	1.7623	-52.361	-62.249	.7662	.875	7.382	.2467
35,000	.3099	1.7964	-54.342	-65.816	.7594	.871	7.041	.2353
36,000	.2981	1.8315	-56.323	-69.382	.7525	.867	6.712	.2243
36,089	.2971	1.8347	-56.500	-69.700	.7519	.867	6.683	.2234
37,000	.2844	1.8753					6.397	.2138
38,000	.2710	1.9209					6.097	.2038
39,000	.2585	1.9677					5.811	.1942
40,000	.2462	2.0155					5.538	.1851
41,000	.2346	2.0645					5.278	.1764
42,000	.2236	2.1148					5.030	.1681
43,000	.2131	2.1662					4.794	.1602
44,000	.2031	2.2189					4.569	.1527
45,000	.1936	2.2728					4.355	.1455
46,000	.1845	2.3281					4.151	.1387
47,000	.1758	2.3848					3.956	.1322
48,000	.1676	2.4428					3.770	.1260
49,000	.1597	2.5022					3.593	.1201
50,000	.1522	2.5630					3.425	.1145
51,000	.1451	2.6254					3.264	.1091
52,000	.1383	2.6892					3.111	.1040
53,000	.1318	2.7546					2.965	.0991
54,000	.1256	2.8216					2.826	.0944
55,000	.1197	2.8903					2.693	.0900
56,000	.1141	2.9606					2.567	.0858
57,000	.1087	3.0326					2.446	.0818
58,000	.1036	3.1063					2.331	.0779
59,000	.09877	3.1819					2.222	.0743
60,000	.09414	3.2593					2.118	.0709
61,000	.08972	3.3386					2.018	.0675
62,000	.08551	3.4198					1.924	.0643
63,000	.08150	3.5029					1.833	.0613
64,000	.07767	3.5881					1.747	.0584
65,000	.07403	3.6754	-56.500	-69.700	.7519	.867	1.665	.0557

REMARKS:
(1) One in. of Hg = 70.732 lb per sq ft
    = 0.4912 lb per sq in.

(2) ICAO Standard Sea Level Air
    t. = 15°C
    p. = 29.921 in. of Hg
    a. = 661.8 knots
    ρ. = .0023769 slug per cu ft

DATA BASIS: NACA Technical Note No. 3182

Figure 11-4. ICAO Standard Altitude Table

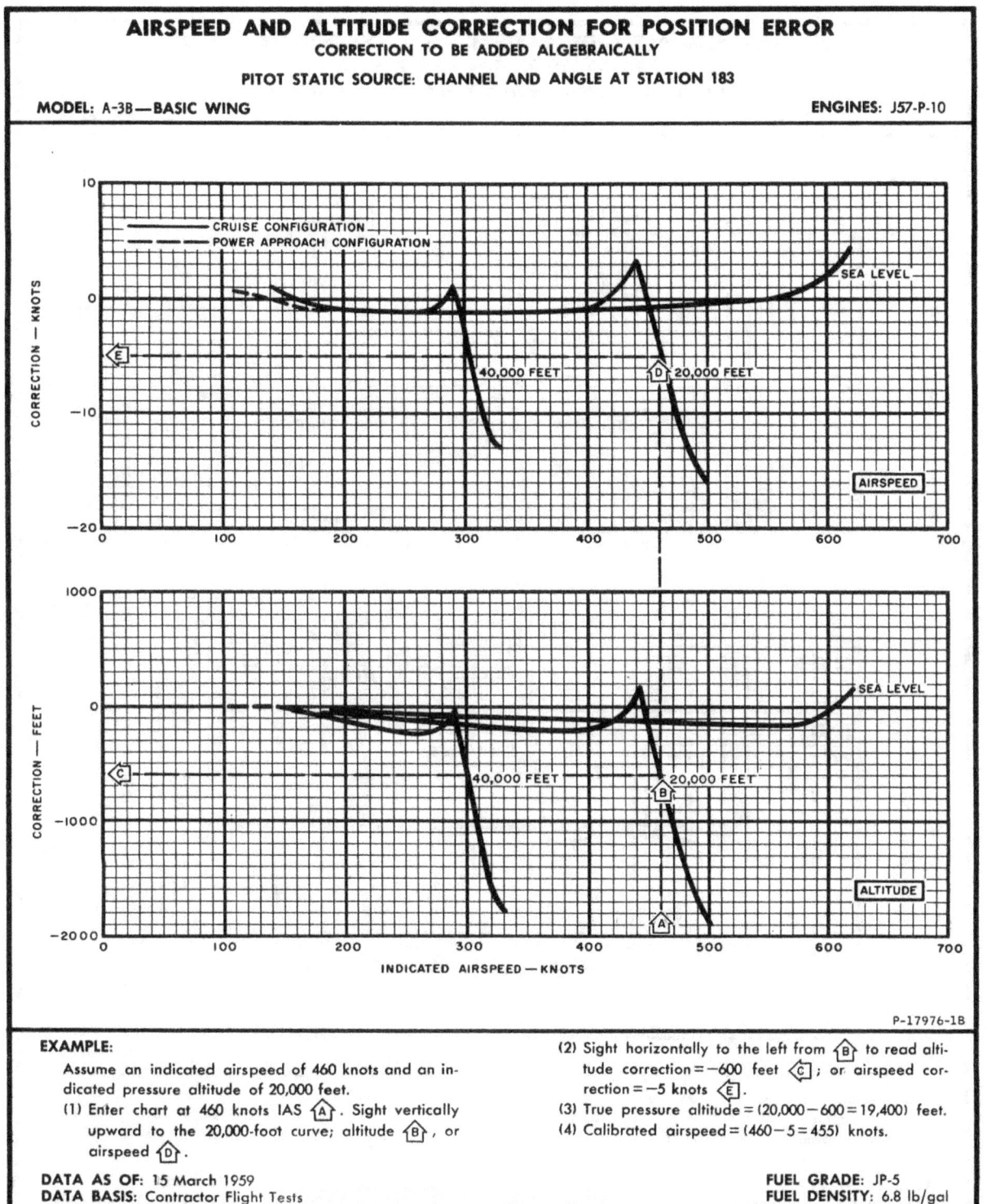

Figure 11-5. Airspeed and Altitude Correction for Position Error (Sheet 1)

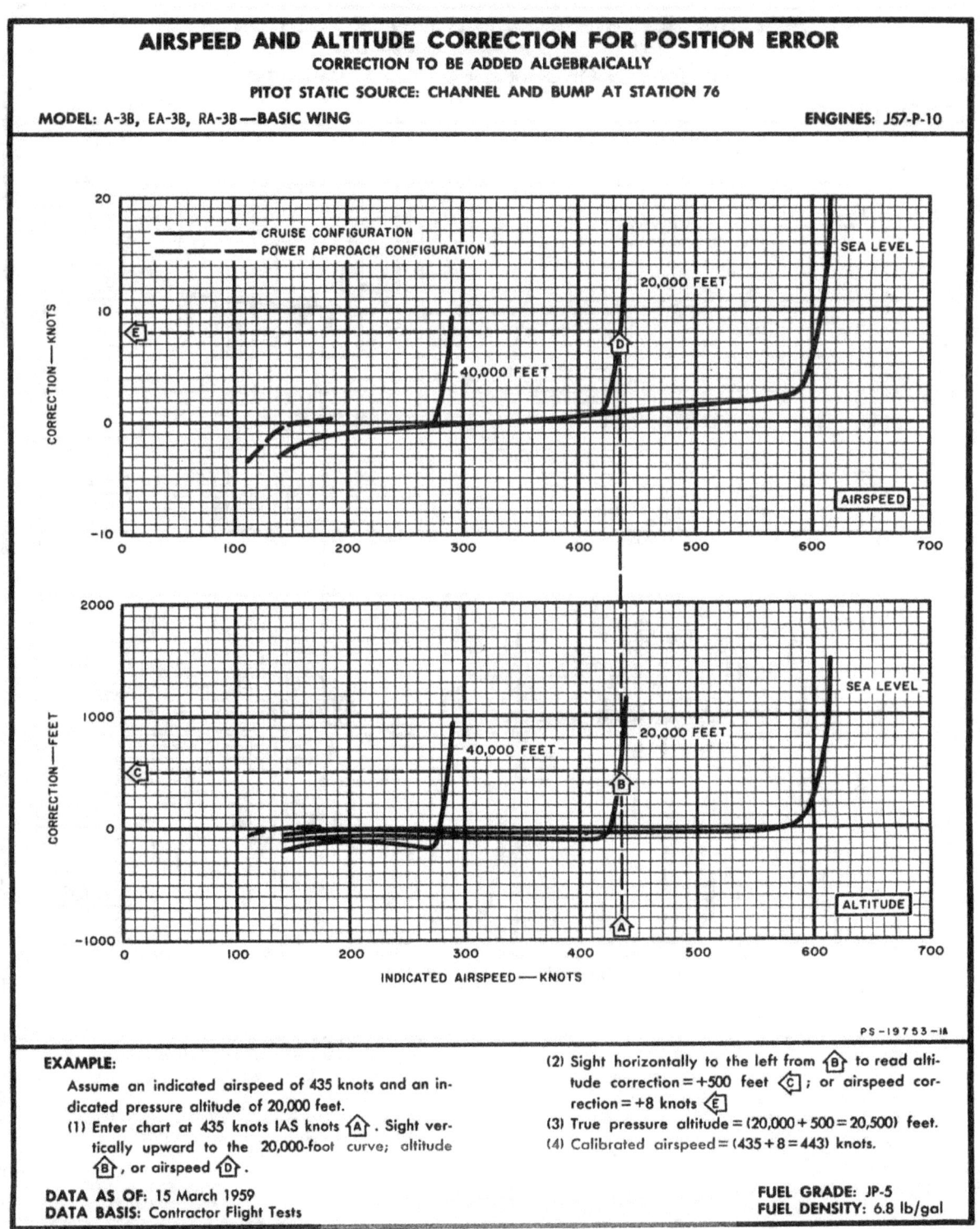

Figure 11-5. Airspeed and Altitude Correction for Position Error (Sheet 2)

NAVAIR 01-40ATA-1

Section XI
Part 1

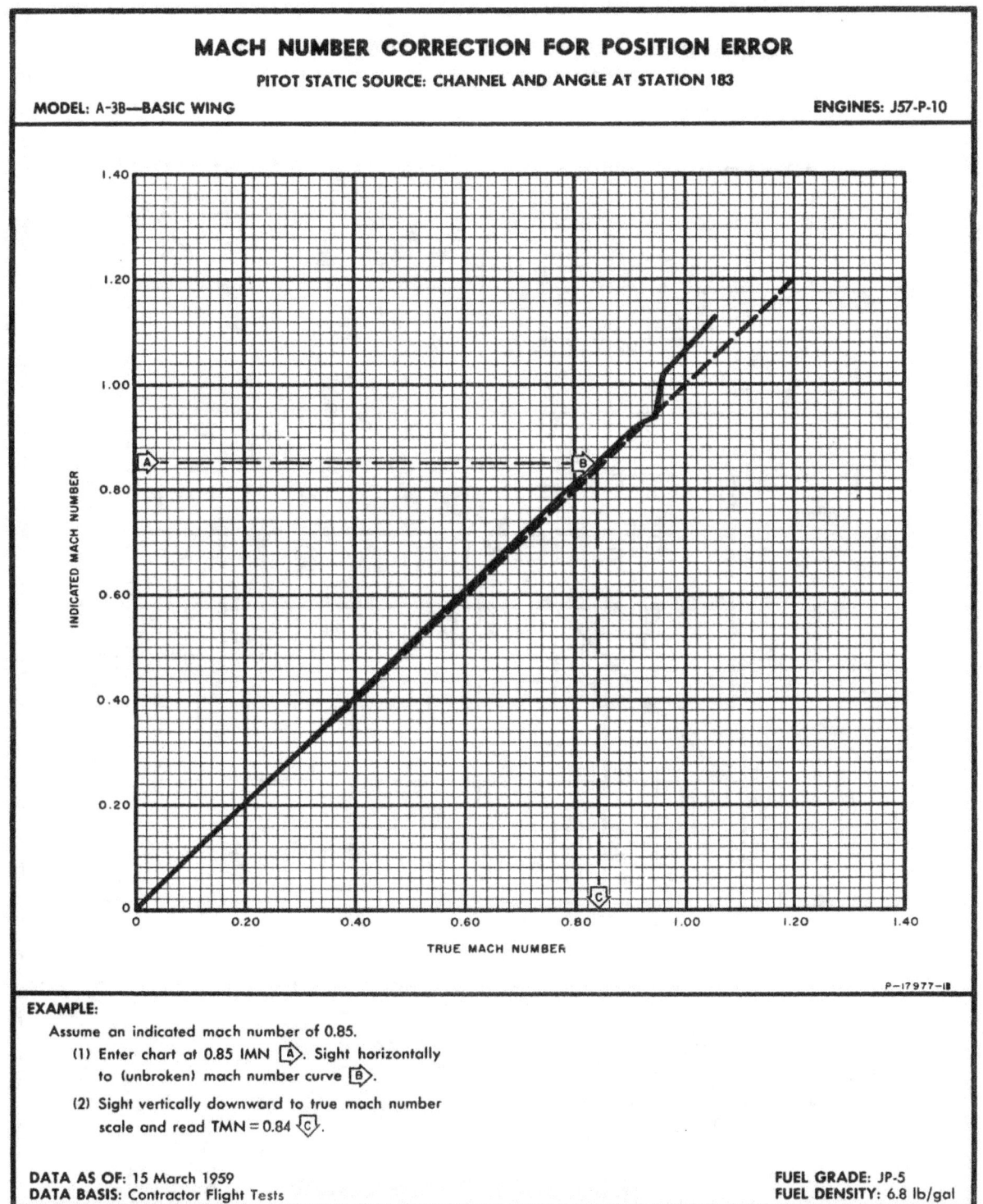

Figure 11-6. Mach Number Correction for Position Error (Sheet 1)

11-13

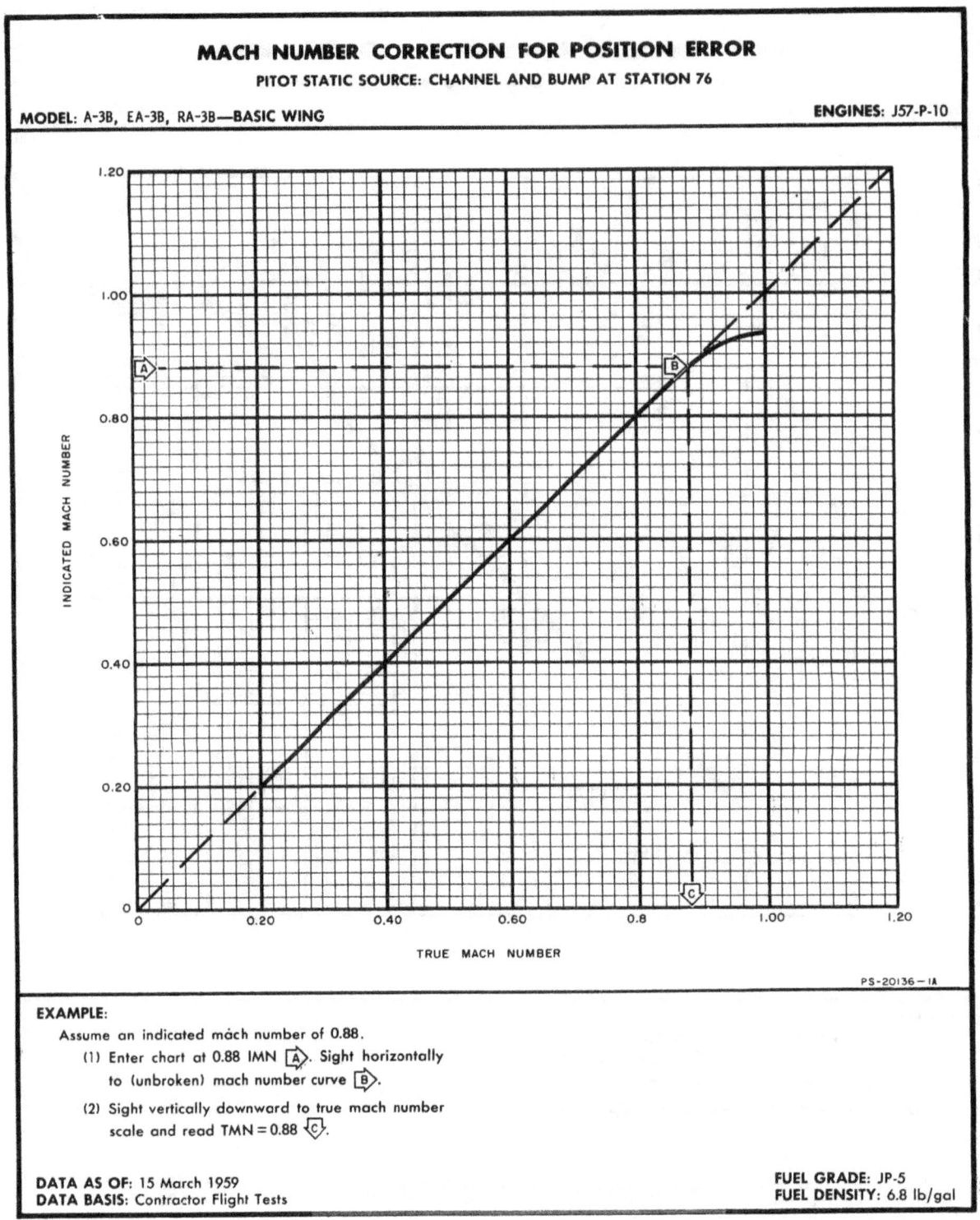

Figure 11-6. Mach Number Correction for Position Error (Sheet 2)

NAVAIR 01-40ATA-1

Section XI
Part 2

PART 2
TAKEOFF

TABLE OF CONTENTS

TEXT

	Page		Page
Takeoff Charts	11-15	JATO Firing Delay and Minimum	
Line Speed Check	11-16	Takeoff Distance	11-17

ILLUSTRATIONS

Figure		Page	Figure		Page
11-7	Recommended Lift-Off Speed	11-19	11-18	JATO Takeoff Distance – 12 Units (15° Nozzle)	11-30
11-8	Takeoff Distance	11-20	11-19	JATO Firing Delay – Two Units (30° Nozzle)	11-31
11-9	Maximum Recommended Takeoff Weight	11-21	11-20	JATO Takeoff Distance – Two Units (30° Nozzle)	11-32
11-10	Minimum Single-Engine Control Speed	11-22	11-21	JATO Firing Delay – Four Units (30° Nozzle)	11-33
11-11	JATO Firing Delay – Two Units (15° Nozzle)	11-23	11-22	JATO Takeoff Distance – Four Units (30° Nozzle)	11-34
11-12	JATO Takeoff Distance – Two Units (15° Nozzle)	11-24	11-23	JATO Firing Delay – Six Units (30° Nozzle)	11-35
11-13	JATO Firing Delay – Four Units (15° Nozzle)	11-25	11-24	JATO Takeoff Distance – Six Units (30° Nozzle)	11-36
11-14	JATO Takeoff Distance – Four Units (15° Nozzle)	11-26	11-25	JATO Firing Delay – 12 Units (30° Nozzle)	11-37
11-15	JATO Firing Delay – Six Units (15° Nozzle)	11-27	11-26	JATO Takeoff Distance – 12 Units (30° Nozzle)	11-38
11-16	JATO Takeoff Distance – Six Units (15° Nozzle)	11-28	11-27	Takeoff Refusal Speeds	11-39
11-17	JATO Firing Delay – 12 Units (15° Nozzle)	11-29	11-28	Refused Takeoff Stopping Distance	11-40

Takeoff Charts

The takeoff charts present the ground roll distance to clear a 50-foot obstacle, both with and without JATO assist, and for a hard surface runway. The charts encompass such variables as takeoff weight, lift-off speed, ambient runway air temperature, runway pressure altitude, and headwind. Full flaps and MILITARY thrust are recommended for all takeoffs.

RECOMMENDED LIFT-OFF SPEED WITH AND WITHOUT JATO

Lift-off speeds are based on operational NATC recommended data and are shown on figure 11-7.

EXAMPLE: Given a takeoff weight of 70,000 pounds, a runway air temperature of 30°C, and a runway pressure altitude of 4000 feet:

1. Enter chart at 30°C(A). Sight horizontally to 4000-foot pressure altitude line (B).

2. Sight vertically to right from (B) to a gross weight of 70,000 pounds (C).

3. Proceed horizontally from (C) and read the recommended lift-off speed of 146 KIAS (D).

TAKEOFF DISTANCE – NO JATO

Takeoff distance and total distance to clear a 50-foot obstacle, without JATO assist, is shown on figure 11-8. The takeoff distances are based on operational NATC flight test data.

Note that there is a region in the temperature and altitude correction boxes where takeoff is marginal. This region represents an area where rate of climb

Changed 1 June 1969

11-15

Section XI
Part 2
NAVAIR 01-40ATA-1

after takeoff may be between 800 and 400 feet per minute and climbout capability is marginal. Since temperature and altitude are not independent, the boundary lines in these boxes are shown for extreme altitude-temperature combinations. To determine accurately if the rate of climb is less than 800 fpm, when operating in this region, refer to figure 11-9. A more detailed explanation of the marginal region is given in the following paragraphs under Maximum Recommended Takeoff Weight.

The method of obtaining the ground roll distance, total distance to clear a 50-foot obstacle, and a linespeed check from the takeoff chart is described in the following examples:

EXAMPLE: Given a takeoff weight of 70,000 pounds, a runway air temperature of 30°C, and a runway pressure altitude of 4000 feet. To determine takeoff ground roll distance and total distance to clear a 50-foot obstacle proceed as follows:

1. Enter figure 11-8 at 146 KIAS (D) as determined from figure 11-7, and continue horizontally to right to line representing takeoff weight of 70,000 pounds (E).

2. Sight vertically downward to temperature baseline and follow parallel to guidelines to temperature of 30°C (F).

3. Continue vertically downward to pressure altitude baseline, then parallel to guidelines to pressure altitude of 4000 feet (G).

4. Proceed vertically downward to headwind baseline, then parallel to guidelines to headwind of 10 knots (H).

5. Proceed vertically downward and read ground roll distance of 7650 feet (J).

6. Note that in step 3, point (G) fell in the region where takeoff is marginal.

Therefore, check figure 11-9 to see if the rate of climb is less than 800 fpm. In making this check, note that for this temperature-altitude condition the maximum takeoff weight at 800 fpm rate of climb is 68,800 pounds. Therefore, at a gross weight of 70,000 pounds, the rate of climb is less than 800 fpm and takeoff is marginal in this case.

Line Speed Check

EXAMPLE: To determine a linespeed check at the 2000-foot runway marker:

1. Enter the takeoff distance chart figure 11-8 at ground roll distance of 2000 feet and proceed vertically upward to a headwind of 10 knots, then parallel to the guidelines to the headwind baseline.

2. Continue vertically upward to pressure altitude of 4000 feet, then parallel to guidelines to altitude baseline.

3. Proceed vertically upward to temperature of 30°C, then parallel to guidelines to temperature baseline.

4. Proceed upward to takeoff weight of 70,000 pounds, then horizontally to left and read linespeed of 88 KIAS.

MAXIMUM RECOMMENDED TAKEOFF WEIGHT – WITH AND WITHOUT JATO

The maximum takeoff weight shown on figure 11-9 is given as a function of rate of climb after takeoff. The data basis for this chart assumes that the landing gear is fully extended, the aircraft is climbing out with MILITARY thrust and without the assist of ground effect.

A rate of climb of 800 fpm, which corresponds approximately to an excess thrust to weight ratio of 0.05, is considered as a minimum acceptable climbout rate where obstacle clearance is required. Takeoff weight limitations and rate of climb less than 800 fpm are shown for conditions where the climbout is made over flat terrain or over the water. Note that in this region the additional horizontal distances to clear a 50-foot obstacle are 2000 to 3000 feet. If flat terrain condition exists at the end of the runway for a considerable distance, takeoffs may be extended into the marginal region. The required technique would be to lift the aircraft off the runway, accelerate and build up climbing speed while the gear is being retracted. After 10 to 15 seconds, the gear will be fully retracted and the reduced drag will permit a more reasonable climbout. Rates of climb of less than 400 fpm are considered insufficient for attempted takeoff.

EXAMPLE: Given a runway air temperature of 30°C, a pressure altitude of 4000 feet, and flat terrain at the end of the runway which would permit a minimum rate of climb after takeoff of 700 fpm.

1. Enter figure 11-9 at temperature of 30°C (A) and sight vertically upward to pressure altitude of 4000 feet (B).

2. From 4000-foot pressure altitude line (B), continue horizontally to right to rate-of-climb baseline (C), represented by 800 fpm, then parallel to guidelines to point (D).

11-16
Changed 1 June 1969

3. Point (D) is determined by entering at rate of climb of 700 fpm and proceeding vertically upward to the intersection of imaginary line drawn in step 2.

4. From point (D) proceed horizontally to right and read maximum permitted takeoff weight, of 72,200 pounds.

5. Note that for rate of climb of 800 fpm (C) with same configuration, maximum permitted takeoff weight is 68,800 pounds.

MINIMUM SINGLE-ENGINE CONTROL SPEED

Minimum single engine control speeds independent of flap position are shown in figure 11-10. The indicated minimum control speed is the speed that a straight course can be maintained with a bank angle of 5 degrees or less, utilizing rudder as necessary to overcome the yaw due to asymmetric thrust.

CAUTION

Avoid permitting aircraft to overrotate upon firing of JATO units in order to preclude scraping drag chute doors.

TAKEOFF REFUSAL SPEEDS

Takeoff refusal speed, figure 11-27, is that speed at which the pilot can cut the power and still stop the aircraft on a runway of a specified length.

EXAMPLE: Assume a takeoff is to be made from an airfield 6500 feet long (A) (dry concrete runway) at 70,000 pounds gross weight (B) under the following conditions: 4000-foot pressure altitude (C), 10°C air temperature (D) and 28-knot headwind (E). To determine the refusal speed enter chart (figure 11-27) at (A) 6500-foot runway length, proceed horizontally to (B) 70,000 pounds gross weight, then vertically downward to pressure altitude baseline. Follow guideline to point where it intercepts 4000-foot pressure altitude line (C). Proceed vertically downward to temperature baseline, then follow guideline up to intersection of 10°C air temperature line (D). Then downward again to headwind baseline, follow guideline to point where it intersects 28-knot headwind line (E). Proceed downward again to 111 knots refusal speed CAS (F). This is maximum speed that can be reached and still enable the pilot to stop the aircraft on a 6500-foot runway.

REFUSED TAKEOFF STOPPING DISTANCE – NO JATO

The refused takeoff stopping distance, figure 11-28 is that distance required to stop an aircraft after it reaches a specified speed. The flight conditions to be taken into consideration are ground speed, gross weight, pressure altitude and air temperature. Two

stopping distances can be obtained; one as the result of using a drag chute and the second distance without the use of the drag chute.

EXAMPLE: Assume a ground speed of 82 knots CAS (A) is reached, during takeoff, at a pressure altitude of 4000 feet (B) with an air temperature of 6°C (C), takeoff weight of 65,000 pounds (D) and a headwind of 10 knots (E). Refer to figure 11-28, and enter graph at refusal speed of 82 knots (A), follow guideline to 4000 foot pressure altitude (B), proceed horizontally to temperature baseline, follow guideline to point where it meets air temperature line of 6°C (C). Proceed horizontally once more to aircraft takeoff weight of 65,000 pounds (D) without drag chute, follow graph line down to the headwind baseline, then follow guideline to where it intersects 10-knot headwind line (E). Follow graph line down to stopping distance of 2500 feet (F). The stopping distance with drag chute deployed is 2000 feet (G).

JATO Firing Delay and Minimum Takeoff Distance

The minimum ground run distance and total distance to clear a 50-foot obstacle may be realized by firing the JATO bottles so that burnout occurs just prior to liftoff. This method is recommended for the following reasons:

1. It produces the shortest takeoff distance.

2. A misfire can be detected early and the takeoff can be aborted well before the refusal point.

3. Special trim settings are required for airborne JATO operation because of the pitching moments generated by JATO thrust.

4. The burnout transient due to thrust reduction, the trim change, and the altitude change necessary to maintain airspeed after burnout would be avoided.

Recommended positioning for alternate JATO combinations are listed below. JATO stations are numbered from 1 to 6, starting at the top:

Number of JATO units	Station numbers
2	3
4	2 and 3
6	2, 3, and 4
12	1, 2, 3, 4, 5, and 6

It is recommended that the JATO firing point be established by distance markers alongside the runway since firing the JATO bottles using a time interval after brake release is too inaccurate. The airspeed at which the JATO would be fired using this technique is generally below the speed at which the airspeed indicator begins to register.

5KS-4500 MK 7 MOD 2 JATO UNITS (15° NOZZLE)

Figures 11-11, 11-13, 11-15, and 11-17 are presented to show the ground run distance covered from brake release to JATO ignition for loadings of 2, 4, 6, and 12 JATO units respectively. Both the ground run distance and the total distance to clear a 50-foot obstacle are presented on figures 11-12, 11-14, 11-16, and 11-18 for the same JATO loadings.

5KS-4500 MK 7 MOD 1 JATO UNITS (30° NOZZLE)

Figures 11-19, 11-21, 11-23, and 11-25 are presented to show the ground run distance covered from brake release to JATO ignition for loadings of 2, 4, 6, and 12 JATO units respectively. Both the ground run distance and the total distance to clear a 50 foot obstacle are presented on figures 11-20, 11-22, 11-24, and 11-26 for the same JATO loadings.

Note that on figures 11-12, 11-14, 11-16, 11-18, 11-20, 11-22, 11-24, and 11-26 there are regions labeled TAKEOFF IS MARGINAL. In these regions the climbout characteristics are marginal. Since JATO burnout occurs prior to liftoff, climbout is similar to takeoff distance NO JATO and the maximum takeoff weight is limited to that shown on figure 11-9.

EXAMPLE JATO FIRING DELAY USING 2 5KS-4500 MK 7 MOD 2 JATO UNITS

To determine the distance at which JATO units are to be fired, assume takeoff is to be made at 70,000 pounds gross weight, runway temperature 30°C, pressure altitude 4000 feet, wind of 10 knots, and runway gradient -1 percent.

1. Enter figure 11-11 at 146 knots (D) as determined from figure 11-7. Proceed horizontally to the right to the line representing 70,000 pounds (E).

2. Sight vertically downward to temperature baseline and follow parallel to guidelines to temperature of 30°C (F).

3. Continue vertically downward to pressure altitude baseline, then parallel to guidelines to pressure altitude of 4000 feet (G).

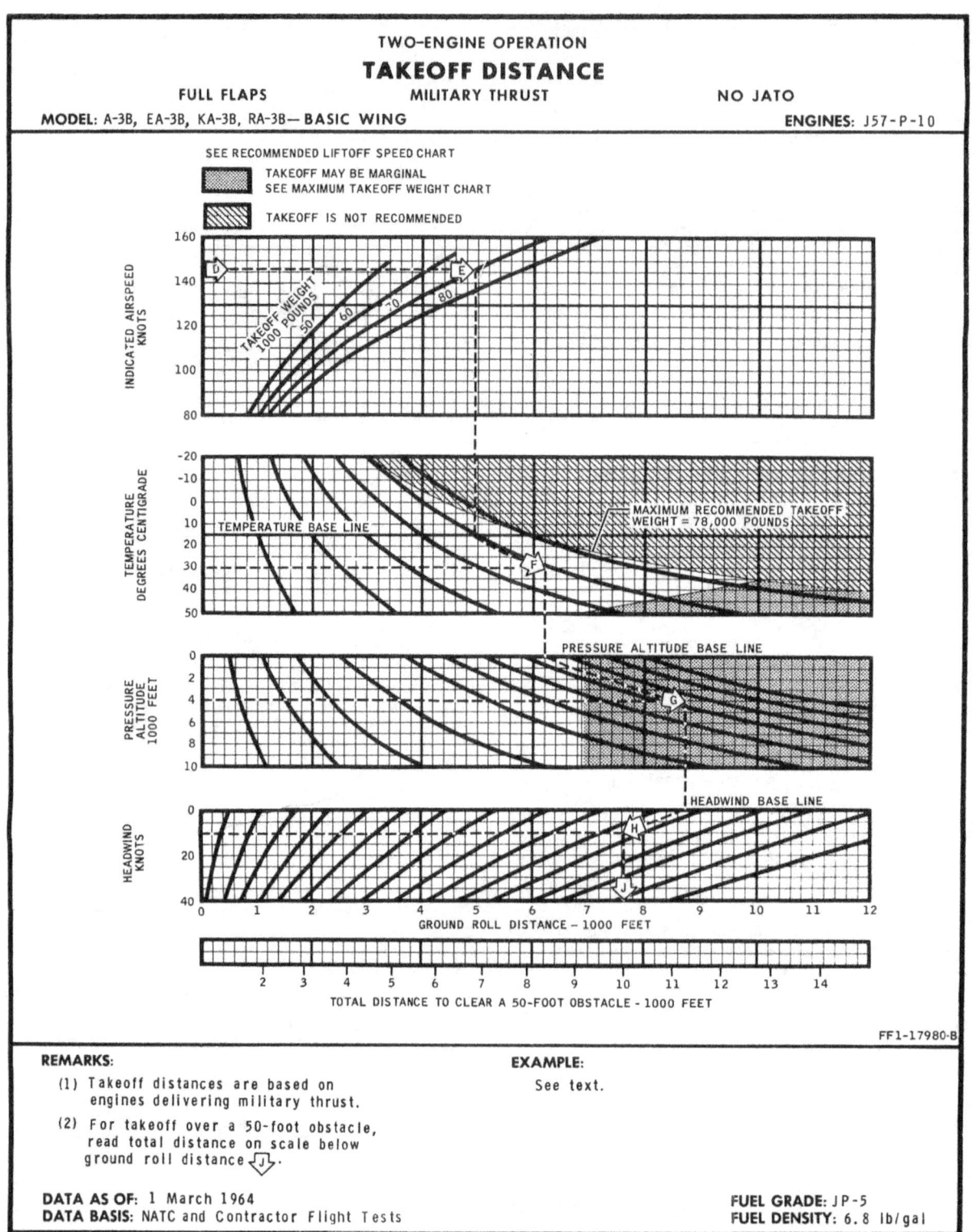

Figure 11-8. Takeoff Distance

NAVAIR 01-40ATA-1

Section XI
Part 2

MAXIMUM RECOMMENDED TAKEOFF WEIGHT

FULL FLAPS—MILITARY THRUST—WITH AND WITHOUT JATO

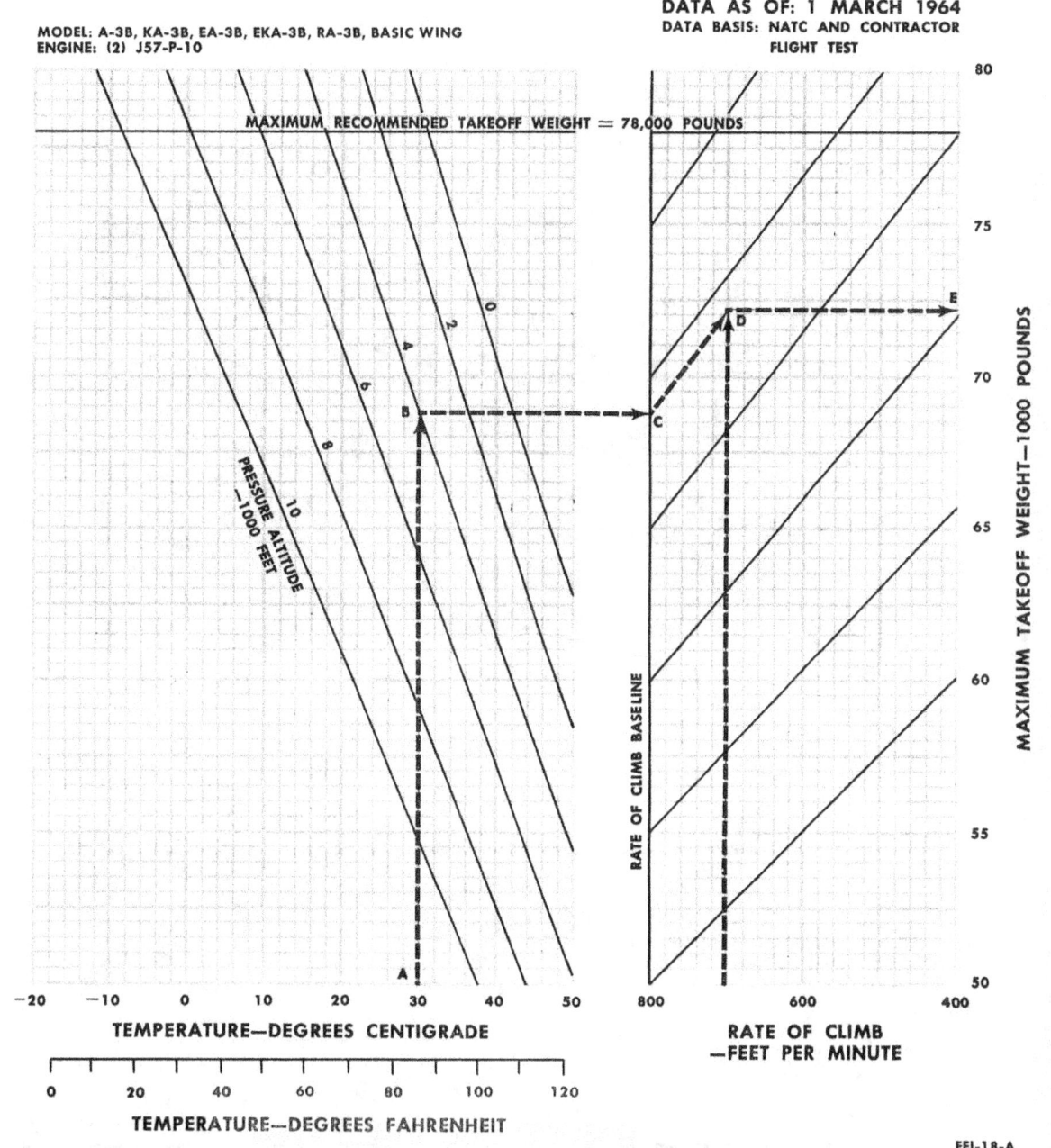

Figure 11-9. Maximum Recommended Takeoff Weight

11-21

Section XI
Part 2

NAVAIR 01-40ATA-1

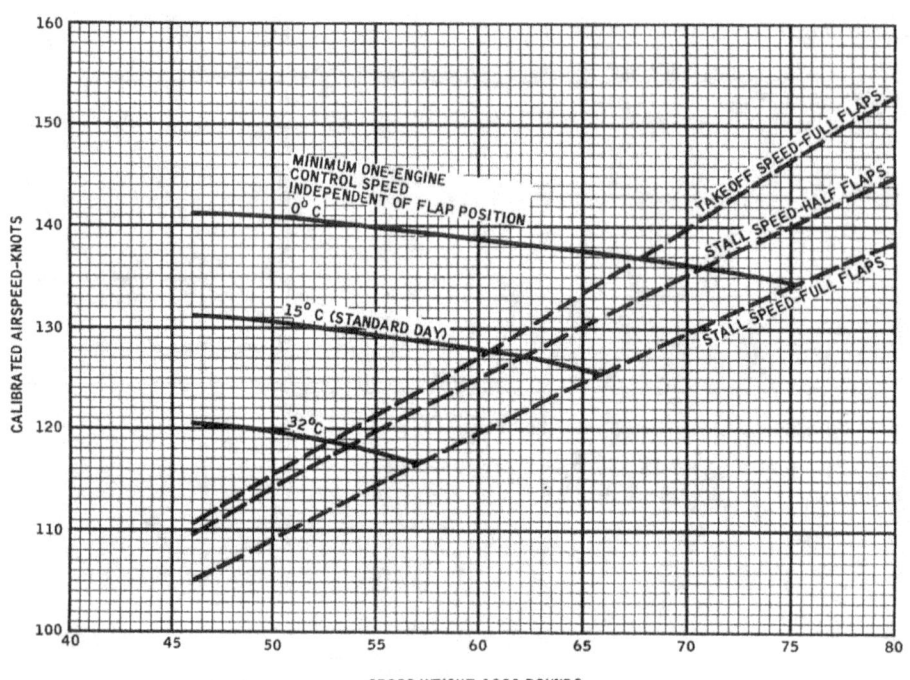

Figure 11-10. Minimum Single-Engine Control Speed

11-22

NAVAIR 01-40ATA-1

Section XI
Part 2

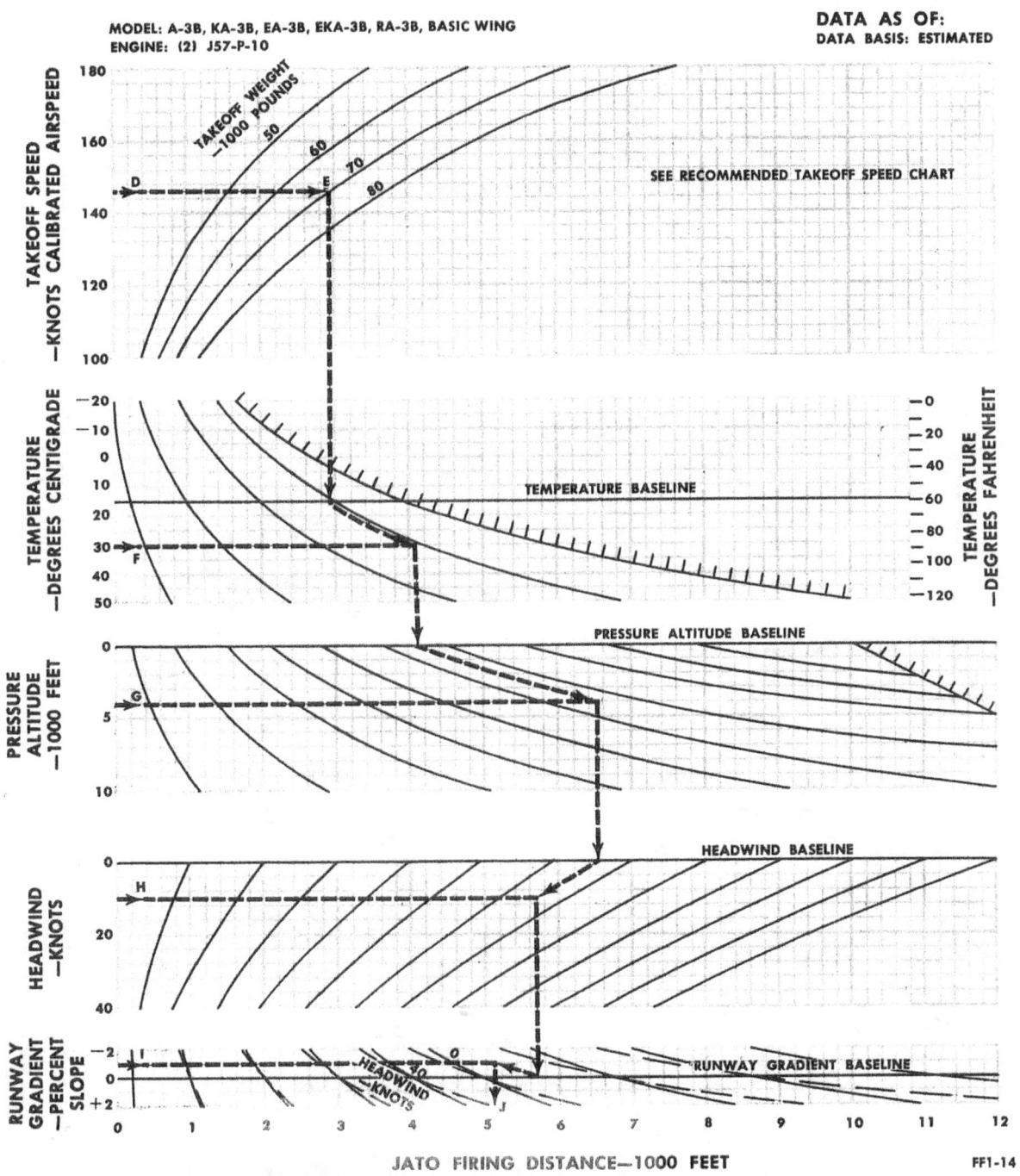

Figure 11-11. JATO Firing Delay — Two Units (15° Nozzle)

Section XI
Part 2

NAVAIR 01-40ATA-1

JATO TAKEOFF DISTANCE
TWO 5KS-4500, MK 7, MOD 2, JATO UNITS (15° NOZZLE)
FULL FLAPS

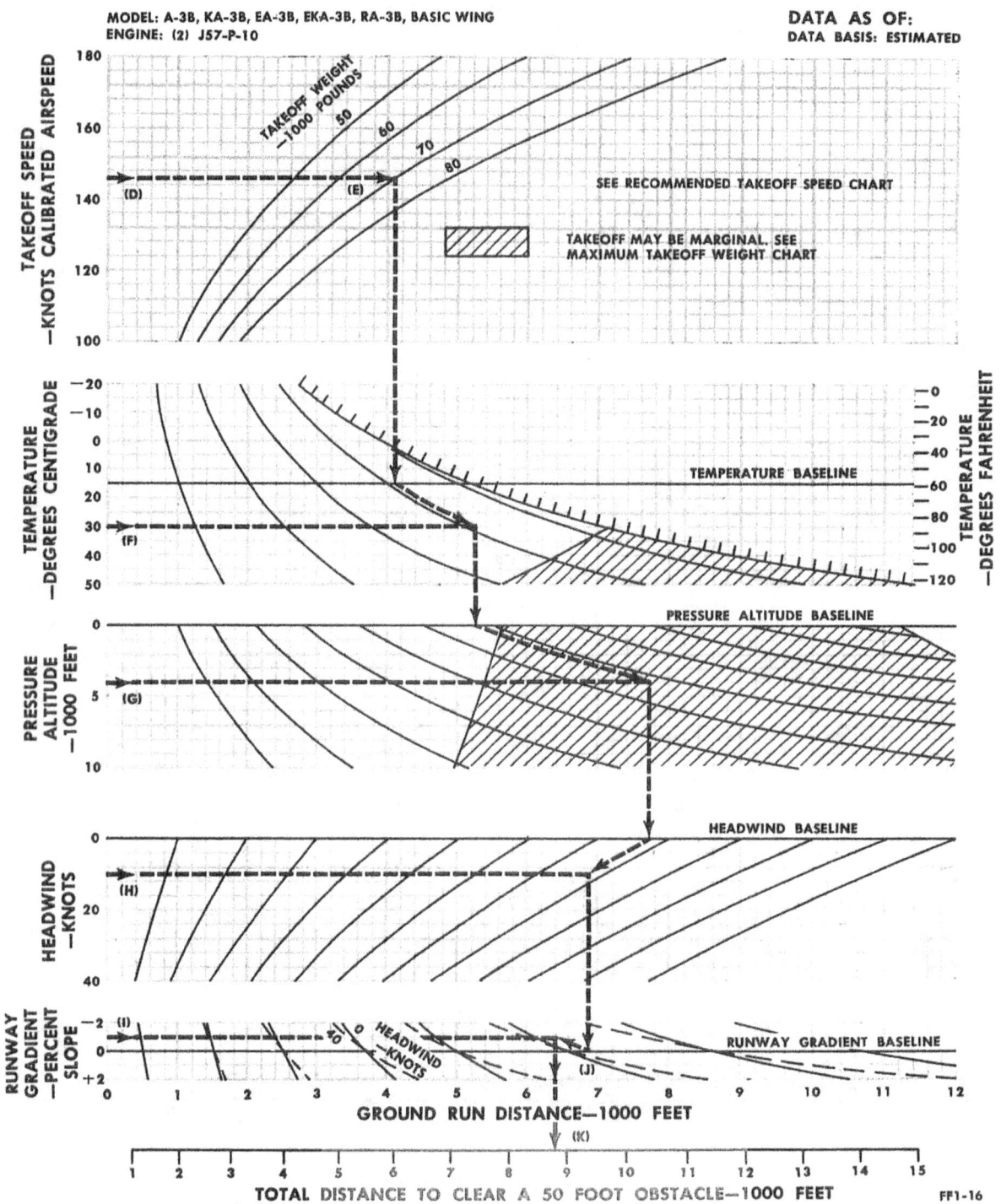

Figure 11-12. JATO Takeoff Distance — Two Units (15° Nozzle)

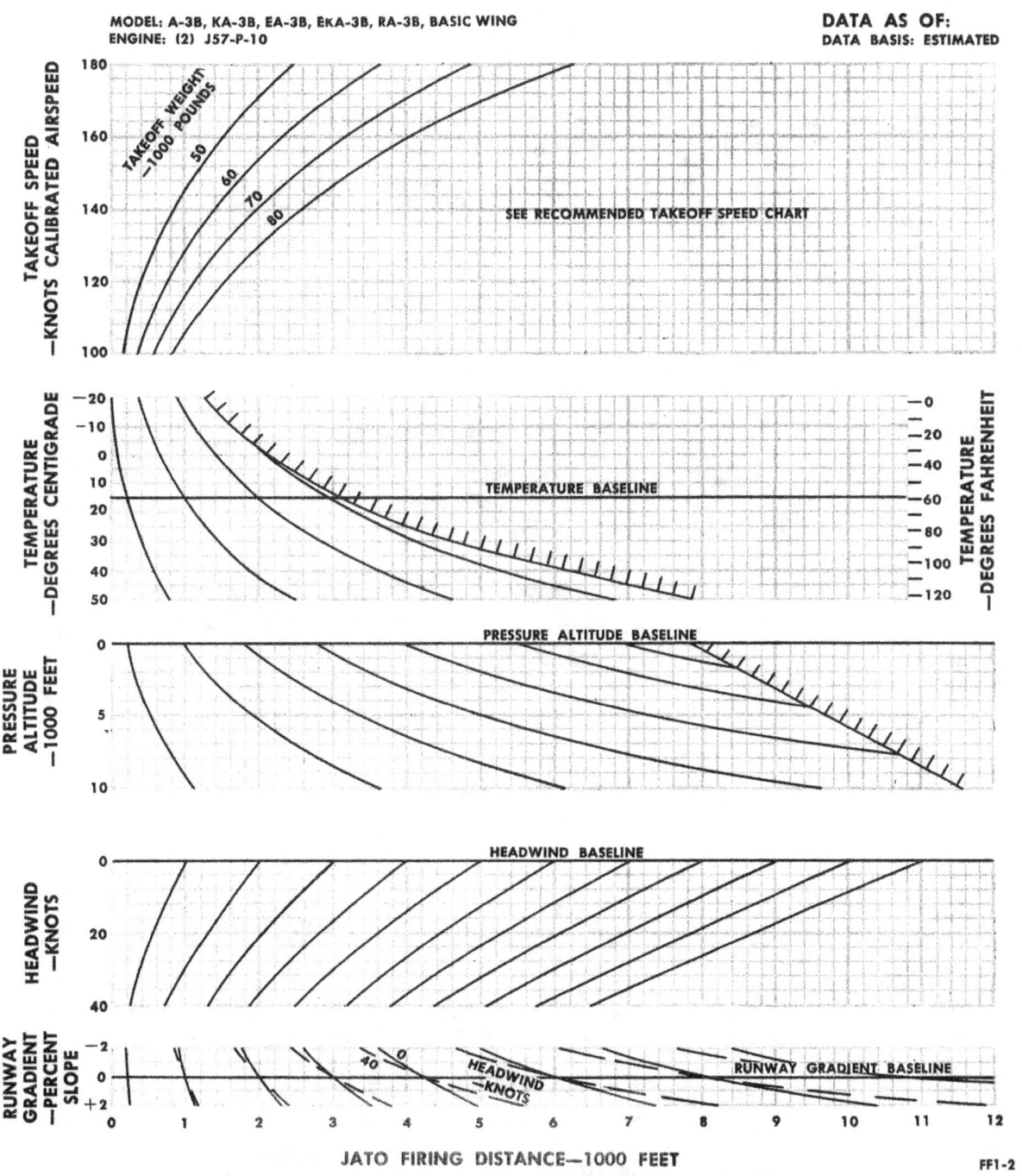

Figure 11-13. JATO Firing Delay — Four Units (15° Nozzle)

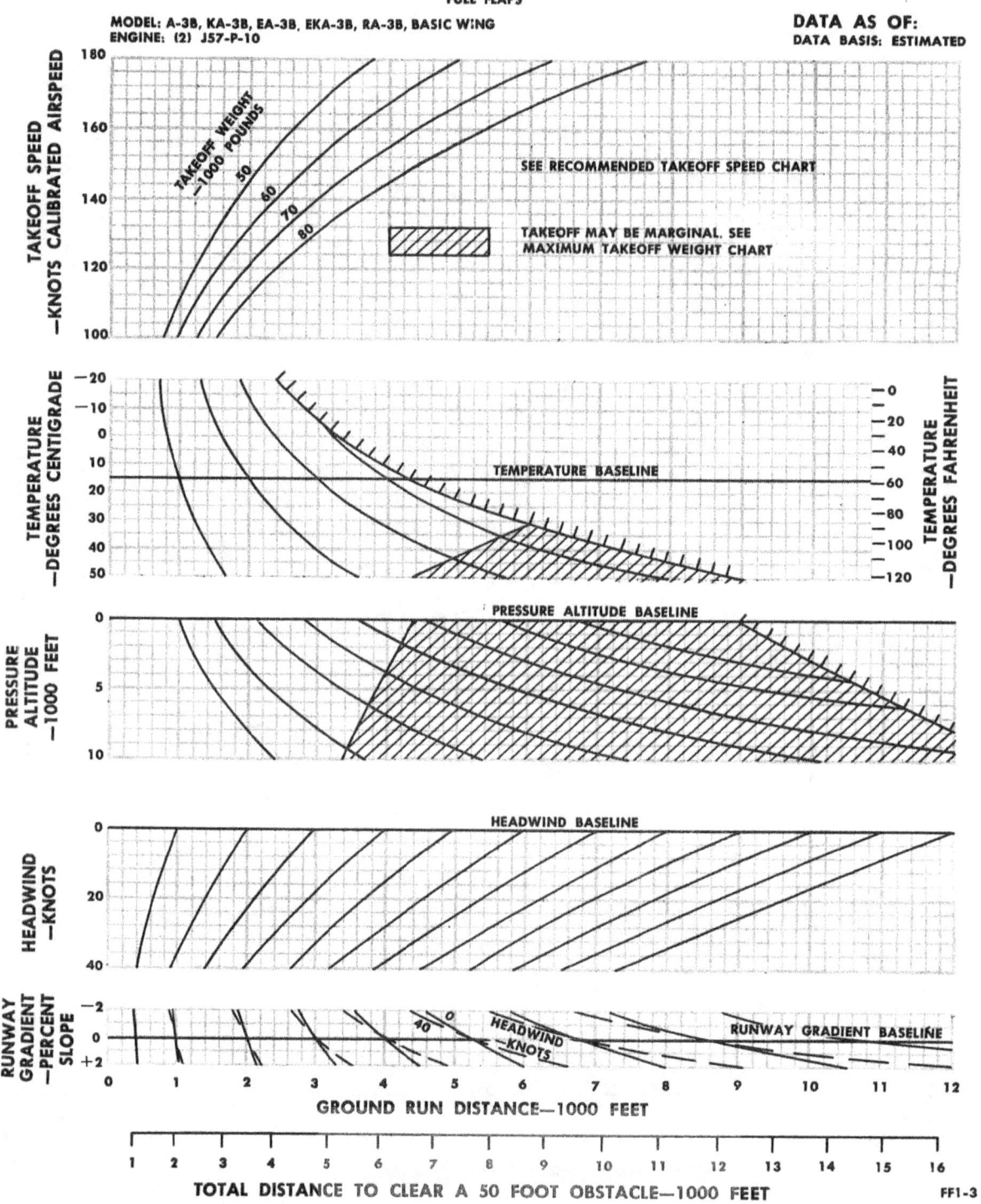

Figure 11-14. JATO Takeoff Distance — Four Units (15° Nozzle)

NAVAIR 01-40ATA-1

Section XI
Part 2

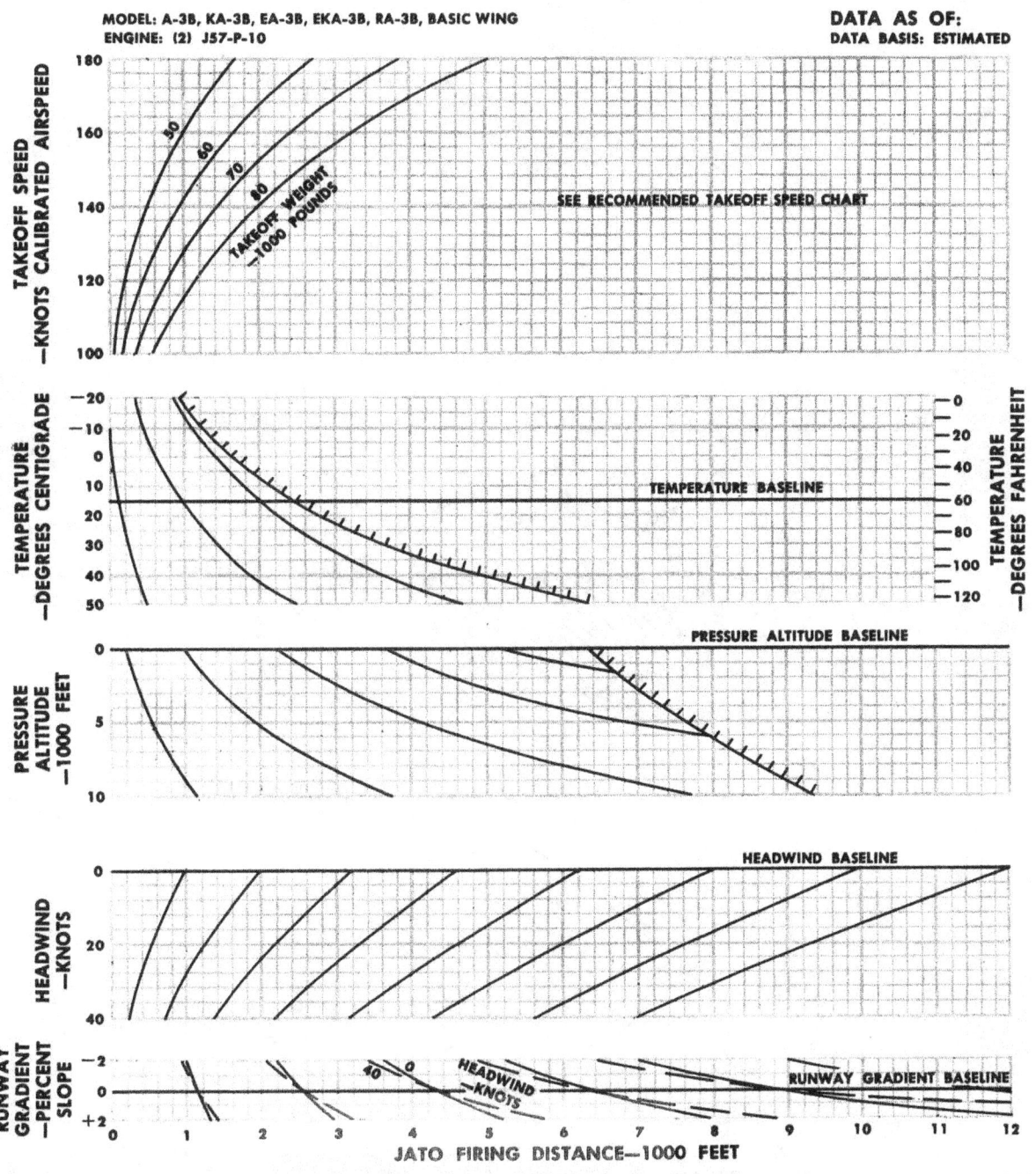

Figure 11-15. JATO Firing Delay — Six Units (15° Nozzle)

Section XI
Part 2

NAVAIR 01-40ATA-1

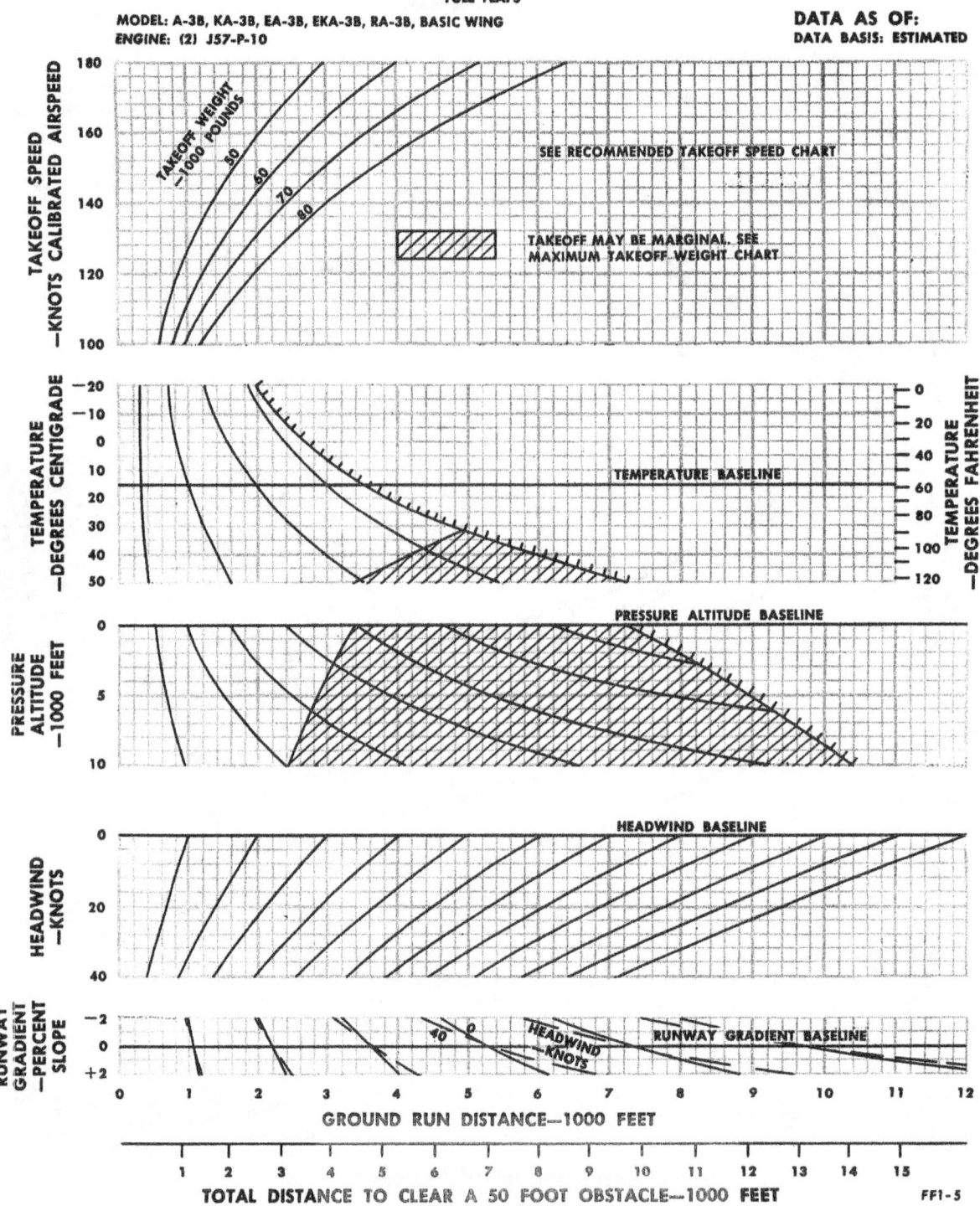

Figure 11-16. JATO Takeoff Distance — Six Units (15° Nozzle)

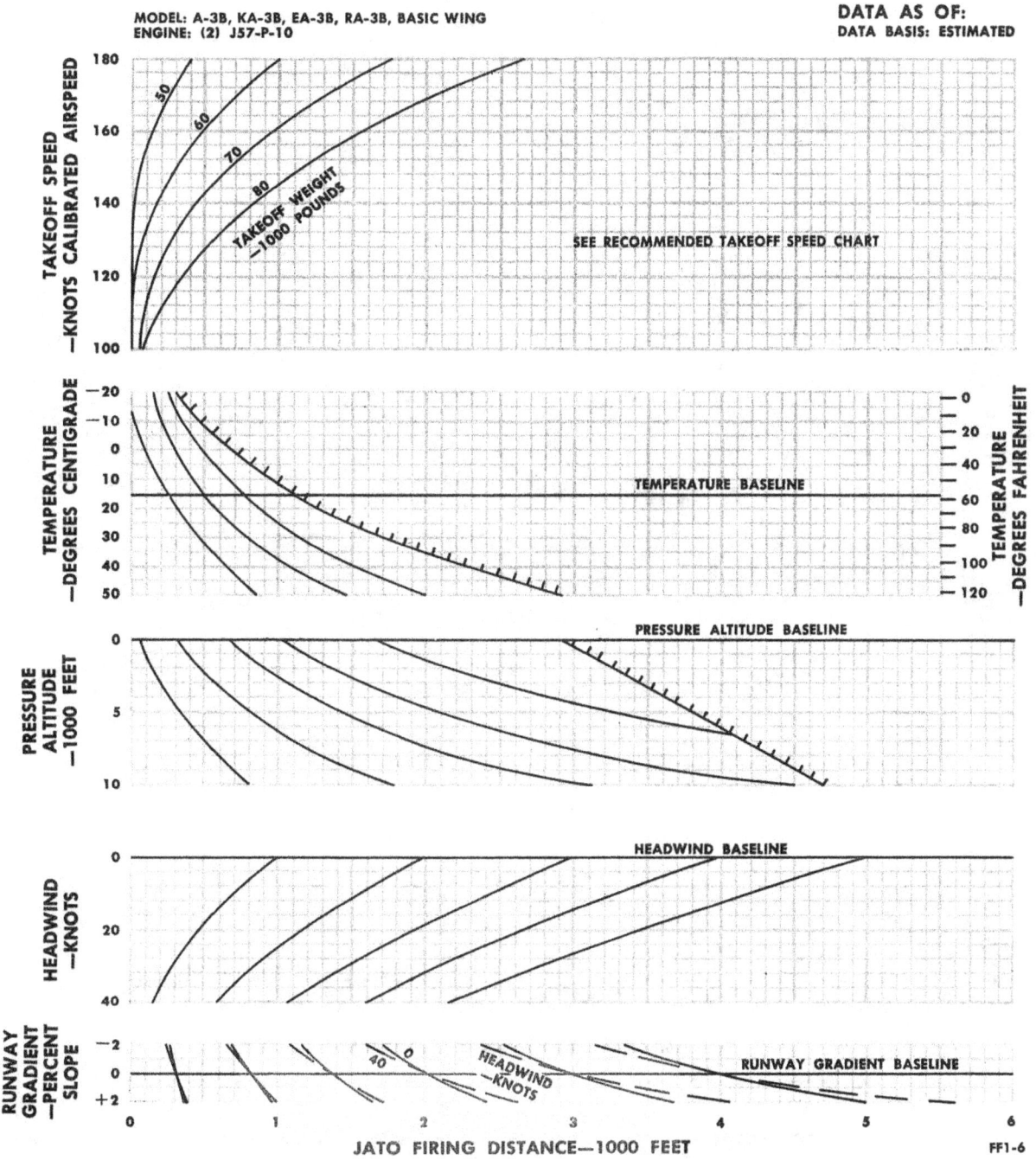

Figure 11-17. JATO Firing Delay — 12 Units (15° Nozzle)

Section XI
Part 2
NAVAIR 01-40ATA-1

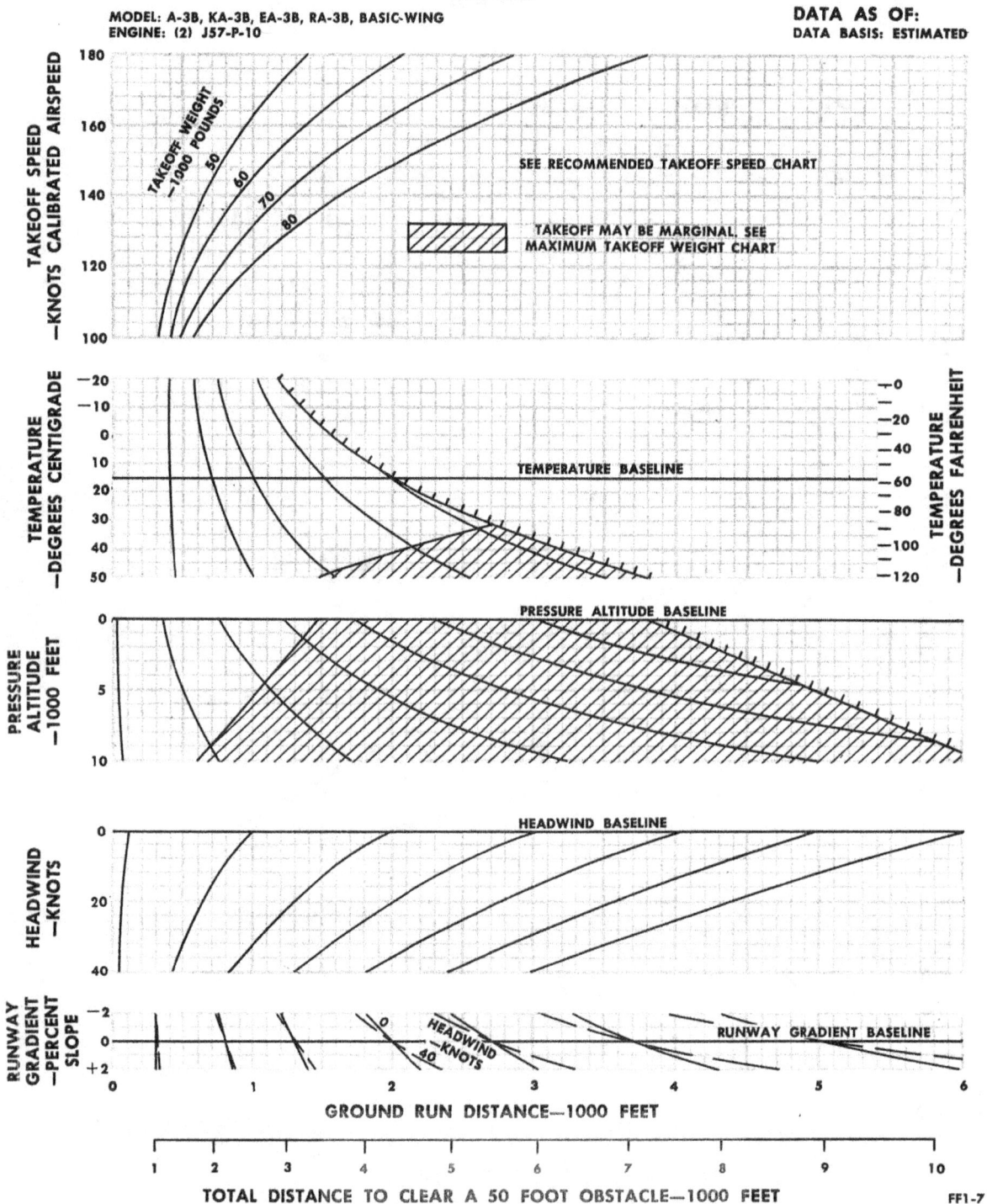

Figure 11-18. JATO Takeoff Distance — 12 Units (15° Nozzle)

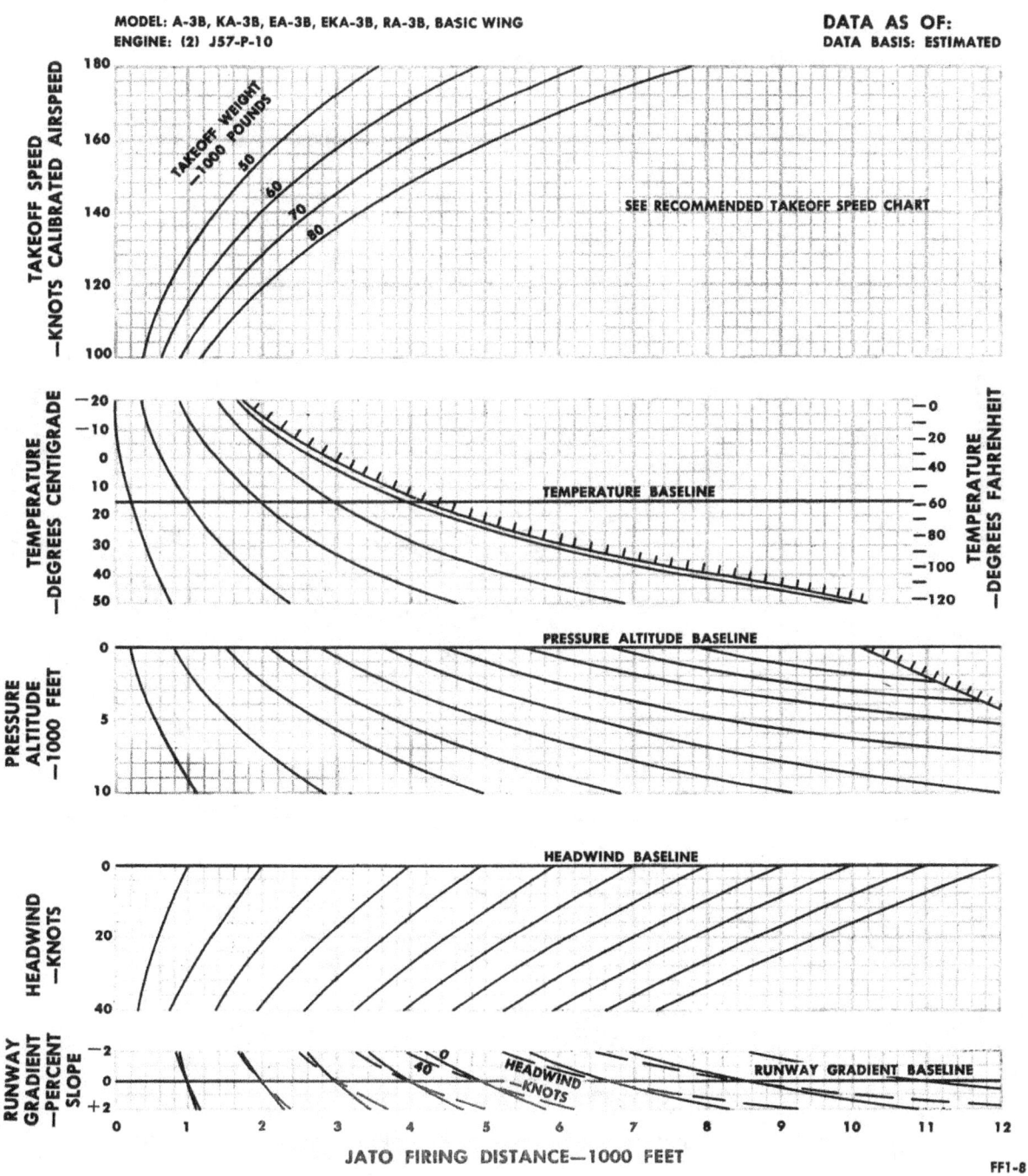

Figure 11-19. JATO Firing Delay — Two Units (30° Nozzle)

Section XI
Part 2
NAVAIR 01-40ATA-1

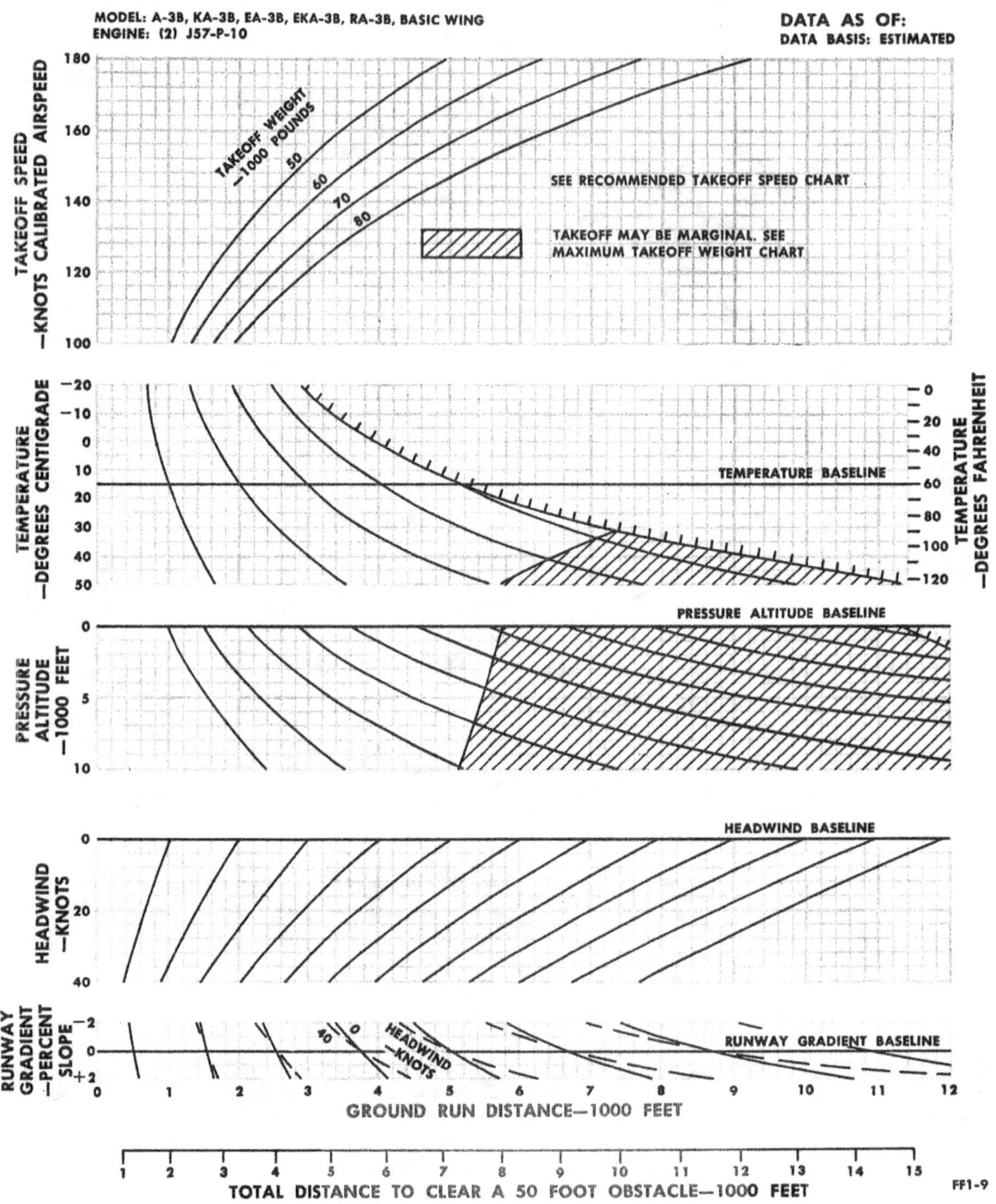

Figure 11-20. JATO Takeoff Distance – Two Units (30° Nozzle)

NAVAIR 01-40ATA-1

Section XI
Part 2

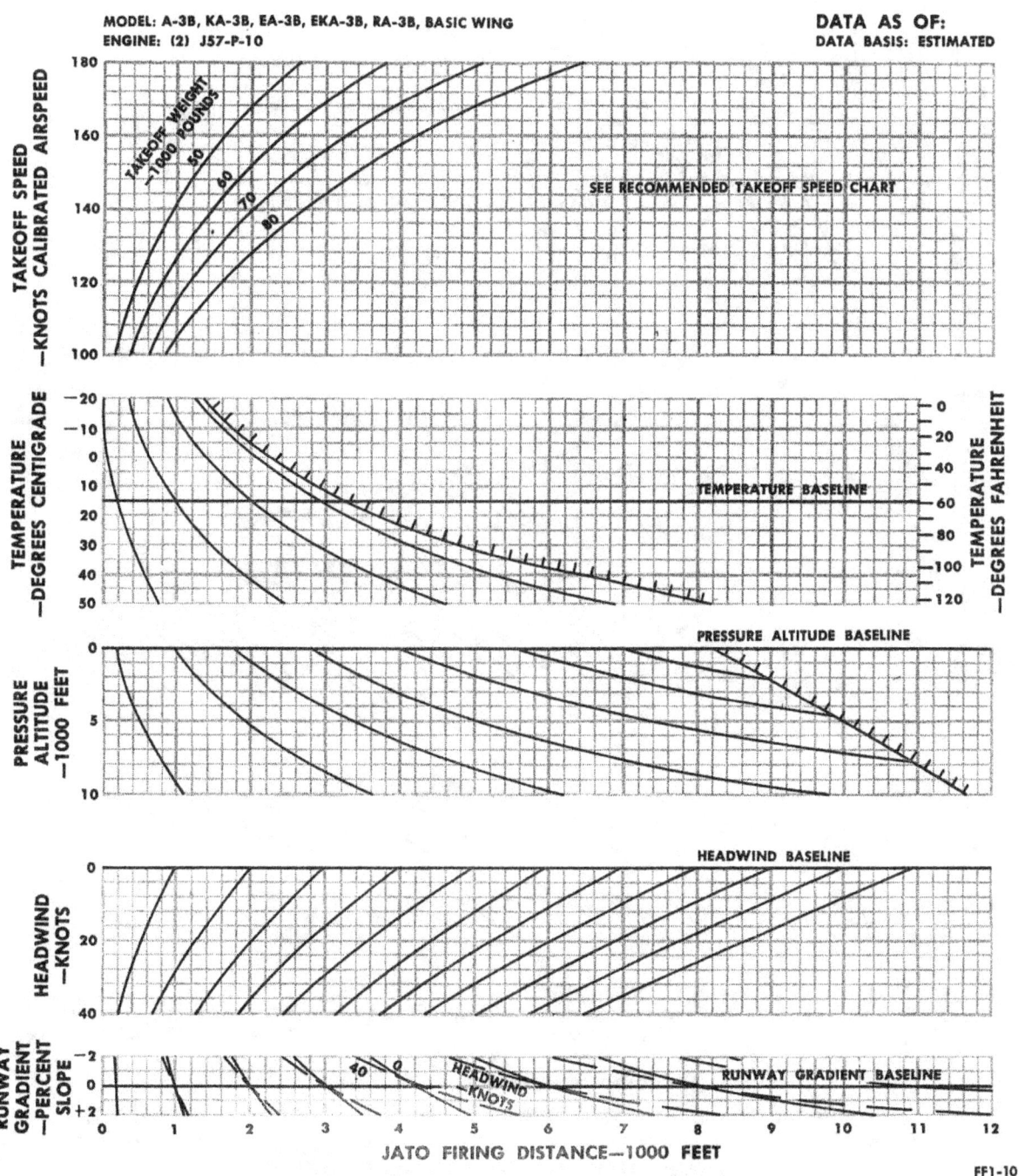

Figure 11-21. JATO Firing Delay — Four Units (30° Nozzle)

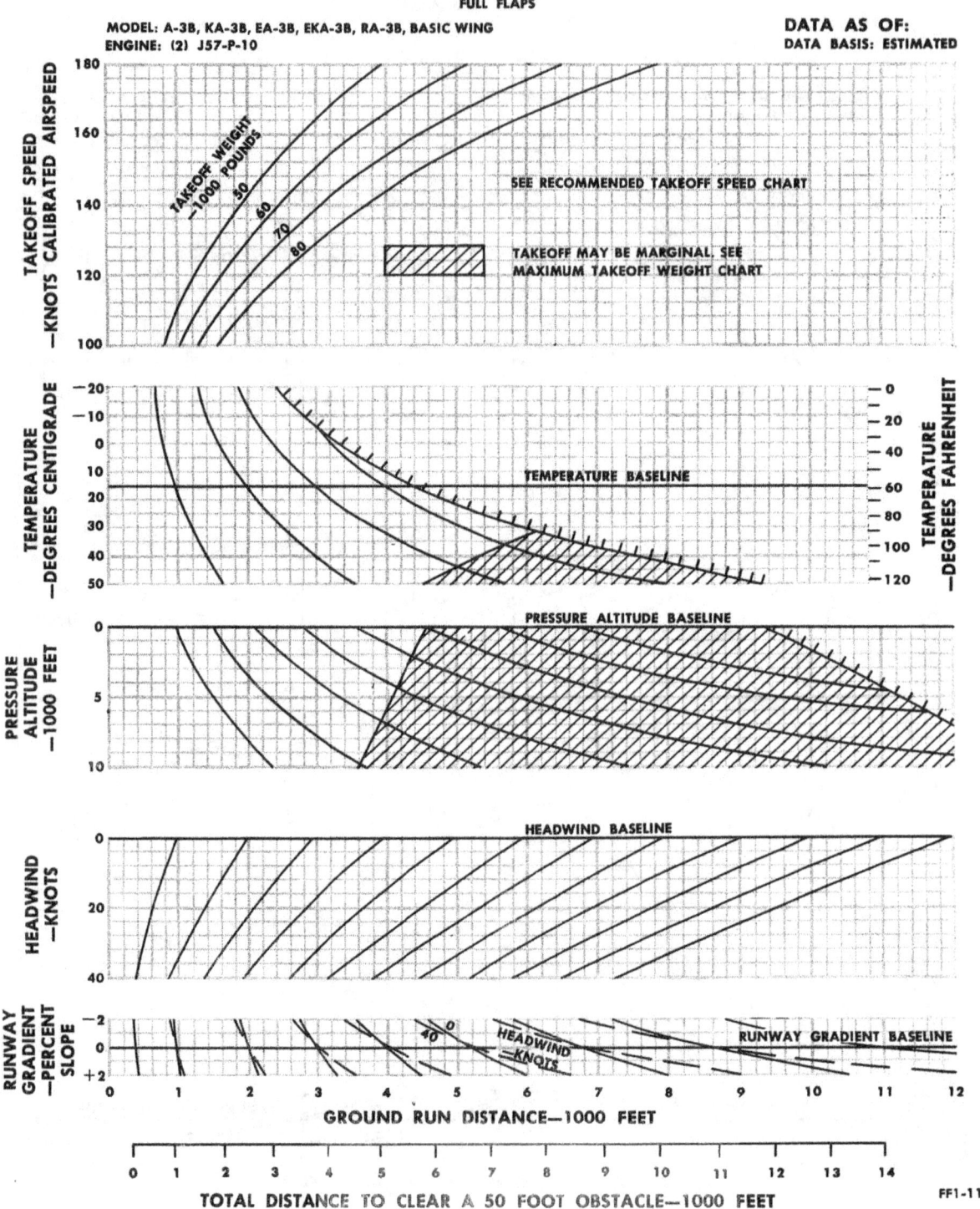

Figure 11-22. JATO Takeoff Distance – Four Units (30° Nozzle)

NAVAIR 01-40ATA-1

Section XI
Part 2

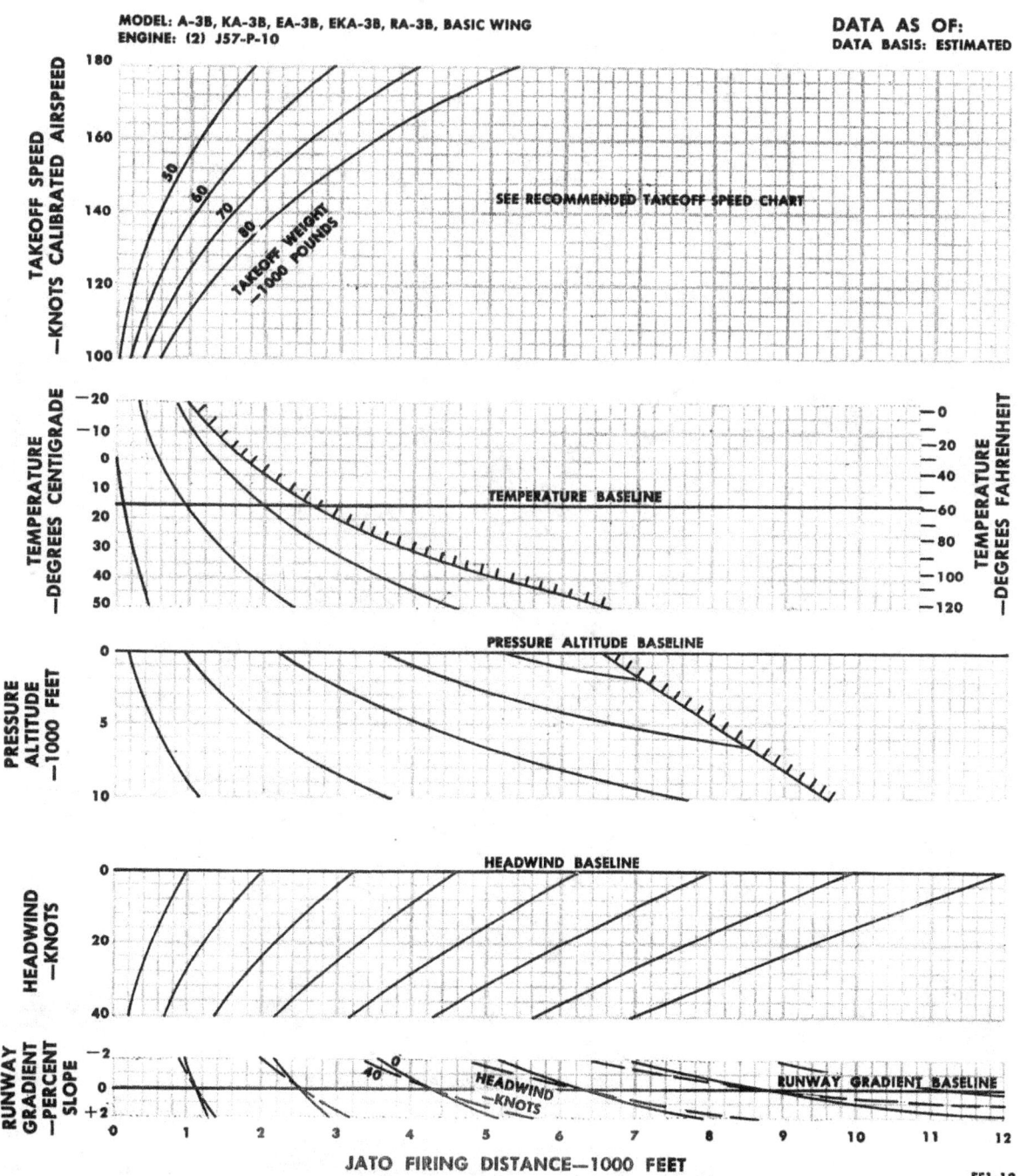

Figure 11-23. JATO Firing Delay — Six Units (30° Nozzle)

Section XI
Part 2
NAVAIR 01-40ATA-1

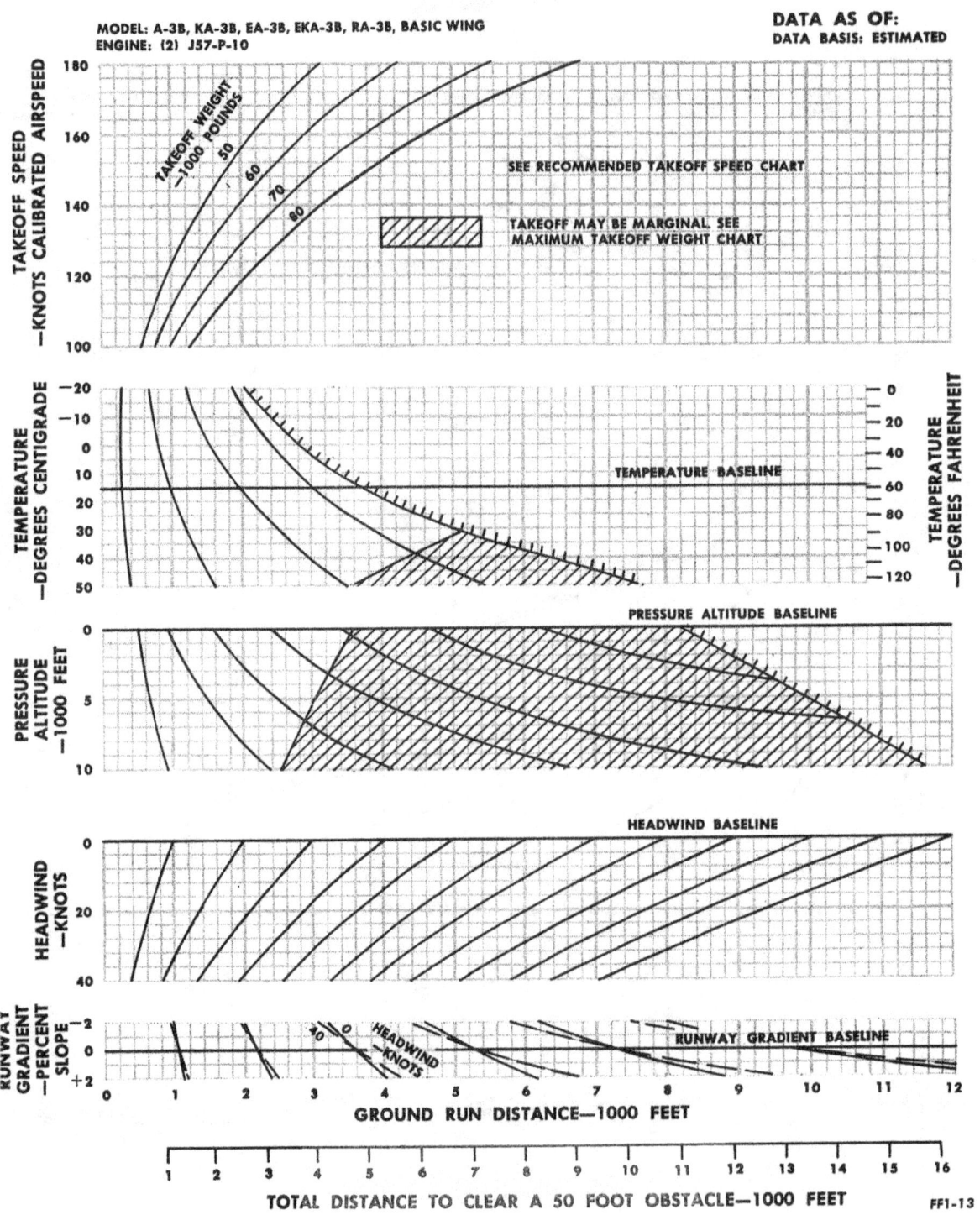

Figure 11-24. JATO Takeoff Distance – Six Units (30° Nozzle)

NAVAIR 01-40ATA-1

Section XI
Part 2

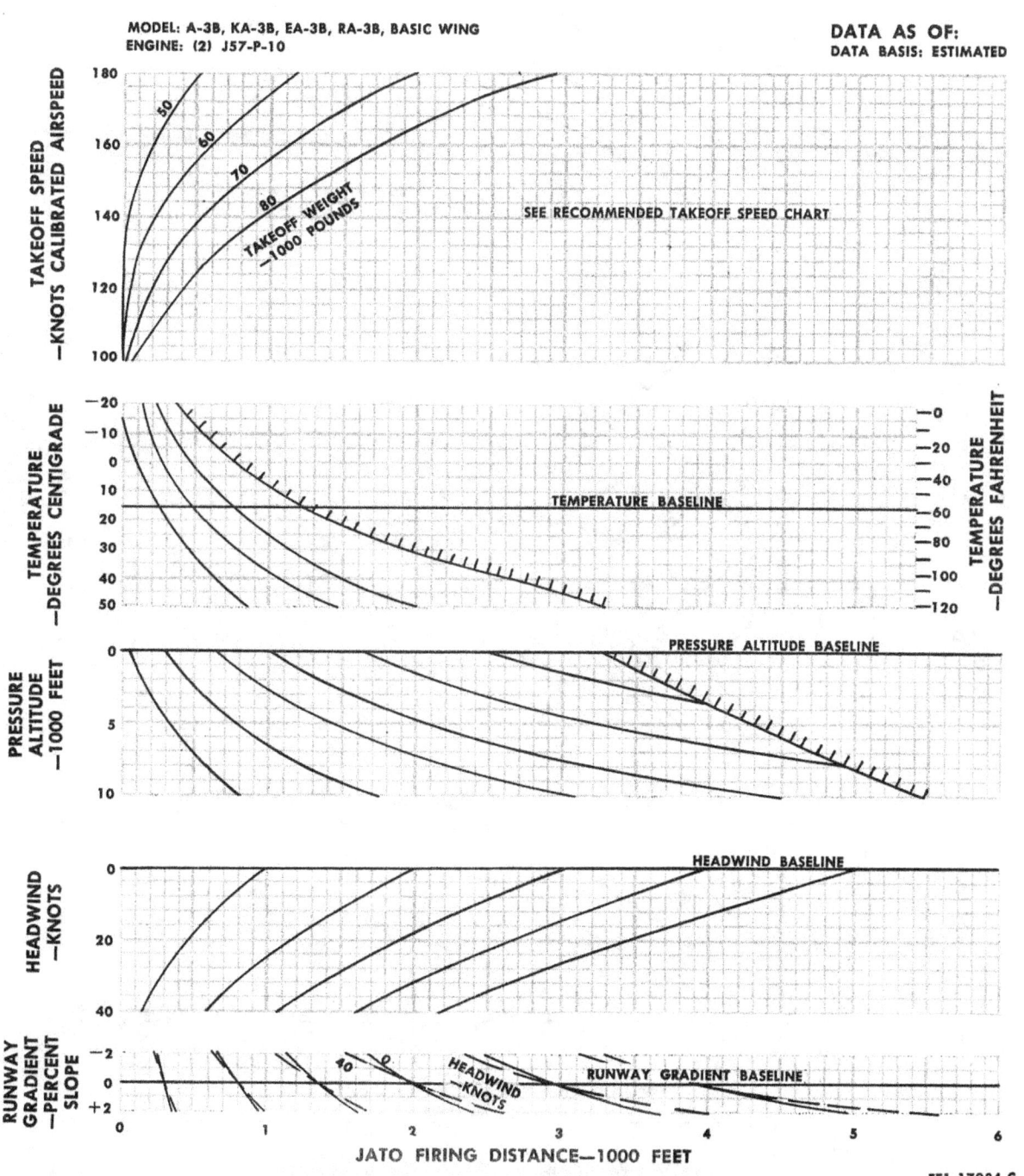

Figure 11-25. JATO Firing Delay — 12 Units (30° Nozzle)

11-37

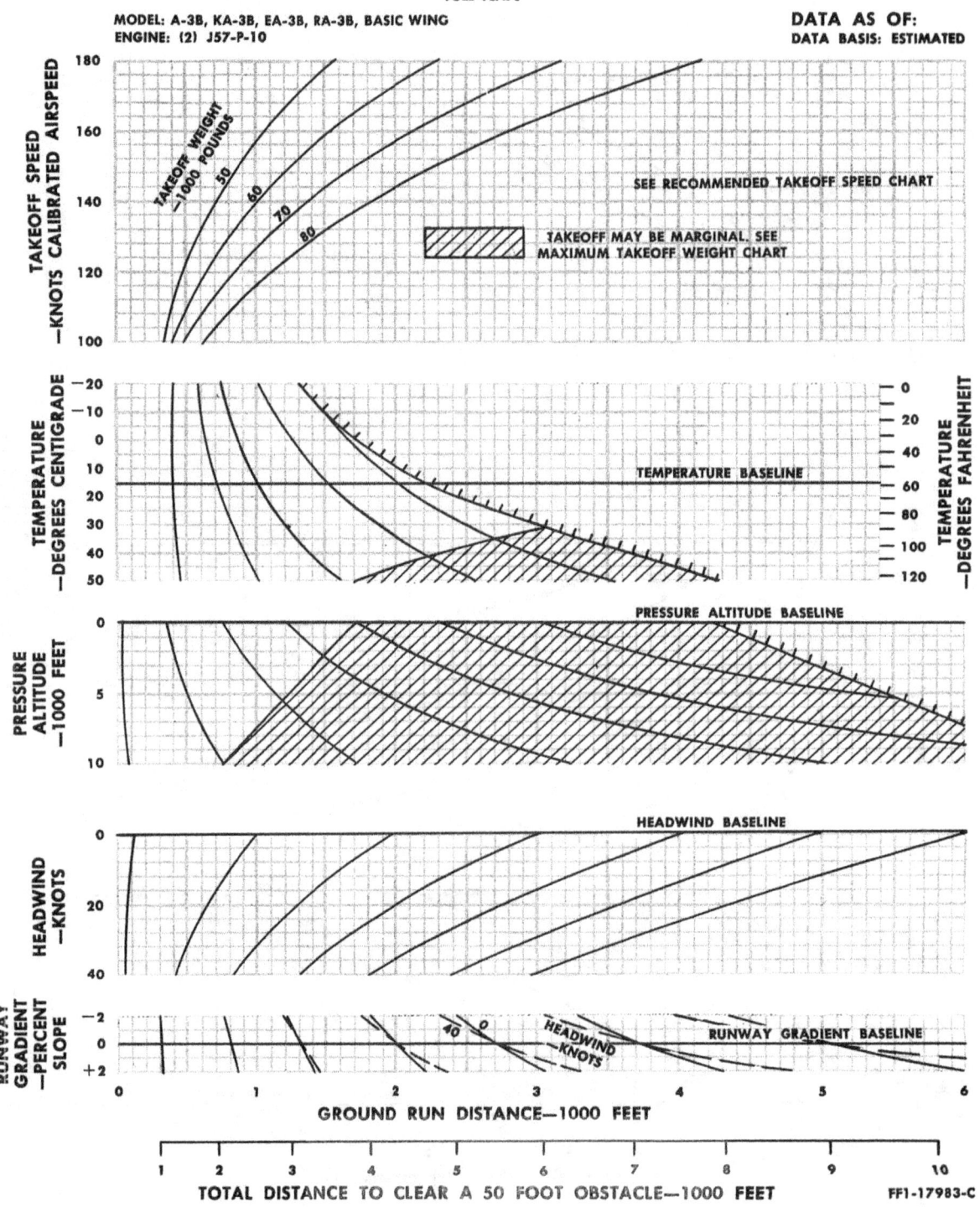

Figure 11-26. JATO Takeoff Distance — 12 Units (30° Nozzle)

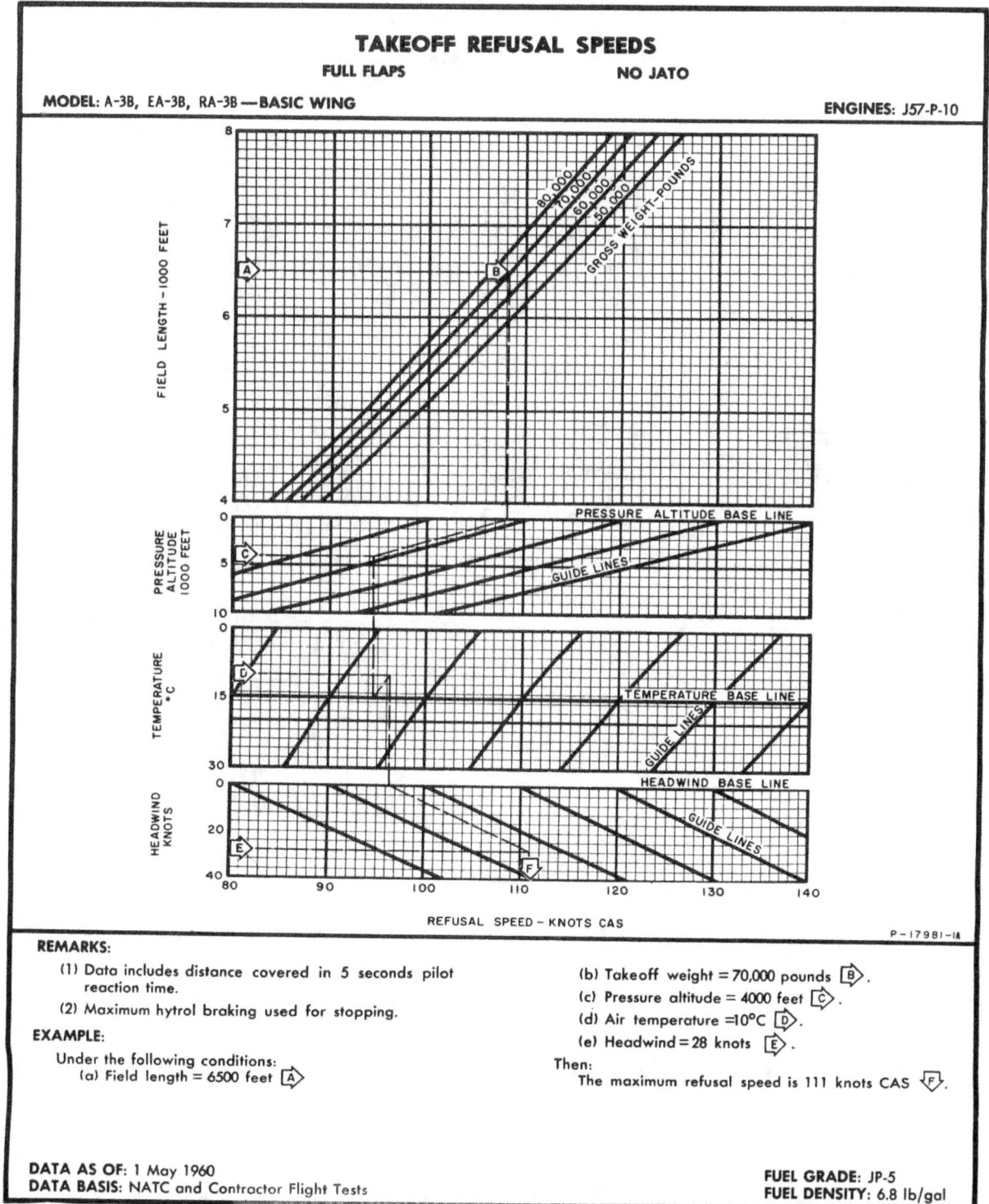

Figure 11-27. Takeoff Refusal Speeds

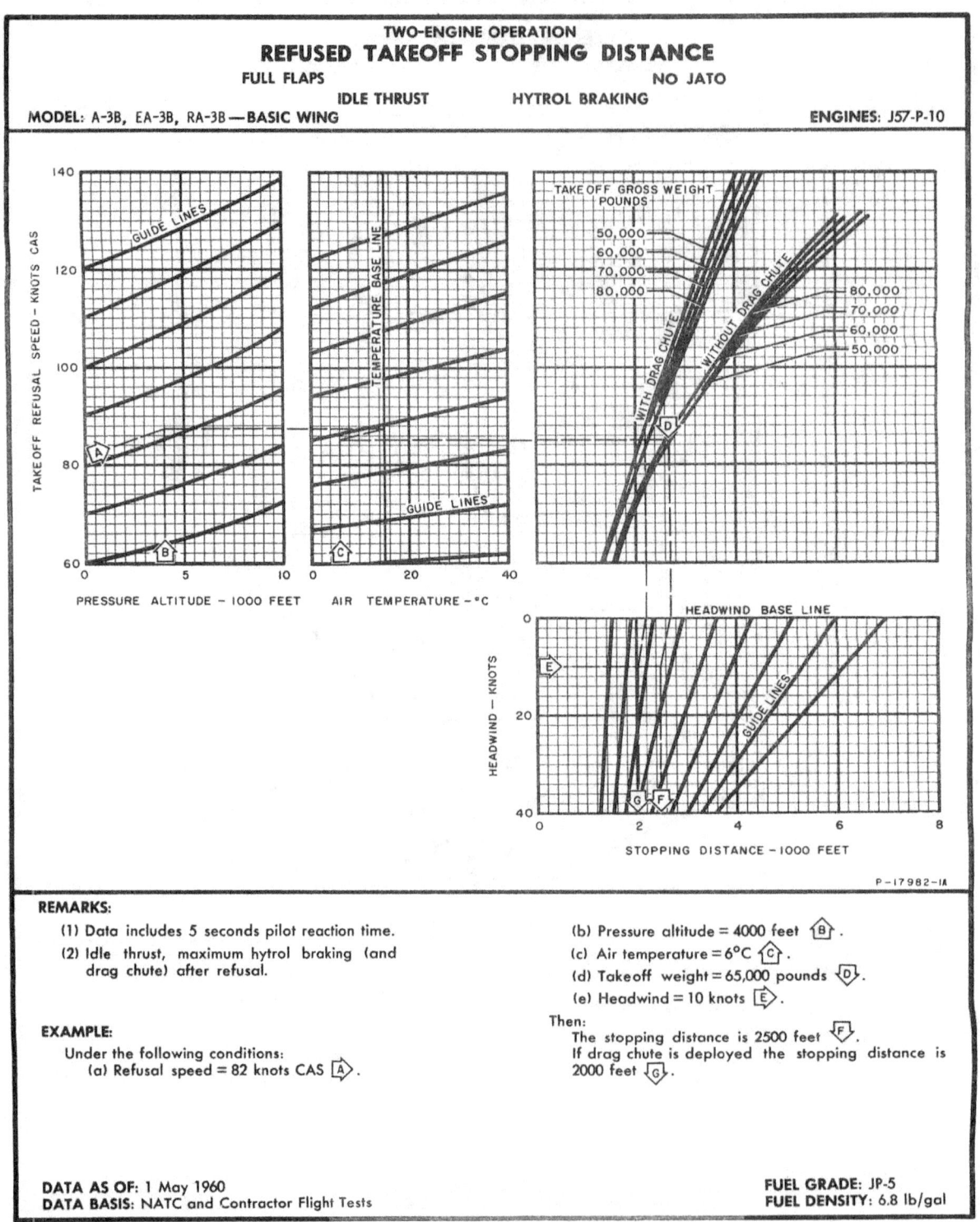

Figure 11-28. Refused Takeoff Stopping Distance

NAVAIR 01-40ATA-1

Section XI
Part 3

PART 3
CLIMB

TABLE OF CONTENTS

TEXT

Page

Climb Performance 11-41

ILLUSTRATIONS

Figure		Page
11-29	Climb Performance After Takeoff	11-44
11-30	Climb Performance for Waveoff	11-45
11-31	Fuel Consumed During Climb	11-46
11-32	Climb Distance	11-47
11-33	Time To Climb	11-48
11-34	One-Engine Rate of Climb – 60,000 Pounds	11-49

Figure		Page
11-35	Temperature Effect of One-Engine Rate of Climb – Military Thrust	11-53
11-36	Fuel Consumed During Climb	11-54
11-37	Climb Distance	11-55
11-38	Time To Climb	11-56

Climb Performance

CLIMB PERFORMANCE AFTER TAKEOFF

Figure 11-29 shows the climb characteristics of the aircraft immediately after takeoff at sea level pressure altitude and a takeoff gross weight of 70,000 pounds. These data show the effects of airspeed, flap position and landing gear extension on the maximum rate of climb with takeoff power. Rates of climb for each landing gear and flap configuration at airspeeds below the recommended airspeed are included.

NOTE

This chart shows maximum rates of climb available at zero acceleration (i.e., stabilized airspeed). Upon achieving a given climb airspeed, the pilot can obtain the corresponding rate of climb shown on the chart if no attempt is made to increase the airspeed.

It is readily apparent from this chart that the landing gear should be raised immediately after takeoff. Also, from the airspeed, the flap retraction time, and rate-of-climb relationships, it is recommended that flap retraction be initiated only after the aircraft has accelerated to an airspeed approximately 30 to 40 knots above the recommended takeoff airspeed.

Two additional curves are provided on the chart. The dashed line in the center of the grid can be used to estimate the loss of rate of climb should one engine fail immediately after takeoff. This curve shows the absolute necessity of increasing the forward speed of the aircraft as well as raising the landing gear and flaps before any attempt is made to gain altitude with one engine inoperative. The curve at the bottom of the grid can be used to estimate the effect on available rate of climb which results from deviations in ambient temperature from the standard temperature of 15°C at sea level. Note that except at low takeoff airspeeds with full flaps (i.e., minimum ground roll) the aircraft has excellent climb-out performance on two engines, even with ambient temperatures considerably above standard.

EXAMPLE: A field takeoff (full flaps) is to be made at 70,000 pounds gross weight with no wind, with sea level pressure altitude, and an ambient temperature of 5°C. Find the rate of climb at 164 knots for a normal climb-out; and for climb-out following engine failure after the landing gear has been retracted.

1. Enter the Climb Performance After Takeoff chart, figure 11-29, with 164 knots CAS, (A), read vertically to the intersection with the solid line (full flaps and gear down). Opposite this point on the left-hand scale (E), read approximately 2380 feet per minute available rate of climb for normal Standard Day operations. From the temperature correction curve note that the available rate of climb is increased by 400 feet per minute for each 10°C temperature decrease from standard day. The correction then is:

$$\left(\frac{15-5}{10}\right) \times 400 = 400 \text{ feet per minute.}$$

This results in:

2380 + 400 = 2780 feet per minute actual rate-of-climb. Assume the landing gear is fully retracted at

Changed 1 June 1969

11-41

175 knots CAS. From the chart, the rate of climb at this point is determined to be:

2875 + 425 = 3300 feet per minute.

2. Assume that with the landing gear retracted and full flaps extended, one engine fails at 175 knots CAS. As shown on the chart, the loss in rate of climb due to failure of one engine at this airspeed is approximately 2425 feet per minute. If the climb-out is continued, the maximum available rate of climb of one engine then becomes:

3300 - 2425 = 875 feet per minute.

CLIMB PERFORMANCE FOR WAVEOFF

Figure 11-30 shows the climb capability of the aircraft after waveoff with military thrust at a gross weight of 50,000 pounds. The chart uses the same format as figure 11-29, Climb Performance For Takeoff. Inspection of the chart will show that, in the event of waveoff, the wheels should be retracted immediately. Acceleration to higher climb speed will improve climb performance. Delay flap retraction until sufficient flight speed is attained. If speedbrakes are open, they should be retracted before the wheels.

ALTITUDE CLIMB PERFORMANCE CHARTS

Clean configuration climb performance with respect to time, fuel, and distance from sea level to altitude may be determined from the data presented in three charts identified as Time to Climb (figure 11-33), Climb Distance (figure 11-32), and Fuel Consumed During Climb (figure 11-31). Climb with throttles set at military thrust, since a military thrust climb to a given altitude requires less total fuel than a normal thrust climb. Climbs may be made with military thrust to cruise ceiling (that altitude at which the rate of climb is 300 feet per minute with normal thrust) at any operating gross weight up to 70,000 pounds without exceeding the engine operating time limit of 15 minutes. It is best to maintain the airspeed schedule shown in the table on each climb chart, although variations in climb airspeed up to 10 knots above or below the scheduled airspeed will not materially affect climb performance, except at altitudes near the ceiling.

The Altitude Climb Performance charts may also be used to determine elapsed time, distance, and/or fuel used in climbing from one altitude to another in flight by taking the difference between the values at the initial and final altitudes, as illustrated on the chart.

EXAMPLE: Assume that a climb is required from 10,000 feet pressure altitude to 25,000 feet pressure altitude, with a momentary gross weight at 10,000 feet of 65,000 pounds. On the time, fuel and distance plots, read the initial values at the intersection of the 65,000 pound gross weight line with the 10,000-foot pressure altitude line. Next, determine the final values at the intersection of the weight guide line with the 25,000 foot pressure altitude line. From these data, the following computations are made:

(figure 11-30) Fuel used during climb = 1375 - 550
= 825 pounds

(figure 11-32) Climb Distance = 39 - 12 = 27 nautical miles

(figure 11-33) Climb Time = 5.7 - 1.8
= 3.9 minutes

ONE-ENGINE RATE OF CLIMB

The one-engine rate of climb charts, figure 11-34 (sheet 1 through 4), and figure 11-35, are presented for emergency usage in the event of engine failure on takeoff. Minimum single-engine control speeds, figure 11-10, are shown on the graphs for the lower gross weights where control speeds are critical. Two-engine lift-off speeds, figure 11-7, are shown on the higher gross weight curves where lift-off speed is higher than minimum single-engine control speeds. The figures include data for gear down and gear up with the flaps positioned at full up, half, and fully extended. The figures indicate that the gear should be retracted immediately but the flaps should not be raised until sufficient airspeed is built up to produce a greater rate of climb with the flaps positioned at half or full up. Figure 11-35 shows the effect of outside air temperature on rate of climb at sea level.

EXAMPLE: If the gross weight is 60,000 pounds, the outside air temperature is 15°C (59°F), and the indicated airspeed is 150 knots, then the rate of climb in feet per minute is:

Figure 11-34 (sheet 2)

	Gear Down	Gear Up
Full Flaps	510	740
Half Flaps	-260	50
Flaps Up	-1460	-1220

Figure 11-35. If the outside air temperature is 10°C higher (25°C) reduce the above tabulated rate of climb by 185 feet per minute.

EMERGENCY CLIMB CHARTS

The Emergency Climb charts, figures 11-34 through 11-38, are presented for use in emergency operation only (one-engine windmilling), since, in normal procedure, climbs are always made with both engines operating.

The use of military thrust during a climb to altitude is restricted to 15 minutes, due to engine operating limitations. If the climb time will exceed 15 minutes, use military thrust during the early stages of the climb and normal thrust during the last portion.

Follow the airspeed schedule shown on the chart as closely as possible. Climb time, fuel and distance data for in-flight climbs with one engine operating on military thrust may be calculated by taking the difference between the time, fuel, and distance values at the initial and at the final altitudes.

EXAMPLE: Assume that a climb is made at 55,000 pounds gross weight on one engine with military thrust from 10,000 feet pressure altitude to 20,000 feet pressure altitude. As indicated on the Emergency Climb chart, the climb time is:

15.1 - 5.9 = 9.2 minutes.

The climb distance is equal to:

76 - 28 = 48 nautical miles.

Fuel used during climb = 1700 - 760 = 940 pounds.

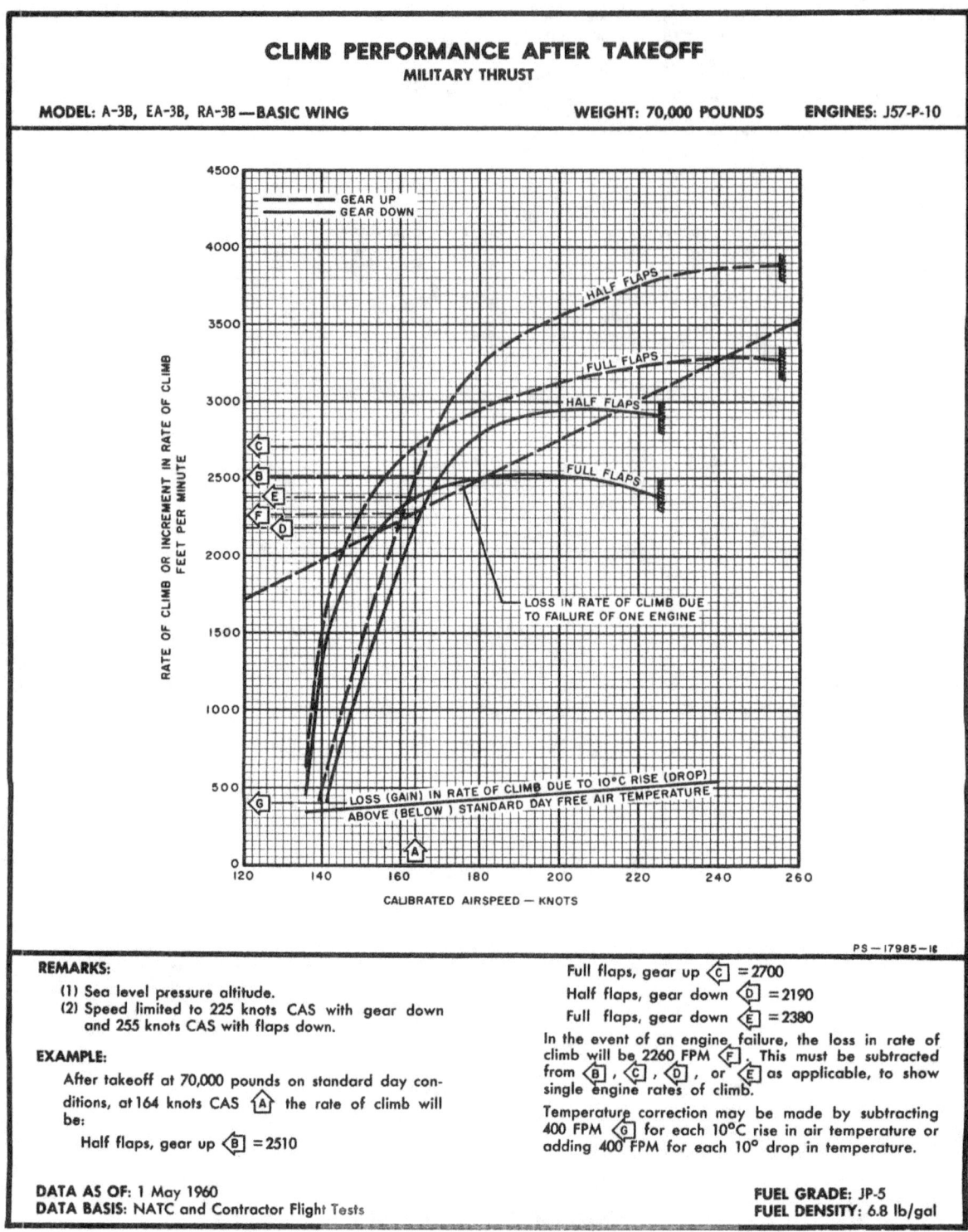

Figure 11-29. Climb Performance After Takeoff

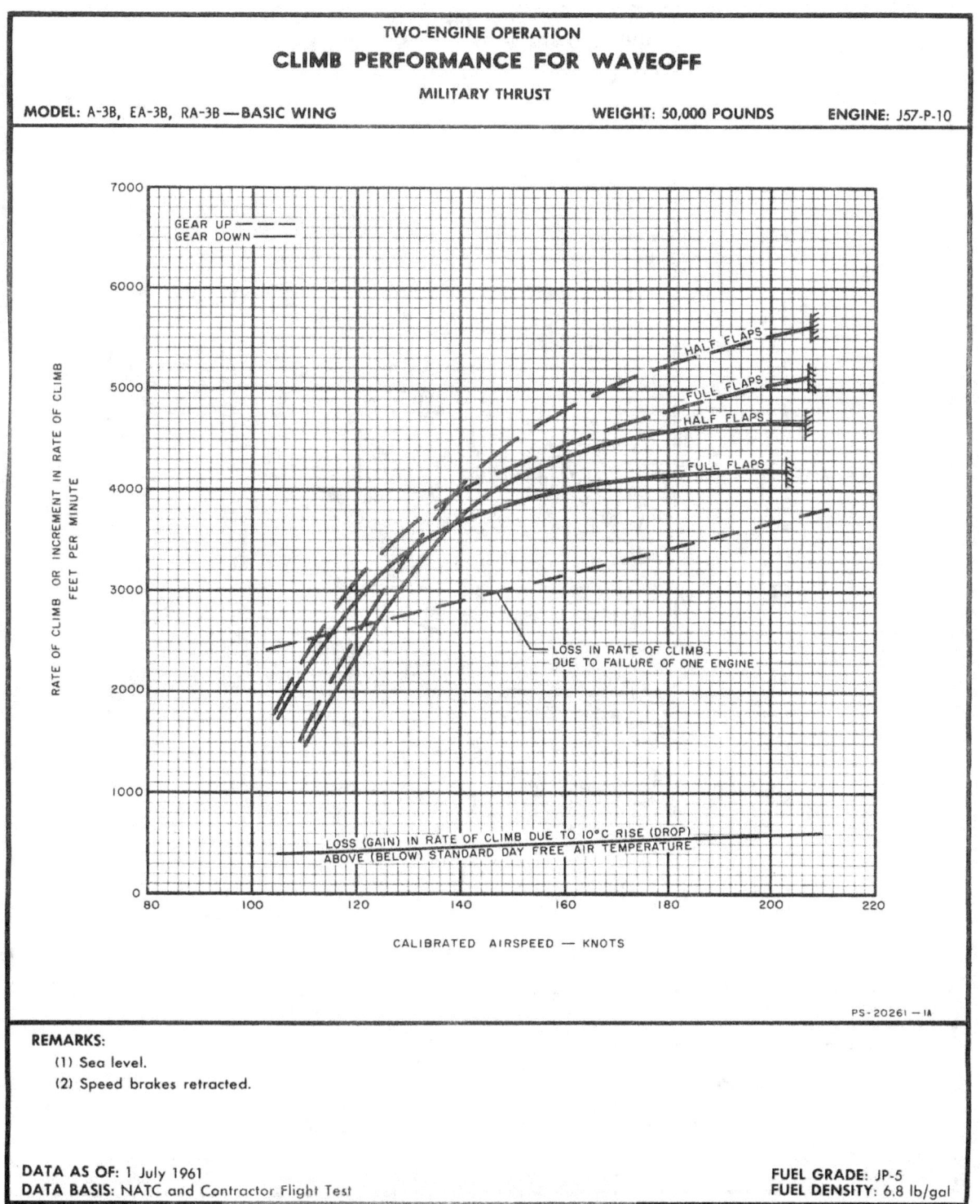

Figure 11-30. Climb Performance for Waveoff

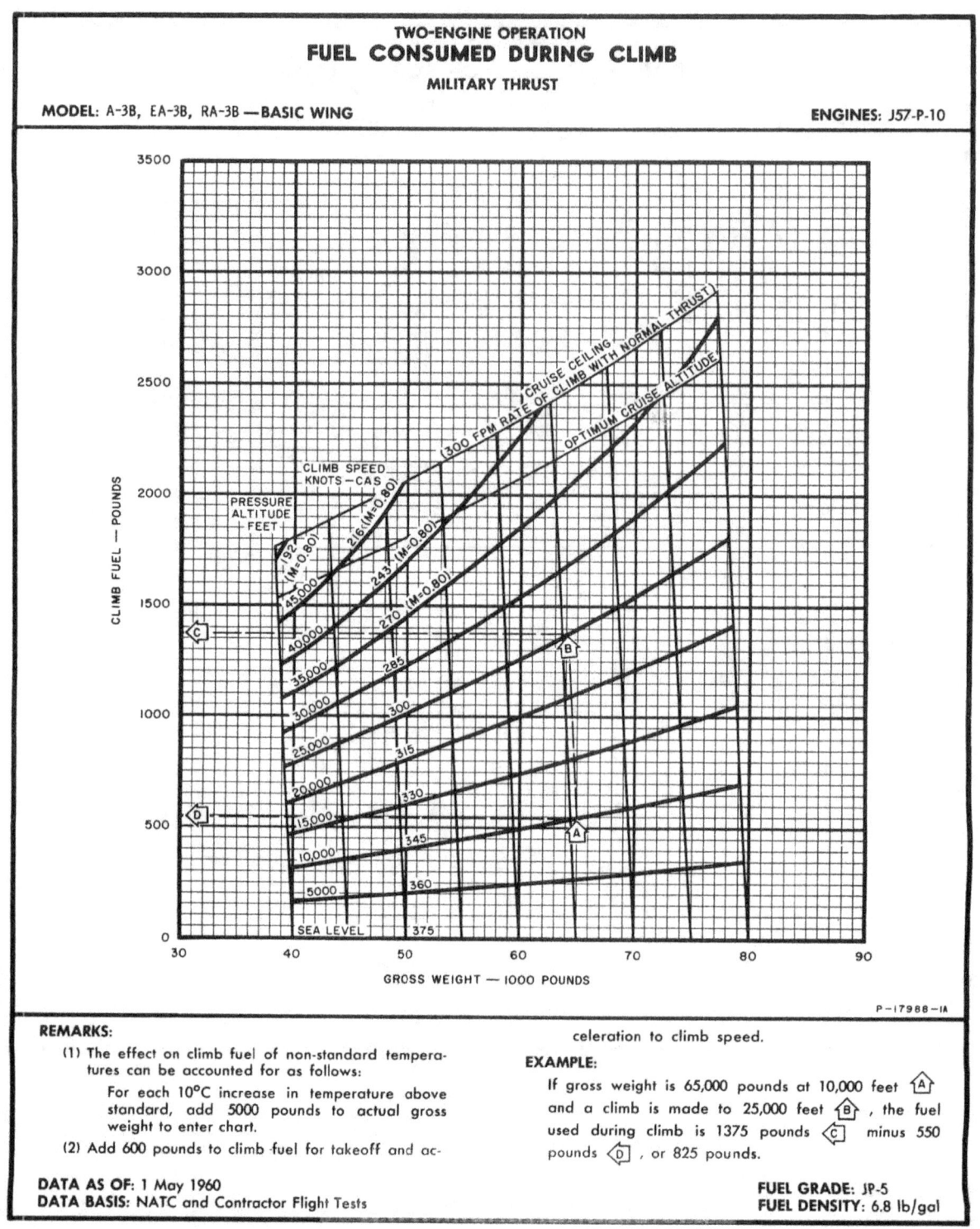

Figure 11-31. Fuel Consumed During Climb

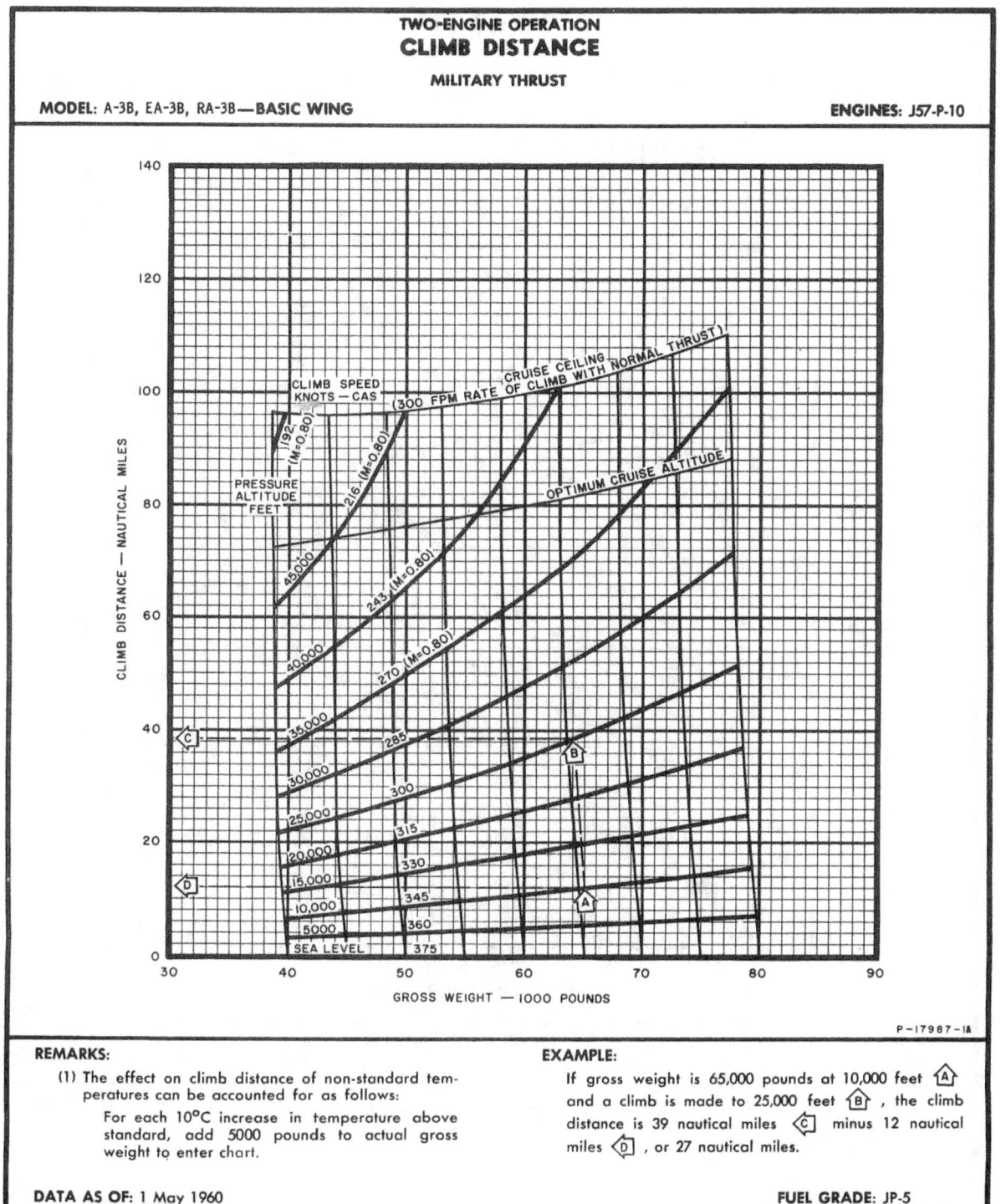

Figure 11-32. Climb Distance

Figure 11-33. Time To Climb

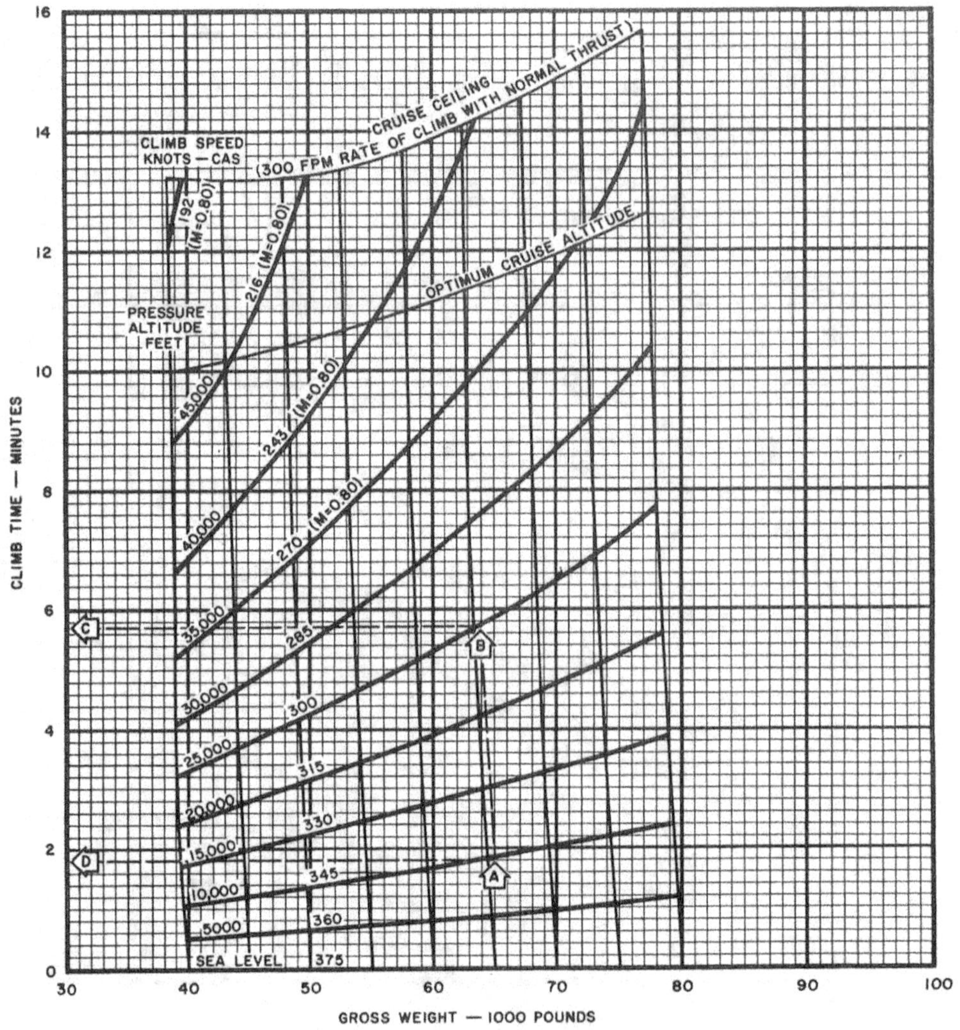

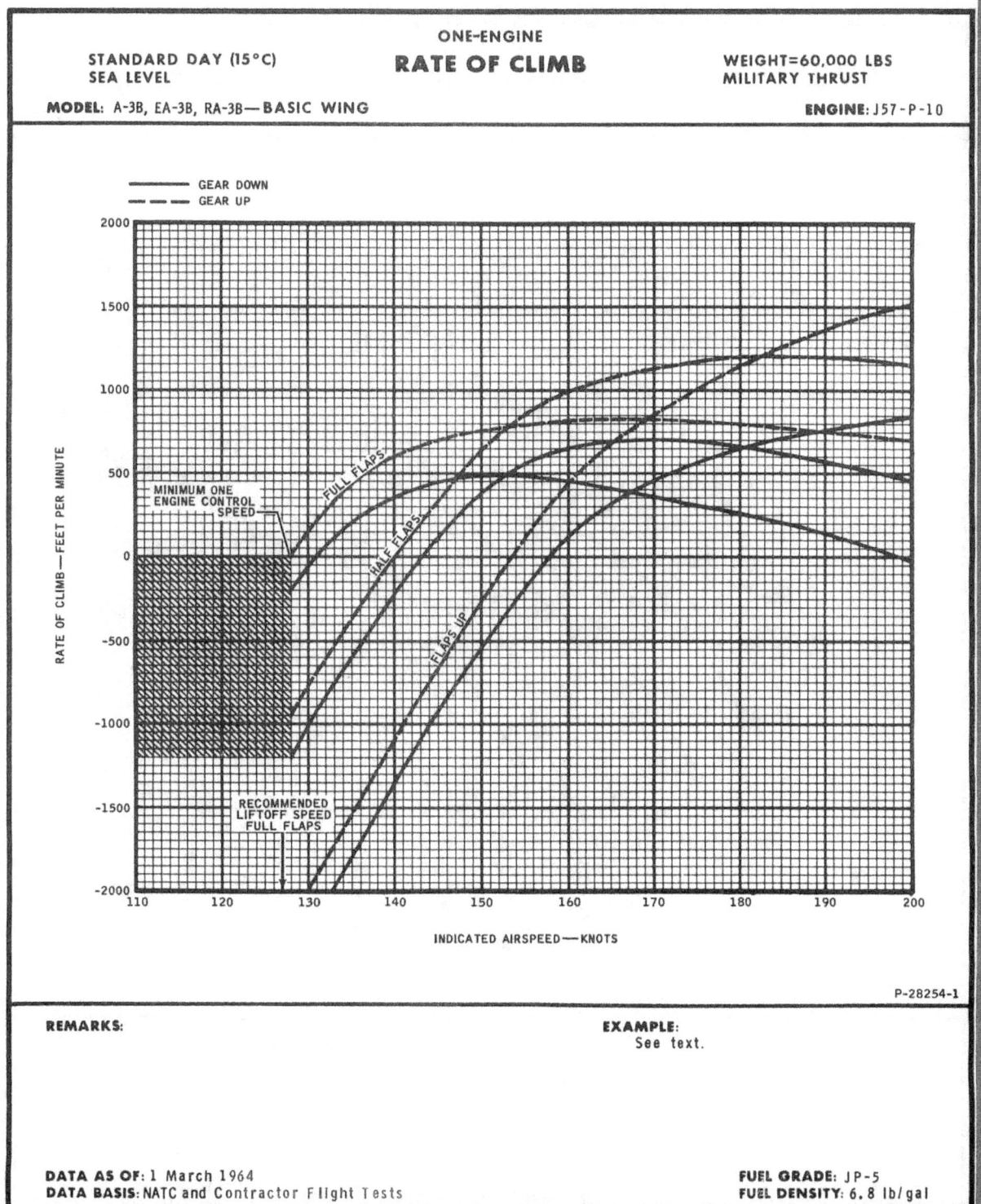

Figure 11-34. One-Engine Rate of Climb – 60,000 Pounds (Sheet 1)

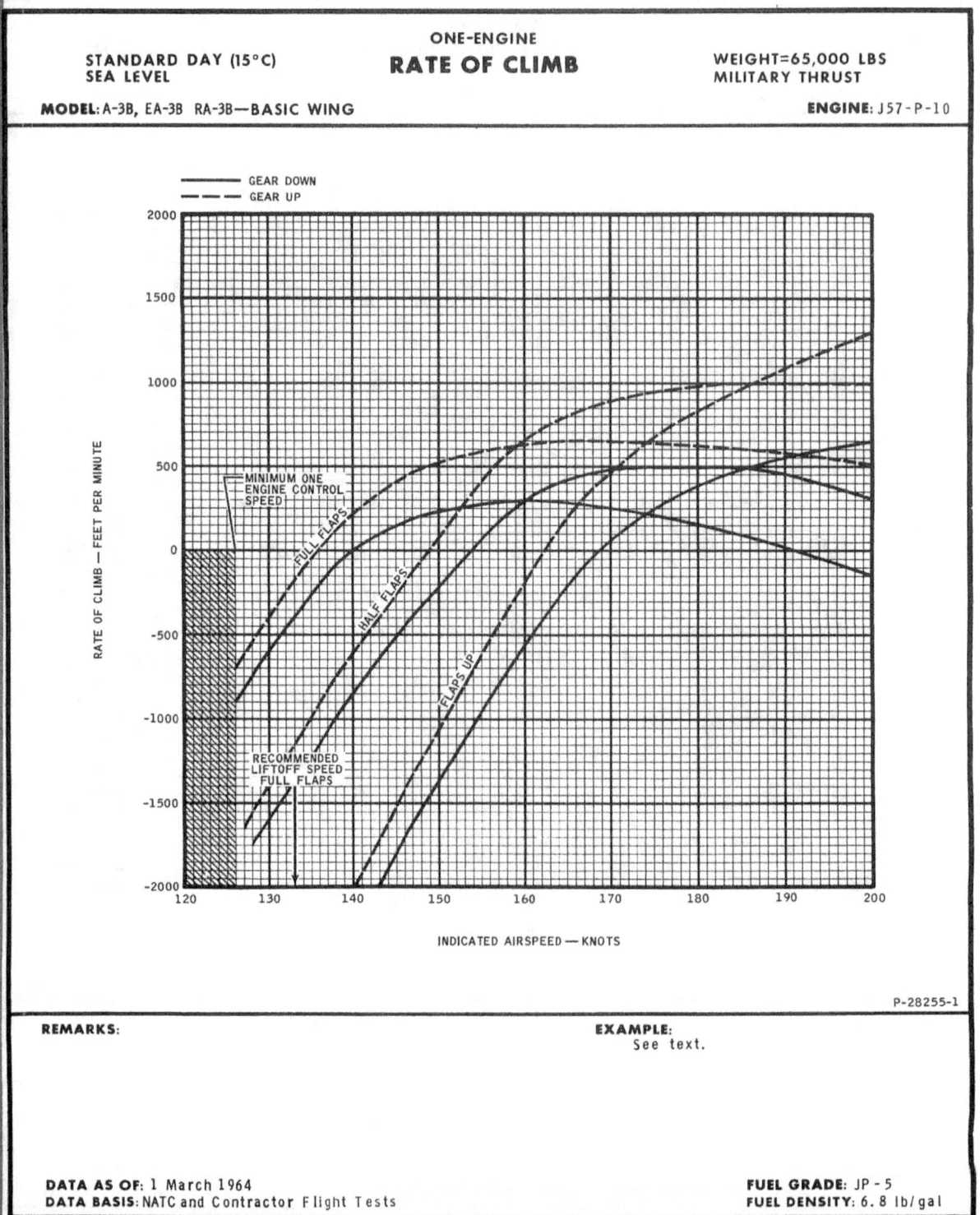

Figure 11-34. One-Engine Rate of Climb — 65,000 Pounds (Sheet 2)

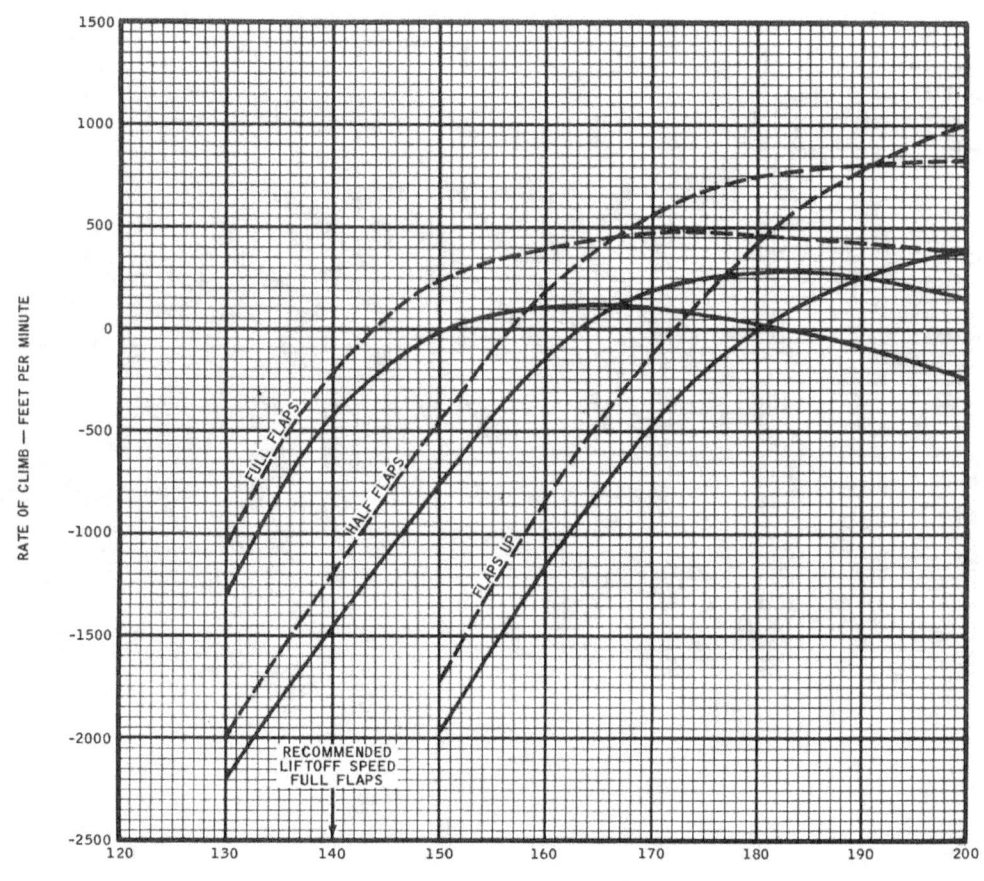

Figure 11-34. One-Engine Rate of Climb — 70,000 Pounds (Sheet 3)

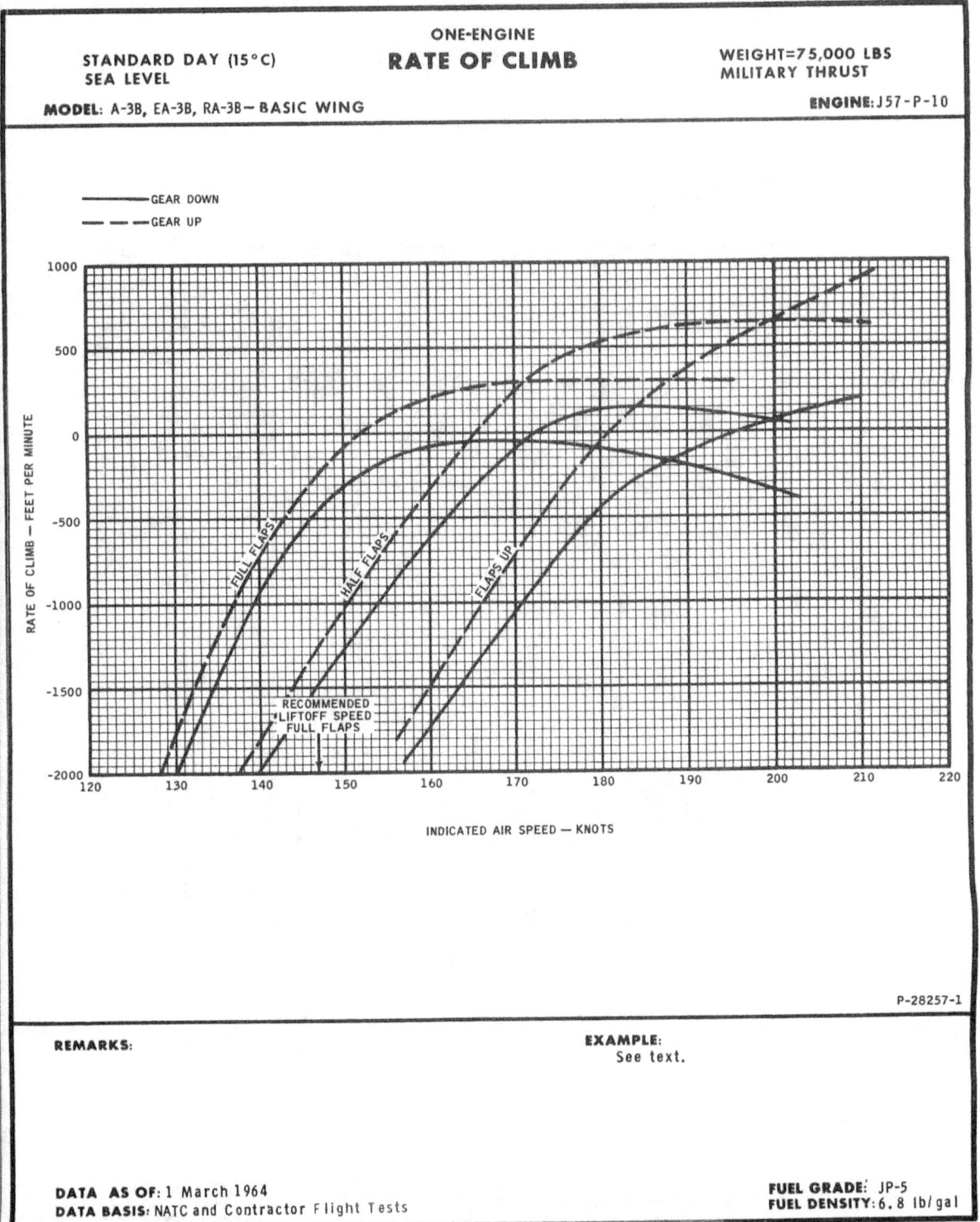

Figure 11-34. One-Engine Rate of Climb — 75,000 Pounds (Sheet 4)

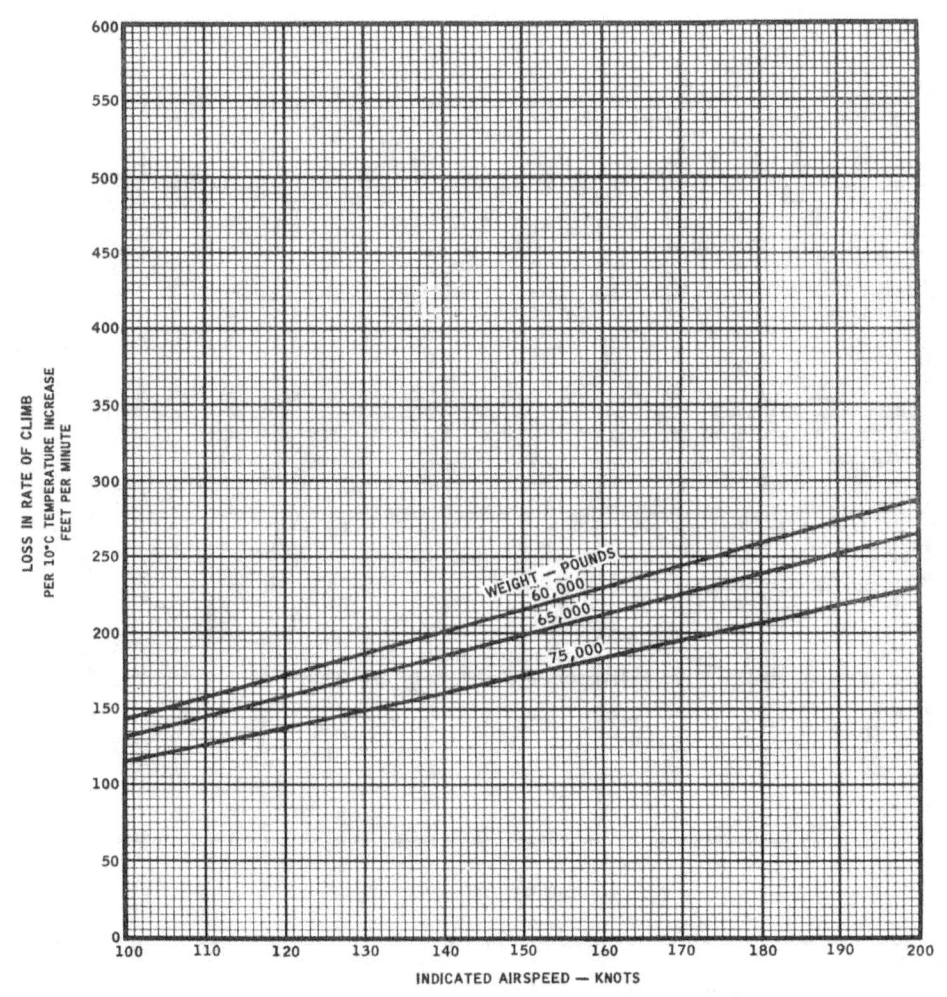

Figure 11-35. Temperature Effect on One-Engine Rate of Climb – Military Thrust

ONE-ENGINE OPERATION
FUEL CONSUMED DURING CLIMB
MILITARY THRUST

MODEL: A-3B, EA-3B, RA-3B — **BASIC WING** **ENGINES:** J57-P-10

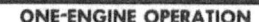

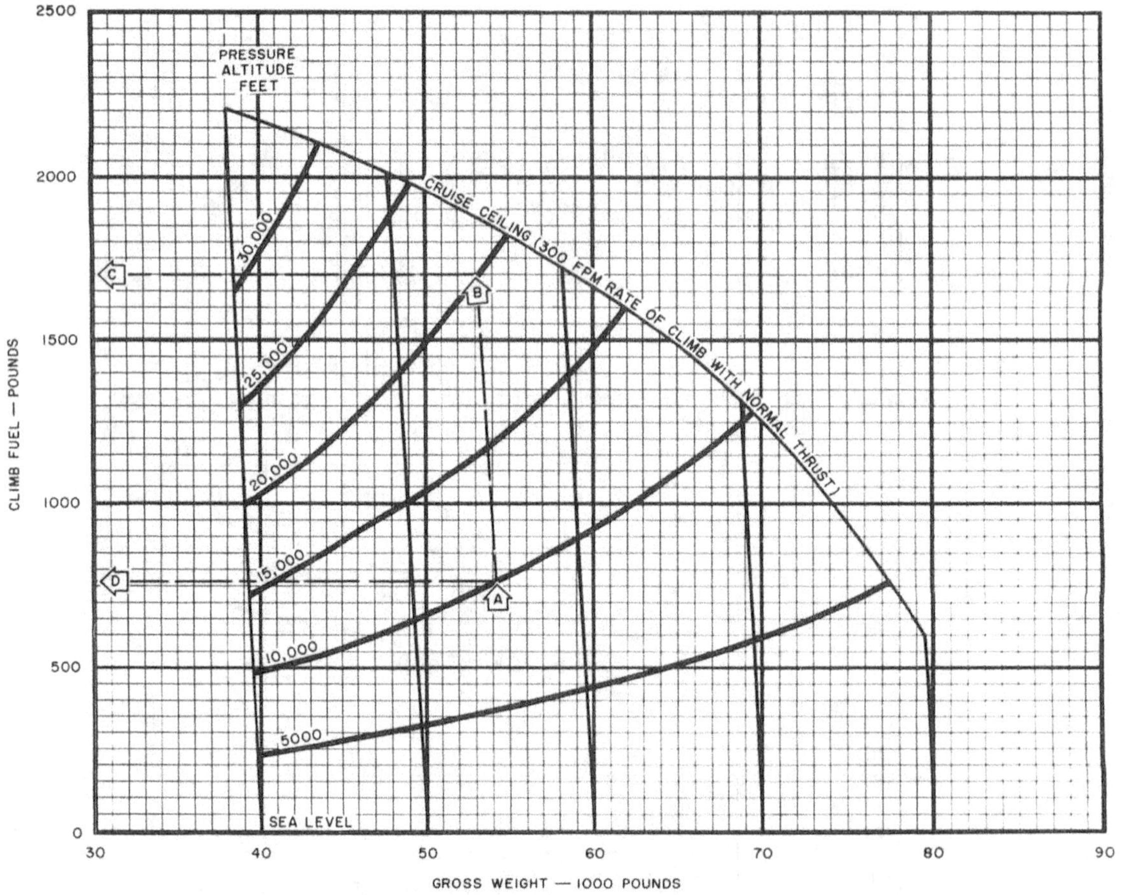

Figure 11-36. Fuel Consumed During Climb

REMARKS:
(1) Inoperative engine windmilling.
(2) Climb speed is 280 knots CAS at sea level decreasing 2 knots per 1000-foot increase in altitude.
(3) The effect on climb fuel of non-standard temperatures can be accounted for as follows:

For each 10°C increase in temperature above standard, add 5000 pounds to the actual gross weight to enter chart.

EXAMPLE:
If gross weight is 55,000 pounds at 10,000 feet ⓐ and a climb is made to 20,000 feet ⓑ the fuel consumed is 1700 pounds ⓒ minus 760 pounds ⓓ or 940 pounds.

DATA AS OF: 1 May 1960
DATA BASIS: NATC and Contractor Flight Tests

FUEL GRADE: JP-5
FUEL DENSITY: 6.8 lb/gal

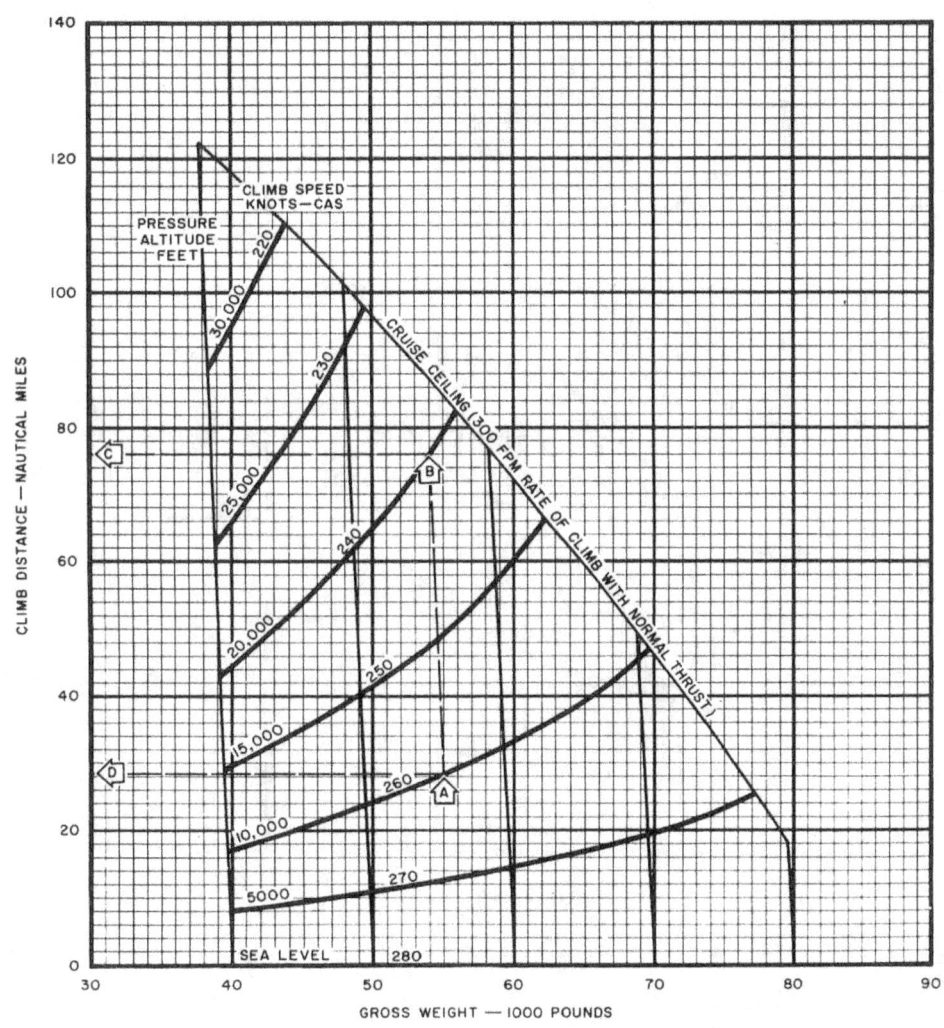

Figure 11-37. Climb Distance

Section XI
Part 3

NAVAIR 01-40ATA-1

ONE-ENGINE OPERATION
TIME TO CLIMB
MILITARY THRUST

MODEL: A-3B, EA-3B, RA-3B — BASIC WING

ENGINES: J57-P-10

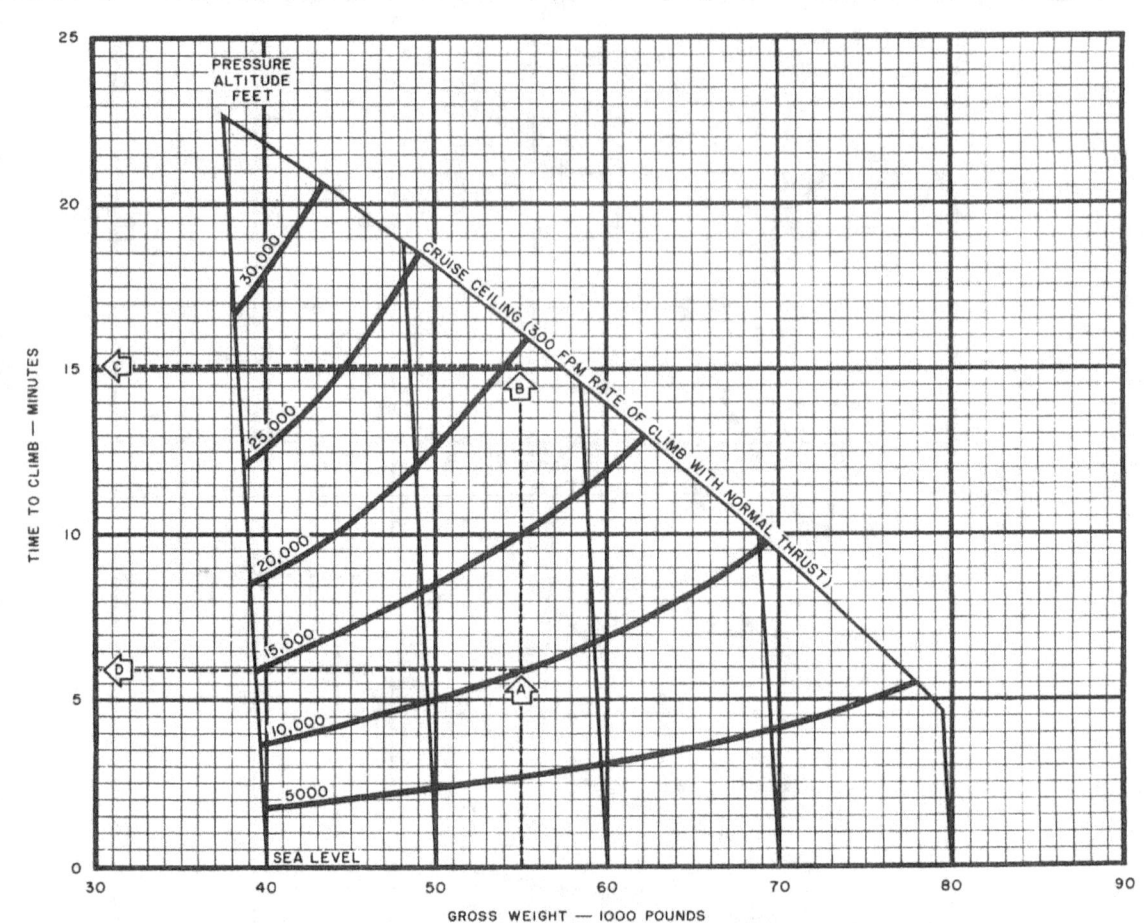

REMARKS:

(1) Inoperative engine windmilling.

(2) Climb speed is 280 knots CAS at sea level, decreasing 2 knots per 1000-foot increase in altitude.

(3) The effect on time to climb of non-standard temperatures can be accounted for as follows:

For each 10°C increase in temperature above standard, add 5000 pounds to the actual gross weight to enter chart.

EXAMPLE:

If gross weight is 55,000 pounds at 10,000 feet ⟨A⟩ and a climb is made to 20,000 feet ⟨B⟩, the time to climb is 15.1 minutes ⟨C⟩ minus 5.9 minutes ⟨D⟩, or 9.2 minutes.

DATA AS OF: 1 May 1960
DATA BASIS: NATC and Contractor Flight Tests

FUEL GRADE: JP-5
FUEL DENSITY: 6.8 lb/gal

Figure 11-38. Time To Climb

NAVAIR 01-40ATA-1

Section XI
Part 4

PART 4
RANGE

TABLE OF CONTENTS

TEXT

Page

Range Charts.................. 11-57

ILLUSTRATIONS

Figure		Page
11-39	Fouled Deck Range – VFR........	11-61
11-40	Fouled Deck Range – IFR.........	11-62
11-41	Fouled Deck Range – Gear Down....	11-63
11-42	Fouled Deck Range – Gear and Flaps Down..................	11-64
11-43	Fouled Deck Range – VFR........	11-65
11-44	Flight Test Fouled Deck Range – IFR......................	11-66

Figure		Page
11-45	Fouled Deck Range – Sea Level.....	11-67
11-46	Maximum Specific Range vs Altitude	11-68
11-47	Specific Range – Sea Level........	11-70
11-48	Specific Range – Sea Level........	11-80
11-49	Mission Profile	11-87
11-50	Combat Radius Profile	11-88
11-51	Mission Return Profile	11-90

Range Charts

The range data for the Model A-3B/KA-3B basic wing aircraft are divided into four different types of presentation. These are:

   1. Fouled Deck Range (figures 11-39 through 11-45).

   2. Maximum Specific Range vs Altitude (figure 11-46).

   3. Specific Range (figures 11-47 and 11-48).

   4. Profile charts (figures 11-49, 11-50, 11-51).

These range data are presented for the aircraft in the clean configuration and are representative of the cruise performance which may be obtained during normal service operation. All data are given for an ICAO standard day.

At a given altitude and gross weight, the maximum range of the aircraft is obtained at the recommended airspeed for maximum range. This airspeed should be primarily established by Mach number (or CAS since Mach number and CAS are directly related at a given altitude). If desirable at altitude of 40,000 ft and below, penalties in the range of the aircraft may be tolerated by increasing the recommended cruise speed such that the range penalty is no greater than 1 percent. This increase in cruise speed will result in significant reductions in elapsed time.

NOTE

The characteristics of the J57 engine are such that engine rpm cannot be used for cruise control. However, as an aid in establishing proper cruise control, engine pressure ratio and engine fuel flow data are provided.

A description of the four types of range presentation follows:

FOULED DECK RANGE ("BINGO CARDS")

The Fouled Deck Range charts (figures 11-39 through 11-42) for two-engine operation and figures 11-43 through 11-45 for one-engine operation are provided to indicate the available range, for low values of fuel remaining, at optimum cruise altitudes. Both VFR and IFR charts are included for one-engine and two-engine operation with the flaps and gear retracted. Also included for two-engine operation are VFR charts for gear down and gear and flaps down (full flaps). A one-engine sea level fouled deck range chart is also included.

Fuel allowances of 300 pounds for two-engine operation and 200 pounds for one-engine operation are included for raising the gear and flaps (where applicable), making a turn, and accelerating to climb speed. A 3000-pound reserve fuel allowance is included at the point where descent is commenced for the VFR charts and at the approach fix for the IFR charts. The charts are based on a basic aircraft weight of 41,000 pounds with a percentage correction factor for additional fuel required at heavier basic weights. Climb, cruise, and letdown speeds are provided together with the letdown time, fuel required, and distances where applicable.

Figures are for a no-wind standard day. Add 1 percent for each 5 knots of head wind for rough calculations.

MAXIMUM SPECIFIC RANGE VS ALTITUDE

The maximum specific range characteristics are summarized for two-engine and one-engine operation in figure 11-46. These data present the specific range as a function of altitude and gross weight that

Changed 1 June 1969

11-57

is attainable at the recommended speed for maximum range. Cruise Mach numbers corresponding to the recommended airspeed for maximum specific range are superimposed on these plots together with the corresponding fuel flow. Cruise ceilings are indicated for both two-engine and one-engine operation. The optimum cruise altitude is provided for two-engine operation.

SPECIFIC RANGE

The specific range charts, figure 11-47, for two-engine operation and figure 11-48 for one-engine operation, present the nautical miles per pound of fuel, or specific range, as a function of Mach number for every 5000 feet of altitude from sea level to 45,000 feet for two-engine operation and 30,000 feet for one-engine operation. The recommended airspeed for maximum range is indicated on each of the charts. The Mach number corresponding to this speed should be used as the primary indication of proper cruise control. In addition, lines of fuel flow and engine pressure ratio are superimposed to provide additional checks on proper cruise control. At low power settings, the intercompressor bleed valves on the J57 engine are scheduled to open. This results in an increase in the fuel consumption at these power settings which in turn reduces the nautical miles per pound of fuel. Therefore, at the lower altitudes the specific range curves are presented to include this effect. The scheduled opening of these valves will vary from engine to engine and, therefore, the data in figure 11-47 should be considered approximate. For flight planning purposes, however, it is recommended that these data be used to predict the cruise characteristics for these conditions. The specific range data are provided for speeds between the recommended speed for maximum endurance and maximum speed with maximum thrust. The specific range data obtained from these charts can be used for all ambient air temperatures as long as the specific range is determined for a given Mach number or CAS. The corresponding TAS, however, for nonstandard conditions will have to be obtained from figure 11-1. Sub scales on each chart show the relationship between Mach number and TAS for standard day conditions only. The relationship between Mach number and CAS is also provided and is independent of ambient conditions.

EXAMPLE: A request is received to escort another aircraft which is returning from a mission at 20,000 feet pressure altitude at 300 knots CAS. If the initial gross weight is 50,000 pounds, including 10,000 pounds of available cruise fuel after allowances for descent and/or reserve, determine the range available and fuel consumption with no wind.

1. Enter the 20,000-foot specific range (Nautical Miles Per 1000 Pounds of Fuel) chart for two engines operating (figure 11-47, sheet 5) at 300 knots CAS. At 50,000 pounds initial cruising gross weight, the specific range is 79 nautical miles per 1000 pounds of fuel. At the final cruising gross weight,

50,000 - 10,000 = 40,000 pounds.

the specific range is 84 nautical miles per 1000 pounds of fuel.

2. The specific range during cruise, based on an average gross weight of 45,000 pounds, is 82 nautical miles per 1000 pounds of fuel. By multiplying this number by the available cruise fuel in thousands of pounds, the range is:

$$82 \times \frac{10,000}{1000} = 820 \text{ nautical miles.}$$

3. The initial fuel flow at 20,000 feet (at 50,000 pounds) is approximately 2550 pounds per hour per engine multiplied by two, or 5100 pounds per hour. During the cruise, fuel flow will decrease due to decreasing gross weight, and at the end of the flight the fuel flow will be approximately:

2 x 2300 = 4600 pounds per hour.

4. True airspeed (also ground speed in this example) and Mach number are 4000 knots and 0.65, respectively.

5. When large amounts of cruise fuel are considered, or when range is critical, greater accuracy may be obtained by computing the range in steps using the above procedure. The degree of accuracy will depend on the number of incremental values of fuel weight used. For the purpose of determining whether operation on one engine would provide a better maximum range performance, follow the same procedure through the specific range chart for single-engine operation.

EXAMPLE:

1. Enter the 20,000-foot specific range (Nautical Miles Per 1000 Pounds of Fuel) chart for single-engine operation (figure 11-48, sheet 5) at 300 knots CAS. At 50,000 pounds initial cruising gross weight, the specific range is 79 nautical miles per 1000 pounds of fuel. At the final cruising gross weight (40,000 pounds), the specific range is 84.5 nautical miles per 1000 pounds of fuel.

2. The specific range during cruise, based on an average gross weight of 45,000 pounds, is 81.8 nautical miles per 1000 pounds of fuel. By multiplying this number by the available cruise fuel in thousands of pounds, the range is:

$$81.8 \times \frac{10,000}{1000} = 818.0 \text{ nautical miles}$$

3. A comparison of the single-engine specific range with that obtainable during two-engine operation reveals a disadvantage in proceeding with one engine shut down. A study of the single-engine chart will reveal that greater than normal rated power must be maintained on the single-engine for a period of time exceeding 2 hours in order to follow this flight plan. For these reasons, two-engine operation should be used for this particular flight.

MISSION PROFILE

The mission profile chart (figure 11-49) presents the total available range on a one way mission as a function of cruise altitudes from sea level to the optimum (cruise climb) altitude. The ranges are presented with a 3000-pound fuel reserve and with zero fuel remaining. A 1000-pound fuel allowance for start, taxi, or takeoff is included. Fuel used and elapsed time lines are included on the chart in order to provide check points during the mission. These range data are presented for a takeoff weight of 76,000 pounds with 34,584 pounds of fuel on board. No allowances are included for wind effects.

The heavy line to the left edge of the shaded area shows the distance traveled during a military thrust climb from sea level to the desired cruise altitude. The climb should be conducted at the climb schedule shown in the lower right-hand corner of the chart. The heavy line at the top of the shaded area represents the optimum or cruise climb altitude. Cruise at the optimum cruise altitude is obtained by maintaining a constant cruise Mach number of 0.75 with an approximate constant throttle setting. The variation of altitude with distance results from the decrease in aircraft weight due to fuel usage during cruise. By use of the fuel usage and elapsed time lines, the optimum cruise altitude can be checked during the mission. Cruise at a fixed altitude should be conducted at the recommended cruise Mach numbers shown in the lower right-hand corner of the chart and will require periodic reduction in throttle setting as fuel is consumed to maintain the particular Mach number.

EXAMPLE: The chart may be entered with one or more of the four range factors: time, fuel distance, and altitude. By entering the chart with the known factors the other factors may be readily determined.

   1. Determine the maximum range with 25,000 pounds of fuel available for climb and cruise, with an average 50-knot headwind.

      a. Enter the chart at 25,000 pounds of fuel. Directly below the intersection of the fuel and optimum cruise climb line, read maximum still air range (air miles) . . . . . 2100 NM

      b. Time required . . . . 4 hr 36 min

      c. Wind effect (time x wind) . . . . . 230 NM

      d. Calculate maximum range with wind (2100 - 230) . . . . 1970 NM

   2. Determine the fuel required, elapsed time, recommended airspeed, and Mach number to cruise 1500 nautical miles at 30,000 feet with a headwind of 75 knots. To determine wind effect upon time, fuel and distance, compute the average true airspeed (distance ÷ time) no wind, and apply wind to TAS to obtain groundspeed (GS). Then compute the time with wind (distance ÷ GS). Reenter the profile at the cruising altitude and computed time with wind to determine the fuel required with wind.

      a. Enter the chart at 1500 nautical miles and proceed upward to the 30,000-foot line to determine time (no wind) . . . . . 3 hr 24 min

      b. Average TAS (1500 ÷ 3.4 hr) . . . 441 knots

      c. Apply wind to obtain average groundspeed (441 - 75) . . . . 366 knots

      d. Calculate time with wind (1500 ÷ 366) . . . . 4 hr 10 min

      e. Re-enter chart at the intersection of cruise altitude and time with wind. Fuel required with wind . . . . 23,000 lb

      f. Recommended tabular cruise speed . . . . 275 CAS 0.74 Mach

COMBAT RADIUS PROFILE

The combat radius profile (figure 11-50, sheet 1) presents the radius capability of the aircraft for cruise altitudes from sea level to the optimum cruise altitude and for combat times of 0 to 20 minutes. The radius is shown for a reserve fuel of 3000 pounds and for no reserve fuel. A fuel allowance of 1000 pounds is included for start, taxi, takeoff, and descent. Lines of fuel used are superimposed on the chart for flight checks during the mission. The profile data are based on a takeoff weight of 73,000 pounds with 28,558 pounds of fuel and a bomb load of 4100 pounds aboard.

The heavy line at the left of the shaded area shows the distance traveled and the fuel consumed during a military thrust climb from sea level to the desired cruise altitude. The climb speed schedule is shown in the lower right hand corner of the chart. The heavy line at the top of the shaded area represents the optimum cruise-out altitude which corresponds to a cruise climb obtained at a constant cruise Mach number of 0.75 and an approximate constant throttle setting. Cruise at a selected constant altitude should be conducted at the recommended cruise Mach numbers shown in the lower right hand corner of the chart and will require periodic reductions in throttle setting as fuel is consumed to maintain the particular Mach numbers. It is assumed that the 4100-pound bomb load is dropped at the end of the cruise out.

The heavy dashed lines to the right of the chart show the radius available for various combat times and for the mission return at the same constant altitude at the cruise-out or at the optimum cruise-back altitude. Allowances for a military power climb from the optimum cruise-out altitude to the optimum cruise-back altitude are included.

The optimum cruise-back altitude is shown as the uppermost heavy line on the chart and corresponds to a cruise climb conducted in the same manner as the optimum cruise-out altitude.

Section XI
Part 4

NAVAIR 01-40ATA-1

EXAMPLE: Determine the combat radius with (figure 11-50, sheet 1) 28,558 pounds of fuel available at an altitude of 30,000 feet and anticipated combat time of 15 minutes with 3000 pounds reserve fuel over base.

1. Climb at military thrust to 30,000 feet observing recommended climb schedule.

2. Cruise at 30,000 feet at recommended cruise speeds . . . . 275 CAS 0.74 Mach

3. Range at 15 minutes combat time . . . . 990 NM

4. Return at . . . . 275 CAS 0.74 Mach

5. Begin idle letdown (220 knots) . . . . 70 NM from base

11-60

NAVAIR 01-40ATA-1

Section XI
Part 4

FOULED DECK RANGE (VFR)

Two-Engine Operation

Model: A-3B, KA-3B, EA-3B, RA-3B - Basic Wing   Engines: J57-P-10

Dist	Fuel Req	Alt	Climb			Cruise			Fuel Flow lb/hr/Eng	CAS	Descent			Total ETE
			ETE	Fuel	Dist	ETE	Fuel	Dist			ETE	Fuel	Dist	
40	3730	10	1	640	7	1	90	6	3000	328	7	165	27	9
60	3940	15	2	820	12	2	120	9	2520	302	10	240	39	13
80	4085	20	3	990	18	1	95	8	2140	275	13	310	54	16
100	4255	25	4	1165	24	1	90	9	1830	248	15	375	67	20
120	4400	30	5	1340	32	1	55	6	1720	240	18	430	82	24
140	4535	35	6	1525	41	0	10	1	1700	240	21	490	98	27
160	4705	35	6	1530	42	3	175	21	1700	240	21	490	98	30
180	4795	40	8	1725	55	1	70	9	1710	235	23	550	117	32
200	4950	40	8	1730	55	4	220	29	1710	235	23	550	117	35
220	5040	45	10	1965	74	1	75	10	1740	215	26	605	136	37
240	5200	45	10	1975	75	4	225	30	1740	215	26	605	136	40
260	5360	45	10	1985	75	6	375	49	1750	215	26	605	136	43
280	5520	45	10	1995	76	9	525	69	1750	215	26	605	136	45
300	5675	45	10	2000	76	12	675	89	1760	215	26	605	136	49
320	5840	45	11	2015	77	14	825	107	1760	215	26	605	136	50
340	6000	45	11	2020	77	17	980	128	1760	215	26	605	136	53
360	6155	45	11	2030	77	19	1125	147	1760	215	26	605	136	55
380	6315	45	11	2030	78	22	1285	167	1770	215	26	605	136	58
400	6490	45	11	2050	78	24	1440	187	1770	215	26	605	136	61

Remarks:

(1) Fuel required includes 300 pounds for cleanup, turn, and acceleration.

(2) Provides 3000 pounds fuel at point where descent is commenced. No wind conditions.

(3) Climb schedule is 370 KCAS at sea level decreasing 30 knots per 10,000 feet altitude to 36,000 feet. Climb at M = 0.80 above 36,000 feet.

(4) Idle descent to sea level at 220 KCAS.

(5) Aircraft operating weight is 41,000 pounds.

(6) For each 1000-pound increase in basic aircraft weight, increase fuel required by 1 percent.

Data as of: 1 March 1964   Fuel Grade: JP-5
Data Basic: NATC and Contractor Flight Tests   Fuel Density: 6.8 lb/gal

Figure 11-39. Fouled Deck Range – VFR

FOULED DECK RANGE (IFR)
Two-Engine Operation

Model: A-3B, KA-3B, EA-3B, RA-3B — Basic Wing Engines: J57-P-10

Dist	Fuel Req	Alt	Climb			Cruise			Fuel Flow lb/hr/Eng	CAS	Total ETE
			ETE	Fuel	Dist	ETE	Fuel	Dist			
40	4145	10	1	640	8	5	505	32	3000	328	6
60	4470	15	2	820	12	8	650	48	2520	300	10
80	4705	20	3	990	18	10	715	62	2130	276	13
100	4950	25	4	1180	25	13	770	75	1830	248	17
120	5150	25	4	1185	25	17	970	95	1830	248	21
140	5345	30	5	1370	33	17	980	107	1750	242	22
160	5525	35	6	1560	42	17	965	117	1720	243	23
180	5700	35	6	1565	43	20	1135	138	1720	242	26
200	5865	35	6	1570	43	22	1295	157	1720	242	28
220	6040	40	8	1775	56	22	1270	164	1730	235	30
240	6200	40	8	1780	57	25	1420	183	1730	235	33
260	6365	40	8	1790	57	28	1575	203	1730	235	36
280	6525	40	8	1790	57	30	1735	223	1740	235	38
300	6690	40	8	1800	57	33	1890	243	1740	235	41
320	6855	40	8	1805	58	36	2050	263	1740	235	44
340	7020	40	8	1810	58	39	2210	283	1740	235	47
360	7185	40	8	1820	58	41	2365	302	1750	235	49
380	7350	40	8	1825	58	44	2525	322	1760	236	52
400	7510	40	8	1830	59	47	2680	342	1760	236	55

Remarks:

(1) Fuel required includes 300 pounds for cleanup, turn, and acceleration.

(2) Provides 3000 pounds fuel at approach fix. No wind conditions.

(3) Climb schedule is 370 KCAS at sea level decreasing 30 knots per 10,000 feet altitude to 36,000 feet. Climb at M = 0.80 above 36,000 feet.

(4) Aircraft operating weight is 41,000 pounds.

(5) For each 1000-pound increase in basic aircraft weight, increase fuel required by 1 percent.

Data as of: 1 March 1964 Fuel Grade: JP-5
Data Basis: NATC and Contractor Flight Test Fuel Density: 6.8 lb/gal

Figure 11-40. Fouled Deck Range — IFR

NAVAIR 01-40ATA-1

Section XI
Part 4

GEAR DOWN FOULED DECK RANGE (VFR)
Two-Engine Operation

Model: A-3B, KA-3B, EA-3B, RA-3B — Basic Wing

Engines: J57-P-10

Dist	Fuel Req	Alt	Climb			Cruise			Fuel Flow lb/hr/Eng	CAS	Descent			Total ETE
			ETE	Fuel	Dist	ETE	Fuel	Dist			ETE	Fuel	Dist	
40	4130	10	2	765	7	4	365	17	2655	209	5	130	16	11
60	4420	20	4	1260	18	2	160	9	2490	208	10	235	33	16
80	4725	25	6	1535	26	2	190	11	2445	204	12	284	43	20
100	5010	30	8	1845	37	2	165	11	2445	202	14	330	52	24
120	5340	30	8	1860	37	6	480	31	2465	203	14	330	52	28
140	5580	35	11	2235	54	4	345	24	2565	208	16	373	62	31
160	5885	35	11	2260	55	7	625	43	2570	208	16	373	62	34
180	6170	35	11	2280	56	10	890	62	2580	208	16	373	62	37
200	6490	35	12	2300	56	14	1190	82	2590	208	16	373	62	42
220	6800	35	12	2325	57	17	1475	101	2600	208	16	373	62	45
240	7100	35	12	2350	58	20	1750	120	2610	209	16	373	62	48
260	7410	35	12	2380	59	23	2030	139	2620	209	16	373	62	51
280	7720	35	12	2395	59	26	2325	159	2625	209	16	373	62	54
300	8022	35	12	2420	60	30	2600	178	2640	209	16	373	62	58
320	8335	35	12	2445	61	33	2890	197	2650	209	16	373	62	62
340	8646	35	13	2470	62	36	3175	216	2660	209	16	373	62	65
360	8965	35	13	2500	63	39	3465	236	2670	210	16	373	62	68
380	9284	35	13	2525	63	42	3755	255	2680	210	16	373	62	71
400	9609	35	13	2555	64	45	4055	274	2690	210	16	373	62	75

Remarks:

(1) Fuel required includes 300 pounds for trim and acceleration at end of climb.

(2) Provides 3000 pounds fuel at point where descent is commenced. No wind conditions.

(3) Climb speed is 225 KCAS to 15,000 feet decreasing 15 knots per 10,000 feet altitude above 15,000 feet.

(4) Idle descent to sea level at 175 KCAS.

(5) Aircraft operating weight is 41,000 pounds.

(6) For each 1000-pound increase in basic aircraft weight, increase fuel required by 1.1 percent.

Data as of: 1 March 1964

Data Basis: NATC and Contractor Flight Test

Fuel Grade: JP-5

Fuel Density: 6.8 lb/gal

Figure 11-41. Fouled Deck Range — Gear Down

FOULED DECK RANGE (VFR) GEAR AND FLAPS DOWN
Two-Engine Operation

Model: A-3B, KA-3B, EA-3B, RA-3B – Basic Wing
Engines: J57-P-10

Dist	Fuel Req	Alt	Climb			Cruise			Fuel Flow lb/hr/Eng	CAS	Descent			Total ETE
			ETE	Fuel	Dist	ETE	Fuel	Dist			ETE	Fuel	Dist	
40	4,385	15	4	1230	12	2	155	6	2800	162	9	230	22	15
60	4,905	20	6	1585	19	4	320	13	2720	157	12	290	29	22
80	5,320	25	8	1970	28	4	350	15	2680	156	15	350	37	27
100	5,730	30	12	2425	40	3	305	14	2710	156	18	405	46	33
120	6,175	30	12	2465	41	8	710	33	2720	156	18	405	46	37
140	6,610	30	12	2500	42	12	1110	52	2740	157	18	405	46	42
160	7,080	30	12	2535	43	17	1545	71	2750	157	18	405	46	47
180	7,530	30	13	2570	44	21	1960	90	2770	158	18	405	46	52
200	8,000	30	13	2620	45	26	2380	109	2780	158	18	405	46	56
220	8,455	30	13	2660	46	30	2795	127	2800	158	18	405	46	61
240	8,915	30	13	2695	47	34	3220	146	2810	159	18	405	46	65
260	9,405	30	14	2740	48	39	3665	166	2830	159	18	405	46	70
280	9,875	30	14	2780	49	43	4095	185	2850	160	18	405	46	75
300	10.660	30	14	2830	50	48	4530	204	2860	161	18	405	46	79
320	10,850	30	14	2880	51	52	4970	223	2880	161	18	405	46	84
340	11,340	30	15	2935	52	56	5405	242	2890	161	18	405	46	88
360	11,830	30	15	2980	53	60	5850	261	2910	161	18	405	46	93
380	12,325	30	15	3035	54	65	6290	280	2920	162	18	405	46	98
400	12,810	30	16	3090	55	69	6720	298	2940	162	18	405	46	102

Remarks:

(1) Fuel required includes 300 pounds for turn and acceleration.

(2) Provides 3000 pounds fuel at point where descent is commenced. No wind conditions.

(3) Climb speed is 180 KCAS at sea level decreasing 11 knots per 10,000 feet altitude.

(4) Idle descent to sea level at 124 KCAS.

(5) Aircraft operating weight is 41,000 pounds.

(6) For each 1000-pound increase in basic aircraft weight, increase fuel required by 1 percent.

Data as of: 1 March 1964
Data Basis: NATC and Contractor Flight Test
Fuel Grade: JP-5
Fuel Density: 6.8 lb/gal

Figure 11-42. Fouled Deck Range – Gear and Flaps Down

NAVAIR 01-40ATA-1

Section XI
Part 4

FOULED DECK RANGE (VFR)
One-Engine Operation

Model: A-3B, KA-3B, EA-3B, RA-3B — Basic Wing
Engines: J57-P-10

Dist	Fuel Req	Alt	Climb			Cruise			Fuel Flow lb/hr/Eng	CAS	Descent			Total ETE
			ETE	Fuel	Dist	ETE	Fuel	Dist			ETE	Fuel	Dist	
40	3580	5	3	465	9	2	115	8	3620	233	6	210	23	11
60	3870	5	3	465	9	7	405	28	3630	234	6	210	23	16
80	3940	10	4	750	20	3	190	15	3480	231	12	400	46	19
100	4205	10	4	755	20	8	450	34	3490	232	12	400	46	23
120	4270	15	7	1050	34	4	220	18	3390	226	17	570	68	27
140	4505	15	7	1050	34	8	455	38	3390	227	17	570	68	32
160	4595	20	10	1380	51	4	215	20	3330	224	21	705	89	35
180	4820	20	10	1390	52	8	430	39	3340	225	21	705	89	39
200	4900	25	15	1775	77	2	125	12	3310	222	26	825	111	42
220	5120	25	15	1800	78	6	320	31	3320	222	26	825	111	46
240	5325	25	15	1805	78	9	520	51	3340	222	26	825	111	50
260	5540	25	15	1825	80	13	715	69	3350	222	26	825	111	53
280	5750	25	15	1840	80	16	910	88	3350	222	26	825	111	57
300	5965	25	15	1845	80	20	1120	109	3360	222	26	825	111	61
320	6175	25	15	1855	81	24	1320	128	3370	223	26	825	111	64
340	6390	25	15	1875	82	27	1515	146	3380	223	26	825	111	68
360	6610	25	16	1890	83	30	1720	166	3380	223	26	825	111	72
380	6825	25	16	1900	83	34	1925	185	3390	223	26	825	111	75
400	7040	25	16	1915	84	38	2125	204	3400	224	26	825	111	79

Remarks:

(1) Fuel required includes 200 pounds for cleanup, turn, and acceleration.

(2) Provides 3000 pounds fuel at point where descent is commenced. No wind conditions.

(3) Climb schedule is 280 KCAS at sea level decreasing 20 knots per 10,000 feet.

(4) Descend at 220 KCAS using 85 percent rpm.

(5) Aircraft operating weight is 41,000 pounds.

(6) For each 1000-pound increase in basic aircraft weight, increase fuel required by 1 percent.

Data as of: 1 March 1964

Data Basis: NATC and Contractor Flight Test

Fuel Grade: JP-5

Fuel Density: 6.8 lb/gal

Figure 11-43. Fouled Deck Range — VFR

FOULED DECK RANGE (IFR)
One-Engine Operation

Model: A-3B, KA-3B, EA-3B, RA-3B – Basic Wing Engines: J57-P-10

Dist	Fuel Req	Alt	Climb			Cruise			Fuel Flow lb/hr/Eng	CAS	Total ETE
			ETE	Fuel	Dist	ETE	Fuel	Dist			
40	3850	S.L.	0	200	0	10	650	40	3820	237	10
60	4175	S.L.	0	200	0	15	975	60	3820	237	15
80	4500	S.L.	0	200	0	20	1300	80	3830	237	20
100	4805	5	2	470	9	22	1335	92	3650	234	24
120	5075	10	4	765	21	22	1310	99	3510	232	27
140	5335	15	7	1075	35	22	1260	105	3420	228	29
160	5590	15	7	1090	36	26	1500	124	3430	228	33
180	5845	20	11	1435	54	25	1410	127	3380	226	36
200	6070	20	11	1445	54	29	1625	146	3390	226	40
220	6305	25	15	1870	82	25	1430	138	3370	224	41
240	6515	25	15	1880	82	29	1635	158	3380	224	45
260	6735	25	16	1905	83	32	1830	177	3390	224	48
280	6955	25	16	1910	84	36	2045	197	3390	224	52
300	7175	25	16	1925	84	40	2250	216	3400	224	56
320	7395	25	16	1945	85	43	2450	235	3410	224	59
340	7615	25	16	1960	86	47	2655	254	3420	225	63
360	7835	25	16	1970	87	50	2865	274	3430	225	67
380	8055	25	17	1980	87	54	3075	293	3440	225	70
400	8275	25	17	1990	88	57	3285	313	3450	225	74

Remarks:

(1) Fuel required includes 200 pounds for cleanup, turn, and acceleration.

(2) Provides 3000 pounds fuel at approach fix. No wind conditions.

(3) Climb schedule is 280 KCAS at sea level decreasing 20 knots per 10,000 feet altitude.

(4) Aircraft operating weight is 41,000 pounds.

(5) For each 1000-pound increase in basic aircraft weight, increase fuel required by 1 percent.

Data as of: 1 March 1964 Fuel Grade: JP-5

Data Basis: NATC and Contractor Flight Test Fuel Density: 6.8 lb/gal

Figure 11-44. Flight Test Fouled Deck Range – IFR

NAVAIR 01-40ATA-1

Section XI
Part 4

SEA LEVEL FOULED DECK RANGE
One-Engine Operation

Model: A-3B, KA-3B, EA-3B, RA-3B – Basic Wing   Engines: J57-P-10

Dist	Fuel Req	Flow lb/hr	CAS	ETE
40	3850	3820	237	10
60	4175	3830	237	15
80	4500	3830	237	20
100	4825	3840	238	25
120	5150	3860	238	30
140	5475	3860	238	35
160	5800	3880	238	40
180	6125	3890	238	45
200	6460	3900	239	50
220	6795	3910	239	55
240	7125	3910	239	60
260	7460	3920	239	65
280	7790	3930	240	70
300	8120	3930	240	75
320	8460	3940	240	80
340	8790	3950	240	85
360	9130	3960	240	90
380	9460	3970	241	94
400	9805	3990	241	100

Remarks:

(1) Fuel required includes 200 pounds for cleanup, turn, and acceleration.
(2) Provides 3000 pounds fuel reserve for landing. No wind conditions.
(3) Aircraft operating weight is 41,000 pounds.
(4) For each 1000-pound increase in basic aircraft weight, increase fuel required by 0.6 percent.

Data as of: 1 March 1964   Fuel Grade: JP-5
Data Basis: NATC and Contractor Flight Test   Fuel Density: 6.8 lb/gal

Figure 11-45. Fouled Deck Range – Sea Level

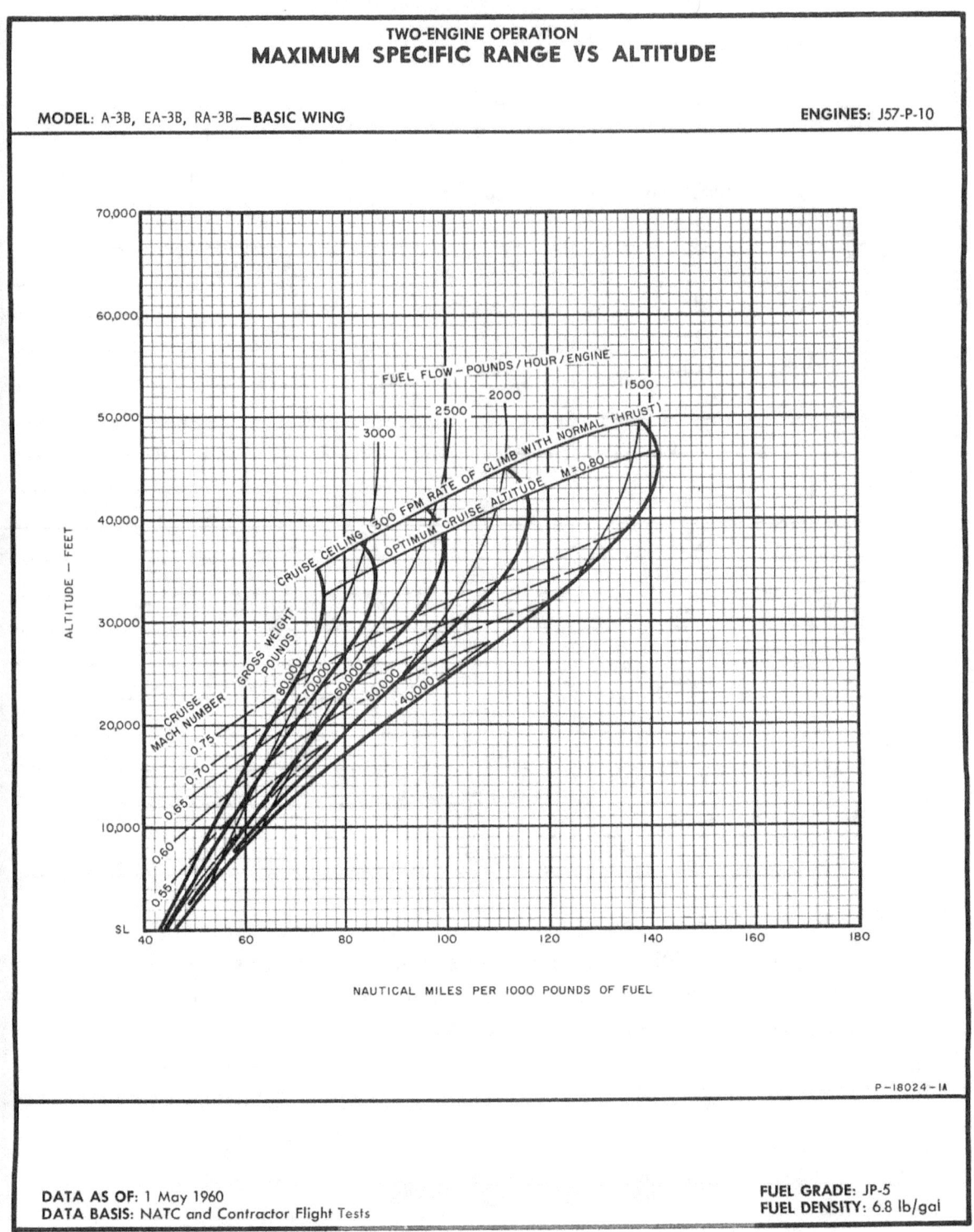

Figure 11-46. Maximum Specific Range vs Altitude (Sheet 1)

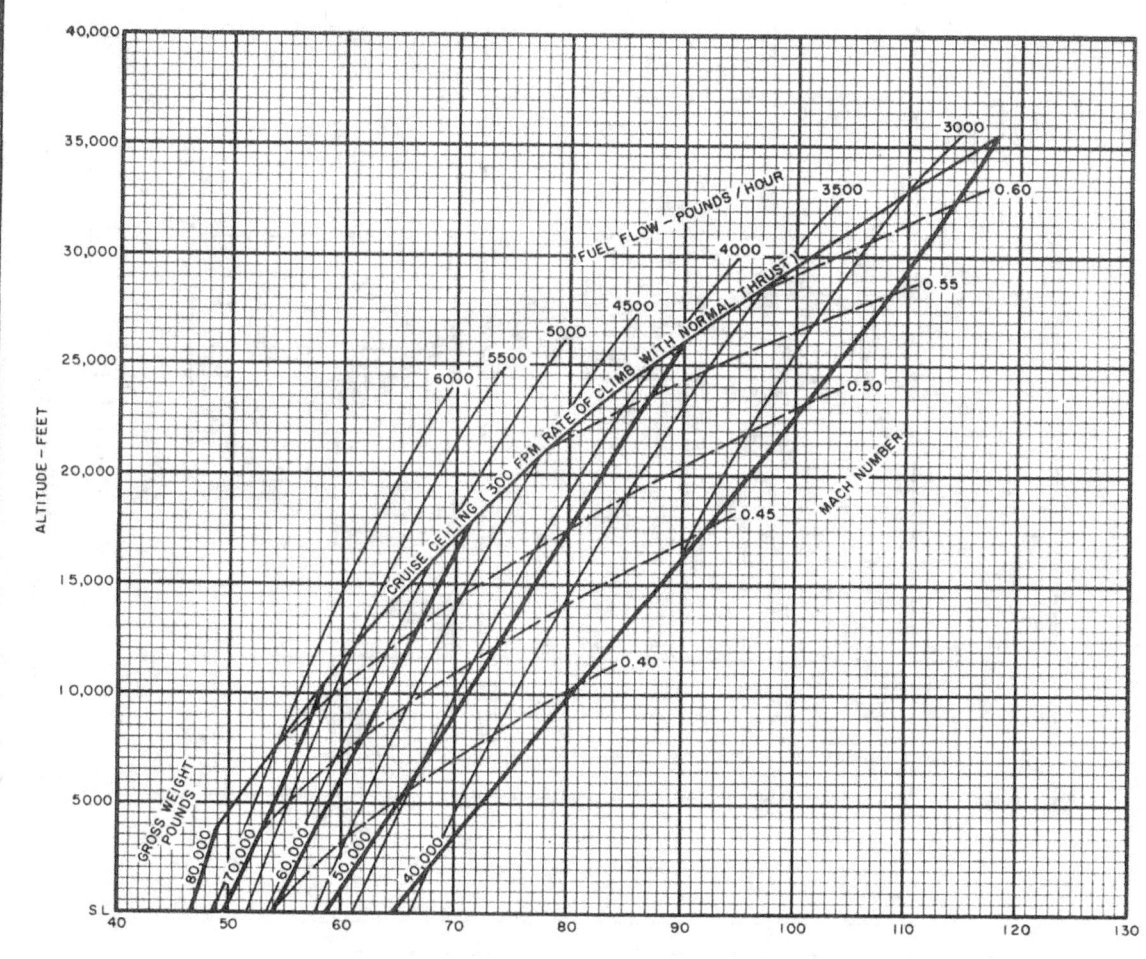

Figure 11-46. Maximum Specific Range vs Altitude (Sheet 2)

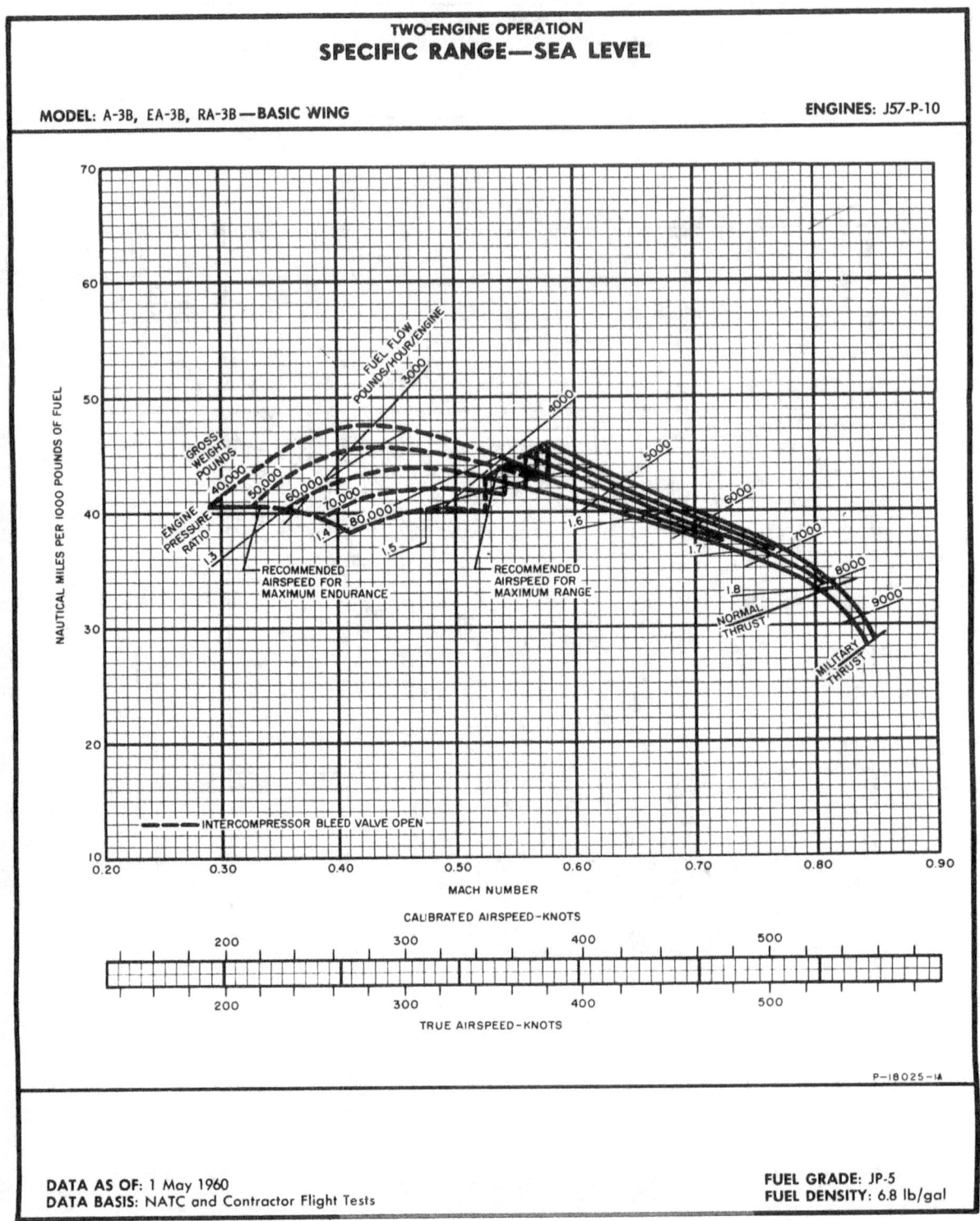

Figure 11-47. Specific Range – Sea Level (Sheet 1)

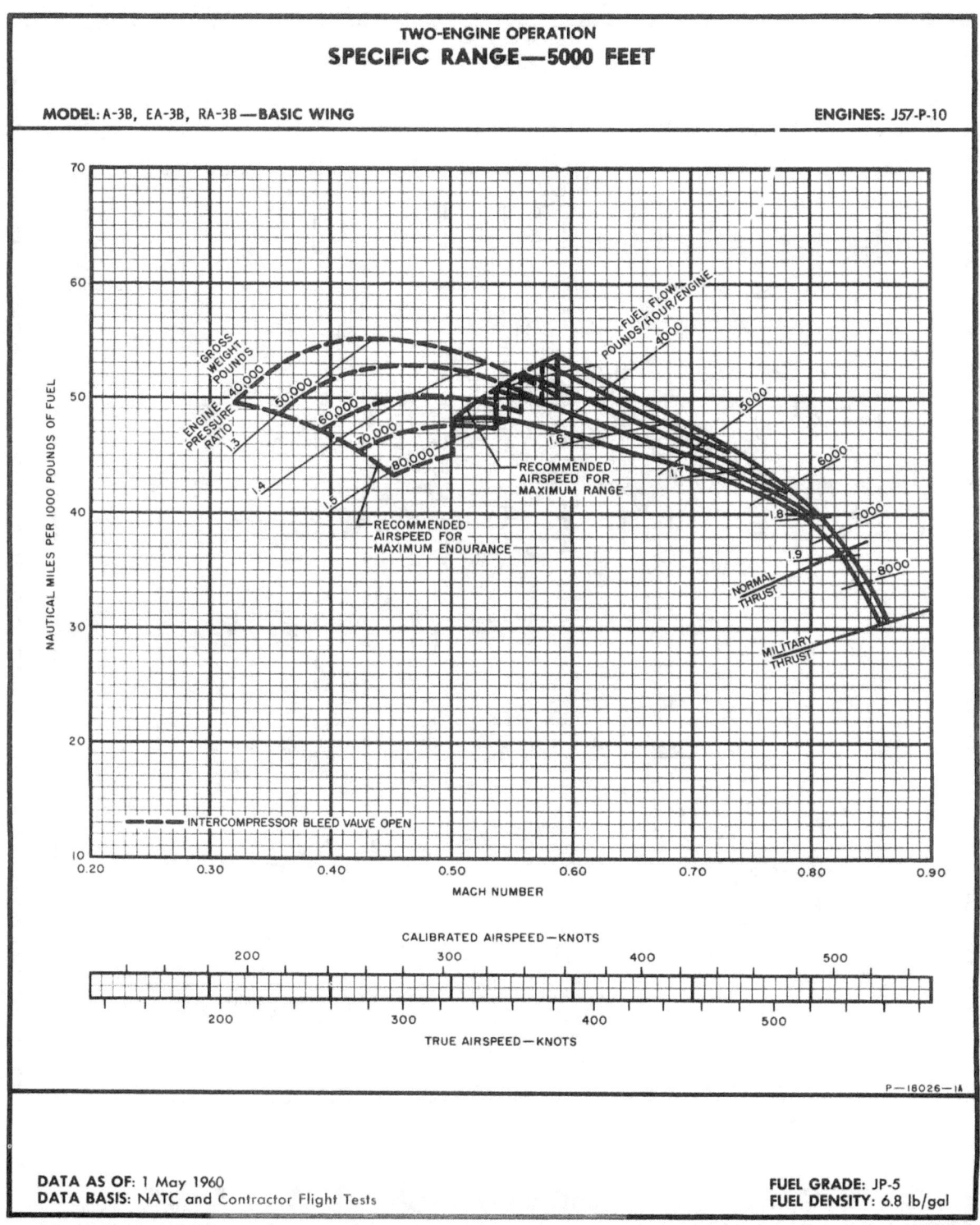

Figure 11-47. Specific Range — 5000 Feet (Sheet 2)

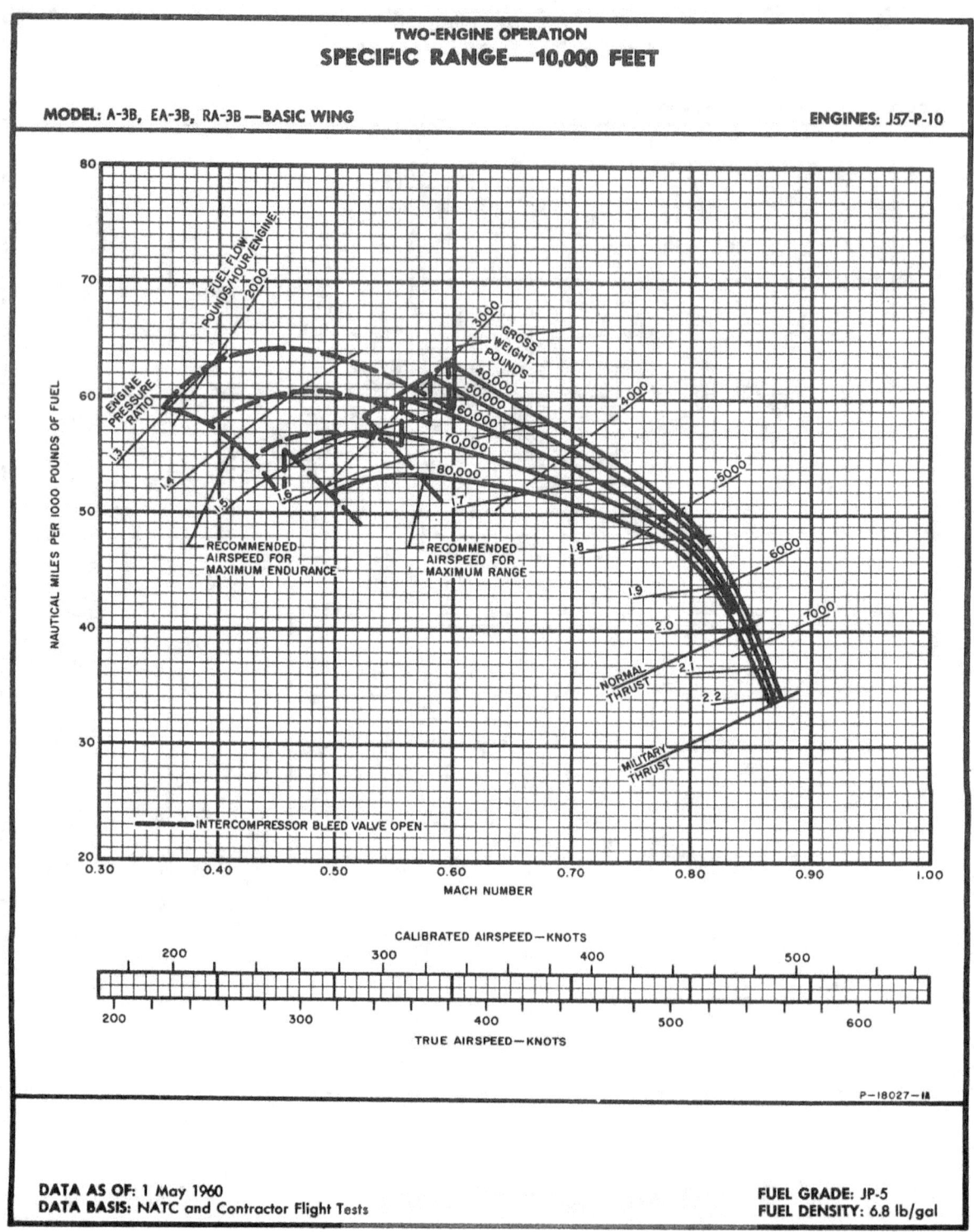

Figure 11-47. Specific Range — 10,000 Feet (Sheet 3)

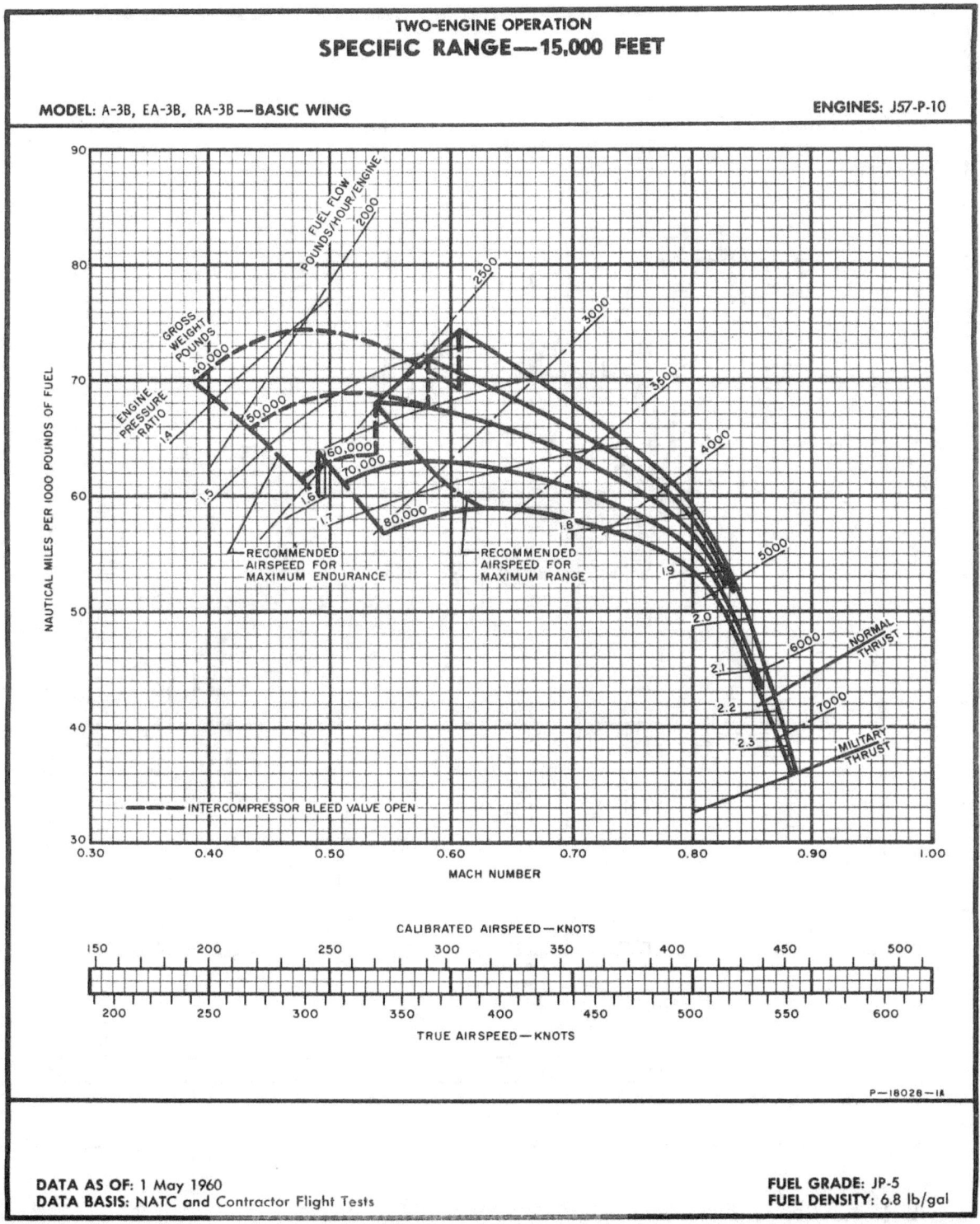

Figure 11-47. Specific Range — 15,000 Feet (Sheet 4)

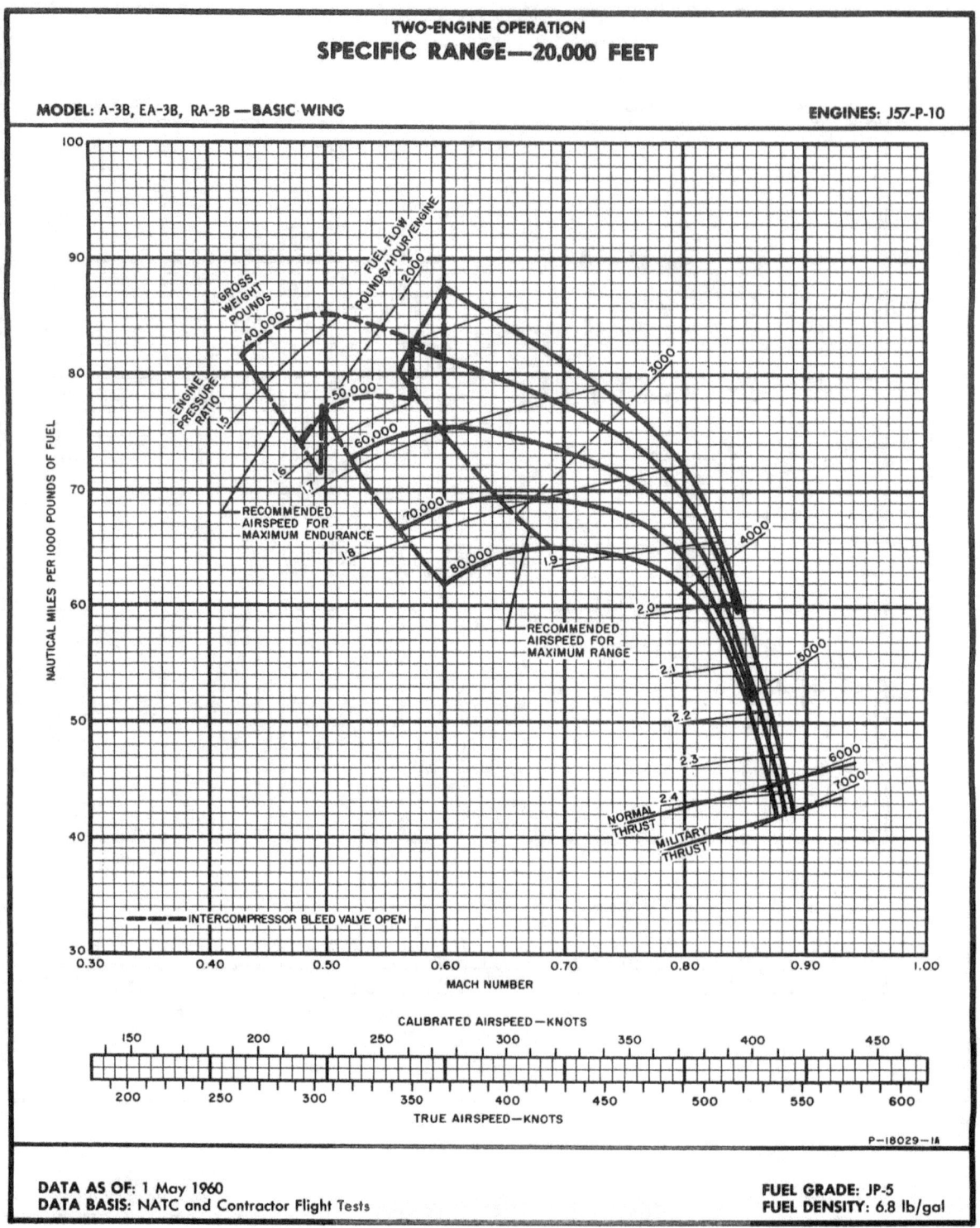

Figure 11-47. Specific Range — 20,000 Feet (Sheet 5)

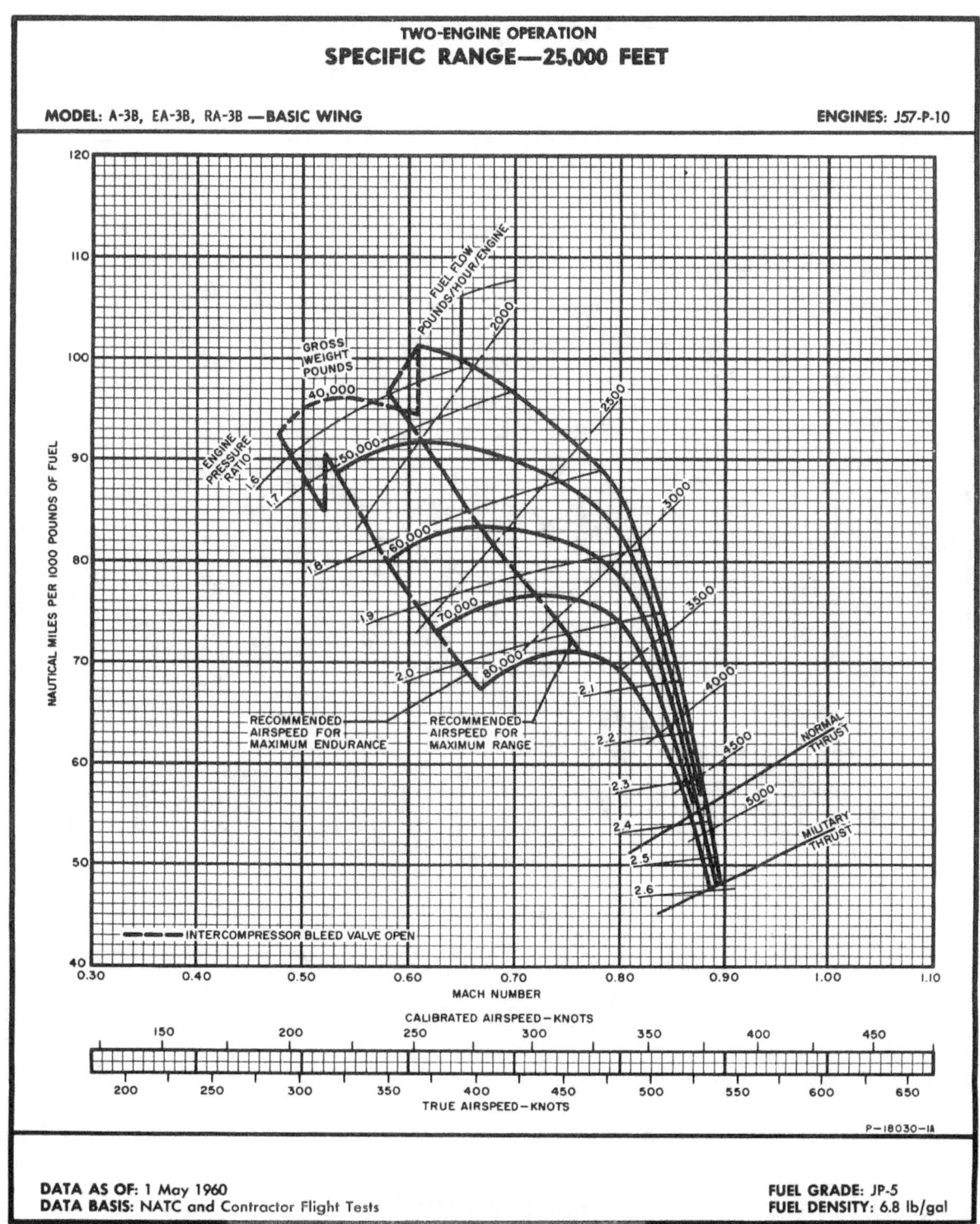

Figure 11-47. Specific Range – 25,000 Feet (Sheet 6)

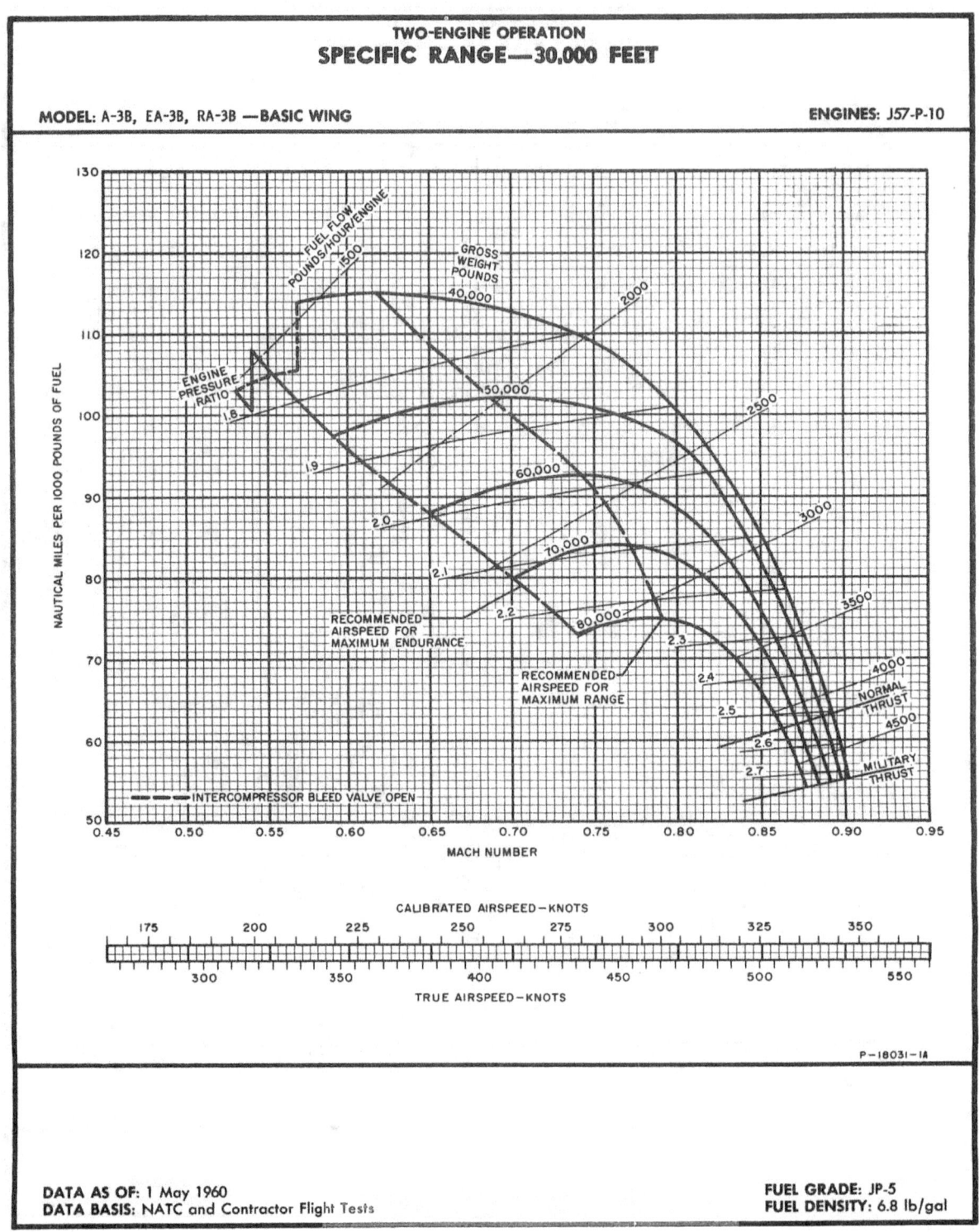

Figure 11-47. Specific Range – 30,000 Feet (Sheet 7)

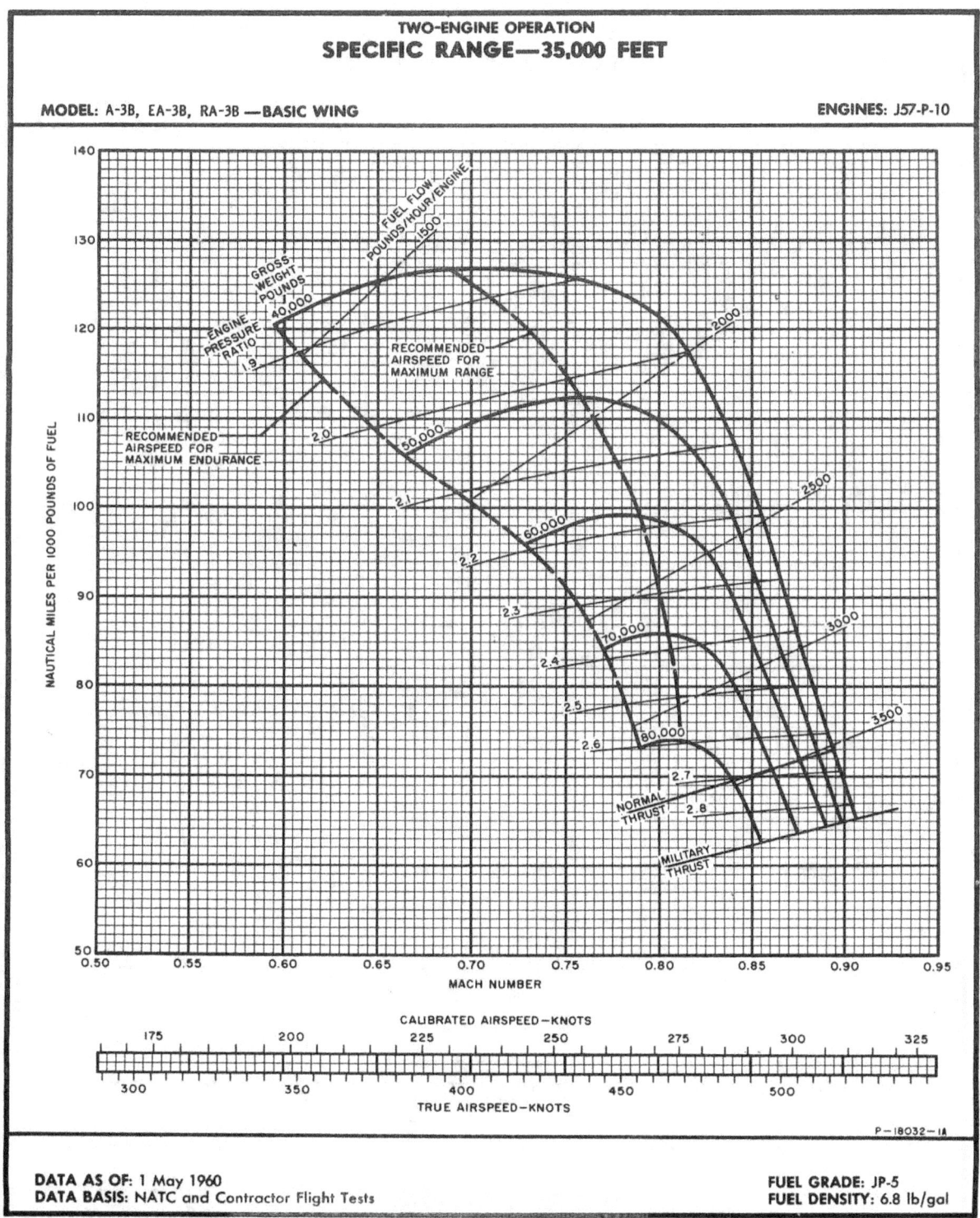

Figure 11-47. Specific Range — 35,000 Feet (Sheet 8)

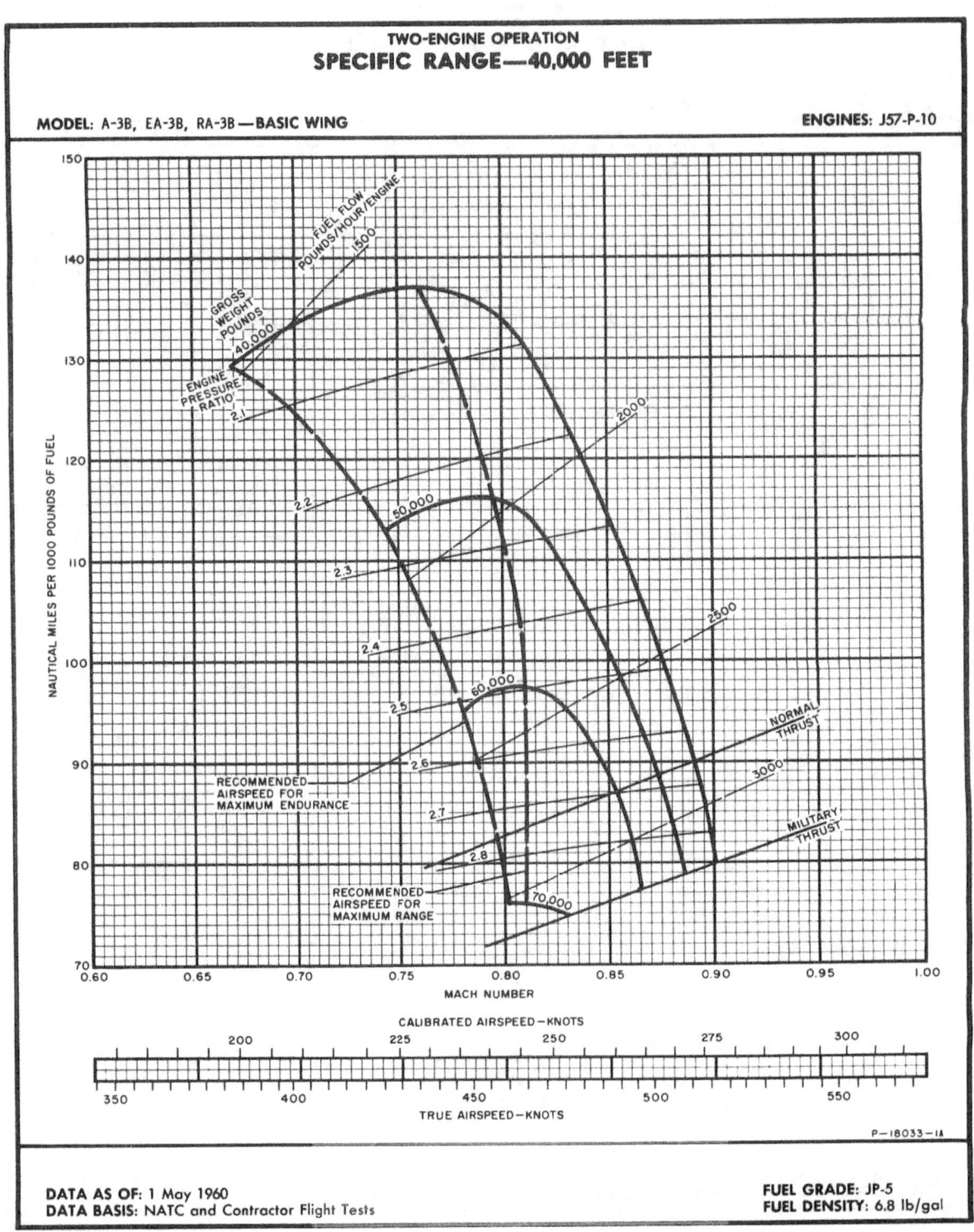

Figure 11-47. Specific Range — 40,000 Feet (Sheet 9)

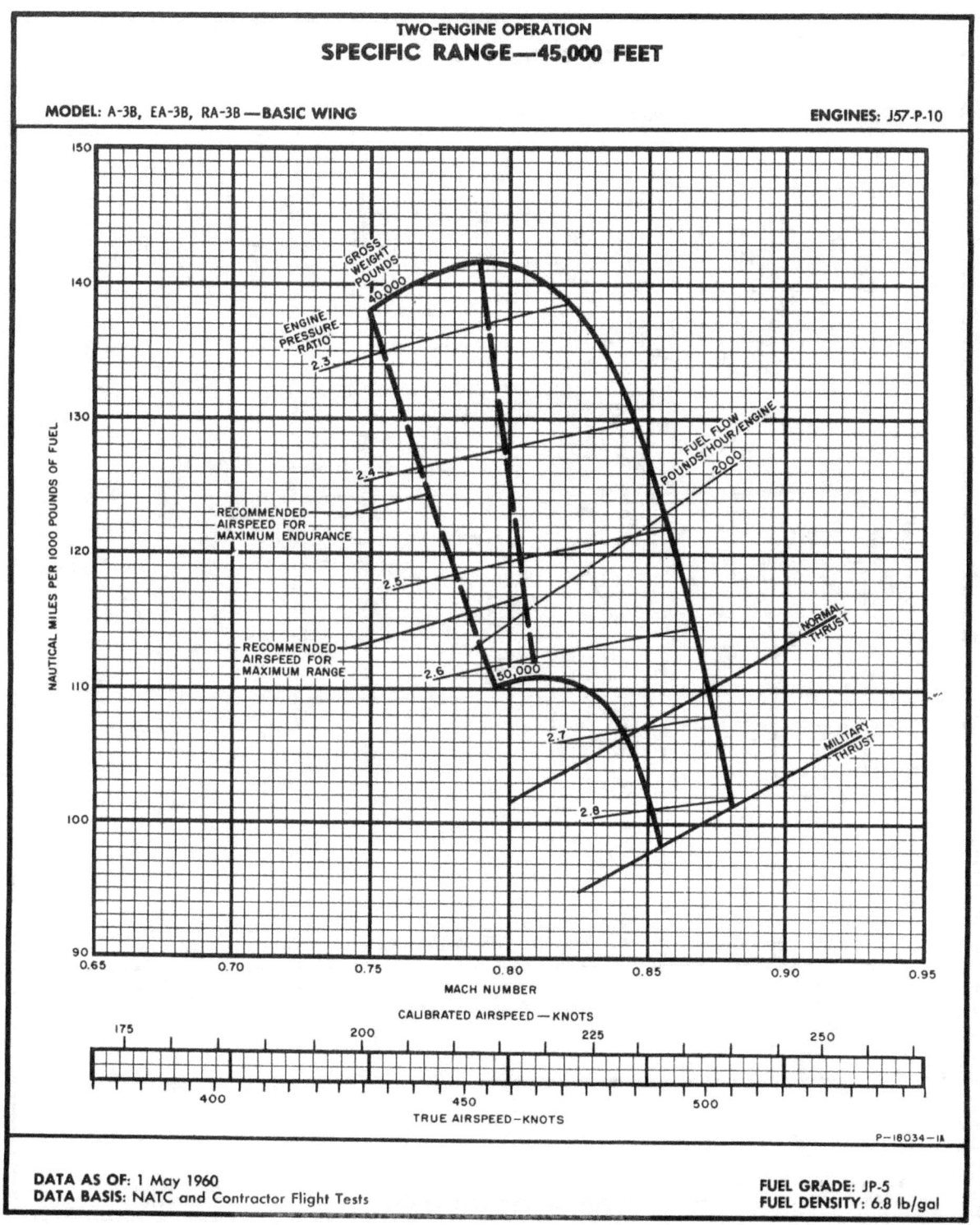

Figure 11-47. Specific Range — 45,000 Feet (Sheet 10)

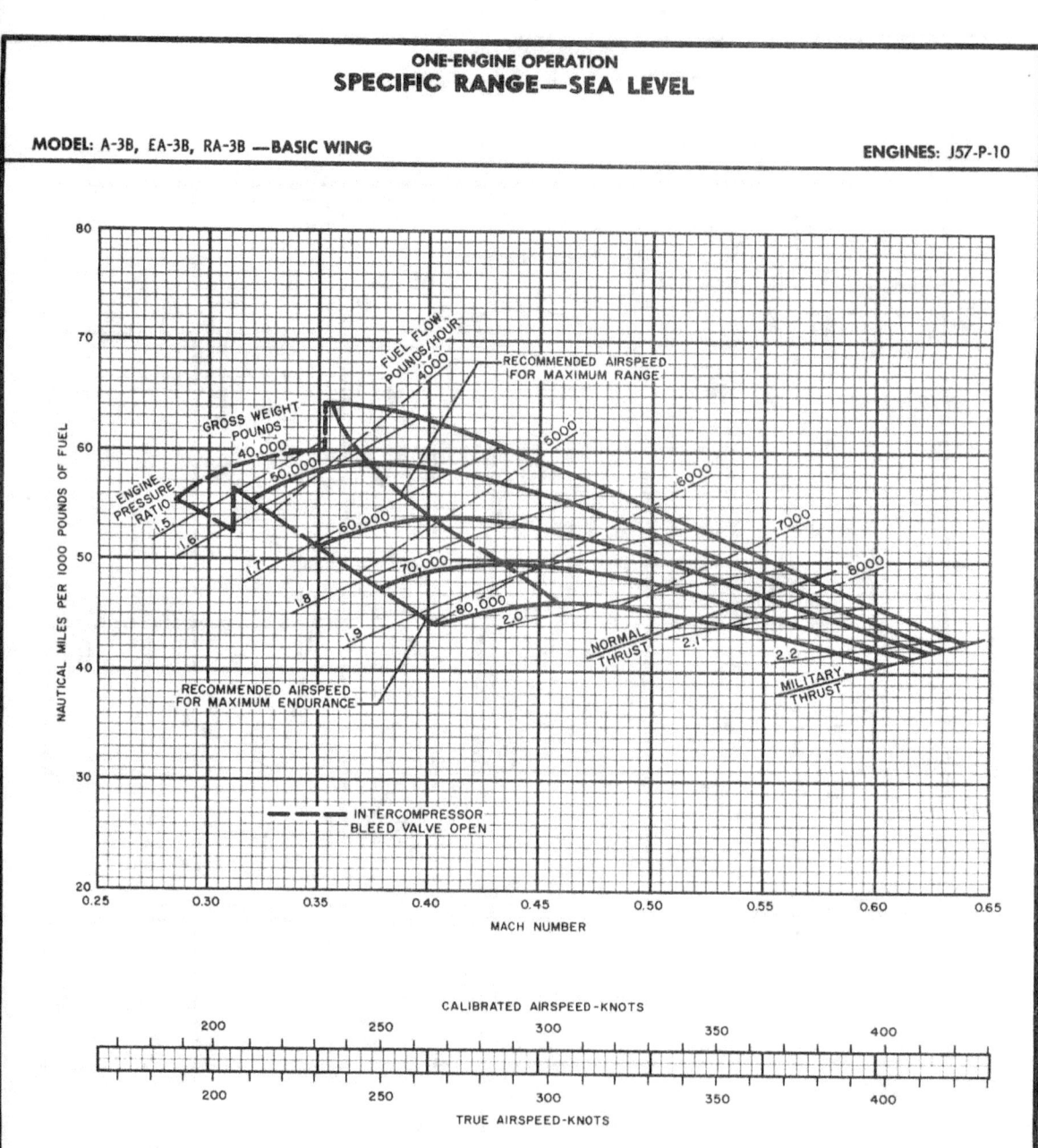

Figure 11-48. Specific Range — Sea Level (Sheet 1)

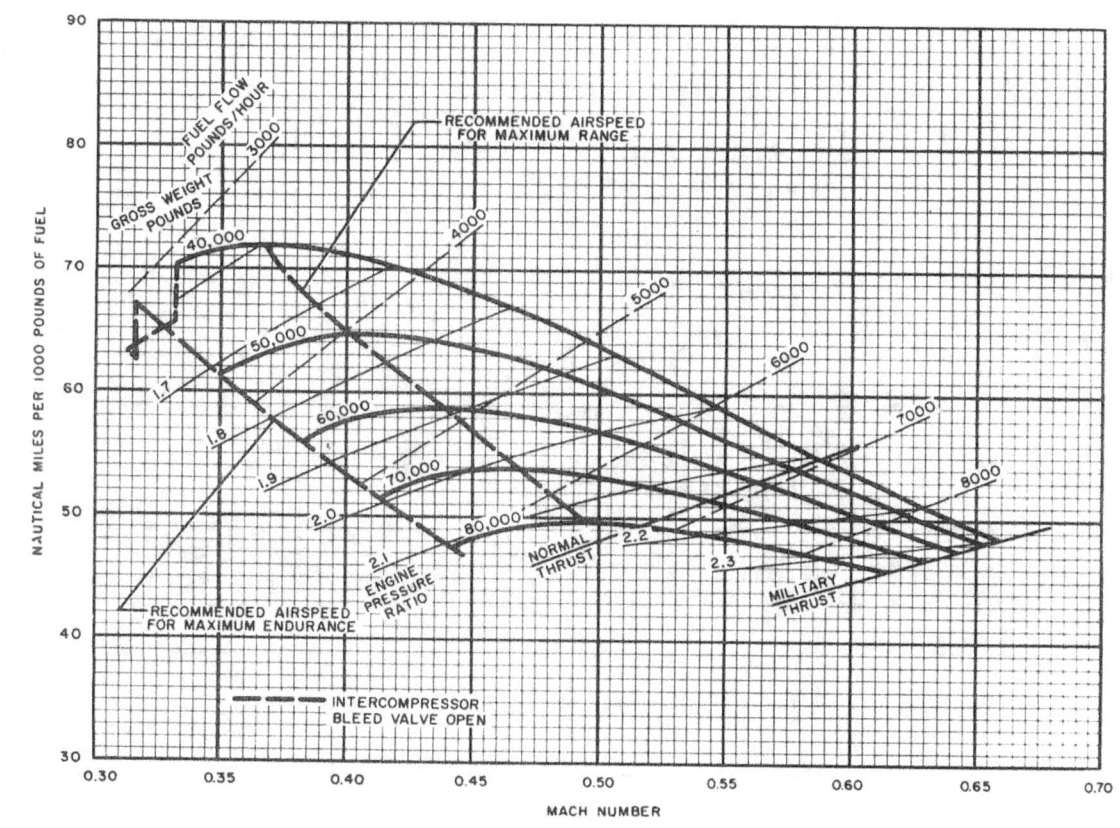

Figure 11-48. Specific Range – 5000 Feet (Sheet 2)

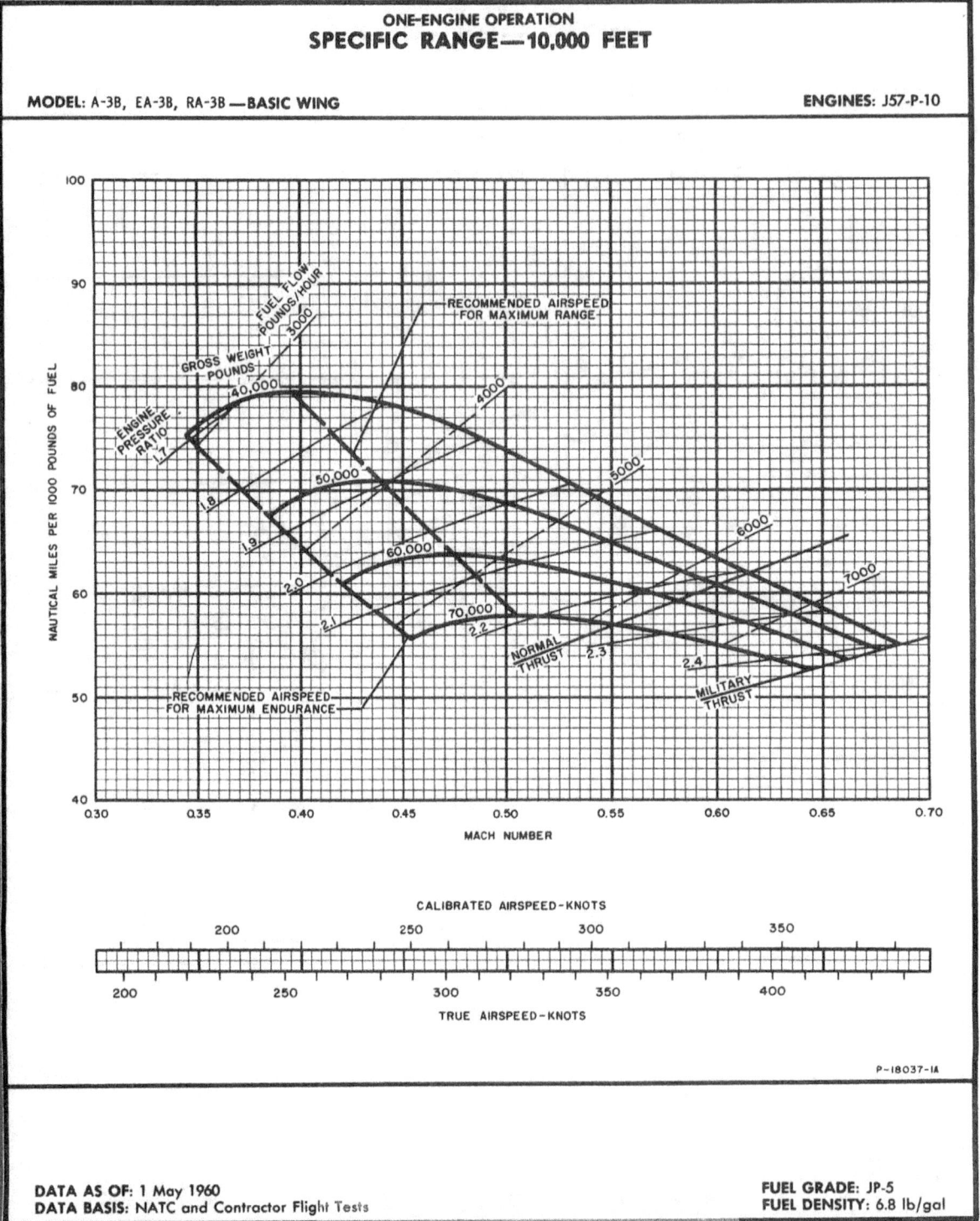

Figure 11-48. Specific Range — 10,000 Feet (Sheet 3)

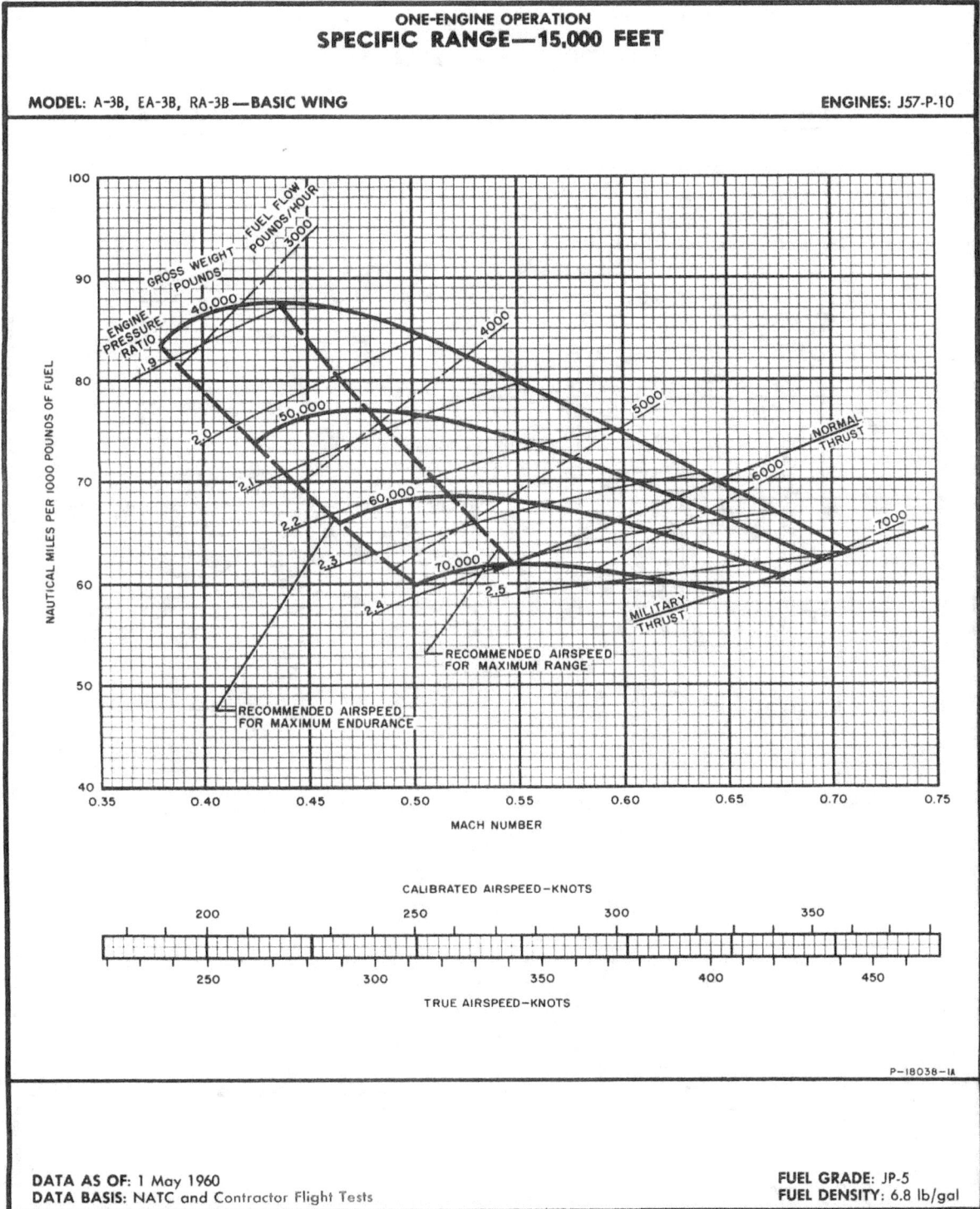

Figure 11-48. Specific Range – 15,000 Feet (Sheet 4)

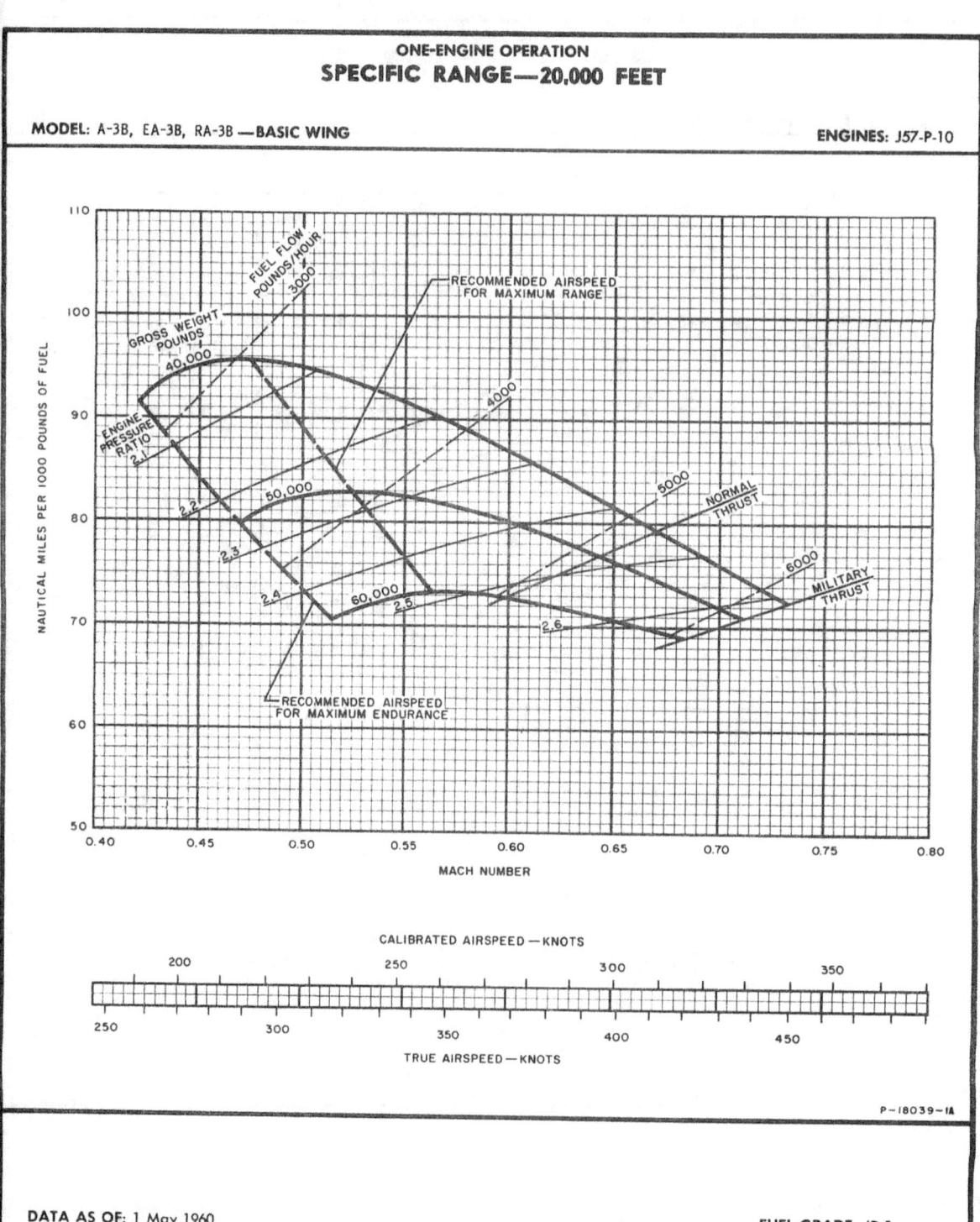

Figure 11-48. Specific Range — 20,000 Feet (Sheet 5)

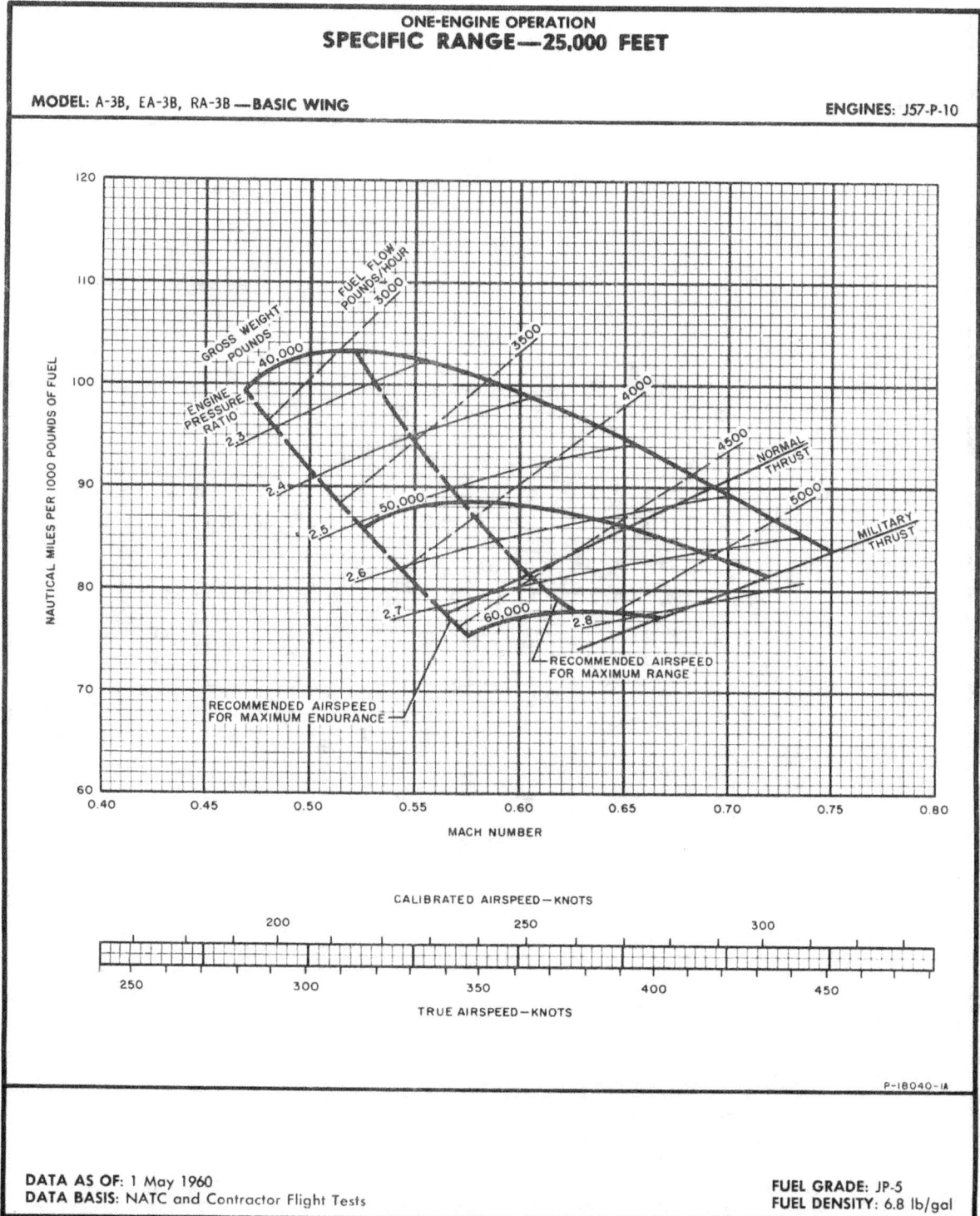

Figure 11-48. Specific Range — 25,000 Feet (Sheet 6)

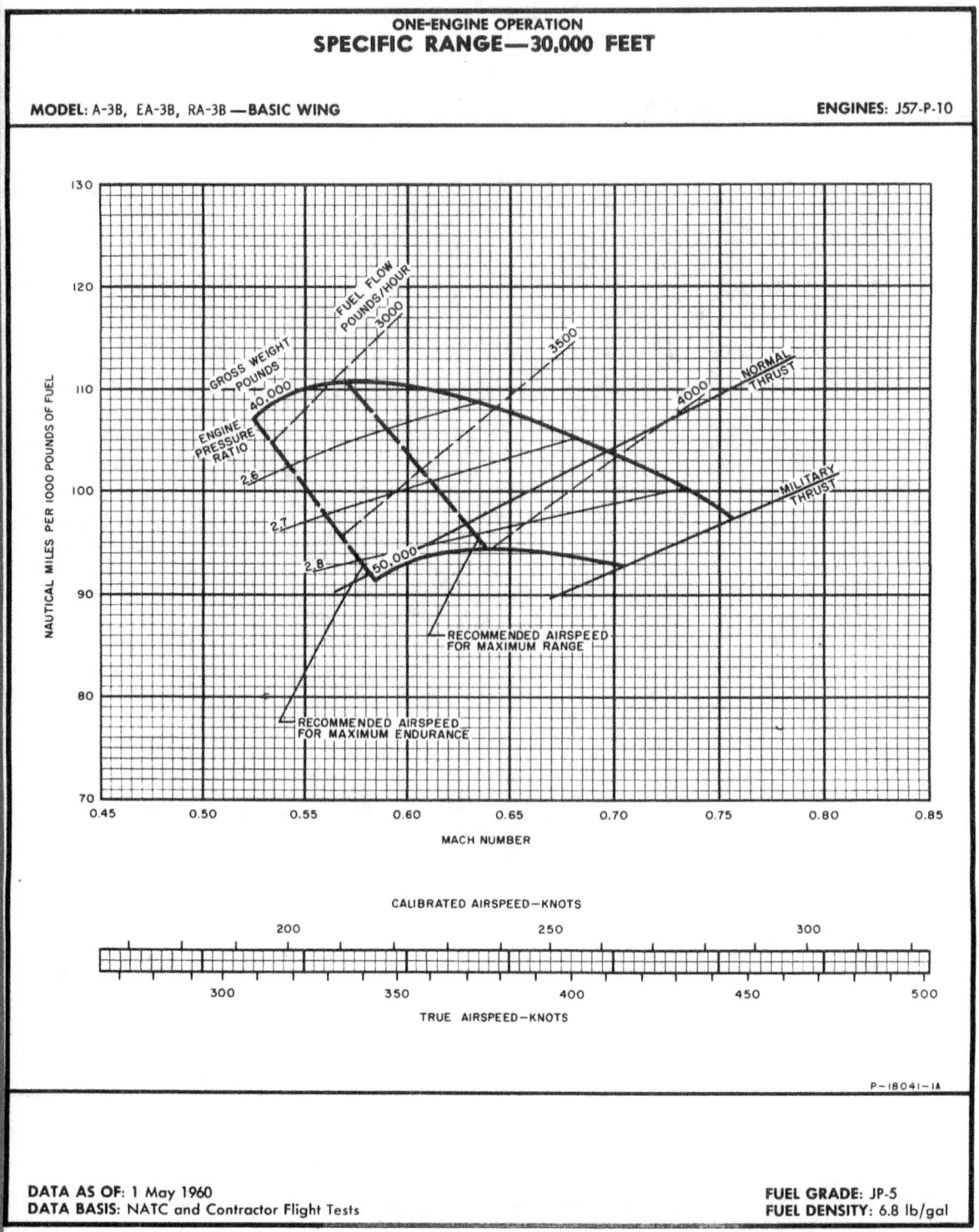

Figure 11-48. Specific Range — 30,000 Feet (Sheet 7)

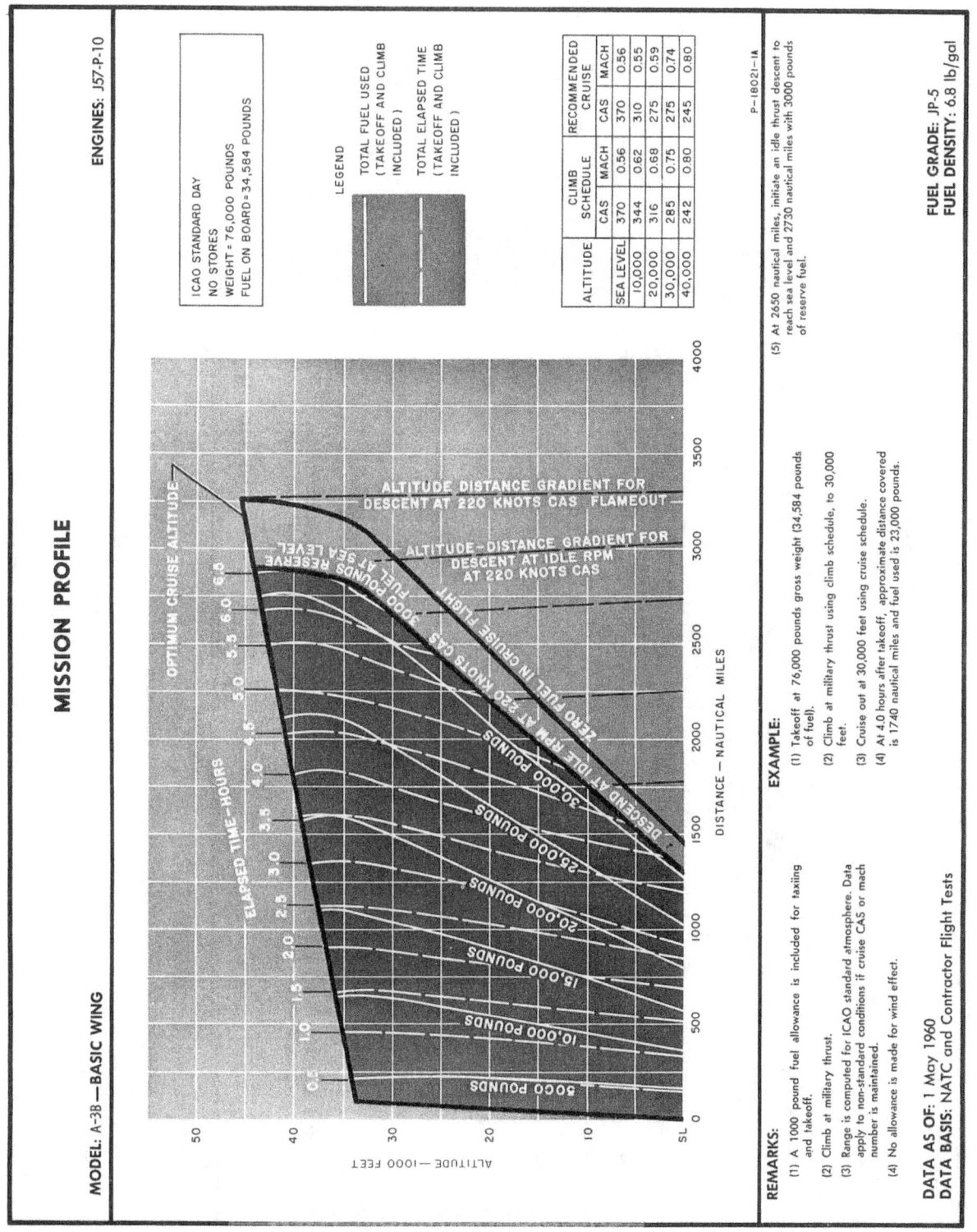

Figure 11-49. Mission Profile

Section XI
Part 4
NAVAIR 01-40ATA-1

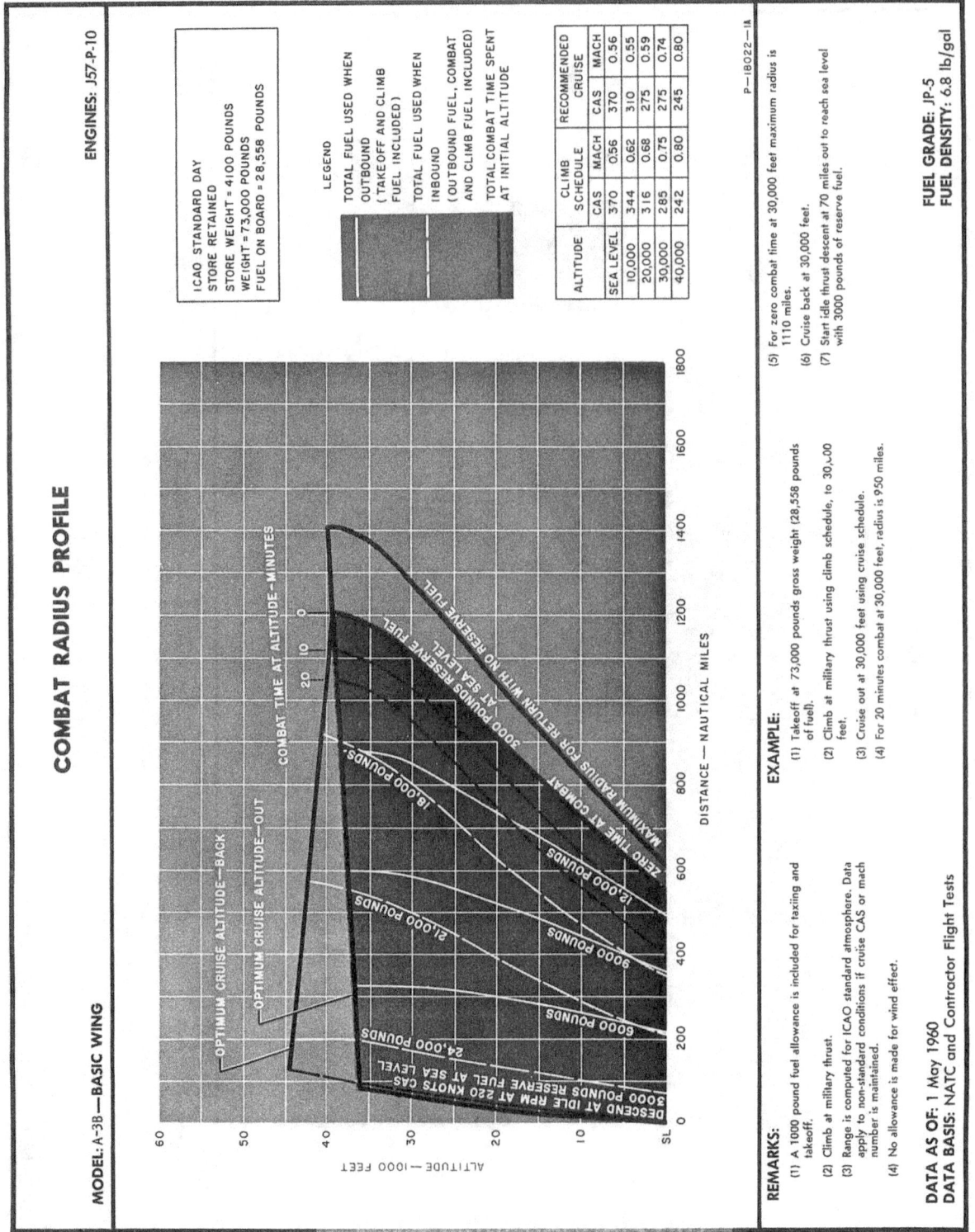

Figure 11-50. Combat Radius Profile (Sheet 1)

NAVAIR 01-40ATA-1

Section XI
Part 4

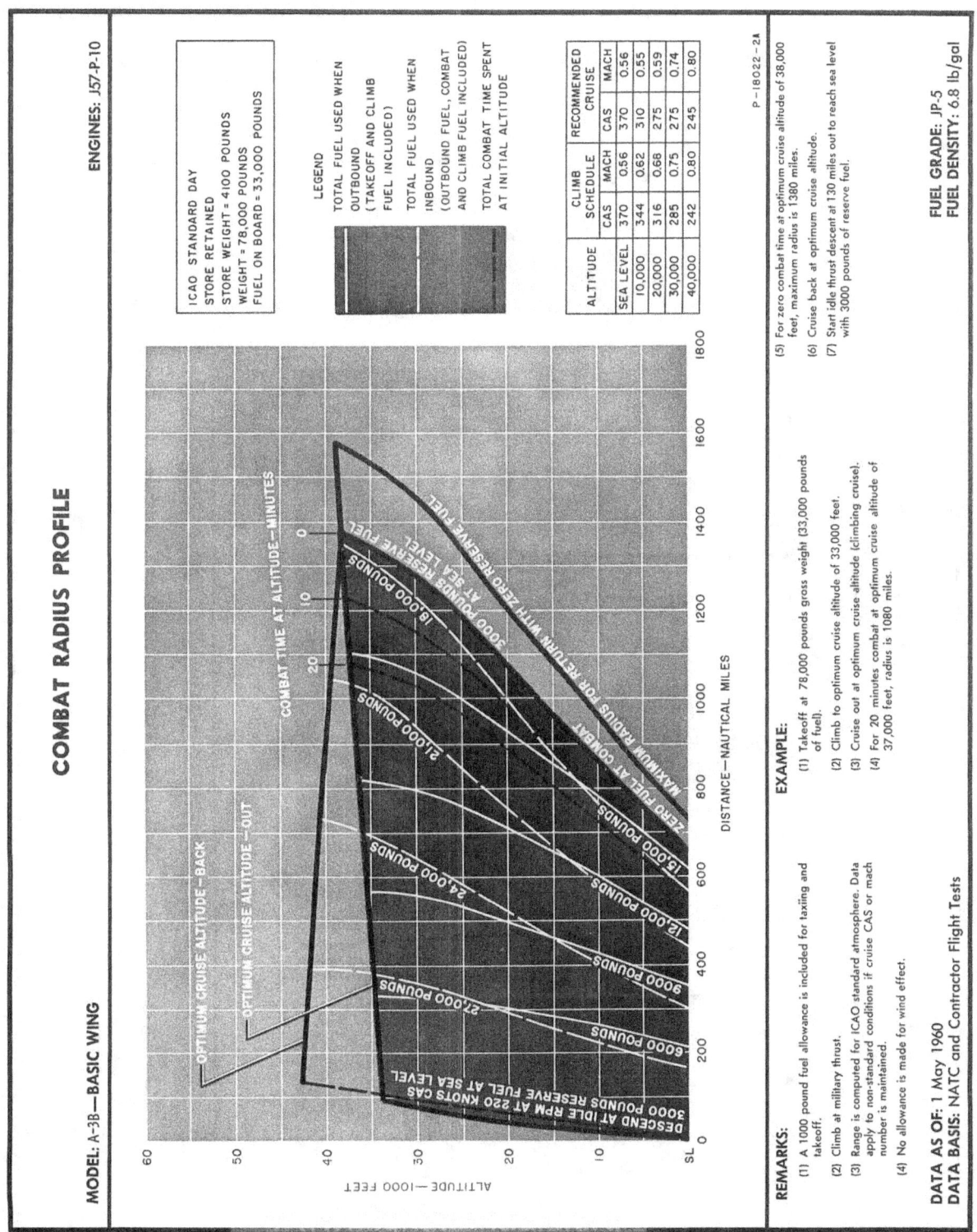

Figure 11-50. Combat Radius Profile (Sheet 2)

11-89

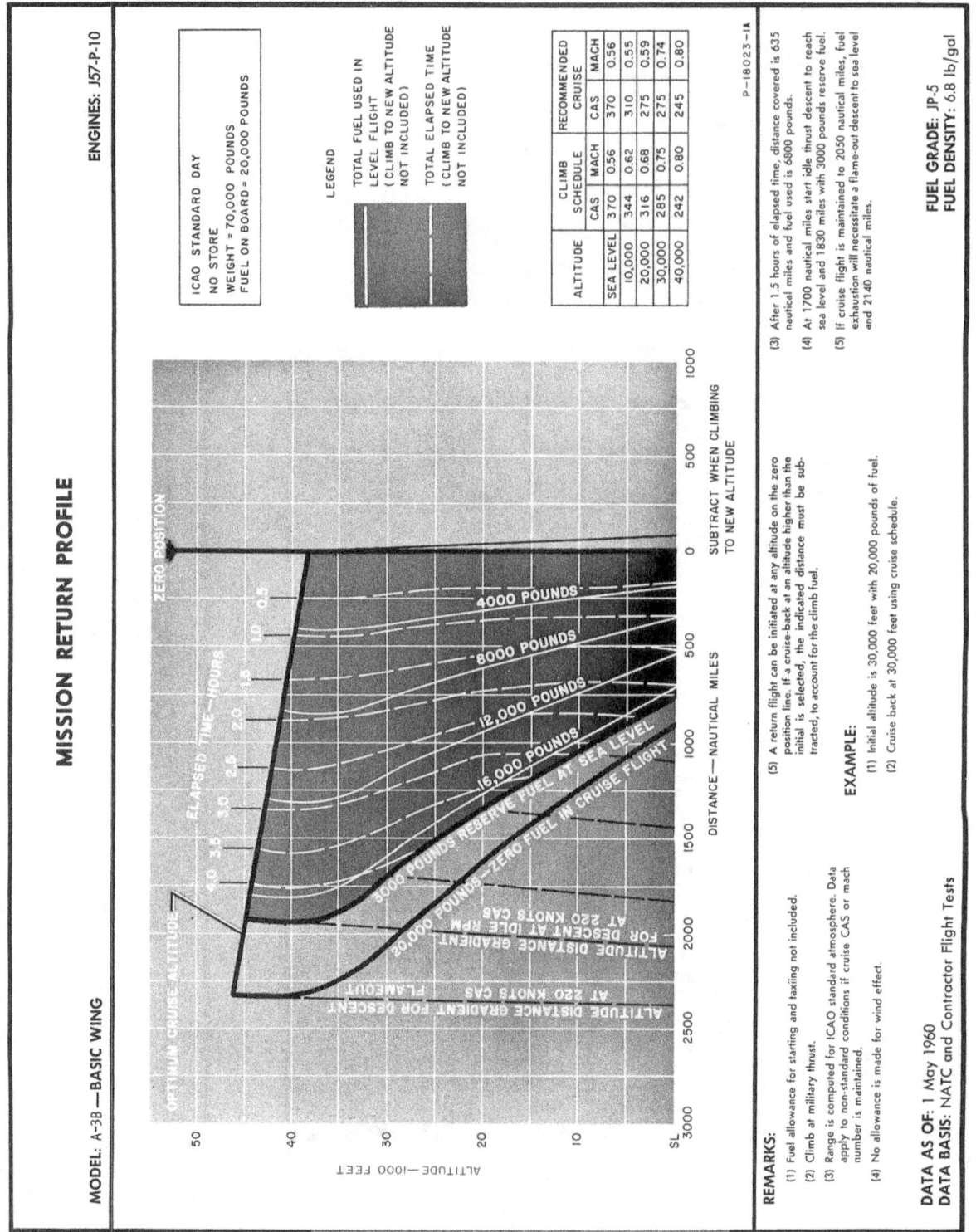

Figure 11-51. Mission Return Profile

NAVAIR 01-40ATA-1

Section XI
Part 5

PART 5
ENDURANCE

TABLE OF CONTENTS

TEXT

Page

Endurance Charts 11-91

ILLUSTRATIONS

Figure		Page	Figure		Page
11-52	Fouled Deck Endurance.........	11-93	11-54	Maximum Endurance Profile..................	11-97
11-53	Maximum Specific Endurance vs Altitude	11-95			

Endurance Charts

When maximum endurance operation is required during flight, such as holding at altitude while awaiting clearance to land, the recommended airspeed to be maintained is approximately 10 percent higher than that at which minimum fuel flow is obtained. The higher airspeed will result in generally better handling characteristics for the aircraft, particularly in mild or moderate turbulence, with only a slight increase in fuel consumption. The endurance data presented in this appendix are based on using the recommended airspeeds. These airspeeds should be maintained by occasional adjustment of the throttle(s) as fuel is consumed.

FOULED DECK ENDURANCE

The fouled deck endurance charts for two-engine operation (figure 11-52, sheet 1) and one-engine operation (figure 11-52, sheet 2) are provided to indicate the maximum available endurance at low values of fuel remaining for various altitudes. For each initial altitude, the endurance at optimum altitude and the optimum altitude are provided. Climb and loiter speed are indicated. A 3000-pound fuel allowance for landing is included.

ENDURANCE FACTORS WITH GEAR AND FLAPS DOWN

These endurance factors are applicable when attempting to loiter with gear down, flaps down, and speedbrakes closed. Multiply the values in the fouled deck endurance appendix charts by the appropriate factors.

SEA LEVEL ENDURANCE		
	Endurance Factors	KCAS
A-3B Basic Wing		
Single Engine	0.70	120 to 130
Two Engine	0.75	120 to 130

MAXIMUM SPECIFIC ENDURANCE VS ALTITUDE

Maximum specific endurance vs altitude charts present specific endurance (hours per 1000 pounds of fuel) as a function of momentary gross weight and altitude for two-engine operation (figure 11-53, sheet 1) and single-engine operation (figure 11-53, sheet 2). The recommended airspeed for maximum endurance is indicated on the charts. The broken lines included in the charts reflect the increase in fuel consumption resulting from opening of the intercompressor bleed valves. It will be noted that the specific endurance increases as the gross weight decreases due to the consumption of fuel. To obtain accurate endurance values under certain conditions, it may be necessary to reenter the chart frequently with small increments to take full advantage of the endurance capabilities of the aircraft. To determine the specific endurance for any given altitude and gross weight, enter the chart at that altitude and move to the right to the applicable momentary gross weight curve, directly below read the specific endurance (hours per 1000 pounds of fuel).

EXAMPLE: Given an altitude of 30,000 feet, a gross weight of 70,000 pounds and 20,000 pounds of fuel available for loiter; find the maximum loiter time.

1. Specific endurance at initial gross weight .... 0.20 hr/1000 lb of fuel

2. Specific endurance at final gross weight (70,000 lb - 20,000 lb = 50,000 lb) .... 0.278 hr/1000 lb of fuel

3. Specific endurance at average gross weight (70,000 lb - (20,000 lb ÷ 2) = 60,000 lb) .... 0.235 hr/1000 lb of fuel

4. Maximum loiter time (0.235 hr/1000 lb of fuel x 20,000 lb) .... 4.7 hr

MAXIMUM ENDURANCE PROFILE

The maximum endurance profile (figure 11-54) presents the loiter time in hours for various quantities of fuel on board as a function of altitude. These data are presented for two conditions, namely:

1. The aircraft initially at the selected loiter altitude (solid lines), and

Changed 1 June 1969

2. The aircraft initially at sea level and climb to a selected loiter altitude (dashed lines).

The calibrated airspeed for loiter does not vary with altitude and is indicated for each value of fuel on board. The climb schedule is noted in the lower right hand corner of the chart. The climb and descent time is not included in the loiter time shown. The indicated fuel is the fuel available for climb and loiter, thus fuel for descent, landing, and reserve must be subtracted from fuel on board to obtain the indicated fuel. The recommended descent speed is 200 KCAS.

To determine the time available for a given amount of fuel with the aircraft initially at the desired loiter altitude, enter the chart at the loiter altitude and proceed horizontally to the right to the amount of fuel available for loiter (solid line). Directly below, read the loiter time available. The chart should be interpreted in the same manner as if the aircraft is initially at sea level and it is desired to loiter at an altitude other than sea level. In this instance, the broken lines should be used as an indication of the fuel available for climb and loiter.

To obtain the fuel required to loiter a given time, enter the chart at the desired loiter altitude and note the initial time, also the amount of fuel on board at the start of loiter. Reenter the chart at the time when loiter ends (initial time less loiter time) and read the final fuel on board. The difference between the initial and final fuel on board is the fuel required for loiter.

EXAMPLE: Determine fuel required to loiter at 25,000 feet for 2 hours with 15,000 pounds of fuel on board.

1. Initial time at 25,000 feet and 15,000 lb . . . . 4.4 hr

2. Final time (4.4 hr - 2 hr) . . . . . 2.4 hr

3. Fuel on board at end of loiter (2.4 hr at 25,000 feet) . . . . 8500 lb

4. Fuel required to loiter (15,000 lb - 8500 lb) . . . . 6500 lb

5. Recommended loiter CAS . . . 212 to 225 knots

NAVAIR 01-40ATA-1
Section XI
Part 5

FOULED DECK ENDURANCE
Two-Engine Operation

Model: A-3B, KA-3B, EA-3B, RA-3B — Basic Wing   Engines: J57-P-10

Fuel on board – pounds		If You Are at sea level					If You Are at 20,000 feet				
		Endurance at sea level	Optimum altitude	Endurance at optimum altitude	Mach at optimum altitude	CAS at optimum altitude	Endurance at 20,000 feet	Optimum altitude	Endurance at optimum altitude	Mach at optimum altitude	CAS at optimum altitude
		Minutes	Feet	Minutes	Mach	Knots	Minutes	Feet	Minutes	Mach	Knots
	6500	38	30,000	46	0.56	206	54	30,000	57	0.56	207
	5500	27	15,000	29	0.41	204	38	30,000	38	0.56	206
	4500	15	5,000	15	0.34	204	21	20,000	21	0.45	205
	4000	9	SL	9	0.30	201	13	20,000	13	0.45	204
	3500	2	SL	2	0.30	200	4	20,000	4	0.45	204
	Climb CAS	370 KCAS					316 KCAS				
	Letdown	30° Dive, speedbrakes open					30° Dive, speedbrakes open				
	Start letdown with fuel on board – pounds	3000					3000				
		If You Are at 25,000 feet					If You Are at 30,000 feet				
		Endurance at 25,000 feet	Optimum altitude	Endurance at optimum altitude	Mach at optimum altitude	CAS at optimum altitude	Endurance at 30,000 feet	Optimum altitude	Endurance at optimum altitude	Mach at optimum altitude	CAS at optimum altitude
		Minutes	Feet	Minutes	Mach	Knots	Minutes	Feet	Minutes	Mach	Knots
	6500	56	30,000	59	0.56	207	61	30,000	61	0.56	208
	5500	39	30,000	41	0.56	207	43	30,000	43	0.56	206
	4500	22	25,000	22	0.50	204	24	30,000	24	0.55	206
	4000	13	25,000	13	0.50	204	15	30,000	15	0.55	205
	3500	5	25,000	5	0.50	204	5	30,000	5	0.55	204
	Climb CAS	301 KCAS					286 KCAS				
	Letdown	30° Dive, speedbrakes open					30° Dive, speedbrakes open				
	Start letdown with fuel on board – pounds	3000					3000				
		If You Are at 35,000 feet					If You Are at 40,000 feet				
		Endurance at 35,000 feet	Optimum altitude	Endurance at optimum altitude	Mach at optimum altitude	CAS at optimum altitude	Endurance at 40,000 feet	Optimum altitude	Endurance at optimum altitude	Mach at optimum altitude	CAS at optimum altitude
		Minutes	Feet	Minutes	Mach	Knots	Minutes	Feet	Minutes	Mach	Knots
	6500	61	30,000	62	0.56	208	59	30,000	62	0.56	207
	5500	42	30,000	43	0.56	207	41	30,000	43	0.56	207
	4500	24	30,000	24	0.55	206	23	30,000	24	0.55	206
	4000	15	30,000	15	0.55	205	14	30,000	15	0.55	205
	3500	5	35,000	5	0.62	206	5	35,000	5	0.62	206
	Climb CAS	No climb required					No climb required				
	Letdown	30° Dive, speedbrakes open					30° Dive, speedbrakes open				
	Start letdown with fuel on board – pounds	3000					3000				

Remarks:
(1) Fuel required includes 300 pounds for cleanup, turn, and acceleration.
(2) Provides 3000 pounds fuel at point where descent is commenced.
(3) Descent at idle thrust.
(4) Aircraft operating weight is 40,342 pounds.

Data as of: 1 March 1964   Fuel Grade: JP-5
Data Basis: NATC and Contractor Flight Tests   Fuel Density: 6.8 lb/gal

Figure 11-52. Fouled Deck Endurance (Sheet 1)

FOULED DECK ENDURANCE
One-Engine Operation

Model: A-3B, KA-3B, EA-3B, RA-3B — Basic Wing   Engines: J57-P-10

Fuel on board – pounds	If You Are at sea level					If You Are at 20,000 feet				
	Endurance at sea level	Optimum altitude	Endurance at optimum altitude	Mach at optimum altitude	CAS at optimum altitude	Endurance at 20,000 feet	Optimum altitude	Endurance at optimum altitude	Mach at optimum altitude	CAS at optimum altitude
	Minutes	Feet	Minutes	Mach	Knots	Minutes	Feet	Minutes	Mach	Knots
7000	65	SL	65	0.30	199	71	20,000	71	0.45	204
6500	57	SL	57	0.30	199	62	20,000	62	0.45	203
5500	38	SL	38	0.30	198	44	20,000	44	0.44	202
4500	22	SL	22	0.30	197	26	20,000	26	0.44	200
3500	5	SL	5	0.30	196	7	20,000	7	0.44	199
Climb CAS	No climb required					Climb CAS	No climb required			
Letdown	30° Dive, speedbrakes open					Letdown	30° Dive, speedbrakes open			
Start letdown with fuel on board – pounds	3000					Start letdown with fuel on board – pounds	3000			

	If You Are at 25,000 feet					If You Are at 30,000 feet				
	Endurance at 25,000 feet	Optimum altitude	Endurance at optimum altitude	Mach at optimum altitude	CAS at optimum altitude	Endurance at 30,000 feet	Optimum altitude	Endurance at optimum altitude	Mach at optimum altitude	CAS at optimum altitude
	Minutes	Feet	Minutes	Mach	Knots	Minutes	Feet	Minutes	Mach	Knots
7000	70	20,000	71	0.45	204	70	20,000	71	0.45	204
6500	62	20,000	62	0.45	203	61	20,000	62	0.45	203
5500	44	20,000	44	0.44	202	44	20,000	44	0.44	202
4500	25	20,000	26	0.44	200	25	20,000	26	0.44	200
3500	7	25,000	7	0.49	200	7	30,000	7	0.55	202
Climb CAS	No climb required					Climb CAS	No climb required			
Letdown	30° Dive, speedbrakes open					Letdown	30° Dive, speedbrakes open			
Start letdown with fuel on board – pounds	3000					Start letdown with fuel on board – pounds	3000			

Remarks:

(1) Fuel required includes 200 pounds for cleanup, turn, and acceleration.

(2) Provides 3000 pounds fuel at point where descent is commenced.

(3) Descend at idle thrust

(4) Aircraft operating weight is 40,342 pounds.

Data as of: 1 March 1964   Fuel Grade: JP-5

Data Basis: NATC and Contractor Flight Tests   Fuel Density: 6.8 lb/gal

Figure 11-52. Fouled Deck Endurance (Sheet 2)

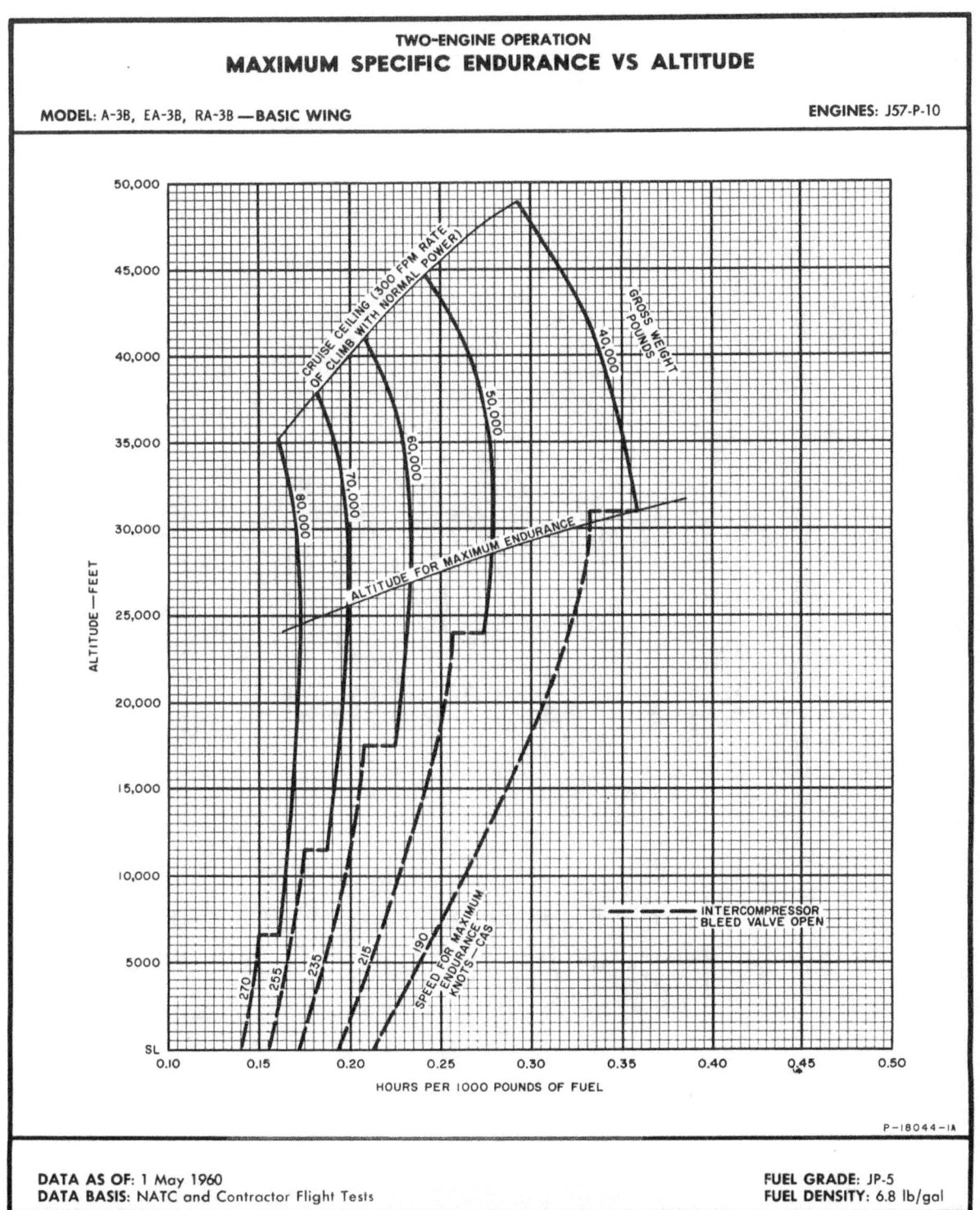

Figure 11-53. Maximum Specific Endurance vs Altitude (Sheet 1)

ONE-ENGINE OPERATION

MAXIMUM SPECIFIC ENDURANCE VS ALTITUDE

MODEL: A-3B, EA-3B, RA-3B — **BASIC WING**

ENGINES: J57-P-10

DATA AS OF: 1 May 1960
DATA BASIS: NATC and Contractor Flight Tests

FUEL GRADE: JP-5
FUEL DENSITY: 6.8 lb/gal

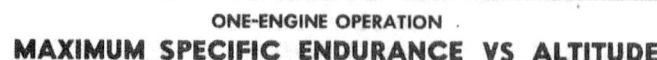

Figure 11-53. Maximum Specific Endurance vs Altitude (Sheet 2)

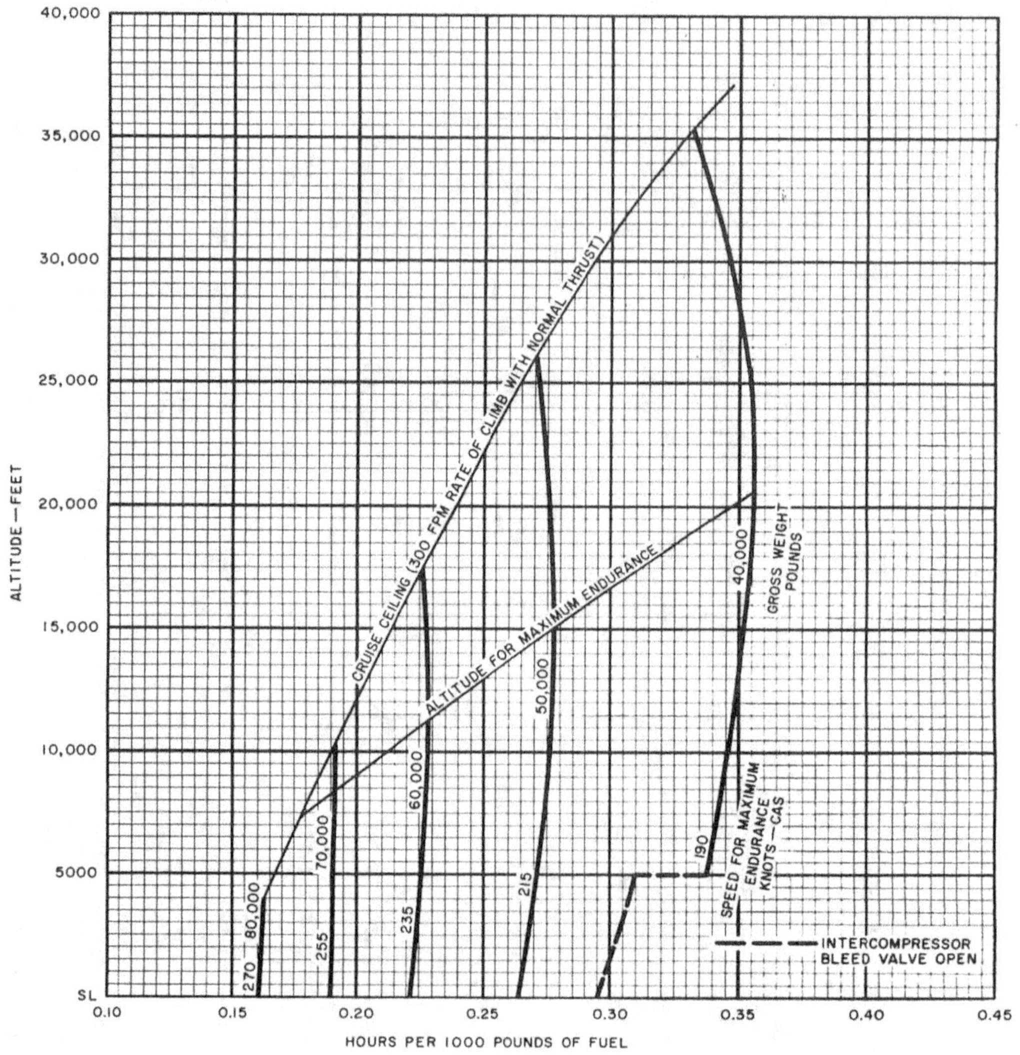

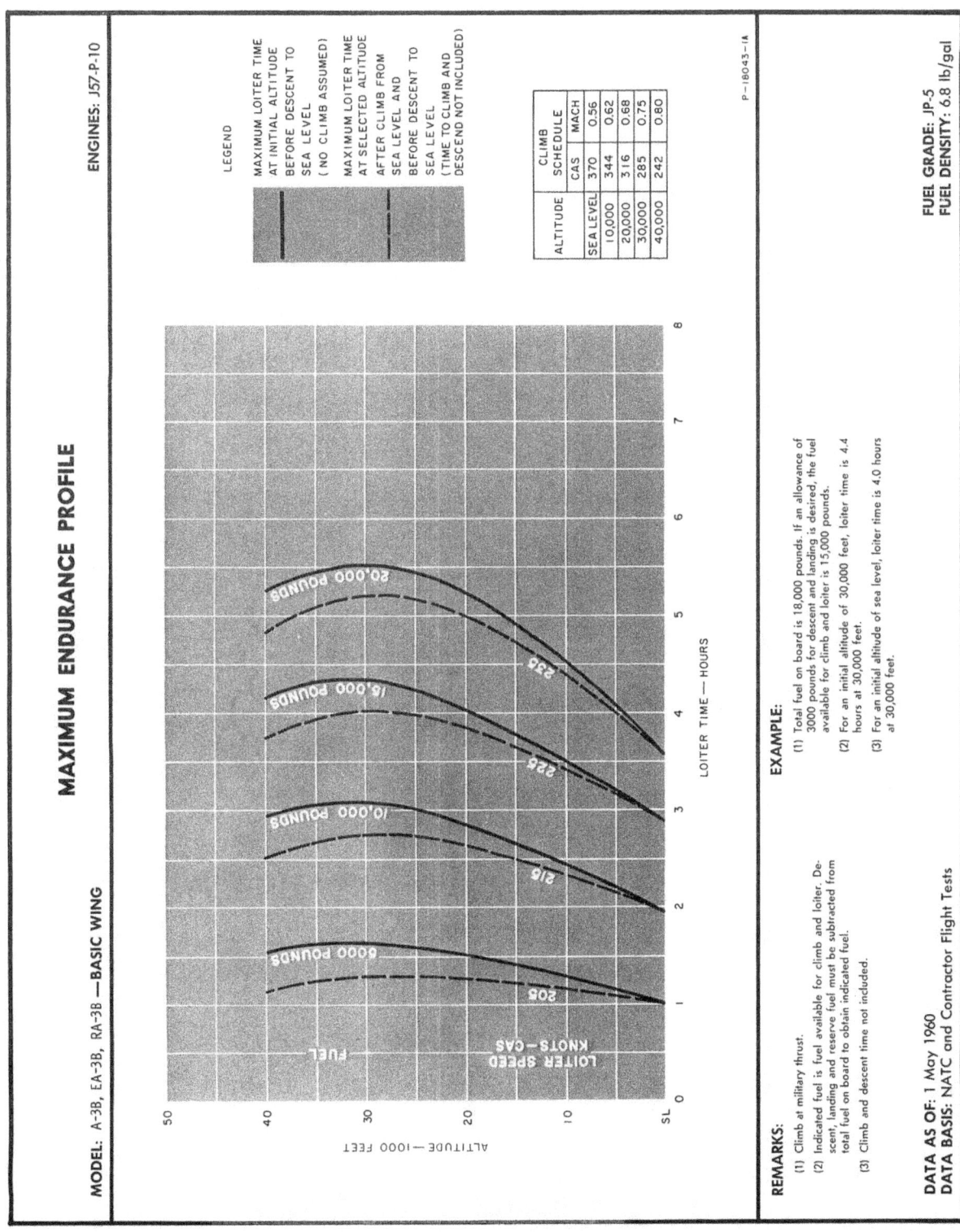

Figure 11-54. Maximum Endurance Profile

NAVAIR 01-40ATA-1

Section XI
Part 6

PART 6
DESCENT

TABLE OF CONTENTS

TEXT

Page

Descent Charts 11-99

ILLUSTRATIONS

Figure   Page

11-55   Maximum Range Descent   11-100

Descent Charts

A maximum range descent should be made with idle power, flaps and gear retracted, and speedbrakes closed. The Maximum Range Descent chart, (figure 11-55) shows descent performance which will be obtained in the above configuration when the recommended airspeeds (CAS) shown in the chart are maintained in the descent. These data may be used for determining rates of descent, elapsed time, distance and/or fuel consumed in descending from any altitude to sea level or from one altitude to another by taking the differences in the desired values at the initial and at the final altitudes.

EXAMPLE: A descent is made from 30,000 feet pressure altitude to 10,000 feet pressure altitude at 40,000 pounds gross weight. Using the data provided on the Maximum Range Descent chart, the descent range is found to be: 81 nautical miles - 27 nautical miles = 54 nautical miles. The elapsed time is:

19 minutes - 7 minutes = 12 minutes

The fuel consumed is:

440 pounds - 160 pounds = 280 pounds.

Descent is made at 220 KCAS.

NOTE

- Distance, time, and fuel consumed in descent with one engine operating at idle power and the other engine completely shut down may be obtained similarly from figure 11-55.

- Distance data with both engines inoperative are presented in Emergency Procedures, Section V.

Changed 1 June 1969

11-99

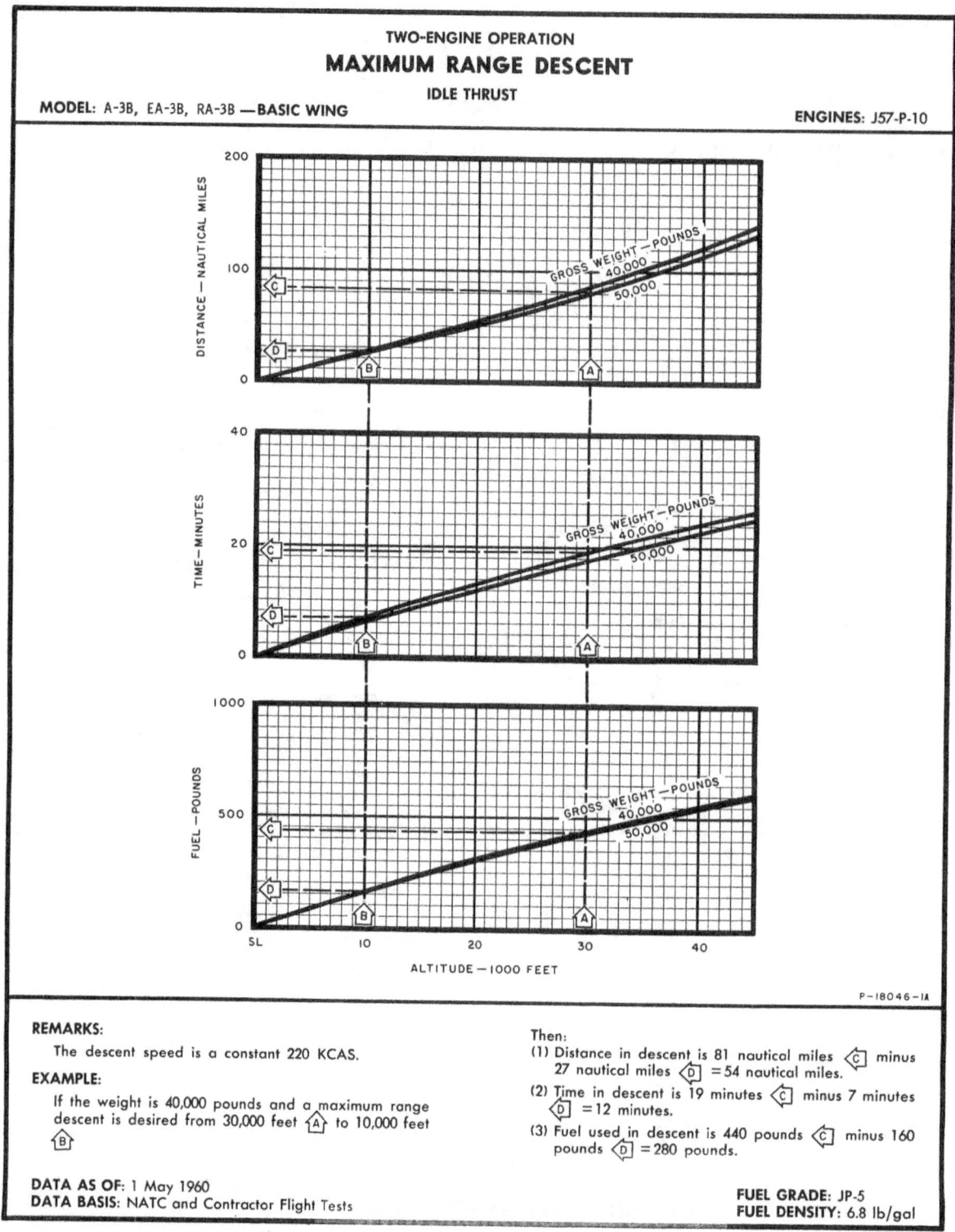

Figure 11-55. Maximum Range Descent (Sheet 1)

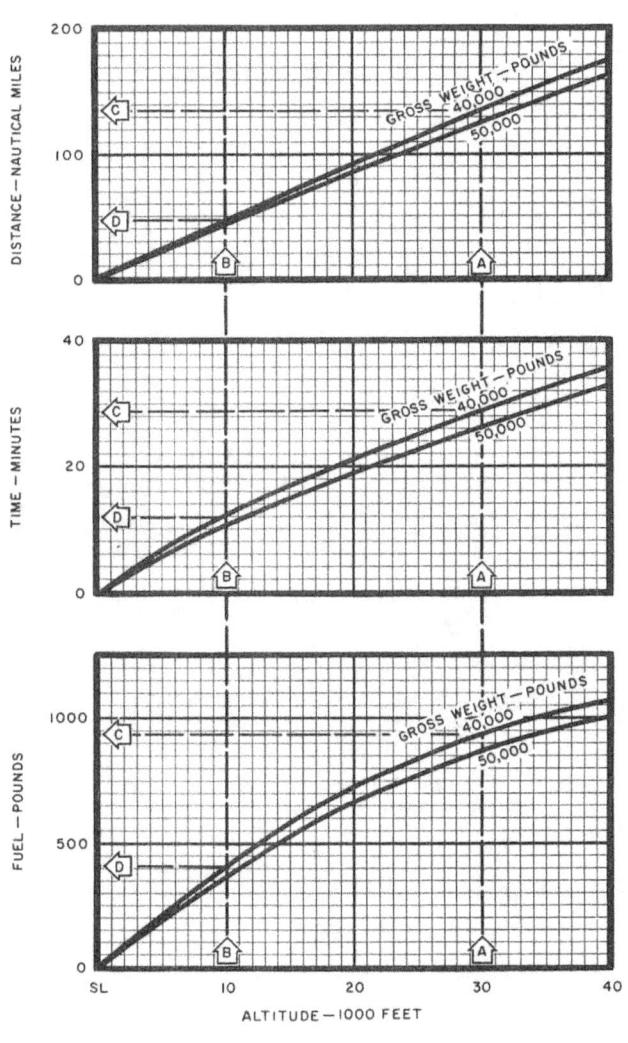

Figure 11-55. Maximum Range Descent (Sheet 2)

PART 7
LANDING

TABLE OF CONTENTS

TEXT

	Page		Page
Approach Charts	11-103	Landing Charts	11-103

ILLUSTRATIONS

Figure		Page	Figure		Page
11-56	Recommended Approach Speeds and Stall Speeds	11-104	11-57	Landing Ground Roll	11-105

Approach Charts

RECOMMENDED APPROACH SPEEDS AND STALL SPEEDS

The recommended approach and stall speed chart (figure 11-56) represents approach and stall speeds, along with the corresponding angle-of-attack units, as a function of gross weight. Figure 11-56 also shows the effect of bank angle on stall speed. Fifteen units for full and half flaps on a properly calibrated angle-of-attack indicator represents the correct approach speed. It is recommended, however, that the angle-of-attack indicator be checked against the aircraft indicated airspeed reading during the approach on each flight. If the 15 units do not indicate the airspeeds shown on figure 11-56, disregard the angle-of-attack indicator and make the approach at the proper indicated airspeed.

EXAMPLE:

Basic Wing Approach Speed
(For figure 11-56)

(A) Gross weight . . . . 44,000 lb

(B) Approach Speed (Half Flaps) . . . . 129.5 kts
Angle of attack . . . . 15 units

Landing Charts

LANDING GROUND ROLL

The landing ground roll distance of the aircraft is dependent upon outside air temperature, runway pressure altitude, aircraft gross weight, flap setting, headwind, runway gradient, runway surface condition, and braking action. Minimum distance requires that the throttles be reduced to idle power at touchdown and maximum braking, without skidding the tires, maintained during the entire ground roll. Ground roll distances for a dry, wet, and snow and ice covered hard runway surface, using drag chute, are presented on figure 11-57, sheets 1, 2, and 3 respectively. These distances are calculated based on the assumptions that the drag chute is actuated at touchdown and that 2 seconds are required for the drag chute to deploy. Figure 11-57, sheets 4, 5, and 6, presents ground roll distances for the same runway conditions without the drag chute. To clear a 50-foot obstacle, an additional 715 feet must be added to the total ground roll distance.

EXAMPLE:

Landing Distance
(For figure 11-57)

(A) Outside Air Temperature . . . . . . 10°C

(B) Runway Pressure Altitude . . . . 2000 ft

(C) Landing Gross Weight . . . . 44,000 lb

(D) Flap Deflection . . . . Half

(E) Headwind . . . . 20 kts

(F) Runway Gradient . . . . -1 percent

(G) Landing Ground Roll Distance . . . 5050 ft

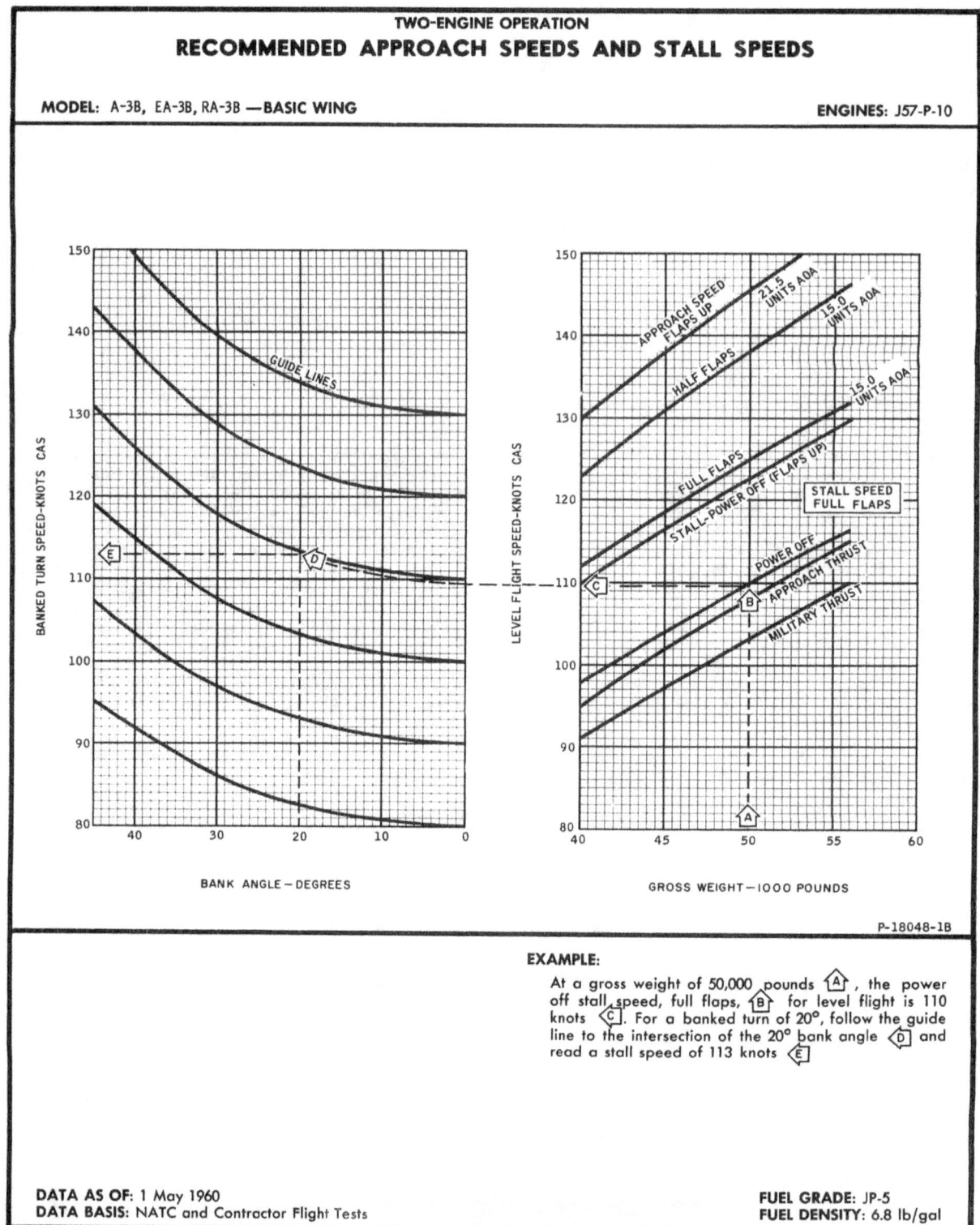

Figure 11-56. Recommended Approach Speeds and Stall Speeds

NAVAIR 01-40ATA-1
Section XI
Part 7

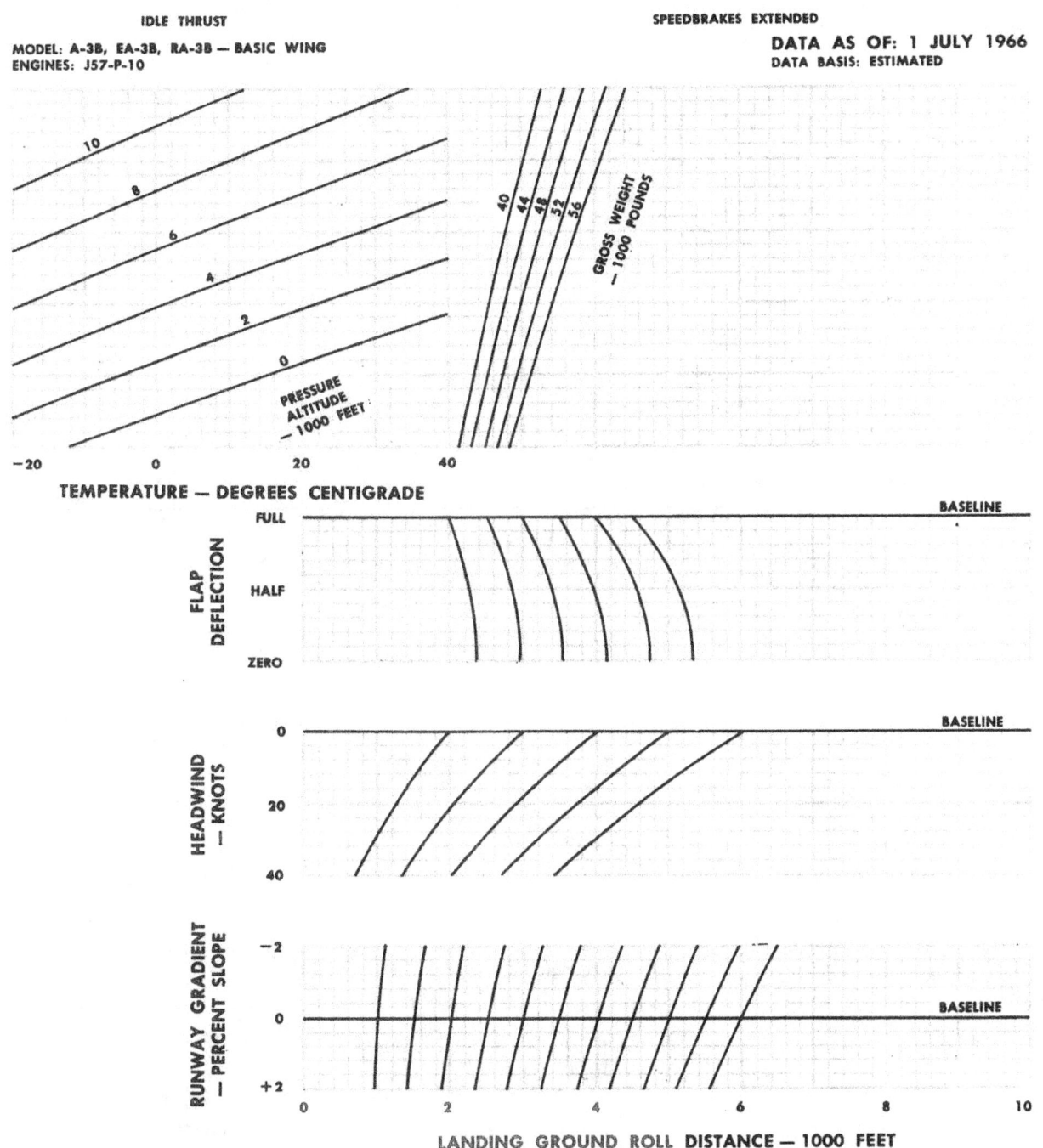

Figure 11-57. Landing Ground Roll (Sheet 1)

11-105

Section XI
Part 7

NAVAIR 01-40ATA-1

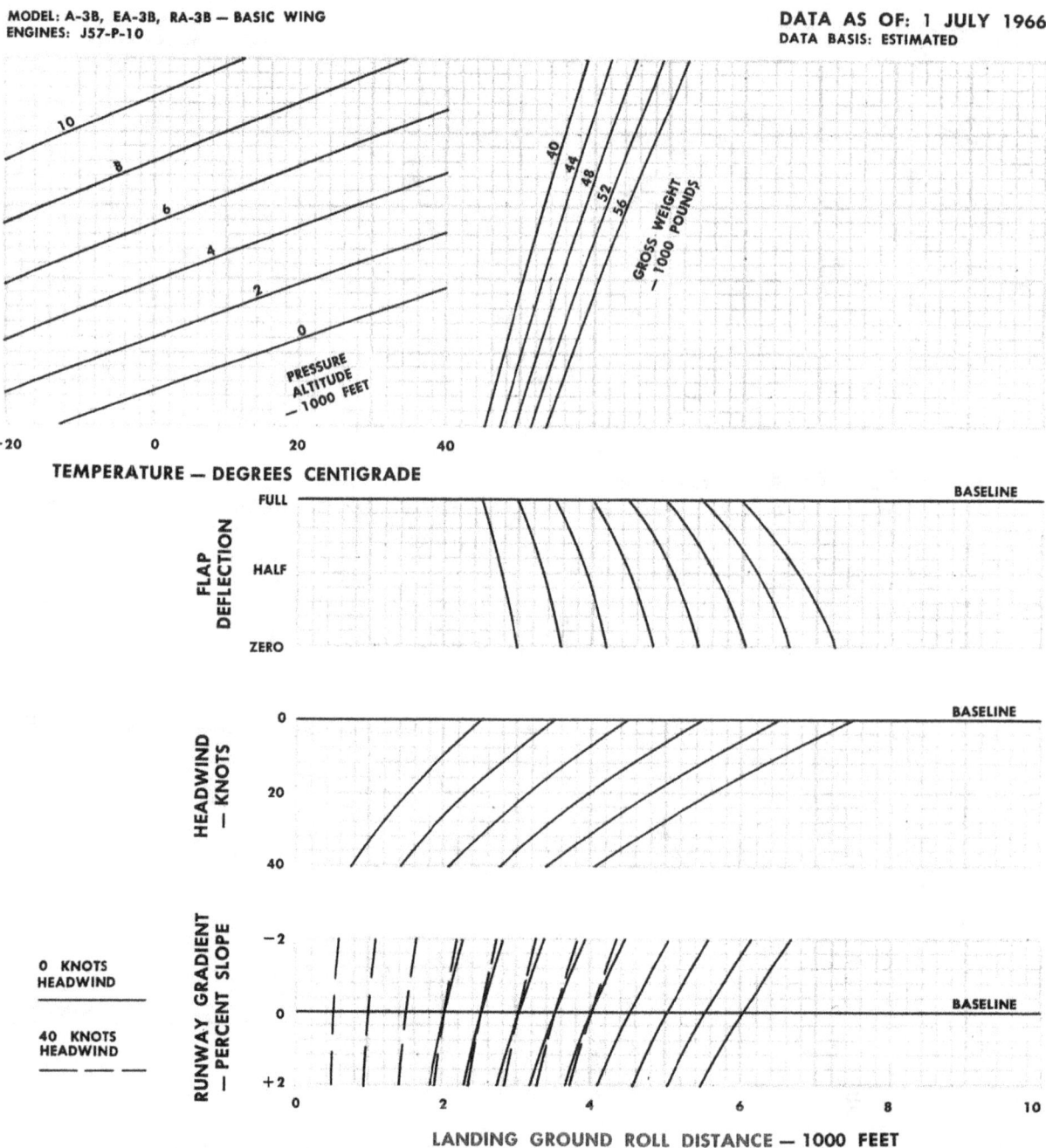

Figure 11-57. Landing Ground Roll (Sheet 2)

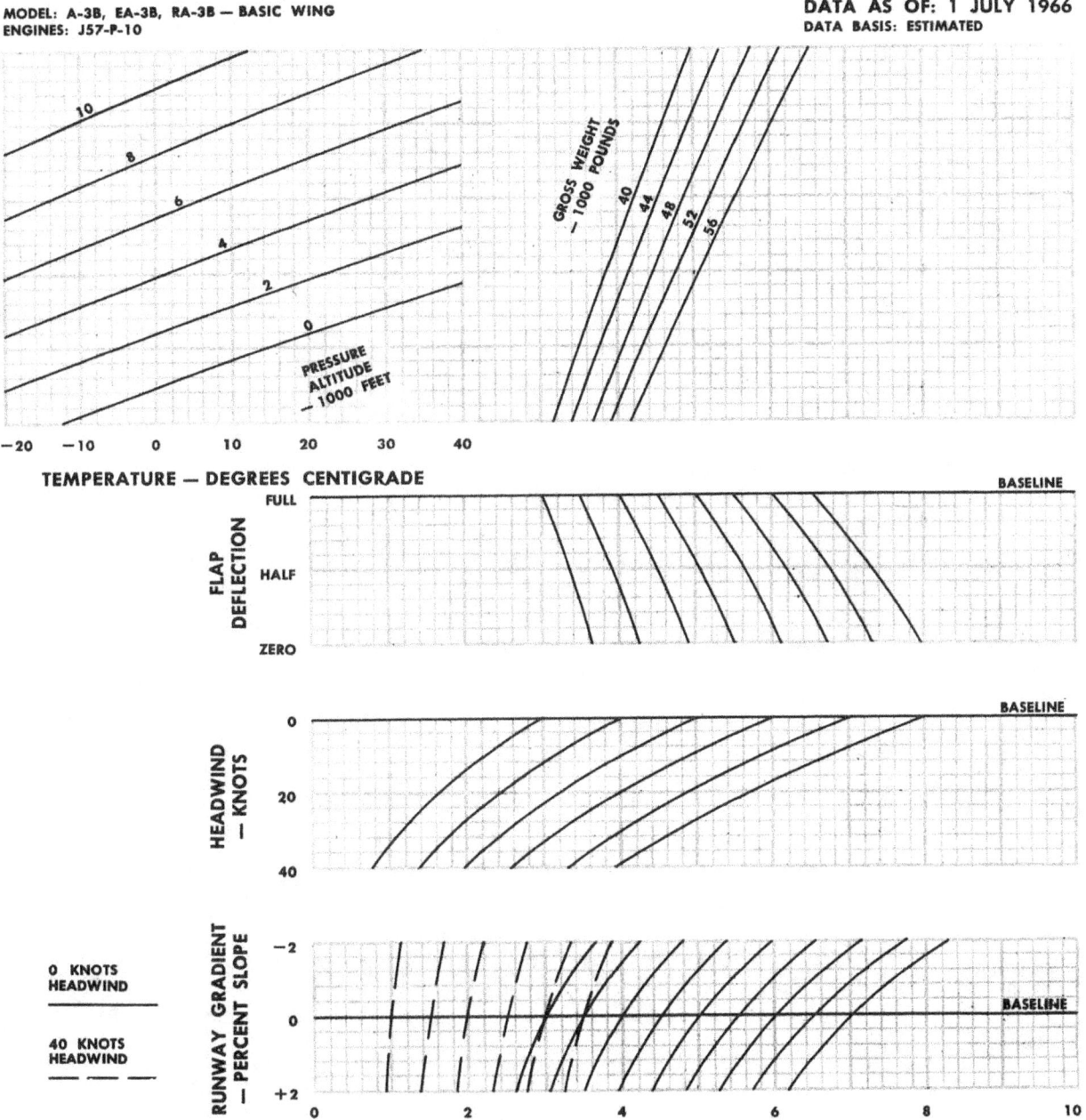

Figure 11-57. Landing Ground Roll (Sheet 3)

Section XI
Part 7

NAVAIR 01-40ATA-1

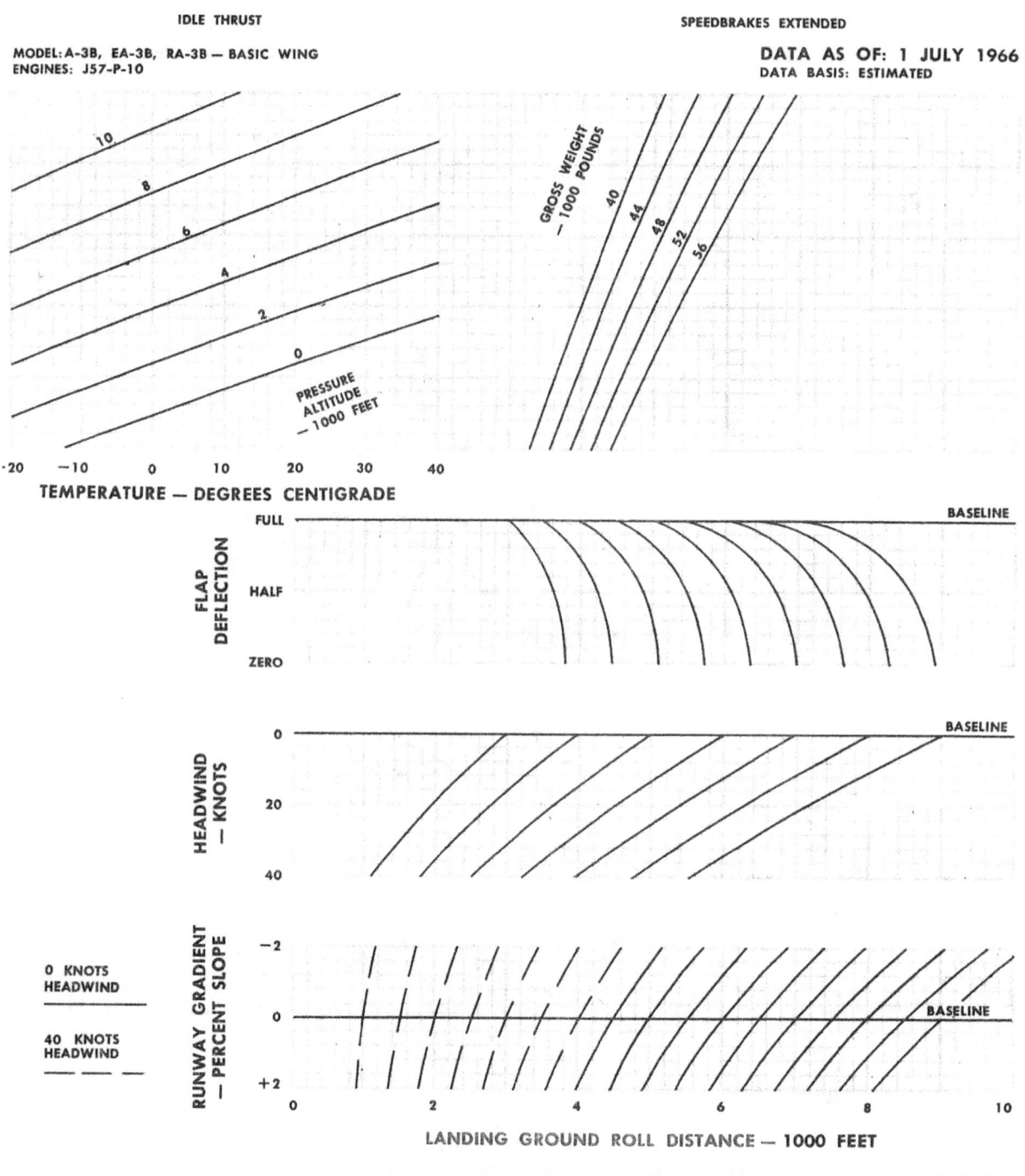

Figure 11-57. Landing Ground Roll (Sheet 4)

11-108

NAVAIR 01-40ATA-1

Section XI
Part 7

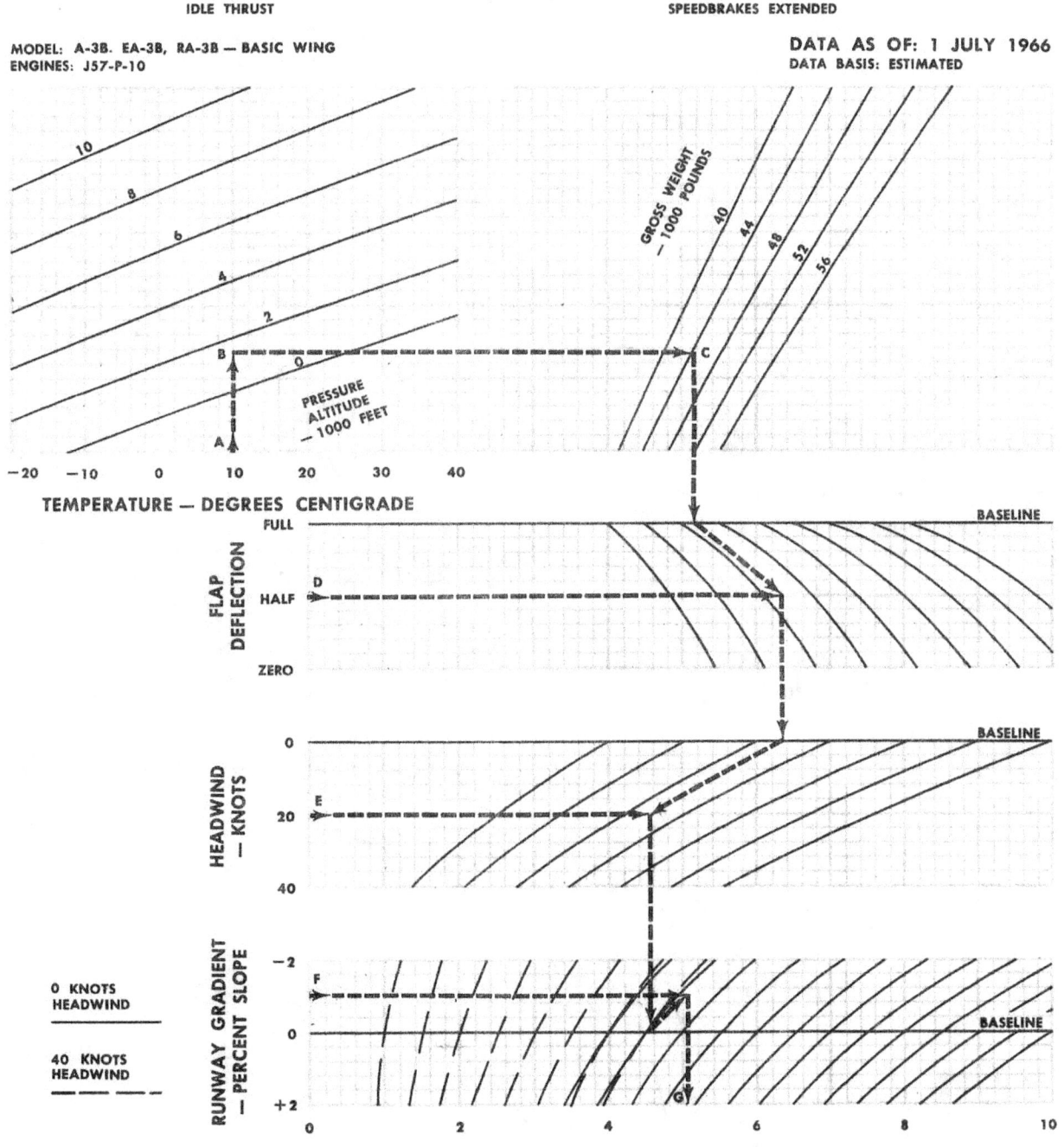

Figure 11-57. Landing Ground Roll (Sheet 5)

Section XI
Part 7

NAVAIR 01-40ATA-1

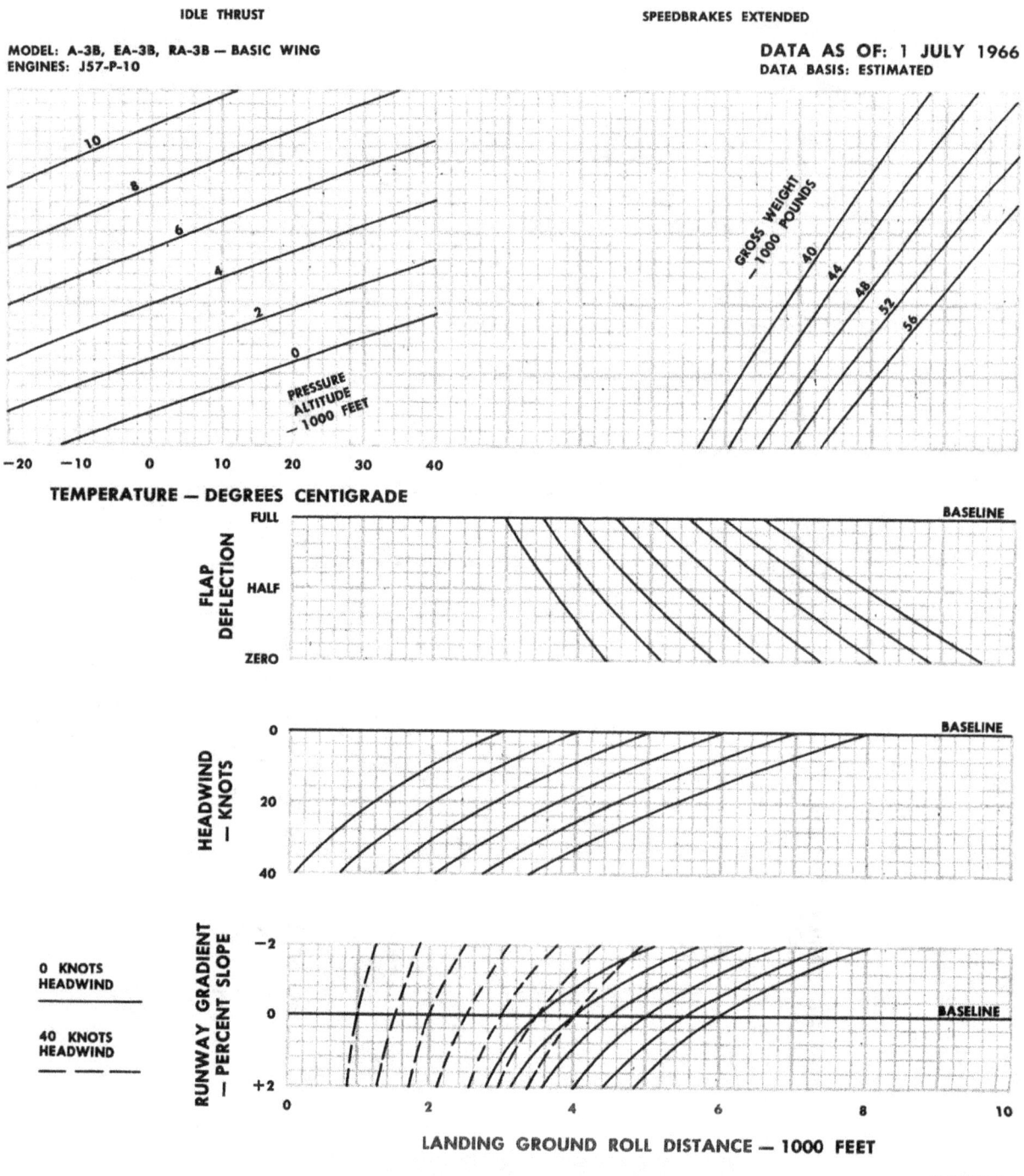

Figure 11-57. Landing Ground Roll (Sheet 6)

NAVAIR 01-40ATA-1

Section XI
Part 8

PART 8
COMBAT PERFORMANCE

TABLE OF CONTENTS

TEXT

	Page		Page
Combat Performance Charts	11-111	Maximum Continuous Power Summary Charts	11-111

ILLUSTRATIONS

Figure		Page	Figure		Page
11-58	Combat Allowance Chart	11-112	11-59	Maximum Continuous Power Summary	11-113

Combat Allowance Chart

Figure 11-58 presents the combat time available for various quantities of combat fuel as a function of altitude. These data are given for both military and normal thrust.

Maximum Continuous Power Summary Charts

These charts, shown in figure 11-59, sheets 1 and 2, are a summary of operating data for both one-engine and two-engine operation at maximum continuous power (normal thrust) for several gross weights. The airspeeds (CAS and TAS) and corresponding fuel consumption figures in pounds per hour per engine are representative of maximum speed in level flight at various altitudes with throttle(s) set at normal power.

Changed 1 June 1969

11-111

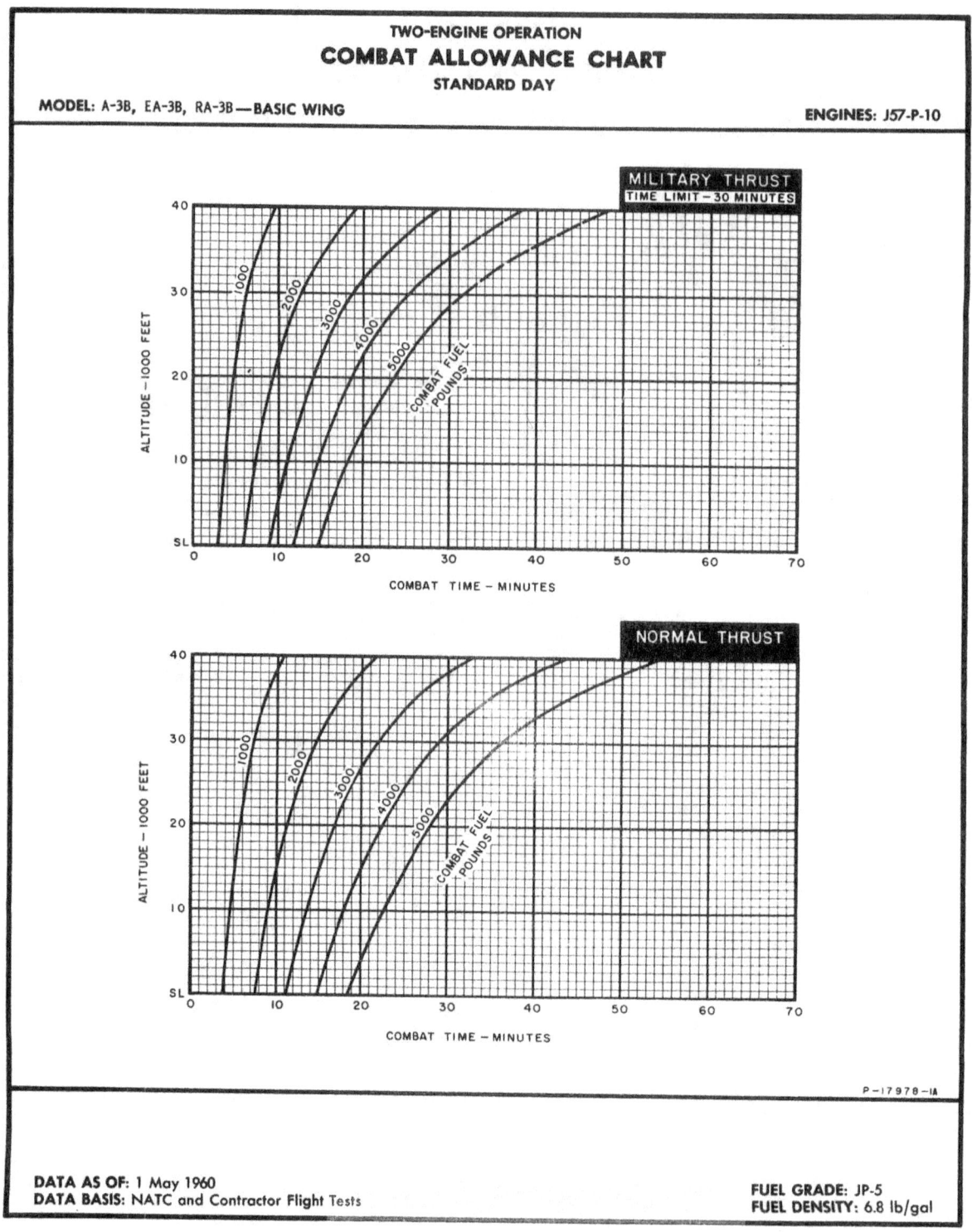

Figure 11-58. Combat Allowance Chart

MAXIMUM CONTINUOUS POWER SUMMARY
Two-Engine Operation

MODEL: A-3B, KA-3B, EA-3B, RA-3B — Basic Wing   Engines: J57-P-10

Clean Configuration Weight: 80,000 Pounds				Clean Configuration Weight: 70,000 Pounds		
Approximate			Pressure Altitude Feet	Approximate		
Pounds/Hour /Engine	TAS Knots	CAS Knots		CAS Knots	TAS Knots	Pounds/Hour /Engine
8200	535	535	Sea Level	535	535	8200
6600	535	470	10	475	540	6600
6050	535	440	15	440	535	6050
5650	530	405	20	405	530	5650
4850	520	370	25	370	525	4800
4150	510	330	30	335	515	4150
3400	485	285	35	295	495	3450

Clean Configuration Weight: 60,000 Pounds				Clean Configuration Weight: 50,000 Pounds		
Approximate			Pressure Altitude Feet	Approximate		
Pounds/Hour /Engine	TAS Knots	CAS Knots		CAS Knots	TAS Knots	Pounds/Hour /Engine
8200	540	540	Sea Level	540	540	8200
6600	540	475	10	475	540	6600
6050	535	440	15	440	540	6050
5650	530	405	20	410	535	5650
4750	525	370	25	375	530	4750
4150	520	340	30	340	520	4150
3400	505	300	35	305	510	3400
2750	490	260	40	265	500	2750
–	–	–	45	225	480	2050

Data as of: 1 May 1960
Data Basis: NATC and Contractor Flight Tests

Fuel Grade: JP-5
Fuel Density: 6.8 lb/gal

Figure 11-59. Maximum Continuous Power Summary (Sheet 1)

MAXIMUM CONTINUOUS POWER SUMMARY
One-Engine Operation

MODEL: A-3B, EA-3B, RA-3B — Basic Wing Engines: J57-P-10

Clean Configuration Weight: 80,000 Pounds				Clean Configuration Weight: 70,000 Pounds		
Approximate			Pressure Altitude Feet	Approximate		
Pounds/Hour /Engine	TAS Knots	CAS Knots		CAS Knots	TAS Knots	Pounds/Hour /Engine
7650	345	345	Sea Level	355	355	7650
6250	345	295	10	305	355	6250
–	–	–	15	275	340	5550

Clean Configuration Weight: 60,000 Pounds				Clean Configuration Weight: 50,000 Pounds		
Approximate			Pressure Altitude Feet	Approximate		
Pounds/Hour /Engine	TAS Knots	CAS Knots		CAS Knots	TAS Knots	Pounds/Hour /Engine
7700	365	365	Sea Level	370	370	7750
6300	370	325	10	335	385	6350
5650	375	300	15	315	390	5700
5000	380	275	20	295	395	5050
–	–	–	25	270	390	4350

Remarks:

(1) Inoperative engine windmilling.

(2) Normal thrust on operating engine.

Data as of: 1 May 1960
Data Basis: NATC and Contractor Flight Tests

Fuel Grade: JP-5
Fuel Density: 6.8 lb/gal

Figure 11-59. Maximum Continuous Power Summary (Sheet 2)

NAVAIR 01-40ATA-1

Section XI
Part 1A

A-3A AIRCRAFT
PERFORMANCE DATA CHARTS (J57-P-6B ENGINES)
TABLE OF CONTENTS

Part	Page	Part	Page
1A General	11-115	5A Endurance	11-177
2A Takeoff	11-123	6A Descent	11-183
3A Climb	11-135	7A Landing	11-187
4A Range	11-145	8A Combat Performance	11-189

PART 1A
GENERAL

TABLE OF CONTENTS

TEXT

	Page		Page
Introduction	11-115	Sample Problem Illustrating Use of	
Airspeed and Altitude Correction	11-115	Graphic Data	11-116

ILLUSTRATIONS

Figure	Page	Figure	Page
11-60 Airspeed and Altitude Correction for Position Error	11-120	11-61 Mach Number Correction for Position Error	11-121

INTRODUCTION

Section XI, Part 1A contains general data applicable to all A-3A aircraft equipped with J57-P-6B engines. The operating data charts contained in Section XI, Parts 1A through 8A, provide the pilot with information pertinent to the maximum performance capabilities of the aircraft.

CRUISE CONTROL COMPUTER

A cruise control computer is available for use with this aircraft. Its use provides a means for the rapid solution of mission planning problems and in-flight problems involving the determination of Range, Endurance, Speed and Time quantities. Operating instructions are packaged with each computer. A supply of REST Computers is provided each Navy operating activity upon first procurement of each new design computer. Additional supplies may be ordered from the Naval Supply Center. For the manufacturer's part number, see REST Computers listing.

Airspeed and Altitude Correction

AIRSPEED CORRECTIONS

To obtain true airspeed, several corrections must be applied to the airspeed indicator reading. Instrument error, which varies for each airspeed indicator as a result of manufacturing tolerances, is noted on the instrument calibration card. This error is usually small and normally may be disregarded, in which case the instrument reading is the actual indicated airspeed (IAS).

The position error correction determined for each location of the static pressure source is added to indicated airspeed to obtain calibrated airspeed, or CAS as indicated in figure 11-60. A Mach number correction for position error is included in figure 11-61.

The A-3A aircraft has the static source located at station 76, with the exception of BuNo. 135407,

REST COMPUTER

Aircraft	Federal Stock No.	Manufacturer's Part No.	Configurations
A-3A	RM6605-606-5848-V170	APN-51	A. Gross Weight — 45,000 B. Gross Weight — 55,000 C. Gross Weight — 65,000

Changed 1 June 1969

11-115

135409, and 135410. If there is any doubt as to the location of the static source, it may be necessary to inspect the aircraft to determine the location. Station 76 has the plate and bump or the channel and bump. Station 183 has the channel and angle static source. After determining the above, the proper calibration curve can be selected.

True airspeed (TAS) and Mach number are read directly from figure 11-1, using known calibrated airspeed, outside air temperature and true pressure altitude. To obtain equivalent airspeed (EAS), true airspeed is multiplied to $\sqrt{\sigma}$ corresponding to pressure altitude and ambient temperature.

True ambient temperature is obtained by applying a temperature correction increment, which includes installation and compressibility error, to the cockpit temperature indicator reading (which is always high). This temperature correction increment may be obtained from figure 11-2, Temperature Correction for Compressibility.

Using the corrected temperature, the value for $\sqrt{\sigma}$ may then be obtained from figure 11-3. Similar data may be obtained from the Standard Altitude Table, figure 11-4, when standard atmospheric conditions are desired.

EXAMPLE: Assume the aircraft is at a pressure altitude of 25,000 feet, with an airspeed indicator reading of 360 knots and a temperature indicator reading of +37°C. Assuming zero instrument error, correct ambient temperature and true airspeed are then found as follows:

Airspeed indicator reading . . . . 360 knots

Correction for instrument error . . . . . . 0 knots

Indicated airspeed . . . . 360 knots

Correction for position error
(figure 11-60) . . . . 0 knots

Calibrated airspeed . . . . 360 knots

Temperature indicator reading . . . . +37°C

Correction for instrument error 0

Indicated temperature . . . . +37°C

Correction for compressibility
(see figure 11-2, sheet 2) . . . . -27°C

Ambient temperature . . . . +10°C

Then Mach No. = 0.85 and true airspeed = 512 knots under standard day conditions. (figure 11-1.)

At 25,000 feet pressure altitude with an ambient temperature of +10°C, true airspeed = 556 knots. (figure 11-1.)

Conversely, the indicated pressure altitude required to establish a selected true pressure altitude can be determined by subtracting algebraically the position error correction provided by figure 11-60, as follows:

Selected true pressure altitude . . . . 20,000 feet

Instrument error (assumed) . . . . 0 feet

Indicated airspeed . . . . 425 knots

Altitude correction . . . . 250 feet

Required indicated pressure
altitude 20,000 - (250) . . . . 19,750 feet

ALTITUDE CORRECTIONS

Instrument error and position error corrections similar to those applied for airspeed indicator readings, must be applied to the indicated altimeter readings to obtain true pressure altitude. Figure 11-60 provides the correction necessary to compensate for the installation.

EXAMPLE: Assume the A-3A aircraft is at an indicated pressure altitude of 20,000 feet with an airspeed indicator reading of 430 knots. The true pressure altitude, assuming zero instrument error, is obtained by the following method:

Altimeter reading . . . . 20,000 feet

Correction for instrument error
(assumed) . . . . 0 feet

Indicated airspeed . . . . 430 knots

Altimeter correction for position
error (figure 11-60) . . . . +500 feet

True pressure altitude . . . . 20,500 feet

MACH NUMBER CORRECTIONS

Instrument error and position error corrections must be applied to the indicated Mach number readings (IMN) to obtain a true Mach number reading (TMN). Figure 11-61 incorporates the position error correction to make possible direct reading of true Mach number. For all flight in the permissible airspeed range, this correction is virtually zero.

Sample Problem Illustrating Use of Graphical Data

Preflight planning for a complete mission will, in practical operations, be subject to variable factors such as wind conditions and tactical requirements. In the following sample problem, the constant cruise-out altitude coincides with the bomb run altitude to simplify calculations.

BASIC FLIGHT PLAN: With a takeoff weight of 70,000 pounds and a fuel load of 22,000 pounds, deliver an 8700-pound bomb load 800 nautical miles from base and return. Make a 15-minute bomb run on course with military thrust at 35,000 feet.

FIND: Total mission time and fuel reserve if the cruise is made at a speed for maximum range with a cruise-out altitude of 35,000 feet and cruise-back altitude of 40,000 feet.

SOLUTION

1. The fuel allowance for starting engines, taxiing, takeoff, and acceleration to best climb airspeed is 1050 pounds (based on 5 minutes static sea level operation with normal power). The initial climb weight is:

70,000 - 1050 = 68,950 pounds.

2. Climb to 35,000 feet. From the Climb charts (figures 11-72 and 11-73) the following climb data are obtained for 68,950 pounds initial climb gross weight at sea level:

Time = 14.1 minutes, Fuel = 2390 pounds, Distance = 95 nautical miles.

Maintain the climb airspeed schedule shown on the charts.

NOTE

Since the bomb run in this example is made on course at military thrust, the distance covered in the bomb run must be determined before the fuel required for cruising the remaining distance on the outbound leg can be calculated.

3. Bomb Run. The average gross weight during bomb run may be estimated by taking the gross weight before takeoff less 50 percent of the usable fuel, as follows:

$$70,000 - \frac{22,000}{2} = 59,000 \text{ pounds}$$

From the applicable Specific Range chart (Nautical Miles Per 1000 Pounds of Fuel), figure 11-85, sheet 8, the maximum airspeed during the bomb run is 305 knots CAS (510 knots TAS or 0.886 Mach). The distance covered during the bomb run is equal to:

$$510 \times \frac{15}{60} = 127 \text{ nautical miles}$$

The Combat Allowance chart (figure 11-94) shows the fuel used at maximum thrust to achieve the desired airspeed. The fuel used at 35,000 feet, at maximum thrust, for a period of 15 minutes, can be determined from the graph. The result will be the amount of fuel used by both engines. Total fuel required for the bomb run is 1900 pounds.

4. Cruise Out. The required cruise-out distance is equal to:

800 - 95 (climb distance out, figure 11-72, sheet 2) - 127 (bomb run) = 578 nautical miles.

The gross weight at the start of cruise is equal to:

68,950 - 2,390 (fuel consumed, figure 11-71) = 66,560 pounds.

For a cruise at maximum range airspeed, the fuel required for cruise out is calculated from the Specific Range chart, figure 11-85, sheet 8. For 66,560 pounds initial cruise weight at 35,000 feet pressure altitude, the distance per 1000 pounds of fuel as shown on the chart is 91 nautical miles.

The estimated cruise-out fuel is obtained by dividing the required cruise-out distance of 578 nautical miles by 91 nautical miles per 1000 pounds of fuel; this results in 6350 pounds of fuel required for cruise out. To obtain the average cruise-out weight it is necessary to use the estimated 6350 pounds of fuel required for cruise out and divide by 2. The result subtracted from the initial cruise-out weight of 66,560 pounds will give the average cruise-out weight.

$$66,560 - \frac{6350}{2} = 63,385 \text{ pounds}.$$

Read the Specific Range chart, figure 11-85, sheet 8, at 63,385 pounds. This will result in 95 nautical miles per 1000 pounds of fuel. Cruise-out fuel is:

578 nautical miles ÷ 95 nautical miles = 6090 pounds.

The cruise-out time is computed from the Specific Range chart, figure 11-85, sheet 8, at the average weight of 63,385 pounds. The TAS of 63,385 pounds at 35,000 feet is 448 knots as read from the Specific Range chart. Cruise-out time is obtained in the following manner:

578 nautical miles ÷ 448 KTAS = 1.29 hours, or 1 hour and 17.4 minutes.

5. Climb to 40,000 feet. After dropping the bomb load, the gross weight will be:

66,560 - 6090 - 1900 - 8700 = 49,870 pounds.

From the Climb chart (figures 11-71, 11-72, and 11-73) for 49,870 pounds initial climb gross weight at 35,000 feet, the following data are obtained for a climb on course to 40,000 feet:

Climb time = 11.5 minutes (to 40,000 feet) - 8.9 minutes (at 35,000 feet) = 2.6 minutes.

Climb distance = 80 nautical miles (at 40,000 feet) - 60 nautical miles (at 35,000 feet) = 20 nautical miles.

Climb fuel = 1800 pounds (at 40,000 feet) - 1550 pounds (at 35,000 feet) = 250 pounds.

6. Descent. In order to find the fuel required for the cruise back, the descent at the end of the flight must first be determined. This information can be obtained from the Maximum Range Descent chart (figure 11-91, sheet 1). Descent should be made at 220 KCAS, descent range is 112 nautical miles, descent time is 24 minutes, and fuel required is 550 pounds.

7. Cruise back. The required cruise-back distance is equal to:

800 - 20 (climb distance) - 112 (descent distance) = 668 nautical miles.

The initial cruise-back gross weight is equal to:

49,870 - 250 = 49,620 pounds.

The fuel required for cruise back is calculated from the Specific Range chart, figure 11-85, sheet 9. For 49,620 pounds cruise-back gross weight at 40,000 feet pressure altitude, the distance per 1000 pounds of fuel as shown on the chart is 116 nautical miles. The estimated cruise-back fuel is obtained by dividing the cruise-back distance of 668 nautical miles by 116 nautical miles per 1000 pounds of fuel. The result is:

668 ÷ 116 x 1000 = 5750 pounds.

To obtain the average cruise-back weight, it is necessary to use the estimated 5750 pounds of fuel required for cruise back and divide by 2. This amount subtracted from the initial cruise-back gross weight of 49,620 pounds will give the average cruise-back weight

$$49,620 - \frac{5750}{2} = 46,745 \text{ pounds}.$$

Read the Specific Range chart, figure 11-85, sheet 9 at 46,745 pounds. This will result in 122 nautical miles per 1000 pounds of fuel. Cruise-back fuel is:

668 ÷ 122 x 1000 = 5460 pounds.

The cruise-back time is computed from the Specific Range chart, figure 11-85, sheet 9 at the average weight of 46,745 pounds. The TAS at 40,000 feet is 445 knots. Cruise-back time is obtained in the following manner:

668 nautical miles ÷ 445 KTAS = 1.5 hours or 1 hour and 30 minutes.

Total mission time (excluding takeoff, acceleration to climb speed at sea level, and time available with reserve fuel) is:

14.1 + 1:17.4 + 15 + 2.6 + 1:30.0 + 24.0 = 3 hours 43 minutes.

8. Reserve. The fuel remaining after a maximum range descent to sea level is computed as follows:

22,000 - 1050 - 2390 - 6090 - 1900 - 250 - 5460 - 550 = 4310 pounds.

If maximum flight time at sea level for this quantity of fuel is desired (after allowing 1000 pounds of fuel for landing), refer to the Specific Range chart (figure 11-85, sheet 1). The gross weight at the end of the descent is:

49,620 - 5460 - 550 = 43,610 pounds

and the gross weight at the end of this maximum endurance period is:

43,610 - 3310 = 40,300 pounds.

An average gross weight for the endurance period is determined by deducting half the weight of the fuel reserve from the gross weight at the end of descent:

$$43,610 - \frac{3310}{2} = 41,960 \text{ pounds.}$$

From figure 11-85, sheet 1, at 41,960 pounds average gross weight, the maximum endurance speed is 195 knots, from figure 11-90, sheet 1, the specific endurance is 0.253 hours per 1000 pounds of fuel. Applying the fuel reserve to this figure, maximum endurance time is found to be:

$$0.253 \times \frac{3310}{1000} \times 60 = 50.2 \text{ minutes.}$$

From the specific endurance, the fuel flow per engine is:

$$\frac{1000}{0.253} \times \frac{1}{2} = 1975 \text{ pounds per hour per engine.}$$

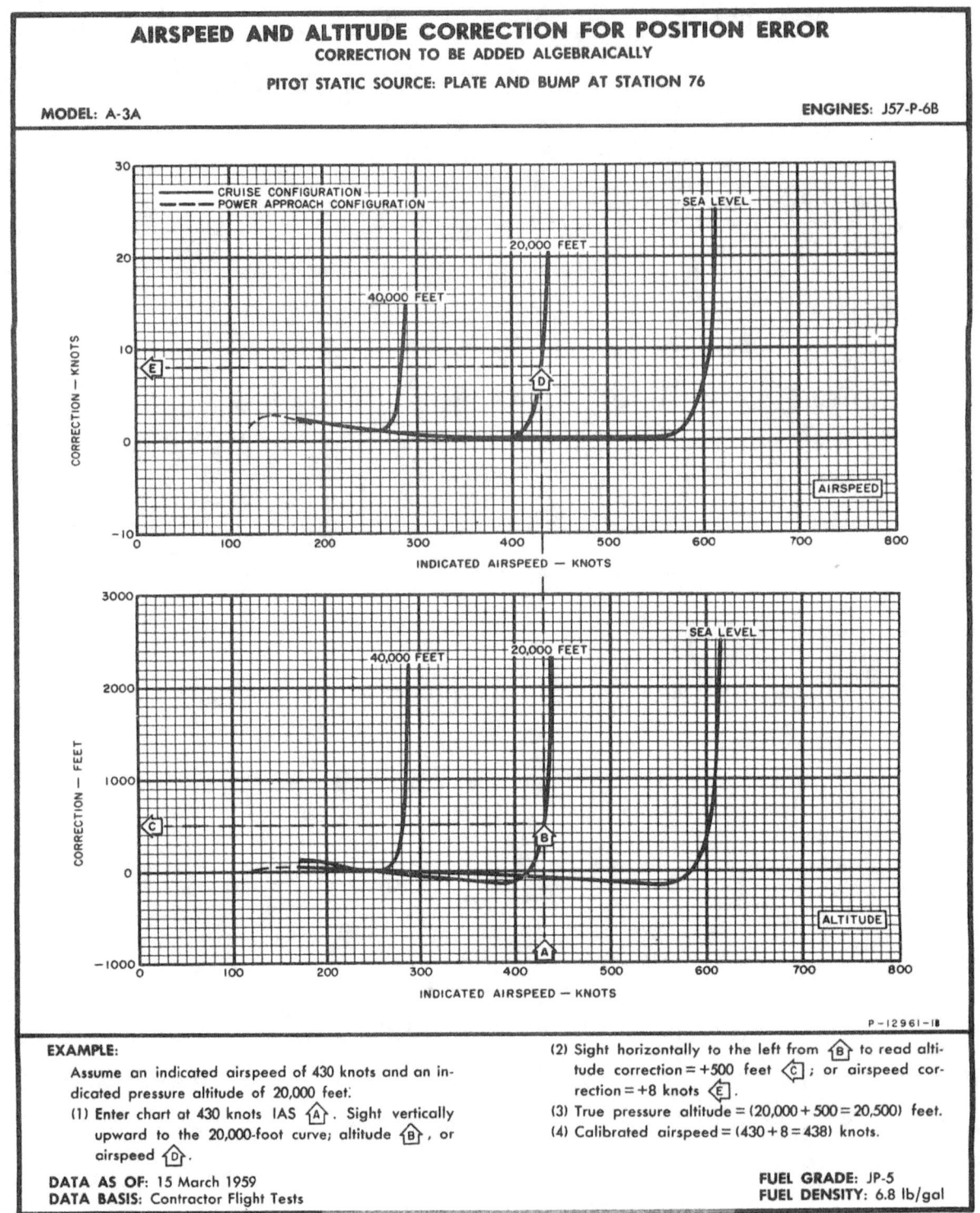

Figure 11-60. Airspeed and Altitude Correction for Position Error

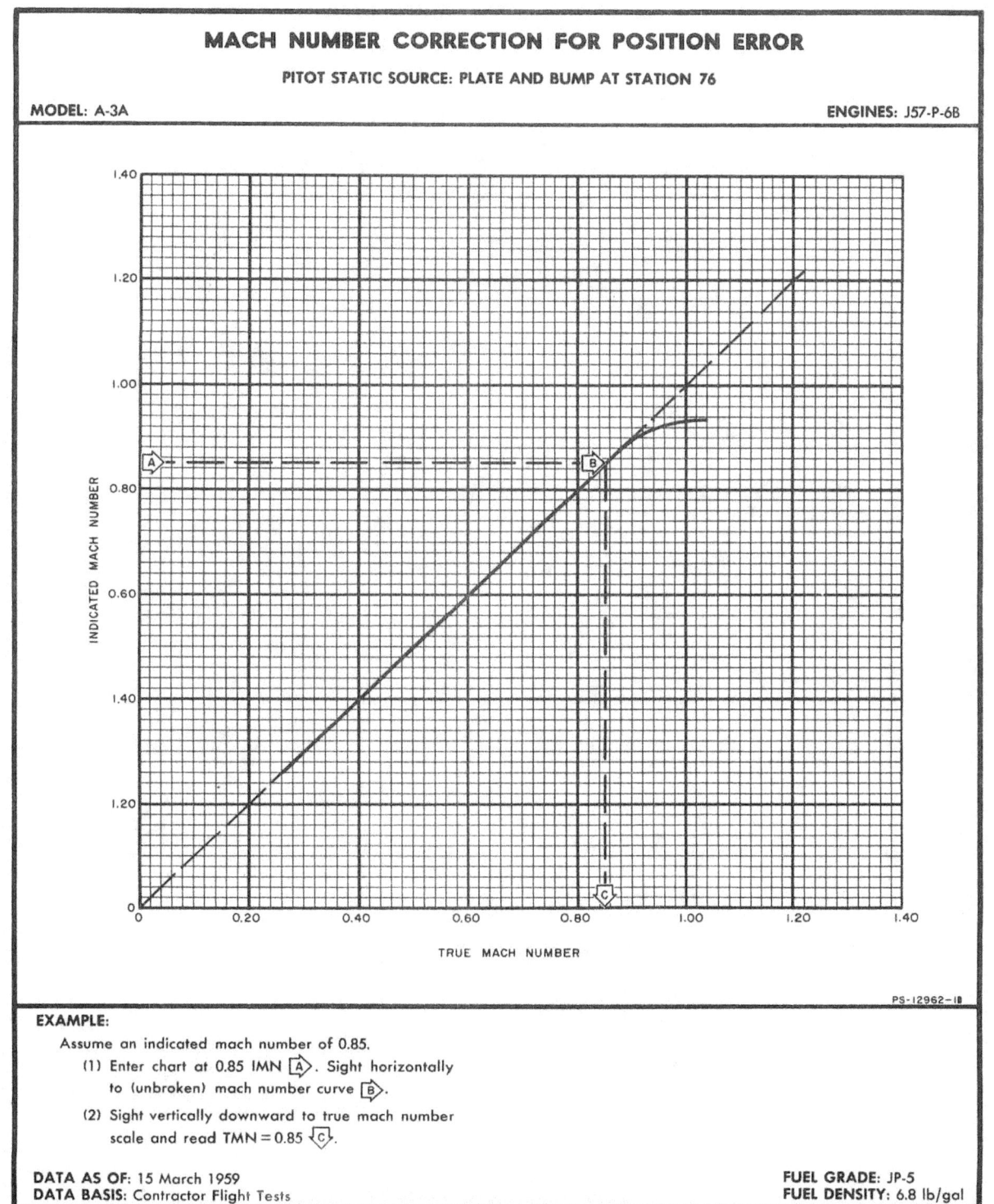

Figure 11-61. Mach Number Correction for Position Error

NAVAIR 01-40ATA-1

Section XI
Part 2A

PART 2A
TAKEOFF

TABLE OF CONTENTS

TEXT
Page

Takeoff Charts 11-123

ILLUSTRATIONS

Figure		Page
11-62	Recommended Liftoff Speed	11-126
11-63	Takeoff Distance	11-127
11-64	Maximum Recommended Takeoff Weight	11-128
11-65	Takeoff Distance Minimum Ground Roll – Four JATO Units (30° Nozzle)	11-129

Figure		Page
11-66	Takeoff Distance Ground Roll – Eight JATO Units (30° Nozzle)	11-130
11-67	Takeoff Minimum Ground Roll – 12 JATO Units (30° Nozzle)	11-131
11-68	Refusal Speeds	11-132
11-69	Refused Takeoff Stopping Distance	11-133

Takeoff Charts

The takeoff charts present the ground roll distance to clear a 50-foot obstacle, both with and without JATO assist, and for a hard surface runway with a zero runway gradient. The charts encompass such variables as takeoff weight, lift-off speed, ambient runway air temperature, runway pressure altitude, and headwind. Full flaps and MILITARY thrust are recommended for all takeoffs.

RECOMMENDED LIFT-OFF SPEED – NO JATO

Lift-off speeds are based on operational NATC recommended data and are shown on figure 11-62.

EXAMPLE: Given a takeoff weight of 65,000 pounds, a runway air temperature of 30°C, and a runway pressure altitude of 4000 feet:

1. Enter chart at 30°C (A). Sight horizontally to left to 4000-foot pressure altitude line (B).

2. Sight vertically from (B) to a gross weight of 65,000 pounds (C).

3. Proceed horizontally to right from (C) and read the recommended liftoff speed of 140 KIAS (D).

TAKEOFF DISTANCE – NO JATO

Takeoff distance and total distance to clear a 50-foot obstacle, without JATO assist, is shown on figure 11-63. The takeoff distances are based on operational NATC flight test data.

Note that there is a region in the temperature and altitude correction boxes where takeoff is marginal. This region represents an area where rate of climb after takeoff may be between 800 and 400 feet per minute and climbout capability is marginal. Since temperature and altitude are not independent, the boundary lines in these boxes are shown for extreme altitude-temperature combinations. In order to determine accurately if the rate of climb is less than 800 fpm, when operating in this region, refer to figure 11-64. A more detailed explanation of the marginal region is given in the following paragraphs under Maximum Takeoff Weight.

The method of obtaining the ground roll distance, total distance to clear a 50-foot obstacle, and a line speed check from the takeoff chart is described in the following examples.

EXAMPLE: Given a takeoff weight of 65,000 pounds, runway air temperature of 30°C, runway pressure altitude of 4000 feet, to determine takeoff ground roll distance and total distance to clear a 50-foot obstacle, proceed as follows:

1. Enter figure 11-63 at 140 KIAS (D) as determined from figure 11-62, and continue horizontally to the right to line representing takeoff weight of 65,000 pounds (E).

2. Sight vertically downward to temperature baseline and follow parallel to guidelines to temperature of 30°C (F).

3. Continue vertically downward to pressure altitude baseline, then parallel to guidelines to pressure altitude of 4000 feet (G).

4. Proceed vertically downward to headwind baseline, then parallel to guidelines to headwind of 10 knots (H).

5. Proceed vertically downward and read ground roll distance of 7150 feet (J).

6. Note that in step 3, point (G) fell in the region where takeoff is marginal. Therefore, check figure 11-64 to see if the rate of climb is less than 800 fpm. In making this check, note that for this temperature-altitude condition the maximum takeoff weight at 800 fpm rate of climb is 67,400 pounds. Therefore, at a gross weight of 65,000 pounds, the rate of climb is greater than 800 fpm and takeoff is not marginal in this case.

Changed 1 June 1969

11-123

Section XI
Part 2A

NAVAIR 01-40ATA-1

LINE SPEED CHECK

EXAMPLE: To determine a line speed check at the 2000-foot runway marker:

1. Enter the Takeoff Distance chart (figure 11-63) at ground roll distance of 2000 feet and proceed vertically upward to headwind of 10 knots, then parallel to guide lines to headwind baseline.

2. Continue vertically upward to pressure altitude of 4000 feet, then parallel to guidelines to altitude baseline.

3. Proceed vertically upward to temperature of 30°C, then parallel to guidelines to temperature baseline.

4. Proceed upward to takeoff weight of 65,000 pounds, then horizontally to left and read line speed of 87 KIAS.

MAXIMUM RECOMMENDED TAKEOFF WEIGHT – NO JATO

The maximum takeoff weight shown on figure 11-64 is given as a function of rate of climb after takeoff. The data basis for this chart assumes that the landing gear is fully extended, the aircraft is climbing out with MILITARY thrust and without the assist of ground effect.

A rate of climb of 800 fpm, which corresponds approximately to an excess thrust to weight ratio of 0.05, is considered as a minimum acceptable climbout rate where obstacle clearance is required. Takeoff weight limitations and rates of climb less than 800 fpm are shown for conditions where the climbout is made over flat terrain or over the water. Note that in this region the additional horizontal distances to clear a 50-foot obstacle are 2000 to 3000 feet. If flat terrain condition exists at the end of the runway for a considerable distance, takeoffs may be extended into the marginal region. The required technique would be to lift the aircraft off the runway, accelerate, and build up climbing speed while the gear is being retracted. After 10 to 15 seconds, the gear will be fully retracted and the reduced drag will permit more reasonable climbout. Rates of climb of less than 400 fpm are considered insufficient for attempted takeoff.

EXAMPLE: Given a runway air temperature of 30°C, a pressure altitude of 4000 feet, and flat terrain at the end of the runway which would permit a minimum rate of climb after takeoff of 750 fpm.

1. Enter figure 11-64 at temperature of 30°C (A) and sight horizontally to left to pressure altitude of 4000 feet (B).

2. From 4000 foot pressure altitude line (B), continue vertically to rate-of-climb baseline (C), represented by 800 fpm, then parallel to guidelines to point (D).

3. Point (D) is determined by entering at rate of climb of 750 fpm and proceeding horizontally to left to intersection of imaginary line drawn in step 2.

4. From point (D), proceed vertically and read maximum permitted takeoff weight, of 69,000 pounds (E).

5. Note that rate of climb of 800 fpm (C) with same configuration, maximum permitted takeoff weight is 67,400 pounds.

TAKEOFF DISTANCE MINIMUM GROUND ROLL – WITH JATO

Minimum ground roll distances shown in figure 11-65 will be obtained by stabilizing the power on both engines with the throttles in "full power" position before releasing the wheel brakes. Fire the JATO units 5 seconds before actual takeoff. Takeoff at the CAS corresponding to the takeoff weight as indicated on the chart (figure 11-67).

Corrections for the effects of wind on the ground run takeoff are shown. Lines of constant JATO firing speed are included to facilitate the determination of the optimum speed for firing the JATO units.

This chart also may be used to determine the necessary headwind for a given ground run with a specific takeoff weight and ambient temperature. Using the figure in this manner, the guidelines in the lower chart are followed to intersect the given deck run in feet and then the required headwind can be read on the lower left-hand scale.

EXAMPLE: Assume a takeoff is to be made at 70,000 pounds gross weight at pressure altitude of 3000 feet and an ambient temperature of 30°C. Enter chart vertically (figure 11-67) at 30°C (A), proceed to 3000 feet pressure altitude (B) and then proceed right to 70,000 pounds (C). Here read the takeoff speed at 135 knots CAS and interpolate for JATO firing speed, here 66 knots. Then move downward into air

11-124

temperature grid and follow guideline to intersection with the 30°C temperature line (A). From this point, move vertically downward to read zero wind takeoff distance of 2080 feet (D). For added condition of 30 knot headwind, move along guideline in headwind grid to intersection with the 30 knot headwind line (E) and then vertically to read ground roll of 1090 feet (F).

> **CAUTION**
>
> Avoid permitting aircraft to overrotate upon firing of JATO units in order to preclude scraping drag chute doors.

FIELD TAKEOFF – WITH JATO

The optimum firing time and aircraft velocity at firing vary with takeoff weight and number of JATO (MK 7 Mod 1, 5KS-4500 30° nozzle) units in the following manner:

Takeoff Weight In Pounds	No. of JATO Units	Firing Time From Brake Release In Seconds	Aircraft Speed At Time Firing In Knots Ind ±
55,000	4	8	54
	8	3	32
	12	0	0
60,000	4	11	68
	8	6	45
	12	3	23
70,000	4	20	93
	8	15	69
	12	12	50

The following takeoff speeds are minimums and should be increased by 5 knots for initial operation.

Takeoff Weight In Pounds	Takeoff Speed In Knots Calibrated
45,000	105
50,000	113
60,000	126
70,000	137

REFUSAL SPEEDS – NO JATO

Refusal speed is that speed at which the pilot can cut the power and still stop the aircraft on a runway of a specified length.

EXAMPLE: Assume a takeoff is to be made at 60,000 pounds gross weight (A) (dry concrete runway) under the following ambient conditions: 15°C air temperature (C) and 4000-foot pressure altitude (B). To determine the refusal speed enter the chart (figure 11-68) at (A) 60,000 pounds gross weight. Proceed horizontally to 4000 feet pressure altitude (B) then vertically down the grid to 15°C air temperature (C). Follow the line horizontally to the 8000 foot runway length (D) and vertically down again to 114 knots refusal speed (E). This is the maximum speed that can be reached and still enable the pilot to stop the aircraft on an 8000-foot runway.

REFUSED TAKEOFF STOPPING DISTANCE – NO JATO

The refused takeoff stopping distance is that distance required to stop an aircraft after it reached a specified speed. The flight condition to be taken into consideration are ground speed, gross weight, pressure altitude and air temperature.

EXAMPLE: Assume a ground speed of 112 KCAS (A) is reached, during takeoff, at a pressure altitude of 3000 feet (B) with an air temperature of 30°C (C) and takeoff weight of 70,000 pounds (D). Refer to figure 11-69 and enter the graph at the refusal speed of 112 knots (A), follow the guideline to 3000-foot pressure altitude (B), proceed horizontally to the temperature baseline, follow the guideline to the point where it meets the air temperature line of 30°C (C). Proceed horizontally once more to the aircraft takeoff weight of 70,000 pounds (D). Follow the graph line down to the stopping distance of 6900 feet (E).

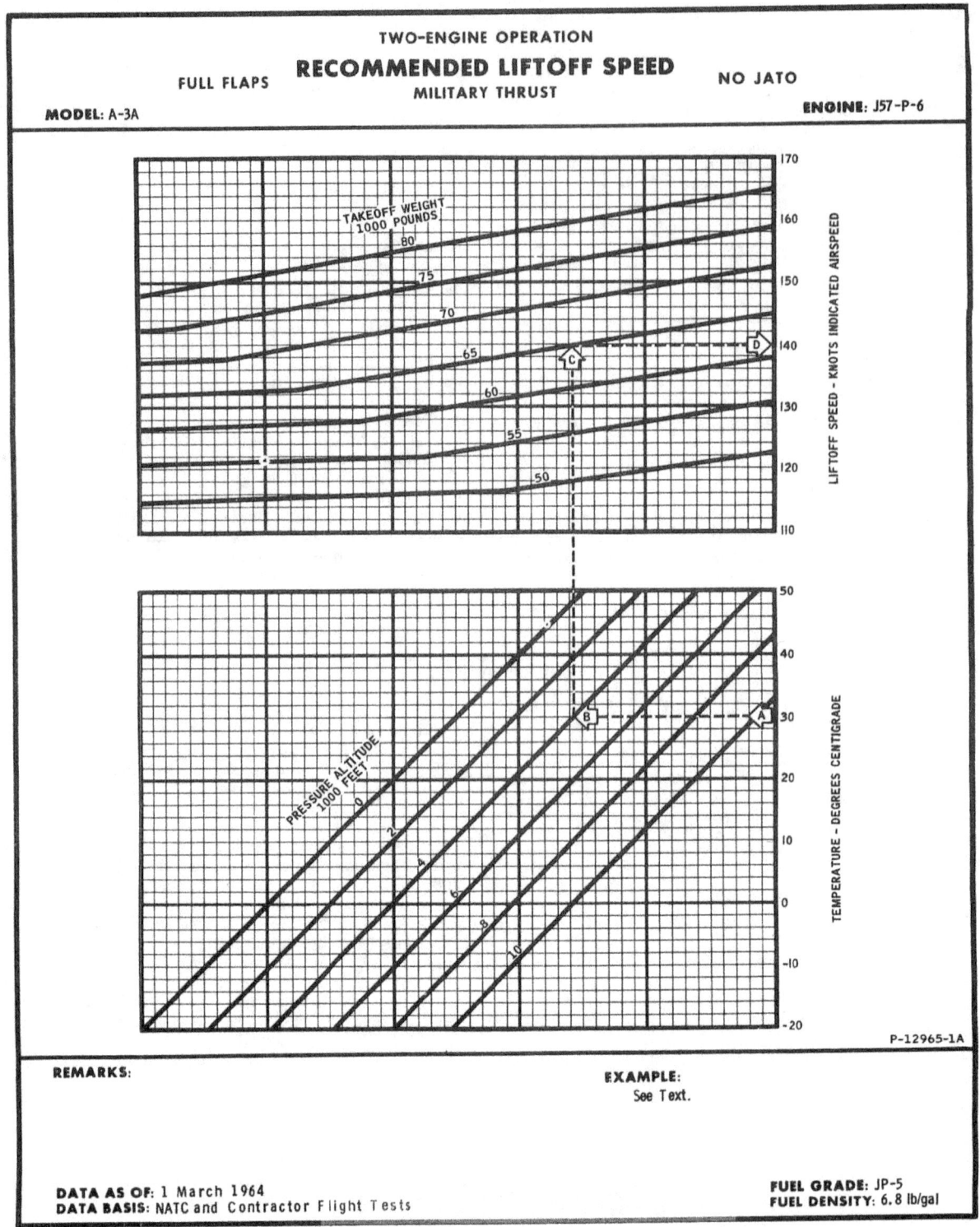

Figure 11-62. Recommended Liftoff Speed

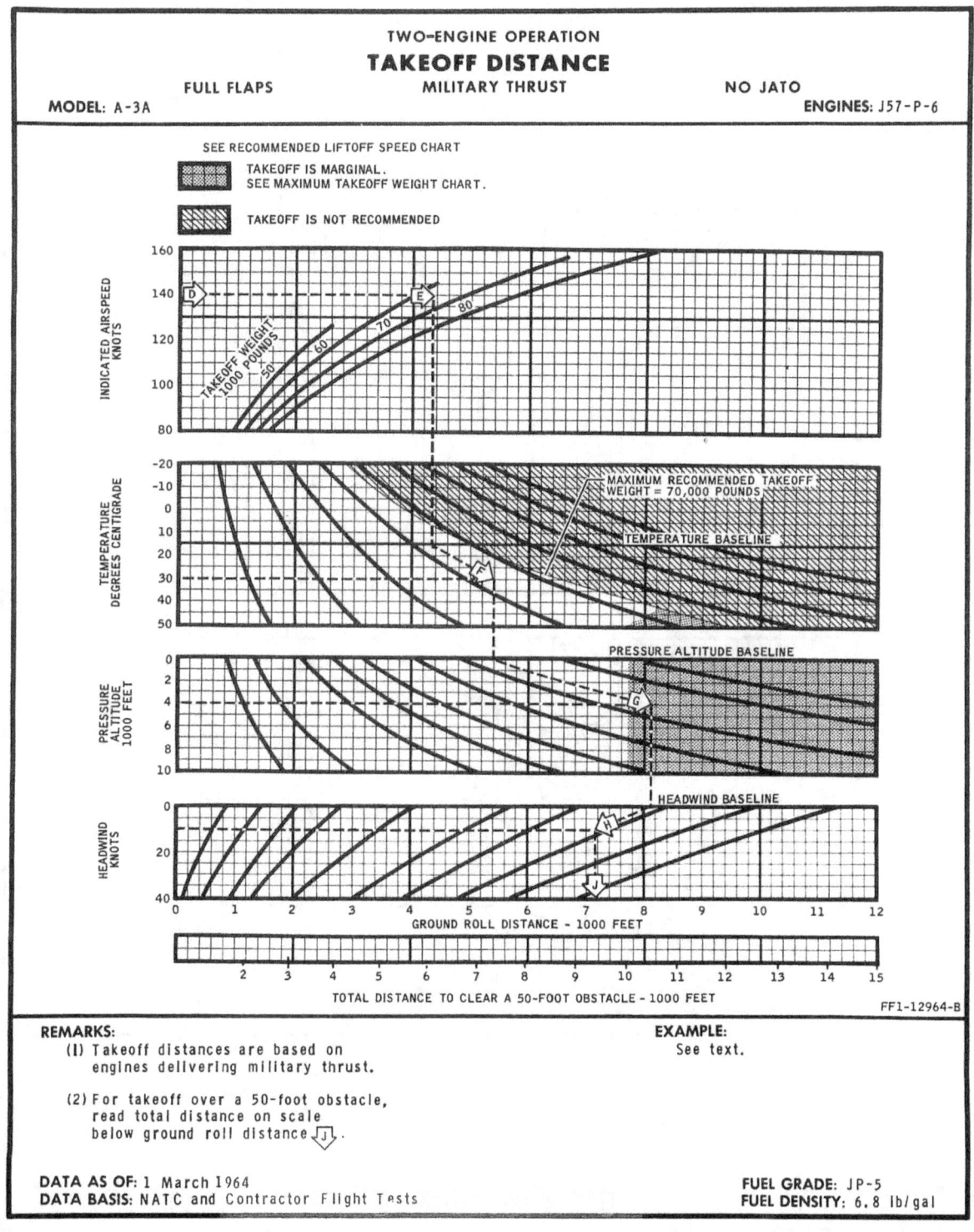

Figure 11-63. Takeoff Distance

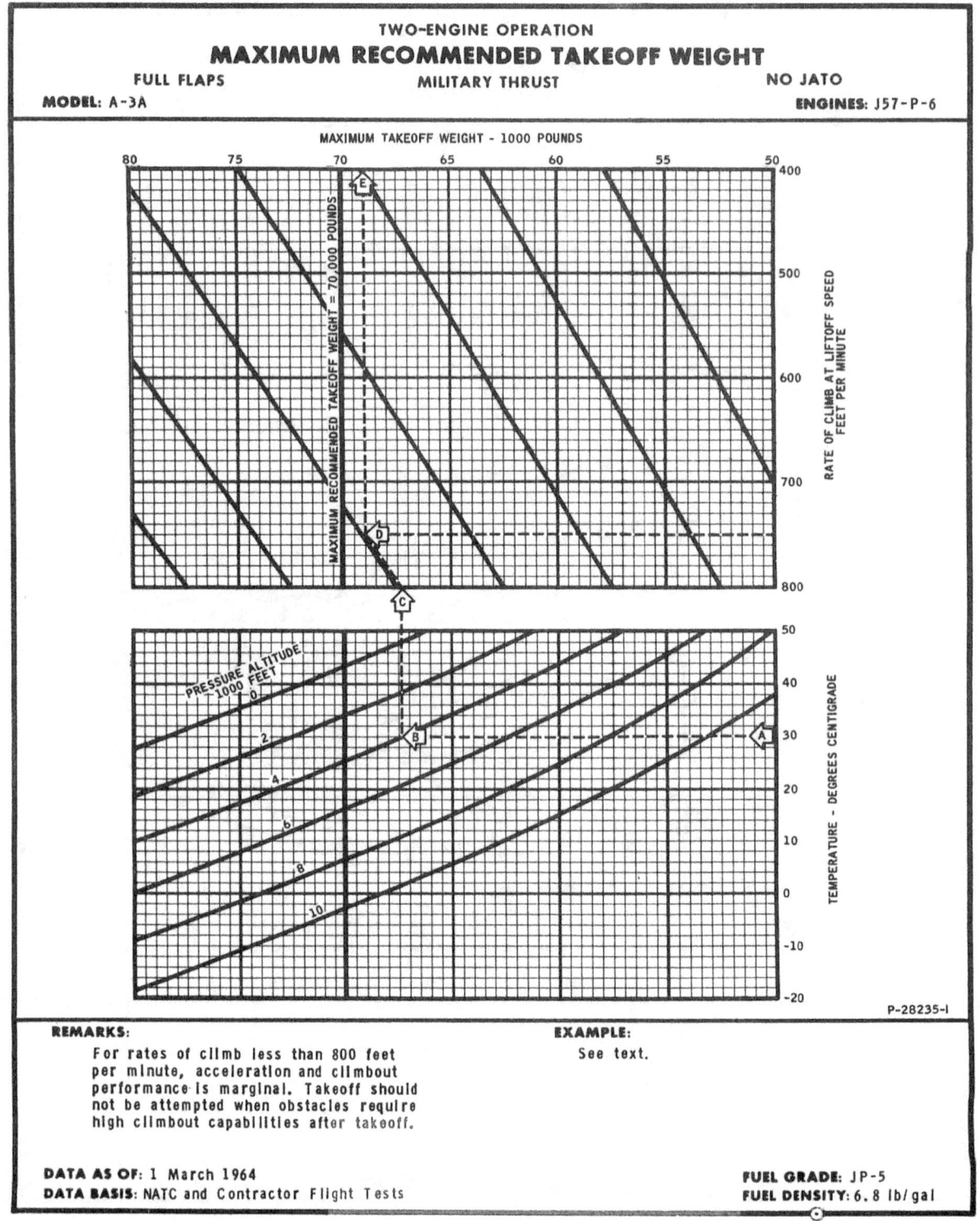

Figure 11-64. Maximum Recommended Takeoff Weight

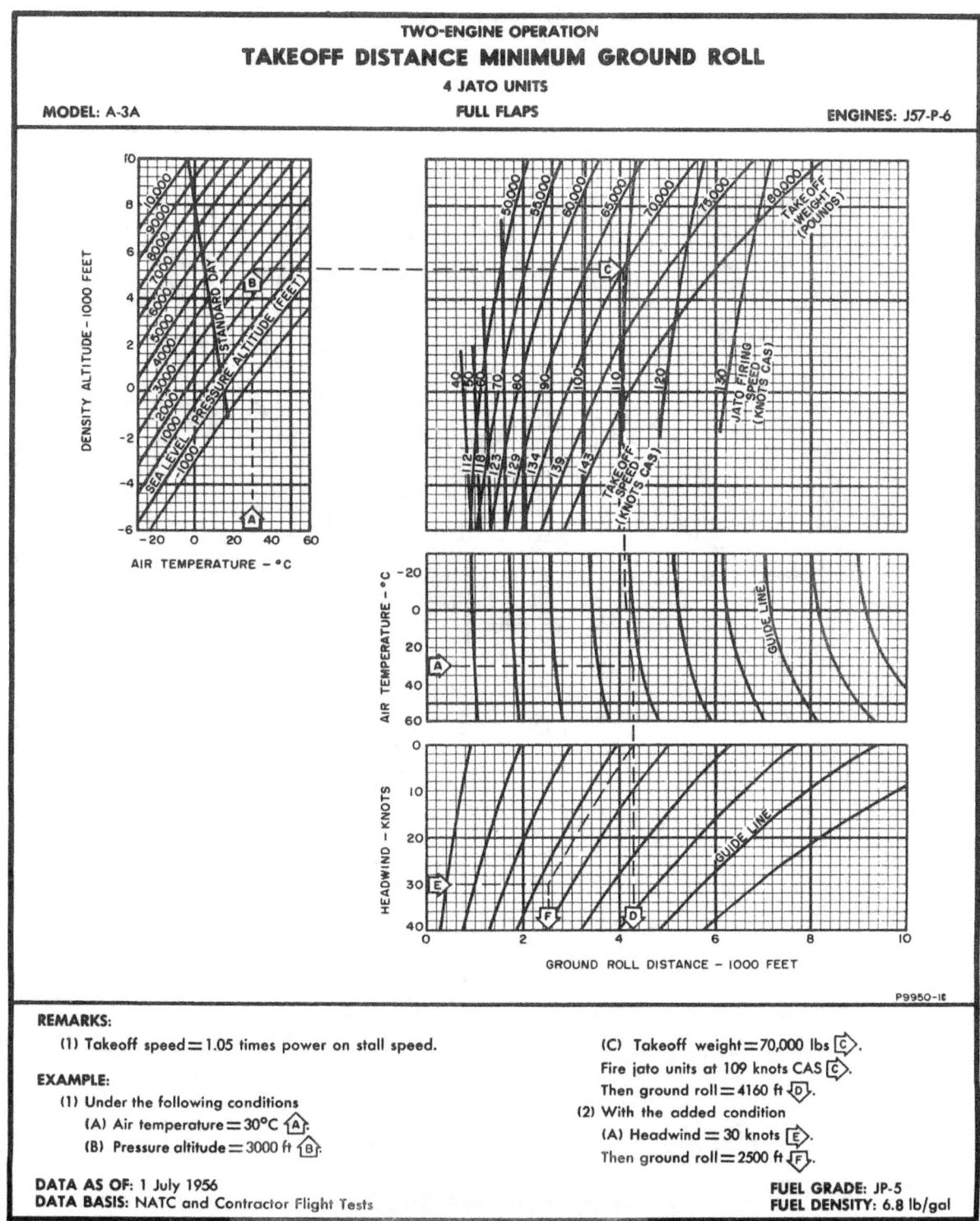

Figure 11-65. Takeoff Distance Minimum Ground Roll – Four JATO Units (30° Nozzle)

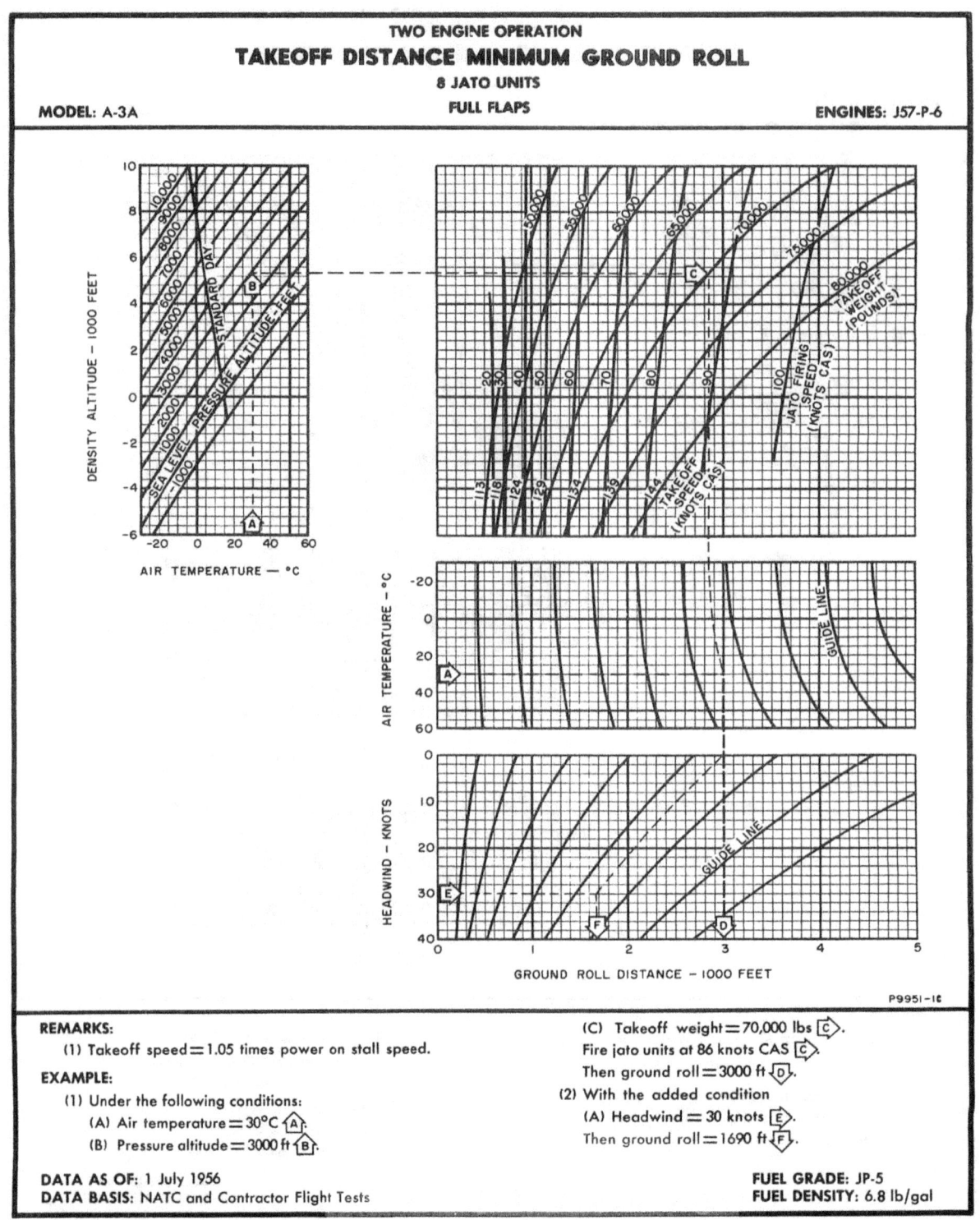

Figure 11-66. Takeoff Distance Minimum Ground Roll — Eight JATO Units (30° Nozzle)

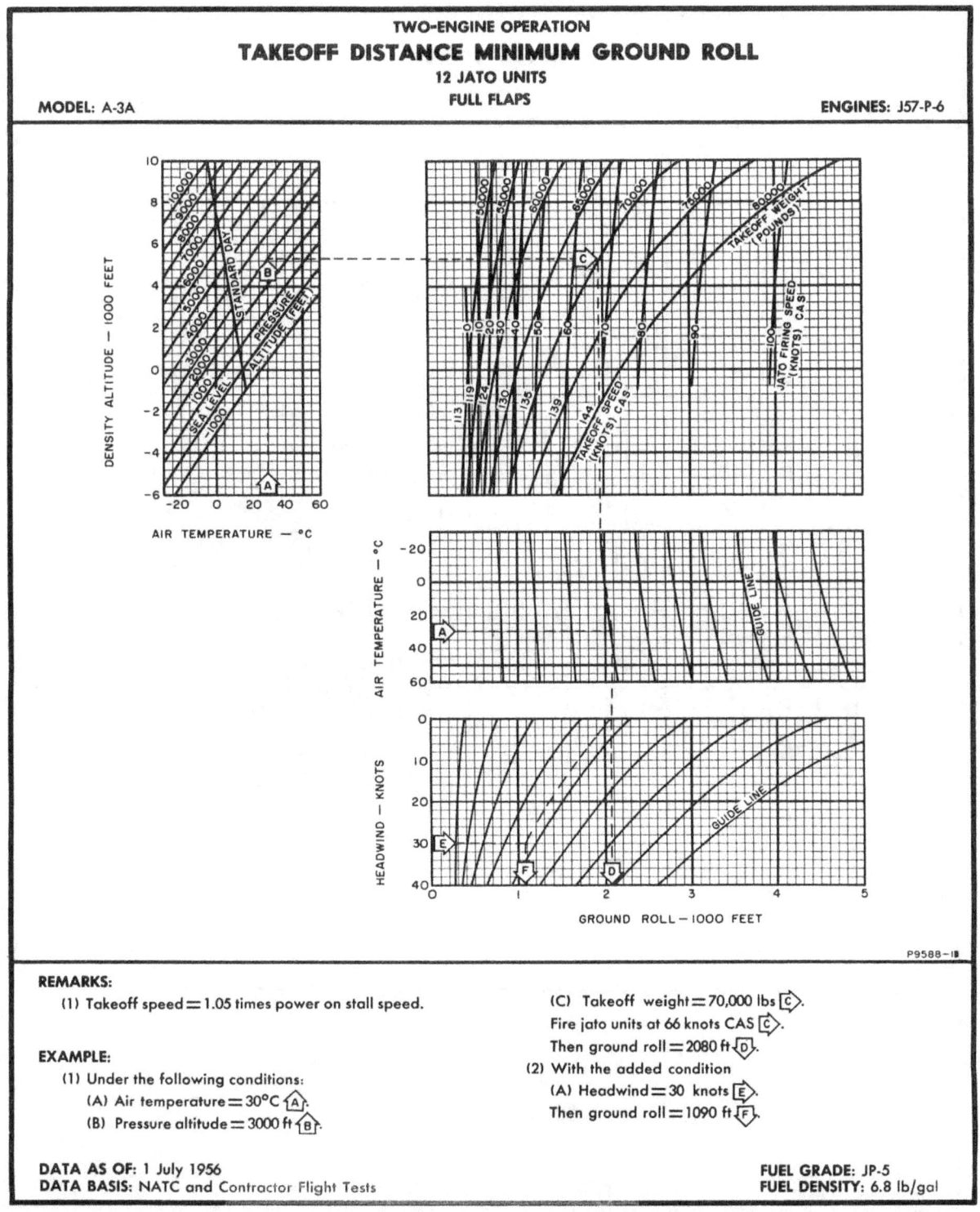

Figure 11-67. Takeoff Distance Minimum Ground Roll – 12 JATO Units (30° Nozzle)

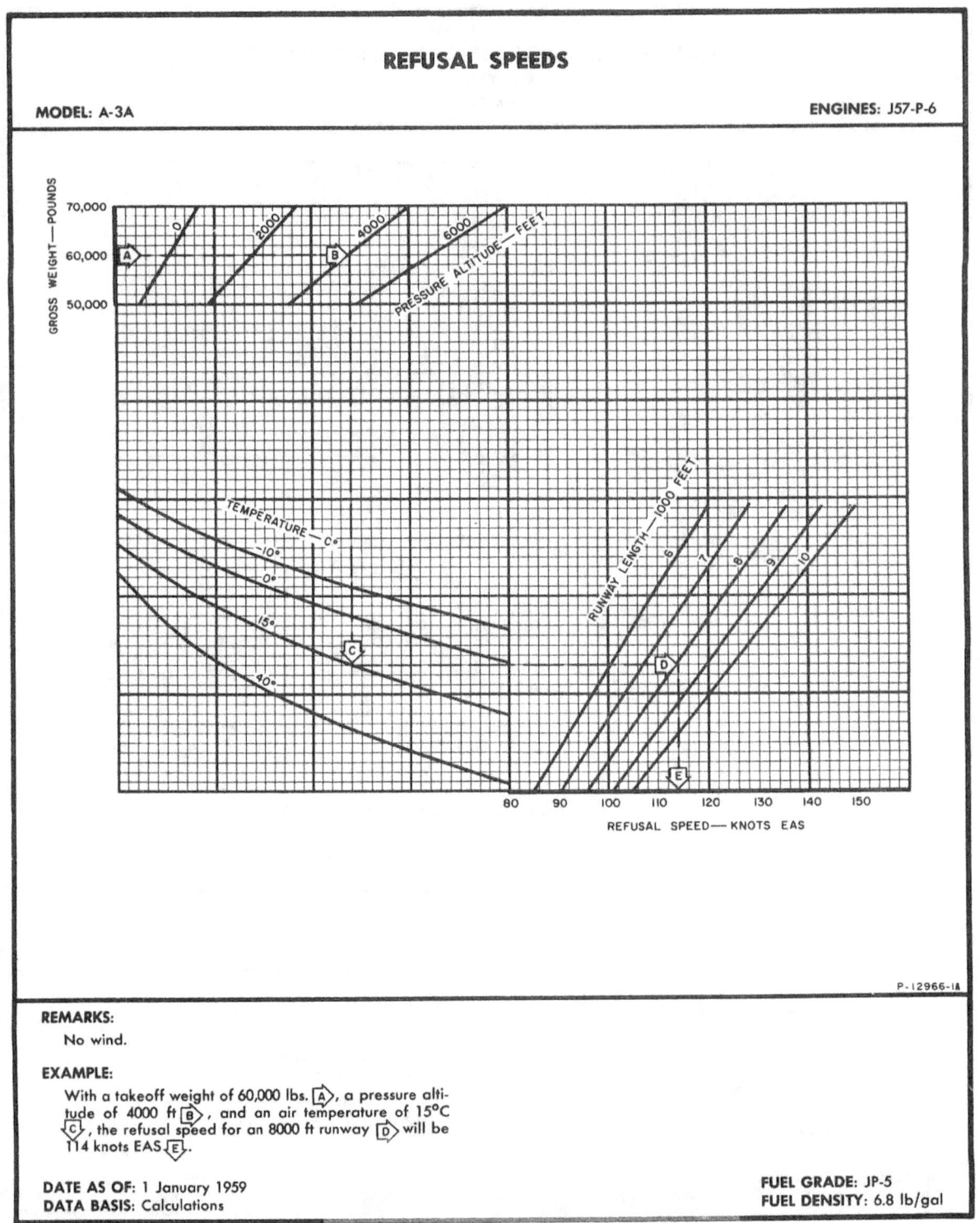

Figure 11-68. Refusal Speeds

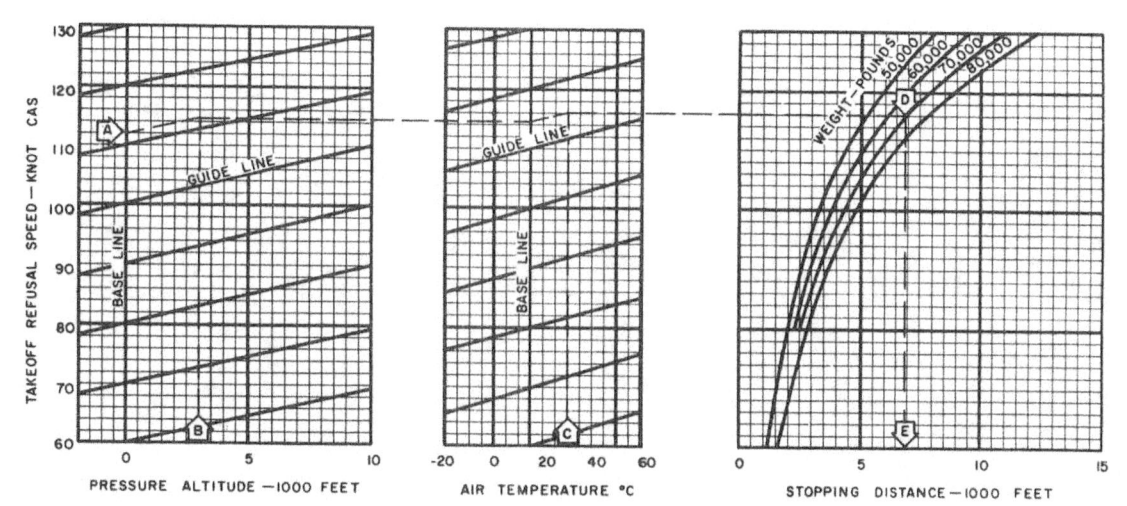

Figure 11-69. Refused Takeoff Stopping Distance

NAVAIR 01-40ATA-1

Section XI
Part 3A

PART 3A
CLIMB

TABLE OF CONTENTS

TEXT
Page

Climb Charts 11-135

ILLUSTRATIONS

Figure		Page
11-70	Climb Performance After Takeoff	11-137
11-71	Fuel Consumed During Climb	11-138
11-72	Climb Distance	11-139

Figure		Page
11-73	Time to Climb	11-140
11-74	Fuel Consumed During Climb	11-141
11-75	Climb Distance	11-142
11-76	Time to Climb	11-143

Climb Charts

CLIMB PERFORMANCE AFTER TAKEOFF

Figure 11-70 shows the climb characteristics of the aircraft immediately after takeoff at sea level pressure altitude and a takeoff gross weight of 70,000 pounds. These data show the effects of airspeed, flap position and landing gear extension on the maximum rate of climb with takeoff power. Rates of climb for each landing gear and flap configuration at airspeeds below the recommended airspeed are included.

NOTE

This chart shows maximum rates of climb available at zero acceleration (i.e., stabilized airspeed). Upon achieving a given climb airspeed, the pilot can obtain the corresponding rate of climb shown on the chart if no attempt is made to increase the airspeed.

It is readily apparent from this chart that the landing gear should be raised immediately after takeoff. Also, from the airspeed, the flap retraction time, and rate of climb relationships, it is recommended that flap retraction be initiated only after the aircraft has accelerated to an airspeed approximately 30 to 40 knots above the recommended takeoff airspeed.

Two additional curves are provided on the chart. The dashed line in the center of the grid can be used to estimate the loss of rate of climb should one engine fail immediately after takeoff. This curve shows the absolute necessity of increasing the forward speed of the aircraft as well as raising the landing gear and flaps before any attempt is made to gain altitude with one engine inoperative. The curve at the bottom of the grid can be used to estimate the effect on available rate of climb which results from deviations in ambient temperature from the standard temperature of 15°C at sea level. Note that except at low takeoff airspeeds with full flaps (i.e., minimum ground roll) the aircraft has excellent climb-out performance on two engines, even with ambient temperatures considerably above standard.

EXAMPLE: A field takeoff (full flaps) is to be made at 70,000 pounds gross weight with no wind, with sea level pressure altitude and an ambient temperature of 5°C. Find the rate of climb at 160 knots for a normal climb-out; and for climb-out following engine failure after the landing gear has been retracted.

1. Enter the Climb Performance After Takeoff chart, figure 11-70, with 160 KCAS (A), read vertically to the intersection with the dashed line (full flaps and gear down). Opposite this point on the left-hand scale (C), read approximately 1800 feet per minute available rate of climb for normal standard day operations. From the temperature correction curve note that the available rate of climb is increased by 250 feet per minute for each 10°C temperature decrease from standard day. The correction then is:

$$\frac{15 - 5}{10} \times 250 = 250 \text{ feet per minute.}$$

This results in:

1800 + 250 = 2050 feet per minute actual rate of climb. Assume the landing gear is fully retracted at

Changed 1 June 1969

11-135

Section XI
Part 3A

175 KCAS. From the chart, the rate of climb at this point is determined to be:

2390 + 290 = 2680 feet per minute.

2. Assume that with the landing gear retracted and full flaps extended, one engine fails at 175 knots CAS. As shown on the chart, the loss in rate of climb due to failure of one engine at this airspeed is approximately 2225 feet per minute. If the climb-out is continued, the maximum available rate of climb of one engine then becomes:

2680 - 2225 = 455 feet per minute.

ALTITUDE CLIMB PERFORMANCE CHARTS

Clean configuration climb performance with respect to time, fuel, and distance from sea level to altitude may be determined from the data presented in three charts identified as Time to Climb (figure 11-73), Climb Distance (figure 11-72), and Fuel Consumed During Climb (figure 11-71). Climb with throttles set at maximum thrust, since a maximum thrust climb to a given altitude requires less total fuel than a normal thrust climb. Climbs may be made with maximum thrust to cruise ceiling (that altitude at which the rate of climb is 300 feet per minute with normal thrust) at any operating gross weight up to 70,000 lbs without exceeding the engine operating time limit of 15 minutes.

It is best to maintain the airspeed schedule shown in the table on each climb chart, although variations in climb airspeed up to 10 knots above or below the scheduled airspeed will not materially affect climb performance, except at altitudes near the ceiling.

The Altitude Climb Performance charts may also be used to determine elapsed time, distance, and/or fuel used in climbing from one altitude to another in flight by taking the difference between the values at the initial and final altitudes, as illustrated on the chart.

EXAMPLE: Assume that a climb is required from 20,000 feet pressure altitude to 35,000 feet pressure altitude, with a momentary gross weight at 20,000 feet of 61,000 pounds. On the time, fuel, and distance plots, read the initial values at the intersection of the 61,000 pound gross weight line with the 20,000-foot pressure altitude line. Next, determine the final values at the intersection of the weight guide line with the 35,000-foot pressure altitude line. From these data, the following computations are made:

(Figure 11-71) Fuel used during climb = 1670 - 1060 = 610 pounds

(Figure 11-72) Climb Distance = 80 - 31 = 49 nautical miles

(Figure 11-73) Climb Time = 11.7 - 5.0 = 6.7 minutes

EMERGENCY CLIMB CHARTS

The Emergency Climb charts, (figures 11-74, 11-75, and 11-76) are presented for use in emergency operation only (one engine windmilling), since, in normal procedure, climbs are always made with both engines operating.

The use of maximum thrust during a climb to altitude is restricted to 15 minutes, due to engine operating limitations. If the climb time will exceed 15 minutes, use maximum thrust during the early stages of the climb and normal thrust during the last 15 minutes.

Follow the airspeed schedule shown on the chart as closely as possible. Climb time, fuel, and distance data for in-flight climbs with one engine operating on maximum thrust may be calculated by taking the difference between the time, fuel, and distance values at the initial and at the final altitudes.

EXAMPLE: Assume that a climb is made at 55,000 pounds gross weight on one engine with maximum power from 10,000 feet pressure altitude to 20,000 feet pressure altitude. As indicated on the Emergency Climb chart:

Fuel used during climb = 2030 - 870 = 1160 pounds.

The climb distance is equal to:

94 - 31 = 63 nautical miles.

The climb time = 20.5 - 7.5 = 13 minutes.

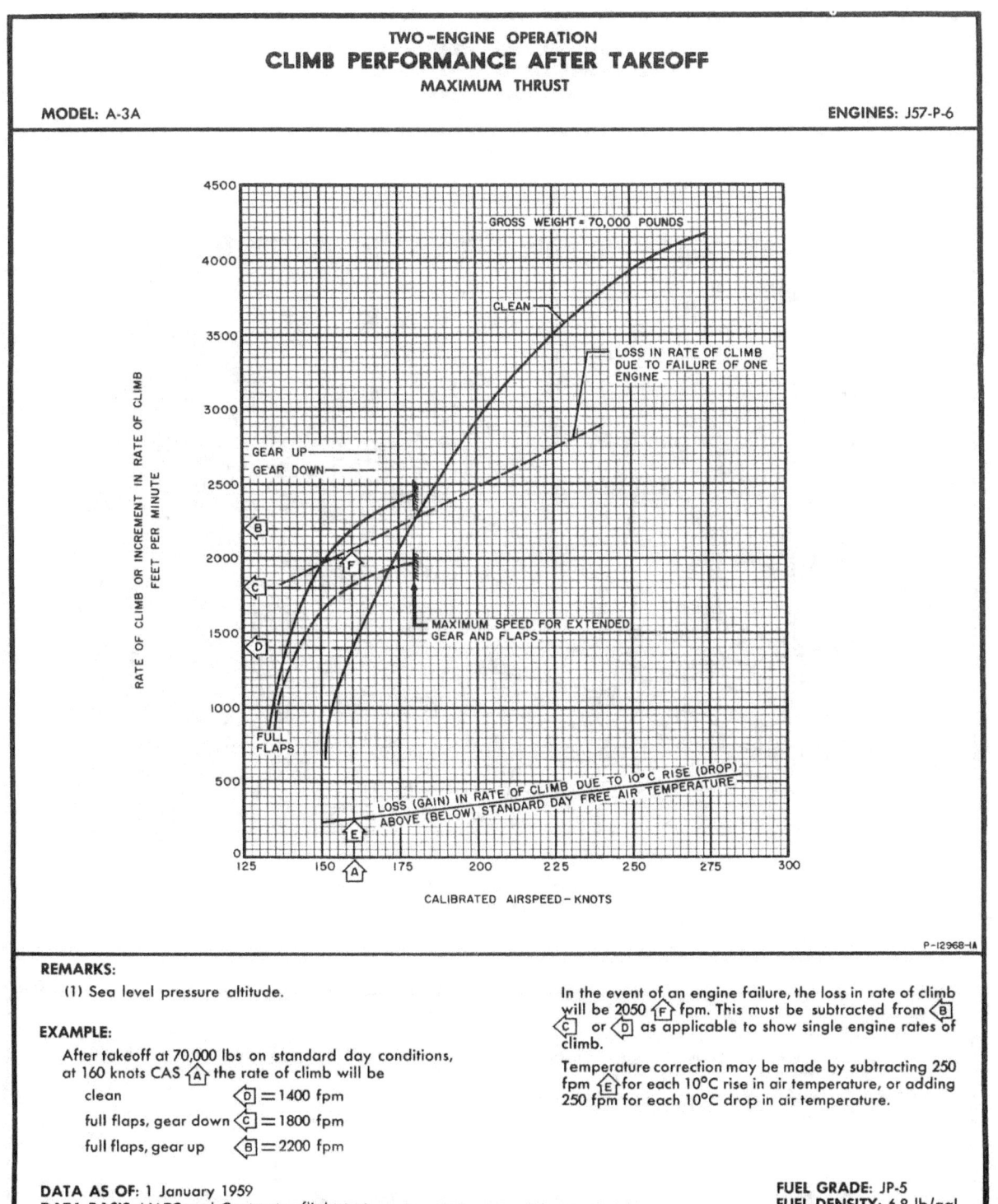

Figure 11-70. Climb Performance After Takeoff

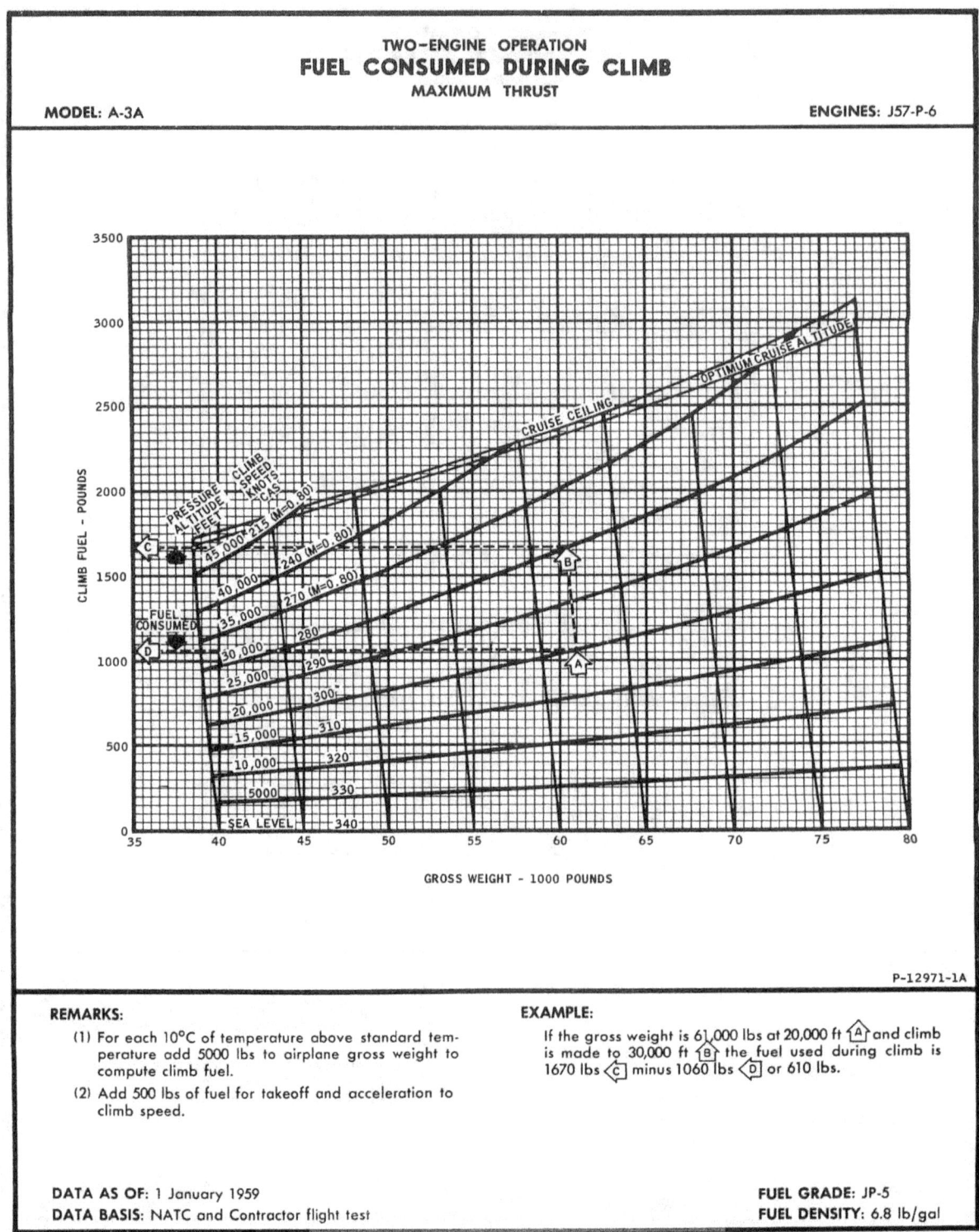

Figure 11-71. Fuel Consumed During Climb

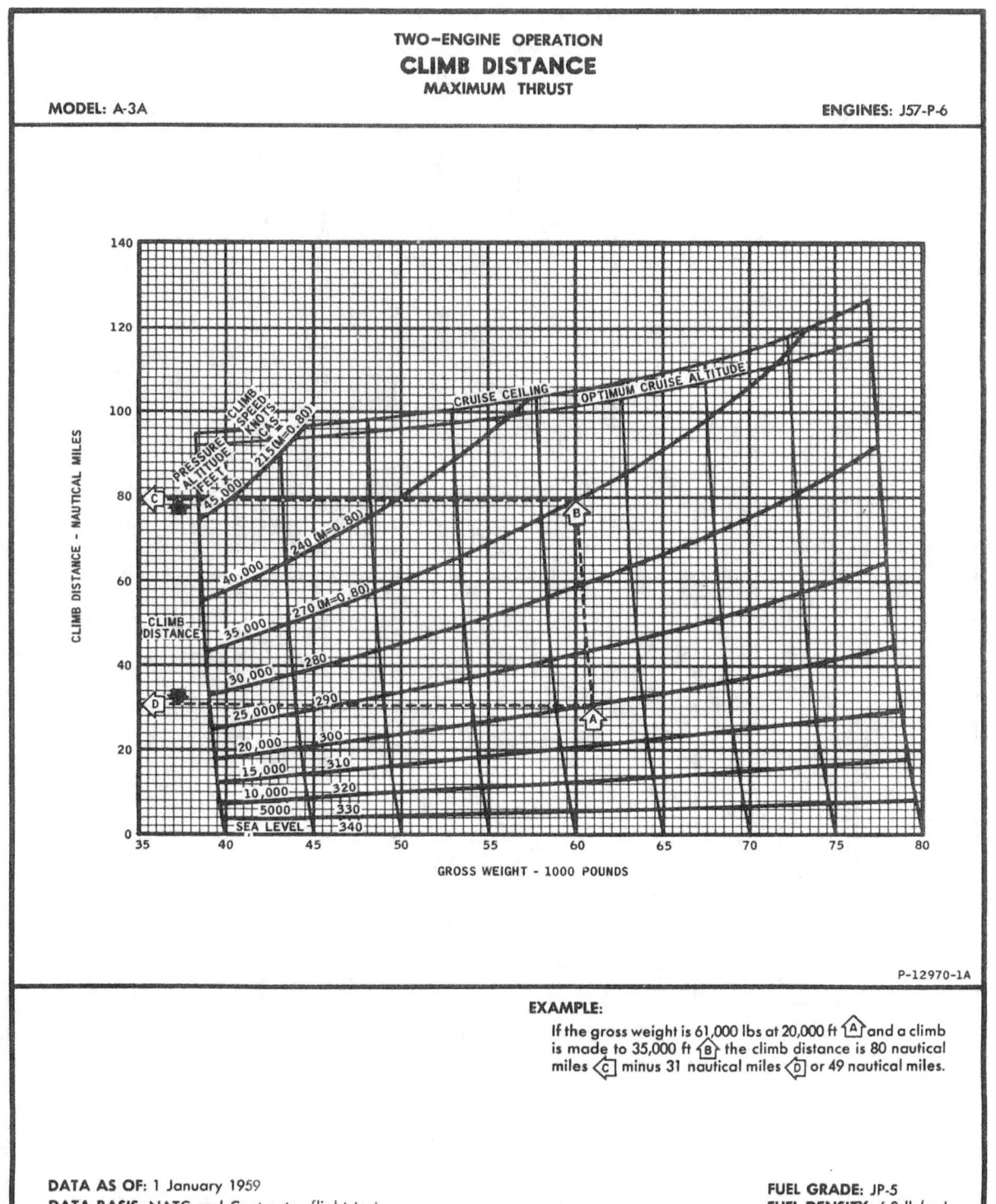

Figure 11-72. Climb Distance

Section XI
Part 3A

NAVAIR 01-40ATA-1

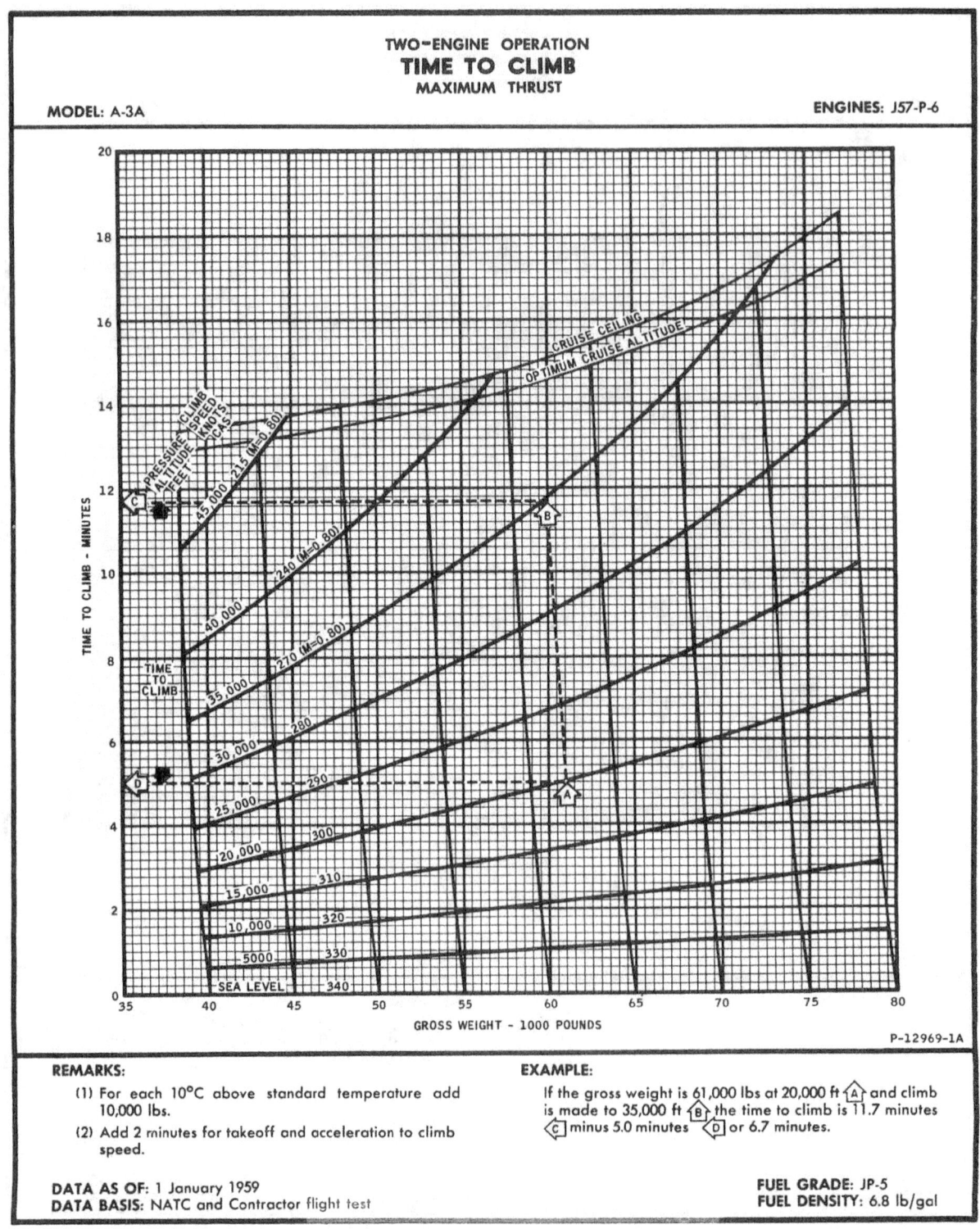

Figure 11-73. Time to Climb

11-140

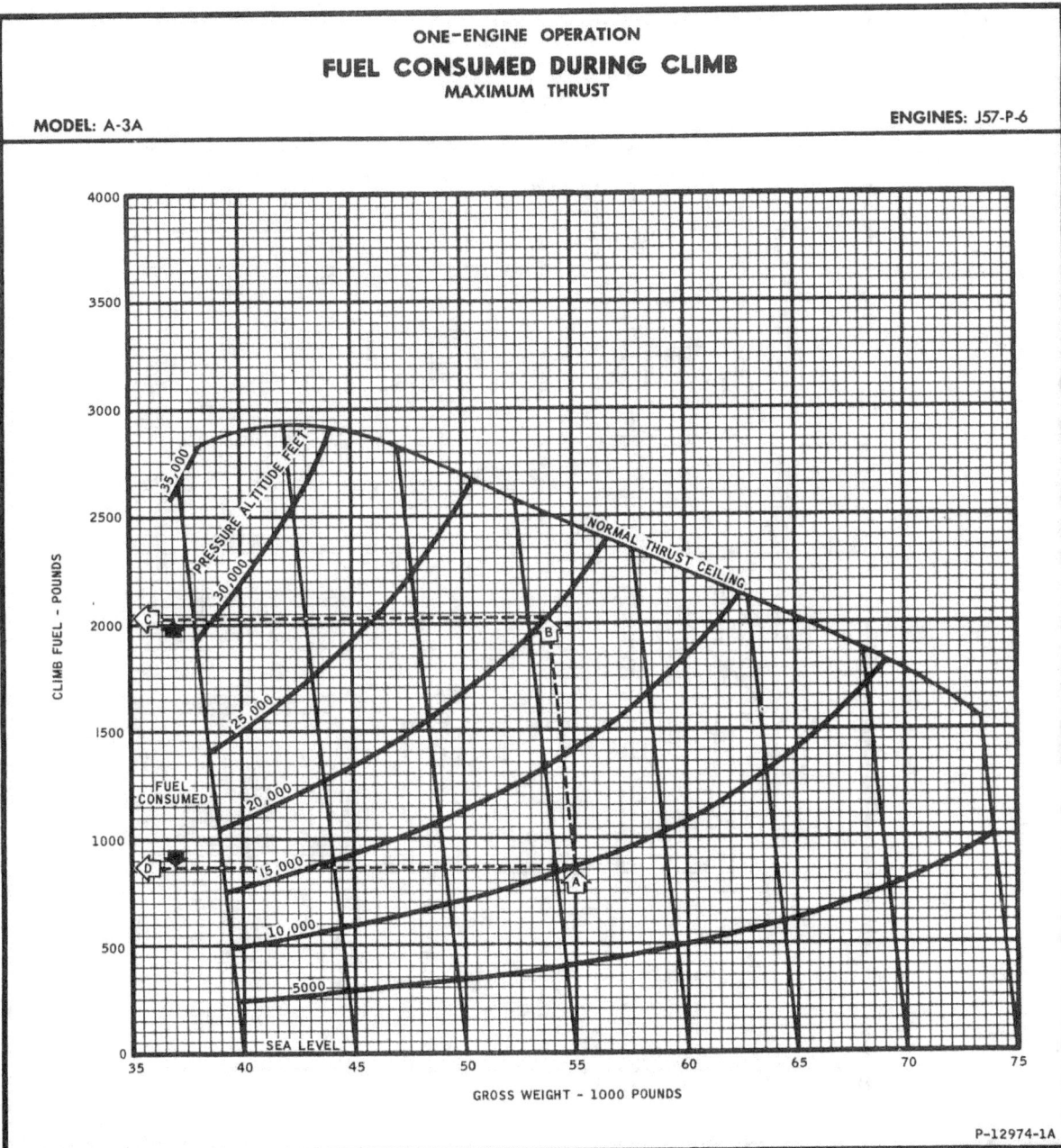

Figure 11-74. Fuel Consumed During Climb

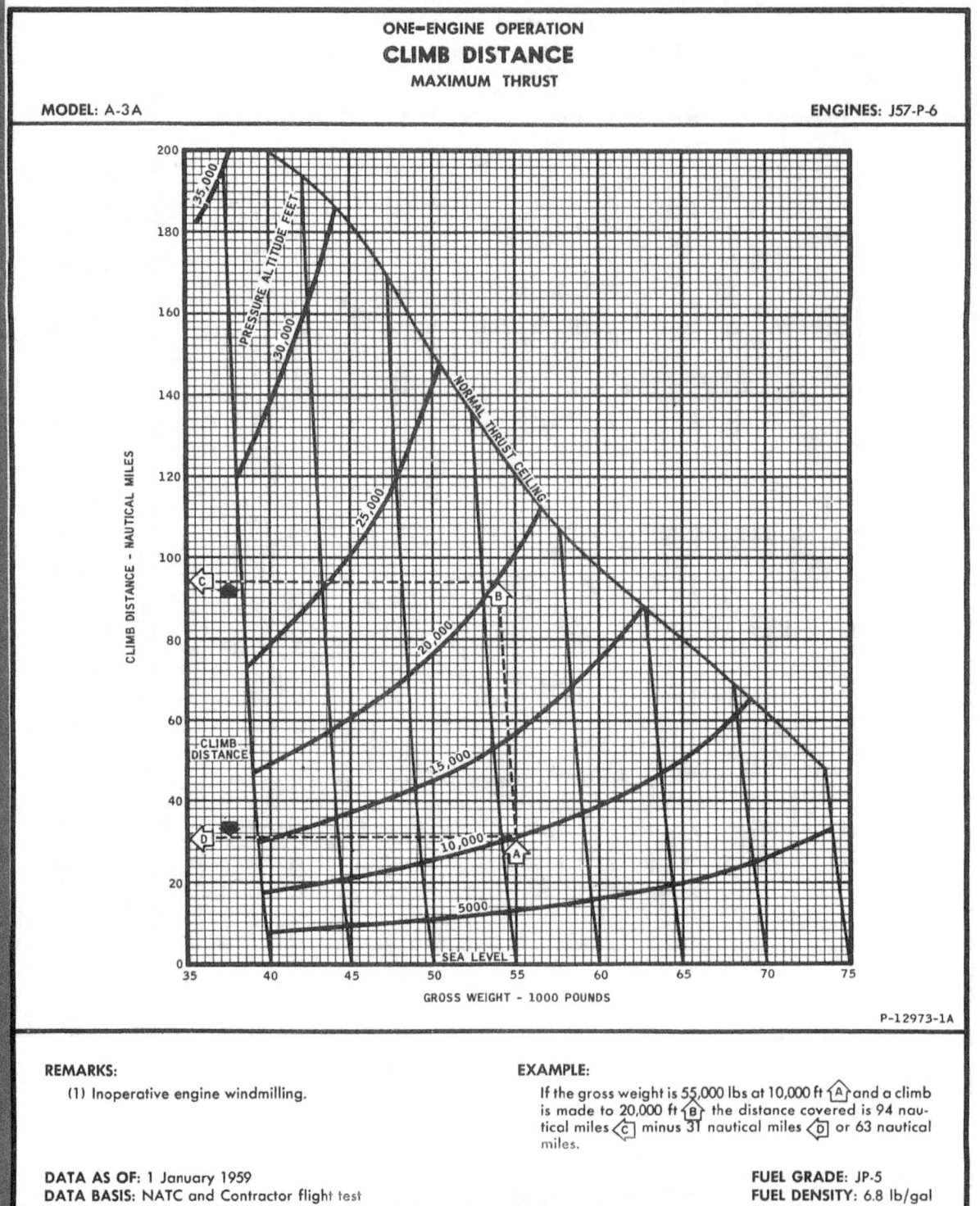

Figure 11-75. Climb Distance

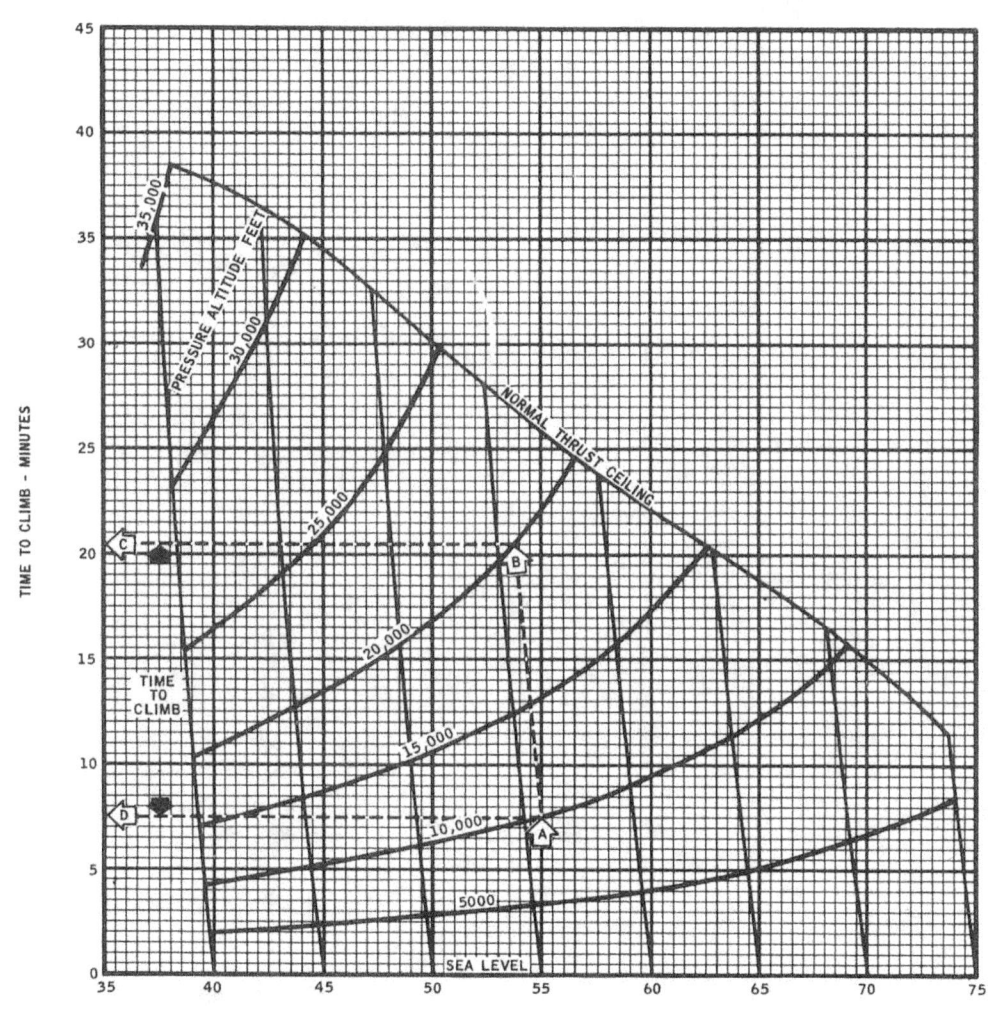

Figure 11-76. Time to Climb

NAVAIR 01-40ATA-1

Section XI
Part 4A

PART 4A
RANGE

TABLE OF CONTENTS

TEXT
Page

Range Charts 11-145

ILLUSTRATIONS

Figure		Page
11-77	Fouled Deck Range – VFR	11-149
11-78	Fouled Deck Range – IFR	11-150
11-79	Fouled Deck Range – Gear Down	11-151
11-80	Fouled Deck Range – Gear and Flaps Down	11-152
11-81	Fouled Deck Range – VFR	11-153
11-82	Fouled Deck Range – IFR	11-154

Figure		Page
11-83	Fouled Deck Range – Sea Level	11-155
11-84	Maximum Specific Range vs Altitude	11-156
11-85	Specific Range – Sea Level	11-158
11-86	Specific Range – Sea Level	11-168
11-87	Mission Profile	11-174
11-88	Combat Radius Profile	11-176

Range Charts

The range data for the Model A-3A are divided into four different types of presentation. These are:

1. Fouled Deck Range (Figures 11-77, 11-78, 11-79, 11-80, 11-81, 11-82, and 11-83)

2. Maximum Specific Range vs Altitude (Figure 11-84)

3. Specific Range (Figures 11-85 and 11-86)

4. Profile charts (Figures 11-87 and 11-88)

These range data are presented for the aircraft in the clean configuration and are representative of the cruise performance which may be obtained during normal service operation. All data are given for a ICAO standard day.

At a given altitude and gross weight, the maximum range of the aircraft is obtained at the recommended airspeed for maximum range. This airspeed should be primarily established by Mach Number (or CAS since Mach number and CAS are directly related at a given altitude). If desirable at altitudes of 40,000 ft and below, penalties in the range of the aircraft may be tolerated by increasing the recommended cruise speed such that the range penalty is no greater than one percent. This increase in cruise speed will result in significant reductions in elapsed time.

NOTE

The characteristics of the J57 engine are such that engine rpm cannot be used for cruise control. However, as an aid in establishing proper cruise control, engine pressure ratio and engine fuel flow data are provided.

A description of the four types of range presentation follows.

FOULED DECK RANGE ("BINGO CARDS")

The Fouled Deck Range Charts (figures 11-77 through 11-80) for two-engine operation and figures 11-81 through 11-83 for single-engine operation are provided to indicate the available range, for low values of fuel remaining, at optimum cruise altitudes. Both VFR and IFR charts are included for single-engine and two-engine operation with the flaps and gear retracted. Also included for two-engine operation are VFR charts for gear down and gear and flaps down (full flaps). A single engine sea level fouled deck range chart is also included.

Fuel allowances of 300 pounds for two-engine operation and 200 pounds for one-engine operation are included for raising the gear and flaps (where applicable), making a turn, and accelerating to climb speed. A 3000-pound reserve fuel allowance is included at the point where descent is commenced for the VFR charts and at the approach fix for the IFR charts. The charts are based on a basic aircraft weight of 38,153 pounds with a percentage correction factor for additional fuel required at heavier basic weights. Climb, cruise, and let-down speeds are provided together with the let-down time, fuel required, and distances where applicable.

Figures are for a no-wind standard day. Add one percent for each 5 knots of head wind for rough calculations.

MAXIMUM SPECIFIC RANGE VS ALTITUDE

The maximum specific range characteristics are summarized for two-engine and one-engine operation in figure 11-84. These data present the specific range as a function of altitude and gross weight that

Changed 1 June 1969

11-145

is attainable at the recommended speed for maximum range. Cruise Mach numbers corresponding to the recommended airspeed for maximum specific range are superimposed on these plots together with the corresponding fuel flow. Absolute ceilings are indicated for both two-engine and one-engine operation. The optimum cruise altitude is provided for two-engine operation.

SPECIFIC RANGE

The specific range charts, figure 11-85, for two-engine operation and figure 11-86 for one-engine operation, present the nautical miles per pound of fuel, or specific range, as a function of Mach number for every 5000 ft of altitude from sea level to 45,000 ft for two-engine operation and 30,000 ft for one-engine operation. The recommended airspeed for maximum range is indicated on each of the charts. The Mach number corresponding to this speed should be used as the primary indication of proper cruise control. In addition, lines of fuel flow and engine pressure ratio are superimposed to provide additional checks on proper cruise control. At low power settings, the intercompressor bleed valves on the J57 engine are scheduled to open. This results in an increase in the fuel consumption at these power settings which in turn reduces the nautical miles per pound of fuel. Therefore, at the lower altitudes the specific range curves are presented to include this effect. The scheduled opening of these valves will vary from engine to engine and, therefore, the data in figure 11-85 should be considered approximate. For flight planning purposes, however, it is recommended that these data be used to predict the cruise characteristics for these conditions. The specific range data are provided for speeds between the recommended speed for maximum endurance and maximum speed with maximum thrust. The engine rpm corresponding to normal and maximum thrust is provided in each chart for standard conditions. The specific range data obtained from these charts can be used for all ambient air temperatures as long as the specific range is determined for a given Mach number or CAS. The corresponding TAS, however, for non-standard conditions will have to be obtained from figure 11-1. Sub scales on each chart show the relationship between Mach number and TAS for standard day conditions only. The relationship between Mach number and CAS is also provided and is independent of ambient conditions.

EXAMPLE: A request is received to escort another aircraft which is returning from a mission at 20,000 feet pressure altitude at 300 KCAS. If the initial gross weight is 50,000 pounds, including 10,000 pounds of available cruise fuel after allowances for descent and/or reserve, determine the range available and fuel consumption with no wind.

1. Enter the 20,000 foot specific range (Nautical Miles Per 1000 Pounds of Fuel) chart for two engines operating (figure 11-85, sheet 5) at 300 KCAS. At 50,000 pounds initial cruising gross weight, the specific range is 82.2 nautical miles per 1000 pounds of fuel. At the final cruising gross weight,

$$50,000 - 10,000 = 40,000 \text{ pounds.}$$

The specific range is 87 nautical miles per 1000 pounds of fuel.

2. The specific range during cruise, based on an average gross weight of 45,000 pounds, is 84.8 nautical miles per 1000 pounds of fuel. By multiplying this number by the available cruise fuel in thousands of pounds, the range is:

$$84.8 \times \frac{10,000}{1000} = 848 \text{ nautical miles.}$$

3. The initial fuel flow at 20,000 feet (at 50,000 pounds) is approximately 2400 pounds per hour per engine multiplied by two, or 4800 pounds per hour. During the cruise, fuel flow will decrease due to decreasing gross weight, and at the end of the flight the fuel flow will be approximately:

$$2 \times 2300 = 4600 \text{ pounds per hour.}$$

4. True airspeed (also ground speed in this example) and Mach number are 400 knots and 0.65 respectively.

5. When large amounts of cruise fuel are considered, or when range is critical, greater accuracy may be obtained by computing the range in steps using the above procedure. The degree of accuracy will depend on the number of incremental values of fuel weight used.

For the purpose of determining whether operation on one engine would provide a better maximum range performance, follow the same procedure through the specific range chart for single engine operation.

EXAMPLE:

1. Enter the 20,000 foot specific range (Nautical Miles Per 1000 Pounds of Fuel) chart for single-engine operation (figure 11-86, sheet 5) at 300 KCAS. At 50,000 pounds initial cruising gross weight, the specific range is 79 nautical miles per 1000 pounds of fuel. At the final cruising gross weight (40,000 pounds), the specific range is 84.5 nautical miles per 1000 pounds of fuel.

2. The specific range during cruise, based on an average gross weight of 45,000 pounds, is 81.8 nautical miles per 1000 pounds of fuel. By multiplying this number by the available cruise fuel in thousands of pounds, the range is:

$$81.8 \times \frac{10,000}{1000} = 818.0 \text{ nautical miles.}$$

3. A comparison of the single-engine specific range with that obtainable during two-engine operation reveals a disadvantage in proceeding with one engine shut down. A study of the single-engine chart will reveal that greater than normal rated power must be maintained on the single engine for a period of time exceeding two hours in order to follow this flight plan. For these reasons, two-engine operation should be used for this particular flight.

MISSION PROFILE

The mission profile chart (figure 11-87) presents the total available range on a one way mission as a function of cruise altitudes from sea level to the optimum (cruise climb) altitude. The ranges are presented with a 3000 lb fuel reserve and with zero fuel remaining. No time or fuel allowances for start, taxi, or takeoff are included. Fuel used and elapsed time lines are included on the chart in order to provide check points during the mission. These range data are presented for a takeoff weight of 70,000 pounds with 29,800 pounds of fuel on board. No allowances are included for wind effects.

The heavy line to the left edge of the shaded area shows the distance traveled, fuel consumed and the elapsed time during a military thrust climb from sea level to the desired cruise altitude. The climb should be conducted at the climb schedule shown in the upper right hand corner of the chart. The heavy line at the top of the shaded area represents the optimum or cruise climb altitude. Cruise at the optimum cruise altitude is obtained by maintaining a constant cruise Mach number of 0.8 with an approximate constant throttle setting. The variation of altitude with distance results from the decrease in aircraft weight due to fuel usage during cruise. By use of the fuel usage and elapsed time lines, the optimum cruise altitude can be checked during the mission. Cruise at a fixed altitude should be conducted at the recommended cruise Mach numbers shown in the upper right hand corner of the chart and will require periodic reduction in throttle setting as fuel is consumed to maintain the particular Mach number.

EXAMPLE: The chart may be entered with one or more of the four range factors: time, fuel, distance and altitude. By entering the chart with the known factors the other factors may be readily determined.

1. Determine the maximum range with 25,000 pounds of fuel available for climb and cruise, with an average 50 knot headwind.

    a. Enter the chart at 25,000 pounds of fuel. Directly below the intersection of the fuel and cruise climb line, read maximum still air range (air miles) . . . . . . 2450 N. miles

    b. Time required. . . . . 5 hr 24 min

    c. Wind effect (time x wind). . . . .270 N. miles

    d. Calculate maximum range with wind (2450 - 270) . . . . 2180 N. miles

2. Determine the fuel required, elapsed time, recommended airspeed and Mach number to cruise 1500 nautical miles at 30,000 feet with a headwind of 75 knots. To determine wind effect upon time, fuel, and distance, compute the average true airspeed (distance ÷ time) no wind, and apply wind to TAS to obtain ground speed (GS). Then compute the time with wind (distance ÷ GS). Re-enter the profile at the cruising altitude and the computed time with wind to determine the fuel required with wind.

    a. Enter the chart at 1500 nautical miles and proceed upward to the 30,000 foot line to determine time (no wind). . . .3 hr 42 min

    b. Average TAS (1500 ÷ 3.7 hr). . . . . 405 knots

    c. Apply wind to obtain average ground speed (405 - 75) . . . . 330 knots

    d. Calculate time with wind (1500 ÷ 330) . . . . 4 hr 30 min

    e. Re-enter chart at the intersection of cruise altitude and time with wind. Fuel required with wind . . . . 21,500 lb

    f. Recommended tabular cruise speed . . . . 260 CAS 0.70 Mach

COMBAT RADIUS PROFILE

The combat radius profile (figure 11-88) represents the radius capability of the aircraft for cruise altitudes from sea level to the optimum cruise altitude and for combat times of zero to 20 minutes. The radius is shown for a reserve fuel of 3000 lbs and for no reserve fuel. A fuel allowance of 1000 pounds is included for start, taxi, takeoff and descent. Lines of fuel used are superimposed on the chart for flight checks during the mission. The profile data are based on a takeoff weight of 70,000 pounds with 25,145 pounds of fuel and a bomb load of 6200 pounds aboard.

The heavy line at the left of the shaded area shows the distance traveled and the fuel consumed during a military thrust climb from sea level to the desired cruise altitude. The climb speed schedule is shown in the upper right hand corner of the chart. The heavy line at the top of the shaded area represents the optimum cruise-out altitude which corresponds to a cruise climb obtained at a constant cruise Mach number of 0.8 and an approximate constant throttle setting. Cruise at a selected constant altitude should be conducted at the recommended cruise Mach numbers shown in the upper right hand corner of the chart and will require periodic reductions in throttle setting as fuel is consumed to maintain the particular Mach numbers. It is assumed that the 6200 lb bomb load is dropped at the end of the cruise out.

The heavy dashed lines to the right of the chart show the radius available for various combat times and for the mission return at the same constant altitude at the cruise-out or at the optimum cruise-back altitude. Allowances for a military power climb from the optimum cruise-out altitude to the optimum cruise-back altitude are included.

The optimum cruise-back altitude is shown as the uppermost heavy line on the chart and corresponds to a cruise climb conducted in the same manner as the optimum cruise-out altitude.

EXAMPLE: Determine the combat radius with 25,145 pounds of fuel available at an altitude of 30,000 feet and anticipated combat time of 15 minutes with 3000 pounds reserve fuel over base.

1. Climb at maximum thrust to 30,000 feet observing recommended climb schedule.

2. Cruise at 30,000 feet at recommended cruise speeds . . . . 260 CAS 0.70 Mach

3. Range at 15 minutes combat time . . . . 890 N. miles

4. Return at . . . . 260 CAS 0.70 Mach

5. Begin idle let-down (220 knots) . . . . 80 N. miles from base

NAVAIR 01-40ATA-1

Section XI
Part 4A

FOULED DECK RANGE (VFR)
Two-Engine Operation

Model: A-3A

Engines: J57-P-6

Dist	Fuel Req	Alt	Climb			Cruise			Fuel Flow lb/hr/Eng	CAS	Descent			Total ETE
			ETE	Fuel	Dist	ETE	Fuel	Dist			ETE	Fuel	Dist	
40	3775	10	1	640	6	2	135	10	2080	265	6	153	24	9
60	3945	15	2	800	11	2	145	12	1780	236	10	224	37	14
80	4080	20	3	965	20	2	115	11	1690	235	13	293	50	18
100	4230	25	4	1155	27	1	75	8	1650	233	16	358	65	21
120	4350	30	6	1330	36	0	20	2	1610	233	19	417	81	25
140	4540	30	6	1340	36	4	200	23	1590	233	19	417	81	29
160	4650	35	7	1525	48	2	125	16	1560	230	21	475	97	30
180	4765	40	9	1715	61	1	50	7	1600	225	24	531	113	34
200	4920	40	9	1725	61	4	195	26	1600	225	26	531	113	39
220	5020	45	12	1990	85	1	30	4	1640	212	26	587	131	39
240	5175	45	12	2000	85	3	175	24	1640	212	26	587	131	41
260	5320	45	12	2010	86	6	310	43	1650	212	26	587	131	44
280	5475	45	12	2015	86	8	460	63	1650	212	26	587	131	46
300	5615	45	12	2020	87	11	595	82	1650	212	26	587	131	49
320	5770	45	12	2030	87	13	740	101	1660	212	26	587	131	51
340	5920	45	12	2035	88	16	885	121	1660	212	26	587	131	54
360	6070	45	12	2050	88	19	1020	142	1660	212	26	587	131	57
380	6225	45	12	2055	89	21	1170	160	1670	212	26	587	131	59
400	6375	45	12	2070	90	23	1305	177	1670	212	26	587	131	61

Remarks:

(1) Fuel required includes 300 pounds for cleanup, turn, and acceleration.

(2) Provides 3000 pounds fuel at point where descent is commenced. No wind conditions.

(3) Climb speed is 340 KCAS at sea level decreasing 20 knots per 10,000 feet altitude to 36,000 feet. Climb at M = 0.8 above 36,000 feet.

(4) Idle descent to sea level at 220 KCAS.

(5) Aircraft operating weight is 38,152 pounds.

(6) For each 1000-pound increase in basic aircraft weight, increase the fuel required by 1%.

Data as of: 1 March 1964

Data Basis: NATC and Contractor Flight Tests

Fuel Grade: JP-5

Fuel Density: 6.8 lb/gal

Figure 11-77. Fouled Deck Range – VFR

11-149

FOULED DECK RANGE (IFR)
Two-Engine Operation

Model: A-3A
Engines: J57-P-6

Dist	Fuel Req	Alt	Climb			Cruise			Fuel Flow lb/hr/Eng	CAS	Total ETE
			ETE	Fuel	Dist	ETE	Fuel	Dist			
40	4060	SL	1	300	0	8	760	40	2960	312	9
60	4360	15	2	810	14	9	550	46	1780	238	11
80	4630	15	2	815	14	14	815	66	1790	238	16
100	4860	20	3	985	20	17	875	81	1700	235	20
120	5077	25	4	1180	28	16	897	92	1690	234	20
140	5265	25	4	1180	28	20	1085	111	1690	234	24
160	5440	30	6	1370	37	20	1070	123	1630	234	26
180	5610	35	7	1560	49	20	1050	131	1580	232	27
200	5770	35	7	1565	49	23	1205	151	1580	232	30
220	5940	35	7	1570	49	26	1370	171	1580	232	33
240	6100	35	7	1580	50	29	1520	190	1580	232	36
260	6265	40	9	1785	64	27	1480	196	1630	225	36
280	6420	40	9	1790	64	30	1630	216	1630	225	39
300	6575	40	9	1795	65	33	1780	235	1630	225	42
320	6730	40	9	1795	65	36	1935	255	1640	226	45
340	6890	40	9	1805	66	38	2085	274	1640	226	47
360	7045	40	10	1810	66	42	2235	294	1640	226	52
380	7210	40	10	1820	66	45	2390	314	1640	226	55
400	7360	40	10	1825	66	46	2535	334	1640	227	56

Remarks:

(1) Fuel required includes 300 pounds for cleanup, turn, and acceleration.

(2) Provides 3000 pounds fuel at approach fix. No wind conditions.

(3) Climb speed is 340 KCAS at sea level decreasing 20 knots per 10,000 feet altitude to 36,000 feet. Climb at Mach = 0.8 above 36,000 feet.

(4) Aircraft operating weight is 38,153 pounds.

(5) For each 1000-pound increase in basic aircraft weight, increase fuel required by 1%.

Data as of: 1 March 1964
Data Basis: NATC and Contractor Flight Test

Fuel Grade: JP-5
Fuel Density: 6.8 lb/gal

Figure 11-78. Fouled Deck Range – IFR

NAVAIR 01-40ATA-1

Section XI
Part 4A

GEAR DOWN FOULED DECK RANGE (VFR)
Two-Engine Operation

Model: A-3A

Engines: J57-P-6

Dist	Fuel Req	Alt	Climb			Cruise			Fuel Flow lb/hr/Eng	CAS	Descent			Total ETE
			ETE	Fuel	Dist	ETE	Fuel	Dist			ETE	Fuel	Dist	
40	4090	15	3	695	13	1	95	5	2380	200	8	185	22	12
60	4370	20	5	920	19	1	150	8	2330	200	10	242	33	16
80	4670	25	6	1195	27	2	175	11	2330	201	12	298	42	20
100	4930	30	9	1480	38	2	150	10	2330	201	14	349	52	25
120	5200	35	12	1850	56	1	50	3	2360	201	16	400	61	29
140	5490	35	12	1870	56	4	320	23	2370	202	16	400	61	32
160	5770	35	12	1890	57	7	580	42	2370	202	16	400	61	35
180	6050	35	12	1920	57	10	830	61	2380	203	16	400	61	38
200	6350	35	12	1940	58	14	1110	81	2390	203	16	400	61	42
220	6640	35	13	1960	59	17	1380	100	2400	203	16	400	61	46
240	6910	35	13	1980	60	20	1630	119	2410	203	16	400	61	49
260	7200	35	13	2000	60	23	1900	139	2420	203	16	400	61	52
280	7500	35	13	2030	61	27	2170	158	2420	203	16	400	61	56
300	7790	35	13	2050	62	30	2440	177	2430	204	16	400	61	59
320	8080	35	13	2080	63	33	2700	196	2440	204	16	400	61	62
340	8380	35	14	2100	64	36	2980	215	2450	204	16	400	61	66
360	8675	35	14	2130	65	40	3245	234	2460	204	16	400	61	70
380	8970	35	14	2160	66	44	3510	253	2480	204	16	400	61	74
400	9260	35	14	2180	67	46	3780	272	2480	204	16	400	61	76

Remarks:

(1) Fuel required includes 300 pounds for turn and acceleration.

(2) Provides 3000 pounds fuel at point where descent is commenced. No wind conditions.

(3) Climb speed is 225 KCAS at sea level; decreasing 12 knots per 10,000 feet altitude.

(4) Idle descent to sea level at 172 KCAS.

(5) Aircraft operating weight is 38,153 pounds.

(6) For each 1000-pound increase in basic aircraft weight, increase the fuel required by 1.1%.

Data as of: 1 March 1964
Data Basis: NATC and Contractor Flight Test

Fuel Grade: JP-5
Fuel Density: 6.8 lb/gal

Figure 11-79. Fouled Deck Range – Gear Down

GEAR AND FLAPS DOWN FOULED DECK RANGE (VFR)
Two-Engine Operation

Model: A-3A   Engines: J57-P-6

Dist	Fuel Req	Alt	Climb			Cruise			Fuel Flow lb/hr/Eng	CAS	Descent			Total ETE
			ETE	Fuel	Dist	ETE	Fuel	Dist			ETE	Fuel	Dist	
40	4,345	15	4	1210	13	2	135	5	2620	155	9	230	22	15
60	4,775	20	6	1530	20	3	245	10	2550	155	12	300	30	21
80	5,205	25	9	1910	29	3	295	13	2550	152	15	360	38	27
100	5,665	25	9	1940	30	8	725	32	2570	153	15	360	38	32
120	6,150	25	9	1970	30	14	1180	52	2590	155	15	360	38	38
140	6,615	25	9	2000	31	19	1615	71	2610	157	15	360	38	43
160	7,100	25	9	2025	31	24	2075	91	2640	158	15	360	38	48
180	7,750	25	9	2050	32	28	2520	110	2660	159	15	360	38	52
200	8,060	25	9	2075	32	33	2985	130	2690	160	15	360	38	57
220	8,545	25	9	2110	33	38	3435	149	2710	160	15	360	38	62
240	9,040	25	9	2150	34	43	3890	168	2730	161	15	360	38	67
260	9,550	25	9	2175	34	48	4375	188	2760	161	15	360	38	72
280	10,035	25	9	2210	35	52	4825	207	2770	162	15	360	38	76
300	10,560	25	9	2245	35	57	5315	227	2810	162	15	360	38	81
320	11,055	25	9	2280	36	62	5775	246	2820	162	15	360	38	86
340	11,555	25	9	2320	37	66	6235	265	2850	164	15	360	38	90
360	12,050	25	9	2350	38	70	6700	284	2850	164	15	360	38	94
380	12,595	25	9	2390	38	75	7205	304	2890	166	15	360	38	99
400	13,120	25	9	2430	39	79	7690	323	2920	167	15	360	38	103

Remarks:

(1) Fuel required includes 300 pounds for turn and acceleration.

(2) Provides 3000 pounds fuel at point where descent is commenced. No wind conditions.

(3) Climb speed is 180 KCAS at sea level; decreasing 15 knots per 10,000 feet altitude.

(4) Idle descent to sea level at 122 KCAS.

(5) Aircraft operating weight is 38,153 pounds.

(6) For each 1000-pound increase in basic aircraft weight, increase the fuel required by 1%.

Data as of: 1 March 1964   Fuel Grade: JP-5

Data Basis: NATC and Contractor Flight Test   Fuel Density: 6.8 lb/gal

Figure 11-80. Foulded Deck Range – Gear and Flaps Down

NAVAIR 01-40ATA-1

Section XI
Part 4A

FOULED DECK RANGE (VFR)
One-Engine Operation

Model: A-3A

Engines: J57-P-6

Dist	Fuel Req	Alt	Climb			Cruise			Fuel Flow lb/hr/Eng	CAS	Descent			Total ETE
			ETE	Fuel	Dist	ETE	Fuel	Dist			ETE	Fuel	Dist	
40	3700	5	2	460	8	6	240	17	3320	224	4	92	15	12
60	3870	10	5	720	19	3	150	12	3250	225	8	171	29	16
80	4130	10	5	725	19	7	405	32	3260	225	8	171	29	20
100	4285	15	8	1020	33	5	265	23	3170	220	12	243	44	25
120	4440	20	11	1360	53	2	80	8	3170	220	16	307	59	29
140	4665	20	11	1370	53	6	295	28	3160	220	16	307	59	33
160	4875	20	12	1380	53	9	495	48	3150	220	16	307	59	37
180	5025	25	18	1830	86	4	235	20	3170	221	19	360	74	41
200	5235	25	18	1840	86	7	395	40	3180	221	19	360	74	44
220	5235	25	18	1860	87	11	575	59	3180	221	19	360	74	48
240	5645	25	18	1880	88	14	765	78	3180	221	19	360	74	51
260	5760	30	29	2600	152	3	160	18	3200	223	22	410	90	54
280	5950	30	30	2610	154	6	340	37	3210	224	22	410	90	58
300	6140	30	30	2640	156	9	500	54	3220	224	22	410	90	61
320	6330	30	30	2680	159	12	650	71	3230	224	22	410	90	64
340	6520	30	30	2700	160	15	820	90	3240	224	22	410	90	67
360	6720	30	31	2740	163	18	980	107	3240	224	22	410	90	71
380	6935	30	31	2785	165	21	1150	125	3250	225	22	410	90	74
400	7120	30	32	2800	166	24	1320	144	3250	225	22	410	90	78

Remarks:

(1) Fuel required includes 200 pounds for cleanup, turn, and acceleration.

(2) Provides 3000 pounds fuel at point where descent is commenced. No wind conditions.

(3) Climb speed is 255 KCAS at sea level; decreasing 15 knots per 10,000 feet.

(4) Descent at sea level at 190 KCAS with 85% rpm.

(5) Aircraft operating weight is 38,153 pounds.

(6) For each 1000-pound increase in basic aircraft weight, increase the fuel required by 1%.

Data as of: 1 March 1964

Data Basis: NATC and Contractor Flight Test

Fuel Grade: JP-5

Fuel Density: 6.8 lb/gal

Figure 11-81. Fouled Deck Range — VFR

Section XI
Part 4A

NAVAIR 01-40ATA-1

FOULED DECK RANGE (IFR)
One-Engine Operation

Model: A-3A Engines: J57-P-6

Dist	Fuel Req	Alt	Climb			Cruise			Fuel Flow lb/hr/Eng	CAS	Total ETE
			ETE	Fuel	Dist	ETE	Fuel	Dist			
40	3805	SL	0	200	0	11	605	40	3450	225	11
60	4125	SL	0	200	0	16	925	60	3460	225	16
80	4480	5	2	460	8	18	1020	73	3350	226	20
100	4760	10	5	730	19	19	1030	81	3290	226	24
120	5020	10	5	740	19	23	1280	101	3300	226	28
140	5285	15	8	1050	34	23	1235	106	3210	223	31
160	5525	15	8	1060	34	27	1465	126	3210	223	35
180	5735	20	12	1420	54	25	1335	126	3170	223	37
200	5970	20	12	1430	55	29	1540	145	3200	223	41
220	6180	20	12	1440	56	33	1740	164	3200	223	45
240	6385	25	19	1920	92	27	1465	148	3200	223	46
260	6640	30	31	2730	161	16	910	99	3240	225	47
280	6830	30	31	2755	163	20	1075	117	3250	225	51
300	7040	30	32	2810	165	23	1230	135	3250	225	55
320	7220	30	32	2820	167	26	1400	153	3260	225	58
340	7430	30	32	2860	169	29	1570	171	3270	225	61
360	7575	30	33	2870	171	32	1725	189	3270	225	65
380	7800	30	33	2900	172	35	1900	208	3270	225	68
400	7970	30	33	2920	176	37	2050	224	3270	225	70

Remarks:

(1) Fuel required includes 200 pounds for cleanup, turn, and acceleration.

(2) Provides 3000 pounds fuel at approach fix. No wind conditions.

(3) Climb speed is 255 KCAS decreasing 15 knots per 10,000 feet.

(4) Aircraft operating weight is 38,153 pounds.

(5) For each 1000-pound increase in basic aircraft weight, increase the fuel required by 1%.

Data as of: 1 March 1964 Fuel Grade: JP-5

Data Basis: NATC and Contractor Flight Test Fuel Density: 6.8 lb/gal

Figure 11-82. Fouled Deck Range — IFR

NAVAIR 01-40ATA-1

Section XI
Part 4A

SEA LEVEL FOULED DECK RANGE
One-Engine Operation

Model: A-3A   Engines: J57-P-6

Dist	Fuel Req	Flow lb/hr	CAS	ETE
40	3805	3450	225	11
60	4125	3460	225	16
80	4445	3460	225	21
100	4760	3470	225	27
120	5050	3490	226	32
140	5365	3500	226	37
160	5670	3500	226	42
180	5995	3500	226	48
200	6310	3520	227	53
220	6630	3540	227	58
240	6940	3560	228	63
260	7260	3560	228	68
280	7580	3570	228	74
300	7900	3570	228	79
320	8215	3570	228	84
340	8535	3590	229	89
360	8880	3620	229	94
380	9210	3620	229	100
400	9520	3640	230	104

Remarks:

(1) Fuel required includes 200 lbs for cleanup, turn, and acceleration.

(2) Provides 3000 pounds fuel reserve for landing. No wind conditions.

(3) Aircraft operating weight is 38,153 pounds.

(4) For each 1000-pound increase in basic aircraft weight, increase the fuel required by 0.6%.

Data as of: 1 March 1964   Fuel Grade: JP-5
Data Basis: NATC and Contractor Flight Test   Fuel Density: 6.8 lb/gal

Figure 11-83. Fouled Deck Range — Sea Level

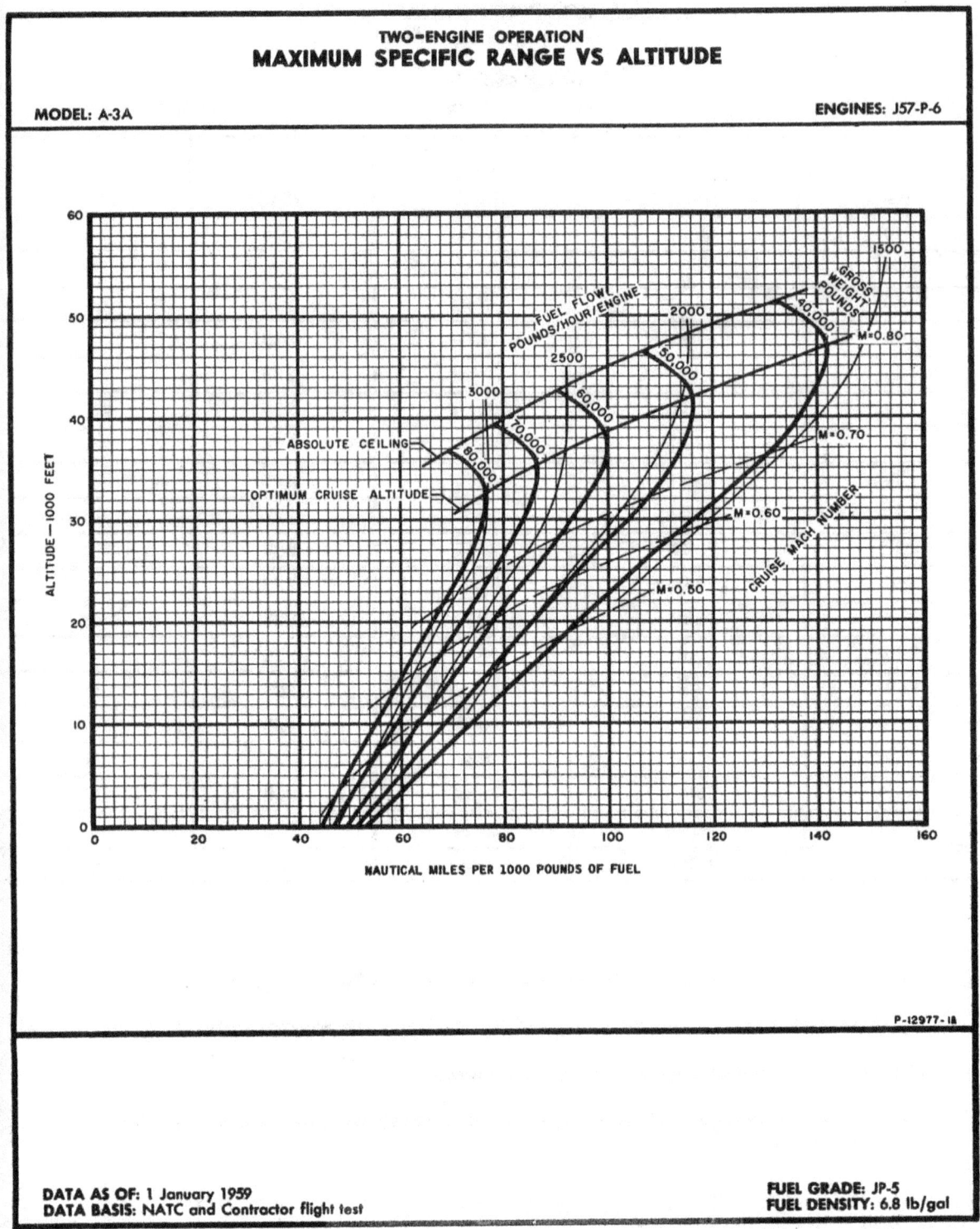

Figure 11-84. Maximum Specific Range vs Altitude (Sheet 1)

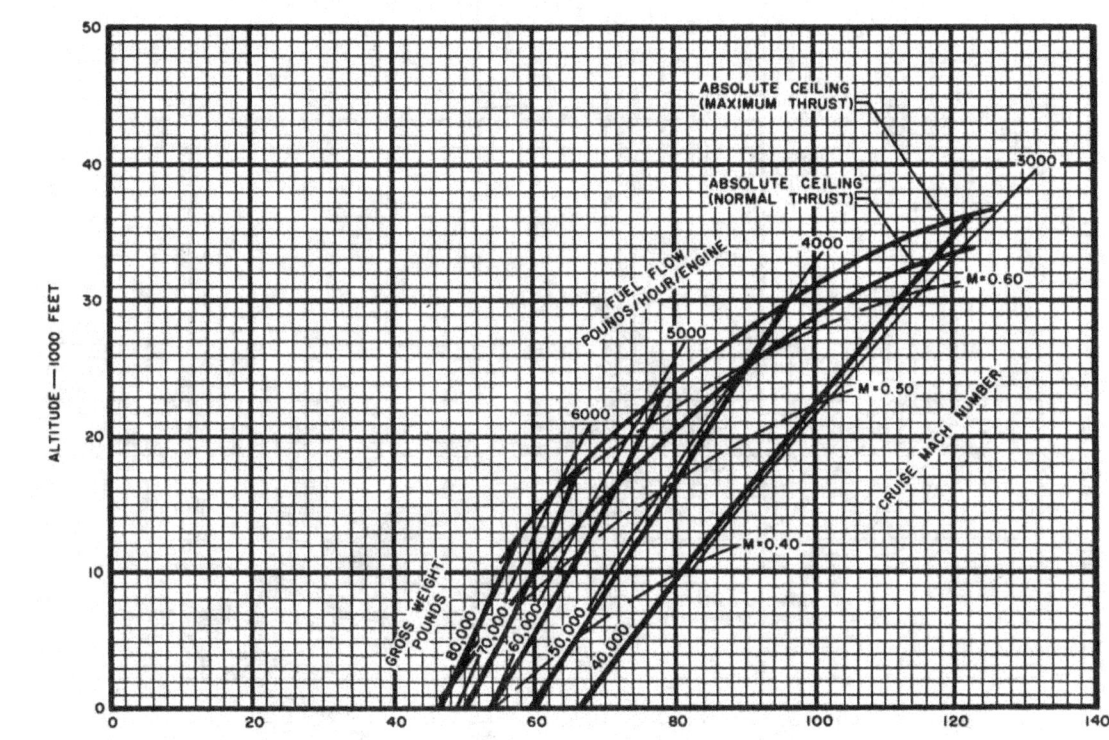

Figure 11-84. Maximum Specific Range vs Altitude (Sheet 2)

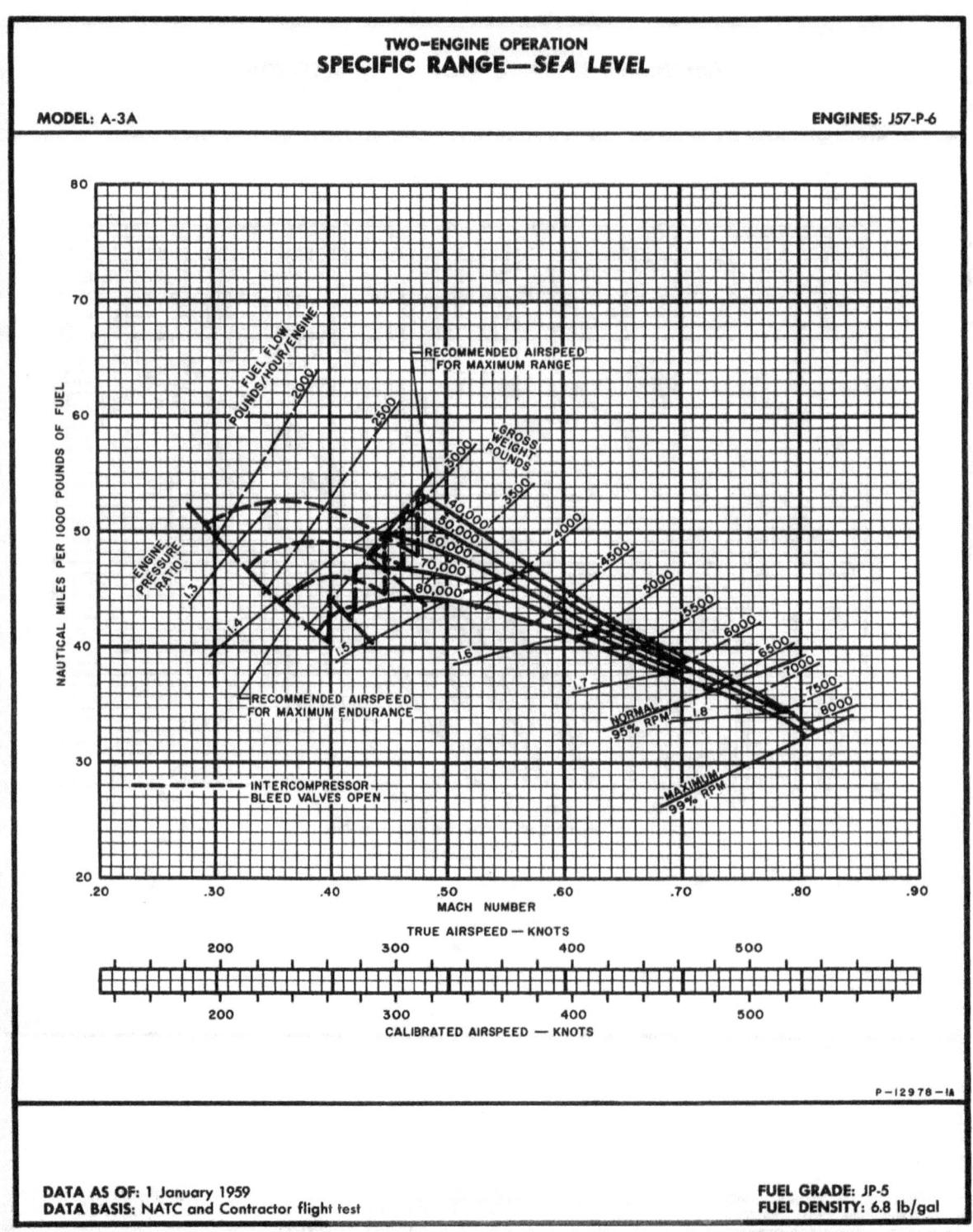

Figure 11-85. Specific Range — Sea Level (Sheet 1)

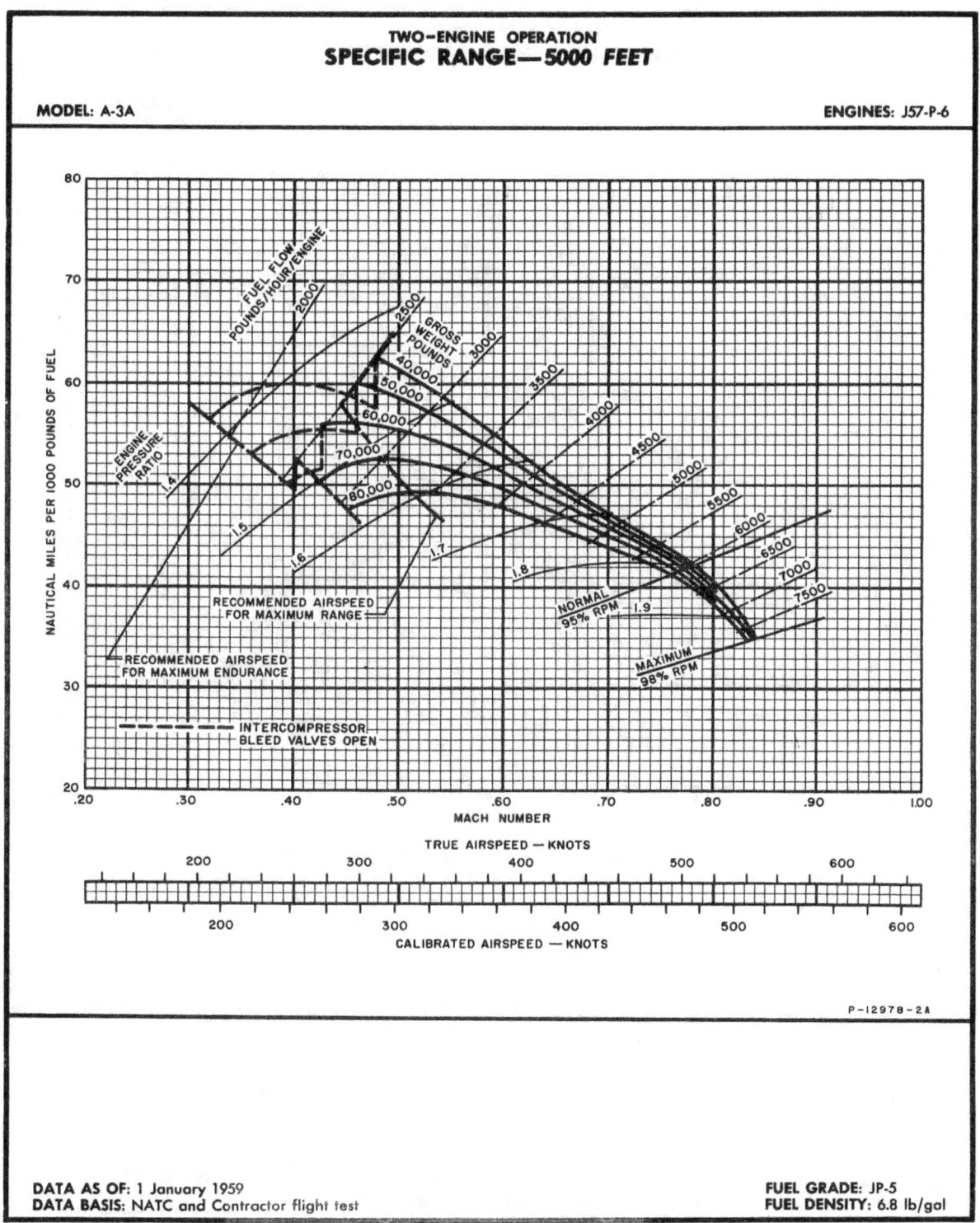

Figure 11-85. Specific Range — 5000 Feet (Sheet 2)

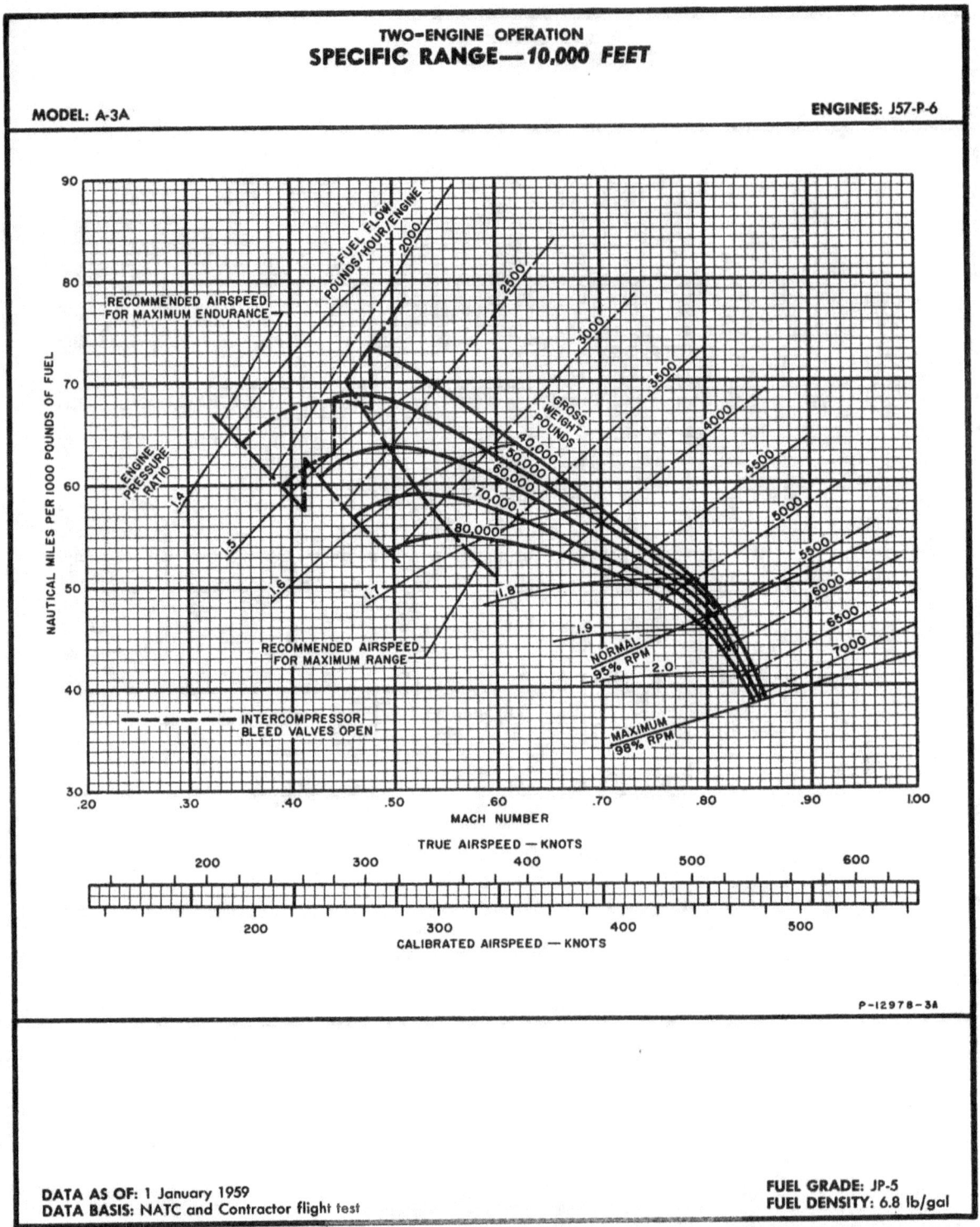

Figure 11-85. Specific Range – 10,000 Feet (Sheet 3)

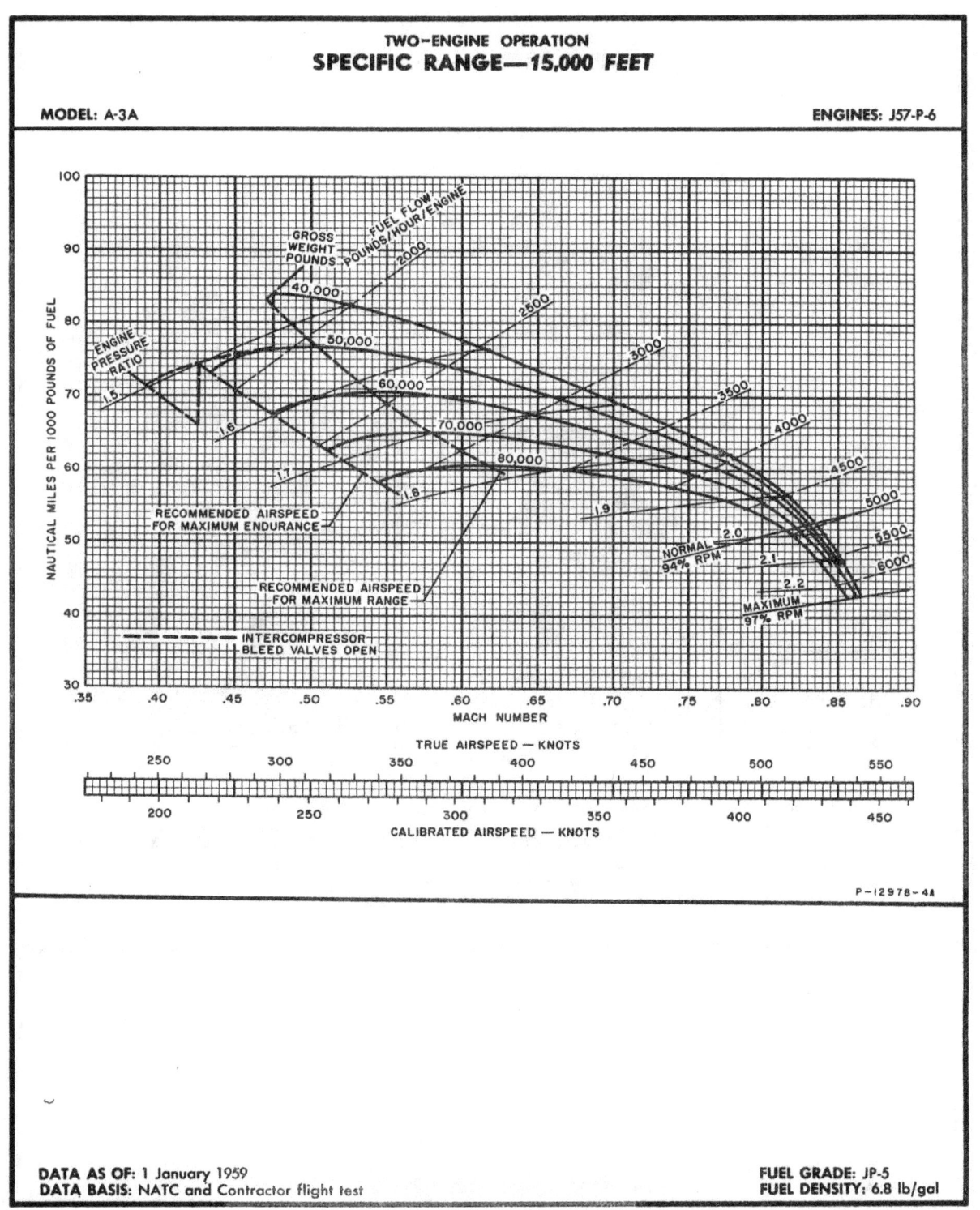

Figure 11-85. Specific Range — 15,000 Feet (Sheet 4)

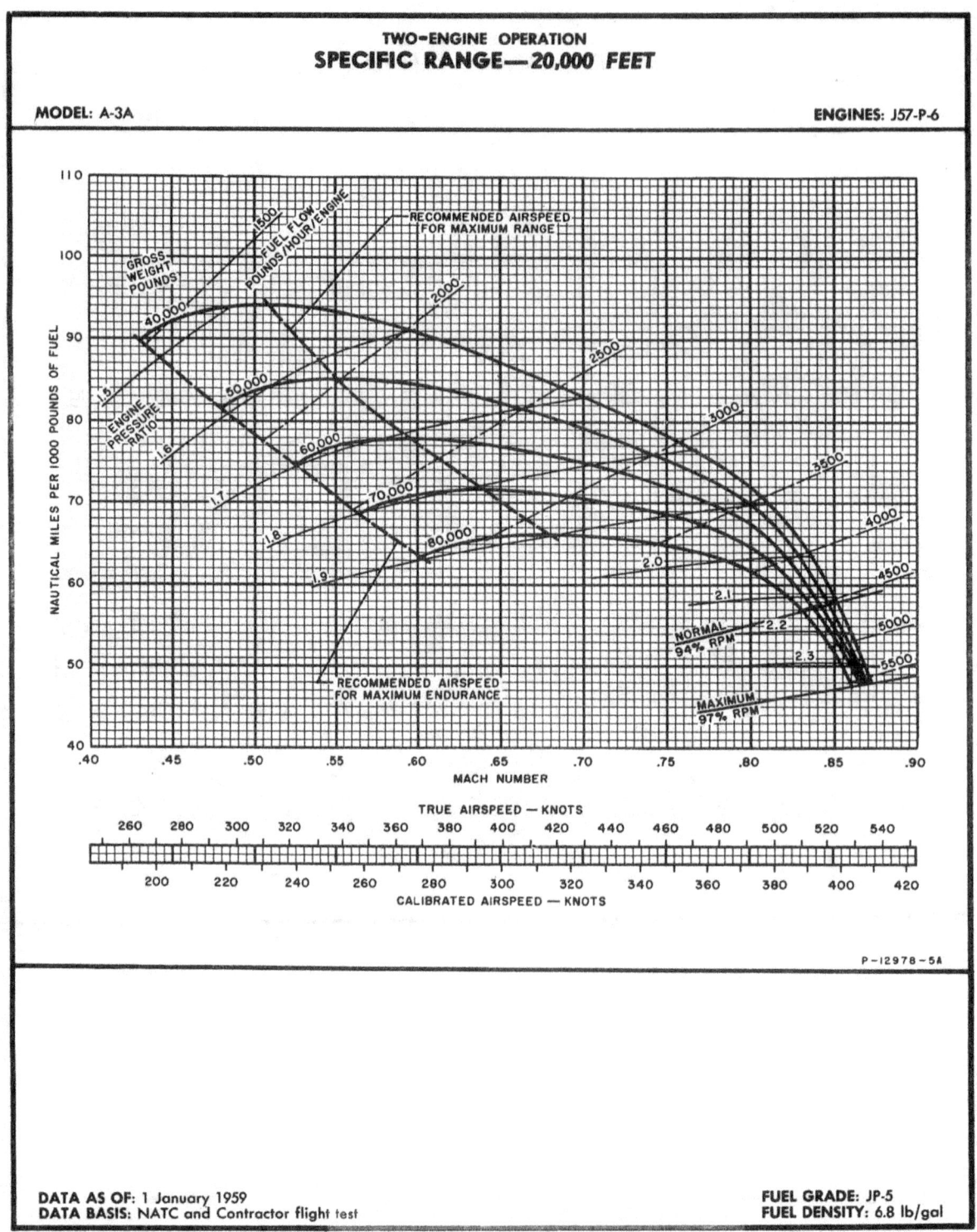

Figure 11-85. Specific Range — 20,000 Feet (Sheet 5)

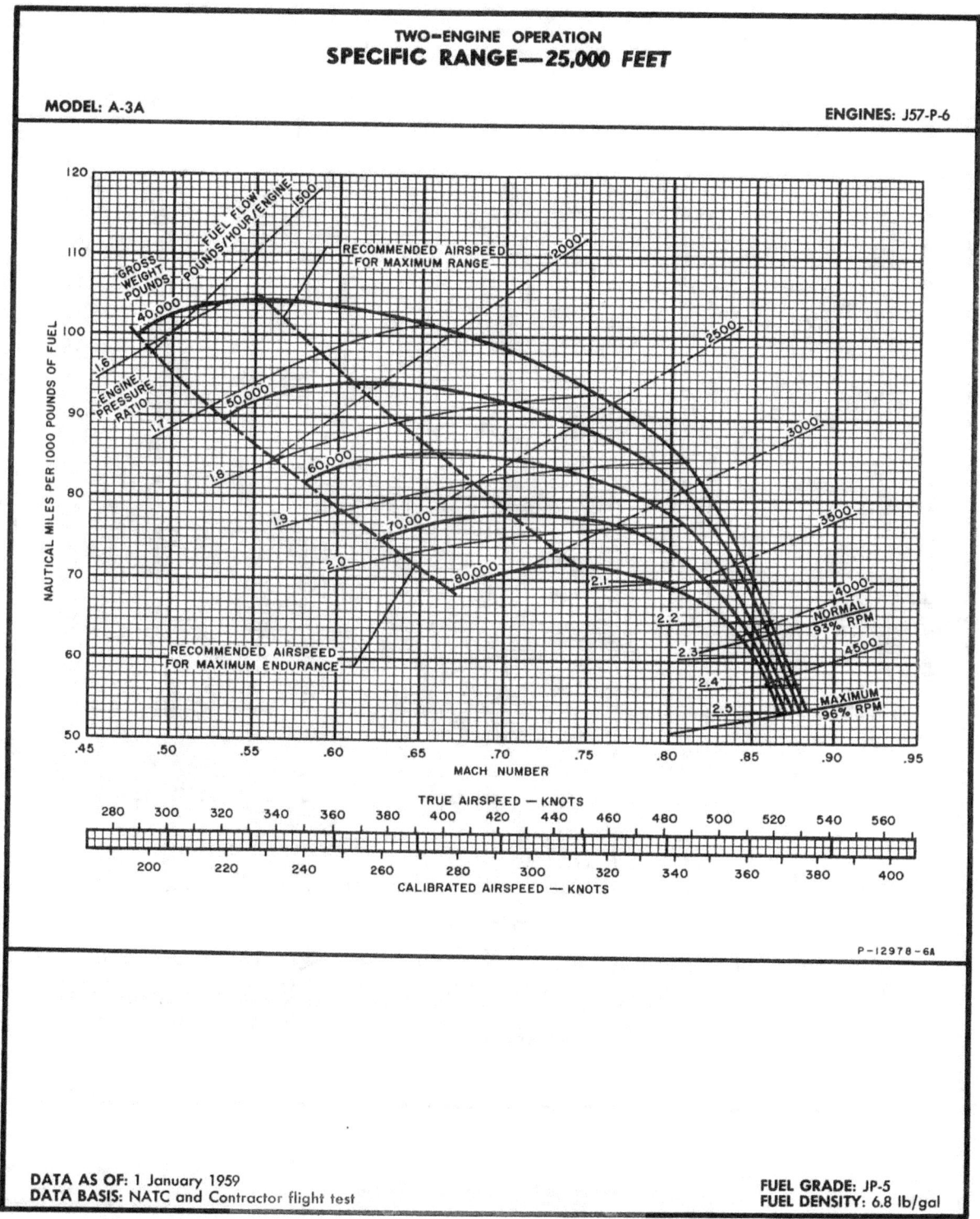

Figure 11-85. Specific Range — 25,000 Feet (Sheet 6)

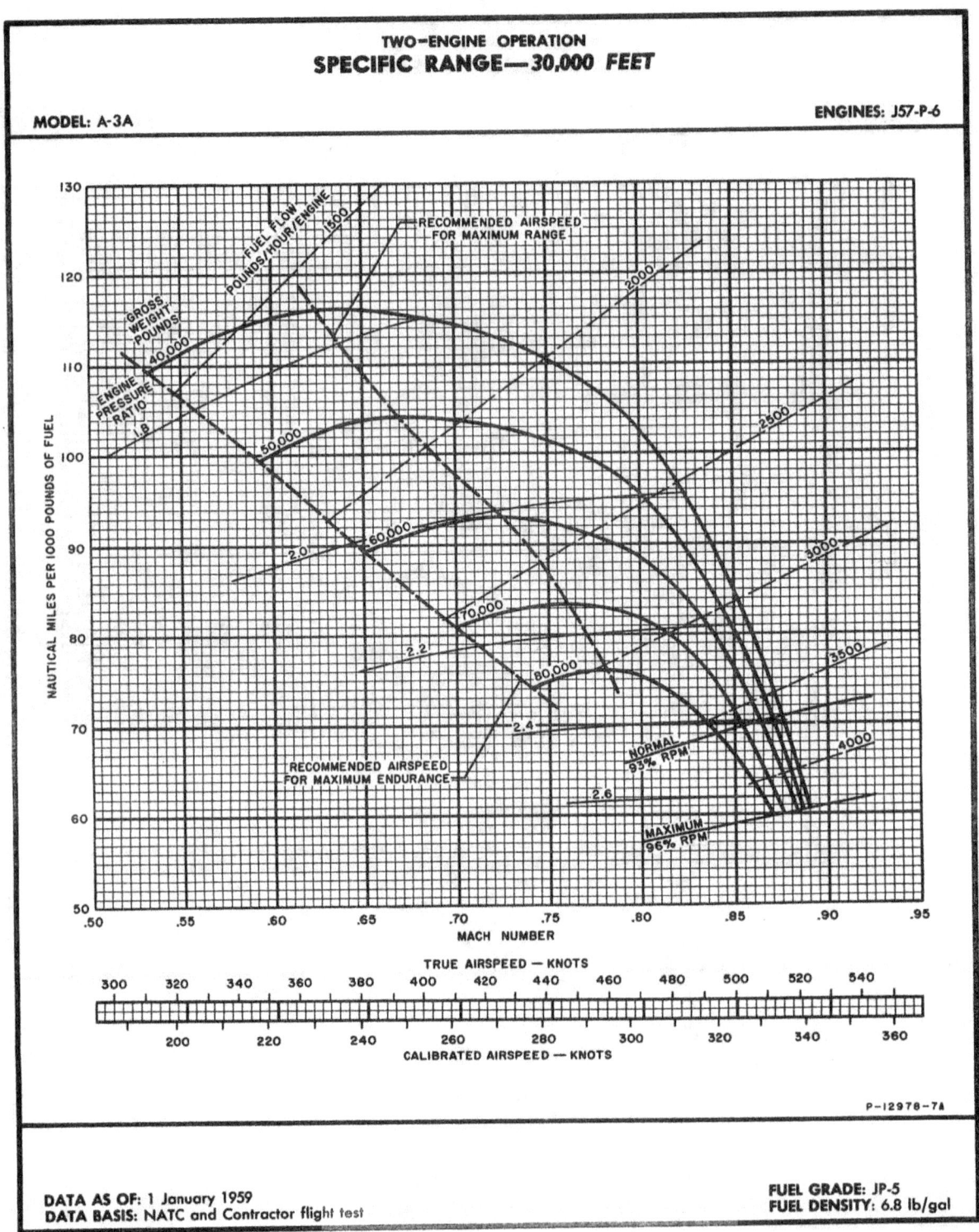

Figure 11-85. Specific Range — 30,000 Feet (Sheet 7)

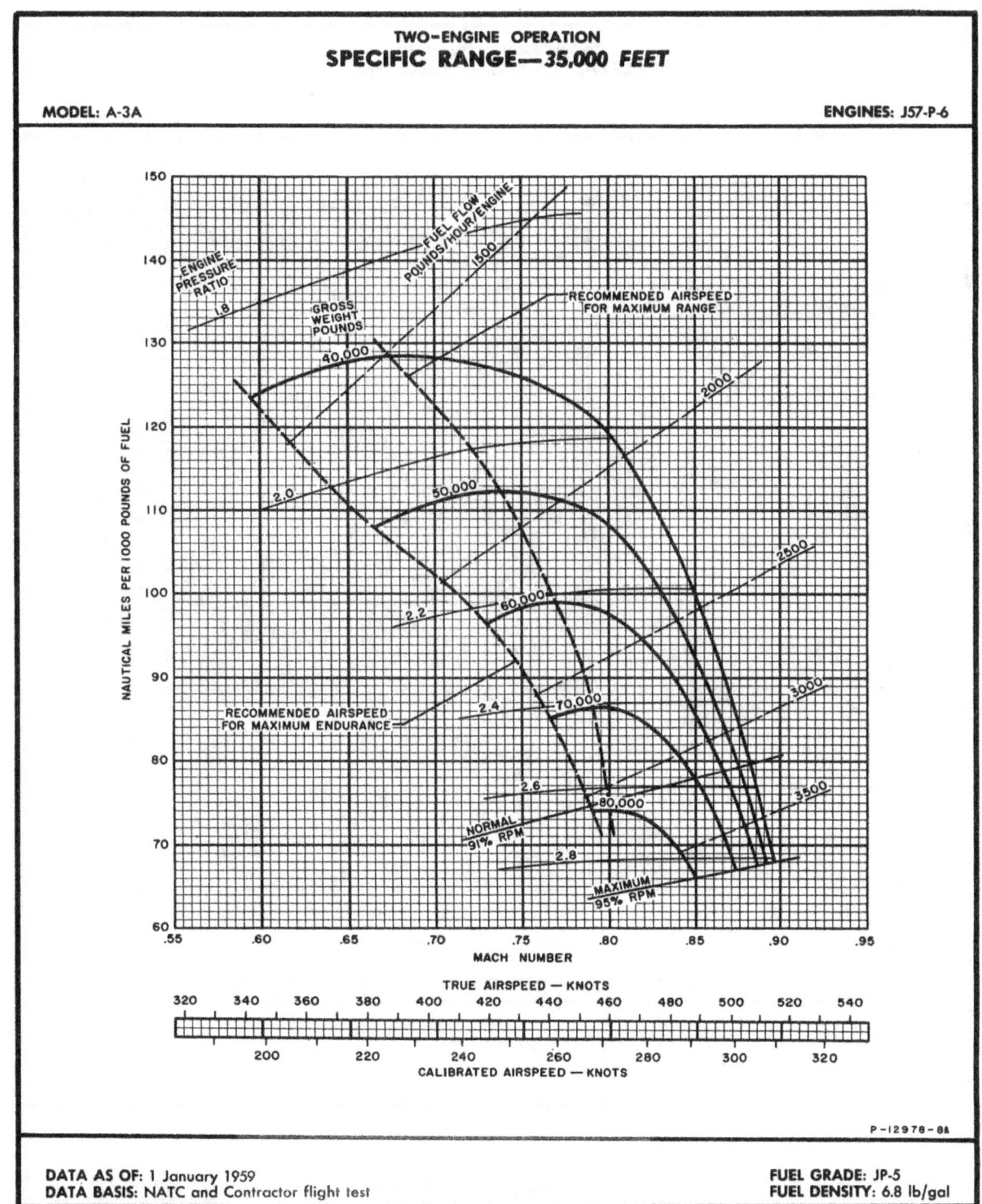

Figure 11-85. Specific Range — 35,000 Feet (Sheet 8)

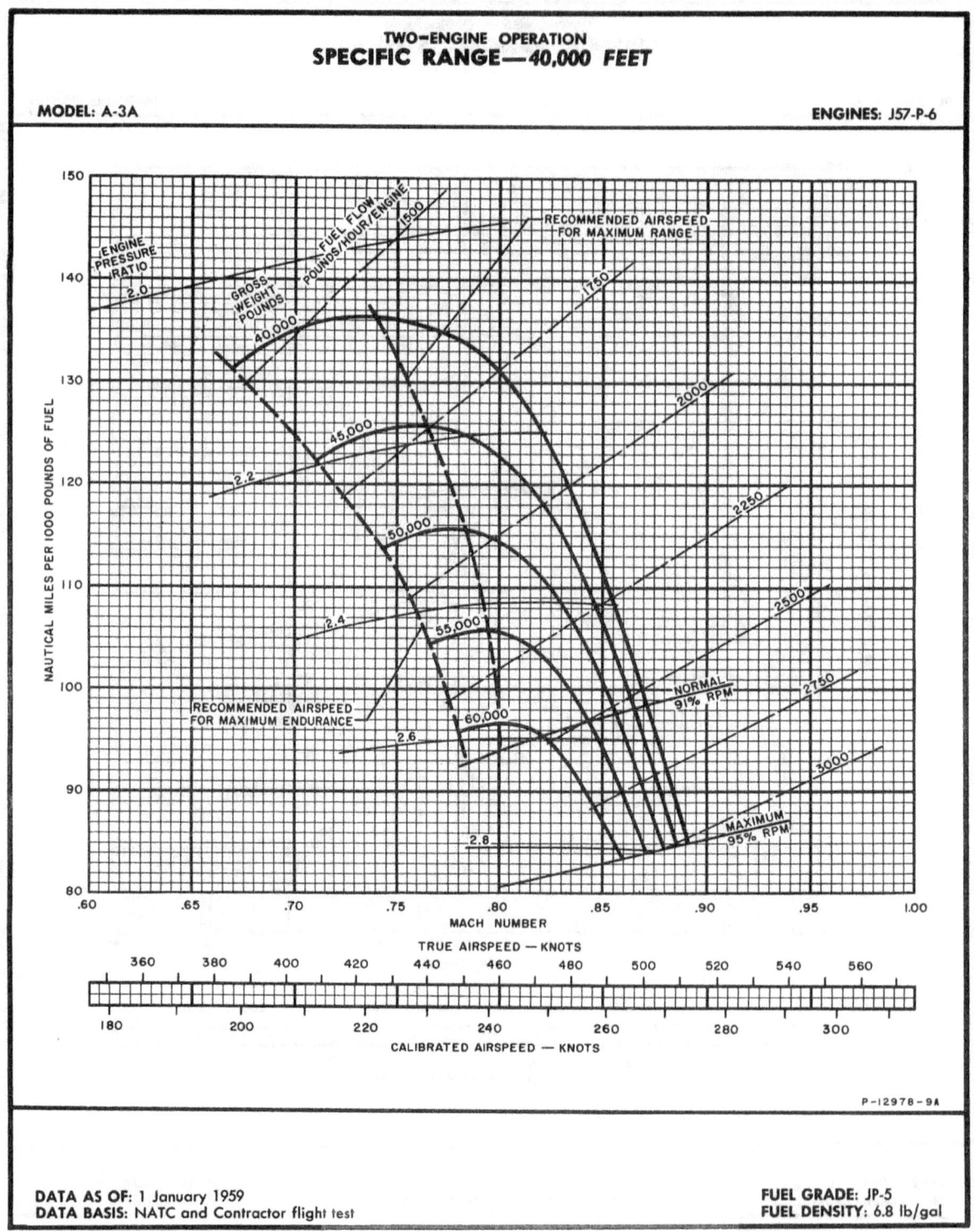

Figure 11-85. Specific Range — 40,000 Feet (Sheet 9)

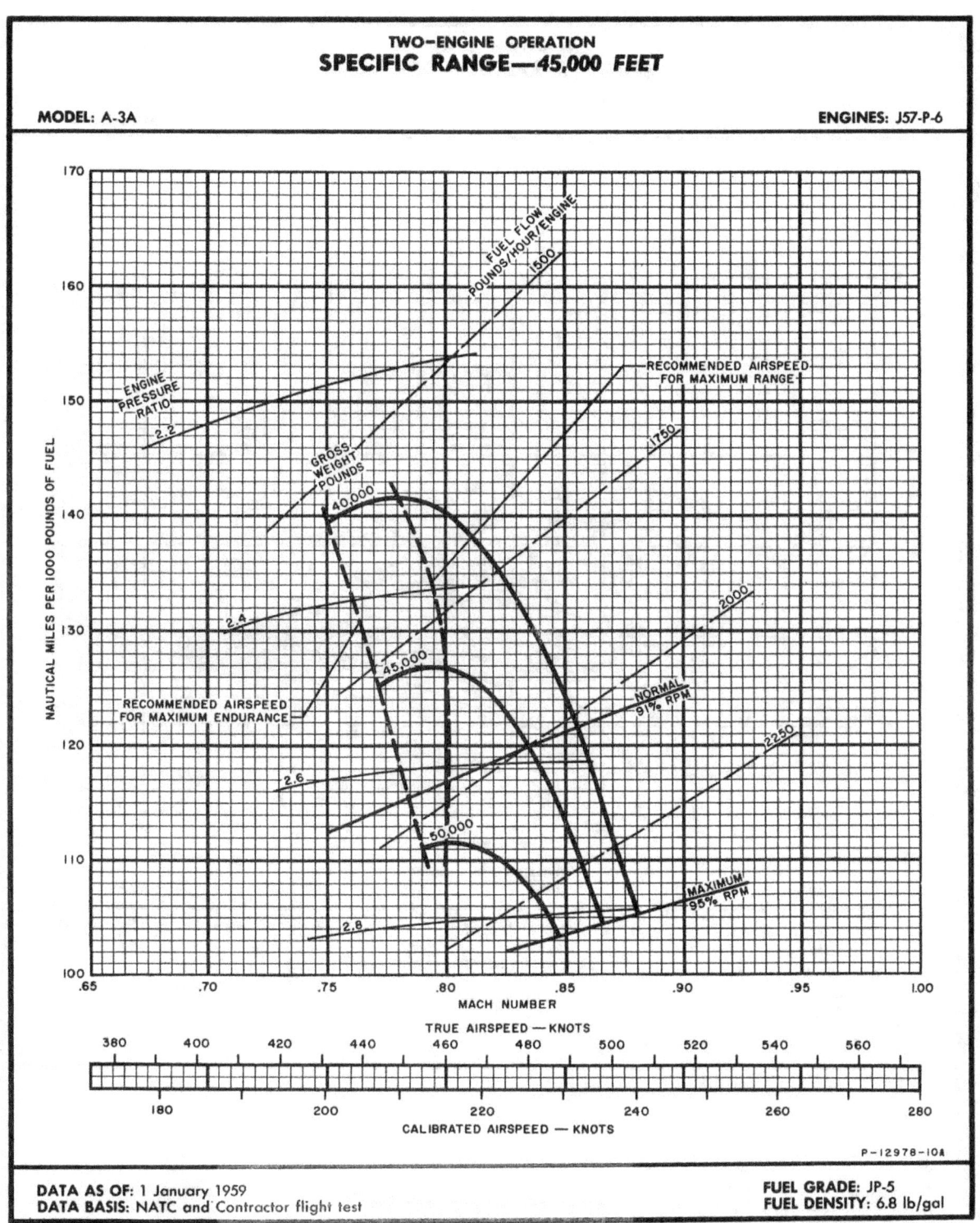

Figure 11-85. Specific Range — 45,000 Feet (Sheet 10)

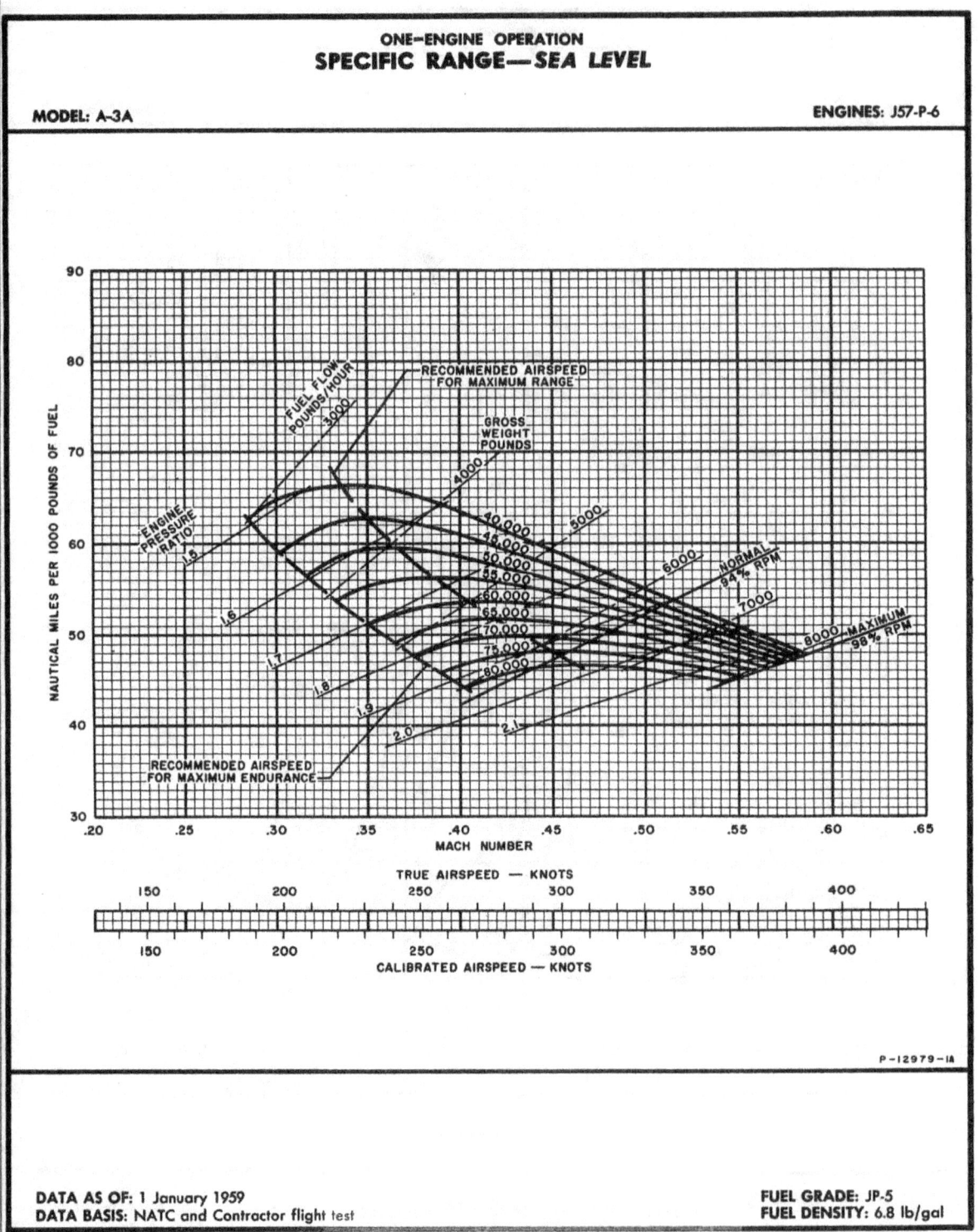

Figure 11-86. Specific Range – Sea Level (Sheet 1)

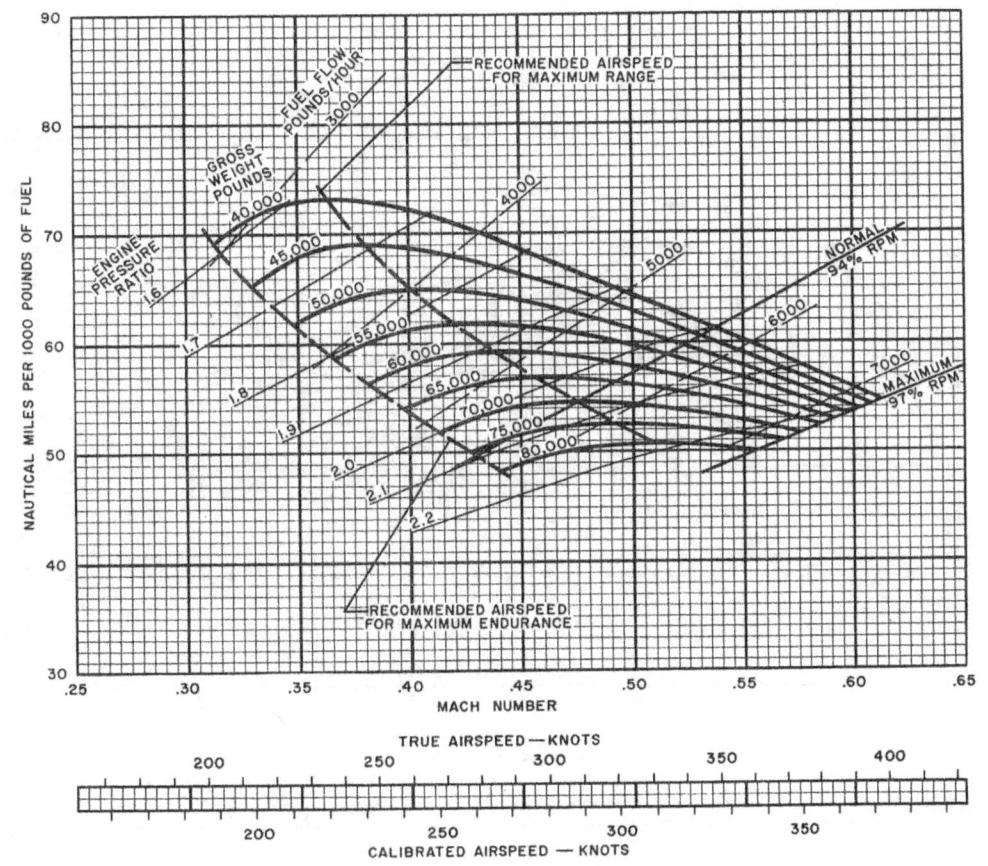

Figure 11-86. Specific Range — 5000 Feet (Sheet 2)

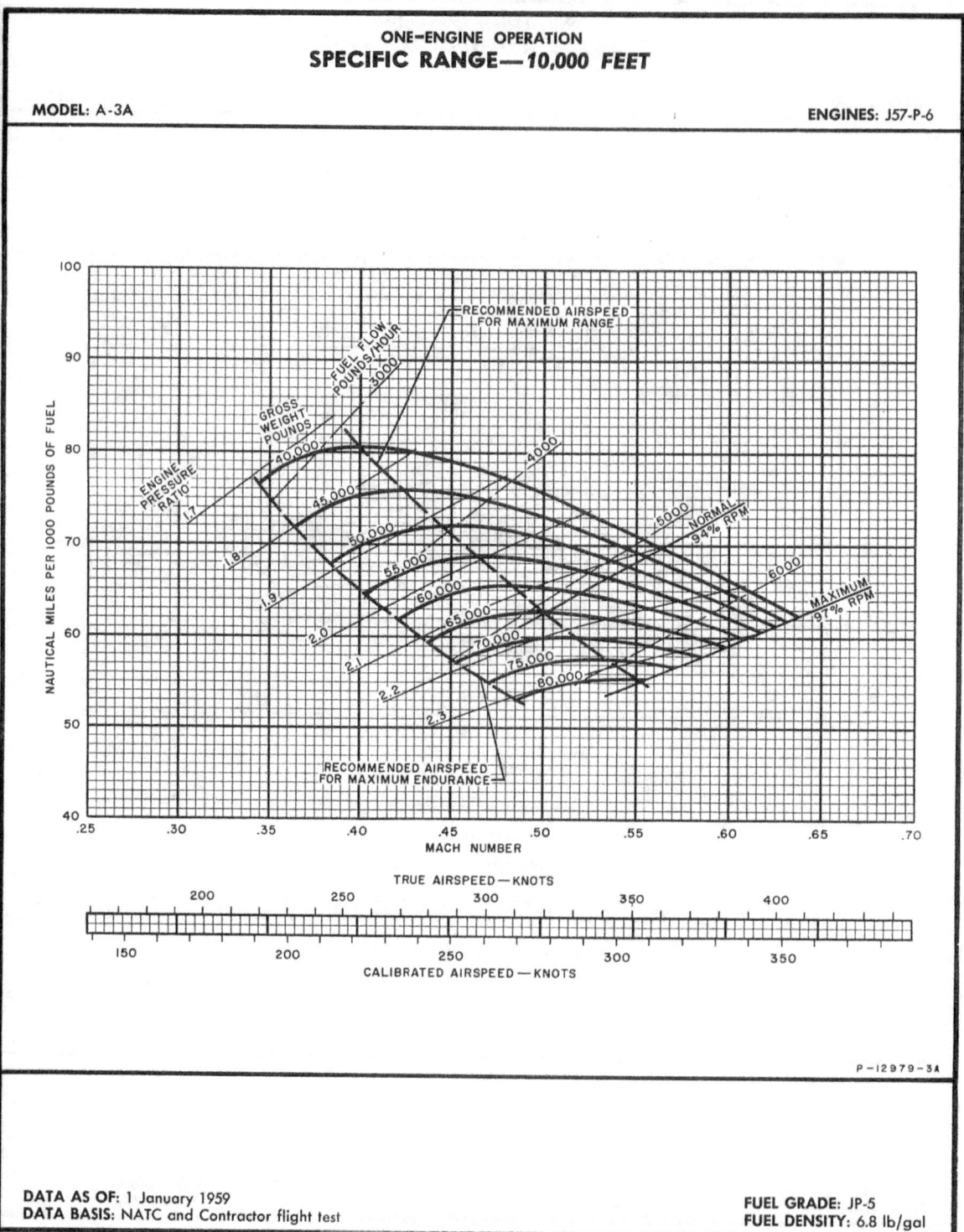

Figure 11-86. Specific Range — 10,000 Feet (Sheet 3)

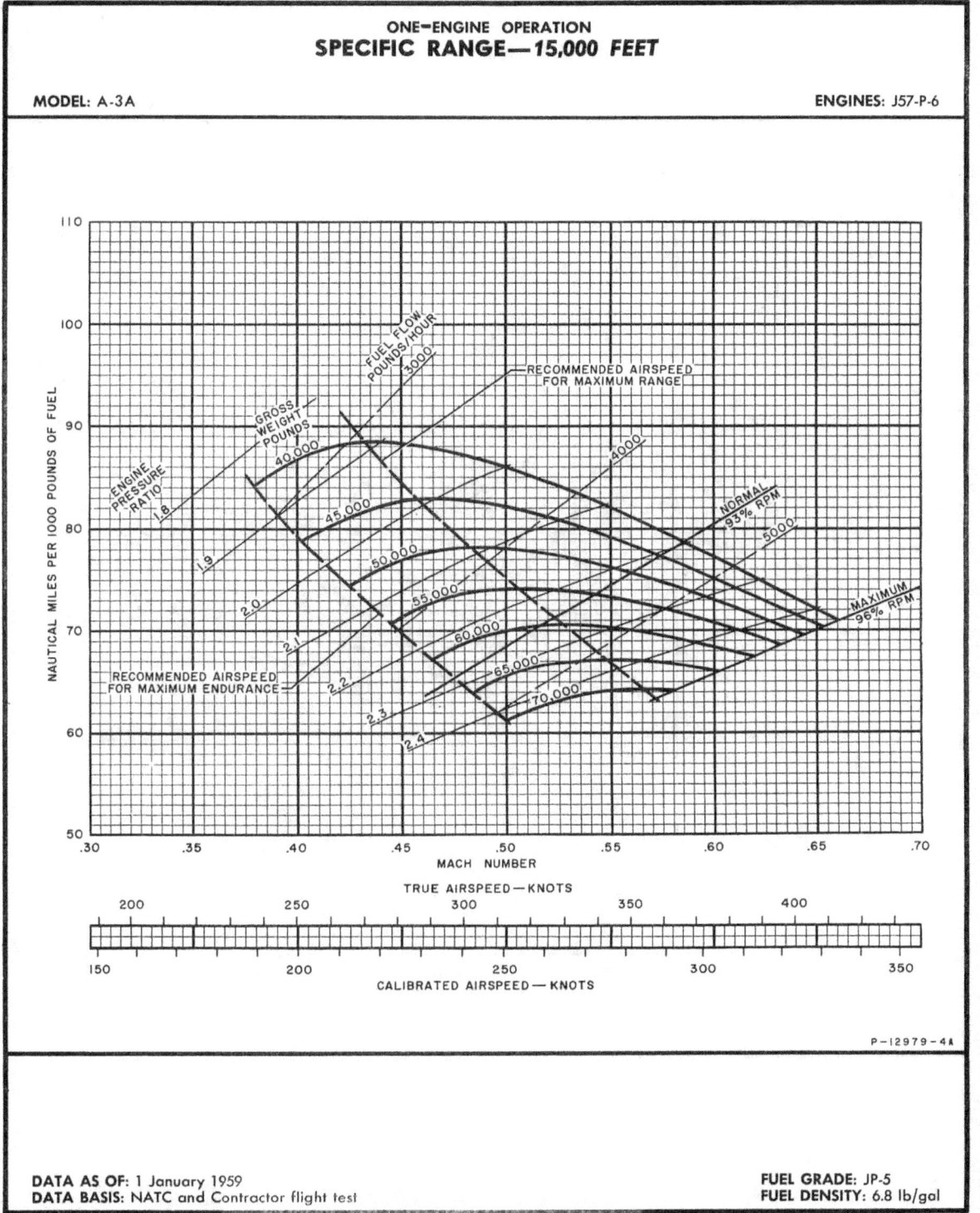

Figure 11-86. Specific Range — 15,000 Feet (Sheet 4)

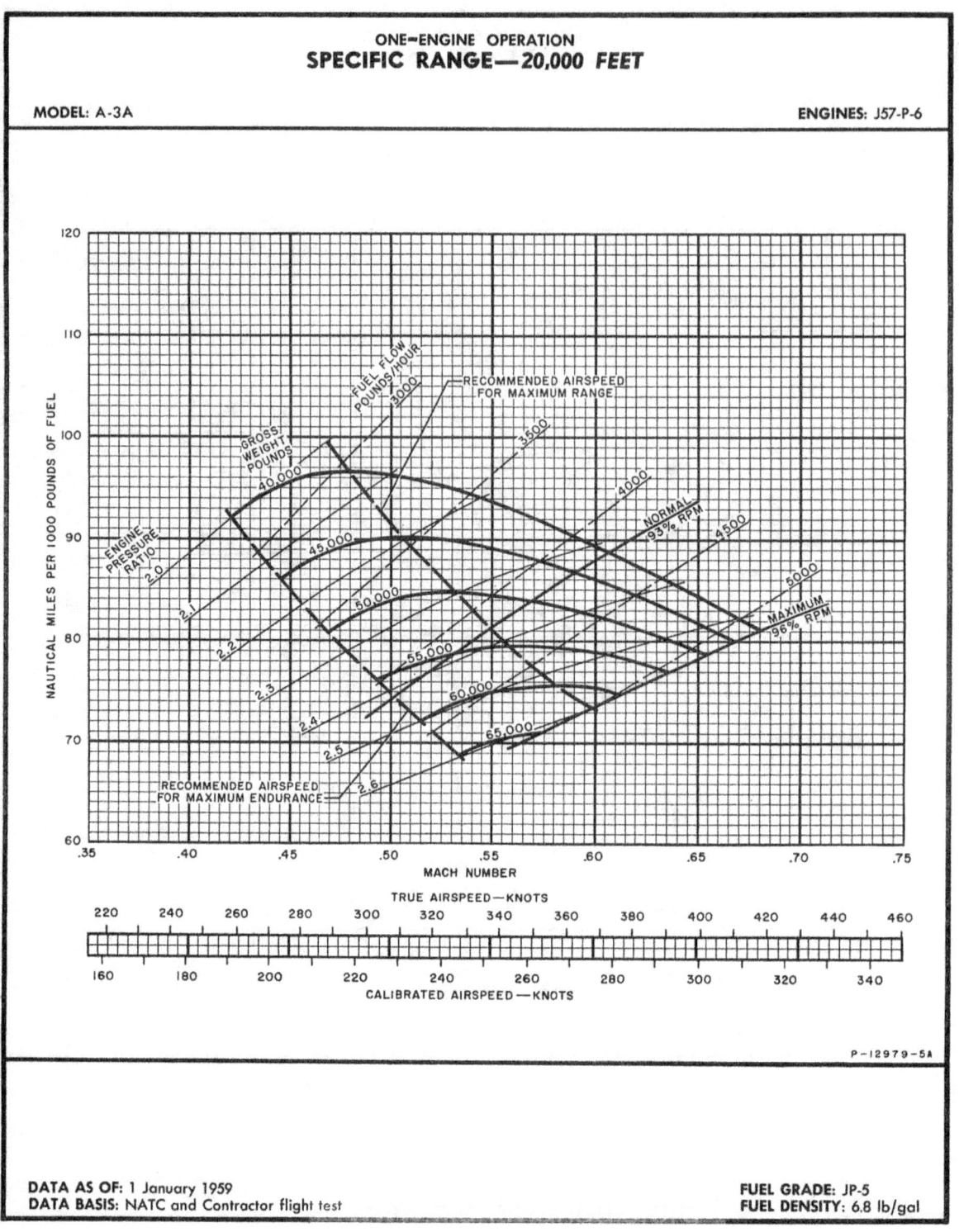

Figure 11-86. Specific Range – 20,000 Feet (Sheet 5)

ONE-ENGINE OPERATION

SPECIFIC RANGE—25,000 FEET

MODEL: A-3A

ENGINES: J57-P-6

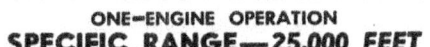

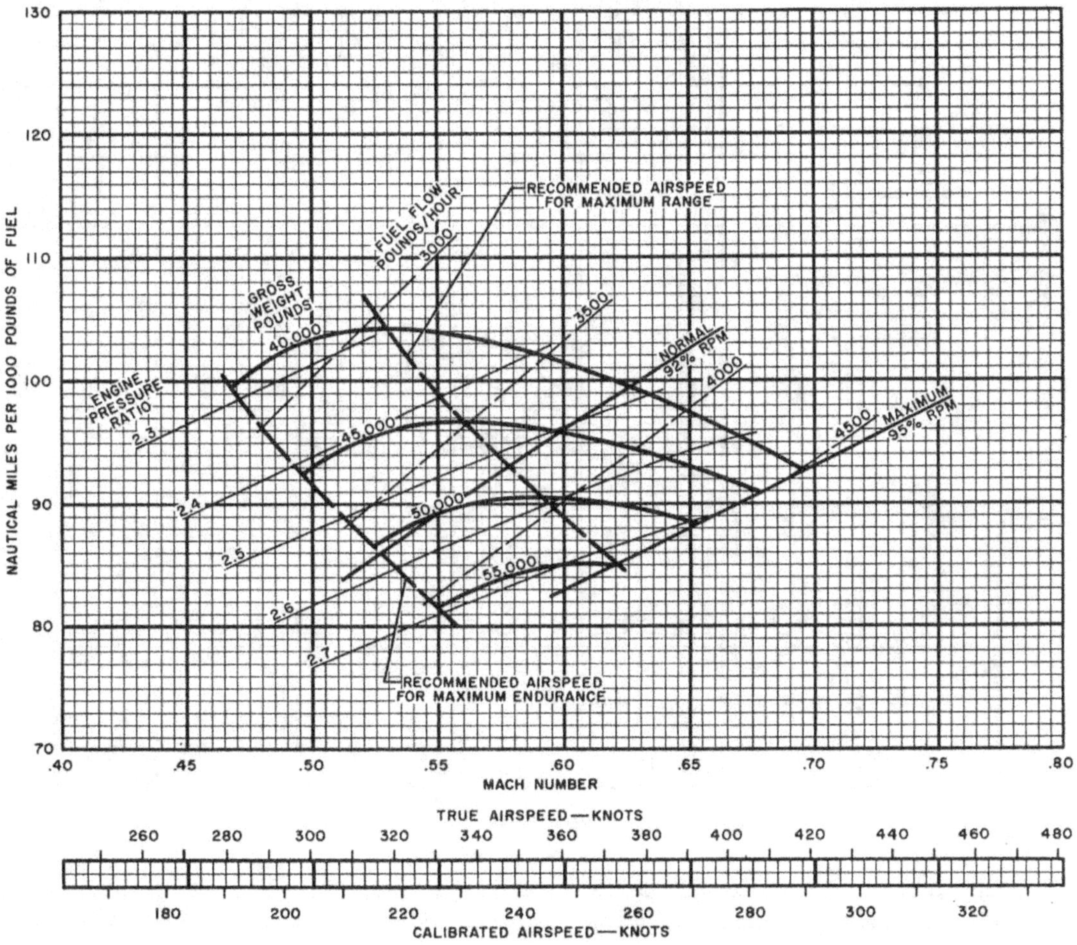

DATA AS OF: 1 January 1959
DATA BASIS: NATC and Contractor flight test

FUEL GRADE: JP-5
FUEL DENSITY: 6.8 lb/gal

Figure 11-86. Specific Range – 25, 000 Feet (Sheet 6)

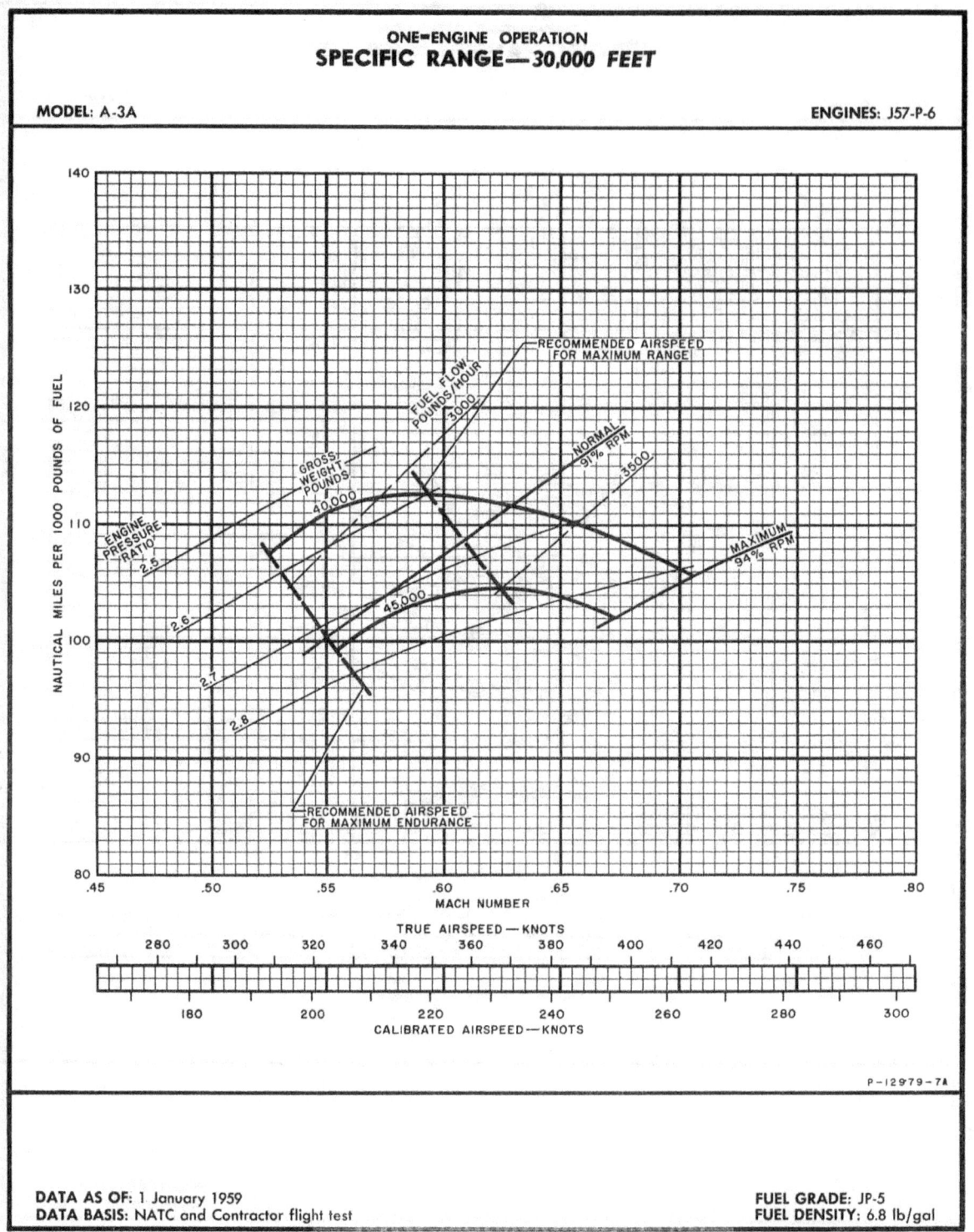

Figure 11-86. Specific Range — 30,000 Feet (Sheet 7)

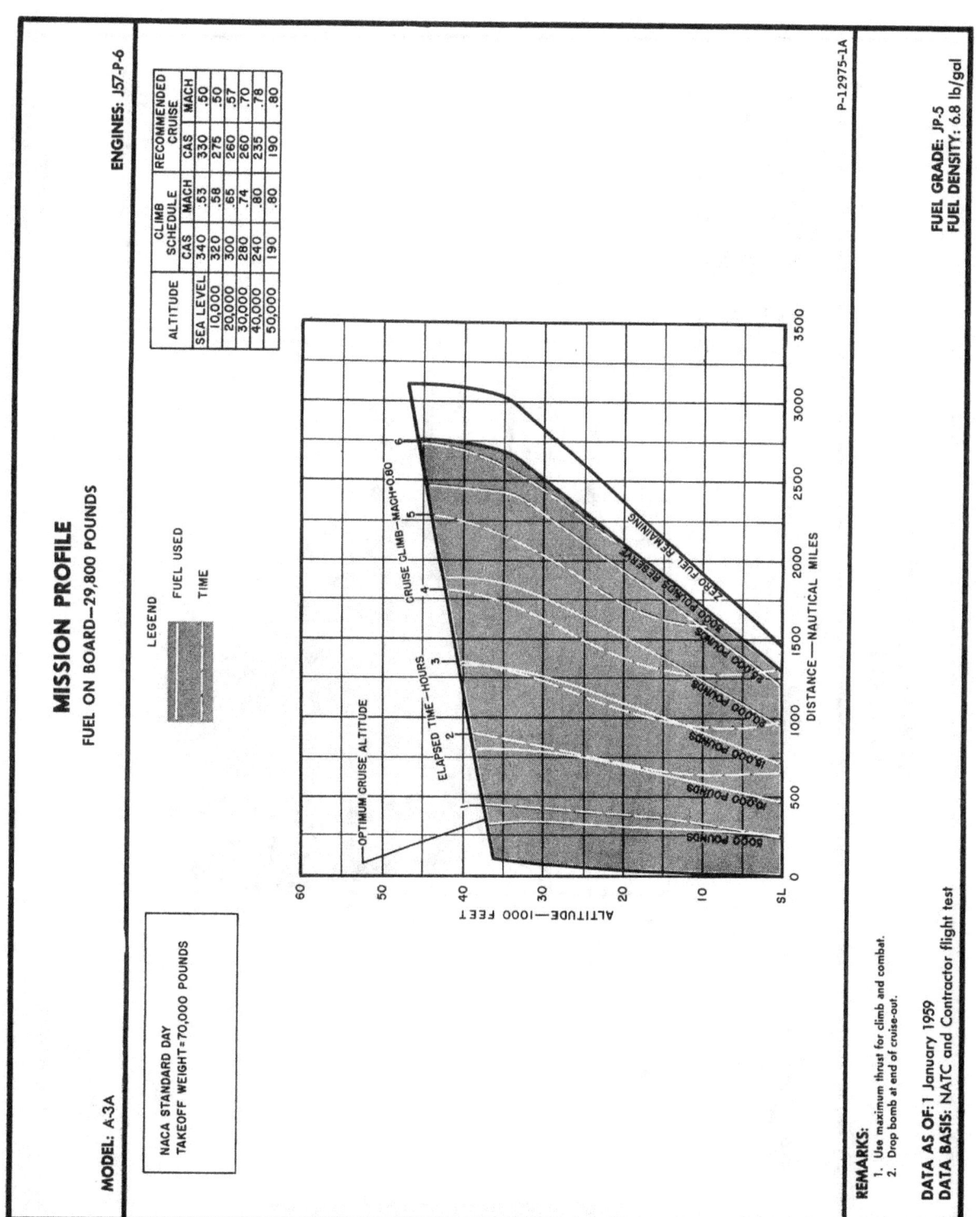

Figure 11-87. Mission Profile

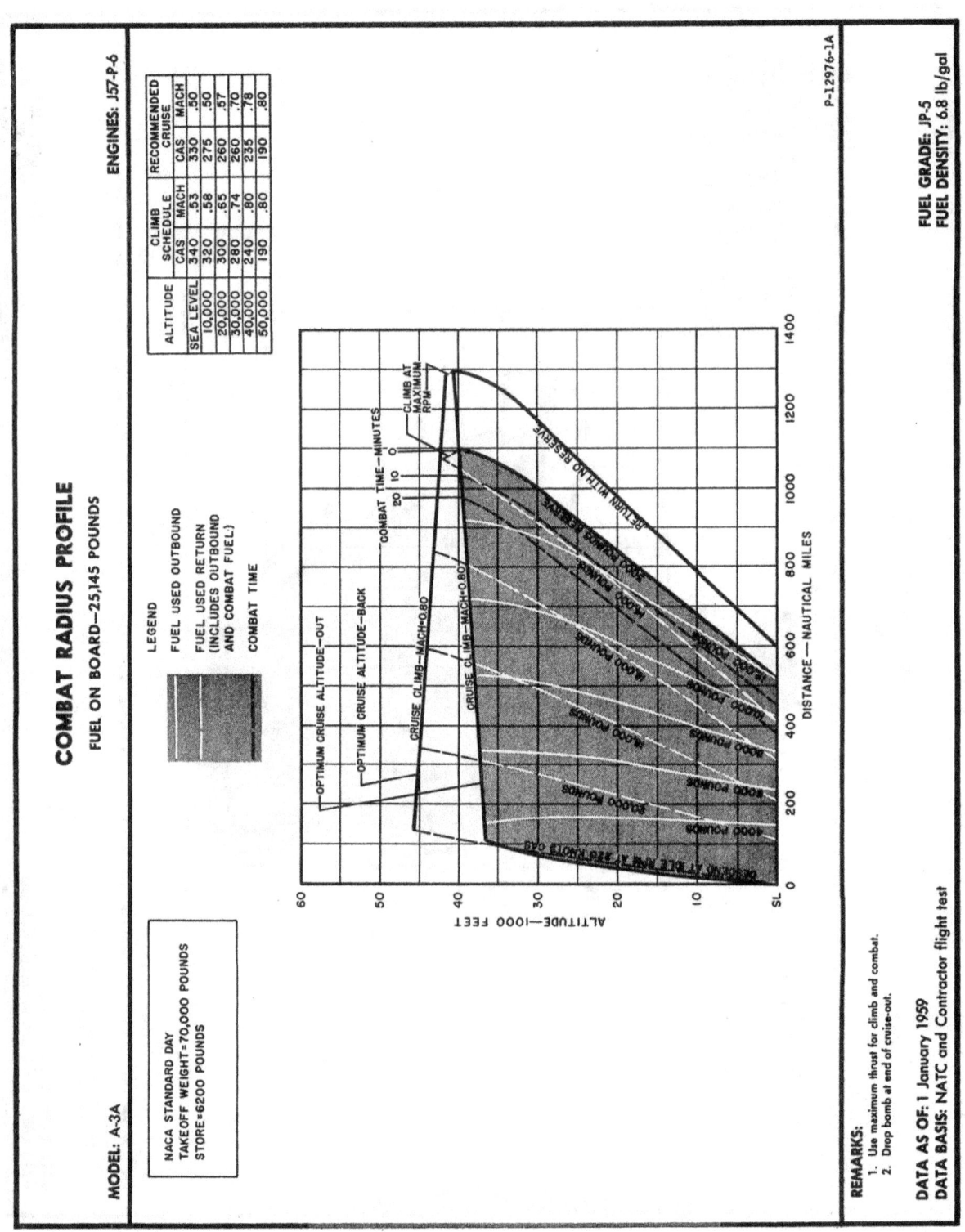

Figure 11-88. Combat Radius Profile

NAVAIR 01-40ATA-1

Section XI
Part 5A

PART 5A
ENDURANCE

TABLE OF CONTENTS

TEXT

	Page
Endurance Charts.	11-177

ILLUSTRATIONS

Figure		Page	Figure		Page
11-89	Fouled Deck Endurance	11-178	11-90	Maximum Specific Endurance vs Altitude	11-180

Endurance Charts

When maximum endurance operation is required during flight, such as holding at altitude while awaiting clearance to land, the recommended airspeed to be maintained is approximately 10 percent higher than that at which minimum fuel flow is obtained. The higher airspeed will result in generally better handling characteristics for the aircraft, particularly in mild or moderate turbulence, with only a slight increase in fuel consumption. The endurance data presented in this appendix are based on using the recommended airspeeds. These airspeeds should be maintained by occasional adjustment of the throttle(s) as fuel is consumed.

FOULED DECK ENDURANCE

The fouled deck endurance charts for two-engine operation (figure 11-89, sheet 1) and one-engine operation (figure 11-89, sheet 2) are provided to indicate the maximum available endurance at low values of fuel remaining for various altitudes. For each initial altitude, the endurance at optimum altitude and the optimum altitude are provided. Climb and loiter speeds are indicated. A 3000-pound fuel allowance for landing is included.

ENDURANCE FACTORS WITH GEAR AND FLAPS DOWN

These endurance factors are applicable when attempting to loiter with gear down, flaps down, and speedbrakes closed. Multiply the values in the fouled deck endurance appendix charts by the appropriate factors.

SEA LEVEL ENDURANCE

	Endurance factors	KCAS
Single Engine	0.65	120-130
Two Engine	0.70	120-130

MAXIMUM SPECIFIC ENDURANCE VS ALTITUDE

Maximum specific endurance vs altitude charts present specific endurance (hours per 1000 pounds of fuel) as a function of momentary gross weight and altitude for two-engine operation (figure 11-90, sheet 1) and single-engine operation (figure 11-90, sheet 2). Mach numbers corresponding to the recommended airspeed for maximum endurance are superimposed on the charts. The broken lines included in the charts reflect the increase in fuel consumption resulting from opening of the intercompressor bleed valves. It will be noted that the specific endurance increases as the gross weight decreases due to the consumption of fuel. To obtain accurate endurance values under certain conditions, it may be necessary to re-enter the chart frequently with small increments to take full advantage of the endurance capabilities of the aircraft.

To determine the specific endurance for any given altitude and gross weight, enter the chart at that altitude and move to the right to the applicable momentary gross weight curve directly below, read the specific endurance hours per 1000 pounds of fuel. Interpolation between the Mach number lines will allow determination of the recommended Mach number corresponding to the recommended airspeed for maximum endurance.

EXAMPLE: Given an altitude of 30,000 feet, a gross weight of 60,000 pounds and 20,000 pounds of fuel remaining; find the maximum specific endurance.

1. Specific endurance at initial gross weight. . . . . 0.235 hours/1000 pounds of fuel

2. Specific endurance at final gross weight = 60,000 pounds - 20,000 pounds . . . . 0.35 hours/1000 pounds of fuel

3. Specific endurance at average gross weight = 60,000 pounds - (20,000 pounds -2) = 50,000 pounds . . . . 0.285 hours/1000 pounds of fuel x 20,000 pounds of fuel

4. Maximum endurance = 0.285 hours/ 1000 pounds fuel x
(20,000 - 10,000) . . 5.7 hours

Changed 1 June 1969

FOULED DECK ENDURANCE
TWO-ENGINE OPERATION

Model: A-3A   Engines: J57-P-6

Fuel on board – pounds

	If You Are at sea level					If You Are at 20,000 feet				
	Endurance at sea level	Optimum altitude	Endurance at optimum altitude	Mach at optimum altitude	CAS at optimum altitude	Endurance at 20,000 feet	Optimum altitude	Endurance at optimum altitude	Mach at optimum altitude	CAS at optimum altitude
	Minutes	Feet	Minutes	Mach	Knots	Minutes	Feet	Minutes	Mach	Knots
6500	47	20,000	53	0.44	200	63	20,000	63	0.44	200
5500	33	20,000	34	0.44	200	44	20,000	44	0.44	200
4500	18	SL	18	0.30	197	24	20,000	24	0.44	199
4000	11	SL	11	0.30	197	15	20,000	15	0.44	199
3500	3	SL	3	0.30	196	5	20,000	5	0.44	198
Climb CAS	340 KCAS					300 KCAS				
Letdown	30° Dive, speedbrakes open					30° Dive, speedbrakes open				
Start letdown with fuel on board – pounds	3000					3000				
	If You Are at 25,000 feet					If You Are at 30,000 feet				
	Endurance at 25,000 feet	Optimum altitude	Endurance at optimum altitude	Mach at optimum altitude	CAS at optimum altitude	Endurance at 30,000 feet	Optimum altitude	Endurance at optimum altitude	Mach at optimum altitude	CAS at optimum altitude
	Minutes	Feet	Minutes	Mach	Knots	Minutes	Feet	Minutes	Mach	Knots
6500	64	25,000	64	0.50	203	63	30,000	63	0.55	202
5500	45	25,000	45	0.49	202	44	30,000	44	0.54	201
4500	25	25,000	25	0.49	201	25	30,000	25	0.54	200
4000	15	25,000	15	0.49	200	15	30,000	15	0.54	200
3500	5	25,000	5	0.49	200	5	30,000	5	0.54	199
Climb CAS	No climb required					No climb required				
Letdown	30° Dive, speedbrakes open					30° Dive, speedbrakes open				
Start letdown with fuel on board – pounds	3000					3000				
	If You Are at 35,000 feet					If You Are at 40,000 feet				
	Endurance at 35,000 feet	Optimum altitude	Endurance at optimum altitude	Mach at optimum altitude	CAS at optimum altitude	Endurance at 40,000 feet	Optimum altitude	Endurance at optimum altitude	Mach at optimum altitude	CAS at optimum altitude
	Minutes	Feet	Minutes	Mach	Knots	Minutes	Feet	Minutes	Mach	Knots
6500	66	35,000	66	0.61	204	63	35,000	66	0.61	204
5500	47	35,000	47	0.61	202	44	35,000	47	0.61	202
4500	26	35,000	26	0.61	202	25	35,000	26	0.61	202
4000	16	35,000	16	0.61	201	15	35,000	16	0.61	201
3500	6	35,000	6	0.60	201	6	35,000	6	0.60	201
Climb CAS	No climb required					No climb required				
Letdown	30° Dive, speedbrakes open					30° Dive, speedbrakes open				
Start letdown with fuel on board – pounds	3000					3000				

Remarks:
(1) Fuel required includes 300 pounds for cleanup, turn, and acceleration.
(2) Provides 3000 pounds fuel at point where descent is commenced.
(3) Descend at idle thrust.
(4) Aircraft operating weight is 38,153 pounds.

Data as of: 1 March 1964   Fuel Grade: JP-5
Data Basis: NATC and Contractor Flight Tests   Fuel Density: 6.8 lb/gal

Figure 11-89. Fouled Deck Endurance (Sheet 1)

NAVAIR 01-40ATA-1

Section XI
Part 5A

FOULED DECK ENDURANCE
ONE-ENGINE OPERATION

Model: A-3A

Engines: J57-P-6

Fuel on board — pounds

	If You Are at sea level					If You Are at 20,000 feet				
	Endurance at sea level	Optimum altitude	Endurance at optimum altitude	Mach at optimum altitude	CAS at optimum altitude	Endurance at 20,000 feet	Optimum altitude	Endurance at optimum altitude	Mach at optimum altitude	CAS at optimum altitude
	Minutes	Feet	Minutes	Mach	Knots	Minutes	Feet	Minutes	Mach	Knots
6500	62	SL	62	0.29	194	67	20,000	67	0.43	196
5500	44	SL	44	0.29	193	47	20,000	47	0.43	195
4500	25	SL	25	0.29	192	35	20,000	35	0.43	194
4000	16	SL	16	0.29	192	17	20,000	17	0.43	193
3500	6	SL	6	0.29	191	7	20,000	7	0.43	192
Climb CAS	No climb required					Climb CAS	No climb required			
Letdown	30° Dive, speedbrakes open					Letdown	30° Dive, speedbrakes open			
Start letdown with fuel on board — pounds	3000					Start letdown with fuel on board — pounds	3000			
	If You Are at 25,000 feet					If You Are at 30,000 feet				
	Endurance at 25,000 feet	Optimum altitude	Endurance at optimum altitude	Mach at optimum altitude	CAS at optimum altitude	Endurance at 30,000 feet	Optimum altitude	Endurance at optimum altitude	Mach at optimum altitude	CAS at optimum altitude
	Minutes	Feet	Minutes	Mach	Knots	Minutes	Feet	Minutes	Mach	Knots
6500	66	20,000	67	0.43	196	65	20,000	67	0.43	196
5500	47	20,000	48	0.43	195	46	20,000	48	0.43	195
4500	27	20,000	28	0.43	194	27	20,000	28	0.43	194
4000	17	20,000	18	0.43	193	17	20,000	18	0.43	193
3500	7	20,000	7	0.43	192	7	20,000	7	0.43	192
Climb CAS	No climb required					Climb CAS	No climb required			
Letdown	30° Dive, speedbrakes open					Letdown	30° Dive, speedbrakes open			
Start letdown with fuel on board — pounds	3000					Start letdown with fuel on board — pounds	3000			

Remarks:

(1) Fuel required includes 200 pounds for cleanup, turn, and acceleration.

(2) Provides 3000 pounds of fuel at point where descent is commenced.

(3) Descend at idle thrust.

(4) Aircraft operating weight is 38,153 pounds.

Data as of: 1 March 1964

Data Basis: NATC and Contractor Flight Tests

Fuel Grade: JP-5

Fuel Density: 6.8 lb/gal

Figure 11-89. Fouled Deck Endurance (Sheet 2)

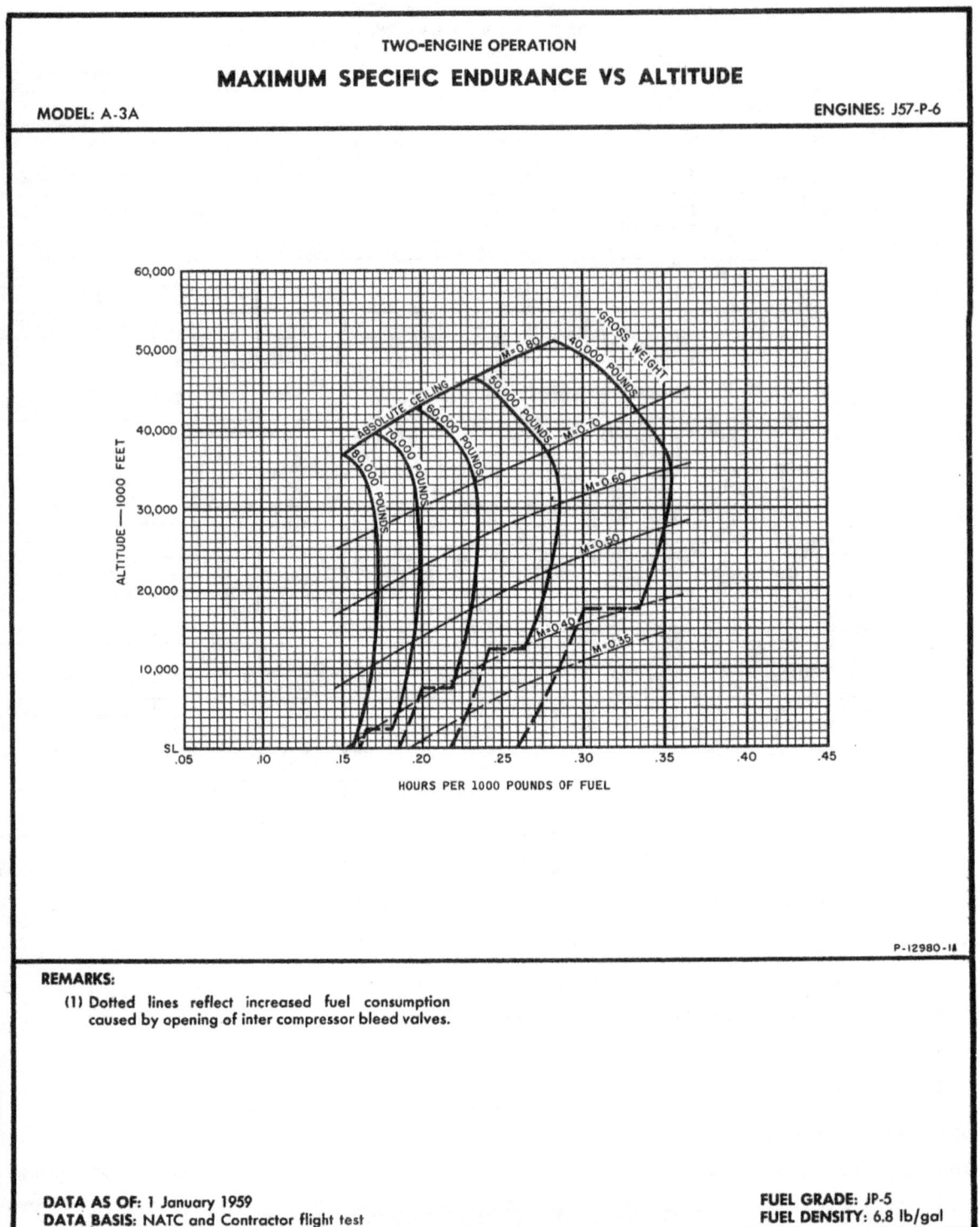

Figure 11-90. Maximum Specific Endurance vs Altitude (Sheet 1)

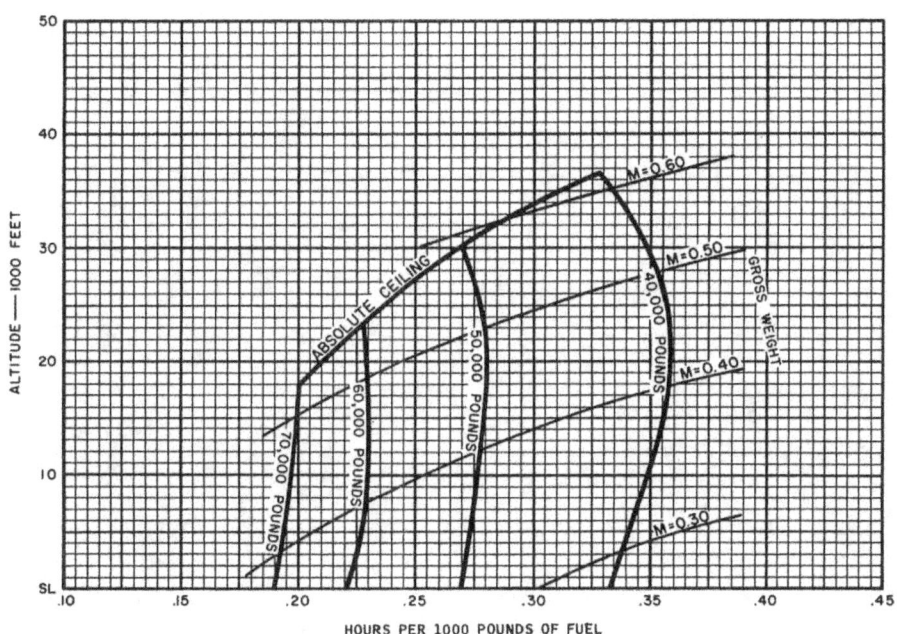

Figure 11-90. Maximum Specific Endurance vs Altitude (Sheet 2)

NAVAIR 01-40ATA-1

Section XI
Part 6A

PART 6A
DESCENT

TABLE OF CONTENTS

TEXT
Page

Descent Charts 11-183

ILLUSTRATIONS

Figure		Page	Figure		Page
11-91	Maximum Range Descent	11-184	11-92	Maximum Rate Descent	11-186

Descent Charts

A maximum range descent should normally be made with idle power, flaps and gear retracted, and speed brakes closed. The Maximum Range Descent chart, figure 11-91, sheet 1, shows descent performance which will be obtained in the above configuration when the recommended airspeeds (CAS) shown in the chart are maintained in the descent. These data may be used for determining rates of descent, elapsed time, distance and/or fuel consumed in descending from any altitude to sea level or from one altitude to another by taking the differences in the desired values at the initial and at the final altitudes.

EXAMPLE: A descent is made from 30,000 feet pressure altitude to 10,000 feet pressure altitude at 40,000 pounds gross weight. Using the data provided on the Maximum Range Descent chart, the descent range is found to be:

80 nautical miles - 23 nautical miles = 57 nautical miles

The elapsed time is:

19 minutes - 6 minutes = 13 minutes.

The fuel consumed is:

420 pounds - 150 pounds = 270 pounds.

Descent is made at 220 KCAS.

NOTE

- Distance, time, and fuel consumed in descent with one engine operating at idle power and the other engine completely shut down may be obtained similarly from figure 11-91, sheet 2.

- Descent data with both engines inoperative are presented in Emergency Procedures, Section V.

The Maximum Rate Descent chart, figure 11-92, gives time and distance used in a maximum rate (30° dive) descent from any altitude.

Changed 1 June 1969

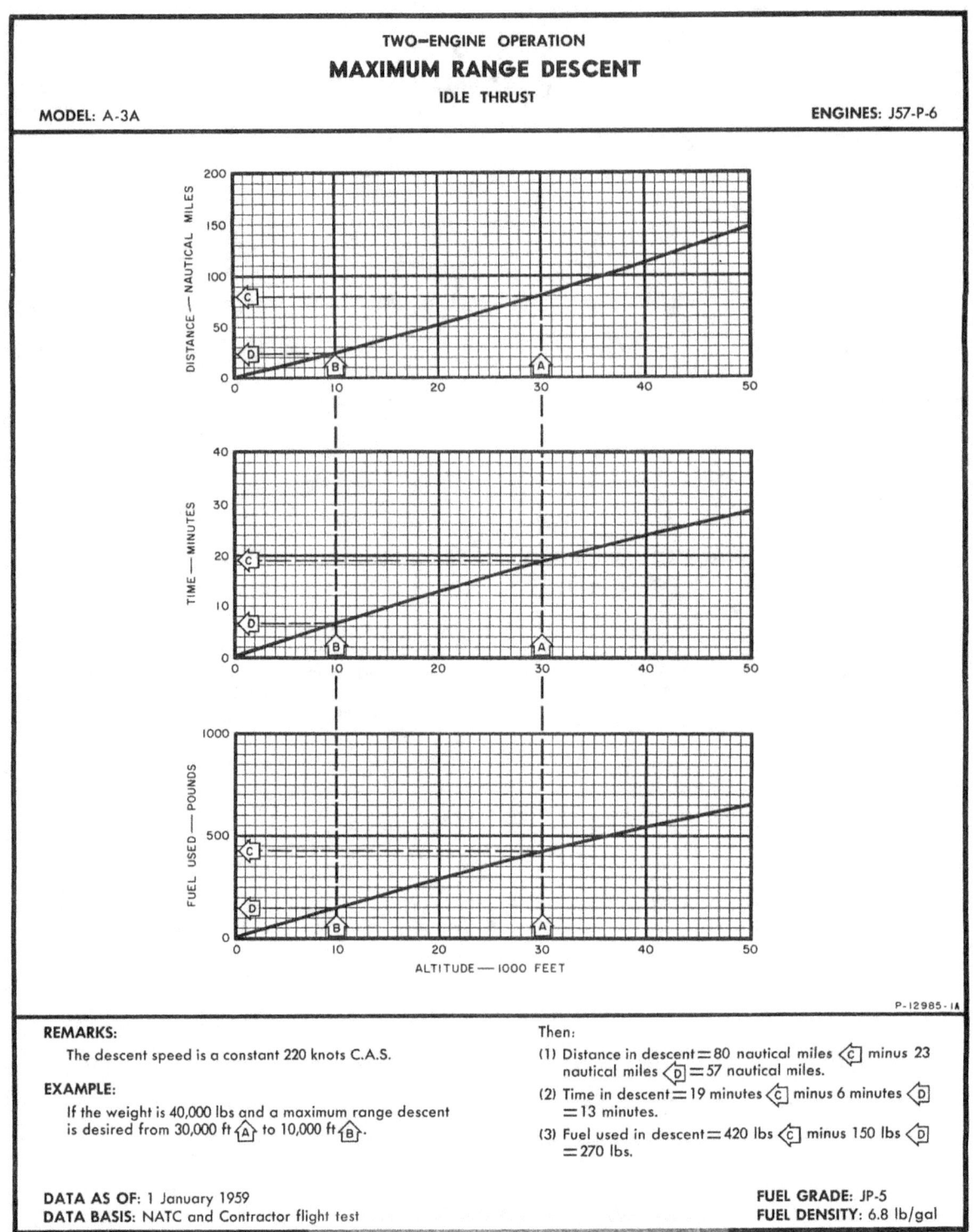

Figure 11-91. Maximum Range Descent (Sheet 1)

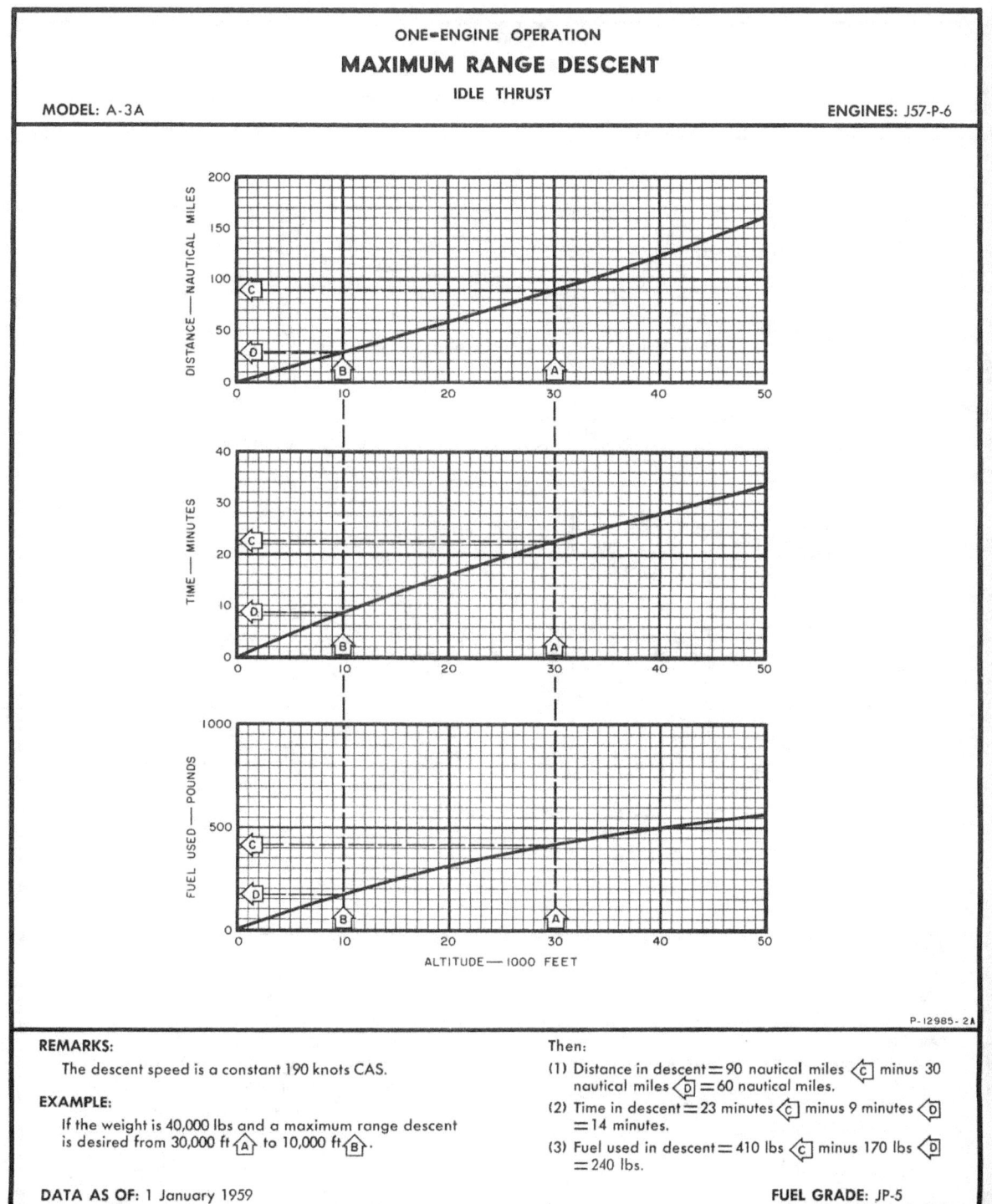

Figure 11-91. Maximum Range Descent (Sheet 2)

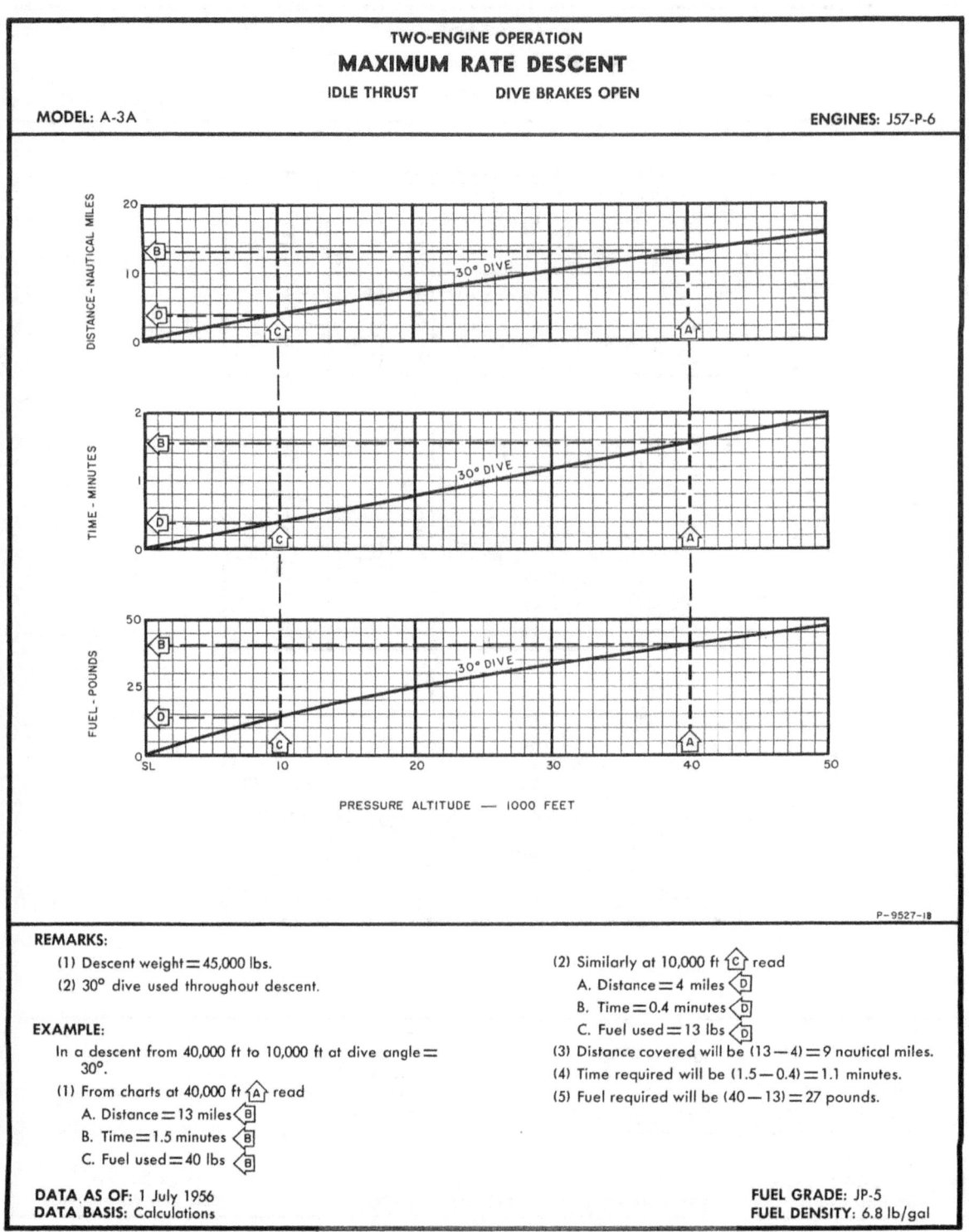

Figure 11-92. Maximum Rate Descent

NAVAIR 01-40ATA-1

Section XI
Part 7A

PART 7A
LANDING

TABLE OF CONTENTS

TEXT

Page

Approach Charts 11-187

ILLUSTRATIONS

Figure   Page

11-93   Recommended Approach
        Speeds and Stall Speeds 11-188

Approach Charts

The recommended approach and stall speed chart (figure 11-93) represents approach and stall speeds, along with the corresponding angle-of-attack units, as a function of gross weight. Figure 11-93 also shows the effect of bank angle on stall speed. Fifteen units for full and half flaps on a properly calibrated angle-of-attack indicator represents the correct approach speed. It is recommended, however, that the angle-of-attack indicator be checked against the aircraft indicated airspeed reading during the approach on each flight. If the 15 units do not indicate the airspeeds shown on figure 11-93, disregard the angle-of-attack indicator and make the approach at the proper indicated airspeed.

EXAMPLE:

Basic Wing Approach Speed
(For figure 11-93)

(A) Gross Weight . . . . 44,000 lb

(B) Approach Speed (Half Flaps) . . . . . 129.5 kts
Angle of attack . . . . 15 units

Landing Charts

The landing ground roll distance of the aircraft is dependent upon outside air temperature, runway pressure altitude, aircraft gross weight, flap setting, headwind, runway gradient, runway surface condition, and braking action. Minimum distance requires that the throttles be reduced to idle power at touchdown and maximum braking, without skidding the tires, maintained during the entire ground roll. Ground roll distances for a dry, wet, and snow and ice covered hard runway surface, using drag chute, are presented on figure 11-57, sheets 1, 2, and 3 respectively. These distances are calculated based on the assumptions that the drag chute is actuated at touchdown and that 2 seconds are required for the drag chute to deploy. Figure 11-57, sheets 4, 5, and 6, presents ground roll distances for the same runway conditions without the drag chute. To clear a 50-foot obstacle, an additional 715 feet must be added to the total ground roll distance.

Landing Distance
(For figure 11-57)

(A) Outside Air Temperature . . . . 10°C

(B) Runway Pressure Altitude . . . . 2000 ft

(C) Landing Gross Weight . . . . 44,000 lb

(D) Flap Deflection . . . . Half

(E) Headwind . . . . 20 kts

(F) Runway Gradient . . . . -1 percent

(G) Landing Ground Roll Distance . . . . . 5050 ft

Changed 1 June 1969

11-187

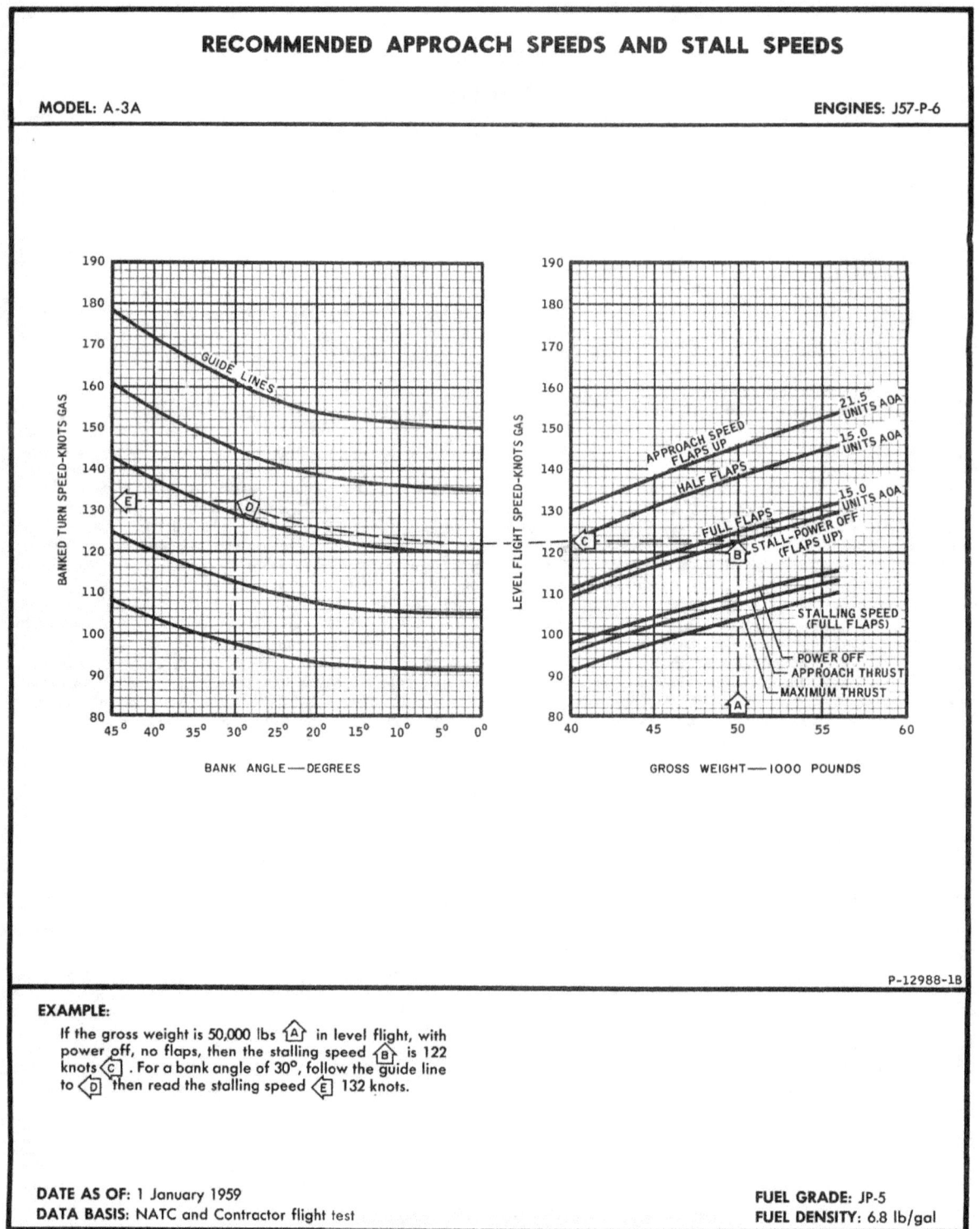

Figure 11-93. Recommended Approach Speeds and Stall Speeds

NAVAIR 01-40ATA-1

Section XI
Part 8A

Part 8A
COMBAT PERFORMANCE

TABLE OF CONTENTS

TEXT

	Page
Combat Allowance Chart	11-189

ILLUSTRATIONS

Figure		Page	Figure		Page
11-94	Combat Allowance Chart	11-190	11-95	Maximum Continuous Power Summary	11-191

Combat Allowance Chart

Figure 11-94 presents the combat time available for various quantities of combat fuel as a function of altitude. These data are given for both maximum and normal thrust.

Maximum Continuous Power Summary Charts

These charts, shown in figure 11-95, sheets 1 and 2, are a summary of operating data for both one-engine and two-engine operation at maximum continuous power for several gross weights. The airspeeds (CAS and TAS) and corresponding fuel consumption figures in pounds per hour per engine are representative of maximum speed in level flight at various altitudes with throttle(s) set at normal power.

Changed 1 June 1969

11-189

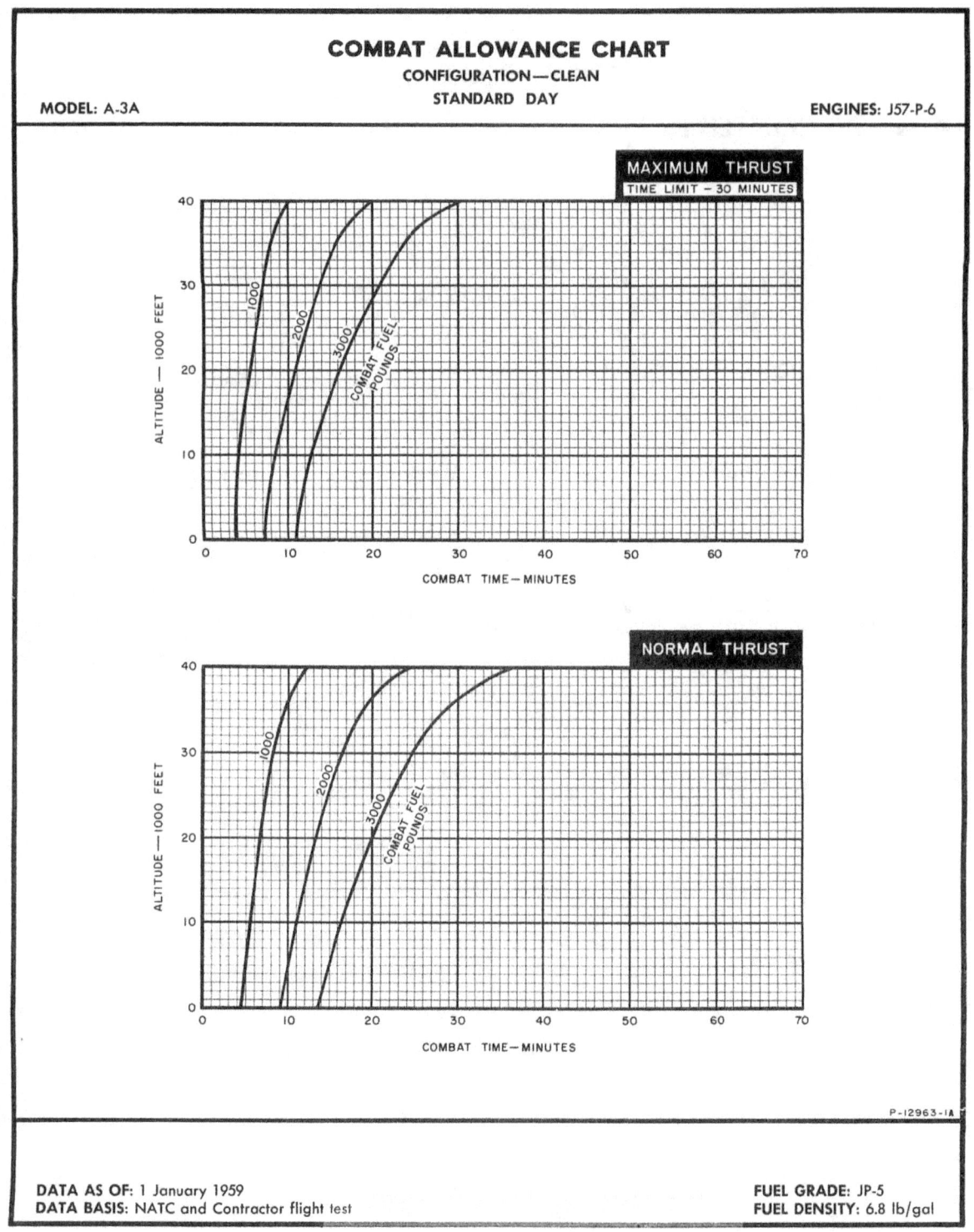

Figure 11-94. Combat Allowance Chart

NAVAIR 01-40ATA-1

Section XI
Part 8A

MAXIMUM CONTINUOUS POWER SUMMARY
Two-Engine Operation

MODEL: A-3A

Engines: J57-P-6

Clean Configuration Weight: 80,000 Pounds				Clean Configuration Weight: 70,000 Pounds		
Approximate			Pressure Altitude Feet	Approximate		
Pounds/Hour /Engine	TAS Knots	CAS Knots		CAS Knots	TAS Knots	Pounds/Hour /Engine
6950	490	490	Sea Level	495	495	7000
6300	505	475	5000	475	505	6300
5650	510	450	10,000	450	510	5700
5150	510	420	15,000	420	510	5150
4700	510	390	20,000	390	510	4700
4250	505	355	25,000	360	510	4250
3750	495	320	30,000	325	500	3800
–	–	–	35,000	285	480	3250

Clean Configuration Weight: 60,000 Pounds				Clean Configuration Weight: 50,000 Pounds		
Approximate			Pressure Altitude Feet	Approximate		
Pounds/Hour /Engine	TAS Knots	CAS Knots		CAS Knots	TAS Knots	Pounds/Hour /Engine
7000	500	500	Sea Level	500	500	6700
6300	510	480	5000	480	510	6300
5700	510	450	10,000	455	515	5700
5150	515	420	15,000	420	515	5150
4700	515	390	20,000	390	515	4700
4250	510	360	25,000	365	515	4250
3800	505	330	30,000	330	510	3800
3300	495	295	35,000	300	500	3300
2550	460	240	40,000	260	490	2600

Data As Of: 1 July 1956
Data Basis: Calculations

Fuel Grade: JP-5
Fuel Density: 6.8 lb/gal

Figure 11-95. Maximum Continuous Power Summary (Sheet 1)

11-191

Section XI
Part 8A
NAVAIR 01-40ATA-1

MAXIMUM CONTINUOUS POWER SUMMARY
One-Engine Operation

Model: A-3A
Engines: J57-P-6

Clean Configuration Weight: 80,000 Pounds				Clean Configuration Weight: 70,000 Pounds		
Approximate				Approximate		
Pounds/Hour /Engine	TAS Knots	CAS Knots	Pressure Altitude Feet	CAS Knots	TAS Knots	Pounds/Hour /Engine
6600	315	315	Sea Level	325	325	6600
5900	305	285	5000	310	330	5950
–	–	–	10,000	280	325	5350

Clean Configuration Weight: 60,000 Pounds				Clean Configuration Weight: 50,000 Pounds		
Approximate				Approximate		
Pounds/Hour /Engine	TAS Knots	CAS Knots	Pressure Altitude Feet	CAS Knots	TAS Knots	Pounds/Hour /Engine
6650	335	335	Sea Level	345	340	6650
5950	340	320	5000	330	350	6000
5350	345	300	10,000	310	360	5400
4850	345	280	15,000	295	365	5900
4350	335	250	20,000	280	370	4400
–	–	–	25,000	255	370	3950

Remarks:

(1) Inoperative engine windmilling.

(2) Normal thrust on operating engine.

Data As Of: 1 July 1956
Data Basis: Calculations

Fuel Grade: JP-5
Fuel Density: 6.8 lb/gal

Figure 11-95. Maximum Continuous Power Summary (Sheet 2)

ALPHABETICAL INDEX

	Page No. Text	Page No. Illus
A		
Abbreviations, Symbols and Definitions	11-3	
Abort Computations, Takeoff	3-3	
Abort Procedures, Takeoff	5-2	
AC		
electrical system		1-78
generator malfunction/failure	5-11	
generator no. 1 bus	1-76	
generator no. 2 bus	1-76	
high-speed stabilizer trim	1-92	
power distribution	1-76	
powered instruments	1-101	
power failure	1-81	
power panel		1-77
power system	1-76	
Accelerated Stalls	4-5	
Acceleration	1-36	
Acceleration Limitations	1-175	
Accelerometer	1-102	
Access, Bomb Bay to Main Gear	1-97	
Access, Companionway	3-13	
Access and Crew Evacuation, Emergency	5-29	
Access, Emergency and Crew Evacuation		5-30
Accumulator		
aileron system	1-153	
brake	1-153	
charging	1-153	1-154
nose gear steering	1-153	
spoiler system (two)	1-153	
Actuator Gangbar, Horizontal Stabilizer	1-94	
Aft Cockpit — A-3A		1-18
Aft Cockpit — A-3B		1-19
Aft Fuselage Tank, Fuel	1-137	
Aft Power Panel		1-76
Aileron	4-2A, 4-9, 4-13	
control	1-85	
control system	1-85	
manual control caging hook	1-87	
power boost assembly		1-88
and rudder-elevator	1-91, 4-13	
spoiler and surface control pressure	1-91	
spoilers	4-1	
system accumulator	1-153	
trim	4-2B	
Air Check, Bleed (Toggle Switches)	3-17	
Air-conditioning		
cabin air contamination	1-69	
cockpit vs aircraft altitude comparison		1-70
control	1-69, 1-71	
pressurization, and defrosting procedures	3-22	
electronic temperature controller	1-66	
and pressurizing system	1-66	1-68
turbine failure	5-7	
upper bomb bay hot bleed air leaks (light on)	5-7	
Air Contamination, Cabin	1-69	
Aircraft, The	1-1	
A-3A aircraft performance data charts (J57-P-6B engines)	11-115	
aft cockpit — A-3A		1-18
aft cockpit — A-3B		1-19
arrangement, general	1-3	1-6
before entering	6-4	
circuit breaker and fuse panels — A-3A		1-26
circuit breaker and fuse panels — A-3B		1-27
vs cockpit altitude comparison		1-70
description	1-3	
dimensions	1-5	1-4
emergency signals between		7-8
and engine operation		7-8
entrance to the		3-13
entrance door	1-5	
general (all)	1-37	
on entering	6-5	
operating limitations	1-171	
plane captain's station — A-3A		1-21
inspection	3-35	
main differences	1-3	
manning	3-9	
navigator's station — A-3A/B (typical)		1-25
navigator's typical right-hand console — A-3A		1-16
navigator's typical right-hand console — A-3B		1-17
operating limitations	1-170A	
penetrations and approaches by dissimilar	4-17	
performance data charts, A-3A (J57-P-6B engines)	11-115	
pilot's center console — A-3B		1-15
pilot's circuit breaker panel — A-3A		1-28
pilot's circuit breaker panel — A-3B typical		1-29
pilot's instrument panel — A-3A/B — typical		1-10
pilot's left-hand console — A-3A		1-11
pilot's left-hand console — A-3B		1-13
plane captain's console — A-3A		1-23
plane captain's console — A-3B		1-24
plane captain's station — A-3B		1-22
seats	1-5	
securing	1-165	
servicing	1-128A	
starting	3-14	
systems	1-31	
upright or inverted	5-27	

Changed 15 July 1970

Index 1

Index
Airfield to Approach

	Text	Illus		Text	Illus
Airfield Landing, Boost-Off	4-14		vs endurance, maximum		
Air Inlet, Engine	1-71		specific	11-91, 11-177	11-180
Air Intelligence and Special Instructions	3-4		high (above 10,000 feet AGL)	5-4	
Air Leaks, Hot Bleed	5-6		hold operation	1-124	
Air Refueling	4-18	7-8	low (3000 feet AGL and below)	5-4	
altitude, airspeed, and engagement procedures	4-18		low and low airspeed dual-engine failure	5-18	
air refueling checklist	4-22		medium (between 3000 and 10,000 feet AGL)	5-4	
communications and signals	4-22		monitoring	6-2	
emergency breakaway procedures	4-22		vs range, maximum specific	11-57, 11-145	11-68, 11-156
receiver capability	4-22		table, ICAO standard	11-10	
tanker light identification signals	4-22		Ammeters	1-81	
probe light	1-118		AN/ARC-27A UHF Radio Receiver-Transmitters	1-105	
speed		4-19	Angle-of-Attack Approach Light System	1-103	
rendezvous procedures	4-18		Angel-of-Attack Indicator	1-103	
Airspeed	4-18		AN/AIC-4A Interphone	1-113	
and altitude correction charts	11-4, 11-115		AN/APA-89 (SIF)	1-113	
and altitude correction for position error		11-11, 11-120	AN/APN-22 Radar Altimeter	1-114	
			AN/APX-6B Transponder (IFF)	1-112	
altitudes, and engagement procedures	4-18		AN/ARA-25 Automatic Direction Finding System	1-109	
corrections	11-4, 11-115		AN/ARC-1 Receiver-Transmitter	1-116	
indicator	1-101		AN/ARC-27A UHF Radio Receiver-Transmitter Installation, Dual	1-109	
limitations	1-171				
low and low altitude dual-engine failure	5-18		AN/ARC-38A HF Radio Receiver-Transmitter	1-111	
vs Mach number		11-6	AN/ARN-14E Receiver (VOR)	1-114	
Air Starting	4-7, 5-3		AN/ARN-21B TACAN	1-115	
engine failure under specific conditions	4-8		AN/ASB-1A Modified Radar	8-1	
immediate	4-8, 5-3		AN/ASB-1A Modified Radar System-- Cockpit Arrangement		8-2
maneuvering flight	4-9		AN/ASB-7 Modified Radar System-- Cockpit Arrangement		8-4
normal	5-3		AN/ASB-7 Radar--Control Panel		8-6
Air System, Escape Hatch	1-99		Angle-of-Attack Relationship	4-9	
Air Systems, Emergency -- Servicing		1-156	angle-of-attack, approximate indicated		4-10
Air-To-Air Ranging, TACAN	1-116		angle-of-attack relationship -- A-3A		4-11
Air-To-Ground Communications	7-1				
Air Turbine Motors (ATM's)	1-63		angle-of-attack relationship -- A-3B		4-12
Air Valve, Oxygen	1-119				
All Weather Operation	6-1		approximate indicated angle-of-attack relationship		4-10
cold weather operation	6-4		boost-off airfield landing	4-14	
hot weather and desert operation	6-6		boost-off carrier landing	4-13	
weather considerations	6-3		boost-off flight	4-9	
Allowance Chart, Combat	11-111, 11-189	11-190	boost-off single-engine landing	4-15	
			pitchup characteristics	4-9	
Altimeter, AN/APN-22 Radar	1-114		probe	1-72	
Altimeter, Counterpointer Pressure	1-101		Antennas and Radio and Radar Equipment		1-106
Altitude	4-18		Anticollision Lights	1-118	
airspeed correction charts	11-4, 11-115		Antiexposure Suit Ventilation	1-72	
			Antifogging Compound	1-161	
airspeed correction for position error		11-11, 11-120	Anti-Icing System	1-71	
			control	1-71	
airspeed, and engagement procedures	4-18		engine air inlet	1-71	
			operation	6-1	
chart, density		11-9	Antiskid Brake System	1-98	
climb performance charts	11-42, 11-135		Antiskid Braking Techniques	3-30	
			Approach	6-3	
comparison, cockpit vs aircraft		1-70	charts	11-103, 11-187	
corrections	11-5, 11-116		GCA	6-3	
			landing, single-engine	3-29	

NAVAIR 01-40ATA-1

Index
Approximate to Boost

	Page No. Text	Page No. Illus
light	1-104, 1-118	
light system, angle-of-attack	1-103	
and penetration by dissimilar aircraft	4-17	
speeds and stall speeds, recommended	11-103	11-104, 11-188
Approximate Indicated Angle-of-Attack		4-10
APX-6B Operation	1-112	
Arming Switch, JATO	1-128	
ARN Radio Selector Switch (3)	1-105	
Arrangement, General	1-3	1-6
Arrested Landings	5-27	
Arresting Gear Data, Field		5-26
Arresting Hook	1-98	
Arrestments, Field	3-32	
emergency	5-24	
long	5-26	
short	5-26	
Arrestment and Taxiing	3-38	
ASB-1A Radar Equipment Checklist	8-7	
ASB-1A Radar Malfunction Checklist	8-8	
ASB-1A Radar Prelanding and Shutdown Checklist	8-8	
ASB-1A Radar Taxi and Pretakeoff Checklist	8-8	
ASB-7 Modified Radar System	8-1	
ASB-7 Radar Equipment Checklist	8-8	
ASB-7 Radar Malfunction Checklist	8-10	
ASB-7 Radar Prelanding and Shutdown Checklist	8-9	
ASB-7 Radar Taxi and Pretakeoff Checklist	8-9	
Assembly, Aileron Power Boost		1-88
Assist Handle, Pilot's	1-8	
Associated Electronics and Communications Equipment		1-110
ATM, Air Turbine Motors	1-63	
compartment fire or hot bleed air leaks	5-7	
compartment temperature warning light	1-65	
failure	1-66	
malfunction/failure	5-10	
monitor panel	1-64	
oil sump — servicing	1-157	1-158
restart		1-67
restart after a negative G condition	1-66	
switches	1-64	
Attitude Indicator, Vertical Gyro (VGI)	1-102	
Automatic Direction Finding System, AN/ARA-25	1-109	
Automatic Fuel Trim Control	1-45	
Automatic Jury Strut	1-95	
Automatic Trimming	1-121	
Autopilot	1-120	
altitude hold operation	1-124	
automatic trimming	1-121	
to disengage	1-124	
emergency procedures	1-125	
to engage	1-124	
engaging and disengaging controls	1-122	
pedestal controller	1-121	1-123
stabilizer trim	1-93	
use following boost disconnect	1-125	
preflight check	3-20	
Autopilot Use Following Boost Disconnect	1-125	
Auxiliary Tank Fuel Transfer Control	1-42	
Auxiliary Tank, Upper Bomb Bay and Forward Fuselage	1-137	
Auxiliary Upper Bomb Bay Tank	1-39	

B

Bailout		
controlled	5-18	
controlled — escape routes	5-21	
ditching doctrine	5-18	
ditching procedures	5-18	
emergency	5-20	
escape routes, emergency	5-21	
Barricade Engagement	3-39	
Barrier, Field	3-33	
Battery Complete ac and dc Failure Including	5-12	
Bingo Cards (Fouled Deck Range)	11-57 11-145	
Bingo Fuel (Minimum Fuel)	3-38	
Bleed Air		
check (toggle switches)	3-17	
hot, and companionway check	3-18	
leaks, hot	5-6	
leaks, hot, or fire, ATM compartment	5-7	
leaks, hot or fires, bomb bay/companionway	5-7	
leaks, hot (light on) air-conditioning/upper bomb bay	5-7	
rotary shutoff switch	5-6	
schematic, engine compressor, A-3A/B and KA-3B		1-61
shutoff system (rotary switch)	1-63	
shutoff system (toggle switches)	1-48	
system, engine compressor	1-48	
toggle shutoff switches	5-7	
Bleeding and Filling Brake System Reservoir Master	1-149	
Bleeding Main Landing Gear Brake	1-152	
Bleeding Power Brake Valves	1-149	
Bomb Bay	1-127	
auxiliary tank, upper and forward fuselage	1-137	
companionway fires or hot bleed air leaks	5-7	
doors	1-127	
doors control	1-127	
doors warning horn	1-127	
to main gear access	1-97	
tank, auxiliary upper	1-39	
upper or air conditioning hot bleed air leaks (light on)	5-7	
Boost		
assembly, aileron power		1-88
disconnect, autopilot use following	1-125	

Changed 15 July 1970

Index 3

Index
Boost-Off to Check

	Page No. Text	Page No. Illus		Page No. Text	Page No. Illus
failure with accompanied engine flameout, fuel	1-38, 5-13		C-2549/ASB-7 Radar Control Panel	8-5	
			Cabin Air Contamination	1-69	
			Cabin Dome Light	1-117	
failure with continued engine operation, fuel	1-38, 5-13		Caging Hook, Aileron Manual Control	1-87	
			Capability, Receiver	4-22	
mechanism, frozen elevator	1-91		Carqual Checklist	3-38	
pressure indicator, fuel	1-34		Carrier-Based Procedures	3-35	
pump control, fuel	1-38		Carrier Landing	3-36	
pump failure	5-13		boost-off	4-13	
schematic, flight controls		1-90	no-boost	5-17	
Boost-Off Airfield Landing	4-14		no-flap	5-17	
Boost-Off Carrier Landing	4-13		no-slat	5-18	
Boost-Off Flight	4-9		pattern, typical		3-37
Boost-Off Single-Engine Landing	4-15		single-engine	3-38, 5-16	
Brake System					
accumulator	1-153		Carrier Operations Limitations	1-175	
antiskid	1-98		Carrier Operations, Night	3-36	
emergency operation, wheel	1-99		Cartridge Start	3-15	
main landing gear — bleeding	1-152		Cartridge Starter	1-34	
master reservoir — filling and bleeding	1-149		Catapult Equipment	1-128	
			Catapult Handgrip	1-128	
power brake valves — bleeding	1-149		CCA Night Recovery	3-38	
servicing	1-149	1-152	Center Console, Pilot's — A-3B		1-15
wheel	1-98		Cg Fuel Control Valve, Manual	1-44	
wheel, emergency	5-18				
wheel, operation after utility	5-10		Cg/Icing	3-25	
Brake System — Servicing	1-149		Cg Indicator	1-44	
main landing gear brake — bleeding	1-152		Cg Limitations	1-175	
			Cg Position vs Elevator Trim Setting	3-23	
master reservoir — filling and bleeding	1-149		Changing Lead, Takeoff, Leaving Formation, Breakup, Landing	7-3	
power brake valves — bleeding	1-149		Characteristics, Flight	4-3	
Braking, Antiskid Techniques	3-30		Charts		
Braking Procedures	3-21		airspeed and altitude correction	11-4	
Breakaway Procedures, Emergency	4-22		altitude climb performance	11-42, 11-135	
Breaker Relay, Bus Tie	1-80		approach	11-103, 11-187	
Breakup and Landing	3-35				
Breakup and Landing, Night	3-34				
Breakup, Landing, Takeoff, Changing Lead, Leaving Formation		7-3	A-3A aircraft performance data charts (J57-P-6B engines)	11-115	
			climb	11-135	
Briefing/Debriefing	3-3, 3-5		combat allowance	11-111, 11-189	11-112, 11-190
Buffet Onset, Load Factor for		4-4	density altitude	11-9	
Bus			descent	11-99, 11-183	
ac generator no. 1	1-76				
ac generator no. 2	1-76		emergency climb	11-42, 11-136	
battery	1-72				
monitor	1-72		endurance	11-91, 11-177	
primary	1-72				
radio	1-72		landing	11-103, 11-187	
secondary	1-72				
tie breaker relay	1-80		maximum continuous power	11-111, 11-189	
Bypass Switch, Arresting Hook	1-104				
			range	11-57, 11-145	
C					
			takeoff	11-15, 11-123	
C-760A/A Control Panel	1-115		Check		
C-852B/ASB-1A Radar Control Panel		8-3	autopilot preflight	3-20	
			bleed air (toggle switches)	3-17	
C-865/ARC-1 Radio Control Panel	1-116		companion way and hot bleed air	3-18	
C-866/ARN-21B NAV Control Panel	1-115		controls	3-19	
			full power	3-23	
C-1159/APX-6B Control Panel (IFF)	1-112		horizontal stabilizer trim	3-20	
			oxygen system	1-160	
			radar control panel	8-7	

NAVAIR 01-40ATA-1

Index
Check to Communications

	Page No. Text	Page No. Illus		Page No. Text	Page No. Illus
voltage (3 minutes after initial power application)	8-7		performance charts, altitude	11-42, 11-135	
voltage	8-9		performance after takeoff	11-41, 11-135	11-44, 11-137
Check Line Speed	11-16, 11-124		performance for waveoff	11-42	11-45
Checklist			schedule	3-25	
air refueling	4-22		temperature effect on one-engine rate of climb		11-53
ASB-1A radar equipment	8-7		time to		11-48, 11-56
ASB-1A radar malfunction	8-8				
ASB-1A radar prelanding and shutdown	8-8		Climb (J57-P-6B-Engines)	11-135	
ASB-1A radar taxi and pretakeoff	8-8		distance		11-139, 11-142
ASB-7 radar equipment	8-8		fuel consumed during		11-138, 11-144
ASB-7 radar prelanding and shutdown	8-9		performance after takeoff		11-137
ASB-7 radar taxi and pretakeoff	8-9		time to		11-140, 11-143
carqual	3-38		Clocks	1-104	
descent	3-26		Cloud Flying	4-17	
landing	3-26		Cockpit	8-7	
level-off/in-flight	3-26		aft — A-3A		1-18
mission	3-5		aft — A-3B		1-19
post-landing (field)	3-32		vs aircraft altitude comparison		1-70
postlanding (ship)	3-39		arrangement — AN/ASB-1A modified radar system		8-2
post takeoff	3-25				
preflight	3-9		indexer	1-104	
prestart	3-13		pressure control	1-69	
pretaxi/taxi	3-19		Cold Weather Operations	6-4	
shutdown	3-32		before entering aircraft	6-4	
shutdown (ship)	3-39		before starting engines	6-5	
start	3-16		before takeoff	6-5	
takeoff	3-22		descent	6-6	
Chocks, Shutdown In	8-8		during flight	6-6	
Chute, Drag	1-99, 3-29		ice, snow, and rain	6-4	
			landing	6-6	
Chute, Emergency Escape and Entrance	1-8		on entering aircraft	6-5	
			shutdown and postflight	6-6	
Chute, Emergency Escape and Entrance — A-3A	1-5		starting and warmup	6-5	
			takeoff	6-5	
Chute Test Switch, Escape — A-3A	1-8		taxiing	6-5	
Chute Test Switch, Escape	1-8		Combat Performance	11-111, 11-189	
Circuit Breaker and Fuse Panels — A-3A		1-26	allowance chart	11-111, 11-189	11-112, 11-190
Circuit Breaker and Fuse Panels — A-3B		1-27	maximum continuous power summary charts	11-111	
Circuit Breaker Panel, Pilot's — A-3A		1-28	maximum continuous power summary		11-113
Circuit Breaker Panel, Pilot's — A-3B Typical		1-29	radius profile	11-59, 11-147	11-88, 11-176
Circuit Breaker Relays, Generator	1-77		Combat Performance (J57-P-6B-Engines)	11-189	
Clearing Procedures, Engine	3-18		allowance chart		11-190
Climb	6-2, 6-7, 11-41, 11-135		maximum continuous power summary		11-191
			Communications	3-3, 6-2	
charts	11-135		air-to-ground	7-1	
charts, emergency	11-42, 11-136		and associated electronics equipment		1-110
cruise	3-25		and direction finding system, UHF	1-105	
cruise after	4-7				
distance		11-47, 11-55, 11-139, 11-142	electronic and navigation		7-6
			emergency	7-1	
		11-46, 11-54, 11-138, 11-141	procedures	7-1	
fuel consumed during			procedures, visual	7-2	
			radio	7-1	
			and signals	4-22	
one-engine rate of climb		11-49	visual communications procedures	7-2	

Changed 15 July 1970

Index 5

Index
Companionway to Crew

	Page No.			Page No.	
	Text	Illus		Text	Illus
Companionway Hydraulics Panel....		1-86	surface characteristics	4-2A	
Compartment Fire, ATM, or Hot Bleed Air Leaks	5-7		switch, wing flaps	1-95	
Compartment Temperature Warning Light, ATM	1-65		system, aileron	1-85	
Compass Controller	1-125		system, engine fuel	1-33	
Compass Indicator, Radio	1-114		systems, flight	1-85	
Compass, Standby	1-103		unit, fire-detection	1-32	
Compass System, Slaved Gyro Magnetic	1-125		unit, hydromechanical fuel	1-33	
Compressibility, Temperature Correction for		11-7	unit, interphone (ICS), navigator's	1-113	
Compressor Bleed Air System, Engine	1-48		units, interphone (ICS), pilot's and plane captain's	1-113	
Compressor Bleed Air Schematic, Engine, A-3A/B and KA-3B.....	1-61		valve, fuel crossfeed	1-37	
Computer, Cruise Control	11-4, 11-115		valve, manual cg fuel	1-44	
Configuration, Landing, Transition to................	6-3		wing, and fin-folding	1-94	
Console			wing spoiler	1-87	
and instrument lights, pilot's....	1-117		wing tank fuel transfer	1-42	
lights, navigator's	1-117		Controlled Bailout-Escape Routes...	5-21	
lights, plane captain's	1-117		Controller		
navigator's typical right-hand – A-3A		1-16	autopilot pedestal............	1-121	1-123
navigator's typical right-hand – A-3B		1-17	compass	1-125	
pilot's center – A-3B		1-15	electronic temperature	1-66	
pilot's left-hand – A-3A		1-11	Control Panel		
pilot's left-hand – A-3B		1-13	AN/ASB-7 radar		8-6
plane captain's – A-3A		1-23	C-760A/A	1-115	
plane captain's – A-3B		1-24	C-852B/ASB-1A radar		8-3
Contamination, Cabin Air	1-69		C-865/ARC-1 radio	1-116	
Continuous Power Summary Charts Maximum.............	11-111, 11-189		C-866/ARN-21B NAV	1-115	
			C-1159/APX-6B (IFF)........	1-112	
Continuous Power Summary, Maximum	11-113, 11-191		C-2549/ASB-7..............		8-5
			radar, check		8-7
			SIF	1-113	
Control			Controls		
aileron	1-85		autopilot engaging and disengaging................	1-122	
air-conditioning	1-69, 1-71		boost schematic, flight		1-90
anti-icing.................	1-71		check	3-19	
arresting hook..............	1-98		flight	4-2A	
auxiliary tank fuel transfer	1-42		oxygen system (panel-mounted regulator)................	1-119	
caging hook, aileron manual	1-87		pilot's microphone	1-113	
cockpit pressure	1-69		Control Surface Characteristics	4-2A	
computer, cruise	11-4, 11-115		flight controls	4-2A	
			speedbrakes	4-2B	
elevator	1-89		trim devices	4-2B	
engine	1-33		wing flaps	4-2B	
exterior lights	1-117		wing slats.................	4-2B	
fuel boost pump	1-38		Conversation, General		7-2
fuel trim – automatic	1-45		Cooler Door Control, Oil	1-37	
fuel trim – manual	1-47		Cooling Equipment, Ground	1-71	
fuel trim – selective..........	1-45		Corrections		
gust and wing pin lock.........	1-94		airspeed..................	11-4	
horizontal stabilizer trim	1-92		airspeed and altitude	11-115	
landing gear	1-97		altitude	11-5	
malfunction, engine fuel	1-33		charts, airspeed and altitude	11-4	
oil cooler door	1-37		for position error, airspeed and altitude................		11-11, 11-120
pitot heat	1-72				
pressure, aileron/spoiler and surface	1-91		for position error, mach number .		11-13, 11-121
rudder	1-87		mach number	11-5, 11-116	
safety pressure	1-119				
settings, radar (power applied)	8-7		temperature, for compressibility .	11-7	
			Counterpointer Pressure Altimeter ..	1-101	
			Course Indicator ID-249A/ARN	1-115	
			CQ and FMLP	3-33	
			Crew Coordination, Flight	9-1	
			Crew, Emergency Removal	5-27	
			Crew Evacuation and Emergency Access.............	5-29	5-30
speed, minimum single-engine	11-16		Crew, Ground	6-4	
			Crewmembers, Flight, Duties	9-1	
			Crew Movement	1-8	

Index 6

Changed 15 July 1970

Index
Crew to Electrical

	Text	Illus
Crew Movement and Compartment Diagram		1-9
Crew Requirements, Flight	2-1	
Crossfeed Control Valve, Fuel	1-37	
Crosswind Landing	3-27	
Critique	10-15	
NATOPS evaluation forms	10-15	
Cruise Climb	3-25	
Cruise After Climb	4-7	
Cruise Control Computer	11-4, 11-115	
Cruise Procedures	3-25	
Cruising	6-2	
Cruising Flight	4-3	
Cycles, Duty and Start Intervals	3-16	
Cylinder, Portable – Gaseous Oxygen Duration		1-122

D

	Text	Illus
Damping System, Yaw	1-123	
Danger Areas	1-165	1-166
DC		
and ac generator failure, complete	5-12	
electrical system		1-74
generator malfunction/failure	5-11	
generator switches	1-73	
generator warning lights	1-73	
power distribution	1-72	
powered instruments	1-101	
power failure	1-73	
power system	1-72	
slow-speed stabilizer trim	1-93	
Debriefing/Briefing	3-3	
Definitions	10-1	
Definitions, Abbreviations, and Symbols	11-3	
Defogging, Windshield	1-71	
Defrosting-Deicing Fluid	1-161	
Defrosting-Deicing Fluid Application Precautionary Data		1-163
Defrosting, Pressurization and Air-Conditioning Procedures	3-22	
Defueling and Pressure Fueling Basic System	1-129	
Defueling and Fueling, Pressure – Basic System		1-136
Deicing-Defrosting Fluid	1-161	
Deicing-Defrosting Fluid Application Precautionary Data		1-163
Delay, JATO Firing and Minimum Takeoff Distance	11-17	
Delay, JATO Firing – Two Units (15° Nozzle)		11-23
Density Altitude Chart		11-9
Departure, Instrument	6-2	
Description, General	1-3	
Desert Operation and Hot Weather	6-6	
Descent	3-26, 6-6, 11-99, 11-183	
charts		11-99, 11-183
checklist	3-26	

	Text	Illus
and landing	6-7	
maximum range		11-100, 11-184, 11-186
penetration	6-2	
Descent (J57-P-6B-Engines)	11-183	
maximum range		11-184
maximum rate		11-186
Differences, Main	1-3	
Dimensions, Aircraft	1-5	1-4
Direction Finding and Communication System, UHF	1-105	
Direction Finding System, AN/ARA-25 Automatic	1-109	
Direct Pressure Instruments	1-101	
Disengaging and Engaging Controls, Autopilot	1-122	
Distribution, dc Power	1-72	
Ditching		
bailout doctrine	5-18	
bailout procedures	5-18	
emergency – land	5-23	
emergency – sea	5-24	
Dome Light, Cabin	1-117	
Door Control, Oil Cooler	1-37	
Door, Entrance	1-5	
Doors, Bomb Bay	1-127	
Doors Control, Bomb Bay	1-127	
Drag Chute	1-99	
Drag Chute, Minimum Roll With	3-29	
Drag Chute, Minimum Roll Without	3-29	
Dropout	1-114	
Dumping System, Fuel Tank	1-55	
Dumping System, Wing Tank Fuel	1-44	
Duration, Gaseous Oxygen – Portable Cylinder		1-122
Duration, Liquid Oxygen		1-120

E

	Text	Illus
Electrical Fire	5-5	
Electrical Power Loss, Vertical Gyro Attitude Indicator (VGI) Operation After	1-102	
Electrical System	1-72	
ac	1-78	
ac power control	1-77	
ac		1-78
ac power distribution	1-76	
ac power failure	1-81	
ac power panel		1-77
ac power system	1-76	
aft power panel		1-76
dc		1-74
dc generator switches	1-73	
dc power distribution	1-72	
dc power system	1-72	
emergency operation	1-73	
generator warning lights	1-73	
Electrical System Malfunction/Failure	5-11	
ac generator	5-11	
complete ac and dc including battery	5-12	
complete ac and dc generator	5-12	
dc generator	5-11	
fuel vent icing	5-14	

Changed 15 July 1970

Index
Electronic to Engine

	Page No. Text	Illus		Page No. Text	Illus
fuel system	5-13		procedures	1-125, 5-1	
horizontal stabilizer trim	5-12				
oil system	5-13		runaway trim procedure	5-12	
Electronic Communications and Navigation		7-6	servicing completely empty/low systems	1-153	7-8
Electronic Navigation Equipment	7-2		signals between aircraft		7-8
Electronics, Associated, and Communications Equipment		1-110	speedbrake operation	5-10	
			single-engine flameout/ failure	5-4	
Electronics and Radio Equipment	1-104		takeoff abort procedures	5-2	
Electronic Temperature Controller	1-66		transceiver	2-3	
Elements, Heat-Sensing	1-32		unsatisfactory start	5-2	
Elevator	4-2A		wheel brakes	1-99, 5-18	
boost mechanism, frozen	1-91				
control	1-89		wing flap operation	1-95, 5-9	
rudder	4-13				
trim setting vs cg position		3-23	Endurance	11-91, 11-177	
Emergencies	3-4		vs altitude, maximum specific	11-177	11-95, 11-180
abort procedures, takeoff	5-2				
access and crew evacuation	5-29	5-30	factors with gear and flaps down	11-91, 11-177	
air starting	5-4				
air systems — servicing	1-153	1-156	fouled deck		11-93
arresting hook operation	1-98		maximum endurance profile		11-97
bailout	5-20		maximum specific endurance vs altitude		11-95
bailout escape routes	5-21				
breakaway procedures	4-22		profile, maximum	11-91	
climb charts	11-42, 11-136		Endurance (J57-P-6B-Engines)	11-177	
communications	7-1		fouled deck		11-178
crew removal	5-27		maximum specific endurance vs altitude		11-180
disengagement procedures	4-21				
ditching-land	5-23		Engagement, Barricade	3-39	
ditching-sea	5-24		Engagement Procedures, Altitudes, and Airspeed	4-18	
dual engine/flameout failure	5-4		Engagement Procedures, Receiver	4-18	
electrical fire	5-5		Engaging and Disengaging Controls, Autopilot	1-122	
electrical system operation	1-73				
engine fire	5-5		Engine	1-31	
engine malfunction/failures	5-3		and aircraft operation		7-8
escape chute and entrance	1-8		air inlet	1-71	
escape chute and entrance — A-3A	1-5		before starting	6-5	
			clearing procedures	3-18	
exits		5-22	compressor bleed air system	1-48	
exit, secondary		5-23	compressor bleed air schematic — A-3A/B and KA-3B		1-61
field arresting gear data		5-26	controls	1-33	
fire warning indications (lights on)	5-5		dual, flameout/failure	5-4	
			dual, low altitude/low airspeed failure	5-18	
flap retraction	1-96		failure after liftoff	5-3	
fuselage fire	5-5		failure, dual, low altitude/low airspeed	5-18	
ground	3-17, 5-2		failure during takeoff run	5-3	
hook operation	5-10		failure under specific conditions	4-8	
hydraulic system	1-85		fire	5-5	
in-flight	5-3		fire-detection system	1-32	
landing	5-14		flameout, fuel boost failure	1-38, 5-13	
landing-diversion recommendations	5-24	5-25			
landing gear operation	1-97, 5-9		fuel control malfunction	1-33	
			fuel control system	1-33	
(low state)	3-38		fuel pumps	1-34	
maximum glide (two engines inoperative)	5-5		ignition system	1-33	
			instruments	1-34	
nosewheel steering operation	1-98		internal fires and hot start	3-18	
operation	1-71		J57-P-6B		1-174
oxygen bottle	1-160		J57-P-10	1-35, 1-174	
oxygen bottle — servicing		1-161	limitations	1-171	
pneumatic systems	1-99		malfunction/failure	1-31, 5-3	
pneumatic systems schematic		1-100			
preparation, takeoff	5-2		master switches	1-34	

	Page No. Text	Page No. Illus		Page No. Text	Page No. Illus
mounted starters	1-165		Escape Chute and Entrance, Emergency	1-8	
oil system	1-36		Escape Chute and Entrance, Emergency — A-3A	1-5	
oil tank servicing	1-149		Escape Chute Test Switch	1-8	
oil temperature indicator, dual	1-37		Escape Chute Test Switch — A-3A	1-8	
one, rate of climb	11-42		Escape Hatch	1-8	
one, rate of climb — 60,000 pounds		11-49	Escape Hatch Air System	1-99	
operating limitations	1-171		Escape Route		
operating, pressure fueling (hot refueling)	1-140		alternate	5-19	
operation	1-31		controlled bailout	5-21	
operation, continued, with fuel boost failure	1-38, 5-13		emergency bailout	5-21	
			primary and secondary	5-18	
shutdown in flight	4-6		Evacuation, Crew and Emergency Access	5-29	5-30
single, approach/landing	3-29		Exchanger, Fuel Line Heat	1-39	
single, flameout/failure	5-4		Exit, Secondary Emergency		5-23
single, flight characteristics	4-7		Exits, Emergency		5-22
single, minimum control speed	11-16	11-22	Extension, Emergency Wing Flap	5-9	
			Extensions, Microphone Headset	1-113	
starter switch	1-34		Exterior Inspection Diagram		3-10
starting	1-34, 3-35, 6-6		Exterior Lights	1-117	
			Exterior Lights Control	1-117	
			External Power Switch	1-80	
trim card	1-104				
Engine Compressor Bleed			**F**		
Air System	1-48				
air turbine motors (ATM's)	1-63		Failure		
ATM monitor panel		1-65	ac and dc generator, complete	5-12	
ATM restart		1-67	air-conditioning turbine	5-7	
schematic A-3A/B and KA-3B		1-61	boost pump	5-13	
shutoff system (rotary switch)	1-63		dual-engine low altitude/low airspeed	5-18	
shutoff system (toggle switches)	1-48		engine, after liftoff	5-3	
Engine Oil System	1-36		engine during takeoff run	5-3	
dual engine oil temperature indicator	1-37		engine, under specific conditions	4-8	
malfunction	1-37		flameout, dual engine	5-4	
oil cooler door control	1-37		flameout, single-engine	5-4	
oil pressure gage	1-37		fuel boost with accompanied engine flameout	1-38, 5-13	
Entrance	3-12				
Entrance to the Aircraft		3-13	fuel boost with continued engine operation	1-38, 5-13	
Entrance and Chute, Emergency Escape — A-3A	1-5				
Entrance and Chute, Emergency Escape	1-8		landing gear solenoid	5-6	
Entrance Door	1-5		malfunction, ac generator	5-11	
emergency escape chute and entrance	1-8		malfunction, ATM	5-10	
emergency escape chute and entrance — A-3A	1-5		malfunction, dc generator	5-11	
escape chute test switch	1-8		malfunction, engine	1-31, 5-3	
escape chute test switch — A-3A	1-8		malfunctions, fuel system	5-13	
escape hatch	1-8		malfunction, fuel quantity indication	5-13	
Equipment					
catapult	1-128		malfunction, oil system	5-13	
checklist, ASB-1A radar	8-7		pitch trim	1-125	
checklist, ASB-7 radar	8-8		utility hydraulic system	5-8	
communications and associated electronics		1-110	wheel brake operation after utility	5-10	
electronic navigation	7-2		False Start	3-18, 5-2	
ground cooling	1-71				
lighting	1-116		Field Arrestments	3-32	
navigation	1-125		emergency	5-24	
omnibearing (VOR)	1-114		gear data		5-26
oxygen check	2-3		long/short	5-26	
personal, requirements	2-2		Field Barrier	3-33	
radio and electronics	1-104		Field Takeoff — With JATO	11-125	
radio and radar and antennas		1-106	Field Landings		
required for starting	3-14		no-boost	5-16	
security	1-111		no-flap	5-17	

Index
Field to FMLP

	Page No. Text	Page No. Illus		Page No. Text	Page No. Illus
no-slat	5-17		engine shutdown in	4-6	
single-engine	5-14		evaluation	10-3	
Field (Post-Landing) Checklist	3-32		evaluation grade determination	10-15	
Fin-Folding and Wing Control	1-94		high-speed	4-3	
Fin-Folding and Wing System	1-94		low-speed	4-5	
Fin-Unlocked Indicator Light	1-95		maneuvering	4-9	
Fire			and navigation planning	3-3	
detection control unit	1-32		normal	1-171	
detection system, engine	1-32		procedures	4-1	
electrical	5-5		procedures, instrument	6-1	
engine	5-5		strength, operating (VN)		
fighting		5-28	diagrams		1-176
fuselage	5-5		test fouled deck range — IFR		11-66
or hot bleed air leaks,			uncontrolled	5-18	
ATM compartment	5-7		Flight Characteristics	4-3	
or hot bleed air leaks, bomb			cruising flight	4-3	
bay/companionway	5-7		high-speed flight	4-3	
internal engine and hot start	3-18		load factor for buffet onset		4-4
warning indications (lights on)	5-5		low-speed flight	4-5	
warning lights (wing(s) and/or			single-engine	4-7	
air condition)	5-7		spins	4-6	
warning light (wing) LH	5-6		stalls		
warning light (wing) RH	5-7		stalling speeds		4-6
wing, or hot bleed air leak	5-6		Flight Control Systems	1-85	
Firing Delay			ac high-speed stabilizer trim	1-92	
JATO and minimum takeoff			aileron control system	1-85	
distance	11-17		aileron power boost assembly		1-88
JATO — two units (15° nozzle)		11-23	aileron and rudder-elevator	1-91	
JATO — four units (15° nozzle)		11-25	aileron/spoiler and surface		
JATO — six units (15° nozzle)		11-27	control pressure	1-91	
JATO — 12 units (15° nozzle)		11-29	arresting hook	1-98	
JATO — two units (30° nozzle)		11-31	autopilot stabilizer trim	1-93	
JATO — four units (30° nozzle)		11-33	bomb bay to main gear access	1-97	
JATO — six units (30° nozzle)		11-35	companionway hydraulics panel		1-86
JATO — 12 units (30° nozzle)		11-37	drag chute	1-99	
JATO, using 2 5KS-4500 MK 7			emergency pneumatic systems		
MOD 2 JATO units, example	11-17		schematic		1-100
Firing Switch, JATO	1-128		escape hatch air system	1-99	
First Aid Kit	1-128		flight controls boost schematic		1-90
Flameout, Engine, Fuel Boost			horizontal stabilizer trim		
Failure	1-38, 5-13		control	1-92	
Flameout/Failure, Dual Engine	5-4		horizontal stabilizer trim		
Flameout/Failure, Single-Engine	5-4		system	1-92	
Flaps			landing gear emergency		
control switch, wing	1-95		operation	1-97	
emergency operation, wing	1-95, 5-9		landing gear system	1-96	
extension, emergency wing	5-9		nosewheel steering system	1-97	
and gear down endurance			pneumatic emergency		
factors	11-91, 11-177		systems	1-99	
			speedbrakes	1-96	
and gear down — fouled deck			wheel brakes system	1-98	
range		11-64, 11-152	wing and fin-folding system	1-94	
			wing flaps	1-95	
position indicator, wing	1-95		wing slats	1-99	
retraction, emergency	1-96		wing spoiler system schematic		1-89
retraction, emergency wing	5-9		Flight Procedures	4-1	
trim, and fuel trim	3-22		air refueling	4-18	
wing	4-2B		air starting	4-7	
Flight			angle-of-attach relationship	4-9	
boost-off	4-9		control surface characteristics	4-1	
conditions, critical	5-5		engine shutdown in flight	4-6	
conditions, normal	5-5		flight characteristics	4-3	
controls	4-2A		formation	4-15	
controls boost schematic		1-90	single-engine flight		
crew coordination	9-1		characteristics	4-7	
crewmembers, duties	9-1		Floodlights	1-117	
crew requirements	2-1		Flying		
cross-country	3-6		cloud	4-17	
cruising	4-3		night formation	4-17	
during	6-6		simulated instrument	6-1	
			Flowmeter, Fuel	1-34	
			FMLP and CQ	3-33	

Index
Foaming to Fuel

	Text	Illus
Foaming Procedures, Recommended Runway	5-27	
Fold, Wing Spread to Wing	1-95	
Formation	4-15	
basic	4-16	
echelon	4-17	
general	4-15	
maneuvering	4-17	
night flying	4-17	
odd numbers in	4-17	
parade	4-16	
rendezvous	4-15	
and rendezvous, night	3-34	
signals		7-4
tactical	4-17	
wing position	4-16	
Forward Fuselage and Upper Bomb Bay Auxiliary Tank	1-137	
Fouled Deck		
endurance	11-91, 11-177	11-178
range ("bingo cards")	11-57, 11-145	
range, flight test – IFR		11-66
range – gear down		11-63, 11-151
range – gear and flaps down		11-64, 11-152
fouled deck range – IFR		11-62, 11-150, 11-154
range – sea level		11-67, 11-155
range – VFR		11-61, 11-65, 11-149, 11-153
Frequency Meter	1-81	
Frost, Guide to Elimination		1-162
Frozen Elevator Boost Mechanism	1-91	
Fuel		
boost failure with accompanied engine flameout	1-38, 5-13	
boost failure with continued engine operation	1-38, 5-13	
boost pressure indicator	1-34	
boost pump control	1-38	
capacity data pressure fueling		1-135
computations	3-7	
conservation prior to takeoff	3-22	
consumed during climb		11-46, 11-54, 11-138, 11-141
control malfunction, engine	1-33	
control system, engine	1-33	
control unit, hydromechanical	1-33	
control valve, manual cg	1-44	
crossfeed control valve	1-37	
distribution schedule		1-46
dumping system, wing tank	1-44	
float valve and shutoff valve – basic system	1-137	
flowmeter	1-34	
line heat exchanger	1-39	
low-level warning light	1-48	
management	3-5	
measurement stick	1-140	

	Text	Illus
minimum (bingo fuel)	3-38	
planning	3-6	
pumps, engine	1-34	
quantity indicating system	1-44	
quantity indication malfunction/failure	5-13	
quantity indicator	1-48	
quantity measurement	1-140	1-150
reserves	3-6	
system malfunctions/failure	5-13	
system switch panel	1-43	
systems	1-37	
tank, aft or forward fuselage	1-135	
tank pressurizing and venting system	1-45	
tanks	1-39	
transfer	1-47	
transfer control, auxiliary tank	1-42	
transfer control, wing tank	1-42	
transfer rate		4-34
transfer and tanker drogue control	4-22	
trim control-automatic	1-45	
trim control-manual	1-47	
trim control-selective	1-45	
trim control system	1-43	
trim, and flaps	3-22	
trim switch, fuselage	1-43	
vent icing	5-14	
vent mast icing	1-45	
Fueling		
aft fuselage fuel tank	1-137	
and defueling, pressure, basic system	1-129	1-136
forward fuselage and upper bomb bay auxiliary tank	1-137	
gravity		1-149
gravity, procedures	1-140	
multiple point	1-137	
power switch, pressure	1-42	
pressure – basic system	1-134	
pressure with engines operating (hot refueling)	1-140	
pressure, fuel capacity data		1-135
system, pressure	1-39	
wing tanks	1-137	
Fuel System, Basic A-3A/B	1-39	
auxiliary tank transfer control	1-42	
cg indicator	1-44	
fuselage trim switch	1-43	
manual cg fuel control valve	1-44	
pressure fueling system	1-39	
quantity indicating system	1-44	
schematic-basic A-3A/B aircraft		1-40
switch panel	1-43	1-43
tank pressurizing and venting system	1-45	
tanks	1-39	
trim control system	1-43	
wing tank dumping system	1-44	
wing tank transfer control	1-42	
wing tank purge system	1-42	
Fuel System Management – Basic A-3A/B fuel system	1-45	
control – automatic	1-45	
distribution schedule		1-46
low-level warning light	1-48	
quantity indicator	1-48	

Changed 15 July 1970

Index 11

Index
Fuel to Hot

NAVAIR 01-40ATA-1

	Text	Illus		Text	Illus
transfer	1-47		Ground, Equipment Cooling	1-71	
trim control – manual	1-47		Ground Operation, Radar	8-1	
trim control – selective	1-45		Ground Roll, Landing	11-103	11-105
Fuel Systems	1-37		Ground Roll, Minimum, Takeoff Distance – With JATO	11-124	
Full Power Check	3-23				
Fume and Smoke Elimination	5-8				
Fuse and Circuit Breaker Panels – A-3A		1-26	Ground Support Starting Equipment	1-165	
Fuse and Circuit Breaker Panels – A-3B		1-27	Ground Training	2-1	
Fuselage Fire	5-5		Guillotine Procedure	1-59, 4-27	
Fuselage Fuel Tank, Aft	1-137		Gust and Wing Pin Lock Control	1-94	
Fuselage Fuel Tank, Aft or Forward	1-135		Gyro Attitude Indicator, Vertical (VGI)	1-102	
Fuselage Fuel Trim Switch	1-43		Gyro Horizon Indicator, Standby	1-103	
Fuselage and Upper Bomb Bay Auxiliary Tank, Forward	1-137		Gyro Magnetic Compass System, Slaved	1-125	
			Gyrosyn Compass Operational Check	1-126	

G

H

Gage, Oil Pressure	1-37		Handle, Pilot's Assist	1-8	
Gangbar, Horizontal Stabilizer Actuator	1-94		Handgrip, Catapult	1-128	
Gaseous Oxygen Duration – Portable Cylinder		1-122	Hardover Failures	1-125	
GCA Approaches	6-3		Harness, Shoulder and Inertia Reel	1-5	
Gear Access, Bomb Bay to Main	1-97		Hatch Air System, Escape	1-99	
Gear Brake, Main Landing – Bleeding	1-152		Hatch, Escape	1-8	
Gear Control, Landing	1-97		Headset Extensions, Microphone	1-113	
Gear Data, Field Arresting		5-26	Heat Control, Pitot	1-72	
Gear Down – Fouled Deck Range		11-63, 11-64, 11-151	Heat Exchanger, Fuel Line	1-39	
			Heat-Sensing Elements	1-32	
Gear Emergency Operation, Landing	1-97		Height Indicator	1-114	
Gear and Flaps Down Endurance Factors	11-91, 11-177		HF Radio Receiver-Transmitter, AN/ARC-38A	1-111	
			High Crosswind Landings	3-28	
Gear, Landing, Collapsed	5-27		High-Speed Flight	4-3	
Gear, Landing, Emergency Operation	5-9		High-Speed Stabilizer Trim, ac	1-92	
			Holding	6-2	
Gear, Landing, Solenoid Failure	5-6		Hold Operation, Altitude	1-124	
Gear, Nose, Steering Accumulator	1-153		Hook, Aileron Manual Control Caging	1-87	
Gear, Personal		2-4	Hook, Arresting	1-98	
Gear System, Landing	1-96		Hook Bypass Switch, Arresting	1-104	
General Arrangement		1-6	Hook Control, Arresting	1-98	
Generator			Hook Emergency Operation	5-10	
ac, malfunction/failure	5-11		Hook Emergency Operation, Arresting	1-98	
circuit breaker relays	1-77				
dc, malfunction/failure	5-11		Horizon Indicator, Standby Gyro	1-103	
failure, complete ac and dc	5-12		Horizontal Stabilizer		
manual reset	1-73		actuator gangbar	1-94	
no. 1 bus, ac	1-76		trim check	3-20	
no. 2 bus, ac	1-76		trim control	1-92	
switches	1-80		trim malfunction	5-12	
switches, dc	1-73		trim system	1-92	
warning lights	1-73, 1-80		trim system – general	1-94	
warning lights, dc	1-73		Horn, Bomb Doors Warning	1-127	
Glide, Maximum (Two Engines Inoperative)	5-5		Hot Bleed Air and Companionway Check	3-18	
Graphical Data, Sample Problem Illustrating Use of	11-116		Hot Bleed Air Leaks	5-6	
Gravity Fueling		1-149	air-conditioning turbine failure	5-7	
Ground Crew	6-4		air-conditioning/upper bomb bay (lights on)	5-7	
Ground Emergencies	3-17, 5-2		ATM compartment fire	5-7	
			bleed air rotary shutoff switch	5-6	
			bleed air toggle shutoff switches	5-7	

Index 12

Changed 15 July 1970

	Page No.	
	Text	Illus
bomb bay/companionway fires	5-7	
(light on), air conditioning/ upper bomb bay	5-7	
smoke and fume elimination	5-8	
wing fire	5-6	
Hot Refueling, Pressure Fueling with Engines Operating	1-140	
Hot Start	5-2	
Hot Start and Internal Engine Fires	3-18	
Hot Weather and Desert Operation	6-6	
before entering aircraft	6-6	
climb	6-7	
descent and landing	6-7	
on entering aircraft	6-6	
postflight	6-7	
starting engines	6-6	
taxi and takeoff	6-7	
Howgozit	3-6	
Hydraulics Panel, Companionway		1-86
Hydraulic System	1-81	
emergency	1-85	
reservoir servicing	1-149	
servicing		1-151
utility schematic		1-82
utility system	1-81	
Hydromechanical Fuel Control Unit	1-33	
Hydroplaning	3-29	

I

ICAO Standard Altitude Table		11-10
Ice	6-3	
Ice, Guide to Elimination of		1-162
Ice, Snow, and Rain	6-4	
Icing/cg	3-25	
Icing, Fuel Vent	5-14	
Icing, Fuel Vent Mast	1-45	
Icing of Pitot-Static Instruments	6-4	
ICS (Interphone Control Unit)	1-113	
ICS Switch, Fourth Man	1-114	
ID-250A/ARN Radio Magnetic Indicator	1-115	
ID-249A/ARN Course Indicator	1-115	
Identification Signals, Tanker Light	4-22	
IFF AN/APX-6B Transponder	1-112	
IFF C-1159/APX-6B Control Panel	1-112	
IFF/SIF Procedures	7-2	
IFR — Fouled Deck Range		11-62, 11-150, 11-154
IFR — Fouled Deck Range, Flight Test		11-66
Ignition Switch	1-34	
Ignition System	1-33	
Immediate Air Start	5-3	
Indexer, Cockpit	1-104	
Indicated Angle-of-Attack, Approximate		4-10
Indicating System, Fuel Quantity	1-44	
Indication, Fuel Quantity, Malfunction/Failure	5-13	
Indicator		
airspeed	1-101	
angle-of-attack	1-103	

	Page No.	
	Text	Illus
cg	1-44	
dual engine oil temperature	1-37	
fuel boost pressure	1-34	
fuel quantity	1-48	
height	1-114	
ID/249A/ARN course	1-115	
ID-250A/ARN radio magnetic	1-115	
light, fin-unlocked	1-95	
radio compass	1-114	
standby gyro horizon	1-103	
system, limit	1-114	
trim position	1-94	
turbine outlet temperature	1-34	
turn-and-slip	1-102	
vertical gyro attitude (VGI)	1-102	
vertical velocity	1-102	
wing flaps position	1-95	
Indoctrination	2-1	
flight crew requirements	2-1	
ground training	2-1	
parachute	2-3	
personal equipment requirements	2-2	
survival training	2-1	
Inertia Reel and Shoulder Harness	1-5	
In-Flight Considerations, General	3-25	
In-Flight Emergencies	5-4	
In-Flight/Level-Off Checklist	3-26	
Initial Power Application, Voltage Check 3 Minutes After	8-7	
Inlet, Engine Air	1-71	
Inspection		
aircraft	3-35	
diagram, exterior		3-10
Instrument Panel, Pilot's — A-3A/B Typical		1-10
Instruments	1-101	
accelerometer	1-102	
ac powered	1-101	
airspeed indicator	1-101	
angle-of-attack approach light system	1-103	
clocks	1-104	
and console lights, pilot's	1-117	
counterpointer pressure altimeter	1-101	
dc powered	1-101	
departure	6-2	
direct pressure	1-101	
engine	1-34	
engine trim card — typical		1-105
flight procedures	6-1	
flying, simulated	6-1	
engine trim card	1-104	
markings		1-172
pitot static	1-101	
pitot-static, icing of	6-4	
proficiency, pilot	6-1	
self-generating	1-101	
standby compass	1-103	
standby gyro horizon indicator	1-103	
takeoff	6-2	
turn-and-slip indicator	1-102	
vertical gyro attitude indicator (VGI)	1-102	
vertical velocity indicator	1-102	
Intelligence, Air, and Special Instructions	3-4	
Interior Lights	1-116	

Index
Interphone to Landing

	Page No.	
	Text	Illus
Interphone, AN/AIC-4A	1-113	
Interphone Control Unit (ICS), Navigator's	1-113	
Interphone Control Units (ICS), Pilot's and Plane Captain's	1-113	
Intervals, Start and Duty Cycles	3-16	
I/P-OUT-MIC Switch	1-112	
J		
J57-P-6B Engines		1-174
J57-P-6B Engines, A-3A Aircraft Performance Data Charts	11-115	
J57-P-10 Engine		1-35, 1-174
JATO	3-24	
arming switch	1-128	
firing delay and minimum takeoff distance	11-17	
firing delay – two units (15° nozzle)		11-23
firing delay – four units (15° nozzle)		11-25
firing delay – six units (15° nozzle)		11-27
firing delay – 12 units (15° nozzle)		11-29
firing delay – two units (30° nozzle)		11-31
firing delay – four units (30° nozzle)		11-33
firing delay – six units (30° nozzle)		11-35
firing delay – 12 units (30° nozzle)		11-37
firing switch	1-128	
jettisoning	3-24	
jettison switch	1-128	
limitations	1-175	
no – maximum recommended takeoff weight	11-124	
no – recommended lift-off speed	11-123	
no – refusal speeds	11-125	
no, refused takeoff stopping distance	11-16	
no – takeoff distance	11-123	
procedures		7-9
recommended lift-off speed, with and without	11-15	
system	1-127	
takeoff distance, no JATO	11-15	
takeoff distance – two units (15° nozzle)		11-24
takeoff distance – four units (15° nozzle)		11-26
takeoff distance – six units (15 nozzle)		11-28
takeoff distance – 12 units (15° nozzle)		11-30
takeoff distance – two units (30° nozzle)		11-32
takeoff distance – four units (30° nozzle)		11-34
takeoff distance – six units (30° nozzle)		11-36
takeoff distance – 12 Units (30° nozzle)		11-38

	Page No.	
	Text	Illus
units (15° nozzle), 5KS-4500 MK7 MOD 1		11-17
units (30° nozzle), four – takeoff distance minimum ground roll		11-129
warning light	1-128	
with – field takeoff	11-125	
with – takeoff distance minimum ground roll	11-124	
Jet-Assisted Takeoff System	1-127	
catapult equipment	1-128	
JATO arming switch	1-128	
Jet Penetrations	6-2	
Jettisoning, JATO	3-24	
Jettison Switch, JATO	1-128	
Jury Strut, Automatic	1-95	
K		
L		
Landing	3-27, 6-6, 11-103, 11-187	
approach charts	11-103	
approach, single-engine	3-29	
arrested	5-27	
boost-off airfield	4-14	
boost-off carrier	4-13	
boost-off single-engine	4-15	
and breakup	3-35	
and breakup, night	3-34	
carrier	3-36	
charts	11-103, 11-187	
checklist	3-26	
configuration, transition to	6-3	
crosswind	3-27	
and descent	6-7	
diversion recommendations, emergency		5-25
emergencies	5-14	
emergency ditching	5-23	
emergency – diversion recommendations	5-24	
gear collapsed	5-27	
gear brake, main – bleeding	1-152	
gear emergency operation	5-9	
gear solenoid failure	5-6	
ground roll		11-105
high crosswind	3-28	
no-boost carrier	5-17	
no-boost field	5-16	
no-flap carrier	5-17	
no-flap field	5-17	
no-slat carrier	5-18	
no-slat field	5-17	
pattern, typical carrier		3-37
recommended approach speeds and stall speeds		11-104
single-engine	5-14	
single-engine carrier	3-38, 5-16	
single-engine and waveoff pattern (typical)		5-15
takeoff, changing lead, leaving formation, breakup		7-3

	Page No.			Page No.	
	Text	Illus		Text	Illus
and takeoff, low level	5-18		Lights		
or taxi light	1-118		air refueling probe	1-118	
touch-and-go	3-29		anticollision	1-118	
unarrested	5-27		approach	1-104, 1-118	
and waveoff pattern		3-31	ATM compartment temperature		
weight	3-33		warning	1-65	
Landing (J57-P-6B-Engines)	11-187		cabin dome	1-117	
approach charts	11-187		control, exterior	1-117	
landing charts	11-187		dc generator warning	1-73	
recommended approach speeds and stall speeds		11-188	exterior	1-117	
Landing Emergencies	5-14		fin-unlocked indicator	1-95	
aircraft upright or inverted	5-27		fire warning (wing) LH	5-6	
A-3 field maximum engagement (KIAS) vs gross weight X 1000		5-26	fire warning (wing) RH	5-7	
			fire warning (wing(s) and/or air cond)	5-7	
bailout/ditching doctrine	5-18		generator warning	1-73, 1-80	
bailout/ditching procedures	5-18				
emergency access and crew evacuation		5-29	identification signals, tanker	4-22	
			interior	1-116	
emergency crew removal	5-27		JATO warning	1-128	
emergency exits		5-22	navigator's console	1-117	
emergency field arrestments	5-24		ON, fire warning indications	5-5	
emergency landing/diversion recommendations	5-25				
			pilot's instrument and console	1-117	
fire fighting		5-28	plane captain's console	1-117	
no-boost carrier landing	5-17		service	1-117	
			system, angle-of-attack approach	1-103	
no-boost field landings	5-16				
no-flap carrier landings	5-17		taxi (or landing)	1-118	
no-flap field landings	5-17		and thermoswitches, warning	1-63	
no-slat carrier landings	5-18				
no-slat field landings	5-17		Limitations		
recommended runway foaming procedures	5-27		acceleration	1-175	
			aircraft operating	1-170A	
secondary emergency exit		5-23	airspeed	1-171	
single-engine landing and waveoff pattern (typical)		5-15	carrier operations	1-175	
			center of gravity	1-175	
single-engine landings	5-14		engine	1-171	
wheel brakes emergency	5-18		JATO	1-175	
Landing Gear Control	1-97		maneuvers	1-171	
Landing Gear Emergency Operation	1-97		stores	1-175	
			weight	1-175	
Landing Gear System	1-96		Limit Indicator System	1-114	
Leaks, ATM Compartment Fire or Hot Bleed Air			Line Heat Exchanger, Fuel	1-39	
			Line Operations	3-9	
Leaks, Hot Bleed Air	5-6		Line Speed Check	11-16, 11-124	
Leaks, Hot Bleed Air or Fires, Bomb Bay/Companionway	5-7				
			Liquid Oxygen Converter — 8-Liter System, Filling	1-157	
Leaks, Hot Bleed Air (Light On), Air-Conditioning/Upper Bomb Bay	5-7				
			Liquid Oxygen Converters — 20 Liter System, Filling	1-158	
Leaving Formation, Breakup, Landing, Takeoff, Changing Lead		7-3	Liquid Oxygen Duration		1-120
			Liquid Oxygen System	1-118	
			Load Factor for Buffet Onset		4-4
Left-Hand Console, Pilot's — A-3A		1-11			
			Lock Control, Gust and Wing Pin	1-94	
Left-Hand Console, Pilot's — A-3B		1-13			
			Long Field Arrestments	5-26	
Level-Off/In-Flight Checklist	3-26		Lookouts	3-21	
Liftoff, Engine Failure After	5-3				
Lift-Off Speed, Recommended		11-19, 11-126			

M

Lift-Off Speed, Recommended — No JATO	11-123		Mach Number		
			number vs airspeed		11-6
Lift-Off Speed, Recommended, With and Without JATO	11-15		correction for position error		11-13, 11-121
			error		
Lighting Equipment	1-116		corrections	11-5, 11-116	11-116
exterior lights	1-117				
interior lights	1-116				

Index
Magnetic to Navigator's

	Page No.			Page No.	
	Text	Illus		Text	Illus
Magnetic Compass System, Slaved Gyro	1-125		Minimum fuel (bingo fuel)	3-38	
Magnetic Indicator, ID-250A/ARN Radio	1-115		ground roll, takeoff distance — with JATO	11-124	
Main Gear Access, Bomb Bay To	1-97		ground roll, takeoff distance — four JATO units (30° nozzle)		11-129
Main Landing Gear Brake — Bleeding	1-152		roll with drag chute	3-29	
Main Differences	1-3		roll without drag chute	3-29	
Malfunction/Failure			single-engine control speed	11-16	11-22
ac generator	5-11		takeoff distance and JATO firing delay	11-17	
ATM	5-10		Mission Checklist	3-5	
checklist, ASB-1A radar	8-8		Mission Plan, Operational	3-3	
dc generator	5-11		Mission Planning Briefings	3-3	
electrical system	5-11		Mission Profile	11-58, 11-146	11-87, 11-175
engine	1-31, 5-3		Mission Return Profile		11-90
engine fuel control	1-33		MK 7 MOD JATO units (15° nozzle), 5KS-4500	11-17	
fuel system	5-13		MK 7 MOD 1 JATO units (30° nozzle), 5KS-4500	11-17	
fuel quantity indication	5-13		Monitoring, Altitude	6-2	
oil system	1-37, 5-13		Monitor Panel, ATM	1-64	
tanker checklist	4-26		Monitor Bus	1-72	
Management, Fuel	3-5		Mooring		1-169
Maneuvering	4-17		Motors, Air Turbine (ATM's)	1-63	
Maneuvering Flight	4-9				
Maneuvers	1-171		Mc		
Manning the Aircraft	3-9				
Manual Control Caging Hook, Aileron	1-87		N		
Markings, Instrument		1-172	NATOPS Evaluation	10-1	
Master Engine Switches	1-34		critique	10-15	
Master Switch, Radio	1-104		flight evaluation grade determination	10-15	
Mast Icing, Fuel Vent	1-45		navigator flight grading criteria	10-10	
Maximum			pilot flight evaluation grading criteria	10-4	
continuous power summary		11-113, 11-191	plane captain flight grading criteria	10-13	
continuous power summary charts		11-111, 11-189	question bank	10-16	
endurance profile	11-91	11-97	records and reports	10-15	
glide (two engines inoperative)	5-5		NAV C-866/ARN-21B Control Panel	1-115	
range descent		11-100, 11-184	Navigation	3-5	
rate descent		11-186	bag contents	3-6	
recommended takeoff weight		11-21, 11-128	and electronic communications		7-6
recommended takeoff weight — no JATO		11-124	equipment	1-125	
maximum recommended takeoff weight with and without JATO		11-16	equipment, electronic	7-2	
specific endurance vs altitude		11-57, 11-91, 11-145, 11-177	and flight planning	3-3	
			planning	3-6	
			slaved gyro magnetic compass system	1-125	
specific range vs altitude		11-68, 11-95, 11-156, 11-180	Navigator	9-1	
			Navigator Flight Grading Criteria	10-10	
			airmanship	10-12	
Measurement, Fuel Quantity	1-140	1-150	debrief	10-13	
Meter, Frequency	1-81		equipment malfunction	10-12	
Microphone Controls, Pilot's	1-113		mission planning	10-10	
Microphone Headset Extensions	1-113		navigation	10-12	
Microphone Switches, Foot	1-113		prelanding and shutdown procedures	10-12	
Military Thrust — Temperature Effect on One-Engine Rate of Climb		11-53	radar equipment preflight checklist	10-11	
			taxi and pretakeoff	10-11	
			Navigator's Console Lights	1-117	
			Navigator's Interphone Control Unit (ICS)	1-113	

Item	Text	Illus
Navigator's Seat (Nav)	1-5	
Navigator's Station – A-3A/B (Typical)		1-25
Navigator's Typical Right-Hand Console – A-3A		1-16
Navigator's Typical Right-Hand Console – A-3B		1-17
Negative g Condition, ATM Restart After	1-66	
Night		
breakup and landing	3-34	
carrier operations	3-36	
FMLP	3-34	
formation flying	4-17	
formation and rendezvous	3-34	
recovery, CCA	3-38	
taxi, and takeoff	3-34	
taxiing	3-21	
No-Boost Carrier Landing	5-17	
No-Boost Field Landings	5-16	
No-Flap Carrier Landings	5-17	
No-Flap Field Landings	5-17	
Normal Air Start	5-3	
Normal Flight	1-171	
Normal Flight Conditions	5-5	
Normal Procedures	3-1	
briefing/debriefing	3-3	
carrier-based procedures	3-35	
mission planning	3-5	
shore-based procedures	3-9	
Nose Gear Steering Accumulator	1-153	
Nosewheel Steering Emergency Operation	1-98	
Nosewheel Steering Procedures	3-21	
Nosewheel Steering System	1-97	
No-Slat Carrier Landings	5-18	
No-Slat Field Landings	5-17	

O

Item	Text	Illus
Oil		
cooler door control	1-37	
pressure gage	1-37	
sump, ATM – servicing	1-157	
system, engine	1-36	
system malfunction	1-37	
system malfunction/failure	5-13	
system servicing	1-149, 1-157	1-150
tank, engine, servicing	1-149	
temperature indicator, dual engine	1-37	
Omnibearing Equipment (VOR)	1-114	
AN/ARC-1 receiver-transmitter	1-116	
AN/ARN-14E receiver (VOR)	1-114	
AN/ARN-21B TACAN	1-115	
control panel C-760A/A	1-115	
course indicator ID-249A/ARN	1-115	
radio magnetic indicator ID-250A/ARN	1-115	
TACAN air-to-air ranging	1-116	
Oil System – Servicing	1-149	
engine oil tank	1-149	
hydraulic reservoir	1-149	
hydraulic systems	1-151	
Omnibearing Equipment (VOR)	1-114	
Operational Check, Gyrosyn Compass	1-126	
Oscillation, Drogue	4-20	

Item	Text	Illus
Outlet Temperature Indicators, Turbine	1-34	
Oxygen		
air valve	1-119	
bottle, emergency	1-160	
bottle, emergency – servicing		1-161
equipment check	2-3	
converter, liquid – 8-liter system, filling	1-157	
converter, liquid – 20-liter system, filling	1-158	
duration, gaseous – portable cylinder		1-122
duration		1-120
supply valve	1-119	
system	1-118	
system check	1-160	
system controls (panel-mounted regulator)	1-119	
system – servicing		1-159
Oxygen System	1-118	
controls (panel-mounted regulator)	1-119	
gaseous duration – portable cylinder		1-122
liquid	1-118	
liquid duration		1-120
Oxygen System – Servicing	1-157	1-159
emergency bottle	1-160	1-161
filling liquid converter – 8-liter system	1-157	
filling liquid converters – 20-liter system	1-158	
purging	1-160	
system check	1-160	

P

Item	Text	Illus
Panel		
ac power		1-77
aft power		1-76
AN/ASB-7 radar control		8-6
ATM monitor	1-64	
C-760A/A control	1-115	
C-852B/ASB-1A radar control		8-3
C-865/ARC-1 radio control	1-116	
C-866/ARN-21B control, NAV	1-115	
C-2549/ASB-7 radar control	8-5	
check, radar control	8-7	
circuit breaker and fuse – A-3A		1-26
circuit breaker and fuse – A-3B		1-27
companionway hydraulics		1-86
fuel system switch	1-43	
mounted regulator, oxygen system controls	1-119	
pilot's circuit breaker – A-3A		1-28
pilot's circuit breaker – A-3B typical		1-29
pilot's instrument – A-3A/B typical		1-10
Parachute	2-3	
emergency transceiver	2-3	
pararaft deployment	2-3	
pararaft kit	2-3	
personal gear		2-4
Parade Formation	4-16	

Index
Parameters to Power

NAVAIR 01-40ATA-1

	Page No. Text	Page No. Illus		Page No. Text	Page No. Illus
Parameters, Operating – Engine-Mounted Starter		1-165	Pitch Trim Failures	1-125	
Pararaft Deployment	2-3		Pitchup Characteristics	4-9	
Pararaft Kit	2-3		Pitot Heat Control	1-72	
Pattern, Speed, and Technique	3-33		Pitot Static Instruments	1-101	
Pedestal Controller, Autopilot	1-121	1-123	Pitot Static Instruments, Icing of	6-4	
Penetration			Plane Captain	9-1	
and approaches by dissimilar aircraft	4-17		console – A3-A		1-23
descent	6-2		console – A-3B		1-24
jet	6-2		console lights	1-117	
thunderstorm	6-4		and pilot's seats – A-3B (typical)		1-20
transition from	6-3		seat (P, C)	1-5	
Performance Data	11-1		station – A3-A		1-21
climb	11-42, 11-135		station – A-3B		1-22
combat performance	11-111, 11-189		Plane Captain Flight Grading Criteria	10-13	
descent	11-99, 11-183		airmanship	10-14	
endurance	11-91, 11-177		checklist	10-14	
			mission planning	10-13	
landing	11-103, 11-187		postlanding	10-14	
range	11-57, 11-145		preflight	10-13	
			pretaxi and taxi	10-14	
takeoff	11-15, 11-123		Planning Briefings, Mission	3-3	
			Planning, Fuel	3-6	
Performance Data Charts (J57-P-6B Engines)	11-115		Planning, Mission	3-5	
climb	11-135		Planning, Operational Mission	3-5	
combat performance	11-115		Planning, Navigation	3-6	
descent	11-183		Planning, Navigation and Flight	3-3	
endurance	11-177		Pneumatic Emergency Systems	1-99	
landing	11-187		Pneumatic Starts with ATSC 100-83 Starter Installed	3-16	
range	11-145		Pneumatic Systems Schematic, Emergency		1-100
takeoff	11-123		Portable Cylinder – Gaseous Oxygen Duration		1-122
Personal Equipment Requirements	2-2		Position Error, Altitude and Airspeed, Correction for		11-120
Personal Gear		2-4	Position Error, Airspeed and Altitude, Correction for		11-11
Pilot Flight Evaluation Grading Criteria	10-4		Position Error, Mach Number, Correction for		11-13, 11-121
climbout and level-off	10-6				
crew coordination	10-8		Position Indicators, Trim	1-94	
cruise	10-6		Position Indicator, Wing Flaps	1-95	
emergencies	10-8		Postflight	6-7	
instruments	10-6		Postflight and Shutdown	6-6	
mission planning	10-4		Postlanding Checklist (Field)	3-32	
preflight inspection of aircraft	10-5		Postlanding Checklist (Ship)	3-39	
takeoff	10-5		Post Takeoff Checklist	3-25	
turnup and taxi	10-5		Power		
Pilot	9-1		application, initial, voltage check 3 minutes after	8-7	
assist handle	1-8		applied radar control settings	8-7	
center console – A-3B		1-15	boost assembly, aileron		1-88
circuit breaker panel – A-3A		1-28	check, full	3-23	
circuit breaker panel typical		1-29	distribution, ac	1-76	
controlled start (remote)	3-15		distribution, dc	1-72	
instrument and console lights	1-117		failure, ac	1-81	
instrument panel – A-3A/B typical		1-10	failure, dc	1-73	
instrument proficiency	6-1		loss, electrical, vertical gyro attitude indicator (VGI) operation after	1-102	
left-hand console – A-3A		1-11	maximum continuous summary charts	11-111	
left-hand console – A-3B		1-13	off stalls	4-5	
and plane captain's seats – A-3B (typical)		1-20	panel, ac		1-77
responsibility	7-1		panel, aft		1-76
seat	1-5		summary charts, maximum continuous	11-189	
Pin Lock Control, Gust and Wing	1-94				

Index 18

Changed 15 July 1970

	Page No.			Page No.	
	Text	Illus		Text	Illus

	Text	Illus
switch, external	1-80	
summary, maximum continuous		11-113, 11-191
switch, pressure fueling	1-42	
system, ac	1-76	
Powered Instruments, ac	1-101	
Powered Instruments, dc	1-101	
Precautions, Safety	1-134, 3-15	
Preflight		
check, autopilot	3-20	
checklists	3-9	
radar system	8-1	
Prelanding	8-8	
Prelanding and Shutdown Checklist, ASB-1A Radar	8-8	
Prelanding and Shutdown Checklist, ASB-7 Radar	8-9	
Pressure		
aileron/spoiler and surface control	1-91	
altimeter, counterpointer	1-101	
control, cockpit	1-69	
control, safety	1-119	
defueling – basic system	1-135	
defueling – tanker-receiver system	1-141	
gage, oil	1-37	
indicator, fuel boost	1-34	
instruments, direct	1-101	
Pressure Check		
basic system	1-134	
and defueling basic system	1-128A	
and defueling – basic system		1-136, 1-138
with engines operating (hot refueling)	1-140	
fuel capacity data		1-135
power switch	1-42	
safety precautions	1-134	
system	1-39	
Pressurization, Air-Conditioning, and Defrosting Procedures	3-22	
Pressurizing and Air-Conditioning System	1-66	1-68
Pressurizing and Venting System, Fuel Tank	1-45	
Prestart Checklist	3-13	
Pretaxi/Taxi Checklist	3-19	
Pretakeoff	3-22	
shipboard	8-8	
and taxi checklist, ASB-1A radar	8-8	
and taxi checklist, ASB-7 radar	8-9	
Probe Light, Air Refueling	1-118	
Probe, Angle-of-Attack	1-72	
Profile		
combat radius	11-59	
maximum endurance	11-91	11-97
mission	11-58, 11-146	11-87, 11-175
Pump, Boost, Failure	5-13	
Pump Control, Fuel Boost	1-38	
Pumps, Engine Fuel	1-34	
Pushing, Parking and Towing	1-129	

Q

	Text	Illus
Quantity, Fuel Measurement		1-150
Quantity Indication, Fuel, Malfunction/Failure	5-13	
Quantity Indicating System, Fuel	1-44	
Quantity Indicator, Fuel	1-48	
Quantity Measurement, Fuel	1-140	

R

	Text	Illus
Radar		
altimeter, AN/APN-22	1-114	
ASB-1A taxi and pretakeoff checklist	8-8	
AN/ASB-7 – control panel		8-6
AN/ASB-1A modified	8-1	
ASB-1A equipment checklist	8-7	
ASB-1A malfunction checklist	8-8	
ASB-1A prelanding and shutdown checklist	8-8	
ASB-7 equipment	8-8	
ASB-7 prelanding and shutdown checklist	8-9	
ASB-7 taxi and pretakeoff checklist	8-9	
control panel, C-852B/ASB-1A		8-3
control panel, C-2549/ASB-7	8-5	
control panel check	8-7	
control settings (power applied)	8-7, 8-9	
ground operation	8-1	
and radio equipment and antennas		1-106
subsystem, tunable	8-7	
system, AN/ASB-1A modified – cockpit arrangement		8-2
system, ASB-7 modified	8-1	
system preflight	8-1	
systems	8-1	
Radar Systems	8-1	
AN/ASB-1A modified radar system – cockpit arrangement		8-2
AN/ASB-7 modified radar system – cockpit arrangement		8-4
AN/ASB-7 radar – control panel		8-6
C-852B/ASB-1A radar control panel		8-3
Radii, turning	1-165	
Radio		
air-to-ground communications	7-1	
AN/APX-6B transponder (IFF)	1-112	
AN/ARA-25 automatic direction finding system	1-109	
AN/ARC-27A UHF receiver-transmitters	1-105	
AN/ARC-38A HF receiver-transmitter	1-111	
ARN selector switch	1-105	
bus	1-72	
C-1159/APX-6B control panel (IFF)	1-112	
channels, changing	6-1	
communications	7-1	
communications and associated electronics equipment		1-110
communications equipment	7-2	
compass indicator	1-114	
control panel C-865/ARC-1	1-116	

	Text	Illus
control panel, UHF	1-107	
discipline	7-1	
dual AN/ARC-27A UHF receiver-transmitter installation	1-109	
electronic navigation equipment	7-2	
and electronics equipment	1-104	
emergency communications	7-1	
IFF/SIF procedures	7-2	
magnetic indicator ID-250A/ARN	1-115	
master switch	1-104	
and radar equipment and antennas		1-106
receiver-transmitter, AN/ARC-38A HF	1-111	
receiver-transmitter installation, dual AN/ARC-27A UHF	1-109	
receiver-transmitters, AN/ARC-27A UHF	1-105	
selector switch, ARN	1-105	
UHF communication and direction finding system	1-105	
UHF control panel	1-107	
Radius Profile, Combat	11-59, 11-147	11-88, 11-176
Radome and Fuselage, Forward (Area A)	3-9	
Rain, Ice, and Snow	6-4	
Rain Repellent	1-160A	
Range	11-57, 11-145	
vs altitude, maximum specific	11-57, 11-145	11-68
charts	11-57, 11-145	
combat radius profile		11-88
descent, maximum		11-100
flight test fouled deck range — IFR		11-66
fouled deck ("Bingo cards")	11-57, 11-145	
fouled deck — gear down		11-63
fouled deck range — gear and flaps down		11-64
fouled deck — IFR		11-62
fouled deck range — sea level		11-67
fouled deck — VFR		11-61, 11-65
maximum specific range vs altitude		11-68
mission profile		11-87
mission return profile		11-90
specific	11-58	11-70
Range (J57-P-6B-Engines)	11-145	
combat radius profile		11-176
fouled deck		11-155
fouled deck — gear down		11-151
fouled deck — gear and flaps down		11-152
fouled deck — IFR		11-150, 11-154
fouled deck — VFR		11-149, 11-153
maximum specific range vs altitude		11-156
mission profile		11-175
specific		11-158
Ranging, TACAN Air-to-Air	1-116	

	Text	Illus
Rate, Tank Transfer	4-20	
Rate of Climb, One-Engine	11-42	
Rate of Climb, One-Engine — 60,000 Pounds		11-49
Receiver AN/ARN-14E (VOR)	1-114	
capabilities, A-3B	4-31	
capability	4-22	
engagement procedures	4-18	
procedures from tankers other than KA-3B	4-21	
transmitter, AN/ARC-1	1-116	
transmitter, AN/ARC-38A HF radio	1-111	
transmitter installation, dual AN/ARC-27A radio	1-109	
transmitters, RT-178/ARC-27A	1-105	
Reel, Inertia and Shoulder Harness	1-5	
Refueling		
air	4-18	7-8
air, checklist	4-22	
hot, pressure fueling with engines operating	1-140	
operations	4-20	
probe light, air	1-118	
speed, air		4-19
Refusal Speeds		11-132
Refusal Speeds — No JATO	11-125	
Refusal Speeds, Takeoff	11-16	11-39
Refused Takeoff Stopping Distance — No JATO	11-16A, 11-125	
Refused Takeoff Stopping Distance		11-40, 11-133
Regulator, Panel-Mounted, Oxygen System Controls	1-119	
Relay Bus Tie Breaker	1-80	
Relays Generator Circuit Breaker	1-77	
Remote (Pilot Controlled) Start	3-15	
Rendezvous	3-35, 4-15	
circling	4-16	
and formation, night	3-34	
on-top	4-16	
procedures	4-18	
running	4-16	
after takeoff	4-16	
Requirements, Flight Crew	2-1	
Requirements, Personal Equipment	2-2	
Reservoir, Brake System, Filling and Bleeding	1-149	
Reservoir, Hydraulic, Servicing	1-149	
Reserves, Fuel	3-6	
Restart, ATM		1-67
Restart After a Negative G Condition, ATM	1-66	
Retraction, Emergency Flap	1-96	
Retraction, Emergency Wing	5-9	
Right-Hand Console, Navigator's Typical — A-3A		1-16
Right-Hand Console, Navigator's Typical — A-3B		1-17
Roll, Landing Ground	11-103	11-105
Roll, Minimum, With Drag Chute	3-29	
Roll, Minimum, Without Drag Chute	3-29	

Index
Rotary to Spoilers

	Text	Illus
Rotary Shutoff Switch, Bleed Air	5-6	
Rotary Switch, Bleed Air Shutoff System	1-63	
Route, Alternate Escape	5-19	
Routes, Escape — Controlled Bailout	5-21	
Routes, Escape, Emergency Bailout	5-21	
Routes, Escape, Primary and Secondary	5-18	
RT-178/ARC-27A Receiver-Transmitters	1-105	
Rudder	4-2B	
control	1-87	
elevator	4-13	
elevator and aileron	1-91, 4-14	
trim	4-2B	
Run, Takeoff, Engine Failure During	5-3	
Runaway Trim Procedure	5-12	
Running Rendezvous	4-16	
Runway Foaming Procedures, Recommended	5-27	

S

	Text	Illus
Safety Precautions	1-134, 3-15	
Safety Pressure Control	1-119	
Seats	1-5	
fourth	2-2	
navigator's	1-5	
pilot's	1-5	
pilot's and plane captain's seats — A-3B (typical)		1-20
plane captain's	1-5	
shoulder harness and inertia reel	1-5	
Securing Aircraft	1-165	
Security Equipment	1-111	
Selective Fuel Trim Control	1-52	
Selector Switch, ARN Radio	1-105	
Service Lights	1-117	
Servicing Aircraft	1-128A	
accumulator — charging	1-153	
antifogging compound	1-162	
ATM oil sump	1-157	
brake system	1-149	1-152
danger areas	1-165	
deicing-defrosting fluid	1-162	
diagram		1-132
emergency air systems	1-153	1-156
emergency oxygen bottle		1-161
engine oil tank	1-149	
external GTC starter	1-163	
fuel quantity measurement	1-140	
hydraulic reservoir	1-149	
hydraulic systems		1-151
oil system	1-149, 1-157	1-150
oxygen system	1-157	1-159
pressure fueling and defueling — basic system	1-129	
rain repellent	1-161	
securing aircraft	1-165	
towing, pushing, and parking	1-129	
turning radii	1-165	

	Text	Illus
Shore Based Procedures	3-8A	
aircraft inspection	3-35	
carrier-based procedures	3-35	
considerations	5-8	
engine starting	3-35	
familiar and transition	3-9	
field arrestments	3-32	
flight deck operations	3-35	
FMLP and CQ	3-33	
landings	3-27	
line operations	3-9	
starting aircraft	3-14	
taxi	3-21	
Short Field Arrestments	5-26	
Shoulder Harness and Inertia Reel	1-5	
Shutdown	8-9	
checklist	3-32	
checklist (ship)	3-39	
(in chocks)	8-8	
in flight, engine	4-6	
and postflight	6-6	
and prelanding checklist, ASB-7	8-9	
Shutoff		
switch, bleed air rotary	5-6	
switches, bleed air toggle	5-7	
system, bleed air (rotary switch)	1-63	
system, bleed air (toggle switches)	1-48	
valve and fuel float valve — basic system		1-137
Signals		
and communications	4-22	
emergency between aircraft		7-8
formation		7-4
tanker light identification	4-22	
SIF AN/APA-89	1-113	
SIF Control Panel	1-113	
SIF/IFF Procedures	7-2	
Simulated Instrument Flying	6-1	
Single-Engine		
approach/landing	3-29	
carrier landings	3-38, 5-16	
control speed, minimum	11-16	11-22
field landings	5-14	
flameout/failure	5-4	
flight characteristics	4-7	
landing, boost-off	4-15	
landings	5-14	
landing and waveoff pattern (typical)		5-15
Slats, Wing	1-99, 4-2B	
Slaved Gyro Magnetic Compass System	1-125	
Slow-Speed Stabilizer Trim, dc	1-93	
Smoke and Fume Elimination	5-8	
Snow, Guide to Elimination of		1-162
Snow, Ice, and Rain	6-4	
Solenoid Failure, Landing Gear	5-6	
Speed, Air Refueling		4-19
Speedbrake Emergency Operation	5-10	
Speedbrakes	1-96, 4-2B	
Speedbrake Switch	1-96	
Speed, Pattern, and Technique	3-33	
Spins	4-6	
Spoiler Control, Wing	1-87	
Spoilers — Ailerons	4-2A	

Changed 15 July 1970

Index
Spoiler to Systems

	Page No.			Page No.	
	Text	Illus		Text	Illus
Spoiler System Schematic, Wing....		1-89	Stopping Distance, Refused Takeoff		11-40, 11-133
Spoiler System Accumulators (Two)	1-153				
Spread, Wing to Wing Fold	1-95		Stopping Procedure	8-5	
Stabilizer			Strut, Automatic Jury	1-95	
actuator gangbar, horizontal	1-94		Supply Valve, Oxygen	1-119	
horizontal, trim check	3-20		Survival Training	2-1	
trim, ac high-speed	1-92		Switches		
trim, autopilot	1-93		ARN radio selector	1-105	
trim, control, horizontal	1-92		arresting hook bypass	1-104	
trim, dc slow-speed	1-93		ATM	1-64	
trim system, horizontal	1-92		bleed air rotary shutoff	5-6	
trim system, horizontal — general	1-94		bleed air toggle shutoff	5-7	
trim, runaway procedure	5-12		dc generator	1-73	
Stall Speeds and Approach Speeds, Recommended	11-103	11-104, 11-188	engine starter	1-34	
			escape chute test	1-8	
			escape chute test — A-3A	1-8	
Stalls	4-5		external power	1-80	
Stalls, Accelerated	4-5		foot microphone	1-113	
Stalls, Power-Off	4-5		fourth man ICS	1-114	
Stalling Speeds		4-6	fuselage fuel trim	1-43	
Standby Compass	1-103		generator	1-80	
Standby Gyro Horizon Indicator	1-103		ignition	1-34	
Start			I/P-OUT-MIC	1-112	
cartridge	3-15		JATO arming	1-128	
checklist	3-16		JATO firing	1-128	
false	3-18, 5-2		JATO jettison	1-128	
hot	5-2		master engine	1-34	
hot, and internal engine fires	3-18		panel, fuel system	1-43	
immediate air	4-8, 5-4		pressure fueling power	1-42	
intervals and duty cycles	3-16		radio master	1-104	
normal air	5-3		rotary, bleed air shutoff system	1-63	
pneumatic, with ATSC 100-83 starter installed	3-16		speedbrake	1-96	
remote (pilot controlled)	3-15		toggle, bleed air shutoff system	1-48	
unsatisfactory	5-2		wing flaps control	1-95	
wet	3-17, 5-2		Symbols, Abbreviations, and Definitions	11-3	
Starter, Cartridge	1-34		Summary Charts, Maximum Continuous Power	11-111	
Starter, Engine	1-33		Systems	1-31	
engine-mounted	1-165		ac electrical	1-78	
engine-mounted — operating parameters		1-165	ac power	1-76	
			aileron control	1-85	
Starter Installed, ATSC 100-83, Pneumatic Starts	3-16		air-conditioning and pressurizing	1-66	1-68
			AN/AIC-4A interphone	1-113	
Starter Switch, Engine	1-34		AN/APN-22 radar altimeter	1-114	
Starting			AN/APX-6B transponder (IFF)	1-112	
air	4-7, 5-3		AN/ARA-25 automatic direction finding	1-109	
aircraft	3-14		AN/ARC-27A UHF radio receiver — transmitters	1-105	
engine	1-34, 3-35, 6-6		angle-of-attack approach light	1-103	
equipment required	3-14		antiexposure suit ventilation	1-72	
procedure	3-14, 8-5		anti-icing	1-71, 6-1	
and warmup	6-5		antiskid brake	1-98	
Steady-State Operation	1-36		ASB-7 modified radar	8-1	
Steering			autopilot	1-120	
accumulator, nose gear	1-153		basic A-3A/B fuel	1-39	
emergency operation, nosewheel	1-98		basic A-3A/B fuel, management	1-45	
procedures, nosewheel	3-21		bleed air shutoff (rotary switch)	1-63	
system, nosewheel	1-97		bleed air shutoff (toggle switches)	1-48	
Stopping Distance, Refused Takeoff — No JATO	11-16A, 11-125		bomb bay	1-127	
			brake, servicing	1-149	
			check, oxygen	1-160	

	Page No.	
	Text	Illus

	Page No.	
	Text	Illus

T

	Text	Illus
controls, oxygen (panel-mounted regulator)	1-119	
dc electrical		1-74
dc power	1-72	
electrical	1-72	
emergency air — servicing	1-153	
emergency hydraulic	1-85	
emergency operation, electrical	1-73	
engine	1-31	
engine compressor bleed air	1-48	
engine fuel control	1-33	
electrical	1-72	
engine fire-detection	1-32	
engine oil	1-36	
equipment ground cooling	1-71	
escape hatch air	1-99	
failure, utility hydraulic	5-8	
flight control	1-85	
fuel	1-37	
fuel float valve and shutoff valve — basic		1-137
malfunction, oil	1-37	
fuel management — basic A-3A/B	1-45	
fuel quantity indicating	1-44	
fuel tank pressurizing and venting	1-45	
fuel trim control	1-43	
horizontal stabilizer trim	1-92	
hydraulic	1-81	
ignition	1-33	
instruments	1-101	
jet-assisted takeoff	1-127	
landing gear	1-96	
lighting equipment	1-116	
limit indicator	1-114	
liquid oxygen	1-118	
malfunction/failure, electrical	5-11	
malfunctions/failure, fuel	5-13	
malfunction/failure, oil	5-13	
navigation equipment	1-125	
nosewheel steering	1-97	
oil, servicing	1-149	1-150
omnibearing equipment (VOR)	1-114	
oxygen	1-118	
pneumatic emergency	1-99	
pressure defueling, basic	1-135	
pressure fueling	1-39	
radar	8-1	
radio and electronics equipment	1-104	
schematic, emergency pneumatic		1-100
schematic, utility hydraulic		1-82
schematic, wing spoiler		1-89
slaved gyro magnetic compass	1-125	
UHF communication and direction finding	1-105	
utility hydraulic	1-81	
wheel brakes	1-98	
windshield defogging	1-71	
windshield wiper	1-71	
wing and fin-folding	1-94	
wing tank fuel dumping	1-44	
yaw damping	1-123	

	Text	Illus
TACAN AN/ARN-21B	1-115	
TACAN Air-to-Air Ranging	1-116	
Tachometers	1-34	
Tactical	3-5	
Tactical formation	4-17	
Takeoff	6-5, 11-15, 11-123	
abort computations	3-3	
abort procedures	5-2	
before	6-5	
changing lead, leaving formation, breakup, landing		7-3
charts	11-15, 11-123	
checklist	3-22	
climb performance after	11-41, 11-135	11-44, 11-137
distance		11-20, 11-127
emergencies	5-2	
field — with JATO	11-125	
fuel conservation prior to	3-22	
instrument	6-2	
JATO	3-24	
JATO firing delay and minimum takeoff distance	11-17	
JATO — two units (15° nozzle)		11-24
JATO — four units (15° nozzle)		11-26
JATO — six units (15° nozzle)		11-28
JATO — 12 units (15° nozzle)		11-30
JATO — two units (30° nozzle)		11-32
JATO — four units (30° nozzle)		11-34
JATO — six units (30° nozzle)		11-36
JATO — 12 units (30° nozzle)		11-38
and landing, low level	5-18	
line speed check	11-15	
maximum recommended takeoff weight		11-21
minimum ground roll — 4 JATO units (30° nozzle)		11-129
minimum ground roll — 8 JATO units (30° nozzle)		11-130
minimum ground roll — 12 JATO units (30° nozzle)		11-131
minimum ground roll — with JATO	11-124	
minimum and JATO firing delay	11-17	
minimum single-engine control speed		11-22
no JATO	11-123	
post, checklist	3-25	
procedures	3-24	
recommended liftoff speed		11-19
refusal speeds	11-16	11-39
stopping distance, refused — no JATO	11-126	
refused takeoff stopping distance		11-40, 11-133
stopping distance, refused — no JATO	11-16A	
rendezvous after	4-16	
run, engine failure during	5-3	
system, jet-assisted	1-127	
and taxi	6-7	
and taxi, night	3-34	

Changed 15 July 1970

	Page No.			Page No.	
	Text	Illus		Text	Illus
using 2 5KS-4500 MK7 MOD 2, JATO units	11-18		Touch-and-Go Landing	3-29	
weight, maximum recommended		11-128	Towing, Pushing, and Parking	1-129	1-130
			Training, Ground	2-1	
weight, maximum recommended — no JATO	11-124		Training, Survival	2-1	
			Transceiver, Emergency	2-3	
weight, maximum recommended		11-21	Transfer		
			control, wing tank fuel	1-42	
weight, maximum recommended, with and without JATO	11-16		rate, fuel		4-34
			rate, tanker	4-20	
Takeoff (J57-P-6B-Engines)	11-123		Transition and Familiarization	3-9	
distance		11-127	Transponder, AN/APX-6B (IFF)	1-112	
distance minimum ground roll		11-129	Trim		
recommended liftoff speed		11-126	ac high-speed stabilizer	1-92	
maximum recommended weight		11-128	aileron		4-2B
			automatic	1-121	
refusal speeds		11-132	autopilot stabilizer	1-93	
refused stopping distance		11-133	card, engine	1-104	
Tank			check, horizontal stabilizer	3-20	
aft fuselage fuel	1-137		control, fuel — automatic	1-45	
auxiliary upper bomb bay	1-39, 1-137		control, fuel — manual	1-47	
			control, fuel — selective	1-45	
forward fuselage	1-137		control, horizontal stabilizer	1-92	
fuel	1-39		control system, fuel	1-43	
wing	1-137		dc slow-speed stabilizer	1-93	
Tanker			devices	4-2	
light identification signals	4-22		failures, pitch	1-125	
other than KA-3B, receiver procedures	4-21		flaps, and fuel trim	3-22	
			position indicators	1-94	
transfer rate	4-20		rudder		4-2B
Taxi	3-21, 3-35, 6-5, 8-8		runaway procedure	5-12	
			setting, elevator vs CG position		3-23
and arrestment	3-38		switch, fuselage fuel	1-43	
(or landing) light	1-118		system, horizontal stabilizer	1-92	
at night	3-21		Turbine Outlet Temperature Indicators	1-34	
and pretakeoff checklist, ASB-1A radar	8-8		Turn-and-Slip Indicator	1-102	
and pretakeoff checklist, ASB-7 radar	8-9		Turbine Failure, Air-Conditioning	5-7	
			Turbine Motors, Air (ATM's)	1-63	
pretaxi checklist	3-19		Turning Radii	1-165	
procedure	3-21				
and takeoff	6-7		U		
and takeoff, night	3-34				
Temperature Correction for Compressibility		11-7	UHF Communication and Direction Finding System	1-105	
Temperature Effect on One-Engine Rate of Climb — Military Thrust		11-53	UHF Radio Control Panel	1-107	
			UHF Radio Receiver-Transmitter Installation, Dual AN/ARC-27A	1-109	
Temperature Indicator, Dual Engine Oil	1-37		UHF Radio Receiver-Transmitters, AN/ARC-27A	1-105	
Temperature Indicators, Turbine Outlet	1-34		Utility Hydraulic System	1-81	
Temperature Warning Light, ATM Compartment	1-65		Utility Hydraulic System Failure	5-8	
Thermoswitches and Lights, Warning	1-63		hook emergency operation	5-10	
Test Switch, Escape Chute	1-8		landing gear emergency operation	5-9	
Test Switch, Escape Chute — A-3A	1-8		shipboard considerations	5-8	
			shore-based considerations	5-8	
Throttles	1-33		speedbrake emergency operation	5-10	
Thunderstorms	6-4				
Time To Climb		11-48, 11-56, 11-140, 11-143	wheelbrake operation after utility failure	5-10	
			wing flap emergency operation	5-9	
Toggle Shutoff Switches, Bleed Air	5-7		Utility Hydraulic System Schematic		1-82
Toggle Switches (Bleed Air Check)	3-17		Unsatisfactory Starts	5-2	
Toggle Switches, Bleed Air Shutoff System	1-48		Utility Failure, Wheel Brake Operation After	5-10	

Index

Valve to Yaw

	Text	Illus
V		
Valve		
fuel crossfeed control	1-37	
fuel float and shutoff valve — basic system		1-137
manual cg fuel control	1-44	
oxygen air	1-119	
oxygen supply	1-119	
shutoff, tanker-receiver system	1-146	
Velocity Indicator, Vertical	1-102	
Vent Icing, Fuel	5-14	
Ventilation, Antiexposure Suit	1-72	
Venting and Pressurizing System, Fuel Tank	1-45	
Vent Mast Icing, Fuel	1-45	
Vertical Gyro Attitude Indicator (VGI)	1-102	
Vertical Velocity Indicator	1-102	
VFR — Fouled Deck Range		11-61, 11-65, 11-149, 11-153
VFR Landing Pattern	10-9	
postflight debrief	10-10	
postlanding and shutdown	10-10	
Visual Communications Procedures	7-2	
aircraft and engine operation		7-8
air refueling		7-8
electronic communications and navigation		7-6
emergency signals between aircraft		7-8
formation signals		7-4
general conversation	7-2	
JATO procedures		7-9
takeoff, changing lead, leaving formation, breakup, landing		7-3
VN Operating Flight Strength Diagrams		1-176
Voltage Check	8-7	
Voltammeters	1-73	
Voltmeters	1-81	
VOR AN/ARN-14E Receiver	1-114	
VOR (Omnibearing Equipment)	1-114	
W		
Warmup and Starting	6-5	
Warning Horn, Bomb Doors	1-127	
Warning Light		
ATM compartment temperature	1-65	
dc generator	1-73	
fire (wing(s) and/or air cond)	5-7	
fuel low-level	1-48	
generator	1-73, 1-80	
JATO	1-128	
and thermoswitches	1-63	
Waveoff, Climb Performance for	11-42	11-45

	Text	Illus
Waveoff and Landing Pattern		3-31
Waveoff and Single-Engine Landing Pattern (Typical)		5-15
Weight, Maximum Recommended Takeoff		11-21, 11-128
Weight, Maximum Recommended Takeoff — No JATO	11-124	
Weight, Maximum Recommended Takeoff, With and Without JATO	11-16	
Weather Considerations	3-3, 6-3	
ice	6-3	
icing of Pitot-Static instruments	6-4	
thunderstorms	6-4	
Weight Balance	3-5	
Weight, Landing	3-33	
Weight Limitations	1-175	
Wet Starts	3-17, 5-2	
Wheel Brake Emergency Operation	1-99	
Wheel Brakes Emergency	5-18	
Wheel Brake Operation After Utility Failure	5-10	
Wheel Brakes System	1-98	
Windshield Defogging	1-71	
Windshield Wiper	1-71	
Wing		
and/or air cond fire warning lights	5-7	
and fin-folding control	1-94	
and fin-folding system	1-94	
fire or hot bleed air leak	5-6	
fire warning light, RH	5-7	
fire warning light, LH	5-6	
flaps	4-2	
flaps control switch	1-95	
flaps emergency operation	1-95	
flap emergency operation	5-9	
flap extension, emergency	5-9	
flaps position indicator	1-95	
flap retraction, emergency	5-9	
fold to wing spread	1-95	
tank fuel dumping system	1-44	
tank fuel transfer control	1-42	
tanks	1-135, 1-137	
pin lock and gust control	1-94	
position	4-16	
slats	1-99, 4-2B	
spoiler control	1-87	
spoiler system schematic		1-89
spread to wing fold	1-95	
XYZ		
Yaw Damping System	1-123	

HUGHES FLYING BOAT MANUAL

SPRUCE GOOSE

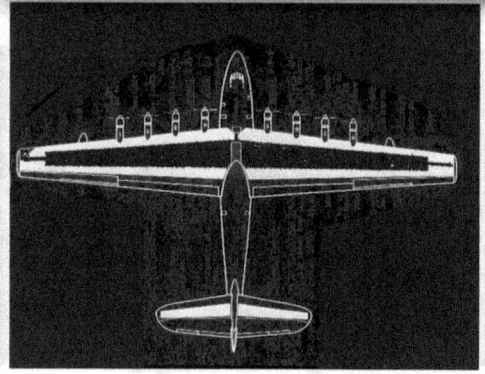

~~RESTRICTED~~

Originally Published by the War Department
Reprinted by Periscope Film LLC

NOW AVAILABLE!

MMS SUBCOURSE NUMBER 151   EDITION CODE 3

NIKE MISSILE
and Test Equipment

NIKE HERCULES

DECLASSIFIED

by U.S. Army Missile and Munitions Center and School
Periscope Film LLC

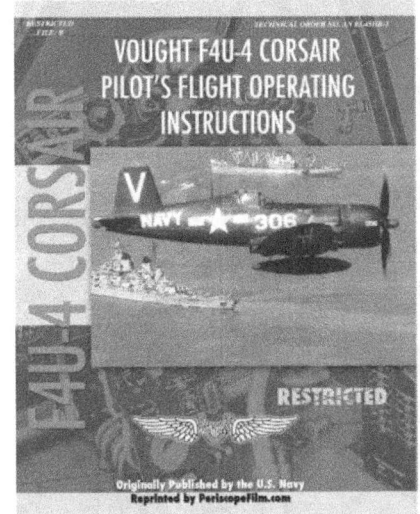
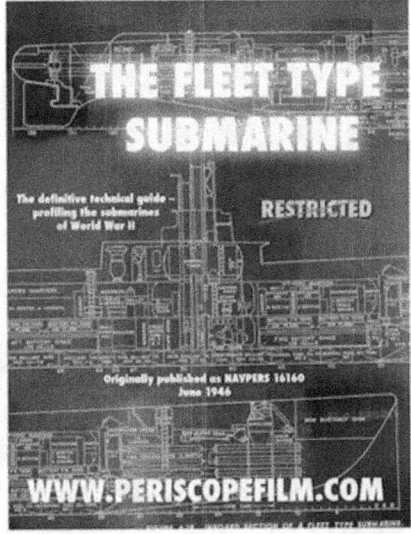

ALSO NOW AVAILABLE FROM PERISCOPEFILM.COM

©2012 Periscope Film LLC
All Rights Reserved
ISBN #978-1-937684-85-3

www.ingramcontent.com/pod-product-compliance
Lightning Source LLC
Chambersburg PA
CBHW080922020526

44114CB00043B/2427